POLAND'S HOLOCAUST

POLAND'S HOLOCAUST

Ethnic Strife, Collaboration with Occupying Forces and Genocide in the Second Republic, 1918–1947

Tadeusz Piotrowski

McFarland & Company, Inc., Publishers
Jefferson, North Carolina, and London

Front and back cover photographs by Andrew Slodkowski; courtesy of Globetrotter Books, Division of International Broadcast Productions, Inc.

British Library Cataloguing-in-Publication data are available

Library of Congress Cataloguing-in-Publication Data

Piotrowski, Tadeusz, 1940–
Poland's holocaust : ethnic strife, collaboration with occupying forces and genocide in the Second Republic, 1918–1947 / Tadeusz Piotrowski.
p. cm.
Includes bibliographical references and index.
ISBN 0-7864-0371-3 (case binding : 50# alkaline paper) ♾
1. Poland—History—1918–1945. 2. Poland—Ethnic relations. 3. World War, 1939–1945—Collaborationists—Poland. 4. World War, 1939–1945—Atrocities. 5. Poland—History—Occupation, 1939–1945. I. Title.
DK4400.P56 1998
943.8'053—dc21 97-26233
CIP

Manufactured in the United States of America

McFarland & Company, Inc., Publishers
Box 611, Jefferson, North Carolina 28640

To the six million
Polish citizens
who perished during World War II

There will come a time when it will be possible to present in great detail an accurate and richly documented account of that scandal, that moral turpitude, that unprecedented jumble of chaos, incompetence, corruption, bad faith, inanity, devastation, falsehood, plunder, decrepitude and ordinary stupidity which characterized the German occupation administration in the years of the present war on Polish soil. It will be a shocking and frightful account.

Field Report from Wilno, 1942
Archiwum Akt Nowych
sygnatura 202/I-31, k.53

In the end I had read a bit of history and I knew that evil takes one incarnation or another in every epoch. And I thought that in the twentieth century evil had incarnated itself in history and that Bolshevism was the devil in history.

Aleksander Wat
My Century

Table of Contents

Abbreviations ix
Tables and Maps xiv
Preface 1

Introduction 3

1. Soviet Terror 7

2. Nazi Terror 21

3. Jewish Collaboration 35
Interwar Years 36
Soviet Occupation 48
Postwar Years 58
German Occupation 66

4. Polish Collaboration 77
Soviet Occupation 77
German Occupation 82
Assistance to Jews 112
Postwar Years 128

5. Belorussian Collaboration 143
Soviet Occupation 144
German Occupation 148

6. Lithuanian Collaboration 159
Soviet Occupation 160
German Occupation 163

7. Ukrainian Collaboration 177
Interwar Years 179
Soviet Occupation 198
German Occupation 204
Ethnic Cleansing 242

Conclusion 259

*Appendix: Documents** 263
Notes 293
Bibliography 389
Index 407

*1: Conference of Ambassadors, 1923. 2: Minorities Treaty, 1919. 3: From Polish Constitution, 1921. 4: Józef Beck, 1934. 5: From NKVD Instructions. 6: Deportations Order, 1939. 7: Beria to Stalin on Katyn. 8: Lynda Brayer, 1993–1994. 9: Kielce Pogrom, 1946. 10: Polish Orthodox Church [1930s]. 11: Petro Pevnyi, 1931. 12: Mykhalo Bachynskyi, 1931. 13: [1930] Report on Poles and Ukrainians.

Abbreviations

AK (Pol.) Armia Krajowa (Polish Home Army)
Polish underground organization under the Polish government-in-exile in London

AL (Pol.) Gwardia Ludowa (People's Army)
Communist-led Polish underground organization, *see* GL

APA (Ger.) Aussenpolitisches Amt (Department of Foreign Politics)
Department of the NSDAP

BBH (Ger.) Bergbauernhilfe (Mountain-Peasants' Help)

BCh (Pol.) Bataliony Chłopskie (Peasant Legions)

BIP (Pol.) Biuro Informacji i Propagandy (Bureau of Information and Propaganda)

BKA (Bel.) Belaruskaya Krayovaya Abarona (Belorussian Home Defense Corps)

BKS (Bel.) Belaruski Kamitet Samapomach (Belorussian Committee of Mutual Assistance)

BNA (Bel.) Belaruskaye Narodnaye Abyednannye (Belorussian National Union)

BNP (Bel.) Belaruskaya Nezalezhnitskaya Partyia (Belorussian Independent Party)

BNS (Bel.) Belaruskaya Narodnaya Samapomach (Belorussian National Organization of Mutual Assistance)

BRL (Bel.) Belaruskaya Republika Ludova (Belorussian People's Republic)

BTsR (Bel.) Belaruskaya Tsentralnaya Rada (Belorussian Central Council)

CIA (Eng.) Central Intelligence Agency

CIC (Eng.) Counter-Intelligence Corps

CKE (Pol.) Centralny Komitet Emigracyjny (Central Emigration Committee)

CKŻP (Pol.) Centralny Komitet Żydów w Polsce (Central Committee of Polish Jews)

Comintern (Eng.) Communist Internation
The international organization of communist parties (1919–1943)

COP (Pol.) Centralny Okęrg Przemysłowy ([Poland's] Central Industrial Area)

DG (Pol.) Dowództwo Główne (Headquarters)

DUN (Ukr.) Druzhyny Ukrainskykh Natsionalistiv (Detachments of Ukrainian Nationalists)

Gestapo (Ger.) Geheime Staatspolizei (Secret State Police)

GG (Ger.) Generalgouvernement (General Government)
Also satirically called Gangstergau (Gangsterland)

GL (Pol.) Gwardia Ludowa (People's Guard)
Communist-led Polish underground organization, predecessor of AL

Hiwis (Ger.) Hilfswillige (willing helpers)
Volunteer auxiliaries in the German Armed Forces

KB (Pol.) Korpus Bezpieczeństwa (Security Corps)

KBW (Pol.) Korpus Bezpieczeństwa Wewnętrznego (Internal Security Corps)

KC PPR (Pol.) Komitet centralny Polskiej Partii Robotniczej (Central Committee of the Polish Workers' Party)

KGB (Rus.) Komitet Gosudarstvennoi Bezopasnosti (Committee for State Security)
Soviet security service, established in 1954; also satirically interpreted as Kontora Grubykh Banditov (Office of Crude Bandits)

KNAPP (Pol.) Komitet Narodowy Amerykanów Polskiego Pochodzenia (National Committee of Americans of Polish Descent)

Komsomol (Rus.) Kommunisticheskii Soyuz Molodezhi (Communist League of Youth)
The communist organization for youth in the Soviet Union

KOP (Pol.) Korpus Ochrony Pogranicza (Frontier Defense Corps)

KP(b)B (Pol.) Komunistyczna Partia (bolszewików) Białorusi ([Bolshevik] Communist Party of Belorussia)
(Rus.) Kommunisticheskaya Partiia (bolsheviki) Belaruskaya ([Bolshevik] Communist Party of Belorussia)

KPP (Pol.) Komunistyczna Partia Polski (Polish Communist Party)

KPRP (Pol.) Komunistyczna Partia Robotnicza Polski (Communist Workers' Party of Poland)

KPZB (Pol.) Komunistyczna Partia Zachodniej Białorusi (Communist Party of Western Belorussia)

KPZU (Pol.) Komunistyczna Partia Zachodniej Ukrainy (Communist Party of Western Ukraine)

Kripo (Ger.) Kriminalpolizei (Detective Forces, Criminal Police)

KRN (Pol.) Komitet Rady Narodowej (Committee of the National Council)

KW PPR (Pol.) Komitet Wojewódzki Polskiej Partii Robotniczej (Provincial Committee of the Polish Workers' Party)

KZMP (Pol.) Komunistyczne Zjednoczenie Młodych Polaków (Communist Union of Polish Youth)

LAF (Lith.) Lietuvių Aktyvistų Frontas (Lithuanian Activist Front)

LVR (Lith.) Lietuvos Vietinė Rinktinė (Lithuanian Local Detachments)

MAP (Pol.) Ministerstwo Administracji Publicznej (Ministry of State Administration)

MBP (Pol.) Ministerstwo Bezpieczeństwa Publicznego (Ministry of State Security)

MO (Pol.) Milicja Obywatelska (Civil Militia)

MON (Pol.) Ministerstwo Obrony Narodowej (Ministry of National Defense)

MOPR (Pol.) Międzynarodowa Organizacja Pomocy Rewolucjonistom (International Organization for Help to the Revolutionaries)

MRN (Pol.) Miejska Rada Nadzorcza (City Supervisory Council)

MTS (Eng.) Machine-Tractor Station, or Motor-Tractor Station

NCO (Eng.) noncommissioned officer

NKGB (Rus.) Narodnyi Komissariat Gosudarstvennoi Bezopasnosti (People's Commissariat for State Security)
Soviet security service, 1941 and 1943–46; predecessor of Soviet Ministry of State Security, 1946–54

NKVD (Rus.) Narodnyi Komissariat Vnutrennikh Del (People's Commissariat for Internal Affairs)
Incorporated State Security 1922–23, 1934–43; predecessor of Soviet Ministry of Internal Affairs

NOW (Pol.) Narodowa Organizacja Wojskowa (National Military Organization)

NRO (Pol.) Naczelna Rada Opiekuńcza (Chief Social Welfare Council)

NSDAP (Ger.) Nationalsozialistische Deutsche Arbeiter Partei (National Socialist German Workers' Party [Nazi Party])

NSW (Pol.) Najwyższy Sąd Wojskowy (Supreme Military Court)

NSZ	(Pol.)	Narodowe Siły Zbrojne (National Armed Forces)
NZW	(Pol.)	Narodwy Związek Wojskowy (National Military Union)
OD	(Ger.)	Ordnungsdienst (Order Service)
OKW	(Ger.)	Oberkommando der Wehrmacht (High Command of the [German] Armed Forces)
ONR	(Pol.)	Obóz Narodowo-Radykalny (Radical Nationalist Group) Offshoot of the SN
ORMO	(Pol.)	Ochotnicza Rezerwa Milicji Obywatelskiej (Volunteer Reserve of the Civil Militia)
OSI	(Eng.)	Office of Special Investigation
OUN	(Ukr.)	Orhanizatsiia Ukrainskykh Natsionalistiv (Organization of Ukrainian Nationalists)
OUN-B	(Ukr.)	The OUN faction led by Stepan Bandera
OUN-M	(Ukr.)	The OUN faction led by Andrii Melnyk
PAP	(Pol.)	Polska Agencja Prasowa (Polish Press Agency)
PBN	(Bel.)	Partyia Belaruskikh Natsianalistov (Belorussian Nationalist Party)
PCK	(Pol.)	Polski Czerwony Krzyż (Polish Red Cross)
PLAN	(Pol.)	Polska Ludowa Akcja Niepodległości (Polish People's Independence Action)
POW	(Eng.)	prisoner of war
PPN	(Pol.)	Polskie Porozumienie Niepodległościowe (Polish Accord of Independence)
PPR	(Pol.)	Polska Partia Robotnicza (Polish Workers' Party)
PPS	(Pol.)	Polska Partia Socjalistyczna (Polish Socialist Party)
PRL	(Pol.)	Polska Rzeczpospolita Ludowa (Polish People's Republic)
PSL	(Pol.)	Polskie Stronnictwo Ludowe (Polish [noncommunist] People's Party)
PUBP	(Pol.)	Powiatowy Urząd Bezpieczeńtwa Publicznego (County Office of State Security)
PZPR	(Pol.)	Polska Zjednoczona Partia Robotnicza (Polish United Workers' Party)
RGO	(Pol.)	Rada Główna Opiekuńcza ([Polish] Main Social Welfare Council)
ROA	(Rus.)	Russkaya Osvoboditelnaya Armiia (Russian Liberation Army)
RONA	(Rus.)	Russkaya Osvoboditelnaya Narodnaya Armiia (Russian National Liberation Army)
RPŻ	(Pol.)	Rada Pomocy Żydom (Council for Aid to Jews) Code name: Żegota
RUP	(Ukr.)	Revoliutsiina Ukrainska Partiia (Revolutionary Ukrainian Party)
SA	(Ger.)	Sturmabteilung (Storm Troopers) Brown-shirt paramilitary units of the NSDAP
SB	(Ukr.)	Sluzhba Bezpeky ([OUN-B] Security Service)
	(Pol.)	Służba Bezpieczeństwa (Security Service)
SBM	(Bel.)	Sayuz Belaruskay Moladzi (Union of Belorussian Youth)
SD	(Ger.)	Sicherheitsdienst (Security Service) Unit of the SS
	(Pol.)	Stronnictwo Demokratyczne ([Polish] Democratic Party)
Sipo	(Ger.)	Sicherheitspolizei (Security Police [Gestapo and Kripo])
SKV	(Ukr.)	Samooboronnyi Kushchovi Viddily (Kushch Self-Defense Units) OUN-B units in Wołyń
SL	(Pol.)	Stronnictwo Ludowe (People's Party)
SMERSH	(Rus.)	Smert' Shpionam, Sovetskii Metod Rozoblacheniia Shpionov (Death to Spies, Soviet Method of Detecting Spies) Soviet military counterintelligence, 1943–46
SN	(Pol.)	Stronnictwo Narodowe (National Party)
SOB	(Pol.)	Socjalistyczna Organizacja Bojowa (Socialist Combat Organization)

SP (Pol.) Stronnictwo Polskie (Polish [communist labor] Party)
(Ger.) Sicherheitspolizei (Security Police)
See Sipo
SS (Ger.) Schutzstaffel (Protection Squad)
Black-shirt unit of the NSDAP
SSR (Eng.) Soviet Socialist Republic
SUNM (Ukr.) Soiuz Ukrainskoi Natsionalistychnoi Molodi (Union of Ukrainian Nationalist Youth)
SZP (Pol.) Służba Zwycięstwu Polski (Service for Polish Victory)
TNRP (Pol.) Tymczasowa Narodowa Rada Polityczna (Interim National Political Council)
TRJN (Pol.) Tymczasowa Rada Jedności Narodowej (Interim National Unity Council)
UB (Pol.) Urząd Bezpieczeństwa (Office of [State] Security)
Predecessor of SB
UDKs (Ukr.) Ukrainskyi Dopomohovyi Komitety (Ukrainian Relief Committees)
Under control of UTsK
UHA (Ukr.) Ukrainska Halytska Armiia (Ukrainian Galician Army)
UHVR (Ukr.) Ukrainska Holovna Vyzvolna Rada (Ukrainian Supreme Liberation Council)
UNA (Ukr.) Ukrainska Natsionalna Armiia (Ukrainian National Army)
(Ukr.) Ukrainska Natsionalna Asambleia (Ukrainian National Assembly)
UNDO (Ukr.) Ukrainske Natsionalne-Demokratychne Obiednannie (Ukrainian National Democratic Union)
UNK (Ukr.) Ukrainskyi Natsionalnyi Komitet (Ukrainian National Committee)
UNR (Ukr.) Ukrainska Narodna Respublika (Ukrainian National Republic)
UNS (Ukr.) Ukrainska Natsionalna Samooborona (Ukrainian National Self-Defense)
OUN-B units in Galicia
UNSO (Ukr.) Ukrainska Natsionalna Samooborona (Ukrainian National Self-Defense)
Paramilitary arm of the Ukrainian National Assembly — UNA
UOT (Ukr.) Ukrainske Osvitne Tovaristva (Ukrainian Educational Societies)
UPA (Ukr.) Ukrainska Povstanska Armiia (Ukrainian Insurgent Army)
URP (Ukr.) Ukrainska Robotnicha Partiia (Ukrainian Labor Party)
USB (Pol.) Uniwersytet Stefana Batorego (University of Stefan Batory)
USDP (Ukr.) Ukrainska Sotsialistychna Demokratychna Partiia (Ukrainian Socialist Democratic Party)
USRP (Ukr.) Ukrainska Sotsialistychna Radykalna Partiia (Ukrainian Radical-Socialist Party)
UTsK (Ukr.) Ukrainskyi Tsentralnyi Komitet (Ukrainian Central Committee)
UVO (Ukr.) Ukrainska Viiskova Orhanizatsiia (Ukrainian Military Organization)
UVV (Ukr.) Ukrainske Vyzvolne Viisko (Ukrainian Liberation Army)
VVN (Ukr.) Viiskovi Viddily Natsionalistiv (Nationalist Military Detachments)
Regiments of the OUN
VZUN (Ukr.) Velykyi Zbir Ukrainskykh Natsionalistiv (Great Conference of Ukrainian Nationalists)
Waffen SS (Ger.) Armed units of the SS, military formations of the SS
WiN (Pol.) Wolność i Niezawisłość (Freedom and Independence)
Last active remnant of the AK
WK PPS (Pol.) Wojewódzki Komitet Polskiej Partii Socjalistycznej (Provincial Committee of the Polish Socialist Party)
WP (Pol.) Wojsko Polskie (Polish Army)
WRN (Pol.) Wolność-Równość-Niepodległość (Freedom-Equality-Independence)
WUBP (Pol.) Wojewódzki Urząd Bezpieczeństwa Publicznego (Provincial Office of State Security)

Żagiew (Pol.) Żydowska Gwardia Wolności (Jewish Guard of Liberty)
Żegota (Pol.) Code name for Rada Pomocy Żydom (Council for Aid to Jews)
See RPŻ
ŻOB (Pol.) Żydowska Organizacja Bojowa (Jewish Combat Organization)
ŻSS (Pol.) Żydowska Samopomoc Społeczna (Jewish Social Welfare Mutual Assistance [Society])
ZUNR (Ukr.) Zakhidno-Ukrainska Narodna Respublika (Western Ukrainian National Republic)
ZWZ (Pol.) Związek Walki Zbrojnej (Union for Armed Struggle)
Predecesssor of the AK
ŻZW (Pol.) Żydowski Związek Wojskowy (Jewish Military Union)

Tables and Maps

Tables

1. Inhabitants of the Soviet-Occupied Provinces by Mother Tongue, 1939–41
2. Number of People Deported to the USSR, 1939–41 (by mother tongue, per thousand)
3. Number of Prisoners and POWs Killed in the Summer of 1941 in Soviet-Occupied Poland
4. Mass Executions of Poles in Ponary According to Polish Underground Reports, 1942–44
5. Execution of the Wilno Jews in 1941
6. Number of Ukrainian Deputies and Senators in the Polish Seym in Relation to Total Membership, 1922–38
7. Number of Votes Cast for Various Lists in the General Elections in Wołyń, 1922–30
8. Mandates Gained by Various Ethnic Constituencies in Eastern Galicia and Wołyń, 1927
9. Number of Elementary Schools in Eastern Galicia, 1924–30
10. Number of Public Schools in Wołyń, 1927–34
11. Prosvita, 1910–35
12. Ridna Shkola, 1900–36
13. Silskyi Hospodar, 1910–36
14. Number of Polish Deaths at the Hands of the Ukrainian Nationalists in Wołyń by Counties between 1939 and 1944
15. National Minorities in Poland, 1995
16. Ethnic Structure of Poland in 1931 (in thousands)
17. Number of Poles Resettled or Evicted Between 1939 and 1944 in German-Occupied Poland
18. Number of Persons Deported from Poland to Germany for Forced Labor, 1939–1945
19. European Losses during World War II (in thousands)
20. Poland's Losses during World War II (in thousands)
21. Number of Jews in Poland, 1931 (in thousands)
22. Number of Belorussians in Poland's Eastern Provinces, 1931 (in thousands)
23. Provinces with Ukrainian Population According to the Official 1931 Census (in thousands)
24. Provinces with Ukrainian Population According to an Adjusted 1931 Census (in thousands)
25. Persons Arrested in Eastern Galicia for Terrorist Activity between July 1 and November 30, 1930

Maps

1. Poland under German and Soviet Occupation, 1939–1941
2. Belorussia under German Occupation, 1942
3. Wilno Region (Okręg Wileński), 1942–1944
4. Provinces and Counties of Southeastern Poland, 1939

Preface

In 1939 a great storm swept over Poland and spread to the rest of the world, killing tens of millions. Of the six million who died in Poland, all but approximately six hundred thousand were noncombatants. They did not all die at German hands. Their tragic deaths cry out for remembrance. *Mortui viventes obligant.* That is why I wrote this book.

In Washington, D.C., the U.S. Holocaust Memorial Museum is dedicated to preserving the memory of some of the victims of that Holocaust, the victims of National Socialism from 1933 to 1945. But if we agree that the Holocaust was an event in historical time involving an officially sanctioned policy of genocide and that *genocide* is the systematic destruction, in whole or in part, of indigenous populations *as such*, then by what rationale should the Soviet Union be excluded from responsibility for its part in either one of these phenomena? Hitler came to power in 1933; Stalin by 1924. One hesitates to venture a guess as to whether more people died under the former or the latter régime. I submit that the term "Holocaust" ought to include the victims of both of these genocidal régimes and their collaborators.

The term "Holocaust," then, embraces more than the wholesale slaughter of Jews, Poles, Gypsies, communists, socialists, trade unionists, Jehovah's Witnesses, homosexuals, and the physically and mentally impaired by the Third Reich. That the Soviet Union turned against its former ally after being invaded by that ally and itself became the object of genocidal policies does not diminish its partnership in the endeavor in the least. Moreover, Soviet genocidal policies both preceded the rise of Nazi Germany and continued after its defeat. Implicit in this expanded definition of the Holocaust is the recognition that such policies were pursued in many countries and that among their victims in many countries were people of numerous nationalities and religious backgrounds. Such is my understanding of the term "Holocaust." This work is about that Holocaust in occupied Poland and those responsible for it, whether they were tried at Nuremberg or not.

Because of the extraordinarily complex nature of the subject matter, this was a difficult book to research and to write. My analysis relies on a wide variety of primary and secondary sources, including memoirs, personal journals, and archival documents, in several languages. I have also tried to incorporate into this work the insights that I have gained about these matters from my informal discussions with survivors, Christians and Jews alike.

The answer to the important question of whether I am a Polish sociologist or a sociologist who happens to be Polish is that I am a naturalized American citizen of Polish descent who happens to be a sociologist—and that I take a great deal of pride in my country of citizenship, my country of origin, and my profession. I do not deny that my family experiences in Eastern Poland—as recounted in *Vengeance of the Swallows: Memoir of a Polish Family's Ordeal under Soviet Aggression, Ukrainian Ethnic Cleansing and Nazi Enslavement, and Their Emigration to America*—have had a profound impact on my thinking about all the issues in this sequel. These experiences have provided me with a certain depth of understanding that I would not otherwise possess. I do not claim to have penned an "objective" account—only that I have made a reasonable effort to do so and that

I have amply documented the evidence upon which my conclusions are based.

For this work, I am grateful to more people than I can possibly name here. My most earnest "thank you" goes to Richard Tyndorf, vice-president of the Adam Mickiewicz Foundation in Canada, for his invaluable research-related assistance, his many helpful suggestions, and his encouragement. I am also grateful to the University of New Hampshire, Manchester, campus librarians — Judy Romein, Mary Jean Colburn, and Cindy Tremblay — for their tireless efforts in my behalf throughout the research, writing, and revision stages of this work. To Ryszard Pedowski, my brother-in-law from Grabowiec, and to Regina Gelb from Starachowice goes a warm "thank you" for allowing me the privilege of conducting in-depth interviews with them. For financial assistance, I am indebted to the University of New Hampshire at Manchester and the Adam Mickiewicz Foundation in Canada. Much of this work was done while on sabbatical in New Hampshire during a wonderfully long and snowy winter.

I thank the following publishers for their kind permission to quote from copyrighted materials: Czytelnik, for sections from Jerzy Tomaszewski, *Rzeczpospolita wielu narodów*; Hoover Institution Press, for Irena Grudzińska-Gross and Jan Tomasz Gross, eds., *War through Children's Eyes*; Institut Littéraire, for Eugenio Reale, *Raporty: Polska 1945–1946*; Kieleckie Towarzystwo Naukowe, for Stanisław Meducki and Zenon Wrona, eds., *Antyżydowskie wydarzenia kieleckie 4 lipca 1946 roku: dokumenty i materiały;* Northwestern University Press, for Emmanuel Ringelblum, *Polish-Jewish Relations during the Second World War*; St. Martin's Press, for Keith Sword, ed., *The Soviet Takeover of the Polish Eastern Provinces, 1939–1941; The New York Review of Books*, for various commentaries by Israel Shahak, Michael Ignatieff, and especially István Deák; (London) *Times Newspapers Limited*, for "The [1930] Report: A Minority in Poland — The Ukrainian Conflict"; University of California Press, for Jaff Schatz, *The Generation: The Rise and Fall of the Jewish Communists of Poland;* Wydawnictwo Interpress, for Jerzy Biernacki, "Silence over the Graves," in *Poland*; Wydawnictwo Karta for Baruch Milch, "Mój testament" and for Krzysztof Popiński, Aleksandr Kokurin, and Aleksandr Gurjanow, *Drogi śmierci*; Wydawnictwo Naukowe Uniwersytetu im. A. Mickiewicza, for Czesław Łuczak, *Polska i Polacy w drugiej wojnie światowej*; and Globetrotter Books for the two photographs by Andrew Slodkowski appearing on the cover. I would also like to thank the following authors: Franciszek J. Proch, *Poland's Way of the Cross, 1939–1945*; Władysław Siemaszko, the co-author of *Zbrodnie nacjonalistów ukraińskich dokonane na ludności polskiej na wołyniu 1939–1945*; Gabriele Simoncini, for his table, "National Minorities in Poland, 1995"; Stanisław Skrzypek, *The Problem of Galicia*; and Maria Wardzyńska, *Sytuacja ludności polskiej w Generalnym Komisariacie Litwy, czerwiec 1941–lipiec 1944.* To Eliza McClennen for her expert cartography and to Rose Grenon and Pat Charron for their help with the index, I am most grateful.

I would also like to mention my students in the "Sociology of the Holocaust" course that I presently teach. They are familiar with some of the themes of this work. The perpetually stunned — but far from disbelieving — look in their young faces tells me that I have a good story to tell. Their wet eyes full of compassion for the victims of the Nazi and Stalinist régimes tell me that the people whose mangled bodies they see on videotape have not died in vain. Their meditative answers to difficult, thought-provoking examination questions — questions that I myself could not answer — tell me that there is hope for the future. I wonder what impact, if any, the content of this course will have on the rest of their lives. Very few of them are Jewish.

Finally, I am eternally grateful to my wife, Terri, and my children — Renia, Ala, and Andrzej — for their patience and understanding. While I was preoccupied with and agonized over the past, they all had to suffer in the present.

Tadeusz Piotrowski
Manchester, 1997

Introduction

After 123 years of partitions by its imperialistic neighbors Russia, Germany (Prussia), and Austria, Poland finally regained its independence in 1918. In the years following World War I, two major problems confronted this young republic: the problem of its forever-straying borders, and the problem of its minorities. The resulting six wars fought concurrently by Poland between 1918 and 1921 taxed both its strength and its resources to the breaking point. The short-lived Polish-Ukrainian War was one of these, the Polish-Soviet War was another, and the Polish-Lithuanian dispute over Wilno was a third.[1]*

By 1921 all the wars were over, and after the Conference of Ambassadors decision regarding Eastern Galicia (see Appendix, Document 1, "Decision of the Conference of Ambassadors, March 15, 1923, on the Subject of the Frontiers of Poland"), a reborn Poland emerged on the maps of Europe.[2] It included some of the territories that had belonged to the first Polish Republic before all the partitions, and more: the province of Wilno, a large part of Belorussia, the western part of Wołyń (Volhynia), all of Eastern Galicia, the "Polish Corridor," a part of Upper Silesia, a sliver of East Prussia, and some contested territories along the Czechoslovak border.

These territorial acquisitions, along with the thousand-year history of conquest and migration that characterized Central and Eastern Europe, resulted in the presence of a substantial ethnic minority population within Polish borders as well as sizeable Polish minorities within the borders of all the neighboring nations: Germany, the Soviet republics of Ukraine and Belorussia, Lithuania, Czechoslovakia, and Latvia.[3]

According to the 1921 census, over 30 percent of all Polish citizens belonged to ethnic minorities. These included Ukrainians/Ruthenians (over 15 percent), Jews (8 percent), Belorussians (4 percent), Germans (3 percent), and small pockets of Lithuanians, Russians, Czechs, and Tatars and even smaller groups of Gypsies, Kashubians, and Karaites.[4] In many regions of Eastern Poland, these minorities, taken collectively, actually constituted a majority of Polish citizens.

Almost half a century before the landmark 1964 civil rights act in America, Poland not only had agreed to the League of Nations June 28, 1919, supplementary Treaty of Versailles on the treatment of minorities (see Appendix, Document 2, "Excerpts from the Minorities Treaty of June 28, 1919") but also had passed its own rather progressive constitution in 1921, in which it voluntarily incorporated many of these same civil rights (see Appendix, Document 3, "Excerpts from the Polish Constitution of 1921"). In post–World War I Poland, there was to be equality under the law for all Polish citizens in respect to their economic, political, cultural, and religious interests irrespective of race, national origin, or creed.

Initially, genuine efforts were made to implement that legislation, though not always with success. In spite of the best of legislative intentions, there was (often officially sanctioned) Polish prejudice toward and discrimination against the ethnic minorities, especially

*See Notes, beginning on page 293.

in the eastern provinces, in almost every category guaranteed by the constitution.

The recitation of this litany of civil-rights transgressions usually begins with the incontestable fact that the 1919 Treaty for the Protection of Minorities was unilaterally abrogated by Poland in 1934. Without a basis of historical context, this statement is often cited as "proof" of Poland's bad-faith attitude toward its minorities.

To begin with, this treaty itself, if not its content, was doomed from the very beginning, since the Poles regarded the Supreme Council's demand for its acceptance — in order to receive the formal recognition of the Polish state — both as an affront and as an infringement on their sovereign rights as a nation to manage their own internal affairs. It was, after all, a matter both of international principle and of national pride.

Second, although many countries had large minorities within their borders, not all were bound by this humanitarian treaty. The exceptions included Germany and the USSR, which, after their entry into the League of Nations, freely availed themselves of their right as member nations to supervise and criticize Poland's track record. Poland expressed its willingness to allow the League of Nations to continue to supervise its treatment of minorities, provided that this procedure was applied to other member countries as well — a fair request for equal treatment and one that would have immensely benefited the oppressed Polish minorities, among others, of Germany and the USSR. This point was brought home by Józef Beck in a statement delivered to the League of Nations on September 13, 1934 (see Appendix, Document 4, "Excerpt from a Statement of Józef Beck").

And finally, the Treaty for the Protection of Minorities, like other such treaties, not only accorded certain rights and privileges to the Polish ethnic groups but also imposed on them certain responsibilities and obligations: cooperation with the legitimately established government, loyalty to the nation that was to be their home, military service, national defense, and the obligation to obey the laws of the land and to preserve public order — civic duties that were often forgotten and, in the case of the radicals, always disregarded.

However, since Poland did not grant autonomy to Eastern Galicia and, furthermore, adopted a centralist rather than the federalist plan initially proposed by Józef Piłsudski[5] (to be sure, Poland had its share of radical nationalists), there may also have been other motives for Poland's abrogation of the treaty. This is borne out by the fact that in the 1930s, many of the policies of the Piłsudski régime were assimilationist. These policies, in turn, led to an escalation of the already existing conflicts between the nationalist leaders and their followers on the one hand and the Polish authorities on the other. Some of the nationalists — the Ukrainian Nationalists — resorted even to sabotage and terrorism. Unfortunately, when all else failed, the Polish government finally (in the early 1930s) attempted to address this public danger by launching a military "pacification action" against the Ukrainian Nationalists, during which action those in charge sometimes failed to distinguish between the innocent and the guilty. Still, far fewer people died in this ten-week pacification campaign in Eastern Galicia than, for example, in the Ukrainian Nationalists' relentless terrorist attacks on Polish citizens between 1921 and 1939.

Moreover, the Polish policies of colonization, agrarian reform, and land grants to Polish veterans of war in the eastern territories produced much bitterness among the land-hungry Belorussians and Ukrainians, who resented the settlers and felt that all of the land, most of which was previously owned by Polish landlords, should go to them. Repressive measures were carried out sporadically against the Eastern Orthodox Church. There was also an effort to Polonize the public school system by decreasing the number of ethnic schools and increasing the number of bilingual ones (attended by both Polish and non–Polish children). And finally, preference was given to ethnic Poles over Jews in the professions that were hitherto overrepresented by the latter, and proportionate quotas were imposed on Jewish university students. These restrictions were also applied to and affected both the Ukrainian and the Belorussian minorities.

Nevertheless, it is also fair to say that, in the words of Jan Tomasz Gross, "despite all of this and more, the material, spiritual and political life of all the national minorities in interwar Poland was richer and more complex than ever before or after."[6] The truth of this statement is borne out by the presence of numerous legal and even illegal political parties, as well as religious, educational, and sociocultural organizations in every major ethnic group. Moreover, the minorities had representation in the Polish parliament, and all of them had access to the "free" press, which, to be sure, from time to time also ran embarrassing blank patches in the pages of various newspapers.

In assessing the nature and extent of Polish interwar prejudice and discrimination, we must beware of judging the situation in Europe during those years by our own contemporary standards. Although the comparison to the contemporaneous plight of the minorities, including the Polish minorities, in the Soviet Union, Germany, or even Lithuania may be too extreme, what was the situation of the minorities in the United States in the 1920s and 1930s? When exactly did our minorities (specifically our Native Americans and African Americans, but others as well) finally achieve that full integration and equality promised by the United States Constitution? The United States, unlike Poland, embraced a prosperous nation of immigrants.

The point is that in spite of the best legislative intentions, these matters take a long time to sort out in any pluralistic society; the new Republic of Poland — ravaged as it was by World War I, a series of continuing wars, and economic depression — was no exception. The cycle is a familiar one. Previous modes of accommodation break down, giving rise to social unrest and upheaval. Then, new forms of accommodation replace the old, only to eventually produce similar results, and so on and so forth until full assimilation, integration, or independence is finally achieved.

In Poland, the root of the problem lay not in the Polish Constitution but in its application and in the understandable impatience of the minorities who wanted justice from the newly established Republic and wanted it *now*. Some nationalist leaders, many of whom were of college age, wanted much more than that. They wanted national independence and the reunification of "their" ethnic territories. Theodore Herzl's words, mutatis mutandis, echo the political aspirations of all the nationalists in interwar Poland: "I do not consider the Jewish question to be a social or religious [one].... It is a national problem. We are a nation."[7] To Poland, the home of ethnic and religious minorities for centuries, the prospect of housing national minorities (i.e., Polish citizens who did not regard themselves as Poles by nationality) constituted a grave danger to its very survival. The political objectives of all radical nationalists were, after all, separatist.

The Ukrainian Nationalists wanted a unified and independent Ukraine, or at least an independent "Western Ukraine." Their ultimate ambitions are best illustrated in both the old and the new maps of "Greater Ukraine," whose boundaries overreach even those of the present-day vast Ukrainian Republic and meander into the Polish heartland, Belarus, Rumania, Czechoslovakia, and the Russian Federation. (The Ukrainian nation had a chance to achieve its independence with the help of the Polish armed forces in 1920 in exchange for Poland's rights over territories that had belonged to it before the partitions. By not supporting the Piłsudski-Petliura alliance, the Ukrainians chose slavery — and paid a heavier price in the blood of millions during the Stalinist purges of the 1930s.)

The Belarusian nationalists also wanted their country reunited, but they dreaded the prospect of being forced to live under the Soviet yoke. Their formula was the same: reunion and independence.

The Lithuanian nationalists wanted the predominantly Polish city of Wilno, the historic capital of the Grand Duchy of Lithuania, "returned" to the Lithuanian Republic.

The German nationalists wanted to continue living in their prewar domiciles, now on Polish soil — but how they wished those domiciles were back in their good old *Vaterland*, where they belonged!

The Jewish nationalists and the Zionists looked to Palestine and meanwhile wanted to be regarded as a national minority in Poland, a nation within a nation. And that segment of the younger generation of politically active Jews who were neither Bundists, nor noncommunist Zionists (as opposed to the Zionists who were "covertly or overtly" pro–Communist[8]), nor assimilationists, nor Agudat Israel[9] in orientation, not having any territorial claims of their own, wanted all the rights and privileges promised by the Communist ideology, which they embraced wholeheartedly. In Eastern Poland, they would have preferred the Soviet to the Polish rule.

As long as Poland remained strong, ethnic conflicts — if not ethnic tensions — were effectively kept in check. Once Poland was weakened by the events of the war, all the safeguards of this fragile and unfinished democracy failed, and the most radical elements of the "oppressed minorities" took advantage of this moment of weakness to settle old scores with the Polish ruling class as well as the underclass and to implement their own political agendas. As the Polish-Jewish intellectual Aleksander Smolar noted: "When the war broke out in 1939, Poles faced two enemies at once: Germany and the Soviet Union. That, however, was not the way certain ethnic minorities saw it. For almost all ethnic Germans and Lithuanians who were Polish citizens, as well as for many Byelorussians, Ukrainians, and Jews, the dual onslaught was an occasion for celebration."[10]

It was the radical members of these minorities who, rather than supporting Poland in its hour of need, chose to side with the enemy and vied with one another in their support of the Soviet Union and Nazi Germany, hoping thereby to achieve their objectives at Poland's expense. One group, the Ukrainian Nationalists, did much more than that: beginning in the fall of 1942, they engaged in a campaign of ethnic cleansing. Meanwhile, both the Soviet Union and Germany attempted to achieve their own military and territorial objectives by taking advantage of and contributing to the ethnic tensions within Poland.

And so, Marshal Piłsudski's worst fears became a reality. "I would not want for anything in the world," he said after the Polish-Ukrainian War, "that Poland would possess spacious territories inhabited by ill-disposed people. History has demonstrated that in the long run such heterogeneous mixture of populations is dangerous."[11] During World War II, it was murderous.

After the first two chapters, which deal in a summary fashion with the Soviet and Nazi reigns of terror in occupied Poland, this work presents a detailed account of just how all these ethnic tensions played themselves out during that terrible war in Eastern Poland. The vast majority of the perpetrators, collaborators, and accomplices of World War II are no longer alive, but the nations they represent live on, and the children of these nations will eventually have to come to terms with the "sins of their fathers."

Chapter 1
Soviet Terror

In a Kremlin speech given on August 19, 1939, a speech that remained top secret until its publication in the German daily *Die Welt* (on July 23, 1996), Stalin told the innermost circle of the Political Bureau of the Central Committee of the Communist Party, which included Vyacheslav Molotov, Lavrenti Beria, Kliment Voroshilov, Lazar Kaganovich, and Georgi Malenkov:

> After we sign the pact with Hitler, Germany will finally attack Poland. Then, England's and France's entrance into the war will be inevitable. A time of unrest and disorder will visit the West and in these circumstances we will be able to enter the war when it is most advantageous to us. The first benefit from signing the pact will be the destruction of Poland and the movement of our borders up to Warsaw....
>
> If we agree to the proposition of England and France, whose delegations are now in Moscow, and sign a friendship pact with them, Hitler may resign from attacking Poland. Then, the war will not break out and Germany will try to seek some kind of an agreement with the West.
>
> Meanwhile, the war is necessary and indispensable to the Soviet Union, since in time of peace Bolshevism is in no position to conquer the western nations. Moreover, peace could constitute a grave danger to the existence of the Soviet Union.
>
> Germany will give us a free hand in the Baltic states and will agree to the annexation of Bessarabia by the USSR. It will also grant us full control over Bulgaria, Rumania and Hungary. The question of Yugoslavia and the remaining states will remain open for now.
>
> What will happen next? Every result of the war will be beneficial to Moscow. In the event of Hitler's defeat, Germany will be Sovietized. But it is in the interest of the USSR that the war lasts as long as possible, otherwise England and France will still have sufficient power to destroy communist Germany. We must, therefore, intensify communist agitation, chiefly in France, in order to demoralize the army and the police. At the same time, we must prepare all communist forces in Western Europe for the protraction of the war.
>
> The possibility exists that Hitler might be victorious. In that case, he will have to control the territories which he will occupy. Then, under the direction of the communists in those countries we will organize a war of national liberation against Hitler.

An order was then issued by the communist leadership for a secret, total mobilization of the USSR. Thus, Stalin's masterplan, like Hitler's, involved the total conquest of Europe. For both leaders, the defeat of Poland was an essential stepping-stone to that grand ambition.

Time will tell whether the above-mentioned document, paid for so dearly by *Die Welt* in western currency, is a genuine commentary on Russia's sordid past or a forgery. In any case, four days later, on August 23, 1939, the Soviet Union and Germany signed a Non-Aggression Pact. In September of that year these two powerful allies invaded and partitioned Poland: Germany from the west; the Soviet Union from the east. Thus began World War II.

At that time, Poland's territory was divided into sixteen provinces (*województwa*—voivodships) which were generally clustered into four groups: western, central, eastern, and southern.

Poland under German and Soviet occupation, 1939–1941

This represented 389,713 square kilometers of land with over 35 million people,[1] a third of whom were ethnic minorities.[2]

Germany formally annexed all of the western provinces (91,902 square kilometers with over 10 million people) as lands belonging to the "New Reich"[3] and, from a part of the more extensive central and southern provinces (95,742 square kilometers with about 12 million people), formed the so-called General Government (Generalgouvernement, or GG). Along the Polish-Slovak line, a few tiny territorial divisions (gminy) that had been annexed by Poland in 1938–39 were then returned to Slovakia with additional Polish territory,[4] perhaps as a concession to the three Slovak divisions, the Swift Group (German: Schnelle Division; Slovak: Rýchla Divizia), and the small air force that fought with Nazi Germany against Poland.[5]

In all, eight provinces, or 187,644 square kilometers (i.e., over 48 percent of Polish territory) containing some 22 million people, fell to Germany.[6] Apart from some 2 million Jews, 1 million Germans, one-half million Ukrainians, and a scattering of other minority groups, the population of these territories was ethnically Polish.

Although the German High Command (in keeping with the secret protocol, signed that

August, for the partition of Poland) wanted the Red Army to synchronize its attack on Poland with that of the Wehrmacht (on September 1), Stalin chose to wait. When, on September 3, Joachim von Ribbentrop inquired about the Soviet plans, Molotov put him off with words like "excessive haste" and assured him that eventually it would be "absolutely necessary for us [the Soviet Union] to start concrete action" at a "suitable time."[7] In all probability, according to the hints from Moscow, Stalin wanted to wait until the fall of Warsaw before joining in the fray. That he attacked Poland when the German campaign was only half complete, that is, when 40–50 percent of the country was still under Polish control, was due to a number of factors: the rapidly deteriorating Polish resistance; the threat of the German army entering that portion of Poland that was to go to the Soviets; the attempt (thwarted by the Germans) to regroup the Polish army in the southeastern regions of Poland near the Rumanian border and continue fighting from there (in mid–September, the Polish High Command was located in Kołomyja); the end of the Soviet campaign against Japan in Mongolia (the Khalkhin-Gol armistice was signed on September 15, hostilities ended on the sixteenth, and to the astonishment of the Japanese, Soviet tanks immediately sped away from the field of battle in a northwestward direction); and finally, the false September 16 communiqué from Berlin stating that Warsaw was already in German hands.[8] (Warsaw did not capitulate until September 27–28, and organized resistance continued until October 6, 1939.)

On September 17, 1939, when virtually all Polish troops were locked in mortal combat with the Germans, the Soviet Union — in a military campaign that lasted fifteen days and in violation of international law and its own pacts and agreements[9] — assumed the "noble role of the hyena to the German lion"[10] and occupied all the eastern provinces of Poland (Wilno, Nowogródek, Polesie, Wołyń), three of its four southern provinces (Lwów, Stanisławów, Tarnopol — provinces known also as Eastern Galicia), and the central province of Białystok.[11] That October, in an outwardly magnanimous but truly perfidious gesture such as only the Soviet mind (with one exception) was capable of engineering, the predominantly Polish city of Wilno and the surrounding borderland areas (Wileńszczyzna, Okręg Wileński) were given to the still independent Republic of Lithuania.

These eight provinces that fell to the Soviet Union were incorporated into the Belorussian and Ukrainian Soviet Socialist Republics on the basis of a carefully engineered "referendum" not worth mentioning[12] and represented 202,069 square kilometers (i.e., almost 52 percent) of Polish soil with over 13 million people.[13] Of this total, about 5 million were ethnic Poles. But there were also about 5 million Ukrainians, about 2 million Belorussians, over 1 million Jews, and somewhat fewer Lithuanians, Russians, Czechs, and Germans.[14] In official Soviet terminology, these territories were now called "Western Ukraine" and "Western Belorussia."

Ever mindful of their grand territorial ambitions, the Soviets knew that there was much to be done between September 17, 1939, and the still unknown date of June 22, 1941— and they were more than prepared for the task that lay ahead. "In many ways," states Norman Davies, "the work of the Soviet NKVD in Eastern Poland proved far more destructive than that of the Gestapo at this stage."[15]

The Soviets, after all, were much more experienced in political terror and murder than their allies. Between 1929 and 1934, during Stalin's unrelenting war against the mythical Kulaks (*kulak*: literally "fist," hence "tightwad" — a class term invented by Lenin) and other "class enemies," 20 million farms were collectivized and 15 million people died — half of them in Siberia, to which they had been deported. In 1932–33 alone, the years of the artificially induced famine, some 4.5 million people starved to death within Ukraine and 3 million outside its borders.[16]

Moreover, the "Great Terror" of 1936–38 struck both at the Ukrainian leadership and at the peasantry and produced mass graves at Vinnitsa; the great purges honed the killer instincts of the Soviet apparatus for the Polish campaign. But who remembers today that the 1.2 million Poles living in the Soviet Union during the interwar years were the first major ethnic group to undergo repression, in 1935–38, by virtue of national rather than class background?[17] In a real sense, September 17, 1939, was simply a continuation of the Soviet policies of the 1930s against the Poles. The ultimate objective of these policies in Eastern Poland was the elimination of all traces of that country's thousand-year history and culture in the borderlands. These policies, in turn, resulted in crimes against peace, crimes against humanity, and war crimes — the three categories of international crimes as defined by the Charter of the International Military Tribunal on August 8, 1945, and used as the basis for judgment by the Nuremberg Tribunal of September 30, 1946.[18]

In "Western Ukraine" and "Western Belorussia," the Polish language was replaced by the Ukrainian and Belorussian languages in official usage. The educational system became a monstrous tool for Soviet indoctrination and included the compulsory study of the Russian language and "history." Polish monuments were razed, streets renamed, bookshops and publishing houses closed, libraries destroyed, books burned.[19] Absolute control and censorship was exercised over all Polish literary productions and the Polish press, which became nothing more than a vehicle for Soviet propaganda. Although religious worship as such was not forbidden, bans were imposed on religious education and the ringing of church bells. Punitive taxation forced thousands of churches, monasteries, and convents to close their doors. Wayside chapels, shrines, and crosses were leveled. "Pray to God," schoolchildren were told, and nothing happened. "Now pray to Father Stalin," and lo, candy fell from heaven, or rather from a hole drilled in the ceiling. The Polish children remember those Godless days very well:

> **Białystok province:** Their [the Russians'] first act was to hang their flag on the president's palace and paint over the bronze statue of Marshal Piłsudski in red.... The "Soviets" behaved seemingly decently, but the jails were becoming full.[20]

> **Lwów province:** The next days the walls of buildings and houses were colored with different posters. But they all had the same substance. "The rule of the Polish masters has ended, the Red Army has liberated Poland." One poster particularly struck me because it hurt me, a Polish eagle was shown wearing a four-cornered Polish soldier's cap all stained with blood and a Soviet soldier stood over it sticking it with a bayonet.
>
> The next day I went to school, I found out that lessons would begin soon. But there was a lot of commotion in the school, soldiers were in the corridors tearing Polish eagles and portraits off the walls.
>
> There was a statue of Marshal Piłsudski in the office, one of the soldiers knocked it down and kicked it and naturally it shattered. And other soldiers were carrying books from the school library and throwing them in a car standing outside the gate like garbage when they were very valuable books. As I found out later from friends the books were burned outside town.[21]

> **Białystok province:** It was a day memorable to all, February 10, 1940.... They had to look through each one of about a thousand Polish books, and then they burnt them.[22]

> **Tarnopol province:** They organized a school system. I started going to school. But what kind of a school could it be without religion and later without the Polish language. Teachers we didn't know continually tried to convince us that Polish teachers taught us badly, that the history they taught us was false and that there is no God and they took down the crosses and in their place hung portraits of Bolshevik leaders. They organized meetings where they forced us to belong to Bolshevik youth associations.[23]

> **Białystok province:** In school they were breaking all the portraits, broke down crosses, arrested teachers for being Polish, and sent their own. Those taught to sing songs against God and against Poland and other unheard-of things.[24]

> **Wołyń province, Sarny county:** They closed the churches.... They removed the pictures and crosses in the school because they began teaching in the Russian language now and against God because later it was forbidden to pray even in silence.... You couldn't find a Polish library, they eliminated the monuments and hard times began.[25]

> **Wołyń province, Równe county:** We saw tearing of the national emblem off the walls, destruction of the library which contained about 200 volumes.[26]

> **Wołyń province, Łuck:** They destroyed most of the library, both the gymnasium and the town library, where we borrowed books, they turned their particular "attention" to books dealing with achievements in the field of labor in the last twenty years and history and science books. Instead brochures appeared dealing with the Soviet system and pseudo-Polish newspapers. The study of the Soviet constitution was introduced and Russian and Ukrainian as compulsory subjects. The teachers were ordered to call us "citizens" and "comrades" or to address us (in Polish!) by given name and patronymic [i.e., after the Russian fashion]. They tried to inculcate atheistic doctrines and forced us to go to school on holidays, but we got out of that everybody sticking together and on religious holidays the school was empty.[27]

> **Wołyń province, Horochów county:** In all the schools they broke the crosses smashed the portraits founded clubs closed churches, they said you shouldn't pray because there is no god, for us stalin is God.[28]

Additionally, the Polish economy in the eastern territories was immediately shattered by the ruse of replacing the zloty with the ruble and equating their value. Then, all businesses were mandated to remain open and sell their goods at prewar prices. Since there was no rationing, the destitute "liberators" who had come to save the "downtrodden masses" first bought up all that their few worthless rubles would allow: "The town [Lwów] swarmed with them, the stores were full of them, they bought everything there was. I saw an officer who bought a big armload of shoe leather and he was happy as a child, saying he would send it right away to his wife in Russia."[29] They then proceeded to steal the rest.[30]

Polish observers described these and other such Soviet policies as "looting," "plunder," and "robbery."[31] *Pravda* reports what happened next — the result of the nationalization decrees of October 1939:

> In order to thoroughly destroy the exploiters, to put an end once and for all to the exploitation of one human being by another, the People's Assembly of the Ukraine, expressing the unanimous will of the people of Western Ukraine and following the example of the Soviet Russia, announces the nationalisation of banks and great industrial concerns in the Western Ukraine.
>
> From now on the deposits of all banks, all great factories, mines and railways will be considered as the property of the people, that is, as state property.[32]

Thus, the confiscation of all Polish private and state property began within a month of the Soviet invasion. Landed property was redistributed to the Ukrainian and Belorussian peasants and then collectivized from under them.[33] Durable goods either went to the support of the Red Army or were shipped off to the Soviet Union. These included entire factory complexes, government establishments, hospitals, and even schools. All were nationalized, dismantled piece by piece, loaded on freight trains, and never seen again.[34] The material losses sustained by the Polish population in Eastern Poland under the Soviet occupation were valued at 2,176 million zloty.[35]

In keeping with the terms of the German-Soviet Boundary and Friendship Treaty, the Soviets helped to break the British blockade of Germany, provided Hitler with navy bases in the USSR, allowed for the passage of raw materials from other nations over Soviet territory, and supplied their ally, Nazi Germany, with plundered Polish goods such as food commodities, cattle, and oil. As a result of the February 10, 1940, German-Soviet pact, the Soviet Union agreed to provide Germany, in twelve months' time, with 800 million reichsmarks' worth of raw materials and food, specifically, 1 million tons of grain, 900,000 tons of oil derivatives, 100,000 tons of cotton, 500,000 tons of phosphates, 100,000 tons of chromium ore, 500,000 tons of iron ore, 300,000 tons of pig iron, 2,400 kilograms of platinum, and many other raw materials.[36]

German military records indicate that until June 1941, the Soviet Union provided the Wehrmacht with English zinc and rubber, 1 million tons of grain, 500,000 tons of wheat, 900,000 tons of oil derivatives, 100,000 tons of flax, 80 million reichsmarks' worth of lumber, and an unspecified amount of manganese and platinum.[37] Each month, for the duration of the Soviet-German alliance, 200–300 Soviet trains carried these goods into the heart of Nazi Germany.[38] How many of these commodities were extorted from the residents of Eastern Poland is unknown.

In addition to all of this, exorbitant taxes were imposed on everyone, as well as fines, corvées (work service, e.g., cutting wood and building roads), and mandated "gifts to the Red Army." The nature of these taxes, corvées, fines, and "gifts" was determined by the various village committees that ran the local governments and from which the Polish people were by and large excluded. Needless to say, this brutal expropriation created severe shortages and long, overnight queues.[39]

Two examples of these practices will suffice. A chemist in Ostróg (Wołyń province) received a tax assessment of 5,600 rubles on a business that was worth only 5,000 rubles. After his shop was confiscated for nonpayment, he was forced to make up the difference of 600 rubles, which the Soviet state claimed it had "lost" in the exchange.[40] Another man, who lived thirteen kilometers from Stołpce (Nowogródek province), was fined twenty zloty. He was then spitefully ordered to pay his fine at the rate of two *grosze* per day, in Stołpce.[41] Meanwhile, entire Polish households were evicted to make room for Soviet soldiers and Soviet families.[42]

As a result of these and similar practices, as well as fear, hundreds of thousands of Polish citizens in the eastern territories were eventually forced to abandon their homes and villages and become refugees, like the homeless refugees streaming in from the interior of Poland. Eventually, this lot was shared by all the ethnic groups residing in the eastern territories of Poland. Corps Commissar S. Kozhevnikov summarized the imaginary consequences of this "sociocultural revolution" after only one year of Soviet occupation:

> The workers of the Western Ukraine and Western Byelorussia, thanks to the fraternal assistance of the Soviet people and its Red Army, were forever liberated from the class and national oppression of the Polish bourgeois. They acquired a homeland for themselves — the land of happiness — the Soviet Union. In the course of the last year the popular masses of the new Soviet regions have made enormous progress under the leadership of the Bolshevik Party and the great Stalin. With each passing day the economy develops, factories grow, dozens — nay hundreds — of schools, libraries, hospitals and cinemas are opened. The cultural life improves, unemployment has been abolished, hundreds of collective farms have appeared, and dozens of machine-tractor stations have appeared. Warmed by the sunrays of Stalin's constitution, people are joyfully building a new life.[43]

The only iota of truth in all of this was the successful establishment of the much-hated collectives and the Machine-Tractor Stations (MTS) which controlled them in the "land of happiness."[44] But the very opposite of these lunatic ramblings was not the worst of it. In September, even before the start of the Nazi atrocities that would horrify the world, the Soviets began their own program of systematic individual and mass executions, especially of Polish officers and policemen. A miller from Tuczyn (the district town where my family milled our grain, Tuczyn was eight kilometers to the south of our village, Ryświanka, in Wołyń) describes one such event in Równe: "I saw with my own eyes how Soviet soldiers caught a Polish colonel in the street, took out his revolver from the holster, shot him with his own revolver, and then left his body lying in the street and went away."[45] On the outskirts of Lwów, several hundred policemen were executed at one time. Near Łuniniec, officers and noncommissioned officers of the Frontier Defense Corps (Korpus Ochrony Pogranicza, or KOP), together with some policemen, were ordered into barns, then were taken out and shot.[46] Sometime in or after December 1939, three hundred Polish priests were killed.[47] And there were many other such incidents. And there are many other such eyewitness accounts of crimes perpetrated by the Soviet régime against the Polish people.

Moreover, during the Soviet occupation, between 1.2 and 1.7 million Polish citizens (resident civilians, refugees from western and central Poland, civilian prisoners, Red Army recruits, and prisoners of war) were deported to the Soviet Union where many of them died.[48] They went to the northern and central regions of the Soviet Union — the area between the Arctic Circle in the North and the Mongolian border in the south. They went to the regions of Archangel: Vołogda, Irkutsk, Sverdlovsk, Kirov, Novosibirsk, Komi. They went to northern Kazakhstan between the Urals and the Altai Mountains: Aktiubinsk, Kustanay, Petropavlosk, Karaganda, Pavlodar and Semipalatynsk.

Except for the sheer volume, such deportations were nothing new to the Poles. Similar removals occurred in 1832, 1864, and 1906, and would reoccur in 1944 and in the postwar period. Jan Plater-Gajewski's family history was shared by many Poles: his great-grandfather spent seven years, his grandfather eleven, his father five, and he himself seventeen years in that Soviet frozen wasteland of bodies and of minds.[49] According to one estimate of Polish authorities, the 1940–41 deportations involved over 1.2 million people. Of these,

> 880,000 were forcibly sent to Russia during the four waves of deportations in February, April, and June of 1940 and in June of 1941; about 150,000 Polish citizens were mobilized into the Red Army; 180,000 were taken into the USSR as prisoners of war; and about 20,000 went there to work. About half of the deportees (440,000) ended up in labor camps and prisons. The other half were dumped into settlements (*posëlki*) all over the Soviet Union. About one-quarter, some 220,000 to 250,000, were children fourteen years of age or younger.[50]

Polish citizens who were deported to the Soviet Union fell into one of the following five categories:

> A. Prisoners of war of all ranks, including those who fell into Soviet hands in the autumn of 1939 as well as those who initially were interned in Lithuania and Latvia, and excluding those who were either allowed to go home or were handed over to the Germans, estimated at 46,000. The total number of POWs remaining in the Soviet hands is estimated at 196,000, or approximately 12 per cent of the total number of Polish citizens deported to the USSR — estimated at 1,646,000.
>
> B. Civilian prisoners, mainly male but some female, who were considered by the Soviet authorities guilty (from the point of view of the Soviet law). These were arrested, imprisoned, submitted to lengthy and severe investigation and sentenced to death or a number of years in corrective labour camps. Their total number is estimated at 250,000 or some 15 per cent of the total number of Polish citizens taken to the USSR.
>
> C. Men, women and children (often whole families) regarded by the Soviet authorities not as guilty, but as suspect, and therefore deported to distant parts of the USSR by an administrative decree, i.e. without the usual legal procedure based normally on arresting, charging and sentencing. This was by far the largest group, estimated at 990,000, or 60 per cent of all Polish citizens deported to the USSR.
>
> D. Young men born in 1918, 1919 and some in 1920 who were called-up into the Red Army or alternatively were sent to work in Soviet industry. Their estimated numbers are 210,000, i.e. 13 per cent of all the Polish deportees.
>
> E. Those who found themselves in the USSR as "free people." Among these there were some voluntary industrial workers, a small group of doctors who volunteered to work in the USSR, several groups of musicians and entertainers, one or two youth summer camps evacuated in front of the advancing German Army, communists and sympathisers who chose not to fall into German hands. Numerically these groups were small and they constituted a negligible percentage of the total number of Polish citizens taken to the USSR at this time.[51]

Ethnic Poles constituted the majority of those deported, but no social category or ethnic group was spared. Zbigniew S. Siemaszko provides a comprehensive breakdown of the deportees (see tables 1 and 2).[52]

TABLE 1. INHABITANTS OF THE SOVIET-OCCUPIED PROVINCES BY MOTHER TONGUE, 1939–1941

Mother Tongue	*Inhabitants in the Soviet occupation zone (incl. Wilno) in thousands*		*Inhabitants and refugees taken to the USSR in 1939–41 (excluding prisoners of war) in thousands (no.) & percentages (%)*					
			Inhabitants		*Refugees*		*Inhabitants & Refugees*	
	no.	%	no.	%	no.	%	no.	%
Polish	5274	39.9	703	63.1	138	41	841	58.0
Yiddish & Hebrew	1109	8.4	83	7.4	198	59	281	19.4
Ukrainian & Ruthenian	4529	34.4	217	19.5	—	—	217	14.9
Belorussian & "local"	1945	14.7	91	8.2	—	—	91	6.3
Russian, Czech, Lithuanian, German & others	342	2.6	20	1.8	—	—	20	1.4
TOTAL	13,199	100	1114	100	336	100	1450	100

TABLE 2. NUMBER OF PEOPLE DEPORTED TO THE USSR, 1939–1941 (BY MOTHER TONGUE, PER THOUSAND)

Mother Tongue	*Taken to USSR (per thousand inhabitants)*
Polish	133
Yiddish and Hebrew	78
Russian, Czech	58
Lith., German, other	48
Belorussian & "local"	47
AVERAGE	84

The social categories of those deported included workers, artisans, peasants, foresters, soldiers, judges, the clergy, professors, scientists, attorneys, engineers, and teachers. But anyone listed in the index of "anti–Soviet elements" could have been deported, and many were (see Appendix, Document 5, "Excerpts from NKVD Instructions Relating to 'Anti–Soviet Elements'"). In spite of the Soviet directives for a well-orchestrated mass exodus (see Appendix, Document 6, "Basic Instructions on Deportations"), the deportation process itself left much to be desired:

> The population of Soviet-occupied Poland was unprepared for the cruelty that characterized the deportations. People were usually awakened in the early morning hours by squads of soldiers and local militiamen, given little time to pack, and quickly driven to the nearest railway station. There, freight trains awaited them. They froze in unheated cattle cars in February and suffocated in the June heat four months later. They were locked in for weeks with only meager rations of food and water, with a hole in the car's floor for all facilities. Men, women, and children of all ages were mixed together. Because even the sick and aged, as well as newborn infants, were put on the trains — there were no exemptions from the deportation order — many died, and the corpses traveled with the living before being discarded at some railway stop.[53]

For the survivors, it is a familiar story. A Canadian-born author details this tragic episode in the life of her own family:

February 10, 1940, 4:00 a.m. Exile. A pounding on the door with rifle butts and shouts of "Open up" in Russian. Because her husband couldn't walk without crutches, Helena went to open the door. Two Russian soldiers with rifles entered, towering over her. "We're going to search your house," they said in Russian....

Then the soldiers said, "Get your things ready because we're taking you far away. Be ready in twenty minutes...."

Now began the first of many dislocations. First the family was taken to the school. Children and the sick rode on the sleighs, while the fit walked in the frigid winter morning air. The colony stretched out for about two miles. By noon everyone from the colony was assembled. People were hungry. Children were crying. Helena's daughter also began to fuss and cry. It was so crowded nobody could move.

In the afternoon the people were herded back onto the sleighs and driven thirty kilometres to the railway station at Parchacz. Luckily Helena had brought some warm comforters. Those people who didn't have quilts had to endure the -30°C temperatures and a biting wind....

Boxcars were waiting at the train station.... There were forty people to a boxcar.... The train must have been a mile long. It was so cold that sounds were distorted....

The train started to move slowly. Everyone was in a state of shock....

The unforgettable journey lasted some twenty-nine days....

At the large train stations along the way, some cars were unhitched, while others were added. When one car hit the next, it felt like the end of the world. It was bitterly cold and snowing when the train reached Moscow....

They passed through the Ural Mountains until finally, days later, seven hundred people were unloaded like cattle in the city of Sośwa, 280 kilometres north of Sverdlovsk.... Countless criminals and political exiles had disappeared without a trace in the vast, frozen, isolated northland. Now it was their turn.[54]

According to a "top secret" Soviet document released to Polish authorities by Boris Yeltsin on October 15, 1992, among the deportees who died in the Soviet Union were most of the 14,700 Polish officers and prisoners of war, as well as 11,000 Polish civilians and prewar state functionaries (almost all of them ethnic Poles) imprisoned in Soviet-occupied Eastern Poland. They were executed on Stalin's orders in April and May 1940 in places like the Katyn forest (those from Kozielsk camp), the inner prison of the People's Commissariat for Internal Affairs (Narodnyi Komissariat Vnutrennikh Del, or NKVD) in Kharkov (those from Starobielsk, buried in Pyatikhatki), and the basement of the NKVD building in Kalinin (those from Ostashkov, buried near Mednoye) (see Appendix, Document 7, "Katyn Document").[55] These statistics do not include the thousands of Polish servicemen who resisted the Soviet takeover and were executed on the spot.

In the first days of the Soviet invasion, some local Polish commanders were confused by the advancing Soviet troops' propaganda that they had crossed the border in order to fight the Germans. None of their terms of surrender were honored by the Soviets. In Lwów, for example, Polish units that had successfully defended the city against the Wehrmacht for ten days surrendered to the Red Army under the condition that they would be allowed to evacuate to Rumania. Instead, the Soviets released the privates and shipped off the officers to the camp in Starobielsk.

After the mid–June 1940 Soviet annexation of Estonia, Latvia, and Lithuania, still other Polish soldiers (about 6,000 interned in the last two countries, including some 800 officers, as well as those who had escaped from Latvian and Lithuanian internment camps, made their way to Estonia and awaited transport to other European countries) were apprehended and deported to the Soviet POW camps in Kozielsk, Pavlishchev Bor, and Griazovets. Fortunately, most of them survived.[56]

Many Polish citizens also died in numerous Soviet prisons, concentration camps, and forced-labor camps established both on occupied Polish territory and in the Soviet Union. Generally speaking, until mid–June 1941 (the beginning of the fourth major deportation) only prisoners of the NKVD wound up in these institutions. These prisoners included the intelligentsia, members of the Polish army and police, businessmen, critics of the Soviet Union, Polish, Ukrainian, Belorussian, and Zionist activists, those who belonged to the underground, those who crossed any Soviet border in any direction, former members of the Communist Party, registered prostitutes, and those denounced by anyone for whatever reason.[57] As Aleksandr Solzhenitsyn put it, "*The heart of the matter is not personal guilt, but social danger.* One can imprison an innocent man if he is socially hostile. And one can release a guilty man if he is socially friendly."[58] The Soviet Penal Code noted, "Departure from or entry to the Union of SSR without either the prescribed passport or permission of the respective authorities is punishable by detention in a camp for a term of from one to three years."[59] Regarding denunciations, one writer noted:

> People acquired great power. Everyone could destroy everyone else. All he needed to do was go to the authorities and make a deposition. The man whom he accused was as a rule done for. In the past bearing false witness was punishable and ineffectual. One had to be careful not to harm oneself with hasty accusations. Now the matter was simpler: a few accusations and your enemy is lost.[60]

The prisoners included not only the residents of Poland but also the Polish citizens who for one reason or another wound up in the USSR or Soviet-occupied Lithuania and the Baltic states. In the USSR, the prisoners were often those who went voluntarily to work in the Soviet Union, those who refused Soviet passports, those who wound up in any of the Soviet camps, those who were mobilized to serve in the Red Army, those who received "amnesty" (on August 12, 1941) for crimes never committed, and even those who served as the official representatives of the Polish Embassy.[61]

At the beginning of 1941, there were 712 prisons in the Soviet Union, including the occupied Polish territories. Although their capacity was 238,000 persons, they held 481,572.[62] In the Wilno area alone, the NKVD arrested between 31,000 and 35,000 Poles.[63]

There were also many POW camps in the Soviet Union. One hundred of them (out of a total of 150) were located in Eastern Poland. In June 1941, they held 30,000 to 40,000 Polish soldiers and NCOs, 14,135 of whom (according to NKVD reports) were kept for forced labor in the Polish occupied territories.[64]

The tragic story of the Polish soldiers streaming eastward, whether escapees from Nazi POW camps or veterans of recently lost battles, still begs the telling.[65] After September 17, 1939, those captured by the Red Army (which purportedly entered Poland as an ally), those caught by the NKVD, and those denounced by the local Ukrainian and Jewish collaborators were taken near Równe — where later a sea of Soviet POWs would themselves be interned, without food or water, by the Germans. There, the officers were separated from the rest and, together with many noncommissioned officers and privates, shipped off to the Soviet Union. (As we have seen, during the liquidation of the Soviet POW camps in the spring of 1940, many of them were subsequently executed.)

Those not deported were shipped by train to transit camps such as the ones in Szepietówka and Nowogród Wołyński and from there marched to one or another forced-labor camp in Eastern Poland. In exchange for their work, they were promised freedom on December 15, 1939. When that day arrived, however, only the Volksdeutsche (Polish citizens of German ancestry, or German nationals) were released.

The interned soldiers worked in groups of twenty to eighty men in heat and cold with only aspirin and thermometers for their medical needs. They constructed airports, built roads, worked in quarries, erected bridges, hewed timber, worked as carpenters, and in winter, shoveled tons of snow. Life in these work camps scarcely differed from that in the Gulag. The staff in charge of the labor brigades was always Russian or Jewish. Their subordinates were Ukrainians, Jews, and a few Poles. Discipline was severe, the threat of deportation constant.

The liquidation of Soviet prisons and forced-labor camps in Eastern Poland began with the German invasion of the Soviet Union. From information available thus far, we know that 2,200 Polish POWs died during this time. Those who lived to march were driven headlong without food or water. (Some bread was distributed once a day; they drank from the pud-

TABLE 3. NUMBER OF PRISONERS AND POWS KILLED IN THE SUMMER OF 1941 IN SOVIET-OCCUPIED POLAND

	Prisoners	*POWs*
Province of Lwów		
Lwów	about 4,000	1,834
Borysław	dozens	
Bóbrka	9–16	
Czerlany		180
Drohobycz	dozens–1,000	
Gródek Jagielloński	3	
Jaworów	32	
Oleszyce	?	
Przemyśl and Dobromil	500–1,000	
Rudki and Komarno	200	
Sambor	616–720	
Sądowa Wisznia	about 70	
Skniłów		200
Szczerzec	about 30	
Żółkiew	30–60	
Province of Stanisławów		
Stanisławów	1,500–2,500	
Horodenka	?	
Kałusz	?	
Kołomyja	?	
Mikołajów by Dniestr	?	
Nadwórna	about 80	
Ottynia	300	
Pasieczna	?	
Stryj	100–few hundred	
Żydaczów	?	
Province of Tarnopol		
Tarnopol	hundreds–1,000	
Brzeżany	over 220	
Busk	about 40	
Czortków	?	
Kamionka Strumiłowa	about 20	
Łopatyn	12	
Przemyślany	?	
Zaleszczyki	?	
Złoczów	650–752	
Province of Wołyń		
Łuck	1,500–4,000	
Dubno	500–550	
Krzemieniec	100–1,500	
Równe	150–500	
Sarny	70–100	
Włodzimierz Wołyński	?	
Zborów	6–9	
Province of Polesie		
Pińsk	dozens–hundreds	
Province of Białystok		
Białystok	hundreds	
Augustów	30	
Ciechanowiec	about 10	
Grodno	dozens–100	
Siemiatycze	15	
Wołowysk	7	
Province of Nowogródek		
Lida	?	
Słonim	?	
Wołożyn	about 100	
Province of Wilno		
Wilno	hundreds	
Berezwecz near Głębokie	1,000–2,000	
Oszmiana	52	
Wilejka	500–800	

dles, marshes, and rivers.) The strongest were placed at the head of the column; the weakest — the old, the sick, the injured — walked in the rear. These were followed by the NKVD, who shot anyone lagging behind. It is not known how many of them survived the death march to the Soviet Union.

> **Stefan Łagowski:** They drove us in a column surrounded by an escort which made contact with the populace impossible ... after a few dozen kilometers a day ... we slept under the naked sky when frost already covered the ground ... many were ill from dysentery.
>
> **Henryk Polak:** We marched 40 kilometers a day ... to Złoczów where we were loaded on a train and taken to Starobielsk.
>
> **Franciszek Gochniak:** In our retreat from Olszanica to Starobielsk, they executed those who from emaciation and nyctalopia could not keep up with the column ... in the camp near Zborów several of my friends were shot when they were found hiding under some boards ... the convoy was alerted that the

> Germans were nearing ... we were marched to a field, told to lie down next to one another, and were surrounded by guards with machine guns ... it proved to be a false alarm; the guards explained that they were not allowed to hand us over to the Germans alive.[66]

The attack on the Soviet Union, Hitler's partner in crime, took place on June 22, 1941. Surprised by the swift advance of the German armies, the NKVD began to write the last horrid chapter of this brutal occupation by evacuating thousands in death marches and death trains into the heart of Russia and by slaughtering additional thousands of prisoners whom they did not have time to evacuate from Eastern Poland (Kresy Wschodnie).[67] Of those evacuated, the weak were killed along the way; when evacuation efforts failed, all were slaughtered. Many also died from hunger, thirst, German bombs and lack of air in congested boxcars.

The prisons, by province, where known summary executions took place just before the arrival of the German armies are listed in Table 3. The toll for the POWs executed in Lwów comes from NKVD documents.[68]

According to Władysław Siemaszko, an eyewitness, out of about 2,000 inmates in the Łuck prison, only 90 survived.[69] In the Brygidki prison in Lwów, of 13,000 inmates, all but 600–700 were executed.[70] According to Krzysztof Popiński, between 20,000 and 30,000 Polish citizens (mostly Poles and Ukrainians but also a small group of Jews) died in prisons and in the course of the evacuations.[71] According to Sławomir Kalbarczyk, the June 1941 evacuation of all Soviet prisons claimed anywhere from 50,000 to 100,000 victims.[72] According to Jan Tomasz Gross, in Eastern Poland alone, some 150,000 prisoners were either moved into the Soviet interior or killed, or both.[73] The execution of the prisoners was often brutal:

> In Bóbrka, many inmates were scalded with boiling water; in Berezwecz, people's noses, ears, and fingers were cut off, and there were also children's corpses in the prison compound; in Czortków, female prisoners' breasts were cut off; in Drohobycz, prisoners were fastened together with barbed wire; in Łuck, a drum lined with barbed wire stood next to one of three mass graves unearthed in the prison yard; in Przemyślany, victims' noses, ears, and fingers were cut off and their eyes put out; similarly in Sambor, Stanisławów, Stryj, and Złoczów.[74]

The following occurred in Borysław, just after the German invasion:

> Ukrainians wearing armbands and carrying rifles immediately appeared in the streets. They dragged Jews out of their houses, presumably to work. What kind of work was this? We were brought to the NKVD building—I was taken together with a friend—where there were already about 300 Jews, and we were ordered to bring corpses out of the cellars and to segregate them. Heaps of corpses. We had to wash some of the bodies. I went once into this cellar. Corpses were not really buried. They were covered with five to ten centimeters of dirt. These were fresh corpses. Those were the bodies of people arrested during the past week or ten days. This fellow Kozłowski and his sister were among them. The girl's nipples, she was about sixteen years old, were torn out as if with pliers, her face was burned—people said it was done after the executions so that victims couldn't be recognized but I think not. Kozłowski had only one eye and it was swollen, his lips were sewn together with barbed wire, his hands were crushed and also burned, the skin was peeling off as if they poured boiling water all over. She was naked, he wasn't. They had no shoes. The impression was horrible. I didn't look at any more corpses, because I simply couldn't. But these were my friends. So I washed their bodies. There were several dozen corpses altogether. I remember a very long row. The majority of these people were not normally killed, with a shot, but badly maimed.[75]

Similar evacuations and murders of prisoners occurred in all Soviet-occupied territories threatened by Nazi conquest, namely, Lithuania, Belorussia, and Ukraine. The NKVD and the NKVD border patrol carried out the evacuations and did the killing. The Red Army, however, also engaged in a whole range of atrocities and at times assisted the NKVD in quelling prison riots, as in Brygidki in Lwów. In Brzeżany, passing Russian soldiers threw grenades into people's homes. In the Prawieniszki prison in Lithuania, soldiers of the Red Army murdered 500 prisoners and their Lithuanian guards. In Rumszyszki near Kaunas, 300 prisoners were shot.[76]

But prisoners were not the only ones executed in that final rampage of the NKVD. In their continuing efforts to liquidate the Polish Catholic clergy,[77] the Soviets attacked the Dominican monastery in Czortków and murdered four priests, three brothers, and a tertiary. Then, on July 4, 1941 (the German troops arrived on the sixth), the monastery was put to the torch.[78]

On January 4, 1944, when Soviet troops crossed the Polish frontier near Sarny for the second time (now as liberators, as Polish allies in pursuit of the retreating Wehrmacht), the killings and the deportations in the eastern territories of Poland began all over again. Between July 1944 and June 1945, more than 50,000 Poles were arrested in the Lublin area alone.[79] Perhaps the saddest case of all was the roundup, internment, and even murders of the members of the Polish Home Army (Armia Krajowa, or AK), who had fought so bravely against Nazi Germany alongside the Soviet partisans. This was the tragic fate of the AK at Wilno, Lwów, Białystok, and Wołyń. In the first few months of 1944, at least twenty Polish AK commanders were hanged and three were shot.[80] In Lublin, in late summer of 1944, AK members were actually interned at Majdanek, the former Nazi extermination camp.[81]

But a much greater betrayal and a far worse tragedy awaited the Polish people that fall. When the Warsaw Uprising began on August 1, 1944, Soviet troops stood idly by for five full weeks on the eastern bank of the Wisła (Vistula) River, which divides Warsaw, and watched and waited as between 150,000 and 200,000 civilians died in the throes of a lost battle. The Soviets even denied the Allied Air Force permission to use their bases for the relief efforts to this beleaguered, dying city until mid–September. Unwilling to fracture the Soviet alliance over Poland, Winston Churchill and Franklin Roosevelt did not press the issue and did not render assistance themselves. Almost a month before the end of the uprising, Roosevelt said, "There now seems to be nothing we can do to help them." After the city's surrender on October 2, over one-half million people were taken to the Pruszków concentration camp or deported to Germany for forced labor. In accordance with Hitler's wishes, what remained of the city was then razed. When the Soviet army finally occupied Warsaw on January 17, 1945, the city of almost 1.3 million inhabitants was empty, and 93 percent of this great center of culture and civilization lay in ruins.[82]

Clearly, the Soviet deportation policies of 1939 and 1944, the massive execution of Polish officers and other "counterrevolutionaries" following 1939; the reestablishment of the Polish Communist Party in early 1942, with its orders to destabilize the Polish Home Army by denouncing its members to the Gestapo (Geheime Staatspolizei — Secret State Police); the severing of diplomatic relations with the Polish government-in-exile over the mass executions at Katyn; the creation of Zygmunt Berling's army; the June 22, 1943, Moscow order to combat the Polish underground in the eastern territories of Poland "with every possible means"; the recently released July 14, 1944, order of Stalin to liquidate the members of all Polish underground forces, which resulted in the execution of thousands of Polish soldiers and the arrest and deportation of tens of thousands; the withholding of military assistance during the Warsaw Uprising; the postwar strategy of using promises of complete amnesty to lure Polish underground members into revealing themselves, followed by their massive arrest, "prosecution," imprisonment and/or execution; the 1945 kidnapping and Moscow "trial" of sixteen wartime Polish political leaders associated with the London-based Polish government-in-exile; the creation of the communist military and political organizations (the Union of Polish Patriots and the Polish Committee of National Liberation) in Moscow to take over the reins of legitimate Polish government after the war; the swift introduction of the major Soviet organs of oppression in every city, town, village, and hamlet throughout Poland immediately after liberation; and the illegal seizure of Poland's eastern territories — all leave little doubt that Stalin never had any intention of allowing the reemergence of an independent Polish state.

During the course of World War II, between 1.2 and 1.7 million Polish citizens (volunteers, deportees, evacuees, Red Army conscripts, prisoners, and POWs) found themselves in the USSR. Some of them are there still.

By the time the war was over, some 1 million Polish citizens — Christians and Jews alike — had died at the hands of the Soviets,[83] and the whole of pre–September 1939 Poland, the only country in the anti–Nazi coalition whose territory was significantly diminished, lay in Soviet hands. The communist reign of terror, which had already twice visited the eastern territories of Poland during the war, was about to embrace the whole of the Polish People's Republic.

Chapter 2
Nazi Terror

If the Germans, in comparison with the Soviets, were inexperienced in wholesale political terror in September 1939, by the time of their invasion of the USSR they had learned a great deal. In fact, the Germans not only caught up to the Russians but soon surpassed them.

While the Soviets were wreaking havoc with the economy of Eastern Poland, the Germans were doing exactly the same with the much greater resources of central and western Poland. Here too, the zloty was devalued. To make sure it would be kept in its place, the Germans simply took over the Bank of Poland. Here too, taxes were raised, village food quotas were imposed, and homes, personal possessions, and private and state properties were confiscated at will — either to be turned over to German settlers or to be used for the conduct of the war.

Here too, shortages were chronic, food lines were long, and hundreds of thousands were homeless. Here too, factories were disassembled and sent piecemeal to the west; those that remained were Nazified, as were Polish hotels, restaurants, small retail businesses, and even cafés. In Łódź, for example, out of 2,387 textile factories, 2,000 were administered by the Treuhandstelle Ost. According to German records, as of February 1941, 264 large, 9,000 medium-sized, and 76,000 small industrial establishments, as well as 9,120 large and 112,000 small commercial businesses, fell under the control of the Treuhänder, which turned over its holdings, as well as many other businesses, to German citizens.[1] During the war 33 percent of Poland's industry, 56 percent of its transportation, 65 percent of its trade, 28 percent of its forestry, and 35 percent of its farming enterprises were destroyed.[2] In all, Polish material losses during the Nazi occupation are said to have exceeded 62 billion zloty.[3]

Considering themselves a people endowed with a historical consciousness, the Germans liquidated Polish libraries, razed historical monuments and markers, forbade the teaching of history and geography, and ransacked most of the Polish archives:

> Thus was concluded the work of destruction of the Warsaw archives during World War II. The Archives of the Age of Enlightenment, the Treasury and the Municipal Archives lost 100 percent of their records; the Archives of Recent Records — 97 percent; the Central Archives of Earlier Records — 90 percent; the Archives of Earlier Records — 80 percent. All the Archives combined lost a total of 92.8 percent of their archive store. No Tartar invasion of the Middle Ages had resulted in such devastation.[4]

Considering themselves a cultured people, the Germans raided the museums and looted Poland's national art treasures. Of the 175 public museums in Poland, 105 survived, but only 33 were in any shape to open their doors to the public after the war. Music by Polish composers was banned. With the exception of some small movie houses that featured Nazi-imposed pornography, all legitimate theaters were shut down.[5]

In this war on Polish culture, Poland's educational, scientific, artistic, and literary establishments were closed outright. "The Poles," said Hans Frank, "do not need universities or secondary schools: the Polish lands are to be changed into an intellectual desert."[6]

In short order the Polish press, which put out 2,250 periodicals (250 in foreign languages), was reduced to nothing more than a Third Reich propaganda machine. While the Germans were liquidating the Jewish ghettos, this Nazi-controlled press was telling the world that the Poles were responsible,[7] an often-repeated lie that unfortunately, after fifty years, still finds an echo in the world today.

Heinrich Himmler's insidious Generalplan Ost called for the expulsion of 31 million people from the eastern territories and for the colonization, by 10 million ethnic Germans, of 700,000 square kilometers of land. (The size of the Reich in 1938 was 583,000 square kilometers.[8]) To this end, in the early days of the war, 630,000 Poles were expelled from the Wartheland or Kraj Warty (of these, 460,000 were sent packing to the General Government), along with 265,000 from Silesia, Pomerania, and the Ciechanów Regency. In all, 923,000 Poles were forcibly removed from the annexed territories to make room for Volksdeutsche and German settlers from Germany, Soviet Latvia, Estonia, and other territories.[9]

In two separate pacification actions (November 1942 to March 1943, and June-July 1943), 116 and 171 villages, respectively, were emptied in the Zamość area for German settlement. In all, 110,000 (31 percent) of the Poles who lived in that region were expelled by the "SS, Gestapo, Wehrmacht, and Ukrainians in German service."[10] Among these were 30,000 children, 4,454 of whom — those with blue eyes and blond hair — were taken to the Reich for Germanization.[11] Throughout the war, about 200,000 Polish children were kidnapped for this sinister program;[12] only about 15 to 20 percent of them could be reclaimed by their parents or the Polish government after the war. In addition, 1.8 million residents of Silesia and Pomerania were Germanized simply by being placed on the so-called Deutsche Volksliste. It is estimated that in all, some 2.2 million Poles were subjected to some form of Germanization.[13]

Moreover, 171,000 persons were displaced from their homes and properties in the General Government and 28,000 from the district of Białystok[14] in order to make room for the needs of the Wehrmacht and the Waffen-SS, and countless thousands were displaced throughout occupied Poland to make room for the resettlement of Jews into ghettos. The Warsaw ghetto, for example, was established between October and November 1940 to accommodate 138,000 Jews. For this, 113,000 Poles had to be evicted.[15]

In all, approximately 1 million Polish citizens (including 300,000 Polish POWs) from the annexed territories and 1,281,000 from the General Government were deported to Germany for forced labor.[16] Similar brutal resettlement and deportation policies and similar Nazi terror would characterize the German occupation of Poland's eastern provinces after June 1941. The lot of the forced laborers was particularly hard:

> The so-called *Poleneinsatz* (employment of Poles), was still perceived as offending against the racial principles of National Socialism. The national and political dangers arising therefrom, as Himmler stated in 1940, were to be counteracted by suitably stringent measures. Accordingly, a vast system of repressive regulations was brought to bear on the Poles. They had to live in hutted camps (which, in the countryside, soon proved to be impossible), received smaller wages, were not allowed to use public facilities (ranging from express trains to public baths), nor attend German church services; they had to work longer hours than Germans and were obliged to wear a badge — the "Poland-P" — pinned to their clothing. Outside work, contact with Germans was forbidden; any Pole involved in sexual relations with German women was punished by public execution. In order to protect "German Blood" it had also been decided that at least half of the civilian workers recruited must be women.[17]

Until the German invasion of the Soviet Union, Poles constituted the largest group of forced laborers in Germany, at times reaching 60 percent of all foreign workers. After mid-1941, they ranked second after the citizens of the Soviet Union. In September 1944, Polish and Soviet citizens accounted for 67.7 percent of all foreign workers in Germany. Of these,

235,192 were Ukrainians from the General Government and the annexed territories.[18]

From the very beginning and without any respite, the Nazis conducted a systematic program of genocide; they were murdering the people of Poland. On September 7, 1939, Reinhard Heydrich stated that all Polish nobles, clergy, and Jews must be killed. On September 12, 1939, Wilhelm Keitel added the intelligentsia to the list. At the end of 1940, Hitler called for the physical liquidation of the "leading elements in Poland," and soon all the major political leaders of Nazi Germany echoed these sentiments. On March 15, 1940, at a meeting of the commandants of the Nazi camps, Himmler said: "All Polish specialists will be exploited in our military-industrial complex. Later, all Poles will disappear from this world. It is imperative that the great German nation considers the elimination of all Polish people as its chief task."[19]

The execution of the Polish intelligentsia began in mid–September 1939 in the annexed territories under the designation "political cleansing of the territory" (Politische Flurbereinigung). On November 6, 1939, 115 professors from the Jagiellonian University in Kraków were arrested and taken to the Sachsenhausen concentration camp, from which many never returned.[20] During the Aktion A-B (Ausserordentliche Befriedungsaktion, or Extraordinary Pacification Action) from 1939 to mid–1941, several thousand people died in Warsaw — in the Seym gardens, on university grounds, on the outskirts of the city, and in the Kampinos woods near the village of Palmiry.[21] Most of these, about 3,500, were members of the Polish intelligentsia.[22] Richard Lukas noted the results:

> The Nazis were so thorough in their grim work that when Dachau was liberated at the end of the war, there were only 50 Polish physicians, 100 lawyers, 50 engineers, and 100 teachers still alive there, in contrast to 5,000 farmers and 3,600 artisans. Testimony of just how successful the Germans were in their resolve is revealed by the fact that during the war Poland lost 45 percent of her physicians and dentists, 57 percent of her attorneys, more than 15 percent of her teachers, 40 percent of her professors, 30 percent of her technicians, and more than 18 percent of her clergy. The majority of her journalists also disappeared — 73 were murdered, 77 died in concentration camps and jails, 50 died in the ghetto, and 12 perished in the Warsaw Uprising.[23]

During the German military occupation — the "merciless and systematic campaign of biological destruction of the Poles"[24] — entire towns and villages were completely destroyed. By the end of 1939, over 40,000 people had died in the annexed territories and some 5,000 in the General Government. The losses were fewer in the latter because fewer local citizens of that area were willing to provide the Germans with lists of those to be exterminated. (In the early days, about 90 percent of the names of those to be sent to concentration camps were provided by German nationals.) By 1940, over 52,000 persons had died in occupied Poland, many by execution.[25]

The executions were generally carried out by the "Operational Groups" (Einsatzgruppen and Einsatzkommando units, consisting of Gestapo members who trailed the regular German armies) and by the Selbstschutz (self-defense police units made up of Volksdeutsche.[26]) But the Wehrmacht was also guilty of atrocities. The first of these occurred in September 1939 when German soldiers killed over 1,000 Polish POWs. In addition, several hundred Polish POWs, including 100 officers, were handed over by the German army to the Gestapo for execution. In this toll of war crimes, over 1,200 members of the Polish National Defense (Obrona Narodowa) and of other Polish organizations captured by the Wehrmacht were murdered. So were 38 postal workers in Danzig (Gdańsk, in November 1939) and hundreds of other civilians as well. By February 6, 1940, the German army had conducted 100 executions on Polish soil. These atrocities continued throughout the war. From January 1, 1943, to July 31, 1944, the Wehrmacht conducted 1,106 pacification actions. Some Polish officers captured in 1944 in Hungary and several hundred POWs from the Polish People's Army captured in 1944–45 were also killed. In February 1945, 32 of them were burned alive in Podgaje.[27]

Of all the cities in Poland, Warsaw suffered the most. According to the Main Commission for the Investigation of Nazi Crimes in Poland, between October 16, 1943, and February 15, 1944, there were 33 street executions in Warsaw, in which 1,528 randomly selected persons were shot.[28] This total does not include the executions conducted at this time for a variety of reasons, and for no reasons at all, in the Warsaw ghetto, where some 9,500 people lost their lives.[29] As we have seen, some months later Warsaw itself would be reduced to a heap of rubble by the Germans; up to 200,000 were killed and over one-half million of the remaining citizens were condemned to death in concentration and slave-labor camps.[30] Throughout the war, Warsaw lost 700,000 of its citizens — more than the combined war losses of the United Kingdom and the United States of America.[31]

Palmiry, Pawiak, Wawer, and Józefów also occupy a special place in the memory of the Polish nation. Janusz Gumkowski and Kazimierz Leszczyński describe the killing operations at Palmiry:

> Beyond the little village of Palmiry, a little to the south of the asphalt road leading from Warsaw to Modlin, there is an expanse of sandy ground covered with fir trees. It was here, several kilometres from the nearest habitation, that an artillery dump had been set up before the war belonging to the old fortress in Modlin. This dump was dismantled by the Germans right at the beginning of the occupation. Even the railway tracks of the siding leading to it were removed.
>
> This desolate spot among the woods was selected by the Gestapo in Warsaw as an execution site. A clearing in the wood was enlarged by cutting down the trees around it. Before each execution a pit of the required size was dug in the sandy ground, usually in the form of a ditch about 3 metres deep. The victims were brought from Warsaw by lorry. They were taken from the Pawiak prison which the Gestapo had used since the beginning of 1940 to detain all its "political prisoners." The prisoners never realized that they were being taken on their last journey. The Nazis did everything to preserve their illusions. The victims were allowed to take small parcels with them, and often their papers and personal belongings deposited in the prison were returned to them. They were also permitted to take food parcels sent from home and were even issued with a ration of bread "for the road."
>
> All these preliminaries allayed any suspicions or misgivings the prisoners might have had. This is quite understandable. Although they had been interrogated by the Gestapo, who had accused them of various things, usually regarding their pre-war activities, no court had passed any sentence on them. In these conditions the prisoners, making allowances for the ruthlessness of German methods, presumed that they were being taken to concentration camps.
>
> The transports were usually taken from the prison in the early morning. The Polish staff was kept away from this action, and working prisoners were not allowed out of their cells or were pulled out of their working parties. Eventually the Polish prison staff and the prisoners who had spent any length of time in Pawiak were able to tell by these signs which transports were being taken away for execution.
>
> In the prison registers the names of these who had been taken off for execution were marked with a "T" — for transport, without any indication given that they had been murdered.
>
> The lorries taking the prisoners were accompanied by a heavy escort. Near Palmiry they turned off the highway, and a few kilometres down the side road they stopped near the clearing in which graves had already been dug. The prisoners were unloaded and blindfolded. They had to leave their baggage in the lorries, but their clothing and personal belongings were not removed. Presumably the Germans had not yet been struck by the practical advantages of killing their victims naked or at best in clothing made of paper tissue, as they did later, and confiscating their belongings and clothes for the "Great Reich." The blindfolded victims were led into the clearing. There they were lined up on the edge of the pit and machine-gunned. If there was a greater number to be executed the victims were split into groups.[32]

Postwar exhumations in Palmiry by the Polish Red Cross and the Main Commission for the Investigation of Nazi Crimes in Poland produced 800 skeletons. From personal possessions and other distinguishing marks, approximately one-half of these victims have been identified by name. About 170 of them were women.[33] Some of these, no doubt, came from the women's prison in Pawiak, another site of frequent executions.

Pawiak was the name of a prison in Warsaw at 24/26 Dzielna Street. From October 1939 until it was blown up by the Germans in July 1944, this prison was used by the Security Police (Sicherheitspolizei, or Sipo) for brutal interrogations and investigations. About 100,000 people, Christians and Jews alike, passed through its gates. Of these, about 37,000 were executed (some just before the 1944 Soviet advance, including forty-two Jews employed in the prison workshops), and 60,000 were deported to concentration camps.[34]

The village of Wawer was also located near Warsaw. On December 27, 1939, 107 persons were executed in Wawer after two noncommissioned German officers were killed by two criminals, who had also shot a Polish policeman the day before.[35] One of the civilian victims was Daniel Gering, a forty-year-old bank official who, although of German extraction, maintained he was Polish — to the great embarrassment of Reich Marshal Hermann Göring, no doubt. When Gering refused to say that he was German, he was beaten to death. Subsequently, a group of 400 scouts took the name of "Wawer" and managed to carry out 150 small and some not-so-small acts of sabotage against the Germans.[36]

The Germans conducted many such retaliatory massacres. On April 13, 1940, the family of Adolf Kastner, a German settler, was murdered in the village of Józefów, located in the county of Łuków, the province of Lublin. The motive was robbery, and the culprits were apprehended three weeks later.

Meanwhile, according to the Nazi version of "collective responsibility," hundreds of Polish civilians from six villages and ten small hamlets were rounded up and executed for the crime, with which they had absolutely no connection. Captain Franciszek Dobromirski, head of the Polish police for the county of Łuków, recalled this tragic episode:

> Just before dusk, when the men were already lined up in a square in the clover field and surrounded by a cordon of SS men, two heavy machine guns were mounted behind the square at a distance of about thirty paces and opened fire. The rear ranks were felled by the hail of bullets, there were cries and screams for help. As they tumbled over, the men at the back forced the ranks in front of them forward by the weight of their falling bodies. The men in front, still unhit by the bullets, rushed forward into the open field in the direction of Chordzieżka, assisted by the fact that the Nazi guards had moved to one side as soon as the massacre began. When the victims started to flee — dusk had already fallen — the Nazis standing to one side began to chase the runaways and shoot at them; in the meantime the officer in charge had given orders to the machine-gunners to hold their fire, and the guards surrounded those who were still unhurt or not yet dead. They were then finished off with small arms, mainly pistols....
>
> As far as I remember, when I asked the commandant of the station in confidence to give me the number of victims the figure was more than 200. The wounded who managed to escape and who subsequently attended to themselves in hiding, came to about 100.[37]

The wife of Józef Kalinowski, one of the victims, noted: "I was forbidden even to take the body of my husband who was buried in a common grave, or to exhume it later. The common grave was ploughed over and levelled."[38]

The above-mentioned mass executions are generally known to people familiar with the Polish experience during the war, but the first large scale Nazi atrocity on Polish soil, the prelude to all the rest, is unfortunately also the least known of all.[39] From the middle of October 1939 until mid-December, in a forest near Piaśnica Wielka in Pomerania (the Gdańsk–West Prussia area), from 12,000 to 14,000 people were slaughtered by the Gestapo and German field gendarmerie. Among them were Polish teachers, clerks, priests, nuns, patriots, as well as Jews, Germans unsympathetic to the Nazi cause, and many psychiatric patients.[40] The victims came from the surrounding areas and from the villages, towns, and cities in the "Polish Corridor," including Gdynia, Gdańsk, Wejherowo, Puck, Kartuzy, Kościerzyna, and the Hel Peninsula. But some came also from the interior of Germany, like the 1,200 German citizens brought there by order of Reichsführer SS Himmler, from various psychiatric wards of Lauenburg, Treptow, Stralsund, and Ückermünde. Here is a sequential account of that tragedy from witness depositions:

> During potato digging time in 1939 Oberwachmeister Wittke from Wejherowo came to our village with the forester Stöckel from the forestry of Warszkowo and called me and my son Werner, Emil Reiner and Paul Lietzow and all the workers from Leśniewo to report for work in the woods.... It was at twilight; the forester took us to the woods belonging to the Piaśnica forestry and personally marked an area 8 meters long and 4 meters wide and ordered us to dig a ditch 2.5 meters deep.... Stöckel ... warned us to keep quiet about this work.... We dug such a ditch in one night to the light of a campfire. In the morning Stöckel paid each of us 10-15 zlotys for digging the ditch.... The same group of people dug about 10 such ditches.... Two or three days later, around noon, rifle shots could be heard and afterwards machine-gun fire. The shooting went on for an hour. The shots came exactly from the site where we had dug the ditches. I guessed that Poles were being executed at those ditches. That was what the entire German population of our village thought.
>
> In the evening Stöckel again came to us and took us, carrying shovels, to that ditch, ordering us to fill it up. The ditch was already partly covered with earth and there remained about a meter and a half to fill. From under the sand there slightly protruded human limbs or parts of civilian clothing. Around the ditch, within a radius of 10 m. I noticed blood, teeth, pieces of jaws with teeth, and even pieces of bone from human skulls. On the trunks of the trees near the ditch I saw bits of human brain, at a height of about a meter and a half.... For sodding the graves they paid us 5 zlotys each.[41]
>
> I have to admit that I had learned, while I was still in prison, from a German guard, some of the details of the way the execution in Piaśnica took place. I don't know the guard's name; he got a short prison term (three days) for drunkenness and a brawl and was put into my cell. This guard, who had qualms of conscience, told me that he had taken part in the execution in Piaśnica and that these executions took place in this way—the victims were lined up at the edge of previously dug collective graves, and then they were shot with machine guns and repeaters.[42]

When the war broke out, I was living in Orle, Wejherowo County, situated along the road to Piaśnica. As soon as the Germans entered they started to arrest people in Orle. I remember when they took the teacher Henryk Zimkiewicz; the others I can't recall; the one I mentioned died in Stutthof. The local people knew that the Germans were murdering Poles. Around October, 1939, I learned that mass murder was being committed in the Piaśnica woods. Perhaps at the end of October 1939—I don't remember the exact date—I went to visit my mother-in-law, in Leśniewo. To get there I had to cross the Piaśnica forest. I was walking alone. When I reached the woods near Piaśnica, I was stopped by a German Wehrmacht soldier, who asked me where I was going. Before, while I was approaching the soldier, I had heard some moaning and crying. But I didn't know where the sounds were coming from, because there was a very strong wind. When I explained to the soldier that I was bound for Leśniewo, he asked me whether I didn't know that entrance to the forest along this road was forbidden. He told me to wait there until he returned and then the soldier went into the woods. Waiting there, I looked around and noticed trucks standing some distance away in the wood. About 100 m. from where I was I noticed people crawling around near ditches. I guessed that an execution was taking place. It was then around 9 a.m. Next, I saw, near the crawling people I mentioned before, one SS-man in uniform, who held a small child by its legs. This SS-man then tore the child apart and threw it against a tree. While I noticed that shocking scene two SS-men approached me with the soldier to whom I had talked before. The Germans asked me why I had come along that road, whether I didn't know that the road was closed. They also asked me whether I knew them and what kind of uniform they were wearing. I said I didn't know them and also had no idea what kind of uniform they were wearing. Next they asked me whether I had noticed trucks in the wood or anything else, which I denied. After that talk, one of the SS-men declared that he was going to take me along; but the other one interfered, saying that they had no more ammunition. They wrote down my personal data and when I told them that I lived in the village of Orle, one of them said that it was a German village. Then they told me to stay where I was and they left while I was to wait with the soldier. When the SS-men had left the soldier told me to return home. I did not tell anybody what I had gone through because I feared reprisals from the Germans. I remember that, while standing in the forest, after the soldier had stopped me, I saw some distance away the priest from Mechowo, named Witkowski, hung on a tree. I did not hear any shooting in the forest. With the exception of the evidence I have given here I know no other facts. I also do not know the names of the Germans who committed crimes in our area.[43]

When ... Nazi power was collapsing ... the SS criminals... tried to efface the traces of this monstrous murder. At the end of the summer and beginning of the autumn of 1944 (according to evidence given by Walter Mahlke) they started burning the corpses of the people murdered in 1939.

A group of prisoners with their legs in chains, was brought to Piaśnica from the concentration camp of Stutthof. These prisoners dug up the graves, unearthed the corpses and burnt them in two crematoriums built in the earth. During the burning, which lasted for a number of weeks, day and night, nobody was permitted to enter the forest. At the edge of the forest were tablets with inscriptions: *Wer weiter geht, wird ohne Anruf erschossen* (Who goes further will be shot without warning!)

The smoke rising above the forest was visible in the vicinity and the stench of burning bodies was carried by the wind, while at night the glow of fires could be seen above the forest.

The prisoners who burned the corpses lived in lairs dug in the earth, with the ground covered by straw. There also remained traces of a field latrine and paths leading from the lairs to the latrine. Jan Angel, a worker from Pryszniewo, who in the autumn of 1944 was in the Piaśnica forest, saw three prisoners in striped prison garb, who were in chains and led by a gendarme to gather wood. He noticed that their movements were restricted, they could only take short steps because of the chains.[44]

According to reliable witnesses, thirty five mass graves exist in Piaśnica. In 1946, the Court Medical Commission uncovered thirty graves and examined twenty-six of them. In 1962 another grave was discovered and, near it, two places where the bodies (perhaps from the remaining graves) had been cremated. Of the 427 victims whose names are known, 300 were members of the intelligentsia. Most of the exhumed victims were naked, many of their skulls were shattered, and some were found in a kneeling position indicating that they had been buried alive.[45]

Many of the victims in Piaśnica were part of the euthanasia (Gnadentod) program that had been launched in the fall, even before Hitler's official "mercy-killing" order, officially dated November 1, 1939, but actually given at the end of that month. Similarly cruel murders occurred in Białystok in the second half of 1941 and in the General Government in 1941-42. Sometimes the victims were shot, as in Piaśnica. Sometimes they were gassed in specially built vans. Sometimes they died by injection, like the worst of common criminals.[46] The Germans emptied many state psychiatric hospitals in this way. In Chełm near Lublin, for example, 420 patients were shot by the German security police on January 12, 1940. In Dziekanka in Poznań, 1,172 mental patients were evacuated and killed.[47]

But the Nazi euthanasia program embraced other types of people as well, namely the old, those with incurable diseases, and invalids. Hundreds of Polish children were given lethal injections in the annexed territories because they belonged to the last two categories. In all, about 12,000 Polish people died in the occupied territories as a result of the Nazi euthanasia program. Of this total, 10,000 were from hospitals for the mentally impaired.[48]

That this was only the beginning of the Nazi plan for achieving a superior race of human beings is borne out by Gauleiter Arthur Greiser's intention to exterminate 25,000 to 35,000 Poles in Kraj Warty because they suffered from tuberculosis. The plan was approved by Himmler in 1942 but was scrapped after Dr. Kurt Blome from the NSDAP (Nationalsozialistische Deutsche Arbeiter Partei, or National Socialist German Workers' Party) health bureau and several others objected — not because of the killing involved but because of fear of world public disapproval. Supposedly, a similar plan to exterminate 70,000 old people and children from Zamojszczyzna (the Zamość area) was abandoned for the same reason.[49] Had Germany won the war, there is no doubt that the scope of the Nazi euthanasia program would have been eventually broadened to include all those who, for whatever reason, were not able to contribute to the economic well-being of the Third Reich.

On February 6, 1940, Governor General Hans Frank in an attempt to explain the difference between the Protectorate of Czechoslovakia and Moravia and his Generalgouvernement (GG, initials that some people quipped stood for Gangstergau — Gangsterland), revealed a ghastly truth to a correspondent for the *Völkischer Beobachter*. "I can give you a vivid illustration of the difference," he said. "In Prague large red notices were posted to inform everyone that 7 Czechs had been shot. At the time I said to myself: If I wanted to have notices posted to announce every shooting of 7 Poles, there would not be enough forests in Poland to produce the paper for these posters."[50] These numerous executions, both known and as yet unknown, had nothing to do with crime and punishment. Their purpose was to cower the native population into submission and to contribute to their eventual extinction.

In addition to the thousands who died in the Nazi executions, virtually every Polish family mourned someone who had been tortured and murdered in the 1,200 extermination, concentration, hard-labor, penal, prisoner-of-war, and transit camps that dotted the landscape.[51] Nearly 1 million Christian Poles were interned in these camps: 150,000 in Auschwitz; 100,000 in Majdanek; 40,000 in Mauthausen; 35,000 in Dachau; 34,000 in Ravensbrück; 30,000 in Sachsenhausen; 23,000 in Buchenwald; and 16,000 in Płaszów, to name but a few. There was even a special camp for Polish children (ages eight to sixteen) in Łódź, where 12,000 of the 13,000 young inmates died. Many people do not know, even today, that Poles constituted the largest group of inmates at both Stutthof and Auschwitz until 1942.[52]

The lot of the Catholic clergy and religious was especially hard:

> Losses among the Catholic clergy and religious, especially the diocesan clergy, were proportionately higher than among the Christian population as a whole. Almost 2,800 out of approximately 18,000 Polish priests and monks were killed, which represents almost 16 percent of their total number. Some 4,000 of them (and an additional 400 clerics) were interned in concentration camps; thousands more suffered other forms of internment or repression. Of the almost 17,000 Polish nuns, more than 1,100 were imprisoned in camps and 289 were killed. Of the 38 bishops in Poland at the outbreak of the war, thirteen were exiled or arrested and sent to concentration camps (six of them were killed). Poles constituted the vast majority of the Christian clergy persecuted by the Nazis; in Dachau, the principal camp employed to imprison clergy from all of Europe, Poles constituted 65 percent of the total clergy population, and about 90 percent of those clergymen were put to death. Of all the Christian clergy in Dachau, Polish priests were especially selected for medical experiments.[53]

One survivor, Iwo Cyprian Pogonowski, recalled such an experiment: "My friend Paul survived the longest among the Jews in Sachsenhausen. His shinbones were broken and set experimentally; the major shinbone was connected to the minor one, leaving the other two stubs unconnected. Paul had to be X-rayed every few weeks so that the Germans could follow up their experiment. I remember many cases of such 'scientific' experiments, performed mostly on Polish Christian inmates."[54]

Among the Polish citizens who died in these concentration camps were the Gypsies, who, like the Jews, were slated for total extermination. Although the king of the European Gypsies and president of the Gypsies in the General Government, Rudolf Kwiek, in 1942 offered collaboration in exchange for better treatment of his people, his proposal went unanswered. Of the 75,000 to 85,000 Gypsies in prewar Poland, over 50,000 died.[55]

The tragic fate of the Jews during World War II occupies a special place in the Holocaust that engulfed the Polish nation as a whole. The history of that tragedy can be divided into four periods: from September 1, 1939, until the end of 1939; 1940–41; 1942–August 1944; and September 1944–liberation.

In the first four months of the war, the disposition of the Jews was left in the hands of the Nazi military and police commandants and the civil authorities. In addition to the general curtailment of liberties and outright discrimination, the Jews were forced to wear the Star of David. By the end of 1939, over 7,000 of them had died in pogroms and executions. The first ghetto was established in October 1939 in Piotrków Trybunalski, and the first forced-labor camps were set up at this time in Kraj Warty.[56]

The years 1940–41 saw the first major concentration of Jews in ghettos and forced-labor camps. By 1941 there were already 300 of the former and 437 of the latter in occupied Poland. Initially, the conditions in the camps were worse than in the ghettos. Tens of thousands of Jews in the forced-labor camps died from hunger, hard work, lack of medical care, and epidemics generally followed by executions. In some of these camps, the "turnover rate" reached 50 percent.[57]

The ghettos, on the other hand, had the Judenräte (Jewish Councils), a thriving black market, financial support from abroad, and Polish assistance. The worst of the ghettos was located in Warsaw, which housed from 360,000 to 450,000 Jews between October 1939 and April 1941. Throughout its existence, about 96,000 Jews died there from "hunger and misery," the form of death prescribed by Ludwig Fischer, the *Gauleiter* or governor of the Warsaw district. Heinz Rolf Höppner, the chief of the security forces in Poznań, thought that sterilization of the healthy workers would be better and that a method of extermination "more humane" and quicker than starvation should be used to dispose of those incapable of working.[58] His method involved the use of gas and open-air shootings. Already in 1940–41, tens of thousands of Jews were executed in Kraj Warty and, as we will see, in Poland's eastern territories after the invasion of the Soviet Union.[59]

Before the official implementation of the "Final Solution," another method of "disposing of the Jews" was considered: placing them in a temporary Jewish "reserve" in the Lublin area (the Reichsgetto) and from there shipping them off to the French Island of Madagascar. When that plan failed, it was thought that perhaps after the swift conquest of the Soviet Union, Siberian exile might be just as effective.[60] These plans were abandoned in favor of genocide. The gassing of Jews began in 1941 and reached its greatest intensity in 1942 after the January 20, 1942, Wannsee Conference, during which the decision was made for the "final resolution of the Jewish question" (Endlösung der Judenfrage).[61]

Most Polish Jews died in 1942. Those brought to Poland from western and southern Europe were exterminated mostly in 1943 and in the first half of 1944. Most of the Jewish deaths occurred in the German extermination camps set up on Polish territory. About (minimum estimates) 1.1 million Jews died in Auschwitz-Birkenau, 900,000 in Treblinka, 600,000 in Bełżec, 250,000 in Sobibór, 152,000 in Chełmno (Kulmhof), and 60,000 in Majdanek.[62] By September 1944 all the Jewish ghettos in Poland had been liquidated (the last, in Łódź, in August 1944), and only a few minor Jewish forced-labor camps remained. Most of the tens of thousands of Jews remaining in the concentration camps died just before the end of the war.

Although still incomplete in some of its

sordid details, the story of the Jewish Holocaust, both in Poland and in the other Nazi-occupied territories, is now generally known — thanks to the thousands of histories, memoirs, oral histories, testimonies and depositions at various trials of war criminals in the last fifty years. The sheer enormity and horror of that attempt at genocide will forever haunt mankind.

Besides dying en masse in the concentration camps and extermination camps, thousands of Polish citizens also died in prisons, in civilian internment camps (Zivilinterniertenlager), and in transit camps (Durchgangslager) such as those in Poznań and Działdowo. Additional thousands died in the forced-labor camps in Poland and in Germany. Still others were killed in untold numbers in the immoral and counterproductive bombardment — by Germany and the Allies — of cities, towns, and villages. (Would that only a few of those bombs had been dropped by the Allies on the death camps at the beginning of their gruesome operations!) Many people simply gave out from extreme duress, hunger, cold, typhus, and tuberculosis.

After the German invasion of the Soviet Union, the Polish province of Białystok (now called Bezirk Białystok), together with Eastern Galicia (Distrikt Galizien, assigned to the GG), became a part of the so-called Grossdeutschland (Greater Germany). The provinces of Wilno, Nowogródek, and Polesie were placed in the Reichskommissariat Ostland (the Eastern Reich Commissariat) under Reichskommissar Heinrich Lohse, and Wołyń became a part of the Reichskommissariat Ukraine (the Ukrainian Reich Commissariat, spanning some 330,000 square kilometers of land). The GG was ruled by Reichskommissar Hans Frank. The Reichskommissariat Ukraine was placed under the command of Reichskommissar Erich Koch.[63]

We already know what could be expected from Frank, but what about Koch? "Gentlemen: I am known as a brutal dog," said Koch in September 1941 at his inaugural in his chosen capital of the Ukraine, Równe, a county seat in Wołyń twenty kilometers from my house. "Because of this reason I was appointed as Reichskommissar of the Ukraine.... Gentlemen: I am expecting from you the utmost severity towards the native population."[64]

In another speech eighteen months later (March 5, 1943) in Kiev, he continued:

> We are the Master Race and must govern hard but just.... I will draw the very last out of this country. I did not come to spread bliss.... The population must work, work, and work again.... We definitely did not come here to give out manna. We have come here to create the basis for victory.
>
> We are a master race, which must remember that the lowliest German worker is racially and biologically a thousand times more valuable than the population here.[65]

By "population" he meant all non-Germans, the Untermenschen, the subhumans: the Jews, the Gypsies, and the Slavs.

To start, with the help mostly of the Ukrainian police, the Germans rounded up all the Jews in Poland's eastern territories and placed them in ghettos — like the one in our nearest town, Tuczyn, eight kilometers from my house. Once there, the Jews were systematically, again with the help of the Ukrainian police,[66] either killed there by the Einsatzgruppen or taken to the nearest forest or village (like Rzeczyca, for example, a small Ukrainian village a few kilometers to our south), shot in the back of the head, and buried unceremoniously in mass graves. A local resident described the creation and liquidation of the Tuczyn ghetto:

> In the summer of 1942, the Germans decided to create a ghetto in Tuczyn. It was one of those days in my life which one can never forget. It was sundown and I was just returning with our two family cows which I had been pasturing. The day was torrid and dust hung in the air. The setting sun shone through the dust in unreal violet rays.
>
> When I entered the township, I saw a group of Jews surrounded by Ukrainian militiamen and German gendarmes. The militiamen were running around like stallions and were pulling out of houses those who managed to hide there. In the middle of this pandemonium and commotion, I found myself engulfed by a profound stillness. Everything appeared as if in some surrealistic painting.

> (I became acquainted with surrealistic art at a much later date and did not know the word at the time.) The Jews were all herded into the marketplace. This was a part of Tuczyn inhabited almost exclusively by Jews, although there was a Catholic church nearby and one of the two Greek Orthodox churches as well.
>
> The liquidation of the Jews began in the fall of that year. For a span of a few days I observed the massive influx of Ukrainian militiamen and German gendarmes, not SS but the regulars with those brown collars, who cordoned off the ghetto. The ghetto was not enclosed by either a wall or even a fence. The militiamen led the Jews out in large groups to the village of Rzeczyca, about three kilometers from the river Horyń. There they were told to dig ditches, to get undressed, and as they were kneeling along these ditches, they were shot in the back of the head.
>
> The ditches, filled to the brim with bodies, were then covered with lime and a thin layer of earth. The stench from the decaying cadavers which pervaded the entire area was simply indescribable. No one knows whence came the myriad of hungry dogs which circled these massive graves and fed on the human flesh.[67]

At times, sealed trucks ("gas vans") were used as mobile killing units. The "gas" was not Zyklon B but the exhaust: carbon monoxide. Unlike in Germany and western Poland, in our area the Germans did not bother to build a sprawling network of concentration and extermination camps, but the solution to the Jewish question —"gas vans" and open-air shootings — proved to be just as final.[68]

Shortly after the invasion of the Soviet Union, over 300,000 Jews died in Wołyń and Polesie. In Stanisławów, 40,000–50,000 Jews were killed between August 1941 and February 1942. By October of that year, except for those in hiding and the 2,000–3,000 needed by the Germans, all the Jews were murdered in that province. In Lwów, only 11,000 Jews remained in 1942. By December 1 of that year, about 50 percent of all the Jews in Galicia had died; by June 1943, almost 90 percent had been killed.[69] By the summer of 1943, all Jews in all Nazi-occupied territories were said to have "officially" ceased to exist. In Ukraine proper, they had ceased to exist long before that. "In the principal occupied Ukrainian cities east of Volhynia and Galicia," states Raul Hilberg, "there were not even remnant ghettos at the end of 1941."[70]

Although the Germans planned to transfer 5 million people from the eastern provinces of Poland to Germany, the full magnitude of that deportation is still unknown. For example, 500 prominent citizens were executed and 40,000 deported from Białystok alone in mid-July 1943.[71] Various estimates for deportees from these provinces range from 400,000 to 518,000 Polish citizens.[72] An excerpt from a report written by a member of the Political Department in the Ostministerium on October 25, 1942, gives us a pretty good idea of what was going on: "In the usual limitless mistreatment of Slavic peoples there were applied the 'enlistment methods' which recall the darkest pages of the slave trade. There started a regular man hunt, and without regard to health, condition, or age, the people were deported to Germany."[73] (In Równe, the trains — their boxcars full of human cargo — were running westward day and night for the entire duration of the German occupation. I and my fractured family found ourselves on the passenger lists of four such transports out of that former largely Jewish city.)

To these half-million or so deportees must be added another 300,000 to 500,000 people (predominantly Poles, like my family) who fled in terror in 1943-44 before the Ukrainian Nationalists, who on their own, under passive German gaze, began a systematic program of ethnic cleansing, of genocide.[74] On the eve of the war Hitler said: "The destruction of Poland is our primary task. The aim is not the arrival at a certain line but the *annihilation* of living forces.... Be merciless! Be brutal.... It is necessary to proceed with maximum severity.... The war is to be a war of *annihilation*."[75]

In October 1942, Otto Thierack, the Nazi minister of justice, forwarded a letter to Martin Bormann, head of the Party Chancellery, whereby the jurisdiction over certain native populations would be handed over to Himmler's SS (Schutzstaffel — Elite Guard or Blackshirt units). The letter reads:

> With the intent of cleansing the German nation of Poles, Russians, Jews and Gypsies and with the thought of cleansing the eastern territories joined to the Reich as territories to be settled by Germans, I intend to instruct the Reichsführer of the SS to execute the sentences against Poles, Russians, Jews and Gypsies. I am proceeding under the assumption that the Ministry of Justice will be able to make only a small contribution to the *extermination* of these people.[76]

In addition to the Polish citizens who died during the war, a number of citizens of other nations were brought to Poland. They were brought there to die. Among these were the Gypsies from Germany and German-occupied territories, the 784,000 Soviet POWs, the 22,000 Italian POWs who would not swear allegiance either to Hitler or to Benito Mussolini, the tens of thousands of POWs from France, Great Britain, the United States, and other countries, the 93 Czech children (gassed at Chełmno) from the town of Lidice, the 4,000 psychiatric patients from Germany, and the 1 million Jews from other European countries. In all, about 2 million people from twenty-nine countries and belonging to fifty different nationalities were also exterminated by the Germans on Polish soil. In no other country did so many citizens of so many other nations die at the hands of the Germans.[77]

By the time the war had run its course, Poland's great cities lay in ruin,[78] about 2.8 million Polish citizens had been deported to Germany and other occupied countries for forced labor, over 2 million had been forced from their homes, about 1 million found themselves in various camps and prisons, and some 5 million Polish citizens—Jews and Christians alike—had been killed by the Germans.

Thus, after almost six years of war and several brutal occupations by Germany and the Soviet Union, Poland lost about 6 million of its Jewish and Christian citizens—about 17 percent of its total population of just over 35 million. (About half of the 6 million were non-Jewish losses. Jewish wartime losses in Poland were between 79 percent and 85 percent of their population; ethnic Polish losses were between 9 percent and 10 percent.) In all, this was one of the highest ratios of losses to population of all countries in Europe.[79]

In the preceding statement, the word "losses" means "deaths." The overall losses, however, need to be interpreted in terms of the overall attrition of Polish citizens between 1939 and 1945. According to Jerzy Holzer, in 1939 there were 35.1 million citizens in the Republic of Poland. At the end of the war, only 19.1 million remained within its new borders.[80] Furthermore, as a direct result of the war, 800,000 Polish citizens became invalids, 80,000 developed various psychiatric disorders, and over 1 million succumbed to various diseases.[81]

These are awesome statistics; beneath them lie the unfathomable depths of human misery and degradation, on the one hand, and human depravity, on the other. As Richard Lukas put it: "Every nation under enemy occupation during World War II experienced a reign of terror by the Nazis. But no nation suffered more than Poland."[82] Thus, the inhuman policies of both Hitler and Stalin were clearly aimed at the total extermination of the Polish citizens, both Jews and Christians. Both régimes endorsed a systematic program of genocide.

Hidden in this Nazi-Soviet attempt at genocide and eclipsed by its grand scale are the efforts of some Polish citizens to collaborate in the tragic fate of their nation. In varying degrees, these collaborators and accomplices must share the responsibility for the overall war losses of Poland. In this work, the designation of wartime "collaborator" or "accomplice" will be applied to any Polish citizen who *voluntarily* offered services to Nazi Germany at any time throughout the war, to the detriment of Poland or its citizens, or who *voluntarily* cooperated with the Soviets between September 17, 1939, and June 22, 1941, or who *voluntarily* worked for the destruction of the Polish underground, citizens and state throughout the war, especially in any of the Soviet organs of oppression in Poland after 1944. The services include military, paramilitary, police, political, economic, literary, and other types of assistance, as well as any assistance given to the Soviets or the Germans in the conduct of genocide.[83]

The terms *collaborator* and *accomplice*, therefore, are being defined from the perspective of the Second Republic of Poland and its citizens. Needless to say, from another perspective, some of these collaborators and accomplices may be hailed as "freedom fighters" and "heroes" who, despite all odds, attempted to secure a measure of independence and/or equality for their respective constituencies. This was, after all, in the words of Thomas Hobbes, a "war of all against all."

It is imperative to remember that even from the perspective of the Polish nation, much of what follows clearly does not apply to the vast majority of Jews, Poles, Belorussians, Lithuanians, and Ukrainians who lived in Poland during that terrible war — only to that small fraction of people who took a stand against Poland, its interests, and its people by collaborating with the enemy, with the two nations that unleashed the terrible fury ever lurking beneath ethnic tensions in every pluralistic society. From this perspective, the vast majority of Polish citizens were not perpetrators, or collaborators, or accomplices. They were victims.

Chapter 3
Jewish Collaboration

The history of the Jews in Poland spans seven hundred years. In comparison with the horrific treatment of the Jews in most other medieval and early modern European countries, relative tolerance prevailed in Poland. This is astounding when one considers that the norm of the day in all of Europe was ethnic and religious exclusiveness and that this norm was adhered to by both Christians and Jews. To be tolerant, therefore, was to *deviate* from the norm. This "abominable vice of tolerance," as the Jesuit Piotr Skarga (1536-1612) called it, clearly existed in Poland, as substantiated by the fact that 75 percent of the Jews in the world today can trace their origins to the old Polish Commonwealth.[1] "As long as Poland was powerful," remarked one prominent rabbi, "Polish Jewry enjoyed an inner autonomy and freedom equalled by no other contemporary Jewry. Furthermore, it cannot be too often repeated that to Poland belongs the priority among European peoples in religious and cultural toleration."[2] There is a beautiful story that goes along with this assessment:

> The place is specially intended for Jews. When the Gentiles had greatly oppressed the exiled Jews, and the Divine Presence saw that there was no limit and no end to the oppression and that the handful of Jews might, God Forbid, go under, the Presence came before the Lord of the Universe to lay the grievance before Him, and said to Him as follows: "How long is this going to last? When You sent the dove out of the ark at the time of the flood, You gave it an olive branch so that it might have a support for its feet on the water, and yet it was unable to bear the water of the flood and returned to the ark; whereas my children You have sent out of the ark into a flood, and have provided nothing for a support where they may rest their feet in their exile." Thereupon God took a piece of Eretz Yisroel, which he had hidden away in the heavens at the time when the Temple was destroyed, and sent it down upon the earth and said: "Be My resting place for My children in their exile." That is why it is called Poland (Polin), from the Hebrew *poh lin*, which means: "Here shalt thou lodge" in the exile. That is why Satan has no power over us here, and the Torah is spread broadcast over the whole country. There are synagogues and schools and Yeshivahs, God be thanked.
>
> "And what will happen in the great future when the Messiah will come? What are we going to do with the synagogues and the settlements which we shall have built up in Poland?" asked Mendel....
>
> "How can you ask? In the great future, when the Messiah will come, God will certainly transport Poland with all its settlements, synagogues and Yeshivahs to Eretz Yisroel. How else could it be?"[3]

All of this is not to say that, for the Jews, Poland was always the "land of milk and honey"—only that they suffered less there and preferred Poland to any other European country as a place of residence. For many centuries, then, Poland was a true sanctuary to the Jews. And so, in 1939, there was little doubt where the allegiance of many Jews lay. On the eve of the war, 100,000 of them were mobilized for the Polish army, and the Bund kept reminding the Polish Jews that Poland was their home. At the end of August 1939, *Nasz Przegląd* stated: "The

Zionist organization and the Jewish people stand on the side of Poland, ready to fight for their own dignity and freedom. This declaration ought to be the guide-post for world Jewry. The place of the Jews throughout the whole world is on the side of Poland."[4]

The capitulation of Warsaw on September 27–28 and the laying down of arms in Polesie on October 6, 1939, ended the Polish struggle. The Polish losses were 66,000 killed, 133,000 wounded, and 400,000 in captivity. According to Jewish historians, the corresponding Jewish losses were 7,000 killed, 20,000 wounded, 61,000 in German captivity, and 20,000 in Soviet captivity. Before the war, the ratio of Christians in western Poland was 1:9; in all of Poland 1:10. Jews had done their part to defend their country. Under the military administration of Poland by the *Wehrmacht,* which ended with the creation of the General Government and the annexation of Poland's western territories by Germany, the Polish and Jewish civilian losses were also, proportionally speaking, even.[5] General Władysław Sikorski stated in November 1939: "It must be emphasized that our land was deeply moved by the proofs of loyalty to Poland manifested by the Slavic and Jewish minorities. This is irrefutable proof that the Polish national bond emerged in tact out of this terrible ordeal cast upon our land."[6]

The task before us, then, is to try to account for the elevated rates of anti–Jewish sentiment in Poland during the interwar years, the war years, and the postwar years — sentiment that, in the extreme, led to Jewish deaths in pogroms carried out by some Polish citizens and executions carried out by some Polish organizations.

In light of the tragic history of the Jews during World War II, this will appear as a hard saying, but a part of the blame for that Polish antipathy must surely rest on the shoulders of the Jews themselves. "Polish-Jewish relations deteriorated sharply on each of the three occasions when the Soviet Red Army has invaded Poland — in 1919–1920, in 1939[–1941], and in 1944–1945," states Norman Davies.[7] In 1939 and 1944, some Polish Jews became coparticipants in the Soviet reigns of terror, a regrettable fact that has now become a part of both Polish and Jewish history.

Interwar Years

It is no secret that the Communist Party in Poland has always had very strong support among the Jews. Aleksander Smolar notes, "The Jews were part of the communist movement from its very beginning."[8] For those readers who may agree with these statements but feel inclined to dismiss this support because of the insignificance of the Polish communist movement in interwar Poland, Jaff Schatz's words may serve as a caution:

> Western analysts who deem the membership of the Polish Communist party as insignificantly small often commit the mistake of forgetting that the movement acted underground, that membership was punishable by a severe prison sentence, that the devotion of the movement's cadres made up for much of its quantitative weakness, and, finally, that the movement had significant influence on a relatively large group of sympathizers and supporters. More serious, a frequent and embarrassing mistake is to disregard [i.e., not include in the tally] those individuals who at different times served prison sentences for their participation in the movement. Still another mistake is to fail to take into account or to diminish the qualitative and quantitative importance of the Communist youth movement.[9]

According to Andrzej Zwoliński, in Polish court proceedings against communists between 1927 and 1936, 10 percent of those accused were Polish Christians and 90 percent were Jews.[10] According to Henryk Cimek, out of the fifteen leaders in the central administration of the Polish Communist Party (Komunistyczna Partia Polska, or KPP) in 1936, eight were Jews and seven were Poles. Jews constituted 53 percent of the members of the "active center" (*aktyw centralny*), 75 percent of the KPP publication apparatus, 90 percent of the International Organization for Help to the Revolutionaries, and 100 percent of the "technical apparatus" of the Home Secretariat.[11] Before the dissolution of the KPP in 1938, Jews accounted for 25 percent of its membership. In the urban centers of central Poland, that membership rose to 50 percent.

According to Isaac Bashevis Singer, nearly all the Warsaw communists were Jews.[12] When Stalin revived the party in Poland at the beginning of 1942, the Warsaw Jews constituted its nucleus. Jaff Schatz presents the following summary of Jewish participation in the prewar Polish communist movement:

> As previously noted, throughout the whole interwar period, Jews constituted a very important segment of the Communist movement. According to Polish sources and to Western estimates, the proportion of Jews in the KPP was never lower than 22 percent. In the larger cities, the percentage of Jews in the KPP often exceeded 50 percent and in smaller cities, frequently over 60 percent. Given this background, a respondent's statement that "in small cities like ours, almost all Communists were Jews," does not appear to be a gross exaggeration.
>
> The proportion of Jewish membership in the KPP reached its peak in 1930 at 35 percent. During the remainder of the 1930s, the proportion is said not to have exceeded 24 percent. However, there are data suggesting that it might have increased further in the large cities: Jewish membership in the Communist organization in Warsaw increased dramatically, from 44 percent in 1930 to over 65 percent in 1937.
>
> All in all, most estimates put the proportion of Jews in the KPP at an average from 22 to 26 percent throughout the 1930s. In the semiautonomous KPZU and KPZB, the percentage of Jewish members was at least similar to that in the KPP.
>
> In the Communist youth organizations, the proportion of Jewish members was even higher than in the party itself. In 1930, Jews constituted 51 percent of the KZMP [Komunistyczne Zjednoczenie Młodych Polaków, or Communist Union of Polish Youth], while ethnic Poles were only 19 percent (the remaining number was composed of Ukrainians and Byelorussians). And in 1933, Jews made up 31 percent as compared to ethnic Poles who made up 33 percent. If we assume that Polish-Jewish Communists constituted between one-third and one-fourth of the total membership of the whole movement (KPP, KPZB, KPZU, and their youth organizations) in the 1930s, this would approximate between 5,000 and 8,400 Jewish Communists, without counting those in prison. If we include those imprisoned, the total number of Jews in the Communist movement in Poland during that period would probably rise to between 6,200 to 10,000 individuals. In addition, Jews were in an overwhelming majority in the Polish MOPR (*Międzynarodowa Organizacja Pomocy Rewolucjonistom*, International Organization for Help to the Revolutionaries), which collected money for and channeled assistance to imprisoned Communists. In 1932, out of 6,000 members in the MOPR, about 90 percent were Jews.
>
> The qualitative significance of Jewish Communists was even larger than their sheer numbers would indicate. Despite the fact that party authorities consciously strove to promote classically proletarian and ethnically Polish members to the cadres of leaders and functionaries, Jewish Communists formed 54 percent of the field leadership of the KPP in 1935. Moreover, Jews constituted a total of 75 percent of the party's *technika*, the apparatus for production and distribution of propaganda materials. Finally Communists of Jewish origin occupied most of the seats on the Central Committees of the KPRP and KPP.[13]

For this very reason, Schatz states, "Jewish Communists, even those who in their messianic fury expressly denied their Jewish roots, form an integral and ... fascinating part of the modern Jewish historical experience."[14] The crucial question, of course, is just how widespread was the Jewish support of communism in prewar Poland. Schatz provides one answer:

> Was, then, the stereotype of Żydokomuna basically correct? Even if we were to accept the claim made by Jewish Communists after the war that "of the highest number of votes the Communists ever polled in Poland, i.e., of the 266,528 votes collected on several lists of front organizations at the Sejm elections of 1928, two-fifths were cast by Jews," it would mean that Communist ideals were sympathetic to only about 5 percent of all Jewish voters. The total picture that emerges is thus one of the very important role Jews played in the Polish Communist movement of the time and, at the same time, a general Jewish community far from sympathetic to communism.[15]

Stanisław Krajewski (pseudonym "Abel Kainer," a Polish-Jewish intellectual who presently serves as the cochair of the Polish Council of Christians and Jews) is of the same opinion: "In prewar Poland, communists neither enjoyed much popularity among the Jewish masses nor had any real influence on the Jewish community's leadership."[16] Yet, 5 percent of the over 3 million Jews in interwar Poland is still a very large number, and we still need to explain, in the words of Krajewski, "the disproportionately large participation of Jews in the communist movement, especially in Poland, both before and after the war."[17]

Needless to say, there must have been a reason these Polish citizens espoused the teachings of communism. Unlike the Ukrainians, Belorussians and Lithuanians, the Jews had no territorial claims of their own. No doubt some of them, particularly the youth, thus became communists for ideological reasons — in the hope of achieving equality (i.e., equality with those in superior status positions) under a system that purported to fight the "enemies of the people," the "class enemies," the bourgeoisie (many of whom were Jews, those who "owned the buildings if not the streets"), rather than specific ethnic or religious minorities. Communism was the "home of the workers," not a haven for the exploitative "leisurely classes." Communism was the utopian land of progress, reason, and modernity, not the home of stifling ancient traditions, religious mandates of intolerance and nationalism. They expected "equal rights" under communism and "equal suffrage." But in the twenty-one months of Soviet occupation of Eastern Poland, what they achieved was only "equality in suffering."[18] To be sure, others joined the communist movement for less noble reasons. This flight to communism within the Polish borders, together with anti-Semitism, may account in part for the persecution of the Jews in Poland during the interwar years, especially after Piłsudski's death in 1935. (The arrest of Polish communists continued after the dissolution of the KPP and lasted until the beginning of World War II.)

But how was Poland different in this respect from the rest of Europe? In some other countries with sizeable Jewish populations, the situation was much worse. Even in the United States, whose constitution guaranteed religious freedom to one and all, there was a great deal of anti-Semitism. For example, voting restrictions on Jews were not lifted in Rhode Island until 1842, in North Carolina until 1868, and in New Hampshire until 1877. There was a wide perception in this country, as in Britain after the 1917 Bolshevik Revolution, that communism and Judaism were synonymous. As in Poland, quotas were imposed on Jewish students at Harvard, Princeton, Ohio State, and other universities across the country, and in spite of their qualifications, Jewish professors in the United States were few and far in between.[19] During the Great Depression, clubs and resorts routinely banned Jews. Between 1933 and 1941, over one hundred anti-Semitic organizations emerged, and by 1938, forty-five radio stations carried Father Charles Coughlin's weekly anti-Semitic "sermons." Even the U.S. Congress was a haven for outspoken anti-Semites. Thankfully, America never had a tradition of pogroms (at least not for Jews — the routine lynching of downtrodden African Americans is another matter), but that was little comfort to Leo Frank, lynched in 1915.[20] As we all know, the situations of the Native Americans and the African Americans were far worse, and some still remember the shop-window signs that read: "Help wanted. Irish need not apply." However, given America's healthier economy, life there was more tolerable for the minorities than in the war-ravaged, poverty-stricken, underdeveloped and chaotic Second Republic of Poland. To single out and humiliate Poland for its real or manufactured anti-Semitism is, therefore, grossly unfair.

Ethnocentrism in Poland was a two-way street. A Jew who married a Christian was anathema in both social circles. "The Jews regarded the Poles with contempt and caution," states Samuel Oliner, a Jewish scholar, "but we had still been on good terms."[21] Unlike the Jews in many other countries, the Jews in Poland chose to remain aloof from the culture in which they found themselves. The reason for this, as Lucien Steinberg put it, was their "underlying fear of losing substance,"[22] or their own cultural and religious identity. Rachmiel Frydland, a yeshiva student, tells us what it was like growing up among Christians in Chełm:

> Our relations with the non–Jewish population were never very good, but at least the opposition was divided. There were the Polish-speaking Gentiles who were Roman Catholics, some more pious than others. We were most afraid of them. We considered them idol worshipers.... I had no contacts with Christianity at all. On the way to school we passed a Roman Catholic church and a Russian Orthodox church, and we spat, pronouncing the words found in Deuteronomy 7:26, "...thou shalt utterly detest it, and thou shalt utterly abhor it; for it is a cursed thing."[23]

Who taught young Rachmiel to utter "such horrible words"? "The people looked so pious," he recalls. "They came from surrounding villages to worship, and they never bothered us."[24] Abraham Sterzer, from Eastern Galicia, tells us about his teachers: "I received the traditional education in a 'heder' (religious school). Our rabbi insisted that we Jewish children spit on the ground and utter curses while passing near a cross, or whenever we encountered a Christian priest or religious procession. Our shopkeepers used to say that 'it was a Mitzveh (blessed deed) to cheat a Goy (gentile).'"[25]

Dora Kacnelson, from Białystok, explains: "There are tolerant Jews, like my father for instance, but there are also fanatical ones, holding on tight to old traditions. They think that the Christians are something beneath them."[26]

Anna Lanota remembered: "The [Jewish] community [in which I lived] had a somewhat unfavourable attitude toward other nations—maybe even contemptuous. There prevailed the feeling that we were the chosen people. In school there was that same atmosphere that Jews were the chosen people. We did not pay attention to what others might be saying about us."[27]

In the 1920s Antoni Słominski, a Polish poet of Jewish origin, stated: "I know very few Jews who are not convinced of the superiority of the Jewish race. For that reason this nation ... does not neglect even the smallest of reproaches.... Those Jews who complain about the lack of tolerance of others are the least tolerant."[28]

After seven hundred years in Poland, most Jews still clung to their own language. According to the 1931 Polish census, Yiddish was the mother tongue of 79 percent of the Jews, Polish of 12 percent, and Hebrew of 9 percent. The actual proportion of those who spoke Polish, however, was probably much higher.[29]

Jewish ethnocentrism, according to Israel Shahak, is not merely the product of Christian persecution: "Judaism is imbued with a very deep hatred towards Christianity, combined with ignorance about it. This attitude was clearly aggravated by the Christian persecutions of the Jews, but is largely independent of them. In fact, it dates from the time when Christianity was still weak and persecuted (not least by the Jews), and it was shared by Jews who had never been persecuted by Christians or who were even helped by them."[30] Richard Lukas adds: "Jews maintained their own lifestyle and values and preferred to have only limited contact with the Poles, usually confined to business dealings. Little wonder, then, that Poles and Jews did not really know each other very well, even though they had lived side by side for centuries."[31]

In Poland this voluntary isolationism was made possible by the sheer numbers of Jews and by the partitions that delayed the process of assimilation. No one, of course, knows what would have happened to the Polish Jews had the war not intervened. Given the large Jewish presence in Poland, tensions would inevitably have escalated as the Jews began to leave their shtetlach and establish contacts with the surrounding Christian population. But the judgment, so often expressed by Jewish scholars, that Poland's increasingly anti–Semitic policies would have driven them out of the country seems to be unwarranted. Jaff Schatz notes:

> Among upper and middle class youth, Polish was becoming the dominant language and, as a second language—after Yiddish—was making inroads even among those from lower strata. Thus, half of Jewish students declared in 1929–30 that they spoke Polish at home; in 1939, half of the Jewish high school students called Polish their mother tongue. Polonized first names became increasingly popular among younger members

> of the middle class and the intelligentsia, and there was a clear shift toward Polish values and norms of behavior. Had not the Holocaust occurred, within one or two generations Hebrew and Yiddish schools would most probably have declined, Polish would have replaced Yiddish and become the main language for Jewish cultural creativity, distinct Jewish dress would have more or less disappeared, and the Polonization of the bulk of Polish Jewry would have been fully comparable to the acculturation of Jews in Western countries.[32]

Be that as it may, the contemporary record of the State of Israel in respect to human rights bears eloquent witness to the difficulties surrounding the full integration of minorities in any country (see Appendix, Document 8, "Affidavit of Lynda Brayer, December 5, 1993"). Many impartial scholars must be astonished that so many of the most strident critics of Poland's interwar policies regarding the treatment of the Jews live in or identify with the State of Israel, which, after all, has had over twice as much time as the Second Republic of Poland to sort out its own ethnic and religious problems.

But we must return to Europe. In *The Holocaust*, Martin Gilbert wrote that just after the First World War, "more than fifty Jews were killed by local Ukrainians in the eastern Polish city of Lvov.... In the city of Vilna, the 'Jerusalem of Lithuania,' eighty Jews were murdered during April 1919; in Galicia, five hundred perished."[33] Israel Gutman and Shmuel Krakowski state: "Most of the murders were perpetrated in a whole line of cities and towns [in Eastern Poland] during the Polish-Soviet War of 1919–20. Jews were accused of favoring communism, of treason, and of espionage." Their account of the Lwów tragedy, however, differs in important details: "In Lwów, a city whose fate was disputed, the Jews tried to maintain their neutrality between Poles and Ukrainians, and in reaction a pogrom was held in the city under the auspices of the Polish army, in which seventy-two Jews were killed and hundreds were injured." The authors continue:

> In a long list of cities and towns in Eastern Poland pogroms and riots were carried out. An incident which occurred in the city of Pińsk caused a deep shock. A group of Jews gathered in the People's Palace in the city on April 5, 1919, to divide the aid sent them by their relatives and by organizations in the U.S.A. The army broke into the building, accused those present of holding a communist conspiratorial gathering, and without conducting any sort of investigation or inquiry summarily executed thirty-five Jews.[34]

According to various Jewish historians, renewed waves of persecutions began in 1936. In March of that year a pogrom occurred in the village of Przytyk, just south of Warsaw.[35] "As for violence, suffice it to say that according to Polish sources, in 1936, 21 pogroms and 348 individual acts of violence took place in the Białystok region alone; according to Jewish sources, seventy-nine Jews were killed and approximately five hundred were wounded from October to April that year."[36] In 1937, 350 physical assaults against the Jews were recorded in Poland in the month of August alone.[37] Between 1935 and 1937, in sixteen pogroms, 118 Jews died.[38] Emanuel Ringelblum, the chronicler of the Warsaw ghetto, attributed such facts to Poland's prewar "united anti-Jewish front, *Endeko-Sanacja.*" He concluded, "Poland before the war became the leading anti-Semitic country in Europe, second to Germany alone."[39] Ben-Cion Pinchuk adds:

> The Polish government followed a systematic policy designed to curtail Jewish economic activity. Anti-Semitism in inter-war Poland was a respectable ideology and culminated in an official policy of ridding Poland of its Jews. Poland's leaders after 1935 used anti-Semitism to direct public attention away from the country's real problems. Overt discrimination in all government institutions and enterprises, limitation of the number of Jewish university students, as well as physical harassment and bloody pogroms were among the manifestations of Polish pre-war anti-Semitism.[40]

The pogroms and killings referred to above represent the worst-case scenarios in Polish-Jewish relations during the interwar years. Aside from the fact that all of these accounts fail to consider the ordinary criminal motives (e.g., robbery) of the perpetrators, as well as the role of the Jewish victims (they were not all innocent bystanders), they paint a grim and severely biased picture of the situation in the Second Republic of Poland. For the most part, interaction between Poles and Jews was quite uneventful, even distantly cordial. Rachela Walshaw described her (more common) experiences in "Wonchok" (Wąchock, near Starachowice), a typical small town in central Poland:

> The community was clearly divided between Poles and Jews. There were about 500 Polish families and only about one hundred Jewish ones, but we all lived and worked in relative peace. There were no ghettos then. Jews could live anywhere in town, but generally chose to live together ... among their own kind.... Though I went to school with Christians, my knowledge of the private workings of the Christian world was limited. The Catholic priests who ran our school were strict but fair and excused us from participating in their prayers. On the whole, my gentile classmates were a decent lot with whom we remained distant but friendly. We were not invited to their homes; nor were they invited to ours.[41]

The conclusions of Ringelblum, Pinchuk, and other Jewish historians must be understood in light of Ezra Mendelsohn's honest assessment of Jewish historiography as it relates to the interwar situation in Poland:

> The attitude of most Jewish scholars has been, and continues to be, that interwar Poland was an extremely anti-semitic country, perhaps even uniquely anti-semitic. They claim that Polish Jewry during the 1920s and 1930s was in a state of constant and alarming decline, and that by the 1930s both the Polish régime and Polish society were waging a bitter and increasingly successful war against the Jewish population. The impression sometimes gained from reading the works of these authors is that Jewish life in Poland was a nightmare of almost daily pogroms, degradation and growing misery.[42]

Indeed, after reading such scholarly accounts, the unwary reader cannot help but garner the distinct impression that the Poles had nothing better to do with their time and their newly won independence than to plan and carry out Jewish pogroms, their chief and perhaps only preoccupation, predilection, and mania until World War II. This line of thinking leads nicely to the conclusion that the Jewish Holocaust on Polish soil was inevitable. Of course, the allegations of continuous pogroms, as well as many Jewish scholars' sweeping conclusions about interwar Polish-Jewish relations, have not gone without challenge. Lukas argues:

> Anti-Semitism existed both in prewar and wartime Poland. In prewar Poland, however, Jews had to contend more with economic and bureaucratic discrimination than with physical assaults.... American and British observers discredited western reports of widespread pogroms in the early years of the Polish Republic. For instance, an alleged pogrom in Lwów was a military massacre in which more Christians than Jews perished. Another reported pogrom in Pińsk in 1919 was in reality the execution of thirty-five Bolshevik infiltrators, a judgment an American investigator considered justified in the circumstances. The brief internment of Jews in Jabłonna in 1920 did not result either in mistreatment or deaths. Moreover, in some places, as in Vilna in 1919 and 1920, the Jews put themselves in a vulnerable position by collaborating with Poland's enemies — Lithuanians and Bolsheviks.[43]

We should note a fine point: of all the "Polish" towns in which the 1918–19 "pogroms" occurred, only Kielce and Częstochowa lay within Polish borders. Lwów was still a part of Austrian Galicia, and Gutman and Krakowski's "long list of towns in Eastern Poland [where] pogroms and riots were carried out" belonged to tsarist Russia. The Polish population in all of these cities and towns, except for Lwów and Wilno, was relatively small.

After investigating 37 places in Eastern Galicia where alleged anti-Jewish excesses were said to have occurred, a Polish Settlement Commission (Polska Komisja Likwidacyjna), reduced Gutman and Krakowski's "long list" to just six towns: Lwów, Kolbuszowa, Pińsk, Lida, Wilno, and Minsk.[44]

On December 8, 1919, a Polish National Committee (Komitet Narodowy Polski) report analyzed all the "so-called pogroms" that had occurred in Poland up to that date and concluded that, "none of the occurrences which took place in Poland in which the Jewish people suffered had the character of a 'pogrom' organized by the Polish people against an unarmed population."[45]

The Anglo-American Investigating Commission sent to Poland in 1919 and headed by two Jews, Henry Morgenthau (American) and Sir Stuart M. Samuel (British), concluded that these excesses were of a political rather than anti-Semitic nature and that the term *pogrom* was inapplicable to the conditions existing within a war zone.

Adam Ciołkosz, a socialist politician married to a Jew and respected by the Jews, arrived in Lwów on November 21, 1918. He later recalled that although the Polish soldiers were fired on from rooftops (by Ukrainian riflemen, he believed, though rumor implicated the Jews as well), "the Polish army not only did not take part in the pogrom, but rather, to the best of its ability, intervened in the defense of the Jewish quarter, and finally quelled the pogrom." He discredited the outlandish report in the *Jewish Chronicle* (December 6, 1918) that 3,200 Jews were massacred in Lwów (it was 72), as well as the February 14, 1919, report, in the same *Jewish Chronicle*, that a *numerus clausus* existed at the Jagiellonian University in Kraków.[46]

In 1919 the Nobel prize-winning author Władysław Reymont reported on the Wilno pogrom: "There were no anti-Semitic disturbances in Wilno on May 5 despite the reports coming from Kaunas. When the Polish army entered the town on Easter Sunday, a number of Jews perished either from fighting in the streets or because many [Polish] soldiers fell from shots emanating from houses inhabited exclusively by Jews."[47]

Józef Piłsudski corroborated this statement: "When I arrived in Wilno on the second day of the holidays, I witnessed how the whole town wept with emotion and joy.... It was considerably worse with the Jews who constituted the governing class under the Soviet rule. With great difficulty was I able to contain the pogrom which hung in the air due to the fact that Jewish civilians were shooting [at the Polish soldiers] from windows and housetops and dropping hand grenades."[48] According to the Morgenthau Commission, Poles also died at the hands of Jews, in Wilno as elsewhere.

In 1990, Adam Penkulla analyzed the March 9, 1936, "Przytyk incidents" on the basis of available archival documents and published his findings in *Polin*. According to this scholarly analysis, the documents reveal the following: there was an escalation of anti-Jewish feeling that was connected to the activities (boycotts of Jewish businesses on market days and direct attacks on Jews and on Poles dealing with Jews) of the local branch of the National Party (Stronnictwo Narodowe, or SN); the "authorities failed to act decisively enough, were unable to prevent the incidents from taking place, or did not realize the consequences of an inevitable direct clash" during the annual horse fair; various political parties and organizations, as well as the court, condemned discrimination against the Jewish population; and after being tried in a court of law, thirty-five people out of fifty-seven accused received sentences. "It is probably significant," states Penkulla, "that they [the Christian and Jewish participants in the incidents] were mainly young men who certainly knew each other and had dealings with each other. Of the 42 Poles named in the indictment, 73.8 percent were aged between 20 and 30 and 14.3 percent between 31 and 40 years.... The Jews indicted were also young. Of the fourteen, 42.9 percent were aged between 20 and 30, and 28.6 percent between 30 and 40." The police report (March 14, 1936) stated: "It has been established beyond doubt, that only Jews used firearms during the events, while peasants used mainly stones and clubs."[49] The March 18, 1936, report of the head of the Social and Political Section of the Provincial Department in Kielce provides some additional details:

> Police constables immediately went there and found that Jews and Christians were throwing stones at each other. Jews were throwing stones from their houses and side streets,

> while Poles were throwing ones found in the streets. There was a large crowd on the bridge trying to break through the Jews towards the square. The police therefore prevented this by attacking both Jews and Christians.
>
> ...several peasants still managed to get into the square. Reinforced by those peasants who returned from the cattle market, they then started to throw stones at the windows of Jewish apartments in the square and on Warszawska Street. At that point the police again attacked the peasants, who started to flee in panic. Then several pistol shots were fired from a window of the first-floor apartment of Leska Moszek, which killed Stanisław Wieśniak, from the village of Wrzos, on Warszawska Street. Kubiak Stanisław from the village of Słowików was also badly wounded and a few peasants slightly wounded by these shots. Of the Jews, Josek Mińkowski was killed, and his fatally-wounded wife, Chaja, died after being carried to the Radom hospital. In addition, 24 Jews were slightly wounded....
>
> These events took place over a relatively short period of time, about 45 minutes, as the mob moved from one place to another at lightning speed. It has been proved beyond any doubt that only Jews used firearms, while the peasants used stones and clubs.[50]

In 1936, the population of this town in the county of Radom was about 3,000, of whom almost 90 percent were Jews. The Poles in the area were mainly farmers; the Jews were mainly engaged in crafts and trade.

As for the Kielce and Częstochowa incidents, the first was sparked by a massive demonstration involving 300 young Jews who marched up and down the town streets chanting: "Long live Lenin! Long live Trotsky! To hell with Poland!"[51] The second was precipitated by the shooting of a Polish soldier by a Jew.[52]

Perhaps no one will ever know the full truth about Polish-Jewish relations during those fateful twenty years of Polish independence. But a *part of that truth* lies in the migratory settlement patterns during the partitions of Poland. As a result of Russian discriminatory policies, an estimated 800,000 "Litvaks" (Litwaki: Jews from Russian territories, notably Belorussia and Lithuania) went to Poland—Jews who were eventually given full Polish citizenship but who were not always welcomed either by the Poles or by the indigenous Jews because they were strangers, because they contributed to population pressures, and because they were perceived as competitors for scarce resources in a modernizing society. At the turn of the twentieth century, these Jews became a political problem as well.

A *part of that truth* also has to do with the sheer enormity and complexity of the ethnic problems confronting this young republic after World War I and with the unrealistic expectations of those minority groups that believed that Poland could have and should have solved these problems in the short twenty years of its existence, during a time of worldwide depression.

A *part of that truth* relates to the state of war in which Poland found itself immediately after World War I. The incident in Lwów, for example, occurred in the context of the Polish-Ukrainian War, in which 340 civilians died, 72 of them Jews. The "pogroms" and "riots" in that "long list of cities and towns in Eastern Poland" (i.e., along the Soviet border) occurred in the context of the Polish-Soviet War. Norman Davies has written:

> The state of war prevailing in Poland from November 1918 to October 1920 was the most important cause of the excesses. This explanation, advanced at an early stage by Polish apologists, was never accepted by liberal and Jewish opinion in England.... In a wartime situation it was impossible to disentangle acts of gratuitous antisemitism from the commonplace looting and brutality of the soldiery. Certainly, "pogrom" in the accepted sense of the deliberate lynching of Jewish civilians, cannot be applied to the great majority of incidents. Where the word does seem relevant, as at Chrzanów in October 1918, the facts did not become known to the British public until much later. As soon as the war ceased, so did the excesses.
>
> The scale of Jewish casualties was minimal considering the conditions in which they occurred.... That fewer than one thousand Jewish civilians perished, when the Polish army during the same period suffered over 250,000 casualties, is a fair indication of the scale of the disaster.
>
> Poland was the target for Jewish publicity

> in 1918–19 partly because the Ukraine, Rumania, and Hungary were not accessible to Western investigators. In the Ukrainian Civil War and the Hungarian White Terror, which raged alongside the Polish-Soviet war, Jewish casualties were incomparably greater. Jewish deaths in the Ukraine have been estimated at 100,000. Thus Horace Rumbold's conclusions in this context still ring true: "the condition [of the Jews] in Poland, bad as it may have been or may still be, has been far better than in most of the surrounding countries. It is giving the Jews very little real assistance to single out as is sometimes done for reprobation and protest, the country where they have perhaps suffered least."[53]

Yet the deaths of "fewer than one thousand Jewish civilians" in Poland cannot be relegated to insignificance by comparison with the Polish losses at this time, or with events in other countries, or with the Holocaust that would follow later — and this is also a *part of that truth*.

A *part of that truth* lies in the contradictory demands made on the Polish government by competing Jewish political parties representing a variety of ideologies: the Orthodox Jewry, resolved to live in its self-imposed isolationism and to pursue its traditional identity based on religion; the assimilationists, resolved to integrate Jews into the general Polish society as quickly as possible; the left- and right-wing Zionists, resolved to establish an Eretz Israel (Land of Israel) outside of Poland; the Jewish Socialists (the Bund), resolved to struggle for equality, secularism, and a Yiddish-based Jewish cultural autonomy; and the Jewish communists, resolved to destroy the prevailing system of "capitalist exploitation" by a grass-roots social revolution. "What united them," states Jaff Schatz, "was their rejection of the world as it was; what divided them were their different prescriptions for Jewish, universal, or Jewish and universal emancipation."[54] What government could meet all these demands?

A *part of that truth* concerns the public perception of the events in Poland, a perception fashioned by the irresponsible use of the phrase "Polish pogroms" by militant Zionist circles and especially by British journalists — in the same years that the infamous *Protocols of the Elders of Zion* was rolling off English presses. The American press was no better. Unfortunately, that faulty perception has now become a "fact of history."

A *part of that truth* is touched on by Ezra Mendelsohn:

> The "Jewish experience" in interwar Poland is often regarded as having represented a crucial, indeed fateful, test for the major political and cultural positions that had developed in the Jewish world during the nineteenth century. Poland in this sense is regarded as a kind of battleground on which the various Jewish proposals to "solve the Jewish question" waged war, the framework in which, for example, the question as to whether the Jews could prosper "here," in the east European diaspora, or whether they should do everything in their power to remove themselves and to resettle "there," in Palestine, was posed in its sharpest form. The reasons why Poland was singled out for this "honour" by Jewish historians, publicists, and ideologues are fairly obvious: there were more Jews there than anywhere else in Europe, they were free to organize (as they were not in the Soviet Union), and they were not undergoing a rapid process of integration into state and society, as were the Jews of the United States. It was on Polish soil that Orthodoxy and secularism, socialism and anti–socialism, nationalism and "assimilationism," Hebraism and Yiddish-ism, Zionism and diaspora nationalism, sought to impose their way of life and their "solutions" on the Jewish population.
>
> There is, of course, yet another reason for the passions aroused by the assessments of the interwar period, namely the question of the relationship between the periods 1918-39 and 1939-45. It is extremely difficult even for the most objective scholar to write about the Jews in interwar Poland without considering what happened in that country during the Nazi occupation ... the mass murder of Jews on Polish soil during the war. This attitude naturally colours Jewish historians' treatment of the interwar period.[55]

Behind these insights lurks a terrible truth: for the State of Israel to be born, Poland — the traditional home of diaspora Jews — had to be compromised with allegations of widespread "Polish anti-Semitism," "Polish pogroms," and "Polish concentration camps."

A *part of that truth* is contained in the following words of Konstanty A. Jeleński, words as descriptive of Poland as of any other country, as applicable to the Jews as, mutatis mutandis, to any other minority the world over, including the Palestinian, Lebanese, and Christian minorities in the present-day State of Israel:

> Since, with the exception of the ONR and Falange (discounting those in the ranks of the National Party), the "consequent" fascist theories modeled after the German Nuremberg Laws did not exist in Poland — one can, on this basis, claim that anti-Semitism did not exist in Poland. Poles came out against the Jews not "because they were Jews," but because they are filthy, avaricious, liars, have sideburns, speak Yiddish, do not wish to assimilate; and also because they are becoming assimilated, are ceasing to speak Yiddish, are elegantly dressed, want to be Poles. Because they are uncultured; and because they are very cultured. Because they are prejudiced, backward and unenlightened; and also because they are infernally capable, progressive and ambitious. Because they have long, crooked noses; and because it is sometimes difficult to distinguish them from "pure Poles." Because they crucified Christ, practice ritual slaughter, and pore over the Talmud; and because they have spurned their own religion and are atheists. Because they are weak, diseased, born milksops and victims; and because they are athletic, have fighting units, and "chutzpa." Because they are bankers and capitalists; and because they are communists and agitators. In any case, because they are Jews.[56]

And finally, a *part of that truth* relates to the following facts: that in the interwar years, the majority of Jews and Poles lived side by side in relative peace; that all considered themselves to be Polish citizens; that in comparison with the general population, Jews were on the average better off than Christians during the entire interwar period; that there were numerous Jewish publications as well as Jewish political parties and Jewish social and cultural institutions; and that interwar Poland, in the words of Aleksander Smolar, was "the land of the largest and the most culturally and politically dynamic Jewish community in Europe."[57]

As for the "on the blood of martyrs" argument voiced by so many Jewish scholars, it can be more truthfully said that Jewish sociocultural life (educational, economic, political, literary, religious, community) prospered in Poland as in no other European country at this time not only because Polish prejudice, discrimination, and persecution existed but also, and more important, because this emerging independent nation was a relatively tolerant, liberal, open, and democratic society. Ezra Mendelsohn understood this when he wrote, "The experience of Polish Jews between the wars was a combination of suffering, some of which was caused by anti-semitism, and of achievement, made possible by Polish freedom, pluralism and tolerance." The specifically Jewish character of all this creativity had as much to do with the "refusal of Polish society to allow for Jewish integration"[58] as it did with the unwillingness of the Jews to become assimilated or, to put it another way, with their conscious choice to retain their language, their religion, their traditions — in a word, their special culture.

These are not arguments, of course, for excusing or promoting the mistreatment of indigenous minorities in pluralistic, democratic societies. Many Jews in Poland did not become more creative; they simply left the country. Between 1921 and 1937, 395,223 Polish Jews emigrated.[59] Stymied by increasingly restrictive immigration quotas imposed by Western countries, 3,679 (according to an early table prepared by the Research Centre for a Solution to the Jewish Problem),[60] or 3,636 (according to a 1938 "Memorandum on the Development of the Jewish National Home"),[61] or 8,856 (according to a 1943 table in *Jewish Social Studies*)[62] emigrated in 1937. According to the above-mentioned Research Centre, out of a total of 270,674 Jewish immigrants to Palestine between 1923 and 1937, 111,502 (or 41.2 percent) came from Poland.[63] It must be remembered that during the interwar years, emigration as a solution to the "Jewish problem" was embraced by a number of Polish as well as

Jewish political organizations, albeit perhaps for very different reasons.[64]

The following non–partisan analysis (dated June 30, 1946) of the "Jewish Problem in Poland" was written by the first secretary of the Italian Embassy in Warsaw. It was forwarded by Ambassador Eugenio Reale along with his own report to the Ministry of Foreign Affairs in Rome, in the hope that this "report dedicated to one of the most characteristic problems of this land may fill out the picture of the major political, social and agricultural problems confronting Poland in the first phase of her postwar existence." A part of that report addresses the history of the Jews in Poland and the nature of and reasons for Polish anti–Semitism during the interwar years.

> The Jews have been in Poland for 700 years. They first appeared here around 1,200 A.D. when, having been thrown out of Germany, they were greeted in Poland with a friendly reception. King Kazimierz III, who surmised that their presence might redound to the benefit of the country, granted them various guarantees and privileges. In the course of the following centuries the Jews, who fall victim to numerous persecutions in almost every European country, continue to arrive in Poland. The last great immigration, which took place toward the end of the nineteenth century, was the result of anti–Semitic riots in the southern provinces of Russia as well as the decree which forbade the Jews to live in the territory of Russia itself; at that time they moved from the East onto Polish lands which were then under the authority of the Tsars.
>
> In Poland, that is to say, in a land which in comparison to Western Europe was economically and socially backward as well as mostly agricultural, the Jews were able to engage in their pursuits without exposing themselves to competition in the sphere which suited their character the best, namely, in industry, trade and financial speculation.
>
> In this long period of time to which we refer in such a cursory fashion, Poland, of course, was also beset with violent anti-Semitic manifestations; but in comparison to the situations which generally forced them to emigrate to Poland, in comparison to the suffering to which they were exposed in other parts of Europe, Poland emerged as the land of the greatest tolerance. The waves of pogroms which visited Russia, the other nations of East Europe, and the Balkans toward the end of the nineteenth and the beginning of the twentieth centuries never reached Poland at all. In reality, relations between Poles and Jews began to deteriorate only from 1912 on, when the first major boycott of Jewish businesses occurred—an action intended to punish the Jews who stood accused of carrying on intrigues during the time of the elections.
>
> Under the Russian, German and Austrian partitions the Polish people were subjected not only to severe rigors of the occupation authorities but also to actions intended to divest them of their national character. And so, while the Poles attempted to safeguard their national rights by fighting bravely against the partitioning powers, the Jews were rather inclined to cooperate with them.
>
> This phenomenon appeared most vividly in that part of Poland which found itself under the German partition, where the Jews were fascinated by German might and where they could greatly benefit from the impressive economic development of that country and its expansion in trade.
>
> In effect, Polish Jews together with German Jews held a monopoly over all exports and imports of goods between Germany and Russia. Certain branches of manufacture in Poland were also under their control, particularly the textile industry in Łódź.
>
> It is of little wonder, then, that the Jews often manifested their true, undeniably existing feelings of solidarity with the Prussians. In Pomerania, during the 1848 insurrection, groups of Jews greeted the insurgents with shouts such as, "We do not want Poland, we are Prussians." Almost a half century later, during the Warsaw manifestations in favor of Polish autonomy in the Russian sphere, the Jews took a similar position against the demonstrators shouting, "Why should Poland exist? Down with Poland! Down with the white eagle!"
>
> During the First World War, a large segment of Polish Jews identified itself with the central powers; many underscored joint Jewish and German interests and demanded the acknowledgement of the fact that Poland is inhabited by two separate nationalities; others supported the idea of an autonomous Poland while maintaining close ties with the

central powers within the context of Mitteleuropa. Finally, still others — these belonged to the adherents of international socialism — relegated themselves to reproaching the Germans with a lack of understanding of their true mission which, they were convinced, consisted in the conduct of war with the aim of bringing about a social revolution.

After the conclusion of the peace at Brest Litovsk, the Polish Jews continued to conduct their anti–national action by supporting the independence of [Western] Ukraine and by advocating that the Polish territories of Chełm be joined to her. At the end of the war, they came out against the Polish takeover of Gdańsk [Danzig], Poznań, Opole [Oppeln], Cieszyn [Teschen], Lwów and Wilno.

In the new Polish Republic which emerged in 1918, the Jewish people lived, in contrast to their Israelite counterparts in Western Europe and America, in almost complete isolation from the Poles, cut off and almost hermetically sealed within themselves; the period between the two wars is characterized by the rise of anti–Semitic dispositions, particularly among the youth which assumed the guise of a notable lack of tolerance. All the political parties, with the exception of the communist (illegal) and socialist, either attempted to ignore this state of affairs or supported it in secret; only the National Party, consisting mainly of young people, spoke openly of the idea of fighting the Jews. The Poles, therefore, maintain a position at this time with respect to the Jews which is inconsistent with the traditions of tolerance and hospitality so characteristic of them in the course of so many centuries.

The Polish government, especially until the death of Piłsudski, did not sympathize at all with this position which, it could be said, was quite prevalent; not only did this government manifest a genuinely friendly attitude toward the Jews, it also attempted to improve their conditions of life and with great energy suppressed all acts of violence directed against them. After the death of the Marshal, the situation clearly worsened. The economic boycott of Jews begins all over again; numerous university departments introduce a *numerus clausus* and some of them even a *numerus nullus*. This decision is motivated chiefly by the desire to reduce their numerical preponderance in the learned professions, for example, among doctors and lawyers.

Polish anti–Semitism. It should be emphasized that anti–Semitism in Poland has never assumed a character of an organized movement. Except for a few attempts on the part of the members of the National Party to work out a theory of anti–Semitism, a true racial theory of the German type has never emerged in Poland. Polish anti–Semitism is primarily an emotional response; among the reasons which called it forth, perhaps the most important was that passive and even hostile position of the Jews towards Poland's national problems. Such a posture of necessity was bound to call forth national indignation on the part of a people as sentimental and patriotic as the Poles.

Modern Polish anti–Semitism can be explained, if not justified, by other factors as well: the downfall of the majority of the European nations and with them also of democracy; the contamination of the minds, particularly of the youth, by Nazi anti–Semitic propaganda; and the flow in the last years of Jews persecuted by the Germans into Poland who left the Poles with an impression that they may pose a dangerous competitive threat in the social and economic areas. In contrast to the Poles who were primarily agriculturalists, the Jews lived predominantly in towns and engaged in industry.

This economic aspect of the Jewish problem in Poland which, without doubt, played a central role in the reasons which called forth anti–Semitism in this land, deserves a closer scrutiny.

Before the war, the 3.5 million Jews, in terms of their numerical strength, constituted the second largest ethnic minority group in Poland. The first were Ukrainians (5 million), third were Germans (over one million), fourth were Belorussians (about half million), fifth were the Lithuanians (about 70,000).

While all of these ethnic groups were concentrated in specific regions, the Jews were scattered throughout the entire territory of Poland.

The Polish middle class which emerged at the end of the last century and constituted the middle strata between the mass of peasants and landowners, consisted predominantly of Jews and Germans. It was this class which built and peopled the towns of Poland both large and small. Before the Second World War, the Jews constituted one-third of town dwellers in all of Poland. Over 80 percent of the Jews lived in towns; the remainder lived in the villages where they had a monopoly on small trades, small industry and the crafts. Before the war, Warsaw itself numbered about 300,000 Jews who constituted a third of its inhabitants. Warsaw was, therefore, a city with the largest concentration of Jews in Europe; in the world, it was second after New York.

Already at the beginning of the twentieth century one-third of Poland's industry and over one-half of its commerce was in Jewish hands. Before the Second World War, three-quarters of all Polish Jews were engaged in trade and industry whereas 80 percent of non–Jews were farmers. In trade, in banking, for every non–Jew there were 35 Jews; in industry and the crafts, for every 8 non–Jews there were 32 Jews; in the learned professions, for every non–Jew there were almost 4 Jews. In agriculture, on the other hand, for every Jew there were 8 non–Jews.

One-third of Polish Jews were engaged in industry and the crafts. Although 80 percent of Jewish workers were employed in industry as skilled craftsmen, a significant part of non–Jewish workers were also forced to work in the crafts. As a result of the monopolistic and closed-shop nature of the Jewish enterprises, non–Jewish workers were naturally unable to advance in industries where they should have, in keeping with logic, replaced the Jewish skilled workers who, in turn, would have been freed to engage in still more profitable enterprises. This state of affairs constituted a catastrophic anomaly in Poland's industry not only because this ill-advised use of the labor force diminished productivity, but also because the employment of skilled workers where other laborers could have been used halted industrial advance. In reality, the Jewish mass of laborers engaged in old-world enterprises, in cottage industries, which not only made more difficult but also actually impeded the industrial development and renewal desired both by the townspeople and the Polish government.

Over 60 percent of Polish citizens worked in agriculture and only 26 percent in trade and industry. A very large segment of the villagers wanted to abandon farming in favor of trade and industry and to move into the towns. Alas, on the road to the realization of this desire a roadblock emerges anew in the form of the Jews who, as we saw, ruled in the towns and extended their control over a very large segment of trade, industry and the learned professions. It was this which impeded industrial development and the desire to modernize the nation and, at the same time, made it difficult to raise the general standard of living.[65]

And it was this state of affairs, more than anything else, that was responsible for the rise in anti–Jewish sentiments in Poland during the interwar years. To put it in Marxist terms, these sentiments were directed not at the Jews as such but at the social class that stood in the way of modernization and progress.

Soviet Occupation

As indicated above, before 1939, especially after the introduction of the Nuremberg Laws of 1935, many German Jews sought refuge in Poland. With the German invasion, these Jews, together with many Polish citizens, continued to head eastward in advance of the German armies. According to one estimate, some 300,000 Jewish refugees (predominantly youths and political activists) arrived in Eastern Poland from the Nazi-occupied territories after September 1939.[66] Those who came within the first few weeks of the war were greeted by the Soviet armies and vice versa. A child from Białystok described the reaction of the major ethnic groups in Eastern Poland to the Soviet invasion: "The arrival of Russians in Poland was sad, and joyful. For some Jews, Byelorussians, and Ukrainians it was joyful. And for the Poles it was sad and hard."[67] Irena Grudzińska-Gross and Jan Tomasz Gross note:

> Even before the Soviets entered, citizens' committees or militias were spontaneously formed in many places to replace the local

> Polish administration, which had either fled or lost the ability to enforce order.... These committees often acted as hosts to Red Army units ... the Soviet commanders relied on such welcoming committees and militias.... Their primary immediate task involved ferreting out hiding Polish officers and policemen.
>
> These first militias were a strange lot. In some areas, particularly in the larger towns where the majority of the 1.7 million Jews living in this territory dwelt, they were predominantly Jewish, often organized by communist sympathizers.[68]

Shmuel Spector wrote of the situation in Wołyń: "Polish-Jewish relations worsened with the onset of the Soviet occupation in 1939. At that time from forty to fifty thousand Poles, mostly city residents working for the Polish administration, were rounded up and exiled. The Soviet authorities replaced many of them with Jews, although Jewish visibility in Soviet local officialdom turned out to be rather short-lived."[69]

According to Arnold Zable, the following occurred in Białystok, on September 22, 1939, Friday, Yom Kippur Eve, after a week of Wehrmacht mayhem:

> Towards evening the Red Army marches into a city decorated with red flags. Communal delegations greet them with flowers and speeches of welcome. Thousands of elated Białystoker throng the streets. Jewish youths embrace Russian soldiers with great enthusiasm. On this, the holiest of nights, the culmination of the Days of Awe, orthodox Jews pack the synagogues and pray with renewed fervour. It is as if a miracle has taken place. Białystok had been granted a reprieve.[70]

The following three testimonies came from the archives of Yad Vashem, the Israeli organization that recognizes Gentiles who assisted Jews during the Holocaust. "The encroaching Red Army was received by the Jews with joy"; "The Jews greeted the Soviet armies with joy, the youth spent their nights and days among the soldiers"; "The Jews welcomed the encroaching Russians enthusiastically."

Other testimonies follow:

> In Grodno: "When the Bolsheviks entered the Polish territories they displayed a great distrust of the Polish people, but with complete faith in the Jews ... they filled all the administrative offices with Jews and also entrusted them with top-level positions."
>
> In Lwów: "I must note that, from the very first, the majority of positions in the Soviet agencies were taken by Jews."
>
> In Żółkwia: "The Russians rely mainly on the Jewish element in filling positions, segregating, naturally, the bourgeois from the proletariat."
>
> In Wielkie Oczy, near Jaworów: A Jewish doctor recalled how local Jewish youths, having formed themselves into a "*komsomol*," toured the countryside, smashing Catholic shrines.[71]

In Pińsk, Polish women locked themselves in a church to prevent Jewish policemen from profaning it.[72] In Siedlce, the Jewish population greeted the Soviet invaders with red armbands and ribbons and, as in Pińsk, with an *arc de triomphe.* A Jewish observer of the pro–Soviet demonstrations in Lwów noted, "Whenever a political march, or protest meeting, or some other sort of joyful event took place, the visual effect was always the same — Jews."[73] Abraham Sterzer, a Jewish doctor from Lwów, later stated:

> But back in 1939, when the Red Army marched into Lviv [Lwów] and other cities of Western Ukraine the Jews behaved as if Messiah had arrived. They flocked to sign up for various communist-front organizations, joined the NKVD secret police, and helped the Russians oppress and fight legitimate Ukrainian nationalism. Today, when Russian imperialism is the mortal enemy of Jews and the Jewish State, it is difficult to believe. But 25 years ago, it was the gospel truth."[74]

Some of these pro–Soviet and anti–Polish Jews said "our armies have arrived" no doubt because of the presence of so many Jewish officers within the Soviet ranks.[75] Others quipped, "You wanted Poland without Jews, so now you have Jews without Poland."[76] Still others insisted, insolently but prophetically: "Your Poland will never resurrect here again."[77] Aleksander Smolar stated: "The evidence is overwhelming: large numbers of Jews welcomed the Soviet invasion, implanting in Polish memory the image of Jewish crowds greeting the invading Red Army as their liberator."[78] That image, delineated more precisely, was one of Jews dancing on Polish graves. A Jew from Rohatyn in Eastern Galicia described the first part of this dance:

> But when on September 17, 1939 the Soviet Army entered the eastern regions instead of the Germans, the Jews without exception welcomed them as liberators and protectors against the Germans and the local population. The Jews welcomed the Soviet soldiers openly and the new power began to deal with the Jews with the same trust with which it dealt with its own brothers — the Ukrainians.
>
> Jews were employed by the Soviet officials in the administration and even in the local militia. Jews went gladly to these tasks since there were very many unemployed craftsmen and intellectuals.
>
> Meanwhile the reorganization of trade, industry and economy on a Soviet basis had begun. Cooperatives of shoemakers, tailors, tinsmiths, and bakers were organized. Each of these artels or cooperatives was headed by a leader with previous craft experience — in most cases a Jew. Raw materials were brought from Stanisławów, Lemberg [Lwów] and Tarnopol. In these cities, too, Jews played an important role as the most experienced craftsmen. The Jewish and non–Jewish workers in the artels worked under the guidance of Jewish directors. Control over the factories was in the hands of the Party, which again had greater trust in the Jews than in the non–Jews.[79]

An entry in a Jewish memorial book from Sambor, near Lwów, also reveals: "Many Jews joined city and government services. The Russians trusted the Jewish population more than the Poles and the Ukrainians, and, therefore, the higher posts were allotted to the Jews."[80] In Soviet-occupied Włodzimierz, a telling Jewish jingle made the rounds:

> *Nasi żydki sięady tędy,*
> *Wszystkie pójdą na urzędy,*
> *Ukraińcy do kołchozu,*
> *A Polaki do wywozu.*[81]

A Jewish testimony from Rożyszcze, Wołyń, reads:

> The communist youth had packed their things planning to proceed towards the Russian border. In the middle of the night the rumour spread that the Russians were coming. We all returned to our homes. The immediate danger had passed.
>
> The following morning found the communist youth, Jews and Ukrainians, rejoicing in the streets. We, members of Betar, immediately went to the clubhouse to burn the membership registry and destroy other documentation which may prove incriminating.
>
> The communists set up a militia of local youth. They enthusiastically decided to form a guard of honour to welcome the Red Army, decorating the square with pictures of Stalin and the communist greats and bringing the fire brigade orchestra. But instead of the victorious Red Army, a train arrived bearing a load of Polish troops who apparently had not heard of the Molotov-Ribbentrop agreement. The newly-formed militia enthusiastically set out to capture the Polish troops. Shooting and general chaos followed with all those in the vicinity taking cover, including those who had gathered to welcome the Reds.[82]

In this same work another Jew noted, "The relations between the Jews and the local Gentile population, which was mostly Polish, had been very good until the outbreak of the war."[83]

Meanwhile, from the very beginning of the war, pro–Soviet sentiments continued to be voiced by the leftist Zionist press in German-occupied Poland. These Jewish political activists saw their liberation linked to a communist victory and the downfall of Poland as a nation. Hashomer Hatza'ir, for example, applauded the German-Soviet Non–Aggression Pact of 1939 and the partitioning of Poland.

Mordechai Anielewicz, one of the leaders of the Warsaw Ghetto Revolt, was the editor of a publication that openly embraced communism and the Soviet Union over Poland and its democratic government.[84]

Thousands of Polish survivors' testimonies, memoirs, and works of history tell of Jewish celebrations, of Jewish harassment of Poles, of Jewish collaboration (denunciations, manhunts, and roundups of Poles for deportation), of Jewish brutality and cold-blooded executions, of Jewish pro–Soviet citizens' committees and militias, and of the high rates of Jews in the Soviet organs of oppression after the Soviet invasion of 1939.[85] The Poles perceived all of this as ingratitude and betrayal; the Jews saw it as retribution and revolution. Aleksander Wat, a Polish prewar communist author of Jewish origin, described the situation in Lwów:

> At that time, however, the Jews constituted a certain class, not the ruling class, but a well-placed one in Russia. In Lwów, there were jailers, denouncers, quite a few Jewish denouncers, a very large number. Jews were more inclined to cooperate with the Soviet authorities. Many prewar communists appeared on the scene, like mushrooms after a rain, and the prewar communists for the most part were Jews.[86]

"The Jews were involved in robbery, rape, and pillage. Often Poles were victims," states Richard Lukas.[87] Norman Davies adds: "Among the informers and collaborators, as in the personnel of the Soviet security police at the time, the high percentage of Jews was striking."[88] It was Jews who, along with the Ukrainian collaborators, prepared the lists on the basis of which Polish "class enemies" were deported to the USSR or executed by the NKVD. Ben-Cion Pinchuk wrote about this postinvasion collaboration:

> State, city and police archives were among the first institutions to be occupied and guarded by the new rulers. They were curious to discover the secrets guarded in the archives. Local collaborators translated from Polish and prepared detailed lists of suspects, to be used in the future. A fine net of informers was spread throughout the territories, in every institution, factory, enterprise and tenement. Local Communists and new recruits were included among the informers ... local Jewish Communists played an important role in locating former political activists and compiling the lists of "undesirables" and "class enemies." The NKVD tried, often with success, to recruit people who had previously been active in Jewish institutions and political organizations and thus created an atmosphere of mutual suspicion and fear among former friends and colleagues.[89]

Among these "friends and colleagues" were a good number of Poles. Among them also were fellow Jews. Max Wolfshaut-Dinkes, who "never knew a non–Jewish communist" in his town of Przemyśl, wrote: "The Jews lived in fear, haunted by the prospect of expropriation and deportation to Siberia. They mistrusted one another and, above all, they feared the Jewish communists. These latter were fanatical supporters of the régime, zealous servants of the authorities. Faithful to their 'duty,' they fought unscrupulously against the 'terrible' class enemy, composed of shopkeepers and craftsmen." Most of the "enemy" were Jews. "I must confess," he concluded, "that I found the conduct of the Jewish communists during the Soviet occupation terribly repugnant."[90]

Statements made by people from various counties in the province of Lwów were gleaned from the Władysław Sikorski Archives and Museum. An editorial comment in the introduction reads:

> I have not found a single entry attesting to a friendly disposition of the Jews to the Polish population. On the contrary, the testimonies indicate that from the first moment of the Soviet occupation the Jewish people greeted the occupant with enthusiasm, occupied the ranks of the militia in great numbers, as well as every possible administrative post. The testimonies speak of the great suffering on the part of the Polish people because of the cooperation of the Jews with the Soviet authorities.[91]

The extensive archives of the Polish Government Collection, the Władysław Anders

Collection, and the Poland, Ambasada (USSR) Collection at the Hoover Institution on War, Revolution and Peace at Stanford University contain similar testimonies for all the eastern provinces.

In February 1940 the following report, entitled "The Situation of the Jews on Territories Occupied by the USSR," was filed by Jan Karski, decorated in Israel after the war for his valiant attempt to warn the world about the Holocaust:

> The Jews are at home here, not only because they do not experience humiliations or persecutions, but [also because] they possess, thanks to their quick-wittedness and ability to adapt to every new situation, a certain power of both a political and an economic nature.
>
> They are entering the political cells; in many of them they have taken over the most critical political-administrative positions. They play quite a large role in the factory unions, in higher education, and most of all in commerce; but above and beyond even all this they are involved in loansharking and profiteering, in illegal trade, contraband, foreign currency exchange, liquor, immoral interests, pimping, and procurement....
>
> The attitude of the Jews toward the Bolsheviks is regarded among the Polish populace as quite positive. It is generally believed that the Jews betrayed Poland and the Poles, that they are basically communists, that they crossed over to the Bolsheviks with flags unfurled.
>
> In fact, in most cities the Jews greeted the Bolsheviks with baskets of red roses, with submissive declarations and speeches, etc., etc....
>
> Certainly it is so that Jewish communists adopted an enthusiastic stance toward the Bolsheviks, regardless of the social class from which they came. The Jewish proletariat, small merchants, artisans, and all those whose position has at present been improved *structurally* and who had formerly been exposed primarily to oppression, indignities, excesses, etc., from the Polish element — all of these responded positively, if not enthusiastically, to the new regime.
>
> Their attitude seems to me quite understandable.
>
> However, there are worse cases, where they (the Jews) denounce the Poles, Polish nationalist students, and Polish figures, when they direct the work of the Bolshevik police force from behind their desks or are members of the police force, when they falsely defame the relations (between Poles and Jews) in former Poland. Unfortunately it is necessary to state that such incidents are quite common, more common than incidents which reveal loyalty toward Poles or sentiment toward Poland.[92]

Having studied the matter of Jewish collaboration during the Soviet occupation, Aleksander Smolar wrote:

> In no other European country was there such a dramatic conflict of interests and attitudes during the war between the Jews and the population among whom they lived as under the Soviet occupation [of Eastern Poland] in 1939-1941. Elsewhere, Jews were at odds with segments of the population (for example with collaborating factions), but in solidarity, in unison with everyone else. In Eastern Poland, however, Jews were themselves viewed as collaborators. One should keep that in mind in any honest assessment of mutual relations [between Poles and Jews].[93]

In a 1944 conference with the representatives of the Polish Jews, General Władysław Anders distinguished between the Jews from western Poland and those from the eastern borderlands. "The latter," he was reported to have said, "in the difficult days of Poland's downfall, sometimes behaved in the worst possible way. They disarmed Polish soldiers and tore off Polish eagles from their hats." Ksawery Pruszyński, who kept the minutes of the meeting, continued:

> The General told how in Lwów, despite the announcement of the capitulation agreement, the Soviet authorities gathered Polish soldiers in a certain place in order to deport them later. The Jewish people (a group of about 1,500) showered abuses upon these prisoners of war. At a later date, Poles and Jews found themselves together in penal camps. And again we have Polish recriminations as to the behavior of the Jews toward

them. Such things do not remain without a trace. Moreover, when the situation became inflamed by actual suffering, the former complaints rankled all the more. The General issued orders to all his subordinates. He will not tolerate anti–Semitism, but he cannot prevent the possibility of this danger from occurring.[94]

In response to allegations of anti–Semitism in his army, General Anders noted the reasons:

> The tearing off of eagles and marks of military distinction by the Jews from off the uniforms of Polish soldiers after their arrest by the Soviet authorities, their participation in the Red militias, their denunciations of Poles, the placement of Jews in all important positions and their behavior toward the Poles, for example, in Brygidki prison in Lwów, the behavior of arrested Jews in prisons ... the behavior of Jews in prisons and camps.[95]

A statement attached to a 1940 report to London reads:

> The Jews welcomed the Soviet armies enthusiastically last September. The Jewish proletariat continues not to be ill-disposed to the Bolsheviks, and to be ill-disposed to Poland. However, the Jewish middle class and the intelligentsia are as oppressed as the Poles. These Jews say that they'd rather be beaten regularly by the Germans morning, noon and night than bear the completely irregular oppression of the Soviets.[96]

Jan Stańczyk, a socialist whom no one can accuse of anti–Semitism, stated to the representatives of Polish Jews in July 1943:

> I do not want to hide it and admit that among the people who returned from Russia as well as in the army there is an anti-Semitic frame of mind. I confess this with a heavy heart, but one cannot remedy this by an order. The reason for all of this lies in the fact that when the Bolsheviks came to Poland, the Jewish militiamen walked around with lists and pointed out those to be deported from among the Poles. Therefore, it seems to every Pole that, were it not for that Jewish militiaman, he would have been able to remain at home on his farm.[97]

According to a statement by Prime Minister General Władysław Sikorski in a Polish government-in-exile meeting that took place in Anvier, France, on January 9, 1940, only about 30 percent of the Jews identified with the communists in Eastern Poland and engaged in provocations against the Poles; the other 70 percent "behaved decently."[98] Yet 30 percent, or even 10 percent, of the over 1 million Jews in the eastern territories of Poland is still a very large number.

The following are but some of the thousands of testimonies that could be cited regarding this Jewish-Soviet collaboration. The first passage comes from the Grodno area in north-Eastern Poland, where a communist-inspired insurrection, led largely by "young Jews," was crushed by the Polish military.[99] The second comes from the Lwów area in southeastern Poland. The speaker in the third passage is a Polish brigadier-general from Wołyń; he was subsequently deported to the Gulag. The fourth account comes from a small town called Gwoździec, located near Kołomyja in the province of Stanisławów. The fifth comes from Brześć and the sixth from Mołodów, near Pińsk.

> [1] I lived in Grodno near Legionowa Street.... In the afternoon I went out with my aunt in order to buy something. Suddenly some shots rang out on Brygidzka Street. We look; on the balconies Jews with red armbands are shooting at people in the streets.... Near our home, someone said that the USSR had crossed our border.[100]

> [2] After several days of traveling by all feasible means toward the Romanian frontier, under incessant vicious attacks by low-flying Nazi planes, news reached us on September 17, 1939, that the Soviet forces had crossed the border and were racing toward the Romanian frontier to cut off that escape route. A rapid confirmation of this shattering news came soon from the skies, when a small flight of Soviet planes bombed the Polish columns. Faced with this we had to turn back and flee in the direction from which we had come — toward Lwów. For a while we

traveled by train, but after the Ukrainians blew up the tracks, the remaining two-thirds of the journey had to be on foot.

As we approached every Ukrainian village, we were fired upon. In towns, we were also shot at by the Jewish militia, armed with stolen Polish army rifles and wearing red arm bands. As we approached the outskirts of Lwów, we came upon a tragicomic spectacle: In a meadow beside the main road, about ten of the Jewish militiamen were guarding a sizeable squadron of one of the élite Polish cavalry regiments. Soviet tank forces had disarmed the Polish regiment and had assigned their new "allies," the Jews, to guard the Poles. I recall a feeling of pain and disgust that those who were Polish citizens should behave so treacherously.[101]

[3] On September 28 [1939] ... we received orders to "pack up" and leave our cells. In the prison yard we met up with most of the officers of our platoon and many others from various military formations.

We were escorted in a column to the barracks by a civilian guard with red armbands and former Polish soldiers — unfortunately all of them were Polish Jews.

We moved out.... Our escort consisted of the same (Jews) with armbands and Polish rifles.... After a time, a rabble of young Jews gathered on each side of our column, marching along with us on the sidewalks and shouting: "Strong! Compact! Prepared! ... ugh!" (*silni, zwarci, gotowi—pfuj!*) What is worse, they soon began to spit at us and here and there even pelted our column with rocks.[102]

[4] Then came the unusually snowy and harsh winter of 1939-1940, and with it the tragic dawn of February 10, 1940 when entire Polish families, including children and the elderly, were loaded on cattle cars. Order was maintained by local Jews and Ukrainians who not so long ago constituted, or so it seemed, a friendly contingent of our township community.[103]

[5] I will never forget the sight of the handcuffed Polish policeman which the militia was leading down Jagiellońska Street, and all around him Jews shrieking inhumanly, spitting on him, pelting him with garbage, rocks and abusing him terribly.[104]

[6] I shall tell here a story from the circle of my own acquaintances.

I knew very well Mr. Henryk Skirmunt, who was the chairman of the Catholic Action of the Roman Catholic diocese of Pińsk, a well known Polish Roman Catholic intellectual, author and social activist....

When the Russian Army crossed the Polish frontier on 17th September 1939, Mr. Skirmunt and his sister — they were [the] only two on the spot — took a car and left their manor house, understandably not having the intention to be caught in their own home by the Soviets. But when passing through the nearby almost purely Jewish townlet of Motol, they were stopped and arrested by a Communist group of local Jews. There was no question of giving them help by people who were, after all, their neighbours. On the contrary, their Jewish neighbours prevented their escape. A few hours, or a few days afterwards they [were] both executed, I do not know exactly by whom, by the same local people who stopped them in the car, or by Soviet authorities to whom they were handed over.

They were good people. The Motol Jews had certainly no grudges or complaints against them. Their only guilt was that they were Poles, aristocrats and reasonably rich.[105]

My brother-in-law, Ryszard Pedowski, was born in 1926 in the over seven-hundred-year-old town of Grabowiec, located in the county of Hrubieszów, the province of Lublin. During the war, Ryszard was a member of the local AK. He estimates that in 1939, about 50 percent of the population of Grabowiec was Polish, 30 percent Ukrainian, and 20 percent Jewish. According to Ryszard, the local Ukrainians and the Poles got along well right through the war — neither killing each other nor betraying each other either to the Soviets or to the Germans. (The town was first occupied by the Soviets in 1939.) It was a different story, however, with the Ukrainians who began to arrive there, under the German occupation, from other parts of the county and Zamość. These strangers proved to be a major headache to all the local residents.

In 1939, the Jews owned most of the stores and buildings in the market square of Grabowiec. Many of them were relatively well off, but there were also poor Jews living in the town, and these were largely pro-communist in their sympathies. Under the Soviet occupation, the red armbands that they proudly wore distinguished them from the rest.

That fall, before the Germans arrived, twelve Polish officers who were dressed in civilian clothing and who were in hiding among the local Polish population were brutally murdered in the bakery of a rich Jew called Pergamen. Later, another Jew — known locally as "Kuka," a *woziwoda* (one who transported and sold water) — took the bodies to the cemetery and left them in a ditch. After being discovered on the following day, the slain officers were given a proper Christian burial by the residents. The officers were dressed only in their underwear and dog tags. Still later, "Kuka" was poisoned.

According to Ryszard, it was the poor Jews, the communist sympathizers, who murdered these officers and poisoned the *woziwoda.* "Were you an eyewitness to either one of these events?" I asked.

"No," he responded. "I only saw the graves after the burial."

"Then how do you know that it was the Jews who killed them?" I asked.

"That's what everyone said," he replied.

"The Ukrainians too?" I asked.

"Yes," he said.

"And what did the Jews say? Did they deny it?" I asked.

"They said nothing," was his response.

"Why was 'Kuka' poisoned?" I continued.

"Because he must have said something," responded Ryszard.

"Could anyone else have killed these officers?"

"Who else was there?"

"How about the Russians?"

"There were no Soviet units stationed in Grabowiec at the time," he replied. "They passed through and continued on to the front. But there were communist sympathizers in our town — both Poles and Jews. As I recall, they did not mix together but formed their own separate groups and established a militia."

This serious allegation based on local hearsay should be investigated further. Unfortunately, I have not been able to uncover any other facts about this event or find people from the area who could shed more light on the cruel execution of those twelve Polish officers in Grabowiec in 1939. At the same time, I cannot pretend that I did not hear what my own brother-in-law told me in Chicago in 1995.[106]

On September 17, 1939, a Jew, Szulman by name, led the Soviets in an attack on the township of Dzisna in the province of Wilno. He was the son of the owner of a large textile store in Dzisna and was prosecuted before the war for his communist activities.[107] In Wilno the Soviets, with the help of local communists, mainly Jews, seized Polish administrative, agricultural, and financial institutions.[108]

In Skidel, near Grodno, on September 18, 1939, local Jews and Belorussians attacked and arrested the Polish administration and participated in the murder of Poles in the Grodno region.[109] Jews also operated Soviet tanks in the attack on Grodno. To everyone's amazement, one of them, after being wounded and apprehended, pleaded: *"Nye ubyvaitye, ya pryiekhal vas osvobodit'"* (Do not kill me, I have come to liberate you).[110]

In Białystok, Herschel Wajnrauch, a Soviet civilian journalist imported to work on a Jewish newspaper, recalled: "The Soviet police did not have enough people to carry out the mass arrests [of Poles], so ordinary Soviet citizens were used to help [as well as local communists]. Our newspaper was asked to provide two people, and I was one of them. We were given weapons and went with the Police to arrest these people and send them to Siberia."[111]

Elsewhere, disarmed Polish soldiers were marched to Łuck by the Soviets, assisted by a hastily mobilized militia consisting of Jews and Ukrainians.[112] Additionally, Polish conspiratorial efforts were often hampered by Soviet infiltrators and the collaborative activities of Jews and Ukrainians.[113]

In Nadwór, about fifty kilometers south of Stanisławów, the entire city administration was taken over by the local Jews.[114] And according to one report, under the Soviet occupation 75 percent of all administrative positions in

Lwów, Białystok, and Łuck were in the hands of the Jews.[115]

The death of Rev. Wacław Rodźko, pastor of Traby, located in the archdiocese of Wilno, was attributed to local Jews. He was murdered in May 1940 in the village of Rosalszczyzna while he was visiting a sick parishioner.[116]

Three Jews — Kramer (a cabdriver), Dawid Kümel, and Dawid Rosenberg — participated in the atrocities against the inmates of the Tarnopol prison just before the entry of the German armies.[117]

Finally, according to witnesses, the previously mentioned last-minute execution of the Dominicans in the Czortków monastery on the night of July 1, 1941, just before the arrival of the Germans was, in part, the work of local Jews in the service of the NKVD.[118]

Needless to say, all of this and much more did not go over very well with the Poles. Norman Davies states:

> What I wrote, and can now confirm, amounts to this: firstly, that among the collaborators who came forward to assist the Soviet security forces in dispatching huge numbers of innocent men, women, and children to distant exile and probable death, there was a disproportionate number of Jews; and secondly, that news of the circumstances surrounding the deportations helped to sour Polish-Jewish relations in other parts of occupied Poland.... These reports about the conduct of Jews do not necessarily make pleasant reading, especially when one reflects on the appalling fate of those same Jewish communities following the Nazi invasion of the Soviet-occupied zone in June 1941. But one should not for that reason discount them, or try to read history backward.[119]

Under the Soviet occupation, the Polish people's perception was that they were the victims of a genocidal policy aided and abetted at every turn by the Jews and other Polish minorities. A June 1940 Polish report from Stryj puts the matter straightforwardly: "The relations between Poles and Jews are at present markedly worse than before the war. The entire Polish population adopted a negative attitude towards the Jews because of their blatant cooperation with the Bolsheviks and their hostility against the non–Jews.... The people simply hate the Jews."[120]

Whatever the reasons for the Jews' extensive collaboration with the Soviets,[121] the argument by David Engel,[122] Shmuel Krakowski,[123] and other Jewish authors — that the Jews welcomed the Soviets simply to protect themselves from the Germans — is rather tenuous. These events that began on September 17, 1939, had absolutely nothing to do with the events that would follow in the summer of 1941. This is confirmed by the fact that many Jews who left Poland before Hitler's Polish campaign decided to return to German-occupied Poland after it was over.[124] At that time, few in the eastern territories knew what was in store for the Jews except Hitler, who probably came up with the idea for the "Final Solution" in September 1939 but did not issue his order for its implementation until June 1941.[125] One Jewish account from Kowel reads:

> In September 1939, I escaped from Ostrow-Lubleski, which, at that time was occupied by the Germans ... to the other side of the Bug River to the territories occupied by the Soviets ... in June 1940 ... my sisters and brother-in-law tried to find a place in Kovel but it was not easy to find a decent place to live and work, and, like so many refugees, they decided to register to go back to German-occupied Poland. Unfortunately, the Kovel Jews [20,000] did not show any sympathy or hospitality for the refugees — they were unable to understand or to believe what the Nazi murderers were capable of doing.
>
> I obtained [Soviet] citizenship and started to work at the railroad station.[126]

Juliusz Górski remembers, "In 1940, about 100,000 Jews, who had arrived in Lwów in flight from German occupation, demanded from a relevant German commission the right to return to the occupied zone."[127]

At Biała Podlaska, when two trains carrying refugees in both directions encountered one another, a telling exchange of vital information took place. "When the Jews coming from Brisk saw Jews going there, they shouted: 'You are insane, where are you going?' Those coming from Warsaw answered with equal astonishment: 'You are insane, where are you going?'"[128] Samuel Tennenbaum reported from Złoczów, "We had heard no reports of pogroms in the western part of Poland occupied by the Germans since 1939."[129]

Meanwhile, although the Soviets knew about the growing excesses of the Nazis in the west and could easily have informed their "citizens" through their elaborate propaganda ministry, they did not. The Nazi-Soviet alliance — sealed by the Secret Supplementary Protocol to the German-Soviet Boundary and Friendship Treaty of September 28, 1939, which called for the suppression of "all beginnings" of "Polish agitation" in both "spheres of influence" — had to be maintained at all costs. Throughout their occupation of Eastern Poland, the Soviets were under strict orders from Stalin not to say or do anything to provoke a German attack.[130] A confirmation (Jewish) of this conspiracy of silence comes from the province of Wilno:

> In 1939 Poland was cut in half.... The Jews welcomed the Red Army with great joy, with flowers, bread and salt. Chayim Band of Brasław tells how the draper Aharon Zeif brought out and distributed rolls of red cloth among all who wanted to make flags.
>
> *The Jews under Soviet rule knew nothing about the condition of their fellow Jews under German occupation.* Only here and there faint echoes would reach them from the other side of the Bug of the deplorable situation of the Jews under Nazi rule. Trickles of refugees would bring sad tidings of the happenings on the western side of the river.[131]

This testimony is borne out by an August 4, 1941, statement of a German intelligence officer noting the situation in the Belorussian provinces:

> To an amazing extent, the Jews are remarkably ill-informed about our attitude toward them. They do not know how Jews are treated in Germany, or for that matter in Warsaw, which after all is not so far away. Otherwise their questions as to whether we in Germany make any distinction between Jews and other citizens would be superfluous. Even if they do not think that under German administration they will have equal rights with the Russians, they believe, nevertheless, that we shall leave them in peace if they mind their own business and work diligently.[132]

But whether or not they knew, and whether or not they welcomed the Soviets simply to protect themselves from the Germans, are beside the point. Nothing justified the excesses of these Polish citizens, these communist Jews, against the Polish population. What is worse, one can only speculate as to the reason for the total absence of any condemnation by the Jewish community and leaders, either then or now. (One possible answer is that to condemn is to admit.) To manifest pro–Soviet sympathy was one thing; to betray, deport, abuse, and murder neighbors, schoolmates, clients, and the soldiers of Poland under the guise of "self-protection from the Germans" was quite another. This was not a case of "do or die." There were no penalties for not volunteering.

After the Soviet invasion, the Jews did initially reap some benefits for their collaborative efforts. As a result of their administrative prerogatives at all levels of government, their general well-being improved immediately under the Soviet occupation. They acquired the use of some monasteries and convents. Their educational opportunities increased dramatically; for example, their prewar enrollment of 15 percent at the University of Lwów rose to 85 percent under the Soviet occupation.[133] They found employment in factories, in schools, and in the militia.

The reader must not infer, however, that the Jewish population *continued* to receive favorable treatment in the Soviet zone as the result of the collaboration of that "30 percent." Just as the Soviets stabbed their Polish allies in the back soon after the July 1941 agreement with Sikorski, so they eventually stabbed the Jews as well.[134] To quote again from Norman Davies:

> The Jewish communes, which flourished under Polish rule, were peremptorily abolished. The Jewish middle class was reduced to penury. Hebrew schools, Zionist clubs, all independent Jewish organizations were

> closed down overnight. Conditions were so bad that thousands of Jewish refugees swarmed westward toward the Nazi zone, passing swarms of other refugees fleeing in the opposite direction. Gross even reports one incident, where a visiting Nazi commission was greeted by crowds of Jews chanting "*Heil Hitler*" in the hope of getting permission to cross the frontier. And on the frontier bridge over the River Bug, they were met by a Nazi officer shouting: "Jews, where on earth are you going? We are going to kill you."[135]

According to Zbigniew S. Siemaszko, 19.4 percent, or 281,000, of the 1.45 million civilian deportees from Poland's eastern territories to the Soviet Union were Jews. The largest number of Jews was not deported until the third large-scale deportation in late June 1940,[136] and most of them were refugees from western and central Poland.[137]

Was the lot of these Jews in the Soviet Union comparable to that of the Poles? Probably. The following comment, though perhaps representing Zdzisław Adamowicz's personal experience in the Soviet Union, also provides a good example of the general belief entertained by many Polish people, especially those from the eastern territories: "There were among us Poles and Ukrainians, but not a single Jew. Can you believe it? Never in my five-year sojourn through Soviet prisons and camps did I encounter a Jew. And so many of them, after all, 'fell' into the hands of the Soviet authorities during their exodus from the territories occupied by the Germans."[138] In any case, those Jews who actively collaborated with the Soviet régime and who voluntarily left for the Soviet Union with the retreating Red Army most certainly did not share the lot of the forcibly deported Polish citizenry.

With the German invasion of Eastern Poland, the remaining Jews had three options: to die; to live in perpetual hiding either with courageous Christian families or as individuals or family units in forest camps; or to join the partisans, preferably Jewish partisans. More often than not, they joined the Soviet partisans or the communist People's Guard/People's Army (Gwardia Ludowa/Armia Ludowa, or GL/AL). Like the Poles who sometimes joined forces with the Soviets at this time, these Jews should not necessarily be construed as collaborators. The common enemy was now Nazi Germany.

However, there was a major difference between joining the Soviet partisans or even the GL/AL to fight the German invaders and willingly participating in the Soviet roundup, imprisonment, execution, or deportation of members of the Polish underground who were also fighting the Germans. As we will see, Stalin ordered these actions in July 1944. But the orders to destabilize the AK by denouncing its members to the Gestapo were issued to Soviet agents in Poland as early as December 1941, when the war was far from over, and in 1943 additional orders were given to Soviet partisans (which included Jews) in Poland's eastern territories to liquidate the Polish underground. The participation of some Jews in these Soviet campaigns (discussed in the following chapter) certainly did not endear them to the Poles during the war.

Postwar Years

Some of the Jews who survived the Nazi and the Soviet reigns of terror welcomed the communist takeover of Poland once more in 1944. Aleksander Smolar notes: "It is a cruel paradox that even deportations did not necessarily dampen Jewish sympathies for the U.S.S.R."[139] Whereas the Polish population despised the new régime, these communists saw it as a protection of their life and liberty. According to Andrzej Paczkowski, between 1944 and 1956 — when Jews constituted less than 1 percent of Poland's population — out of 447 persons occupying positions of leadership in the headquarters of Poland's Ministry of State Security (Ministerstwo Bezpieczeństwa Publicznego, or MBP), 131 (just over 29 percent) were Jews. (We can only wonder who constituted the remaining 71 percent, the other 316 members of the party leadership!) Many of these Jews, claims Paczkowski, were associated with the Communist Party before the war and spent the war years in Moscow, in the Soviet partisans, or in the GL/AL.[140] Stanisław Krajewski noted:

> Those "old" communists ... when they were in exile in the USSR, as the majority of them were, they had witnessed the pervasive terror and often had experienced it themselves simply because they belonged to the Communist Party of Poland [KPP] which had been dissolved and whose leaders had been put to death [by the Soviets]. Undeterred, they arrived in Poland at the side of the Red Army in order to build socialism. In their fanaticism they believed that civilized Poland could avoid what they called Soviet degeneration. Their prescription for putting out the fire was faithfulness to Stalin and his doctrines — that is, pouring gasoline on the fire.[141]

Czesław Miłosz wrote:

> The first *cadres* of the Polish Communist Party in 1945, it must be remembered, were composed of men in uniform, a very large proportion of them intellectuals of Jewish descent. The Russians regarded them as more reliable instruments of Soviet desires in the belief that they would be less inclined to Polish patriotism because of the discrimination to which the Polish rightists had subjected them before the war.[142]

Aleksander Smolar stated:

> The Jews became very visible indeed, especially in the central nodes of power. Popular imagination multiplied their numbers, sensing the existence of Jews under newly adopted Polish names everywhere. For the man in the street, this "Jewish flood" was a shocking new phenomenon, more shocking than certain other more essential and more durable aspects of the new communist reality. It seemed to be a resumption and indeed a continuation of the Soviet occupation of Eastern Poland in 1939-1941, but also a continuation of the "cold civil war" between the "Polish element" and the "Jewish element," which in the minds of right-wingers had been waged in Poland even before the war. Official posters, appearing in April 1946, read "Honor to the heroic defenders of the ghetto," and "Shame to the fascist knaves of the AK army."
>
> To many Poles, it seemed as though the Jews had "won."...
>
> Long before the end of the war, the political elite of the future People's Poland was selected in the Soviet Union, mostly from among the old communists, but not exclusively. Once Poland was occupied, the expanding apparatus of domination absorbed anyone willing to cooperate, calling primarily for educated people, who were then in very short supply. Many educated Poles were ready to help in the rehabilitation of their country; they were not, however, ready to participate in the ruling of the country under communists. The new authorities, for their part, were deeply suspicious of the intelligentsia, a group rich in long and lively patriotic traditions.
>
> The Jewish response was quite different. Grateful to the Soviet Union for saving their lives, emerging from an almost complete isolation, the Jews were culturally uprooted, acutely aware of the distrust felt toward them by the rest of Polish society. Dreaming of brotherhood and equality, and at the same time quite willing to give the "reactionaries" a lesson, they were ideal candidates for the new men in power. Independent of that, many were convinced communists of long standing....
>
> There is no doubt that Jews were favored by the new authorities.[143]

In mid-1949, there were an estimated 70,000 to 80,000 Jews in Poland, and at the end of the 1940s, an estimated 10,000 Jews (20,000 if family members are included) belonged to the Polish United Workers' Party (Polska Zjednoczona Partia Robotnicza, or PZPR).[144] In the ensuing years, as more and more Jews emigrated, the Jewish PZRP members formed an increasingly larger proportion of the remaining Jewish population.

According to various authors, in postwar Poland communist Jews, often with changed names, served in the major Soviet organs of oppression; held key positions in the Ministry of Foreign Affairs, the Ministry of Justice, the Parliament, the National Council, the Ministry of Education and the press; were commandants in Soviet-run concentration camps on Polish soil; accused and delivered Polish citizens into the hands of the People's Commissariat for State Security (Narodnyi Komissariat

Gosudarstvennoi Bezopasnosti, or NKGB); fingered the elites and those who needed to be eliminated; and imprisoned, tortured, and murdered thousands of Polish civilians and members of the Polish anticommunist resistance movement. Stefan Korboński, one of the leaders of the Polish underground state and a Yad Vashem medal recipient, provides us with a few of their names and positions:

> The team assembled by Jakub Berman [a Soviet citizen] at the beginning of his rule consisted of the following dignitaries, all of them Jewish:
>
> 1. General Roman Romkowski (Natan Grünsapan-Kikiel) ... vice-minister of State Security.
>
> 2. General Juliusz Hibner, born Dawid Schwartz ... aide to the minister of State Security ... commander of the internal military forces ... vice-minister of the Interior.
>
> 3. Luna [Julia] Brystygier ... director of the fifth department of the Ministry of State Security...the former wife of Dr. Nathan Brystygier, a Zionist activist in the prewar period.... Immediately after the arrival of the Red Army in Lwów in 1939 Brystygier started denouncing people on such a scale that she antagonized even Communist Party members....
>
> 4. Colonel Anatol Fejgin ... director of the tenth department of the Ministry of State Security....
>
> 5. ... Józef Światło [Licht, Lichtstein, Fleischfarb] ... deputy director of the tenth department.... Two massive steel closets in his office contained material which incriminated every important personality from Berman down and was kept for purposes of blackmail.... [Out of fear for his life, Światło defected to the United States on December 5, 1953, and in ten months' time, he told all. This resulted in the liquidation of the Ministry of State Security in Poland.]
>
> 6. Colonel Józef Różański (Goldberg) ... director of the investigation department of the Ministry of State Security.... [Judges, eager to stay on the right side of the secret political police, would call Różański to ask him what sentence he would suggest for a person charged by his office. Różański's replies were laconic: "five years...ten years...life...death."] It was rumored that he settled in Israel....
>
> 7. Colonel Czaplicki (fictitious name) ... headed the third department of the Ministry of State Security, was charged with the prosecution of the Home Army....
>
> 8. Zygmunt Okręt [Okrent] ... director of the archives department of the Ministry, in charge of records and personal files.
>
> The above dignitaries were far from being the only Jewish officials of the Ministry. Wiktor Kłosiewicz, a Communist and member of the Council of State, stated in his interview conducted by Teresa Torańska: "Accounts had to be settled in 1955 and it was unfortunate that all the department directors in the Ministry of State Security were Jews."
>
> The reason was Stalin's decision not to use Poles, whom he did not trust....
>
> Hence the hierarchy: Stalin in Moscow at the pinnacle, issuing orders to Berman orally during his visits and all-night feasts or by direct telephone line; Berman assigning duties to the directors of the various departments of the Ministry, every one of them Jewish. Since the Ministry of State Security exerted at the time the power of life or death, it held Poland under a reign of terror in the years 1945–1955, at the cost of many lives.... That task was assigned to the Jews because they were thought to be free of Polish patriotism, which was the real enemy.
>
> Aside from leadership in the Ministry of State Security, which played a role analogous to the Gestapo in Hitler's Germany, the Jews also held leading positions in other government departments of the Communist regime...Hilary Minc...Roman Zambrowski, born Rubin Nussbaum...Tadeusz Zabłudowski...Roman Werfel...Leon Kasman ...Jerzy Borejsza (brother of Józef Różański)...Wiktor Grosz...Eugeniusz Szyr... Artur Starewicz...Adam Schaff....
>
> The major part of that leadership group of Jewish prominence came to Poland from Russia, where it had fled during the war. It exerted totalitarian rule over Poland from 1945 to about 1955 and the "Polish October" of 1956.[145]

John Sack, a Jewish-American investigative reporter and author of the controversial *An Eye for an Eye,* provides us with some additional thought-provoking information:

Of the Jews in the Office [Urząd Bezpieczeństwa Publicznego, or Office of State Security] ... [a list of names follows].

Barek Eisenstein estimated that 90 percent of the Jews in the Office in Kattowitz [Katowice] changed their names to Polish ones. Barek said one was even buried in a Catholic cemetery. Pinek Mąka, the Secretary of State Security for Silesia in 1945, estimated that 70 or 75 percent of the officers in Silesia were Jews. Barek Eisenstein estimated that 75 or more percent were, Stanisław Gazda that "most" were, Adam "Krawecki" that 70 to 80 percent were, and Moshe Mąka that 70 or 75 percent "maybe" were. Józef Musiał, the Vice Minister of Justice for Poland in 1990, said, "I don't like to talk about it," but most officers in the Office in all of Poland were Jews.... Pinek estimated that two or three hundred officers worked for the Office in Silesia, and three fourths would be 150 to 225.

Stanisław Gazda, who was secretary to Chaim Studniberg, the Director of Prisons and Camps for Silesia, said there were twenty to thirty prisons in Silesia, as did Efraim Lewin, the commandant at Neisse [Nysa]. Among them, Pinek, Stanisław Gazda, Shlomo Morel and Colonel Wacław Kożera, the Director of the Department of Criminal Institutions in Katowice in 1989, remembered prisons in Będzin, Beuthen [Bytom], Bielsko-Biała, Breslau [Wrocław], Częstochowa, Hindenburg [Zabrze], Jastrzębie, Kattowitz, Königshütte [Chorzów], Nikolai [Mikołów], Myslowitz [Mysłowice], Neisse, Oppeln [Opole], Schwientochlowitz [Świętochłowice], Sosnowiec (three prisons), Tarnowitz [Tarnowskie Góry] and Zawiercie. Among the Jewish commandants in Silesia were Major Frydman at Beuthen, Jacobowitz at an unidentified camp, Shmuel Kleinhaut at Myslowitz, Efraim Lewin at Neisse, Shlomo Morel at Schwientochlowitz, Oppeln and Kattowitz, and Lola Potok Ackerfeld at Gleiwitz [Gliwice]. Czesław Gęborski, the commandant at Lamsdorf [Łambinowice], was probably a Catholic, but I was told of no other gentile commandants.[146]

For reasons such as those above, Krajewski states:

The archetype of the Jew during the first ten years of the Polish People's Republic was generally perceived as an agent of the secret political police. It is true that under Bierut and Gomułka (prior to 1948) the key positions in the Ministry of State Security were held by Jews or persons of Jewish background. It is a fact which cannot be overlooked, little known in the west and seldom mentioned by the Jews in Poland. Both prefer to talk about Stalin's anti-Semitism (the "doctors" plot, etc.). The machine of communist terror functioned in Poland in a manner similar to that used in other communist ruled countries in Europe and elsewhere. What requires explanation is why it is operated by Jews. The reason was that the political police, the base of communist rule, required personnel of unquestionable loyalty to communism. These were people who had joined the Party before the war and in Poland they were predominantly Jewish. This is not all. Due to the dearth of old, faithful comrades, anyone whose loyalty was beyond question would do, especially the unattached — those without the supportive structures of family, neighbors and friends — and those who were attracted to socialism and wanted to make the Party their frame of reference. Many Jews, but by no means only they, met such qualifications.[147]

The reader should not get the impression, however, that life for the Jews in Poland was easy. After all, the vast majority of them did not identify either with the régime or with the Jewish communists. As one survivor explained: "People used to say — it was easy for Jews in the old regime because there were so many Jews in it. But that was only true if you gave yourself over to them. If you wanted to be yourself, it was just as hard on the Jews as on the Poles."[148]

Between 1944 and 1948, an estimated 150,000 people were arrested and imprisoned by the Soviet régime in Poland, and between 1945 and 1956, perhaps as many as half a million people passed through the dungeons of the Soviet organs of oppression. Supposedly the communist guards told the prisoners protesting their innocence: "We have the person, the paragraph will be found" (*Człowiek jest, paragraf się znajdzie)*; "Here, no one is innocent, everyone must sign a confession" (*Tu nie ma niewinnych, każdy musi się przyznać*)"; and "You will sit it out, you'll get used to it—and if you don't, you'll die like a dog" (*Posiedzisz, przywykniesz—a jak nie przywykniesz, to zdechniesz*).[149] Poland, in short, came to resemble the Soviet Union, where, it was said, there were only three categories of people: "those who were in prison, those who are in prison, and those who will be in prison."[150] The victims were overwhelmingly ethnic Poles. The persecution was often racially motivated: Poles were called "*ty polska świnio*" (you Polish pig), in the Nazi fashion, and Jewish jailers—such as Shlomo Morel—spoke openly of revenge.[151]

Torture during interrogations included breaking ribs, stomping bodies, knocking out teeth, pulling out fistfuls of hair especially that of women, mashing and cutting off fingers, forcing the prisoner to stand naked at attention by an open window in winter or to stand on one foot, dousing the prisoner with buckets of freezing water, tying up and beating the prisoner, issuing a sudden blow to the back of the head of a prisoner facing the wall so that the face smashed into the wall, pressing some metal object to the back of the head to give the impression of a gun, impaling the prisoner through the rectum by having him sit on the leg of an upturned stool and then suddenly kicking the stool out from under him, inserting metal objects or wire into the penis or rectum, or ordering solitary confinement, starvation, or sleep deprivation—and a hundred other physical and psychological indignities learned from the Gestapo and perfected to a fine science by the Soviets and their sadistic collaborators.[152]

According to Jerzy Poksiński, between 1944 and 1955 tens of thousands of cases were heard by the Stalinist military tribunals (called Stalinist Ministry of [*In*]Justice, by Poksiński) in Poland and tens of thousands of sentences were handed out, without much ado. Of these, 6,700 were death sentences—70 percent of which were carried out. Begining in 1946, regional military courts were established in Poland, and regional prosecutors were appointed to try civilians for predominantly political crimes. According to information provided by the chief of the Department of Service to Justice (Department Służby Sprawiedliwości MON), Colonel Henryk Holder, out of 538 positions in the military tribunals in mid–1946, 52 were occupied by Jews or people of Jewish origin and 17 by Red Army officers.[153]

On the basis of lists provided by local spies (including Poles like Leon Zubiak) in Grabowiec, my brother-in-law, Ryszard Pedowski, was rounded up with fifty-nine other Poles by the NKVD/UB (Urząd Bezpieczeństwa—Office of [State] Security) after the Soviet liberation in 1944. Of the sixty, thirteen were identified as AK members and sent to a prison in Hrubieszów. The rest were interrogated, beaten, and released. In Hrubieszów prison, Ryszard was interrogated nine times, tortured thrice, and released after thirteen weeks of imprisonment.

"Who conducted the interrogations and beat you?" I asked.

"Mainly Jewish officers," he replied.

The following testimony comes from Canada:

> I was a leader of a Home Army unit which sheltered Jews with individual families (including my own) and provided food to Jews confined in the ghetto. With the help of parish priests who issued false birth certificates, the unit fabricated over 500 identity documents to assist Jews to hide out.
>
> Three members of the unit were caught by the Germans. One was shot trying to escape, the others died in a concentration camp. As in many other Home Army units, several Jews also served as partisan fighters.
>
> I am aware of other former members of the Polish Home Army living in Canada who also provided assistance to Jews in the ghettos.
>
> After my capture by Soviet troops in 1939 I was guarded by a Jewish militia, who often treated former Polish officers with the utmost brutality.
>
> In post-war Stalinist Poland, when I, along with tens of thousands of anti–Nazi Polish Home Army members, was prosecuted as an "enemy of the people," Jews figured prominently in all stages and levels of my prosecution and internment. Fortunately, I was able to survive 10 years of harsh prison life.[154]

Stefan Korboński maintains that the postwar reign of Soviet terror, carried out with the help of the Jews, claimed tens of thousands of lives — mostly of Poles who belonged to the resistance movement during the war and who became the avowed enemies of the communist régime in Poland after it was over. When these Jewish communist élites were finally dismissed from the party and left Poland along with other Jews, a wail of protests was raised by the world Jewish community, including a thousand American professors, over this "anti–Semitic" purge. No attempt was made to distinguish the true Jewish victims of communism from the purged Jewish communists. This purge, this internal struggle within the Communist Party, did not concern the vast majority of Poles. Who can blame them for not speaking out in defense of those who not only attained their positions on the basis of patronage rather than merit but also grossly abused their authority? Korboński ends this black chapter of Polish history as follows:

> The ten years of Jewish [i.e., Stalinist] rule in Poland could not be easily forgotten. It was an era of the midnight knock at the door, arbitrary arrests, torture, and sometimes secret execution. Most of those responsible for that reign of terror left Poland and upon arrival in the West represented themselves as victims of Communism and anti-Semitism — a claim which was readily believed in the West and earned them the full support of their hosts.[155]

In other words, these executioners were transformed into victims.

Some people have said that these Jews were not Jews at all but communists (who just happened to have been Jewish).[156] If so, then why did most of them emigrate to Israel in the successive waves of 1946-48, 1956-57, and 1958-59? And why did those who wound up in the West generally lose no time in identifying themselves with the Jewish community, joining Jewish organizations, and representing themselves as "victims of communism and anti-Semitism"? These people cannot have it both ways; and neither can the Jewish leadership, both in postwar Poland and abroad, which, while failing to contain (or at least condemn) the excesses of the Jewish communists, tried to exert its influence on the Catholic Church officials to speak out against Polish anti–Semitism.[157] John Sack replies:

> They were "more Communist than Jewish," a University of California professor wrote — they were "Communists from Jewish families," "Communists from Jewish backgrounds," "Communists of Jewish origin." Now, I'd known these people seven years, and I'd never thought I would read that. I'd interviewed twenty-three Jews who'd been in the Office, and one, just one, had considered himself a communist in 1945. He and the others had gone to Jewish schools, studied the Torah, had been bar-mitzvahed, sometimes worn *payes*. In German camps, at the risk of their lives, some had made *matzo* on Pesach, and in 1945 they had lighted candles on Shabbas, held seders on Pesach, stood under *huppas* at weddings, sounded *shofars* on Rosh Hashanah, and fasted on Yom Kippur. By whose definition weren't they Jews? Not by the Talmud's, certainly not by the government of Israel's or the government of Nazi Germany's. Had they died in the Holocaust, I'd have guessed that the world would count them among the six million.[158]

Krystyna Kersten believes that not only the communists of Jewish origin were considered to be Jews — and not only by the Polish society. "In public opinion anyone who cooperated with the authorities could be a Jew, and those Poles of Jewish heritage and the large group of people who found themselves somewhere on the road between Jewish cultural society and the Polish national community, most certainly were. What is more, they were considered to be Jews in the eyes of the Jews, of the Americans, and of the world."[159]

Of course it would be instructive now to specify *exactly* how many Jews served in the Polish communist régime, particularly in the Office of State Security, in comparison with Poles and people of other ethnic background. One answer comes from Daniel Jonah Goldhagen, in his vitriolic review of Sack's *An Eye for an Eye*:

> For we *know* how many Jews were in the Office of State Security. According to a

> tabulation of November 21, 1945, by Bolesław Bierut, then President of Poland, the Office of State Security had 25,600 members, of whom 438 were Jews. 438! Not Sack's 75 percent, but 1.7 percent of its members were Jewish. There were sixty-seven Jews among the 500 people in leading positions. Moreover, the Polish historiographical literature shows that those Jews who were in the Office of State Security did not act as Jews but as Polish Communists (many of them had scarcely any attachment to their Jewishness), and did not act in a manner different from the 25,000 non-Jewish Police Security officers. Finally, the Office of State Security was not ultimately run by Jewish Poles or non-Jewish Poles. It was run by the Soviets.[160]

John Sack replied:

> I must ask, does Goldhagen really accept the statistics of Bolesław Bierut? Does Goldhagen really believe that if Bierut, Stalin or Mao gives us a statistic, then we *know* it? In 1945 many Poles felt (and not without reason) that Jews ran the Office of State Security, and Bierut's interest in mollifying the Poles went well beyond his devotion to statistical truth. In fact, almost none of the Jews in the Office told the Office, or Bolesław Bierut, or anyone except other Jews, that he or she was a Jew. Almost all of them changed their names to Polish ones like General Romkowski, Colonel Rozanski, Captain Studencki and Lieutenant Jurkowski, and some, when they died, were even buried in Catholic cemeteries. So how did Bierut conjure up his 438?[161]

Goldhagen replied: "The president of Poland was not trying to lie to the Poles; the document, a purely internal, top-secret, handwritten note based on a report submitted to Bierut by the minister of public security [Stanisław Radkiewicz], was merely informing Bierut about the ethnic composition of his security services."[162]

If so (and perhaps the document was written in November 1945, before the massive influx of Jews from the Soviet Union), why was this handwritten note "top-secret"? Why wasn't this information promulgated far and wide to dispel the myth of the Jewish conspiracy against Poland? Why *wasn't* it used to mollify the Poles, if those figures were absolutely accurate? Was it because of the offices held by those sixty-seven? Does anyone doubt that 67 — out of 500 (a nice round number), that is, 13.4 percent — strategically placed Jews could, in effect, run the Office of State Security, which was in turn controlled by Moscow? Does anyone familiar with the *modus operandi* of the Soviet system doubt that a even just a handful would be sufficient? As far as I know, it was Krystyna Kersten who first reported this "find" in 1992. Her information, in turn, came from Andrzej Paczkowski, who provided her with a copy of Bierut's note.[163] And it should come as no surprise that neither Goldhagen nor anyone else has accused John Sack ("I am a Jew") of being guilty of anti-Semitism.

But we need not rely on Bierut's note alone. Schatz has already told us that at the end of the 1940s, about 10,000 Jews (20,000 counting family members) belonged to the PZPR. We also have Paczkowski's statement that between 1944 and 1956, 131 (out of 447, over 29 percent) MBP leaders were Jews. Another historian, Andrzej K. Kunert, estimates that about 10 percent of the leading positions in the Polish communist organs of oppression, including Informacja and the judiciary, consisted of Jews. Finally, a most revealing work on this topic has recently been written by Henryk Pająk and Stanisław Żochowski, who name hundreds upon hundreds of Jewish operatives in postwar Poland.[164]

In any case, all of these figures and estimates — without exception — indicate that the Jews were clearly overrepresented, especially in the upper ranks, in the Polish Communist Party apparatus. Introductory statistics tell us that such overrepresentation is unlikely to occur by chance alone. Reason tells that the reality behind these statistics was bound to have a profound and adverse effect on Polish-Jewish relations in the postwar years, in the present, and in the future. Such was Stalin's intention, no doubt. He used similar techniques to consolidate power in other Soviet-occupied territories, namely Czechoslovakia, Rumania, and Hungary — with similar results and, ultimately, similar postwar Stalinist purges of the communist Jews themselves.

Following the events of 1956, some 40,000 Jews left Poland. With the emigration of some 20,000 Jews after March 1968, the long history of Judaism in Poland virtually ended. During and after these communist purges, the stereotype of the Jew as the "eternal enemy of Poland" was promulgated far and wide by the communist organs of propaganda. In this way, the Communist Party, which had first put some of the Jews in visible positions of power and used them, along with other Polish citizens, to break the spirit of the nation, now attempted to exonerate itself by placing all the blame for the excesses of the Stalinist régime on the shoulders of the Jews.

In conclusion, then, in postwar Poland the Jewish communists constituted a small but privileged and powerful minority not so much in the rank and file as in dominant party positions and in organs of oppression. The victims of these organs of oppression were almost always Poles. (Scholarly literature, testimonies, and memoirs are silent on the issue of Stalinist repressions aimed against Jews in the immediate postwar years.) The Jewish communists were also well paid: "Already in the first year of their reign," states Zbigniew Błażyński, "they invested in houses, bought automobiles, clothes, suits, looked around for servants." Those in the Office of State Security were even better off than their colleagues in other party offices. In the words of Józef Światło, they had "considerably better privileges and considerably more money" and lived "better than the most affluent prewar capitalists."[165]

In a thought-provoking passage, Władysław T. Bartoszewski addresses some of the arguments advanced by apologists for the postwar role of the Jewish communists in Poland:

> Most Poles particularly resent the application of this double standard to those Jewish individuals who were active in, and high-ranking members of, the Communist Party, and especially of the security police. These are sometimes excused on the grounds that Communist ideology offered them hope of achieving equal status with the Gentile population and of living in a country free of antisemitism where social justice and liberal ideals would prevail. It is often suggested that the Jews, being more vulnerable because of their ethnic background, had no choice but to participate in the construction of the new order. This view is offensive both to the majority of the Jews who did not want to live under Communism and left Poland, and because it implies that different moral standards can be applied to judge Jewish and Gentile moral behaviour. It is important to make a distinction here between those who supported and joined the Communist Party and even became its propagandists and activists for whatever misguided reason, and those who were directly involved in the security apparatus. The latter involved active participation in arrests and interrogations, and thus torture, deportations, and, in some instances, killing of the civilian population. One can treat the former cases with some sympathy and understanding, but it is not possible to excuse the latter. Whatever the conditions existing in Poland between 1945 and 1956, no one — Gentile or Jewish — can claim that he or (very often) she *had* to be a member of the Stalinist political police or the judiciary and, for one reason or another, had no choice but to torture and kill their innocent political opponents. After all, no one looks for extenuating circumstances for ex-members of the Gestapo.[166]

In the interest of truth, just as Polish prejudice, discrimination, and anti–Semitism should not be swept under the rug of history, so too Jewish-Soviet collaboration should not be excluded from the overall history of the Jews in the Second Republic of Poland and during the two Soviet occupations. Since adjectives seem to stand in the way of that truth, "some" may be the only modifier acceptable to both sides. *Some* of the 23 million ethnic Poles were anti–Semitic, and *some* of the 3.3 million Jews in Poland collaborated with the Soviets before and during the war, to the detriment of the Polish nation and citizens. For the sake of peace and reconciliation, let us also reach the same conclusion for the situation after the war.

German Occupation

Initially, not knowing what was in store for them, the Jews in some of the towns in central Poland sent delegations to welcome the German invaders. On September 8, 1939, for example, Jewish community leaders and rabbis met the German troops on the flower-strewn Mikołaj Rej Street in Radom and offered them the keys to the town, as well as bread and salt.[167] In his Warsaw diary, Chaim Kaplan viewed the Germans as avengers: "This is a civilization which merits annihilation and destruction ... the Poles themselves will receive our revenge through the hands of our cruel enemy ... both sides are murderers, destroyers and plunderers, ready to commit any abomination in the world."[168]

During the Nazi occupation of Poland, while millions of Jews died, there were cases of individual Jews collaborating with the Germans and informing on their fellow countrymen, Jews and Poles alike.[169] There were the Jewish *szmalcowniki* (blackmailers).[170] There was a Gestapo-sponsored Jewish militia (Żagiew—Żydowska Gwardia Wolności, or Jewish Guard of Liberty, led by Abraham Gancwajch) and the Society of Free Jews (Towarzystwo Wolnych Żydów, under Captain Lontski), whose members spied on the Jewish underground. There were the Jewish Gestapo brigades and Jewish Sonderkommando units. There was a Jewish police force (Jupo). There were camp "trusties" (Kapos), retrievers (Abholer), raiders (Ordner), stool pigeons (Spitzel), scouts (Fahnder), and catchers (Greifer) of Jewish descent, such as the infamous blond-haired, blue-eyed Stella Goldschlag of Berlin, who ferreted out and handed over to the Gestapo even her best friends and former schoolmates.[171] There were the Jewish prostitutes who worked the SS guardrooms.[172] Naturally, the Jewish community considered all of these the scum of the earth. There were also the concentration-camp inmates who cooperated with the Germans; they will be discussed in the following chapter. And there were the Jewish Councils (Judenräte) with their own militias; those who benefited from them regarded the councils as a blessing—those who did not, as a curse.

At his trial Adolf Eichmann testified that the Nazis regarded Jewish collaboration as "the very cornerstone" of their anti-Semitic policy. Alois Brunner, Eichmann's assistant, was credited by Simon Wiesenthal, the Nazi hunter par excellence, as having invented Jewish collaboration because of his fervor and success in enlisting the Jews to carry out their own Shoah.[173] According to Tadeusz Bednarczyk: "Collaboration and betrayal among the Jews reached an alarming proportion in the Warsaw ghetto. There was, proportionately speaking, a substantially greater number of them than the number of collaborators and traitors in the Polish nation and perhaps in other occupied nations.... The conclusion is sad. There were many Jewish Gestapo agents, traitors, *szmalcowniki* and collaborators."[174]

In *Holocaust Memoirs,* Maximilian T., a survivor, tells us exactly how the Jewish blackmailers plied their trade, in conjunction with their Polish counterparts in Warsaw:

> Life in Warsaw was very hard, and the population in general lived on meager food rations. But among the millions of Polish residents were many bandits, cold-blooded cads, who found a way to profit from the misfortune of the Jews. Hunting for Jews and blackmailing them became a lucrative business. The blackmailers, who preyed on the misfortune of Jews, reaped where they had not sown and made fortunes....
>
> These hyenas, working hand in glove with Jews who, for the price of letting them live when they were themselves discovered, cooperated with the *szmalcowniki*, supplying them with addresses and other details about Jews living in hiding as Aryans....
>
> [He then describes how, after his arrival in Warsaw, he gave his address to a Jewish friend also living under an assumed name. He was soon visited by *szmalcowniki,* who accepted a bribe instead of turning him in.]
>
> These *szmalcowniki* liked the way I behaved, that I didn't bargain and even treated them to vodka and a snack. One of them, who had more vodka than he probably could bear, came back after the others left and said that he liked me very much and had come back to warn me that I should change our apartment. When I asked him who had given them my name, he said that

> I was not the only one on their list of Jews living in Warsaw under Polish names. I asked him to show me the list, but he laughed, saying, "Oh no, I can't do that!"
>
> ...the next evening he came with a bottle of vodka, buns, butter, and other delicacies, and said, "I wanted to show you that I am a real friend. I brought not only vodka and appetizers, but also the list you asked for...."
>
> I was beside myself when I saw the list. It contained quite a number of Jews, among them about ten from my hometown, all registered by their assumed Polish names, their addresses in Warsaw, their real names, and also their means, the size of their families, their profession before the war, and finally, the place where they were working in Warsaw, if one held a job....
>
> Although I had my suspicions about who the author of the list was, I still was not sure and asked my friend to tell me who he was. My friend, the *szmalcownik*, gave me a few names of Jews who belonged to their gang. I was stunned to learn that, among others, there were two colleagues of mine whom I mentioned earlier. They both came from so-called good Jewish families, and who would have believed that they could have been the source of information given to the blackmailers, by which they betrayed a fellow Jew, their former class-mate?[175]

Jews betrayed their own for many reasons: sometimes, as we have seen, for profit; sometimes, out of fear for themselves or someone dear to them; sometimes, under cruel torture; and sometimes, for petty revenge. Dana I. Alvi provides an example of the last category:

> When the [Warsaw] uprising was crushed, we all went into hiding, anticipating the arrival of the Soviet Army.
>
> In November, 1944, one of the Jewish women we saved argued with a group of Jews and brought the Germans who then killed 18 people, including her nephew and her elderly sister. One man survived. He came at night to the place where I and 10 others were hiding, informed us of the tragedy and warned us of our own imminent danger, probably saving our lives. For us, and the Jews who passed through our home, the greatest fear was that someone from the ghetto would betray [us]. The names of Jewish traitors are a record in history books authored by Jews. The photos of Jews being pulled out of their hidings in the ruins of the Warsaw ghetto are testimonials to such betrayals. No other people but their own Jewish acquaintances knew of those hidings.[176]

Except, perhaps, the Polish *szmalcowniki*.

The Jewish police, called Order Service, consisted of volunteers who were at the disposition of the Nazis and who patrolled the Jewish ghettos run by German-appointed Jewish Councils. According to one estimate, 2,500 Jewish policemen were in the service of the Nazis in the Warsaw ghetto, containing 500,000 Jews at its peak.[177] According to Raul Hilberg's incomplete listing, there were 2,000 Jewish policemen in Warsaw, 600 in Łódź, 500 in Lublin, and "volunteers were plentiful."[178]

The Jewish police, in conjunction with the Polish "Blue Police," also participated in Nazi-mandated roundups of Jews hidden throughout Poland for purposes of deportation to extermination camps, concentration camps, forced-labor camps, or execution.[179] Zygmunt Klukowski, the meticulous chronicler of the Zamość region, wrote in his diary:

> May 7, 1942. Today the "blue police," along with the Jewish police and with help from a few Polish civilians, arrested five Jews and eight women.... No one knows the reasons for these arrests.

> October 31, 1942. Still some Jews are hiding. Besides the gendarmes and the "blue police," four members of the Jewish police are very active in hunting the Jews. They know the hiding places, and they hope they will survive. One thing is sure: they will be the last ones shot.[180]

When their services were no longer needed, the Jewish policemen also became victims of the "Final Solution." Some died sooner, for example the thirty-seven Jewish policemen who refused to take part in a roundup of children in Kaunas, Lithuania, and so were shot by their Nazi masters.[181] The role of the Jewish policemen as collaborators has been assessed by both Aleksander Bieberstein and Emanuel Ringelblum:

> Bieberstein: After the resignation from service of decent people who, in the conditions created by the OD [Ordnungsdienst—Order Service], could not act in keeping with their conscience, there remained in the OD spies, denouncers, sadists, blind executors of the orders of the occupant having, in due course, the lives of very many Jews on their conscience. Throughout the entire period of occupation, the Ordnungsdienst was an instrument in the hands of the Gestapo, per its instructions fulfilling without reservations the most despicable deeds, often surpassing the ruthlessness of the Germans. In time, the Ordnungsdienst became a terrible monster [*twór straszny*] usurping for itself power over the Jews.[182]

> Ringelblum: The Jewish police had a very bad name even before the resettlement. The Polish police didn't take part in the forced-work press gangs, but Jewish police engaged in that ugly business. Jewish policemen also distinguished themselves with their fearful corruption and immorality. But they reached the height of viciousness during the resettlement. They said not a single word of protest against this revolting assignment to lead their own brothers to the slaughter. The police were psychologically prepared for the dirty work and executed it thoroughly. And now people are wracking their brains to understand how Jews, most of them men of culture, former lawyers (most of the police officers were lawyers before the war), could have done away with their brothers with their own hands. How could Jews have dragged women and children, the old and the sick, to the wagons—knowing they were all being driven to the slaughter?...
>
> In the presence of such nihilism, apparent in the whole gamut of our society, from the highest to the lowest, it is no surprise that the Jewish police executed the German resettlement orders with the greatest of zeal. And yet the fact remains that most of the time during the resettlement operation the Jewish police exceeded their daily quotas. That meant they were preparing a reserve for the next day. No sign of sorrow or pain appeared on the faces of the policemen. On the contrary, one saw satisfied and happy individuals, well-fed, loaded with the loot they carried off in company with the Ukrainian guards.
>
> Very often, the cruelty of the Jewish police exceeded that of the Germans, Ukrainians, and Letts. They uncovered more than one hiding place, aiming to be *plus catholique que le pope* [more Catholic than the Pope] and so curry favor with the Occupying Power. Victims who succeeded in escaping the German eye were picked up by the Jewish police. I watched the procession to the wagons on the Umschlagplatz for several hours and noted that many Jews who were fortunate enough to work their way toward the spot where the exempted people were standing were forcibly dragged back to the wagons by the Jewish police. Scores, and perhaps hundreds, of Jews were doomed by the Jewish police during those two hours. The same thing happened during the blockades. Those who didn't have the money to pay off the police were dragged to the wagons, or put on the lines going to the Umschlagplatz....
>
> For the most part, the Jewish police showed an incomprehensible brutality. Where did Jews get such murderous violence? When in our history did we ever before raise so many hundreds of killers, capable of snatching children off the street, throwing them on the wagons, dragging them to the Umschlag? It was literally the rule for the scoundrels to fling women on to the Kohn-Heller streetcars, or on to ordinary trucks, by grabbing them by the arms and legs and heaving. Merciless and violent, they beat those who tried to resist. They weren't content simply to overcome the resistance, but with the utmost severity punished the "criminals" who refused to go to their death voluntarily. Every Warsaw Jew, every woman and child, can cite thousands of cases of the inhuman cruelty and violence of the Jewish police. Those cases will never be forgotten by the survivors, and they must and shall be paid for.[183]

Blanca Rosenberg comments not on the "inhuman cruelty and violence of the Jewish police" but on their sadism in her ghetto: "Members of the Jewish Auxiliary Police—the Judische Ordnungsdienst—seemed to take a special pleasure in their grisly duties."[184]

The Jewish Councils, established by Reinhard Heydrich in 1939, have been the subject of a bitter debate ever since Hannah Arendt published her controversial *Eichmann in Jerusalem: A Report on the Banality of Evil* in 1965. Their mandate consisted of two divergent sets of responsibilities: to provide for the general well-being of their charges and to carry out Nazi orders. The former category included such tasks as the procurement of food, clothing, fuel, housing, and other necessities for those in need; religious and cultural education; mail deliveries, fire control, sanitation, funeral arrangements; and the general maintenance of law and order. The second category included such responsibilities as the procurement of various material quotas (furniture, furs, etc.) imposed by the Germans; assistance in the resettlement of Jews from the GG and of those who came into Poland from Germany and other conquered nations; and the delivery of a specified number of Jews to work camps outside the ghetto, to forced-labor camps, and finally to extermination camps.

One Judenrat leader was Mordechai Chaim Rumkowski, the "Elder of the Jews" of Łódź. He put thousands of Jews on trains to death camps, suppressed strikes and resistance in the ghetto, and handed over to the Gestapo those trying to hide or those hiding others. To this day he is hailed by some Jews as a tragic hero and vilified by others as a despotic and contemptible collaborator.[185] Rumkowski gave encouraging speeches even in the darkest hours of the ghetto: "Representatives of the new population, I appeal to you again to finally accept the ghetto's conditions of life." "I am certain that if the ghetto does its work in earnest and does it well, the authorities will not take repressive steps. Nothing bad will happen to people of goodwill." "My expectation, based on authoritative information, is that the deportees' fate will not be as tragic as is expected in the ghetto. They will not be behind wire, and they will work on farms."[186] Leaving his Łódź kingdom to its destiny, Rumkowski himself eventually went to work on one of those unfenced farms.

Other Jewish Council leaders of the larger ghettos — who thought they could save their people and their own skins by cooperating with the Nazis — included Mojsze Merin in Upper Silesia, Efraim Barasz in Białystok, and Jakub Gens in Wilno. "We know how the Jewish officials felt when they became instruments of murder," states Hannah Arendt, "like captains 'whose ships were about to sink and who succeeded in bringing them safe to port by casting overboard a great part of their precious cargo'; like saviors who 'with a hundred victims save a thousand people, with a thousand ten thousand.'"[187]

In his review of the film *Schindler's List*, H. R. Shapiro states:

> The Nazis formed the *Judenrate* to implement Nazi policy in the Jewish community and, more importantly, to divide and conquer the Jews and to crush any resistance to the Nazis. The Jews who worked with Schindler were all leaders of the *Judenrate*....
>
> Hannah Arendt, in her great study of the Jewish Holocaust, *Eichmann in Jerusalem*, informs us: "Wherever Jews lived, there were recognized Jewish leaders, and this leadership, almost without exception, cooperated in one way or another, for one reason or another, with the Nazis. The whole truth was that if the Jewish people had really been unorganized and leaderless, there would have been chaos and plenty of misery but the total number of victims would hardly have been between four and a half and six million people."
>
> The *Judenrate* were simulated state governments. Each had its own instruments of terror, the *Ordnungsdienst* and *Zivilabteilung* (Nazi-Jewish and Secret Police), ministries of housing, food and welfare, etc., as well as the power to tax their communities and provide slave labor, at no charge, to the Nazi war machine. These Nazi-Jewish councils divided privileged Jews from non–privileged....
>
> The function of the *Judenrate* was to contain and register all Jews in the old and newly formed ghettos. The obvious objective was to save the "better Jews" (themselves, to begin with) by selecting others among their own people to be sent to their deaths. "To a Jew, this role of the Jewish leaders in the destruction of their own people is undoubtedly the darkest chapter of the whole dark story," Arendt concluded.

Isaiah Trunk, in *Judenrat,* writes that "for ghetto inmates the Jewish Councils were the visible organs of oppression.... Small wonder that all the pent-up hatred for the relatively remote Nazi enemy was aimed at the one visible adversary, the hated Councils."

News of the genocide of the summer of 1941 reached Warsaw almost overnight, and the great majority of Jews by the end of that year. The *Judenrate,* however, through secrecy and lies, convinced the Jewish masses that reports of horrors to the east were only rumors, and that Jews were merely being "resettled." With potential opposition thus neutralized, the Nazis were able to deport and exterminate most of the Warsaw Jews. By contrast, those who had some connection to the *Judenrate* and their associates, especially the privileged and the wealthy, survived the war.

The *Judenrate* leaders, writes historian L. Yahil, "perceived Jewish resistance as a threat to the existence of the ghetto or as a personal threat." Thus the Jewish communities at large lost the organizational means and spirit to defend themselves. This is what enabled the Nazis to blindside and murder most of the Jews in Eastern Poland, the Baltic states and in the occupied USSR. M. Tenenbaum-Tamaroff, a young resistance leader who participated in revolts in Warsaw and other cities to the north, led a 1943 revolt in Białystok to free the Jews who were on their way to the trains. The young Jews who were trying to effect the escape of the people of the city were thwarted by the *Judenrate* and most lost their lives in battle with the Nazis....

One of Schindler's contacts, Dr. R. Kastner, in Hungary (a member of the *Judenrate* in Pest, and an agent of the Jewish agency in Palestine) also saved some Jews — saved exactly 1,684, including his relatives and friends, according to Arendt. Kastner's privileged Jews survived through deals with Eichmann and the Zionist Jewish Agency, while almost 500,000 unsuspecting Jews in Hungary were exterminated.

Kastner was later tried in Israel for selecting who should and who should not survive. Zionist courts, of course, whitewashed Kastner — that is, the *Judenrate*— but, according to an Israeli army officer, Israeli agents assassinated him, no doubt to remove him from history.[188]

Joseph Kermish and Shmuel Krakowski lump the Judenräte into the same category as the Jewish police and paint an equally grim picture of their collaborative activities:

> As time passed, the *Judenrat* and the Jewish Police cut themselves off more and more from their own people, whom they had previously said they were serving. In the last resort, little by little, they became the willing instruments of those who had vested authority in them and they carried out the will of the rulers. They began by standing on street corners and controlling the movement of passers-by. Then they went on to bring in Jews who had not presented themselves for work, and finally it came to breaking into shelters and hide-outs to fetch out women and children and hand them over to the hangmen during the "action." If a policeman did not produce five "head" of victims for the Germans, they would take his wife, his children, and him too, and it was for this — to sacrifice the lives of innumerable people in order to save his own — that he was trained by those who gave him authority. Some individuals who realized in time what was happening drew back and resigned, while later on it became impossible to retreat. As time passed, the only people who stayed in the force were pliable characters who became the actual executors of all the German operations and the direct instrument of extermination. Every new anti–Jewish decree of the authorities the Jewish police turned into a source of income for itself. The vilest of all were the blackmailers among the police, including many brutes among them who decided the next victims for the torture camps.[189]

The use (twice) of the words "as time passed" in the passage above is subject to dispute. Klukowski records some of the activities and privileges of the Judenräte in the Zamość area beginning in 1940:

> July 17, 1940. This day was very hard for the Jews ... last night we received a notice that Jews from Szczebrzeszyn must provide five hundred men for labor camps in Germany. This notice started a riot.... Lublin eventually reduced the number of "requests" from 500 to 130. Just this morning the recruit-

ment of Jews began. The so-called *Judenrat* assigned 130 young men to be recruited but only 98 showed up. The rest went into hiding.[190]

August 26, 1940. New regulations were posted in town.... "All affairs of the Jewish community will be handled by the mayor in the quarters of the *Judenrat*.... These regulations are not binding for members of the *Judenrat* or workers in German barracks."[191]

December 31, 1941. Here in Szczebrzeszyn there is new action against the Jews. On December 26 it was announced that under penalty of death all Jews must surrender all fur coats, fur hats, fur collars, fur gloves, fur muffs, and any other clothing made of fur. Now most Jews are trying to hide all fur articles, but some are giving them away. Dr. Bolotny took to the *Judenrat* about 12,000 zloty worth of his own and also his wife's furs.[192]

April 4, 1942. ...During some fighting in the forest in Zakłodzie a German gendarme, Himler, was killed.... [Entry continues on April 8, 1942.] On April 6 the funeral of gendarme Himler took place.... Most of the people attending the funeral were gendarmes, Germans in civilian clothing, and the entire city council. Flowers were sent by city hall, the "blue police," and the *Judenrat.*[193]

May 8, 1942. ...Around 3 P.M. a real hell started in town. From Zamość there arrived a group of gestapo. They ordered the *Judenrat* to provide 100 Jews for forced labor, giving only one hour for this to happen.[194]

August 8, 1942, 11 A.M. ... All Jews must report at 8 A.M. across from the *Judenrat*.... The mayor informed me the 2,000 Jews will be deported east to the Ukraine. Railroad workers said that a large train with fifty-five cars is ready at the station. So far there are no volunteers, so the Germans began mass arrests. I asked a gendarme what would happen if the Jews did not show up. His answer was, "We will kill them here."

It is 7 P.M. Without interruption, throughout the entire day, patrols of gestapo, gendarmes, *Sonderdienst,* "blue police," along with members of the *Judenrat* and the so-called Jewish Militia, patrolled the city. They searched houses, including basements and attics. Any Jews that were found were moved to the marketplace. Most Jewish houses are empty now. [Entry continues on August 8, 9 P.M.] ...No one believes that the Jews will be moved to the Ukraine. They will all be killed. [Entry continues on August 10.] ...I learned that the train carrying the Jews went to Belzec. They have probably been killed by now.[195]

October 21, 1942. ... This was the beginning of the so-called German displacement of Jews, in reality a liquidation of the entire Jewish population in Szczebrzeszyn....

By 3 P.M. more than 900 Jews had been assembled. The Germans began moving them to the outskirts of the city. All had to walk except for members of the *Judenrat* and the Jewish police; they were allowed to use horse-drawn wagons.[196]

A more damaging assessment of the work of the Judenräte comes from the Łukacze ghetto and Świniuchy in Wołyń:

> It was daylight again. The *Judenrat* went to the chief of police once more.... At noon the *Judenrat* returned to report that the police chief had received a new required number from the regional commissioner, 322....
>
> At 5:00 AM the militia moved quickly from home to home silently distributing notification slips. Soon thereafter everyone knew who was called. The notices made it clear that favoritism and not fairness was the determining factor in reaching a decision. The 322 people included mothers, and fathers of 5 children with weak and/or sick mothers or wives, quite often 3 and 4 adults from the same family. Those who had someone serving in the *Judenrat,* police or other official connections were not called upon even if there were 2 or 3 able bodied men in the family.
>
> The *Judenrat* did not dare show its face outside....
>
> It was 7:00 AM and there was no one at the gathering site. The Jewish militia, holding sticks, accompanied by their Ukrainian equivalents, went looking for the people. Walking between the homes the Jewish

militiamen would point out a person to the Ukrainians, who seized him. Those who refused to go were beaten. Many hid in various places but the Jewish militia who knew all of those hiding spots, found them and turned them over to the Ukrainians. Loud name-calling and cursing was heard everywhere.[197]

Samuel Tennenbaum comments on the Judenrat and Jewish militia in Złoczów, in the province of Tarnopol:

> A Jewish militia was organized, supposedly to keep order among the Jewish population, but it soon became clear that its function was much more sinister — collaboration with the German destruction of the Jewish community. With few exceptions, the job attracted the dregs of society....
>
> News filtered through gentiles that the Jews, allegedly going to camps in Russia, were in fact being executed en masse in a camp in Belzec. The news was disbelieved at first. Our Judenrat firmly denied it and spread the word that letters had been received from the deported families, but nobody ever saw such a letter and no deported person ever came back.[198]

A Jewish account from Czortków states:

> The Judenrat served also as the executive agency of the Nazi authorities, being forced meticulously to carry out their orders....
>
> The Judenrat emptied the Jewish population of their property, in order to fulfill the demands of the Nazis. The Judenrat never tried to make use of the large sums and means at its disposal, to do something in order to ease the terrible situation of the Jews in Czortkow....
>
> As is known, a Jewish Police Force existed which was at the disposal of the Judenrat. The Jewish Police, "Ordnungs-Dienst" (Order-Service) in German, consisted of 20 men headed by the Officer Hungar of the municipality. The Order-Service received orders from the Judenrat, and carried out with loyalty and strictness all the requirements, like collection of taxes, the confiscation of valuables, furniture, utensils and so on, in order to complete the imposed quotas....
>
> Both the Judenrat and the Order Servicemen never shrank back from helping in snatching Jews to be sent to labour camps, which were in fact death camps....
>
> Despite the incessant demands of the Nazi authorities from the Judenrat for the supply of valuables as well as large sums of money, it never happened that the Judenrat did not meet a demand to the last penny....
>
> All the Judenrats faultlessly fulfilled their assignment, however, the Judenrat of Czortkow exceeded all others, especially in its chairman, Dr. Ebner. This man managed his treacherous activities mercilessly, with disgusting German punctuality, and the Jewish population was full of powerless anger against the chairman of the Judenrat who served with so much brutality his Nazi masters.
>
> I emphatically declare that some of the members of the Judenrat became rich and benefitted from special privileges granted to them at the expense of the Jewish population which was doomed to extermination.[199]

Perhaps the most devastating testimony regarding the activities of the *Judenräte* and the Jewish police comes from Baruch Milch, a Jewish doctor from Tłuste, a small town located in the county of Zaleszczyki, the province of Tarnopol in Eastern Galicia. The following is a selection from his work, entitled "My Testament," dated July 15, 1943.

> A Judenrat was instituted for the Jews in every town and thus began our introduction to a deeper gehenna. In our locality, I was also selected for the Judenrat. I did not realize as yet the nature of this endeavor (*czym to pachnie*) and participated very intensively in bringing help to those in need as well as in securing a certain measure of safety for the Jewish people. I had almost complete access to the local authorities, and the local Aryan population treated me with respect for the medical treatment I imparted and for my disinterested dedication....
>
> As soon as I became convinced that the Judenrat was created not to help and protect the Jews but to destroy and eradicate them — according to Hitler's saying, "*Um Juden zu vernichten, muss man Juden haben*" [To exterminate the Jews, one must use Jews] — I slowly began to back out of the Judenrat....

In any case, the Judenrat became an instrument in the hands of the Gestapo for the extermination of the Jews; it became, as the [Judenrat] members would later say, "the Gestapo on the Jewish street." Everywhere they surrounded themselves with the Ordnungsdienst to carry out their orders. This police was made up of the worst social elements such as demolishers, butchers, horse-dealers, and train porters who — as if for the sake of amusement — were dressed in uniforms, wore a Star of David on their caps, and were given sturdy clubs instead of arms. And this was supposed to be the Jewish police which would maintain order on the Jewish street.

In point of fact, the Judenrat began to play a game of political robbery in order to fill their own pockets and also to bribe the authorities and the Gestapo with these funds — but only to secure their own fortune and that of their nearest family members. I do not know of a single instance when the Judenrat helped some Jew in a disinterested manner. And if it should happen that the Judenrat would help a poor soul from time to time and give him a few zloty, that tossed bone would stick in his throat, and these poorest folks, being a burden to the Judenrat, would be the first to be rounded up or sent to the camps. So much so, that these unfortunates were afraid to ask for help, preferring instead to die [*zdychać*: the word "to die" applied to animals] from hunger and cold.

To accomplish their disreputable objectives — such as the gathering of taxes and requisitions, roundups for camps, searches and attacks on Jewish homes — the Judenrat would use their Ordnungsdienst to whom they would give a percent of the take and these in turn, in groups of ten to fifteen at a time, would attack the people and beat them mercilessly while destroying and robbing whatever was available and doing this with terrible ruthlessness. They received the power to do this from the Gestapo who, in addition, warned them that if they did not treat the Jews like this, they [the Gestapo] would, and the Jews would be the worse off for it.

For the major undertakings the Judenrat would often invoke the help of the Ukrainian police, and sometimes the Germans. It is a fact that the Judenrat were responsible for huge Besstelung or requisitions that the specially installed Besstelungsmann could exact at any moment. But for every requisition or expense incurred they would demand ten times as much, and the most important thing to note is that all the extortions perpetrated by the Judenrat did not relieve the Jewish society from any of the other plagues in the least. The Ukrainian police, Gestapo, every German, all public officials and every Aryan having the least bit of authority also harassed us, made us work, conducted searches, put us in prison, beat us up, and often killed us. In the end, when nothing was left to take from anyone and just about everyone was exterminated, it was the Judenrat's turn. Only then did they realize that this strategy was a bad one and that they were on the wrong road. But it was too late.... Only here and there was it possible for some of them, for huge sums of extorted money, to hide or to slip away abroad. History and the world will square accounts with them. I myself would very much like to survive this war and meet up with these individuals....

In the third month of my membership in the Judenrat I quit.... When certain things brought by the poorest Jews began to disappear as a matter of policy, I became very irritated, started a quarrel and quit.

This affected me drastically, since from that moment on they began to persecute me, harass me with taxes and take various things from my house. Later, in addition to this, a doctor appointed as Judenaltester proceeded to settle his own professional scores with me and ruined me completely. It was he, alas, who in large measure contributed to the final tragedy of my family....

Gradually, they began to liquidate the Jews completely in individual districts with the help of the specially organized brigades of the mobile Sonderdienst, assisted in turn by the local Gestapo with the Judenreferent at the head, the Ukrainian police, from time to time the Judenrat, and in certain locations the Ukrainian civilian population....

For the time being the doctors and the families of the Judenrat were left in peace....

[An unexpected roundup occurs.] Although our town lived in constant fear and expectation, this action in broad daylight caught the people completely off guard. Since this action did not involve our town as such but was needed to complement a contingent of a neighboring town, the Judenrat agreed to deliver the 300 people required in three hours time to the murderers. The Jews themselves had to catch and deliver their own brothers and sisters into the hands of the executioners who stood in the public square across the street from our house, greeted those brought with clubs or whips, and later transported them to Bełżec. The action began at 9 o'clock in the morning. The Judenrat and the Ordnungsdienst with the help of the Ukrainian police and a few Germans who were even paid so that they would work quickly, ran up and down the streets like mad dogs and fanatics; sweat poured from them in streams.... At 12 o'clock the Gestapo counted their victims and since the required total of 300 lacked twenty-some persons, they demanded 100 more.

Then the biggest, most despicable crime in the whole world took place. About three kilometers from town there was a seasonal farm-camp of girls from various Galician towns who worked at a rubber plant. They were beautiful girls, about 80-100 in all, the very flowers of youth, the majority of whom were high school graduates.... A devilish thought hatched instantly in the brains of the Judenrat and the Sonderführer [Lauterbach] ... it was decided to add them all to that transport. And that's how they were paid for their half year of labor, with the currency called Bełżec.[200]

Baruch Milch also tell us that when major actions against the Jews were in the air, the Judenrat would not convey the information to their own people. On the contrary, the Judenrat would assure them that there was no need to worry. Only by observing the behavior of the families of their leaders, of the Judenrat, did the Jews of Tłuste learn what to expect and when. Milch's is a particular account of a particular place and time. Needless to say, the behavior of Judenräte members was not uniform.

The Jewish militia, otherwise known as Żagiew, the previously mentioned "Jewish Guard of Liberty," consisted of Jewish Gestapo agents. At the end of 1941 and the beginning of 1942, the Gestapo had around 15,000 such Jewish agents in the General Government.[201]

Tadeusz Bednarczyk, a Polish resistance fighter in Warsaw and chronicler who came to the Warsaw ghetto on a daily basis until April 18, 1943, commented that in addition to the 6,000 Jews employed by the Judenrat in Warsaw and the 2,500 Jews who joined the ghetto police, the Germans had in their service over 1,000 Jewish Gestapo agents in the German-sponsored Żagiew organization. Some 300 of these agents continued to reside in the Gestapo premises on Szucha Street after the liquidation of the ghetto and, during 1943-44, were employed in ferreting out Jews. It was likely because of these agents that so many Jews in hiding were captured. Previously these agents had hampered the smuggling of food to the Warsaw ghetto and had been instrumental in organizing the Hotel Polski affair, in which wealthy Jews were lured to come out of hiding on false promises of obtaining foreign passports and permission to leave occupied Poland. Instead they were robbed and murdered. Polish archives hold documentation with an incomplete list of 1,378 Jewish collaborators and betrayers. One of them, Hening, directed a seventy-member team at the Gestapo premises on Szucha Street and was charged with the task of obtaining information about Polish underground organizations. Another Jew at the Gestapo premises interrogated suspect Jews on their knowledge of Catholicism and performed physical examinations.[202]

For reasons such as these, a secret Jewish court in the Warsaw ghetto executed fifty-nine Żagiew collaborators.[203] The Polish underground killed the collaborators as well.[204] So did the Gestapo — because the collaborators "knew too much" and because rival Gestapo groups often killed the agents of their competitors.[205] In time, their numbers dwindled, and the remainder, together with the decreasing number of members of the Society of Free Jews, were incorporated into the Jewish Gestapo brigades, formed in 1941 by Hauptsturmführer Alfred Spilker. Spilker was appointed by Hans Frank to head up the special Sonderkommando AS, which, in conjunction with the Abwehr, attempted to counter the efforts of the Polish underground. Sonderkommando AS consisted of groups of renegades from various nationalities. Among them were 820 Jews, who formed the Jewish brigades. During the Warsaw uprising, "Spilker's boys" were assigned the task of "cleansing" the areas captured by the Germans.[206]

Generally, however, the Jewish Sonderkommando consisted of prisoners whose tasks included working at the gas chambers and burning bodies in pyres and crematoria. "Jewish *Sonderkommandos* (special units)," states Hannah Arendt, "had everywhere been employed in the actual killing process, they had committed criminal acts 'in order to save themselves from the danger of immediate death.'" For this reason they were later exempted from "Sections 10 and 11 of the Nazis and Nazi Collaborators (Punishment) Law of 1950 [which] had been drawn up with Jewish 'collaborators' in mind."[207]

Władysław Bartoszewski, a Polish historian, cofounded the Polish wartime Council for Aid to Jews and was later decorated by Yad Vashem. He wrote: "Aside from the German police and the informers and extortionists, who were recruited from the dregs of the Christian Polish and Ukrainian populations, it was the Jewish confidence men who represented the greatest threat to Jews living in hiding. Seduced by false hopes and promises, they frequently helped the Germans to track down fellow Jews who were hiding in the 'Aryan' sector [of Warsaw]."[208]

Commenting on this Jewish-Nazi collaboration in the Warsaw ghetto, Israel Shahak, professor and human rights activist, stated:

> Of course there were Polish policemen who rounded up Jews and Poles, who blackmailed Jews whom they recognized as such.... But who of the Jewish survivors does not know ... that there were also Jewish blackmailers, some of them even quite famous by name, outside the Ghetto, who were neither better nor worse than the Polish ones, and also Jewish policemen in the Ghetto whose duty in the first weeks of the extermination of summer 1942 was to deliver, each of them a specified number, Jewish victims to "be sent" to extermination. *Now*, I hold that both kinds of murderers or accessories to murder are fully equal and that the abhorrence in which one should hold them does not depend on nationality, but my memories (and memories of all the survivors who are honestly "talking among themselves") tell me that at the time we Jews hated the Jewish policemen, or the Jewish spies for the Nazis in the Ghetto, much more than we hated anybody else.[209]

The Jewish-Soviet collaborators in Eastern Poland, and certainly the Jewish-Nazi collaborators in all of occupied Poland, were not numerous in proportion to the over three million Jews. Yet they too must bear the burden of guilt for contributing to the death toll of Polish citizens. Simon Wiesenthal's words provide a sobering commentary on the postwar treatment of Jewish-Nazi collaborators by the very people they betrayed: "We have done very little to condemn Jewish collaboration with the Nazis. When, after the war, I demanded that those who had abused their office in ghettos or concentration camps be removed from Jewish committees, I was told that 'this would diminish the guilt of the Nazis.'"[210]

Chapter 4
Polish Collaboration

Soviet Occupation

In the mid–1930s the leaders of the Polish Communist Party were called to Moscow for their eternal reward. In other words, they were to be killed. Most of those who escaped this fate did so because they were sitting in Polish jails at the time and hence were unable to travel. The Communist International dissolved the Polish Communist Party in 1938.

Few Polish people, therefore, welcomed the Soviet invasion of September 1939. Among these few were the undaunted former members of the Communist Party (both Christians and Jews) who gathered in Lwów and hoped for better days, people like Edward Ochab, Zenon Kliszko, Hilary Minc, and Władysław Kruczek. For their faithfulness and efforts in behalf of the Soviet government during the occupation of Eastern Poland, those who survived the war were rewarded with prominent positions in the Polish Workers' Party (Polska Partia Robotnicza, or PPR); people like Władysław Gomułka, Edmund Pszczółkowski, Czesław Domagała, Wacław Lewickowski, Janina Bier, Wacława Marek, and Jan Krasicki.[1]

In the October 1939 elections to the "People's Assembly of Western Ukraine," in which practically all the deputies handpicked by Moscow were Ukrainians, were 44 Poles.[2] Among the 926 deputies in the same election to the "People's Assembly of Western Belarus" (many of them former members of the Communist Party of Western Belorussia which claimed a multinational membership but which actually consisted predominantly of Belorussians and Jews),[3] 127 Poles were placed on the ticket.[4] The honeymoon did not last long. In 1940, even the remnants of the Polish Communist Party in the east headed toward the Nazi zone to escape the Soviet purges.[5] Needless to say, Moscow did not trust the "Polish communists."

Besides the political collaborators — who out of fear or conviction sided with the Soviets and helped to implement Soviet policies in Eastern Poland — a number of Polish writers also contributed their talent to the Soviet cause.[6] Many of these writers were refugees from Nazi-occupied Poland. Many of them were Jewish. Among the latter was Aleksander Wat, the onetime editor of the Polish Communist *Miesięcznik Literacki* (1929) and later (1939) an employee of the *Czerwony Sztandar* in Lwów. Wat described the exodus: "The autumn of 1939 was the last autumn of autocratic Poland, that Poland which oppressed classes and nationalities. During this autumn not only the left-wing, but all honest writers ran away from the disgrace and shame of their fatherland; they all became 'fugitives to socialism,' as the poet S. Kirsanov put it."[7]

In Lwów, the refugee "oppressed classes and nationalities" numbered some 100,000; the "honest writers" totaled over one hundred. In this same article, Wat provides his readers with the names of thirty such writers who resided in the Lwów area at the time. Surprisingly, on their arrival, the Soviet authorities displayed a most benevolent attitude to these potential (in the words of Stalin) "engineers of human souls." Repeated radio announcements urged displaced writers to gather in Lwów, they were spared the wave of arrests that swept the land in the fall of 1939, a Literary Club in the city provided them with food and drink, various meetings were arranged in their behalf with Soviet, Ukrainian, and Jewish writers, and the general secretary of the Union of Ukrainian Soviet Writers, Aleksandr Korneychuk, made a personal effort to recruit as many of them as possible for the communist cause.

Among the refugee writers eventually recruited were Jerzy Borejsza, Władysław Broniewski, Emil Dziedzic, Mieczysław Jastrun, Leopold Lewin, Adam Polewka, Jerzy Putrament, Julian Przyboś, Ewa Szemplińska, Lucjan Szenwald, Wanda Wasilewska, Aleksander Wat, Adam Ważyk, and Tadeusz Boy-Żeleński. To these can be added a number of residential Lwów literati such as Jan Brzoza, Aleksander Dan, Halina Górska, Karol Kuryluk, Leon Pasternak, and Stanisław Wasylewski. Borejsza, Jastrun, Lewin, Szenwald, Wat, Ważyk, Górska, and Pasternak were of Jewish origin.[8]

A number of pragmatic reasons lay behind the Soviet interest in the Polish writers. After the liquidation of the Polish intelligentsia in the Soviet Union and the members of the Communist Party of Poland, there was a desperate need to staff Polish communist newspapers with people fluent in the Polish language. These publications included the following: *Słowo Żołnierza; Czerwony Sztandar*, whose chief editor was Roman Werfel and later I. Mankovskyi from Kiev; *Prawda Wileńska*, which employed such writers as Teodor Bujnicki, Kazimierz Hałaburda, Józef Maśliński, Jerzy Odra, and Professor Stanisław Zajączkowski and whose chief editor (Antoni Fiedorowicz) was replaced by an arrival from Moscow (Władysław Sokołowski) who did not read Polish and consequently had to have the entire paper translated into Russian for his benefit; and *Nowe Widnokręgi*, a Lwów literary monthly existing from January to June 1941 under Wanda Wasilewska and such writer-editors as Helena Usiejewicz, Tadeusz Boy-Żeleński, Janina Broniewska, and Zofia Dzierżyńska.[9]

Another reason for the Soviets' interest in the Polish writers was the immediate need to use their talent for the upcoming "referendum" and to use their names for an aura of legitimacy. Fourteen writers actually signed a statement, published in the *Czerwony Sztandar*, supporting the unification of Ukraine. They were also needed to edit new textbooks in Polish history and literature (sixteen authors participated in this venture, including Boy-Żeleński, Wasylewski, Werfel, Henryk Schiller, Melania Kierczyńska, and Jan Kott),[10] to establish ties with the working class, to participate in mass mobilization campaigns, to promulgate official Soviet policies, to propagandize Soviet ideology, and to appear in public with Soviet writers and dignitaries. Two writers, Adam Polewka and Halina Górska, were even put up as official candidates and were elected to serve on the People's Assembly. Irena Grudzińska-Gross and Jan Tomasz Gross describe Polewka's selection process:

> Adam Polewka...a writer who later fled to the Generalgouvernement was visited one morning by three grim-looking Soviet officers. He was convinced that they had come to arrest him. They proceeded to interview him, checking his answers against a file they had brought along. When they finished, the senior Soviet inquisitor shook Polewka's hand and announced proudly to him, "You will be a deputy to the National Assembly!"[11]

Not all the Polish writers who "escaped to socialism" remained under Soviet rule. After a time, some made their way to Rumania or Lithuania, and some, like Adam Polewka, actually returned to the Nazi-occupied territory.

Of those who chose to remain, not all were converted to the Soviet cause; some, both refugee and resident Lwów writers, continued to think and act as if they were free agents. Above all, contrary to the official Soviet line, they continued to criticize Nazi Germany. As a result of this lack of total internal conversion (a sine qua non requirement of party affiliation), but also as a result of the Soviet denunciation policy applied by and to the writers, and the demand of the Ukrainians for a full implementation of the policy of Ukrainization, these Polish writers, dubbed contemptuously by the Soviets as the "London Poles," found themselves under arrest on January 24, 1940, and were soon deported. Among them were Herminia Naglerowa, Teodor Parnicki, and Beata Obertyńska.

This purge, which lasted until the middle of 1940, was followed by a renewed Soviet interest in cultivating the friendship of the remaining Polish literary community. In the fall of 1940, Polish writers were permitted to commemorate the first anniversary of the "liberation" of Poland's eastern territories, as well as the eighty-fifth anniversary of the death of Adam Mickiewicz, a native son born in Nowogródek, in the Belorussian SSR; they were invited to Kiev and Moscow; they were honored for their literary achievements; twenty-two of them were admitted to the Lwów branch of the Union of Ukrainian Soviet Writers; they were allowed to publish new periodicals in the Polish language; and having willingly collaborated with the Soviets during the occupation of Poland in 1939, these same writers were recruited again to participate in the subsequent Sovietization of Poland after 1944.

Meanwhile, during the war years, the Polish-American community, consisting of some 4 to 5 million people, split along three different lines on the question of the Soviet claims over Eastern Poland.[12] The largest group was centered in Chicago, home of the Polish National Alliance and the Polish Roman Catholic Union. These "Chicago Poles" supported the Polish government-in-exile and Prime Minister Władysław Sikorski's efforts (after the Polish-Soviet Agreement of July 30, 1941) to reach some sort of an accommodation with the Soviet Union regarding these territories.

The second faction, known as the National Committee of Americans of Polish Descent (Komitet Narodowy Amerykanów Polskiego Pochodzenia, or KNAPP), operated out of New York. Although they too supported the Polish government-in-exile, they were inflexible on the issue of the eastern territories and insisted on the return of these territories to Poland after the war. Furthermore, they continued to regard the Soviet Union not as Poland's ally but as an enemy on a par with Nazi Germany. As a result of deteriorating Polish-Soviet relations, by mid-1944 many of the "Chicago Poles" took this position as well.

The third contingent was a very small but vocal group of Polish-Americans associated with Detroit's communist *Głos Ludowy* (People's Voice). This pro–Soviet faction castigated the Polish government in London for seeking a return of the eastern territories to Poland and was often quoted by the American communist *Daily Worker* as well as (after the April 25, 1943, rupture of relations between Moscow and the London Poles over the Katyn executions) by *Izvestia* and *Pravda*. These "Detroit Poles" were hailed by the Soviet press as heroic leaders and were portrayed as genuine spokespeople for the entire Polish-American community.

Among these Polish-American collaborators were Leo Krzycki, the American-born Socialist labor leader, vice-president of the Amalgamated Clothing Workers Union and president of the American Slav Congress, founded in 1941; the American-born Reverend Stanisław Orlemański, characterized by Alexander Werth as "either a well-meaning simpleton or else a practical joker," a parish priest from Springfield, Massachusetts, and the organizer of the Kościuszko League, whose views coincided with the leftist American Slav Congress; and a University of Chicago professor, Oskar Lange (1904–65), a Polish-born (in Tomaszów Mazowiecki) and educated (at the Jagiellonian University) economist of Jewish origin and a personal friend of Wanda Wasilewska, who was one of the Lwów pro–Soviet writers and head of the Moscow-based Union of Polish Patriots (Związek Patriotów Polskich), established in 1943, which was being groomed by the Soviets to take over the Polish government.[13]

Stalin was so impressed with the work of these Polish-American collaborators that he not only prevailed on President Franklin Roosevelt to obtain a passport for Lange and Orlemański to visit the Soviet Union to speak with him personally but also proposed offering all three of them positions in the future Polish cabinet. The idea of three American citizens serving as cabinet members in a foreign government struck Averell Harrison, the American ambassador to Moscow, as "fantastic," and he advised Roosevelt to completely ignore this absurd offer.

The Lange-Orlemański trip to Moscow caused a great furor in the Polish-American community, galvanizing it into a staunch anti–Soviet coalition under the Polish American Congress. Unaware of Roosevelt's December 1943 Teheran decision to let Stalin have Eastern Poland, the Polish American Congress condemned Lange and Orlemański, defended the Polish government-in-exile, and demanded postwar Polish independence in prewar Polish boundaries. The American Polish press, meanwhile, let it be known in no uncertain terms that neither Lange nor Orlemański had the right to speak in the name of American Polonia, and the Polish ambassador, Jan Ciechanowski, registered his complaint to the State Department by asking whether it was standard practice for the American government to send private citizens abroad "to engage in a discussion of matters which involved the relationship of governments friendly to the United States," especially when "it was quite evident from the purpose and basis of such a visit that the results would be inimical to the interests of [the Polish government.]"[14] The State Department's reply was its earlier prepared rationale: the two went to Moscow as "private citizens" and not as the representatives of the American government — a very lame argument in light of how and why the visit was arranged in the first place.

After their return from the Soviet Union, Orlemański (who had gone to Moscow without informing his ecclesiastical superior) was promptly silenced by his bishop and relegated to a monastery. Lange continued to espouse positions no different from those of Stalin and continued to be quoted by the *Daily Worker, Głos Ludowy, Izvestia,* and *Pravda.* An American citizen, he was also appointed as Polish ambassador to the United States.[15]

In voicing his leftist views, Lange, together with the other pro–Soviet Polish-American activists, not only undermined the work of the Polish government-in-exile but also helped to inaugurate and legitimize the Polish People's Republic and the new wave of Soviet terror on Polish territory. After his short-lived and ineffective tenure as ambassador, Lange gave up his American citizenship and returned to the People's Republic of Poland, which, until his death in 1964, treated him much better than had the United States, awarding him with honor after academic honor and position after political position. The death of this "exponent of creative, innovating Marxism" was eulogized with superlatives in communist Poland: "Poland has said farewell to a man who needs no superlatives of praise, for his whole life, work, and achievement have won him a place in our memory.... [Poland] has bid farewell to a political man in the best tradition of the Polish working-class movement and a scholar in the manner of Poland's greatest thinkers."[16] In America, few Polish people mourned his death.

The Soviets left no stones unturned in their efforts to find suitable collaborators among the Poles in the occupied territories. After the slaughter of the POWs in 1940, about 450 older army officers from the Kozielsk, Starobielsk, and Ostashkov POW camps were sent to the Pavlishchev Bor POW camp for possible conversion.[17] From Pavlishchev Bor, some were then sent to the Moscow prison of Butyrki, and some were placed in Lubianka. From there, at the beginning of November, some were transferred to the "Villa of Happiness" (also known as the "Villa of Pleasure") in Malakhovka, near Moscow. Of the 450, however, only 13 officers were deemed suitable for the work that lay ahead: the formation of a Polish division under Soviet control. These officers were Zygmunt Berling, Eustachy Gorczyński, Leon Bukojemski, Kazimierz Dudziński, Leon Tyszyński, Kazimierz Rozen-Zawadzki, Roman Imach, Janusz Siewierski, Włodzimierz Szumigalski, Michał Tomala, Tadeusz Wicherkiewicz, Stanisław Szczypiorski, and Franciszek Kukliński.

Three days after the outbreak of the German-Soviet war, these thirteen officers were transferred from the "Villa of Pleasure" to Moscow, where they were kept under guard. Except for Berling and Wicherkiewicz, who chose to remain in Krasnovodsk, and Bukojemski, who wound up in prison, the officers were allowed to join General Władysław Anders' army. This experiment was summarized aptly by Lavrenti Beria's second-in-command: "*My sdelali s nimi bolshuyu oshibku*" (We made a big mistake regarding them). By "big mistake," he meant that they should have been shot along with the rest.

The second group that the Soviets attempted to use to their advantage consisted of younger Polish officers interned in the POW camps in Lithuania and Latvia. After the Soviet occupation of these republics, some of these officers were brought to Kozielsk and divided into two groups: those who professed to be communists and those who favored Polish-Soviet cooperation. The first group was led by Andrzej Adryan, the second by Mikołaj Arciszewski. Later both groups were joined into one and became known as the Democratic Left (Lewica Demokratyczna).

After the German invasion of the Soviet Union, the Democratic Left supported collaborative military action, and about thirty to forty members immediately volunteered as parachutists for diversionary work behind enemy lines. In the second half of 1941, they were transported to a training camp in Skhodni. Their camp was located near another training center for Soviet partisans where two high-ranking Jews, Marceli Nowotko and Paweł Finder, were being prepared for a secret mission.

In all, twenty-eight members of the Democratic Left parachuted into Poland and operated in the regions of Baranowicze, Białystok, Wilno, Kielce, and Warsaw. According to Zbigniew S. Siemaszko, their task surpassed simply gathering anti–German intelligence and espionage. They also rendered assistance to the GL, supplied information regarding the AK to the Soviets, and maintained channels of communication between the PPR and the Soviet Union. In light of the future Soviet mandates first to destabilize and then to liquidate the Polish underground, these activities constituted acts of treason.

The heavily guarded "Villa of Pleasure" in Malakhovka was also the home of thirteen Polish POW rank-and-file soldiers, many of whom were radio-telegraph operators. They were brought from various Soviet prison camps to the "Villa" at the end of August 1941 and told that their services were required to establish radio contact between Polish and Soviet army headquarters. Out of this group, which was also being prepared for parachuting into Poland, two were willing, one protested, and the rest were noncommittal. Later, five of them were sent to Moscow, where they established contact with the Polish Embassy, which, in turn, demanded their release. All of them eventually joined the Polish army. Clearly, this Soviet venture also produced meager results.

Finally, some of the deportees who were granted "amnesty" were persuaded to become informers for the NKVD after their release, and they signed papers to this effect. For some, this was the price of freedom. General Zając divided the "few officers and rank and file soldiers" who manifested communist tendencies or who were required to sign declarations of collaboration into the following categories: (1) Those who were Communist idealists; (2) those who, for the sake of their careers and their future, established contact with the NKVD and, after being partially coerced, signed the agreements, by which they felt bound; and (3) those who broke under pressure and wanted to back out of their agreements. In General Zając's opinion, those in the first category were less harmful to the Polish cause than those in the second.

In addition, there were a few Polish opportunists willing to derive some profit from human misfortune. A fourteen-year-old from my province, Wołyń, tells of one such incident:

> At 4:00 AM on the seventeenth of September, 1939, Soviet troops crossed the Polish border.... At once the colonists were arrested and imprisoned. The arrests were made by Ukrainian peasants and a few local Poles. These Poles, together with the Ukrainians, took from the colonists not only: cattle, horses, pigs, poultry, inventory of dry goods, furniture from homes, but one was not even allowed to keep for oneself the grain needed for bread.... At so-called "skhody" or meetings, which were held at the marketplace ... they would tell untrue stories about the colonists and demand their death or exile.[18]

After the July 1941 Władysław Sikorski-Ivan Maisky Agreement, when the two sides became uneasy allies in the fight against Nazi Germany, 167,727 Poles served under Red Army command[19] (in Berling's army, for example[20]), and many served in the Red partisan groups as well. To accuse the Polish side of military collaboration with the Soviets after that date simply for fighting alongside the Soviet Union is to accuse all the Western Allies of the same. (When the Soviet army crossed the Polish frontier for the second time in 1944, the NKGB rode in U.S. jeeps.) This, however, does not exclude the possibility of individual collaborators who may have worked against Polish interests.

In 1944, as we have already seen, the Soviets stabbed their Polish allies in the back; they continued to twist that rusty bayonet for almost half a century. Unfortunately, this was done with the help of some Polish citizens, both Christians and Jews.[21] Władysław T. Bartoszewski noted of this situation after the war:

> There was a tendency among the Poles to concentrate on the fact that these [the Communist Party and security apparatus] contained a disproportionate large number of Jewish Communists who, nevertheless represented only a small percentage of the Jewish community as a whole. (This tendency glossed over the fact that the majority of Communist Party members and secret policemen were actually Polish Gentiles. This insistence, wholly without moral justification, of applying to another ethnic grouping standards of behavior which they were unwilling to apply to themselves, enabled the Poles to ignore their own participation in Stalinist crimes, and also encouraged the idea that no "real Pole" could ever have committed such crimes against his or her own nation. Few Poles reflect on the fact that the creator of the largest and most bloody secret police organization in history, the Cheka and its successors the NKVD, KGB and so on, was a Polish nobleman, Feliks Dzierżyński, as was his successor Henryk Yagoda [Jagoda]. After all, thousands of Jews left Poland in 1945–47 because, other factors apart, they disliked and feared communism.[22])

All these Polish opportunists, accomplices, and collaborators, whatever their number, who willingly served the Soviet Union throughout the war to the undoing of Poland and its citizenry, are just as guilty as (and even more so than) their brutal masters of contributing to the Polish genocide.

German Occupation

After September 1, 1939, and throughout the remainder of the war, German propaganda stated time and time again that the majority of Poles collaborated with the Germans, and 32 million German brochures and pamphlets were disseminated encouraging the remainder to do the same.[23] But as Norman Davies put it, "For the Poles, there was no question of collaboration."[24]

In spite of repeated German proposals for united military action against the Soviet Union before the war,[25] German offers to restore Polish autonomy under German rule during the war, and even German promises of creating an independent Poland after the war, in spite of some Poles' opinion that Germany was the lesser of the two evils confronting Poland, in spite of voiced desires from abroad for some sort of a modus vivendi, in spite of the constant barrage of Nazi anticommunist and anti–Semitic propaganda, and in spite of Katyn, *there was never an organized Polish response to the German overtures either at home or abroad.*[26]

Polish soldiers fought the Germans on most Allied fronts: at sea, in the air, and on land; in Norway, France, the Battle of Britain, Normandy, the Lower Rhine, the Soviet Union, the Mediterranean, Italy, and North Africa. Poland's formidable underground, the largest in all of Europe, tied down 500,000 German troops, and according to German records, the Poles prevented one in every eight Wehrmacht transports from reaching the Russian front.[27]

Not only did Poland have the best intelligence-gathering organization in Europe, but the underground also furnished the Allies with a V-2 rocket. It was the Polish cryptoanalysts (Marian Rejewski, Jerzy Różycki, and Henryk Zygalski) who cracked the supposedly insoluble *ENIGMA* ciphers used by the German army and navy and handed their French and British counterparts — in July of 1939 — a copy of the machine as well. G. Bertrand of the French intelligence appraised this feat: "As for the Polish cryptologists, to them alone all the merit and all the glory for having carried out, technically, thanks to their knowledge and their tenacity, this incredible adventure, unequalled in any country in the world."[28] "Experts agree," says Kazimierz Stys Nepean, himself an expert in cryptography, "that the solution of the ENIGMA ciphers was the most influential single factor, besides the atom bomb, that changed the course of the war. They also agree that the war in Europe was shortened by at least a year, and possibly two years, thus saving hundreds of thousands of lives and preventing immense material destruction."[29] How could there have been an organized Polish response to the German overtures?[30]

Before continuing, we should distinguish between the term *conscription* and the (already defined) term *collaboration*. Contrary to appearances, people in the former category should not be considered as collaborators. For example, the Nazis tried to Germanize the Wasserpolen, Masurian, Kashub, and Silesian Polish nationals simply by placing their names on the Racial Register (Volksliste).[31] In addition, in Silesia, Bishop Stanisław Adamski directed his harassed clergy and parishioners to assume the status of Volksdeutsche in order to save churches and lives. He himself never did so. Although he was severely criticized for his action by the High Command of the AK — in part because the laity who followed his advice wound up being conscripted into the German army[32]— the resulting casualties among the priests in Silesia, comparatively speaking, were minimal. (Forty-three died in concentration camps and two in resistance work, and thirteen were deported to the General Government, including Bishop Adamski.[33]) In Gdańsk (Danzig) and Pomerania, all Poles were automatically registered as Germans by Gauleiter Albert Forster.[34] None of these people deserve the designation of "collaborator." Even the Polish underground, which condemned and executed genuine Volksdeutsch[35] collaborators, did not consider them to be such.

Neither should we include in the list of collaborators the hundreds of thousands of Poles who were forced into the German army, whether they carried arms or were used in auxiliary functions (the usual case). By war's end there were 400,000 Poles in the Wehrmacht and the Organisation Todt (a technical paramilitary organization), compared with 380,000 in the AK.[36] According to one authority on the subject, Stefan Korboński, in 1942 all Poles of military age in the western territories that had been incorporated into the Reich were rounded up, placed on the Volksliste, and automatically drafted into the German army.[37] General Władysław Sikorski addressed the plight of these unfortunate, involuntary conscripts: "The determined resistance to and the mass desertion from this press-gang conscription, unheard of in the 20th century, have already led to numerous death sentences in the home country."[38] It is little wonder, then, that after their capture by the Allies, some 90,000 of these "press-gang" conscripts served willingly under the British command.[39]

Concentration camp victims who became spies constitute a special case. One should ponder the matter before placing them all, whether Jews or Christians, indiscriminately into the category of "collaborators." Speaking of the informers at Auschwitz, Józef Garliński wrote:

> There were large numbers of them in the camp.... The informers were recruited from various nationalities; they were on every Block, almost in every *Kommando*. A prisoner's social class, pre-war position, political opinion, religion — none of these were decisive in the camp, nor were they a guarantee of how he would behave. Titles, honours, hereditary privileges were all left outside the gate and a man entered the camp stark naked, dressed only in his own dignity, and his own character, which made itself known in the hours of trial. How many misunderstandings there were in this respect, how many surprises!
>
> The informers represented various nationalities and generally concentrated on the groups they knew best: Poles on Poles, Germans on Germans, Jews on Jews. They were recruited in many ways. Most often it happened during interrogation, when by means of physical torture and the threat of it, as well as by mental pressure, the prisoners were forced to co-operate and to inform on their fellows. Once a man had broken down, there was no way back. The Political Department kept a firm hold on the victim, on the one hand threatening fresh torture or even death, and on the other giving small privileges, like extra food and easier conditions of work, which in the camp were of the utmost importance. These advantages, offering a chance of prolonging one's existence, attracted many volunteers who of their own accord sought secret contact with the SS-men.[40]

Among the most notorious of these concentration camp spies was Stefan Ołpiński, a Pole who, after receiving a prison sentence in Poland before the war, fled to Germany and declared himself a Reichsdeutsche. At Auschwitz, in exchange for various privileges from the Gestapo, Ołpiński organized a group of spies who reported all illegally organized camp activities as well as escape plans, the punishment for which was death. For his voluntary collaboration, Ołpiński was "tried" by the camp underground court and sentenced to death. After receiving a sweater full of typhus-infected lice, he became ill, was taken to the hospital, and died sometime in January 1944 — probably with assistance, or perhaps lack of assistance, from Dr. Wirth, a German doctor sympathetic to the plight of the inmates. Other methods of execution included adding castor oil to soup which induced diarrhea and resulted in the same one-way trip to the hospital, or switching a spy's chest X-rays with those of a tubercular patient, qualifying the spy for one of Dr. Josef Klehr's lethal injections.[41]

Before passing judgment on these unfortunate concentration-camp accomplices, one should bear in mind the words of Adeleide Hautval, a former Auschwitz prisoner: "I don't think anybody in the world to-day has the right to judgment or decision as to what he himself would have done in those completely improbable conditions with which one stood face to face in places like Auschwitz."[42]

Finally, we should not include in the category of "collaborators" any forced laborers who "worked for Hitler" no matter what their nationality, or any members of the Polish Red Cross who cooperated with the Germans for humanitarian reasons, or any of the tens of thousands of kidnapped Polish children who were drafted into Nazi youth groups such as the Hitlerjügend.

As one studies World War II literature, two facts — both very important markers of the nature and extent of collaboration with the Germans — become perfectly clear: The Poles never produced either a Quisling or any specifically Polish SS divisions. In contrast, almost all other European countries provided Nazi Germany with both.[43] As Aleksander Smolar put it: "In Poland, Poles worked for the Germans for money, out of spite, in fear of blackmail or torture. However, there was no collaboration based on the belief that national interests would be served by cooperating with the occupying power. There was no [Henri Philippe] Pétain or [Vidkun] Quisling in Poland."[44]

There was an attempt, however, to create an SS legion from the Polish highlanders known as Górale. Of the three hundred men recruited for this unit, most deserted immediately, and some were disqualified for service in the SS. The handful that remained did not justify a formation of a "legion," and the mission was aborted.[45]

One weakly documented instance of Poles serving in the Waffen-SS can be found in Jerzy Turonek's otherwise well-documented work dealing with Belorussia under the German occupation. According to Turonek, Obersturmbannführer Siegling's *30.* Waffen-Grenadier-Division der SS (russiche Nr 2.), organized in 1944, consisted of predominantly Belorussians but had "quite a few Russians, Poles, Ukrainians and others" within its ranks. "After a brief training," continues Turonek, "the 30th was sent to the western front, where it quickly dissipated due chiefly to frequent desertions. A substantial number of the deserters, predominantly Poles and Belorussians, joined General Anders' army in the fall of 1944."[46]

In addition, at the end of 1944, some of the detachments of the 30th were transferred to General Andrei Vlasov's pro–Nazi Russian Liberation Army (Russkaya Osvoboditelnaya Armiia, or ROA). On January 28, 1945, the remnant of the 30th was reinforced with fresh Belorussian recruits, and the division changed its name to 30. Waffen-Grenadier-Division der SS (weissruthenische Nr 1). According to Turonek, the manning of this newly named division was never completed, and it was never used at the front. In April 1945, the division surrendered to the Americans. At the time of its capitulation, it consisted of three battalions with a total of 1,094 men including 182 officers and noncommissioned officers.[47]

Interestingly, neither George Stein nor Gerald Reitlinger nor even *The Oxford Companion to World War II*, published in 1995, mentions Poles as belonging either to the 30th or to any other SS division. Judging from their desertion, perhaps these Poles were not volunteers. A personal testimony comes from Piotr Wandycz, who stated: "In the last years of the war people were included in the *Waffen-SS* by force. I knew Poles who were included even though they had nothing in common with the Nazis."[48]

Although they may not have been politically motivated by national interests, there were genuine collaborators and accomplices among the Polish people: those who preyed on victims in the larger cities, especially near the ghettos, and robbed them of their possessions; the *szmalcowniki,* or blackmailers, who extorted payment from Jews, their Polish protectors, and members of the underground in exchange for not reporting them to the Gestapo; the professional, paid confidants of the Detective Forces/Criminal Police (Kriminalpolizei, or Kripo)—Volksdeutsche, Poles, Belorussians, Lithuanians, Ukrainians, and even Jews—who, for a price, denounced everyone;[49] those who belonged to the Polish auxiliary police (*policja granatowa*—the "Blue Police"); sporadically, some wildcat AK detachments in the Nowogródek and Wilno areas; the NSZ Brygada Świętokrzyska; those Polish citizens of German ancestry who voluntarily became Volksdeutsche for some material advantage and who formed a fifth column on Polish soil to assist the Wehrmacht;[50] those local volunteers who assisted the Nazis in the liquidation of the smaller ghettos;[51] some members of the Polish Main Social Welfare Council; and those who served as writers and editors for the Nazi-controlled Polish "Adder Press" (*prasa gadzinowa*)[52]—as well as the Polish prostitutes who serviced the Nazis and sometimes acted as agents for the Polish underground.

One Polish collaborator was Wacław Krzeptowski, the "mountaineer prince" who attempted to found a separate "mountaineer nation" (Goralenvolk) but was hanged instead by order of the underground court in Zakopane, the intended capital of the new "nation." Another was the famous film actor Igo Sym, who became a Volksdeutsch, worked for Paul Joseph Goebbels' propaganda department, and was shot on March 7, 1941. Ferdynand Goetel worked in the same office as Sym and tried to recruit other writers as well. He managed to quit his post just before the establishment of the underground court and wound up joining the underground movement. For this reason his case was postponed by the court until after the war. Among other writers who collaborated with the Germans were Feliks Burdecki, Jan Emil Skiwski, Czesław Ancerewicz, and Józef Mackiewicz. The first two survived the war but fled Poland. The second two were condemned to death by the underground court, but only Ancerewicz was executed. After the war Mackiewicz denied that he had ever collaborated with the Germans.[53]

But none can match Bronisław (or Mieczysław) Kamiński, the degenerate SS Brigadeführer of mixed ethnic heritage[54] who ingratiated himself with the Germans in Lokot (in Belorussia) and eventually recruited a pro–Nazi militia from among local peasants, partisans, and prisoners of war to fight the partisans. Although he referred to this militia as the Russian National Liberation Army (Russkaya Osvoboditelnaya Narodnaya Armiia, or RONA), the official name of his unit was "SS Brigade Kaminski." By 1943–44 his army—consisting of Russians, Belorussians, some Ukrainians, and some Jews—numbered between ten thousand and twenty thousand Nazi collaborators.

With the Soviet advance, Kamiński moved his men first to Lepel in Belorussia and then to Upper Silesia. At the time of the Warsaw Uprising in 1944, Kamiński was a brigadier general, and by Himmler's personal order, his infamous unit was officially incorporated into the Waffen-SS. It distinguished itself from the very beginning by rape, pillage, and murder, and together with the SS (Oskar) Dirlewanger Police Brigade made up of criminals, it achieved the record for perpetrating the worst crimes of all units in Warsaw during the uprising. The man appointed to quell the Warsaw Uprising, General Erich von dem Bach-Zelewski, was so appalled at the undisciplined nature of Kamiński's unit (if not the nature of its crimes) that he had Kamiński arrested and executed by the Gestapo.[55] His men were then incorporated into General Andrei Vlasov's army.

Joseph Kermish and Shmuel Krakowski comment on the vile *szmalcowniki*, among them ethnic Poles, who plagued all Jewish ghettos and whose primary motive was greed:

> The greatest danger threatening Jews in hiding and those who gave them shelter was the plague of blackmailers and informers. Whole gangs of blackmailers went around in Warsaw and its environs trying to trap Jews. These gangs included Polish police, Polish agents of the Gestapo and the Kripo, smugglers, speculators, criminal underworld types and members of the Polish anti-Semitic and Fascist movements as well, such as "Szaniec," "Miecz i Pług" and others, who did this work for its own sake and not for reward. These blackmailers and informers (popularly called *Schmalzowniks*) brought disaster to thousands of Jews who had succeeded in escaping from the clutches of Hitler's murderers.

Noticeably missing in this list of "blackmailers and informers" are the numerous Jewish Gestapo agents and *szmalcowniki*. These authors state that the Polish underground "conducted an energetic fight against Polish traitors who collaborated with the Nazi invaders or worked for them. Thus, for example, just in the period of only a year and a half from January 1943 and June 1944, more than 2,000 [this high figure is questionable, see below] death sentences were carried out on informers and agents among the local Polish population." They also claim that the Polish underground "displayed far less determination in fighting the plague of blackmailers who attacked Jewish fugitives from the Ghettos and the camps." After a protest by leaders of the Jewish resistance, "the Polish *Komitet Walki Cywilnej* (Committee for Civilian Struggle) issued a warning to blackmailers (published in the clandestine journal, *Biuletyn Informacyjny*, of 18 April 1943), and consequently about ten [this low figure is also questionable] death sentences were carried out for the murder or persecution of Jews in hiding."[56]

According to Korboński, of the thousands of cases brought before the underground courts (established in December 1942) no more than two hundred death sentences were pronounced and carried out. Other forms of punishment included flogging and head-shaving. Many cases ended in acquittal, and many were deferred until after the war. However, in many instances death sentences were also passed and carried out by organizations other than the official underground courts.[57]

Generally speaking, the hierarchy of the Roman Catholic Church did not collaborate or cooperate with the German occupation authorities. Several Polish bishops, however, in the interest of protecting the Church from further repressions, did enter into compromising arrangements with the Germans in local matters of secondary importance and were considered to be "collaborators" by some elements of the Polish resistance. The bishops in question were Czesław Kaczmarek in Kielce, Czesław Sokołowski in Siedlce, Jan Kanty Lorek in Sandomierz, and Teodor Kubina in Częstochowa.[58] An exceptional case was Antoni Skoczyński, the vicar of Luborzyce in the county of Miechów, who was responsible for the arrest and subsequent execution of twenty-three Poles. For his role in their apprehension, the Special Civil Courts of Warsaw and Kraków Regions sentenced him to death.[59]

To ensure the uninterrupted flow of the various quotas (the "product contingents") imposed on the peasants and to assert further control over their lives, the Germans had decided early in the war to liquidate all existing social welfare agencies and to establish a German-controlled umbrella organization to oversee the three largest groups in the General Government, namely Poles, Ukrainians, and Jews. When the Polish Red Cross (Polski Czerwony Krzyż, or PCK) refused this dubious honor, the Germans created their own Chief Social Welfare Council (Naczelna Rada Opiekuńcza, or NRO) in May 1940. Under the NRO were the Polish Main Social Welfare Council (Rada Główna Opiekuńcza, or RGO, headed by Count Adam Ronikier until October 1943, then by Konstanty Tchórznicki), the Ukrainian Main Social Welfare Council coordinating the activities of the Ukrainian Relief Committees (Ukrainskyi Dopomohovyi Komitety — UDKs), and the Jewish Social Welfare Mutual Assistance Society (Żydowska Samopomoc Społeczna, or ŻSS). The Polish and the Ukrainian Councils lasted until the end of the war. The work of the ŻSS ended with the liquidation of the Jews.[60]

Although under Nazi control, all three organizations performed a range of important social-welfare functions for their respective constituencies: the poor; the forced laborers; the children; in the case of the first two, the POWs; and in the case of the ŻSS, the ghetto dwellers. However, many of the Ukrainian Main Social Welfare Council members, together with their nationalist leaders, and some members of the RGO also performed valuable services for the Germans. These collaborators agitated in favor of forced labor quotas, made sure that the product contingents were delivered on time, declared their loyalty to the occupation authorities, spoke out against the attacks on Germans, and participated in local festivities organized by the Germans. In addition, the Ukrainian Main Social Welfare Council encouraged young Ukrainian men to volunteer for the SS-Galizien.[61]

According to some reports, in the summer of 1941 some Poles, like some Jews, welcomed the Wehrmacht, especially in "Western Belorussia" and the Wilno area. Like the Jews, they, were unaware of what was happening in western Poland and were only too glad to be rid of the Soviets.

> The non–Jewish inhabitants welcomed them [the Germans] with bread and salt, thereby manifesting their joy at having been liberated from the Russian yoke.
>
> The Poles elected a special council to facilitate collaboration with the Germans. Among its members noted for their antisemitic activity were the Chief of Police, Jasinski, the mayor, Kowalski, the prison superintendent, Szliachczik, a Volksdeutsch (local German) and notorious sadist, as also the teacher Pawlik and his wife, both local Germans, and others.[62]

In "Western Belorussia," unlike anywhere else, the entry of the German army also meant the return of the Polish activists and functionaries who had fled to Wilno or to the General Government between 1939 and 1941. Relying on German, Belorussian, and Polish sources, Jerzy Turonek states that in the initial stages of the German occupation — in the Białystok, Lida, and Wilejka regions, in Grodno, in Brześć, in Baranowicze and Słonim — the Poles had a virtual monopoly on almost all the key positions in local and district offices. In addition, the local auxiliary police was mainly under their control.[63] There were, of course, exceptions especially in predominantly Belorussian areas such as, for example, in Derewno, where the Jewish police of the Soviet occupation was replaced by the Belorussian police under the Nazi occupation.[64]

This German restitution of the offices to their former (pre-1939) Polish occupants (a temporary arrangement due to the dearth of qualified Belorussians) was followed by the "settling of accounts" dating back to the days of the Soviet occupation. As a result, some Belorussians, especially the members of the intelligentsia, were denounced to the Gestapo by some Poles for their real or manufactured Bolshevik tendencies. Toward the end of July 1941, under pressure from the German Security Service (Sicherheitsdienst, or SD) of the SS, an unsuccessful attempt was made to replace the Poles with Belorussians. Under a deluge of protests and new denunciations, many of the recent Belorussian appointees were dismissed.[65]

A Chief of the SP (Sicherheitspolizei — Security Police — also called Sipo) and SD report dated August 12, 1941, states of Grodno, where the administrative apparatus was almost entirely in Polish hands and where the Order Police was exclusively Polish: "The posts of mayor and vice-mayor are occupied by Belorussians. These measures are aimed at preventing further penetration of Polish elements into the municipal administration."[66]

During a July 1942 parley between the representatives of the Polish Home Army and the Belorussian Nationalist Party (Partyia Belaruskikh Natsianalistov, or PBN), the head of the PBN, Ian Stankevich, not only accused the local Poles of collaborating with the enemy but added that the Polish government-in-exile and the underground were promoting this "two-faced policy." Zofia Dobrzyńska ("Ewa"), a representative of the Chief Command of the AK, issued a response: "I answered that I give my word of honor that this is not only not the action of the central command but quite the opposite, that such a course of action is a betrayal of Poland, and that the legitimate authorities of Poland will punish such people for betraying the state.... I demanded a register of the places where such incidents took place and another list of the Poles who were in the service of the Germans."[67] As we shall see, due to Nazi occupation policies and Belorussian collaboration, by the end of 1941 the political situation in these territories changed drastically in favor of the Belorussians.

Stankevich's reference to the collaboration of the underground, specifically the AK with the Germans is not entirely without foundation. Pressed by the Soviet partisans, the Germans in the Nowogródek and Wilno areas offered the AK units a deal that some of them simply could not refuse: arms and provisions in exchange for antipartisan warfare against the Soviets. Moreover, as we will see shortly, at this time the Soviet partisans were under orders to liquidate the AK forces. These were, therefore, purely tactical, short term arrangements and did not constitute the type of ideological collaboration evidenced in the Vichy régime or in Quisling's Norway. The Galician Ukrainian Nationalists also accepted German arms but with two major differences: (1) besides using the arms on the Soviets, they also turned the weapons against unarmed civilians; and (2) their initial intention was to maintain the German occupation, to press for a German victory, and to forge a lasting alliance with the victorious Third Reich.

On December 9, 1943, AK Captain Adolf Pilch ("Góra") in the Nowogródek area, followed on December 24 by Lieutenant Józef Świda ("Lech") in Lida, entered into one such "arms for anti–Soviet warfare" agreement with the Germans. Pilch received supplies from Minsk until the very end of the German occupation, and Świda received five transports between January and March 1944. Although both claimed that their actions were approved by the leadership of the AK in Nowogródek district, such practices were condemned by the Chief Command AK in Warsaw and by the Polish Supreme Commander in London, who on January 17, 1944, ordered them discontinued and the guilty parties disciplined. In March, Świda was removed from Nowogródek, but Pilch ignored the order and continued to collaborate.[68] In all probability, Pilch and Świda were correct in their contentions that their actions were approved by the Nowogródek AK leadership. Under public pressure, the AK in Warsaw and, more so, the Polish government-in-exile considered the Soviets as allies. Officially, there was but one enemy: Nazi Germany. However, the local AK commanders in Belorussia, considered, with good reason, both Germany and the Soviet Union as the enemy.

Similar efforts were made to strike a deal with the AK in the Wilno area at this time as well. Talks between Aleksander Krzyżanowski ("Wilk," an AK leader) and the Seidler von Rosenfeld of the SD near Wilejka (January 19, 1944) and later (February 10) the chief of the Wilno Abwehr, Julian Christiansen, seemed to produce some results. According to Curt von Gottberg, acting general commissar of Belorussia, at the end of January and the beginning of February, "three sizeable Polish detachments [*Banden*] came over to our side and initially also fought well."[69] The units were not specified, but according to Turonek, they "probably consisted of the AK units from Wilno."

Christiansen's proposal of February 10 has been preserved in the AK archives. It reads as follows:

> 1. This agreement has a military character, not a political one; its aim is to clear the land of Soviet bands.
>
> 2. No change in the administration of the land or administrative policies are anticipated. The Polish side will obligate itself not to harass the German army or the German and Lithuanian administration. The delivery of product quotas to the army must take place without interference.
>
> 3. In each region only a single authorized individual is to step forward in the name of the partisans. Liaisons between the Polish and German commands will be appointed.
>
> 4. Polish detachments will receive full combat equipment, including light artillery.
>
> 5. Polish detachments have the right to take food supplies from designated regions.
>
> 6. Certain kinds of arms may be given

only for the time of battle with the obligation to return them upon its termination.

7. Polish-German cooperation in combat is possible.[70]

Although Krzyżanowski rejected this proposal because of the state of war between Poland and Germany, a clandestine arrangement was agreed to: in exchange for AK support against the Soviet partisans, the Germans would leave weakly guarded arms and provisions that the AK could then "capture." In addition, German military supplies were simply left where they could be found in regions occupied by the AK. In this way, both the Nowogródek and the Wilno AK units—specifically the Wilno brigades of Lieutenant Gracjan Fróg ("Szczerbiec") and Lieutenant Zygmunt Szendzielarz ("Łupaszka")—were outfitted by the Germans.[71]

The evidence for collaboration is strengthened by the fact that when Gottberg called for the mobilization of the Belarusian Home Defense Corps (Belaruskaya Krayovaya Abarona, or BKA) on February 23, 1944, the entire region of Lida and certain areas of the Wilejka and Głębokie regions were excluded from his mobilization order, that is, were left to the disposition of the AK. In these territories, the AK began its own mobilization campaign in the first half of 1944. By June of that year, there were 7,700 AK members in the Nowogródek region; 40 percent of them were Orthodox Belorussians. Of the 7,700, 6,500 belonged to the AK in the Lida area. The AK mobilization efforts in regions other than those approved by Gottberg fared less well by comparison.[72]

Additional facts argue for collaboration. For example, the Germans withdrew from a series of Nowogródek counties that were then taken over by the AK. Also, when the Lithuanian police inspector, Marijonas Podabas, was assassinated by the AK, not a single AK member was among the ten Poles who were executed in reprisal. German spies and agents were often spared by the AK, for no apparent reason. For example, why was there no death warrant for Jerzy Orłowski, a known Gestapo agent who arrested and murdered even his former friends, destroyed the youth organization of the Alliance of Free Poles (Związek Wolnych Polaków) in Wilno by arresting the leadership, and sent more than fifty Poles to their death in Ponary? Six editors (i.e., two-thirds of all the editors) and some other employees of the *Goniec Codzienny*, a German publication in the Polish language, were members of the AK, and although the editor-in-chief, Czesław Ancerewicz, a non-AK member, was shot by the AK for "collaboration," no AK employee met a similar fate. The Wilno anti-Soviet AK counterintelligence unit called "Cecylia," headed by Mirosław Głębocki, worked hand in glove with the Abwehr through the AK's liaison, Henryk Borowski. And finally, in the 1944 military action ("Ostra Brama") against German-occupied Wilno, only 5,500 AK soldiers (out of the available 16,000) assisted the Soviets in liberating the city. Shortly thereafter, Gebeitskommissar Wilna-Land Horst Wulff was shot by the SS for his part in providing the AK with arms.[73] Józef Mackiewicz, a Wilno publicist and observer of these events, wrote in 1969:

> For now there is an agreement. The Germans give us arms in secret—it's said that we capture them, but they do not lift a finger to stop us. In return, they want us to drive out the Soviet partisans. When our detachment meets gendarmes on the road, we look to one side, they to the other, and so we pass like puppets. Recently, the Lida Gebeitskommissar [a high-ranking German official in charge of a geographical district called Gebeit] gave us his entire "Gebeit" in exchange for clearing the Bolsheviks out of his district. And we "clear them out," just like that.... It even came down to this, that our commandant, in full uniform, three stars on his four-cornered hat, "Mauser" in his belt, a Polish soldier in a nice hat, arrives in broad daylight before German command headquarters in town. The German commandant comes out, salutes, and is saluted back. They go in for a conference. They come out, salute, our man sits down, departs for the forest. Well, that's how it's done.
>
> ...In 1943/44 a situation came about that a whole line of districts in the Nowogródek area is entirely in Polish hands. The Germans, seeing the anti-Bolshevik activity, have taken advantage of the Polish army to secure their own safety. They do not bother

> the Polish detachments; in many instances they even offer them their assistance.... Warsovians ... believe that there is no better place in all of Poland to create an underground army than in Szczuczyn. This is facilitated not only by the friendly predisposition of the people but also by the tolerant attitude of the Germans as well. In Szczuczyn, the Germans released nine boys from prison telling them that they would gain their independence if they joined the "whites."[74]

On July 3, 1944, with the approaching Russian front, the Germans made another tempting offer to the AK. In a meeting between Lubosław Krzeszowski ("Ludwik") and General Poel, the latter proposed that in exchange for a unified action in the defense of Wilno against the Soviets, the administration of the city would be placed in Polish hands, eventually the city itself would be given to Poland, and moreover, the Germans would release all Poles imprisoned by the Gestapo. Krzeszowski rejected the offer. But as we have seen, although the AK did not help the Germans defend the city, only a third of the available AK forces fought with the Soviets for its liberation.

Documents released after the war revealed why the Germans were so anxious to strike this deal. On July 3, General Poel had only about 500 soldiers at his disposal with which to defend Wilno against the Soviet onslaught. Moreover, SD reports indicated that 18,000 (an exaggeration) "Polish bandits" were on their way to attack the city as well (Operation "Ostra Brama"). A few days later, on Hitler's personal orders, General Rainer Stahle arrived in Wilno with a veritable army. On July 7, Wilno AK brigades and Nowogródek battalions attacked the city. Later that afternoon, the Soviet army joined in the fray. On July 13, the Soviets announced that Wilno had been liberated.[75]

In conclusion, the foregoing instances of military "tactical collaboration" must not be generalized to the AK as a whole. As Joseph Rothschild has noted, "The Polish Home Army was by and large untainted by collaboration."[76] Although specific units of the Polish Home Army may have cooperated with the enemy in the ways stated above, the honor of the AK as a whole is beyond reproach.[77]

Jewish authors often state that the Polish underground collaborated with the Germans in another way: by killing Jews. Was the Polish underground,[78] including the Home Army, involved in anti–Semitic atrocities? The answer is yes, according to one Jewish memoir from Jody in "Western Belorussia."

> There was no official stance on the fate of Poland's three million Jews. In fact the AK were extremely anti–Semitic. In many parts of Poland they actually participated in the mass executions of Jews. In other places they killed Jews for their valuables. When it finally became clear that the Germans had lost the war, many AK units entered the forests where they managed to murder thousands of helpless Jews. We knew nothing of this in May 1942.[79]

When exactly did the author of the above memoir (published in 1992) actually find out about all of this, and what was the nature of the historical sources at his disposal? Israel Gutman and Shmuel Krakowski state:

> Organized murders of Jews committed by various underground formations began toward the end of 1942, and occurred quite frequently thereafter. They did not stop entirely at the moment of termination of the Nazi occupation, but continued for some time afterwards. The largest number of such murders were perpetrated by the units of National Armed Forces [NSZ]; but some groups of the Home Army also shared this guilt. Obviously most of these units may have belonged to that part of the National Armed Forces which joined the Home Army.
>
> ...Our file contains cases of murder of Jewish fugitives by Polish underground groups from 120 different localities or forest ranges.[80]

The authors provide some instances of these murders. In an editorial note in Emanuel Ringelblum's *Polish-Jewish Relations during the Second World War,* Krakowski, this time with coeditor Joseph Kermish, accuses the Government Delegate's Office and the Home Army of embarking on "a way that led to the extermination of the Jewish survivors in the forests." The editors continue, "On 12 September 1943, General [Tadeusz] Bór-Komorowski, Commander-in-Chief of the Home Army, issued Order No. 116 to the units under his command directing them to take active measures against the Jews in the forests." They add, "In fact the Order in question was a weapon aimed at the Jews in the first place."[81] This unfair interpretation has not gone without challenge.[82]

In his postscript to the above-mentioned work by Ringelblum, Kermish states:

> [Polish-Jewish] Relations reached a peak of tension when a report was received that a unit of the Jewish Combat Organization in a village near Koniecpol in the Częstochowa province had been attacked by the "Eagle" unit of the N.S.Z. or the A.K. and eleven of its twenty-four members killed. The Jewish Combat Organization learnt that similar bands in the Częstochowa, Radom and Kielce areas had murdered some 200 Jews who had been in hiding. Further facts were also uncovered later concerning the collaboration of N.S.Z. bands with the *Gestapo,* the *Gendarmerie* and the *Wehrmacht* in an "action" to kill "Jews and Communists". N.S.Z. bandits even murdered Democratic personalities connected with the A.K., especially those of Jewish origin. N.S.Z.-men organized a special group at Józefów near Warsaw to hunt down Jews and kill them off. The alarmed protests of the Jewish Combat Organization over the murder of a group of 18 Jews in the village of Wygoda and other such murders produced no results.[83]

Clearly, the less disciplined units of the Home Army engaged in some anti-Semitic atrocities in the regions mentioned above. Częstochowa is a case in point. There seems to have been no apparent reason for the attack on this Jewish Combat Organization (Żydowska Organizacja Bojowa, or ŻOB) unit, which intended to establish a partisan group in the Koniecpol region and enjoyed good relations with the surrounding populace. On September 10, 1943, an AK group under the leadership of Leon Szymbierski ("Orzeł") enveloped the unit and cut it down. So far this account matches the one above. But the impression given by Kermish — that nothing was done about such incidents — is wrong. Not only were those responsible condemned by the command of the AK, but sanctions followed. After a hearing, Szymbierski was sentenced to death by the district leader of the AK in Kielce. He was executed in June 1944.[84] I do not recall reading, however, that Jewish military authorities took similar actions against those who denounced, attacked and murdered AK members and other Poles in Eastern Poland. Perhaps I have not read enough. In any case, we should not judge either side by the actions of the few. Moreover, the imposition of severe penalties by the AK leadership for anti-Semitic actions argues eloquently against the charge of officially sanctioned anti-Semitism in the AK, as well as for the fact that some such incidents did indeed occur.

Another account implicating AK members in anti-Semitic atrocities, this time against civilians, comes from an eyewitness from Ejszyszki. It appeared most recently in an article by Richard Z. Chesnoff in the April 3, 1995, edition of *U.S. News and World Report*:

> Holocaust historian Yaffa Sonenson Eliach, one of only 29 Jews who survived the slaughter of the 3,500 Jews of the Polish town of Eishyshok [Ejszyszki] by SS directed Lithuanian guards, remembers the chilling taunts of Christian villagers when she and her family finally came home after liberation. "You are like cockroaches creeping out from all the cracks," they yelled. Four months after liberation, a gang of Polish partisans, accompanied by a neighbor, stormed the family house. Yaffa, then 7 years old and hiding in a closet, watched through a crack in the closet as her mother held Yaffa's infant brother in her arms and pleaded: "Kill me first, not my baby." In reply, the partisans fired nine bullets into the baby's body before pumping another 15 rounds into Yaffa's mother.
>
> Similar scenes were repeated all across Eastern Europe.[85]

The Sonenson family, it may be noted, survived the Holocaust in part because they were sheltered by various Poles, including Kazimierz Korkuć who hid and assisted scores of Jews.[86]

In 1939, of the population of the town of Ejszyszki (about 70 kilometers south of Wilno — and immortalized in Yaffa Eliach's "Tower of Faces" in the U.S. Holocaust Memorial Museum), 65 percent was Jewish.[87] In October 1944, in the above account, the "Christian villagers" were undoubtedly Poles, the "gang of Polish partisans" was undoubtedly a small unit of the Nowogródek AK, and the "liberation" was the Soviet liberation. At this time, as we will see, the Soviets were liquidating the AK, and the surviving groups of the AK responded by turning on the members of the Soviet organs of oppression, spies and informers. In his later memo to Merrill McLoughlin (editor of *U.S. News and World Report*), Chesnoff stated:

> It is true that in their campaign to take over Poland after it was liberated from the Nazis, the Soviets dealt brutally with many Polish nationalists. My article, however, was about the fate of those Jews who survived the Holocaust. And there is ample historical data that indicates many survivors encountered virulent anti–Semitism, even pogroms, when they tried to return to their pre-war homes in Eastern Europe. The murder of Professor Eliach's mother and infant brother is an example of that....
>
> In fact, according to Professor Eliach's account, the murders were not part of a retaliation against informers. They were motivated by anti–Semitic anger that Professor Eliach's family had returned to its village alive — and by greed (according to Professor Eliach, the Polish neighbor who led the killer band to the family home had been a pre-war business competitor of her father's). This account has been verified by the Holocaust Museum and is accepted by historians such as Nechama Tec.[88]

What is difficult to comprehend in this account is that a remnant of the AK (which by that time had officially laid down arms in that region) would make its way to Ejszyszki — where a Soviet garrison consisting of several hundred prison-camp guards, militia, NKVD-NKGB members, and soldiers was stationed[89] — with the sole purpose of murdering a specific Jewish family. Leon Kahn, a communist partisan who later became an NKVD official, provides one answer to this riddle:

> On a number of occasions we combined forces with the green hats to halt the activities of the Polish renegades and the Lithuanian partisans. One day we received a call to go to the rescue of a small Russian [Soviet] garrison in Eiseskes [Ejszyszki] who were under siege by the Polish partisans.
>
> In a battle with a large group of Poles, the Russians had captured forty or fifty of them and imprisoned them in the old Eiseskes post office which had been converted into a jail. The Russians then retired to their own quarters directly across the street, but very soon the remaining Poles laid siege to these quarters. Under cover of the renewed battle, they released their comrades from the jail.
>
> Once liberated, they roamed the streets looking for blood ... some of Eiseskes' Jews had returned home determined to build their lives again. Among these were Moishe Sonenzon [Sonenson] and his wife, Faigl....
>
> Moishe grabbed the other children and ran. Faigl picked up her baby and fled to the attic, but the Poles heard the baby's cry and dragged Faigl and her child downstairs. Then Faigl recognized one of her captors, a pharmacist who had known her father who was also a pharmacist. The man pretended not to know her....
>
> He turned away and the others shot her and the child.
>
> Two truckloads of green hats and our police group drove the twenty miles to Eiseskes, but we had been called too late. The A.K.'s had fled. We entered the Sonenzon house and I stared down at the floor stained with the blood of the poor victims.[90]

In this version, there were no surviving witnesses. The account notes the presence of a "small" Soviet garrison that, in "a battle with a large group of Poles [the AK]," had "captured forty or fifty of them and imprisoned them." In other words, there was a *large* Soviet garrison in Ejszyszki. From this account we also gather that the objective of the first attack was the Soviet garrison. The reason for the second attack was to free the imprisoned AK members ("they released their comrades from the jail"). After that, "they roamed the streets looking for blood." Were they after Jewish blood, or the blood of those they had come to attack in the first place and of those who had put them in prison — the Soviet soldiers and the NKVD officials stationed in Ejszyszki — or both?

The Polish neighbor may indeed have "led the killer band to the [Sonenson] family home" because of "anti-Semitic anger that Professor Eliach's family had returned to its village alive" and because of greed. The neighbor may also have done so because there were Soviet officers on the premises. According to Michał Wołłejko, an official NKVD document states that a captain of the Soviet SMERSH (*Smert' Shpionam/Sovetskii Metod Rozoblacheniia Shpionov*, or Death to Spies/Soviet Method of Detecting Spies), whose prime objective was to liquidate the Polish underground, was in the house. During the fight on the night of October 19, 1944, he was wounded, was taken prisoner by the AK (according to the NKVD document, his secret archive, *sekretnooperatsionnyie dokument,* also fell into AK hands), and after a hearing by a Polish field underground court, was sentenced to death and was killed.[91]

Yitzhak Sonenson, Yaffa's older brother, confirms the presence of Soviets on the premises:

> After liberation, we returned to Ejszyszki. There were 30 of us, the remnant of the 2,000 Jews who lived in that country town before the war.
>
> We kept together. We took a few flats in neighboring houses. We did our best to rebuild our lives. On October 20, 1944, the AK, who were called "White Poles," attacked the Jewish homes and began to murder and to steal. My mother, my baby sister, and *two soviet soldiers* were killed.
>
> The Jews wanted revenge. They go hold of some arms and attacked the Poles. But the Soviet authorities arrested these Jews, among them my father, who wanted to avenge the death of his wife and child. My father was deported to Kazakhstan and served five years in jail.
>
> The Jews left Ejszyszki. I left with my cousin's family for Wilno.[92]

On August 23, 1996, *Głos Polski* (Toronto) published the following statement by the World Federation of Soldiers of the Home Army regarding the Ejszyszki incident:

> The action on Ejszyszki, in reality the two actions of October 19/20 and December 6/7, 1944, are known to historians studying the history of the Wilno District of the Home Army: Dr. Jarosław Wołkonowski, Dr. Piskunowicz of the Institute of Military History, and Dr. Kazimierz Krajewski of Warsaw. They are also reflected in memoirs and documents.... All of these differ fundamentally from the account of Professor Eliach, at that time a seven-year-old girl. Furthermore, Professor Eliach confuses her facts, joining up two distinct actions as one event.
>
> As we know, after the Wilno region fell under the control of the Red Army in July 1944, soldiers of the Home Army began to be persecuted. Home Army units, including those who had taken part in the "Ostra Brama" operation along with the Soviet army, their supposed ally, were surreptitiously disarmed and their members sent to camps in the interior of the Soviet Union, imprisoned, shot, or at best forcibly inducted into the Soviet army. The socially and politically active segments of the Polish population suffered a similar fate.
>
> These actions sparked the spontaneous emergence of Polish self-defense units which were subsequently suppressed by NKVD units in which thousands served and which employed an ever growing network of informers. The repressions also forced many endangered soldiers of the Home Army back into the forests. In his extensive monograph about the Wilno District of the Home Army, Dr. Krajewski writes: "On the night of the 19th and the morning of the 20th of October, 1944, units of the Home Army mobilized from the local self-defense network, under the command of M. Babul ("Gaj"), took control of the town of Ejszyszki. The documentation found in the "selsovet" was destroyed, seals and blank forms which the Polish cell issuing false documents needed to save endangered Poles were taken, and official documents found in the Regional Action Committee were also destroyed.... A much sought after captain of the NKVD — an agent of the army counterintelligence "Smersh" who organized a network of informers in the region — was also captured.

> During this action, a sergeant of the NKVD was killed and a Red Army soldier was disarmed. In the cross fire that took place during the disarming of the NKVD officer, two civilians were killed in the home where the officer was living, a Mrs. Sonenson and her young child. The fact that this NKVD officer and Mrs. Sonenson were both Jews by nationality did not play any part in this action." ... Dr. Wołkonowski, referring to various documents, relates a similar unfolding of events.
>
> That the events in Ejszyszki clearly had a military purpose, typical of partisan warfare — yet one that entailed a tragic and dramatic episode and not a planned "pogrom," as alleged by Professor Eliach — is attested to by this simple fact: of the over 30 Jews living in the besieged building, no one perished or was wounded apart from Mrs. Sonenson and her child.

Were the mother and the son simply the victims of the exchange of gunfire in the house, or were they executed by the AK unit led by Mikołaj Babul? In my opinion, it is pointless to question the truth of Professor Eliach's vivid recollections. After fifty years, memory may fail regarding specific dates, names, places, and circumstances — but not regarding the central facts surrounding the murder of family members.[93] I therefore respect Professor Yaffa Sonenson Eliach's account of what happened to her mother and her infant brother, despite all the different versions and unresolved complexities of that story. It is now up to the historians to figure out *why* this unfortunate incident happened and to sort out the surrounding circumstances. In cases involving the death of Jewish children, the claim that the Polish underground was simply liquidating members of the PPR and the Soviet organs of oppression is indefensible.

Members of the Polish National Armed Forces (Narodowe Siły Zbrojne, or NSZ), who are said to have begun a "campaign at the end of 1942 against Jewish partisans and Jewish fugitives in hiding in the forests,"[94] should also be mentioned in the list of those who contributed to Polish (citizen) losses during the war — if not as collaborators, then as perpetrators. The NSZ, as opposed to the AK, was an independent, self-supporting, radical, right-wing military organization that split from the moderate right-wing National Military Organization (Narodowa Organizacja Wojskowa, or NOW, the military wing of the National Party, Stronnictwo Narodowe, or SN) when the latter (some 70,000 men) became subordinated to the Union for Armed Struggle (Związek Walki Zbrojnej, or ZWZ) or, as it was later called, the Home Army. The official founding date of the NSZ was September 20, 1942, although the formation probably began in July of that year. In short order it became a rather large military force drawing members from twelve major and several minor Polish conspiratorial groups. Although it operated mostly in the Kielce and Lublin districts, NSZ units were also stationed in Częstochowa, Białystok, Podlasie, and Mazowsze.[95] The NSZ subordinated itself to the AK on March 7, 1944, but many of its members remained unmerged until the NSZ's dissolution on July 5, 1945. A remnant of the NSZ as well as the Home Army continued to fight the communist security forces in Poland for a number of years afterward.[96]

After the war, most NSZ officers and rank-and-file members were either killed or imprisoned, and the Soviet propaganda machine, mixing fact and fancy, did everything in its power to discredit this organization, which Moscow loathed. These facts, the inaccessibility of Soviet archives, and the reluctance of former NSZ members to release, before 1989, any documents that may have been in their possession, combined with the fact that the NSZ as a rule did not publish its exploits during the war for security reasons, make it extremely difficult to objectively assess the nature and activity of this organization or to gauge the full extent of its alleged anti-Semitic agenda. That the NSZ killed Jews — but not always simply because they were Jews — during the war and afterward, however, is beyond dispute.

The NSZ took an uncompromising stand on two crucial, interrelated issues: Poland's postwar borders as established by the Treaty of Riga (exemplified in its directive "March East"); and the communist threat, which it considered to be as serious to Poland's future as that of Nazi Germany. "Poland does not have Enemies No. 1 and No. 2. There is only one enemy irrespective of whether he is called German or Bolshevik."[97]

The NSZ political platform is clearly enunciated in its February 1943 "Declaration": "Our eastern borders, established by the Treaty of Riga, are not a subject matter for discussion.... At the present time, over and beyond organizational and training work, NSZ also conducts a conspiratorial battle with the occupant and liquidates communist diversionary forces."[98] The battle against the communists included fighting with the GL-AL, which contained Jewish partisans. The underground publication *Szaniec* stated:

> The organ of the AK "Informational Bulletin" of November 18 [1943], includes an official communiqué which reads as follows: "The Commandant of the National Forces of Poland [Siły Zbrojne w Kraju—not the NSZ] informs that it has been ascertained with absolute certainty that National Forces of Poland units had nothing in common with the heinous murder on August 5 [1943] of the unit of the so-called People's Army [AL] near Borów in the Lublin province."
>
> What is this heinous crime from which the government organ of the AK distances itself? In September of this year a forest unit of the NSZ liquidated a communist band, led by a major of the Soviet Officers' Corps which, in mockery of our Polish feelings, adopted the name of a national hero....
>
> Hired assassins, monsters and scoundrels, bandits and cut-throats who, like the German criminals, also established for themselves the objective of the extermination of the Polish people, disinterred the names of our honored national heroes: Kościuszko, Głowacki, Kiliński.... With these names the Soviet diversionary forces, appearing under the name of People's Guard [GL] or People's Army [AL], baptized their own units.[99]

The "Polish partisans" who killed the 120 Jews in Worczyn in March 1944 may have been members of the NSZ.[100] It is certain that the NSZ wiped out the GL unit named "Waryński" on July 22, 1943. But it is also certain that the GL-AL killed members of the Polish underground. The NSZ attack on "Waryński" (in which seven people died), for example, was in reprisal for an earlier action by the GL unit "Lew," led by Julian Ajzenman (Kaniewski, "Julek"), whose Jewish unit was responsible for the bloody events in Drzewica on January 22, 1943, in which eleven people died. The "Waryński" unit was composed of the remnant of the "Lew" unit.[101] Other GL-AL attacks on the Polish underground include Owczarnia, where on May 4, 1944, an AL unit killed eighteen AK soldiers, and Stefanówka, where on July 2, 1944, the AL murdered several dozen AK members.[102]

Clearly, then, the NSZ attacked and killed GL-AL members and took pride in these "patriotic" actions. Since these units contained Jews, Jews were also killed. But whether the NSZ also killed Jews under the *pretext* of liquidating the communist underground is another question. This brings us to the numerous accusations leveled against the NSZ: that they were rabidly anti-Semitic and that they killed Jews out of racial motives, that is, simply for being Jews.

This, of course, has been the communist postwar line, but neither can one dismiss the many accounts of survivors whose attestations are strikingly similar, namely, that the NSZ attacked helpless Jews in the forests and either killed them outright or turned them over to the Gestapo. Many Jewish historians and some Polish ones as well make similar claims. If true, and there is no reason to doubt at least some of the testimonies, this would certainly indicate a very strong anti-Semitic (i.e., racist) streak in the ranks of the NSZ. Korboński states:

> Various units of the National Armed Forces were also responsible for instances of murder of Jews, who were hiding in the forests. And on June 13, 1943, a squad of the National Armed Forces, bent on "cleaning out the Jews" from the Bureau of Information and Propaganda of the High Command of the Home Army, killed two officers of the High Command—Professor Ludwik Widerszal and Jerzy Makowiecki, an engineer, whose wife was also killed. Another worker of the Bureau of Information and Propaganda, an engineer by the name of Czarnomski, was also murdered by the National Armed Forces storm troopers. Finally, on July 14, 1944, two other BIP [Biuro Informacji i Propagandy—

> Bureau of Information and Propaganda] workers — Professor Marceli Handelsman and a well-known writer, Halina Krahelska — were abducted from their office by the National Armed Forces and delivered to the Germans, who put them in prison.[103]

However, it is still not clear that, apart from its extreme factions, the NSZ as a whole sought to eliminate Jews as such. Richard Lukas, for example, states that some members of the NSZ rendered assistance to Jews.[104] According to *The Jewish Voice* (June 19, 1986), the Holy Cross Brigade, led by a Polish army colonel, Antoni Bohun-Dąbrowski, rescued about 1,000 persons — including 280 Jews — from the women's concentration camp in Holiszów. More convincing are the (rare) reports that place Jews in NSZ units. One such testimony comes from a former NSZ veteran.[105] Leszek Żebrowski maintains that a Jewish doctor served in Captain Władysław Kolaciński's ("Żbik") NSZ group after leaving the AK, that a few Jews were in the Holy Cross Brigade, and that accounts of Jews serving in the NSZ are in the Yad Vashem archives. Moreover, Żebrowski notes that one NSZ captain, Edward Kemnitz, now living in Montreal, was awarded a medal by Yad Vashem for rescuing Jews and that the wife of Zbigniew Stypułowski, the secretary general of the Interim National Political Council (Tymczasowa Narodowa Rada Polityczna, or TNRP) and the political leader of the NSZ, was of Jewish origin and that their son, a Jew by Jewish religious law, served in the NSZ.[106]

The clearest evidence that Jews served in the NSZ comes from Feliks Pisarewski-Parry, a Jew who served in Major Mieczysław Osmólski's ("Kozłowski") NSZ group in Warsaw after being freed from Pawiak prison.

> Around 3 o'clock in the afternoon a car with one policeman and one civilian came for me at the hospital.
>
> We drove in the direction of the Great Unknown which awaited me.
>
> My destiny, however, was not death but life!
>
> Somewhere on the corner of Piękna Street, a small truck halted in front of the police car. Two or three young men with revolvers in hand broke into our car; the muzzles were pointing at the escort. I jumped out into the street and not looking around tore in the direction of the gate whose number was previously given to me. Someone ran in front of me; someone else behind me. They were friends, safeties....
>
> Vodka. I drank a few glassfuls. I shuddered within and without. After a year, I found myself again among normal people, among trusted friends, in a private household....
>
> I have not stood near a young woman in nearly a year and it was strange. The female prisoners in Pawiak were to us comrades in suffering; we did not notice their femininity.
>
> "Wanda" invited me to a cup of tea....
>
> Suddenly, footsteps were heard in the hallway. Knocking at the door. I grabbed for a revolver.
>
> "Who's there?"
>
> "Mietek."
>
> "Pietia" [Osmólski] my savior.
>
> I embraced him until his ribs cracked....
>
> I received a real shock shortly thereafter when I discovered that "Pietia's" organization belonged to the NSZ! To be sure, the NSZ was shortly to become a part of the AK, but that didn't change anything. I was probably the only Jew in the ranks of the NSZ and for that reason rescued by the NSZ! Afterwards, I became convinced that many members of the NSZ didn't have the slightest notion of the ideological underpinnings of their organization. I dare to make the claim that at least 50 percent of the defenders of Poland did not know the political ambitions or the party affiliation of their leaders. The participation in any organizational unit was chiefly a question of personal contacts, chance, or circumstance. Many nameless heroes would never have understood the labyrinth of personal positions or organizational structures in the underground. And so, an opponent of the ONR [Obóz Narodowo-Radykalny, or Radical Nationalist Group), fascism and racism, I became an officer in the NSZ, and at a relatively high level!
>
> Dear God, who through long ages with so much patience has led the Jews to disasters and glory, forgive me!
>
> Let us return to reality. For the time being I will live here and will spearhead the "Pawiak project." I am to work up a plan for the liberation of the prisoners from Pawiak.[107]

This remarkable account, so deftly written, draws one into believing the impossible: a rescue of a Jew by the NSZ, his willing service in the organization, his promotion to a high-ranking office, and the ambivalent sentiments of one who finally realized the nature of the organization to which he owed his life and allegiance.

Feliks Pisarewski-Parry's statement that not everyone who served in the NSZ knew or shared its ideology leads one to draw the following general conclusion at this stage of the research on the NSZ: the NSZ did not have a uniform policy regarding the Jews in the forests, and as a result, the more radical members of the NSZ did turn Jews over to the Gestapo and did even kill them out of racist motives, right from the beginning of the organization's existence.

Some people also argue that initially, the bulk of the NSZ attacks were directed primarily against the Soviet partisans and the GL-AL, in whose ranks a number of Jews served, and that after the Soviet liberation of Poland, these attacks became more focused on individual Jews who were placed in highly visible positions of authority in the PRL and in the organs of oppression. Although most of the available material on the activities of the NSZ (based almost exclusively on testimonies) leads in the direction that the NSZ should probably be condemned as an anti–Semitic organization, the final judgment must await a more thorough study of the documents that are just now becoming available to scholars. As is usually the case in such matters, no one should expect to find a smoking gun, an order or policy statement encouraging the killing of Jews, but "by their deeds we shall know them."[108]

The absence of a clear-cut condemnation of the NSZ by the Polish government-in-exile makes this judgment all the more difficult today. When the Council for Aid to Jews demanded that the Polish Government Delegation for the Homeland issue a formal declaration in the underground press condemning the NSZ murders as well as all anti–Semitic displays, a government delegate formally replied (May 1944) that the time was not "opportune" for such a pronouncement but that measures would be taken against the NSZ and all blackmailers and extortionists. He then proceeded to explain, without excusing them, the reasons for these anti–Jewish "actions": the memories of Jewish collaboration with the Soviets in 1939–41 in Eastern Poland; Jews' betrayal of Polish protectors; the plunder by Jewish partisans of Polish peasants' provisions in order to survive; and finally, the news of desertions of Jews from the Polish army, especially in the Middle East where nearly 3,000 of the 4,200 Jews (about 6 percent of all personnel) in General Anders' army deserted in 1943.[109] Similar incidents occurred between January and March 1944 in England, where over 200 Jews deserted from the Polish armed forces.[110]

Another important reason, not stated by the delegate, was the perceived Jewish-communist (the *żydokomuna*) connection before and throughout the war. Lukas notes: "There is a great deal of ambiguity among Jewish writers on the question of Jewish affiliation or cooperation with the Communists as a major factor in Polish hostility toward the Jews. Anti-Semitic motivations of the Poles are stressed without referring to or emphasizing Jewish connections with the Communists."[111] We have already considered the extent and nature of that Jewish-Soviet collaboration between 1939 and 1941. One example of the Polish reaction to this treasonous behavior of the Jews is provided by Bishop Wincenty Urban:

> After the Russian armies entered Poland in 1939, the Jews in Krasne, fugitives from the western parts of Poland, immediately organized "meetings" during which they attacked Polish authorities, hung red flags on masts, and established local communist control. The reaction of the listeners, both Polish and Ukrainian was dreadful. The Jews were pelted with rocks, they were beaten with their own rifles, the flag was cut down and stomped under foot. That they survived was due only to their escape by wagons.[112]

The following passage from the Jewish author of the memoir from Jody in Belorussia gives us a unique insight into how these Polish-Jewish-communist relations worked themselves out in the heat of the battle. Under the first general commissar of Belorussia, Wilhelm Kube (a known anti-Semite), the Jews, especially those in the western part of Belorussia, which he controlled, were initially spared wholesale extermination. According to an SD report, 75 percent of the Jews in Belorussia (i.e., 128,000 out of 169,828) remained alive at the end of 1942. Kube's policies, based in part on economic considerations, enabled tens of thousands of Jews to escape from ghettos and seek shelter in the forests.[113] Many of them joined the ranks of the Jewish or the Soviet partisans. The account from Jody reads:

> During the summer of 1943, Yacov and I were members of a Soviet partisan brigade named after its commander Ponomarenko. A large group of partisan detachments, including the Markov Brigade, were assembled in the forest. The Markov Brigade was a strong force and had steady contact with Moscow, both through radio connections and airplane (Kukuruznik) drops. Nearby was a Polish partisan base known as Kmicic. One of their officers was Porucznik Mruckowski. At this time there was an atmosphere of cooperation between the Russian and Polish partisans as they fought their common enemy, the Germans.
>
> There were many Jewish boys in the Markov Brigade. One of them was Sleima Shapiro. At this time the Jews and Polish partisans were still friendly....
>
> We were curious as to the reason for the sudden assembly of so many partisan groups. We heard rumours that we were preparing an attack on the German garrison in Miadziel. We lay in ambush position and within a few hours shots could be heard nearby. We soon discovered what had happened. The leaders of a unit of Polish partisans of the AK (Armia Krajowa) Land Army had been arrested by Soviet partisans on orders from Moscow. Some of them had taken their own lives. Their partisans had been separated and assigned to several Soviet detachments. They kept their weapons, but their commanders were arrested and though some may have escaped the rest were shot.
>
> At the first chance they got, the Polish partisans deserted the Soviet brigades and reformed their own AK units. They were now our enemies. The Germans, pleased by this turn of events, planted spies in the AK who helped organize their attacks — attacks now aimed at the Soviet partisans and, especially, at the Jews hiding in the forests. Jews in the family camps were at great risk, as was every Jewish partisan. If the AK came across a non-Jewish partisan they were disarmed and stripped of their clothing but left alive. If they found Jews, they were shot.
>
> I was with a liaison group and travelled frequently to deliver messages from district party command headquarters. The danger posed by the AK created a major problem for us. We usually travelled in groups of three. Now we had to worry about our safety both day (from the Germans) and night (from the AK). Many Jews lost their lives to these AK partisans, especially the unit of General Kaminiski [*sic*]. These were Polish, Belorussian, and Ukrainian collaborators and were actually working for the Germans.[114]

Oswald Rufeisen, a Jew who spent the war in the Nowogródek area, remembered the summer of 1943:

> When I entered the forest the Polish partisans were being liquidated, disarmed, subdivided, and placed into different units. I don't know if the purpose was to finish them off or simply to subordinate them to the Soviets. Perhaps only later on someone gave an order to liquidate them. After they were dispersed they could not have become Russian enemies because they were disarmed. The few I had met in our unit were shot in the back, in an underhanded way. This happened when they were supposedly being transferred to another place. Someone who sat behind them, one by one.... This was not decent. I think that it was a part of a conscious effort to liquidate the Polish underground.... This was a dirty job of the Soviets, the same way as Katyn was or the Polish uprising in Warsaw.[115]

After breaking off diplomatic relations with the Polish government-in-exile (April 1943) over Katyn, Moscow ordered — on June 22, 1943, at a meeting of the Central Committee of the Communist Party of Belorussia, Lithuania, and Ukraine — the Soviet partisans to "combat with every possible means bourgeois-nationalist units and groups [i.e., the Polish partisans]." In Belorussia, these orders were implemented by Pantelemon Ponomarenko, the first secretary of the Communist Party of Belorussia and later chief of general staff of the partisan movement with headquarters in Moscow. In "Western Belorussia," the only legitimate partisan units in the territories "which formed an integral part of the Belorussian Republic" were to be Soviet or "those oriented to Soviet interests."[116] The Soviets, then, increased their partisan strength in "Western Belorussia" from 11,100 to 36,800 men in 1943.[117]

As a result of the above-mentioned order, the partisan unit led by Antoni Burzyński ("Kmicic") was liquidated, at the end of August 1943, as was, later, Kacpar Miłaszewski's unit as well. The technique was always the same: leaders of the Polish partisans were invited for talks, during which they were disarmed and their units liquidated.[118] Similar events occurred in the Wilno area, in Lublin, in Wołyń, and in Eastern Galicia, including Lwów itself, where the regional AK leaders under Lieutenant Władysław Filipkowski, as well as a group of members of the regional Polish Government Delegation for the Homeland, were arrested and sent to the USSR.[119]

On February 18, 1944, Deputy Ivan Serov of the First Belorussian Front, the chief officer in charge of the mopping-up operations aimed against Polish resistance, reported to Beria that he had arrested 5,191 Poles. On July 14, 1944, Stalin issued his Order No. 220145 to General I. D. Cherniakovsky of the Third Belorussian Front and to Serov.[120] This new order called for an "immediate and energetic action against Polish armed underground formations." On July 17, Beria informed Stalin:

> Today, we called upon the so-called general — major "Wilk" (Kluczycki) [Aleksander Krzyżanowski]. We informed "Wilk" that we were interested in the combat abilities of Polish formations and that it would be good if our officers could become acquainted with these tactics. "Wilk" agreed and revealed to us six locations of the whereabouts of his regiments and brigades. We were also interested in his officers corps and proposed a meeting with all the leaders of his regiments and brigades, their deputies, and chiefs of staff. "Wilk" also agreed to this and gave corresponding orders to his liaison officer who promptly left for headquarters.
>
> Later, we disarmed "Wilk"....
>
> On the basis of the information provided by "Wilk," we came up with the following plan....
>
> [Beria's July 19, 1944 report:] The action lasted two days.
>
> Yesterday [July 18] ... as of 4:00 P.M., we disarmed 3,500 persons, including 200 officers and NCOs.

That July, Beria reported to Stalin that 60,000 Polish soldiers had been disarmed, including 15,000 AK members. Beria and Cherniakovsky then requested Stalin's permission to hand over to the NKVD, the NKGB, and SMERSH the officers with an "operative value" (i.e., with potential for collaboration with the Soviets) and to direct the remaining officers to various NKVD camps "lest they undertake the organization of numerous Polish underground formations."

In another report based on Serov's field report, Beria informed Stalin: "In the course of our work in the liberated territories of the Lithuanian SSR [i.e., the Wilno area], from July to December 20, 1944, the NKVD and NKGB arrested 8,592 persons. 1,589 bandits were killed. From December 20, 1944, to January 1, 1945, 3,857 persons were arrested. 985 were killed. Thus, the NKVD and NKGB in the Lithuanian SSR arrested 12,449 persons in all and killed 2,574 bandits as of January 1, 1945."

After these successes Serov was sent to the Lublin area, where, under the direction of the NKVD, the NKGB and SMERSH, further "actions" were carried out. In December 1944, Serov informed Beria that 15,000 AK members had been detained in Lublin.

Meanwhile, on November 14, 1944, Lavrenti Tsanava (of the Second Belorussian Front and the People's Commissar of Internal Affairs in Belorussia) and Viktor S. Abakumov informed Beria: "On November 12, 1944, we sent a second transport (no. 84180) consisting of 1,014 active members of the AK and other Polish underground organizations to the NKVD camp in Ostashkov. During the operation, 1,044 persons in all were arrested and deported."

On January 11, 1945, Beria issued Order No. 0016 instructing his commanders to dispatch with "hostile elements in the liberated territories." On January 11, 1945, Serov informed Beria that 13,000 members of the AK and other Polish organizations had been arrested. In a report issued one week later, Serov told Beria of the arrest of an additional 10,000 people, including over 5,000 participants in the Warsaw Uprising.

In April 1945, Beria's Order No. 00315 called for the execution of "hostile elements." This order also specified that county officials, town and regional civil servants, editors of newspapers and journals, and authors of anti-Soviet publications be arrested and deported to the USSR. At the end of that month, Serov informed Beria that 50,000 people had been detained in his sphere of operation.

Several of the high-ranking operatives in this territorial cleansing of anti–Soviet forces were Jews — for example, Serov's deputy Aleksander Vadis and Tsanava and his deputy Yakov Yedunov. Both Vadis and Yedunov served as chiefs of SMERSH.

The Soviet battle against the Polish underground continued for the remainder of the war and beyond. According to General Leopold Okulicki, commander of the Home Army, between July and December 1944, some 30,000 AK members east of the Vistula found themselves under Soviet arrest. (In Lublin province the number was 15,000, in Białystok province, 12,000.[121]) According to Czesław Łuczak, of the 70,000 AK members who participated in Operation "Burza" ("Tempest," the 1944 attempt to liberate the Polish territories), 5,000 were killed in action and 50,000 were deported to the USSR, where many more died.[122] Meanwhile, oblivious to this treacherous turn of events in the summer of 1943, the Polish government-in-exile in London, and consequently the leadership of the AK, continued for a time to encourage the members of the Polish underground to cooperate with the Soviet army and partisans in the war against the Germans.[123] It is against this background that one must view and assess the "tactical collaboration" of individual AK units in Wileńszczyzna and Nowogródek, mentioned earlier.

In addition to such provocation and irrespective of the claims of Krakowski and others, at least *some* of the recorded anti–Jewish actions had nothing to do with anti–Semitism. Some of the Jewish victims were *szmalcowniki.* Others, because they lived in the forests and stole peasants' provisions to stay alive, were branded as members of "gangs" or "bandits."[124] Still others were traitors: either Nazi or Soviet agents or collaborators.

The second and third categories above need comment. To fully appreciate the complexity of the situation in the forests, we must remember that the forests at that time were literally crawling with all kinds of people. There were the tens of thousands of Jews who had escaped from the camps and ghettos, as well as the local homeless populace and the refugees (from both the Nazi zone and the Soviet zone), representing a variety of ethnic groups — all trying to find salvation from the Nazis, the auxiliary police, and the murderous Ukrainian Nationalists. Some fended for themselves. Others lived primarily in family units in underground hideouts. Still others sought protection in family camps, such as the 900-person family camp guarded by Tuvia Bielski's 300 soldiers, or the family camp defended by Jechiel Grynszpan's unit of 50 men in the Naliboki forest.[125] (Both of these leaders were corporals in the Polish army before the war.) Others, like the Poles, established refugee and civil-defense centers, usually in villages or towns, which sometimes housed thousands. Still others were completely unprotected.

Then there were the partisans: the Polish partisans, including the AK, the Peasant Legions (Bataliony Chłopskie, or BCh), the Socialist Combat Organization (Socjalistyczna Organizacja Bojowa, or SOB), the NSZ, and others; the Soviet partisans; the Jewish partisans; the Ukrainian partisans; the Ukrainian Nationalist "partisans"; the communist GL-AL, which included units of mixed nationalities (Polish-Jewish, Polish-Russian-Jewish, and Russian-Jewish); and the Belorussian nationalists. Many of these groups fought not only the Germans but each other as well.

Criminal gangs also inhabited the forests: the opportunists, the robbers, and in general, all those who were unattached to partisan groups and who preyed on the weak and the helpless.

And they all had to live. And they all turned to the local peasants for their daily bread. As a rule, only the AK paid for the provisions; the rest either received or took what they needed by force. To give weight to their demands, some — including Jews, especially those with "Aryan" features — posed as AK members. After escaping from camps and ghettos, recalled one Jewish lieutenant, they turned to the peasants for provisions. "We naturally told them that we belonged to the Polish army which is operating in secret."[126]

The peasants, poor as they were and already burdened with harsh German quotas, initially were willing to share their meager provisions with those in need, including the Jews.[127] With time, however, choices had to be made if they and their families were to survive. Inevitably, the Jews and the Russians, being "strangers" and without money, were turned away; they were compelled to take what they needed by theft or force — not always without resistance. Hersz Broner, a cook in the Jewish "Adolf" partisan unit located in the southern part of Lublin province, recalled: "Jews from the nearby villages made up the bulk of the unit. They often fought battles, they robbed in order to gain provisions. The food was generally good, due to the energy of the partisans."[128]

In Belorussia, the situation reached such alarming proportions that the local peasants turned to the Germans for help against the "swamp and forest people," or the *lesaviki* (wood demons) as they called them.[129] One Jewish partisan in Polesie recalled, "Our partisans called these excursions 'economic action,' but the peasants regarded it as robbery and immediately felt inclined to report our whereabouts to the Germans."[130] The provisions robbed by the partisans (at least by Soviet partisans in Belorussia) included not only food but almost every household necessity imaginable, which often later appeared in the marketplaces of local towns, having been sold for "pocket money."[131] How many Jews needed provisions? In the GG were the tens of thousands of camp and ghetto escapees, in Belorussian areas were 12,000 to 15,000 Jewish combatants, in Lithuanian areas were 850 jews, and in Wołyń, 2,000.[132]

The peasants, moreover, suffered grave consequences for any anti–Nazi actions by any of the partisan groups or bandits. For example, after the assassination of one German officer and two German officials in Święciany, 1,200 Polish people were murdered in May 1942. In Polesie twenty villages, together with the residents, were burned in reprisal for Soviet partisan action; in the province of Białystok, seventy villages were torched. Similar incidents occurred in the GG as well.[133] Filip Ożarowski explains the consequences awaiting the Polish peasants in Wołyń who, willingly or not, assisted the Soviet-Jewish partisans:

> At night, a group of uninvited guests visit a household. They consist predominantly of Soviet soldiers who escaped from [POW] camps or Jews [who escaped from the ghettos]. Under the threat of the use of arms they demand to be let into the house for the purpose of getting some food. What is the Pole, living in the forested terrain of Wołyń, to do? In fear, he opens the door and gives them a loaf of bread and some rancid pork fat. As a rule, such guests demand some cooked food as well. The host and hostess then cook up some cabbage and potatoes. In many instances such guests, especially the Soviet soldiers, rob the premises of sheepskin coats, boots, warm clothing and provisions. In the morning, they depart for the forest together with the booty.
>
> The Ukrainian Nationalists, particularly those neighbors who were in the service of the Germans as confidants, would report such instances. The Germans, as a rule, regarded this as collaboration with the Soviet partisans. They would then send out the Ukrainian policemen who would shoot the entire family or pacify the village.[134]

The Polish communist GL-AL often pursued an aggressive policy toward the Germans, with little concern for the local population that had to bear the brunt of the German reprisals. Are the following words from *Szaniec* mere anti-Semitic propaganda?

> What are the Bolshevik diversionary units and the GL with its central headquarters in

> Moscow doing in Poland? They attack our villages and towns, rob estates, presbyteries, peasants; murder those guarding their possessions; conduct diversionary activities; blow up bridges, railroad tracks; burn sawmills and ... habitually refrain from direct contact with the Gestapo and German gendarmerie. And the result? These heroes withdraw to a safe place and meanwhile the Gestapo and German gendarmerie murder the innocent and peaceful population whose only crime is that it lives in the vicinity of the perpetrated sabotage.[135]

As a general rule, the Polish underground was much more circumspect in its anti–German diversionary and sabotage activities, trying whenever possible not to place the local population in harm's way.

In addition, Soviet partisans with Jewish units, such as the "Pobieda" Brigade and the Bielski Brigade, also called "Jerusalemites" (Jerozolimy) by local inhabitants, sometimes conducted murderous raids, such as that of May 8, 1943, on the eastern town of Naliboki:

> Everyone is in tears. The plunderers did not omit a single homestead. Something was taken from everyone. Because he resisted, they killed the father of my schoolmate and cousin, Marysia Grygorcewiczówna. The "soldiers of Pobieda" and "Jerusalemites" took with them the pigs and chickens which they shot, flour, as well as other provisions. They wanted to live! But they took the lives of others. They did not come to fight....
>
> In the space of almost two hours, 128 innocent people died, the majority of them, as eyewitnesses later testified, at the hands of the Bielski and "Pobieda" assassins.[136]

This was the situation that prompted General Tadeusz Bór-Komorowski to issue his Order No. 116, aimed solely against the "plundering or subversive bandit elements" inhabiting the forests or, more precisely, their leaders. It was left up to the Polish underground unit commanders to distinguish between "civilians," "partisans," and "bandits" (not between Poles, Russians, and Jews) in carrying out that order. Undoubtedly this order was variously interpreted and probably misinterpreted by some commanders. Mistakes were also made, and innocent people died. No one wore signs in those days stating: "I belong to such and such unit" or "I am a bandit." The leader of the Wilno-Nowogródek district (the area subjected most heavily to the Jewish partisan "economic action") instructed his units to protect the civilians irrespective "of whether the bandit is Polish, German, Russian, Lithuanian, Latvian or Uzbek."[137] In this listing of nationalities, Jews are not mentioned. Those who criticize the issuance of this order should try to put themselves in the shoes of the civilian population that it was intended to protect.

As for the accusation that the Polish underground killed Jewish concentration camp and ghetto escapees who joined the partisans, the following example may illustrate the complexity of the situation and the pitfalls of leaping to any unverified conclusions. The case in point is the alleged murder of sixteen Jewish ghetto escapees in the Wyszków forest by Polish partisans (according to Marek Edelman)[138] or by the AK/NSZ (according to Shmuel Krakowski).[139]

To begin with, according to Leszek Żebrowski, no Polish partisan units were in that area at the time of the murders (summer 1943).[140] Moreover, a communist pamphlet entitled *The Warsaw Ghetto Revolt 1943: A Collection of Documents*—published in Warsaw in 1945, at a time when there was a veritable witch hunt for Polish underground members—is silent on the alleged role of the AK/NSZ in this incident. However, according to recently-released Soviet documents, there was a GL unit in the Wyszków forest consisting of Ukrainian concentration-camp guards who deserted their posts in Treblinka. Supposedly, this unit was so corrupt that it finally had to be destroyed by the Soviet partisans.[141]

According to a June 25, 1943, GL field report, 158 people were sent in the direction of the Wyszków forest, where a group of 17 gravediggers, who distinguished themselves by a lack of discipline and robbery, broke away from the main body and roamed the territory for several days.[142] These gravediggers were not ghetto combatants (i.e., ŻOB members) but were men who buried cadavers and, in the process, helped themselves to the belongings.

In the ghettos these types ranked just above the *szmalcowniki*.

Another GL document, "A Report from Wyszków Regarding the Partisan Unit," dated July 7, 1943, speaks of these former Warsaw ghetto gravediggers, or Pinkertons (Pinkertowcy), in the Wyszków forest with the utmost disdain, referring to them as "blackguards of the lowest order [*kanalie ostatniego rzędu*] who arrived with their wives and children and were received with amazement and indignation," who claimed that they had been sent by Central Headquarters, who behaved "as if, for money meant for the party, they bought the right to survival in the forest under the protection of the 'mercenary partisans,'" and who "strengthened their position as the 'occupants of the forest' by favoring particular leaders (such as Kraczek [Stanisław Gaik] and others) with gold." This report from the leader of District 1 GL states: "The unit is more like the black market than a partisan detachment. When the unit does not have enough to eat, the Pinkertons—in addition to their portion of rations—have their own reserves on which they gorge themselves in secret. The hatred towards them is so great that the partisans are inclined to get rid of them at any price and to liquidate them."[143]

This report also states that the partisans believed that only a portion of the valuables, whose worth was estimated at 2 million zloty (a huge sum by 1943 standards), remitted by the Pinkertons wound up in the proper hands and that, in their present condition, the units in Wyszków forest avoided all real military actions and relegated themselves to the "action" of securing provisions. Neither of the above-mentioned GL reports mentions the presence of any Polish partisans or, in spite of the expropriations, a negative disposition toward the Jews on the part of the indigenous population. The second report concludes by asking Warsaw Headquarters to

> 1. Clarify the situation of the Pinkertons. [Their claim to have been sent by Warsaw often silenced all complaints.]
>
> 2. Conduct an investigation regarding the alleged affair of the [missing] jewelry.
>
> 3. Appoint decisive leaders in charge of the units and one chief leader in charge of the entire operation.
>
> 4. Assign a few "Aryans" to specific units.
>
> 5. Send a suitable individual from DG [Dowództwo Główne, or Headquarters] here to see to it that this purge [*czystka*] is carried out.

As for the Polish underground's efforts to eliminate Soviet agents, it is noteworthy that in December 1941 squads of Polish NKVD agents, the "initiative groups" led by Marceli Nowotko, Paweł Finder (both Jews), and Bolesław Mołojec, were parachuted into Poland by Stalin to revive the Communist Party under the name of the Polish Workers' Party. After the mysterious death of Nowotko and Mołojec in November 1942, Władysław Gomułka and Bolesław Bierut (both Poles) were named as their replacements.

The PPR was formally established in Warsaw on January 5, 1942. Its military arm, which was to rival the AK, was the GL, established that March under the leadership of Franciszek Jóźwiak and Marian Spychalski. Its military strength was about 3,000 men. In 1944 the GL was renamed the AL and placed under General Michał Żymierski ("Rola"). According to communist sources, the numerical strength of the AL was between 50,000 and 60,000 men.[144]

Nowotko's secret mission had been to destabilize the Home Army by denouncing AK partisans to the Gestapo.[145] A Polish intelligence report dated March 24, 1944, states: "In the area of the town of Lubartów, it has been determined from evidence found on a killed communist that he possessed a list of AK members which was addressed to the Gestapo. The communists have an order to denounce members belonging to Polish organizations."[146] During his interrogation, Władysław Gomułka revealed that according to Marian Spychalski, such denunciations were approved at a staff conference attended by Paweł Finder.[147]

The most damaging evidence comes from the testimony of Józef Światło:

> I know from documents to which I have access and investigations which I have conducted, that Marceli Nowotko—who was parachuted into Poland by Moscow—brought with himself unambiguous Soviet

> instructions to establish contact and to collaborate with the Gestapo. The chief and only purpose of this collaboration was to make a thorough study of the Polish underground network of liberation and to liquidate it by the hand of the Gestapo....
>
> I accuse Bolesław Bierut of one of the greatest crimes which he committed in his dismal career as an agent of Moscow. I accuse Bolesław Bierut and his clique of the planned and systematic liquidation of the Home Army and the entire Polish underground movement of liberation.[148]

The liquidation of the Polish resistance, according to Światło, followed a chronological, three-pronged approach: Phase I, liquidation through collaboration with the Gestapo; Phase II, liquidation by Soviet "operational groups," which followed the Soviet army of liberation; Phase III, exposure (*ujawnienie*) and liquidation of the underground once the war was over.

Phase I involved a vigorous campaign of disinformation — the handing over of lists of names and addresses of AK members who were said to be communists — as well as the recruitment of the worst anti-Semites (such as those belonging to "Miecz and Pług") to destroy the Polish underground, after which they themselves were destroyed.

Phase II consisted of massive arrests by the Soviet "operational groups," followed by internment in the concentration camp at Rembertów and exile to camps in the Soviet Union. Światło was attached to one such "operational group" in Warsaw.

Phase III was the *ujawnienie* plan — the process of drawing out underground members with promises of due process, equal rights, and total amnesty. "We should wait," said Roman Romkowski, the first vice-minister of the Security Service, "until every member of the Home Army comes forward. Then, we can liquidate them all at once."[149] That is why he discouraged premature arrests and liquidation of surfaced AK members. Such was the welcome that the Polish heroes of World War II received at home, from their ally and liberator, the Soviet Union.

Meanwhile, in the summer of 1943 even the commander of the Polish underground, General Stefan Grot-Rowecki, was betrayed. After being arrested by the Gestapo (June 30), he was spirited away to Berlin and was murdered in Sachsenhausen in August 1944. General Bór-Komorowski was his successor.[150]

In 1944 the so-called AL "sham units" (*oddziały pozorowane*) were created by the Soviets to fight the Polish underground and to compromise it by committing political and common murders for which the AK was often blamed. A December 4, 1945, order from the minister of the Office of State Security, Stanisław Radkiewicz, to the provincial cells states:

> In the last few weeks, the activity of the reactionary and conspiratorial bands has intensified throughout the land. We are in the possession of documents proving that this action is supported by legal opposition parties who sympathize with it.... In conjunction with this, I order the Directors of the UB outposts to prepare in great secrecy an action aimed at the liquidation of the members of these parties and to make it appear as if it was done by the reactionary bands. For this action use the special squads created last year. This action should be accompanied by a press campaign aimed against the terrorist bands on whom will fall the responsibility for these deeds.[151]

According to German counterintelligence, by the summer of 1944 there were 20,000 Soviet agents behind German lines, and they were increasing at the rate of 10,000 every three months.[152] It was these agents who provided the Soviet Einsatzgruppen, the "operational groups," with the names of the AK members to be arrested and liquidated.[153]

This is the historical context in which the liquidation of traitors, spies, collaborators, blackmailers, "bandits," Soviet agents, and other such types — whether they were Russians, Poles, Ukrainians, Jews, or members of any other nationality — was ordered and carried out by the Polish underground.[154] The Jewish Combat Organization (ŻOB) also killed Jews, yet no one calls it anti-Semitic.[155]

The GL-AL did too. According to Piotr Jakucki, one GL-AL leader, Eugeniusz Iwańczyk ("Stary Jakub," "Wiślicz"), habitually denounced both Jews and Poles to the Gestapo in Kielce.[156] A Jewish survivor noted the "treacherous murder of our valorous brothers, the partisans and forest Jews, by their 'comrades in arms,' the AL partisans or with their knowledge and consent."[157] Józef Światło sheds much light on two such incidents that occurred while the Germans were liquidating the Warsaw ghetto:

> Certain AL squads were priceless partners of the Gestapo in the bloody and massive liquidation of Jewish partisan units which fought with the German occupant....
>
> Two Jewish partisan units operated in Lasy Janowskie in the Lublin area. One of these was quartered in the village of Ludmiłówka.
>
> These units were formed from Jews who, during the liquidation of the ghettos, fled from the German camps. The Chief-of-Staff of the People's Army at that time was Witold Jóźwiak; the Party Secretary was Paweł Finder. On the instructions of Jóźwiak, General [Grzegorz] Korczyński, the commandant of the AL in the Lublin area, established contact with these units and promised to equip them with arms under the condition that the arms be paid for in cash. There would be no drops. We will provide the arms, said Korczyński, but you must pay for them. Both units of the Jewish partisans garnered considerable sums of money which Korczyński took and left, ostensibly to purchase the arms.
>
> General Korczyński went to Warsaw and handed the money over to Jóźwiak. After this he returned to the Lublin area with instructions from Jóźwiak and Finder which mandated the liquidation of the units. Both units numbered about 50 persons. Jóźwiak instructed them to gather in two separate locations in order to claim the supposedly delivered arms. He sent three or four men armed with machine guns to each of these units. In a word, they really did bring the weapons and immediately made good use of them. They shot the unarmed people gathered in the forest with salvos from the machine guns. The women and children who were with their husbands and fathers also fell victims in this murder. Officially, both units were shot under the pretext that Jews who escape from a German camp are Gestapo agents, and that knowing the whereabouts of the People's Army, they would report this to the Gestapo....
>
> The second instance of the liquidation of a Jewish partisan unit took place under the occupation in Pruszków in the province of Warsaw. The leader of the AK in that district ... was Hilary Chełchowski.... In the region of Pruszków, the leader of the People's Army was Major Beck. And there in Pruszków operated a small unit of Jewish partisans of eight or nine men under a former employee of the town's slaughter-house. The extermination of this unit was carried out personally by Beck on the express orders of Chełchowski. It happened in this way: Beck reached an understanding with the unit supposedly for an action. He moved along with the unit with his helper but in the rear. And from the rear he wiped out the entire unit with a machine gun. After this he and his helper immediately robbed the cadavers completely, down to the boots.[158]

Światło knew these details and more because during the Gomułka trial, when all of this was being aired, he was the chief investigator. Zbigniew Błażyński, who interviewed Światło in the mid–1950s, adds that these were by no means sporadic attacks and that the Soviet partisans conducted similar actions.

Faye Schulman (née Fayna Lazebnik), for example, a partisan "woman of the Holocaust," places the AK "bandits" in the same category as the infamous "Bulbovces, Bandarovces and Vlasovces" and thus cannot be accused of harboring Polish sympathies. In her revealing memoir of Polesie, where the AK was a weak force in comparison with the Soviet partisans, she states:

> Hundreds of Jews were killed by our own Soviet partisans. In 1941 the partisan movement was struggling. Spies, traitors and Nazi collaborators among the populace abounded. Many partisans were ambushed and killed. In frustration, the commander of the Pinsk partisan units issued an order to kill every stranger in the woods who was not attached to a partisan group.
>
> Unaffiliated strangers were immediately shot. Most were Jews who escaped from ghettos or camps and were hiding in the

> woods. They did not belong to any combat unit because the partisans did not want them. How cruel that those lucky enough to have escaped from the Nazis into the forest survived only to be shot as spies. Hundreds were killed before the commander realized his error; he was targeting innocent Jews and not Nazi spies. By the time he called off the order, it was too late for too many.[159]

Oswald Rufeisen comments on the reasons behind the Soviet partisan attacks on the Jewish fugitives:

> At first these Russian partisans were poorly organized. Among the runaway Jews many were older people, children, and women. The Russians were afraid that when the Germans would catch such people they might in turn tell about the Russians' whereabouts. To prevent this from happening, and for their own safety, the Russians would deliver to the authorities the unarmed, helpless Jews, or they would themselves kill them. These were the laws of the jungle.[160]

Thus, not anti–Semitism but the "laws of the jungle" guided these anti–Jewish actions. Speaking of the Soviet anti–Jewish purges at the beginning of the war, Ben-Cion Pinchuk states:

> Jews were disproportionately represented among those that the new regime and communist ideology considered "class enemies" who had to be eliminated. The relatively large proportion of Jewish refugees, a group which the authorities did not know how to assimilate into Soviet society, contributed its share to the high percentage of Jewish victims. *It should be noted, however, that from the evidence available, anti–Semitism played no manifest role in the imprisonments and deportations.*[161]

Are the Poles, who caused much less harm to the Jewish people, religion, and culture than the Soviets, to be judged by a different, less discriminating standard? Were all of the almost 300,000 Jews (and their children) who were deported to the Soviet Union in 1939–41 "class enemies"? How would the following paraphrase of the postwar situation in Poland sound to Ben-Cion Pinchuk and Jewish scholars in general?

> Jews were disproportionately represented among those citizens whom the Polish underground considered "enemies of the nation" who had to be eliminated after the war. The relatively large proportion of Jews in the Polish People's Republic in the top levels of the communist régime and organs of oppression contributed its share to the high percentage of Jewish victims. *It should be noted, however, that from the evidence available, anti–Semitism played no manifest role in these anti–Jewish actions.* Jews were eliminated not because they were Jews but because they were the enemies of Poland.

If the Polish underground's (including the Home Army's) assistance to the Jews is sometimes exaggerated, so is its "anti–Semitism." Those who accuse the Polish underground, as a whole, of anti–Semitism should also consider its transmission of information to the Allies about the extermination of the Jews, its role in Żegota, and its many documented, valiant efforts to help the Jews.

But if the AK was not anti–Semitic, why did it not accept Jews into its ranks? Or to put it another way, why didn't the Jews, with some exceptions, join the Polish underground? First, their initial welcome of the Soviets did not endear them to the Poles, especially in the eastern half of Poland. As the commandant of the Polish Legion in Belorussia, Lieutenant Kacpar Miłaszewski, told some willing Jewish volunteers: "*Panowie* [Gentlemen], those of you who hail from central or western Poland we accept to the Legion most willingly. We know that you are patriots. We cannot, however, accept any locals. The local Jews sympathize with the Soviets; we, therefore, do not have confidence in them."[162]

Second, the Soviet partisans and the GL-AL, which ethnic Poles did not join as a rule, needed reinforcements and accepted the Jews with open arms. Third, some Polish underground members were anti–Semites. Fourth, there was, generally speaking and in spite of the examples above, a lower level of anti–Semitism in the Soviet-communist resistance.

Fifth, for security reasons only those people personally known were accepted by the Polish underground. Understandably, the Polish underground was extremely wary about accepting just anyone into its ranks, especially minorities, without personal recognizance and recommendation. Both Nazi and Soviet agents, after all, were on the prowl. Because of their consciously elected, unassimilated status in prewar Poland, few Jews were "personally" known enough to be trusted.

Sixth, the majority of Polish partisan units did not accept volunteers without arms. This disqualified many Jewish escapees from the camps and ghettos.[163] According to Faye Schulman, who served in the Molotov Brigade, the Soviet partisans in Polesie, acting on orders from headquarters, expelled Jews who did not have rifles.[164]

And finally, since Polish and Soviet partisans had agreed not to recruit each other's men, even armed Jews requesting admittance were not accepted by the Polish partisans if they belonged to the Soviet partisans.[165]

For all these reasons, no welcoming order was issued by the leaders of the Polish underground to accept Jews, and few Jews sought acceptance. And yet, in spite of all these obstacles and precautions, at least several hundred Jews did serve in the AK—some under their own names, some under assumed "Aryan" names.[166] Some served in the AK in the Kresy Wschodnie (the eastern territories of Poland).[167] Some were even unit leaders.[168]

One thing is perfectly clear: the leadership of the Polish government-in-exile's underground never embarked on an anti–Jewish campaign during the war. Like the vast majority of the Polish people, including many prewar anti-Semites, the Polish underground was horrified by the wholesale liquidation of the Jews and sympathized with their plight.[169] Numerous AK reports and underground press releases eloquently testified to the full extent of that national horror. One did not have to be a saint to be shocked—only a decent human being. Those who, in spite of all evidence to the contrary, claim otherwise are guilty of bad scholarship, bad faith, or both.

The major task of the Polish military and paramilitary organizations was *not* protection of the Polish minorities (including the Jews), *not* the protection of the Polish people, *not* engagement with the occupying forces, and *not* diversion and sabotage. Although they did all these things and more,[170] their chief assignments, on orders from the Polish government-in-exile, were to gather intelligence, to stockpile arms and ammunition, to train cadres of military personnel, and to stay alive until the moment of Germany's greatest weakness *and* the anticipated Soviet march on Warsaw, the seat of the Polish government. That moment in history is called the 1944 Warsaw Uprising. That is why the Home Army did not throw its full support behind the Warsaw Ghetto Revolt in 1943, when Germany was still strong. Doing so would have been heroic but suicidal and therefore militarily inadvisable; nor did the responsible leaders of the Jewish underground expect the AK to participate in this symbolic gesture of resistance and heroism. The soundness of that judgment is borne out by the fact that the Polish forces failed to accomplish their objective even during the 1944 Warsaw Uprising. The Home Army, by that time better prepared and equipped and actively assisted by a thousand Jews,[171] was crushed. Had that plan succeeded, the course of history would undoubtedly have been altered in favor of Poland and the free world. As we have seen, however, the Warsaw Uprising, without external assistance, ended in a colossal disaster, twice surpassing that of Hiroshima and Nagasaki. The subsequent communist takeover of Poland went virtually unchallenged.

For over fifty years now, the AK has been unjustly criticized, mostly by non–military types, for "not rendering assistance" or "not rendering enough assistance," especially arms, to the insurgents in the Warsaw Ghetto Revolt. It will not hurt, therefore, to repeat what has been said many times before by the Polish side in response to these unfair accusations and to add a little. Let us begin with the fair assessment of Marek Edelman, the last surviving leader of the revolt: "We didn't get adequate help from the Poles, but without their help we couldn't have started the uprising. You have to remember that the Poles themselves were short of arms."[172]

Lukas presents a listing of the materials provided by the Polish underground:

> According to the official Polish history of the AK, Rowecki's organization gave the following arms and supplies to the ŻOB prior to the Ghetto Uprising of April 1943: 90 pistols with magazines and ammunition, 500 defensive hand grenades, 100 offensive grenades, 15 kilograms of explosives with fuses and detonators, 1 light machine gun, 1 submachine gun, and material to make Molotov cocktails and sabotage material such as time bombs and safety fuses. The AK and its affiliates aided the ŻOB in purchasing arms on the black market, a practice in which the AK also engaged. *Żegota* also allocated some of its funds for the purchase of arms for the Jewish resistance.
>
> In addition, two organizations, part of the AK—the Polish People's Independence Action [Polska Ludowa Akcja Niepodległości] (PLAN) and the Security Corps [Korpus Bezpieczeństwa] (KB)—gave the Jewish Military Union [Żydowski Związek Wojskowy] (ŻZW), an independent Jewish resistance group, aid in acquiring arms and ammunition. According to Henryk Iwański, who distinguished himself along with other members of his unit, the KB provided the ŻZW with 2 heavy machine guns, 4 light machine guns, 21 submachine guns, 30 rifles, 50 pistols, and over 400 grenades. The PLAN also managed to supply the ŻZW with an assortment of pistols, rifles, ammunition, and on one occasion a case of 60 grenades.[173]

In terms of the need, all of this was but a drop in the bucket. But then the Home Army did not have much to begin with, much of what it had was unusable (having been buried in the ground since 1939), and most of what it had was in the hands of individual soldiers, not stockpiled in some depot. That the Home Army shared *any* of its equipment with the Jews is a wonder in itself, not because of their connection to the PPR and the GL but because the AK simply did not share its arms with anyone, not even other Polish military formations. The real surprise in all of this, however, is that the GL contribution to the Revolt was only 25 rifles and 2 boxes of ammunition.[174]

According to Teresa Prekerowa, in the spring of 1943, the AK possessed 11,000 hand grenades, 1,100 revolvers, 1,182 rifles, 62 light machine guns, and 25 heavy machine guns. At that time 20,000 trained soldiers were in the AK. Thus, approximately one in every 10 Polish soldiers could be equipped with a revolver or a rifle, one in 230 soldiers with a machine gun. Needless to say, this is no way to fight a war.

At the time of arms negotiations between the AK and the ŻOB in preparation for the Warsaw Ghetto Revolt, the ŻOB had about 200–300 men at its disposal in Warsaw. (The number of men reached about 500 by the time of the uprising.) This Jewish proportion (1 to 1.5 percent) of all the soldiers in the Warsaw district received 8 percent of all revolvers possessed by the district AK, 5.5 percent of all grenades, and 2.3 percent of all the automatic weapons. On the average, then, each ŻOB soldier was four to five times better armed than a soldier in the AK.

A year later, during the Warsaw Uprising, General Command of the AK could scarcely equip 20 percent of its own soldiers. One in eight front-line AK soldiers received a revolver, every fortieth (every fourteenth, according to some sources) received a rifle, and the grenades averaged out to a mere 1.4 for each fighting man. In terms of automatic weapons, the ŻOB soldiers in 1943 were five times better equipped than the Polish insurgents in 1944.[175] Enough said.

Regarding the collaboration of the Polish auxiliary police with the Nazis, Hilberg states:

> Of all the native police forces in occupied Eastern Europe, those of Poland were least involved in anti-Jewish actions. Territorially, Polish police were confined in the main to the four original districts of the Generalgouvernement, where they numbered about fourteen thousand. The Germans could not view them as collaborators, for in German eyes they were not even worthy of that role. They in turn could not join the Germans in major operations against Jews or Polish resistors, lest they be considered traitors by virtually every Polish onlooker. Their task in the destruction of the Jews was therefore limited.[176]

Emanuel Ringelblum's assessment is quite different: "The Polish Police, commonly called the Blue or uniformed police in order to avoid using the term 'Polish', has played a most lamentable role in the extermination of the Jews of Poland. The uniformed police has been an enthusiastic executor of all the German directives regarding the Jews." He then lists the various functions of the "Blue Police" in Warsaw: "(1) guarding the exit gates of the Ghetto as well as the walls and fences enclosing the Ghettos or the Jewish districts; (2) participating in 'resettlement actions' in the capacity of catchers, escorts, etc.; (3) participating in tracking down Jews who were in hiding after the 'resettlement actions'; (4) shooting Jews sentenced to death by the Germans."[177]

The Polish police did not always follow orders. On June 3, 1942, when ordered to shoot 110 Jews in Warsaw in the prison on Gęsia Street, they simply refused. One eyewitness stated that after being made to watch the executions, several of them wept.[178] A priest from Opole Lubelskie, near Puławy, reported that the "Blue Police" refused to take part in the execution of the Jews during the liquidation of the ghetto on October 23, 1942.[179] Klukowski: recalled "September 17, 1942 ... I was told that the 'blue police' assisting the gendarmes in searching the houses helped some people to escape. The policemen tried to make plenty of noise by shouting on the streets and breaking doors to give enough time for some people to escape or hide."[180]

Other such reports indicate that the Polish police sometimes used their privileged position to assist those persecuted by the Germans in and outside of the ghettos: delivering food, arms, and ammunition to ghetto dwellers; providing training to members of the Jewish resistance movement; warning Jews of denunciations; failing to arrest denounced Jews; liquidating Gestapo agents and *szmalcowniki*; providing "Aryan" documents; assisting Jews to escape from the ghettos, sometimes in exchange for payment, sometimes disinterestedly (one Jewish girl recalled how she was carried out of the Warsaw ghetto in a potato sack by *pan policjant*, and a five-year-old girl was brought to the convent of the Albertine Sisters in Bochnia by Wojciech Pacula, a guard in the Kołomyja ghetto); hiding Jews (e.g., Second Lieutenant Ryszard Stołkiewicz hid several Jewish families in May 1943, for which he was denounced, sent to Pawiak, and executed, and Warsaw "Blue Police" District Chief Mieczysław Tarwid sheltered Benjamin Mandelkern and his wife);[181] and providing protection for Jewish children in hiding (e.g., two hundred Jewish children lived in the Warsaw "Home of Father Boduen").[182]

The Germans not only distrusted the Polish police but executed some of them for their pro–Semitic views and for rendering assistance to the Jews.[183] In his July 16, 1941, address to the officers of the Polish police, Major Franciszek Augustyn Przymusiński stated: "In contacts with German authorities one constantly hears of complaints against the Polish police. Policemen not only do not fulfill their obligations adequately, but outright facilitate criminal behavior, for example, they protect the smugglers in the Jewish quarter from capture by German functionaries."[184]

On the other hand, in March 1941, on orders of the commissioner for the Jewish District, Heinz Auerswald, the "Blue Police" executed a number of Jews in the Warsaw ghetto for the "crime" of smuggling on the Aryan side.[185] On November 17, 1941, eight Warsaw Jews were executed for leaving the ghetto without permission. One witness reported: "The execution squad was composed of Polish policemen. After carrying out their orders, they wept bitterly."[186] A similar execution took place in the fall of 1942.[187] In October, a unit of the Polish police executed a group of prisoners from Pawiak in Kabacki Forest. Two of the policemen refused to participate in the execution and were themselves shot by the Germans. In the same year, the "Blue Police" executed fourteen Poles near Piaseczne. Similar incidents took place in 1943.[188]

The Polish police were also used by the Gestapo in the roundups of Jews; for example, on September 1, 1942, in Działoszyce, 2,000 Jews were killed on the outskirts of the town and 8,000 were deported to Bełżec, where they were gassed.[189] The "Blue Police" participated in the roundups of Gypsies as well and sometimes even in their murders outside of the ghettos.[190]

Klukowski, in his entries of August 6, 1941, and May 7, August 8, September 17, October 11, 21, 23, 24, and 26, 1942, reported the use of the Polish police in the roundup of Jews. The last two entries read:

> October 24, 1942.... Additional gestapo agents came from Biłgoraj. With the help of gendarmes, "blue police," and some citizens they looked everywhere for Jews. All cellars, attics, and barns were searched. Most Jews were killed on the spot, but some were taken to the Jewish cemetery for public execution.
>
> I witnessed a group of Jews being forced to march to the cemetery. On both sides of the prisoners marched gendarmes, "blue police," and so-called Polish guards dressed in black uniforms. To speed things up the Jews were beaten on their heads and backs with wooden sticks. This was a terrible picture.[191]

> October 26, 1942.... I feel it is correct to give some names of the German gendarmes and members of the "blue police" who were very active in the killing of the Jews. Gendarmerie Commandant Meister Frymer; gendarmes Pryczing and Schultz; Polish-speaking gendarmes Mendykowski, Wisenburg, Bot, Prestlaw, and Syring; and "blue police" Muranowski, Tatuliński, Hajduczak, and Jan Gal. The cruelest of all is Gal, who is even teaching his teenage son how to kill Jews.[192]

For reasons such as these, many "Blue Police" members were condemned to death and executed by the "executive" of the underground courts of the Directorate of Civil Resistance. The first such execution was carried out in Warsaw on Roman Leon Święcicki, a lieutenant in the "Blue Police."[193] Yet interestingly, the "Blue Police" enjoyed a decidedly better reputation than the Jewish ghetto police, *even among the Jews.*[194]

Ethnic Poles in the Kripo numbered 1,790 in the General Government at the end of 1942 and 2,800 by mid–1944. In addition, about 600 Polish Kripo members were serving in Eastern Galicia at the end of 1942, a figure that would remain constant until the end of the occupation.[195] The official assignment of the Criminal Police, which operated under the German Security Police (Sipo), was to apprehend common criminals — murderers, thieves, bandits, and in general, all "trouble makers." Unofficially, however, the Polish Kripo was also used, in conjunction with a network of agents, to ferret out Jews in hiding and to participate in actions against Gypsies and even members of the Polish resistance. Often, those apprehended were handed over to the Gestapo for "special treatment."[196]

One case of special interest involved the use of the Polish Kripo in foiling the May 15, 1943, robbery attempt on the "Społem" Bank in Warsaw. In the exchange of fire, all the robbers were killed, together with one bystander and three Polish policemen, and one bystander was wounded. No one knew at the time that the robbery — or rather, the "expropriation" — was carried out by the GL.[197]

There were incidents of Polish civilian collaboration as well. Klukowski reported some of these on May 7, August 8, October 22, 23, and 26, 1942. The last two entries read:

> October 23, 1942.... While I was gone, the gestapo, local gendarmes, "blue police," and some street people in Szczebrzeszyn again started to hunt for Jews. Particularly active was Matysiak, a policeman from Sulowo, and Skorzak, a city janitor. Skorzak had no gun, only an ax, and with the ax he killed several Jews. The whole day people hunted and killed Jews, while others brought corpses to the cemetery for burial.

> October 26, 1942.... I witnessed how Jews were removed from a hiding place in the ropemaker Dym's house. I counted approximately fifty Jews as they were taken to the jail. A crowd looked on, laughing and even beating the Jews; others searched homes for more victims.[198]

The Zamość area that Klukowski wrote about had been in Soviet hands for a month or so in September-October 1939, and the Jewish pro-communist sympathies there were very strong.

Another account comes from a Jewish eyewitness who described the participation of young Polish hooligans in the 1940 pogrom in Warsaw during Passover:

> The Passover pogrom continued about eight days. It began suddenly and stopped as suddenly. The pogrom was carried out by a crowd of youths, about 1,000 of them, who arrived suddenly in the Warsaw streets. Such types have never before been seen in the Warsaw streets. Clearly these were young ruffians specially brought from the suburbs....
>
> The Polish youngsters acted alone, but there have been instances when such bands attacked the Jews with the assistance of German military. The attitude of the Polish intellectuals toward the Jews was clearly a friendly one, and against the pogrom. It is a known fact that at the corner or Nowogródzka Street and Marszałkowska a Catholic priest attacked the youngsters participating in the pogrom, beat them and disappeared. These youngsters received two złotys daily from the Germans.[199]

In *The Holocaust*, Martin Gilbert documents still other cases of Polish collaboration. He quotes from Klukowski's diary: "Many Poles, particularly youths, are enthusiastically assisting in the searches [in Szczebrzeszyn] after the Jews."[200] This same entry for August 8 (11 A.M.), 1942, in the 1993 English edition of Klukowski's chronicle reads: "Some Poles are helping the Germans search for Jews."[201]

Gilbert also cites Klukowski's November 26, 1942, entry:

> "The peasants," noted Zygmunt Klukowski in his diary on November 26, "for fear of repressive measures, catch Jews in the villages and bring them into the town, or sometimes simply kill them on the spot." Klukowski added: "Generally, a strange brutalization has taken place regarding the Jews. People have fallen into a kind of psychosis: following the German example, they often do not see in the Jew a human being but instead consider him as a kind of obnoxious animal that must be annihilated with every possible means, like rabid dogs, rats, etc."[202]

The entry for November 26, 1942, in the 1993 English edition reads: "There are several Jews active with the bandits. The villages have turned against the Jews because of this and try to find them in the fields and forests. It is hard to believe but the attitude toward Jews is changing. There are many people who see the Jews not as human beings but as animals that must be destroyed."[203]

In addition, Gilbert quotes two other sources:

> "On 5 November, I passed through the village of Siedliska. I went into the cooperative store. The peasants were buying scythes. The woman shopkeeper said: 'They'll be useful for you in the round-up today.' I asked, 'What round-up?' 'Of the Jews.' I asked, 'How much are they paying for every Jew caught?' An embarrassed silence fell. So I went on, 'They paid thirty pieces of silver for Christ, so you should also ask for the same amount.'
>
> Nobody answered. What the answer was I heard a little later. Going through the forest, I heard volleys of machine-gun fire. It was the round-up of the Jews hiding there. Perhaps it is blasphemous to say that I clearly ought to be glad that I got out of the forest alive.
>
> In Burzec, one go-ahead watchman proposed: 'If the village gives me a thousand zloty, I'll hand over these Jews.' Three days later I heard that six Jews in the Burzec forest had dug themselves an underground hide-out. They were denounced by a forester of the estate."[204]

> It was a "frequent occurrence," [Emanuel] Ringelblum wrote, "for Polish children playing there [in the Łuków woods] to discover groups of these Jews in hiding: they had been taught to hate Jews, so they told the municipal authorities, who in turn handed the Jews over to the Germans to be killed."[205]

Gilbert concluded: "Most Poles accepted Jewish help in the [Warsaw] uprising, and Poles and Jews fought side by side as the German trap closed in upon them. But the murder, by Poles, of more than a hundred Jews during those same heroic weeks, gave a bitter twist to the Jewish fate."[206]

These are but a few examples of denunciation, betrayal, and murder of Jews by Poles.[207] Few will deny the fact that *some* Poles, including members of the NSZ and of the Polish underground, did despise, persecute, betray, and murder Jewish people simply because they were Jews both during and after the war. Yet, this fact needs to be placed beside another truth: that *many* Poles risked their lives to help Jews in the ghettos and to save Jews on the outside.

Assistance to Jews

In Poland, during the German occupation, assistance to the Jews came from many quarters. Rescue operations, whether by organizations or by individuals, always involved supreme efforts and great personal risk. The outcomes were uncertain. Surprisingly, among the more notable rescuers were self-professed anti–Semites: the Polish writer Zofia Kossak-Szczucka, the cofounder of the Council for Aid to Jews (Żegota), to whom dozens of Jews directly owed their lives;[208] Jan Dobraczyński, who, as head of the Warsaw Social Services Department, placed some five hundred Jewish children in Polish convents, where they survived the war;[209] Jan Mosdorf, the fascist who helped the Jews in Auschwitz; and Father Marceli Godlewski, who cared for the Jews in the Warsaw ghetto.[210]

Perhaps G. K. Chesterton put it best when he said in 1935: "The Jews are now being jumped on very unjustly in Germany itself, and old Victorians like Mr. Belloc and myself, who began in the days of Jewish omnipotence by attacking the Jews, will now probably die defending them."[211] Neither he nor Mr. Belloc was called on to sacrifice his life in behalf of the Jews, but many Polish people were asked to do precisely that. As Kossak-Szczucka, Dobraczyński, Mosdorf, Godlewski, and others demonstrated, dislike of the Jews and compassion for their plight to the point of risking one's life in their behalf are not necessarily mutually exclusive categories. The following words of a rescued Jew are thought-provoking indeed:

> In the small houses in Warsaw's Żoliborz district inhabited mostly by the Polish intelligentsia there were hidden many Jews who had escaped from the ghetto. I was in such a home which belonged to a known prewar Endek. Having learned that he was sheltering two Jewesses I asked with surprise: "You who before the war were an anti–Semite are now harboring Jews in his home???" He replied: "We have a common enemy and I am fighting in my way. They are Polish citizens and I have to help them."[212]

But Zofia Kossak-Szczucka, in her eloquent "Protest," put it best: "He who remains silent in the face of murder becomes an accomplice of the murderer. He who does not condemn, condones."[213]

Using Polish and Jewish testimonies, Israel Gutman and Shmuel Krakowski wisely deal with "Crimes Against the Jews" and "Forms of Help to the Jews" in the same chapter of their work *Unequal Victims*.[214] And Martin Gilbert has not been the only one to ponder this enigma: "Rescue and denunciation: the historian is overwhelmed by the conflicting currents of human nature."[215]

Emanuel Ringelblum — the famed historian of the Warsaw ghetto who was saved twice by the Polish underground[216] before taking up residence with over thirty other Jews in a "bunker" built by a Pole under a greenhouse,[217] whom the London-based Polish government-in-exile offered to rescue through the Home Army,[218] who refused salvation so that he could "fulfill [his] duty to society," who was betrayed (according to Tadeusz Bednarczyk) by a Jewish Gestapo agent,[219] and who was tortured and executed, together with his wife and his son, by the Nazis[220] — was also ambivalent. His chronicle stands both as a testament to the heroism of the Polish people and as an indictment. He notes of the Warsaw pogroms:

> No one will accuse the Polish nation of committing these constant pogroms and excesses against the Jewish population. The significant majority of the nation, its enlightened working-class, and the working intelligentsia, undoubtedly condemned these excesses, seeing in them a German instrument for weakening the unity of the Polish community and a lever to bring about collaboration with the Germans.[221]

He comments on the Poles who helped the Jews:

> Idealists from among both the educated and the working classes, who saved Jews at the risk of their lives and with boundless self-sacrifice — there are thousands such in Warsaw and the whole country. The names of these people, on whom the Poland to come will bestow insignia for their humane acts, will forever remain engraved in our memories, the names of heroes who saved thousands of human beings from destruction in the fight against the greatest enemy of the human race.[222]

And Ringelblum criticizes the Poles for not having done enough to help the Jews:

> It is difficult to estimate the number of Jews hiding in Poland.... Probably no more than fifteen thousand Jews are in hiding in the capital, located with approximately two or three thousand Polish families. If we take into account that these two or three thousand families are acting with the knowledge and approval of their nearest relatives we reach the conclusion that at least ten to fifteen thousand Polish families in Warsaw are helping to hide Jews — reckoning four persons to a family, a total of about forty to sixty thousand persons. In the whole country including Warsaw, there are probably no more than 30,000 Jews hiding. Among the Polish families hiding Jews there are doubtless some anti–Semites. It is, however, the anti–Semites as a whole, infected with racialism and Nazism, who created conditions so unfavourable that it has been possible to save only a small percentage of the Polish Jews from the Teuton butchers. Polish Fascism and its ally, anti–Semitism, have conquered the majority of the Polish people. It is they whom we blame for the fact that Poland has not taken an equal place alongside Western European countries in rescuing Jews. The blind folly of Poland's anti–Semites, who have learnt nothing, has been responsible for the death of hundreds of thousands of Jews who could have been saved despite the Germans. The guilt is theirs for not having saved tens of thousands of Jewish children who could have been taken in by Polish families or institutions. The fault is entirely theirs that Poland has given asylum at the most to one per cent of the Jewish victims of Hitler's persecutions.[223]

Is this criticism, appearing in the last paragraph of his "Conclusion," justified? Let us begin with the penultimate sentence about the Jewish children. When the Warsaw clergy and religious made an offer to shelter several hundred Jewish children in Catholic institutions, the Jewish leaders vehemently objected to the idea on the basis of "soul-snatching" and greed. Here is Ringelblum's analysis of the situation:

> For the sake of history, we mention a project to settle a few hundred Jewish children in convents, in accordance with the following principles: the children would be aged ten and upwards; the annual charge of 8,000 zloty would be paid in advance; a card-register would be kept of the children, recording their distribution throughout the country, so that they could be taken back after the war. This project was discussed in Jewish social spheres, where it met with opposition from Orthodox Jews and certain national groups. The objection was raised that the children would be converted and would be lost to the Jewish people for good. It was argued that future generations would blame us for not rising to the necessary heights and not teaching our children *Kiddush Ha-Shem* (martyrdom for the faith), for which our ancestors died at the stake during the Spanish Inquisition. The discussion on the matter among social workers reached no agreed conclusions, no resolutions were accepted. The project was not carried out because of a variety of difficulties, but mainly because the Polish clergy was not very much interested in the question of saving Jewish children.[224]

Ringleblum's conclusion was wrong and purposefully deceptive. "For the sake of history," let it be said that these children were not saved because of the opposition of the rabbis and other Jewish leaders. Why would the Catholic clergy propose a dangerous and daring plan of rescue if they themselves were "not very much interested in the question of saving Jewish children"? It was the Jewish leaders who were "not very much interested"! Besides, numerous convents and monasteries were already sheltering hundreds of Jewish children brought there by various agencies and sometimes by their parents and continued to save them in spite of the objections of that Jewish leadership. We need but ask those who were thus saved whether their parents, the "soul-snatchers," and people like Jan Dobraczyński or their leaders had more sense? Where is the evidence that conversion to Christianity was ever a prerequisite for Jewish salvation?[225]

In this context, Ringelblum's hypothetical "fact" that "tens of thousands of Jewish children" could have been saved in Poland needs to be placed beside the documented fact that thirty thousand Jewish children in the care of the Organization to Help Children and both Catholic and Protestant clergy in southern France could have been saved by being granted American visas to Switzerland but were not.[226]

Furthermore, was Ringelblum, hiding in the Warsaw ghetto, aware of just how much the Polish people had done and were doing to help the Jews not only in the ghetto but throughout all of Poland? What was the statistical basis for his final sweeping generalization and harsh judgment? After all, who among the Poles would admit in those days to the "crime of harboring the Jews," and what Jews would admit to being harbored by the Poles? How many Jews were saved in the years before Ringelblum's 1943–44 estimate and how many after his death? How many died together with their saviors? Even after all these years, we still do not know the full extent of that heroic assistance.

Finally, was Ringelblum in a position to know the record of those Western European countries he compared with Poland? Were the conditions in those other countries the same as those in Poland? Should he, then, be taken as the final authority on these aspects of "Polish-Jewish Relations during the Second World War"? The answer is given by Ringelblum himself at the very beginning of his work, the second paragraph:

> The material on which this work is based is as yet too fresh, too unripe, to permit objective judgment by a historian. Much official information, press material and the like, which will be needed to supplement this work after the war—all this is lacking. The views given here express the feelings of certain circles among the handful that were rescued from the slaughter of a whole people. As such they will be a contribution to the future historian's history of the Jews in Poland during the World War.[227]

Let us examine these Polish-Jewish relations in the light of some of that historical evidence that has surfaced since Ringelblum wrote his famous Warsaw diary. The words of Richard Lukas provide a good point of departure. During World War II, he states, "The Polish record of aid to Jews was better than many Eastern Europeans—Romanians, Ukrainians, Lithuanians, Latvians, and even French."[228] (In France, more men volunteered for the Waffen-SS than for the division of "Free Frenchmen." Moreover, thousands of Frenchmen and foreigners, mostly Jews, were willingly handed over to the Gestapo.[229]) Some would say that the Polish record was even better than that of the Jews themselves and was certainly better than that of the Jews of the diaspora, whom the Polish underground kept well informed about the nature and extent of the Holocaust.[230]

Unlike in most other German-occupied countries, where fines or imprisonment was the normal penalty, in Poland the death penalty was prescribed for rendering assistance (even a cup of water) to the Jews. In Poland, this penalty was routinely and summarily imposed on the offenders *and* their entire family. In Poland, it was dangerous to talk to Jews. In Poland, the "criminal offense" of bearing arms was punishable by death. An example of the measures taken by the Germans is the following circular issued on September 21, 1942, by the SS and police chief in Radom district:

> The experience of the last few weeks has shown that Jews, in order to evade evacuation, tend to flee from the small Jewish residential districts in the communities above all.
>
> These Jews must have been taken in by Poles. I am requesting you to order all mayors and village heads as soon as possible that every Pole who takes in a Jew makes himself guilty under the Third Ordinance on restrictions on residence in the Government General of October 15th, 1941.
>
> As accomplices are also considered those Poles who feed run-away Jews or sell them

> foodstuffs, even if they do not offer them shelter.
>
> Whatever the case, these Poles are liable to the death penalty.[231]

This is but one of the reasons why Ringelblum's comparison of rescue efforts in Poland with those in the Western European countries — even if the comparison were statistically verified, which it was not — lacks all validity.

So, why didn't the Polish people do more to save the Jews? Lukas answers: "The wonder is not how few but how many Jews were saved in Poland during the German occupation."[232] Adam Ciołkosz provides another answer: "We cannot accept as true the point of view that 'Polish Fascism and its ally, anti–Semitism, have conquered the majority of the Polish people' [Ringelblum's words], which consequently resulted in the death of hundreds of thousands of Jews who could have otherwise been saved. In this context we may ask: Who was there to save the three million Poles who fell victims to the Germans and whom should the Polish people blame for their death?"[233] In Norman Davies' interesting twist to this question, we have still another answer. "To ask why the Poles did little to help the Jews is rather like asking why the Jews did nothing to assist the Poles."[234] All Poles, both Christian and Jewish, were slated for total annihilation.

On August 22, 1939, just before the German army crossed the Polish border, Hitler personally instructed the top Wehrmacht officers in what was to be done with the Poles:

> Our strength lies in our speed and our ruthlessness. Genghis Khan caused the death of millions of women and children deliberately and without any qualms. But history sees him only as a great founder of a state. I do not care what the helpless civilization of Western Europe thinks about me. I have issued orders to shoot anyone who dares utter even one word of criticism of the principle that the object of war is, not to reach some given line, but physically to destroy the enemy. That is why I have prepared, for the moment only in the East, my "Death's Head" formations with orders *to kill without pity or mercy all men, women and children of Polish descent or language*. Only in this way can we obtain the living space we need."[235]

As we have already seen, Himmler was just as outspoken. "All Poles will disappear from this world," he said. "It is imperative that the great German nation considers the elimination of all Polish people as its chief task."[236]

In fact, until 1941 it was not at all clear whether the Jews or the Poles would be annihilated first. Prekerowa notes:

> In the course of the first year of occupation and even later, the Polish population did not have the impression that the Jews were more oppressed than they. Quite the contrary. It was mainly the Poles who were arrested, tortured in Gestapo prisons, executed, sent to concentration camps in Auschwitz, Buchenwald and Sachsenhausen. The Jews were more circumscribed in the respect to the economy, they were more and more sharply removed from participation in the agricultural life of the country, but the majority of the Polish people considered this to be the lesser of evils.[237]

The situation of the Poles at this time was symbolized by places like Auschwitz, Oranienberg and Mauthausen; the Jews' condition was symbolized by the ghetto.

Czesław Madajczyk states that whereas more Jews than Poles died in the districts of Kraków, Warsaw, and Rzeszów as the result of the Einsatzgruppen terror of 1939, the opposite was true in the remaining districts.[238] According to the estimate of Szymon Danter, longtime director of the Jewish Historical Institute in Warsaw, for every Jew who died between 1939 and 1941, ten Poles were killed by the Nazis.[239] Although this ratio almost matches the population ratio (1:9) of Jews (2 million) to ethnic Poles (18+ million) in German-occupied Poland, the common perception among the Poles *and the Jews*, in those first years of war was that the former were more endangered than the latter.[240] The Poles, it was thought, were slated for extermination, the Jews for economic expropriation.[241] It was simply a question of more blood, not statistics. To escape the murderous campaign of the Nazis, one Polish officer in the Home Army, Olgierd Szczeniowski, changed into civilian clothes and saved his life by placing the Star of David on his arm.[242] Philip Friedman reports that a brisk trade arose between Poles and Jews for the Stars of David.[243] Ringelblum notes in his May 8, 1940, entry: "Horrifying day. At twilight, Poles were seized in every street. Jews had their papers checked to make sure they weren't Christians. Stopped streetcars, dragged everyone in them off to the Pawia Street prison; from there, it is said, they are sent to Prussia. Dozens of autos drove off toward Dzielna Street and the Pawia Street prison."[244]

I clearly recall that for years after the war, the question for the Jewish community and the world was not "Why didn't the Polish people help the Jews?" or "Why didn't the Poles do more to help the Jews?" The agonizing question then was "Why were the Jews so passive?"[245] Ironically, individuals who view Jewish passivity (their resignation, their fear of resolute action because of the risks involved) with a great deal of understanding and compassion are able, in the same breath, to condemn without reservation this same behavior in the equally threatened Poles in German-occupied Poland. Was not self-defense as important as rescue? When the 250,000 Warsaw Jews were being "resettled in the East" in the massive Aktion of the summer of 1942, who was more guilty of "passivity": the majority of the Jewish leaders who chose to take no action, or the Polish community that failed to rescue the Jews bound for Treblinka? This Jewish apathy often proved to be a stumbling block to Polish attempts at rescue. Both Christian Poles and Jews, after all, found themselves in an impossible predicament. Both lost millions of people in Poland (Jews, three million; ethnic Poles, over two million). Both lost extraordinarily large numbers of children.[246]

How could the Poles — whose territory was both annexed and occupied by the Nazis, with a free hand to do as they pleased in almost total isolation from the world, whose government and decimated regular army were in exile, and whose underground Home Army was not consolidated until well after the Jews officially "ceased to exist" — have saved more Jews when they could not even save their own capital or themselves?

How many German soldiers were needed to keep Denmark in submission? A few hundred. How many soldiers were required to govern Lithuania? About 6,000. How many Nazis were stationed in occupied France, where some 40,000 Frenchmen were on the Gestapo's payroll? Only several thousand. And how many Hitlerites were there in Poland — in every city, town, village, and hamlet? According to Władysław Bartoszewski, on April 6, 1944, in one raid in "Aryan" Warsaw, 3,000 Germans were deployed from four in the morning until nine at night in a house-to-house search for Jews.[247] Lukas notes, "The Germans regularly maintained fifty thousand to eighty thousand SS and police forces in Poland, infamous for the severity of their subjugation."[248]

In addition, the German population of Poland grew from a prewar total of some 800,000 to 2.2 million by mid-1944. In the General Government alone, in December 1940, Germans constituted 0.9 percent of the population; by the end of 1942, they represented 2.5 percent of all the inhabitants.[249]

How could the Poles have prevented the Germans from having their way either in the Nazi-built extermination camps or in the killing fields, when all of the combined forces of Europe, the Soviet Union, the United States, and Canada could not stop them for almost *six years*? And yet the Polish people *did* help the Jews and, by their heroic efforts, achieved not only one of the best records in all of Europe for the number they assisted and saved, but also an unsurpassed record for the number of the ultimate sacrifices they had to make in doing so. How does this record compare with that of the United States and Great Britain, which the Polish underground bombarded with constant news of the Holocaust and with urgent pleas for help? How does it compare with that of the Soviet Union, discounting those thousands of Jews "saved" by being deported to the Gulag, where thousands also died? Lukas states: "At least hundreds of thousands and probably several million Poles were directly or indirectly involved in giving some sort of help to Jewish people. The assistance included food, shelter, false documents, and medical aid."[250]

Many Jews survived thanks to Żegota. To assist the Jews in their hour of need, the Polish Government Delegation for the Homeland established the Provisional Committee of Konrad Żegota on September 27, 1942. Zofia Kossak-Szczucka and Wanda Krahelska-Filipowiczowa were copresidents. On December 4 of that year, the name of the committee was changed to the Council for Aid to Jews (Rada Pomocy Żydom, or RPŻ, code name Żegota). Headquartered in Warsaw but with affiliates in other cities as well, and supported by Polish government funds and Jewish émigré organizations, Żegota's leadership was recruited from two Jewish groups — the Bund and the Jewish National Committee (Żydowski Komitet Narodowy) — and from three Polish political parties: (the Polish Socialist Party/Freedom-Equality-Independence (Polska Partia Socjalistyczna/Wolność-Równość-Niepodległość, or PPS/WRN), the People's Party (Stronnictwo Ludowe, or SL), and the Democratic Party (Stronnictwo Demokratyczne, or SD). In horrendous, death-threatening situations, the members of Żegota performed the following functions:

- Provided financial assistance. In 1944, four thousand Jews were receiving 500 zloty on average per month, the same allocation as that received by AK members — just enough to keep one from starving.
- Forged "Aryan" documents. In 1943–44, about fifty thousand such documents were provided, usually free of charge, to Jews in hiding.
- Located safe houses and constructed camouflaged hiding places.
- Provided medical assistance and food to the needy.
- Cared for and placed children in Polish homes, orphanages, and boarding-schools administered by the Main Social Welfare Council (Rada Główna Opiekuńcza, or RGO) or by orders of nuns. About twenty-five hundred children were hidden in Warsaw by Żegota.
- Maintained contacts with certain forced-labor camps and delivered correspondence and funds through Jewish agencies. In a few instances Jewish prisoners — for example, Ringelblum and Michał Borwicz — were actually rescued from these camps.
- Facilitated escapes to Hungary for a few dozen Jews from Kraków.
- Carried on an active campaign against blackmailers, informers, and the anti-Semitic Nazi press. In its time, Żegota put out three widely disseminated flyers in the Polish language encouraging people to help the Jews. It also produced a German-language flyer that appealed to the conscience of soldiers and the occupation authorities and warned them of the consequences for committing atrocities. The brochure was issued in the name of the fabricated secret organization Erwachendes Deutschland.

Less known for its humanitarian efforts is the Zamość-Lublin Committee for Rendering Assistance to Jews (Komitet Zamojsko-Lubelski Niesienia Pomocy Żydom), founded in Warsaw in the winter of 1942. This organization, headed by Stefan Sendłak, worked hand in glove with Żegota and consisted of about one hundred members and a few Polish organizations, such as the Association of Polish Syndicalists (Związek Syndykalistów Polskich) and the Community Self-Defence Organization (Społeczna Organizacja Samoobrony), which included help to the Jews on their action agendas.[251]

Other Polish organizations included the Special Committee for Assistance to Jews, established by the Polish Workers Party and headed by Władysław Gomułka, the Polish Red Cross, and the Polish Main Social Welfare Council. The Roman Catholic Church, through hundreds of its monasteries, convents, and parish churches, also assisted the Jewish community by providing birth certificates, food, clothing, and shelter.[252] In addition, many Polish people brought packages of food, medicine, and clothing to the ghettos and forced-labor camps, provided the Jews with money, and helped them to establish contacts with their families both in Poland and abroad.[253]

Throughout the war, the Polish government-in-exile, the Home Delegation, the majority of the Polish underground organizations, and the intellectuals protested vehemently —

both at home and abroad—against the Jewish Holocaust. All the Allies and neutral nations of the world, as well as the Vatican, were well-informed by the Polish community as to what was going on inside Poland. What all these countries and the Vatican did or could do about the situation is another matter.

Lukas notes, "Out of 100,000 to 120,000 Jews who survived the war in Poland, approximately half were aided in some way by the clandestine organization known as Żegota." According to Czesław Łuczak about 30,000 received such assistance.[254] Other estimates of the number of Jews who survived the war in Poland run lower: 50,000 to 70,000, according to the Jewish Historical Institute of Warsaw.[255] Still other estimates run higher, as do estimates of the number of Jews saved by Poles. Szymon Danter commented: "Among historians there is controversy over the number saved. The divergence is large: from fifty thousand according to Friedman to one hundred and twenty thousand in the opinion of Kermish from Yad Vashem Institute in Jerusalem. My estimate, also intuitive to some degree, is that eighty to one hundred thousand were saved."[256]

As a teenager, Joseph S. Kutrzeba served in the resistance under Mordechai Anielewicz. Dr. Kutrzeba was later a Polish officer, a United Nations Information Officer, a staff member at CBS-TV, and an award-winning producer-director for "Children in the Holocaust." In 1996 he stated:

> [The number of Jews saved by Poles] has long been a subject of disputation among historians—chiefly due to inadequate and insufficient extant sources. E.g. Joseph Kermish, the eminent historian at Yad Vashem, and a friend of my murdered Father, believes that the documented number of Righteous Christians in Poland could approximate 100,000. This may still be a very conservative view, for it is generally ascertained that it was impossible for anyone to singly save a Jew during World War II in Poland; rather, it had taken the cooperation of a number of persons to achieve this—Poland being the only country in Nazi-occupied Europe where a death penalty was mandated for assisting a Jew in any way. In my own case, it had taken the cooperation of nine persons to save my life, not including some 20 who'd aided me along the way. Only one had been recognized by Yad Vashem. Thus statistics.[257]

Hanna Krall, a Polish-Jewish journalist, has identified forty-five Poles who helped to shelter her.[258] Szymon Danter noted: "We sometimes forget that saving one Jew often took several or even a dozen or more people, with actions that generally lasted for long years. On the other hand, one person and one moment were enough to betray a Jew. Second, many attempts to aid ended in failure. Both the Jew and the Pole sheltering him dies, and this is not counted in the positive statistics."[259]

Those in hiding sometime during the war must surely have numbered in the hundreds of thousands. How many of them, both "saved" and "not saved," were given shelter at one time or another by the Polish people? According to Władysław Żarski-Zajder, the answer is as many as 450,000—an estimate questioned by scholars.[260] However, the number of those who received other forms of assistance during the war in all probability surpassed this figure.

By way of comparison, in Holland some 7,000–16,000 Jews (out of a total Jewish population of 140,000, with 25,000 in hiding) were saved by a Christian population numbering 9 million. The larger estimate (16,000) includes those Jews exempt from deportation, for example, those married to Christians. Such categories did not exist in Poland.[261] Philip Friedman estimates that 15,000 Dutch Jews survived out of the 40,000 who tried to save themselves by "passing."[262] In Czechoslovakia, 500 Jews were rescued by a Christian population of 7 million, and only 424 Jews survived in hiding.[263] István Deák commented on the records of Denmark and Norway, countries with very small Jewish populations and with direct access to nearby safe havens in neutral Sweden:

> It has become a habit to compare Poland unfavorably with Czechoslovakia or some Western European country, often Denmark.... But Denmark allowed the German army to cross its border in 1940 without firing a shot,

> and it joined the Anti-Comintern Pact, thereby legally becoming a German ally.[264]
>
> Following the invasion, Denmark was occupied by a single German infantry division and even that division was withdrawn, in May 1940, to participate in the campaign against France and the Low Countries. Allowed to retain its king, ministry, parliament, political parties, army, and police forces, Denmark was supervised by eighty-five German civilian officials and an additional 130 employees.[265]
>
> True, an admirable resistance movement developed there, and brave Danes saved the lives of most Danish Jews. Yet we must ask: which country was more useful to the anti-Nazi cause during World War II, Denmark, or the Czech Protectorate, where German troops were sent for rest and recreation, or Poland, where the Germans got killed? As for good King Christian X ... he did not ride the streets with a yellow star on his breast.... Certainly, the legend has helped to distort our understanding of the phenomena of collaboration, resistance, and the Holocaust.[266]
>
> In that book [Leni Yahil, *The Rescue of Danish Jewry*] Yahil explains how, during the initial stages of the rescue operation, in 1943, only well-to-do Danish Jews could afford the short voyage to Sweden. Private boatmen set their own price and the costs were prohibitive, ranging from 1,000 to 10,000 kroner per person ($160 to $1,600 in the currency of that period). Afterward, when organized Danish rescue groups stepped in to coordinate the flight and to collect funds, the average price per person fell to 2,000 and then 500 kroner. The total cost of the rescue operation was about 12 million kroner, of which the Jews paid about 7 million kroner, including a 750,000 kroner loan which the Jewish community had to repay after the war. The rescue operation took place with the connivance of the local German naval command. Consequently, there were no casualties either among the Jews or among the boatmen.[267]
>
> *Norway's Response to the Holocaust,* by Samuel Abrahamsen, is a book sponsored by the "Thanks to Scandinavia" Foundation ... but having read this eminently objective account, I wonder why Jews should be particularly thankful, at least in the case of Norway. Nearly half of that country's minuscule Jewish population of 1,600 (0.05 percent of the total population) was killed during the war and, as Abrahamsen, a professor emeritus at Brooklyn College in New York, points out, none would have died without Norwegian collaboration. Norway had only a few convinced Nazis but enough anti-Semites and law-abiding policemen and bureaucrats to make the Final Solution a near-success. To begin with, the small number of Jews in Norway was the result of a long and, at least to me, astonishing tradition of anti-Semitism combined with an extremely restrictive interwar immigration law that kept out nearly all refugees from Nazi terror. During the war, many Norwegians who would otherwise not have helped the Germans, took part in registering, arresting, and handing over Jews to the German authorities. As for the powerful Norwegian resistance movement, it resembled all the other European resistance movements in caring little about what happened to the Jews. Just as elsewhere, there were thousands of decent Norwegians who helped hundreds of Jews escape, for the most part across the Swedish border.[268]

In Poland, moreover, perhaps several thousand people — clergy, laymen, women, children, families, communities — of the hundreds of thousands of people who rendered assistance were summarily executed, burned alive, or murdered in Nazi concentration camps specifically for the "crime" of helping Jews. Gilbert states:

> In Poland, where helping Jews meant certain death, if caught, individuals continued to defy the threat of execution. Indeed, the help given to Jews by non–Jews had led, in Cracow, to an increase in the number of special courts set up to try Poles accused of helping Jews. A report of the German Chief of Police in the Government General, dated October 7 [1943], recommended that cases of Poles helping Jews should be dealt with by the police "without the necessary delay of court hearings."[269]

Scores of people died while providing military assistance to the heroes of the Warsaw Ghetto Revolt. The following is a very brief chronology selected from over eight hundred recorded instances of Christian Poles executed for helping Jews.[270]

September 7, 1939. In Limanowa, near Kraków, the Germans executed nine Jews together with a Catholic mailman, Jan Semik, who intervened in their behalf.

January 14, 1940. The Germans found the broken shackles of a Jewish prison escapee in the Warsaw apartment of Maria Brodacka, a Catholic Pole. She was executed.

July 1–12, 1940. The Gestapo arrested and deported to Auschwitz the Board of Directors of the Polish Bar Association in Warsaw (eighty Polish lawyers) for refusing to disbar Jewish lawyers. Practically all of them died.[271]

May 1941. German plans for the starvation of the Warsaw ghetto were systematically sabotaged by illegal deliveries of about 250 tons of flour a day. Józef Dąbrowski and several other Poles were shot by the Germans for making such deliveries.

November 1941. The German commandant of Warsaw, Ludwig Fischer, issued a decree that made the act of providing "Aryan" identity documents to Jews punishable by death. At least eleven Polish municipal employees in the registry office were murdered by the Gestapo for giving false papers to thousands of Jews during the war.

February 21, 1942. In Lwów, two Catholic priests were shot to death by the Germans for providing shelter in their monastery to two Jewish families. On December 14, 1943, a German notice in Lwów contained the names of fifty-five Poles who were executed. Eight of these were shot for hiding Jews.

April 1942. In Mława, the Gestapo conducted a public execution of fifty Jews. A Polish bystander shouted, "They are spilling innocent blood!" For those words, he was murdered along with the Jewish victims.

May 1942. In Tarnów, fifteen Polish farmers, together with the twenty-five Jews whom they sheltered, were executed by the German military police. Their homes and farm buildings were burned to the ground.

July 1, 1942. In Białobrzegi, near Opoczno, German military police executed a Pole, Maksymilian Gruszczyński, for letting Jews bake bread in his home.

July 20, 1942. In Warsaw, Polish socialists Tadeusz Koral and Ferdynand Grzesik were arrested by the Germans for teaching tactics of sabotage and diversion in the ghetto; Koral was executed and Grzesik sent to a concentration camp.

July 21, 1942. In Warsaw the Germans murdered Dr. Franciszek Raszeja, a noted professor of medicine at the University of Poznań, together with his assistant, Dr. Kazimierz Polak, and his nurse — for providing medical assistance to a Jewish patient.

July 1942. During the liquidation of the ghetto in Kielce, twenty Poles were rounded up and shot by the Nazis.[272] One Pole was shot while taking some water to fainting Jews locked up in the railway cars.

October 6, 1942. In Bidaczów Nowy, near Biłgoraj, the Germans murdered twenty-two Polish farmers for sheltering Jews. Their homes and farm buildings were burned to the ground.

October 20, 1942. Rev. Edward Tobaczkowski, the pastor of Tłumacz, was tortured to death in Stanisławów prison for smuggling food into the ghetto, encouraging his parishioners to shelter Jews, and providing Jews with false baptismal certificates. According to a resident of Tłumacz, Szlomo Blond, Tobaczykowski was betrayed to the Gestapo by a Jewess.[273]

October 1942. German military and Ukrainian auxiliary police massacred over seventy inhabitants, from twenty-two families, in the Polish hamlet of Obórki, near Łuck, for feeding and giving shelter to Jews.[274]

Autumn 1942. During the deportation of Jews from the town of Chmielnik, two Poles found near the ghetto were executed. One of them had been turned over to the German police by a Jewish Gestapo agent.

November 19, 1942. A Polish farmer from Nasutów, near Lubartów, was hung for sheltering a Jew and his son, whom four German soldiers spotted leaving the farmer's barn. The farmer's barn was also burned to the ground.[275]

December 1, 1942. In Studzieniec, near Rzeszów, German military police executed five

Jews and eleven Poles. The Jews, who received help and supplies from the Poles, betrayed them under torture.

December 4, 1942. In Przeworsk, six Catholics were executed by the Germans in reprisal for aid given to Jews by Polish Christian townspeople.[276]

December 6, 1942. In Ciepielów Stary, near Kielce, a motorized detachment of the SS burned alive twenty-one Poles for harboring Jews.

December 6, 1942. In Klamocha Forest, near Kielce, Polish partisans battled German forces surrounding a hideout of Jews. Twenty Poles were killed; two captured Jews died without betraying the names of the Polish game wardens who had helped them.

December 14, 1942. A Polish farmer and his wife, from Bidaczów Nowy, near Biłgoraj, were executed for sheltering a Jewish family in their attic. The homestead was then burned to the ground. Although forewarned by the village reeve of an impending German raid, the Jewish charges nevertheless had returned to the Polish home from the woods, where they were staying temporarily.[277]

December 28, 1942. Seven Polish villagers from Majdan Nowy, near Biłgoraj, were shot by the German police for assisting Jews hiding in nearby forests. The villagers were betrayed by a young Jewish woman who was apprehended by the Germans.[278]

December 1942. In Warsaw, two members of the Polish Underground Scouting Organization called "Szare Szeregi" were arrested by the Gestapo for bringing aid and weapons to the Jews in the ghetto. Zdzisław Grecki was publicly executed in Warsaw; his friend was tortured in the Pawiak prison and then executed.

January 15, 1943. In Pilica-Zamek, German policemen executed Maria Rogozińska and her one-year-old son for harboring Jews. A local Polish policeman was also executed because he did not report the presence of Jews in the village.

Mid-January 1943. A Polish farmer from Gunatów, near Puławy, who had repeatedly sheltered Jews, was executed. A Jewish tailor who had benefited from the farmer's hospitality led a patrol of German gendarmes to the farm, where he had been sheltered.[279]

January 29, 1943. In Wierzbica, near Miechów, a Jew betrayed the hideouts of a number of other Jews, including his own in-laws. They and six members of another Jewish family were executed. This also precipitated the execution by the Germans of three Polish families consisting of fifteen people.

March-July 1943. Julius Gebler, the head of the Gestapo in Dębica, near Rzeszów, personally led raids on farms in the vicinity to trap Polish families sheltering Jews. He ordered the executions of seventy Poles and the burning of their homes and farm buildings.[280]

March 1943. In Zarzetka, near Węgrów, sixteen Polish farmers were tortured and murdered by the Gestapo during the investigation of aid given to Jewish escapees from Treblinka. The Germans had been led there by a Jewish communist by the name of Rubin, from Wołomin, who had been given shelter by the local residents.[281]

March 13, 1943. In Przewrotne, near Rzeszów, thirty Poles were murdered for hiding Jews. On May 5, 1943, sixteen additional victims were added to the toll.

March 25, 1943. In Sterdyń, near Sokołów, the German SS executed forty-seven Polish farmers and deported 140 to concentration camps for the "crime" of Judenherbergerung, or harboring of Jews. Two Jews — one from Warsaw, the other a communist from Sterdyń — showed the Germans where and from whom they had received assistance.[282]

May 1943. In Brody, near Tarnopol, German military police surrounded a house where two Jewish guerrillas had found shelter. The Polish inhabitants were shot for refusing to show where the two Jews were hiding. Both Jews committed suicide.

June 8, 1943. In Zwięczyce, near Rzeszów, nineteen Polish farmers were executed by the German Gestapo and the Ukrainian SS-Galizien for aiding Jews and communists.

June 10, 1943. In Hucisko, near Głogów Małopolski in the province of Rzeszów, twenty-one Poles were massacred for sheltering Jews. Seventeen homes of the executed Poles were burned, together with a large number of farm buildings.

June 28, 1943. In the village of Ciesie, near Minsk Mazowiecki, a raid was conducted by the Gestapo, SS, and German military police to search for Jewish escapees from a death train to Treblinka. Twenty-one Poles and three Jews were burned alive, and the village was set on fire. Several Polish families were executed; one Jew escaped.

July 4, 1943. In Bór Kunowski, near Starachowice, Germans murdered forty-three Poles for helping Jews who had escaped from the ghetto and formed a partisan unit in the nearby forest. Twenty-three Poles were burned alive; twenty were shot to death.

September 18, 1943. In Białystok, twenty-one Poles from five families were murdered for assisting Jews. One of the charges of which they were accused was the making of "Aryan" documents.

September 1943. The townspeople of Tarnopol were herded into the marketplace by the Gestapo to watch a Polish family being hanged alongside the Jewish family they had sheltered. This public display was meant as a warning of what would happen to those befriending Jews.[283]

October 1943. In Warsaw, the Gestapo arrested the rector of the Catholic seminary, Monsignor Roman Archutowski, for rendering assistance to Jews. He was sent to Majdanek concentration camp, where he died after being tortured.

November 11, 1943. In Kraków, a member of the "Blue Police" who was also a soldier of the Home Army was executed for providing Jews with "Aryan" papers.

1943. Aleksander Zielonkiewicz, a lieutenant in the Home Army, was executed by the Germans for giving shelter to a Jewish family by the name of Szapiro in his home in Ossów, near Warsaw. The head of the Jewish family led the German police to the Zielonkiewicz house. When Mrs. Szapiro saw her husband approaching with the Germans, she took her child and escaped through the back door.[284]

January 29, 1944. In Kraków, the head of the SS and German military police condemned seventy-three Poles to death for helping Jews. The names of those who were executed were listed on an official German poster displayed in Kraków.

February 22–23, 1944. The Polish village of Huta Pieniacka (near Tarnopol, in Eastern Poland) and its inhabitants were annihilated by the Nazis, with the help of the Ukrainian Nationalists, for assisting Jews.[285]

March 7, 1944. The extended family of the gardener Władysław Marczak, as well as Mieczysław Wolski, cared for a group of thirty-four Jews, including Emanuel Ringelblum, in a "bunker" built under a greenhouse at 84 Grojecka Street in Warsaw. Six of the Poles who had provided shelter to these Jews were executed.[286] A Catholic midwife who had come to the hideout to deliver a baby was also executed in the ruins of the ghetto. As we have seen, according to Bednarczyk the hideout had been betrayed by a Jewish Gestapo agent.

March 23, 1944. The Polish village of Huta Werchobuska (near Tarnopol, in Eastern Poland), together with its inhabitants, was destroyed by the Nazis and their Ukrainian auxiliaries for assisting Jews.[287]

Spring 1944. A street peddler by the name of Marczak gave shelter to a group of eight to ten Jews in an underground hideout under his home at 14 Nowiniarska Street in Warsaw. In the spring of 1944 a young, well-dressed Jewish woman came to the house seeking admission into the group and threatening otherwise to inform the Gestapo. Several days later she returned with the Gestapo, who seized the Jews. Unable to find Marczak, the Germans took a large group of Poles as hostages and threatened to shoot them if Marczak did not surrender. Marczak gave himself up and was promptly executed. The Jewish woman was suspected of being a Gestapo agent, one of many in Warsaw specializing in seeking out Jewish hideouts.[288]

September 1944. In Warsaw, the Germans executed eight Catholic nuns from the order of the Sisters of Charity for refusing to surrender Jewish children sheltered in their orphanage. (The majority of Catholic religious orders in occupied Poland are known to have sheltered Jews in their convents and monasteries.)

As some of the above entries indicate, even in Eastern Poland, where the bitter 1939–41 memories of Jews "dancing on Polish graves" were never erased, Poles did not refrain from rendering assistance to the Jews. In Gwoździec, for instance, where Jews and Ukrainians had helped the Soviets load Polish people onto cattle cars for deportation to Siberia, several Poles hid Jews from the Germans. "Among them was Stefania Krasnodębska, my mother," states J. Rokicka, "as well as Janina and Karol Krzeszowicz. They hid five Jews under their stable: Mendel, Moszek and Frydel Bergman together with Preszel and Stella. Aniela and Piotr Nosal hid the Jewish family named Neubarger who survived the war and emigrated to the United States."[289] The Krzeszowicz and Nosal families are now numbered among the "Righteous Among the Nations." As noted by one Jewish critic of the Poles, Reuben Ainsztein, Polish aid to the Jews in the eastern territories was so extensive that the Germans wiped out two entire Polish villages in retaliation: the aforementioned Huta Pieniacka (near Brody) and Huta Werchobuska (near Złoczów).[290] Finally, among these murders of exemplary human beings, sixty priests who were known to render assistance to Jews were executed.[291]

This is no fanciful tale of heroism spun by Polish patriots and Polonophiles. As of January 1, 1996, 4,688 Poles (among them, hundreds of children) have been decorated by Yad Vashem, the Israeli organization that recognizes gentiles who assisted Jews during the Holocaust. These Polish Righteous Christians represent over 34 percent (the largest single national group) of all those officially recognized (13,618) by Yad Vashem, Martyrs' and Heroes' Remembrance Authority in Jerusalem. In 1996, about 100 additional names of Poles were added to this list.

Given the historical evidence for Polish sympathy for and assistance to the Jews during World War II, there is no rational explanation for the accusation of massive Polish complicity in the Holocaust of their own citizens, the Polish Jews. Many such accusations were voiced in former years not so much by the Jews who survived in Poland as by those who spent the war years in the Soviet Union and returned to Poland after the war was over.

In wartime Poland, neither the Jewish nor the Polish nor any other collaborators were responsible for the conduct of the Holocaust. The killers were the Germans, who, in open-air shootings, also relied on the auxiliary police to do some of their dirty work. As Adolf Berman put it:

> Accounts of the martyrdom of Poland's Jews tend to emphasize their suffering at the hands of blackmailers and informers, the "blue" police and other scum. Less is written, on the other hand, about the thousands of Poles who risked their lives to save the Jews. The flotsam and jetsam on the surface of a turbulent river is more visible than the pure stream running deep underneath, but that stream existed.[292]

The heroic record of Polish assistance to the Jews must be clearly borne in mind when speaking about Polish collaboration in the destruction of the European Jews during World War II. Israel Gutman, a leading historian in Holocaust studies, director of research at Yad Vashem, and editor of the four-volume work *Encyclopedia of the Holocaust*, states:

> I should like to make two things clear here. First, all accusations against the Poles that they were responsible for what is referred to as the "Final Solution" are not even worth mentioning. Secondly, there is no validity at all in the contention that ... Polish attitudes were the reason for the sitting of the death camps in Poland.
>
> Poland was a completely occupied country. There was a difference in the kind of "occupation" countries underwent in Europe. Each country experienced a different occupation and almost all had a certain amount of autonomy, limited and defined in various ways. This autonomy did not exist in Poland. No one asked the Poles how one should treat the Jews.[293]

More recently he added:

> I want to be unequivocal about this. When it is said that Poles supposedly took part in the extermination of Jews on the side of the Germans, that is not true. It has no foundation in fact. There was no such thing as Poles taking part in the extermination of the Jewish population. There were minor exceptions where the [Polish] "blue" police and the Jewish police took part in the expulsion and extermination of Jews. Moreover, it is the

> case that the Poles did assist the [Warsaw] ghetto insurgents. One has to remember, however, that at that time the Poles themselves did not have sufficient quantities of arms and were also under the occupation of the German Reich.[294]

Perhaps this is as good a place as any to address the moral requirements involved in civilian rescue operations under the conditions obtaining in Poland during World War II. For the purposes of illustration, a simple hypothetical scenario may suffice. In a midwestern town in America a house stands engulfed by flames, and in it a family is trapped. Out of the throng of passersby going about their daily business, a crowd gathers, and out of that crowd a single individual rushes in — either to come out alive with or without those he went in to save or to perish in the flames. In this scenario, moreover, a few people are throwing gasoline on the fire, and some are rejoicing, both in secret and out loud, because they despise the occupants. How should we judge the heroic actions of that individual, the "passivity" of the crowd, and the actions of those who add fuel to the fire as well as those who rejoice?

Sound moral judgment requires us to condemn the gas-throwers and the rejoicers and to applaud the hero. But what about the passive bystanders? Is there a moral imperative that *requires* heroic action? No. We do not condemn the crowd. The heroic ethic is for the heroes of this world alone. It is extraordinary, exceptional, over and beyond what we consider to be required moral conduct. Moreover, it goes against the grain of our genetic programming for survival. That is precisely why it is "heroic" — like the heroic resistance of some Jews when faced with hopeless odds.[295]

To truly reflect the conditions in Poland during World War II, the above scenario of the burning house needs a few added details: this midwestern town is under the control of skinheads; it is effectively cordoned off from the rest of America; the town is without either a law-enforcement agency or a functioning fire department; the family in question was targeted simply because its members had long hair (this is also why the gas-throwers in the crowd despise the family, though neither do they identify with the skinheads, by whom they are also terrorized); and finally, to prevent attempts at rescue, land mines have been planted around the house, and terrorist guards armed with grenades and uzies are patrolling the perimeter — never mind the secret skinhead agents who are planted in the crowd of onlookers and who are just itching to turn someone in, producing a psychological, but real, atmosphere of mistrust and fear.

If the reader is troubled by this analogy, the sobering words of Emanuel Ringelblum may attest to its appropriateness:

> The life of a Pole who is hiding Jews is not an easy one. Appalling terror reigns in the country, second only to Yugoslavia [Serbia?]. The noblest among the people and the most self-sacrificing individuals are being sent *en masse* to concentration camps or prisons. Informing and denunciation flourish throughout the country, thanks largely to the *Volksdeutsche.* Arrests and round-ups at every step and constant searches for arms and smuggled goods in the trains are common in the city streets. Every day the press, radio, etc. infect the masses of the population with the venom of anti-Semitism. In this atmosphere of trouble and terror, passivity and indifference, it is very difficult to keep Jews in one's home. A Jew living in the flat of an intellectual or a worker or in the hut of a peasant is dynamite liable to explode at any moment and blow the whole place up.... Jewish flats are constantly "burning" [i.e., are no longer safe].[296]

Such is the dilemma that confronted the "passive" Polish people during World War II. The dilemma was the Polish version of *Sophie's Choice*: choose the Jew or your own family. If you choose the Jew, you risk sacrificing your loved ones. The question of whether the record of the Jews would or would not have matched the record of the Poles, were their roles reversed, is academic. (In circumstances much less threatening to rescuers, how many Jews rendered assistance to Poles during the 1939–41 Soviet purges in Eastern Poland?) Again, morally speaking, no one is *required* to be a hero. Szymon Danter addresses this moral dilemma:

> Approximately a quarter of a million people looking for help—were a problem for the Poles. They tapped on the window of a cottage or the door of an apartment, and a question appeared alongside them: To save them or not? And how to do it? Would even a piece of bread help, or should I pretend not to hear anything? Or should I go inform the Germans, which is what the law enjoins? Every form of aid was forbidden under pain of death for oneself and one's whole family.
>
> To us today the choice seems altogether clear. And yet I was shocked not long ago by a woman I know, a Jew. She is a person my age, someone I value highly for her honesty and courage. And she told me, "I am not at all sure I would give a bowl of food to a Pole if it could mean death for me and my daughter."
>
> It was a truly satanic moral trial that Poles were subjected to. I do not know if anyone else would have emerged victorious from it.
>
> On the other hand, to speak correctly of the attitude of Poles toward Jews: the majority of Poles behaved passively, but that can be explained by the terror and also by the fact that Poles, too, were being systematically murdered on a mass scale by the Germans.
>
> On the other hand, aside from passivity, which I regard as entirely justified by a situation in which every action was heroic, there also existed an indifference that I regard as negative—although even here one could look for a psychological explanation. Next, as if on parallel lines, come two active groups. Those who betrayed, attacked, or murdered either from a desire for gain or out of pure hatred, and those who sheltered Jews and aided them in various ways. The second group was more numerous and more representative of the Polish underground. Yet the first group was more effective.[297]

As for those who were secretly or overtly glad that Jews died, that "Hitler was doing the job for them," Israel Shahak's answer (the answer of a survivor of the Warsaw ghetto) is as good as any other:

> It is of course true that there was another small group which either helped the Nazis, or expressed, quite loudly too, their satisfaction that the Jews "are gone." ... But in justice it should be pointed out that on many, perhaps most, of those occasions, there was also a verbal opposition to such a statement.... I had, by the way, many occasions to think about this and similar occasions, when I heard completely similar statements made by Israeli Jews in the summer of 1982, when a minority (but a greater one I am sure than in conquered Poland of 1943) expressed delight in every report of the death of Palestinians and Lebanese.[298]

Such immoral behavior on the part of Jews or Gentiles needs no commentary.

I have given some thought to the question of whether my family could have hidden some Jews during the war while we were still in Poland. Our humble abode in Ryświanka, Wołyń—a four-room peasant domicile with a thatched roof, no attic, no basement, no electricity, and no running water—housed a family of nine. We also had a small barn and perhaps a cowshed or a pigsty. Ours was a typical Polish peasant home. If some Jew or a Jewish family tapped on our window, I am certain my mother would have been able to provide them with lodgings but not to "hide" them. We could have put them in our potato cellar (basically, a hole in the ground) if we were forewarned of an impending search (and who was?), but they could not have lived there for any length of time. Any search of the premises would have turned them up immediately. (Any household could be and often was searched by almost anyone in authority at any time, and at least half a million Nazis, Gestapo agents, spies, and collaborators were employed full-time in the nasty business of the "Final Solution," which involved ferreting out and murdering the Jews.[299]) Most homes in Poland were not built with secret rooms, passageways, and hiding places. The idea is preposterous that had they only wanted to, Poles in German-occupied Poland could have "hidden" Jews from the Gestapo and their collaborators: the Einsatzgruppen and their SS auxiliaries; the German, Ukrainian, Lithuanian, Latvian, Belorussian, Polish, and Jewish police; the Kripo; the Volksdeutsche; the *szmalcowniki*; and sometimes ill-disposed neighbors of various ethnic backgrounds.

My own family was never called on to take

a stand on the issue of rendering assistance to the Jews, since we ourselves needed assistance. But there is no doubt in my mind that my mother, who had a good heart and who even in our last extremity would always share whatever we had with others, would not have failed this satanic test of character — and that, since we were surrounded by Ukrainian Nationalist collaborators, I would not be writing these words here and now.

Here is a replay of that scenario of the burning house, this time taken from a real-life situation in 1943. The narrator is the previously mentioned Dr. Baruch Milch of Tłuste, who had just lost his only son in an "action" — one of several attacks on the town's Jewish community. This particular "action" was carried out by "over 300 bandits consisting of Germans (about 150) and Ukrainian policemen (over 200)."

> Worthy of note are the voices and disposition of the Aryan society during this action. It is true that a part of that society, predominantly the Poles, looked upon all of this with abhorrence, did not eat, could not fulfill the work responsibilities of daily life, and as far as possible helped and hid the poor martyrs. But the majority followed the daily routines of their lives as if nothing was happening around them. Often at the last, most dangerous moment, they would abandon to fate [i.e., chase out] those hidden on their farms, even though they knew [about the attack] beforehand or took great sums for hiding them....
>
> There were also those who laughed and with satisfaction said: "The Jews deserved this. This is God's punishment for their sins." Others again would reprimand the Jews saying: "Why didn't they defend themselves or run away" knowing full well how much can be achieved by attacking the sun with a hoe [*rzucać się motyką na słońce*]. Besides, they also knew that against these defenseless children, women, old people and dispirited youth there presently stands a mighty military power from hell, which for the time being holds all of Europe and perhaps the world in check.
>
> They did not know the meaning of the phrase *Kiddush ha-Shem*, which is so deeply imbedded in the consciousness of every Jew (*Kiddush Ha-Shem*, an offering to God).[300]

The refusal of Christians to harbor Jewish families with small children instinctively provokes the severest of moral condemnations in any healthy mind — today. The testament of Baruch Milch addresses this issue as well. The following simple yet powerful account written by a country doctor must certainly rank among the most poignant "works of literature" produced during those terrible, hopeless times. The scene occurs in the attic of a certain "Mr. B," whom Milch describes as follows: "He gave the appearance of being resolute, brave, enterprising, poor, frugal, and although a Ukrainian, did not manifest a negative disposition toward the Jewish question, all the more so since his brother was the head of the *silrada* [village council] during the Soviet occupation for which reason both he and his wife were murdered by the local Ukrainian *Sich*."

Remember that Milch was a medical doctor who dedicated himself wholeheartedly to saving lives and that his only son had just been murdered by the Nazis. This passage follows a description of the incredible tensions that by then characterized the lives both of the saviors and of those being saved.

> When the mother with her only son returned from the dark shelter (they had run out of kerosene) on June 18 [1943] around 7 o'clock in the evening, exhausted and wild in appearance, the child bolted from his mother's grasp and began to jump and run around the attic like a bird freed from his cage or a wild stallion. Loud words of joy and happiness came pouring out of his mouth. It was then that the proprietor came upstairs and warned us that unless we dealt with the child today, we would all be thrown out. And we all, instead of rejoicing at this beautiful sight of the happy child, frightened as we were, had to discipline him and call him to order.
>
> No sooner did we sit down, each in a different place, to consider the matter, than the child became boisterous again and would not be quieted, driving us to the edge of madness with exasperation. It was at that moment that my brother-in-law suddenly rose up and in an instant determined the fate of the child. With a single lunge of his right hand he grasped the delicate neck of his son

in order to quiet him down. The child's eyes immediately bulged out, his tongue came out of his mouth, and he fell silent. His appearance at that moment was terrible, even horrible. Everyone stood aghast. I paced here and there and finally ran up to my brother-in-law and when I grabbed his hand, he asked me: "Shall I let him go or not?" I responded several times: "Yes...no...yes... no"—not knowing myself what to do. My brother-in-law, however, did not remove his hand from his son's throat. Kneeling in one position over the child he was white as a ghost and would not take his eyes off the choking child whose face with every passing moment was turning bluer and bluer. Later when I took the child's hand, I could scarcely feel his pulse which subsequently vanished completely. The father then released him, placed a blanket over his face which assumed a horrible expression, and sitting down in a corner began to tear out his hair. He said: "I will be condemned as a child murderer for all eternity, but I have saved him much suffering and at least he did not perish at the hands of the Teutonic executioners."

And so in the space of about two minutes, without the slightest sound, perished this greatest comfort of parents at the hands of his own father, in the presence of the mother and closest family members. At the time his father was holding him, there was no possibility of releasing him because the child would have made a terrible noise and, given the disposition of the proprietor and the fact that just then a mass of people were returning from work, we would all have been lost. But it was not only the thought of saving ourselves and of improving our situation which led to this deed. More importantly, it was done with the intention of diminishing his torments, of subjecting him to the most unexpected form of death, but not at the hands of these bandits.

This deed was sudden, unexpected, but the intention had been germinating within us for several days now. The first to propose this criminally heroic thought was the father himself. We often discussed it and deliberated on the form and means which would cause the child the least amount of suffering. We did not have an ample supply of narcotics at our disposal; we did not want to shoot him. And so, choking him by means of a firm grasp on the vagus nerve and central neck artery (carotid), turned out to be the best means of imparting a quick death and of causing the least amount of suffering.

Before reaching this conclusion we considered the question of the child from various angles. We could not remain here with the child and we would not be able to find another place with him. People with children were not admitted to camps. To make our way with him to some border or to wander through fields and forests would mean torment and certain death. We did not know of any refuge where he could be dropped off and even if we had known of one, from the unfortunate characteristic of his body (circumcision), he would have been recognized as a Jew and his fate would have been uncertain. And even if a person could be found who would nestle him to her bosom, even if my acquaintance would have been willing to take in a strange child for a huge sum of money, either she would have become tired of him or the child would have betrayed himself and fallen into the hands of the police or the Germans. And even if this didn't happen, such a child—being used to having a good mother and life—would become emaciated from longing and the lack of proper domestic care and would in the end die in great suffering.

In addition, recently the proprietor had urged us and tried to persuade us to do away with the child lest we all die along with him. There was no other way out. According to him, what was the life of Jews worth these days anyway? Although he himself was a father of three children, he said this to himself quite naturally with a light heart, whereas we were not a little hurt by it all.

The mother of the child and my wife cried and lamented terribly, spilling entire streams of tears. But at the same time, one could not pour out one's grief nor cry out loud. Every one of us was as if in a trance, spewing out a deluge of blasphemous words against everyone and everything that existed in this world. We were only comforted by the thought that our end would be no better. Later the mother came over to the child, uncovered his face, which now took on the appearance of peaceful slumber, began to kiss it fiercely, cut off a tuft of hair from his golden locks, and swore to avenge his death. In that moment

> we all felt that we were no longer normal people, that we were capable of everything, even murder.
>
> My wish to all German parents, to those who support them or prolong the war is that they at least once in their lifetime would find themselves in the same predicament as we find ourselves tonight.[301]

"We were no longer normal people," wrote Dr. Milch in 1943. If the Jewish victims felt that way in those dark days, so did the "unequal victims." Perhaps my sister, Janina Piotrowski, spoke in the name of many Polish survivors when she said:

> There is much more to be told, but that belongs to my private sphere. About these matters I do not wish to speak because no one would believe me anyway. I was never sent to an extermination camp because I always bore patiently come what may. I witnessed how they would hang Polish people in the city streets for the merest infractions, or how they would send them off to the gas ovens. No, I survived because I became that to which I was reduced in Nazi Germany: *pokorne cielę* [a submissive calf].[302]

If this is what is meant by Polish or Jewish "passivity," so be it.

I know of no better assessment of wartime Polish-Jewish relations, and none more pleasing to Polish rescuers, than that issued by the Jewish National Committee on July 22, 1944:

> We have especially deep and sincere ties with the fighting, democratic Polish underground. Our eyes are open. We know that a certain segment of Polish society is still infected with anti–Semitism.... All the more brightly and beautifully stand out numerous acts of self-sacrificing and selfless assistance on the part of the democratic and working class elements in Polish society. The deeply humanitarian stance of a significant portion of the Polish educated classes, activists of many movements, and many good, simple people will be forever etched in the minds of Polish Jewry.[303]

This, however, does not let the collaborators off the hook. How many Polish collaborators were there? That is unknown. Lukas states:

> No precise data exist concerning the number of collaborators during the war, but the number does not appear to have loomed large in relation to the total population. Emmanuel Ringelblum, the famous Jewish chronicler who lived through much of this period, said that most of the denunciation and informing in wartime Poland was done by the *Volksdeutsch*, who were considered traitors by the overwhelming majority of Poles. One report [*Komisja Polskiego Sztabu Głównego w Londynie*] suggested that in the period January 1943 to June 1944, underground authorities pronounced 2,015 death sentences on informers and collaborators. Postwar statistics of the Israeli War Crime Commission indicated that only 7,000 Poles out of a population of over twenty million ethnic Poles collaborated with the Nazis.[304]

Although no cause for celebration, I submit that this is a record of which any other European nation of those times would be proud. Be that as it may, these thousands (whatever their number) of Polish informers, blackmailers, denouncers, accomplices, and collaborators should also be counted among those who were responsible for the total war losses of Poland.

Postwar Years

Unfortunately, the killing of Jews in Poland did not end with the end of the war. According to Shmuel Lerer, 350 Jews were killed in Poland within seven months after the end of the war.[305] Gilbert documents some of these incidents.

On May 20, 1945, four Jews were murdered by "Polish anti–Semites."

On May 22 of the same year, Polish thugs attacked a train, beat Mejer Sznajder, and took him away, never to be seen again.

On September 1, 1945, Yaakov Waldman was killed near Turek.

In October, eight Jews were killed by a Polish underground group in Bolesławiec.

In December, eleven Jews were killed in Kosów Lacki.

In February 1946, four Jewish delegates were murdered on their way to a Jewish convention in Kraków.

In that same month and year, four Jews were killed in the Parczew Forest, and four more were taken out of a car flying a Union Jack, shot, and left by the side of the road.

On March 28, the British Foreign Office learned that several Jewish leaders traveling from Kraków to Łódź were murdered after being tortured.

On Easter Sunday, April 21, five Jewish survivors of Auschwitz, Buchenwald, and Mauthausen were shot on the outskirts of Nowy Targ by "members of the former underground forces of the Polish Home Army." Six days after the funeral of these five, another seven died in almost the same location.

In May, Eliahu Lipszowicz, a former officer in the Red Army, was murdered in Silesia.

In June, two Jews were murdered in Biała Podlaska.

On March 19, 1946, according to Gilbert, "one of only two survivors of the death camp at Belzec, Chaim Hirszman, gave evidence in Lublin of what he had witnessed in the death camp. He was asked to return on the following day to complete his evidence. But on his way home he was murdered, *because he was a Jew.*" Gilbet adds, "No Polish town was free from such incidents."[306]

By far the most infamous attack took place on July 4, 1946, when, again according to Gilbert, forty-two Jews were killed in Kielce by a mob of Poles. "Following the Kielce 'Pogrom,'" states Gilbert, "one hundred thousand Polish Jews, more than half the survivors, fled from Poland, seeking new homes in Palestine, Western Europe, Britain and the United States, Latin America and Australia."[307] Maurice Goldstein, president of the International Committee of Auschwitz, described the exodus somewhat differently: "The anti–Semitic campaign ... drove out of Poland 100,000 Jews who decided to rebuild Poland from its wounds after the war."[308] The Poland in question was the Polish People's Republic. Stanisław Krajewski put it a third way:

> After the war, there were more Jews repatriated from the east than Jews who somehow managed to survive in Poland. Although their experiences differed, the Holocaust hovered over them in the same way. With each step they confronted graves and the sharp absence of Jewish life. This caused the majority of them to emigrate to the West and to Israel.... There was, however, one other reason that they left — a sense of insecurity. As studies by Irena Nowakowski reveal, the reason for leaving most frequently mentioned, besides the impossibility of living "in a graveyard," was precisely the threat of anti–Semitism.... The stereotype of Polish anti–Semitism contains an unjust generalization. However, this stereotype was a fundamental determinant of Jewish self-consciousness in occupied Poland and directly afterward."[309]

In 1946, just before the Kielce incident, the first secretary of the Italian Embassy in Poland provided, by way of an anecdote, another reason why some Jews left postwar Poland: "When one Jew was asked recently why he had decided to leave Poland, he replied: when the Jews ran the businesses and non–Jews governed it was possible to live in Poland, but now when the Jews govern and the non–Jews run the businesses it is better to emigrate."[310]

In addition to all these considerations, two more reasons can be added for the mass exodus of the Jews from Poland: the influence of the Zionist pro–emigration movement (Poland was the center of the Zionist movement); and the disenchantment of the vast majority of the Jews who had returned to Poland from the Soviet Union and who wanted nothing to do with the Soviet system that they had come to know so well. George Lenczowski pointed out these reasons in 1952:

> The press in Western countries either misunderstood or was unwilling to face the realities of the situation in Eastern Europe in 1945 and 1946. It was thought that the Jews were emigrating because of acute anti–Semitism, which lingered even after Hitler's downfall. There was anti–Semitism in that area, but two reservations should be made. First, anti–Semitism was not a new phenomenon in Eastern Europe. It had existed

> before the war and it had been expressed in anti-Jewish legislation. But it had never caused a mass exodus of Jews; such an exodus was without doubt a result of Soviet occupation of the area in question. Secondly, some new acute manifestations of anti-Semitism were partly attributable to the role individual Jewish Communists played in the establishment of the puppet regimes in Eastern Europe [e.g., those of Jakub Berman in Poland, Rudolf Slánský in Czechoslovakia, Ana Pauker in Rumania, and Mátyás Rákosi in Hungary].... The teeming camps of displaced persons in Western Germany confronted the West with a major political and humanitarian problem and added considerably to the pressure that the Zionist organization was exercising for a favorable solution in Palestine.[311]

For all these reasons, over 25,000 Jews had left Poland by January 1946. In 1946, the year of the Kielce pogrom, 150,000 left the country.[312]

Kielce is often regarded as the crowning point of the Polish "anti-Semitic campaign" that began soon after the German retreat and gradually intensified in the following years. This time period also happens to coincide with the Stalinist consolidation of power in Poland and the civil strife that brought death to an estimated 1,500–2,000 Jews between 1944 and 1947. However, this figure represents but 2 to 3 percent of the total victims of the postwar Stalinist era in Poland. While not forgetting these 2 to 3 percent, we should also from time to time pay homage to the other 97–98 percent (the tens of thousands of Christians) as well and remember why and how they died.

A number of unrelated reasons lay behind the Polish action against the Jews in those days: the continuing anti-Semitism compounded by many years of Nazi anti-Semitic propaganda, sometimes veiled as a response to the *żydokomuna* threat; an unwillingness to relinquish Jewish real estate and property to the rightful owners, or just plain greed; fear of retribution for Polish treatment of the Jews during the war years; and the already discussed postwar role of the Jews in Poland, a role that included the liquidation of the AK and the Polish underground.[313] No justification whatsoever can be found for the first three reasons. With respect to the fourth reason, we must remember that the Soviet takeover of Poland, which began in 1944, was very swift and that it was accomplished with the visible assistance of the Jews. In the second half of August 1944, all the communists operating in Poland were melded with those who arrived with the Red Army. Among the former were Władysław Gomułka and Bolesław Bierut. Among the latter were Jakub Berman, Hilary Minc, and Aleksander Zawadzki.

By the end of February 1945, Civil Militia (Milicja Obywatelska, or MO) and UB headquarters existed in every province, every county, and every commune (*gmina*) throughout Poland. By April 1945, the MO numbered 40,000 and the UB around 10,000. In March, the Internal Army (Wojsko Wewnętrzne) was reconstituted into the Internal Security Corps (Korpus Bezpieczeństwa Wewnętrznego, or KBW), which commanded three brigades and 28,000 soldiers. Most of the leaders of the AL found employment in the MO. For example, the chief of the AL in the Lublin area, Grzegorz Korczyński — who murdered the members of the two units of Jewish partisans in the Janowskie Forest and passed a death sentence on Shlomo (Solomon) Morel's brother — became the MO commandant in Lublin, and the chief of the AL in the Kielce area, Mieczysław Moczar — who in 1968 spearheaded the party purges of Jews — became the director of the Provincial Office of State Security (Wojewódzki Urząd Bezpieczeństwa Publicznego, or WUBP) in Łódź.[314]

As we have seen, in an attempt to "divide and conquer," Stalin placed some Jews in highly visible positions of authority in the PRL and in the organs of oppression. This diabolical strategy was purposefully engineered to put Poles and Jews directly on a collision course. Many, if not most, of these Jews — whether local or imported — were, at least nominally, communists. The American ambassador in Warsaw, Arthur Bliss Lane, wrote in his report of July 15, 1946:

> One of the principle reasons for the increasing hostility towards the Jews, which

> is evidenced by many acts of violence, including assassinations by anti–Government armed groups, is the estimated opposition of eighty to ninety percent of the Polish people against the Government and especially against the small, but controlling group, composed of Jews who have received their indoctrination in the Soviet Union and who are believed responsible for the repressive measures of the Security Police, the lack of freedom of the press and the present lack of independence of the nation.[315]

Just after the Kielce pogrom, Primate August Hlond expressed the opinion of a large segment of the Polish people when he declared:

> The fact that conditions are worsening should in large part be attributed to the Jews today occupying leading positions in the Polish government and attempting to introduce a governmental structure which the majority of the nation does not desire.... It is regrettable that some Jews are losing their lives in deadly armed struggles and on the political front in Poland, but a disproportionately larger number of Poles are losing their lives.[316]

That is also the position of Father Andrzej Zwoliński, who stated in 1994: "The actual participation of the Jews in the establishment of the new system of government constituted one of the reasons for the stirring of anti–Semitic attitudes within the [Polish] society." He counseled that in "cases involving the murder of Jews ... one should look for political motives (armed groups, called 'bands' by the communists, resisted the 'new government' and murdered members of the PPR)."[317]

At the end of 1945, 80,000 members remained in the Polish underground. Of this total, 30,000 belonged to Freedom and Independence (Wolność i Niezawisłość, or WiN, founded on September 2, 1945) and 20,000 belonged to the NSZ and the National Military Union (Narodowy Związek Wojskowy, or NZW). These were the "armed groups," the "bands," that conducted the attacks on the functionaries of the PRL/PPR and the Soviet organs of oppression, which in turn were desperately trying to eliminate them as well.[318] On January 17, 1945, Mikołaj Demko (a.k.a. Mieczysław Moczar) issued a special order to "shoot the AK murderers on sight." The first concentration camp set up by the NKVD for AK members (March 1945) was located in Rembertów near Warsaw. According to information from local communist sources and Józef Światło, in 1945 alone, the Soviets rounded up and deported some 50,000 members of the Polish underground to various camps in the Soviet Union.[319]

I have already quoted the controversial statements of Stefan Korboński, John Sack, Józef Światło, and others who noted that the Jews were overrepresented in the upper strata of the PRL government, the security forces, the police, and even the judiciary. Gerald Keith, the American chargé d'affaires in Warsaw, also commented that postwar Poland found itself "under a very marked Jewish governing and industrial influence." He added, "I consider it difficult to estimate what proportion of the resentment towards the government may be attributed to the part played by the Jews in the government and government-controlled industry, but it is surely of considerable consequence."[320] The attempt of the communist régime to camouflage the background of these Jews did not help in the least. As a result, the repressive institutions run by the Soviet-controlled Office of State Security were filled with Polish political prisoners, and the rivers of bitterness, resentment, and revenge ran high. The ruthless persecution by the communist régime in postwar Poland embraced not only members of the Nazi-era Polish underground[321] but also ordinary citizens and even prominent members of Żegota.

Writing in 1946, Wanda Lisowska, a teacher from Nowogródek before the war and a courier in the Polish underground, told of Soviet roundups *(łapanki)*, of crowded jails, of brutal interrogations and mass deportations of Poles in the summer of 1944 from Soviet-occupied northeastern Polish territories, with the assistance of the Jews:

> They [the Soviets] conducted massive roundups. It happened this way: they would arrive around 2:00, 3:00 o'clock in the morning,

> surround the village and conduct house-to-house searches looking for arms and taking away the men. The prisons in the neighboring towns of Raduń and Ejszyszki were overflowing.... The NKGB interrogations were savage; they were conducted mainly at night. The informers were mostly recruited from among the Jews who occupied positions in the military, NKVD, and NKGB and worked as confidants.... Partisan [Polish Home Army] units, not wanting the civilian population to suffer on account of these denunciations, liquidated Soviet confidants....
>
> Right after the battle of Surkonty, I was arrested. I was bringing civilian clothing to the soldiers in a hideout. ... They took us to Raduń. The men were locked in a stable and I, in a dark chamber. They held me for two weeks. The interrogations took place at night. On the first night I was interrogated seven times. ... The interrogations were ordinary: one was beaten. Their purpose was to elicit information about AK detachments. The men were treated much worse. They were tortured, beaten, their ribs were broken, their teeth knocked out. ... In towns, the prisoners were held for up to two weeks, then they were taken to Wilno or Lida for trial. Trains departed for Siberia every two weeks....
>
> In December 1944, in Wilno, the arrests were so massive that the NKVD were stationed in almost every apartment building arresting anyone who entered. In Wilno, there were sixteen prisons; in Łukiszki there was tremendous overcrowding. It was very difficult to get information about those arrested. They took them away and they disappeared like a rock in water. The families brought packages to all the prisons and received the same answer — "not here."
>
> Christmas 1944 was a very sad day all over the Wilno district. On the second day of the holidays a large transport filled with Poles left for Siberia.[322]

On the night of April 12, 1945, about seventeen Polish young people — some of them members of the AK and the NSZ — were dragged out of their homes in Siedlce by the UB and shot. The perpetrators, among whom were said to have been some Jews, were never brought to trial. Similar murders occurred in Węgrów, Mińsk Mazowiecki, and Kalisz.[323] The kidnapping and Moscow "trial" of the sixteen Polish underground leaders took place that year as well.[324]

Among the persecuted members of Żegota were Zofia Kossak-Szczucka and Władysław Bartoszewski.[325] Teresa Torańska comments on this tragic state of affairs through a conversation with Jakub Berman, a member of the Presidium of the Council of Ministers since 1945, a member of the Politburo since 1948, and the chief puppeteer of the Ministry of State Security:

> *In 1948–49 you arrested members of the Home Army Council of Aid to Jews, the "Żegota."*
>
> Yes well, all organizations connected with the Home Army were included; the scope was wide.
>
> *Mr. Berman! The security services, where all or nearly all the directors were Jewish, arrested Poles because they had saved Jews during the occupation, and you say that Poles are anti-Semites. That's not nice.*
>
> It was wrong that that happened. Certainly it was wrong. At that time I didn't have any facts about what this "Żegota" did [he thanked Zofia Kossak-Szczucka soon after the war for rescuing his brother's children]; it was later that my brother [Adolf, secretary to Żegota] told me about it.... We later released them all.
>
> *Władysław Bartoszewski was in prison almost seven years.*
>
> I don't know how long he was imprisoned, but I certainly don't deny he was persecuted; he did his time.
>
> *And what did your brother have to say about it?*
>
> Adolf told me about the Żegota, but not until many years later [incredible: the arrests in question were made in 1948–49], and then, in 1950, he emigrated to Israel....
>
> *Everyone from the "Żegota" group was rehabilitated after 1956.*

Certainly; it was a group of extraordinarily noble people.

Is that all?

Look, you must understand: that was 1949–50. I already had some idea of my situation and Stalin's attitude towards me. So I thought that if I got involved in certain things, if I acted against the wishes of the Soviet advisers, then reports about my activities would reach Stalin, who would say, what kind of behavior is this? So I had a choice: either leave or manoeuvre.[326]

Berman did not leave; he "manoeuvered" instead. The nature of this "manoeuvering," which began in 1944, is best described by Sack:

> In time, all of Poland and 44,000 square miles of Germany were rid of Germans, were *Deutscherein,* and the Office's institutions were full of Poles, 150,000 Poles from the antecedents to Solidarity. In places like Gleiwitz [Gliwice], the Poles stood against the prison wall as Implementation tied them to big iron rings, said, "Ready!" "Aim!" "Fire!" shot them, and told the Polish guards, "Don't talk about this." The guards, being Poles, weren't pleased, but the Jacobs, Josefs and Pineks, the Office's brass, stayed loyal to Stalin, for they thought of themselves as Jews, not as Polish patriots. And *that's* why the Good Fairy Stalin, the man who didn't hate the Germans but who abhorred the Enemies of the People, the Agents of Reactionary Elements, the Oppressors, Imperialists and Counterrevolutionaries, be they the Germans, Russians or Poles, had hired all the Jews on Christmas Eve, 1943, and had packed them into his Office of State Security, his instrument in the People's Republic of Poland.
>
> And now, 1945, the Poles went to war with the Office, shooting at Jews in Intelligence, Interrogation and Imprisonment, the Jews concluding that the Poles were antisemitic, the Poles contending that no, they were only anti the Office.[327]

Lukas adds:

> In the years immediately following World War II there were sporadic anti–Semitic outbreaks in Poland, most of which were the work of criminal elements associated with the nationalistic right wing of the Polish underground. The scope and effect of the attacks were exaggerated in the western press. [Stanisław] Mikołajczyk [leader of the non-communist Polish People's Party], who was not an anti–Semite, pointed out that he was in Radom and Kraków at the time when the western press reported that pogroms had occurred in these cities. What he had witnessed, on the other hand, were political riots against the communists. In view of the large number of Jews who were members of the [communist] PPR, including the universally despised security police, it is little wonder that there was a revival of anti–Jewish feeling in postwar Poland. Since most Poles regarded the regime as an alien-imposed system, the obvious prominence of Jews within the government, along with those who returned to Poland from the Soviet Union after the war, created an extremely tense situation.[328]

As a result, to quote Foreign Minister Wincenty Rzymowski, Polish hostilities were "aimed primarily against the present regime in Poland and only in the second place against the Jews."[329]

Such is the context in which the pogrom in Kielce occurred, but this was far from being a plain, old-fashioned pogrom. Of the 25,000 Jews who had lived in Kielce before the war, fewer than 500 survived the Holocaust by escaping, often with Polish assistance, from the Kielce ghetto and either going into hiding in the surrounding villages and forests or joining the partisans. (The Kielce ghetto housed 25,000 Jews: locals, those resettled from Łódź and Poznań, and about 1,000 from Vienna. On August 20–24, 1942, the ghetto was liquidated with the help of the local police, the *Bahnschutz* (railway security police), and units made up of Ukrainians. The Jews were then sent to Treblinka.[330] According to town records, by January 25, 1945, 79 of the local Jews had returned to Kielce. Later, other Jews arrived there from Kraków, Lwów, and Wilno. Starting in February 1945, 203 transports brought 136,000 Jews from the Soviet Union to Poland; about 300 settled in Kielce.[331]

By the end of 1945, about 2,000 Jews,

gathered in 45 Jewish enclaves, lived in the entire province of Kielce. According to town records, on July 1, 1945, Kielce itself counted 53,560 inhabitants, including 212 Jews.[332] As elsewhere in Poland, throughout this time some of the Kielce Jews chose to emigrate, and some decided to remain in their hometown and rebuild their lives.

At the beginning of 1946, 304 Jews lived in Kielce. In May of that year, that number fell to 163. Except for a few families who lived in private residences in town, the rest lived in a Jewish Center located at 7 Planty Street, regarded by some as a UB domicile.[333] Some of these were local residents waiting to reclaim their properties; most were outsiders.[334] Some joined the Communist Party, and some were employed by the Soviet-controlled security apparatus.

By 1946 the town's governance structure was, in part, in the hands of Jews, who did not hide their ancestry. Several of the associates of Voivode (Provincial Governor) Eugeniusz Iwańczyk-Wiślicz were of Jewish origin. (According to Piotr Jakucki, the GL-AL leader Eugeniusz Iwańczyk—"Stary Jakub," "Wiślicz"—habitually denounced both Jews and Poles to the Gestapo in Kielce during the war.] The head of the WUBP was Adam Kornecki, the deputy-chief of the County Office of State Security (Powiatowy Urząd Bezpieczeństwa Publicznego, or PUBP) was Albert Grynbaum, the first secretary of the Provincial Committee of the Polish Workers' Party (Komitet Wojewódzki Polskiej Partii Robotniczej, or KW PPR was Józef Kalinowski, the secretary of the Department of Civil Servants was Edka Eisenman, the director of the Organizational Department of the PPR was Julian Lewin, the town president was Tadeusz Zarecki.[335]

A leaflet disseminated by the Polish underground during an attack on the Kielce prison stated: "The present government is not the government of national unity.... At the helm are found Jews and Soviet lackeys (*sługusy*) who take their orders from Stalin."[336] That "helm," it may be supposed, was in the hands of people like Jakub Berman, Hilary Minc, and Roman Zambrowski. Although Bierut and Radkiewicz were often included on that list as well, they were the "Soviet *sługusy*." Indeed, the system was full of Soviet "advisors," "specialists," "instructors," and "observers." In Kielce, as elsewhere in Poland, the communist régime was often equated with the "rule of the Jews"—and the Jews with the rule of the communist régime—hence the stereotype, the dominant idea, the perception, and the mythical reality: "All Jews are communists and all communists are Jews."

In fact, even the local Polish communists complained of favoritism when it came to the Jews. For example, when Zarecki was thrown out of the party by the Kielce chapter of the PPR for his corrupt practices, he was immediately reinstated by the Central Committee (KC) of the PPR.[337] Indeed, the local Polish communists' resentment toward the Jewish communists has led Krzysztof Kąkolewski, who has been gathering information on the Kielce pogrom for the past five years and who published his findings in a work, *Umarły cmentarz* (Dead Cemetery), just before the fiftieth anniversary of this tragic episode, to conclude that this was the main reason Kielce was selected by the Soviet authorities as the site for the 1946 pogrom.[338]

Moreover, the UB was not well disposed toward the Poles of Kielce, and vice versa. The provincial governor noted in a report dated October 1945, "...The functionaries of the Security Office in Kielce express themselves inappropriately towards the Polish population using, for example, such words as, 'I will shoot all of you Poles here' (*Ja tu was Polaków wszystkich powystrzelam*)."[339]

On April 19, 1945, Kielce observed the second anniversary of the Warsaw Ghetto Revolt. Unfortunately, the communist press took advantage of this occasion to launch another smear campaign against the AK—a double message not lost on the patriotic readers. When Ludwik Krzymiński and Kazimierz Markwita entered the domicile of Felicja Kwiatkowska (Fajgel Krongold) in Ostrowiec Świętokrzyski and opened fire, killing four and wounding others, their deed was attributed to the NSZ and "fascist elements in the AK."[340]

Tension mounted. That same April, eighteen Jews were murdered in five attacks throughout the province of Kielce. In June, thirteen more died in ten attacks. In October 1945, a grenade was thrown into the Jewish Center at Planty Street in the town of Kielce, and some people were injured.[341]

On June 30, 1946, a referendum — essentially a vote of confidence/no confidence in the new régime — was held in Poland. According to unofficial PPS and even PPR sources, the result was a 70 to 83 percent vote against the PPR, a count that was subsequently falsified by the communist régime, which said just the opposite. On July 6, Gomułka proclaimed a victory for the "democratic camp."[342]

Just before the pogrom (July 4) and the official announcement of the results, a majority of the formidable KBW forces deployed in Kielce and the vicinity to ensure order during the referendum were withdrawn, and vicious rumors of blood-libel, so characteristic of Russian-inspired pogroms, and of missing children were circulated in Kielce.[343] On July 1, a nine-year-old Kielce boy, Henryk Błaszczyk, disappeared, only to reappear on the evening of July 3 — the eve of the day on which the falsified results of the referendum were to be officially reported[344] and on which the Nuremberg Tribunal was to begin its hearings on Katyn. Among the evidence to be considered by the tribunal was the material, provided by officers of General Anders' army, implicating the Soviets in the massacre.[345]

After his return, Henryk was manipulated by two people (Antoni Pasowski and Jan Dygnarowicz) and stated that he had been abducted by the Jews. At 11:00 P.M. (July 3) Henryk's father took his son to the local police station and reported the incident. He was told to return with the boy in the morning. (For the rest of the "official" story, see Appendix, Document 9, "Chronology of the Kielce Pogrom, July 4, 1946").[346]

On July 4, as Western diplomats and correspondents in Poland gathered at Hotel Polonia for festivities in commemoration of America's independence, they were informed about the events occurring in Kielce.[347] The pogrom lasted from 10:00 A.M. until 5:00 P.M. By the time it was over, 42 Jews and 2 Poles were dead, over 50 people were injured, fewer than 100 were arrested, and 12 were indicted. Of the last group, 9 were executed, 1 received a life sentence, and the other 2 received prison terms of ten years and seven years. Meanwhile, as news of the alleged abduction and blood-libel spread, some 30 other Jews were killed in train stations and on trains in the Kielce area on the day of the pogrom at 7 Planty Street.

Interestingly enough, in 1946, neither the Polish communist régime nor the opposition had considered the July 4 events in Kielce to have been a result of spontaneous mob action. Ambassador Arthur Bliss Lane noted, "Although the violence of the pogrom might have given the impression that the tragic happening was due primarily to uncontrolled racial passions, both government and antigovernment sources admitted that it was not spontaneous, but a carefully organized plot."[348]

According to Gomułka, Berman, Korczyński, and others, the pogrom was staged by the Polish underground (including the NSZ and the WiN) in conjunction with the opposition Polish (noncommunist) People's Party (Polskie Stronnictwo Ludowe, or PSL) and the western Polish émigrés (including members of Anders' army), who, in their disappointment over the referendum results, attempted to launch a civil war. Since the trial that followed produced no evidence to implicate any of the above-mentioned organizations and since, as we will see shortly, this thesis would have required the close cooperation of the anti-communist underground and the very forces established by the communist régime to liquidate it, this position was quickly abandoned.[349]

On the other hand, PSL representatives such as Stefan Korboński and Stanisław Mikołajczyk — together with PPS activists such as Adam Pragier — accused the UB of organizing the pogrom, with the full knowledge and consent of Moscow, in order to compromise Poland in the international arena and to draw attention away from the falsified referendum. This position was also taken by Arthur Bliss Lane.[350]

Iwo Cyprian Pogonowski gives yet another reason for the staging of the Kielce pogrom by the communists: "It is well known that the Soviets systematically used to their advantage the desire of Jews to fight for the establishment of the state of Israel. The Soviet aim was to get rid of the British mandate in Palestine and play a more active role in the oil-rich Middle East. Towards this end they committed numerous acts of terror to pressure Jews to emigrate and join the struggle for Israel."[351]

Among those said to have been responsible for orchestrating the Kielce pogrom were the chief of the UB in Kielce, Major Władysław Sobczyński (a.k.a. Spychaj, a prewar Soviet spy known as "Władek" and "Jurand" in the AL), and Mikhail A. Dyomin (or Demin), a high-ranking Soviet intelligence officer and expert in Jewish affairs who "just happened" to be present in Kielce at the time. Sobczyński was the organizer of the failed pogrom in Rzeszów and probably of the one that occurred Kraków. (These Soviet-organized pogroms failed to make international headlines because of a much larger story: the dropping of the atomic bomb on Hiroshima and Nagasaki on August 6 and 9, 1945, respectively.) Sobczyński was also implicated in the murder of Władysław Kojder, a member of the executive committee of the PSL. Dyomin had been sent to Kielce several months before the pogrom, and he left two weeks after it was over.[352]

Other important officers in the employ of the Soviets were also in Kielce at the time of the pogrom: Sztablewski and Adam Humer, from the Ministry of State Security (Ministerstwo Bezpieczeństwa Publicznego, or MBP); Shpilevoi, a Soviet advisor to the Kielce UB; and Hilary Chełchowski and Władysław Buczyński, two special envoys of the Central Committee of the Polish Workers' Party (Komitet Centralny Polskiej Partii Robotniczej, or KC PPR) — to name but a few. The first two came to Kielce as referendum advisors. The last pair came to Kielce straight from Warsaw to observe the pogrom. Judging by the time of their arrival in Kielce (around noon on July 4), they would have had to have left Warsaw between 9:00 and 9:30 A.M. — at a time when the "spontaneous" pogrom they went to observe had not yet begun.[353]

Additional circumstantial evidence links the UB to the pogrom. According to the evidence presented by Michael Checinski (a former counterintelligence officer who emigrated from Poland to Israel in 1969), Henryk's father — Walenty Błaszczyk — may have been a paid UB informant and possibly an NSZ infiltrator as well. The pogrom, according to Checinski, was planned by the Soviet advisors present in Kielce at the time.[354]

During the pogrom, the communist-controlled militia, the military, and the UB seemed to do everything possible not to avert a tragedy but rather to ensure its occurrence. As if to guarantee the presence of a mob, the militia sent to investigate the allegations against the Jews residing on Planty Street told people they met along the way about the "abduction" of the nine-year-old boy by the Jews.[355]The pogrom began not on the street but the minute that the soldiers and militia entered the Jewish Center — yet at the trial that followed, nothing was said about their role in the pogrom. The militia and military first disarmed, then beat, bayoneted, and shot the Jews, threw them out of second-story windows and off the balcony, and forcibly led them from the building and handed them over to the waiting crowd.

According to Kąkolewski, the following militia-military units were present in Kielce during the action against the Jews at the Jewish Center: two partially filled companies of the KBW; individual units of the 4th infantry regiment; two infantry divisions from Kielce; functionaries of the Commissariat of the Civil Militia (MO) located at Sienkiewicz Street and other commissariats; county and provincial MO units; members of the militia and UB schools; an élite guard platoon in charge of protecting UB buildings; Information (Informacja) officers of the WP; and prison guards. "It was, therefore," states Kąkolewski, "a full mobilization of forces. Not all of them entered the building; most of them formed a cordon around it."[356]

The following testimonies shed additional light on just who was responsible for the murder of the Jews at 7 Planty Street. The first of these witnesses, Albert Grynbaum, was himself, later murdered, while returning home from testifying at a follow-up trial in Warsaw. At first, the authorities attributed his murder to the WiN. When it became known that the WiN no longer existed at the time of his murder, the deed was attributed to the WiN remnants who were trying to rebuild their organization. According to Kąkolewski, however, "everything points to the fact that the murder was committed by the UB dressed like partisans."[357]

> *Albert Grynbaum:* I gathered about 40 Jews in a room [on the first floor] and did not allow the soldiers to enter. I turned to [the soldiers] and told them that their task was to keep order on the street not to conduct searches. After checking the stock [of firearms] the soldiers together with their subordinates went to the second floor. A few minutes later two Jews came to me and said that the soldiers were killing the Jews and robbing their belongings ... the first victims were on the second floor to which only the soldiers had access.[358]
>
> *Mordko Grinewize:* I heard yelling on the street and after a while bullets came flying through the door.... [There is some controversy as to whether it was the soldiers or the Jews who fired the first shot.] I was on the second floor. After penetrating the door, the bullets hit two Jews (killing one and wounding another). They called to us from behind the closed doors to give ourselves up or else they would throw grenades [into the room]. ... I answered that we would surrender.... When I went outside, the soldiers beat me.[359]
>
> *Berek Fajtel:* [Out on the street] the soldiers began to beat me ... with rifle butts until I fell to the ground.[360]
>
> *Baruch Dorfman:* ...The others who were led out with me were pierced by bayonets, shot, hit by rocks. I fell, lost consciousness, regained my senses from time to time.... One of them wanted to shoot me ... but I heard the voice of another: "Don't shoot. He'll die (*zdechnie*) anyway."[361]
>
> *Grynbaum:* A man was thrown onto the street from the second floor. A soldier came over to the dead victim and kicked him in the head in the presence of the crowd. Then among the gathered ... people, shouts were heard: "Don't be afraid of the soldiers, they're on our side."[362]
>
> *Ewa Szuchman:* The militia threw two Jewish girls over the balcony on the second floor into the street and the crowd below finished them off.[363]
>
> *Israel Terkieltaub:* Soon three army lieutenants arrived. At that moment I was in the room of Dr. [Seweryn] Kahane, the chairman of the congregation [Jewish Community]. When the officers entered the room, Dr. Kahane had the [telephone] receiver in his hand and was trying to get in touch with the city, but by then the telephone was out of order. The officers said they had come to take away the arms, which some of the Jews had permission to carry. One of them came to Dr. Kahane and told him to keep calm because everything would soon be over ... and then he crept up on him from behind and shot him at close range through the head.[364]
>
> *Ewa Szuchman recalled that after the Jews were taken to the stadium, one of the military types said:* "Why did you bring them here? You should have wiped them out."[365]
>
> *A witness:* [Markiewicz] ...himself... pushed people away, and at a certain moment proposed that the crowd would choose a delegation to investigate whether there were any murdered [Polish] children in the [Jewish] building. This suggestion of Markiewicz resulted in the crowd surging into the interior of the building.[366] [Many witnesses reported the presence of civilians on the first floor of the building.]
>
> *Jechiel Alpert to Shpilevoi on the phone:* I tell him there is danger, something might happen. I beg for help. And he says that he can do nothing because he does not have any units in Polish uniforms, only Russian, and that later it would be said that the Russians were killing the Poles — he cannot send anyone.[367]

Kąkolewski maintains that uniformed strangers (i.e., people unknown to the locals) appeared in the crowd at 7 Planty Street in "battle dress." Some of the uniforms had the word "Poland" (in English) on the upper arm. He has thus far identified only three of these strangers by name. One of them was a UB functionary, another was the son of a UB functionary, and the third was a prison guard. Kąkolewski notes Shpilevoi's answer to Jechiel Alpert and asks, "Why was there a dearth of Polish uniforms and where were those who wore them?"[368]

Moreover, among the crowd were also strangers in civilian clothes. Two of these were women who mingled in the crowd, asked questions about referendum voting, and placed chalk marks on people's backs. Those so marked were later discreetly removed by the UB. One of these women was from Warsaw; the other later admitted that she took part in "operational work during the pogrom in Kielce." "Even as the crimes were being committed," notes Kąkolewski, "alibis were being prepared and victims were being selected to stand in front of the firing squad in lieu of the real murderers."[369]

In that crowd, again according to Kąkolewski, were also two special units of men organized by the communist régime to commit murders for which the Polish underground was to bear the blame. They too were dressed in civilian clothes. The first group was an MBP unit founded in the summer of 1945; the second, founded on June 17, 1946, consisted of officers and NCOs of the Polish army. They were sent to Kielce ostensibly to "safeguard the referendum." Nevertheless, they were not withdrawn after the referendum was over. It was these "civilians" who were allowed inside the Jewish Center on 7 Planty Street, which was under heavy military guard.[370]

Sobczyński and Shpilevoi were at the scene of the pogrom. Sobczyński, who arrived there around 10:30, soon returned to his office. When two UB officers, Edward Kwasek and Jan Mucha, came to tell him about the behavior of the crowd and the soldiers and to find out why, in spite of all the phone calls and pleas for help, no reinforcements had been sent, they found him sitting, completely relaxed, on the sofa. They asked him: "And what is the Major doing? After all we are all going to have to answer for it; there's a mass of people out there!" Then they observed, "Major Sobczyński who always gave the impression of being an energetic person, was quite calm and collected on that day."[371]

While all this was going on, the militia also went to the home of Regina and Abram Fisz at 15 Leonarda Street, where a crowd had gathered, to search for arms. One of them wore a military uniform. Stefan Mazur was in charge of the search. After the search, members of the Fisz family, together with Abram Moszkowicz, who was in the house that day, were led outside. Regina (twenty-four years old) pleaded for her life, offered money and jewelry, and promised never to return to Kielce. The money was taken from her, and as the militia consulted on the matter, the family attempted to escape. Moszkowicz witnessed how Mazur shot Regina (Abram Fisz was also killed) and her three-week-old child. Asked in court whether he aimed or fired blindly, Mazur replied: "I aimed. I am a good shot. I can hit a man at half a kilometer." Asked why he killed the child, he replied cold-bloodedly: "Although it was sad, it had to be done. What's to be done when there's no mother? Must the child cry?"[372]

The soldiers and the militia were aided by the agitated mob, which also beat and killed some of the Jews. The arrival (around 12:30 P.M.) of the 600 steelworkers from "Ludwików" resulted, according to Grynbaum, in another fifteen to twenty deaths.[373] According to Kąkolewski, the workers who were allowed to break through the cordon around 7 Planty Street consisted of handpicked members of the PPR-ORMO (Ochotnicza Rezerwa Milicji Obywatelskiej, or Volunteer Reserve of the Civil Militia) from the steelworks factory. Some of them were hired just before the pogrom and never returned to work after it was over. They were organized by the factory ORMO leader and were given instructions to arm themselves with steel rods and to go to the Jewish Center in order to settle accounts with the Jews. "That this group had a paramilitary character and was under the direction of the ORMO," states Kąkolewski, "becomes clear due to the fact (one of many) that when the director of the factory, engineer Soból, placed himself at the gate in the way of the marching unit, he was removed to the side without being injured. He was a Jew, and they all knew it." Apparently, the victims of the factory workers were not to be just any Jews but the Jews at 7 Planty Street. Moreover, the size of this marching unit was greatly exaggerated. According to Kąkolewski, there were not 600 but about 60. Among them, at least one of the recent factory hirees carried a TT-type revolver. In those days, the penalty for bearing arms without authorization was five years to life.[374]

Unbelievable as it may sound, the UB officers — and there were many of them of various ranks present throughout the day — refused to take charge of the situation either before or after the arrival of the steelworkers and gave no orders. Public prosecutor Jan Wrzeszcz, who was in the middle of it all, described the diabolically planned chaos:

> When I asked who was in charge, I was told that there are several units and each of them is acting on its own. Colonel Kuźnicki introduced me to some lieutenant-colonel of the Polish army [Wojsko Polskie, or WP] but he told me that that was no concern of a prosecutor and to stay out of it. I turned to the officer standing beside me and said that the crowd should be dispersed. One should be prepared to use firearms. I was told rather brusquely that no one will issue such an order and that the soldiers would not carry it out anyway. The soldier standing near the officer verified this by saying that enough blood had already been spilled. It dawned on me that one could not count on any energetic action on the part of the army and so I suggested that all the threatened Jews should be taken away in cars. They would not agree to this either.[375]

In other words, no one was in charge, and very little was done to quell the riot (aside from the attempt to use fire hoses, which were soon cut by the mob). And yet, a glance at the street map of Kielce reveals that all the essential elements of effective crowd control were present literally within blocks of 7 Planty Street: the Commissariat of the Civil Militia (MO), the Provincial Office of State Security (WUPB), the headquarters of the 2nd Infantry Division, the fire department, and the Militia School with its cadets, which was the farthest away — a mere ten-minute march.[376]

According to various witnesses, a crowd of 200 to 300 people gathered in front of 7 Planty Street, on the bridge over Silnica River, and on the other side of that river as well. This in itself is both remarkable and incredible, since from the end of the war until 1956 it was illegal for civilians to gather in unauthorized crowds no matter what the reason. (One characteristically Polish cartoon from those days portrays a policeman telling an individual standing idly on a street corner to "disperse.") Evidently, the Kielce crowd was allowed to gather at 7 Planty Street because it was *needed* there. The authorities knew full well the danger that the crowd posed to the occupants of the Jewish Center.

To this incomplete listing of circumstantial evidence for Soviet involvement in the pogrom can be added the manifold courtroom improprieties that occurred during the first trial, which began only five days after the pogrom: the trial of civilians by a (Supreme) Military Court, which deliberately steered clear of implicating any military types in the crimes; the appointment of defense attorneys by the court to represent all the accused at once; the beating and terrorization of the accused (two of the accused, Józef Pokrzywiński and Józef Kukliński, stated as much in court);[377] the deliberate miscount of the victims who had been shot during the pogrom (the official court records state that ten persons sustained gunshot wounds, but in reality there were seventeen, and of these, nine — including two Poles — died[378]); the inability of defense attorneys to contact the accused, to call defense witnesses, to review the case, to make proper preparation, or to question any military types appearing as witnesses; the coercion of the defense attorneys into submitting an immediate appeal and plea for a reprieve, in violation of standard procedures; the swiftness of the proceedings and the verdict, which was rendered outside the courtroom (two and a half days in all, from July 9 to July 11, 1:15 P.M.); the arrival of a firing squad from Warsaw even before the sentence was rendered; the closed Military Court session the following day in Warsaw, during which, in the absence of the defense attorneys, the appeal and the plea for mercy were denied; the quick execution of the eleven prisoners that same day; and the failure to notify the attorneys or the families of the condemned of the execution.

There were also improprieties in the court sessions that followed. For example, in the November 18 trial, five of the accused—Henryk Symkiewicz, Eugeniusz Krawczyk, Jan Soboń, Michał Stępień, and Kazimierz Redliński—were beaten and terrorized.[379] Soon after the proceedings, a veil of silence regarding the Kielce incident was imposed on all publications—a silence that remained unbroken until Krystyna Kersten's December 4, 1981, article on Kielce in *Tygodnik Solidarność*.[380] Finally, at least four persons who "knew too much [about the Kielce pogrom] and did not want to keep it to themselves" have mysteriously disappeared, and in 1989—the year of Poland's liberation—the Kielce Security Service [Służba Bezpieczeństwa, or SB] archives from 1945–54 were destroyed during a suspicious twelve-hour blaze.[381]

On September 19, 1946, Ambassador Lane informed the secretary of state in Washington, "On September 1, 1946 Monsignor Kaczmarek, Bishop of Kielce, handed [me] an eighteen-page report in Polish giving the point of view of members of the Roman Catholic Hierarchy with regard to the Kielce incident." With the memorandum, Ambassador Lane enclosed a summary prepared by a member of his staff and added that it "should be of interest to the Department in view of the conclusions contained therein." The summary of the Polish memorandum reads as follows:

CONFIDENTIAL

September 6, 1946

MEMORANDUM FOR THE AMBASSADOR:

In accordance with your instructions I have examined the 18-page memorandum prepared by the Polish clergy concerning the incident at Kielce on July 4, 1946.

This document gives an entirely different picture of the incident, of the background leading up to it and the aftermath than that given by the Polish press. It gives a picture similar to that which Mr. Dillon and I brought back from Kielce as the result of our visit to that city on the Saturday following the incident, which we described to you in a separate memorandum, at that time.

The present document goes into much greater detail and describes the events leading up to the incident, the incident itself and the aftermath step by step with dates, times, names and places but does not change the story as we have it.

The memorandum points out that there was no anti–semitism in Poland during the German occupation, on the contrary the Polish population often aided the persecuted Jewish population to avoid mistreatment by the Germans. However, the memorandum points out, this changed when the Jews commenced taking over important posts in Poland in Government offices, in the U.B., in factories, the censorship bureau, Polish Embassies and Consulates, the press. The additional fact that Jews are the chief propagators of Communism in Poland has created an antipathy in Poland to the Jews who have remained in the country or recently arrived in it.

In addition, a number of children actually disappeared from Kielce during the months preceding the July 4 incident and rumors ascribed this to Jews. The fact that the militia, to which the disappearances were reported, seemingly took no action, confirmed the suspicion that Jews in Poland were inviolable.

The memorandum points out that the court procedure violated the regulations governing court procedure in many ways and endeavors to prove that the entire trial was prearranged and not in accordance with ordinary and regular requirements. The boy, who made the original complaint, was not at the trial, a special team of military judges was brought from Warsaw to Kielce in connection with the trial and foreign newspaper correspondents were also brought to watch the allegedly well-rehearsed proceedings in the courtroom. In order to increase the number of accused, those accused for the Kielce incident were tried at a joint trial with others, accused of banditism but who had no connection with the Kielce affair.

The lawyers, appointed by the authorities to defend the accused, were given only 24 hours to prepare a defense and the accused heard the text of the indictment only an hour prior to commencement of the trial. The court refused to examine witnesses suggested by the defense and refused to permit discussion of extenuating circumstances. The tribunal was a military court but three of the defense lawyers were civil court lawyers not familiar with military court procedure. One of the accused was wounded and another stated he had been beaten during grilling.

The memorandum goes to considerable length to explain the role of the Roman Catholic clergy, its continual condemnation of violence, its attempts to quieten the populace, its proclamations to the people of Kielce.

The conclusions of the memorandum are that "certain Jewish communist factors" in collaboration with the local U.B. decided to arrange a pogrom to show that Poland is unsafe, that it is anti–semitic, that the Church is reactionary, that it is urgent to arrange for emigration of Jews from Poland. Instead of stopping the small original commotion on Planty Street, the authorities are accused of practically throwing the Jews in the building out in the street into the hands of an excited mob, which beat them and tore them from limb to limb. The murderers in the mob included militiamen, soldiers, workers from a nearby factory and incidental passersby, PPR members. Since revelation of the truth would compromise the government in the eyes of the domestic population and in the eyes of foreign countries, many details had to be omitted in the court procedure. The press and the government, according to the memorandum, prearranged all the details.

In the opinion of the memorandum those that created the circumstances which led up to the Kielce incident should also have been on the defendants' bench. Polish opinion knows who they are and they are condemned for creating division among the Polish people and giving Poland a bad name abroad.

[Signature]
S. D. Zagórski[382]

In due time, the 1979 report of the Polish Accord of Independence (Polskie Porozumienie Niepodległościowe, or PPN), an underground organization of intellectuals founded in 1976, may yet prove to be correct in its assessment of the Kielce pogrom: that it was part of a long-range Soviet policy in Poland to discredit the Polish underground and the Polish nation with charges of anti–Semitism. This report states:

> The latter [anti–Semitism] was revived in 1946 when, in order to justify the failure of the U.S.S.R. to honor the obligations it had entered into with the Western powers, the NKVD (Soviet Security Service) and the UB (Polish Security Service) organized the so-called Kielce pogrom, a mass murder of Jews. Their intention was to represent Poland as a nation of racists, quite incapable of governing themselves.[383]

In 1990 the director of the infamous Tenth Department of the Ministry of Internal Affairs, Anatol Fejgin, a close associate of Bierut, Berman, and Radkiewicz, was asked by Henryk Piecuch about the 1946 referendum, the pogroms in Rzeszów and Kielce, and the methods used in combating the PSL and Mikołajczyk. He responded as follows:

> There are no holds barred if one wants to defeat an uncompromising opponent. After the war, after those terrible experiences of Poland and the Poles, we could not forgo this great trump card which would gain us new followers. Anti-German leaflets, posters and slogans appeared.... We exploited anti-Semitic moods in yet another way. It is still not the time to talk about it. We counted on a mistake by our opponents. Eventually, they had to make it. But we could wait no longer. We needed some catalyst [*przyspieszacz*]. Hence the pogroms and other stratagems.[384]

So there we have it! Kielce was a mere stratagem in the struggle for political power, whose victims were both Jews and Poland. Michał Borwicz notes, "If, as much of the circumstantial evidence seems to suggest, the postwar pogroms, with the Kielce incident at their head, were the consequence of Soviet provocation, intended to turn Western opinion against Poland during those crucial and difficult years, then it must be admitted that the provocations succeeded, and beyond the hopes of the provocateurs."[385]

But perhaps the incidents were the result not so much of Soviet "provocation" as of a deliberately planned and executed *program* of pogroms in Poland and other captive nations (e.g., in Hungary and Czechoslovakia).[386]

Meanwhile, the thousands who gaze daily on the Kielce pogrom mural, so prominently displayed in the U.S. Holocaust Memorial Museum's permanent collection, will continue to wonder how the Polish people could have done such a terrible thing to the survivors of the Holocaust.

A related question is often asked by those who readily admit the possibility of Soviet complicity in the Kielce pogrom: How was it possible to incite the Polish people to do such a terrible thing? The answer to that question lies in the wealth of information provided by the social sciences on the art of propaganda, persuasion, and crowd manipulation — a topic on which the Soviets were experts. Once the specific details are known, Kielce may yet prove to be a classic example of the plying of that art and of the successful coverup that followed and that continues to this day.

At the end of January 1996, the Polish minister of foreign affairs, Dariusz Rosati, a former communist, apologized to the World Jewish Congress for Polish anti-Semitism and Kielce. "The new democratic Poland deeply regrets and mourns all the injustice suffered by the Jewish people," said the minister. "In 1996, we shall shed tears over the victims of the infamous Kielce pogrom which was committed 50 years ago during the chaos of the Polish civil war."[387] What Polish civil war? asks Kąkolewski.[388] And more important, who will apologize to the Polish people for the long, absolute, despotic, and cruel communist rule that made events like Kielce possible?

Just before the Kielce incident, during the exchange of populations between the Soviet Union and Poland, a Polish representative in Biłka Szlachecka, a Jew, thanked the Soviet Union in the name of the Polish people for allowing them to live on Russian soil, for providing them with the opportunity to work there, and for saving them from the Germans. (This was just before the Poles of Biłka Szlachecka were forced to apply for Soviet passports. Because they refused, they were not given any food rations for ten days. When they arrived in central Poland, they were filthy, in rags, shirtless, and hungry.[389]) Biłka Szlachecka was located in Poland's eastern territories. During the war, the Poles in this village, at the risk of their own lives, had hidden five Jewish families from the murderous Ukrainian policemen who were then exterminating the Biłkan Jews on Łysa Góra (Bald Mountain).[390]

Earlier, in February 1945, Piotr Sender — a Jew in the uniform of a Polish officer, a member of the Union of Polish Patriots in Moscow — said to the crowd gathered in Biłka Szlachecka: "This is the Ukraine. A good Pole goes back to Poland.... He who does not return to Poland willingly will be sent to Siberia by force."[391]

Perhaps Simon Wiesenthal's summary of wartime collaboration and postwar Polish-Jewish relations is the best:

> Then the war came. It is in times like these that the lower elements in society surface — the *szmalcownicy* (blackmailers) who would betray Jews for a bottle of vodka or a pair of shoes. That was one aspect. On the other hand the 30 or 40,000 Jews who survived, survived thanks to help from Poles. This I know. But on the other hand, whenever I am talking on this subject I always say that I know what kind of role Jewish communists played in Poland after the war. And just as I, as a Jew, do not want to shoulder responsibility for the Jewish communists, I cannot blame 36 million Poles for those thousands of *szmalcownicy*.[392]

After all these years, what should we Poles and Jews, we who now have so little in common, tell our children about Polish-Jewish relations during World War II and the decade that followed? Perhaps only this: that we suffered together — and that some of us were bitter enemies and some of us were dear friends, but that most of us just worried about today and tomorrow and tried to get by as best we could in the land we both called home.

Chapter 5
Belorussian Collaboration

The 1921 Soviet-Polish Treaty of Riga divided Belorussia into two parts, the larger of which — containing the majority of the Belorussian population — fell to the Soviets. According to Jerzy Tomaszewski's 1931 adjusted census figures, there were 5,108,700 people in the four northeastern provinces of Poland, namely Polesie, Nowogródek, Białystok, and Wilno. Of these, 2,251,000 were Polish, 1,948,000 were Belorussian, 505,000 were Jewish, 101,000 were Russian, 83,000 were Lithuanian, and 9,000 were German. The Belorussians, then, represented about 38 percent of the total population in the Polish territories that later became, in part or in whole, annexed to the Belorussian SSR. They were distributed as follows: Polesie, 654,000; Nowogródek, 616,000; Wilno, 409,000; Białystok, 269,100. In Nowogródek and Polesie, the number of Belorussians exceeded the number of Poles. In Białystok and Wilno, the case was just the opposite. According to the official, but unreliable, census for 1931, Poles exceeded Belorussians in all four provinces.[1] In September 1939, these Soviet-occupied territories increased the total area of Soviet Belorussia by 85 percent (from 127,000 to 235,000 square kilometers) and almost doubled its population.

The Belorussians were mainly poor peasants who lived on the land. At this time, they were untroubled by nationalistic aspirations. The Poles, loyal to their country, inhabited the towns, especially Wilno, but also owned large estates and lived in the villages. The Russians lived in the far northern reaches of the province, although there was also a sizeable colony of them in Wilno itself. The Lithuanians inhabited small villages strung out along the Polish-Lithuanian border. As in the rest of Poland, the Jews lived in the towns and prospered.

After their success in Russia, the Bolsheviks wasted no time in spreading their revolution abroad. The Communist Workers' Party of Poland (Komunistyczna Partia Robotnicza Polski, or KPRP) was founded in December 1918. At its second convention in 1923, the KPRP created two autonomous political parties, the Communist Party of Western Ukraine (Komunistyczna Partia Zachodniej Ukrainy, or KPZU) and the Communist Party of Western Belorussia (Komunistyczna Partia Zachodniej Białorusi, or KPZB). The unofficial name of "Western Belorussia" hails from that date. In 1925 the name of the KPRP was changed to the Polish Communist Party (Komunistyczna Partia Polski, or KPP).[2]

Life for the Belorussians in the Polish portion of Belorussia may have left a lot to be desired during the interwar years, but in comparison with life in the eastern portion at this time and what was to follow, the situation in Polish Belorussia was sheer paradise. According to the estimate of Zenon Pozniak, in Soviet Belorussia during the Stalinist *proces monstrum* of the 1930s, over half a million people, mostly Belorussians, lost their lives.[3]

Surprisingly, many devoted communists, members of the KPZB who sought shelter in the USSR, were also purged. For example, in October 1935, an NKVD special forces unit surrounded a KPZB party-sabotage school on the outskirts of Minsk and, after arresting everyone, shot all of the leaders and most of the "students" as well.[4] In the mind of the Soviets, the

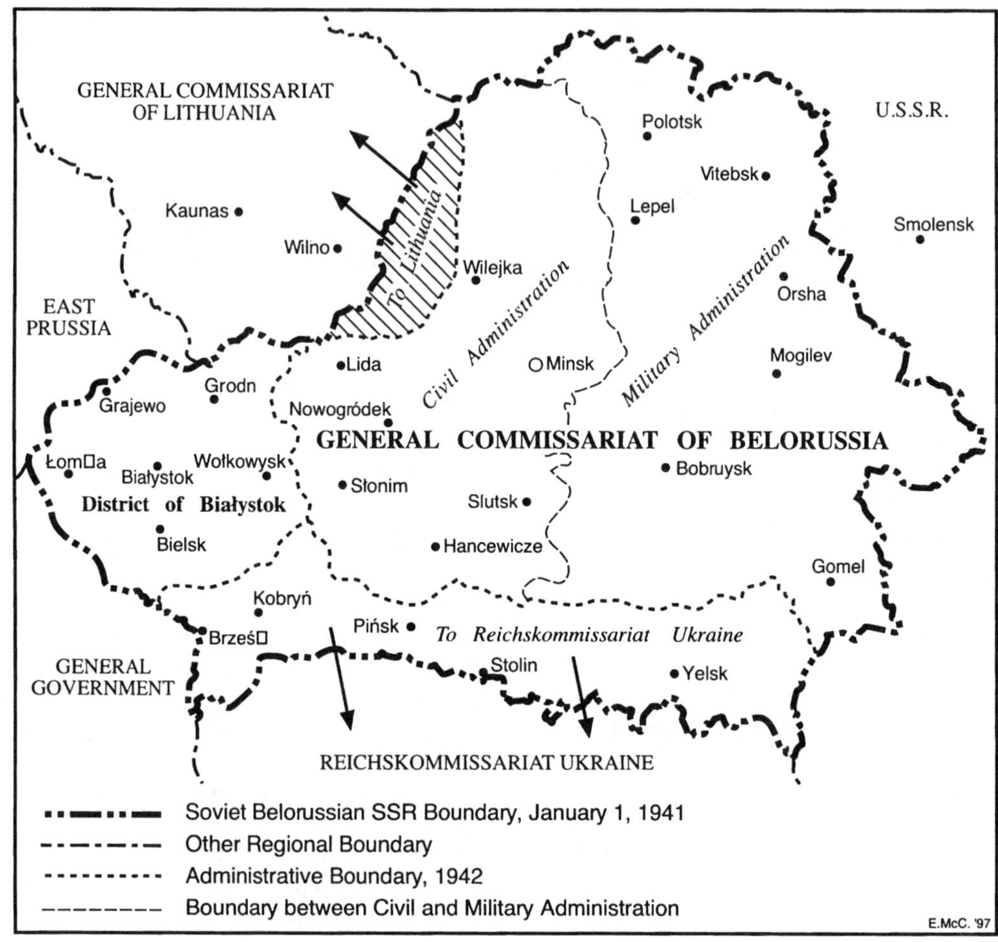

Belorussia under German Occupation, 1942

KPZB was seen as a child of Polish counterintelligence. That the KPZB was also persecuted by the Polish authorities did not seem to matter. Undoubtedly, the real and only reason for the purges was simply to terrorize the eastern Belorussians into absolute conformity. By 1938, the membership of communist parties in Poland was so low that they were all dissolved by the Comintern.

Soviet Occupation

By September 17, 1939, the pacification of Soviet Belorussia was over, and thanks to both Soviet and Polish policies, the emergent Belorussian national movement, including its communist offshoot, was considerably weakened, though it did not quite expire. After a nine-day struggle between the Red Army and the Polish armed forces, Belorussia was reunited and, together with substantial tracts of ethnically Polish territory, on the basis of a carefully orchestrated referendum, became another Soviet Socialist Republic.[5] Those nine days of struggle were portrayed by Soviet historians as a "victory of socialist revolution in the western regions of Belorussia."[6] A year after that "historic campaign," Corps Commissar S. Kozhevnikov wrote:

> The working population of the Western Ukraine and Western Byelorussia immediately perceived the arrival of the Red Army as a liberation from the oppression of the Polish Pans. Therefore every meeting of the

> workers with our units turned into a thrilling demonstration of solidarity and fraternity. The population gave great assistance to its liberator — the Red Army. The workers and peasants repaired bridges destroyed by the departing Polish army, caught the provocateurs and spies, and disarmed soldiers and officers.[7]

Although this depiction is surely a product of Soviet hype and propaganda, it does point to a curious truth: at least some Belorussians welcomed the Soviet invasion and even actively participated in the "liberation" of "Western Belorussia" from the Polish "*pany.*" The previously quoted child's recollections of his experience in Białystok are worth repeating: "The arrival of Russians in Poland was sad, and joyful. For some Jews, Belorussians, and Ukrainians it was joyful. And for the Poles it was sad and hard."[8]

Many sources, both Soviet and non-Soviet, note that the Red Army was enthusiastically greeted by the Belorussian population, that triumphal arches were erected, and that local Belorussians (referred to in Soviet literature as Belorussian "partisan units") overpowered the Polish authorities in Skidel (20 kilometers east of Grodno), arrested Polish people, and fought at the side of the Red Army in Grodno, in the Zelwa region, in Polesie, and in other places as well.[9] They willingly assisted the Soviets in disarming captured Polish military units.[10] Jan Wszędobył recalled how in Nowa Ruda (Grodno county), "Belorussian bands" ambushed Polish soldiers. General Stefan Grot-Rowecki explained why the situation of the Poles in the east was worse than that of the Poles in the GG: "In the Soviet-occupied territories, the work is significantly more difficult than in the General Government. This is due most of all to the fact that the Bolsheviks have at their disposal a significantly more numerous police apparatus, understand the Polish language, and receive much help from the local elements: Ukrainians, Belorussians, and especially Jews."[11] Jan Tomasz Gross notes:

> For the record it must be stated unambiguously: throughout the Western Ukraine and Western Belorussia, in hamlets, villages, and towns, the Red Army was welcomed by smaller or larger but, in any case, visible, friendly crowds. These were largely composed of young people from the so-called ethnic minorities — Belorussians, Jews, and Ukrainians. But since ethnic minorities were a majority in these lands, such welcoming committees were truly scattered all over the invaded territory. The crowds had built triumphal arches and put up red banners (it was enough to cut off the white stripe from the Polish national flag to make one) or yellow-and-blue ones; in Kleck a mixed crowd came out hoisting a church banner, and "in the confusing elation communist songs mixed with religious hymns." Entering troops were sometimes showered with flowers, embraced, and kissed; even tanks were kissed (Jews seemed to have a predilection for kissing tanks; somehow no one mentions Ukrainians or Belorussians doing this). They were greeted sometimes with bread and salt, a traditional gesture of hospitality.[12]

The tragic and largely unknown history of Grodno bears witness to the consequences of this collaboration. The city fell to the Red Army on the night of September 21, 1939. According to that day's Soviet communiqués, three Polish infantry divisions, two cavalry brigades, and various other units were captured and disarmed.[13] Then, according to witnesses, the Red Army began to apprehend and execute not only the remaining military personnel who did not evacuate Grodno or surrender but also ordinary civilians, especially the Polish youth who had taken part in the defense of the city. Among those killed were 130 Polish officers, soldiers, and high school students.[14]

> *Romuald Czuszel:* They [the Polish soldiers who remained in the city and were caught] were taken into captivity by the Soviets. They were led under heavy guard to the Franciscan monastery. The same fate befell the foresters and the railway employees.... Some of the prisoners, for reasons unknown but probably only because they were Polish, were shot by the monastery wall.[15]

> *Paweł Juszkiewicz:* Anyone who showed the least bit of resistance was shot.[16]

> *Janina Lenk:* I saw how they attached a young student by his feet to a tank and dragged him, head to the pavement, through the entire city. He died as a martyr.... That's how it was in the first few days.... I saw near Grodno, in a small forest called Poniemuń, very many cadavers of young cadets and students, shot because supposedly they took an active part in the defense of Grodno.[17]

> *Lesław Kiszyński:* Schoolchildren caught after 7:00 p.m. were taken to a jail and not even allowed an explanation. After a few days, they were led under convoy to the so-called "Dog's Hill" (Psia Góra). They were told to dig ditches, then they were all shot and another party covered the cadavers with dirt.[18]

> *Józef Repucha:* The Bolsheviks began the executions on the night of September 23. These executions were carried out on a massive scale with machine guns. Among those killed were women from PCK [Polish Red Cross] and school youth over 14 years of age.[19]

> *Karol Szlamka:* School youth and soldiers were shot on the streets of the city and in the region of the village Przesiółka. I saw the bodies of very many people who were not buried until October 4, 1939.[20]

According to witnesses, the perpetrators of these crimes were the Soviets and although the local communists (Belorussians and Jews) may have participated in some of the atrocities, they were mostly used to round up the victims. Bronisław Dowgiałło stated, "The local communist rabble was assigned the task of catching the youth."[21] Jews were reported to have shot at passers-by. According to Karol Liszewski (Ryszard Szawłowski), in some areas of "Western Belorussia" the local communists actually took part in the atrocities:

> We must also note the murders committed in these days and weeks in the district of Grodno and in further regions. They were perpetrated—with Soviet "blessing"—by local Belorussians and Jewish communists as well as the Soviets themselves. Supposedly, at that time, the Bolsheviks gave the local communists two weeks time in which to freely murder the so-called class enemies, in any case in the villages.[22]

How are we to explain this misguided (in light of what was bound to follow) enthusiasm and collaboration on the part of these Belorussians? In part, the reaction was due to the Polish interwar policies in "Western Belorussia," policies that were assimilationist and that, after 1924, became repressive. In 1924, there was strong reaction to the Belorussian separatist movement. Later, three hundred Belorussian schools were Polonized. In 1928, the Belorussian Hramada (Commune: a left-wing organization consisting of liberals, socialists, and communists) was brutally suppressed and its leaders were arrested. In the 1930s, Belorussia experienced Piłsudski's Sanacja (Sanitation) repressions, which included the imposition of martial law, arrests, and summary trials. Some political parties were banned and some restrictions imposed on the Orthodox Church.[23] In 1935, more schools were closed, along with some cultural organizations.[24] The Polish authorities even made a futile attempt to re-Polonize the peasant minor nobility (*szlachta zagrodowa*). However, the peasants (whether they were former nobles or not) resisted this divisive form of patriotism.[25]

In part, the Belorussian reaction was also due to the Polish government's disastrous land-grant policies in the eastern territories, where farmland was given to the "military settlers" from western and central Poland. In all, some 9,000 Polish officers and soldiers who fought in the 1914–20 wars of independence became land-grant recipients. In the Nowogródek and Polesie regions, the land set aside for colonization exceeded the land assigned for agrarian reform. For the most part these colonists were regarded by the local population, who had expected to receive the land, as squatters, thieves, and enemies of the people. Some of the new arrivals had no agricultural qualifications; the land was sometimes left derelict and was sometimes even sold or rented out.[26] (This was not always the case, however, and some Polish agricultural colonies in the eastern territories did quite well.[27]) As Adolf Warski, a Seym (parliament) deputy, put it in his speech of April 28,

1926: "In the Ukraine and Western Belorussia ... sits the Polish *szlachta*, transplanted alive from the seventeenth century to Poland in general and to the Ukraine and Western Belorussia in particular."[28] Of course, this transplanted *szlachta* had few feudal rights of the sort the seventeenth-century *szlachta* had exercised. Although the land-grant policy was discontinued in 1924, its political fallout lingered until the beginning of the war and beyond. In addition to the "military settlers," many civilian colonists arrived throughout the interwar period in these territories as well.

In part, the Belorussian reaction was due to the massive Soviet propaganda that portrayed the invasion as a "liberation" and promised to place the previous Polish governance structure and land in the hands of local Belorussians. In part, it was due to fear and the hope that "good deeds" would be remembered when the purges came. And finally, the reaction was also due to a blind faith in the socialist vision of a "united Belorussia"—a vision entertained by the seven thousand former members of the KPZB who somehow managed to escape both Polish repression and NKVD terror and probably mobilized the masses and organized the grand receptions for the Red Army.[29]

Yet even though many Belorussians genuinely supported the Soviets, joined the workers' guards, and manned the peasants' volunteer militias, the Russians never trusted the "Polish Belorussians." It is true that the Soviet "liberators" deported all the Polish military and civilian settlers, all the hated foresters, all the officials and the police—often with joyful Belorussian collaboration and frequent denunciations. And it is true that the Soviet authorities redistributed the land among the local peasants, advanced the cultural life of the Belorussians, and gave the Belorussian language national prominence by introducing it into the school system and by publishing a Belorussian newspaper.[30] But it is also true that soon the landholdings of the peasants were subjected to economic exploitation and forced collectivization[31] (49,000, or 6.7 percent of all farms were collectivized by June 1941, and the rate was rapidly increasing), that remaining political activists in the Belorussian nationalist movement were being liquidated,[32] that Soviet officials were imported to fill top-level administrative posts, and that often the only rewards offered to the local Belorussians for their support were low-level administrative positions and paramilitary posts.[33] For all their trouble, the Belorussians were soon treated almost as badly as the Poles.[34] Even the ever-faithful KPZB felt betrayed. V. P. Laskovich stated:

> The joy felt on the part of the whole nation as a result of liberation was followed as early as the second day by the declaration that all revolutionaries, members of the KPZB, Komsomol members, who had only just been released from Polish prisons, were enemies; the KPZB was considered to be a party founded by Polish military intelligence. Greater madness could not have been expected. Our struggle, our sufferings, our dreams for a happy future were mocked and spat upon. I'll say more: many KPZB members were arrested, and all the rest found themselves under constant surveillance.... Our enemies laughed at these idiotic events.[35]

In fact, until October 1940, everyone *except* the former members of the KPZB were being admitted to the new party organizations established in the occupied territories. Moreover, Ivan Klimov, the director of the propaganda department of the Central Committee of the (Bolshevik) Communist Party of Belorussia [Polish: Komunistyczna Partia (bolszewików) Białorusi; Russian: Kommunisticheskaya Partiia (bolsheviki) Belaruskaya, or KP(b)B], was sent to Wilno to organize repressions against certain former Belorussian activists with nationalistic tendencies. This purge was truncated only by the transfer of Wilno to Lithuania.[36]

By far the worst disaster to befall the Belorussians at the hands of the Soviets occurred shortly after the German invasion. Fortunately, due to the rapid advance of the German armies and to local resistance, the residents of "Western Belorussia" were spared the full brunt of the scorched-earth policy that enveloped the rest of their territory.

To begin with, 500,000 residents were mobilized for the Red Army, and 1,500,000 were evacuated to the interior of the Soviet Union (91,000 from "Western Belorussia," according to Zbigniew S. Siemaszko). This represented about 22 percent of all residents in Soviet Belorussia.[37] In addition, along with the evacuees, everything — literally everything — of economic value was either shipped off to the Soviet Union or destroyed. Stalin's July 3, 1941, radio address to the nation explained the order:

> During the forced retreat of Red Army divisions, all rolling-stock must be withdrawn, not leaving the enemy with a single engine, a single train car, not leaving the enemy with a kilogram of iron, a liter of fuel. Kolkhoz members should turn out all farm animals and relinquish grain to national organs with the objective of evacuating it to the interior of the land. All valuable property, including precious metals, grain and fuel which cannot be evacuated must be unconditionally destroyed.[38]

And so, with the assistance of Soviet "destruction (*istrebitelnyye*) battalions" backed by the Red Army, entire townships such as Vitebsk and Polotsk were demolished. Throughout the land, smoke rose from public buildings, farmsteads, and even private homes.[39] When the Soviets left, the residents of Belorussia were left without even the barest necessities of life. After the war, in typical Soviet style, these brutal acts were vociferously attributed to the conquering German armies, which in their own time conducted 60 brutal pacifications, liquidated 692 villages, and murdered hundreds of thousands of people in Belorussia. But in the beginning, the Belorussians were glad to see the German armies as agents of change and welcomed them with bread and salt. Anything would be a welcome relief from that Soviet hell.[40]

German Occupation

After the German invasion of the Soviet Union, on August 1, 1941, the province of Białystok (68,000 square kilometers), renamed Bezirk Bialystok, was incorporated into the Grossdeutschland. Belorussia, together with the three Baltic republics of Lithuania (including the Wilno region), Latvia, and Estonia, now became a part of Reichskommissariat Ostland. That fall, the southern (Polesie) territories of "Western Belorussia" including Brześć, Pińsk, Stolin, and Jelsk became a part of the Reichskommissariat Ukraine, and on April 1, 1942, the counties of Ejszyszki, Oszmiana, and Świr were added to the Wilno region, which now became a part of Lithuania (Generalkommissariat Litauen). After these divestitures, the rest of Belorussia became the General Commissariat Belorussia (Generalkommissariat Weissruthenien). About 75 percent of that territory had belonged to the Soviet Union before September 1939. Wilhelm Kube (assassinated by his mistress on September 22, 1943, and replaced by Curt von Gottberg) was appointed General Commissar of Belorussia, but in reality his power was limited to only the western part (henceforth, Belorussia-West), which was placed under civil administration and consisted of 53,700 square kilometers, about 78 percent of which (including the regions of Baranowicze, Głębokie, Hancewicze, Lida, Nowogródek, Słonim, and Wilejka) had belonged to Poland before the war and the rest (including the regions of Minsk, Borisov, and Slutsk) to the USSR. The remaining larger portion of the commissariat (henceforth, Belorussia-East) was placed under a military administration and remained thus until the end of the occupation.[41]

The German connection with the Belorussian minority in Poland actually began in 1933, when the Department of Foreign Politics (Aussenpolitisches Amt, or APA) of the National Socialist German Workers' Party (NSDAP) under Alfred Rosenberg established contact with Fabian Akinchyts, the leader of a small group of Belorussian national socialists. With APA's backing, Akinchyts' group put out a newspaper (*Novy Shlakh*) in Wilno, established the Belorussian National Socialist Party, and founded in Berlin, the Alliance of Belorussian Students in Germany.[42] Rosenberg's aim was to win over the Belorussians with tantalizing hints of possible future autonomy under the Third Reich and to create in Belorussia, as in Ukraine, a German base for the future destruction of the Soviet Union. These early ventures, however, met with little success.

Initially, the KPZB (led by communists operating out of legal leftist organizations), the centrist Belorussian National Union (Belaruskaye Narodnaye Abyednannye, or BNA), and the nationalist group of Father Wincenty Godlewski rejected the fascist propaganda spewed out by the *Novy Shlakh*. By 1939, however, with more intense propaganda, which now began to speak of Belorussian independence and the "protection of the interests of small nations and minorities," the BNA became less critical of Nazi Germany, and Godlewski's nationalists began to base their hopes for freedom more and more on Germany. After the Soviet invasion of Poland, many of these Belorussian activists relocated to Wilno, and shortly before the city was handed over to Lithuania, they moved to the German-occupied territories of Poland.[43]

In addition to the émigrés, small pockets of Belorussians already existed in Warsaw, Łódź, and Prague. In November 1939, the German ministry of internal affairs in Berlin created the Weissruthenische Vertrauenstelle, commonly known as the Belorussian Representation or the White Ruthenian Nazi Party, with Akinchyts as director. The following summer, the Belorussian Committee of Mutual Assistance (Belaruski Kamitet Samapomachy, or BKS) in Germany was established under Andrei Boroŭski, the consul of the Belorussian People's Republic in Berlin. Concomitantly, committee cells emerged in Munich, Leipzig, Prague, Toruń, and elsewhere. Meanwhile, independently of the German-based BKS, in January 1940 a Belorussian Committee was established under Mikola Shchors in the GG, with headquarters in Warsaw and delegations in Biała Podlaska and Kraków. The mission of all these committees was ostensibly sociocultural — to establish libraries, to organize artists' groups, to sponsor public readings, and so forth.[44] In reality they were also recruitment agencies for future Nazi collaborators.

Building on the above committees, other groups of a more political nature soon emerged and presented themselves as the representatives of the Belorussian people and as potential partners with the Third Reich. One of these groups was led by Ivan Jermachenko, an activist in Prague. With Vasil Zakharka, the symbolic émigré leader of the Council of the Belorussian People's Republic, Jermachenko addressed a letter to Hitler requesting a clarification of the Belorussian question in the anticipation of the attack on and dissolution of the Soviet Union. On August 3, 1939, both he and Zakharka were invited to attend a conference in Berlin, where they outlined their program of Belorussian-German cooperation.[45]

A second group was led by Akinchyts, the founder of the "Akinchyts School" in Berlin where young Belorussian activists were indoctrinated and prepared to assume positions of leadership in Belorussia after the German invasion.[46]

A third émigré group with political ambitions was established under the leadership of Shchors, head of the Belorussian Committee in Warsaw and, in the 1930s, an active member in the Alliance of Belorussian Students in Germany. Father Godlewski was his right-hand man. The mission of this group was also to prepare members, with the help of the SD, for the administrative takeover of Belorussia.[47] In addition, Shchors contacted the Abwehr in the second half of 1940, recruited volunteers for its diversionary units, and on June 18, 1941, after providing them with a training course in Lamsdorf (Łambinowice) near Oppeln (Opole), sent fifty of his people across the Soviet border for diversionary action along the Stołpce-Baranowicze railway line. Three days before the invasion of the Soviet Union, on June 19, 1941, Shchors' group formed an organization called the "Center," whose ostensible mission was to coordinate émigré activities but whose real mission was to become the interim administration and police in Belorussia.[48]

All of these Belorussian émigré groups counted on Nazi Germany to further the goals of their own organizations and the cause of Belorussian independence. In contradistinction to these nationalist groups, the Belorussian Nationalist Party (Partyia Belaruskikh Natsianalistov, or PBN), founded in Warsaw in 1940 by Ian Stankevich, with Vatslaŭ Ivanoŭski as its idealogue, banked on the Western Allies and hoped for a federalist resolution of the Belorussian question in the international forum.

Like the other émigré groups, it too intended to take advantage of the German occupation to establish its own administrative control over Belorussia and to build up an armed force that would survive the war.[49]

Such was the political situation in Belorussia on the eve of the German invasion. Amid various German proposals — ranging from granting "a certain degree of autonomy" to Belorussia (Rosenberg's plan) to including Belorussia in the GG (the plan of the Reichsstelle für Raumordnung) — no decision was made by Hitler regarding the future disposition or administration of Belorussia in his plan for "Barbarossa," the invasion of the Soviet Union.

In the first few weeks after the invasion, the whole of the General Commissariat of Belorussia found itself under German military control. Both Poles and Belorussians initially welcomed the German armies, as we have already seen; nevertheless, due to a lack of qualified specialists,[50] the administration of Belorussia-West was handed over mostly to the prewar functionaries, the Poles, many of whom returned to their former homes after the German invasion. Needless to say, this did not go over very well with the above-mentioned Belorussian organizations, which were eagerly preparing their own members for this task. In Belorussia-East, where only a feeble effort was made to create a civil administration, Volksdeutsche and even Russians were just as likely to be given administrative posts as Belorussians.[51]

The Polish administration in Belorussia-West proved to be ephemeral. A November 26, 1942, Nazi document relating to the treatment of Poles by the German occupation authorities simply restated the policy already in force throughout Eastern Poland. This document instructed Nazi administrators to ensure that, "in particular, mayors, district and regional chiefs of Polish nationality or pro–Polish leaders of large industrial plants and estates will be dismissed and replaced by members of other nationalities (Lithuanians, Belorussians, Ukrainians).... The Polish language ... must neither be put on the same level nor be preferred to Lithuanian, Belorussian, or Ukrainian."[52]

By the end of 1941 the new political order in the General Commissariat of Belorussia consisted predominantly of the German occupation authorities, the Belorussian groupings of Jermachenko, Akinchyts, and Stankevich/Ivanoŭski, and those of Radaslaŭ Astroŭski. Astroŭski — the former minister of education of the Belorussian (1918) Republic, a member of the Hramada, and the head of the Belorussian Committee of Mutual Assistance in Łódź — would become the future president of the German-controlled Belorussian Central Council (Belaruskaya Tsentralnaya Rada, or BTsR). The military arm of the BTsR was the BKA. The total life span of the BTsR and the BKA was six months.[53]

During the Nazi occupation, then, three sets of actors appeared on the Belorussian war scene: the Soviet partisans subservient to Moscow, who had 143,000 members by June 1944 and who wanted a return to the status quo existing prior to June 22, 1941; the Belorussian pro–Nazi and anti–Nazi nationalists, who wanted an independent and unified Belorussia; and the Polish underground members, who wanted to return to the status quo existing prior to September 1, 1939.[54] Each vied with the others to achieve its own postwar objectives.

In this war of all against all, it was not always clear at any given time just who "the enemy" was. For example, the Poles fought the Germans but initially also attempted to win the Germans' favor. They opposed the Belorussian nationalists but also held meetings with Belorussian representatives — meetings that, were it not for the question of postwar boundaries, might have produced a unified anti–Nazi front.[55] They despised the Russians, but in 1941 the two became allies; after Moscow's June 22, 1943, order to liquidate the AK, they were enemies once more. All of this played directly into the "divide and conquer" strategy of the Germans.

To add to the confusion, the battle lines did not always depend on ethnic affiliation. Both Belorussians and Poles belonged to the Soviet partisans. Poles belonged to the Belorussian police, and Belorussians could be found among the AK, especially in the Wilno and Nowogródek areas.[56]

There were three major reasons for Belorussian ("White Russian") antipathy toward the "White Poles" (Białopolacy) during the German occupation: the initial Polish monopoly on administrative power; the return of the Polish landlords, who demanded the restoration of their property that had been redistributed by the Soviets, then collectivized, then reredistributed again to the peasants by the Germans; and most important, the question of the postwar status of this area.

When the Germans began to deport Poles to forced-labor camps in 1941, some Belorussians were only too willing to lend a helping hand. Among the collaborators were some members of the Orthodox clergy who betrayed Catholic priests and nuns because they saw in the "Polish" church not only a threat to their own faith but also a stumbling block to Belorussian postwar independence. One Orthodox priest's September 1941 denunciation reads as follows:

> The Roman Catholic clergy is conducting an active propaganda campaign in order to rebuild an independent Polish nation. It is attempting to recruit people and plans, after the departure of the German armies, to create partisan groups to free the occupied territories from the enemy of Poland, in this case, from the Germans. The ringleaders of this movement are the Roman Catholic priests from the churches in Oszmiana, Holszany, Granosieckie, Boruny, Senorgoje [probably Smorgonie], Krew, Draby, Soły, Żuprany, etc.[57]

As a result of such denunciations, in November 1941 several Polish Catholic priests were shot, including a missionary, Father Henryk Hlebowicz. So were Fathers Dionizy Malets and Stanislaŭ Hlakoŭski — both Belorussian Catholic priests. The SD was informed by the Belorussian Orthodox clergy that even their Catholic counterparts were being used by the Catholic hierarchy to further the Polish cause. No one could have accused Father Hlakoŭski of this. He was a well-known prewar Belorussian patriot in Wilno and in 1941 even published a badly needed Belorussian catechism in the language of his people.[58] The April 7, 1944, edition of *Belaruski Holas* in Wilno stated that the Belorussian Orthodox were forbidding the Belorussian Catholics from calling themselves Belorussian and that the Orthodox considered all Catholics to be Poles.[59]

The Nazi purges of Polish intellectuals began in 1942. In the fall of that year, 84 Poles were shot in Słonim, and by war's end, in Słonim and the surrounding vicinity, 1,000 had been dismissed from their jobs — due, in part, to Belorussian denunciations — and replaced by Belorussians. The differential treatment of Poles and Belorussians is revealed by the fact that over 500 Poles in that region petitioned the authorities for Belorussian nationality status and by the fact that the use at work of "any other" language except Belorussian and German was forbidden.[60]

In Nowogródek, several dozen Poles, including several priests, were shot on July 31, 1942, and Poles were often betrayed by Belorussians and removed from work. (The regional commissar in Nowodródek estimated — perhaps with some exaggeration — that 80 percent of the Belorussian population in that region was adversely disposed toward the Poles. He personally regretted their removal from work and complained about the hardships endured as a result of having to hire less-capable replacements.) Similar incidents occurred in the Wilejka region, where over one hundred Poles were executed in the summer of 1942.[61]

On August 1, 1943, eleven Sisters of the Holy Family of Nazareth were brutally murdered on the outskirts of the town of Nowogródek. Did Belorussian collaborators have a hand in this crime? In the absence of real or even fictitious charges against the nuns, Rev. Aleksander Zienkiewicz, who knew the Sisters, proposes the following explanations for the death sentences:

> It proved impossible to discover the Gestapo's immediate reasons or pretext for murdering the Sisters. Rumors circulated that the whole thing was a mistake. It was said that the Pallotine Sisters who had a house in Nowogródek and another in a village named Rajca, were the ones to have been executed. The Rajca convent happened to be in the district controlled by Soviet guerrillas and

the Sisters were suspected of contacts with them and of giving first aid to the wounded. This gave rise to talk among the White-Russians [Belorussians] that the Pallotine Sisters were in sympathy with the "red bandits." On the basis of this accusation, the Germans may have intended taking action against them but the Gestapo's ignorance of the local situation caused the Sisters of the Holy Family of Nazareth to be the victims instead—victims of a mistake.

Such a supposition is not improbable and this very conclusion could be reached from the words "They were innocent," uttered by the Gestapo officer after the execution. Yet, it must also be understood that the occupying forces would never have pardoned the "guilt" incurred by the Sisters who taught catechism and whose sympathies were with the Church and with their suffering fatherland.

It is known, in fact, that the Sisters from "Fara" [the Polish word for "parish church"] had for a long time been on the black list of the White-Russians who were collaborating with the Gestapo. Under orders from the Germans, committees of the White-Russian Welfare Society had been compiling and keeping up to date, lists of names of the more prominent Poles and even of White-Russian Catholics, submitting them to the secret police, who in their turn, on the slightest provocation, transferred certain names from these to other lists on which names were replaced by numbers given to those who were to be exterminated.

The Sisters of the Holy Family of Nazareth in charge of "Fara" represented for the White-Russian activists and for the Germans a nucleus of religious and national life, and had therefore incurred their hatred. Threats and forecasts of the extermination of that "nest" of Polish nationalism were heard occasionally. Yet White-Russian collaborators, such as Regula, Jakucewicz and Romanowicz were utterly bewildered and horrified by the cynicism of this wanton crime on the part of their overlords. Stranger still was the fact that the murder caused surprise even to the German police stationed in the locality.[62]

To this day no one knows who betrayed the nuns to the Gestapo or why they were executed.

The antipathy toward the Poles was also promulgated in the Belorussian press. In largely Polish-speaking Białystok, the newspaper *Novaya Daroha* (New Way) urged greater Belorussian participation in the "cleansing" of Poles. "These *panowie* from before 1939, occupying this or that position in the administration," states the article, "evidently forget whose bread they are now eating and imagine themselves in their former roles."[63]

No wonder, then, that some Belorussians, especially those in administrative positions and the police, became involved in anti-Polish atrocities; so did some organizations—for example, the Belorussian National Organization of Mutual Assistance (Belaruskaya Narodnaya Samapomach, or BNS), whose members assisted the Germans in deporting both Polish and Belorussian Catholics to forced-labor camps in 1942.[64]

The lieutenant of the Wilno AK, Aleksander Krzyżanowski, reported in October 1942: "Just as the Lithuanians, the Belorussians do not expect anything from the Germans, but cooperate with them because they feel that the extermination (*wyniszczenie*) of the Polish element will be of benefit to them. They consider this action as a cleansing of the territory for their future activity."[65] The "cleansing" of Poles was quite effective. In 1943, the Belorussians constituted 80 percent of the administrative workforce and 60 percent of the police force in the Belorussian Commissariat.[66]

In response to this Nazi-Belorussian terror, the AK began an anti-Belorussian campaign. According to Belorussian sources, 1,200 Belorussians had died in the Lida region by mid-February 1944. The 500 men in the Polish auxiliary police in that region did little to prevent these murders. According to the regional commissar, the police were completely unreliable and were probably themselves connected with the Polish underground. But Lida was the exception. In other areas under Belorussian control, such actions were sporadic and limited in scope.[67]

In the neighboring Nowogródek region, 300 Belorussians were executed by the AK, and 80 were denounced to the Gestapo and German field police as "members of the Communist Party." Some of them were shot, some deported.[68] Jerzy Turonek notes:

> In anticipation of the withdrawal of the Germans, the AK in Nowogródek achieved not a little in the domain of combating the potential opponents of rebuilding the Polish statehood in these territories. As [Adolf] Pilch stated, from December 1943 to the end of June 1944, the members of his unit killed 6,000 "Bolsheviks." We can surmise that the vast majority of them consisted of the civilian Belorussian population suspected of collaborating with the Soviet partisans. The extermination of the Belorussians in the district of Lida also escalated. According to Belorussian estimates, from mid–February to mid–April 1944, several thousand people died at the hands of the AK, including 480 in one Bielicka commune [*gmina*].[69]

Evidently, after the Soviet June 22, 1943, order to liquidate the Polish underground in Belorussia and after the agreements between the Germans and some AK units to exchange arms for anti–Soviet partisan warfare, no holds were barred — but whether the "vast majority" of the "Bolshevik" casualties were Belorussian civilians is highly questionable. According to the statistics provided by Turonek himself, in mid-June 1944, the Nowogródek region contained 7,700 AK members, of which almost 85 percent (6,500) belonged to the AK in the Lida area. Of the total AK members, 40 percent were Orthodox Belorussians.[70] Turonek does not state how many of the remaining 60 percent (undoubtedly Catholics) were Belorussians, but if any Belorussians were inclined to join the AK, surely it would have been the Catholics. If Turonek's conclusion — that the "vast majority" of those killed were innocent Belorussian civilians — is correct, is it conceivable that so many Belorussians would have joined an organization that was betraying and murdering their people in such great numbers? The more likely conclusion is that the AK units in question, as Pilch said, were killing the Soviet partisans, who were killing them in turn. Turonek's statistics take us only to June 1944. On July 14, Stalin himself would issue an order aimed at the total annihilation of all Polish underground forces in Soviet-occupied Poland — an order that would never be rescinded. The AK, therefore, had good reasons for slaughtering the Bolsheviks, of whom there was no lack in Belorussia. Already in the fall of 1941, 4,650 Russian and Belorussian graduates of Soviet espionage schools were sent into the German-occupied territories.[71] In addition, as we have seen, in 1943 there were 36,800 Soviet partisans in "Western Belorussia."

Among Belorussian collaborators under the German occupation, the following deserve special mention: the Belorussian auxiliary police; the Belorussian police battalions; the ill-fated antipartisan fortified villages (Wehrdörfer) set up by the Germans; the BTsR-BKA; the Belorussian Independent Party (Belaruskaya Nezalezhnitskaya Partyia, or BNP); some gullible members of the Union of Belorussian Youth (Sayuz Belaruskay Moladzi, or SBM); and the Belorussian volunteers in Siegling's 30. Waffen-Grenadier-Division der SS (russiche Nr 2).[72]

Members of the Belorussian auxiliary police were known as "Ravens." There were 20,000 of them in Belorussia-West and probably as many in Belorussia-East.[73] Their task was to keep order and to assist the Nazis in the liquidation of the Jewish ghettos and the roundups of the Jews for executions. Sometimes, they did the shooting. The largely Jewish town of Borisov was the first to fall. On October 20, 1941, on orders of Stanislaŭ Stankevich, the "Butcher of Borisov" and its ruler, about 7,000 Jewish men, women, and children were brutally murdered.[74] John Loftus describes the conduct of the collaborators during these executions:

> The SS professed to be shocked by the Borissow massacre — not at the slaughter of the Jews but at the carnival aspects of it. Over the next three years, as the Belorussian holocaust increased in intensity and dimension, the *Einsatzgruppen* supervised the actual shooting themselves. Then, at least, the moment of execution would be devoid of the demonic games favored by the collaborators. But even after the sport of pulling the trigger at the pits had been taken from them, hundreds of collaborators guarded the roads,

> chased fugitives, and forced the living down into the graves. Children were thrown into wells and hand grenades dropped down upon them, and Belorussian policemen swung infants by the heels and smashed their heads against rocks.[75]

On November 15, 1941, the Jews of the Minsk ghetto were trucked outside the city and killed.[76]

On the feast of Purim in 1942, the Baranowicze ghetto was liquidated. During the roundup, Belorussian police "would strike at random with their rifle butts at the stomachs of those being given their [work] cards."[77] On March 5 of that year, the Jews were assembled by the German, Lithuanian, and Ukrainian police brought to Baranowicze to assist the local "Ravens." After being separated, those marked for execution were carted off in lorries to a railway line some 3 kilometers away. There, about thirty-three hundred Jews were murdered and buried in pits dug by Russian prisoners of war and by ten Jewish policemen who were among those killed.[78]

On September 3, 1942, the Lachwa ghetto was surrounded by Belorussian police and, after a heroic resistance, was burned to the ground by the Gestapo the next day. A thousand Jews perished.[79] In Nowogródek, by 1943 only five hundred Jews remained out of the earlier Jewish population of five thousand. These had been saved to work in the ghetto labor camp. According to one Jewish survivor, half were killed later by the Germans and the Belorussian police.[80]

Various authors of the previously mentioned Jody memoir refer to the use of the Belorussian police in the liquidation of the Jews:

> The police department in Jody came under German supervision. Its members were composed of Belorussians, Russians and a few Poles.[81]

> In December 1941, there were 450 Jews who remained in Jody, plus a number of refugees from Lithuania and from Latvia who escaped massacres.
>
> It was December 16. Neither the Judenrat nor most of the males of Jody went to bed. Everyone else went to sleep in their clothes. Later that night the local Chief of Police [a Pole], a man friendly to the Jews, had warned the Judenrat of impending doom.... Local police, mostly Belorussians, Russians and some Poles, most of them drunk, carried out the executions.[82]

> There was also a band of gypsies who had managed to escape the massacre of gypsies that spring. While in the forest they decided to perform a traditional gypsy wedding, replete with music and dance. Because they congregated in an open area during the day, they were discovered, and all one hundred of them were murdered by the Germans and their Belorussian helpers.[83]

Nicholas Vakar stated, "The anti–Semitic position of the Belorusssian collaborationists is acknowledged, among other things, by a large 1944 poster displaying pictures of Astroŭski, [A.] Kalubovič, and other nationalist leaders, with quotations from Astroŭski's speech about the 'Judaistic (*ažidavely*) Kremlin,' 'Jewish hirelings,' and the like."[84]

In time, all the Belorussian Jewish ghettos were liquidated, always by the Einsatzgruppen with the active assistance of the auxiliary police and, at times, some local collaborators. According to Vakar, only 20 percent of the Jews in Belorussia survived the war.[85] But there were also heroic Belorussian rescuers.[86]

In addition to this type of police work, Belorussian collaborators performed duties as SS auxiliary prison and camp guards — for example, in the Maly Trostenets camp near Minsk — and served in the Criminal Police in the territory of the GG.[87]

With the partisan threat on the rise, foreign police battalions (Schutzmannschaften) were brought to Belorussia: Lithuanian, Latvian, Ukrainian, Russian, and even one Polish police battalion (no. 202). Moreover, in 1943 an effort was made to form specifically Belorussian police battalions. By February 1944, seven such battalions, totaling 2,167 men, had been formed in Belorussia-West. In Nowogródek, one volunteer police battalion was recruited from among the students of a local teachers' school. The success of these ventures can be gauged by the fact that by the beginning of 1944, at least

50,000 people were in the various military-police formations of the commissariat — excluding the foreign detachments.[88] These Belorussian police battalions were used primarily for punitive military expeditions against Soviet and, especially, Polish partisans.[89]

The Germans also attempted to fortify a string of villages (Wehrdörfer) and to use them as bases for antipartisan warfare. On October 19, 1943, Gottberg ordered the police authorities to clear such villages of undependable political elements and to supply each of them with fifty to one hundred rifles. Dozens of such villages appeared in Belorussia-West and, after 1943, some in the eastern part as well. In the Baranowicze area fourteen such villages were organized; five also appeared in the eastern part of the Białystok district. These efforts, however, met with little success. Lack of manpower (due to deportations for forced labor and conscription), resistance on the part of the villagers, and fear of partisan reprisals conspired to produce meager results.[90]

More positive results were obtained by Gottberg's December 21, 1943, announcement in Minsk to form the BTsR, followed by his February 23, 1944, order for the formation of the BKA. Astroŭski, the Nazi-appointed president of the BTsR, not only expressed his gratitude to the Third Reich but also urged all Belorussians to join the fight for "ultimate victory." With the backing of the BNS as well as the Orthodox Church, the result of the mobilization order surprised even the Germans: forty thousand volunteers showed up! An AK leader observing this disturbing phenomenon stated, "The Belorussians are wholly united in behalf of the Germans by virtue of these concessions and the majority enter the army willingly."[91]

Not prepared to organize and arm so many recruits, the regional commissars sent half of them back home. By March 15, 19,000 men were accepted into the BKA. By the end of March, the BKA consisted of 22,000 men, to which several police battalions were added, for a total strength of about 24,000 to 25,000 soldiers. In mid–April they were divided into thirty-nine infantry battalions and six battalions of engineers (*sapery*) and placed under the command of Frantsishak Kushel. On June 15, two weeks before evacuation, a BKA officers' school was opened in Minsk.[92]

Bolstered by the success of its military formation, the BTsR convened a General Belorussian Congress in Minsk and on June 27, its 1,039 delegates from Belorussia, Lithuania, Latvia, Poland, Austria, and Germany reaffirmed the March 25, 1918, declaration of independence by the Belorussian People's (National) Republic (Belaruskaya Republika Ludova, or BRL). By the end of that month, however, the BKA — without having engaged in a single battle — ceased to exist, and Astroŭski's efforts to create a Belorussian military force that would survive the war and continue to fight for Belorussian independence came to an end.[93] The BTsR was to continue for a while longer, in Berlin.

In addition to the BTsR, the BNP, created in July 1942 in Minsk, also presented itself as a patriotic organization fighting for Belorussian independence. Its leaders (Vsyevolod Rodzhko, Mikhal Viryušhka, and others), however, worked behind the scenes with the Abwehr. Under the slogan, "We will either secure an independent Belorussia, or perish in battle," the BNP was able to recruit a substantial number of Belorussians for diversionary and espionage activities behind the lines of the Red Army. The efforts of this organization continued well after the Soviet takeover of Belorussia. In July 1944, a special training camp was established for BNP commandos by the Abwehr in Dahlwitz, West Prussia. Meanwhile, Kamiński's criminal brigade was given a free reign in the regions of Nowogródek and Słonim.[94]

Among Gottberg's other ambitious plans for garnering Belorussian assistance in the conduct of the war was his effort to recruit teenagers from the SBM. This patriotic youth organization, which by mid–1944 had some 100,000 members with centers in Baranowicze and Minsk, was run along military lines: uniforms, military drills, marches to patriotic Belorussian songs, a course of studies in "political science," and vacations to Germany. These were the youth, then, that Gottberg tried to recruit for the Luftwaffe. Before long, 1,000 young men between the ages of fifteen and twenty-one were sent to Dessau. In June 1944, 5,000 more went to Germany. The largest contingent (2,000) of the latter group were from Głębokie; 500 were from Baranowicze.[95]

One example of the kind of recruitment tactics that were used to lure unsuspecting teens from Mołodeczno was given by Mikhal Luzhynski. An SBM member associated with the middle-school in that town, Luzhynski stated that in May 1944 two men, the regional director of SBM and a Luftwaffe lieutenant called Fermann, came to his school. Fermann addressed the students:

> Today the destiny of entire Europe hangs in the balance, and also of your fatherland. The Belorussians have already created their army, the Belorussian Home Defense Corps [BKA]. However, this new army cannot be effective without its air force. I call upon you, boys, to voluntary service in the airborne armed forces. Some of you will become pilots, others — navigators or aviation mechanics.[96]

And so, forty-six youngsters from the Mołodeczno middle-school eagerly signed up for the Nazi Luftwaffe.

In a report dated October 19, 1944, Hauptbannführer Siegfried Nickel, the former leader of the Belorussian Hitler Youth and chief of the recruitment action (Heu-Aktion) for the eastern territories, provided the following breakdown for his charges: SS auxiliaries (SS-Helfer)—1,383 Russian, 5,953 Ukrainian, 2,354 Belorussian; air force auxiliaries (Luftwaffen-Helfer)— 3,000 Estonian, 3,614 Latvian; naval auxiliaries (Marine-Helfer)— 346 Estonian; air force auxiliaries (female)— 2,000 from all nationalities; Todt Organization auxiliaries (O.T.-Helfer)— 2,000 males from all regions, 700 females from all regions.

These youth wore brassards in their national colors and were employed mostly in noncombatant functions (e.g., transport, signals). Some, however, manned guns in Flak units. According to Nickel, forty-one of the latter had been killed to date and two were awarded the Iron Cross Second Class. The recruitment and training of these youth was in the hands of the SS and the Hitler Youth.[97]

A plan to organize a Belorussian SS brigade — the Waffen-SS Grenadier-brigade "Weissruthenian" — never materialized. Many Belorussians, however, were thrown in with Siegling's 30. Waffen-Grenadier-Division der SS (russiche Nr 2) which after being depleted by desertions and Andrei Vlasov's army, was transformed into the 30. Waffen-Grenadier-Division der SS (weissruthenische Nr 1). The reinforcements for that renamed division came from Astroŭski's Belorussian battalion-in-training.[98]

But all the plans were in vain. Certain German observers found all these efforts to be beyond belief. The regional commissar in Baranowicze observed, "Half of the peasants in the defense villages evacuated and the BKA battalions ran away."[99]

In mid–July 1944 the leaders of the BTsR were called to Berlin. There Rosenberg finally acknowledged that this organization was to be "the exclusive and only political representative of the Belorussian nation," a prerogative generally decided by the voice of the people, not an occupying power. In Berlin, Gottberg and Rosenberg hammered out the last futile assignments of the BTsR — in Germany, not in the Soviet-occupied territories of Belorussia. The BTsR was to organize the 378,000 Belorussian laborers brought there by force, the several thousand youth volunteers from the SBM, the refugees, and the small number of Belorussian prewar émigrés — some 500,000 Belorussians in all — into a pro–Nazi movement, at a time when the war was hopelessly lost.[100]

What happened to all of the Belorussian collaborators after the war? John Loftus, a former member of the Office of Special Investigation (OSI), the U.S. Justice Department unit established to prosecute Nazi war criminals, answers this question:

> Ostrowsky [Astroŭski] decided that the best chance for safety lay with the Polish government-in-exile in London and its anticommunist leader, General Władysław Anders....
>
> With the help of Abramtchik's [Mikola Abramchyk] contacts in Paris and Switzerland a deal was quickly made. General Anders, a bluff professional soldier without political guile, agreed to welcome the Belorussia Brigade [Belorussian members of the Waffen-SS unit] as part of a Free Polish

> army to liberate his country from what he feared would become a long Communist occupation. It is one of the ironies of history that the Poles, who had recently suffered so much at the hands of the Belorussians, were first to give them shelter from the avenging Russians....
>
> In the spring of 1945, as the Third Reich was collapsing, Ostrowsky ordered Kushel to march the Belorussia Brigade toward General Patton's Third Army ... [to] provide temporary shelter for the Belorussians until they could link up with Anders. The brigade members removed the double cross from their collar tabs, hid their flags and records, and disguising themselves as escaping POWs, marched toward the sanctuary of the American lines. The Belorussia SS settled down as prisoners in an American internment center just outside the city of Regensburg.[101]

There, they listed their place of birth as prewar Poland in order to avoid repatriation. Some passed themselves off as Polish prisoners of war; others carried false identity cards that certified them as discharged Polish officers.[102] Eventually, most of them wound up in the United States. "Between 1948 and 1950," states Loftus, "over 200 Belorussian Nazis, together with their families, arrived in South River [New Jersey]." On June 25–26, 1949, the remaining Belorussian collaborators held a conference at a displaced-persons camp near Stuttgart, Germany, where they passed a motion to "transfer the whole organization to the United States, inasmuch as all the officers were there." Astroŭski, who emigrated to Argentina, was the last to arrive in South River. He lies buried near many of his comrades in the cemetery of St. Euphrosynia's Church on Whitehead Avenue. A tall monument proclaims: "Glory to those who fought for the freedom and independence of Belorussia." A small circle of iron enclosing a double-barred cross adorns the monument.[103]

The Belorussian people as a whole cannot be blamed for their "rotten apples." The vast majority of them did not support the Nazi régime. Like the Poles, they were subjected to German pacification actions, mass exterminations, and deportations to concentration camps. By the end of 1944, of the 9.2 million residents (not only ethnic Belorussians) living in the borders of Soviet Belorussia and "Western Belorussia" before the German occupation, only 6.3 million remained, an attrition of 2.9 million people. Of these still unaccounted-for, displaced-deceased people, an estimated 750,000 civilians were murdered by the Soviets and the Germans.[104]

The Belorussian collaborators, then, who assisted both the Soviets and the Nazis during their murderous occupations of Eastern Poland, must also take their stand alongside those responsible for Poland's overall war losses.

Chapter 6
Lithuanian Collaboration

Generally speaking, a great deal of sympathy characterized Polish-Lithuanian relations from the days of the great Polish-Lithuanian Commonwealth until the late nineteenth century. By 1914, however, the ever-widening chasm between Polish and Lithuanian nationalistic aspirations had laid the foundation for the interwar conflict and wartime tragedy.[1]

The focal point of this bitter contention during the interwar years was the city of Wilno — the capital of the Grand Duchy of Lithuania, object of both Polish and Lithuanian pride, seedbed of nineteenth- and twentieth-century Lithuanian and Belorussian cultural awakening, target of tsarist depolonization and Russification efforts, and home of the miraculous "portrait" of Our Lady of Ostra Brama, renowned by Poles, Lithuanians, and Belorussians alike — in short, a center of cultural and intellectual life with museums, theaters, churches, research institutes, and one of Poland's six major prewar universities.

The various names of the city bear witness to its tragic history: *Wilno* in Polish, *Vilnius* in Lithuanian, *Vilna* in Russian and Belorussian, and *Wilna* in German. These nations, then, along with the Jews — who claimed Wilno as their "cultural Jerusalem" and set up their great archive, YIVO, in its midst — were the players in the tragic fate of that city and its residents.

The trouble began after World War I, when both Poland and Belorussia laid claim to Wilno — and when the Republic of Lithuania, whose Lithuanian-speaking citizens in Wilno numbered no more than 5 percent, declared the city to be its capital. In the next few years, Wilno was occupied and reoccupied time and again until October 9, 1920, when Marshal Józef Piłsudski reclaimed it for Poland just two days after the Polish government recognized Lithuanian independence. After the March 15, 1923, Conference of Ambassadors decision, Wilno, the capital of Lithuania, was officially incorporated into the Republic of Poland.

During the interwar years, Wilno experienced a tremendous growth in population, which rose from 129,000 residents in 1919 to 209,000 in 1938. On the eve of the war, it was the sixth-largest city in Poland and ranked second, after Kielce, in terms of growth. Its inhabitants included over 137,000 Poles, 58,000 Jews, 7,000 Russians, 1,600 Belorussians, 1,500 Lithuanians, and a small number of Germans, Gypsies, and Karaites.[2]

By December 2, 1939, 18,311 war refugees had settled in Wilno. Of these, 7,728 were Poles, 6,860 were Jews, and 3,723 were Lithuanians. As of February 25, 1940, about 36,000 refugees resided in Wilno. Forced out of the city, some of the Polish refugees (assisted by Lithuanian Polonia) settled temporarily in Lithuania, especially near its borders with Latvia and Germany.[3]

The region bordering Wilno — a strip of land from 20 to 80 kilometers wide running 220 kilometers along the Lithuanian border, 6,880 square kilometers in all — was called Wileńszczyzna, or Ziemia Wileńska. Its population in 1939 was 548,000. Of this total, 321,700 were Poles, 107,600 were Jews, 75,200 were Belorussians, 31,300 were Lithuanians, 9,000 were Russians, 1,100 were Germans, and 2,100 belonged to other nationalities.[4]

Wileńszczyzna formed a part of the

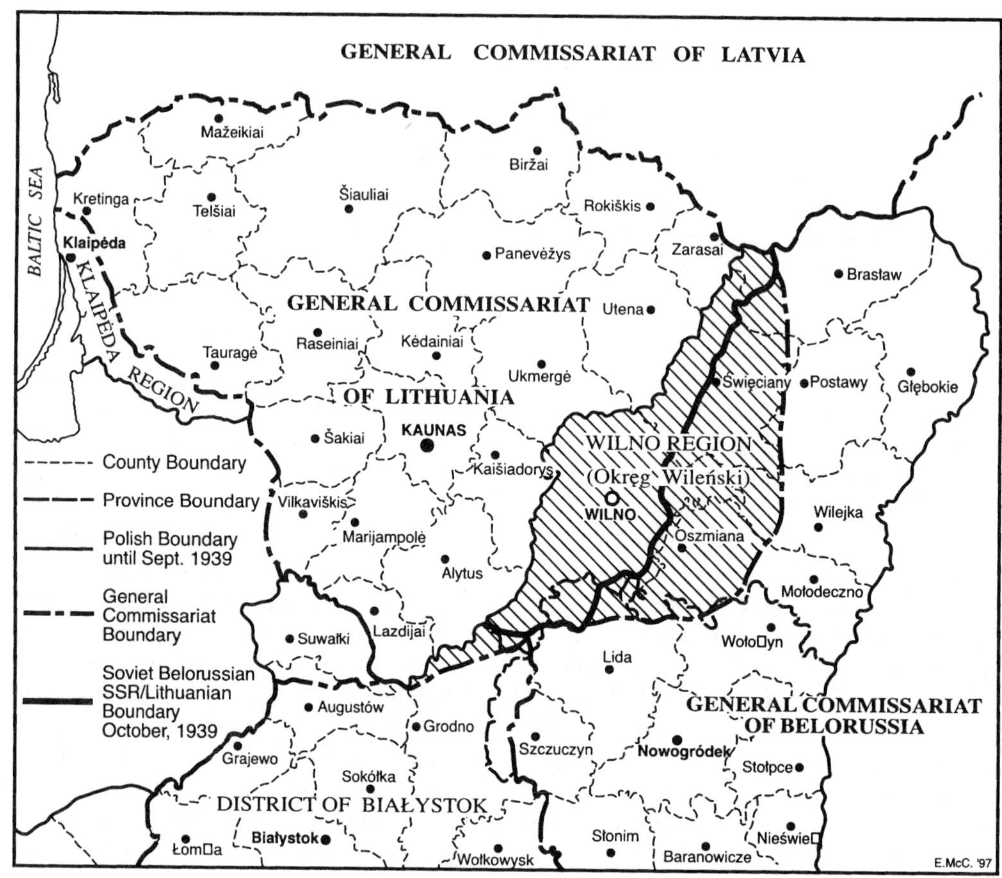

Wilno Region (Okręg Wileński), 1942–44

province of Wilno, an area of 29,000 square kilometers of land with a 1931 population of 1,275,900. Of this total, 641,000 were Poles, 409,000 were Belorussians, 111,000 were Jews, 67,000 were Lithuanians, 43,000 were Russians, and 1,000 were Germans. Another 13,000 Lithuanians inhabited the province of Białystok, and some 3,000 lived in the province of Nowogródek. In all of Poland, then, in 1931 there were approximately 83,000 Lithuanians—all of them living in the three northeastern provinces near the Republic of Lithuania.[5]

Soviet Occupation

In accordance with the August 23, 1939, German-Soviet Non-Aggression Pact, the province of Wilno fell within the Soviet "sphere of influence." Lithuania itself was to go to Germany. On September 28, 1939, however, Stalin decided to trade the province of Lublin and the rest of the province of Warsaw to the Bug River for Lithuania. All of this was done with the utmost secrecy. The exchange may have been due to Stalin's unwillingness either to break up ethnically Polish territory or to incorporate too much of it for fear that his stated reasons for occupying Eastern Poland (to liberate the oppressed Ukrainian and Belorussian population) might sound too hollow to Western ears. This move was perhaps facilitated by Joachim von Ribbentrop's disappointment over the fact that the deer he wanted to hunt so badly in the Augustów Forest (the reason he coveted the region so avariciously), were simply engaged in their annual migration. "The Foreign Minister now requests you to tell either Mr. Molotov or Mr. Stalin himself that there are no stags in

Augustów," reads the telegram from the chief of protocol to Friedrich Werner Schulenburg.[6]

The Soviet army entered Wilno on the night of September 17, 1939; on September 20, Moscow set up its provisional administration there. Although Belorussians and Russians found themselves on the list of that provisional government, not a single Lithuanian name appeared on it. The Soviet army and administration then proceeded, during a forty-day rampage, to plunder and transport everything of value to the interior of the USSR: food products, factory goods and installations, typewriters, linotypes, and both Polish and foreign gold and other valuables from bank vaults. Beginning on September 25, with the assistance of local Lithuanian and Jewish communists, a number of Polish soldiers, political activists, policemen, administrators, foresters, settlers, and landlords were arrested, subjected to interrogations, and deported to the Gulag.[7]

The Lithuanian government's initial response to the rape of Eastern Poland was mixed. On the one hand, the government was well-disposed toward the few thousand Polish refugees who wound up in its republic. In secret, it even helped them resettle in France and England. On the other hand, from September 19 to September 24, 1939, 2,500 officers, 9,000 soldiers, and 2,300 members of the Polish police who also wound up in Lithuania were disarmed and interned, together with all young Polish male civilians, in various camps and forts.[8]

On October 10, 1939, supposedly neutral Lithuania, a member of the League of Nations, became an accessory (not as an equal partner, but as a willing one) to the partition of Poland. On that day, a deal was struck between the Lithuanian government and the Soviet Union (the Soviet-Lithuanian Friendship Treaty) whereby in exchange for Soviet military bases and the placement of Soviet garrisons on Lithuanian soil (for "defense" purposes), the occupied, ravaged, predominantly Polish city of Wilno (with a Lithuanian population of less than 1 percent), together with the Wilno region (with a Lithuanian population of 5.7 percent), was handed over by the Soviets to Lithuania (officially on October 29). That region (Wileńszczyzna) was now called "Vilniaus Kraštas" in Lithuanian and "Okręg Wileński" or "Kraj Wileński" in Polish. The remainder of the province of Wilno was then incorporated into the Belorussian SSR.

Unaware of the fate that awaited it, Lithuania welcomed the return of "its" city and the borderland territory. On October 27, 1939, the Soviet armies marched out of Wilno, and Lithuanian troops marched in. That they were heckled by crowds of angry Poles who accused them of betrayal should surprise no one. Eventually, in addition to the 30,000 Lithuanian refugees from Polish territories occupied by the Soviet Union, about 20,000 Lithuanians arrived from the interior of the republic in the Wilno region. These included soldiers as well as those who would become the police and the regional administrators of Vilniaus Kraštas.[9]

Anticipating the mutual destruction of Hitler and Stalin, the Lithuanian authorities began preparations for the permanent retention of Wilno after the war. The Lithuanianization of Wileńszczyzna and specifically of Wilno (opposed even by some local Lithuanians) assumed many guises. Perhaps the greatest blow to Polish pride involved the liquidation on December 15, 1939, of the Polish University of Stefan Batory (Uniwersytet Stefana Batorego, or USB) with its 84 professors, 39 assistant professors, 245 teaching assistants, and over 3,000 students.[10] By December 20, all Polish university employees had been dismissed, and only some were rehired in subsequent months.

Although the university, with substantial changes in curriculum, organizational structure, and personnel, continued to limp on as a Lithuanian institution until the Soviet occupation,[11] the imposition of the requirement that instruction was to be given in the Lithuanian language was by itself enough to destroy it. As USB Professor Konrad Górski put it, "The Polish language, known to all nationalities studying in Wilno such as the Poles, Russians, Belorussians and Jews, is now to be replaced by the Lithuanian language which no one understands." He goes on to compare the Lithuanian takeover of USB to the proverbial dog who would neither eat his bone nor surrender it to another. "The Lithuanians destroyed 20 years of work and diligent management of USB," he wrote, "and themselves fail to take advantage of what they illegally acquired."[12]

Furthermore, in this process of Lithuanianization, Polish books were removed from bookstores. Polish schools were taken over by Lithuanian administrators — by June 1940 only two academic institutions offered instruction in the Polish language, the National Adam Mickiewicz Gimnazjum and the Mieczysław Karłowicz Conservatory of Music. Polish civil authorities were replaced by Lithuanians. Over 4,000 Polish teachers and officials lost their jobs. Lithuanian became the official language, and streets were renamed. Polish offices, stores, and businesses were closed. Except for a few charitable organizations, most (a total of 118) social and cultural and all political institutions were disbanded. Banks were robbed once more. Some members of religious orders and the diocesan clergy were resettled in Lithuania, and as of February 28, 1940, the services in eleven Roman Catholic churches (out of thirty-seven) were being held in the Lithuanian language. Attempts were made to drive a wedge between Poles and Jews (some Jews did support the Lithuanian anti–Polish policies, but the majority did not). Peasants were urged to change their nationality on passports and to Lithuanianize their names. Some 12,000 people (including Jews and Belorussians) were granted Lithuanian citizenship, and 150,000 people, mostly Poles, were declared "foreigners" and thereby excluded from many professions. These "foreigners" needed special work-cards in order to work (work-cards that Lithuanian citizens did not need) and were even prohibited from riding on trains. The Polish press was allowed to put out only three, heavily censored newspapers (*Kurier Wileński, Gazeta Codzienna,* and *Nasze Słowo*). All Polish periodicals were liquidated, and the showing of prewar Polish films was forbidden. Ordinary Polish citizens were arrested and beaten; they were attacked both on the streets and in churches during and after services. People were killed. The refugees from western and central Poland, moreover, were not allowed to leave their place of residence without permission from the Lithuanian police, were forbidden to participate in political activities, were not allowed to attend any meetings whatsoever, and were even forbidden to use typewriters. "The list of wrongdoings and pogroms organized by the police, Shaulists [members of a nationalistic group of Lithuanian riflemen serving in German military formations] and the Lithuanian youth," stated Stanisław Lagun, an eyewitness, "is very long."[13]

Life went on thus until June 14, 1940, when the Soviet Union handed Lithuania an ultimatum and the Red Army proceeded to reoccupy (on June 15) not only the Wilno region but the whole of the twenty-three-year-old Lithuanian Republic — according to the amended Soviet-German August agreement. The Soviets then expanded Okręg Wileński by adding to it the regions of Święciany-Hoduciszki, Dziewie-niszki, and Druskieniki-Marcinkańce. Consequently, the population of this area increased once more — not only because of the citizens who were residents of the incorporated territories but also because of the Russian functionaries and political commissars who came streaming into Wilno (and Kaunas) along with their relatives and friends. (The territory of Okręg Wileński would again be increased, this time under the German occupation, by the inclusion of Oszmiana, Świr, and Ejszyszki in April 1942, thus adding about 200,000 more people. With this addition, the total area of Wileńszczyzna came to 15,840 square kilometers.[14])

On July 21, 1940, the newly elected, Moscow-controlled Lithuanian "People's Diet" passed a resolution to include Lithuania among the Soviet socialist republics. The Soviet government willingly accepted the resolution, and on August 3 the Republic of Lithuania, with Wileńszczyzna, officially became the Lithuanian SSR. Sweeping changes were quick to follow, among them a new constitution, a dramatic increase in the membership of the Communist Party (from 1,500–1,800 on the eve of the war to 4,625 at the end of 1940), and the reorganization of the Lithuanian army into the 29th Territorial Corps of the Red Army.[15]

In Wileńszczyzna, under the renewed Soviet reign of terror, all Polish newspapers ceased to function and all Polish institutions, even charitable ones, were liquidated. In the spring of 1941, members of the Polish underground, especially the leaders of the Service for Polish Victory and the Union for Armed Struggle (Służba Zwycięstwu Polski- Związek Walki Zbrojnej, or SZP-ZWZ) were arrested in Wilno and Kaunas. That June, the last of the mass deportations that swept Poland's eastern territories also visited Lithuania and Wileńszczyzna. The transports to the Gulag continued unabated to within literally hours of the German invasion. During this time some 31,000 to 35,000 Poles and some 40,000 (German estimate) to 60,000 (Lithuanian estimate) Lithuanians were arrested and deported by the NKVD.[16] (Zbigniew S. Siemaszko's estimate for the category that included Lithuanians, Czechs, Russians, Germans, and others was 20,000.) In Wilno, out of the 7,602 deportees (including 2,380 women and 1,036 children), about 5,000 were Poles.[17] Finally, just before the German invasion there were death marches to the Soviet Union and last-minute executions of political prisoners.[18]

When the Red Army marched out of Wilno and Wileńszczyzna for the second time, it was harassed not only by the Poles but by the Lithuanians as well. The Wehrmacht entered the city on June 24, 1941. "Many of the same Lithuanians who professed to be fervent communists in the days of the Soviet occupation," stated Lagun, "now became confirmed fascists."[19]

German Occupation

Not all Lithuanian Nazi collaborators lived in their homeland. Before the German invasion, many Lithuanian activists and functionaries sought a haven in Germany, where they were warmly welcomed. There they encountered the émigré followers of former minister Kazys Škirpa, the Lithuanian deputy in Berlin known for his anti–Polish, pro–German orientation, as well as the followers of the former prime minister of Lithuania, Augustinas Voldemaras, whose party, after its failed 1934 coup, sought the backing of the Germans.

As a result of Škirpa's efforts, on November 17, 1940, the Lithuanian Activist Front (Lietuvių Aktyvistų Frontas, or LAF) was established in Berlin with a network of branches in Lithuania. Under its wing gathered the representatives of almost every prewar Lithuanian party: Voldemaras, the National Unionists (Tautininkai), the Peasant Populist Union, the Christian Democrats, and the Social Democrats. Far from considering the Nazis a threat, the LAF hoped that in exchange for its offer of collaboration, Germany would grant Lithuania at least the same amount of freedom as it had granted Slovakia on March 14, 1939.

The LAF parties with the largest representation were the National Unionists, whose prewar slogan was "Lithuania for Lithuanians," and the Christian Democrats, founded by Rev. Mykolas Krupavičius. (The Lithuanian clergy played a major role in the political life of the young republic and continued to do so under the German occupation — not as a force opposed to the new régime but as its supporter. It was no coincidence that when the Wehrmacht was forced to evacuate Lithuania, 250 Lithuanian clergymen followed in its footsteps.[20])

In anticipation of the German invasion of Lithuania, the LAF began to organize pro–Nazi intelligence and diversionary groups in Germany under the Shaulists, to recruit a Lithuanian army, and to instruct those in the homeland in what was to be done once the German armies arrived. One such directive, dated March 19, 1941, reads as follows:

> The hour of Lithuanian freedom is nigh. You will be informed by radio or in some other way regarding the beginning of the march from the West. At that moment local uprisings should occur in the enslaved Lithuanian towns, settlements and villages — in other words, take over the administration ... organize yourselves in small groups.... After the military operations, take over the bridges, important railways junctions, airports, factories, and so forth.... Paratroopers will be dropped in the rear at the time of the military operations. Establish contact with them immediately and render whatever help is needed.[21]

The Lithuanian population was furthermore instructed to receive the German army with genuine enthusiasm: "The German army will march through villages, towns and cities. In their ranks there will be many of your fellow-countrymen whom you will recognize. Receive them all with equal enthusiasm and give them your assistance. By that time, a temporary Lithuanian government would already be in place."[22]

The German invasion of Lithuania was accompanied by a general uprising. "About 100,000 guerrillas took part in this insurrection," stated a September 15, 1941, LAF memorandum to the "Government of the Reich." "Over 4,000 Lithuanian youths died in the battle with the Bolsheviks"—a figure the Germans thought to be rather inflated. That plaintive memorandum continues: "When the German army marched into Lithuania, it found very friendly Lithuanian government organs everywhere, not Bolshevik offices. Lithuanian army units and Lithuanian guerrillas everywhere helped the German army marching through Lithuania as much as they could. Lithuanians fought with Germany, not against it."[23]

Avraham Tory's Kaunas ghetto diary makes it clear that the Lithuanian people welcomed the Germans as liberators and were more than willing to collaborate with them.[24] Flowers were strewn before the German tanks, and the Lithuanians rejoiced at the prospect of regaining their prewar independence. Indeed, they did recognize some of those who marched with the Wehrmacht: those in the LAF military units reinforced later by thirty-six hundred deserters from the 29th (Lithuanian) Territorial Corps of the Red Army.[25]

On entering Wileńszczyzna, the LAF units distinguished themselves by committing murder, rape, and pillage. They called themselves "Lithuanian partisans," but even the Germans referred to them as "organized bands of robbers" *(organisierte Räubenbande)* whose rape and plunder belonged to the daily order of things (*Plünderungen und Notzüchtigungen gehören schon zur Tagesordnung dieser Einheiten*).[26] Sometimes, as in Wilno, the Roman Catholic clergy was the object of their cold-blooded rampage.[27]

The Lithuanian Provisional Government, presided over by Juozas Ambrazevičius (Brazaitis),[28] was established by the LAF on June 23, 1941—just one day after the invasion. With the approval of the German military authorities, all Soviet structures were quickly dismantled and replaced by Lithuanian ones administered by LAF members. Daily order was maintained by the LAF police. For a time, it seemed that Lithuania had indeed achieved the status of Slovakia. The Germans, however, had no intention of granting autonomy to Lithuania. The illusion of freedom lasted but one month.

On July 25, 1941, the General Commissariat of Lithuania, as Lithuania and Okręg Wileński were now called, was placed under German civil administration, and the LAF government, which was never recognized by Germany, was systematically liquidated. In its place, a seven-member Lithuanian Generalräte (Directorate or "General Counselors"), headed by General Petras Kubiliūnas, was appointed to help the Nazi authorities administer the commissariat.[29] On August 16 and 17 of that year, a letter from the bishop of Kaunas, Vincentas Brizgys, was read in Lithuanian churches urging the faithful to cooperate with Kubiliūnas and the new administration.[30] A July 23, 1941, Chief of the SP and SD report states: "The control of the sermons in Vilnius has resulted in a generally positive political attitude."[31]

To prevent the buildup of an indigenous army, the LAF military units and the police were dispersed among the various pro–Nazi organizations that would form the heart of the Lithuanian collaborative structures for the remainder of the war: the Lithuanian Detective Forces/Criminal Police (Kripo), the secret security police (Saugumo), the special security police units (Sonderkommando), the auxiliary police units (Hilfspolizeitruppe) and guard units (Wachmannschaften) incorporated into the Schutzmannschaften, the so-called Lithuanian Aufbaudienst forces, and the Lithuanian Legion or "Local Detachments" (Lietuvos Vietinė Rinktinė).

Throughout the Nazi occupation, the Lithuanian Criminal Police prowled about in every city and town of the commissariat. Their main task was to apprehend criminals and to hunt down and arrest anyone suspected of opposing the new régime. These arrests were often conducted on the basis of information provided by the Saugumo police, which was affiliated with the Gestapo and relied on its tactics as well. Among the veritable army of spies were Rev. J. Bartomaitis (the confessor of the Łukiszki prison in Wilno) and the pastor from Jęczmieniszki (in Wileńszczyzna), Rev. A. Jakavonis. Another clergyman, Rev. Žeidzina of Oszmiana, worked directly for the Gestapo.[32]

The Lithuanian Sonderkommando der Sipo und SD performed guard duties and, together with the SS, conducted the mass executions at the Seventh Fort in Kaunas and in Ponary. There were 205 former Lithuanian partisans in the Kaunas Sonderkommando and 150 in the one stationed in Ponary. The latter were also known as the Ypatingas Būrys, or "Ponary Riflemen" (Polish: *strzelcy ponarskie*). Formed in June 1941, they would remain in the general area of Wileńszczyzna until July 1944, when the SD was evacuated from Wilno. Their leader was Hauptscharführer SS Martin Weiss, who commanded two officers and a few dozen NCOs of the former LAF army. Initially, they wore the uniform of the Lithuanian army — later, that of the SD. They were armed with pistols, hand machine guns, and rifles. They were required to sign an oath of secrecy regarding the activities of their unit, were paid, and received free provisions. In addition to the executions in Ponary, the Sonderkommando committed unspeakable atrocities in other areas of Wileńszczyzna as well.[33]

The remaining LAF officers and enlisted men who were not assigned to police formations, together with the Lithuanian POWs from the Red Army, became a part of the Lithuanian Aufbaudienst. This organization, which operated in battalion formations, was subdivided into self-defense units (Selbstschutzabteilung), order-keeping units (Ordnungsabteilung), and work units (Arbeitsabteilung). Seven such battalions were stationed in Kaunas, one in Šiauliai, and one in Panevėžys. Of the five battalions established in Wilno, Battalion 2 (18 officers and 450 enlisted men) was sent to perform guard duty in Majdanek, Battalion 1 (10 officers and 334 enlisted men) and Battalion 4 (8 officers and 253 enlisted men) remained in Wilno, Battalion 5 (22 officers and 288 enlisted men) performed railroad guard duty in the Wilno area, and Battalion 3 (24 officers and 607 enlisted men) was sent to Minsk.[34]

In November 1941, all existing auxiliary police and guard units were incorporated into the Schutzmannschaften, and additional Schutzmannschaften battalions, numbered 251–265 and 301–310, were added. The Lithuanians who became concentration and forced-labor camp guards (Wachmannschaften) received their training in Trawniki along with the Ukrainians, Russians, Latvians, and Volksdeutsche from Poland.[35] According to the Lithuanian Generalräte, in mid–1942 there were 16,000 Lithuanians in the Schutzmannschaften units: 6,000 in the police (Hilfspolizei) and 10,000 in various battalions (Schuma-Bataillonen).[36] Hilberg states:

> When Lithuanian Schutzmannschaft battalions were set up, many of these units were sent out from their homeland to other regions. The first of the border crossers were the Lithuanian companies of Major Lechthaler's 11th Reserve Police Battalion, which killed thousands of Jews in Belorussia. During August and September 1942, two Lithuanian battalions took part in "Operation Swamp Fever," which covered the marshes of Belorussia and Ukraine. In this expedition, more than eighty-three hundred Jews were killed. Two other battalions were posted in succession to the death camp of Maydanek (Lublin). Lithuanian battalions ranged all the way to the southern Ukraine, eight hundred miles from the Lithuanian frontier, where they guarded Jewish laborers.[37]

One Lithuanian battalion was also used to quell the Warsaw Ghetto Revolt,[38] but the Lithuanians were there much earlier. During the "resettlement" of the Warsaw ghetto in 1942, states Martin Gilbert, "many Jews, resisting or fleeing, were killed on the spot, often by Ukrainian, Latvian and Lithuanian volunteers, or their German SS officers."[39]

Like Metropolitan Andrei Sheptytsky, who provided chaplains for the Ukrainian Nationalist SS-Galizien, Archbishop Juozapas

Skvireckas and Bishop Vincentas Brizgys provided the Lithuanian Schutzmannschaften battalions with chaplains. Both of these high-ranking prelates were among the 250 clergymen who evacuated the Lithuanian Commissariat with the German army in 1944.[40]

In subsequent years, German efforts to form other Lithuanian military formations met with varying degrees of success. The attempt to create a Lithuanian Waffen-SS division comparable to the Latvian, Estonian, and Ukrainian (Galician) SS divisions floundered and was discontinued on March 17, 1943. That summer, an "All Lithuanian Conference" sponsored by the German authorities paved the way for a more successful mobilization campaign. On February 16, 1944, the anniversary of Lithuanian independence, the Germans announced the formation of a 10,000-man Lithuanian Legion, or "Local Detachments" (Litauische Sonderverbände, in German, and Lietuvos Vietinė Rinktinė, or LVR, in Lithuanian), under General Povelas Plechavičius; some 30,000 young Lithuanians volunteered for its ranks.[41] The mission of this legion was to combat the Polish underground as well as the Soviet partisans in Wileńszczyzna. The legion also perpetrated atrocities against Polish civilians in Pawłów, Graużyszki, and Sieńkowszczyzna.[42]

During its battles and skirmishes with the AK, the LVR was so weakened that after the fiasco at the fortified city of Murowana Oszmianka, Plechavičius and his officers were relieved of command and were arrested by the Germans. Plechavičius was sent to the concentration camp of Sulaspils (Kircholm) near Riga in Latvia for a short time; after his release he was sent to Germany. With his arrest, many of the LVR officers and soldiers deserted, and the Germans sent others to Ponary to be executed by their fellow countrymen. The remnant of the legion was reformed and placed under a Colonel Birontas. Categorically denied permission to transform the legion into an SS unit, Birontas organized it into several infantry battalions, which were then sent to the eastern front. About 3,500 men were also transferred to Germany to perform guard duty at various airports.[43] Another interpretation of these events is presented by Romuald Misiunas and Rein Taagepera:

> In May [1944], the transfer of the new units into the Auxiliary police Services of the SS was initiated. However, it triggered an immediate self-demobilization of the remaining units, most of whose personnel managed to slip away into the woods. General Plechavičius and his staff were arrested on 15 May, and some 100 of his men were indiscriminately shot. Those who did not succeed in escaping (about 3,500) were transferred for *Luftwaffe* ground duty in Germany and Norway.[44]

Finally, in May 1944, mobilization efforts got under way in the Lithuanian Commissariat to reinforce the failing German defenses by providing Army Group North with 50,000 Lithuanian soldiers, the navy with 40,000, and the air force with 30,000 men.[45] As Maria Wardzyńska points out, the willing participation of the Lithuanians in the Nazi military, police, and administrative structures made it possible for Germany to maintain in Lithuania one of the smallest occupation forces in all of its captured territories: 6,000 Germans at the end of 1943.[46]

The manifest reason for the German invasion of the Soviet Union was to provide additional living space for its population. This required cleansing the conquered territories of their indigenous hostile populations. In Lithuania and Wileńszczyzna these were thought to be the communists, the Jews, and the Poles — in that order. A July 1, 1941, Chief of SP and SD order to all operational groups reads as follows: "The cleansing action must first and foremost be conducted against the Bolsheviks and the Jews. With respect to the Polish intelligentsia, the matter can be resolved later. In the event that this postponement may result in danger, and the incident is not sporadic, remedial steps will be taken immediately."[47]

Thus, unlike in central and western Poland, in Lithuania and Wileńszczyzna there was no concerted effort, initially, to exterminate the Polish intelligentsia, which was in any case already decimated under the Soviet rule. The Germans also expected that the Poles would contribute to the extermination of the Jews and the Bolsheviks and that the Lithuanians would contribute to the extermination of

Table 4. Mass Executions of Poles in Ponary According to Polish Underground Reports, 1942-1944

Year	*Number of Persons*
1942	
May 4, 5	About 50 Polish prisoners from Łukiszki
May 6	A group of intellectuals
May 9, 17	About 300 prisoners mainly from Łukiszki, including 80 male and 5 female students
July 2	About 150 people
July 5	60 persons, including 47 women and 1 ten-year-old girl
July 15	26 Poles from Łukiszki; some reports say 60
July 16	18 Poles
July 18	100+ Polish political prisoners
July 19	Another 100+ Polish political prisoners
September 2	51 persons
December 2	120 members of the Polish underground
1943	
January	19 Polish prisoners from Łukiszki
July 17	27 women
July 28	30 prisoners from Łukiszki
September 17	10 Poles
1944	
April 18, 20	100 Poles

the Jews, the Bolsheviks, and the Poles. They were right about the Lithuanians but wrong about the Poles.

Very few Lithuanian communists could be found in Lithuania and Wileńszczyzna after the entry of the Germans because most of them, in accordance with the LAF directive to "spare Lithuanian blood," had become anti–Bolshevik partisans. For example, one Lithuanian member of the NKVD who went by the name of "Pavlov" under the Soviet occupation became "Požėlas" under the German occupation; to prove his loyalty he even headed up one of the volunteer units that exterminated Jews. Shortly thereafter he was hung.[48]

For the Poles, the German occupation of Wileńszczyzna began with arrests, especially the arrests of the Polish youth. According to Einsatzkommando 3 reports, just after the invasion about six hundred prisoners were interned in every county town.[49] Certain prisoners — political activists, communists, administrative functionaries — were slated for immediate execution. Others were given prison sentences.

Under the Ambrazevičius administration, as well as under the directorate of Kubiliūnas, the Lithuanianization of Wileńszczyzna followed the same pattern as before, except that now there was much more anti–Polish rhetoric and violence. Some clergy called from the pulpit for Polish pogroms, stating that the Poles were worse than the Jews.[50] There were reports that Lithuanian priests were offering indulgences for the killing of Poles.[51] At least one enterprising Lithuanian professor devoted a paper to the theme "Why We Should Hate the Poles,"[52] and the LAF called for the erection of Polish ghettos, for the establishment of ordinances requiring Poles to wear identification badges, and for the reduction of food rations to Poles — while bragging that under the Soviets they had exterminated 50 percent of the Poles and that under the Germans they planned to exterminate the other 50 percent.[53]

Although not initially on a massive scale, murders of Polish people were reported — murders committed by the Wilno Sonderkommando in Niemenczyn, Nowa Wilejka, Orany,

Troki, Rzesza (Rieše), Ejszyszki, Siemieliszki, Jaszuny, and Święciany. On September 27, 1941, 320 Poles from the prison at Łukiszki were executed in Ponary.[54] But the real terror against the Polish people began in November 1941, when a wave of "preventive" arrests swept Okręg Wileński. People suspected of collaborating with the resistance were rounded up by the Lithuanian police, interrogated by the Saugumo, and handed over to the Gestapo. Often their destination was the Łukiszki prison, then Ponary. (See Table 4.[55])

On March 3 and 4, 1942, mass arrests of the Polish clergy and members of religious orders took place in Wilno and all of Wileńszczyzna, followed by the closure of monasteries and convents. This was done with the assistance of the Lithuanian police.[56] According to Czesław Łuczak, sixteen such institutions were closed in Wilno between March 23 and April 4, 1942, and a portion of the 253 religious evicted from them were imprisoned.[57] A document dated March 27, 1942, lists the names of 196 members of religious incarcerated in Łukiszki prison.[58] Some of the spiritual leaders of Wileńszczyzna were also sent to forced-labor camps, including the one in Pravieniškės, 22 kilometers south of Kaunas. The Lithuanian bishops did not intervene in the arrests or call for a halt to the robberies committed in their course.

At this time, just as during the entire period of the German occupation, the Lithuanian police seemed to have a free hand. On March 25, 1942, the police killed two Poles for talking in Polish on the street. A week later, they broke the hand of Kasper Czecowski because he answered them in Polish.[59] In September 1942 they shot a young Pole on the streets of Wilno. In nearby Mickuny, a Lithuanian policeman shot a teenager for refusing to hand over his bicycle. Near the Ponary brickyard, a man brought from Wilno by the Lithuanian police was clubbed to death. In Draskienki, the Lithuanian police, which routinely removed Poles standing in food lines, shot a boy for taking some sugar from a store.[60]

Aside from such incidents and the formal executions in Ponary and elsewhere, many Polish people died in reprisals for the assassinations of Germans, Lithuanian policemen, or Nazi spies—no matter which partisans did the killing. On May 19, 1942, the Soviet partisans assassinated Kreislandwirtschaftsführer Joseph Beck, his designated successor, and another officer of the Wehrmacht on the road between Stare Święciany and Łyntupy near the village of Wygoda. Several hours later, 200 Poles were executed in their homes and on the streets, and orders were given to arrest 1,000 more. By the time this reprisal action—carried out by the commandant of the Lithuanian police, Jonas Maciulevičius, and the Ponary execution squad—was over, 1,200 Poles had been murdered in Nowe Święciany, Łyntupy Stare, and the surrounding regions. In addition, Captain Zehnpfenig of the German Wilno field command ordered the execution of 150 Polish prisoners in the Łukiszki prison.[61]

On September 15, 1943, the inspector of the Lithuanian police, Marijonas Podabas, was assassinated by the AK, which, except for this incident, was generally careful to plan its activities so as not to provoke reprisals against civilians. As a result of Podabas' death, the commandant of the secret police ordered the arrest of 100 Poles, 10 of whom were executed two days later in Ponary; the rest were detained and told that they would be killed in the event of another assassination attempt.[62] Actually, 140 hostages were taken by the Wilno Lithuanian police on the night of September 16. Among them were 14 professors of USB, the university head librarian, 4 doctors, 9 officers, 3 teachers, 4 lawyers, 2 priests, a few engineers and chemists, a school director, a theater director, and many other members of the Polish intelligentsia, including some of the wives.[63]

Sometimes both Polish and Lithuanian civilians died in mutual reprisals of warring partisan groups. On the night of June 19, 1944, in a skirmish over provisions between the AK and a Lithuanian paramilitary unit in Glinciszki, the Lithuanians lost 4 men. In reprisal, they decided to kill 40 Poles—10 for every one of their comrades. The Poles they planned to kill were civilians. On the morning of September 20, a party of 100 Lithuanian policemen murdered 38 innocent civilians—men, women, and children—in and around Glinciszki.[64] In their turn, according to one account, the 5th Brigade of the AK, Zygmunt Szendzielarz's "Łupaszka," decided to exact revenge on the Lithuanian village of Dubinki, which housed the families of some of the Lithuanian policemen involved in the Glinciszki incident. In defiance of the April 12, 1944, AK order no. 5 of Aleksander Krzyżanowski ("Wilk")—an order that forbade AK units to engage in reprisal actions against civilians—the "Łupaszka" group attacked the citizens of Dubinki on June 23 and slaughtered 27 Lithuanian men, women, and children. "Wilk," meanwhile, sent two AK brigades, "Narocz" and "Brasławska," under "Węgielny," into the area as a show of force and as a warning to refrain from further anti-Polish actions.[65] According to another (more probable) version, the reprisal action involved all three brigades under the leadership of "Węgielny."[66] Fortunately, the Soviet offensive that began on that very day put an end to this sad chapter of Polish-Lithuanian relations during World War II.

In addition to the executions and reprisals in which thousands of Poles died at the hands of the Lithuanian police, the Sonderkommando, and the SS, a number of Polish families were resettled from the Lithuanian Commissariat in order to make room for German families as well as for those Lithuanian families previously displaced from the Suwałki and Klaipėda (Memel) regions annexed by Germany. Just how many Poles were resettled is not known, but an October 1942 report from the Eastern Bureau to the Polish government-in-exile states that between mid–September and the end of October of that year, about 1,500 Polish families were given fifteen minutes to two hours in which to pack. After this, they were placed under arrest in transit camps and then either set free, sent to other counties to live with relatives and friends, or shipped to forced-labor camps. At the end of 1943, when this action was brought to a halt, 30,000 Germans (including 16,000 former residents) and an unknown number of Lithuanians were settled in the General Commissariat of Lithuania on predominantly Polish farmsteads and in predominantly Polish domiciles. This action was carried out by the Lithuanian police, which routinely attacked and beat the Polish people in the process.[67]

In total, about 40,000 people, mostly Poles, were also deported from the commissariat to Nazi Germany for supplying forced labor and to Leningrad for building fortifications. (According to an August 25, 1942 report of the Polish Government Delegation for July 16 to August 25, about 20,000 people were deported to the Third Reich from Wilno and the surrounding areas.[68]) Another 50,000 or so were used for forced labor inside the commissariat. The need for forced labor intensified with the progress of the war, and in January 1944 the Germans demanded 50,000 workers by the end of February and another 50,000 by October 1. These deportation actions, which included rounding up people on the streets and dragging them out of their houses, always involved the Lithuanian police and even the Saugumo when it came to the "recruitment" of the "most undesirable elements" among the Poles.[69]

Władysław Pobóg-Malinowski provides a good summary of the Polish tragedy in Wileńszczyzna and of the part played by the Lithuanian collaborators:

> The Lithuanians who cooperated with the Germans oppressed, pestered, and harassed the Polish people, plagued and persecuted them, and with cool determination destroyed and exterminated all that was Polish in language, agricultural establishments, and culture. They Lithuanianized children in schools, disseminated Polonophobic propaganda in the press. The Lithuanian police was brutal, rapacious, boorish, and cruel in its frequent searches, arrests, and interrogations. Often, it surpassed the Gestapo in its treatment, interrogations, and demands for confessions from prisoners. The inspections, night raids, and street roundups carried out with the help of the Lithuanians went beyond the demands of the Nazis. Thousands of Poles, among them women and children, died from Lithuanian bullets, from butt-ends of rifles and bayonets.... Polish literature does not speak of this ghastly terror aimed at the destruction of all that was Polish.... But a crime is always a crime and this one—the Lithuanian—in Wileńszczyzna must be acknowledged as representing a frightening example of the most predatory instincts liberated by the immunity from

> punishment, not of animals, but of human savagery. The Lithuanians not only besmirched their historical good name by their actions against the Polish people; they also helped in the persecution and destruction of the Jews in local ghettos and in Ponary where, in the course of several months, the most monstrous slaughter of the Jews brought there for that purpose from all over transpired.[70]

The task of liquidating the Jews was assigned to the German motorized operational groups known as the Einsatzgruppen der Sicherheitspolizei und des SD. Einsatzgruppe A and its Einsatzkommando 2 and 3 operated in the Baltic countries including Lithuania. Okręg Wileński was the domain of Einsatzgruppe B, with its Einsatzkommando 9. On July 2, 1941, Einsatzkommando 3 took over the anticommunist and anti–Jewish actions in Okręg Wileński. On August 9, it took over the function of the security police as well.[71]

After the German invasion, bolstered by Nazi anti–Semitic propaganda that continually reminded the Lithuanians of the role played by the Jews during the Soviet occupation, the LAF called for a final resolution of the Jewish question, stating in its various proclamations that Lithuania must be liberated not only from "Bolshevik Asiatics" but also from "longstanding Jewish pressure." One of these proclamations told the people to inform the Jews that their days were numbered, so that those who were able to leave Lithuania would do so immediately, in order to avoid unnecessary victims. Another proclamation stated that traitors would be forgiven if they could prove that they had killed at least one Jew.[72] As a result, Jewish pogroms (as distinct from Einsatzkommando executions) were staged in every city and town across the former Lithuanian Republic just after the German invasion. In Kaunas, for example, 2,500 Jews died. Michael Ignatieff notes, "Many Lithuanians enthusiastically took part in the Final Solution."[73]

The Lithuanian partisans also killed Jews. An Einsatzkommando report for June 28, 1941, confirmed that a group of Lithuanian partisans had shot several thousand Jews in the previous three days. By July 2, the victim toll of those shot by the partisans was about 4,000 Jews. In all, together with those who died in Lithuanian pogroms, about 7,000 Jews died at this time.[74]

Initially, the situation in Okręg Wileński was somewhat different. Although the Germans fully expected the "anti–Semitic" Polish population to engage in spontaneous Jewish pogroms, it did not. Meanwhile, the LAF was concerned more with establishing its self-proclaimed Lithuanian government there and with re–Lithuanianizing the area than with carrying out the "Final Solution."

The liquidation of the Jews in Wileńszczyzna began on July 2, 1941. It was carried out by Einsatzkommando and the Lithuanian Sonderkommando unit. The Lithuanian police, under the auspices of the Saugumo, first arrested the Jews (8,000 in Wilno alone), then interned them in Łukiszki prison, and finally took them to Ponary. By July 28, 1941, 35,000 Jews were crammed into the Kaunas ghetto; by September of that year, 60,000 found themselves in the ghetto in Wilno. Hilberg states:

> By the beginning of July, 1,150 Lithuanians in Vilnius [Wilno] were employed by Einsatzkommando 9 to round up and shoot 500 Jews a day. When the Jews of Vilnius were subjected to ghettoization two months later, Lithuanian police and freelancing "Selbstschutz" in the city lent a hand. At 6:00 A.M. on September 6, 1941, the police conducted the Jews to the ghetto site and the Selbstschutz formed a cordon around the ghetto to prevent escapes.[75]

The first execution of the Jews in Ponary took place on July 4, 1941: 54 Jews. On July 5, 93 others were killed. By July 8, 321 had been murdered. At the end of August, the Wilno Jews were confined in a ghetto from which, one group at a time, they were taken to Ponary and shot.[76] Gilbert describes one of these massive roundups of the Jews for Ponary, occurring in October of that year: "Thousands of Jews hid in cellars, or in attics but groups of Lithuanians went from house to house in search of them, often returning several times to the same house.... In many of the cellars, Jews resisted the Lithuanian 'hunters,' and refused to leave. They were shot dead on the spot."[77]

Ponary was located about 10 kilometers from Wilno. The place of execution was about 3 kilometers from the Ponary railway station — a secluded, wooded area where deep fuel pits dug during the Soviet occupation made ideal mass graves. The entire area was surrounded by a barbed-wire fence and was guarded by ten to twelve Sonderkommando lackeys. "No Trespassing" signs warned that violators would be shot. Those to be executed were often brought by rail and by truck, but just as often they were marched to their graves.

Generally speaking, even when guarded by a handful of Lithuanian policemen, the Jews went there without resistance. They were told that they were being taken somewhere for "work," and sometimes this was the case. Moreover, severe reprisals awaited the desperate and the brave. On September 2, 1941, some shots were fired by Jews at German soldiers. In reprisal, 3,700 Jews died in the largest single execution at Ponary. On another occasion (November 2, 1941), in the course of their death march the Jews of Žagarė (near the Latvian border) drew out weapons and, amid shouts of "Long Live Stalin" and "Down with Hitler," attacked their Lithuanian guards, wounding seven. For this, 150 of them were shot immediately, and the remaining 2,000 were killed at the execution site.[78] The killing process at Ponary is described by Gilbert: "A hundred Jews at a time were brought from the city to Ponary, to a 'waiting zone.' Here, in what had once been a popular holiday resort for Vilna Jewry, they were ordered to undress and to hand over whatever money or valuables they had with them. They were then marched naked, single file, in groups of ten to twenty at a time, holding hands, to the edge of the fuel pits, and shot down by rifle fire."[79]

A more chilling and detailed description of daily events at Ponary is provided by the diary of Kazimierz Sakowicz. Before the war, Sakowicz was the owner of the newspaper *Przegląd Gospodarczy* in Wilno. During the occupation, he moved his family to Ponary, near what turned out to be the execution site, and began to keep a journal on the atrocities committed there. The entries begin on July 11, 1941, and end on October 25, 1943. As a Polish army officer, Sakowicz belonged to the underground. He died in the general Polish uprising of 1944 called Operation "Tempest" ("Burza"). The journal was discovered after his death — in bottles that he had buried in his garden. Some of the text was illegible. Here are selections from his entries:

1941

July 11. The weather is rather nice, warm, white clouds, wind, some gunfire coming from the woods. Probably training exercises ... found out that many Jews were brought there. And they are shooting them....

July 23. Day of Atonement, about 500 Jews are brought. The shooting goes on until late. Yells: "I'm not a communist!" "What are you doing?" They began to run away, there's shooting throughout the woods, throughout the night and morning catching, shooting, finishing off. Many intelligentsia....

From July 23. ... All together about 5,000 persons have been shot in July....

From August 22. The Germans are taking all the valuables, leaving the clothing for the Lithuanians....

In August there was shooting on the following days: 1, 2, 6, 8, 11, 16, 22, 23, 26, together then ten days, 2,000 persons were shot. Already last week, i.e., August 17–25, the Shaulists were saying that in the following week, in the course of a single day there will be as many executed as there were in all of August....

September 2. They brought 2,000 Jews, among them many women and children.

September 12. Again, about 2,000 were shot.

Tuesday, October 21. They brought about 1,000 exclusively women and small children of both sexes....

Note. October 25. One Jewess hearing shots tries to escape. They catch her and on the order of the officer she is murdered on the road. The officers also beat and taunt her. The Germans are now conveying the clothes to Wilno by truck....

November. On November 1, the pious representatives of the murderous Lithuanian nation [*bogobojni przedstawiciele katowskiego narodu litewskiego*] liquidated four lorries of Jews. They are shooting in their army uniforms. November 1 (Saturday) was All Saints Day. That did not prevent them from shooting.

1942

On Tuesday, May 5. ... 47 people were killed, not Jews but Poles and members of the Red Army....

May 13. Thursday. ... Among those shot—some 70 persons—were 6 women, several Jews and Jewish policemen, and evidently 2 clerics ... [illegible].... Today Shaulist Gailiūnas ... brought a partially torn [priest's] robe to the railway hut ... and wanted 50 rm. for it....

July 15, Wednesday. Red Army soldiers and Poles were shot; 4 truckloads (about 70 persons)....

July 30. They brought 150 old Jews on trucks through the gate on the strategic road.

In Ponary, the railwayman, policeman and a woman from the post office, in general, the entire Ponary "Lithuanian colony" is in close contact with the Shaulists (in point of fact, they are no Shaulists but soldiers)....

August 25, Tuesday. ... The Lithuanians, as usual, are doing the shooting....

September 10. ... A covered automobile; the Germans are going to the base with some person. They chased out the Lithuanians from the base, shot and buried him themselves. When the Lithuanians returned, they uncovered [the body] in order to take the clothes and later sell them....

October 10, Saturday. One transport (bus); the Lithuanians are sitting on the benches and the condemned are lying on the floor. In this way they attempt to camouflage the fact of the executions ... [illegible] one could surmise that the Lithuanians are on their way to fill in old ditches....

December 2, Wednesday. ... A condemned man ran to the woods; he was already wounded.... The Lithuanians began firing frantically. The condemned man crashed to the earth. One of the Lithuanians ran up and smashed the lying man in the head with the butt of his rifle. Then they halted a wagon, placed the remains (the head was one big mass of brains and blood) on it and took it to the base....

1943

January 28, Thursday. Three transports from the direction of the strategic road, including several women, among them Jewesses. The Lithuanians did the shooting. There were two Germans....

Leningrad, Rostov, Kursk, Kharkov ... on the Caucasus the Germans are surrounded ... only now a foretaste of the disaster which awaits the Lithuanians who, as no other nation in the world, have so many murders on their conscience....

18 ... [illegible], Thursday. ... After one hour the executioners return loaded down with the belongings of the murdered people.... [The Lithuanian] tells about his worries; in his hands, Polish engineer boots (wants 4,000 rubles). The boots are still warm....

March 5, Friday. ... I could not remain by the hut because one of the Germans began to eye me keenly....

April 4, Sunday. At 5 o'clock p.m. four lorries arrived from Wilno with Lithuanian police dressed ... [illegible], i.e., gray overcoats or ... [illegible], i.e., in German and 3 in Gestapo uniforms ... [illegible] with them arrived two crates of liquor....

The Gestapo went to the base, we see that they are examining the closest pit.... To pass the time the Lithuanians are touring Ponary, singing, trying to initiate conversations with the locals, mostly without success since to every question in Lithuanian people reply, "I don't understand".... Suddenly, there's a news flash that they're going to bring a trainload of Jews from Wilno ... and shoot them....

Around 6 o'clock the next morning ... Gestapo opened four train cars and the Jews were told to get out.... Soon they were surrounded by a dense chain of Lithuanians and Gestapo ... nervous ... when they entered the barbed-wire gate they saw ... understood what awaited them ... the young and even the women began to flee ... they were told to remove their clothes by the first pit. There's crying, sighing, pleading, begging on knees....

They tried to hide their children under the [discarded] clothes. Evidently, they hoped that when the clothes were taken away ... their children hidden in this way would be saved.... Some woman is showing the Lithuanians a small child, obviously still an infant, one of them grabs the woman and pushes her into the pit with the child. There's a large group of men and women who are still dressed; they are hurried into the pit in their scanty clothes. They are beginning to shoot from above. Finally, they stand seven women in their underclothes at the pit, shots ring out. Again, they hurry a new party into the pit, again shots. Again, on the other side of the pit ... ten men and women by the pit. Shots again. Four men are left in their underclothes. They're told to place all the clothes in a pile. Another child. A Lithuanian orders it to be thrown into the pit. A Jew is carrying it and at a certain moment he bolts with the child into the woods. They chase him, shots ring out. The Jew disappears in the thicket of trees, more shots ring out. In a while the Lithuanians return. Did he get away!? One of the Lithuanians is saying something to the remaining three Jewish men and they are taken to the forest in the company of two more policemen, ten minutes pass. In that time a third party arrives preceded by a loud shooting noise and the same undressing begins, some woman, it's plain to see, spits in the face of the German, at that moment a Lithuanian strikes her with the butt-end of a rifle, the woman falls.... In this way, in less than four hours, about 2,500 people are killed ... a few escaped, about 50....

April 5, Monday. ... about 200–300 people are coming, mainly children, women, a few old people, youths.... The women have many toddlers ... they are driven mercilessly by the Lithuanians.... A terrible impression is created among the rest of the condemned who are no further than 10–15 meters from the shooting. They, therefore, see what is happening to their dear ones and [know] what awaits them. Three men, and two women; one of them with a child in her arms tries to flee. A Lithuanian chases her down and strikes her in the head with his rifle butt. The woman collapses. The Lithuanian seizes the child and carries it by its legs. He nears the pit and flings it in....

From the first day of April 1943, the Lithuanians on the base have been dressed in Gestapo uniforms....

May 3, Monday. ... On the other side stood three Lithuanians with rifles and shot the condemned man. They brought, it seems, 11 persons in all. Mostly young people ... the condemned were not undressed. Two to three hours later, the Lithuanians were already selling the clothes....

The Lithuanians are saying that they will have a lot of work yet, since Jews are going to be brought from across the border. It seems that Jews brought from France, Belgium, etc. under the pretext of being taken to Sweden were shot in the Fourth Fort in Kaunas....

July 15, Thursday. ... around 10 o'clock, one salvo and that's it....

P.S. Until — more or less — 1943, the Jews hiding in the forests conducted themselves properly. Now, however, in 1943 they are becoming bandits, falling on individual homes in villages and even on entire villages (Zwieczyniec). They also attack people on the roads.... They grab boots, food and are relentless. The villagers are enraged and are beginning to protect themselves by turning the Jews over to the Lithuanians....

August 14, 1943, Saturday. Around five o'clock they brought 5 persons to the Rudziński pit. They led people out one at a time and shot them. The victims were 2 women, a few Bolsheviks, and the rest were from the Łukiszki prison. There was not a single Jew among them. Since one month ago the police are also doing the shooting....

August, 1943. ... the naked are going to their death, after a while the Shaulists return from the base.... It seems that they were shooting

TABLE 5. EXECUTION OF THE WILNO JEWS IN 1941

Date	*Number of Jews Killed*	*Date*	*Number of Jews Killed*
Aug. 12–Sept. 1	440	Oct. 25	2,578
Sept. 2	3,700	Oct. 27	1,203
Sept. 12	3,334	Oct. 30	1,533
Sept. 17	1,267	Nov. 6	1,341
Oct. 4	1,983	Nov. 19	171
Oct. 16	1,146	Nov. 25	63
Oct. 21	2,367		

Polish lawyers and doctors. They shot them two at a time. They held out quite well ... [illegible] they did not beg, only wished each other farewell and making the sign of the cross proceeded....

September 17. On Friday ten hostages [were brought]. The Shaulists, who came for the changing of the guard, are continually saying that the hostages, and generally all Poles, hold up very "honorably," do not cry like the Jews who kiss their feet and beg for their lives to be spared.

September 27, 1943, Monday. ... all together there were 26 shots, then in the course of 10 to 15 minutes another seven one after the other. I don't know what this means. Although I usually watched the executions from Rudziński Street (near the fence), this time the car stopped in such an unfortunate way that, besides the trees, the car itself hid the condemned who were being executed.

They were probably not Jews but Poles from the Gestapo prison. It all lasted one hour.

September 29, 1943, Wednesday. Today another car arrived, they were from the Gestapo prison. A Lithuanian says that there were 25 people, mostly Poles....

October, 1943. ... On October 1 and 2 at night, a band is robbing, stealing wagons and taking them into the wilderness. Today, on the night of October 2, the following [villages] were robbed: Pułstoki, Wejsiaty, Jacewicze, Podborze. When Pułstoki was being robbed ... [illegible] one girl ... recognized one of the bandits, a "good" Lithuanian acquaintance from the village of Krusze. When the bandits left, they were talking among themselves in the yard in Lithuanian. Among the bandits there were also Bolsheviks who ... [illegible]....

October 12, 1943, Tuesday. It seems that the ghetto is finished....

October 25, 1943, Monday. At 9 o'clock in the morning there's sudden, rapid firing on the base. The shots are quick, chaotic, do not come from a single point over the pit as usual but are dispersed throughout the base, even close to the fence and the road.... It was a car of victims who ran off in all directions on the base. Unfortunately, it seems that no one was able to escape. Who it was, I do not know for certain, but it seems, that it was the remnants of Jews hiding in the ghettos.[80]

From reports of Einsatzkommando 3 we know of the above executions carried out against the Wilno Jews in 1941. (See Table 5.[81])

Of the approximately 170,000 Jews murdered in the General Commissariat of Lithuania throughout the war, about 60,000 died at Ponary.[82] According to István Deák, from 70,000 to 100,000 people, including Jews and Poles, died there between 1941 and 1943.[83] According to Roman Korab-Żebryk, the Ypatingas Būrys shot more than 100,000 people in Ponary over three years. Longin Tomaszewski uses the same estimate and adds that of these, 75 percent were Jews and the rest consisted of Soviet and Polish POWs, Tatars, Gypsies, Belorussians, and even some Lithuanians. The Soviet POWs were all Polish citizens. His estimate for ethnic Poles is "several thousand."[84] Zdzisław A. Siemaszko states that among the victims were approximately 1,700 Poles, including many AK members.[85] Speaking of these atrocities, one Sonderkommando member testified at his postwar trial:

> This was horrible both for the victims and for us. Our shoulders ached from the rifle butts, our fingers from loading, and our ears swelled from the shooting and the despairing pleas [of the victims]. We shot them in the back of the head. There was a rule, however, that whoever had a child in arms had to stand before us face to face. Then, one shot went to the bearer of the child and a second one to the child.[86]

At the end of 1941, the head of Einsatzkommando 3 wrote in his report to Berlin: "I can today confirm that the objective of solving the Jewish problem in Lithuania has been accomplished by Einsatzkommando 3. Except for the Jewish workers [Arbeitsjuden] and their families, there are no more Jews in Lithuania."[87] At the end of 1941, the spared Jews in the Kaunas ghetto numbered 15,000—all that remained of the 35,000 who had been there in July 1941 and those brought thereafter. Out of the 60,000 in the Wilno ghetto in September 1941 and those brought there later (all together 90,000, according to a Polish Government Delegation report), also 15,000 remained alive. An additional 4,500 Jewish workers were kept alive in Šiauliai.[88] In the course of 1943, almost all of these workers died. In August (16-22) of that year, the Wilno ghetto was liquidated by the Sonderkommando, whose inebriated members slaughtered all the old men, women, and children, sparing only the younger men capable of working.[89]

In September 1943, in order to destroy the evidence of their crime against humanity in Ponary, the Germans sent an eighty-man team consisting of seventy Jews, nine Russians, and one Pole (imprisoned because he had hid a Jewish child) to dig up and burn the bodies of the victims. This "Special Commando 1005" unit was headed by SS Colonel Paul Blobel. These eighty prisoners, chained at the waist and ankles, were supervised by thirty Lithuanian and German guards and fifty SS-men. Their macabre task did not end until April of the following year.

> The first grave opened by the "Blobel Commando" at Ponar contained the corpses of eight thousand Jews, five hundred Soviet prisoners-of-war and several hundred Catholic priests and seminarists. Most of the corpses were blindfolded and had their hands tied behind their backs. The second grave contained the corpses of 9,500 Jewish children, women and men. In the third grave the prisoners counted 10,400 corpses. Hardly any of the children's remains showed marks of bullets, but their tongues were protruding. In the fourth pit the prisoners found twenty-four thousand corpses, among them many Soviet prisoners-of-war, a number of Poles, Catholic priests and nuns, and one German soldier. In the fifth grave they found 3,500 women, children and men, all naked, and all shot in the back of the head. In the sixth grave they counted five thousand naked corpses. In the seventh grave they found several hundred political prisoners, and in the eighth and ninth graves they found five thousand naked corpses of Jews from the rural ghettos in the Vilna region.[90]

But not quite all of the Lithuanian Jews were killed by the Nazis and their collaborators, whether in Ponary, in the Fourth, Seventh, and Ninth Forts of Kaunas, or in the many towns and villages across the General Commissariat of Lithuania. Some of them managed to escape from the ghettos into the forests, where they either formed survival groups or joined the Soviet partisans. They were among these who, in the struggle for existence, were sometimes reduced to robbery and even murder of the local population.

Others survived because they were helped by individual Poles, the clergy, the underground, Polish families, and Polish institutions. Among these institutions were the religious orders, especially of nuns (e.g., the Dominican Sisters in Kolonia Wileńska[91]), who not only hid Jews but also provided arms for the Jewish resistance in the Wilno ghetto. In their sermons, priests spoke out vehemently against the murders of the Jews, and the Polish "Legalization Department" (Legalizacja) in Wilno cranked out "Aryan" documents for Jews to use. For their assistance to the Jews, some Poles paid with their lives, such as those who were hanged in a public execution in the square of the Wilno Cathedral. The Germans also used the assistance rendered to the Jews by the clergy and nuns as a pretext for liquidating the Wilno monasteries and convents in March 1942 and imprisoning the members.[92] Still other Jews survived because of compassionate Lithuanian assistance.[93]

But all this heroism did little to prevent the ultimate catastrophe in the General Commissariat of Lithuania, for which the Lithuanian people, as a whole, cannot be blamed. Deák's words may serve to put the matter of Lithuanian collaboration and rescue efforts in proper perspective:

> That many Lithuanians participated in the early spontaneous killings, and that many volunteered for militia service under the Germans, does not make the Lithuanian situation any different in these respects from that prevailing in the Ukraine, Belorussia, Hungary, Romania, Croatia, Slovakia, Austria, or France. Most of the countries that were occupied by the Nazis or were allied with them produced roughly the same proportions of butchers, of the indifferent, of sympathizers, and of active rescuers. But it was not the same thing to offer to help the Jews in the East and in the West. In Lithuania and Poland, gentiles who tried to rescue Jews were routinely executed and so, often, were their families.[94]

On March 9, 1995, a short article appeared in the *Canadian Jewish News*:

> Jerusalem — The president of Lithuania offered a public apology to the Jewish people for the mass murder of Lithuania's Jews by his country's citizens during World War II.
>
> Addressing the Knesset last Wednesday, the second day of a state visit, Algirdas Brazauskas sought forgiveness for the role his people played in the murder of more than 200,000 Lithuanian Jews.
>
> Several Lithuanian survivors were present during the speech. One of them, former Knesset member Gustav Badyan, was overcome by emotion and was taken to the hospital with chest pains, Israel Television said.
>
> Prime Minister Yitzhak Rabin told the Knesset that Israel would hold Brazauskas to his pledge to repeal a blanket pardon given to Nazi criminals in 1991, when Lithuania became independent.

Although it is too late to prosecute most of the Lithuanian collaborators who contributed to the deaths of so many Polish and Lithuanian citizens, President Brazauskas' apology to the Jewish people represents an indispensable first step in the process of healing. To the same end, a similar apology to the Polish people, together with a resounding condemnation of the collaborators, would be most welcome. After all, the Poles and the Lithuanians had been friends for centuries past.

Chapter 7
Ukrainian Collaboration

If Polish-Lithuanian relations were marred by the struggle for a single city and its environs, Polish-Ukrainian relations were marred by a dispute over four of the eight eastern provinces of Poland as well as parts of three others: the southeastern half of Polesie, a part of the Lublin province, and the Łemko area. For the Polish people, the events in Wileńszczyzna pale in comparison with the tragedy in "Western Ukraine," the Soviet designation for the territory that included the province of Wołyń and the three provinces of Małopolska Wschodnia, or Eastern Galicia: Lwów (exclusive of the far western counties around Rzeszów), Stanisławów, and Tarnopol.

Neither the dispute nor the bloodletting involved Ukraine as a nation, as a territory, or as a people. Rather, the struggle was mainly localized to the four above-mentioned provinces and chiefly involved the Polish civilians and about 40,000 (at their height) Ukrainian Nationalists, trained and armed by Germany, who claimed to represent "their" nation (the some 5 million Ukrainians in Eastern Poland, the over one-half million in central Poland, and the approximately 24 million Ukrainians east of the river Zbrucz) and who were able to mobilize a part of the largely illiterate, land-hungry Ukrainian peasants of Wołyń and Eastern Galicia for the task of ethnic cleansing.

When did this "fratricidal conflict" begin? In the twentieth century, it began in 1919 with the formation of a small Ukrainian terrorist organization called "Volya"[1] that provided the blueprint in 1920 for the UVO (Ukrainska Viiskova Orhanizatsiia — Ukrainian Military Organization). The conflict worsened in 1929 with the founding of the OUN (Orhanizatsiia Ukrainskykh Natsionalistiv — Organization of Ukrainian Nationalists), which subsumed the UVO, and turned murderous in September 1939 when several thousand people, including scores of known Polish officers and soldiers returning from the war, were brutally killed.[2] The struggle became unbearable in the fall of 1942 (and in 1943) during the massive Nazi resettlement of Poles from the Zamość area (Zamojszczyzna), carried out with the assistance of Ukrainian collaborators, and it turned sadistic in Wołyń that same fall at the hands of the UPA (Ukrainska Povstanska Armiia — Ukrainian Insurgent Army). The "undeclared Polish-Ukrainian war" continued raging there all through 1943, engulfed the whole of Eastern Galicia and some regions of Chełm and Przemyśl later that year and throughout the remainder of the war, and finally ended in the Carpathian Mountains in 1947 with the liquidation of the UPA by Polish, Soviet, and Czech communist forces.

As will become clear, none of this would have been possible without Germany's active support of the Ukrainian Nationalists during the interwar years, without the Soviet Union's approval and encouragement during its occupation of Eastern Poland, and without the tacit approval of the German occupation forces after June 1941. Both powers, after all, were doing exactly the same thing to the Poles during the war — but on a much grander scale. All of this and more was part of their *divide et impera* wartime strategy.

Much of the blame for the general lack of knowledge about this unknown attempt at genocide lies on the shoulders of the Polish

Provinces and Counties of Southeastern Poland, 1939

émigrés who, unconstrained by communist censorship, failed for one reason or another to speak out and to document this lost war story, this sad part of their tragic national history. Meanwhile, for fifty years now, the émigré Ukrainian neo-Nationalists have been spinning their own, virtually unchallenged version of these events—justifying interwar terrorism against the Polish Republic, turning wartime collaborators into helpless victims, and elevating murderous war criminals to the status of national heroes, all the while claiming, "We fought Hitler and Stalin." The breakup of the Soviet Union has enabled Polish scholars to

TABLE 6. NUMBER OF UKRAINIAN DEPUTIES AND SENATORS IN THE POLISH SEYM IN RELATION TO TOTAL MEMBERSHIP 1922-1938

	Total number		*Ukrainians*	
Period	***Deputies***	***Senators***	***Deputies***	***Senators***
1922–28	444	111	25	6
1928–30	444	111	46	11
1930–35	444	111	28	4
1938–	208	96	19	6

TABLE 7. NUMBER OF VOTES CAST FOR VARIOUS LISTS IN THE GENERAL ELECTIONS IN WOŁYŃ, 1922-1930

Year	***Number of Votes Cast***	***For Polish Lists, Including Government Bloc***		***For Ukrainian Lists, Including List of Other National Minorities***	
		Votes	*%*	*Votes*	*%*
1922	430,955	84,613	19.6	320,398	74.3
1928	583,219	245,652	42.1	239,627	41.1
1930	596,033	486,342	81.6	69,121	11.6

TABLE 8. MANDATES GAINED BY VARIOUS ETHNIC CONSTITUENCIES IN EASTERN GALICIA AND WOŁYŃ, 1927

	Eastern Galicia		***Wołyń***	
		%		*%*
Poles	33,568	36	443	26
Ukrainians	50,691	54	961	55
Jews	4,861	5	266	15
Others	4,158	5	69	4
Total	**93,278**	**100**	**1,739**	**100**

begin their investigation of the Ukrainian Nationalists' ethnic cleansing campaign aimed at all foreigners in "Western Ukraine," and it does not make for pleasant reading. How did this brutal campaign come about?

Interwar Years

In 1931, there were just over 2 million people in Wołyń. Of these, 69.3 percent were Ukrainians, 15.6 percent Poles, almost 10 percent Jews, and the remaining 5.1 percent Germans, Czechs, Russians, and other ethnic groups. The three Polish provinces of Eastern Galicia contained about 3.3 million Ukrainians, 2.3 million Poles, and 616,000 Jews. Thus, although a total of about 4.7 million Ukrainians inhabited these four provinces in 1931, the overall character of these *ethnically mixed* lands was also determined to a large extent by the presence of about 2.6 million Poles and 824,000 Jews whose upper strata gravitated toward the Polish language and culture.[3]

The Ukrainians, by and large, lived in the villages; the towns were occupied mostly by Poles and Jews. The cultural center of Lwów, like that of Wilno, was predominantly Polish. The majority of the Poles, however, also lived in villages, a pattern that did not characterize the Jews, who found the towns much more to their liking and especially suitable to their various professions. In Wołyń, for example, in the 1930s, although there were only 745 Polish villages, the Polish people lived in 5,200 settlements out of a total of 6,800.[4]

Whereas the Polish people in all four provinces were predominantly Latin-rite Roman Catholics, the Ukrainians in Wołyń were, with few exceptions, members of the Eastern Orthodox Church. In the three provinces of Eastern Galicia, the Ukrainians belonged almost entirely to the Eastern-rite (Uniate) Catholic Church.

Aside from the presence of a large number of political parties (in itself an indicator of civil liberties), the Ukrainians had representatives in all the Polish Seyms except the first.[5] Members of various Ukrainian parties, both favoring and opposing cooperation with Poland, also sat on the Chamber of Deputies and the Senate. (See Table 6.[6]) The voting patterns in the General Elections in Wołyń are particularly revealing. (See Table 7.[7])

Thus, Ukrainians in Poland had representation at the highest levels of government. (The vice-marshal of the Polish *Sejm*, Vasyl Mudryi, was Ukrainian.) That they did not hold more seats was due in part to the fact that a good number of the Ukrainian people voted for Polish lists, especially in the 1930 parliamentary elections. In addition, about 10 percent of the Ruthenian population tended to vote for lists put forth by Ruthenian groups, who did not consider themselves Ukrainians and were opposed to the Ukrainian separatist movement. These groups were always loyal to Poland.[8]

In terms of local government, the statistics in Table 8 show that the Ukrainians were not adversely represented, at least not in 1927.[9]

In general, Ukrainians fared better in villages than in towns. This to be expected, since in the towns of Eastern Galicia, Ukrainians ranked third in population after Poles and Jews, and in Wołyń, they ranked third after Jews and Poles.[10]

By 1939, however, the situation, at least in Wołyń, seems to have changed drastically in favor of the Polish minority, and we may rightfully suspect foul play. Out of 103 chief officers of a cluster of villages (*wójt*), 81 were Polish and 19 were Ukrainian. In village or commune councils (*gmina*), 69 percent of the offices were controlled by the Poles and 26 percent by the Ukrainians. On the county level (*powiat*), the proportion was 75 percent to 16 percent in favor of the Poles. Still greater disparities existed in the towns.[11]

Polish land reform policies in the eastern provinces have been a subject of much discourse and criticism. As we have seen, these policies involved parceling out land, belonging mostly to large Polish estates, among the landless peasants, as well as distributing land grants to Polish soldiers and officers, the "military settlers." According to one 1939 estimate, out of a total of 872,000 acres of land parceled out in Eastern Galicia between 1919 and 1938, 495,000 acres went to Ukrainian peasants.[12] The Polish policy stated that Ukrainians and Poles were to be treated equally in the distribution of land. That the Ukrainians received more is explained by their proportionately larger numbers. If this estimate is correct, the Ukrainians received 57 percent of the land, the Poles 43 percent. According to Jerzy Tomaszewski's adjusted census figures for 1931, there were 3.25 million Ukrainians and 2.3 million Poles in Eastern Galicia (58.6 percent and 41.4 percent, respectively). Myron Kuropas states that by the beginning of the war, Polish colonization policies had resulted in the resettlement of about 300,000 additional Poles in the primarily Ukrainian rural areas of "Western Ukraine."[13]

In 1931, 16.1 percent of all landholdings in Eastern Galicia fell into the category of "over 50 hectares" (125 acres).[14] In 1938, that figure dropped to 14.4 percent. According to the 1931 census, Poles owned 1,300 such properties. Although Poles thus owned more large estates than any other group, Poles with large estates constituted only about .5 percent of the total 2.3 million Poles inhabiting these regions. (This is a point worth remembering in reference to the argument that the vehemence of the Ukrainian Nationalists in 1942–44 was turned primarily against large Polish landowners. In any case, how many of them were left after the Stalinist deportations of 1940–41?) According to estimates for 1938, Jews owned over 20 percent of these estates, and the Greek Catholic (Uniate) Episcopate owned large tracks as well.[15]

In 1939 in Wołyń, for every 1,000 farmsteads in the 30–50 hectare range, 8 were owned by Poles and 2 by Ukrainians; for every 1,000 farmsteads of 10 hectares or more, there were 185 Polish ones and 66 Ukrainian ones. What irked the Ukrainians more than this unequal distribution of land was that more and more of these farms went not to local Poles but to settlers from the interior of Poland. In 1939, there were 7,796 farms in Wołyń in the 10–50 hectare range. Between 1921 and 1939, 7,047 Polish settlers had arrived in that province; as a rule, they had received 10 or more hectares of land.[16]

If the Ukrainian peasants felt that all of this land should have been distributed to them instead, so did the Polish peasants — and with perhaps greater cause, since the land in question was expropriated from the Polish landlords.[17] Poland's colonization policy did not end with the abrogation of the land-grant act in 1924. It continued unobtrusively until the beginning of the war. Not all of the settlers, of course, were large or even small landowners, and many who began in the country wound up in the towns. This represented but a small percentage of the 5 to 6 million people that Poland considered bringing into its eastern territories, for obvious reasons.[18] Whether this could have been done in the already overcrowded Kresy Wschodnie without somehow displacing the ethnic minorities already living there is another question. Such was, however, the standard practice in Eastern Europe whenever any of its borders got rearranged! Germany followed this policy in pre-World War I western Poland, as did Lithuania and democratic Czechoslovakia. When the Soviet Union invaded Poland in 1939 it followed suit, but it had the Gulag to absorb those displaced. As we have seen, Himmler's Generalplan Ost also called for the expulsion of some 31 million people from the eastern territories and for the subsequent colonization by 10 million ethnic Germans.

The majority of the Ukrainians in Poland were Eastern-rite Catholics in union with Rome, and no restrictions were imposed on them by the government. The Orthodox Church was also a legal entity protected under Polish law, but due to the legacy of the tsarist rule, unlike the Uniate Church, the Orthodox Church ran afoul of the Polish government. An unpublished 1938 article by Józef Gieysztor stated the case:

> At the beginning of March, district administrators received instructions to "regulate" the holdings of the Eastern Orthodox Church so that, in keeping with the intent of the instructions received, in five districts in the province of Lublin (Biłgoraj, Chełm, Hrubieszów, Tomaszów and Włodawa) 39 operational churches were closed and sealed, and 41 churches and houses of prayer which were not considered permanent (*etatowe*) were demolished or completely taken apart. In conjunction with this, "superfluous" Eastern Orthodox priests were banished or relegated to an inferior position and cemeteries deprived of caretakers were closed with the result that today, in order to avail oneself of religious or burial services, one has to travel several dozen kilometers to a village that still has an Eastern Orthodox Church, a priest (*pop*), and cemetery. This state of affairs reminds those over fifty years of age from the former Russian sector of their childhood. Then, too, one heard about the closing of churches and the demolition of chapels and crosses. Then, too, there were heated exchanges about the teaching of religion in schools and preaching of sermons in the language of the State. At that time, like today, the terrain of that action, among others, was Podlasie. The difference lies in this alone, that then it was the Tsarist, despotic and backward Russia that oppressed the Catholic or the Uniate Church in such a defiant way, and now it is the free and cultured Polish Republic that "regulates" the affairs of the Eastern Orthodox faith.[19]

According to official information received in London from Warsaw and dated August 4, 1938, in June and July of that year 91 Eastern Orthodox churches, 10 chapels, and 26 houses of prayer were demolished in the Lublin province.[20] Myron Kuropas presents the Ukrainian position:

> While the Rome-Warsaw Concordat protected the Ukrainian Catholic church from open discrimination, the Ukrainian Orthodox Church enjoyed no such advantage. Numerous attempts were made by Poles to induce the Ukrainian Orthodox to accept Catholicism. When these endeavors proved unsuccessful, an effort was made to introduce the Polish language and the Gregorian calendar into Orthodox practices and observances. Ukrainian Orthodox later came under the jurisdiction of the Autocephalous Orthodox church of Poland, a religious institution controlled by the Polish government. When Orthodox resistance increased, a number of churches were simply closed. Of the over 300 Ukrainian Orthodox churches in existence in 1914, only 51 survived until 1939.[21]

Of course as Jerzy Tomaszewski points out, one could argue that such actions by the Polish government were intended to remove the advantage that the privileged Eastern Orthodox obtained before 1914 under the Russian rule — but this was little comfort to those who lost their churches, clergy, and cemeteries.[22]

Under tsarist rule, the Uniate population had been forcibly converted to Orthodoxy. In 1875, at least 375 Uniate churches were converted into Orthodox churches. The same was true of many Latin-rite Roman Catholic churches. In 1905, when voluntary conversion was allowed (but not to the Uniate rite), some 200,000 Orthodox reverted to Latin-rite Catholicism. Hence the Polish "revindication campaign" — the closing and even destruction of old, often abandoned, Orthodox churches or their reconversion into Roman Catholic churches during the interwar years.[23] A contemporary (1942) publication dealing with the Eastern Orthodox Church in Poland presents the Polish perspective on these matters (see Appendix, Document 10, "Nationalist Tendencies and Programmes in the Polish Orthodox Church").

In a July 21, 1938, complaint to the president of the Council of Ministers, Deputy Stefan Baran enumerated 109 locations spanning 7 counties in the province of Lublin where 107 Orthodox places of worship (*świątynie*) and 7 chapels (*kaplice*) were demolished and 3 churches were burned. In two informative articles, Father Janusz Kania of the Catholic University of Lublin has analyzed these claims and has commented on the role of the Roman Catholic Church in all of this. According to his analysis, of the 107 places of worship, 16–19 were houses of prayer (wooden sheds, barracks, peasant huts, etc.) and about 90 were churches and chapels built before 1915. The 7 "chapels" were most probably wayside shrines or simply figurines of which no records exist in any of the Uniate or government sources. Of the 117 Orthodox holy places, 52 were former Uniate churches, 29 were built on sites of Uniate churches, 32 were Orthodox churches, and the rest were of undetermined origin. Since 1923, 20 of the 117 were in ruins, and many of these were beyond repair. By 1938 that number may have doubled, since many of the churches were simple wooden structures. In 1938, therefore, as a rule, the Polish government destroyed those churches that were dilapidated and abandoned, or illegally constructed between the years 1929–30 and 1936–38, or built during the tsarist rule between 1905 and 1914, when many Uniate churches had been destroyed.[24]

Moreover, this "action" was carried out by the Piłsudski dictatorial Sanacja régime (with the assistance of the army) against the wishes of the Roman Catholic Church as expressed by the bishop of Lublin, Marian Leon Fulman, on June 2, 1938 (i.e., at the very beginning of this government action). In a directive to the Catholic clergy under his jurisdiction, Bishop Fulman wrote: "The demolition, burning or dissolution of former Uniate churches being carried out in the territory of our diocese is transpiring without any consultation with the Curia of Bishops. This is being done by government agents on their own and they are responsible for it." He also condemned the methods used: "In general, the methods used in the dissolution and destruction of the houses of God, from our point of view, are not acceptable." Furthermore, Bishop Fulman forbade local priests and deacons to receive government agents who made it a practice to inform (either before or after) the clergy of their deeds. "These messengers," wrote Bishop Fulman, "should be referred to the Curia of Bishops which alone is competent to deal with such matters."[25]

The aforementioned 1942 publication on the Eastern Orthodox Church in Poland summarized the status of the Church after the events of 1938 until the beginning of the war:

> Shortly after the painful incidents just referred to, a Decree concerning the relations of the State with the Autocephalous Orthodox Church in Poland was issued by the President of the Republic (November 1938). In December of the same year an ordinance appeared recognising its internal laws. These two edicts laid the foundation for the legal organisation of the Orthodox Church in Poland, which, in the light of the rich past of Polish Orthodoxy throughout the ages, must be regarded as an event of considerable interest....
>
> The new organization provided to the fullest extent the internal unity of the Church, i.e. the co-operation of the hierarchy, the clergy and laity. In addition the traditions of the Orthodox Church's heyday in the old Polish Republic were maintained. It was, in fact, an organisation that fitted in with the past of Polish Orthodoxy and at the same time satisfied the demands of the canons of the Orthodox Church. In the old Polish State, as we have seen, the Orthodox Church combined the principles of Synod government with the participation of the laity in church life, and it showed remarkable proficiency in learning. The Mohylan Academy of Kiev, founded by the Metropolitan Peter Mohyla, was a shining light not only for South-East Poland where it implanted West European learning; its influence was felt throughout the whole of Muscovy, far beyond the Polish frontiers. Orthodox ecclesiastical manuals, printed in Polish, and models of monastic learning, reached far-off Moscow, as fruits of the civilising labours of the Mohylan Academy.
>
> The tragic events of September 1939 interrupted the work of rebuilding the Polish Orthodox Church on new foundations which were to have provided for a long and prosperous future.
>
> At present it is subjected to the arbitrary decisions and dealings of the German authorities which never hesitate ruthlessly to exploit for their political aims everything that comes within their grasp.[26]

After the Soviet liberation of 1944, the Orthodox Church contiued to be exploited by the communists. Stanisław Skrzypek noted what happened to the Uniate Church in "Western Ukraine":

> After the Soviet had taken over the control of Eastern Galicia anew in 1944, the most brutal persecution of the Greek Catholic Church began. The Head of this Church, the Metropolitan of Lwów, as well as all the bishops and many of the priests were imprisoned and deported into Russia, where some of them died and where the others have never been heard of since. A further act, carried out under pressure on the part of the Soviet authorities, was the "fusion" of the Greek Catholic Church of Eastern Galicia and the former Rumanian province of Northern Bukovina with the Russian Orthodox Church. This "fusion" was carried out by violence—against the will of the great majority of the Greek Catholic Clergy, who had no opportunity at all of stating their views.
>
> In this another step has been taken in the direction of the sovietization and russification of the Ukrainian population in Eastern Galicia and the severing of the last ties by which it is still bound to Western Europe.[27]

After 1944, the situation of the Catholic Church was but a little better in "Western Belorussia."

The following analysis of the Ukrainian public school system under the Polish rule may leave many American readers wondering what all the fuss was about. In the United States of the 1920s and 1930s, as now, not only was it unthinkable that ethnic schools would be supported at taxpayers' expense but most Americans would not want their children to attend such schools, that is, schools in which the entire curriculum was taught in a foreign language. Ethnic schools did exist in America, but they were all privately funded, and eventually all of them adopted English as their official language. Publicly funded bilingual programs had to await a more progressive era.

The situation in Eastern Poland was much different. The minorities in these newly acquired territories were not immigrants but were local people who had lived there for many centuries—

like the Native American population of the United States in the "Nation of Immigrants." As such, they had a right to an education in their own language, if they so chose. This right was guaranteed by the Minorities Treaty.

Under Austrian rule, there were 2,919 Polish and 2,450 Ukrainian elementary schools in Eastern Galicia. There were no Polish schools under the tsars in Lithuania, Belorussia, and Wołyń. In these territories, the use of the Polish language for instruction had been strictly forbidden since 1864 "in every school, under any form, and under whatsoever pretext."[28] The Second Republic of Poland did not follow either of these models. In the provinces of Lwów, Stanisławów, Tarnopol, Wołyń, Polesie, and Nowogródek and in the districts of Grodno and Wołkowysk in the province of Białystok, instructions, in keeping with the minimal requirements of the Treaty of Minorities, were generally to be bilingual. However, the act of July 31, 1924, provided for other possibilities as well.

In elementary schools, if there were at least 40 students in a given school district whose parents wanted instruction in their own language, and if the school was located in a village where at least 20 percent of the inhabitants belonged to that nationality, that language would be introduced into the school as the only language of instruction if there were no Polish children in that school. If there were Polish children, instruction would be bilingual. If the parents made no such request, classes would be conducted in the Polish language — even if there were no Polish children in the school. This was, after all, Poland, and the official language was Polish.

In the case of secondary schools, the petition of 150 parents of Ukrainian or Belorussian children was required; in state technical schools, the request of parents of students representing 40 percent of the pupils at that school was necessary. Other provisions were mandated by the Order of the Ministry of Education (No. 2334/27) of April 12, 1927, in all state and "infant" (kindergarten) schools in which instruction was conducted in other than the state language. These provisions stated:

> *a.* Notices and instructions issued to pupils or their parents may be made in both the languages used for teaching;
>
> *b.* At the request of parents or guardians certificates and advices [notices] may be issued in both languages;
>
> *c.* Answers by the management to applications and to letters written in other than official tongue must be in the same tongue;
>
> *d.* Meetings of Pedagogic Councils and other school conferences may be conducted in the language in which the pupils are taught and reports of speeches must be drawn up in the same language. Records and other school documents must be written in two languages.
>
> Private schools and kindergartens where other than the official language is used for teaching may use this language in all internal affairs, in all notices, inside or outside, in all documents, and in correspondence with parents, or other persons and institutions in accordance with Art. 110 of the Polish Constitution.[29]

It is debatable whether these provisions met, failed to meet, or exceeded the Treaty of Minorities education provision, which mandated that "in the primary schools, the instruction shall be given to the children of such Polish nationals through the medium of their language," and which added, "This provision shall not prevent the Polish Government from making the teaching of the Polish language obligatory in the said schools" (see Appendix, Document 2, "Excerpts from the Minorities Treaty of June 28, 1919," Article 9).

In all fairness, however, it must be added that there were differences between the "laws on the books" and their local application, which was often beyond the control of the legislators. For example, in the eastern territories, the signatures of parents requesting instruction in their own language for their children had to be notarized — not by the local *sołtys* (village administrator) but by some notary public, a court, an administrator of a commune council (*urząd gminny*), or some district *starosta* (higher-up). In addition, local school administrators often imposed other requirements, such as the inspection of parental records by school authorities. The summons were delivered to the parents by

TABLE 9. NUMBER OF ELEMENTARY SCHOOLS IN EASTERN GALICIA, 1924–1930

Type	*1924–25*	*1925–26*	*1929–30*
Polish	2,598	2,452	2,223
Ukrainian	2,176	1,199	716
Bilingual	9	1,102	1,794
Other	82	84	88

TABLE 10. NUMBER OF PUBLIC SCHOOLS IN WOŁYŃ, 1927–34

Year	*Number*	*Polish*	*Polish with Ukr. Language*	*Bilingual*	*Ukrainian*
1927–28	1,185	412	350	419	14
1928–29	1,312	406	329	498	9
1929–30	1,383	426	417	524	9
1930–31	1,679	627	417	534	11
1931–32	1,651	558	584	606	11
1932–33	1,686	616	546	530	4
1933–34	1,782	545	631	539	11

a policeman. All of this required a great deal of traveling and was extremely intimidating to the peasants. Meanwhile, the parental requests of only 20 Polish students would be sufficient to introduce the Polish language in a given elementary school, and none of the above-mentioned bureaucratic tape was required. The education would then be conducted in both languages.[30] The result of such uneven practices can be clearly seen in Table 9.[31]

Thus, we see a reduction of both Ukrainian and Polish schools and a rise of bilingual schools, called *szkoły utrakwistyczne*. However, whereas the Ukrainian schools decreased by 1,460 between 1924-25 and 1929-30, there were only 375 fewer Polish schools in 1929-30. In this same time period, 1,785 bilingual schools were established. By 1938, there were 2,485 bilingual schools in Eastern Galicia and only 452 Ukrainian schools.[32] The situation in Wołyń is presented in Table 10.[33]

In 1936 in Wołyń, out of 1,732 elementary schools, only 11 were strictly Ukrainian. Whereas 96 percent of the Polish children attended classes, only 69 percent of Ukrainian children did so.[34] At the secondary level, whereas there was one Polish *gimnazjum* for every 16,000 Poles in 1931, there was only one Ukrainian *gimnazjum* for every 230,000 Ukrainians.[35]

The situation was even worse at the university level. The Ukrainians wanted their own university to be established in Lwów. Perhaps because of the active role of students in political affairs (they constituted the backbone of the OUN) and the anticipated Polish protest due to the memories of the Ukrainian attempt to seize the city in 1918, Poland offered to establish a Ukrainian university in Kraków instead. Since the Ukrainians objected to this proposal, no state Ukrainian university was founded during the interwar years. Nevertheless, a secret Ukrainian University was established in Lwów; it had 54 professors and 1,500 students before it was shut down in 1925 by the Polish authorities.[36]

There were Ukrainians on the faculties of the Universities of Lwów, Kraków, and Warsaw, together with 2,175 (in 1929–30) Ukrainian students in various Polish universities.[37] There was also a Greek Catholic Theological Academy in Lwów as well as a Ukrainian National Museum, the Museum of the National House, and the Shevchenko Scientific Society with

TABLE 11. PROSVITA, 1910–1935

Year	*Branches*	*Members (in thousands)*	*Reading Rooms*	*Central Reading Rooms*	*Libraries*
1910	64	—	2,376	114	2,290
1925	81	6.9	2,020	121	978
1935	83	31.1	3,017	295	2,915

TABLE 12. RIDNA SHKOLA, 1900–1936

Year	*Branches*	*Members*
1900	10	943
1910	51	4,298
1926	337	20,520
1936	1,980	92,000

TABLE 13. SILSKYI HOSPODAR, 1910–1936

Year	*County Branches*	*Village Groups*	*Members (in thousands)*
1910	85	317	12.5
1930	81	1,122	28.0
1936	63	1,683	107.2

three departments (philosophy, history, and natural sciences), nine commissions devoted to various branches of the sciences, and a library that, in 1926, housed 184,974 books and 1,452 manuscripts. A similar society, the Ukrainian Scientific Institute, existed in Warsaw.[38] All of these were state-subsidized institutions.

In addition, two important private Ukrainian organizations filled the educational void: Prosvita (Enlightenment) and Ridna Shkola (Native School). The 1936-37 *Ukrainian Statistical Yearbook* showed the development of Prosvita, as seen in Table 11.[39]

The same *Yearbook* provided the statistics for Ridna Shkola. (See Table 12.)

By 1938, Ridna Shkola had 107,332 members organized into 2,049 groups, maintained 33 elementary schools, directed 684 libraries housing 67,008 books, and operated 126 theatrical companies. Another society, Silskyi Hospodar (Village Husbandman), was primarily concerned with promoting agricultural education. The *Yearbook* noted its progress. (See Table 13.)

Other Ukrainian societies proliferated: the Soiuz Ukrainek (Union of Ukrainian Women), Sokil (a gymnastic society), Luby (a paramilitary organization), the Union of Ukrainian Lawyers, the Society of Ukrainian Secondary School Teachers, the Union of Ukrainian Merchants, and the Ukrainian Medical Society, to name but a few.

The Ukrainian press during the interwar years poses somewhat of an enigma. Before 1910 there were only 72 publications in the Ukrainian language. According to the *Yearbook*, in 1926 there were 149 papers and periodicals, 129 of which were published in Eastern Galicia (88 in Lwów). In 1929, the only daily newspaper, *Dilo*, had a circulation of a mere 4,600 copies (compared with the 16 German dailies with a circulation of 98,000 copies and the 20 Jewish dailies with a circulation of 220,000 copies in Poland). By 1936, 223 additional scientific (31), literary (60), popular (121), and other (11) publications appeared.[40] Still, why were there so few for the some 5.5 million Ukrainians who lived in Poland at that time? This sad state of affairs cannot be blamed on Poland, which imposed no restrictions in this regard. The obvious answer is that the vast majority of the Ukrainians lived in rural Eastern Poland, where the overall illiteracy rate was quite high. In Wołyń, for example, the rate was 77.4 percent among the Ukrainians and 68.9 percent among the entire population.[41]

Yet, in spite of all the lost opportunities in "Western Ukraine," all the Polish prejudice and discrimination, all the terrorist activities of the Ukrainian Nationalist extremists, and all the bitterness and frustration, ordinary Poles and Ukrainians still seemed not only to get along fairly well and even become friends but also to fall in love and marry. In 1927, 16.2 percent of the total number of marriages in Eastern Galicia were between Poles and Ukrainians.[42] In all probability, the percentage of these types of mixed marriages was even higher in "peaceful" Wołyń — a fact that, during the ethnic cleansing campaign of the Ukrainian Nationalists often led to tragic consequences for both spouses and their "half-Polish" children.

Writing in 1948, Stanisław Skrzypek divided the history of interwar Polish-Ukrainian relations into the following stages:

> 1919: Struggles between the Poles and Ukrainian separatists in Eastern Galicia.
>
> 1919–1921: The end of military operations. Ukrainians *émigré* elements conduct anti-Polish activities in the international sphere. Boycott of the population census in 1921 and proclamation of the boycott of elections to the second Polish Seym.
>
> 1920: The Piłsudski-Petlura Agreement on Polish-Ukrainian co-operation in the war against the Bolsheviks.
>
> 1923: Statement of the first Ukrainian Program in the Polish Seym by Father Mikołaj Ilkow [Mykola Ilkov], in the name of the Ukrainian Peasant Party, and Deputy Podhirski [Podhirskyi], in the name of the Ukrainian Party, on the question of normalizing Polish-Ukrainian relations.
>
> 1928: The cessation of tendencies to boycott elections to the Seym and the emergence of Ukrainian groups in the Seym and Senate.
>
> 1931: Discussion for an understanding, conducted between representatives of the Ukrainian Parliamentary Representation and the Government *Bloc*, and the pastoral letter issued by Bishop Chomyszyn [Khomyshyn] on the necessity of Ukrainian-Polish co-operation.
>
> 1933: Polish-Ukrainian Accord (beginning of the normalization period).
>
> 1939: UNDO's [Ukrainian National Democratic Union] manifesto and that of the Greek Catholic Episcopate, calling on Ukrainians to defend the Republic in the approaching war and the declaration of Vice-Marshal M. [*sic*] Mudry [Vasyl Mudryi], after the outbreak of war, on Ukrainian solidarity with Poland in the war against the Germans. Ukrainians voluntarily join the Army. They fight side by side with the Poles against the Nazi invaders.[43]

Skrzypek added, "Undoubtedly the general evolution was in the direction of establishing a *modus vivendi* between the two peoples, and if it had not been for the war and the occupation of Poland by foreign troops in 1939, Polish-Ukrainian relations would have continued to improve."[44]

That may have happened, but three political trends emerged among the Ukrainians in Poland's eastern provinces during the interwar period. One of them was indeed accommodation. The other two were nationalism and, to a much lesser degree, communism. Generally speaking, a large number of Ukrainians would have preferred an independent Ukraine or at least an autonomous "Western Ukraine" under Poland. Unfortunately, the short-lived Western Ukrainian National Republic [Zakhidno-Ukrainska Narodna Respublika, or ZUNR], established by the Ukrainian National Rada in Lwów on November 1, 1918, was doomed from the start and was not recognized by the League of Nations.[45] This republic was established at a time when the Ukrainian National Republic (Ukrainska Narodna Respublika, or UNR), proclaimed by the Ukrainian Central Council (Rada) in Kiev on January 25 (backdated to January 22), 1918, already existed. In January 1919, a union of the two states was ratified and proclaimed but was never implemented, and each government continued to operate independently of the other. Under Symon Petliura, the UNR recognized the Polish rule west of the River Zbrucz. The ZUNR did not. According to its constitution, the ZUNR was to encompass the following territories:

> The whole Ukrainian ethnographical area within Austria-Hungary, especially Eastern Galicia to the River San as a boundary, together with the Lemki [Łemko] territory, north-western Bukovina, with the towns of Czernowitz, Storozinetz and Seret, as well as the Ukrainian portion of northeastern Hungary, form one undivided territory. This national Ukrainian territory is hereby constituted the Ukrainian State.[46]

In considering these proposed boundaries, we must keep two things in mind: (1) the ownership of these territories had not as yet been determined either by force of arms or by the League of Nations, and (2) these territorial boundaries were modest in comparison with the overall territorial ambitions of the OUN-UPA. The OUN-UPA's understanding of "Ukrainian ethnographical areas" included, and still includes, parts of the territories of Russia, Belorussia, Rumania, Czechoslovakia, the already mentioned Polish territories of Łemkowszczyzna (the sub-Carpathian region), and the additional Polish territories of Chełmszczyzna (Chełm region), Wołyń, and Podlasie. Some of these areas now lie within the borders of independent Ukraine.[47]

Polish resistance, the Polish-Ukrainian War (November 1918 to July 1919), the Treaty of Riga, and finally the various decisions of the Great Powers ended these territorial ambitions. On June 25, 1919, the Supreme Council of the Four Powers informed Warsaw:

> With a view to protecting the persons and property of the peaceful populations of Eastern Galicia against the dangers to which they are exposed by the Bolsheviks, the Supreme Council of the Allied and Associated Powers decided to authorise the forces of the Polish Republic to pursue their operations as far as the river Zbruch [Zbrucz] (which separates Galicia from East Ukraine).
>
> This authorisation does not, in any way, affect the decision to be taken later by the Supreme Council for the settlement of the political status of Galicia.[48]

The Treaty of Riga of March 18, 1921, established Poland's sovereign rights over these territories:

> Article 2. The two Contracting Parties, in accordance with the principle of national self-determination, recognize the independence of the Ukraine and of White Ruthenia and agree and decide that the eastern frontier of Poland, that is to say, the frontier between Poland on the one hand, and Russia, White Ruthenia and the Ukraine on the other, shall be as follows: [Description of frontier follows.]
>
> Article 3. Russia and the Ukraine abandon all rights and claims to the territories situated to the west of this frontier laid down by Article 2 of the present Treaty....
>
> Article 5. Each of the Contracting Parties mutually undertakes to respect in every way the political sovereignty of the other Party.[49]

The March 15, 1923, decision of the Conference of Ambassadors (see Appendix, Document 1, "Decision of the Conference of Ambassadors, March 15, 1923, on the Subject of the Frontiers of Poland"), recognized by the United States on April 5, approved Poland's de facto occupation of the eastern provinces it had owned before the partitions. But the dream of the Galician nationalists, of independence and reunification of all ethnic Ukrainian lands, lived on.

When it became clear that the possibility of "Western Ukrainian" independence was out of the question and that Poland could not or would not honor its recognition of the need for an autonomous Galician régime under its administration (for reasons stated eloquently in the December 12/18, 1930, London *Times* report, quoted in full in the Appendix), political savvy dictated an ethnic policy of accommodation. Myron Kuropas notes:

> Following the 1923 Council of Ambassadors' decree, most Ukrainians in eastern Galicia reconciled themselves to Polish rule, believing that accommodation through political and economic action was the only reasonable course of action. A number of political parties were created, the largest of which was the Ukrainian National Democratic Union (UNDO). In the 1928 election, some seventy Ukrainians were elected to the Polish National Assembly, twenty-three of whom were members of UNDO.[50]

This commonsense approach was even more promising in Wołyń, where the communist influence was on the wane. (For examples of accommodationist thinking, see the Appendix, Documents 11 and 12: Speeches by Deputy Petro Pevnyi, a Ukrainian from Wołyń, and Deputy Mykhalo Bachynskyi, a Ruthenian from Małopolska Wschodnia.)

Although the UNDO (Ukrainske Natsionalne-Demokratychne Obiednannie, or Ukrainian National Democratic Union), which tended toward accommodation, was the major political party in southeastern Poland, numerous other parties also emerged. Among the various left-wing parties, those that followed a policy of self-reliance included the Ukrainian Radical-Socialist Party (Ukrainska Sotsialistychna Radykalna Partiia, or USRP) and the Ukrainian Socialist Democratic Party (Ukrainska Socialistychna Demokratychna Partiia, or USDP), which was in tactical collaboration with the Polish Socialist Party. Those that pursued a policy of reliance on the Soviet Union included the Ukrainian Labor Party (Ukrainska Robotnicha Partiia, or URP), the Ukrainian Peasants' and Workers' Socialist Organization (Sel-Rob), the Ukrainian Peasants' and Workers' Socialist Union (Sel-Rob Union), and the Communist Party of Western Ukraine (KPZU). Because the KPZU was illegal, it often conducted its affairs through the other, legal parties listed above.[51]

As news of the Soviet terror against the Ukrainians east of the Zbrucz River in the 1930s began to reach Poland, KPZU party membership and influence declined drastically, and finally in 1938 the party was dissolved by the Comintern.[52] (After the Soviet invasion, the Ukrainian Communist Party was revived and became the *only* party in southeastern Poland. According to Article 58 of the Criminal Code of the Ukrainian Soviet Socialist Republic, membership or activities in any other party or even a social agency was a criminal offense subject to punishment and even death.[53] More than a few Ukrainians, therefore, longed for the civil liberties they had enjoyed in the "good old days" under the "tyranny" of Poland.)

In the final analysis, none of these parties in themselves represented the Ukrainian people as a whole. In 1931 M. Feliński stated, "It is remarkable how many declarations and petitions there are on record addressed to international public opinion by particular Ukrainian parties, each one usurping to itself the privilege of speaking in the name of the whole Ukrainian body."[54] In addition, from 1920 until 1939, the UNR government-in-exile also found a home in Poland.

Meanwhile, during the interwar years, another movement grew steadily and became virtually unchallenged after 1939: the Ukrainian Nationalist movement. More than anything else, the radical nature of this movement and the repressive reaction that it called forth poisoned Polish-Ukrainian relations during these formative years of Poland.[55] It would be a grave mistake, however, to believe that the illegal organization at the forefront of this movement represented the will of the Ukrainian people.

A proper understanding of the nature of twentieth-century radical Ukrainian nationalism must begin with Dmytro Dontsov's nihilistic political testament presented in his *Natsionalizm*—a work that was printed in, of all places, the printery of the Greek Catholic Basilian Fathers. That ideological framework had several facets: *ultra-nationalist*—"Ukraine for Ukrainians"; *ethnocentric*—"never give minorities cultural-national autonomies"; *Nitzschean*—"will to power" of the "strong man" (*sylna liudyna*); *Social Darwinian*—"Life makes him [right] who proves himself morally and physically stronger"; *amoral*—the "amorality of the person of action"; *elitist*—"in place of democracy—the principle of initiative-minority (superior people) and of creative violence"; and *racist*—Jews were "hyenas," "a cowardly and slavish race," and "About pogroms ... what pogroms? There were no pogroms in the Ukraine." In short, integral Ukrainian nationalism was built upon a *fascist* ideology.[56] Unfortunately for all the minorities in southeastern Poland, that ideology—endorsed uncritically by large segments of Ukrainian youth and by students in particular—was adopted by the UVO. Dontsov never joined either the UVO or the OUN, since he was primarily a theoretician, a "man of words" rather than a "practical man of action."[57]

Founded in Prague on August 30, 1920 (the same year that the National Socialist German Worker's Party, founded in 1919, received its name), by a group of embittered Galician war veterans, the UVO (led by Ievhen Konovalets) simply dismissed the 1919 decision of the Allied Supreme Council, the 1921 Treaty of Riga, and the 1923 decision of the Conference of Ambassadors regarding Poland's eastern border. The UVO refused to accept defeat and determined to continue, by means fair or foul, the 1918–19 Polish-Ukrainian War through its underground military cells in "Western Ukraine."[58] The following "great commandments" of the "revolutionary-fighter" can be found in the UVO Organ *Surma* (1927):

> 1. Never do anything that may benefit the enemy.
> 2. Always and everywhere do what will bring harm to the enemy.
> 3. Consolidate your spiritual and physical forces.
> 4. A struggle without arms must be waged not only by individual groups of revolutionary-fighters, but also by the entire people. The revolutionary-fighters are only the advance guard in this protracted conflict.[59]

The "Decalogue" (*Dekaloh*) of Stepan Lenkavskyi appeared in *Surma* in 1928.[60] These ten commandments were used as a set of guidelines by the Union of Ukrainian Nationalist Youth (Soiuz Ukrainskoi Natsionalistychnoi Molodi, or SUNM), established in 1926:

> 1. Attain a Ukrainian State or die in battle for It.
> 2. Do not allow anyone to defame the glory or the honor of Your Nation.
> 3. Remember the Great Days of our efforts.
> 4. Be proud of the fact that you are an heir of the struggle for the glory of Volodymyr's [St. Vladimir's] Trident.
> 5. Avenge the death of Great Knights.
> 6. Do not speak of the cause with whomever possible, but only with whomever necessary.
> 7. Do not hesitate to commit the greatest crime, if the good of the Cause demands it.
> 8. Regard the enemies of Your Nation with hate and perfidy.
> 9. Neither requests, nor threats, nor torture, nor death can compel You to betray a secret.
> 10. Aspire to expand the strength, riches, and size of the Ukrainian State even by means of enslaving foreigners.[61]

Another article, entitled "Permanentna revoliutsiia" (Permanent Revolution), appeared in the October 1930 edition of the same UVO organ:

> By means of individual assassinations and occasional mass actions, we will attract large circles of the population to the idea of liberation and into the revolutionary ranks. The broad masses must become interested in the cause of revolution and liberty.... Only with continually repeated actions can we sustain and nurture a permanent spirit of protest against the occupier and maintain hatred of the enemy and the desire for final retribution. The people dare not get used to their chains, they dare not feel comfortable in an enemy state.[62]

The goal of the UVO, then, was to create a state of "constant revolutionary boiling," which would prepare the masses for the "final reckoning with the enemy" at the "appropriate moment."[63]

The successor of the UVO was the OUN. Founded at the First Congress of Ukrainian Nationalists (January 28–February 3, 1929) held in Vienna, the OUN, also led by Konovalets, would eventually replace the UVO. It too would pursue a policy of violence toward the Polish government.[64] At this very first gathering of the OUN, the previously cited

"Decalogue" was accepted verbatim (i.e., OUN members were required to swear to it)—except for the word "efforts" (in commandment no. 3) which was replaced by the phrase "struggle for freedom," and except for the phrase "even by means of enslaving foreigners" (in commandment no. 10), which was deleted.[65]

More important, two pivotal documents emerged from that meeting, documents that would provide the ideological basis for the removal of the non–Ukrainian population from Eastern Poland in the 1940s. They read as follows:

> **Proclamation:** Only the complete removal of all occupants from Ukrainian lands [i.e., ethnic cleansing] will create the possibility for an expansive development of the Ukrainian people in the borders of their own nation.... In its internal political activity, the Ukrainian nation will strive to attain borders encompassing all Ukrainian ethnographic territories.
>
> **Resolution:** The complete removal of all occupants from Ukrainian lands [i.e., ethnic cleansing], which will follow in the course of a national revolution and create the possibility for an expansive development of the Ukrainian people in the borders of their own nation, will be guaranteed by a system of our own military formations and goal-oriented political diplomacy.[66]

The important point to ponder is the *ultimate* end of this political agenda, namely the establishment of an autonomous Western Ukrainian state wedded to *samostiina Ukraina,* independent Ukraine. But exactly what was to be the nature of that future Western Ukrainian state envisioned by the Nationalists, and how was total Ukrainian independence to be achieved?

According to the ideological framework for the Ukrainian Nationalist movement fashioned so brazenly by Dmytro Dontsov and incorporated by the OUN directorate into its political platform, the nation-state was to be fascist[67] (a "national dictatorship")[68] and led by a supreme *vozhd* (führer or leader) whose authority was unlimited and unquestionable.[69] It was to be ethnically pure[70] ("Ukraine for Ukrainians").[71] It was to be established on all ethnic Ukrainian lands ("Greater Ukraine").[72] And it was to be achieved through compulsory mass action ("creative coercion")[73] in an armed struggle first with Poland and then with the Soviet Union.

It just so happened, however, that most of the Ukrainians did not share either the Nationalist fascist vision or its agenda, were not fanatically proindependence, did not support either the UVO or the OUN in spite of, or perhaps because of, the "join or die"[74] recruitment policy, and certainly did not want another war, especially a two-front war with the Polish Eagle and the Russian Bear. It is possible that the OUN and its brand of radical nationalism may have grown stronger in Poland in the 1940s had there been no war. It is also possible that with continuing legal action against its leaders and concerted Polish efforts to curb terrorism, it may have eventually expired under the weight of its own unrealistic expectations. But then Nazi Germany came along, and the war, and suddenly everything became possible, or so it seemed to the Nationalists.

The trail of political terror of these two youth-oriented, militant organizations during the interwar years is well documented, as are the Polish reactions to it.[75] Although the Ukrainian neo–Nationalists, like their predecessors, never fail to list the Polish repressions during the interwar years, they always "forget" to mention the reasons for the repressions. Although the Polish ten-week (September 16–November 30, 1930) pacification was brutal and often failed to distinguish between the innocent and the guilty, the number of Poles who died under the UVO-OUN terror was much greater than the handful of Ukrainians who died under the resulting Polish crackdown.[76] Moreover, although many Ukrainian Nationalists were arrested and some found guilty and sentenced, no terrorist was ever executed, and none "died" in Polish prisons. All, together with all the common criminals, were eventually released by the Soviets and the Nazis, who had a great deal in common with both types and used them to good advantage.[77]

This record stands in stark contrast to the numerous acts of the Ukrainians: robbery ("expropriating" mail vans, post offices, and letter carriers); acts of sabotage (cutting telegraph wires and felling telegraph posts); bombings (five successful ones of newspaper offices, administrative buildings, and a railroad station and one foiled attempt on the Soviet consulate in Lwów); arson (burning Polish households, haystacks, granaries, and barns, some belonging to Jewish farmers — 470 incidents in the first few weeks of 1922 alone); assaults; and cold-blooded political assassinations and attempted assassinations of the Polish police, other Ukrainian "collaborators," and prominent Polish and Ukrainian political figures.[78] Alexander Motyl comments on these killings conducted during the interwar years, in the prevailing tradition of fascism:

> The OUN was particularly active in eliminating its real and perceived political opponents. At least sixty-three actual or attempted killings are known to have occurred between 1921 and 1939. (The real figure is probably higher, since unreported killings in backwater regions must have also taken place.) Of this number, at least two-thirds were the work of the OUN. Only eleven cases can be considered significant as assassinations or attempted assassinations of prominent Polish and Ukrainian figures. The vast majority of the remaining 52 killings and attempted killings were of Ukrainians believed to be collaborators (informers and minor officials enjoying good relations with the authorities, or publicly opposed to nationalist tactics) and of Polish policemen, undercover agents, and suspected informers. A breakdown by nationality reveals that successful and unsuccessful attempts were made on the lives of 36 Ukrainians, 25 Poles, one Russian, and one Jew. Of this number, two Communists — one Ukrainian and one Russian — were assassinated.[79]

These mafia-type executions and planned executions included the unsuccessful attempts on the life of Marshal Józef Piłsudski (1921), President Stanisław Wojciechowski (1924), and school superintendent Godomski (1933) and the successful assassination of the minister of the interior, Bronisław Pieracki (1934), as well as of Stanisław Sobiński (1926), Tadeusz Hołówko (1931), Emilian Czechowski (1932), and Jerzy Ciesielszuk (1933). The attaché at the Soviet consulate in Lwów, Aleksei Mailov (1933), was also killed. Among the Ukrainians labeled as "traitors" and executed on OUN command were Sydor Tverdokhlib (1933), a writer, and Ivan Babii (1934), the well-known and respected director of the prestigious Ukrainian Gymnasium in Lwów.[80] (Later, similar fascist tactics would characterize the OUN *internal* struggle for power. Such tactics would continue even after the war in the displaced persons camps, where intimidation, beatings, and even killings were carried out by the Bandera faction against its own people. [81])

These terrorist attacks continued throughout the 1920s and 1930s but reached their greatest intensity during the sabotage campaigns of 1922 and 1929–30. The latter involved some 2,200 "serious" acts of sabotage.[82]

An interesting article that was published in the periodical *Ukraina* in Chicago (no. 19, October 17, 1930) illustrates the translation of policy into practice. The editorial note indicates that the article came from the inner circle of the UVO:

> The Part Action of the U.W.O. [UVO]
>
> For the second time the U.W.O. has resorted to so-called part action. The object of this part action is to promote, by organized activities, disquiet in the country and panic among the Polish population, to break the Polish spirit of expansion, to breed distrust of the Government as their protector against Ukrainian attacks, now or in the future. It is to encourage a state of mind extremely hostile to the Polish State and nation among the Ukrainian masses. Finally, its object is to foster uncertainty and anarchy so as to deepen the impression abroad that the frontiers of Poland are not permanent, that the Polish State is not consolidated, and that the feelings of the Ukrainian population are manifestly anti–Polish.
>
> It began with sporadic acts of sabotage committed against the property of well-known Poles, such as generals, former voivodes, former ministers, and so on. In a short time its action was extended against all Polish proprietors without exception, against colonists and Government property. Why was particular attention paid to Polish landlords and settlers? Firstly, because the

> colonization of our countryside by landless Polish peasants, under the protection of the Polish State, is one of our greatest dangers, and so we must make Polish colonists afraid of settling on Ukrainian lands. Secondly, because a mass attack has the best psychological effect upon the Ukrainian peasants as a whole. Fires which can be clearly seen from a score of villages, fires destroying what belongs to the enemies of the Ukrainian peasant, who are robbing him of his land, have a greater effect upon him than, for instance, attacks upon organs of governmental authority or upon individuals unknown to him.[83]

Such a shameless confession needs no commentary. Among the contemporary sayings of the Ukrainian Nationalists were the following slogans, so characteristic of all terrorists: "Blood is needed — we will provide a sea of blood! Terror is needed — we will make it hellish." "We are not ashamed of murders, robbery and burnings. In war there are no ethics."[84] "The worse it is, the better."[85] Clearly, the Ukrainian Nationalists were not interested in improving the lot of their people under the Polish rule. On the contrary, they *wanted* the situation to deteriorate. No concessions from the Polish side would have appeased them. They wanted revolution, not reform. The following revealing and even more disturbing admission can be found in the April 17, 1932, edition of the Ukrainian newspaper *Meta*: "Ukrainian Nationalism must be prepared to employ every means in the struggle ... not excluding mass physical extermination, even if millions of human beings, physical entities, are its victims."[86]

During the interwar years, the acts of violence were calculated to elicit a strong reaction from the Polish authorities. In tandem with the countermeasures, the Nationalists, according to plan, would then proceed to lodge "protests" with the League of Nations and try to elicit international sympathy and support for their cause. One OUN report of the day reads as follows:

> All branches of the O.U.N. were ordered to establish committees of protest in their own areas, composed of representatives of various groups and associations. These branches were the first to send telegrams of protest to the League of Nations and to various governments and to begin the preparation of extensive memoranda for circulation to the same quarters. Similar orders were given to all branches of the O.U.N. in other countries. Nationalist Press Bureaux function in Switzerland, Berlin (two Bureaux), Lithuania and Belgium. The chief propaganda department of the U.W.O. sends immediate information about events in the country to all branches of the O.U.N. in Europe, and also to American periodicals.... In Lithuania the wireless is used to report events taking place in Eastern Galicia. In Prague a bulletin is issued in the Czech tongue, under the editorship of Ukrainian nationalists.... The propaganda services of the O.U.N. are constantly in touch with American Ukrainians. Agents of the O.U.N. have left for America to organize protests, which seem to be developing on a large scale. Their instructions are that every local association must begin by sending a telegram demanding that an International Commission be sent to Galicia. Then they must collect funds, hold meetings of protest and make demonstrations before Polish Consulates.[87]

In spite of these protests, by the end of that twenty-year period, many OUN leaders found themselves behind bars in Bereza Kartuska, a relatively small (in comparison with the German camps and the sprawling network of camps in the Soviet Gulag) Polish concentration camp for political prisoners. Clearly, no legitimately established government can allow such subversive activities within its commonwealth. Anticipating events unlikely to occur in the first place, some governments have gone to extremes. During the Second World War didn't both Canada and the United States intern their Japanese populations in concentration camps and confiscate Japanese property merely on the *suspicion* of possible disloyalty? Didn't Canada do the same thing with its Ukrainian citizens ("enemy aliens") in 1914–1920?[88] How do we feel about terrorism today? Consider the American reaction to the 1994 bombing of the New York World Trade Center or to the 1995 bombing of the Federal Building in Oklahoma City. President Bill Clinton noted in a speech on May 5, 1995, "There is no right to resort to violence when you don't get your way."

But terrorists, by definition, have never understood the "art of compromise." In the interwar years, it has been argued, neither did the Polish government. Could that government have done anything to assuage the demands of the Nationalists? Short of granting them an independent state, the answer is "no." The question, then, was not one of "rights" but of territory, an issue on which the UVO-OUN took an uncompromising position. So did Poland. As "one of the most representative of Ukrainian leaders" told a reporter for the *Times* (London) in 1930: "We are fundamentally disloyal. We do not want peace. If our people are allowed to enter into friendly cooperation with the Poles they may cease to cherish the dream of an independent Ukraine, which we hope to realize in 30 or 40 years' time. Whatever is done for us, we must always be discontented."[89]

The League of Nations, in its January 30, 1932, response to the barrage of Ukrainian Nationalist protests regarding the 1930 pacification by the Polish authorities, did not approve the methods used but recognized that it was the Ukrainian Nationalists themselves who were to blame for consciously inviting this response by their "revolutionary actions." The league stated that this was not a governmental policy of persecution of the Ukrainian people.[90] In effect, the January 1932 decision of the League of Nations Council branded the OUN as a terrorist organization. In light of the repressive actions that inevitably followed, during the interwar years, the "Enemy No. 1" of the Ukrainian citizens of Poland was not the Polish government, but the terrorist organization: UVO-OUN.

Most Ukrainian authors and John A. Armstrong will surely disagree with this characterization of the UVO-OUN. Armstrong's depiction of the UVO also represents his assessment of the nature of the OUN:

> After the collapse of the UNR, the unit [Sichovi Striltsi — Sich Sharpshooters — under Konovalets] disbanded in Galicia; many of its members united in (1920) in an illegal, para-military organization known as the Ukraïns'ka Viis'kova Organizatsiia (Ukrainian Military Organization — UVO). In the bitter struggles with the Poles in the twenties, this group was harshly treated and retaliated with some deeds of violence. Basically, however, it was a military protective group rather than a terrorist underground.[91]

A remarkably candid and informative document (a report) was written by Osyp Dumyn in May 1926: *Die Warheit über die ukrainische Organisation* (The Truth about the Ukrainian [UVO] Organization). The report bears the stamp of Auswärtiges Amt (Ministry of Foreign Affairs) in Berlin and the date when it was received, June 17, 1926. Dumyn was the director of the UVO intelligence unit on behalf of the Germans and therefore was privy to all the innermost secrets of this organization.[92]

Clearly, this document was meant for the eyes of his Abwehr superiors alone and represented an act of treason against the UVO. That it was never shared with the UVO leadership is indicated by the fact that Dumyn was not assassinated either by the UVO or by the OUN (he disappeared without a trace in 1944 after the Soviet conquest of East Prussia) and by the fact that he is regarded by authors of Ukrainian encyclopedias as a deserving activist and fighter. It is doubtful that Dumyn would have dared to falsify any information in this report meant to be read by Abwehr officials to whom he was indebted and who had both his career and his life in their hands. No scholar can ignore Dumyn's report, a primary source on the inner workings of the UVO until 1926. The two-paragraph section entitled "Program and Military Plans of the UVO" reads:

> The mission of the UVO was to conduct an incessant and uncompromising war with Poland. The objectives of the UVO were to destroy Polish rule in all Ukrainian spheres, to undermine Polish national influence, the material and moral annihilation of the Polish national organs of authority, and finally the attainment and institutionalization of its own independent Ukrainian nation. In the course of the first two years of the existence

> of the UVO, this work unfolded according to plan, the proof of which were many deeds.
>
> By instituting its own detachments, the UVO was to create a real, although secret, Ukrainian army which could at the appropriate moment initiate an open war against the Polish occupant.[93]

If this is not a working definition of a terrorist organization operating within a legally constituted government, I don't know what is! To refer to the UVO as a "protective group" (à la Armstrong) is to whitewash history. That future "independent Ukrainian nation" to which Dumyn refers would undoubtedly be ruled by the fascist UVO élites: the "initiative-minority" (superior people) led by their all-powerful *vozhd*. Dumyn continued:

> Unfortunately, the leadership of the organization by no means fulfilled their mission. At the end of 1925 the founders of the UVO realized that the leadership avoided war on purpose and did everything possible to quiet the war-like disposition of the masses. All of this can be proven with facts. Even the leaders of the UVO said: "if it now came to war and if we were to initiate the course of action expected of us — we would be entirely compromised."[94]

And so the acts of terror committed by the UVO and by the masses it agitated into a fever pitch subsided in 1926 — in good measure because of the massive arrests by the Polish government. Dumyn — who was reporting all of this to his Abwehr contacts or, rather, masters — did not know in 1926 that three years later the reorganized UVO-OUN would again resume its campaign of terror against the Polish government and people in Eastern Galicia and Wołyń in the hope of launching that long-talked-about revolutionary war of independence. The new leaders, with the reenergized Konovalets at the helm, then fully intended to carry out the mission of the founding fathers. (For a contemporary, third-party assessment of the Eastern Poland situation, which finally culminated in the Polish pacification of 1930, see the December 12 and 18, 1930, report of the *Times* [London] in the Appendix, Document 13: "The [1930] Report: A Minority in Poland — The Ukrainian Conflict.")

Significantly, the OUN did not operate in and had no impact on Soviet Ukraine. Its very presence there would have been suicidal. Its frame of reference was Nazi Germany. The tactics of the "brownshirts" were its tactics: "Fiercely nationalistic, desperate, unencumbered by democratic scruples, the West Ukrainian youth of the 1930s could only take cheer from the rise of Hitler in Germany."[95] In these words of John-Paul Himka, however, the descriptive adjectives are misapplied. It was not so much the "Boy Scouts" who were "fiercely nationalistic, desperate [and] unencumbered by democratic scruples" as the "Galician schoolmaster's son" from Berlin and his cohort of "hardened conspirators" [from the *Times* (London) report], who put these ideas into their young brains and sent them first on their missions of pyromania on bicycles and trolley cars and then, when they were twelve years older, on their missions of ethnic cleansing.

Who financed the UVO-OUN during the interwar years? Who provided the Nationalists with the requisite training and the necessary supplies to carry out their program of bombings, sabotage, and murder? The answers to these two important questions have a direct bearing on Ukrainian Nationalist–Nazi collaboration during World War II.

Although martyrs were produced by the eighteen known "expropriations" (the attacks on mail carriers and postal trucks),[96] the few zloty that were so dearly acquired in the process were scarcely worth the effort.[97] Terrorist activities, as we know, require enormous sums. In the interwar years, these sums came predominantly from Germany, but other countries contributed to "the cause" as well. Among them were the Ukrainian émigrés in the United States, Canada, and various Western European countries, as well as the governments of Czechoslovakia, Lithuania, and the Soviet Union. Some funds also came from the Ukrainian people in Eastern Galicia and Wołyń.[98] In short, during these times of inflation, the UVO possessed ample funds to carry out its mission.

The UVO was founded in Prague[99] because Czechoslovakia was willing to provide this illegal organization with financial assistance and with a base camp, Josefov, where new recruits could be trained and military material stored.[100]

Lithuania supported the Ukrainian Nationalists in several ways: backed their complaints to the League of Nations; granted passports to UVO-OUN activists (Ievhen Konovalets, Volodymyr Martynets, Roman Sushko); made funds available to the organization and specific individuals (e.g., in 1923, the UVO received $1,000 per month from the Lithuanians,[101] and Osyp Reviuk, a former officer in the Ukrainian army and director of Lithuanian espionage, received a quarterly government subsidy of $2,000); and published the UVO organ *Surma* after it was moved out of Berlin in 1928 to offset Polish complaints that the UVO was on Germany's payroll.[102]

According to Dumyn, the "Belorussian Affair," which first and foremost involved Lithuanian dollars, was hatched by the UVO directorate in 1922. UVO members were dispatched to Kaunas and told to portray themselves as the representatives of a secret Ukrainian army that was ready at any moment to launch a general uprising against Poland. (At this time the whole UVO organization consisted of only a few disgruntled veterans and the students whom they were able to influence so effectively.) The plan was to persuade the Lithuanian government to provide funds so that the UVO might be able to create a similar "army" in the Belorussian territories that were also under Polish control. To prove its genuine intentions, the UVO sent its delegate to Wilno. The Lithuanians took the bait and shelled out. Yet although the UVO kept reassuring the Lithuanians that the work was progressing and that the conspiratorial web was embracing the whole of "Western Belorussia," nothing was being done in this regard with the Lithuanian funds. The charade lasted until 1924, when the Lithuanians demanded a consolidated Lithuanian-Ukrainian-Belorussian attack against Poland. When the UVO directorate launched its excuses for why this was quite impossible, the Lithuanians, realizing they had been duped, cut off the funds, at least for the time being.[103]

Soon after this, the UVO turned to the Bolsheviks in Berlin and Kharkov for financial assistance and received a monthly stipend of $500 to $600. In Kharkov, the deal was made with the condition that the UVO endorse the reunification of "Western Ukraine" with the Soviet Union. The UVO accepted this condition and the money. The Russian subsidy was later reduced and then discontinued when the Bolsheviks found out what kind of an organization they were dealing with.[104]

Finally, the UVO attempted to secure funds by selling Polish documents both to the Lithuanians and to the Bolsheviks. Dumyn recorded one aspect of this venture as practiced by the UVO. During the training courses in Preussisch-Holland, the German instructor brought in some secret Polish documents on the Polish army to show the trainees what such documents looked like; Richard ("Riko") Jary photographed them, made copies, and sold them to the parties mentioned above. "Later," said Dumyn, "three to five copies were made of all documents received from the Germans, including those brought simply for purposes of translation, and sold on orders of Konovalets and Jary."[105]

The interest of German military circles in Ukrainian nationalism preceded World War I, spanned the entire interwar era, and continued throughout World War II.[106]

In 1921, Jary — a military and political leader of mixed Ukrainian-Austrian descent, a cavalry officer in the UHA (Ukrainska Halytska Armiia — Ukrainian Galician Army), the chief of UVO intelligence, a founding member of the OUN, a future member of the OUN Provid, and together with Sushko, its Berlin liaison — established contact with the Reichswehr and with Alfred Rosenberg, Hermann Göring, and Ernst Röhm.[107] Later, Jary was placed on the German intelligence payroll.[108]

In 1922, Konovalets began courting the German General Staff and moved his place of residence from Eastern Galicia to Berlin, then to Geneva and Rome, where he remained until 1929. Later, he received 110,000 German marks per month for his organizational needs.[109]

In 1923, an espionage course was founded in Munich by the intelligence branch of the UVO.[110]

In 1924, Abwehr's interest in supporting

the intelligence-gathering service of the UVO prompted the UVO leadership to initiate a request for financial assistance through Jary. To convince Germany of the UVO's usefulness, a decision was made to assassinate Poland's head of state, President Stanisław Wojciechowski. Since no qualified or willing assassin could be found, a young student, Teofil Olshanskyi, a son of a Uniate priest, was recruited for the job. He was given a badly designed bomb (which failed to explode) and a revolver without a firing pin. Since no money was given him for cab fare, he had to use the trolley. After the unsuccessful assassination attempt, he received political asylum in Germany. Stanisław Steiger, a Jew, was accused of the assassination attempt, tried and found innocent. Only later did Germany (not the UVO) reveal Olshanskyi's role in this affair.[111]

In 1925, a Berlin-sponsored officers' school was established in the Free City of Danzig (Gdańsk) and graduated 110 active UVO members.[112] German arms, military equipment, and explosives were easily funneled into Nationalist hands simply by being transported over the bridge connecting Poland and Germany.[113]

In 1926, the UVO Supreme Command moved its headquarters to Berlin and received political and financial support from the German General Staff.[114]

Between 1922 and 1927, training courses were established by German military and intelligence circles in Munich (1922–23), Preussisch-Holland (1924–25), Breslau (1926), and near Berlin (1927).[115] The intent of these training courses was to prepare young Ukrainian intellectuals for espionage service before their recruitment into the Polish army.

In 1927, *Surma* was published in Berlin.

In 1933, Jary signed a contract with Röhm; on this basis, a number of Ukrainians were accepted into the SA (Sturmabteilung — Storm Troopers). Konovalets and Jary officially engaged in talks with the Gestapo regarding collaboration and financial support.[116]

In 1938, extensive training centers were established by the Abwehr (German military counterintelligence service headed by Wilhelm Canaris), such as, for example, the one near Lake Quenz in Austria in the Wiener-Neustadt region.[117]

Ukrainian centers appeared in Berlin, Munich, Hamburg, Bremen, Hawelland, Delmenhorst, Hemelingen, and elsewhere.[118] In February 1939, the leader of the OUN, Andrii Melnyk, wrote: "Today ... at our side stand other nations — Germany, Italy, Spain, Japan — whose victories aim at the final annihilation of the common enemy. In this battle the leading task falls to Ukraine. The quick conclusion of this battle depends on the strength and tenacity of the Ukrainian nation."[119] Meanwhile, the OUN sent Hrytsko Kupetskyi, a fugitive from Polish justice, to Japanese-occupied Manchuria. Kupetskyi, together with Valentyn Moroz and another OUN member, took part in a diversionary course in preparation for the Japanese attack on the Soviet Union; the attack never materialized.[120] And finally, in April 1939 the OUN proclaimed: "Ukrainians and Germans are natural allies. Besides Germany, Ukraine has no other active ally in the whole world against all occupants of the Ukraine."[121]

Melnyk, Konovalets' successor, was known in German counterintelligence circles as "Consul I," Stepan Bandera as "Consul II." Jary served both as an agent of the Abwehr and as a member of Bandera's OUN Provid.[122]

These are but a few indicators, based on documentary evidence, of the extent of interwar Ukrainian Nationalist-German collaboration, the aim of which was to produce a bloody revolution in "Western Ukraine" and force Poland to grant it independence. As far as the Germans were concerned, however, the funds, the arms, the military equipment, and all that training of the UVO-OUN cadres were to serve a more important purpose: to further the future war effort, the first victim of which was to be the Republic of Poland.

All this was foreseen in 1927 by none other than, in the words of William Shirer, that "muddled party 'philosopher'"[123] Alfred Rosenberg, who wrote, "Once we have understood that the elimination of the Polish State is the first demand of Germany, *an alliance between Kiev and Berlin* and the creation of a common border become a necessity of people and state for a future German policy."[124]

And if a "muddled 'philosopher'" drew this conclusion twelve years before the great war, at least some clearheaded Nazi plotters must have figured it out as well — and made the necessary preparations for the attainment of that future German state "in close [and] indissoluble alliance" with Ukraine, as Rosenberg put it on April 7, 1941.[125] "If there had been no Ukraine," sighed some Berlin politicians, "Germany would have had to invent one."[126] In other words, Ukraine was God's gift to Germany, and of all the people in Europe, no other were more suited for the task that lay ahead than the young and gullible cohort that pined for Ukrainian independence and freedom from the "tyranny" of the Polish rule: the Galician Ukrainian Nationalists of the OUN. For them, Germany was God's gift to Ukraine.

With the prospects of war on the horizon, the OUN abandoned its prewar strategy of achieving Western Ukrainian independence by means of a popular revolt. The road to freedom, it thought, lay in a German victory over Poland. In exchange for an independent Ukraine, the OUN was now prepared to collaborate fully with Nazi Germany in the destruction of Poland. Of course, Hitler had his own view on these matters, and although he welcomed Ukrainian assistance in whatever form, he promised nothing. Neither did he inform the Nationalists of his previous agreement with Stalin, to whom he had promised that "Western Ukraine" would fall to the Soviet Union.

This was the state of affairs as of September 1939, when both Hitler and Stalin invaded Poland. On the eve of the war, the OUN had approximately 20,000 members.[127]

Soviet Occupation

When the Soviet armies crossed the Polish frontier in 1939, they were greeted with bread and salt, flowers, *arcs de triomphe*, and blue-and-yellow flags waving in the wind. The Ukrainian peasants thought the Soviets came to rescue them from the Polish *pany*. Anti-Polish sentiments were vigorously expressed at village meetings throughout Eastern Poland: "We Ukrainians have been under the Polish yoke for these past twenty years, but now the hour of freedom has struck." "Just as the dead will not rise, so too, Poland will never resurrect again." "Remember, your rule has ended. The Pole-Lakh [*polak-lakh*] can no longer be a teacher or a civil servant; he [*lakh*] must now be an ordinary laborer." Such phrases were mouthed by Vasyl Hryshchenko, a well-known Ukrainian Nationalist from Ostrówki, at meetings in Huta Stepańska, Siedlisko, and Wyrka — Polish settlements in the county of Kostopol.[128] Even Metropolitan Andrei Sheptytsky, head of the Greek (Ukrainian) Catholic Church, expressed similar sentiments. At the news of the Soviet invasion he stated: "We occupied only a few rooms on the ground floor until recently and now we have it all to ourselves. There is still a tenant on the first floor, but when we push him out the entire house will finally be ours."[129]

This widespread exuberance of the Ukrainian masses and the subsequent Ukrainian-Soviet collaboration in "Western Ukraine" pose somewhat of an enigma. As early as September 20, 1926, the UNDO broke with pro–Soviet tendencies and, together with various Ukrainian political parties and organizations, including the Ukrainian Greek Catholic Church, condemned Soviet policies in Eastern Ukraine. In a May 13, 1929, article, *Novyi Chas* lamented the widespread "pauperization and a general feeling of depression" among the Ukrainians east of the River Zbrucz. On March 25–26, 1932, the UNDO National Congress passed an anti–Soviet resolution: "The National Congress calls upon the whole Ukrainian population, and in particular all the party organs and the whole Ukrainian national Press to a ruthless struggle with Communism in all its open or masked (pro–Soviet) forms."[130]

On April 24, 1933, the Ukrainian Socialist Radical Party condemned the persecutions in Soviet Ukraine. On July 25, 1933, a Ukrainian Committee for Help to the Suffering Ukraine was set up by twenty-five organizations and institutions. "Let us ring the great bell in alarm, O Ukrainian Nation!" began its declaration.

On August 28, 1933, the Greek Catholic Church issued a manifesto entitled "The Ukraine in Death-Throes." On September 16, 1933, the Ukrainian Socialist Radical Party, the Ukrainian Social Democratic Party, and the

Ukrainian Social Democratic Labor Party issued an anti–Soviet manifesto:

> We Ukrainian Socialists protest in the face of the whole cultured world against this barbarous destruction of the Ukrainian working classes by the Bolshevik dictatorship, against the trampling underfoot of those rights which the Ukrainian nation has gained through long years of revolutionary struggle, and we protest against the mass executions, against the infamy of the concentration camps.

On October 21, 1933, the Soviet consulate in Lwów was attacked. On August 3, 1936, the pastoral letter of Metropolitan Sheptytsky railed against communist activities and pro–Soviet tendencies:

> He who helps the Communists in their work, even purely political, is a traitor to the Church.... He who helps the Communists in the realization of their plan of a common "people's" front with the Socialists and the Radicals, betrays his nation.... everywhere the one goal and the one tactic point to one leader.... We have, too, in Galicia not a few proofs that this leader is Red Moscow, that the "people's front" whether here or in Volhynia or in White Ruthenia is aiming at the same goal as were the Bolsheviks in the Greater Ukraine when they condemned to death by starvation millions of Ukrainians.

Finally, on January 4–5, 1938, the National Congress of UNDO passed an anti-Soviet resolution: "In the Soviet Union, in the ancestral Ukrainian lands, the Ukrainian nation is enduring fearful persecution in national, religious, social, cultural and economic spheres. Bolshevik terror has there become the only method of ruling the Ukrainian nation."

In September 1939, did *anyone* believe that the Soviet Union invaded Eastern Poland merely to "protect" the rights of its "downtrodden minorities"? How, then, are we to explain the phenomenon of Ukrainians rejoicing and collaborating with the Soviets? Who were these Ukrainians? That they were Ukrainians is certain, but were they communists, Nationalists, unattached peasants? The answer is "yes"— they were all three. Referring to the entire war period, one of the foremost authorities on this subject matter, Władysław Siemaszko, states:

> The first manifestations of hatred and depolonization policies took place in 1939, not only after September 17 under the influence of Soviet agitation, but right after the eruption of the Polish-German War. Polish soldiers, the police and everyone in uniform, settlers, local residents, government employees, and those fleeing central Poland were murdered. The perpetrators were Ukrainians with a *pro–Bolshevik* orientation, *nationalists*, as well as *peasants* without any ideological affiliation. Robbery and denunciations of Poles to the NKVD were a daily occurrence. Poles conversing in the streets of Zdołbunów were threatened by the Ukrainians: "Do not speak in that foul (*psim*— dog-like) language, your day has passed, we will show you pigs...." Whether these Ukrainians were communists or Nationalists, the witnesses did not know.[131]

Of the thirteen attacks in September 1939 documented by Siemaszko in his major work, ten were said to be the work of "Ukrainian Nationalists," one of "local Ukrainian peasants," one of "Ukrainian peasants," and one of "local Ukrainians." Siemaszko does not use these terms indiscriminately. In this important matter, he is very careful to record the actual words found in 350 testimonies (documenting 1,600 incidents of atrocities), which deal only with Wołyń. (As of May 9, 1992, he had received 160 additional accounts. These 510 accounts speak of atrocities occurring in one-third (1,039) of all the locations inhabited by the Polish people in the province of Wołyń.) Other designations appearing in his work are "Nationalists," "Nationalist bands," "*Banderowcy*" (OUN-B members), "*Bulbowcy*" (members of Taras Bulba-Borovets' gang), "Ukrainian neighbors," "Ukrainians," and "Ukrainian police."[132] One of the thirteen September accounts reads as follows:

> September 1939. In the unpopulated forests between the village of Smerdyń in the township of Trościaniec, county of Łuck, and the town of Sokul, a band of *Ukrainian*

> *Nationalists* murdered 22 Poles in a bestial manner. In that number were 9 women between ages 20–30 who had all been raped. Also raped were two girls between the ages of 11–13. The victims included four children, five boys between ages 10–14 and a couple in their eighties.[133]

That some Ukrainians, like some Jews, welcomed the Soviets was verified by Samuel Lipa Tennenbaum:

> On his last day of office our starosta issued a public proclamation ordering a display of white flags and calling for a friendly greeting of the Soviet Army. The majority of the population followed the starosta's orders. However, the Ukrainians showed their nationalist blue and yellow flags and a handful of local Communists (newly emerged from hiding) and their sympathizers displayed red flags. The starosta, the mayor and members of the city council went to the outskirts of the city to meet the incoming army of occupation. A separate unofficial delegation showed up, with the tiny enthusiastic group of local Communists.
>
> I was not present at this encounter, but I heard about it from workers in our factory. The Russian commander rebuffed the official group led by the starosta in a rude language; he ignored the Communists, but warmly greeted the Ukrainians. Photographs were taken of Ukrainian girls embracing Russian soldiers and giving them flowers; these were later displayed prominently on the front pages of Russian newspapers. Little did our local Ukrainians know that they were moving from the frying pan into the fire.[134]

Although the Ukrainian Communist Party had been dissolved in 1938, it should not surprise us that its diehard members supported the invasion and hoped for better days. That the common man helped the Soviets should not surprise us either. By doing so, he helped himself as well. Clearly, the extent of the Ukrainian peasants' collaboration was directly related to their own material well-being and, what is worse, greed. Whatever their misgivings, they looked forward to their improved status in the "dictatorship of the [ethnically cleansed] proletariat" with their newly acquired wealth and their expanded (formerly Polish) territorial holdings.

> November, 1939. Nawóz — Ukrainian village in the township of Rożyszcze, county of Łuck [in Wołyń], Popowski Ostrów. *Local Ukrainian peasants* murdered around 200 persons of Polish nationality from among the refugees from central Poland who had paused in and around the village of Nawóz, the township Sokul and in other places. The murderers posed as members of the Refugee Aid Committee and offered the refugees better accommodations. At a predetermined hour in the evening, they were taken in the direction of Popowski Ostrów, murdered, and dispossessed of their belongings.[135]

But the Nationalists? Did they collaborate with, as they themselves put it, their "Enemy Number 1"? The obvious answer is that in 1939, the chief backers of the Ukrainian Nationalists and the Soviet Union were *allies*. Thus, collaboration with the Soviets was indirect. Ultimately, however, the early murders in the Soviet zone committed by the Ukrainian Nationalist–Nazi collaborators were but a prelude to the *intended* ethnic-cleansing campaign that the OUN had proposed in 1929 but was unable to carry out on a full scale until the summer of 1943, when the confluence of historical events presented it with the opportunity to do so.

Relying on a regional Polish Government Delegation report dated June 14, 1944, Jerzy Węgierski states that in September and October 1939, the Ukrainians murdered 200 local Poles in the county of Przemyślany and that in June and July 1940, another 100 were killed. Moreover, about 2,000 Poles — refugees from other territories — were killed by Ukrainians in 1939 in the counties of Przemyślany, Rohatyn, Brzeżany, Podhajce, and Buczacz.[136] All of these counties, with the exception of Rohatyn, which was in the province of Stanisławów, were in Tarnopol. Similar murders occurred in the provinces of Lwów and Wołyń.

In his memoir *Under Assumed Identity*, Yitzhak Sternberg wrote: "When the Polish army began to retreat from the Germans in September 1939, it encountered, among others, Ukrainian groups. The Ukrainians, as allies of the Germans, were convinced that their moment had arrived, and they began to disarm the Polish army. There were places where the Ukrainians wearing yellow-blue bands with the 'Trizub' ... seized power with a view to declaring their independence."[137] In this passage, Sternberg was undoubtedly referring to the Ukrainian Nationalists.

Ukrainian Nationalists also fought with the retreating Polish army units. One such battle took place in Gródek Jagielloński, with heavy losses incurred by the Nationalists.[138]

In October 1939, Stanisław Kot, the Polish ambassador to the USSR, wrote from Rumania to General Władysław Sikorski: "Regarding the territories under the Soviets: Unimaginable despair. It's as if all that is Polish (*polskość*) has simply collapsed. The Ukrainians under Konovalets have taken over everything, in part also members of the UNDO and the Jews (not the bourgeois, these are cautious), and all of these are in the hands of the Stalinist element from Kiev."[139]

As we have seen, the Ukrainians along with the Jews played a vital role in the pro-Soviet citizens' militias whose members were allowed to carry weapons and whose primary task was to protect their communities from "class enemies." That meant, first and foremost, ferreting out and arresting Polish soldiers and policemen. These militias, formed spontaneously before the arrival of the Soviets, were later placed under the NKVD and participated in the deportation of Poles by preparing lists of those to be deported, rounding them up, and escorting them to the transports.[140] Many of the militiamen were either common criminals or political prisoners whom the Soviets had recently released from Polish jails. "The Red Army broke open jails along its way — Who else could have been kept there but class enemies of the Polish 'masters'? — a logical deduction since during the first days of the war scores of Ukrainian nationalists and communist sympathizers had been arrested in Poland."[141]

A child from the province of Lwów, Lubaczów county, recollected: "And only in two weeks they came to us and started letting the worst criminals and murderers, who were awaiting them and greeted them with great joy, out of prisons. After letting these criminals out they started giving them the authority of so-called militiamen who together with the Russian militia helped to oppress Polish citizens."[142]

That the Ukrainians (including the Nationalists) ran for the Nazi border in 1940 (as did tens of thousands of Jews) says nothing about their initial welcome, celebration, and collaboration. After the purges, those collaborators who remained were in the full employ of the Soviets, and their very life as well as material well-being depended on doing their job and doing it well.

What was gained by that collaboration? In the beginning, a great deal for both sides.

> The initial collaboration of ethnic minorities allowed for the effective penetration of local society. The effect of this collaboration on the occupier's administration cannot be overestimated. And it is to the Soviet's credit as practitioners of revolution that they were able to appreciate and nurture such local support as long as they needed it. They were carrying out a social revolution in Eastern Poland, which could not be accomplished without *local* support, as experience in their own country had shown. A battle could be won or pacification achieved with imported manpower, but not a social revolution.[143]

What did the Ukrainians get in exchange? To begin with, the freed prisoners, along with other non–Polish peasants, were put in charge of local government.

> Naturally, prisoners of the Polish government were more trustworthy than those who had not been in jail; a coachman was a better candidate for town office than a civil servant or a politician; a doorman was better fit to run a large enterprise than an engineer; a porter made a perfect railroad stationmaster; and the poorest peasants were promoted over everyone else to village committees.[144]

Ukrainian now became the official language. Lands expropriated from Polish landlords were turned over to Ukrainian peasants. The schools of higher education were Ukrainianized,[145] meaning that the students, the teachers, the curriculum, and the language of instruction were Ukrainian. (The University of Lwów was renamed after Ivan Franko.) By mid–June 1940, some six thousand Ukrainian elementary schools existed in "Western Ukraine."[146] There too, new teachers were hired, new administrators were installed, new curricula were introduced, and all traces of information on Polish culture and history disappeared.[147] In the words of a well-known American cliché, "reverse discrimination" (radically applied) became the order of the day.

For these and other such benefits and privileges accorded to the Ukrainians and for the sake of the Soviet "social revolution," the Polish people had to suffer and die. There was no other way to achieve these goals simultaneously. And so the Poles were harassed by the Ukrainians: communists, Nationalists, and peasants alike.[148]

I can think of no better way to document the role of the Ukrainians in the pacification of Eastern Poland, including the massive deportations of the Polish people to the Gulag, than through the words of the Polish children who wound up in the Gulag as well.

> *Białystok province*: The arrival of Russians in Poland was sad, and joyful. For some Jews, Belorussians, and Ukrainians it was joyful. And for the Poles it was sad and hard.[149]
>
> *Lwów province*: In schools Russian and Ukrainian languages were introduced.... On the night of April 12/13 I was awoken by energetic ringing and knocking at the doors. I sprang to my feet and opened it. A Soviet officer, a Ukrainian militiaman, and two soldiers with bayonets stood in the doorway.[150]
>
> *Nowogródek province*: During the first days after the Bolshevik invasion, some Ukrainians and some Jews were threatening the Poles, and even assaults and robberies took place.[151]
>
> *Polesie province*: After the invasion ... we were persecuted a lot by the soviet authorities and by the ukrainians. Every day the ukrainians would come in riding bicycles with small red flags.... Ukrainian bands kept raiding us and breaking paintings from the walls they took our Polish books away from us.[152]
>
> *Stanisławów province*: In was a cold night, the snow fell and the wind blew. It was on February 10 at three in the morning, when everyone slept soundly. Suddenly there was a loud knocking. I jumped up from my bed it frightened me very much and also my mummy. Daddy got up put on the light and opened the door, four Russians rush into the apartment and two Ukrainians with rifles drawn, at this sight I became even more frightened and rushed out from bed got dressed and sat down. After a moment they gathered the whole family into one room daddy, mommy, my brother, sister, and me. They asked daddy where we want to go to Russia or to Germany, daddy said to America. Then they became very angry.[153]
>
> *Tarnopol province*: From the moment the war broke out, great changes took place that were most unpleasant for the Poles. When, as everyone knows, Russia occupied Polish territory, it seemed that she was coming to the assistance of the Poles. In the first days they treated the Poles very gently and protected them from attacks by the local Ukrainians. But soon the Ukrainians bribed the Soviet authorities and then they attacked the Polish communities together, robbing and pillaging, taking men into prison. In the settlement where I lived the Ukrainians began to torment us badly. They attacked at night, killing farmers. In the settlement neighboring ours it happened that in the evening the farmers were sitting down to dinner when a whole bunch of armed Ukrainians attacked and killed one of the men through the window and in many other houses, wounding others, robbed the more valuable belongings, leaving behind abandoned houses. On another evening they attacked a certain farm, where they completely destroyed the house and practically killed the people, ripping the clothes off them and everything that had been in the house only rubble remained and in it those who had been seriously wounded and left naked. They broke all their kitchenware over the people's heads and as they were leaving they threatened that if they reported them to the authorities they would come back and finish them off and would destroy the whole settlement. They tormented us dreadfully.... And they even took all the cows, horses, and pigs.... They also took everything from the barns. There was empti-

ness everywhere. Russians soldiers stood with rifles and watched that the Poles should not resist these robberies.... During this time the Ukrainians and the Soviets made population lists several times although we did not know what they needed it for.[154]

Polish soldiers came back from fighting the Germans but how they came back. Ukrainian bands attacked the returning Polish soldiers and robbed them of their clothes and let them go home beaten and naked.[155]

There were two Polish officers on the road going home to their wives and children. Some Ukrainians and Bolsheviks grabbed them. After three days of real murder they were shot, and the Ukrainians took their shoes and clothing. Before he died one said to tell his wife he was alive no more.[156]

Wołyń province: When the Ukrainians heard that the Soviet army was coming they began to revenge themselves on the Poles.... The next evening the Ukrainians came and took away our cows, horses, pigs etc. and even small things even my rabbits. And so they came every evening to revenge themselves on the people.[157]

With the invasion of Soviet troops, the Poles experienced a period of cruelty at the hands of the Ukrainians.[158]

When the Soviets came to our village then the ukrainians started taking everything away from our homes and afterwards they started distributing our land among themselves.... Afterwards the Soviets gave the Ukrainians 24 hours to do what they pleased with the Poles, so then the ukrainians from the village of Nawóz came to our settlement and started plundering and killing the colonists, they killed the following five colonists.[159]

The Ruthenian population of the nearby villages (in accord with the leaflets dropped from Soviet planes) came to "settle accounts with the Polish masters...." People often came to blows over their place in line, and the militia rarely intervened, composed as it was for the most part of Jews and Ruthenians.[160]

Well there were some Ukrainians who were in the prison at P. for theft and murder so they came with a written order that they have an order from the Soviets to drive us out wearing whatever we had on, and so they drove us out.[161]

This initial period of active Ukrainian-Soviet collaboration was short-lived. A child eloquently recorded the beginning of the end of that grace period:

> *Tarnopol province*: At the beginning the Ukrainian population was favorably inclined to the Bolsheviks and also to the first elections [October 22, 1939]. After the first elections, after voting for the annexation of "Western Ukrainia" to the USSR, they began to arrest Ukrainian leaders. You no longer saw hordes of Ukrainians with red bands on their arm and rifles and proudly and haughtily strutting around town. They didn't spit any more when they saw a Pole and with pity they nodded their heads in mutual understanding.[162]

And so, especially in 1940, the Soviets began to introduce their "downtrodden masses" to the joys of communal existence. The land that the Ukrainian peasants owned, as well as the Polish land that had so generously been given to them, was now "collectivized." (This collectivization had cost millions of lives in Soviet Ukraine. The peasants hated it with a passion.) Libraries and reading rooms were closed. Cooperatives were either eliminated entirely or restructured on the Soviet model. All former social organizations and political parties were abrogated. Both the Ukrainian Greek Catholic Church and the Eastern Orthodox Church (untouched initially) were now subjected to various restrictions aimed at curtailing their autonomy. Worst of all, the Ukrainian people were being shipped off in boxcars to frozen wastelands of the Gulag. As we have seen, according to Zbigniew S. Siemaszko, 14.9 percent, or 217,000, of the 1.45 million inhabitants and refugees deported to the Soviet Union from Poland's eastern territories were Ukrainian (or Ruthenian). To be sure, some Ukrainian collaborators continued to ply their trade until the bitter end, but most of the initially pro–Soviet Ukrainians early on recognized the "evil empire" for what it really was.

In the meantime, while the Soviets turned on the Ukrainians, some Ukrainians turned on the Jews.

> At Lubieszow, Jews armed themselves with axes, hammers, iron bars and pitchforks, to await the arrival of local Ukrainians intent upon murder as soon as the Red Army withdrew, and before the Germans had arrived. The Ukrainians came, and were beaten off. But then, retreating to the nearby village of Lubiaz, they fell immediately upon the few isolated Jewish families living there. When, the following morning, the Jews of Lubieszow's self-defense group reached Lubiaz, "they found the bodies of twenty children, women and men without heads, bellies ripped open, legs and arms hacked off."[163]

As in the cases of the other collaborators already considered, we do not know either the number of Ukrainians who assisted the Soviets during the occupation of Eastern Poland or the number of their victims. One thing is certain, however: given a little more time, Stalin's goal of exterminating the Poles with the help of Poland's own citizens would have been achieved. Much of that work had already been accomplished in just twenty-one months! The "oppressed minorities" whom he had come "to protect" would then have shared the lot of their enslaved eastern brothers and sisters.

As the world held its breath, the Soviet program of ethnic cleansing ended on June 22, 1941. On July 30 of that same year, the Soviet Union — which, with the help of local collaborators, had decimated the Polish civilian population and murdered the soldiers and officers of the Polish army — declared itself an ally of Poland.

German Occupation

The Nazi occupation of Eastern Poland was much worse. Under the Nazi occupation, the Polish population was exposed to the "organized and intentional effort aimed at the physical extermination of the Polish population."[164] These words do not refer to the devastation wrought by the Nazi war machine or Generalplan Ost but to the Ukrainian genocide program that assisted the German war effort. This program was carried out by the Ukrainian Nationalists. Like the Soviets, they mobilized the Ukrainian peasants for the task of their own "social revolution" along with its integral component: ethnic cleansing. (Perhaps this is the real meaning of the term "integral nationalism.")

Peasants so inclined, meanwhile, simply continued to rob, pillage, and murder the Polish people — and now also the Jews.[165] What did it matter to them whether the marching orders came from Moscow, Berlin, or Lwów? While the petty masters kept changing, their one and only true Master — greed — remained the same. The idea, planted in their brains by the Nationalists, that they were doing their patriotic duty may have helped to ease their conscience somewhat, as did the "join or die" policy of the Nationalists. In any case, by now they were used to it.

Despite assertions to the contrary on the part of the Ukrainian neo-Nationalists, the close ties to Germany so carefully cultivated for twenty-one years were never entirely severed, not even by the OUN-B (the Bandera faction) during World War II.[166] The often-repeated phrase "limited collaboration" describes the OUN-B's position *after* June 30, 1941, better than its position *before* that date. The OUN-M (the Melnyk faction) cannot claim even that much.

What is the evidence for the collaboration between the Ukrainian Nationalists and the Third Reich throughout the war?

1939–June 30, 1941

The cordial relationship between the Ukrainian Nationalists and Germany during the interwar years was rather one-sided, with the Nationalists getting the better end of the deal. In the months preceding the attack on Poland, however, Germany began to extract its pound of flesh. In March 1939, the Ukrainian Nationalists surfaced in the ephemeral Transcarpathian government.[167] According to a German document, on the eve of the war four thousand Galician Ukrainian Nationalist agents trained by the Abwehr in sabotage and diversion infiltrated central and southern Poland, incited the minorities, and participated in acts of violence against the Polish people.[168] Then, in the summer of 1939, a regiment of OUN members, known as the Nationalist Military Detachments (Viiskovi Viddily Natsionalistiv, or VVN) but officially called Bergbauernhilfe (Mountain-Peasants' Help — BBH) by the Abwehr, who organized it, was placed under the command of Roman Sushko in Austria.[169] This secretly formed unit of some two hundred men (sometimes also referred to as Sushko's "Ukrainian Legion"), working hand in glove with the Abwehr and the SD, was to participate in the war effort both as a legion and as the instigator of a bloody uprising (Flurbereinigung) in the east directed against communists, Jews, and Poles after the attack on Poland. In such a case, Wilhelm Canaris noted in his diary, "I would have to make appropriate preparations with the Ukrainians so that, should this alternative become real, the Mel'nyk Organization (OUN) can produce an uprising which would aim at the annihilation of the Jews and Poles."[170]

The revolt never materialized because, by virtue of the August Agreement, Eastern Poland fell to the Soviet Union. Sushko's Ukrainian Legion was subsequently incorporated into the 14th German Army Group under Wilhelm List and participated in the attack on Poland on September 1.[171] After the Polish campaign, the legion was reorganized into a Ukrainian police unit, served as a border patrol (Grenzschutz) in the Carpathian Mountains (the Polish-Slovak border, mainly to prevent Poles and Jews from escaping and to attack Polish civilians and straggling Polish soldiers),[172] and then demobilized. Its members were given a choice either to continue serving in the police or to join a special Ukrainian Company of Instructors in Zakopane.[173]

That December (1939), a secret Gestapo police-espionage training school was established in Zakopane. Among its "students" were 120 Ukrainians. The training lasted five months, after which the graduates were deployed to various districts as prison and camp guards. The school was run by Walter Krüger and his assistant, Wilhelm Rosenbaum. Mykola Lebed was in charge of the Ukrainian unit.[174]

At this time, the OUN, through Richard Jary and Roman Sushko, planned to spread propaganda and to gather intelligence. It was also prepared to engage in sabotage if necessary through its followers not only in Poland but in Canada, the United States, and Britain as well.[175]

The Polish campaign was short. In preparation for the attack on the Soviet Union, the help of the Nationalists was enlisted once more. A German Abwehr officer responsible for subversive activities revealed in Nuremberg:

> It was pointed out in the order that for the purpose of delivering a lightning blow against the Soviet Union, Abwehr II ... must use its agents for kindling national antagonisms among the people of the Soviet Union.... In carrying out the above-mentioned instructions of Keitel and Jodl, I contacted Ukrainian Nationalist Socialists who were in the German Intelligence Service and other members of the nationalist fascist groups.... Instructions were given by me personally to the leaders of the Ukrainian Nationalists, Mel'nyk [Code Name "Consul I"] and Bandera [Code Name "Consul II"] to organize ... demonstrations in the Ukraine in order to disrupt the immediate rear of the Soviet armies.... Apart from this, a special military unit was trained for subversive activities on Soviet territory.[176]

John Armstrong notes:

> As early as 1940 the Germans surreptitiously formed military training units for Ukrainians. Their enlistment was concealed by official statements that the units were for *Volksdeutsche* (ethnic Germans) only, and the purpose of the units was disguised by designating the Reichsarbeitdienst (Reich Labor Service) to be the supervising agency in the Generalgouvernement. Years later, a Ukrainian informant mentioned ... that "fifteen thousand Ukrainians served in the German Army in 1941 as scouts, parachutists, saboteurs, and interpreters." Many were also trained for police duties.[177]

While these preparations for the invasion of the Soviet Union were going on and just when the Abwehr thought it had a firm control over the Nationalists, a disturbing (to the Germans) event took place in the ranks of the OUN. After his release from a Polish prison, Stepan Bandera, with the backing of some other young radicals such as Mykola Lebed, Roman Shukhevych, and Iaroslav Stetsko, challenged the leadership of Melnyk[178] and, in February 1940, established a rival Revolutionary Directory, with himself in charge. After a bitter conflict, the OUN split into two uncompromising and mutually antagonistic factions. Bandera's group came to be known as the OUN-B, Melnyk's as the OUN-M. Although the ensuing hostilities produced bloodshed and victims on both sides, Bandera was clearly headed for victory — that is, until June 30, 1941.

On April 19, 1940, in a meeting between representatives of both factions of the Ukrainian Nationalists and Hans Frank in Kraków's Wawel Castle (there were several such meetings), the Nationalists issued a declaration of loyalty to the Third Reich and, to prove it, donated thirty-eight church bells to German foundries, participated in various festivities organized by the Germans in the General Government, and more important, supported the delivery of product contingents demanded by the Germans and assisted in the deportation of people for forced labor.[179]

Meanwhile, another nationalist group, that of Taras "Bulba" Borovets, began operating in 1940 in Wołyń but was unattached either to Bandera or to Melnyk. After the invasion of the Soviet Union, Borovets contacted the Wehrmacht and, in August 1941, secured an authorization to form his *Poliska Sich,* a diversionary military unit that was armed by the Germans and participated in the German pacification of Soviet partisans and Jews in Wołyń in the fall of 1941. This unit consisted of approximately three thousand men. It was officially dissolved by Erich Koch in November of that year but continued operating illegally for a while. In May and June 1942, Borovets formed another group of "partisans" from the remnant of the dissolved Poliska Sich.[180]

In the spring of 1941, an agreement reached between the Wehrmacht and the OUN-B strengthened Bandera's hand even more. Under the terms of that agreement, his faction was allowed to engage in political activities in "Western Ukraine" in exchange for military and clandestine collaboration.[181] The ability to move German-trained Ukrainians to "Western Ukraine" for diversionary and espionage activities before the invasion of the Soviet Union was facilitated greatly by the German-Soviet Boundary and Friendship Treaty, signed on September 28, 1939. This treaty provided for the return of ethnic Germans, Belorussians, and Ukrainians to their respective countries. At the end of the Polish campaign, this agreement was unilaterally amended by Germany to read as follows: "The flow of refugees from the east to the west across the line of demarcation [with the U.S.S.R.] is to be stopped immediately, with the exception of Volksdeutsche elements and Ukrainian activists."[182] As it turned out in this "repatriation" process, although many German-trained diversionary and espionage Ukrainian agents were able to penetrate "Western Ukraine," eventually some twenty thousand Ukrainian Nationalists fled *from* there to the Nazi-occupied territories of Poland.[183]

In April 1941, Germany began recruiting Ukrainian Nationalists into its armed forces and paramilitary organizations. Military and police training was provided by German instructors in Kraków, Krosno, Zakopane, Sanok, and Tarnów.[184] Some of the graduates, with the OUN's agreement, were then placed in Werkschutz (work security) units and concentration camps (as police guards). Others were assigned to paramilitary units, such as the Ukrainischer Heimatdienst (Ukrainian work service), which were often engaged in military construction work. These were later used by the Nazis for police action, pacifications, antipartisan warfare, and roundups of Poles and Ukrainians.[185]

Most important, as the result of a conference between OUN-B representatives and emissaries of German intelligence, at the beginning of 1941 a Ukrainian Legion was organized and equipped by the Abwehr. Its membership was recruited from other Ukrainian units formed earlier by the Wehrmacht (including Sushko's demobilized "Ukrainian Legion")[186] and consisted of seven hundred men. Camouflaged under the harmless name of Reichsarbeitsdienst, it trained in such places as Krynica and Dukla.[187]

That May, the legion was divided into two OUN-B regiments: Nachtigall and Roland.[188] Nachtigall, under Albrecht Herzner and Theodor Oberländer on the German side and Roman Shukhevych ("Tur," "Taras Chuprynka") as head of the Ukrainian staff, wore the uniform of the Wehrmacht; Roland, under the supervision of Jary and the command of Ievhen Pobihushchy ("Rena"), wore traditional Ukrainian uniforms. The former trained in Neuhammer near Breslau (Wrocław), where the representatives of the OUN-B Provid were temporarily located; the latter trained in Saubersdorf near Wiener-Neustadt.[189] Collectively, these two units also went under the name Detachments of Ukrainian Nationalists (Druzhyny Ukrainskykh Natsionalistiv, or DUN).[190]

At the outbreak of the invasion of the Soviet Union, Roland was sent to advance from Rumania to Iaşi and the Odessa area, and Nachtigall marched on Lwów. Among the OUN-B members in Nachtigall were Bandera's chief associates: Iaroslav Stetsko, Lev Rebet, Iaroslav Starukh, Ivan Ravlyk, Stepan Lenkavskyi, and Dmytro Iatsiv.[191]

In addition, early in 1941, under German auspices, both the OUN-B and the OUN-M formed and trained their own *pokhidni hrupy* (marching or expeditionary groups). These formations were recruited from German-occupied Galicia, Rumania, Bukovina, and the Nationalist Central and Western European bases. In all, they numbered between five thousand and eight thousand men. The destination of the OUN-B expeditionary forces (assembled and trained in the San and Łemko regions) was Soviet Ukraine. OUN-M forces (assembled in Hrubieszów, Krystynopol, Jarosław, Radymno, and Sanok) permeated Wołyń and continued eastward as well. Later, some of the leaders and members of the OUN-M forces joined Borovets' partisans. The mission of both units was to follow the Wehrmacht, spread nationalistic propaganda, set up local administrations and militias, organize OUN cells, recruit new members to the OUN, and "combat Jews and Communists."[192]

Ten days before the invasion, the OUN-M forwarded Hitler a detailed plan for its administration of the Ukraine and stated therein that Hitler could rely on his group as the "sole counterweight" to the Russian and Jewish influence.[193] Although the German ambassador to Moscow was never officially forewarned about the impending invasion of the Soviet Union, the Nationalists not only were informed about it months in advance but also had a comprehensive proposal for the governance of Eastern Poland and Soviet Ukraine.[194]

Seven days before the invasion, on June 15, 1941, the "Memorandum of the OUN on the Solution to the Ukrainian Question" clearly stated that the "natural alliance" between Germany and Ukraine (i.e., the Ukrainian Nationalists) demanded not merely "tactical collaboration" on the part of OUN members but "sincere friendship" with the Third Reich: "Since the interests of both nations demand a natural alliance, German-Ukrainian relations must be based on sincere friendship.... Conclusion: An independent Ukrainian military power which corresponds to the spiritual attitude of Ukraine will warrant the German-Ukrainian alliance."[195]

After two years of intense collaboration, even skeptical Germans had changed their mind about the usefulness of the Nationalists. These doubts, for example, had earlier been expressed by Stabsleiter A. Schickedanz to Hans Lammers (head of the Reich Chancellery), von Stutterheim (Chancellery), and Reinhard Heydrich (SD, Gestapo):

> June 15, 1939: That organization [the OUN], which can best be compared with the Croat Ustashi group, is probably still slated by the OKW [Oberkommando der Wehrmacht—High Command of the Armed Forces] to carry out certain intelligence tasks in case of conflict with Poland. It may be suited for that purpose but is entirely unfit to lead a political operation to seize hold of the population.[196]
>
> September 17, 1940: The OUN is nothing but a small terrorist group with a coloration specific to Galicia.[197]
>
> September 18, 1940: The evident discord within this group now shows that the nature

> of this group does not warrant our political support. We have always regarded it as a very limited, purely terrorist organization, without any political influence and without the slightest importance. More precisely, it is nothing more than a national-Galician offshoot of the felled tree of the Great Russian social-revolutionary movement. After the occupation of Galicia by the USSR, this group [the OUN] has lost the remainder of its political importance. At any rate, it is untimely and ill-advised to grant it any importance and to keep it artificially alive, inasmuch as its activity seems to be endangering the security of the state. Therefore, the only right thing to do is to dissolve this political organization.[198]

Now, however, with the prospect of a Soviet war and the need for pacification, sabotage, and diversionary activities behind enemy lines in Eastern Poland, perhaps this "terrorist organization" could be kept "artificially alive" and could be used, if not for a "political operation" then for political organization; but whether the Ukrainian Nationalists could "seize hold of the population" was still very much in doubt. In fact, the vast majority of the Ukrainian people, whom the Nationalists claimed to represent, never supported them, and this the Germans knew. For the remainder of the war, although the Ukrainian Nationalists would be used as servants of the Nazi policy, they would never gain the status of equal partners. Throughout the war each side tried to use the other to its own advantage. In this game, clearly Nazi Germany held all the cards.

And so the German-Soviet War began. At dawn, on June 22, 1941, as the world held its breath, the Nazi war-machine raced across the Ribbentrop-Molotov line of demarcation. On that same day, the Germans permitted the Nationalists to establish a National Ukrainian Committee in Kraków consisting of all nationalist group representatives except Melnyk's.[199] That night, scores of Ukrainian and Belorussian commandos were parachuted by Germany over "Western Ukraine" and "Western Belorussia." Nachtigall crossed the border near Przemyśl and eight days later (June 30, 1941) entered Lwów together with the first battalion of the Brandenburg regiment and other German units, several hours in advance of the regular German army.[200] Ivan Klymiv, an OUN-B commandant, wrote to his subordinates: "The German Army, Deutsche Wehrmacht, entered the Ukrainian lands as a partner.... We should regard it as such and assist it in every possible way.... It is the army of liberation of the Ukrainian nation."[201]

What happened next has been the subject of an unresolved debate for the last half a century. Various authors, especially Polish and Jewish, maintain that while in Lwów, Nachtigall slaughtered innocent Polish and Jewish civilians, murdered many (usually the number given is 25) university professors and their families, and on leaving Lwów, left a similar trail of blood all along its march to Vinnista.

Relying on the work of Aleksander Drożdżyński and Jan Zaborowski as well as Cyprian Sawicki, Antoni Szcześniak and Wiesław Szota state that on entering Lwów, Nachtigall tortured and executed 51 professors and members of their families, as well as 100 Polish students. According to these authors, in the following days the SS, in conjunction with Nachtigall, murdered about 3,000 of the Polish intelligentsia. At the same time there appeared on the streets of Lwów civil patrol units of the OUN, which pretended to be a part of the Ukrainian militia and which proceeded to torture and kill both Polish and Jewish civilians. After Lwów, Nachtigall's trail of pacification and extermination led through Złoczów, Tarnopol, Satanów, Proskurov, and finally Vinnitsa.[202] Saul Friedman stated:

> During the first three days of July 1941, the Nachtigall Battalion, composed almost entirely of Ukrainians under the direction of the Gestapo, slaughtered seven thousand Jews in the vicinity of Lwów (Lemberg). Before their execution, Jewish professors, lawyers and doctors were made to lick all the steps of four story buildings and to carry garbage in their mouths from house to house. Then forced to run a gauntlet of men wearing blue and gold armbands (coincidentally the colors of the Petlurist Republic), they were bayonetted to death in what was officially termed Aktion Petliura.[203]

Gerald Reitlinger noted, "During the occupation of Lwów in July 1941 these Ukrainian leaders [Melnyk and Bandera] cooperated with Heydrich's Einsatzgruppen, who were good enough to help them organise a pogrom which they dedicated to their dead hero as 'Action Petliura.'"[204] Drożdżyński and Zaborowski provide eyewitness accounts of these events.[205]

John Armstrong questions these "alleged eyewitness assertions" and states, "Since, however, the numerous Ukrainian interpreters for German formations like the military field police ... wore similar uniforms, they may well have been the real culprits." Moreover, he believes that Drożdżyński and Zaborowski's work (*Oberländer*) was written to "discredit the German officer Theodor Oberländer, who had supervised 'Nachtigall' and at the time of publication was a member of the cabinet of the Federal Republic of Germany." (Oberländer was dismissed from his post the same year in which the above-mentioned work was published.) He adds, "I have not been able to find any corroborating evidence indicating involvement of 'Nachtigall' members, specifically, in anti-Semitic atrocities."[206]

Martin Gilbert attributes these atrocities to "mobs of Ukrainian hoodlums, incited by German proclamations and pamphlets," "Ukrainian gangs," and the "Ukrainian militiamen."[207] He attributes the July 1941 three-day events of the "Petliura Aktion," which claimed the lives of "at least two thousand" Jews, to "local Ukrainians."[208] Alexander Dallin notes, "During the following days of chaos [in Lwów], it became obvious to the Germans that Bandera's followers, *including those in the 'Nightingale'* regiment, were displaying considerable initiative, conducting purges and pogroms."[209]

Ryszard Torzecki claims that although the execution of the professors was carried out by the Einsatzkommando zur besonderen Verwendung under Brigadeführer Karl Eberhard Schöngarth, on the basis of eyewitness accounts it cannot be ruled out that the Ukrainian police also took part in these atrocities. It is less likely, he thinks, that *Nachtigall* members were involved. Like all other Polish sources, however, he reports that the atrocities against the professors were carried out on the basis of lists prepared in advance by young OUN members (former students?) before the invasion.[210]

Krzysztof Popiński points out that at the end of June and the beginning of July, at least fifty-one pogroms (thitry-one involved deaths) took place in Eastern Poland, mostly in the southeastern provinces. These pogroms were carried out by the "special German police forces and the SS in conjunction with the Ukrainian and Lithuanian military and order-keeping forces as well as the local population." The pogrom in Lwów, according to this author, began on June 30 and lasted for several days. The special German police and the Ukrainian auxiliary police forced some one thousand Jews to recover and bury the bodies of the prisoners murdered by the Soviets. The chief of Einsatzgruppen C, Dr. Rasch, who arrived in Lwów in the first week of July, accused the Jews of the atrocities and ordered them shot in retribution. "Until that time," states Popiński, "it was primarily the Ukrainian police and the unit *Nachtigall*" that were responsible for the pogroms. "The appeal of Archbishop Sheptytsky," he says, "did not lessen the participation of the Ukrainians in the pogrom."[211]

According to Wiktor Poliszczuk, in the first days of the German occupation OUN leaflets appeared on the city streets. They read: "Exterminate the Poles, Jews and communists without mercy. Do not pity the enemies of the Ukrainian National Revolution!" "Nation, know that Moscow, Poland, Magyars [Hungarians], Jews are your enemies! Annihilate them!" Poliszczuk adds that from the very beginning, the Ukrainian auxiliary police that were assigned to the Einsatzgruppen SS and the Einsatzkommando units not only assisted these units but also murdered the Jews — and not only in Lwów.[212]

Simon Wiesenthal states: "Among the strongly anti-Semitic population the rumour was spread by the Ukrainian nationalists that all Jews were Bolsheviks and that all Bolsheviks were Jews. Hence it was the Jews who were really to blame for the atrocities committed by the Soviets."[213] In the editorial preface to his *Justice Not Vengeance*, we read: "His [Wiesenthal's] *via dolorosa* began in June 1941 with

Hitler's attack against the Soviet Union. Eight days later the last Russians left Lvov and the first German uniforms appeared: they were worn by Ukrainian auxiliary troops who celebrated their return by three days and three nights of continuous pogroms. Six thousand Jews lost their lives."[214] Wiesenthal himself attributes the execution of the professors — rounded up on the basis of a list prepared by "Ukrainian deserters"— to a squad of five ethnic German SS men and two Ukrainian police auxiliaries," who were later shot.[215]

Czesław Łuczak claims that the Nachtigall murdered the Polish populace (*ludność polska*) in Lwów.[216] Two eyewitnesses, A. Rzepicki and Wanda Ossowska, recalled that after the Nachtigall and the Wehrmacht entered Lwów, the Jews were used to carry out the bodies of those slain in the prisons by the NKVD. Rzepicki added that these Jews were rounded up and beaten so severely that there was hardly a difference between them and the dead. "For the carrying out of these atrocities, for the roundup of the Jews," Rzepicki concluded, "Ukrainian soldiers were used from the detachment 'Nachtigall,' I believe."[217]

In his 1989 study, Włodzimierz Bonusiak stated:

> From the moment the town [Lwów] was taken, massive Jewish and Polish pogroms began. The arrests and murders were carried out by four different formations. They were: the Ukrainian police, "Nachtigall," Feldgestapo and Einsatzkommando.... On the evening of July 3, 1941 around 10:00 p.m., groups consisting of officers and noncommissioned officers of the Gestapo and field gendarmerie together with soldiers from the Nachtigall battalion moved on to the various streets of Lwów in order to arrest the Polish intellectuals on the basis of lists provided, most probably by the Ukrainian Nationalists.... We can only surmise that it was not by accident that the names of the professors of the University Polytechnical Division — where S. Bandera and R. Shukhevych were students — were on that list.[218]

That this list was prepared well in advance (perhaps already in 1939) is corroborated by the fact that several of the professors whom the Gestapo came to arrest had already died during the war. A wife of one of the murdered professors testified, "Later we arrived at the conviction that the inspiration for the arrest of these professors came from the Ukrainian Nationalists."[219]

On May 2, 1966, the Procurator von Belov, in Hamburg, wrote to Anna Krukowska regarding the massacres in Lwów:

> Findings inside and outside the country produced the following conclusions. Lemberg [Lwów] was taken by German troops on June 30, 1941. Before its departure, the Red Army shot about 3,000 persons, mainly Ukrainian Nationalists, in Lemberg in the courtyard of Brigidki [Brygidki, the old monastery church of St. Brigid] and Lonski [Łącki] prisons. The discovery of that deed led to extended excesses against the Jewish and communist populations in the first days after the German occupation. The Ukrainian militia and the "Ukrainian Liberation Army" took part in these outrages which also involved arbitrary killings.[220]

On October 22, 1959, during a press conference for foreign correspondents in Berlin, Professor A. Norden stated that on the basis of his evidence, between July 1 and July 7, 1941, Nachtigall and the Security Service (Sluzhba Bezpeky, or SB) of the OUN-B, headed by Mykola Lebed, killed three thousand Poles and Jews in Lwów.[221] Finally, Werner Brockdorff wrote of Nachtigall's march on the city of Lwów: "Ukrainian soldiers entered Lwów.... Anyone who fell into their hands during these hours, lost his life."[222]

Ukrainian authors either keep silent about the Ukrainian participation in these pogroms or deny Nachtigall's involvement in them altogether. In any case, it is beyond dispute that thousands of Jews and Poles lost their lives in Lwów in those first few days of July, that most of the professors died (in great secrecy) on July 4, 1941, and that Nachtigall was not withdrawn from that city until July 7. Those who deny Nachtigall's participation in these atrocities must tell us exactly what the regiment did there during that time. In any case, since no one has ever stated that the Ukrainian, pro–Nazi Nachtigall opposed these atrocities or in any way tried to prevent them, its members are guilty at least of the sin of omission.

On the same day that Nachtigall and the Wehrmacht stormed the gates of Lwów, something quite unexpected happened, something about which the Germans were very much disturbed, something that landed many of the OUN-B members in concentration camps and enabled the Ukrainian Nationalists to state, for generations to come, "We fought Hitler." On June 30, 1941, the Bandera faction unilaterally declared Ukrainian independence! This event was preceded by a letter to Hitler from Bandera, who argued the case for an independent Ukrainian state but said nothing about the OUN-B's intended course of action. The letter was dated June 23, 1941, just one day after the German invasion of the Soviet Union.[223] There was no reply from Hitler.

Thus, the Ukrainian Nationalists—in a grand celebration attended by several high-ranking officers of the German army, including Hans Koch who spoke in their behalf—in one swift stroke not only "liberated" the whole of Ukraine from both Polish "tyranny" and Soviet tyranny but gave it a new government as well—one in "close [and] indissoluble alliance with the German Reich."[224]

"The newly created Ukrainian nation," reads one version of the declaration, "will work closely with the national social Germans who, under the leadership of their leader, Adolf Hitler, are creating a new order in Europe and the world." It ends with the following salutation: "Long live free Ukraine. Long live the Great German Reich and its leader, Adolf Hitler!"[225]

During the ceremonies the Rev. Ivan Hryniokh, a chaplain in Nachtigall, offered his regards to the Reich in the name of Roman Shukhevych. Congratulations were forwarded to Stepan Bandera, head of the OUN-B, to Metropolitan Sheptytsky, head of the Ukrainian Greek Catholic Church and a vigorous supporter of the Ukrainian Nationalists, to the "Famous Germany Army," and to Adolf Hitler, "Creator of Great Germany." The telegram to Hitler reads:

> To our Führer.
>
> According to the will of the Ukrainians, the Independence and Unification of all Ukrainian territories is proclaimed today.
>
> The longing wishes of the many sexes have been fulfilled. Your struggle was crowned with success. The Ukrainian Nation is prepared for the continued struggle to achieve complete freedom for the Ukraine under your banners.
>
> We are glowing today with happiness, inspired by the spirit of an idea, and are uniting in thinking with our Volks-comrades of the entire world.
>
> We are rushing to the Ukrainian capital—the golden dome[d] Kiev. In this great moment we are sending you, unshattered Hero of National Revolution, our sincere wishes. We are convinced, that your intentions, and the longing cravings of the entire Ukrainian Nation, regarding re-establishment of a mighty Ukrainian State, will be realized.
>
> Heil the Ukraine.[226]

The Metropolitan was so moved by the gravity of the moment that he wrote a pastoral letter to his faithful Ukrainian people exhorting them to be thankful to their "liberators" and to support the newly established Ukrainian régime. "We greet the victorious German Army," he wrote, "as deliverer from the enemy. We render our obedient homage to the government which has been erected. We recognize Mr. Iaroslav Stets'ko as Head of the State Administration of the Ukraine."[227] On July 10, 1941, the Orthodox archbishop of Łuck, Polikarp (Sikorskyi), appointed by Metropolitan Dionysius, supported the proclamation.[228] And the "Head of State" himself wrote a formal letter to Hitler and sealed it with the "Seal of Ukrainian State."

> To the Führer and the Chancellor, Berlin
>
> 7/4/41, Lvov, Ukrainian Government, No 2/41.
>
> Your Excellence:
>
> It is with an overwhelming feeling of gratitude and admiration for your heroic army which has covered itself with new glory in battles with Europe's worst enemy—

> Moscow Bolsheviks — that we are hereby sending Your Excellence, on behalf of the Ukrainian people and its government which has been created in liberated Lvov, our heartfelt wishes for complete victory in your struggle.
>
> The triumph of German arms, will enable you to extend your planned construction of new Europe also to her Eastern Part. You have thus also given an opportunity to the Ukrainian people as one of the full and free members of the family of European nations to take an active part in the implementation of this great plan in its sovereign Ukrainian state.
>
> On behalf of the Ukrainian government,
> Yaroslav Stetzko,
> Head
> (Seal of Ukrainian State)[229]

In short, a government was being foisted upon some 30 million Ukrainians without their consent or knowledge, headed by a leader most Ukrainians had never heard of and a cabinet of equally unknown Nazi collaborators. To be sure, there would soon be a Ukrainian government in Ukraine, but it would not be headquartered in Lwów, the center of Ukrainian Nationalism, or in "golden domed" Kiev. Its capital would be Równe, and Erich Koch would be its Reichskommissar.[230] Later, Koch declared: "There is no such thing as a free Ukraine. The aim of our work is to ensure that Ukrainians work for Germany."[231]

June 30, 1941–End of 1942

When Hitler, whose mind was set on dealing with Moscow, not Lwów, heard about this surprising turn of events, he issued a threefold order effective immediately: dissolve the Ukrainian "government," arrest the leaders, and bring to heel all Ukrainian Nationalists. Although the Abwehr, with the backing of Rosenberg, tried to soften the blow for the sake of future collaboration with the Nationalists, after an initial period of investigation and interrogation the arrest of the members of the Ukrainian "government" began in the second half of 1941.[232]

The OUN-B leaders (among them Stepan Bandera, who was in Kraków on June 30, 1941, Iaroslav Stetsko, Roman Ilnytskyi, Dmytro Iatsiv, Lev Rebet, and Volodymyr Stakhiv) were all sent to Sachsenhausen and placed in Zellenbau, a special section of the camp for political prisoners, among them such notables as the chancellor of Austria, Kurt von Schuschnigg, the leader of the "Iron Guard," Horia Sima, and, from July 1943, General Stefan Grot-Rowecki. If the Ukrainian neo–Nationalists of today want to take comfort in that thought, let them also remember that the conditions in Zellenbau were a far cry from those endured by the regular inmates of Sachsenhausen. Not all concentration-camp inmates were treated equally. In Zellenbau, the political prisoners not only ate well but also were exempted from the grueling daily roll calls, could receive packages, and had access to newspapers.[233]

Other repressions soon followed. On July 1, 1942, Mykola Maksymchuk-Kardash, the head of the regional Provid of Wołyń, was killed by the Germans. On November 25, 1942, a member of the main Provid and a regional leader, Dmytro Myron, were assassinated in Kiev. Bandera's own brothers, Aleksy and Vasyl, died in concentration camps. Perhaps most devastating was the raid on the Nationalist headquarters in Lwów, where four hundred OUN-B members were arrested.[234] Imprisonment increased dramatically after the September 12, 1941, meeting between representatives of the Abwehr (H. Koch, G. von Mende) and the leaders of the OUN-B (Bandera, Stetsko, and Ievhen Stakhiv), who refused to change their political direction and refused to withdraw the June 30, 1941, proclamation.[235] The purge was so thorough that by November 1941, all legal and quasi-legal Ukrainian organizations that tried to pursue their own agendas independently of Germany were liquidated.[236] By the end of 1942, 80 percent of the OUN-B leadership was in prison.[237]

Perhaps most indicative of the German change in mood toward the Ukrainian Nationalists was the treatment of the Nachtigall and Roland regiments. On July 7, 1941, both regiments were directed to the front by Wilhelm Canaris. The first went to Vinnitsa, the second to Odessa. From there, on August 27, 1941, Nachtigall was sent to Neuhammer in Silesia and Roland to Saubersdorf near Vienna. Both were then directed to Frankfurt on the Oder, and on March 23, 1942, the DUN were placed under Erich von dem Bach-Zelewski, whose Schutzmannschaft Bataillon 201 was then engaged in the brutal pacification of Belorussia.[238]

To fully appreciate the significance of this move, one must remember that von dem Bach-Zelewski was in charge of the anti–partisan war in the east and that both Hitler and Himmler welcomed the partisan challenge as a means of "thinning out" the Slavic population. Hitler stated: "The Russians now have an order for a partisan warfare behind the lines. This partisan warfare also has its advantages. It gives us the chance to eliminate everybody who is against us."[239]

Sol Littman notes: "The [Nachtigall] was responsible for the massacre of thousands of Jews, Poles, and democratically minded Ukrainians in the Lviv region on the heels of the German invasion; the [Roland] assisted the Einsatzgruppen operating in the southern Ukraine. Together, they served as an antipartisan force in Belorussia, where they murdered thousands of innocent villagers."[240]

Such, then, was the nature of the pacification of Belorussia in which the DUN, under SS General von dem Bach-Zelewski, played a part. The OUN-B historian Roman Ilnytskyi, in his *Deutschland und die Ukraine* (1958) stated, without shame or apology, that von dem Bach-Zelewski, the war criminal, considered his "Ukrainian Legion" (under the leadership of Ievhen Bobihushchy and Roman Shukhevych)[241] as "the best of all the sub-divisions under his command."[242]

When the DUN contract (they were paid collaborators) expired on October 31, 1942, it was not renewed by the Germans. Some soldiers went home, many joined the UPA, which was just forming, and the rest were sent to Lwów for police work and guard duty. Except for Shukhevych, who managed to escape, the officers were arrested. The DUN regiments were formally dissolved on December 1, 1942.[243] This was the "thanks" they received from the Third Reich for their collaboration in the German war, which was far from over.

Although not involved in the June 30, 1941, fiasco, the OUN-M was also purged. The roundups of predominantly young OUN-M intellectuals in the Lwów, Prague, and the Dnieper area took place between the end of November 1941 and the beginning of 1942.[244] A good gauge of the repressions launched against the OUN-M was the arrest of Melnyk, as well as the arrests of many of his closest followers — but not until January 26, 1944.[245]

Penultimately, Erich Koch inaugurated his reign over Hitler's Reichskommissariat Ukraine by calling on "Taras Bulba" and his men on November 16, 1941, to lay down their arms and to dissolve the Poliska Sich.[246] Although Borovets and some of his most faithful followers took to the woods, the leader was eventually caught and thrown into Sachsenhausen in the fall of 1943.[247] At the height of their power, the Germans wanted all the Ukrainian Nationalist leaders close to home and continually "on call."

One final blow that befell the Nationalists may or may not have had anything to do with the proclamation of independence. By Hitler's decree, on August 1, 1941, Eastern Galicia became incorporated into the GG — not into the Reichskommissariat Ukraine, as the Nationalists had hoped and agitated for since the beginning of the Nazi occupation.

What was the response of the Ukrainian Nationalists to these failing fortunes and downright misfortunes? Did they avail themselves of this opportunity to part ways with Nazi Germany once and for all? Unfortunately, the evidence indicates a continued but "limited" collaboration for the remainder of 1941 and throughout 1942. They had come a long way on this treacherous road, had taken many gambles they could not afford to lose, and did not want to admit defeat before the war had run its course. Although snubbed and persecuted by the Germans, they were sure that somehow a way could be found for them to derive some advantage for their own cause from the anticipated German victory.

On July 6, 1941, just after that fiasco that pleased the OUN-M to no end, Melnyk sent Hitler a declaration of utmost loyalty. The letter ended with the following words: "We request that we be allowed to march shoulder to shoulder with the legions of Europe and with our liberator, the German Wehrmacht, and therefore we ask to be permitted to create a Ukrainian military formation."[248] On July 10, just four days later, the OUN-M pledged Hitler its "most loyal obedience" in fashioning a Europe "free of Jews, Bolsheviks, and plutocrats."[249] "On 11 and 12 July 1941," stated an SP and SD report,

> all of the Ukrainian party groups in Lviv including the Melnyk group of the OUN — except for the Bandera group — have assured the liaison officer of the Wehrmacht Command of their loyalty to the German authorities and informed them of their willingness to participate in the positive reconstruction of the country. Prof. Koch also contacted the Bandera group regarding this issue. The group stated that the clarification of two points was lacking: 1) the position of the issue of Ukraine's future, 2) the matter of Bandera's release.[250]

That July, OUN-M formed its Bukovinian Battalion of 1,000 men which fought in the ranks of German auxiliary forces against the Soviet partisans in Belorussia.

On August 3, 1941, Stepan Bandera, "Führer der Organisation Ukrainischer Nationalisten — OUN" sent a letter to the Führer of the Third Reich. Bandera expressed his disappointment at the placement of Galicia, North Bukovina, and Bessarabia into the orbit of the General Government and hoped that this "division of the Ukrainian states was a temporary arrangement and that His Excellency would soon reunite these territories with the Motherland."[251]

On August 14, 1941, an OUN proclamation favored a policy of continued cooperation with Germany: "The OUN supports further close cooperation with Germany and is of the opinion that the dissolution, or rather the disavowal, of the Ukrainian government established in Lviv would only place unnecessary burdens on this cooperation."[252]

On August 18, 1941, a chief of the SP and SD report stated "In several places, units were formed by the Ukrainian militia, like 'Ukrainian Security Service,' 'Ukrainian Gestapo,' and others."[253] After the fall of Kiev to German troops in August 1941, Metropolitan Sheptytsky sent a letter to Hitler:

> His Excellency the Führer
> of the Great German Empire,
> Adolf Hitler,
> Reichschancellory, Berlin
>
> Your Excellency,
> As head of the Ukrainian Greek Catholic Church, I send your Excellency my warmest congratulations as regards the occupation of the capital of the Ukraine, the golden domed city of Dnieper — Kiev. In your person, we see the invincible leader of the incomparable and glorious German Army. The aim of destroying and rooting out Bolshevism which you, as Führer of the Great German Reich, have made the target of this campaign, wins your Excellency the gratitude of all the Christian world. The Ukrainian Greek Catholic Church knows the historic meaning of the tremendous progress of the German nations under your guidance. I will pray to God to put his blessing upon the victory which shall be the guarantee of enduring peace for Your Excellency, the German Army and the German nation.
>
> Very respectfully yours.
> Count Andrey Sheptytsky,
> Metropolitan[254]

A blessing for the victory of Nazi Germany when death and destruction surrounded this old cleric on every side — what in God's name was he thinking? Five months later Sheptytsky would write a letter to Himmler to protest the use of the Nationalists for the slaughter of the Jews. On March 27, 1942, and in November of that year he would promulgate two pastoral letters in which he would condemn, threaten with anathema, and excommunicate those who took part in these atrocities. He would also forbid the youth to enter criminal organizations — not the OUN, but the police.[255]

While he was writing his letter of protest to Himmler, he was appending his Christian name to another letter as well, one with a quite different message. The letter — written to the man responsible for all that radical evil, Adolf Hitler — was signed by Metropolitan Sheptytsky, Melnyk, and other Nationalist leaders on

February 2, 1942. In the letter they assured Hitler of their continued loyalty and their desire to do battle by the side of the "great German ally," they explained what great faith they placed in the Nationalist-German alliance, and with great pathos they reminded Hitler, "The war still goes on and the Nationalists desire to fight not only for the German order, but for the New Order in Europe."[256]

A similar letter was sent to Hitler on January 1, 1942, by T. Omelchenko, president of the OUN-M national union of Ukrainian émigrés in Germany, the UNO.[257] But Hitler was no longer listening (did he ever?), and as we have seen, for the remainder of 1941 and all of 1942, things did not go well for the Ukrainian Nationalists. As Governor General Hans Frank put it: "I see the solution to the Ukrainian question to be the same as to the Polish, mainly they must be at our disposal as manpower."[258] The almighty *Wehrmacht*, storming the walls of Moscow itself, no longer needed this old "loyal ally."

The Nationalists, meanwhile, continued their overtures to Nazi Germany: the Melnyk organization observed the second anniversary of the occupation of the Soviet Union with great fanfare; Melnyk, in the name of the Nationalists, wrote a letter to Rosenberg expressing his eternal gratitude to the "great German ally" for "liberating the vast territories of Eastern Europe"[259]; various proposals were submitted and other attempts were made on appropriate occasions with promises for collaboration with Germany in exchange for Ukrainian independence.[260]

A September 19, 1942, Security Police report to Berlin stated, "In Galicia and Volyn, the Bandera group is making vigorous attempts to get some of its members into German administrative departments as interpreters."[261]

An October 29, 1941, Security Police report discusssed a letter sent by the OUN to the Gestapo in Lwów: "The letter questions further Germany's success in this war and states that Germany will not be able to win the war without Ukraine."[262]

An April 10, 1942, Security Police report to Berlin noted:

> There is, however, a notable difference in the attitude of the Ukrainian intelligentsia circles of the older generation on the one hand, and the younger generation on the other. The older generation tends to reach a compromise according to democratic-parliamentary standards and wants to be recruited in any way possible to cooperate with the German authorities. The young activists' circles are in the OUN and have a more revolutionary-oppositional attitude....
>
> During a larger raid, ten more members of the Bandera organization were arrested. They are young adolescent boys, who have no permanent employment and who indulge in secret activity either out of habit or spirit of adventure, have no permanent residence, wander about and conspire.[263]

Such were the youth recruited by the OUN-B![264] In October 1942, when the initially favorable winds of war had turned foul for Nazi Germany, the head of the Ukrainian Central Committee (Ukrainskyi Tsentralnyi Komitet, or UTsK, established in Kraków in the spring of 1940), Volodymyr Kubiiovych, wrote to Otto Wächter, the gauleiter of Distrikt Galizien: "We have fulfilled our obligation to provide product contingents commendably. The Ukrainians can always be counted on."[265] That committee, officially recognized by the German occupation authorities in June 1940, functioned until the end of the war.

It is true that these are simply words and that the Ukrainian Nationalists should not be judged only by their words. In fact, just as many statements in propaganda leaflets (not official letters addressed to Hitler and the German High Command) distributed among the Ukrainian population by the OUN can be produced to "prove" exactly the opposite point: that the OUN took an active stand *against* Nazi Germany at this time. Notably, these types of pronouncements increased in proportion to the likelihood of a German defeat and the need to court the victorious Allies. What, then, did the OUN members *do* in these eighteen months of war between June 30, 1941, and the end of 1942? Did they "fight Hitler," or did they continue to collaborate?

We read in German SP and SD reports, dated 1942, that telephone lines were cut and that telephones were destroyed by "bandits."[266] We read that bombings, derailments of trains,[267] and thefts of dairy products, eggs, grain, and livestock by "bandits" continued into 1943.[268] And there were other such reports. But whether the OUN-B bandits should be credited for *all* these activities is questionable. As we already know, there were many other bandits in that area; even the members of the Polish Home Army were referred to by the German authorities as "bandits." By Himmler's June 1942 order, the term "partisans" was replaced by the term "bandits" in German correspondence.[269] There were, therefore, Russian bandits, Ukrainian bandits, Jewish bandits, Polish bandits, Czech bandits, and perhaps other bandits as well — and none of them belonged to the OUN. All these "bandits" were true partisans whose mission was to weaken the German might. By their own admission in a leaflet entitled "Our Position Regarding the Partisan Warfare," the OUN-B bandits were not partisans. That leaflet stated unequivocally, "The Ukrainians [i.e., the Nationalists, "we"] did not and do not participate in partisan warfare."[270]

This is not to say that the OUN-B did not attack German outposts and convoys. The OUN-B bandits were very active in Wołyń beginning in the fall of 1942. They had an "army" (UPA) to arm and to provide for, after all.

Report No. 32 From
the Occupied Eastern Regions

> The activity of the bandits has not decreased in Ukraine. Within the past eight days, approximately 150 surprise attacks by the bandits have been recorded in the sector of the commander of Rivne and Zhytomyr alone. Their sole aim is to provide the gangs with supplies. There have been numerous bombings and derailments of trains....
>
> During the gun-battles fought against the gangs, 594 bandits were killed, two earth bunkers and thirteen bandit camps were demolished or rather destroyed. German losses were three members of the police and ten Ukrainian policemen.[271]

The Ukrainian police consisted largely of OUN-B members. Was the Ukrainian police, then, killing its own bandits? In short, even if the OUN was angered by the German "betrayal" (after all, Germany never officially promised anything) and was inclined to take an active anti-German stance, the Nationalists were in an extremely precarious position. What could they do? Thus, with a few exceptions (notably the assassinations described below, which ended in disasters for the Nationalists), no significant overt activities were carried out against the Germans by either faction of the OUN in 1941 and 1942.

In October 1942, the OUN-B faction, still smarting from its wounds, tried to make a preemptive strike against further ill treatment by its former ally. When a three-man investigative team from Berlin arrived in Lwów to size up OUN activities, two of them were immediately assassinated. In reprisal, the Germans executed one hundred Ukrainians suspected of having contacts with the OUN-B. A similar incident occurred at the time of the raid on the OUN-B headquarters in Lwów. In reprisal for the death of two Gestapo agents, the Germans shot thirty-two members of the OUN.[272] In early November 1942, two members of the SP and SD Einsatzkommando units of Kiev, along with a Ukrainian "traitor," were killed by two OUN-B militants. Again, repressions followed.[273] For obvious reasons, this course of action was soon abandoned by the OUN-B. Armstrong notes:

> The active resistance that the Bandera organization was unwilling to risk, in spite of the large number of its youthful adherents and the proximity of its Galician base, the Mel'nyk faction obviously could not attempt, even when its break with the Germans might have made resistance desirable. Consequently, the only Ukrainian nationalist organization which could remotely be described as a partisan group during the first year of the Reichskommissariat's administration of Volhynia was the Polis'ka Sich (Polessian stronghold) under Borovets'.[274]

Armstrong adds that it is "extremely difficult to ascertain just what activities the UPA carried out during 1942" other than fighting sporadically with small groups of Soviet partisans and stashing arms. "It is reasonably certain," he continues, "that some of its members had armed encounters — attacking state farms and freeing prisoners—with German security forces in the Sarny region while helping peasants resist oppressive measures." He then states, "But Borovets' asserted that he remained friendly to the Wehrmacht and 'had spilled no German blood.'"[275]

All of this is true. It is also true, as we have seen, that Borovets' "partisan" group had actually *helped* the Wehrmacht to "pacify" Wołyń in 1941! It was only toward the very *end* of 1941 that Borovets had become a thorn in Erich Koch's side. And yet, although he had already spilled much Jewish and Russian blood and would shortly spill much Polish blood as well, by his own admission his hands and conscience were free of German blood both at this time and later, when he would again serve the Third Reich faithfully. Borovets reestablished his contacts with the Wehrmacht in September and again in November 1942.[276]

In answer to the question of whether the Ukrainian Nationalists continued to collaborate in 1941 and 1942, Torzecki states: "In spite of the reversals which befell OUN-B in June, that faction did not renounce collaboration ... [and] the OUN-M served the Germans more loyally than the OUN-B."[277] But what exactly was the nature of that collaboration? Did they continue to serve Germany militarily? Yes, at least until the end of October 1942 in the Nachtigall and Roland. There was no order from the OUN to cease and desist; no command was issued for mass desertion, as there was later for the predominantly OUN-B Ukrainian militia in Wołyń and Podole (the latter region was in Eastern Galicia, east of Lwów) when the OUN needed to fill the ranks of its new "army," the UPA.

How else did the Ukrainian Nationalists continue to assist the Reich at this time? Szcześniak and Szota answer,

> Organized and equipped by the Nazis, the Ukrainian fascist police, guard units, and other formations zealously performed their duty: took part in the battle against the Soviets and Polish partisan units, in [German] extermination actions against the Polish people in the entire territory, in Warsaw among other places, often performing guard duty in concentration camps, extermination camps, and interrogation prisons.[278]

On direct orders from Himmler himself (June 25, 1941), the Germans created the Wachmannschaften des SS- und Polizeiführers im Distrikt Lublin. Members of this unit as well as other Wachmannschaften units were recruited from local police and Soviet POWs and schooled in Trawniki in the Lublin district under the control of Odilo Globocnik. Although Russian, Lithuanian, Latvian, and the Volksdeutsche from Poland were among the camp recruits, Trawniki (established between August and November 1941) was predominantly a training center for Ukrainian guard units. All training (lasting three to four months) was done in the German language under the leadership of Volksdeutsche and the noncommissioned Ukrainian officers from Galicia. After the completion of their training course, the graduates were used as concentration camp guards, as ghetto guards, and as auxiliaries of the SS. In all, about two thousand Ukrainians trained for the SS-ukrainische Wachmannschaften. The recruits who deserted the unit after training were interned in concentration camps. Other training camps, similar to Trawniki, existed in the district of Lublin—for example, Wólka Profecka, where the Schutzmannschaft-Ersatz-Bataillon 203 was stationed. These were also run, in part, by Ukrainians from Galicia.[279]

One of the Trawniki-trained battalions participated in the liquidation of the Warsaw ghetto in the spring of 1943.[280] The Trawniki graduates also constituted the major guard forces at Bełżec, Sobibór, Treblinka, and Trawniki, but other concentration camps employed Ukrainians as well.[281]

Kurt Gerstein recalled that in Bełżec, where the guards were mainly Ukrainian, "two hundred Ukrainians assigned to this work [emptying trains] flung open the doors and drove the Jews out of the cars with leather whips."[282] Another Bełżec survivor maintained, "The Ukrainians employed in the camp treated people even more sadistically than the Germans."[283]

In Sobibór, states Moshe Shklarek, "[SS Staff Sergeant Paul] Grot was the leader of the

Ukrainian 'columns,' between the two rows of whom the camp prisoners were frequently ordered to pass, to be scourged with leaden whips, rubber clubs and all kinds of flagellation instruments with which the servants of the Nazis, who stood on both sides of the row, were equipped."[284]

According to Franciszek Zabecki, an eyewitness at Treblinka railway station, a Ukrainian "promised a Jewess that he would let her and her child go if she put a large bribe in his hand. The Jewess gave the Ukrainian the money. The Jewess walked away from the train, holding her child by the hand; as soon as she walked down the railway embankment the Ukrainian shot her.... Another Ukrainian killed the child with one blow of a rifle butt on its head."[285]

At Chełmno, "Ukrainians and Germans, working in pairs, using pliers, would pull out the gold teeth and take off the rings of the murdered Jews."[286] Meir Peker recalled a murder at a transit camp in Białystok: "The Germans in charge of the Ukrainian guards broke the boy's hands, first one, then the other, joint by joint. This done, two Ukrainians stretched him out on a chair, still half-conscious, and broke his back: they then laid out his lifeless body, like an empty sack, and emptied their rifles into it. I saw these things with my own eyes, and curse the day on which I was forced to witness such bestial atrocities.... It is hard to forget." [287] All of these accounts are from 1942.

Ukrainians were also used for guard duty in the forced-labor camps set up by the Germans throughout Poland. Two of these, Starachowice and Skarżysko-Kamienna, were located in the very heart of Poland's Central Industrial Area (Centralny Okręg Przemysłowy, or COP). With the outbreak of the war, all the residents of these towns expected the worst and headed for the forests. Although the Nazi low-flying aircraft strafed the forests time and again with machine-gun fire, the bombers flew over the towns as if they didn't exist. Two weeks later, the iron-ore smelting factories in both towns began churning out ammunition for the Wehrmacht.

Regina Gelb (née Laks),[288] a former resident of Starachowice, recalled that sometime in late 1939 or early 1940 all the Jews were moved to a poorer section of town. During the liquidation of the ghetto in October 1942, they were assembled in the town square by Ukrainian and Latvian police. Those with factory work-cards and the able-bodied were culled out and marched off to the two slave-labor camps (Strzelnica and Majówka) set up near the factory complex. (Later the two camps were combined into one.) The rest of the Jews, and this was the majority, were put on a train and shipped off to Treblinka. The following (1941) report gives a frightening summary of the conditions of such camps:

> In the forced labor camps, most of which were located in the proximity of the present Soviet border, the conditions are terrible. Barracks are not heated, food is bad, work is hard, beating and harassment go on ceaselessly. Inadequate clothing of the inmates and their lack of previous experience with menial work are the sources of particular hardship. Mortality is enormous: it reaches 10%, thereof 6% from illnesses and 4% by firing squads. Once particular military projects are terminated, the Jews who had been working on them are shot.[289]

The factory where this twelve-year-old worked operated round the clock. The factory overseers were Nazis; the factory guards were Germans and Ukrainians. The camps, on the other hand, were manned solely by Ukrainians, who were also responsible for marching the Jews to and from the factories. These Ukrainians belonged to the Nazi auxiliary police unit called Lagerschutz (camp guard), were volunteers, and wore German uniforms.[290] The Ukrainian commandant was called "Piorun" because he was like lightning: one never knew where he would strike.[291] "They had complete authority," said Regina Gelb, "and if they didn't like the way you looked, they would shoot you or beat you according to their pleasure."

One of their tasks was to round up everyone who looked ill during the typhus epidemics that raged through the camps from time to time. "They even dragged the sick out of their beds," she said. "Then, they marched them off to the woods and shot them." A report (1940) on the camps located in the district of Lublin stated that the temperature of the workers was "checked every day: and those with a temperature exceeding 38 degrees centigrade [were] shot, as a precaution against contamination."[292] The factory labor force, however, remained the same: those shot were replaced by healthier Jews from one or another concentration camp.

Both Jews and Poles worked in the factories. The Poles, who had manned the factories before the war, now constituted the skilled labor force, worked in three eight-hour shifts, were paid, and lived in their own houses. The Jews were used for menial labor, worked in two twelve-hour shifts, were not paid, and lived in the slave-labor camps. This continued until August 1944, and the Ukrainian guards were there from the beginning to the very end.

The story was the same in Skarżysko-Kamienna. Róża Bauminger recalled that in addition to their other tasks, on the morning of November 16, 1943, the Ukrainians rounded up all workers who had collapsed on the job out of sheer exhaustion the night before — and shot them.[293] Over 25,000 Jews passed through this one forced-labor camp. More than 18,000, or 72 percent, died there.[294]

At the end of July 1944, all the Jews of Starachowice were rounded up once more and relocated to a makeshift transit camp near the factory railroad station. Regina Gelb described the last days of her work-camp experience:

> Toward the end of July 1944, Jews from the Starachowice slave-labor camp in the Majówka section of town were transferred to another camp located very near the Starachowice munitions factory. The new compound, adjacent to the factory's railroad terminal, was enclosed by a wooden fence and consisted of barracks built around a courtyard. The camp was guarded by uniformed Ukrainians who also manned the gate and the guard towers. These Ukrainians, who were in charge of us since October 1942 when the Starachowice camp was established, carried out their brutal treatment of the inmates here just as before, the only difference being that now they no longer marched us to and from the munitions factory because work for Jews had ceased there.
>
> Empty cattle-train cars stood at the factory railroad terminal, waiting. Rumors spread quickly that all of us were to be shipped out from this provisional location "somewhere," but nobody knew where or when. When the train, still empty, departed, we wondered what was to become of us. That same night, after curfew, we heard gunfire and blood-curdling screams. Through the small barrack window we saw the tower searchlights crisscrossing the camp grounds. We were terrified because we thought that the Nazis, with Ukrainian help, had decided to put an end to us right then and there.
>
> All through the night, as the heart-rending screams from the direction of the fence continued, we also heard a woman's agonizing cries very near our barrack. It was the voice of a girl from our home town, Starachowice. Her legs were shattered by gunfire when she ran across the courtyard and she was bleeding profusely. She was begging the camp guards to kill her in order to end her agony. But they would not do it. They let her suffer just to teach the rest of us a lesson. She died at dawn.
>
> At that time, my two sisters and I were in one barrack, our father in another, the men's section. We were terrified at the thought that he may have been among the victims because we knew from experience how cruel the Ukrainian guards could be. Throughout that night the screams and moaning continued unabated, as did the Ukrainians' gunfire, cursing and yelling.
>
> When morning came we found out that some young Jewish men had tried to escape from the camp to the nearby forest. In preparation for their breakout, they had pried loose some planks in the fence, just enough so that they could be easily removed when the time came. That night, anticipating the worst, they tore off the loose boards and dove for the opening. Unfortunately, because the opening was very narrow, only a few inmates escaped before the guards realized what was happening. They started shooting, the alarm sounded and reinforcements arrived. The gunfire seemed endless and people died in heaps right in front of the opening in the fence through which they were trying to squeeze through. Like the girl from our home town, those not yet dead were left in mortal agony as punishment ... and warning to the rest of us.

> [In a subsequent interview, Regina's sister, Krystyna, commented that some of the Jewish escapees were later rounded up by the NSZ and delivered to the Gestapo, who brought them back to camp.]
>
> On the day following the massacre, another train with empty cattle cars arrived at the factory terminal. We were marched in formation toward it and, together with other women, shoved inside by the uniformed Ukrainians. My sisters and I saw our father in a group of men who were also being pushed onto the train. He had survived the macabre night. Then, the doors were bolted and our voyage into the unknown began.
>
> German field gendarmerie accompanied our transport. We traveled for several days in those overcrowded cattle cars without any sanitary facilities. In the course of our journey many Jewish people died of thirst, hunger and lack of air. Finally, we arrived at our destination, Auschwitz. When we were being unloaded on the platform near the crematorium, we saw our father once more and for the last time. He saw us too. Father died in the Auschwitz gas chambers shortly thereafter, while my sisters and I lived to become part of the January 1945 death march from Auschwitz.

Regina Gelb and her sisters (Krystyna Lerman and Anna Wilson) were in the women's contingent sent to Ravensbrück. Miraculously, they survived all the vicissitudes of that cruel war.

Ukrainians also guarded the notorious Pawiak prison in Warsaw,[295] as well as the camp and killing grounds of Kampinos woods and Łowicz, both just outside of Warsaw. Yitzhak Zuckerman, a resistance activist and prisoner at the Kampinos woods camp noted the cruelty of the Ukrainian guards there. After ninety-one Jews were murdered in Łowicz, Ringelblum wrote that the "basic cause" was "the terrible treatment of those in the camp by most of the Ukrainian camp guards," and the "starvation" rations. "The seventeen corpses brought to Warsaw from work camp on May 7th made a dreadful impression: earless, arms and other limbs twisted, the tortures inflicted by the Ukrainian camp guards clearly discernible."[296] Shmuel Spector noted of the Wołyń-Podole area: "The size of a detachment assigned guard duty varied from several hundred to over a thousand policemen, according to the scale of the operation. Most of these units consisted of Ukrainians. This is borne out by the survivors' testimonies and the fact that the ratio between Germans and Ukrainians was 1:10."[297]

Furthermore, in 1942–43, an effort was made to recruit young Ukrainians to the Heimatdienst in the districts of Lublin and Galicia. This process was facilitated by the local Ukrainian administrators (*wójty* and *sołtysy*), who encouraged their youth to join the SS-ukrainische Wachmannschaften in accord with the Ukrainian Committee's statement that "all Ukrainians should serve in the armed forces." At this time (1941–42), the Ukrainian population of the district of Lublin was under the strong influence of the pro–German Galician Ukrainian Nationalists. As members of the SS-ukrainische Wachmannschaften (and later as soldiers of the SS-Galizien under Friedrich Beyersdorff), they participated in the German-organized massive resettlement campaigns of the Polish population from this area in November 1941 (involving eight villages) and in November 1942– March 1943 and June-August 1943 (both involving over 100,000 people), as well as in the brutal pacification action of October 1942.[298] Later, many of them joined the UPA.

Above all, throughout all this time and until the Jews "ceased to exist," the Ukrainian Nationalists participated in the "Final Solution" in their capacity as auxiliary police and as members of the units attached to the infamous Einsatzgruppen and Einsatzkommando, which were, at this time, liquidating the Jewish ghettos in the east.[299] Their orders to "combat the Jews" came from the OUN Directorate. The Second General Congress of the OUN-B adopted the following resolution at its April 1941 meeting in Kraków:

> 17. The Jews in the U.S.S.R. constitute the most faithful support of the ruling Bolshevik regime and the vanguard of Muscovite imperialism in the Ukraine. The Muscovite-Bolshevik government exploits the anti–Jewish sentiments of the Ukrainian masses to divert their attention from the true cause of

> their misfortune and to channel them in time of frustration into pogroms on Jews. The OUN combats the Jews as the prop of the Muscovite-Bolshevik regime and simultaneously it renders the masses conscious of the fact that the principal foe is Moscow.[300]

The Jews were hated by the Ukrainian Nationalists not only because they were regarded as "the most faithful support of the ruling Bolshevik regime and the vanguard of Muscovite imperialism in the Ukraine" but also because they were Jews and "foreigners." The following slogan appears in a letter signed by the Bandera group and recorded in the July 16, 1941, Einsatzgruppen report: "Long live a greater independent Ukraine without Jews, Poles, and Germans; Poles behind the River San, Germans to Berlin, and Jews to the gallows."[301] One German eyewitness in Złoczów, Tarnopol province, reported:

> [July 3, 1941] I saw that in the ditches, about 5 meters deep and 20 meters wide, stood and lay about 60–80 men, women, and children, predominantly Jewish. I heard the wailing and screaming of the children and women, hand grenades were bursting in their midst. Beyond the ditches waited many hundreds of people for execution. In front of the ditches stood 10-20 men in civilian clothes, who were throwing grenades into the ditch.... I found out from the SS soldiers, that they were Bandera's people.[302]

A Jewish account reads:

> Kovel was occupied by the Germans. On June 29, 1941, hell broke loose....
>
> Right after the first days of the occupation the Germans and their Ukrainian collaborators began their sadistic actions against the Jewish population. Every day, every night, there were different orders, arrest raids, groups of Jewish people killed. Abraham Silberman was one of the first victims. The Ukrainian police arrested him together with more well-known Jewish citizens and massacred them. They were forced to dig their own graves. I saw this, I was a witness. Malka, the unfortunate widow, the three little orphans, together with the whole family and I, mourned Abraham Silberman's death.[303]

An account from the Rokitno area, Wołyń, 1942, states, "The murdering of Jews in the nearby forests was carried out, as always, by the eager and vengeful Ukrainian police."[304]

The Ukrainian auxiliary police, formed previously by the OUN-B and consisting predominantly of its members, participated in almost every aspect of the "Final Solution," including executions.[305] The Nazis reorganized this police, placed it under German leadership, subordinated it under Sipo, and through it under the SD. Reuben Ainsztein notes:

> Stetsko and Bandera proclaimed the creation of a "free Ukraine" and organized a 31,000 strong militia.... The militia played a most important part in making it possible for the Einsatzkommando to carry out their task of genocide and terror until the middle of August [1941].... The militia was them disbanded and 3,000 cut-throats were allowed to enroll in the Ukrainian Auxiliary police which was to play such an abominable role in the annihilation of the Jews of Eastern Europe.[306]

In Wołyń and Podole, the greater part of the 12,000 Ukrainian militia members were OUN-B people.[307] In Eastern Galicia, Germans took control of 6,000 Ukrainian policemen and placed them under either German officers or the followers of Melnyk and Dmytro Paliiv.[308]

> UKRAINISCHE HILFSPOLIZEI
> (Ukrainian Auxiliary Police)
>
> Ukrainian militia units were set up in the earliest days of the German invasion of the Soviet Union and the occupation of Ukrainian-inhabited areas. The initiative for this step came from the Ukrainian nationalists who accompanied the German forces on their entry into the Ukraine. These units were recruited either as mobile groups (*pokhidni grupy*) or at the initiative of local nationalist activists — in all cases with the full encouragement of the military governors....
>
> On July 27, 1941, on Heinrich HIMMLER's orders, the formation of the mobile Ukrainian Auxiliary Police was launched, under the jurisdiction of the SS and German police commanders in the various Kommissariate

(subdivisions of the German civil administration). The battalions were housed in police barracks in key places, and were deployed in major police operations such as the drive against the partisans. After the civil administration had been installed in August 1941 in the Galicia district and, throughout September, in the other parts of the German occupied Ukraine, the militia units were renamed the Ukrainische Hilfspolizei Schutzmannschaft (Ukrainian Auxiliary Police Constabulary), and the individual policeman was generally referred to as a *Schutzmann* (constable). The units were subordinate to the German police and gendarmerie.

The Ukrainian Auxiliary Police were equipped with captured Soviet light weapons and wore black uniforms. On some occasions a collective fine was imposed upon the Jews in order to defray the costs of providing the police with uniforms and boots. The senior commanders of these units were Germans. In the first few days of the occupation, Ukrainian police, as an organized group or on an individual basis, participated in pogroms against the Jews, in Lvov, in the cities of Eastern Galicia, and in Volhynia. Later, when the Ukrainian police escorted groups of Jews to places of work or were on guard duty in the ghettos, they extorted money from the Jews, harassed them, and frequently shot Jews merely for the sake of killing. When the ghettos were being liquidated, units of the Ukrainian Auxiliary Police took part in *Aktionen*: blockading the ghettos, searching for Jews who had gone into hiding, and hunting those who had escaped. They escorted Jews to their execution in pits and served as the guards surrounding the murder sites, barring access to them. They were known for their brutality and killed many thousands of Jews who could not keep up on the way to the execution sites, or who tried to escape.[309]

Samuel Lipa Tennenbaum provides a shorter and better description of the Ukrainian auxiliary police: "This was an assortment of thugs who soon acquired a reputation for corruption and cruelty matched only, I was told, by units composed of Lithuanians."[310]

Hilberg notes: "Almost all the Jews left behind by the retreating Red Army in Ukrainian territory were killed.... Almost from the beginning, Ukrainian militia were used in these killings as helpers."[311] A case in point is Babi Yar, where over 33,000 Jews were slaughtered by the Einsatzkommando units with the assistance of Ukrainians.[312] Sometimes the Ukrainians were used for the ghastliest of tasks:

> In addition to the Baltic Selbstschutz used by Einsatzgruppe A, a Ukrainian militia (*Militz*) was operating in the areas of Einsatzgruppen C and D. The Ukrainian auxiliaries appeared on the scene in August, 1941, and Einsatzgruppe C found itself compelled to make use of them because it was repeatedly diverted from its main task to fight the "partisan nuisance".... The Ukrainians were used principally for dirty work—thus Einsatzkommando 4a went so far as to confine itself to the shooting of adults while commanding its Ukrainian helpers to shoot children.[313]

The use of the Ukrainian police for the "Final Solution" was common knowledge in those days, as illustrated by Metropolitan Sheptytsky's letter of protest to Himmler in 1942 in which he deplored the use of the Ukrainian auxiliary police for such sinister purposes.[314] Hilberg states:

> The great bulk of the helpers, eventually hundreds of thousands, were placed under the command of the Order Police. Native personnel augmenting the Order Police were designated the *Schutzmannschaft.* Mirroring the organization of the Order Police in Germany, the Schutzmannschaft could be found in cities, rural districts, and battalions. The stationary component of the Schutzmannschaft included Ukrainians, Belorussians, Russians, Estonians, Lithuanians, and Latvians.... [No Poles are mentioned.]
>
> In Ukrainian areas quickly traversed in 1941 there was a second wave of shootings in 1942. This sequel was most intensive in Volhynia, where hundreds of thousands of Jews were living in small ghettos. For the renewed killings, all available SS and Police forces were deployed along with the stationary Ukrainian police, now organized as a Schutzmannschaft.[315]

Oswald Rufeisen, who survived the war with the help of some Polish nuns in Mir in the province of Nowogródek and who later emigrated to Israel, relates: "I spent the war in Eastern Poland where I joined the German Police pretending to be a Pole. I did not see Poles there murdering Jews, although I did see Poles being murdered. Moreover, I saw Belorussians, Latvians, Estonians, and Ukrainians who murdered [Jews], but I did not see Polish units doing that."[316]

In Galicia, the district SS and Police leader wanted a Ukrainian police consisting of 63 officers and 2,900 men. To achieve this end, he established a police school for the Ukrainians in Lwów and within a year used the graduates to round up Jews for Bełżec and to shoot some as well.[317] The director of the school was Ivan Kozak.[318]

In Białystok, an Einsatzkommando report dated August 1941 stated that Ukrainian militia commandos would "have persons shot if they do not please them, as was done before."[319] Maria Halina Horn, an escapee from the deportation to Treblinka, recalls:

> I lay there underneath the train and listened to the loud shouts and cries of the Jews. The Ukrainians were beating them. I could hear the whistling of their whips, the curses flying from the Ukrainians' mouths. I could hear my own mother crying.... There were only Ukrainians left on the platform now. I could hear their footsteps, their voices.... Ukrainians were walking along the length of the train. I could see their feet, their high army-issue boots and pants.... Ukrainians kept passing by beside me. They climbed into each car. "Where has he hidden?" they asked in Ukrainian.... I crawled out from under the train. I looked around me. I saw a sign: "Białystok."[320]

In Belorussia the Schutzmannschaften battalions were staffed by many Ukrainians recruited from POW camps. One German commander, Sturmbannführer Hans-Hermann Remmels, told his men, "Thank God, we are no longer going to have to do the shooting, the Ukrainians are doing it."[321]

The first Schutzmannschaft battalion, Schuma 201, was formed in October 1941 from Ukrainian prisoners freed by the Germans. Schuma-Bataillon 202 was formed in 1942. At the end of that year and the beginning of 1943, battalions 203, and then 204–206 were launched. (Battalions 207–212 were formed in 1944.)[322] The strength of the Ukrainian Schutzmannschaften in Eastern Ukraine stood at 35,000 men in 70 battalions. In addition, in 1942-43 there were over 15,000 Ukrainian Schutzpolizei and some 55,000 Ukrainian gendarmes in the Reichskommissariat Ukraine.[323]

B. F. Sabrin's *Alliance for Murder: The Nazi-Ukrainian Nationalist Partnership in Genocide* contains numerous eyewitness accounts of the role of the Ukrainian Nationalists in the killing of the Jews.

> The same day in the afternoon, groups of Ukrainian Nationalists at once formed their police, the so-called "Hundred Group." The bloody Pogrom started. They attacked the quarter where Jews lived. With iron bars and sticks the Jews were cruelly bludgeoned to death — all those who didn't manage to escape.... The violence of the Hitlerites and the OUN ... almost never stopped for a day.[324]

> Early in September, 1942, there was a large "Action" against Jews in the town. Many tried to run, and the German Gendarmes, with the help of the Ukrainian Police, were shooting.[325]

And there are documents from the Ukrainian SSR State Soviet Archives:

> Ukrainian Police of Lviv: Report of Jewish action 8/20/42. A total of 525 Jews were delivered ... 14 Jews killed.[326]

> Ukrainian Police in Lvov: Report Jewish Action, 8.20.42.... Those trying to run away, and others resisting, were shot.... A total of bribes — money: 1785 Zl. [zloty], plus one gold watch and gold ring was taken.[327]

> Ukrainian Police in the City of Lviv: On the Jewish action carried out on August 14, 1942. I report herewith that ... 2,128 Jews were delivered ... 12 Jews were shot.... Money and valuables given to the policemen as bribes.... Jews were evicted from 37 apartments.[328]

> Ukrainian Police in Lviv City: report on the Jewish Action Carried out on August 15,

1942. I report herewith ... 1,660 Jews were delivered ... 8 Jews killed.[329]

To
Command Ukrainian Police
city Lvov:
Report Jewish Action, 8-21-42

Declare that this day ... during Jewish "action" five bullets were fired. One Jew was killed and 59 were delivered. Some tried to bribe the policemen. The Jew Kranc Leon, residing at ... gave 200 Zl. and a hand watch to the policeman. A Jewess (killed by policeman Chorka W.) gave 234 Zl, a hand watch and a ring. Jew Firger Oziasz, residing at ... gave one stone watch.

Enclosed: 434 Zl, 2 hand-watches, 1 stone watch and one gold ring.

[signature]
Chief 2nd Commissariat
Ukrainian Police
Lutyk Taras[330]

Staff Ukrainian Defense Police
Regional Service — Staff Order Nr 50
Personal thanks:

Expressing gratitude to policeman Kirichuk, Y.W., for stopping one Jew, 27.8.42, in his non-service hour. For this devoted act, he is rewarded with I. kg. fat, and I. kg. flour.

Sign. Kabajda
Commander Staff UOP
Soten Kabajda[331]

These anti-Jewish actions were carried out by the members of the Ukrainian police who eventually joined the UPA. Like the Poles, Lithuanians, and Belorussians, however, the Ukrainians also counted heroic rescuers among their population.[332]

Finally, in 1942, frustrated by their inability to march "shoulder to shoulder" with the "Great German Army" and realizing that the contract of their only military formations, Nachtigall and Roland, was about to expire, the OUN-B — under the leadership of Mykola Lebed ("Maksym Ruban") — made the momentous decision to form, out of the remnants of those formations, the Ukrainian police, and the largely illiterate Ukrainian peasantry of the Wołyñian countryside, its own military arm, the UPA[333] — and to direct it against completely defenseless civilians that very fall. Although it "fought" against these civilians day and (mostly) night for the remainder of the war, this "army" took no prisoners. Thus ended anno Domini 1942, the year of "limited" collaboration between Ukrainian Nationalists and the Nazis.

1943

The anticipated victory over the Soviet Union did not turn out to be as easy as the Germans had expected. After five months of bitter struggle, Stalingrad was still free. At the end of January 1943 the entire German 6th Army was in the hands of the Soviets and the remainder of the German forces began a dishonorable retreat. The tide had turned. It was to be a long fight after all, and in that fight the military and paramilitary assistance of the Ukrainian Nationalists was needed once more. When Melnyk wrote another letter to Hitler, on January 18, 1943,[334] if the Führer himself was not listening, some of his cronies were beginning to. By the end of 1943, in official talks the Ukrainian Nationalists were reaffirming their loyalty to the Third Reich and the Germans were expressing their gratitude to the Nationalists for assistance in the war effort against the Soviet Union.[335]

Initially, Germany's military might in the east consisted of two "racially pure" formations: the Wehrmacht and the Waffen-SS. In April 1941, when Obergruppenführer Gottlob Berger successfully recruited "64 racially suitable and 615 racially unsuitable" Ukrainian volunteers from Poland for a nucleus of what was to become a Ukrainian SS formation, Himmler turned down his request for racial reasons.[336] However, in spite of Hitler's fanatical aversion to the use of foreign soldiers in his armed forces, after Stalingrad the Wehrmacht and the Waffen-SS vied with each other for precisely such military assistance from a variety of Untermenschen groups.[337] As Myroslav Yurkevich put it, "After the disaster at Stalingrad on January 31, 1943, the need for cannon fodder overrode ideological considerations."[338] By the end of the war, some 1 million Osttruppen (excluding military construction workers) were serving in the Wehrmacht.[339]

The Ukrainian cannon fodder for the Waffen-SS was provided by Volodymyr Kubiiovych (called "a principal collaborator during the German occupation of Galicia" by Sol Littman). Kubiiovych once said, "We in the UCK [UTsK] appealed to our people to persevere in their stations, not to provoke the Germans, and to remember that anti–German action helps the Bolsheviks."[340] (According to Kubiiovych himself, the UTsK was on the payroll of the Abwehr. It was essentially a German organized [OUN-M] enterprise, which functioned in the GG and, after 1942, in Eastern Galicia until the Soviet counteroffensive.[341]) On March 8, 1943, Kubiiovych contacted Hans Frank, the *Generalgouverneur*, with the proposition of establishing a voluntary Ukrainian military unit that would fight alongside the Third Reich. Frank promptly contacted his subordinate, Otto Wächter, the *Gauleiter* of Galicia, who contacted Himmler, head of the SS, who gave his consent on March 28, 1943. "I wrote to Governor Wächter on 8 April," stated Kubiiovych, "and informed him that our community was ready and well disposed to the formation of the Galician division."[342]

Of the Galician Ukrainian community's readiness and disposition, Wächter had no doubts. In a letter to Himmler asking that the name of the division include the term "Ukrainian," since the SS-Galizien was "open only to the Ukrainians of Galicia and not the Poles," Wächter reminded the *Reichsführer*, "We have 'Ukrainian committees,' 'Ukrainian delegations,' a 'Ukrainian police,' 'Ukrainian newspapers,' etc., *all officially established and recognized by the German authorities.*"[343] This in 1943!

The Ukrainian press published the *Krakivski Visti*, a German newspaper in the Ukrainian language, *Nashi Dni*, a popular literary journal, and books. There were also various social UDKs and Ukrainian cultural organizations under the UOT (Ukrainske Osvitne Tovaristva — Ukrainian Educational Societies). In Lwów there were medical, pharmaceutical, veterinary, forestry, and agrarian upper-division courses, technically open to both Poles and Ukrainians but in which the latter always had a clear advantage. There were even Ukrainian sports clubs.[344] The Ukrainian community in Eastern Galicia was indeed "ready and well disposed to the formation of the Galician division."

Wächter formally announced the formation of the division on April 28; Kubiiovych wrote his passionate "Appeal to Ukrainian Citizens and Youth by the Central Committee President on the Formation of the Ukrainian Division" on May 6; and the recruitment began that month. Of the 80,000 volunteers, 50,000 were selected, 42,000 appeared before the commission, 27,000 qualified, 25,000 were called up, 19,000 were accepted, and 13,200 reported for duty. Of these, 11,600 received military training.[345] The remainder of the 80,000 volunteers were "absorbed into the German police to form five new Police regiments."[346] In November 1943, in a swearing-in ceremony in France, the Ukrainian soldiers of this Waffen-SS division pledged their personal loyalty to Hitler — not to Ukraine or the OUN. The text of the oath stated, "I swear by God this sacred oath that in the struggle against Bolshevism I will give unconditional obedience to the Supreme Commander of the German *Wehrmacht,* Adolf Hitler, and that, as a courageous soldier, I will always be prepared to give my life for this oath."[347]

In his congratulatory speech, Wächter made a point to clarify the meaning of that solemn declaration: "Since today you pledged your oath to Adolf Hitler, you are now, Galician volunteers, triply obligated to him. In the first place, as the *Führer* and the Leader of the German Armed Forces. In the second place, you are obligated to Adolf Hitler as the *Führer* of the Reich.... In the third place, you are obligated to Adolf Hitler as the *Führer* of the whole of Europe."[348]

In spite of Wächter's pleas, by Himmler's orders the official name of the division was not to contain the word "Ukraine" or "Ukrainian." The soldiers were to be referred to as "Galicians," not as "Ukrainians."[349] Division members were given German uniforms, and their insignia was the Galician lion, not the Ukrainian trident.[350] The first name of the division was SS-Freiwilligen-Division "Galizien" (SS Volunteer Division "Galician"). It was later (June 27, 1944) changed to 14. Freiwilligen-Grenadier-Division der SS (galizische Nr 1) (14th Volunteer Grenadier Division of the SS, 1st Galician) and also 14. Waffen-Grenadier-Division der SS (galizische Nr 1).[351] As George Stein noted, these euphemistic designations "fooled no one, least of all the personnel of the division, who were mostly Ukrainian nationalists."[352]

The first commander of the SS-Galizien was SS Brigadeführer Walter Schimana. On November 20, 1943, he was succeeded by SS Oberführer Fritz Freitag, a former SS officer, an East Prussian once described by a fellow German as "self-seeking, unpleasant and bureaucratic."[353] Its chief of staff (appointed in January 1944) was Major Wolf-Dietrich Heike, a former Wehrmacht officer. Freitag committed suicide at war's end; Heike survived and wrote a sanitized memoir for which, nevertheless, future historians will certainly be grateful because, unlike the records for most other German divisions in the east, the file on the SS-Galizien has been lifted from the original German archives and from the microfilm copy in the U.S. National Archives as well.[354] The chief organizer of the SS-Galizien and highest-ranking Ukrainian officer (the command staff was German) was Dmytro Paliiv.[355]

In his book originally entitled *Sie wolten die Freiheit: Die Geschichte der Ukrainischen Division, 1943–1945* (They Wanted Freedom: The History of the Ukrainian Division, 1943–1945), Heike described the recruits to the SS-Galizien: "Alongside the peasants and workers stood older and distinguished veterans of World War I, soldiers and officers from the Austro-Hungarian army and the Ukrainian Galician Army (UHA), as well as scores of young men of the Western Ukrainian intelligentsia."[356] Roman Krokhmaliuk states that 90 percent of the recruits were between the ages of eighteen and thirty.[357] Among the older recruits were the Nachtigall and Roland officers who had been released from prison to serve in the division.[358]

How are we to explain the fact that so many young Ukrainian men volunteered to serve in a Nazi SS division, that is, to collaborate so willingly with Nazi Germany? That this was genuine collaboration is beyond doubt. Kubiiovych knew this very well; in his "Appeal to Ukrainian Citizens and Youth" he wrote:

> The *long-awaited* moment has arrived when the Ukrainian people will *again* have the opportunity to come out with gun in hand to do battle against its most grievous foe—Bolshevism. The Führer of the Greater German Reich has agreed to the formation of a separate Ukrainian volunteer military unit under the name of SS Infantry Division "Galicia." ... You must stand *shoulder to shoulder with the invincible German army* and destroy, once and for all, the Bolshevik beast.... Side by side with the heroic army of Greater Germany and the volunteers of other European peoples, we too come forth to battle our greatest national foe.... The cause is sacred and just and therefore it demands great efforts and sacrifices.[359]

Wächter also had no doubt that this was collaboration. In his "Appeal to the Able-Bodied Youth of Galicia," he stated:

> *Time and again*, the Ukrainians of Galicia voiced the wish to participate in *Germany's armed struggle*, with weapons in hand. The Führer has acknowledged *the will of the Galician people*, and has allowed for the formation of the SS Infantry Division "Galicia." ... Ukrainian youth of Galicia! You have earned this right. You are called to battle with your deadly enemy, the Bolshevik, to fight for your faith and for your Fatherland, for your families and your family fields, and for the just, new order in Europe.[360]

Heike himself had no doubt either. His book is a heartfelt tribute to that collaboration. In his short (page and a half) preface, Heike tells the reader three times that SS-Galizien fought on the side of Germany:

> It is an incontestable fact that the Ukrainian Division fought on the German side.... They fought with the Germans in good faith and for a cause they considered just.... This work was written by a German who discovered and experienced the history and relations of the Ukrainian Division, the largest self-consciously Ukrainian military unit on the German side during World War II.[361]

These texts read as if they were taken from a common script. They represent high-powered propaganda meant to appeal to the most lofty patriotic sentiments of the Ukrainian people. I assume by 1943 the Ukrainians knew that "SS" did not stand for Sichovi Striltsi (Sich Riflemen). I assume they knew that fighting the Bolsheviks at this time also meant furthering the military objectives of Nazi Germany. I assume they knew that the New Order called for a Europe free of Jews, knew the meaning of the term Untermensch, and appreciated the rhyming sounds of Sklaven and Slaven. I assume they knew that they were collaborating with the enemy.

We are back to the original question: What did it take to get the Ukrainians to volunteer in such great numbers for an SS division? The answer is provided by Armstrong: "To form the Division, virtually all major Ukrainian political factions eventually accepted (at least tacitly) renewed collaboration with the Germans."[362] The Ukrainian church hierarchy accepted the division as well. Coincidently, on April 29, 1943, one day after the announcement of the formation of the division, Metropolitan Sheptytsky's treasury received a generous sum of 360,000 occupation zloty from the Nazi Administration of the GG.[363]

The OUN-M supported the formation of the SS-Galizien not only because it had long been associated with Kubiiovych but also because it saw the division as a way of countering the growing threat of the OUN-B to its own existence — and with good reason; shortly it would be attacked by OUN-B forces. The SS-Galizien was to be Melnyk's answer to Bandera's UPA. Many OUN-M members, therefore, played a leading role in its development and, through their press, in the recruitment process, which lasted twelve months.[364]

For these reasons, today's OUN-B members are all too willing to place the SS-Galizien in the orbit of the OUN-M entirely, in addition claiming that from the very beginning, the OUN-B vigorously denounced both the division and those who supported it. And this is true according to the literature of the day. Yet as Armstrong points out, "It is hard to conceive how recruitment could have proceeded so vigorously in Eastern Galicia if the OUN-B, the most powerful political force among Ukrainian youth there, had opposed the Division as strongly as the underground propaganda implied."[365]

An example of what was going on is the late 1944 UPA (OUN-B) leaflet that protested the forcible recruitment of OUN-B members for the SS-Galizien. As it turns out, a secret German report, based on the testimony of the volunteers, indicates that it was the UPA, controlled by the OUN-B, that had ordered the members to enlist in the first place! In fact, to forestall an OUN-M monopoly over SS-Galizien membership and for other reasons as well, the UPA intended to have half of the Galician youth join the UPA and the other half, under its aegis, sign up for the SS-Galizien.[366] Moreover, Roman Shukhevych — the head of OUN-B military staff since May 1943 and soon to be the supreme commander of the UPA — personally encouraged Ukrainian youth to join the division for the sake of the military training they would receive, and he even ordered "a considerable number" of OUN-B members to enter its ranks, where they were to occupy prominent positions. Other OUN-B members gladly volunteered without authorization.[367]

To secretly support such a Nazi division at the beginning of its formation was one thing, but to actively and openly support its re-formation in 1944 after the great loss of Ukrainian lives at Brody was quite something else. Yet that is exactly what the OUN-B did.[368]

One final piece of evidence for OUN-B support of the SS-Galizien is provided by Heike and confirmed by Wasyl Veryha, an SS veteran and the division's historian. Heike first stated that during the training period, the UPA "opposed the Division and tried to stop the flow of young Ukrainians into the Division." Two sentences later, he wrote: "During each leave the Division's soldiers were used by UPA cadres as instructors for their partisans. Generally, at the end of their leave, the UPA would let the soldiers return."[369] In fact, after the division's horrendous defeat at the battle of Brody, many of its members joined the UPA. Veryha verified this fact and corroborated the statements made above regarding OUN-B's support of the SS-Galizien: "While recalling the fairly well known facts that the personnel trained in the division had become the backbone of the UPA, it should be mentioned that the UPA command also sent groups of its people to the division to receive proper military training."[370]

With this revelation we now have a good picture of the military core of the UPA as well: the German-trained remnant of Nachtigall and Roland, the German-equipped members of Borovets' Poliska Sich who were later forced to join the OUN-B, the German-trained and German-equipped leaders and members of the OUN-M *pokhidni hrupy* who joined Borovets' "partisans" and were later "converted" to OUN-B forces, the 5,000 German-trained and German-equipped Ukrainian policemen who joined up in March 1943, the additional 7,000 to 8,000 Ukrainian policemen who joined subsequently,[371] and now these German-trained and German-equipped officers, instructors, and soldiers from the *SS-Galizien*. It seems, then, that the UPA can best be described as a German-organized, German-trained, and German-equipped deserter, military organization turned guerrilla. Such were the forces that confronted the initially defenseless Polish civilians in that "undeclared Polish-Ukrainian War," a euphemism for the OUN-UPA ethnic cleansing campaign.

Surprisingly, in addition to the secular Nationalist leadership, both the Ukrainian Autocephalous Orthodox Church and the Greek Catholic Church supported this élite Nazi formation, the SS-Galizien.[372] The son of the vicarial bishop of Kiev (Mstislav — Stepan Skrypnyk) joined its ranks. The Uniate bishop of Przemyśl, Iosafat Kotsylovskyi, blessed the volunteers. Bishop Iosyf Slipyi, the successor of Metropolitan Sheptytsky, celebrated the formation with a church service at St. George Cathedral in Lwów. Metropolitan Sheptytsky had told Kubiiovych (in the summer of 1941), "There is almost no price which should not be paid for the creation of a Ukrainian army"; he now not only applauded the formation of the SS-Galizien but also consigned over twenty Uniate priests to it as chaplains — including one of his senior clergymen, Father Vasyl Laba, to oversee them. (Normally, SS divisions did not have chaplains.) Father Laba, in turn, preached a sermon, which was duly filed and preserved by the Germans, calling on Galician Ukrainians to help "Hitler and the German people" destroy Bolshevism.[373] These are the reasons why the Ukrainian youth flocked to join the SS-Galizien.

Kubiiovych noted: "Those Ukrainians who contributed their energies to the organization of the Division ... knew that the Germans would somehow have to be paid for this. They did not approach the matter sentimentally, but with cold political calculation."[374] Part of this payment came in the form of warfare against the Polish partisans before June 1944.[375] The remainder was paid in full at Brody. Between July 13 and July 22, 1944, at the battle of Brody, a little town on the main highway between Równe and Lwów, the Soviet army encircled and decimated the combined German and Ukrainian forces in the Waffen-SS. George Stein comments, "14,000 had gone into the cauldron, 3,000 came out."[376] According to Torzecki, out of 15,300 men (in June 30, 1944) including 1,480 officers and junior officers, the Germans had only 5,075 men including 670 officers and junior officers at their disposal on September 4, 1944.[377] According to Heike, of the 11,000 Ukrainians in the SS-Galizien, 7,000 were killed, wounded, or taken prisoner by the Soviet army. "They paid dearly in blood," he said, "a fact that the German people should never forget."[378] Neither should the Ukrainian people, I may add.

But this is not quite the end of the story of the SS-Galizien. After Brody, on direct orders from Himmler the division was re-formed and reinforced with 8,000 new recruits from the reserve-training regiment and the five police regiments. "The Division did not have any problems with lack of personnel because new volunteers kept arriving," recalled Heike. "There was no lack of Ukrainian soldiers."[379]

In October 1944, the division was ordered to proceed to the occupied Slovak Republic and to participate in the suppression of an anti–Nazi partisan rebellion. In mid–January 1945 it was transferred to Slovenia, where it fought Tito's partisans. At the end of March it was moved to the Austrian front near Gleichenberg and Feldbach, and it finally surrendered to the British on May 8, 1945, near the town of Radstadt, Austria.

But there is still more to be told. Heike ended his preface: "Let this work bring rightful recognition of the worthy deeds of Ukrainians who fought for true democracy, and let it serve as a testament to the courage and rectitude of soldiers who carried their swords honestly, to the end of the war, and put them down unstained."[380] That the Ukrainian Nationalist division, the SS-Galizien, fought bravely is beyond doubt; that its soldiers carried their swords "honestly" and put them down "unstained" is highly questionable. There is a trail of civilian blood to be accounted for, a trail that, according to Polish and Jewish accounts, was left in Eastern Poland by the SS-Galizien.

In his work, Heike referred to the division's antipartisan activity and the "continuous clearing of territory."[381] (The Einsatzgruppen also "cleared the territory.") The division did more, then, than simply engage in major campaigns at the front.

It should be stated at the outset that the earlier Polish claims that the SS-Galizien participated in the quelling of the Warsaw Uprising have now been fairly discredited. Although some German-trained Ukrainian officers and soldiers did participate in this brutal campaign, they were not expressly associated with the SS-Galizien.[382]

There are, however, the claims of Aleksander Korman to be reckoned with: that from 1943 to 1945, subunits of the SS-Galizien took part in extermination actions under the code names of Wehrwolf, Sturmwind I, Sturmwind II, Immergrun, Vagabund, Wilbersturm, Maigewitter, and Wittenmayer. There are also his contentions and those of others, including the testimonies of eyewitnesses, that this trail of blood led through such Polish villages as Chodaczów Wielki in the county of Tarnopol, Huta Pieniacka and Podkamień in the county of Brody, Siemianówka in the county of Lwów, and Wicyń and Huta Werchobuska in the county of Złoczów, as well as dozens of other villages in Wołyń, *Lubelszczyzna* (the Lublin area), Slovakia, and Yugoslavia. In these attacks, thousands of civilians are said to have died. In Huta Pieniacka alone, 500 to 800 people were victims of the combined SS-Galizien and OUN-UPA forces. Names are given, dates are cited, circumstances are described.[383] *Na Rubieży*, the Polish publication dedicated to preserving the memory of those murdered by the Ukrainian Nationalists, contains vivid descriptions of the SS-Galizien atrocities in Huta Pieniacka, Palikrowy, and Podkamień.[384] One of the residents of Huta Pieniacka, Władysław Bąkowski, sent a letter to the Polish Seym:

> I come from Huta Pieniacka. On February 28, 1944 the population of Huta Pieniacka was murdered and the village burned. On that day, among others, my parents were killed.... On that day over 1,000 residents of the village were murdered in an inhuman manner. Not all could be identified; most of them were burned alive. That atrocity was committed by the soldiers and officers of the SS-Galizien and the Ukrainian Nationalists of the OUN-UPA.[385]

Relying on various sources, Littman provides the following examples of atrocities committed by the SS-Galizien and its regiments.

> According to Kiev journalist-historian Valery Styrkul, subunits of the division participated in a variety of death-dealing activities while training in other sites: the execution of prisoners of war at Szebnie, the liquidation of Poles, Gypsies, and Jews in the town of Moderowka, and the reinforcement of German units guarding the concentration camp at Szebnie....
>
> In February 1944 two of the division's three regiments were organized as a special antipartisan battle-group (SS-Kampfgruppe) under the command of SS Obersturmbannführer [Friedrich] Beyersdorff and Battalion Commander Bristot and sent off to fight Soviet partisans in the Chelm area. "Not surprisingly, the aforementioned task force did not perform its duties well," reported the division's chief executive officer, Wolf-Dietrich Heike. "Soon after reports of the unseemly behaviour of the unit began to arrive at the Division."
>
> The Beyersdorff detachment is reported to have joined other police units in attacking the village of Kokhanivka on November 23, 1943. One hundred adults were taken for brief rides in *Gaswagens,* and twenty old people and fifty children were locked in a village house and burned to death. According to Styrkul, "Legal bodies investigating the war crimes of the Nazi occupiers estimated that the special company of the SS Halychyna Division had tortured more than 2,000 civilians to death in Poland, shipped 20,000

persons off to Germany and burned down 20 villages."

By late 1943 the bulk of the Jews had been eradicated in the Ukraine through mass pogroms, mass shootings, and mass "resettlement" in concentration camps. This left the Ukrainian nationalist forces free to concentrate their attacks on the Polish villages that dotted Galicia. Since the Poles were almost entirely Roman Catholic, this meant frequent attacks on Catholic institutions and priests. On Sunday, March 4, 1944, a combined UPA (Ukrainian Partisan Army) and "SS Volunteer Ukrainian Division" rounded up some two thousand people who were hiding in the Dominican monastery in Podkamien parish of Brody. "Altogether, they murdered 600 people in the villages of Palikrowy, Malinska, and Czernicy."

Attacks on Polish villages were apparently marked by special savagery. "Entire Polish villages were wiped out, their inhabitants invariably tortured and raped before being slaughtered with knives and axes, the babies and children murdered with the same cruelty as had been the fate of the Jewish children."

Not far from Lviv lay a triangle of Polish villages, the largest of which was Huta Pieniacka. Small bands of unarmed Jews and poorly armed partisans sometimes visited these villages in search of food and medical supplies. On cold winter nights they took shelter in the villagers' barns and sheds. German intelligence reports identified these villages as partisan havens. According to standing orders, it was required that such villages be razed to the ground and their populations murdered in such a way as to serve as a horrible example to other villages.

On February 27, 1944, a mixed force consisting of a Ukrainian police regiment, a sprinkling of Wehrmacht reserves, and a strong contingent from the SS Halychyna Division was dispatched to "pacify" Huta Pieniacka. "After firing and throwing hand grenades from the outskirts, the murderers went into the village, assembled all the farmers together with their families and locked them up in their barns.... Then they set fire to the entire village.... The village burned all day, and only at night did the murderers finally leave."[386]

Littman states that Pavlo Shandruk, the appointed head of the National Ukrainian Committee formed under German auspices in November 1944, "included a number of additional German-led Ukrainian auxiliary police units in the division's ranks." The author adds:

> Among them was the 31st SD, a Volhynia-based legion that had played a part in cruelly suppressing the 1944 Warsaw uprising. Most deadly of all were the four hundred men of the Brigade for Special Tasks under Commander T. Bulba-Borovets. This "ingathering" resulted in the division including in its ranks prior to its surrender several of the most vicious of the German-led Ukrainian formations, such as the Roland and Nachtigall battalions, the 207th and 201st Police Battalions, the 31st SD, and the [SS Obersturmbannführer Friedrich] Beyersdorff detachment.[387]

Other works, such as that of Józef Fajkowski and Jan Religa, provide a partial listing of villages pacified by various German units with the assistance of Ukrainians from the SS-Galizien in the central Poland provinces of Rzeszów (Zwięczyce on June 8, 1943), Zamość (Majdan Stary on July 2, 1943, and Godzów in March 1944), Tarnobrzeg (Borów on February 1–2, 1944, Szczecyn and Wólka Szczecka on February 2, 1944), Kielce (Kamionka and Przysieka on July 28, 1944), and Tarnów (Jamna on September 24, 1944 and Rajbrot on November 23-24, 1944). All of these killings were in addition to those in the Lublin area, mentioned by Korman. Victim tolls, and even individual names and ages of those murdered, are also provided.[388] Similar charges have been made by Szcześniak and Szota and by Henryk Komański and confirmed by the following AK field reports.[389]

> March 23, 1944: Murders increase especially in Tarnopol. The participation of the SS-Galizien (the name of the Ukrainian unit) in these murders is verified.
>
> May 13, 1944: After the German bombardment in the region of Rejowiec, Ukrainian SS men come and massacre the Poles.
>
> May 17, 1944: Lately, there appeared in the [region] of Hrubieszów units of the division SS-Galizien which began their

terrorist activity by exterminating the people. Six Polish villages were burned.

May 24, 1994: The terrorist activity of the Ukrainian division SS-Galizien and the UPA continues in Chełmszczyzna, restrained only by our self-defense and partisan units.

July 7, 1944: Terrorist activity on the part of the SS-Halychyna Division in Lubelszczyzna has increased ... cruelty of the Ukrainian SS ... in southern Lubelszczyzna during food requisition.

In his speech to the division, Himmler offers another glimpse of the wartime activities of the SS-Galizien: "Your homeland has become so much more beautiful since you have lost — on our initiative, I must say — those residents who were so often a dirty blemish on Galicia's good name, namely the Jews.... I know that if I ordered you to liquidate the Poles ... I would be giving you permission to do what you are eager to do anyway." But the privilege of giving such an order belonged solely to "the savior of Europe, Adolf Hitler, and cannot be presumed by anyone else."[390] Himmler, of course, must have known about the unofficial ethnic cleansing of Poles by the Ukrainian Nationalists which had begun in the fall of 1942.

Who was responsible for the deaths alluded to by the AK reports, Korman, Styrkul, Littman, Fajkowski and Religa, Komański, Szcześniak and Szota, and others? Heike lays the blame for these atrocities on the soldiers of the infamous SS Dirlewanger Brigade and the Osttürkischer Waffenverband (Eastern Turkish Battle Group) under "Prince Harum al Rashid," a German convert to Islam — units that accompanied the SS-Galizien in the Slovak campaign.[391]

That is undoubtedly a part of the picture; it does not, however, explain the atrocities in southeastern Poland. Among the likely suspects for these crimes are the five police regiments, associated with the SS-Galizien, whose members came from among the initial "flood of volunteers" for the division.[392] The mission of such regiments generally was to "clear the territory" in advance of the regular army's arrival. Heike gave a listing of these regiments and their strength:

> The composition of the regiments was as follows: 1,264, Galizischen SS-Freiwilligen Regiment 4; 1,372, Regiment 5; 1,293, Regiment 6; 1,671, Regiment 7; 1,573, Regiment 8. Battalions in these regiments consisted of four companies of about 160 soldiers, and the companies consisted of three infantry platoons and one communications section. All of the officers and NCOs of the police regiments were German.[393]

Heike added that in February 1944, the fourth regiment was sent into action against Soviet partisans in Galicia and the Red Army in Tarnopol.[394]

Could these police regiments, incorporated into the SS-Galizien in the spring of 1944, have been responsible for the reported atrocities perpetrated against the civilians of Eastern Poland, Slovakia, and Yugoslavia?[395] Or could it be that the regular soldiers of the SS-Galizien, before and after the spring of 1944, were the real culprits? Or were they all involved? Since the files of the SS-Galizien have been removed from German and U.S. archives, we may never know for certain which units committed these crimes. After the call of the OUN for the massive ethnic cleansing of Poles (another missing document), which was already in effect at the time of the formation of the SS-Galizien, all the members of this Ukrainian Nationalist SS division were suspect.

Simon Wiesenthal traces the progression of the Ukrainian Nationalists from their role as Soviet collaborators to auxiliary police mass murderers, to reorganized auxiliary police regiment members, and to combatants in the SS-Galizien. "The bulk of these men [Ukrainian auxiliary policemen]," he states, "had previously served in the Soviet militia.... But when the Soviets had to withdraw again it took scarcely twenty-four hours before the same militiamen offered their services to the new Nazi rulers and became their most loyal assistants." It was these same "loyal assistants," in their role as police auxiliaries, who "were reorganized into new police regiments and in the summer of 1944 integrated into the SS Division 'Galicia.' Thus a division, which by and large might be described as a combat unit, suddenly found itself riddled with mass murderers."[396] He had but to add that later, after the defeat at Brody, some of these same "mass murderers" joined the UPA, as their ideological colleagues had done in the spring of 1943. The members of Nachtigall and Roland followed a similar progression: after their divisions were demobilized, they first served under Bach-Zelewski, then in the Ukrainian police, then in the SS-Galizien, and finally in the UPA — where most of the Nationalists eventually wound up.

When Wächter congratulated the members of the SS-Galizien on February 22, 1944, for their valor and uprightness, either he was ignorant of their crimes or he was engaging in a peculiar brand of Nazi cynicism:

> While you, full of hope, openly engage in battle against the Bolsheviks, the enemy of the world, the people from the green cadre [UPA] murder innocent men, women and children. In this way they sink all the more into crimes and chaos, covering their nation's name with shame. In the battle for the future of one's country and a better world, one does not kill in treachery, but fights in the open, in a disciplined way, as a soldier at the front of this unique war.[397]

As for Michael Yaremko's argument that the Germans had agreed that the SS-Galizien would be used only on the Eastern front and not against the Allies, Sol Littman's response is as good as any other:

> There are no documents, either German or Ukrainian, to substantiate the claim. In any event, even if such an agreement was made — which appears unlikely in view of the Nazis' contempt for their Ukrainian allies — it was repeatedly ignored. Ukrainian units manned defenses in Belgium and Norway. Members of the division, while training in France, joined in sweeps of the French countryside for downed British and American fliers.[398]

According to Himmler, as of January 1, 1944, there were some 25,000 Ukrainian soldiers in the Waffen-SS.[399] This means that a substantial number of Ukrainians served in SS divisions *other* than the 14. Waffen-Grenadier-Division der SS or the SS-Galizien. These other divisions included the 24. Waffen-Gebirgskarstjäger-Division der SS, consisting of Italians, Slovenes, Croats, Serbs, and Ukrainians, as well as the two divisions formed from the Russians and Ukrainians serving in Schuma-Bataillone (Security Units): the 29. Waffen-Grenadier-Division der SS (russische Nr 1) and the 30. Waffen-Grenadier-Division der SS (russische Nr 2). Both the 29th and a number of detachments in the 30th were eventually turned over to Andrei Vlasov.[400]

Did the Ukrainian Nationalists collaborate with Nazi Germany in 1943? Judged by their deeds, indeed they did. And some corroborating words exist as well, for example this proclamation issued by the OUN-B in July 1943 in the German language:

> Our Organization is not turned against You. Do not allow yourself to be awakened into battle with us. Spare yourselves the useless loss of blood.
>
> We do not destroy German communications, we do not disturb German armed forces. Do not allow yourselves to be drawn into battle with a peaceful people lest the whole Ukrainian nation turn against You.
>
> Long live the understanding of nations against the Bolshevik threat.[401]

According to SP and SD reports and various Ukrainian authors, in the first few months of 1943, before the formation of the SS-Galizien, OUN-B anti–Nazi propaganda continued to be disseminated among the people, supply trains continued to be sporadically attacked by Ukrainian and other "bandits," prisoners were freed, and one large weapons and ammunition factory in Orżew (Równe county) was taken by the UPA on March 10 and 11. During this attack, about sixty Germans were killed.[402] In addition Wolodymyr Kosyk claims, "The OUN-B did not content itself with verbal condemnation of the personal and collective collaboration with the Germans but it proceeded systematically with liquidation operations of SD and Gestapo agents, of Ukrainian policemen who had taken part in punitive anti–Ukrainian activities, of members of protection units and Soviet agents in German service."[403]

In turn, states Kosyk, "The Gestapo and the SD continued to hunt down OUN-B members."[404] Peter J. Potichnyj maintains that during 1943-44, the UPA "carried on very intensive military and political campaigns against the Germans."[405] Other Ukrainian authors imply that German antipartisan efforts in the east were also directed against the UPA in 1943. Ihor Kamenetsky, for example, states: "In the big action in the summer of 1943, conducted by SS General Bach-Zelewsky against the Ukrainian partisans in Volynia and Polyssa, 50 tanks ... and nearly 10,000 German and auxiliary police were used. In addition, several Hungarian detachments and eastern volunteer battalions participated."[406]

Could it have been that the Germans were waging this kind of fierce battle with the Ukrainian Nationalists while *at the same time* trying to recruit them for the SS-Galizien? Or did Kamenetsky have other Ukrainian partisans in mind: the non-Nationalist partisans in the Soviet units already lost to the Nationalist and German cause? Reuben Ainsztein gives one answer:

> The Germans assembled a 15,000-strong force made up of SS and Wehrmacht troops, Lithuanians, Vlasov units and Ukrainian police, as well as 5,000 Ukrainian nationalists, and in August launched a massive operation against the partisans.... While Fyodorov [Aleksei Fyodorov-Chernigovskiy, a Soviet partisan leader] took the brunt of the fighting against the Germans, Brinskiy's brigade was given the task of engaging the Ukrainian Partisan Army [UPA] battalions, which supported by German bombers and mortar batteries tried to push the partisans into the bag prepared by the Germans.[407]

During this time, the UPA also took credit for the untimely death of Viktor Lutze, chief of staff of the Nazi SA. But the Ukrainian Nationalists and the Germans disagree as to what really happened, as well as where and why. Kamenetsky, for example, claims that Lutze was assassinated by the UPA and died on a highway between Kowel and Brest (Brześć).[408] Kosyk agrees with Kamenetsky as to the cause of death but places Lutze on the road between Kowel and Równe.[409] German authors, on the other hand, maintain that Lutze was injured in a car accident near Berlin and died in a Potsdam hospital, nowhere near Kowel, Równe, or Brześć.[410] According to *The Goebbels Diaries*, as the result of Lutze's death, Hitler told the German leadership to limit the speed of Nazi vehicles to 50 miles per hour.[411] The only point of agreement between the Ukrainian Nationalists and the Germans on this issue seems to be that Lutze did indeed die and was buried in May 1943.

In his memoir, Władysław Kobylański states that toward the end of June or the beginning of July 1943, a group of Ukrainian Nationalists pretending to be Poles from Huta Stepańska wiped out a 30-man contingent of German gendarmes near the Ukrainian village of Melnica. Consequently, a punitive expedition of 250 Germans was sent against the civilian residents of Huta Stepańska but did not attack after learning the truth.[412]

Finally, according to Armstrong, a new and inexplicable wave of German repressions was launched against the Ukrainian Nationalists that fall, and Borovets and some prominent OUN-M leaders were arrested.[413]

One explanation for this turn of events in 1943 is provided by Czesław Łuczak. After the UPA began to attack the German settlers in Eastern Galicia and after the massive exodus of the Polish people created a hiatus in the flow of requisitions, the Germans decided to stop the UPA terrorist attacks against civilians. These counteractions, however, were sporadic, were carried out mainly in the towns, and were generally ineffective.[414] Another explanation is provided by Shmuel Spector. During 1943, the UPA captured "several localities, thereby forcing the Germans to counteract and recapture them."[415]

In conclusion, then, in 1943 the Ukrainian Nationalists did little to impede the German war effort and much to promote it. If the leaders of the Ukrainian Nationalists were really out to get the Germans at this time, as their defenders now claim, why didn't they encourage those 80,000 young and eager volunteers to join the Allied anti-Nazi military organizations, as so many millions of their fellow countrymen had done before them, rather than the SS?

1944 — End of War

On February 4, 1944, Wilhelm Kinkelins (Rosenberg's and Gottlob Berger's associate) wondered: "Why, in the fifth year of the war, should only the Germans bloody themselves, why not utilize the Slavs, above all the Ukrainians? We should follow the example of the English who always protect their own skins with the hands of others."[416]

Równe fell to the Soviets on February 11, 1944, Lwów on July 27. By October, all of Eastern Poland lay in Soviet hands. As the German army began its withdrawal, the UPA began to attack its rear guard and seize its equipment. The Germans reacted with raids on UPA positions. On July 15, 1944, the Ukrainian Supreme Liberation Council (Ukrainska Holovna Vyzvolna Rada, or UHVR, an OUN-B outfit) was formed and, at the end of that month, signed an agreement with the Germans for a unified front against the Soviet threat. This ended the UPA attacks as well as the German countermeasures. In exchange for diversionary activities in the rear of the Soviet front, Germans began providing the Ukrainian underground with supplies, arms, and training materials.[417] A September 4, 1944, Army Group North, Ukraine, report stated, "After the recent events at the front, the leadership of the UPA has recognized that it cannot wage the struggle against the Bolsheviks by itself and has repeatedly asked the Wehrmacht for support in the form of arms."[418] These arms they turned against the Soviets, ambushing and killing officers and soldiers, including Marshal Nikolai Vatutin, commander of the First Ukrainian Front.[419] The arms were also used against innocent civilians during the continuous ethnic cleansing campaign.

In addition to the Ukrainians in the SS-Galizien who cooperated with the Nazis until the end of the war, Ukrainian youth from Eastern Galicia were (sometimes forcibly) recruited by the Germans for the SS antiaircraft defense cadet corps. Wearing the uniforms of the Flakartillerie and organized like the Hitlerjügend, these young men were sworn in on June 1944, withdrawn with the regular army units in July because of the Soviet advance, and exploited by the Germans according to their needs until the end of the war.[420] David Littlejohn states:

> The Ukrainian youths came under the aegis of *H. J. Kriegseinsatz-kommando Süd* with headquarters at L'vov in the General Government. It succeeded in raising 5,933 young persons for the Luftwaffe; most went to its Flak defenses but others were utilized by its signals and transport sections. Two hundred fifty of the Ukrainian lads were later selected as suitable to go on training courses as N.C.O.s for the Waffen SS.[421]

Efforts were also made at this late date to contact and enlist the help of the Ukrainian Nationalist groups in and out of Eastern Poland. In the fall of 1944, all the Nationalist leaders were released from German prisons to assist in the war effort. Among them were the big three: Borovets was freed in August; Bandera on September 25; and Melnyk on October 17.[422]

When Vlasov issued his "Manifesto of Prague" on November 14, 1944, calling into existence his Russian Liberation Army (ROA), the Nationalists — who wanted nothing to do with him or the "peoples of Russia" — issued their own appeal under Melnyk's signature and sent it to Hitler by way of Rosenberg. They pleaded for their own "national military formations ... subject to the German Wehrmacht in operative matters."[423] On the same day that Vlasov's manifesto was issued, Kubiiovych brought a delegation of Ukrainian Nationalist peasants to Hans Frank to underscore his continued loyalty to the German authorities.[424]

In their efforts to bolster their position and to reinforce their ranks, the Nationalists even tried to prevent the 2 million worn-out Ukrainian forced laborers from returning to their fatherland from Nazi Germany.[425] This coincided with the Germans' desperate hopes, or rather illusions, of somehow mobilizing these "reserves," whom they treated as contemptible slaves, into a proud army of Third Reich defenders.[426]

In September, the Germans tried to mobilize the Hilfswillige (Hiwis—auxiliaries — and other "volunteers" representing various nationalities including Ukrainians) into three divisions under the ROA. When Himmler attempted to combine them into an army that could be sent to the front, he ran into stiff opposition from the incredulous Nazi generals, who proceeded to inform him that 900,000 men (they did not know how many Hiwis there were) could not be properly organized for such a venture in so short a time.[427] There was also an attempt to create a Ukrainian Nationalist division under P. Diachenko. This small "division," consisting of some 1,900 volunteers, was incorporated into Schörner's pancer (armored) army group.[428] In November, Shandruk was called to Berlin to form the Ukrainian National Army (Ukrainska Natsionalna Armiia, or UNA).

As the result of all these efforts, two sizeable pro–Nazi armies emerged: Vlasov's ROA, with some 300,000 men of whom 30 to 40 percent were Ukrainians; and General Shandruk's Ukrainian Liberation Army (Ukrainske Vyzvolne Viisko, or UVV).[429]

In the last months of the war, all major Nationalist leaders were called to Berlin to assist the dying Third Reich through the UNK. And finally, toward the end of the war, the Brigade for Special Tasks was formed in Berlin under Borovets.[430] A Nazi officer testified at Nuremberg:

> During the retreat of German troops from the Ukraine, Canaris personally instructed the Abwehr to set up an underground network to continue the struggle against Soviet power in Ukraine, to organize acts of terrorism, subversion and espionage. Competent agents were left behind specially to direct the Nationalist movement. Orders were given to install caches, to store munitions, etc. To maintain liaison with these bands, agents were sent across the front line.[431]

In 1944, as the vanquished Wehrmacht was withdrawing from "Western Ukraine," these collaborators not only provided the German troops with intelligence reports about "the enemy" but also gave them safe passage by blockading the smaller passes in the Carpathian Mountains.[432]

But their efforts were all in vain: the allied advance on the western and eastern fronts could not be halted. Soon the entire prewar eastern territory of Poland was Deutschfrei. Instead of participating in that liberation, the Ukrainian Nationalists evacuated behind the Wehrmacht. The war was lost, and so was the cause of the Ukrainian Nationalists who collaborated with the Nazis to the bitter end. As Major Wolf-Dietrich Heike put it, referring to the surrender of the SS-Galizien and the evacuation of the division members after their capitulation to the Allies on May 8, 1945: "With this relocation [to Rimini in northern Italy and Radstädter Tauern] the Ukrainian involvement in the German war effort came to an end."[433] Alexander Dallin provides a good summary of the alliance between the Ukrainian Nationalists and the Nazis during World War II:

> The nationalist leaders had wished to collaborate with the Germans, on their own terms. Although claiming to speak for the Ukrainian people, they met initially with little popular support in the Soviet Ukraine. They formed partisan units but refrained from attacking the Germans. Their leaders were put in German jails and concentration camps; yet when released in 1944, they again rallied to the Nazi side to resume the struggle against Moscow.
>
> In all likelihood, the prompt eruption of the crisis in L'vov and its aftermath precipitated the inevitable. Short of utter surrender, not even the pliable OUN groups could survive in a climate of German officialdom whose majority espoused the *Untermensch* thesis and whose confused minority floundered between a "pro–Ukrainian" outlook and a stern belief in "Germany first."[434]

David Littlejohn takes the middle road on the issue of UPA-German collaboration:

> "These people" (the Slavs), Hitler had once declared, "have only one justification for their existence — that is to be useful to us." Koch acted on this principle and mercilessly exploited the Ukraine. In face of his callous behavior, the extent of Ukrainian cooperation with the Germans is perhaps surprising. Some became resistors, some active collaborators; a few even contrived to have it both ways, like the U.P.A. (Ukrainian Insurgent Army) which sometimes aided the Germans in actions against Soviet partisans, and sometimes fought against them in revenge for

> Koch's inhuman treatment of their compatriots.[435]

Perhaps this is as good a summary as any other. I would add only that whereas the Ukrainians in Reichskommissariat Ukraine were indeed treated brutally by Erich Koch, the Ukrainians in Eastern Galicia (a part of the GG) were treated significantly better—hence the explanation for the "surprising" extent of Ukrainian Nationalist on-again, off-again collaboration with the Germans until the end of the war.

The best statement on the subject was provided by Melnyk in the November 18, 1944, Nationalist proclamation, which he signed:

> It is therefore not astounding that these peoples [non–Russians] greeted the outbreak of the German-Russian war with the greatest joy. They placed themselves at the side of the German army from the first day on, helped where they could, welcomed the troops with open arms, and with cordial friendship. Standing shoulder to shoulder with the German soldiers in battle, they proved their loyalty to the national idea.[436]

Surely Melnyk is here describing the overwhelming welcome of the German armies in Eastern Galicia, the stronghold of the Ukrainian Nationalist movement. Here are some examples of that welcome by both factions of the OUN. The no. 3, July 10, 1941, issue of *Samostiina Ukraina*—an OUN-B publication from Stanisławów—noted: "The emerging Ukrainian nation will cooperate closely with the National-Socialist Great German Nation which, with its Leader Adolf Hitler, is creating a new order in Europe and the world.... The Ukrainian National Revolutionary Army ... will fight together with the Allied German Army for a new order in the whole world."

The July 16, 1941, OUN issue of *Ukrainski Shchodenni Visti*, from Lwów, stated: "We Ukrainians sincerely wish for a German victory in the fight for the new order ... fate itself has united the Germans and the Ukrainians.... We know well what our Ukrainian people can expect from Stalin, Roosevelt, Churchill and Sikorski."

The OUN leader and editor Ulas Samchuk wrote in the no. 18, November 23, 1941, issue of Równe's *Volyn*: "The power of the spirit! Perseverance, order, discipline! Behold the mottos of our war.... Together with Hitler's army, together with his system, together with his ideals which light our way, we will firmly and unyieldingly bring about a final victory."

The no. 16, July 16, 1944 issue of *Ridna Zemlia*—an OUN-M publication from Lwów—proclaimed:

> The war will last until the Germans will be victorious together with all of Europe, until the dark forces perish, until Bolshevism together with Anglo-American imperialism fall to pieces.... The enemy will not break the spirit of Germany and Europe! ... We Ukrainians must take our example from the German nation, from its spiritual determination to survive until the last battle, the last victory. Away with all hesitation, away with all doubts, away with all resignation! Only the complete dedication to the task at hand will lead to a full victory.

By way of a general summary, World War II pro–Nazi Ukrainian military and paramilitary formations, as well as other pro–Nazi formations with sizeable numbers of Ukrainians, can be listed as follows:

Pokhidni hrupy

Viiskovi Viddily Natsionalistiv (VVN): Nationalist Military Detachments, officially called Bergbauernhilfe (Mountain-Peasants' Help, or BBH) by the Abwehr

Ukrainian Legion camouflaged as Reichsarbeitsdienst; transformed into Druzhyny Ukrainskykh Natsionalistiv (DUN): Detachments of Ukrainian Nationalists consisting of Nachtigall and Roland

DUN members in Bach-Zelewski's Schutzmannschaft Bataillon 201

Poliska Sich of Taras "Bulba" Borovets

Beyersdorff's unit of 2,000 SS-Galizien men

Bukovinian (OUN-M) Battalion of 1941

14. Waffen-Grenadier-Division der SS (galizische Nr 1—the SS-Galizien) and its five police regiments

24. Waffen-Gebirgskarstjäger-Division der SS (along with Italians, Slovenes, Croats, and Serbs)

29. Waffen-Grenadier-Division der SS (russische Nr 1) (along with Russians)

30. Waffen-Grenadier-Division der SS (russische Nr 2) (along with Russians and others)

Vlasov's Russkaya Osvoboditelnaya Armiia (ROA): Russian Liberation Army

Shandruk's Ukrainske Vyzvolne Viisko (UVV): Ukrainian Liberation Army

Ukrainska Natsionalna Armiia (UNA): Ukrainian National Army

Ukrainischer Werkschutz (work security)

Ukrainischer Grenzschutz (border guards)

Ukrainischer Bahnschutz (railway security police)

Ukrainischer Baudienst (compulsory labor service)

Ukrainischer Lagerschutz (camp guards)

Ukrainischer Heimatdienst (work service)

Ukrainischer Hilfswillige or Hiwis (volunteer auxiliaries in German armed forces)

SS-ukrainische Wachmannschaften

Ukrainischer Hilfspolizei Schutzmannschaften (Ukrainian auxiliary police attached to the Einsatzgruppen and Einsatzkommando units)

Ukrainischer Kriminalpolizei (Kripo) (detective forces/criminal police).

Ukrainischer Militz (Ukrainian police, or militia)

SS antiaircraft defense cadet corps (along with others)

Although the UPA fought sporadically against the Germans, it too can be included in this list: it also assisted Germany in the war effort through military actions against the Polish underground, the Soviet partisans, and the Jewish partisans; and it had a policy of ethnic cleansing of people hostile to the Nazis, a policy that also provided Germany with fleeing refugees for forced labor for the conduct of the war. The need to allocate large forces to protect civilians from the UPA also impeded the AK's sabotage and military operations against Germany.[437]

According to reliable Ukrainian sources, in October 1944, some 220,000 Ukrainians were serving in the armed forces of the Third Reich and some 90,000 in the UVV.[438] Whether organized by the Germans or the Ukrainians with the consent of the Germans, many of these formations consisted of or included either OUN people or those sympathetic to their cause. In many instances, the recruits were volunteers — young and old — prodded on by the leadership of the OUN. Irrespective of the above listing, of course, many more non–OUN Ukrainians, in numbers too numerous to count,[439] fought on the side of the Allies *against* Nazi Germany — including those from Canada and the United States. As I. Gartner notes, "Ukrainian Nationalists today who claim they were coerced, or, in an even further stretch of the imagination, forced to cooperate with the Nazis, against their better nature, must not only deny their behavior in World War II, but also much of their prewar history."[440]

John Loftus states:

> The CIC [U.S. Counter-Intelligence Corps] had an agent who photographed eleven volumes of the secret internal files of OUN/Bandera. These files clearly show how most of its members worked for the Gestapo or SS as policemen, executioners, partisan hunters, and municipal officials. The OUN contribution to the German war effort was significant, including the raising of volunteers for several SS divisions.[441]

What happened to the members of these organizations after the war? Although most of the Ukrainian Nationalist leaders had no problem emigrating, a few (like Bandera) decided to live incognito in Germany among their former friends and allies. Of those who were trapped in "Western Ukraine," many were killed by the Soviets. A hard-core remnant of the UPA became entrenched in the Carpathian Mountains. The SS-Galizien, however, marched day and night in order to surrender to the Western Allies, who, instead of returning them to the USSR or trying them as war criminals, after a pro forma screening[442] and despite the vehement protest of the Ukrainian-American League,[443] with Vatican intervention,[444] classified them as displaced persons and released them.

Simon Wiesenthal states, "roughly 8,000 members of the Ukrainian SS division 'Galicia' emigrated to Canada between 1948 and 1951 ... and Canadians accepted them in defiance of the existing laws."[445] In a December 1995 talk in Toronto, John Loftus, a former member of the OSI, told his audience: "It's my belief that next to Buenos Aires, Toronto has the highest per capita residence of Nazi war criminals of any other city in the world.... Let's face it. You ended up as a dumping ground and your government doesn't have the guts to tell you."[446]

In reference to the members of the SS-Galizien, Norman Davies states, "One of the last secrets of the 'Last Secret' is that the survivors of the SS-Galizien were saved from deportation to the USSR and from certain death, by virtue of the claim to be Polish citizens."[447] And, I may add, they were also saved from Polish retribution by virtue of the claim that after the war, their country of origin was no longer Poland.[448] A February 21, 1947, refugee "screening" (very little screening was done) commission report commented on this unique situation of the Ukrainian collaborators just after the war:

> This camp consists entirely of male Ukrainians who were either captured in German uniform or were working in Germany as civilians and attached themselves to the 1st Ukrainian Division shortly before its surrender....
>
> It might be worthwhile noting in this connection that on the nationality issue these men are really having the best of both worlds. They do not qualify as Soviet citizens because their place of birth and/or habitual domicile on 1.9.39 were in Poland, and they therefore by our definition escape all punishment by the Russians for their having assisted the enemy; and they are not presumably eligible now for punishment by the Polish authorities because that part of the country from which they came is no longer part of Poland.[449]

Another "last secret" of the war is that many other Ukrainian Nationalists (i.e., not only the members of the SS-Galizien) who fled to the west after the 1944 Soviet advance were not repatriated because of their vociferous claims that they were citizens of Poland, the country that they had tried so desperately, together with their Nazi allies, to destroy. Eventually, most of them, with the help of the OUN or the United Nations, emigrated.

Should any of the members of the aforementioned military and paramilitary formations have been classified and tried as war criminals? According to the International Military Tribunal, the following organization was declared criminal:

> (4) Die Schutzstaffeln der Natzionalsozialistischen Deutschen Arbeiterpartei (commonly known as the SS), more particularly all persons who had been officially accepted as members of the SS, including:
>
> (a) the members of the Allgemeine SS,
> (b) *the members of the Waffen-SS,*
> (c) the members of the SS-Totenkopf-Verbände, and
> (d) members of any of the different police forces who were members of the SS, but not including those who were only members of the so-called riding units.[450]

All those who "became or remained members of the organization with knowledge that it was being used for the commission of acts declared criminal by Article 6 of the [London] Charter, or ... were personally implicated as members of the organization in the commission of such crimes"[451] were regarded by the Tribunal as war criminals. On the question of whether the volunteers knew that they belonged to a criminal organization, the Tribunal stated:

> Knowledge of these criminal activities was sufficiently general to justify declaring that the SS was a criminal organization to the extent herein described. It does appear that an attempt was made to keep secret some phases of its activities, but its criminal programs were so widespread, and involved slaughter on such a gigantic scale, that its criminal activities must have been widely known. It must be recognized, moreover, that the criminal activities of the SS followed quite logically from the principles on which it was organized.[452]

Excluded from the criminal status were "those members who were drafted into membership by the State in such a way as to give them no choice in the matter and who had committed no such crimes." Finally, the Tribunal determined, "Members of military or paramilitary units raised by the Germans during the war, or which collaborated with the Germans, are only to be excluded [from refugee status] if there are serious reasons for considering that they personally have committed a crime mentioned in Article IF(a)."[453]

For the volunteers to the Waffen-SS (and therefore of the SS-Galizien as well), the criteria for the status of war criminal hinged on membership in and knowledge of the criminal nature of that organization *or* personal commission of a crime.[454] For other military and paramilitary units raised by the Germans, the criterion was membership *and* personal commission of a crime.

Under these criteria, how many Ukrainians of the pro–Nazi organizations listed above were ever charged with war crimes? Very few — or rather, too few. Although Mykola Lebed should be behind bars, serving out the remainder of his life sentence in Poland for his role in the treasonous assassination of Minister Pieracki, he is still at large, in New York, a free man (he was recruited and brought here after the war by the CIA).[455] So is Ivan Demjanjuk who, unlike Lebed, was stripped of his American citizenship, extradited, sentenced to death in Israel, and then released because he was not "Ivan the Terrible" of Treblinka; nevertheless, he had served as a guard in Sobibór and Flossenburg and had been a willing accomplice in the Nazi program of genocide.[456]

In an effort to create a "national dictatorship" over an independent Ukraine, or rather "Western Ukraine," the Ukrainian Nationalists courted Germany for a full quarter of a century. It remains but to recapitulate and evaluate their changing strategy in terms of their primary objective.

In the interwar years, the Ukrainian Nationalists, with mostly German support, did everything in their power to create unrest in Eastern Poland and to elicit sympathy abroad. Their aim was to "rally the masses" and to launch a massive uprising against a legitimately established government in "Western Ukraine." Unfortunately for the Nationalists, the people they claimed to represent distrusted their youthful zeal, resented having to reap what the Nationalists had sown, and abhorred their "join or die" tactics. The Ukrainians of Eastern Poland were simply not ready for another military confrontation with Poland and were wary of an independence that, in the event of political instability, could land them in the Soviet camp. Thus the vast majority of Ukrainians belonged to and voted for the legal Ukrainian parties in Poland. The critical radical mass never materialized. In 1939, after almost twenty years of political activity, the Nationalists constituted but a very small fraction of 1 percent of the Ukrainians in Eastern Poland. During all this time, their strength and support depended not on the Ukrainian people but on Germany. In Soviet Ukraine, their batting average was zero. This, then, was the political strength of the movement that sought to unify and liberate a vast nation of over 30 million people.

But what if the Nationalists had succeeded in rallying the Galician masses in the interwar years? Would the ensuing revolution, which they hoped would spread to Wołyń, Belorussia and Soviet Ukraine, have been successful? A war with Poland, militarily much stronger than in 1918, would have been difficult to win. Since the territories that belonged to Poland for hundreds of years even before the partitions of the late 1700s were recognized as part of its frontiers by the League of Nations, Poland had a right to defend itself against this separatist threat. Without external assistance, the Ukrainians would surely have lost the war, if it had ever come to that. But who would have been there to help them? The Soviet Union — which was all too willing? The émigrés — who were themselves divided on which course to follow? The League of Nations — which had decided against Galician independence to begin with? In short, the plan of launching a "social revolution" in Poland's eastern territories and Soviet Ukraine was strategically flawed from the very beginning.

As it turns out, there was another player in the game: Germany. Its plan to annihilate Poland couldn't have come at a more convenient time as far as the Nationalists were concerned. In response to this new development, they quickly shifted their strategy from "revolution" to "collaboration" with the enemy of Poland. As Germany's "partner," they would to ride to freedom on the crest of a German victory over Poland and the rest of Europe.

How realistic was this new strategy? To be sure, in the beginning Germany's position on the question of Ukrainian autonomy was purposefully ambiguous. There were initial gestures of goodwill, some hints that autonomy might be possible, some veiled promises from Rosenberg and others. But after June 30, 1941, who could possibly have doubted Germany's intentions to enslave the Slavs? Had the Nationalists read *Mein Kampf* (translated into Ukrainian by Dmytro Dontsov), they would have learned what lay in store for them from the very beginning. The strategy of "tactical collaboration," then, was also a serious error of judgment on the part of the Nationalist leaders. If there was to be a German victory, it was not intended to be shared with anyone, least of all the Slavs. There was to be only "one master."

After June 30, 1941, and expecially when it became clear that Germany would lose the war, the Nationalists embarked on a new version of that strategy: "limited tactical collaboration." The idea was to build up, with or without Germany's assistance, a military force that would survive the war and would somehow — in the balance of power, or the chaos, or the Third World War that they expected to follow — seize the moment and liberate all of Ukraine both from Poland and from the Soviet Union. This is why they continued to plead with Germany to allow them to march "shoulder to shoulder" with the "Great German Army" and why they urged their followers to fill the ranks of the SS-Galizien. Kubiiovych stated in April 1943: "Only now do we come to a partial realization of our efforts. Why only now? Because earlier, the Germans had refused to allow Ukrainians into the political arena, even at the lowest level."[457]

This is also why the OUN formed its own military arm, the UPA. German reports trace the genesis of that endeavor:

> May 22, 1942: It has been established that the Bandera movement has managed to gain a solid foothold in Volyn and Podillia [Podole], and to recruit a large number of members.[458]
>
> October 29, 1942: Ukrainian nationalists have combined their forces for the first time into a large bandit group in the Sarny area and are constantly receiving reinforcements.[459]
>
> November 3, 1944: The UPA was born at the end of 1942 in Volhynia through a merging of previously different independent combat groups. It moved into the attack on the territory of Galicia in the beginning of 1944 under the form of the UNS (Ukrainian National Self-Defense).[460]

For the remainder of the war, the main tasks of the UPA were to gather military equipment and supplies and, in preparation for the "final struggle," to clear the territory of all non–Ukrainians. The anti–Nazi propaganda of the OUN-UPA was meant to win over the oppressed (by Germany) Ukrainian masses. An August 20, 1942, SP and SD report noted, "The Bandera movement continues to make every effort in the Reichskommissariat Ukraine to influence the local Ukrainian population by circulating illegal propaganda."[461] The raids on Nazi prisons were a form of recruitment of the most loyal of followers. (The freed prisoners generally joined the UPA.) The purpose of the occasional skirmishes with the Germans was to shore up the military might and supplies of the UPA. Even Erich Koch was surprised at their success: "The Ukrainian national bands have a rigorous and able leadership and an astonishing amount of weapons.... The bandits attack targets vital for the exploitation of the country and provisions for the front, railroads, roads and bridges, state properties, dairies, wheat and hay granaries, as well as assessable industrial enterprises."[462]

Present-day Ukrainian neo–Nationalists state emphatically, "We fought Hitler and Stalin."[463] That they fought with the Soviet and Jewish partisans and the AK — that is, the enemies of Germany — is not doubted. Szcześniak and Szota, however, present another interpretation for the relatively few OUN-UPA anti-Nazi actions that have been recorded: "The activities of the OUN against Germans and their armies were from the beginning demonstrative and propagandistic in nature. Their main objective was not to weaken the German military potential but mainly to gain the backing for the objectives of Ukrainian nationalism of that segment of Ukrainian society which suffered the terror and the economic oppression of the occupant."[464] The only tasks of the Ukrainians in the SS-Galizien were to fight the German war, to survive if possible, and to join the UPA at the first opportune moment during or after the war.

How realistic was this final strategy of the Ukrainian Nationalists? Didn't the Polish government follow a similar strategy with respect to its own armed forces? Yes, but for the Poles — except for the previously mentioned renegade AK units in Nowogródek and Lida and the NSZ Brygada Świętokrzyska — there was never a question of "tactical," "limited," or any other kind of organized collaboration with Nazi Germany. The Poles never embraced the notion of independent Poland "at any price." Unlike the self-appointed OUN "government" of "Western Ukraine," the legitimate Polish government never wrote personal letters of gratitude and obeisance to Hitler and his cronies, never pleaded for military formations under German leadership, never urged its youth to volunteer for German SS or any other divisions, and never condoned the type of excesses that characterized the Ukrainian police, the UPA, and the SS-Galizien. Unlike the OUN, the Polish government never gave an order to its Home Army for the ethnic cleansing of civilians. Unlike the Waffen-SS, and by inclusion the SS-Galizien, no Polish unit was labeled as a criminal organization by the International Military Tribunal.

Moreover, the Polish government had a concrete plan of action: to launch a general uprising in Warsaw at the moment of Germany's greatest weakness and just before the Soviet advance, which they fully expected, in order to save Poland from the threat of Soviet occupation by virtue of that final *combined* victory. Although it ended in disaster, this was at least a sound strategy, one that may have worked with help from the Allies. The mobilized underground was to play a key role in this last desperate struggle against the German invaders. It was to this end that Poland built up and saved its armed forces. They were to be used *against* Nazi Germany.

What was the Ukrainian Nationalist plan of action? An August 20, 1942, SP and SD report states that a captured OUN-B document entitled "Ukraine" contained the following sentence: "All indications point to the fact that Germany will not succeed in establishing world-wide supremacy despite its great military success."[465] After Stalingrad, it became increasingly clear that the Germans would lose the war. By 1944, it was a known fact that the war was already lost. Throughout all this time (from the fall of 1942 until the end of the war), the Nationalists continued to mobilize their forces and to collaborate with Germany either directly or indirectly.

Since a stalemate was out of the question and since it was common knowledge that the anticipated chaos in Poland's eastern territories would soon be ordered by the Soviet régime, what did the OUN plan to do with its German-trained and German-equipped armed forces, which included the UPA? They were to be used in the *Third* World War, between the Western Allies and the Soviet Union. But exactly where would this impressive army, which had no allies except for the Germans, be warehoused while it waited? In Soviet-occupied "Western Ukraine"? In Poland? In vanquished Germany? As we have seen, the Nationalist leaders were the first to abandon the cause and emigrate abroad. Only Roman Shukhevych, with his few thousand faithful UPA members, went underground in the mountainous terrain of the Polish eastern borderlands, there to await the Third World War and there to die. This final strategy, therefore, was also fatally flawed.

Thus ended the Ukrainian Nationalist movement of World War II. The defeat of Germany proved to be the unraveling of the OUN as well, which, in the words of Szcześniak and Szota, was a "road to nowhere." Its precursor, Volya, had been founded in 1919 — the same year as the establishment of the German Workers' Party. The UVO had been founded in 1920 — the year in which the name of the German Workers' Party was altered to the NSDAP.

Throughout the war, whenever the Germans lost ground, the OUN-UPA forces retreated behind them. The year 1945 spelled doom to the NSDAP — and also to the OUN-UPA.

It is most remarkable that after accomplishing little of lasting importance and after leaving its legacy of terror and destruction, this movement has found a score of contemporary émigré adherents, defenders, and mythmakers who continue to glorify its founders, leaders, and followers. B. F. Sabrin notes: "The naked fact remains that the U.S.-born and Canadian-born Ukrainian Nationalist leadership didn't find the courage (almost five decades later) to come out with the truth, to disassociate themselves from the old 'heroes,' and the Nationalist 'patriots' of the past. The old policy remains: No remorse, no regret, and don't admit anything."[466]

The OUN, the progenitor of the UPA, it seems, is alive and well and stronger than ever both abroad and in present-day Ukraine, especially in Lviv. Perhaps its current members are the children of the World War II Ukrainian Nationalists; perhaps they are fresh recruits. If they are proud of the OUN-UPA legacy, it may be because they have been told only about the valiant attempts on the part of their heroes to win Ukrainian independence against all odds. If so, they cannot be blamed for their hero-worship and their devotion to the OUN-UPA. "For two postwar generations of Ukrainians, especially in the West Ukraine and in emigration," states John A. Armstrong, "the Ukrainian Insurrectionary Army is not merely part of the historical record; it is a major constituent of beliefs, transcending history, which form their identity."[467]

But there is another side to that historical record, a macabre story that is just now being told — and it dangles about the neck of the Organization of the Ukrainian Nationalists like the albatross in the *Rhyme of the Ancient Mariner.*

Ethnic Cleansing

The story begins with Mykola Mikhnovskyi's *Independent Ukraine*, published in 1900 in Lwów:

> We know that the struggle will be long and bitter, that the enemy is strong and unsparing. But we also know that this is the final conflict, not to be followed by another opportune moment for a new struggle. The night has been long, but the dawn has approached and we shall not allow the rays of national freedom to shine on our chains: we shall break them before the rising of the sun of liberty. For the last time we shall enter the arena of history and either succeed or die....
>
> Let the cowards and renegades go, as they have in the past, to the camp of our enemies. They have no place among us, and we shall denounce them as enemies of the Fatherland.
>
> All in Ukraine who are not for us are against us. Ukraine for the Ukrainians! So long as a single foreign enemy remains on our territory we do not have the right to lay down our arms.[468]

Dmytro Dontsov, the spiritual father of the OUN if not its founder or even member, took this message one step further in his work *Natsionalizm*:

> To the emotionality and fanaticism of great ideas which move masses must be added another attribute: amorality.[469]
>
> Be ravishers and conquerors before you become stewards and possessors.[470]
>
> Only Philistines can absolutely dismiss and morally condemn war, murder, power.[471]
>
> Ridiculed by Philistines, the philosophy of ... German nationalism: "Deutschland über Alles" should become — mutatis mutandis — our motto as well.[472]

Such glib pronouncements became the very foundation of the OUN ideology and ethic. During the very first gathering of the OUN — the January 28 to February 3, 1929, Congress of Vienna — this "amoral" ideology was translated into a proclamation issued to the Ukrainian people, whom this fledgling fascist organization presumed to represent, and into a concrete OUN resolution to be implemented at the appropriate time:

> **Proclamation:** Only the *complete removal* of all occupants from Ukrainian lands [*povne*

> *usunennia vsikh okupantiv z ukrainskykh zemel*—i.e., ethnic cleansing] will create the possibility for an expansive development of the Ukrainian people in the borders of their own nation.... In its internal political activity, the Ukrainian nation will strive to attain borders encompassing all Ukrainian ethnographic territories.
>
> **Resolution:** The *complete removal* of all occupants from Ukrainian lands [*povne usunennia vsikh zaimantsiv z ukrainskykh zemel*—i.e., ethnic cleansing], which will follow in the course of a national revolution and create the possibility for an expansive development of the Ukrainian people in the borders of their own nation, will be guaranteed by a system of our own military formations and goal-oriented political diplomacy.[473]

These "occupants" included the newly arrived settlers as well as those non–Ukrainians who had lived in these territories for countless generations, people like my father.

The Second Great Conference of Ukrainian Nationalists (II (Velykyi Zbir Ukrainskykh Natsionalistiv, or VZUN, held on August 27, 1939, in Rome) repeated the above sentiments in a more dramatic form and adopted the Nazi "blood and iron" solution to the problem at hand just five days before the invasion of Poland: "Ukraine for Ukrainians. We will not leave one inch of Ukrainian land in the hands of enemies and foreigners.... Only blood and iron will decide between us and our enemies."[474]

On September 1, 1941, in *Volyn*, Ulas Samchuk informed the Ukrainians: "The element that settled our cities, whether it is Jews or Poles who were brought here from outside the Ukraine, must disappear completely from our cities. The Jewish problem is already in the process of being solved, and it will be solved in the framework of a general reorganization of the 'New Europe.'" In the aftermath of these solutions, the beneficiaries would be, said Samchuk, "the true proprietors of the land, the Ukrainian people."[475] This OUN editor knew full well that by September 1, 1941, "the element ... brought here from outside the Ukraine" was already in the Gulag.

The Galician Ukrainian Nationalists said, "*Smert lakham, zhydam i moskalam*" (Death to the Poles, Jews, and Russians), and when their territories were Judenfrei, they said: "We have finished with the Jews, now it's the Poles' turn."[476] They then began on their long-talked-about and planned program of the "complete removal" (*povne usunennia*) of all occupants for the sake of their "free, independent, united" (*vilna, samostiina, soborna*) "Ukraine for Ukrainians" on all "Ukrainian ethnographic territories" under the rule of the "initiative-minority," the superior people of the OUN.[477] As they promised, so they delivered "a sea of blood" and made it "hellish" and employed "every means in the struggle ... not excluding mass physical extermination." And they cleansed their "ethnographic territories" of all "occupants" (*okupantiv/zaimantsiv*), but alas, they were never in a position to give the territories back to the "true proprietors." Just as the Jewish Holocaust was the logical consequence of the Nazi policies and practices of the 1930s (Nuremberg Laws, Kristallnacht, etc.), so too was this genocide the logical consequence of the interwar policies and practices (proclamations, acts of terrorism, etc.) of the UVO-OUN.

One letter from those days, addressed probably to Archbishop Adam Sapieha, metropolitan of Kraków, reads:

> Krzemieniec, June 7, 1943
>
> Most Venerable Father:
>
> An opportunity presents itself to send you a few words through a person who is escaping the knives of the Ukrainians. What is happening here and now, the slaughter and torment of Polish families, defies all words. The descriptions in Sienkiewicz's *With Fire and Sword* or Kossak-Szczucka's *Conflagration* pale in comparison to present events.
>
> Almost all the Poles in the villages of the county of Krzemieniec have been butchered, and those who were able to escape the haydamak knives and bullets have sought shelter in Krzemieniec and Wiśniowiec where there are still German units. In other places such as Szumsk, Dederkały, Kuty, and Łanowce, the weaker units were either destroyed or fled before the larger bands of Ukrainians.

I will submit a few examples in a chronological order so as not to be accused of exaggeration. The murder of Poles began already last November and continued through the winter; but these were sporadic occurrences. For example, in one village a family was butchered, in another two or three more. Massive murders began only after Easter [1943] and with each day gather force. Immediately after the holidays, about 600 people were killed in the villages around Szumsk and the rest sought shelter in Krzemieniec. Later, Kuty was attacked. This was the largest parish (4,000 souls) in Krzemieniec county. When the murders began, the people together with their parish priest barricaded themselves in a church. There, they defended themselves all through the night. In the morning, the women and children went to Krzemieniec and the men remained to defend the church. The following night, more numerous hordes arrived, destroyed the church and butchered the 200 Poles who were in it. Not a single soul remained of those in the parish. The church in Krzemieniec was converted into a shelter for the refugees. Later, the Germans came and deported the young people for forced labor in Germany; the old people continue to suffer in dire poverty.

At the beginning of May, two parish priests from Oleksiniec and Kołodno came to our refuge. Almost all the Polish parishioners from the Oleksiniec parish were robbed and killed. The parish priest, having nothing to do, left us yesterday for the General Government; so did the pastor of Kołodno. Almost daily one can see fires; they are burning Polish settlements and murdering those who do not escape in the most bestial manner.

On the night of May 15, the honorable Kuś family was attacked in Młynów. Two daughters and a 21-year-old son were killed. The rest of the family managed to escape. The attackers, after thoroughly robbing the house, threw the murdered victims into it and burned it down.

All the refugees are fleeing to Wiśniowiec where they are living in the monastery in terrible conditions and utter poverty. One's heart bleeds at the sight of their poverty and over the stories of their experiences.

Every morning there is news: there, they were killed; there, robbed; there, another house was burned together with its occupants. And thus one day follows another in suffering and our nerves are constantly on edge because there is no doubt that on the first night after the German unit leaves Wiśniowiec (castle), all the Poles will be murdered. Whoever can, therefore, flees to the GG because these haydamaks swear that not a single Polish foot will remain in Wołyń. Wiśniowiec, once consisting of Jewish houses, has almost vanished. Every single Jew was killed there last year and the Ukrainians took apart all their houses and sheds. Only the castle, monastery, commune (*gmina*) office and pharmacy still remain — the rest was knocked down. On the outskirts of town, only the homes of the haydamaks remain.

You, Reverend Father, can imagine what our life is like from this description: we are prepared to die, because only a miracle and the special protection of Our Lady can save us now. We therefore plead earnestly for your holy prayers so that the Lord Jesus would have mercy on us and all would quiet down again. The Poles here, whose only fault was that they were born Poles and are Catholics, are truly experiencing a terrible crisis. Even those Ukrainians who converted to Catholicism during Polish times are being killed.

Ending once more, we humbly ask for your holy prayers so that our peace of mind may be restored and that we may be able, in accordance with God's will, to endure these moral and perhaps even physical torments.

I humbly kiss the holy scapular and once more beg for your prayers.

Brother Cyprian[478]

The wholesale slaughter of innocent civilians — men and women, the old, the young, and the unborn, clergy and laity, Poles, Jews, Russians, a few Czechs and Gypsies, and many Ukrainians who refused cooperation, who assisted the Polish citizens at risk, who warned them of impending attacks, and who told them which way and when to run — this slaughter began in the fall of 1942 in the Sarny region of the province of Wołyń, intensified greatly in 1943, spread to Eastern Galicia and even the region of Chełm/Zamość in the province of Lublin, and ended in 1947 with Operation "Vistula" (Akcja "Wisła").[479]

Authors who characterize this massacre as a "fratricidal Polish-Ukrainian conflict" or an "undeclared Polish-Ukrainian War" are either unaware of the facts or are deliberately throwing up a smoke screen to hide the truth. They may as well talk with equal conviction of the "undeclared German-Jewish War." The slaughter, at least in its early stages, was almost entirely one-sided: the German-equipped, German-trained and experienced UPA killers with their local (sometimes forcibly recruited) military Kushch Self-Defense Units (Samooboronnyi Kushchovi Viddily, or SKV) and military Ukrainian National Self-Defense Units (Ukrainska Natsionalna Samooborona, or UNS) against the initially completely unprepared and defenseless civilians. At times, even neighbors participated in the massacres.

It was not until the summer of 1943, when the Poles in Wołyń began to enter the German police (vacated by the Ukrainians) for self-defense and retaliation, that the civilians received some measure of military protection. Aside from the AK Wołyń (the 27th Infantry Division of the AK formed in March of 1944),[480] the Polish underground lent some assistance, as did the Hungarian forces stationed in Eastern Poland (including Wołyń),[481] the Soviet partisans, and the Soviet-organized *istrebitelnyye* (destruction) battalions, which consisted both of Poles and of Ukrainians under Soviet command — about twenty-five men to a village.[482]

Mostly, however, the hundreds of thousands of Polish citizens from "Western Ukraine" who wanted to escape death at the hands of the OUN-UPA were forced to seek refuge not only in the Polish territories to the west, under German control, but also in the Ukrainian lands east of the River Zbrucz, where they were generally well received,[483] or in the surrounding swamps and forests, where hunger, cold, and typhus awaited them, or in the partisan-established civilian camps, which offered an uncertain haven, or in the civil-defense centers (there were 160 of them in Wołyń alone),[484] which were often attacked, or finally, in the larger towns occupied by German garrisons, from which they were involuntarily deported to Nazi Germany for forced labor.

There is no doubt that the marching orders for the OUN-UPA genocidal action came straight from the OUN-B directorate.[485] How else can one explain, for example, the fact that — according to the personal testimonies analyzed by Józef Turowski and Władysław Siemaszko — 20,000 people died in the month of July 1943 in various locations throughout Wołyń. (The count for July 11 and 12 alone was 12,000 victims.[486]) If not a direct order, what other possible explanation is there for such a concerted effort in such a brief period of time against so many people in so many places? The Polish Government Delegation had no doubt that there was such an order: "The murder of the Polish people in Wołyń began on orders of the *Banderowcy*," begins the "conclusion" of one report.[487] One survivor from Ostrówki, Agnieszka Muzyka, reported hearing such an order being read before the executions in her village: "He pulls out a piece of paper and reads that today at this moment all are to be shot."[488]

The clearest indication of the issuance of such an order is the lack of an order from OUN-UPA headquarters to cease and desist after the atrocities had begun or at any time throughout this long and bloody ethnic cleansing campaign. Just as troubling is the lack of any condemnation of this "action" on the part of the Ukrainian leadership, either then or now.

Metropolitan Sheptytsky's pastoral letter "Thou Shall Not Kill" was published in the fall, probably November, of 1942.[489] This was before the massive murders in Wołyń, which occurred in the summer of 1943. That general letter has been interpreted in many ways and has often been invoked as a condemnation of the "fratricidal conflict," the "undeclared Polish-Ukrainian War," which was just then unfolding. That interpretation, however, lies in between the lines. The pertinent phrases read:

> The person who spills the blood of his political adversary or, in general, of his enemy is precisely the same type of murderer as he who murders out of greed, and deserves the same punishment from God and the same condemnation of the Church.... With sorrow we are obliged to speak of those instances of murder which are the result of hatred and discord and which lead brothers

> to a civil war.... What other enemies should Ukraine fear if Ukrainians mutually hate each other and are not even ashamed of this hatred.[490]

In addition to the murder of Ukrainians by Ukrainians (the last sentence above is a clear reference to the *Ukrainian* fratricidal battle *within* the OUN factions),[491] the Metropolitan specifies three other types of murders that he considers particularly abhorrent: the killing of children by parents, abortion, and suicide. There is no unambiguous reference whatsoever in this letter to the Polish-Ukrainian "fratricidal conflict": to the killing of Poles by Ukrainians or to the killing of Ukrainians by Poles. Most troubling of all is the fact that there was no follow-up pastoral letter from the Metropolitan regarding this topic when the real slaughter began. Torzecki states:

> We know that the Metropolitan called on the UPA to desist from battle and to lay down its arms, but this happened only after the passing of the [Soviet] front in Western Ukraine. [Sheptytsky died on November 1, 1944.] The question remains, why didn't he categorically demand this at the moment of the bloody exploits with the Poles. It is true that he called for an end to the fratricidal wars, that he threatened excommunication, but why did he not "break" with those who continued this war? There was no longer a question here of "conversion." Did the Metropolitan have further doubts? In respect to this, what could they have been? These must remain as open questions until such time as new documents come to light, documents which would once and for all allay our doubts.[492]

The order for the ethnic cleansing of all "occupants" of ethnic Ukrainian lands was probably issued by Mykola Lebed ("Maksym Ruban," head of OUN-B from July 1941 to August 1943) and relayed by his commanders, such as Roman Dmytro Klachkivskyi ("Klym Savur," "Okhrym," "Klym," "Krymskyi," "Omelian"—head of UPA North in Wołyń and Polesie) sometime in the fall of 1942 or the spring of 1943.[493] A Soviet partisan report dated March 3, 1943, stated: "The Ukrainian nationalists conducted a bestial action against the unarmed Polish population with the goal of completely eliminating the Poles in Ukraine.... In the Cumań region, UPA units received orders to exterminate all Poles and to burn their villages and settlements by April 15, 1943."[494]

Taras "Bulba" Borovets stated in his *Armiia bez derzhavy*, published in 1981, "The officer corps of the new UPA received the following military assignment from Mykola Lebed's party in June 1943: Without delay and as soon as possible *conclude* the action of completely cleansing the Ukrainian territories of Poles."[495]

Lebed himself stated that the aim of the UPA was "to clear the forests and the surrounding areas of foreign elements."[496] He furthermore explained how this was done: "In the summer of 1943 Wołyń was completely under the control of the UPA. The Poles who received an injunction to leave the territory, generally complied willingly with this order. Their fixed property passed into the possession of the Ukrainian people."[497]

The least of the lies contained in the passage above is that these "injunctions" (nailed to people's doors, basically saying, "Get out, or die!") were issued in Wołyń. No such notice was nailed to my family's door in 1943 before our home was torched in the middle of the night by the Nationalists. No such warnings were given to the Polish residents of Leonówka before the attack that claimed the lives of my relatives. These crude "injunctions" were issued in Eastern Galicia in 1944. Two of them read as follows:

> [1] Because the Polish government and the Polish people collaborate with the Bolsheviks and are bent on destroying the Ukrainian people on their own land, [name] is hereby called upon to move to native Polish soil within 5 days....
>
> [2] You are called upon as a Polish family to leave the village within 48 hours and to depart from Ukrainian lands westward beyond the San [River].
>
> In the event that you do not comply with this order, you bring upon yourself a death sentence and your possessions will be burned.[498]

A secret directive issued and signed by Klachkivskyi in June 1943 reads: "We should undertake a great action of liquidation of the Polish element. We should take advantage of the occasion, before the German forces withdraw, to liquidate the entire Polish population from 16 to 60. ... We cannot lose this battle and, without counting the cost, we should diminish the Polish strength. Forest villages and those near forests should disappear from the face of the earth."[499]

A Soviet partisan report that covers the period from June 19 to August 18, 1943, stated: "The chief task of the Ukrainian nationalists at the present time is to gather forces and cleanse the occupied territories of Poles. The nationalists conduct themselves in a bestial manner with the Poles. They burn, massacre and shoot people, confiscate their belongings and burn the buildings."[500]

According to Władysław Filar, German documents also attest to the Ukrainian Nationalist policies of annihilation (Ausrottung) of the Polish people in Wołyń in July 1943.[501] That July, as we have seen, 20,000 innocent civilians were slaughtered in Wołyń. That same July, when so many people were being killed in such brutal ways, an OUN leaflet addressed "To the Citizens of Poland" stated: "We do not want to enslave any of you. Those of you will remain in the territories of the Ukrainian Nation who will willingly attest to the fact that they want to do so. *We guarantee you full freedom, safety and equal rights on equal footing with all Ukrainian citizens. Our motto: freedom for nations and the individual.*"[502]

We are asked to believe that at the August 21–25, 1943, Third (OUN-B) Great Conference of Ukrainian Nationalists (VZUN), the OUN-B turned "democratic." The OUN-B, we are told, now became an "organization with clearly defined firm democratic principles and with a progressive social program."[503] This assembly, we are told, condemned "internationalist and fascist national-socialist programs and political concepts" and proposed a "system of free peoples and independent states [as] the single best solution to the problem of world order." Its ruling ideology, "Ukraine for Ukrainians," we are told, was now replaced with "rights of national minorities."[504] But the wholesale murder of the "foreigners" in "Western Ukraine" continued without respite.

Right after this conference, on August 30, 1943, the Polish residents of Wola Ostrowiecka were rounded up in the local schoolyard. The men were taken five at a time to a barn, where they were axed to death; the women and children were packed into a school, into which grenades were thrown and which was set on fire. That day, 529 people died in Wola Ostrowiecka, of whom 220 were children under fourteen years of age. The same thing happened on the same day in the neighboring village of Ostrówki, where 438 were killed, including 246 children. In all, about 1,700 people belonging to the "national minorities"—who were granted equal rights by the OUN-B VZUN just a week before—died in that one region. An exhumation was held on August 17, 1992. The reburial of 330 remains took place on August 30, the forty-ninth anniversary of the slaughter. A forensic expert, Dr. Roman Mądro from the Medical Academy of Lublin, examined the remains and wrote a lengthy report. A gruesome videotape was made. Pictures were taken. Witnesses were interviewed. All, living and dead, were the victims of the "new," "reformed" OUN-UPA.[505] Such was the nature of the "undeclared Polish-Ukrainian War" in "Western Ukraine."

This slaughter continued to the very end of the war and beyond. An AK report dated April 20, 1944, stated that the "UPA in Wołyń received an order to hide arms and, at the beginning of [that] summer, to leave the forests and to murder the Poles and Soviets."[506] A letter dated April 12, 1945, from the county elders of Lubaczów to the Ministry of Public Administration in Warsaw pleaded in vain for assistance against the "Ukrainian revolutionary bands of Banderowcy" who were "murdering the remaining [Polish] population in a bestial manner ... and burning their possessions." The letter continued: "Daily there are dozens of murders; the same is true in the eastern part of the county of Jarosław. The battalion of the Polish army stationed in Lubaczów ... is not in a position to control the situation in the county which is getting worse every day. The detachment dare not leave the town even for one moment for fear that it would be immediately attacked by the *Banderowcy* and the unarmed Polish population murdered." The letter noted the burial on that day of two militiamen and twenty-eight Polish soldiers who were attacked by the UPA as they were trying to bring arms and ammunition to the battalion stationed in Lubaczów. "If this situation lasts any longer," concluded the elders, "this entire county and part of Jarosław county will be under the control of the Ukrainian bands and the remainder of the Polish population will perish."[507]

Among the reasons for the extent and the barbarity of the slaughter in Wołyń and Eastern Galicia, as well as the relative absence of defensive strategies among the civilians, the following are noteworthy:

1. The 1940–41 massive deportations to the Gulag by the Soviets. (Of all people deported, ethnic Poles constituted an absolute majority.)
2. The liquidation of the Polish intelligentsia and officers by the Soviets.
3. The massive deportations of able-bodied civilians (Poles and Ukrainians) to Germany for forced labor after 1941. The Ukrainian Nationalists, on the other hand, either were in German uniforms or in the ranks of the OUN-UPA.)
4. The continual recruitment of men into the armed forces on all fronts and into anti-Nazi partisan groups.
5. The complete breakdown of previous governance and criminal-justice structures in towns and villages.
6. The "crime" of bearing arms, punishable by death (while the Ukrainian Nationalists were legally armed).
7. The gullibility of the Polish peasants, who, knowing themselves to be innocent, could not believe that they would be killed without reason. (This is a common refrain in survivors' stories and testimonies, including my mother's.)
8. The Ukrainian Nationalist propaganda, which even while leading them to their death, assured the civilians that they had "nothing to fear" and that "nothing would happen" to them if they cooperated (another common reform).
9. The ability of the Nationalists to mobilize the local Ukrainian inhabitants (not always successfully) for the task of ethnic cleansing through various manipulative techniques (e.g., appeals to patriotism), terror tactics, threat of execution, and murder.
10. And finally, the already stated fact that the gullible, defenseless, and inexperienced civilians were confronted by German-trained Ukrainian military and paramilitary personnel. In addition to the *pokhidni hrupy* who arrived in Wołyń in July of 1941, some members of the Nachtigall and Roland battalions joined the UPA after the expiration of their "service" contract in October 1942. Among these was Roman Shukhevych, the organizer of the Nachtigall, the chief of the Ukrainian auxiliary police, and later the head of the OUN-B and the commander-in-chief of the UPA. It was no coincidence that the first murders in Wołyń began around this time as well. In March 1943, as we have seen, 5,000 members of the Ukrainian auxiliary police joined the UPA (soon to be followed by 7,000 to 8,000 other deserters). Likewise, the first *massive* murders in Wołyń began in that same month and year.

Another question of some importance is why this ethnic cleansing of Poles began in Wołyń instead of Eastern Galicia, the cradle of Ukrainian nationalism. Ukrainian publications offer one explanation, an explanation that at the same time places the blame for initiating the conflict on the shoulders of the Polish underground.[508] Wołyń, so the argument goes, was simply a case of retaliation for the prior Polish massacres of Ukrainians in the province of Lublin (especially in the counties of Zamość, Biłgoraj, Hrubieszów, and Tomaszów), massacres that supposedly began in 1942. In Ukrainian literature, this area is often referred to as being a part of Chełmszczyzna. In Polish literature, it is called Zamojszczyzna, the name Chełmszczyzna being reserved for the more compact region around the city of Chełm to the north.

The major drawback to this argument is that although political assassinations were being carried out against "the enemy" by the Polish underground throughout the war (this included the killing of Ukrainians who, in the service of the Nazi régime, were responsible, directly or indirectly, for the killing of many Poles, especially after the German invasion of Eastern Galicia in the summer of 1941), the first *civilian* massacres of Ukrainians by Poles in the Zamojszczyzna region of Lublin province occurred in May 1943 (not 1942), well after the beginning of ethnic cleansing by Ukrainian Nationalists in Wołyń in the fall of 1942.[509]

Without attempting to justify these massacres, let me just state that the reason behind them seems to have been retaliation against the Ukrainian Nationalists, who — especially in their capacity as members of the militia, as village administrators (*sołtysy*), and later as members of the Ukrainian SS police regiments attached to the SS-Galizien — were assisting the Germans (from November 1942 until the following summer) in the infamous ethnic cleansing of over 100,000 Poles from Zamojszczyzna for German settlers. This is clear from the following Polish underground appeal and warning:

TO THE UKRAINIAN PEOPLE
Living in the Area of
Hrubieszów County

The evacuation and murder of Poles perpetrated by the Ukrainian police and militia on the initiative of the Germans deepens the tragic misunderstanding between Poles and Ukrainians.

We therefore appeal to the conscience and dignity of the Ukrainian people.

Do not be an implement of murder in the hands of the Germans because the road to freedom does not lie in that direction.

Do not look for enemies among the Poles, because you will not find them there.

Our common enemy is the Germans, who for their own ends, are setting Ukrainians against Poles in one district, and in another, Poles against Ukrainians — all the while rejoicing from this mutual war.

Our common enemies are all those, whether Poles or Ukrainians who, by collaborating with the Germans, deepen our misunderstanding. Do not believe in the promises of the Germans since they give away freely that which has been robbed. Poland was and will be. Ukraine was and will be, but not on the soil of Hrubieszów, because it was never here and never will be.

We will not give up the Hrubieszów territory. It will be neither German nor Ukrainian but — Polish.

We will defend it to our last drop of blood.

Our patience is already at an end. We declare in so many words to all those in whose interest lies the deepening of the misunderstanding between Poles and Ukrainians:

1. For every Polish village evacuated with the help of the Ukrainian police and militia, two Ukrainian villages will be burned immediately.

2. For every Pole killed by a Ukrainian, two Ukrainians will be killed immediately.

We issue this appeal on a day when we celebrate Easter in common with a deep belief that it will be understood in the right spirit and that this holiday which we hold in common will be the beginning of our further mutual efforts to reclaim our independence.

25.IV.1943[510]

Zygmunt Klukowski, in his Zamojszczyzna diary, chronicles what was going on in those days:

December 7, 1942. ... In the forests around us more and more people are trying to organize fighting units. Some former Polish officers are forming regular units for the Home Army (A.K.). Many villagers are forming their own units with only one goal, revenge. They are well armed. Some try to burn down and completely destroy the evacuated villages before the new owners, mostly German settlers from Eastern Europe, take possession of them.

I was informed that even in the very well organized and disciplined Home Army officers have a hard time holding down the growing urge for revenge [against Germans but, as the later passages make clear, also against the Ukrainians assisting them].[511]

April 21, 1943. ... During the past few days several evacuated villages have been burned down by the partisans.[512]

June 2, 1943. ... I was told that in Zamość several Germans and German informers who received death sentences by the underground courts were liquidated.[513]

July 21, 1943. ... This morning all Ukrainians were moved from Szczebrzeszyn and other villages to Tarnogród. This was done in a completely different manner from the evacuation of the Poles. Each Ukrainian received a horse-drawn wagon and was allowed to take as much of the household as he or she wished.[514]

July 23, 1943. On Monday, July 19, the Ukrainian mayor of Żółkiewka and Fik, the village administrator of Turobin, were assassinated. Two hand grenades were thrown as they drove along in an official car, killing both instantly. The killing of Fik was a mistake; he was a very good man. On the other hand, the Ukrainian was already the subject of many actions, but he always escaped injury.[515]

March 4, 1944. Around Tarnogród and Biłgoraj, Ukrainian SS units are still fighting and killing Poles.[516]

March 17, 1944. ... I was told about terrible things taking place in Hrubieszów County. Ukrainian nationalists are torturing and murdering Poles, singling out large farmers and ranchers. In retaliation the Polish underground is killing Ukrainians.[517]

May 9, 1944. ... Yesterday and today many Polish escapees from Rawa Ruska arrived in our town. There the Ukrainians are the law. Ukrainians set May 10 as the day by which all Polish families must leave.[518]

In any case, Ukrainian civilians and villages were not targeted by the Polish underground in the Lublin province in 1942 and thus did not provide any justification for the attacks on Wołyń in the fall of that same year. The various *plausible* reasons why the Ukrainian Nationalists began ethnic cleansing in Wołyń and not in Eastern Galicia can be summarized as follows:[519]

1. The marshy, forested terrain of Wołyń was especially suitable for the guerrilla tactics of the UPA. Also of great significance were the 416,000 (in 1938) horses in Wołyń.
2. There were fewer Poles in Wołyń, and their scattered villages were difficult to defend.
3. In Eastern Galicia, the Polish underground was stronger and much better organized.
4. Wołyń was a relatively backward province and housed a large percentage of uneducated people, who could be easily manipulated.
5. The OUN could count on the support of the Orthodox Church because of the wrongs done to it in 1938 in the Lublin province.
6. Borovets' Poliska Sich had formidable forces in the north of Wołyń, forces the OUN-B wanted to incorporate and control — and did so by the fall of 1943. At this time, an internal struggle for power characterized the OUN. Borovets leaned toward the OUN-M.
7. For symbolic reasons, the Ukrainian Nationalists wanted to launch the revolution, whose aim was to create an independent Ukraine, on Ukrainian soil, that is, in Reichskommissariat Ukraine, which included Wołyń, rather than in the GG of Poland, which included Eastern Galicia.
8. Soviet partisans were present in Wołyń, enabling the UPA to represent itself as an antipartisan force and thereby win German approval and support.
9. Expecting a scorched earth in the aftermath of its actions, the OUN opted to destroy "Orthodox" Wołyń rather than its own homeland.
10. And finally, and most important, Eastern Galicia was the home of the organizational and propaganda departments of the OUN. A revolt there may very well have destroyed the organization itself. This area, after all, with its rich petroleum deposits, was under the special protection of Governor Hans Frank. As the corridor to the east and Rumania, it was thought that any disruptive uprising in this area would have been brutally suppressed by the Nazi régime.

But the real and only reason for this ethnic cleansing campaign in Wołyń lay in the will of the leaders of the OUN directorate, who sent their one thousand hardened emissaries to "peaceful Wołyń" in 1942 to mobilize, by force if necessary, the Ukrainian peasants for the task that lay ahead. Meanwhile, as we have already seen, the Ukrainian auxiliary police, consisting mostly of OUN-B members who had been engaged in killing Jews and pacifying Polish villages, joined the UPA in March 1943, and an additional UPA reinforcement arrived in Wołyń from Lwów on July 4 of that same year.[520]

TABLE 14. NUMBER OF POLISH DEATHS AT THE HANDS OF THE UKRAINIAN NATIONALISTS IN WOŁYŃ BY COUNTIES BETWEEN 1939 AND 1944

District	*Documented*	*Estimated*
Dubno	1,900	6,800
Horochów	2,400	4,200
Kostopol	4,400	7,000
Kowel	3,350	7,300
Krzemieniec	3,000	5,100
Luboml	1,856	1,900
Łuck	4,000	11,300
Równe	1,000	7,400
Sarny	1,400	6,100
Włodzimierz	6,500	8,000
Zdołbunów	500	3,600
Total for Wołyń	30,306	68,700

Even during the worst of it, the Polish residents of Wołyń always felt that this UPA was a cancerous transplant form Eastern Galicia and that their own neighbors could not and would not engage in such atrocities — in the killing of women, children, and the aged.[521] Alas, they were right about the former but were wrong, dead wrong, about the latter assumption.

How many Polish citizens died at the hands of the OUN-UPA? That is unknown. The estimates run from 50,000 to 500,000. Few, however, would argue with the estimate for ethnic Poles of 100,000.[522] Some actual figures are also available, as are many recent testimonies and some memoirs.[523] Speaking only of Wołyń, Władysław Siemaszko states:

> In 1939, there were 350,000 Polish people in Wołyń and in 1942, according to the German census, 305,000. "Thanks" to the Soviet occupation, the Polish population of Wołyń declined by 45,000. According to the records of the Polish Government Delegation for the Homeland [Delegatura Rządu na Kraj], 100,000 persons fled Wołyń to escape the atrocities and about 50,000 were murdered. A large proportion fled across the Bug River to the province of Lublin. Therefore, at the present time we can place the decline of the Polish population in Wołyń due to Ukrainian terror, in the vicinity of at least 121,000 to 150,000 persons — both murdered and departed.[524]

Józef Turowski and Władysław Siemaszko, in *Crimes Perpetrated Against the Polish Population of Wołyń by the Ukrainian Nationalists, 1939–1945*, provide a tally of Polish losses for the province of Wołyń in Table 14 above. Their information is based on content analysis of materials that have been collected over the last thirty years by the Main Commission for the Investigation of Nazi Crimes in Poland and by the oral-history project initiated in 1985 by members of the 27th Division AK.[525]

Ethnic cleansing, as we know from the recent incidents in Rwanda and Bosnia, is an ugly form of "radical evil." The way it was conducted in the southeastern provinces of Poland defies description. In province after province, in county after county, in town after town, in village after village, in house after house, people died in hideous ways: eyes were plucked out; teeth were knocked out; fingers, ears, tongues, and breasts were severed; bellies were sliced open; heads were cut off; people were thrown alive down wells, impaled on fence posts, run through with pitchforks, gashed with scythes, stabbed with knives, hacked with axes, sawed in half, nailed to trees, thrown alive into flames, dashed — as in the case of infants — against buildings, raped, molested, and tortured.

These are the stories from people who remember seeing these events and who swear on stacks of bibles that what they are relating is the gospel truth. A person today has nightmares simply from *reading* about such matters. The idea was to "cleanse the territory" in such a way as to strike fear into the hearts of those who would even consider staying behind — or returning after the war. That fear haunts many still. That fear prevents many from returning, even for a visit. That fear is tangible. It is HERE and NOW. It will never go away. It is the fear of the OUN-UPA.

The methods of ethnic cleansing varied from place to place. In the beginning it was done at night, then in broad daylight: some UPA members and SKV/UNS units ride out one night and surround a village or house; men rush in, break windows, knock down doors; sometimes grenades are thrown in; people panic, run; men shoot, go into homes and torture, kill, execute, and rob all that's worth having, set fire to the premises, leave and go home to their wives and children, wash off the blood, perhaps lie awake at night.

At other times people were rounded up in village squares, marched off to buildings, and shot five at a time. And finally, there was the procedure learned from the Nazis while serving as auxiliary police: lead the people away from their homes and villages while assuring them that they have nothing to fear if they do as told, have the victims dig their own graves in some out-of-the-way place in the woods, make them lie face down, and shoot them in the back of the head.

In an autobiographical chapter entitled "Life in the Forests and Liberation" in Wołyń, Michael Diment wrote:

> Gangs [the UPA] disseminated flyers warning that anyone hiding Jews would be exterminated along with his entire family.... Last night the [UPA] gangs attacked the Poles in villages and killed all of them. They were slain by guns, axes and pitchforks. Andrii overheard the killers last night claiming that they had murdered thousands all through the [Polish] Ukraine. Many escaped into the cities and forests. Now what?
>
> The news about the Poles dashed my last hope. The Jews trusted them somewhat. They were a minority like the Jews....
>
> Every day brought news of panic and stories of death. Now, many Polish villages were the prime targets of recent events. There were reports of Ukrainians seizing Polish girls in the woods, raping them and then pushing empty bottles into their vaginas, and torturing them to death. "First they did this dastardly thing to the Jewish girls, then to the Polish ones," Avross commented.[526]

Tennenbaum reported from Złoczów: "The neighboring forest had become thick with Ukrainian national partisans, called Banderowce, after their leader Bandera. They were raiding villages, looting, and killing Poles."[527]

As can be expected, there were individual cases of retaliation by the Poles, as well as some organized reprisals, such as those carried out in the following villages: Deraźne (Kostopol county); Olszanica, where 6 Ukrainians died; Chlebowice Świrskie and Czerepin, where from March 9 to 22, 1944, some 130 Ukrainians died; Sahryń, where, according to Ukrainian sources, on March 10, 1944, from 600 to over 800 Ukrainians were killed and, according to Polish sources, on March 9, 200 Ukrainians were killed in battles between BCh/AK units and OUN units supported by subunits of the *SS-Galizien* and local Ukrainian police; Szołomyja, where on the night of June 10, 1944, from 9 to several dozen Ukrainians were killed; Dobra, where on January 9, 1945, 33 people died; Pawłokoma, where on March 3 or 4, 1945, from 300 (Polish estimate) to 324 (Ukrainian estimate) people died; Saków, where on April 4, 1945, 15 Ukrainians were shot; Rudka, where in April 1945, 6 Ukrainians died; Dobcza, where on May 18, 1945, 40 people died; Piskorowice, where 300 Ukrainians were shot at the beginning of June 1945; and Wierzchowiny, where on June 6, 1945, 194 Ukrainians were murdered either by the NSZ, WiN, or the armed forces of the Polish People's Republic.[528]

Indeed, it would be surprising if there had been no such retaliatory measures. Unfortunately, some of these punitive actions involved the slaughter of innocent Ukrainian civilians as well. But as Wiktor Poliszczuk puts it, these actions "in terms of their extent were but a droplet in the sea of the massive murders which the OUN-UPA carried out against the Poles."[529]

Poles and other non–Ukrainians were not the only victims of the OUN-UPA. This organization, which usurped the power of government and spoke in behalf of the Ukrainian nation, also judged, condemned, and executed its own people as traitors. Stepan Bandera testified at his 1936 trial: "We believe that it is every Ukrainian's duty to subordinate his personal affairs and his whole life to the interests and good of the nation. When someone voluntarily cooperates with the enemy in fighting the Ukrainian liberation movement — and with physical means at that — we believe that such a crime of national treason requires the death sentence."[530]

During the ethnic-cleansing campaign, many Ukrainians were labeled "traitors" by the OUN-UPA for a variety of reasons. The sentences handed down against these "national traitors" were just as ruthless as, and often more so than, the atrocities committed against the non–Ukrainian population. One was considered a traitor simply for not joining the OUN. The following two OUN leaflets,[531] as well as numerous testimonies, attest to this "join or die" policy:

TO UKRAINIANS IN
OFFICIAL POSTS AND THE POLICE

In consideration of the political situation brought about by the Germans which could eliminate the intelligentsia and leadership of the Ukrainian nation, the OUN orders [all persons] to immediately vacate their present posts, link themselves up with the OUN and disappear in the territory. Whoever does not leave his position by April 15, and does not come to an understanding in this matter with the OUN, will be punished in the revolutionary manner.
4.IV.1943

Glory to the Ukraine
Glory to the Heroes
Iaroslav Chornomorets

TO ALL UKRAINIANS,
WHO LEFT THEIR LOCALITIES
AND ARE WANDERING AT LARGE

It has been ascertained that many Ukrainians who left the police and civil service have not joined the OUN and are sitting quietly at home or wandering about the territory not realizing the gravity of the moment.

Therefore, the OUN decrees that:

All Ukrainians, who left the police and civil service and are wandering about the territory, should immediately join the OUN and submit themselves to its orders.

After April 20, 1943, the OUN will catch and shoot as deserters all those who will be wandering about the territory.
5.IV.1943

Glory to the Ukraine
Glory to the Heroes
Iaroslav Chornomorets
Okr. Dca OUN

Ukrainians were also killed by the OUN-UPA for other reasons. Bronisław Janik, a member of the Soviet partisans, declared: "Savage hordes of Banderowcy-Bulbowcy brought about such terror in the Ukrainian villages that even Ukrainians well disposed toward us could not offer us any assistance. More than one of them died only because he offered food to the Soviet partisans or showed them the way."[532]

One of these "traitors" was a young Ukrainian girl who committed the crime of exchanging a few words with a soldier of the Red Army. The Ukrainian Nationalists tied her feet to two saplings, bent to the ground for the occasion, and let her go — thus tearing the poor girl in half. No one bothered to ask whether the soldier she had spoken with was Ukrainian.[533]

Another such "traitor" was Wiktor Poliszczuk's paternal uncle, who was shot through the mouth because he dared to speak ill of the UPA. Poliszczuk's in-laws (father, Czech; mother, Polish) were warned by a young Ukrainian of an imminent UPA attack. For this "act of treason," he was hung in the village square with a sign that read: "This will happen to all traitors." No one was allowed to cut him down for several days.[534]

Then there were poor Vasyl and Anna Gienek, good Ukrainian people who often helped the Poles in Berezów Niżny in the county of Kołomyja, the province of Stanisławów. They raised a fine son by the name of Antek, a Banderowiec by force but one who helped the Polish people and ended up joining the Russian army. That final "act of treason" was a death warrant for his Ukrainian parents. They were executed in the "revolutionary manner." Helena Piotrowiak, whose Polish family was saved on several occasions by Vasyl and Anna, as well as by their son, Antek, told the story:

> Sometime after their house was burnt, I saw two bodies hanging from a weeping willow. I ran over to see who they were because I thought that maybe the Ukrainians killed my mother and my sister. There I saw Vasyl and Anna suspended from a single nail under a weeping willow tree. It was a very large nail, this thick [Helena showed me her little finger] and about this long [she measured off a distance of about 30 centimeters with her hands]. Vasyl was dangling from that nail, his feet barely touching the ground. Dried blood was caked on his face and his long matted whiskers were also drenched with blood. On his chest hung a sign: "*Za zradu batkivshchyny*" [For betraying the fatherland].[535]

Among the "traitors" executed by the OUN-UPA were also those who refused to participate in the murder of Poles and those married to them. The latter type of executions occurred in Rokiny Nowe, Czarna Łoża, Czartorysk, Białozórka, Klepaczów, Rejtanów, Zielony Dąb, Deraźne, Koszów, Łyczki, Sucha Łoża, Maria Wola, Mielnica, Antolin, and Łuczyce.[536] An example of the former comes from Uście Zielone, a small town in the county of Buczacz in the province of Tarnopol. A certain Slavko Hulub was hung and perforated with bayonets by the UPA for refusing to participate in the killing of Poles. On his chest was placed a sign that read: *Khto ne z namy, toi proty nas* (Who is not for us, is against us).[537]

In Netreby, the Ukrainian residents, "having nothing in common with the 'Bulba' brand of nationalism, left their homes and moved out to the forests. Since they refused to join the ranks of the engineers of *samostiina Ukraina*, they had to hide in the forests just like the Polish people. They preferred this, however, to the killing of Poles and Jews."[538] And in turn, they themselves were killed. A case in point is the tragic death of Bohdan Steblychyn, a seventeen-year-old Ukrainian lad who had just returned to Berezów Niżny from a forced-labor camp in Germany, only to be murdered, within hearing of his own despairing Ukrainian mother, because he refused to join the Banderowcy. In Berezów Niżny, as throughout "Western Ukraine," Ukrainians "either had to join or be killed."[539] On August 28, 1943, twelve Ukrainian youths were similarly executed in Szeple, Wołyń, because they also refused to join the UPA.[540]

Sometimes repressions against family members of these "traitors to the nation" would follow. Often the executioners were members of the Gestapo-Cheka-like Security Service of the OUN-B, the infamous SB headed by Mykola Lebed, which was also in charge of assassinating Ukrainian opposition members. According to Zynovii Knysh, the Banderowcy killed about four thousand Ukrainian political opponents alone.[541] The SB also killed its own. According to a Czech account, one SB member personally shot eighteen Banderowcy because in his estimation they had fought badly in an encounter with the Germans, an encounter intended to bring in some arms and cattle.[542]

Maksym Skorupskyi noted: "In general, the SB and its activity constituted the blackest page of history in those years ... that police was the law and the court. The Security Service was organized on the German model. The majority of the leaders of the SB were the graduates of the German police school in Zakopane from the years 1939–40. They were mostly Galicians."[543]

Mychailo Podvorniak recalled: "We remember the Bandera SB (Security Services) very well. Our people feared these two letters no less that they feared the NKVD or the Gestapo, because whoever fell into their hands did not escape alive. They explained this cruelty by the fact that there was a state of war, of revolution which demanded a hard hand, firm authority. But this was no excuse because sadists will always be sadists both in time of war and in time of peace."[544]

This, then, was the OUN-UPA.
Such were its World War II heroic battles.
Such were its victories.

Such is its legacy.

In the summer of 1996, in response to a petition requesting combat status for former UPA members, the Ukrainian parliament appointed a commission to conduct a legal-political assessment of the OUN-UPA. Also in response to that petition, 95 members of that parliament, among them leaders of the parliamentary constituencies of the Socialist Party of Ukraine, the Communist Party of Ukraine, the Agrarian Party of Ukraine, and the Peasants' Party of Ukraine, affixed their signatures to the following appeal:

APPEAL
TO THE NATIONS, PARLIAMENTS
AND GOVERNMENTS OF UKRAINE,
BELORUSSIA, ISRAEL, POLAND, RUSSIA,
SLOVAKIA, AND YUGOSLAVIA:

We, the deputies of the Highest Council of Ukraine, turn to the nations, parliaments, governments, and all patriotic political and social organizations in Ukraine, Belorussia, Israel, Poland, Russia, Slovakia, and Yugoslavia in the hope that they will fully realize the danger of the national fascism which now threatens Ukraine. We turn to all of those who can never forget the hundreds of thousands of innocent victims tortured to death by members of the criminal Organization of Ukrainian Nationalists (OUN) and its military formations, especially the Ukrainian Insurgent Army (UPA), whose organizational and ideological activities and practices provide an ample rationale for qualifying them as a variation of Ukrainian fascism. We turn to all those who do not wish to see the eventual rebirth and empowerment in Ukraine of the nationalist-fascist organizations whose members have never separated themselves from their bloody predecessors, who equate their terrible crimes with heroic deeds, who profess the ideology and practice of "integral nationalism," who create detachments of storm troopers, and who are now making a grab for political power.

The programmatic documents of the OUN-UPA, beginning with the resolutions passed by the First Congress of Ukrainian Nationalists (1929), numerous archival materials, court decisions as well as the testimonies of those who witnessed the criminal activities of the OUN-UPA, the 14th division SS "Galizien," the "Roland" and "Nachtigall" battalions, and numerous works of scholars from various nations fully confirm their criminal, fascist nature. The death of hundreds of thousands of murdered civilians of various nations, including Ukrainians, lie on the conscience of the OUN-UPA which usurped unto themselves the right to speak in the name of the Ukrainian nation. Thus, in Volhynia and Galicia alone, these formations were responsible for the bestial murder of at least 100,000 civilians only because they were Poles. The Ukrainian nationalists also actively participated in the crimes of the occupying fascist regime. On their conscience lie the massive murders of civilians — in Babi Yar and Khatyn [not to be confused with Katyn], for example — and the bloody suppression of the anti-fascist uprisings in Belorussia, Poland, Slovakia and Yugoslavia.

Even after its shameful defeat in the years of the Second World War, Ukrainian nationalism continued to conduct its terrible activity on Ukrainian lands. On its hands is the blood of hundreds and thousands of doctors, teachers, agronomists, as well as other skilled workers who came to Western Ukraine with the idea of rebuilding the farm economy ruined by the war and of raising this region from its many years of poverty and darkness. It was the Ukrainian nationalist gangs who terrorized the civilian population for years sowing blood and death. Their crimes call for a well-justified condemnation on the part of our nation. Moreover, their crimes, constituting genocide, qualify for condemnation by the international community. The activities of a whole range of military formations under this movement place the OUN-UPA in the category of criminal organizations as defined by the International Tribunal in Nuremberg.

However, despite historical truth, despite international law as well as the laws of a number of nations, the contemporary heirs of Ukrainian nationalism — taking advantage of currently favorable conditions — are presently conducting a massive campaign to rehabilitate the OUN-UPA, are engaging in efforts to make heroes out of its members, and are demanding that the warriors of the criminal nationalist formations be equated with the soldiers who fought victoriously in the Great Patriotic War [World War II] waged against fascism.

In many towns, particularly in the territories of western districts, city streets and squares carry the names of notorious nationalist criminals, memorials and commemorative plaques are erected and museum complexes are opened in their honor, dates of evil memory are elevated to festive occasions, etc.

Presently, active nationalistic circles have not distanced themselves from the so-called "idea of a unified Ukraine," which was and continues to be the cornerstone of their political platform. It is, therefore, for this reason that pretentious territorial claims are formulated in an aggressive manner vis-à-vis the neighboring nations of Ukraine: Belorussia, Poland and Russia — claims that are not only inconsistent with the Helsinki Accords [Helsinki Final Act of August 1, 1975] agreement, but which could also constitute grounds for the destabilization of the situation in Western Europe. Presently, attempts are being made to give the idea of "unified Ukraine" an aura of legality.

Under the pressure of those seeking a return of nationalistic forces, the situation in Ukraine is leading to a deep social polarization, to a breach of trust and to mutual suspicion. All the more so because Ukrainian nationalism is intent on monopolizing a special social role: that of its own preeminence in the age-old struggle of the Ukrainian nation for independence.

Without a final resolution to a whole range of exacerbated problems, without a profound assessment of the activities of the OUN-UPA, particularly those dating back to the Second World War and the postwar period, without an unequivocal stand with respect to the activities of the neo–nationalists whose exponents are some right-wing political organizations in Ukraine, it will be impossible to achieve peace and harmony in our society.

This problem reaches beyond the internal borders of a single nation; it assumes an international character. In turning to the nations, parliaments, governments, and the political and social organizations of countries whose citizens have suffered the most as a result of the bloody crimes of the OUN-UPA, we propose the creation of an International Commission whose task will be to compile factual information and to prepare a legal-political report consisting of conclusions regarding the activities of the OUN-UPA during World War II and those subsequent to its termination, with the intent of referring these materials to an International Tribunal.

Work in this area is of paramount importance right now — in conditions of ever deepening social destabilization and the orientation of the specified political forces toward the use of naked force and political extremism. The failure to detect the growing danger of national fascism constitutes not only a crime against the memory of bygone days, but also against the future. Only the combined efforts of those nations and people who proceed along the road of freedom, democracy and historical truth can guarantee the progressive flowering of society and avert the danger threatening the continued existence of mankind.

We turn to these nations and people in the hope that they will not ignore this danger. We request the creation of an International Commission whose decisions may help to deter the spread of national fascism which in this day and age is rearing its head in Ukraine.

Deputies of the Ukrainian Parliament
Kiev, August 1996
[95 signatures follow][545]

On May 21, 1997, Presidents Aleksander Kwaśniewski and Leonid Kuchma signed the following historic declaration:

MUTUAL DECLARATION OF THE PRESIDENTS OF THE REPUBLIC OF POLAND AND UKRAINE REGARDING UNDERSTANDING AND RECONCILIATION

The President of the Republic of Poland and the President of Ukraine, mindful of historical accountability to present and future generations of Ukrainians and Poles, as well as the role of Poland and Ukraine in the strengthening of security and stability in East Central Europe, and also appreciative of the importance of the strategic partnership of both nations, guided by the resolution of the Treaty of Good Neighborliness, Friendly Relations and Cooperation of May 18, 1992, certain that the future of Polish-Ukrainian relations should be constructed on truth and justice, as well as deep and sincere understanding and reconciliation, desiring mutually to overcome the complicated heritage of Polish-Ukrainian misfortunes, so that the shadows of the past may not fall on the present and future friendly and partnership ties between both nations and peoples, hereby declare:

In the centuries-old history of Polish-Ukrainian relations there are many moving examples of genuine friendship, mutual assistance and cooperation between both countries. In it are also threads of brotherly military ties, cultural influences enriching both nations, and neighborly good will.

We should not, however, omit the moments of tragedy, such as the ten-year wars in the seventeenth and eighteenth centuries, the manifestation of anti–Ukrainian policies during the twenties and thirties in the twentieth century, and the persecution of the Polish people in Soviet Ukraine during the time of Stalinist repressions. We cannot forget about the blood of Poles spilled in Volhynia particularly in 1942-43, or about the cruelty of the Ukrainian-Polish conflicts in the first years of the postwar era. A separate dramatic page in the history of our relations was writ by Operation "Vistula," aimed at the general Ukrainian community in Poland. To keep silent about all these facts or to present them from a single perspective does not mitigate the suffering of those wronged or their near ones, does not promote a deepening of understanding between our nations. The road to authentic friendship leads above all through truth and mutual understanding. We acknowledge that no end can constitute a justification for resorting to criminal behavior and the use of force, or the application of collective responsibility. At the same time, we must remember that sometimes the sources of these conflicts lay beyond Ukraine and Poland, that they were occasioned by circumstances unrelated to Poles and Ukrainians and imposed upon our nations against their will by undemocratic political systems. We pay homage to the innocent — those murdered, fallen and forcibly resettled Poles and Ukrainians. We condemn those responsible for their suffering. At the same time, we express our gratitude to all those who, in the course of these difficult years, acted in behalf of bringing our nations closer together.

At the present time, Poland and Ukraine are sovereign nations, good neighbors and strategic partners. For that reason, it is imperative to overcome the bitterness lingering in the memories of many Ukrainians and Poles. This is necessitated not only by our respect for democratic values, human rights, and the basic principles and norms of international law, but also by the desire to see Ukraine and Poland within a unified Europe.

The interpretation of our mutual past and its various periods is a task which should be taken up by specialists who, in an atmosphere of openness, will rigorously investigate the facts and prepare their objective assessments.

For the sake of a better mutual understanding between the Polish and Ukrainian nations, a dialogue should be stimulated within the media. Greater advantage should be taken of the capabilities of the Polish citizens of Ukrainian origin and of Ukrainian citizens of Polish origin who, through their work, make significant contributions to the cultural and economic development of our nations. They should be the animators of a close-knit cooperation between Poland and Ukraine. Both nations, for their part, should look after them and support the well-being of the Polish minority in Ukraine and the Ukrainian minority in Poland.

The Republic of Poland and Ukraine will do their part to make sure that the consciousness of young Ukrainians and Poles will not be burdened by the memory of the tragic pages of history. May future generations live in a common European home in which there will be no room for prejudice and mistrust.

With this conviction we, the Presidents of the Republic of Poland and Ukraine, intend mutually to assume guardianship over the preservation of the idea of Polish-Ukrainian understanding and reconciliation.

In former days, our predecessors poured water on swords as a sign of peace, alliance and brotherhood. And today, we Poles and Ukrainians wish to pour feelings of friendship and solidarity into our hearts.

On the threshold of the twenty-first century, let us remember the past but let us think of the future.

President of the Republic
of Poland,
President of Ukraine

Aleksander Kwaśniewski
Leonid Kuchma
Kiev, May 21, 1997

The signing of the above declaration, noted President Kuchma, "is an event awaited by more than one generation" of Poles and Ukrainians. Referring to the ethnic cleansing campaign (but not using the term) carried out by the OUN-UPA and taking a firm stand against his advisors who attempted to delete or soften the reference to the "blood of Poles spilled in Volhynia," he said: "People's blood is not water and if it was spilled, we must say so openly and sincerely."

In his address to the members of the Highest Council of Ukraine, President Kwaśniewski stated: "We understand how tragic were the consequences of Operation 'Vistula' for the Ukrainian victims.... We also wish for your understanding of the suffering of the Polish people during the tragic occurrences in Volhynia, Eastern Galicia and Podole during the war." Kwaśniewski knows whereof he speaks. His wife Jolanta's family was among those who had to flee from Wołyń before the terror of the OUN-UPA.

In conclusion, the above declaration marks the end to the long debate of whether or not the tragic events described in this chapter had ever occurred in southeastern Poland during World War II. Although the perpetrators were not mentioned by name in that declaration, everyone knows the name of the movement and the organization to which they belonged. The greatest crime of Ukrainian integral nationalism, of the OUN-UPA, was neither its collaboration with Nazi Germany in the conduct of the war, nor its separatist ambitions with respect to the legally constituted Second Republic of Poland. Although guilty on both counts, its greatest crime was the crime against humanity: the indiscriminate slaughter of tens of thousands of Polish citizens in southeastern Poland which included the planned, systematic program of genocide of non–Ukrainians and the equally brutal slaughter of Ukrainians who opposed these practices or who spoke out against the OUN-UPA.

In determining the level of responsibility and guilt in such cases, the Nuremberg principle applied to the Nazi leadership holds true: ones culpability increases in direct proportion to one's power in the system. In the case of the Ukrainian Nationalists, the chief blame for this crime against humanity rests on the shoulders of the members of the OUN Provid.

During World War II, the Ukrainian collaborators did much harm to the Polish nation which was their home and which numbered them among its own. They too must stand before the tribunal of historical justice and take their rightful place among those who contributed to that horror, called the Holocaust, which engulfed the Second Republic of Poland and all its citizens.

Conclusion

Poland was devastated by the Second World War or, more precisely, by the twin evil empires of Nazi Germany and the Soviet Union with the assistance of their various accomplices and collaborators. When the war ended, Poland was still a captive nation.

In addition to sustaining substantial territorial and population losses, many of its citizens became permanently displaced. These joined the Polish communities in countries across the globe. According to Soviet sources, in 1989 there were 1,126,000 ethnic Poles living in all the Soviet Republics, concentrated mostly in Belorussia (417,700), Lithuania (258,000), and Ukraine (219,200).[1] These numbers are regarded as low by some Polish demographers, who claim that in 1995 there were still about 2.5 million ethnic Poles in the former USSR, including 700,000 in Belorussia, 500,000 in Ukraine, and 300,000 in Lithuania.[2]

Conversely, Poland itself became extremely homogeneous. Its Jewish and Gypsy populations were all but annihilated by the Nazis. The surviving Jews (some 100,000 in German-occupied Poland), as well as the 150,000 who returned to Poland from Soviet exile, soon emigrated in successive waves between 1946 and 1958. By the end of the 1950s fewer than 30,000 remained in Poland. More left in the late 1960s because of communist anti-Semitic purges. Many of the 25,000 Gypsies who survived (a third of all the Gypsies in prewar Poland) now live in other countries where they sought shelter from the Nazis. Some have returned to resume their interrupted lives in Poland.

Just before the end of the war, millions of Germans fled Poland in advance of the Red Army. The rest were expelled by the communist authorities in the immediate postwar years in accordance with the decree of the Allied Powers at Potsdam. In all, Germany reclaimed about six million of its citizens and Volksdeutsche.

At the same time, during the massive exchange of populations that followed World War II, Soviet Ukraine reclaimed hundreds of thousands of ethnic Ukrainians from Poland. Poland, in turn, reclaimed over one and a half million ethnic Poles — those who were deported from the lost territories in the east to the smaller, prewar German, western "recovered (*odzyskane*) territories" awarded it by the Allies in compensation for the loss of Eastern Poland. On the basis of the September 9 and 22, 1944, Polish-Soviet agreements, between September 1944 and January 1, 1947, some 784,000 Poles were repatriated from Soviet Ukraine, 170,800 from Soviet Lithuania, and 272,000 from Soviet Belorussia. On the basis of the July 1945 agreement, between 1945 and 1950 about 226,000 Poles were repatriated from the interior of the Soviet Union as well. During Phase II (1956 and 1957), more Polish people were repatriated from all these areas.[3]

In addition to the wartime annihilation of Poland's Jewish citizens and the postwar population transfers, the loss of Poland's eastern territories was the principal reason for the homogenization of Poland's population. The Lithuanians, who had lived predominantly in Poland's northeastern provinces, now found themselves included in the Lithuanian SSR, the Belorussians in the Belorussian SSR, and the Ukrainians of Wołyń and Eastern Galicia in the Ukrainian SSR. Moreover, about 150,000

TABLE 15. NATIONAL MINORITIES IN POLAND, 1995

Ethnic Groups	*Seym Commission Estimates*	*Ethnic Organizations' Estimates*
Germans	350,000	1,000,000
Belorussians	250,000	350,000
Ukrainians	250,000	300,000
Lemkos	50,000	60,000
Roma (Polish only)	25,000	30,000
Lithuanians	20,000	25,000
Slovaks	10,000	20,000
Russians (total)	13,000	
Russians	10,000	
Russians, Old Rite	3,000	
Jews	5,000	10,000
Armenians	8,000	15,000
Tatars	2,500	4,000
Greeks (total)	4,500	
Greeks		
Macedonians	4,500	
Czechs	3,000	
Hungarians	400	
Karaites	200	
Wilamowians (Dutch)	60	
Illegal Aliens	500,000–550,000	

TOTAL POPULATION OF POLAND IN 1995:
38,609,000 (Europa World Year Book)
38,792,442 (The World Almanac)

Ukrainians, Ruthenians, and Lemkos from southeastern Poland were forcibly relocated during Operation "Vistula" (Akcja "Wisła") in 1947 to the northern and western regions of the country. This action, condemned by the Polish Senate on August 3, 1990, finally brought an end to the UPA, which used the villages and settlements of the Carpathian region as bases for its continued anti–Polish and anti–Czech terrorist activities while awaiting World War III.

As a result of all these factors, by the early 1950s there remained "officially" only about 10,000 Germans (an extremely contentious figure), 15,000 Lithuanians, 160,000 Belorussians, and 200,000 Ukrainians within the postwar borders of Poland. In the late 1940s, after the Greek Civil War, about 10,000 Macedonians and Greeks also arrived there. The above table reveals the situation in Poland in 1995.[4]

Under the communist régime, which did not recognize ethnicity as a demographic category, the Polish minorities had little hope for achieving any significant cultural autonomy or political representation. The communist policies were assimilationist: "Poland for the Poles." In the 1960s, some gains were made by the minorities under the watchful eye of the Ministry of the Interior, primarily in areas of funding for education and cultural activities. No elbow room was allotted, however, for any independent political activities. These minimal concessions eroded in the 1970s. Meanwhile, no meaningful dialogue ensued between Poland and the Lithuanian, Belorussian, and Ukrainian Soviet Socialist Republics because Moscow handled all foreign relations.

The year 1980 hailed an era of change spearheaded by Solidarity. As the Communist

Party lost its grip on the nation, minority demands were voiced for political representation, parliamentary seats, greater access to the media, and increased funding for educational, cultural and organizational activities. That all ended in 1981 with the imposition of martial law.

In 1989, the cold war strategy pursued so relentlessly by the West for so many years bore fruit: the whole communist house of cards built on sand tumbled to the ground — thanks in large measure to the Polish workers (for whom it was built) and the inspiration provided by the "Polish Pope." Poland was free once more. In June of that year, in the first multiparty elections in fifty years, a Ukrainian won on the Solidarity ticket, and a Belorussian gained a seat in the Polish Seym.

Unlike the Second Republic, the Third Republic of Poland — in word as well as in deed — took a progressive stand on the issue of minority rights in respect to religious, cultural, educational, and political freedoms. Meanwhile, as the citizens of Ukraine, Belorussia, and Lithuania pressed for their own independence, in Poland the minorities representing these countries pressed for additional government funding and support from the Polish government. By comparison, the Polish minorities in these countries fared, and continue to fare, much worse. At times, their very existence has been threatened by the argument that they are, after all, not Poles but Ukrainians, Belorussians, and Lithuanians who happen to speak Polish. Meanwhile, the revival of the Polish language in these territories is perceived as a linguistic threat to the advancement of the native languages.

Given past grievances and the current plight of the minorities in Poland and the rest of East Central Europe, this recent period of transition has not always been smooth. In Poland, some Ukrainians who resettled on former German properties during Akcja "Wisła," are now calling for the return of their former land and properties seized by the Polish government but are not offering to relinquish the land and properties they had originally received as compensation for their losses. Some Ukrainian neo–Nationalists, mostly outside of Poland, are demanding the incorporation of Polish territories into "Greater Ukraine." Religious tensions mount over the return of Uniate churches lost after the transfer of populations. Interethnic tensions escalate over those Ruthenian Lemkos who want to be considered not as "Ukrainian" but rather as a separate ethnic group.

Conversely, concerns are being raised by Poland over the religious and cultural rights of its minorities in Ukraine, demands are being voiced for at least some (Ukrainian) government funding and support for Polish organizations and publications, calls are being issued for the return of some of the Polish Roman Catholic Church properties seized by the communists and most recently by the Uniate Church, and fears have been expressed over growing anti–Polish and anti–Jewish sentiments in Lviv.[5]

Vilnius is another city for which many Poles still have a genuine attachment and to which some have legal claims: pre-World War II land deeds that the Lithuanian government declines to honor. Before Lithuanian independence, some Lithuanians accused Polish minority leaders of trying to undermine their drive for statehood and of siding with the local communists. In spite of the promising results of a recently released survey,[6] Polish activists, in turn, continue to voice their legitimate concerns about the minority status of Poles in Lithuania and continue to hope for an officially recognized Polish university in Vilnius.

Tensions with Belorussia center on certain Belorussians' wish that a part of Poland inhabited by a substantial number of Belorussians (Białystok province) be declared an "ethnic region." (After gaining its independence, Belorussia staked an official claim to Białystok and its hinterlands.) Polish citizens, meanwhile, continue to express their disappointment over the treatment of the Polish minority in Belorussia and the continued attempts to deny the existence of Polish ethnic areas there.

There are no Polish political parties in either Belorussia or Ukraine.

Yet in spite of all these and other difficulties, a great deal of progress has already been made to normalize relations among these four neighboring countries. The first major step in that direction was Warsaw's signed agreements with Ukraine, Belorussia, and Lithuania to respect the current borders. This is a good beginning. Let us hope that the present-day ultranationalistic trends in these four new republics can be kept in check by the good judgment of their citizens and by the lessons of World War II — and Bosnia.

Appendix: Documents

Document 1: Decision of the Conference of Ambassadors, March 15, 1923, on the Subject of the Frontiers of Poland

(Extract)

The British Empire, France, Italy and Japan, signatories with the United States of America, as the principal Allied and Associated Powers, of the Versailles Treaty of Peace:

Considering that by the terms of Article 87, paragraph 3, of the said Treaty, it is for them to fix the frontiers of Poland, which have not been specified by that Treaty;

Considering that it is recognized by Poland that in so far as the eastern part of Galicia is concerned, the ethnographical conditions necessitate an autonomous regime;

Considering that the Treaty concluded between the principal Allied and Associated Powers and Poland on June 28, 1919, has provided for special guarantees in favour of racial, language and religious minorities in all the territories placed under Polish sovereignty;

Considering that so far as its frontier with Russia is concerned, Poland has entered into direct relations with that State with a view to determining the line;

Have charged the Conference of Ambassadors with the regulation of this question.

In consequence, the Conference of Ambassadors:

Decides to recognize as the frontiers of Poland (description follows):

Decides to recognize all Poland's rights of sovereignty over the territories comprised between the frontiers above defined and the other frontiers of the Polish territory, with reserve to the dispositions of the Treaty of Peace concluded at Saint Germain-en-Laye concerning the charges and obligations incumbent upon the States to which any territory of the former Austro-Hungarian Monarchy is transferred.

Done at Paris, March 15, 1923.

Eric Phipps. R. Poincaré.
Romano Arezzana. M. Matsuda.

The undersigned, duly authorized, declares, in the name of the Polish Government, his acceptance of the foregoing dispositions.

Done at Paris, March 15, 1923.

(Signed) Maurice Zamoyski.

Source: Stanisław Skrzypek, *The Problem of Galicia* (London: Polish Association for the South-Eastern Provinces, 1948), pp. 74-75.

Document 2: Excerpts from the Minorities Treaty of June 28, 1919

Art. 2. Poland undertakes to assure full and complete protection of life and liberty to all inhabitants of Poland without distinction of birth, nationality, language, race or religion.

All inhabitants of Poland shall be entitled to the free exercise, whether public or private, of any creed, religion or belief, whose practices are not inconsistent with public order or public morals.

Art. 7. All Polish nationals shall be equal before the law and shall enjoy the same civil and political rights without distinction as to race, language or religion.

Differences of religion, creed or confession shall not prejudice any Polish national in matters relating to the enjoyment of civil or political rights, as for instance admission to public employments, functions and honours, or the exercise of professions and industries.

No restriction shall be imposed on the free use by any Polish national of any language in private intercourse, in commerce, in religion, in the Press, or in publications of any kind or at public meetings.

Notwithstanding any establishment by the Polish Government of an official language, adequate facilities shall be given to Polish nationals of non–Polish speech for the use of their language, either orally or in writing before the courts.

Art. 8. Polish nationals who belong to racial, religious or linguistic minorities shall enjoy the same treatment and security in law and in fact as the other Polish nationals. In particular they shall have an equal right to establish, manage and control, at their own expense, charitable, religious and social institutions, schools and other educational establishments, with the right to use their own language and exercise their religion freely therein.

Art. 9. Poland will provide in the public educational system in towns and districts in which a considerable proportion of Polish nationals of other than Polish speech are residents adequate facilities for ensuring that, in the primary schools, the instruction shall be given to the children of such Polish nationals through the medium of their language. This provision shall not prevent the Polish Government from making the teaching of the Polish language obligatory in the said schools.

In towns and districts where there is a considerable proportion of Polish nationals belonging to racial, religious or linguistic minorities, these minorities shall be assured an equitable share in the enjoyment and application of the sums which may be provided out of public funds under the State, municipal or other budget, for educational, religious or charitable purposes.

The provisions of this Article shall apply to Polish citizens of German speech only in that part of Poland which was German territory in August, 1914.

Art. 12. Poland agrees that the stipulations in the foregoing Articles, so far as they affect persons belonging to racial, religious or linguistic minorities, constitute obligations of international concern and shall be placed under the guarantee of the League of Nations....

Poland agrees that any Member of Council of the League of Nations shall have the right to bring to the attention of the Council any infraction or any danger of infraction, of any of these obligations, and that the Council may thereupon take such action and give such direction as it may deem proper and effective in the circumstances.

Source: Stanisław Skrzypek, *The Problem of Galicia* (London: Polish Association for the South-Eastern Provinces, 1948), pp. 85–86.

Document 3: Excerpts from the Polish Constitution of 1921

Art. 1, par. 1. The Polish state is the common wealth of all its citizens.

Art. 5, par. 2. The State assures its citizens the possibility of developing their personal capabilities, as also liberty of conscience, speech and assembly.

Art. 7, par. 2. These rights cannot be restricted by origin, religion, sex, or nationality.

Art. 109, par. 1. Every citizen shall have the right to preserve his nationality and to cultivate his language and national qualities.

Art. 110. Polish citizens belonging to national, confessional or lingual minorities shall have equal rights with other citizens to establish, supervise and administer, at their own expense, philanthropic, confessional and social institutions, schools and other educational establishments, likewise freely therein to use their language and to carry out the precepts of their religion.

Art. 111, par 1. Freedom of conscience and of religion shall be guaranteed to all citizens. No citizen shall by reason of his faith or his religious convictions be limited in his enjoyment of rights possessed by other citizens.

Source: Stanisław Skrzypek, *The Problem of Galicia* (London: Polish Association for the South-Eastern Provinces, 1948), p. 44.

Document 4: Excerpt from a Statement of Józef Beck in the League of Nations Assembly, September 13, 1934

The existence of such a system of minority protection as exists today has proved to be a complete failure. The minorities themselves gain nothing from it whilst the system, only too often misused in a manner which is quite incompatible with the spirit of the Treaty, has in a great measure become the tool of a slanderous propaganda directed against the States bound by it; it has also become a means of applying political pressure on the countries which freed of all minority protection obligations benefit by the right and prerogative of participation in control.... Awaiting the entrance into force of an universal and uniform system of minority protection, my Government finds itself obliged to refrain as from to-day from all co-operation with the international organs controlling the application of the minority protection system by Poland.

Quite obviously this decision of the Polish Government is in no event directed against the interests of the minorities. These interests have been and will continue to be defended by the Constitution of the Polish Republic which assures the lingual, racial and confessional minorities freedom of development and equality of rights.

Source: Stanisław Skrzypek, *The Problem of Galicia* (London: Polish Association for the South-Eastern Provinces, 1948), p. 87

Document 5: Excerpts from NKVD Instructions Relating to "Anti-Soviet Elements"

5. Index accounting must embrace all persons who, by reason of their social and political background, national-chauvinistic and religious convictions, and moral and political instability, are opposed to the socialist order and thus might be used for anti-Soviet purposes by the intelligence services of foreign countries and by counter-revolutionary centers.

These elements include:

a) All former members of anti-Soviet political parties, organizations and groups: Trotskyists, Rightists, Socialist Revolutionaries, Mensheviks, Social Democrats, Anarchists, and such like;

b) All former members of national-chauvinistic anti-Soviet parties, organizations and groups: Nationalists, Young Lithuanians, Voldemarists, Populists, Christian Democrats, members of Nationalist terrorist organizations ("The Iron Wolf"), active members of student fraternities, active members of the Riflemen's Association (the National Guard), and the Catholic terrorist organization "The White Steed";

c) Former military police, policemen, former employees of the political and criminal police and of the prisons;

d) Former officers of the Tsarist, Petlyura, and other armies;

e) Former officers and members of the military courts of the armies of Lithuania and Poland;

f) Former political bandits and volunteers of the White and other armies;

g) Persons expelled from the Communist Party and Comm-Youth for anti-Party offenses;

h) All deserters, political émigrés, re-emigrants, repatriates, and contra-bandists;

i) All citizens of foreign countries, representatives of foreign firms, employees of offices of foreign countries, former citizens of foreign countries, former employees of legations, concerns, concessions and stock companies of foreign countries;

j) Persons maintaining personal contacts and correspondence abroad, with foreign legations and consulates, Esperantists and Philatelists;

k) Former employees of the departments of ministries (from Referents upwards);

l) Former workers of the Red Cross and Polish refugees;

m) Religionists (priests, pastors), sectarians and the active worshippers of religious congregations;

n) Former noblemen, estate owners, merchants, bankers, businessmen (who availed themselves of hired labor), shop owners, proprietors of hotels and restaurants.

6. In preparing index accounts of the anti-Soviet element, all sources must be utilized, including: agency (informers') reports, special investigative materials, data of the Party and Soviet organizations, statements of citizens, depositions of arrested persons, and other data. As a rule, statements and other official materials must be verified by means of agents.

Source: Keith Sword (ed.), *The Soviet Takeover of the Polish Eastern Provinces, 1939-1941* (New York: St. Martin's Press, 1991), pp. 306–7.

Document 6: Basic Instructions on Deportations Order No. 001223, Dated October 11, 1939

Instructions Regarding the Procedure for carrying out the Deportation of Anti-Soviet Elements from Lithuania, Latvia, and Estonia.

Strictly Secret

1. General Situation

The deportation of anti–Soviet elements from the Baltic Republics is a task of great political importance. Its successful execution depends upon the extent to which the district operative "troikas" and operative headquarters are capable of carefully working out a plan for executing the operations and for anticipating everything indispensable.

Moreover, care must be taken that the operations are carried out without disturbances and panic, so as not to permit any demonstrations and other troubles not only on the part of those to be deported, but also on the part of a certain section of the surrounding population hostile to the Soviet administration.

Instructions as to the procedure for conducting the operations are given below. They should be adhered to, but in individual cases the collaborators engaged in carrying out the operations shall take into account the special character of the concrete conditions of such operations and, in order correctly to appraise the situation, may and must adopt other decisions directed to the same end, viz., to fulfill the task entrusted to them without noise and panic.

2. Procedure of Instructing

The instructing of operative groups by the district "troika" shall be done as speedily as possible on the day before the beginning of the operations, taking into consideration the time necessary for travelling to the scene of operations.

The district "troika" shall previously prepare the necessary transport for conveyance of the operative groups in the village to the scene of operations.

On the question of allocating the necessary number of motor-cars and wagons for transport, the district "troika" shall consult the leaders of the Soviet party organized on the spot.

Premises for the issue of instructions must be carefully prepared in advance, and their capacity, exits and entrances and the possibility of intrusion by strangers must be considered.

Whilst instructions are being issued the building must be carefully guarded by operative workers.

Should anybody from amongst those participating in the operation fail to appear for instructions, the district "troika" shall at once take steps to replace the absentee from a reserve which shall be provided in advance.

Through police officers the "troika" shall notify to those assembled a division of the government for the deportation of a prescribed number contingent of anti–Soviet elements from the territory of the said republic or region. Moreover, they shall briefly explain what the deportees represent.

The special attention of the (local) Soviet party workers gathered for instructions shall be drawn to the fact that the deportees are enemies of the Soviet people and that the possibility of an armed attack on the part of the deportees cannot be excluded.

3. Procedure for Acquisition of Documents

After the general instructions of the operative groups, documents regarding the deportees should be issued to such groups. The deportees' personal files must be previously collected and distributed among the operative groups, by communes and villages, so that when they are being given out there shall be no delays.

After receipt of personal files, the senior member of the operative groups shall acquaint himself with the personal affairs of the families which he will have to deport. He shall, moreover, ascertain the composition of the family, the supply of essential forms for completion regarding the deportee, the supply of transport for conveyance of the deportee, and he shall receive exhaustive answers to questions not clear to him.

Simultaneously with the issuing of documents, the district "troika" shall explain to each senior member of the operative group where the families to be exported are situated and shall describe the route to be followed to the place of deportation. The roads to be taken by the operative personnel with the deported families to the railway station for entrainment shall be indicated. It is also essential to indicate where reserve military groups are stationed, should it be necessary to call them out during trouble of any kind.

The possession and state of arms and ammunition of the entire operative personnel shall be checked. Weapons must be in complete battle readiness and magazine loaded, but the cartridge shall not be slipped into the rifle breech. Weapons shall be used only as a last resort, when the operative group is attacked or threatened with attack or when resistance is offered.

4. Procedure for Carrying out Deportations

If the deportation of several families is being carried out in a settled locality, one of the operative workers shall be appointed senior as regards deportation in that village, and under his direction the operative personnel shall proceed to the villages in question. On arrival in the villages, the operative group shall get in touch (observing the necessary secrecy) with the local authorities: the chairman, secretary or members of the village soviets, and shall ascertain from them the exact dwelling-place of the families to be deported.

After this, operative groups, together with the representatives of the local authorities, who shall be appointed to make an inventory of property, shall proceed to the dwellings of the families to be deported. Operations shall be begun at daybreak. Upon entering the home of the person to be deported, the senior member of the operative group shall assemble the entire family of the deportee into one room, taking all necessary precautionary measures against any possible trouble.

After the members of the family have been checked in conformity with the list, the location of those absent and the number of sick persons shall be ascertained, after which they shall be called upon to give up their weapons. Irrespective of whether or not any weapons are delivered, the deportee shall be personally searched and then the entire premises shall be searched in order to discover hidden weapons.

During the search of the premises one of the members of the operative group shall be appointed to keep watch over the deportees.

Should the search disclose hidden weapons in small quantities, these shall be collected by the operative groups and distributed among them. If many weapons are discovered, they shall be piled into the wagon or motor-car which has brought the operative group, after any ammunition in them has been removed. Ammunition shall be packed together with rifles.

If necessary, a convoy for transporting the weapons shall be mobilized with an adequate guard.

In the discovery of weapons, counter-revolutionary pamphlets, literature, foreign currency, large quantities of valuables etc., a brief report of the search shall be drawn up on the spot, wherein the hidden weapons or counter-revolutionary literature shall be indicated. If there is any armed resistance, the question of the necessity of arresting the parties, showing such armed resistance, and of sending them to the district branch of the People's Commissariat of Public Security shall be decided by the district "troika."

A report shall be drawn up regarding the deportees in hiding or sick ones, and this report shall be signed by the representative of the Soviet party organization.

After completion of the search of the deportees they shall be notified that by a Government decision they will be deported to other regions of the Union.

The deportees shall be permitted to take with them household necessities not exceeding 100 kilograms in weight.

1. Suit. 2. Shoes. 3. Underwear. 4. Bedding. 5. Dishes. 6. Glassware. 7. Kitchen utensils. 8. Food, an estimated month's supply for a family. 9. Money in their possession. 10. Trunk or box in which to pack articles. It is not recommended that large articles be taken.

If the contingent is deported from rural districts, they shall be allowed to take with them small agricultural stocks — axes, saws, and other articles, so that when boarding the deportation train they may be loaded into special goods wagons.

In order not to mix them with articles belonging to others, the Christian name, patronymic and surname of the deportee and name of the village shall be written on the packed property.

When loading these articles into the carts, measures shall be taken so that the deportee cannot make use of them for purposes of resistance while the column is moving along the highway.

Simultaneously with the task of loading by the operative groups, the representatives of the Soviet party organizations present at the time prepare an inventory of the property and of the manner of its protection in conformity with the instructions received by them.

If the deportee possesses his own means of transport, carts shall be mobilized in the village by the local authorities, as instructed by the senior member of the operative group.

All persons entering the home of the deportee during the execution of the operations or found there at the moment of these operations must be detained until the conclusion of the operations, and their relationship to the deportee shall be ascertained. This is done in order to disclose persons hiding from the police, gendarmes and other persons. After verification of the identity of the detained persons and establishment of the fact that they are persons in whom the contingent is not interested they shall be liberated.

If the inhabitants of the village begin to gather round the deportees' home while operations are in progress, they shall be called upon to disperse to their own homes, and crowds shall not be permitted to form. If the deportee refuses to open the door of his home, notwithstanding that he is aware that the members of the People's Commissariat for Public Security have arrived, the door must be broken down. In individual cases neighbouring operative groups carrying out operations in that locality shall be called upon to help.

The delivery of the deportees from the village to the meeting place at the railway station must be effected during daylight; care, moreover, should be taken that the assembling of every family shall not last more than two hours.

In all cases throughout the operations firm and decisive action shall be taken, without the slightest excitement, noise and panic.

It is categorically forbidden to take any articles away from the deportees except weapons, counter-revolutionary literature and foreign currency, as also to make use of the food of the deportees.

All participants in the operations must be warned that they will be held legally accountable for attempts to appropriate individual articles belonging to the deportees.

5. Procedure for Separating a Deportee's Family from the Head of the Family

In view of the fact that a large number of deportees must be arrested and distributed in special camps and that their families must proceed to special settlements in distant regions, it is essential that the operations of removal of both the members of the deportee's family and its head shall be carried out simultaneously, without notifying them of the separation confronting them. After the domiciliary search has been carried out and the appropriate identification documents have been drawn up in the deportee's home, the operative worker shall complete the documents of the head of the family and deposit them in the latter's personal file, but the documents drawn up for members of his family shall be deposited in the personal file of the deportee's family. The convoy of the entire family to the station shall, however, be effected in one vehicle and only at the station of departure shall the head of the family be placed from his family in a car specially intended for heads of families.

During the assembling (of the family) in the home of the deportee the head of the family shall be warned that personal male effects must be packed in a separate suitcase, as a sanitary inspection of the deported men will be made separately from the women and children.

At the station of entrainment heads of families subject to arrest shall be loaded into cars specially allotted to them, which shall be indicated by operative workers appointed for that purpose.

6. Procedure for Convoying the Deportees

The assistants convoying the column of deportees in horse-carts are strictly forbidden to sit in the said carts. The assistants must follow alongside and behind the column of deportees. The senior assistant of the convoy shall from time to time go the rounds of the entire column to check the correctness of the movement.

When the column of the deportees is passing through inhabited places or when encountering passers-by, the convoy must be controlled with particular care; those in charge must see that no attempts are made to escape, and no conversation of any kind shall be permitted between the deportees and passers-by.

7. Procedure for Entrainment

At each point of entrainment a member of the operative "troika" and a person specially appointed for that purpose shall be responsible for entrainment.

On the day of entrainment the chief of the entrainment point, together with the chief of the deportation train and of the convoying military forces of the People's Commissariat of Internal Affairs, shall examine the railway cars provided in order to see that they are supplied with everything necessary, and the chief of the entrainment point shall agree with the chief of the deportation train on the procedure to be observed by the latter in accepting delivery of the deportees.

Red Army men of the convoying forces of the

People's Commissariat of Internal Affairs shall surround the entrainment station.

The senior members of the operative group shall deliver to the chief of the deportation train one copy of the nominal roll of the deportees in each railway-car. The chief of the deportation train shall, in conformity with this list, call out the name of each deportee, shall carefully check every name and assign the deportee's place in the railway-car.

The deportee's effects shall be loaded into the car, together with the deportee, with the exception of small agricultural inventory, which shall be loaded in a separate car.

The deportees shall be loaded into railway-cars by families; it is permitted to break up a family (with the exception of heads of families subject to arrest). An estimate of twenty-five persons to a car should be observed.

After the railway-car has been filled with the necessary number of families, it shall be locked.

After the people have been taken over and placed in the deportation train, the chief of the train shall bear responsibility for all persons handed over to him and for their delivery to their destination. After handing over the deportees the senior member of the operative group shall draw up a report on the operation carried out by him and briefly indicate the name of the deportee, whether any weapon and counter-revolutionary literature have been discovered, and also how the operation was carried out.

After having placed the deportees on the deportation train and having submitted reports of the results of the operations to be thus discharged, the members of the operative group shall be considered free and shall act in accordance with the instructions of the chief of the district branch of the People's Commissariat of Public Security.

Deputy People's Commissar of Public Security of the USSR, Commissar of Public Security of the Third Rank (signed):

SEROV.

Authentic: (Signature)

Source: Keith Sword (ed.), *The Soviet Takeover of the Polish Eastern Provinces, 1939–1941* (New York: St. Martin's Press, 1991), pp. 301–6. With the exception of point no. 5, the above deportation order was also implemented in the Soviet-occupied Polish territories.

Document 7: Katyn Document from Beria to Stalin, Signed by Stalin and Politburo Members Kliment Voroshilov, Vyacheslav Molotov, and Anastas Mikoyan

TOP SECRET

5 March 1940

USSR People's Commissariat for Internal Affairs
March 1940
Moscow

To Comrade Stalin:

A large number of former officers of the Polish Army, former employees of the Polish police and intelligence agencies, members of Polish nationalist, counterrevolutionary parties, members of exposed counterrevolutionary resistance organizations, escapees, and others, all of them sworn enemies of Soviet authority [and] full of hatred for the Soviet system, are currently being held in prisoner-of-war camps of the USSR NKVD and in prisons in the western oblasts of Ukraine and Belorussia.

The military and police officers in the camps are attempting to continue their counterrevolutionary activities and are carrying out anti-Soviet agitation. Each of them is waiting only for his release in order to enter actively into the struggle against Soviet authority.

The organs of the NKVD in the western oblasts of Ukraine and Belorussia have uncovered a number of counterrevolutionary rebel organizations. Former officers of the Polish Army and police as well as gendarmes have played an active, leading role in all of these organizations.

Among the detained escapees and violators of the state border a considerable number of people have been identified as belonging to counterrevolutionary espionage and resistance organizations.

14,736 former officers, government officials, landowners, policemen, gendarmes, prison guards, settlers in the border region, and intelligence officers (more than 97% of them are Poles) are being kept in prisoner-of-war camps. This number excludes soldiers and junior officers.

They include:

Generals, colonels and lieutenant colonels —	295
Majors and captains —	2,080
Lieutenants, second lieutenants, and ensigns —	6,049

Officers and junior officers of the police, border troops, and gendarmerie — 1,030
Rank-and-file police officers, gendarmes, prison guards, and intelligence officers — 5,138
Government officials, landowners, priests, and settlers in border regions — 144

18,632 detained people are being kept in prisons in western regions of Ukraine and Belorussia (10,685 of them are Poles).

They include:
Former officers — 1,207
Former intelligence officers of the police and gendarmerie — 5,141
Spies and saboteurs — 347
Former landowners, factory owners, and government officials — 465
Members of various counter-revolutionary and resistance organizations and various counter-revolutionary elements — 5,345
Escapees — 6,127

In view of the fact that all are hardened and uncompromising enemies of Soviet authority, the USSR NKVD considers it necessary:

1. To instruct the USSR NKVD that it should try before special tribunals
   1) the cases of the 14,700 former Polish officers, government officials, landowners, police officers, intelligence officers, gendarmes, settlers in border regions, and prison guards being kept in prison-of-war camps
   2) and also the cases of 11,000 members of various counterrevolutionary organizations of spies and saboteurs, former landowners, factory owners, former Polish officers, government officials, and escapees who have been arrested and are being held in prisons in the western oblasts of Ukraine and Belorussia and apply to them the supreme penalty: shooting.

2. Examination of the cases is to be carried out without summoning those detained and without bringing charges; the statements concerning the conclusion of the investigation and the final verdict [should be issued] as follows:
   a) for persons being held in prison-of-war camps, in the form of certificates issued by the Administration for the Affairs of Prisoners of War of the USSR NKVD;
   b) for arrested persons, in the form of certificates issued by the NKVD of the Ukrainian SSR and the NKVD of the Belorussian SSR.

3. The cases should be examined and the verdicts pronounced by a three-person tribunal [*troika*] consisting of Comrades Merkulov, Kabulov, and Bashtakov [head of the first special department of the USSR NKVD].

People's Commissar for Internal Affairs of the USSR

L. Beria

Source: Louisa Vinton, "The Katyn Documents: Politics and History," *RFE/RL Research Report* 2, no. 4 (January 22, 1993): 22.

Document 8: Affidavit of Lynda Brayer, December 5, 1993

I, Lynda Brayer, resident of the City of Jerusalem, Israel, make oath and say as follows:

1. I am the Executive Legal Director of the Society of St. Ives, a legal resource centre for human rights operated under the auspices of the Latin Patriarchate of Jerusalem.

2. I am a member of the Israeli Bar and have been practicing law in Israel, specializing in human rights issues, since 1987.

3. Our legal centre currently focuses on issues relating to Palestinians, both in Israel and the occupied territories. In my years of practice, I have dealt with many human rights issues concerning discrimination against Christians and other non–Jews.

4. My own nationality is Israeli; my religion, Roman Catholic; my ethnic heritage, Jewish.

5. All information contained in this affidavit is given, to the best of my ability without bias in favour of any religious or ethnic group and is based solely on my experience of dealing with human rights issues in the state of Israel.

6. As a generality, it should be understood that Israel is a Jewish state. It is not a democratic

state for heterogeneous population consisting of Jews, Christians, Muslims, Bahais, and others.

7. Israel does not have a constitution. It does have a set of primary laws which do provide a basis for a democratic state. However, there are many normal civil benefits, such as ownership of land, public education, access to housing, employment, and health benefits which are the subject of deep-seated discrimination in the sense that they are not equally available to Jews and non–Jews.

8. As a generality, it can be said that these inequalities are systemic and have not been moderated by the rule of law.

9. There are many reasons why effective protection of non–Jews does not exist. The principal reasons are one or all of the following:

1. Protective legislation does not exist.
2. Protective legislation exists but does not provide an effective remedy.
3. The legislation exists but is not enforced by government agencies.
4. The legislation exists but the courts have not upheld the protections.
5. The legislation exists but no practical access to the courts has been available.

10. When non–Jews have sought equitable remedies in the courts they have invariably been unsuccessful. In Israel, the courts have not protected Christian rights when they have conflicted with Jewish rights. This has been true in virtually every kind of civil dispute whether dealing with custodial rights of children, property claims, or any rights where ethnic or religious identity is relevant.

11. By way of brief but graphic example, in a recent case, where the Jewish spouse in a mixed marriage died, the court granted custody of a young child to the Jewish grandparents in preference to the non–Jewish spouse. There were no extraordinary facts in the case to justify the decision.

12. Where discrimination is acknowledged either by the state or social commentators, the explanation is that there are few "bad" guys in a good system. As stated above, it is my opinion that the discrimination is systemic and the system, by its very nature, is discriminatory.

13. Non–Jews very rarely rise to the higher ranks within the hierarchy of the state including courts, diplomatic service, government or other administrative branches. Apart from international agencies, there are few non–Jewish resources to provide protections against discrimination or to promote change.

14. I emphasize that the nature of the discrimination is usually systemic. It is extremely difficult to isolate legislated discrimination in the way in which the South African government entrenched apartheid. Few laws expressly exclude any religious or ethnic group. Rather, preference is simply given to Jews, as opposed to non–Jews, and there is no popular or political will to either acknowledge the exclusion of non–Jews or effective mechanisms of the state to prevent de facto discrimination from occurring.

15. In other words, the allocation of benefits is always done on an individual and discretionary basis, where it is extremely difficult to isolate patterns of discrimination against any particular groups. Similarly, it is also extremely difficult to gather statistical evidence confirming patterns of discrimination.

16. I will provide specific examples within the context of specific discrimination issues about which [name withheld], legal counsel for the claimants, has asked. They are as follows:

Housing

17. Only seven percent of all land in Israel is privately owned. The rest is controlled by the state. Anyone wishing to buy land, whether a property or an apartment, is restricted to a long term lease. Such a lease or, for that matter any purchase, cannot be effected without the permission of the state's Land Authority.

18. Each application to the Land Authority is individual and confidential. It is clearly understood by anybody working within the state of Israel that the intent and purpose of the permission is to consolidate and maintain exclusively Jewish areas, which tend to be the commercially and residentially valuable areas of the country.

19. I cannot recall an occasion when an application to the Land Authority has been granted to a non–Jew in a Jewish area.

20. At the same time, Jewish applications into heterogeneous areas is extremely common. The overall effect is to slowly whittle away at the availability of adequate housing to non–Jews.

21. In regard to rental housing, [name deleted] has informed me that his clients could not

find either private rental or state subsidized housing unless they hid their Christian identity, which they were not prepared to do.

22. If applicant tenants were known to be Christian, it is quite predictable that they would be refused subsidized housing. Again, any individual refusal of state benefit is difficult to isolate. They would not be told, "You are Christians and therefore cannot have an apartment." Instead, the request would be deferred, postponed or simply not answered. If an outright denial is given, another reason will be given, such as: lack of resources, etc....

23. In regard to the denial of housing by a private landlord, there is no legislation to enforce non–discrimination of private sector housing.

24. I have been informed that the claimants were summarily evicted from both a kibbutz and an immigrants' hostel with state funding, for having associated with a Russian-Orthodox priest on the relevant properties.

25. In regard to evictions on grounds of Christian religion, little practical protection is available. An application might have been made to the Magistrate's Court. However, in practical terms, these claimants would have had no effective remedy. There is no agency which would or could prevent an eviction of non–Jews by Jews.

26. In regard to Christians in particular, it is important to understand that the Jewish perspective has been shaped by the long history of Christian pogroms and persecutions in Europe. In addition, the majority of Christians living in Israel are Palestinians, who of course are also politically suspect.

27. Where housing for non–Jews is quite limited, this couple, if able to rent at all, would almost certainly be forced into renting in one of the non–Jewish, primarily Arabic areas where there are no available apartments.

28. Recent documents have finally confirmed that these regions are drastically under-serviced in most civil amenities including schools, water and sewage systems, roads, and other municipal services in contrast to Jewish regions.

Employment

29. Employment operates in a similar manner to housing. Discrimination in hiring Jews, in preference to non–Jews, is assumed as a normal practice.

30. Equal hiring legislation has recently been introduced into Israel. I am not aware of any cases initiated yet under the new legislation and the laws were neither conceived nor intended to protect non–Jews from discrimination.

31. It is unimaginable, at this time in Israel, that an employer could be effectively charged for either firing or refusing to hire a non–Jew because of his race or religion.

32. I personally know many Christians who hide their Christianity for fear of being fired. I also know of many Christians who have been dismissed from employment. Evidence of the discrimination is of course difficult since other reasons will always be given for the dismissal.

33. I am aware of no dismissal case involving a Jewish employer and non–Jewish employee where the employee was able to recover his or her job or receive compensatory damages. For non-Jews, realistic protection from either the courts or state agencies is not available.

Military Conscription

34. Mr. [name deleted] has informed me that one of the claimants received a military conscription notice, that he objected to military service where he might be required to serve in the West Bank or one of the occupied territories and that his objection was dismissed by the military authorities.

35. This information again is consistent with known practices. No formal provision is made for either alternative service or service restricted to the state of Israel itself.

36. However, geographically limited service or alternative service might be permitted on an individual, discretionary basis. It is unrealistic to expect that such discretion would be exerted in favor of a non–Jew, who is overtly Christian.

37. Favourable conscription treatment would ordinarily only be accorded those with significant influence with state or military authorities. The fact of being Christian would almost ensure that favourable treatment would not be granted.

38. A more likely treatment would be to compel service in one of the occupied territories with, upon refusal, a predictable court martial, imposition of a short jail term followed by a "section 21" release. By way of example, this was the treatment given one Christian who recently refused military service.

39. A "section 21" release indicates mental imbalance which would effectively prevent any prospect of reasonable employment. The application form for most state benefits, including education benefits, subsidized housing, health benefits and state employment enquire about military service.

40. A "section 21" would prevent allocation of any benefit which was discretionary and would, in itself, provide an added basis for discrimination.

41. I am informed that one of the claimants had a notice to report to the military by a specified date which has long ago expired. Almost certainly, for that offence alone, he will be court martialled.

42. An additional comment should be made concerning the moral aspect of conscientious objection to service in the Israeli army.

43. In regard to Israeli military practices in the occupied territories, I have considerable knowledge given the centre's work with Palestinian victims.

44. I can say, without reservation, that the Israeli army has instructed all personnel to treat all hors de combat, unarmed civilians in the occupied territories as armed and hostile. The soldiers have orders to shoot if they, in their own discretion, perceive a physical threat.

45. During the entire course of the Intifada, tens of thousands of unarmed civilians, including women and children, have been shot and wounded without any reasonable justification.

46. In almost all cases, disciplinary proceedings were not taken against the soldiers responsible. Where disciplinary action was taken, Israeli soldiers have received minimal punishments, such as a drop in rank.

47. Although the Israeli army claims the shootings only take place within "humanitarian guidelines," those guidelines are purely discretionary and, again, reviewable only on a case-by-case basis.

48. The army refuses to uphold or recognize any of the normal standards cited by UN Conventions such as the Fourth Geneva Convention for the Protection of Civilians during War or Occupation.

49. The overall attitude and treatment of the Israeli military of Palestinian civilians has been extremely aggressive, abusive and, as stated above, frequently murderous.

50. It is difficult for me to understand how refusal to perform military service in such a situation, could be seen as anything other than legitimate conscientious objection to military action which falls far outside acceptable international standards.

Civil Status

51. It should be understood that, within Israel, Israelis are normally classified on their identity card, not as citizens, but as either Jews or Arabs. Those are the two predominant categories.

52. Other non–Jews may simply not be identified. In other words, a blank is left open where nationality is indicated. On other occasions, the person may be identified by prior nationality, such as "Russian." In either case it would be taken as an indication that the person was not a Jew.

53. As stated above, virtually all state benefits flow from Jewish identity. It is, in a sense, a form of covert apartheid.

54. There is an anomaly between the Law of Return and Jewish nationality. Under the Law of Return, a Jew, or a child or grandchild of a Jew is permitted to enter Israel.

55. However, once admitted into Israel, actual treatment of the person, either by the state or private individuals, will really flow from Jewish identity. Certainly in regard to Russian immigrants, a great deal of public concern has been expressed over the number of non–Jews who have arrived. Some figures put that number as high as forty percent.

56. Although there has been some discussion of it, I am not aware of any case where the Ministry of the Interior has actually returned anyone to Russia.

57. However, it must be stated that the Ministry of the Interior has the power to order a non–Jew to leave Israel, thereby revoking their residency. In my view, a Russian Christian cannot rely on having a safe and non–reversible status in Israel.

58. In addition, the Ministry of the Interior, along with the Ministry of Defense, is subject to the Law of Reasons, which means such administrative decisions can be made without having to provide reasons to the person concerned.

Reporting of Discrimination

59. It should be noted that Israel does not have a meaningful free press.

60. The Arabic press is subjected to severe censorship. Normally the Arab papers send all of their copy to state censors three times a day.

61. The Jewish press, whether Hebrew or other language, is not censored. However the Israeli Journalists Association has formally agreed to impose self-censorship.

62. The censorship also relates to human rights abuses occurring in the occupied territories. However the climate of self-censorship is pervasive.

63. Any story which would tarnish the national image of Israel becomes controversial. Israel is very dependant upon American and western democratic support and is very conscious of the image that is projected to the western democracies.

64. Coverage of any story involving discrimination against Christians would have to be quite inflammatory to see the light of day. Stories involving refusal of housing, housing evictions, refusal of employment or health benefits, would simply not be covered.

Health Benefits

65. I have been informed that health benefits were never granted to these claimants, although several requests for the benefits were made.

66. Again, such an account is completely consistent with government or institutional practice rather than an outright refusal, the applicant will be put off in a thousand ways and will never be given a response, but, in the interim will not be allotted benefits.

Conclusion

67. The above comments have been a brief attempt to cover an extremely complex subject. Certainly it can be said that these claimants, if they are Christians who refuse to hide their religious identity, would continue to suffer severe problems of discrimination in regard to employment, housing, and state benefits. They would not ordinarily be given the protection of the state if they suffered harassment or discrimination from private citizens, except in the most egregious circumstances.

68. Their future and that of their children would be extremely bleak particularly if the husband refused military service and they continued to openly disclose their Christian faith. Institutionalized discrimination would lock them into a cycle of poverty which would be very difficult to escape.

69. On this last point, concerning children, I would add that it will be very difficult for the family to maintain its religious identity. Many Christian youth, who do not have a strong religious viewpoint, convert to Judaism because "it is easier to be Jewish." Given the many pressures that a non–Jew is subjected to, it requires a strong religious commitment for anyone, particularly a young person, to sustain their religious identity.

70. I have provided this information at the request of legal counsel. All of the facts and opinions stated are true to the best of my knowledge. I swear this affidavit knowing it may be given the same force and effect as testimony in a court of law.

71. I would add, since some of this material may be viewed in Canada as controversial, that I hold no personal bias or prejudice against any ethnic or religious group. However, as a practicing human rights lawyer, I certainly feel it is important to report discrimination and oppression where it occurs, regardless of the identity of the oppressor or the oppressed.

SWORN BEFORE ME IN THE CITY OF JERUSALEM, STATE OF ISRAEL, ON THE 5TH DAY OF DECEMBER, 1993.

[Seal] [Signature]

A Notary Public of the State of Israel — Lynda Brayer

The above affidavit was released to the general public by Lynda Brayer on May 3, 1994. The following excerpt is taken from her subsequent lengthy address to the Canadian Immigration and Refugee Board. *Ms. Brayer stated the following:*

In Israel there is an absence of an open discussion about the real problems caused by the Zionist legal and social system.... In fact, even in arithmetic, children do not use the cross sign to indicate addition, but rather an upside-down capital T, because the cross sign is indicative of Christianity which is anathema for Jews.

First of all, it must be reiterated that Israel

does not have a Constitution which guarantees and protects human rights and freedoms. There is no recourse in the courts to such a document. Despite the misleading remarks of an Israeli official to the contrary, the Declaration of Independence which speaks of non–discrimination is NOT, and I repeat, NOT, a legal document and cannot be used in the courts. It has been explicitly rejected by the courts as not being legally binding. It is not, and cannot be a reference point for Israeli officials nor for human rights groups.

There are today basic laws — i.e., laws of a constitutional nature which define the State of Israel as a Jewish State and a State for the Jewish people, i.e., it is a "homeland" for the Jews of the world and any and all Jews are encouraged to make their homes there — including my Canadian fellow speaker, Prof. Irwin Cotler. The Jewish nature of the State is stated in the following laws, of which the following are only a sampling.

1. Basic Law: Dignity of Man and his Freedom

> *1. Purpose*
> *This basic law, the purpose of which is to protect the dignity of the person and his freedom, in order to anchor this basic law in the values of the State of Israel as a Jewish and democratic state....*
>
> *10. This basic law does not effect the validity of all laws which were in place on the eve of its legislation.* (It does not cancel all laws discriminating between Jew and non–Jew — L.B.)

N.B. I want to point out that there is no mention of the principle of equality which is regarded as the cornerstone of democracy in the enlightened world.

2. Basic Law: The Knesset

> *7(a) The following lists are prevented from running for election:*
> > *A list of candidates will not participate in elections to the Knesset if in its aims or actions, explicitly or implicitly, is one of the following:*
> > > *1. Negation of the existence of the State of Israel as the* ***state of the Jewish people.***

The later article was interpreted in a decision of the Supreme Court which is the leading precedent for this issue of the Jewishness of the State of Israel, and what this actually means, and can mean, in practice.

Appeal 2/88 Yehoram Ben Shalom et al v. The Central election committee for elections to the Twelfth Knesset. (Court Decisions M/G 4 p. 224 ff.)

The question at stake was whether it was legal for a group of Israelis, who happened to be both Jews and non–Jews, i.e., Arabs, to run for parliament (Knesset) on a platform advocating equality for all the citizens of the State of Israel, irrespective of their religious or ethnic affiliation, and thus promote the political concept of a "State for all its citizens" as opposed to the concept of a "Jewish state" and a "State for the Jewish people." The Court's finding was that according to the law, Israel can only be a Jewish state and a state for the Jewish people in Israel and in the diaspora, and that it was illegal for a party based on the principle of absolute equality of all citizens within the state to run for the Knesset.

Source: Lynda Brayer: sworn affidavit, Jerusalem, December 5, 1993; address to the Canadian Immigration and Refugee Board, Conference on Israel, Montreal, August 19, 1994. Emphases in the original.

Document 9: Chronology of the Kielce Pogrom, July 4, 1946

The following chronology is based on UB documents released after 1989. It must be kept in mind that all these communist documents, and especially the court proceedings, were prepared to back up the official version of what transpired in Kielce.

July 1, 1946 — Monday

A nine-year-old student of the Grzegorz Piramowicz Elementary School, Henryk Błaszczyk, the son of Walenty, residing at 6 Podwalna Street, hitches a ride on a passing cart to the village of Zaborowice (hamlet of Bielaki near Mniów) without his parents' knowledge. Walenty Błaszczyk, anxious about his son's disappearance, begins to look for him. Around 11 p.m. Walenty reports the incident to the Municipal Civil Militia (MO) Station at 45 Sienkiewicz Street.

July 2 — Tuesday

Walenty Błaszczyk and his wife continue to search for their son. The information about the boy's disappearance reaches ever-widening circles.

July 3 — Wednesday

Henryk Błaszczyk, carrying some cherries given to him by Jan Bartosiński, begins his journey back to Kielce [25 kilometers away]. The boy arrives home at 7:00 p.m. Antoni Pasowski, the proprietor, asks the boy where he had been. According to the statement of the father, Walenty Błaszczyk, the boy replied that "he was at Herbska Street where a certain man gave him a parcel to take to a certain house whose address he did not reveal. This was on July 1, 1946. For his trip, the boy ... received 20 zloty. The man showed him the way.... After he arrived at the destination ... the parcel and the 20 zloty were taken away from him and he was put into a cellar.... He was given no food." Pasowski asks whether these people hadn't been Gypsies or Jews. The boy replies that they must have been Jews.

11:00 P.M.

Walenty Błaszczyk informs the MO about his son's return and that "he was supposedly locked in a cellar by Jews."

July 4 — Thursday

Błaszczyk, together with his son and Jan Dygnarowicz, goes to the MO commissariat. As Błaszczyk testifies later, near a building on Planty Street "his son said that that's where he was locked up, and in response to my question whether he would recognize who it was that locked him up, he said that he would recognize him and pointed to a short Jew wearing a green hat standing in a group of three other men." The father and son are received at the MO commissariat by Warrant Officer Kręglicki who was just then ending his night shift. He refers the matter to Lance Corporal Stefan Kuźmiński who takes them to the MO commissariat commander, Sergeant Edmund Zagórski.

8:30—9:00 A.M.

Zagórski issues an order for the detainment of the Jew. Kuźmiński, together with the father and son and four militiamen, go to Planty Street (about 200 meters from the MO commissariat) and arrest a man pointed out by the boy, Kalman Singer. Dr. Seweryn Kahane, Chairman of the Jewish Committee, comes to the station and asks for Singer's release "since he could not have held the boy in a cellar simply because there were no cellars in that building."

9:00—9:30 A.M.

Zagórski orders Stefan Sędek [Investigation Department Deputy Head] "to send his best detectives and the boy with the objectives of verifying the actual state of affairs, finding out from what cellar the boy escaped ... [and] detaining the proprietor of the home and cellar." He also orders him "to send uniformed militiamen with the detectives to guard the house and cellar." A group of nine militiamen leaves a few minutes later. As the militiamen proceed along the street they tell the passers-by and the gathering groups that the boy had escaped from the Jews after being locked up in a cellar. The detectives enter the building with the boy to search for the cellar. The fact that the building does not have a cellar is verified. The militia patrol surrounds the building.

At that time, there were about 50 people just standing around in front of the building and watching the activities of the militia. By telephone, Zagórski notifies the Deputy Chief Militia Commander for the Province, Major Kazimierz Gwiazdowicz of the existing situation. The Chief Commander, Lieutenant Colonel Wiktor Kuźnicki does not report for work until 10 o'clock. Major Władysław Sobczyński, being informed by Department "A" employees about the search of the Jewish building and its surrounding by the militia, orders the officers from the Ministry of State Security (MBP), Sztablewski and Adam Humer (staying in Kielce as referendum advisers), to go with six UB members to 7 Planty Street in order "to convince the militia to leave, and to place their own men at the entrance of the building and not to let anyone in." Major Sobczyński telephones Major Gwiazdowicz and demands the transfer of the boy and Singer to the Provincial Office of State Security (WUBP) and the withdrawal of the militia. Hearing that "this is a political affair ... this is a provocation," Gwiazdowicz replies: "whether this is a provocation, we'll see, but I have to investigate this matter to the end." Colonel Shpilevoi, the Soviet adviser of the WUBP in Kielce, also phones Gwiazdowicz regarding this matter.

9:30—10:00 A.M.

Seven militiamen from the guard platoon under the command of Captain Jan Mucha from the WUBP go to 7 Planty Street. The crowd around the building increases to about 150 people. A considerable part of it consists of women. After searching the house, the detectives take the boy out into the square in front of the building to search for the cellar. The boy "could not find the place where he had been held; once he said that he was held in a kennel ... a pigsty."

Lt. Tadeusz Majewski arrives at the MO commissariat from the Provincial Militia Headquarters. Major Gwiazdowicz and Lt. Tadeusz Majewski, both present, decide to take control of the situation. Dr. Seweryn Kahane phones Major Sobczyński and asks him for help and the withdrawal of the militia. An attempt to disperse the gathering crowd is not successful since "seeing the small number of the militia, it [the crowd] maintained its position and refused to step back any more." Major Sobczyński places a phone call to the headquarters of the Internal Security Corps (KBW) to the Commander of the 2nd Warsaw Infantry Division, Col. Stanisław Kupsza, in the matter of sending troops to 7 Planty Street. He also orders Major Gwiazdowicz to send more militiamen. He calls upon the city fire brigade and fire brigade from "Społem" to disperse the crowd with water. The gathered multitude in front of the Jewish home begins to bombard the windows of the place with rocks.

10:00—10:30 A.M.

Troops appear in front of the Jewish building: 40 soldiers from the KBW, 30 from the 4th regiment of the 2nd Infantry Division, 5 information officers, 30 military policemen and soldiers from the city headquarters. The sight of troops quiets the crowd for a time. Some of the soldiers and militiamen enter the Jewish building. Lieutenants Marian Rypist and Jędrzejczak order the Jews to relinquish their weapons. Six or seven pistols are collected. Not all the residents surrender their weapons, claiming that they had licenses for them.

Testimonies concerning further events are contradictory. Militiaman Ryszard Sałapa: "the soldiers were bringing the Jews out of their flats whom the people attacked with whatever they could get a hold of—sticks, iron rods, stones ... the people shouted: 'Down with Jews!' 'Beat them for our children!' 'Long live the Polish army!' ... The soldiers themselves, being armed, did not respond but blocking their ears ran off to the side, and some entered the building again and led out other Jews."

Lt. Col. Wiktor Kuźnicki phones the Chief Commander of the MO, Gen. Franciszek Jóźwiak, and asks him for permission to withdraw the troops and the security forces.

Sobczyński, by phone, informs the Minister of State Security, Stanisław Radkiewicz, about the situation in Kielce and requests military assistance. Radkiewicz assures him that soldiers from the Security Brigade from Góra Kalwaria would arrive soon. The fire brigade arrives at Sienkiewicz Street. The people cut the hoses. The following persons arrive at Planty Street: Major Sobczyński; Soviet advisor Col. Shpilevoi; city commandant Markiewicz; division commander Col. Stanisław Kupsza; commander of the Militia School on Zagórska Street, Cpt. Mańkowski.

At this time the first shot is fired.

Special report of Major Kazimierz Konieczny (deputy commander for political affairs and training of the 2nd Warsaw Infantry Division), July 5, 1946: "The crowd followed the militia into the building ... destroying the flats and murdering ... the Jews."

Report to Władysław Gomułka and Roman Zambrowski from Hilary Chełchowski and Władysław Buczyński, July 18, 1946: "Some shots were fired by the Jews in self-defense, which made the crowd furious."

Report to the Chief Prosecutor of the Polish Army (WP) from Major Czesław Szpondarski, prosecutor of the Chief Military Prosecution, July 19, 1946: "The militia began to search the flats; they beat the Jews and threw them out of house no. 7 onto the courtyard where the crowd caught them and subjected them to the Lynch Law of rocks."

Statement of Jechiel Alpert: "The soldiers fired through the closed doors and called for surrender, otherwise they would throw a grenade ... the first victims were on the second floor to which only the troops had access."

Report of Stefan Nabiałczyk, an officer from the WUBP in Kielce, August 2, 1946: "After the troops arrived they immediately started firing into the building."

Report of Major Władysław Siedlecki to the minister of the Ministry of State Security (MBP), Stanisław Radkiewicz, August 23, 1946: "In the process of disarming the Jews, one of the soldiers fired for no reason at all. This fact intensified the general excitement and chaos."

11:00—12:00 A.M.

Col. Kupsza sends a group of soldiers under the command of Major Kazimierz Konieczny (deputy division commander) from Division Headquarters to the site of the events. Konieczny orders the firing of warning shots. With Captain Bronisław Bednarz, he forces the crowd to leave the courtyard and posts soldiers around the building. Captain Surowiec [commandant of the Militia School nearby] interrupts classes and orders a march to Planty Street.... Militiamen from the school bring the dead and injured Jews to the city hospital.

Rev. Roman Zelek, pastor of the cathedral, and Rev. Jan Danilewicz arrive at Planty Street. They stated: "On our way we met a cordon of troops and militia and a machine gun post, which did not let us ... reach the Jewish house ... an officer and two civilians arrived. One of the civilians said: 'The security forces have the situation under control; the soldiers are under orders not to allow civilians to enter the area.'"

Jan Wrzeszcz, prosecutor, arrives at the site intending to begin an investigation. In his memoir he wrote: "When I asked who was in charge, I was told that there are several units and each of them is acting on its own.... I turned to the officer standing beside me and said that the crowd should be dispersed.... One should be prepared to use firearms. I was told rather brusquely that no one will issue such an order and that the soldiers would not carry it out." The riots move from Planty Street to other streets of the city. There's a search for Jews in the streets and in the houses. Cases of accidental beatings of a few Poles also occur.

12:00—1:30 P.M.

Sobczyński is informed by the technical director of the steelworks "Ludwików" engineer, Adam Soból, that his workers are preparing to leave the factory for 7 Planty Street. In order to stop the workers by "means of persuasion" Sobczyński sends over two UB people: Błażejewski and Markiewicz. He phones the first secretary of the Provincial Committee of the Polish Workers' Party (KW PPR), Józef Kalinowski, and asks him to "go to the factory, call a meeting, dissuade the workers, and make them abandon their plan." During lunch break, at 12:30, "about 600 workers opened the gate by force and headed in the direction of 7 Planty Street." On their way they took with them workers from the Sawmill No. 1. They "were armed with sticks, bars, stones; they were shouting that the Jews had murdered children, that the militia was firing into the crowd." The workers break through the cordon of troops and militia, reach the square and enter the building.

A meeting is held in the office of the first secretary of the KW PPR. Present: W. Sobczyński, Józef Kalinowski, Henryk Urbanowicz (vice-governor), Julian Lewin (head of the KW PPR Personnel Department). After a half an hour dispute, no agreement is reached as to who should go to 7 Planty Street and speak to the crowd. Józef Kalinowski does not want to do it because he does not want the PPR to be regarded as a defender of the Jews; Henryk Urbanowicz does not want to do it because he resembles a Jew; Julian Lewin, because he is a Jew.

Forty-seven persons from the UB Security Force School from Zgórsko (8 km from Kielce) arrive at the WUBP building. The School principal, Lt. Tadeusz Seweryński, waits for about an hour-and-a-half for an order to proceed to the Jewish house. A meeting is held in Sobczyński's office. Sobczyński: "I would give an order to open fire." Shpilevoi: "Eta nye budyet kharasho" [That would be out of order]. The first group of instructors from the KC PPR, with Hilary Chełchowski and Władysław Buczyński at the head, arrive in Kielce. They mix with the crowd and observe what is happening.

1:30—2:30 P.M.

Col. Stanisław Kupsza sends a squad of 50 people under the command of the division chief of staff, Col. Pollak, to 7 Planty Street. After firing several warning shots and forming a line of defense, the soldiers push the crowd out of the courtyard and the street. The soldiers, militia and the military police surround the house. Guards are posted. The injured and the dead are taken to the city hospital from the square, the flats and the stairs.

2:30 P.M.

Rev. Roman Zelek and Rev. Jan Danilewicz accompanied by three other priests head again to the site of the incident: "It became evident that there was no longer a crowd on Planty Street and that the people standing in small groups on Sienkiewicz and Piotrkowska Streets were behaving themselves."

2:30—3:30 P.M.

The crowd moves from the square and the streets to the schoolyard. Col. Pollak's unit disperses the gathering.

3:30 P.M.

Troops and tanks appear on the streets of Kielce from Góra Kalwaria. Military patrols continuously canvass the city and check everyone's identity papers. Another meeting is held at the office of Governor Wiślicz [Eugeniusz Iwańczyk-Wiślicz]. In the course of the meeting, a fierce argument erupts between Sobczyński and Kuźnicki who accuses the WUBP of "arresting too many people who are unhappy, and [states] that the today's occurrences are the fault of the UB."

6:00 P.M.

A meeting of political party representatives including Henryk Urbanowicz and Jan Wrzeszcz. The following purport of a proclamation is worked out: "To the people of the city of Kielce. The proclamation prepared by Rev. Danilewicz and accepted by Iwańczyk-Wiślicz is hereby put off till arrival of comrades from the KC PPR."

8:00 P.M.

Col. Kupsza proclaims "a curfew from 8:00 p.m. to 5:00 a.m. from this day forward until further notice. The functionaries of the WUBP are continuing the arrests. Edmund Zagórski and the militia patrol which arrested Singer are being detained. About 50 Jews who lived in different parts of the city have been transported to the WUBP."

July 5 — Friday

President Bolesław Bierut issues a statement on the incident in Kielce at the Committee of the National Council (KRN). Before noon the following fly to Kielce from Warsaw: 1) an investigative group with Gen. Stanisław Steca in order to conduct a preliminary investigation; 2) representatives of the Central Committee of Polish Jews [CKŻP] — Adolf Berman and Paweł Zelicki; and 3) Zenon Kliszko, member of the KC PPR Secretariat. The KC PPR instructors organize a meeting with 1,000 employees of the "Ludwików" steelworks. They pass a resolution "condemning the criminal doings of the reactionaries ... [and] the transference of the Nazi methods to Poland by Anders' flunkeys." The proclamation entitled, "To the people of the city of Kielce" was posted all over the city. It was signed by the representatives of the Polish Workers' Party (PPR), Polish Socialist Party (PPS), Polish People's Party (PSL), Democratic Party (SD), People's Party (SL), Polish (communist labor) Party (SP), and the trade unions. Zenon Kliszko denies permission for publishing the proclamations of the Bishops' Council and the governor. All day long searches and arrests; among others, of firemen and militia patrol members who had conducted the searches [in the Jewish house]. The representatives of the CKŻP meet with the surviving Jews. They imply that the Anders' Army was responsible for the pogrom.

July 6 — Saturday

A special train of the Polish Red Cross (PCK) transports 28 injured and 60 other Jewish people to Łódź. Minister Radkiewicz, prosecutor Dąb (chief of the Prosecutors' Supervision office), a group of officers from the MBP, a MBP Special Commission, and a Ministry of Justice Commission arrive in Kielce. Roman Zambrowski instructs the Special Commission to examine the propriety of the action during the incident on the part of the local authorities. The City Supervisory Council (MRN) in Kielce issues a resolution condemning "the impulse of that part of society which so thoughtlessly let itself be provoked into excesses." The KC PPR instructors organize meetings in "Społem," Kadzielnia, the "Granat" factory, and train stations, which disapprove of the pogrom. The following people are arrested: Col. Wiktor Kuźnicki, Major W. Sobczyński, Major Kazimierz Gwiazdowicz, Lt. Dionizy Sidor, Stefan Sędek, and Edmund Zagórski. UB officers search the MO Militia School. Five militiamen found to possess objects from the Jewish house are arrested.

July 7 — Sunday

A proclamation issued by the Bishops' Council which condemned the crime is read in the churches of Kielce: "To all the pastors of the city of Kielce."

July 8 — Monday, 3:00 P.M.

The funeral of the victims of the pogrom. The route of the funeral procession: City Hospital, Kościuszko Street, Słowacki Street, Marmurowa Street, and Pakosz Street. The trucks carry 42 coffins including two small ones of children murdered during the pogrom. The funeral is attended by about 10,000 people. Present: Michał Kaczorowski, Minister of Reconstruction as representative of the Interim National Unity Council (TRJN); Dr. Adolf Berman; Stanisław Radkiewicz; Col. Dawid Kahane, chief rabbi of the Polish army; Eugeniusz Iwańczyk-Wiślicz; delegations of Jews from abroad; delegation from Joint [Distribution Committee]; and a reporter from *Film Polski* (Polish Film).

July 9 — Tuesday

The Supreme Military Court [NSW] at the session in Kielce begins hearing the case against 12 persons charged with "battery, incitement to batter, and the murder of Jews." Attorneys for the defense appointed by the court: Zygmunt Chmielewski, Stefan Grzywaczewski, Józef Okińczyc, Zenon Wiatr, and Roman Cichowski. Attorney Zygmunt Chmielewski applies for exclusion from the defense because "the Military Court is not competent [i.e., does not have jurisdiction] to try civilians ... [because] having received the indictment only yesterday, he did not have time to become acquainted with it, and [because] even the military code provides for five day grace period in which to become acquainted with the indictment." The motion was rejected.

The indictment states that the pogrom "had been carried out by the WiN, the NSZ, and those reactionary elements who see as the only way out, the negation of the present Polish reality."

July 10 — Wednesday

The second day of the trial. Twenty-two witnesses, including four Jews testify. When Ewa Szuchman begins to speak about the army, she is cut short by Prosecutor Czesław Szpondarski who tells her that, "the trial is only a beginning, the whole matter will be impartially examined, and please do not bring up the subject of the army again."

July 11 — Thursday, 1:15 P.M.

The judgment of the court is announced. Nine persons are sentenced to death. In violation of the procedures, the attorneys are made to submit an immediate appeal and a plea for a reprieve. A joint meeting of the KW PPR and the Provincial Committee of the PPS (WK PPS) is held in Kielce. It is decided to "begin arrests among parasitic elements, to close places of entertainment, and to give the vacated premises to the workers." These actions are intended "to shift the people's anger away from the Jews toward the parasitic elements." The Diocesan Council of Kielce issues its own proclamation condemning the pogrom. Cardinal August Hlond [who was not in Kielce at the time of the pogrom] holds a meeting about the pogrom with the western press.

July 12 — Friday

The judges of the Supreme Military Court, Aleksander Michalewicz presiding, hold a closed session in Warsaw and, in the absence of the defense attorneys, decide to dismiss the appeal.

9:25 P.M.

The convicts are executed by a firing squad in a forest near Kielce. Neither their families nor attorneys are notified of the execution.

August 1946

The following persons are dismissed from their posts in Kielce: Józef Kalinowski (First Secretary of the KW PPR), Henryk Urbanowicz (vice-governor), Aleksander Chachaj (Starosta of Kielce), Major Kazimierz Konieczny (Deputy Division Commander), Zofia Machajek (Head of the WUBP — Office of Information and Propaganda), and Prosecutor Jan Wrzeszcz. Aleksander Żaruk-Michalski, Deputy Minister of Public Administration (MAP), announces that the Province of Kielce will be divided into the Provinces of Częstochowa and Radom.

September 1–20, 1946

The decree on the fight against anti–Semitism was withdrawn from the sessions of the Committee of the National Council (KRN). At the KRN session deputies from the PSL, Adolf Berman, and Emilia Hiżowa pose questions concerning the pogrom.

September 25, 1946

Kielce trial against militiamen charged with theft and battery of the Jews. In January 1947 the court renders a decision of acquittal.

September 26–December 3, 1946

Seven other militiamen charged with theft and battery of the Jews are put on trial. Six of them are acquitted at the end of December 1946. The remaining militiaman is given the maximum prison term — 2 years.

From November 18 to 22: fifteen civilians and militiamen from the Municipal Civil Militia (MO) Station are put on trial by the District Military Court in Kielce.

At the beginning of December, another trial is held involving seven soldiers from the KBW. One of them is sentenced to life. Some officers and soldiers from the 2nd Warsaw Infantry Division (4th regiment of Infantry in Kielce) are also tried.

December 13-16, 1946

Major Sobczyński, Col. Kuźnicki and Major Gwiazdowicz are put on trial before the Supreme Military Court in Warsaw. Col. Władysław Garnowski presides. Attorneys for the defence: Jugo-Grodnicki, Antoni Hryniewicz, Mieczysław Maślanko. Acquitted: Gwiazdowicz and Sobczyński. Kuźnicki is sentenced to one year in prison. He is paroled in October 1947. He dies in Kielce in 1948. Gwiazdowicz is killed in Laos in October 1964. Sobczyński dies in Warsaw in 1988.

Source: Zenon Wrona, "Kalendarium tragedii," *Gazeta Kielecka,* June 29, 1990. The above translation takes into account the English version of Wrona's chronology in Stanisław Meducki and Zenon Wrona (eds.), *Antyżydowskie wydarzenia kieleckie 4 lipca 1946 roku: dokumenty i materiały,* vol. 1 (Kielce: Urząd Miasta Kielce and Kieleckie Towarzystwo Naukowe, 1992), pp. 89–100.

Document 10: Nationalist Tendencies and Programmes in the Polish Orthodox Church

The census returns of 1931 gave a total of 3,762,484 Orthodox in Poland. Of these the Ukrainians numbered 1,540,062, the White Ruthenians 903,557, the natives of Polesia of undefined nationality 696,397, the Poles 497,290, the Russians 99,636, the Czechs 21,672....

There are five Orthodox dioceses in Poland: (1) Wilno-Nowogródek, (2) Polesia, (3) Grodno, (4) Volhynia, and [5] the Metropolitan diocese of Warsaw and Chełm....

The Polish State showed much care for the education of the young Orthodox clergy: a seminary was maintained at Wilno and another at Krzemieniec. In Warsaw there was a faculty of Orthodox theology at the University, the dean of that faculty being the Metropolitan Dionysius. In addition, the State maintained at its own expense a hostel for students of Orthodox theology in Warsaw.

In the provinces of Lublin, Polesia, Wilno, Nowogródek and Volhynia, where most of the Orthodox live, there were 1,500 State-aided parishes, and, wherever the religious needs of the population demanded it, sub-parishes were also created.

The Orthodox Church had also several monasteries and convents, the most famous being that of Poczayov [Poczajów] in Volhynia. Every bishopric, monastery and parish had its own landed property. Every parish and sub-parish were allowed its glebe, which varied according to the fertility of the soil and which often amounted to one hundred acres. Both the parochial clergy and the higher church dignitaries received a salary from the Treasury, in addition to the emoluments accruing from their ecclesiastical functions and the incomes derived from church lands. The State Budget made provision for the Orthodox Church, through the Ministry of Church Affairs and Education. The allowance — over two and a half million zloty in the last pre-war year — was sufficient to elicit the remark from the Catholic Press that, taking into account the relative numerical strength of the two religions, the Orthodox parishes were more generously subsidised than the Roman Catholic.

As a result the Orthodox Church was sufficiently provided for, and enjoyed ample protection from the State, in accordance with Poland's traditional religious toleration and care for her subjects, of whatsoever nationality or creed. A Russian church historian, Professor Budanov, testifies in one of his works that in Catholic Poland the inviolability of the possessions of the Orthodox Church was more carefully observed than in Orthodox Muscovy.

Difficulties and Conflicts

A certain dislike of the Orthodox Church inevitably remained in Polish minds from the prewar days when Orthodoxy, exceeding the religious sphere, lent itself as an instrument to the Russifying policy of the Czarist Governments.

The war-time troubles of 1914–20 did much to hinder the normal adjustment of relations between the Polish majority and the Orthodox minority. And it was only natural if institutions destined solely to reinforce Orthodoxy in the country, but not corresponding to any real needs of the people, were abolished. No sooner had the Polish troops entered the Eastern provinces than popular feeling became aroused against things which reminded the Poles too vividly of their many years of bondage. But it must in justice be mentioned that a large number of places of worship was abandoned by the Russian clergy, who returned to Russia with the Czar's retreating armies. Polish claims were sporadic and did not create much resentment on the part of the

Orthodox, as they themselves were aware that many of these institutions were really superfluous. Claims were only put in for such church edifices which had formerly belonged either to the Roman Catholic or the Greek Catholic Church [Uniate] and which the Russian administration had handed over to the Orthodox Church after the Partitions.

A certain difficulty was brought about by the propaganda for union which began at the same time. For centuries the Holy See has striven to gain for Catholicism the hundred million Orthodox of Russia. In accordance with this policy the Catholic episcopate undertook in the Eastern provinces of Poland a campaign in favour of union on the basis of the Eastern Slavonic rite. A number of Orthodox priests, together with their parishioners, having embraced Catholicism, regrettable incidents took place and a number of outrages were perpetrated by both sides. An atmosphere of excitement prevailed, which called for tactful intervention on the part of the Polish authorities. The Uniate campaign in the East and in the province of Lublin led to the creation of over a dozen Catholic parishes of the Eastern rite, embracing a total population of over 30,000 proselytes....

Still more bitterness was caused by the action taken before the Courts by the Catholic episcopate for the return of over 600 church buildings, formerly belonging to the Roman Catholics and the Uniates. The Orthodox Church opposed this action in various ways, and — as we have already mentioned — the Metropolitan Dyonysius attempted to convoke a Synod in order to raise a solemn protest against this claim.

The action of the Catholic bishops was by no means vexatious, but it was intended to establish by legal decision the rights of the Catholic Church and to prevent their becoming barred by lapse of time.

It may here be remarked that the Roman Catholic Bishops, namely Mgr. Łoziński of Pińsk and Mgr. Jałbrzykowski, archbishop of Wilno, repeatedly expressed their desire for an amicable settlement of the dispute by direct negotiations with the Orthodox Church. The Catholic episcopate declared themselves ready to waive their rights to much church estate that had been seized by the Russians in their campaign against the Uniates, but demanded the restoration of a number of possessions in localities where the Catholics had no religious edifices. The Orthodox bishops did not accept the offer of the Catholics, though some of them seemed to understand its advantages.

In view of the then existing legislation the Law Courts declared their incompetency to deal with the matter. In doing so they referred to a Decree of the General Commissioner for the Eastern Territories, issued in 1919, whereby interdenominational disputes concerning churches were to be settled by the administrative authorities, taking the actual needs of the communities into consideration. But the administrative authorities did not like to make use of their rights and things remained as they were.

Nevertheless, the Concordate concluded on February 10th, 1925, between Poland and the Holy See provided an additional agreement concerning property formerly in the possession of the Uniate Church, and on June 20th, 1938, such an agreement was made. It bore upon those lands, churches, chapels and buildings which had been in former times taken from the Uniates but were not, at present, in the hands of the Orthodox. They consequently formed a category apart, of which the Polish State in fact could freely dispose. In virtue of the agreement in question the Holy See waived all the rights of the Catholic Church to this property in favour of the Polish Republic in exchange for roughly twenty-five thousand acres of land to serve the needs of that church and a sum of money to make up for the deficit in land. The Polish Government further undertook to inquire what was the actual state of churches formerly belonging to the Eastern Uniate Church at present in possession of the State and not being used by the Orthodox Church, and wherever possible to make them over to the Catholic Church as its property.

This whole question, in fact, only affected one particular region of Poland, namely that of Chełm, the religious history of which must be kept in mind....

In this region, therefore, for half a century Orthodoxy received every help and encouragement and the all-powerful Government of the Czars made lavish expenditure for its support. And there is nothing astonishing if, as a result, that area was so rich in churches and chapels that after both Catholic and Orthodox parishes had been reasonably provided, a large number of them appeared to be in excess of existing needs. Especially the Orthodox were well supplied as their number had dwindled in the last generation and some of their parishes contained no more than 150 or 200 souls.

Nevertheless the supernumerary churches and chapels of which there was in the region of Chełm about a hundred, became an object of strong desire especially since it became known that they were definitely to become State property or to be turned over to the Catholics. The Orthodox clergy sought to establish *faits accomplis* and to enter into possession of the vacant chapels, although they were often completely out of repair. Sometimes clever stratagems were used, in other cases outright force was applied to occupy premises or perform religious functions in hitherto closed churches. Nationalist Ukrainian elements were only too willing to lend a hand in these irregular proceedings and Ukrainians were numerous among the priests thus illegally put in charge of churches. The Government evidently could not countenance such methods of dealing with objects which now, by virtue of the agreement with the Holy See, had become State property. Also a part of the Orthodox clergy were opposed to these disorderly undertakings.

But in opposing them, light-headed and irresponsible agents started a counter-movement which was unjustifiable and produced much resentment. Certain men in authority were charged with connivance. In any case the fact remains that in an incredibly short time most of the churches and chapels not yet awarded to any denomination in the eastern districts of the voievodship of Lublin were pulled down and ceased to exist.

This outrage was publicly condemned by the Roman Catholic Episcopate of Poland and became the subject of pastoral letters of both Catholic and Orthodox bishops of the Eastern Rite. It produced much bad blood and was not passed over without mention by the country's ill-wishers in foreign lands. Reports on these "anti-Orthodox" disturbances exaggerated and misrepresented, as will always happen in similar occurrences, contributed to distort the picture of the general conditions under which the Orthodox Church in Poland existed in the last years before the outbreak of the present war. These conditions, on the whole, were favourable and promising.

Source: Polish Research Centre (ed.), *The Orthodox Eastern Church in Poland: Past and Present* (London: Polish Research Centre, 1942), pp. 38–46.

Document 11: The Speech of the Deputy Petro Pevnyi, a Member of the Government Bloc, Delivered to the Seym in Open Session, February 5, 1931

In the history of every nation there are splendid chapters, and one of the splendid chapters in the history of the Ukrainian nation will be that relating the part played by the Ukrainian population of Poland in the life of the Polish Republic.

The presence in the Seym and Senate of representatives from the Ukrainian community, and of other National Minorities, is sufficient evidence that the Polish State in no way tends to denationalise or to belittle them, but, on the contrary, treats them on the basis of full political and national equality before the law. The fact that the Government Bloc includes the representatives of all the nationalities which live within the borders of the Polish Republic, and Ukrainians amongst them, is conclusive proof that the Government of Marshal Piłsudski not only affords them its protection but also desires the National Minorities to take an active and effective part in the consolidation and development of the Polish State, demanding in return only a loyal and honest attitude towards the Republic.

In affording this protection, the State in large measure accommodates the methods of its action and its efforts for the satisfaction of Ukrainian necessities to the attitude which Ukrainian representatives adopt towards Polish rule and to their activities among their people.

Experience has clearly shown that the policy of indiscriminate opposition to all things Polish, adopted some time ago by various political groups among the Ukrainians, is a policy which produces no good results. It did no more than destroy good feeling between Poles and Ukrainians and postpone an honest solution of the Ukrainian problem in Poland.

The Ukrainian Group in the Government Bloc consisting of six deputies and two senators elected from Volhynia, has the honour to declare that, remaining loyal to the ideals of the Ukrainian nation, for which her best sons have fought in the past and are fighting now, and desiring at the same time to solve by peaceful means the Ukrainian problem in Poland, it stands firmly by a policy of full loyalty to the Polish State and Constitution. To show what is our attitude towards Polish rule we now declare that, not only as a matter of party discipline but out of deep conviction, we shall vote for the adoption of the Budget as a whole (with, of course, the amendments introduced by the Budget Committee); though we did not find in it sufficient provisions to satisfy the economic and cultural needs of the Ukrainians in Volhynia and for the expenses connected with the convocation of the Autocephalous Synod of the Greek Orthodox Church in Poland.

We are voting for the Budget in order to emphasise the fact that, as representatives of Volhynia, we desire to act in conformity with the opinion of the large mass of its population, who demand from their delegates constructive work and loyalty to the State. When we vote for the adoption of the Budget we see the beginnings of genuinely constructive work for the State which, as it develops, will lead to the solution of the Ukrainian problem in Poland: the solution of a minority problem according to the principles of democracy upon which modern States are founded.

We maintain that the Ukrainian peasantry, the workers, the intelligentsia — in fact, all the Ukrainian peoples of Volhynia — have bound up their fate and their future with the fate and future of Poland. So while we shall continue to cultivate our own national and regional characteristics, we shall strive together with the Polish nation to strengthen and develop the Polish State.

Boldly and openly, with a full sense of our national dignity and of our responsibility to conscience, we declare from this high tribune, on behalf of the population of Volhynia, that we in Volhynia have not afforded, and do not afford now, opportunities for the propaganda of national extremism — what I might call "zoological" nationalism — which makes chaos of Polish-Ukrainian relations, and allows our enemies to wreak destruction upon us, besides belittling the majesty of the Polish Republic.

Differences of historical conditions in the development of various national groups dictate different methods for the defence of national rights. The Ukrainian intelligentsia of Volhynia regard as very dangerous for their province the methods adopted by those political parties which were established outside Volhynia under different conditions of life. So those parties have been supported neither by the Ukrainian intelligentsia nor by the masses of Volhynia; and their political bankruptcy was declared by the last General Elections to the Seym as well as by the General Elections of 1928.

The native population of Volhynia welcomed the assertion of Polish sovereignty in those parts as their deliverance from the yoke of Moscow, and their attachment to Polish rule has been openly shown on many occasions.

The Ukrainians of Volhynia carry out conscientiously all their duties of citizenship towards the State, by paying taxes, providing recruits to the army, and taking part in the work of local self-government. Volhynia demonstrated its real attitude towards the Polish Republic during the visit of His Excellency the President. On that occasion the spontaneous signs of welcome and enthusiasm were probably more striking than any observed by His Excellency in other voivodeships.

The reason why such excellent relations subsist between Poland and the Ukrainian population of Volhynia are, firstly, the proximity of the Soviet frontier, and, secondly, the reports which have come from refugees of persecution suffered by Ukrainians in the Soviet Hell, of property destroyed and of holy relics desecrated. The Ukrainians who live within the Polish frontiers know well that nobody will lay hands upon their land, their houses or their goods — they know that nobody will dare to invade their church and tear the chalice from the hands of the priest at the moment of consecration. While the Greek Orthodox churches in the Bolshevik Hell have been given over to impious men to be used as clubs, in Volhynia their bells still loudly call the people to prayer at every festival. And if to-day there are still controversies outstanding about ecclesiastical affairs, the reason is that the Autocephalous Greek Orthodox Church in Poland has not as yet emancipated itself from the conditions of the past. Therefore the Greek Orthodox people of Volhynia regard as of great importance the proclamation of His Excellency the Polish President on the convocation of a Synod for the Autocephalous Greek Orthodox Church. For us it heralds the regeneration of our Church, protected from the influences of Moscow, and the restoration of its Synod, which is a prime foundation of the Greek Orthodox Church.

The Ukrainian people of Volhynia have a guarantee that they are secure from the Bolshevik soldiery, that their property and their wealth, the fruit of their own toil, will be protected and safeguarded. This guarantee is the source from which springs their loyalty to the Polish State. Accordingly, every Ukrainian, as a citizen of the Polish Republic, is ready to defend its frontiers, whether in the East or in the West, wherever the need may arise, and to stand in the ranks of its army at the first call of the Government.

The war passed over Volhynia, leaving ruins and desolation no less than in Belgium. To-day, after a decade of Polish rule, it would be difficult to find a trace of the conflict. Volhynia healed her wounds without the help or assistance of political parties. But all the time she has been given the very active aid of Polish official institutions, such as the Bank of Agriculture, the Government Land Office and the local authorities, and especially the aid of the State administration, which has recently been so well organised. The unification of scattered holdings, the distribution of land, the general improvement in the national credit — all these have notably contributed, not only to an increase in the prosperity of the people but particularly to the strengthening of Polish rule in Volhynia. We are sure that this will result in the extension of their rights of local self-government, which will enable Volhynia to develop her cultural and economic potentialities.

During the period when Volhynia was under the rule of Moscow it was against the law for teaching to be conducted in the vernacular, for the whole tendency of that regime aimed at the denationalisation of Ukrainians, no less than Poles. We were forbidden as well to organise any educational or economic societies of our own. To-day the Polish authorities do not interfere in matters which concern our own private schools or our cultural societies, so long as they are not governed by revolutionaries or express hostility towards the Polish State. Only these considerations caused the closing-down of some of the Proswita's branches. But educational and cultural societies conducted by the Ukrainian native element outside the influence of political parties are developing in a healthy and fruitful manner. Side by side with them we see the growth of the Co-operative movement on a large scale, of credit societies and — a recent establishment — of the local union of all these communal movements, which will even more closely identify the interests of the Polish and Ukrainian peoples. Our most urgent desires, which we will formulate on another occasion, are for an increase in the number of Ukrainian schools where our mother tongue is taught, for the nationalisation of private schools, and for the further extension of credit to our Co-operative societies, an urgent necessity in face of the present economic crisis.

We wish to express our deep conviction that now the Ukrainian population of Volhynia shows signs of having restored to it again its old traditions of the days when Volhynia was in the vanguard of Western culture and the Piedmont of Ukrainian life. For that reason we put forward no far-reaching demands and we propose no programme extensive in its scope. All these points must be discussed and studied by a special national committee, in the deliberations of which representatives of the Ukrainian community will take part. We mention now the necessity that such a committee should be convened, because we believe that the Ukrainian problem in Poland can be solved agreeably with the spirit of the age and in accordance with its moral dictates.

The other factor which leads to the more peaceful co-operation of Poles and Ukrainians is their common misfortune in having been for many years under the yoke of Moscow.

For more generations than one the national leaders of Poles and Ukrainians gave their lives under the tortures of the Czars or amidst the snows of Siberia. Ukrainians no less than Poles were directed by all possible means into one and the same "Russian sea" into which, according to Russian policy all the "Slavonic streams" were forced to flow into that sea which tried to swallow up all the national currents making for an independent life, and where, even without the protection of Russia and the Czarist knout, even without the so-called "mission" of Russian Socialism (which has drawn from the ranks of the Ukrainians so many able politicians), the factor of denationalisation proves probably even stronger than the pressure of the Czars.

For this reason there are in Volhynia none of the Ukrainian intelligentsia with a wide political outlook who would be the enemies of the Polish State, for we have been confirmed by many generations of experience in the opinion that the solution of the Ukrainian problem is possible only by the close collaboration and agreement of both nations, Polish and Ukrainian. If there is to be a stabilised peace in Eastern Europe, and after that a solution of the Ukrainian problem, a complete and satisfactory solution, Poland cannot be left out of account.

So, as representatives of the Ukrainian nation and members of the Government Bloc, soberly considering a situation which is the result of past or recent events, we feel it our duty to avoid any irritation of Polish-Ukrainian relations, and to make every endeavour to eradicate gradually from the hearts of both nations that feeling of ill-will detrimental to the agreement and mutual confidence which are so necessary for the prosperity of both nations.

To combat all signs of chauvinism and to work for the satisfaction of the needs of the Ukrainian population in Volhynia — whether national, religious or economic — by means of harmonious and close co-operation with the Polish nation: these are our deepest desires. We are sure that they will bring us to the proper solution of the Ukrainian problem in Poland, that they will enrich the culture and develop the distinctive characteristics of Volhynia, and that at the same time they will assist the process of pacification in Eastern Europe, preparing the way for peaceful co-existence and friendship between Poland and the Ukraine.

For the sake of the glorious future of our nation in which we sincerely believe, we, the Ukrainians of Volhynia, consider it our duty and our obligation to co-operate actively with the Polish people, as citizens of a common state, to strengthen the prosperity, the solidity and the power of the Polish Republic, and to increase its sovereign majesty.

It is for these reasons that we cast our votes, as Ukrainian deputies, in favour of the acceptance of the National Budget.

Source: M. Feliński, *The Ukrainians in Poland* (London, 1931), pp. 62–71. Deputy Pevnyi was a Ukrainian from Wołyń.

Document 12: Extract from a Speech Delivered by Deputy Mykhalo Bachynskyi before the Administrative Commission of the Seym, January 21, 1931

If in this speech I use the term "Ruthenian" I ask you not to take the term as a synonym for "Russian." I shall use the term "Ruthenian" as a generic name for the nation dwelling in former Eastern Galicia, now Eastern Małopolska; so it does not connote "Russians" but Ruthenians of the Greek-Catholic rite.

In the same way, I shall use the terms "the Ukraine" and "Ukrainian" only to describe that part of the Ruthenian nation dwelling in Eastern Małopolska which has admitted their use as a national description. When I speak of the Ukrainians I shall refer to all the members of the three Galician-Ukrainian parties and to the members of the U.W.O. [UVO] (the Ukrainian Military Organization).

As the representative of the loyalist part of the Ruthenian nation inhabiting the south-eastern provinces of the Polish Republic, I rise to speak on the extremely important Ruthenian problem and on the motion proposed by the hon. members who represent the Ukrainian groups.

First of all, I want to take this opportunity of expressing a categorical protest against the statement contained in the former motion of the Ukrainian deputies, that the areas inhabited by a Ruthenian population were annexed to the Polish State by force of arms. From this statement it might have been concluded that these areas have been incorporated in the Polish State against the will of the Ruthenian people. As it happens, nobody in 1918 bothered to ask the opinion of the Ruthenian people on the matter.

It is a historical fact that the fighting which took place in 1918 [against the Poles] was forced on the Ruthenian people. It was not the expression of the people's will; it resulted from the machinations of certain individuals, Ukrainian-Galician politicians, who were at the disposition of Austria. The warfare was begun by the Ukrainian-Galician intelligentsia, who were at that time assembled in Vienna, and in particular by a certain group of Ukrainian representatives in the Austrian Parliament, acting with the sanction and collusion of the Austrian Government.

The Hapsburgs eagerly welcomed the idea of creating an East Galician Ukrainian State, which was to remain under their rule, its throne occupied by one of their House, the Archduke Wilhelm Hapsburg, of Żywiec, who even assumed for that purpose the Ukrainian name of Wasyl Wyszywany.

To this end, Austria placed a general staff composed of officers and subalterns, funds, arms, ammunition, transport, etc., at the disposal of the Ukrainian-Galician politicians, promising that all Greek Catholics serving in the Austrian Army would be withdrawn to form special Ukrainian military units.

Previously, however, Charles I. (the last Austrian Emperor of the Hapsburg dynasty), influenced by the Ukrainian-Galician politicians, issued a proclamation commanding all Greek Catholics without exception, living in the territories of the Austrian monarchy, to adopt the name "Ukrainian" as designating their nationality.

Thus the Imperial Decree in a definite and peremptory way disposed of the traditional and historical name of the Ruthenian nation by a single stroke of the pen. The wrong then inflicted upon the Ruthenian nation by Austria has but lately been redressed by the present Polish Government.

Here was the actual genesis of the Polish-Ukrainian troubles, in which the aggressors were not the Poles but the Austro-Ukrainian politicians. If, in 1918, the Ruthenian nation had been given the opportunity of expressing its views on this matter, it would certainly have declared itself against any fighting.

The Ruthenian people, exhausted by the long years of the World War, crushed by Austrian persecutions, and ruined materially and financially, would never have agreed to a war with Poland, a war begun with the sole object of creating a new Ukrainian State dependent entirely upon the Austrians, without any prospect of either cultural or economic development....

The idea of a Ukrainian State under the protection of Germany is outside the sphere of reality. Ruthenians would only agree to it with the proviso that it be entirely modified and changed by the elimination of all German influences, and that our own territories form no part in it. Otherwise the future has in store for this conception a fate such as we saw overtake that other conception in 1918.

The stability and the security of the Ruthenian nation is most closely bound up with the stability and security of the Polish State. For that reason I hold it my sacred duty to do what I can to free the Ruthenian nation from the noxious and harmful influence of the policies followed by the Galician-Ukrainian leaders. This I will effect not by fighting or opposition, but by coming to agreement and understanding with the fraternal Polish nation. As the representative of the loyal Ruthenian nation I will do everything in my power for its cultural and economic development, and for the complete vindication on behalf of my nation of those rights which the Polish Republic guarantees in its Constitution to other citizens.

Source: M. Feliński, *The Ukrainians in Poland* (London, 1931), pp. 71–75. Deputy Bachynskyi was a Ruthenian from Małopolska Wschodnia.

Document 13: "The [1930] Report: A Minority in Poland—The Ukrainian Conflict"

To revisit Eastern Galicia at the present time is to have a sharp and unpleasant reminder of one of the few latent wars that continue to be waged by a wholly submerged nationality. The conflict is between the Poles, who are sovereign, and the Ukrainians or Ruthenes, who are subject.

There is no clear line of demarcation between the two races because their settlements overlap and are intermixed. Under these conditions the best criterion for estimating their numbers is the difference of religious observance, which, more than any other factor, has enabled the Ukrainian national movement in Eastern Galicia to mature. Both races are Roman Catholic in the widest sense of the term, but, whereas the Poles belong to the Latin Rite and follow the usages and traditions of the Western Church, the Ukrainians of Eastern Galicia possess a Uniat Church of their own which uses the Eastern Rite and the Old Slavonic Liturgy. The three East Galician Provinces of Lwów (Lemberg), Stanisławów, and Tarnopol contain nearly 3,500,000 Uniats, about 2,000,000 Latins, and about 500,000 Jews. It is fair to say that to every four Poles there are six or seven Ukrainians. The East Galician Ukrainians belong to the same race as the Ukrainians of Orthodox faith who inhabit Polish Volhynia and the Soviet Republic of the Ukraine; but, as they were cut off from the Ukrainians of Russia while Galicia was under Austrian rule, their language, culture, and general outlook are on a different level.

A Ukrainophil movement, aiming at the exaltation of a peasant dialect into a literary Ukrainian tongue, was started in the Russian University of Kharkoff about the middle of last century. It was not, however, till 30 or 40 years later that it became a serious political factor in Eastern Galicia. By that time a number of educated people had emerged from the peasant mass, and in 1891 a group of Ukrainian Deputies appeared for the first time in the Austrian Reichsrath. The new middle class was recruited almost exclusively from the sons of the Uniat priests, who were permitted to marry in accordance with the tenets of Eastern Christendom.

The War of 1918

As the movement grew steadily in numbers and influence, the Governments of the three Empires and the various national organizations of the Poles took an increasingly active interest in its possibilities. The Poles, who always regarded it as a danger to themselves, worked in Austria and in Russia to obstruct it. Russians and Poles gave their support to a smaller Russophil party, known as the Old Ruthenes, and the Russian Government developed a vigorous propaganda in Eastern Galicia to counteract the new Ukrainian nationalism. Germany and Austria, on the other hand, made use of the Ukrainians as a weapon against Russia and the Poles. They were thus in sympathy with an ecclesiastical ambition to endow the Uniat Church with a national status and extend it into Russia as an instrument for the conversion of the Orthodox.

After the collapse of Austria-Hungary in 1918 the Ukrainians of Eastern Galicia proclaimed a West Ukrainian Republic and fought a war against the Poles, which they lost. A year later the Poles, in alliance with the Ukrainian Ataman Petlura, with whom they had come to terms, made their ill-fated march on Kieff, the failure of which did not prevent them from establishing their frontier once again on the River Zbrucz, the former eastern boundary of Austria, when they concluded a peace treaty with the Bolshevists. The Allied Powers had conceived a plan of giving Poland a mandate over Eastern Galicia for 25 years, but eventually they recognized the whole of the Polish eastern frontier in the consideration that it was acknowledged by Poland, so far as concerned Eastern Galicia, that ethnographical conditions required a system of autonomy.

When to Promise?

The reason why autonomy has not been granted is a simple one. The relations of the two peoples have continued so strained that there has not been the slightest ground for expecting that autonomous institutions would be made to work, or would do anything but widen the area of friction. While the difficulties of getting the Galician Poles to treat the Ukrainians as equals are admittedly great, the policy and behaviour of the Ukrainians during the last decade have rendered conciliatory intervention by the Central Government futile. Any Government inspired by Marshal Piłsudski — whose belief in the benefits of a Polish-Ukrainian alliance has been proved up to the hilt — would not hesitate to overrule the Polish Nationalists if the Ukrainians showed the will to cooperate. That is being done in Volhynia.

Hostility to the State

The attitude of all but an insignificant minority of the Ukrainian parties and organizations has been one of declared hostility to the Polish State, and the politicians have been avowed secessionists, not home-rulers. I cannot do better than quote the following extract from a conversation with one of the most representative of Ukrainian leaders: "We are fundamentally disloyal. We do not want peace. If our people are allowed to enter into friendly cooperation with the Poles they may cease to cherish the dream of an independent Ukraine, which we hope to realize in 30 or 40 years' time. Whatever is done for us, we must always be discontented."

The effects of this doctrine on the everyday life of the two communities can safely be left to the imagination. What is important is that the forces of intimidation at the command of the extremists have prevented many moderate home-rulers from making their peace with the Poles, whom they recognize to be as indigenous to Eastern Galicia as they are. While this state of affairs lasts a Polish Government can no more introduce an autonomous régime than a British Government could persuade Ulster to unite with a Southern Ireland in which there was a Republican majority. The East Galician Poles, like their northern compatriots of Vilna, are animated by a spirit which is comparable to that of Ulster.

The intimidation of moderates is exercised, at bottom, by the U.O.W. [UVO] (Ukrainian Military Organization), a secret and illegal association which aims at being a sort of CADRE. Its recruits are found among lads in the upper classes of the Ukrainian secondary schools, university students, and peasants of the younger generation, but it is controlled by hardened conspirators. Volunteer fire brigades, athletic clubs, and even an organization modelled on the Boy Scouts have been used locally to screen allegiance to the U.O.W. The commander-in-chief is M. Konovalets, a Galician schoolmaster's son, who is now living at Geneva after a long residence in Berlin, whence the funds and munitions of the organization are largely derived.

The interest of German military circles in Ukrainian nationalism is nothing new; it was well established before 1914.

The U.O.W. which has always counted terrorist action among the weapons in its armoury, embarked for the first time last summer on an intensive campaign, immediately distinguishable from the sporadic outrages of former years. There are three possible explanations of this sudden offensive, none of which excludes the others. It may have been that a more conciliatory temper was becoming faintly discernible, which it was thought necessary to nip in the bud. It may also have been that the German friends of the organization wished to cause a diversion in Eastern Galicia; or that a newly-appointed "commander in the field" was over-anxious to prove his worth.

The campaign, which radiated from well-defined centres where there were Ukrainian secondary schools, consisted in the burning of barns, cornstacks and cottages belonging to Polish landlords and peasants, and is believed to have been executed for the most part by senior schoolboys, who were allotted objects to set on fire at some distance from their homes and accomplished their mission on bicycles after nightfall.

Subsidiary attention was given to the cutting of telegraph and telephone wires, and a successful raid was made on a mail-van carrying a large sum in bank notes, in the defence of which a Polish constable lost his life. Communist agents, often appearing in the guise of Nationalists, joined independently in the work. There were nights when parts of the worst-stricken district, Rohatyn, were lighted by the glare in the sky; demoralized and disaffected villages refused obedience to the police; and it became clear that there was an imminent danger of spontaneous reprisals which might have been followed by an outbreak of anarchy. Early in September 57 Polish cottages were destroyed by a single fire at Kozowa, together with the entire crops of their owners.

The Polish Government then decided on extraordinary measures, as any other Government in a similar emergency must have done.

Counter Measures

One method would have been to introduce martial law and military justice, with summary infliction of the death penalty for certain offences. Another would have been to put some thousands of disaffected persons in gaol or concentration camps. Both would have been open to serious objections, and I would not suggest that either was considered. The method chosen was to send a few squadrons of an East Galician cavalry regiment and 1,000 police, who were specially drafted in, on pacificatory tours of the most disturbed regions.

These expeditions conducted their operations in a narrow belt of country, running from the district of Gródek Jagielloński, a few miles to the west of Lwów, through Bóbrka, south of the same city, Rohatyn, Brzeżany and Podhajce, to the district of Tarnopol. In other words, the operations were local, affecting only those districts in which the campaign of terrorism had been most intense and disaffection most rife in the villages. The places in which the troops and police established themselves, for periods varying from a few hours to five days, were deliberately chosen by the authorities, and lists of persons notoriously disaffected were furnished to the officers commanding.

The main accusations against the expeditions are that they inflicted brutal and promiscuous floggings, and that, on the pretext of searching for hidden arms, ammunition, and terrorist literature, they did reckless damage to house property, and particularly to the premises of cooperatives and cultural institutions. There can be no doubt that they felt themselves entitled to inflict corporal punishment on the persons who had been marked out for attention and on any others who offered them resistance. There can also be no doubt that in certain villages, sometimes under provocation and sometimes not, they committed most culpable excesses. But, having obtained entirely independent information about the procedure of the expeditions in some places where excesses were not committed, and having compared the number of places in which the Ukrainians truthfully or untruthfully allege excesses with my estimate of the total number of places visited, I am bound to conclude that even if all the Ukrainian allegations of pulped flesh were to be substantiated — as some undoubtedly have been — the number of visitations accompanied by gross cruelty would still be a small proportion of the whole. A sufficient number of oiled rifles and machine-guns were discovered, some in the houses of parish priests, to justify the search of every suspected hiding-place, even if partial demolition of a thatch or a chimney was involved. I am satisfied that wanton destruction of institutional buildings was not within the Government's intentions, and that in the relatively few places where anything of the sort occurred it was the work of unauthorized individuals.

II. Reconstruction

It must be made plain that the object of the recent repressions, whatever their faults, was not the destruction of Ukrainian culture. Having spent a fortnight in motoring through Eastern Galicia on routes selected by myself, I can only report that in practically every town and most of the larger villages I noticed a branch of the Ukrainian cultural society or a Ukrainian cooperative without going out of my way to find it.

The cooperatives appeared to be doing a vigorous trade, and the signboards over many of them were painted in the Ukrainian national colours of blue and yellow. I also noticed that the number of signs in the Ukrainian alphabet on private houses and shops was much greater than when I made my last visit.

Economically, the Ukrainians have been free to consolidate themselves very rapidly, and more at the expense of the Poles than the Jews. If they have not got more schools and institutions, it is primarily because they have let so many become hives of sedition. It is difficult to understand the inert tolerance of the Polish administration which permitted the Ukrainian gymnasium towns like Rohatyn and Tarnopol to develop into the centres of a terrorist campaign. Ukrainians hold a fair proportion of judicial posts, in some districts over 40 per cent., but not all the judges and prosecutors have proved dependable. Intimidation or the threat of boycott by their own countrymen has prevented Ukrainians from entering the administrative services in any number.

The Austrian Example

The first condition of any lasting improvement in the relations of the two communities is that order should be guaranteed by a stronger administration and police force. One of the main sources of weakness has been the survival of officials trained in the Austrian school, who have found themselves unable to cope with altered conditions. Men of the type that has been producing good results in the eastern marches from Vilna to Volhynia are now being appointed to responsible posts in Eastern Galicia, where their broader vision is sorely needed. The difference between the two types of administrator is this: Those of the older Austrian school resign themselves to the prospect of perpetual strife; they have not the mental equipment to combat the Ukrainian refusal to cooperate with constructive ideas, and their inheritance of Austrian methods of LAISSER ALLER, combined with the fact that they are out of contact with the central government, makes them weak and hesitant when they are called upon to perform the elementary task of suppressing lawlessness and crime. These men are steadily being pensioned off.

The administrators of the new type understand that their first duty is to keep order and that inertia only makes a bad situation worse. But, instead of despairing of ever inducing the Ukrainians to become useful and loyal citizens, they set out to fight the boycott by protecting Ukrainians who might be willing to cooperate with them from the intimidation of their fellow-countrymen, by showing themselves just, benevolent, and constructive administrators in their personal intercourse with such people, and by improving the economic condition of the peasantry. These methods have had some success in the mountainous districts of the South, where political agitation has always been weaker. It is too early to say whether they are ever likely to succeed in Eastern Galicia as a whole, an over-populated agricultural country, in which both over-population and the poverty attendant on it have been much increased since the War by restriction of emigration overseas. The field for constructive work will certainly be widened by the expected passage in the new Seym of a law to introduce in the former Austrian provinces the more representative forms of district and communal self-government which have proved a very helpful asset in the eastern marches. To sum up, new men and new methods are being given trial.

Towards Cooperation

If terrorism and conspiracy, which are at the root of all ills, cannot be eliminated or at least controlled in any other way, it may be found desirable to recognize frankly that Eastern Galicia is in an unhealthy state and furnish it with a GENDARMERIE somewhat on the lines of the frontier guard. When law and order have been established it may be possible to induce the two races gradually to cooperate by the methods indicated, which means starting from the bottom of the scale in the lowest units of administration and self-government.

At the same time it is necessary to face the fact that most Ukrainians regard the Poles as foreigners in their midst and themselves as forced to live in a foreign State against their will. Whether in the long run they will be content to reserve for a more distant future their ambitions of joining the Great Ukraine or forming a buffer State between Poland and Rumania, conceived as the Piedmont of the Ukrainian race, and accept temporary allegiance to the Polish State, depends to a large extent on the play of external factors. Those ambitions can only be realized in the nearer future by war, and if the Ukrainians ever became convinced that Europe as a whole was not heading for war but for peace they might moderate their hostility towards Poland. At present there are no signs of such a change.

The obvious requirement is that there should be full inquiry into the allegations against soldiers and police and punishment of those who are found guilty. I understand that this is being done. It is also hoped that in time members of the Government's party will be able to discuss the situation with some of the Ukrainian Deputies.

It would be unfair not to add that I believe there to be a firm determination in Warsaw and Lwów to make the recent restrictions the end, not the beginning, of a chapter.

Source: Times (London) *Newspapers Limited,* December 12, 18, 1930.

Notes

Introduction

1. The six wars were as follows: the war with the "Western Ukrainian Republic" (1918–19), the Poznanian War with Germany (1918–19), the Silesian War (1919–21), the Lithuanian War (1919–20), the Czechoslovak War (1919–20), and the Soviet War (1919–20). Norman Davies, *God's Playground: A History of Poland*, vol. 2 (New York: Columbia University Press, 1982), p. 394. In these wars, the only assistance received by Poland from the West came from France in the war against the Soviet Union.

2. The June 25, 1919, decision of the Allied Supreme Council allowed Poland to militarily occupy Eastern Galicia to the River Zbrucz. The Treaty of Riga (March 18, 1921) landed the western part of the historic province of Volhynia and a large part of Belorussia in Poland. The Conference of Ambassadors (March 15, 1923) recognized Poland's sovereignty over the area from Eastern Galicia in the south to Wilno and the adjacent territories in the north, thus fixing the eastern border of Poland. See Annex No. 2, "Decision of the Supreme Council of June 25, 1919, Concerning Eastern Galicia," in Stanisław Skrzypek, *The Problem of Galicia* (London: Polish Association for the South-Eastern Provinces, 1948), p. 65; Annex No. 12, "The Treaty of Peace between Poland, Russia and the Ukraine, Signed at Riga, on March 18, 1921," ibid., pp. 72–74; and Annex No. 13, "Decision of the Conference of Ambassadors, March 15, 1923, on the Subject of the Frontiers of Poland," ibid., pp. 74–75.

3. See Jerzy Tomaszewski, *Rzeczpospolita wielu narodów* (Warszawa: Czytelnik, 1985), pp. 53–66.

4. Janusz Bugajski, *Ethnic Politics in Eastern Europe: A Guide to Nationality Policies, Organizations, and Parties* (New York: M. E. Sharpe, 1994), p. 360.

5. Initially, Piłsudski (1867–1935) opted for a federalist, pluralistic solution to the problem of the Ukrainian, Belorussian, and Lithuanian minorities in Poland. Others, like Roman Dmowski (1864–1939), leader of the National Democratic Party, thought that a homogeneous religio-ethnic community was the answer. After Piłsudski's overtures to the above-mentioned minorities failed, he was forced to abandon the federalist plan but nevertheless retained, until his death, a pluralistic disposition toward the minorities in Poland.

6. Jan T. Gross, *Revolution from Abroad: The Soviet Conquest of Poland's Western Ukraine and Western Belorussia* (Princeton: Princeton University Press, 1988), p. 6.

7. As quoted by Andrzej Chojnowski, "Problem narodowościowy na ziemiach polskich w początkach XX w. oraz w II Rzeczypospolitej," in Andrzej Garlicki (ed.), *Z dziejów Drugiej Rzeczypospolitej* (Warszawa: Wydawnictwa Szkolne i Pedagogiczne, 1986), p. 180.

8. The phrase in quotes, "covertly or overtly," is used by Samuel Lipa Tennenbaum to describe the communist orientation of the Zionist followers of Hashomer Hatza'ir. Samuel Lipa Tennenbaum, *Zloczow Memoir* (New York: Shengold Publishers, 1986), p. 55.

9. "Union of Israel" is a world organization of Orthodox Jews founded in 1912. Until 1947, *Agudat Israel* opposed Zionism on religious grounds. Its main governing body is the "Great Assembly." The "Council of Sages," composed exclusively of rabbis, is responsible for its spiritual guidance.

10. Aleksander Smolar, "Jews as a Polish Problem," *Daedelus*, spring 1987, p. 38. Smolar's essay "Tabu i niewinnosć" first appeared in *Aneks* (London) 41/42 (1986): 89–133.

11. Józef Piłsudski, *Pisma zbiorowe: wydanie prac dotychczas drukiem ogłoszonych*, vol. 5 (Warszawa: Instytut Józefa Piłsudskiego, 1937), p. 147.

Chapter 1: Soviet Terror

1. *Okupacja i rozbiór Polski we wrześniu 1939 r.* (Warszawa: Wojskowy Instytut Historyczny, 1992), a map and text prepared for a historical-military atlas, *Polacy na frontach II wojny światowej*. Władysław Pobóg-Malinowski, *Najnowsza historia polityczna Polski, 1864–1945*, vol. 3 (1939–45), (London, 1983), p. 102, states that in 1939, Poland contained 389,500 square kilometers of land and 35.2 million people.

2. In the southeastern provinces, these minorities constituted a significant majority: over 60 percent of the population. Irena Grudzińska-Gross and Jan Tomasz Gross (eds.), *War through Children's Eyes: The Soviet Occupation of Poland and the Deportations, 1939–1941* (Stanford, CA: Hoover Institution Press, 1985), p. 7. Polish edition: *W czterdziestym nas matko na Sybir zesłali... Polska a Rosja 1939–1942* (London: Aneks, 1983). The exact number of persons belonging to these minorities is still debated, since the last census before the war (1931) involved questionable methodology, especially the use of mother tongue as an indicator of nationality. In his *Rzeczpospolita wielu narodów*, p. 35, J. Tomaszewski provides the following official and adjusted census figures (taking religious affiliation into account) for Poland in 1931.

TABLE 16. ETHNIC STRUCTURE OF POLAND IN 1931 (IN THOUSANDS)

Nationality (mother tongue)	***Official***		***Adjusted***	
Polish	21,993	68.9	20,644	64.7
Ukrainian	4,442	13.9	5,114	16.0
Jewish	2,733	8.6	3,114	9.8
Belorussian	990	3.1	1,954	6.1
German	741	2.3	780	2.4
Russian	139	0.4	139	0.4
Lithuanian	83	0.3	83	0.3
Czech	38	0.1	38	0.1
Local (tutejsi)	707	2.2	—	—
Other	11	0.1	11	0.1
Not Given	39	0.1	39	0.1
Total	**31,916**	**100%**	**31,916**	**100%**

Tables listing the 1931 population of Poland by mother tongue and religious affiliation can be found in Jan Jankowski and Antoni Serafiński (comp.), *Polska w liczbach: Poland in Numbers* (London: Polish Lawyers Association in the United Kingdom, 1941), p. 32. Another table entitled "Comparison of Religious Affiliation and Language: Poland, 1931," is in Paul S. Shoup, *The East European and Soviet Data Handbook: Political, Social, and Developmental Indicators, 1945–1975* (New York: Columbia University Press, 1981), p. 165. Other relevant tables in this work are "National Composition According to Language or Ethnic Affiliation: Poland, 1931–1975," p. 138, and "Religious Affiliation: Eastern Europe — Poland 1931," p. 162.

3. *Okupacja i rozbiór Polski*. The annexed territories included the areas of Pomorze, Wielkopolska, Górny Śląsk, and Zagłębie Dąbrowskie, as well as a part of the provinces of Kielce, Łódź, Warszawa, and Białystok.

4. The *gminy* in question formed a part of the territories of Orawa and Spisz, whose ownership had been a source of contention between Warsaw and Prague since World War I. Between 1920 and 1924, some areas of Orawa and Spisz fell to Poland, others to Slovakia. With Germany's support, on the basis of the November 1 and 30, 1938, agreements between Poland and Czechoslovakia, Poland annexed 226 square kilometers (and 4,280 people) of Orawa and Spisz. The following year, on the basis of an agreement (November 21, 1939) between Germany and Slovakia, these territories, along with some previously Polish sections of Orawa and Spisz (a total of 752 square kilometers of land with 30,000 people), were transferred to Slovakia. Czesław Łuczak, *Polska i Polacy w drugiej wojnie światowej* (Poznań: Wydawnictwo Naukowe Uniwersytetu imienia Adama Mickiewicza, 1993), p. 530.

5. David Littlejohn, *Foreign Legions of the Third Reich*, vol. 3 (San Jose, CA: R. James Bender Publishing, 1985), pp. 57, 60. In preparation for the war on Poland, 115,000 Slovak reservists were called up. Three divisions and the Swift Group, a motorized light infantry unit, were formed from these reservists and fought with General Wilhelm List's 14th German Army. Most of the soldiers were demobilized after the Polish campaign but were remobilized after Hitler's attack on the Soviet Union. The two new divisions and a new Swift Group, consisting of 1,346 officers and 40,393 other ranks, became a part of the 17th German Army (part of Army Group South). In 1940,

the Slovak Air Force consisted of three reconnaissance squadrons, three fighter squadrons, one technical wing, and one reserve wing. The total strength of the air force was around 4,000 inadequately trained officers and men. Most of the aircraft were obsolete and were eventually replaced with German planes.

See also Krzysztof Komar Kielecki, "Letters to the Editor," *Gazeta* (Toronto), July 25, 1995. According to this contributor, during the war the Slovak police imprisoned, tortured, and handed over Polish couriers to the Gestapo. Among the victims was the well-known Polish Olympic skier Helena Marusarzówna.

6. According to Pobóg-Malinowski, p. 102, 189,000 square kilometers with 21.8 million people fell to Germany.

7. *Nazi-Soviet Relations,* Woermann memorandum, June 15, 1939, pp. 20–21, as quoted by John Erikson, "The Red Army's March into Poland, September 1939," in Keith Sword (ed.), *The Soviet Takeover of the Polish Eastern Provinces, 1939–1941* (New York: St. Martin's Press, 1991), pp. 8–9.

8. See ibid., p. 9; Ryszard Szawłowski, "The Polish-Soviet War of 1939," ibid., pp. 29, 31; Davies, *God's Playground,* pp. 439–40, and his "The Misunderstood Victory in Europe," *New York Review of Books,* May 25, 1995, point no. 3, p. 8.

9. In particular, the Soviet attack on Poland violated the following five bilateral and multilateral international treaties.

Bilateral: the 1921 Polish-Soviet Treaty of Riga, which stated that Russia and the Ukraine renounced "all rights and claims to the territory lying west of the border established in Article II of the treaty"; and the Polish-Soviet Non-Aggression Pact of 1932, renewed in 1934 for an additional ten years, which stated that both parties agreed to "renounce war as an instrument of national policy in their mutual relations, and to refrain from conducting any act of aggression or invasion against the territory of the other Party, whether independently, or in concert with other Powers."

Multilateral: the 1919 Covenant of the League of Nations (the USSR became a member of the League in 1934); the 1928 Treaty on the Renunciation of War as an Instrument of National Policy (the Kellog-Briand Pact); and the 1933 London Convention on the Definition of Aggression, which was signed in behalf of the USSR by Foreign Commissar Maxim Litvinov, which defined aggression as the invasion of the territory of one state by another, even without a formal declaration of war, and which warned that, "no political, military or other considerations could serve as a justification for such aggression."

See "Introduction," pp. xvi–xvii, and Szawłowski, in Sword, *The Soviet Takeover,* p. 30. The quoted passages come from *Documents on Polish-Soviet Relations,* vol. 1 (London: Heinemann, 1961), pp. 3–8, 15–16, and 16–17, as quoted in the "Introduction." See also Skrzypek, *The Problem of Galicia,* p. 11.

The Soviet arguments for the invasion of Poland — that Poland no longer existed, that Soviet security was threatened, and that the interests of the Ukrainian and Belorussian minorities needed protection — were completely specious. In light of the events that followed, which ultimately embraced the Ukrainian and Belorussian populations of Eastern Poland as well, the last argument must be reckoned among the most bitter of Soviet political ironies. One wonders why the two evil empires, the Soviet Union and Nazi Germany, felt it necessary to justify their unethical conduct in the first place.

10. This phrase, first appearing in the *New York Times* article "The Russian Betrayal" (September 18, 1939), was echoed in a number of newspapers and periodicals throughout the world.

11. Grudzińska-Gross and Gross, *War Through Children's Eyes,* p. 245.

12. The "elections" were held on October 22, 1939. The Polish territories, now called "Western Belorussia" and "Western Ukraine," were incorporated into the Soviet Socialist Republic on November 1 and 2, respectively. After these dates, all residents in these territories became Soviet citizens, whether they wanted to or not. In the summer of 1940, the hundreds of thousands of refugees, streaming in from the west in advance of the German armies, were given a questionnaire with just two questions: (1) Do you wish to adopt Soviet citizenship? (2) Do you wish to return to your country of origin? That country of origin for most refugees, including the Jews, was German-occupied Poland. Fearing the loss of their Polish citizenship, the majority, including the Jews, elected repatriation. Indeed, those registering as Poles were not returned; instead, they were arrested and deported to Siberia. The "committees of aid to the refugees" conducting this compulsory census were organs of the NKVD. Paweł Korzec and Jean-Charles Szurek, "Jews and Poles under Soviet Occupation (1939–1941):

Conflicting Interests," *Polin: A Journal of Polish-Jewish Studies* 4 (1989): 219–20. The interested reader may also want to consult Gross, *Revolution from Abroad,* pp. 71–113, or the shorter treatment of this infamous plebiscite with record-breaking "turnout," in Grudzińska-Gross and Gross, *War Through Children's Eyes.,* pp. 21–26.

13. *Okupacja i rozbiór Polski.* The Belorussian SSR contained the provinces of Nowogródek, Polesie, and Białystok and part of the Warsaw and Wilno provinces. In the south, Wołyń, Tarnopol, Stanisławów, and part of the Lwów province were incorporated into the Ukrainian SSR.

According to Mikołaj Iwanow, "The Byelorussians of Eastern Poland under Soviet Occupation, 1939–1941," in Sword, *The Soviet Takeover,* pp. 254–55, 108,000 square kilometers (53 percent of the 202,000 square kilometers of Soviet-occupied Polish territory) went to the Belorussian SSR, 88,000 (44 percent) went to Soviet Ukraine, and 6,900 (3 percent) were transferred to Lithuania.

According to Pobóg-Malinowski, p. 102, 200,000 square miles with 13.4 million people fell to the Soviet Union.

14. According to J. Tomaszewski's adjusted census figures for 1931 (*Rzeczpospolita wielu narodów,* pp. 78 and 116), these eight provinces contained 4,920,000 Ukrainians, 4,866,000 Poles, between 1,948,000 and 2,226,000 Belorussians, 1,329,000 Jews, and fewer Russians, Lithuanians, Germans, and Czechs.

According to Zbigniew S. Siemaszko, "The Mass Deportations of the Polish Population to the USSR, 1940–1941," in Sword, *The Soviet Takeover,* table on p. 230, there were 5,274,000 (39.9%) Poles, 4,529,000 (34.4%) Ukrainians and Ruthenians, 1,945,000 (14.7%) Belorussians and "local," 1,109,000 (8.4%) Yiddish and Hebrew, and 342,000 (2.6%) Russians, Czechs, Lithuanians, Germans, and others in these Soviet-occupied territories in 1939–41 as classified by mother tongue. Siemaszko derived these figures from the *Concise Statistical Year-Book* (London: Polish Ministry of Information, 1941) and from PB's *Polska Wschodnia 1939–41.*

For another demographic table for these territories, see *Myśl Polska* 6 (June 15, 1941), reprinted in Łuczak, p. 511. A table that is based on the *Concise Statistical Year-Book* and that presents demographic information on both the Soviet and the German-occupied territories of Poland can be found in Piotr Eberhardt, *Polska granica wschodnia, 1939–1945* (Warszawa: Editions Spotkania, n.d.), p. 49. This undated work was probably published in the early 1990s.

15. Davies, *God's Playground,* p. 447.

16. Ian A. Hunter, "Putting History on Trial: The Ukrainian Famine of 1932–33," in John D. Honsberger (ed.), *Gazette* (Toronto) 26 (1992): 147.

17. Mikołaj Iwanow, "The First Punished Nation: Excerpts from the Study *Poles in the Soviet Union, 1917–1990,*" *Panorama Polska* (Warszawa), 502 (November 1991): 9–11, English section, pp. iv–v. See also Mikołaj Iwanow, *Pierwszy naród ukarany: stalinizm wobec polskiej ludności kresowej 1921–1938* (Warszawa: Agencja Omnipress, 1991). For evidence of Stalin's anti–Polish attitudes during the interwar years, see Nikita Khrushchev, "Khrushchev's Secret Tapes," *Time,* October 1, 1990, p. 47. After being accused by Stalin of being a Pole, Khrushchev recalled, "The hunt for Poles had reached the point that Stalin was ready to turn Russians into Poles!"

18. Szawłowski, in Sword, *The Soviet Takeover,* p. 31.

19. For example, in 1940 the Soviets burned large quantities of Polish books in a public display in northeastern Poland. See Karol Liszewski (Ryszard Szawłowski), *Wojna polsko-sowiecka 1939 roku* (London: Polska Fundacja Kulturalna, 1986), pp. 76–77.

20. In Grudzińska-Gross and Gross, *War Through Children's Eyes,* p. 46.

21. Ibid., p. 71.

22. Ibid., pp. 55–56.

23. Ibid., p. 149.

24. Ibid., p. 50.

25. Ibid., p. 199.

26. Ibid., p. 197.

27. Ibid., p. 195.

28. Ibid., p. 172.

29. Ibid., p. 71.

30. Ibid., p. 12.

31. Keith Sword, "Soviet Economic Policy in the Annexed Areas," in Sword, *The Soviet Takeover,* p. 89 and p. 100 n. 9.

32. Ibid., p. 87.

33. For Soviet land reform and collectivization policies, see David R. Marples, "The Ukrainians in Eastern Poland under Soviet Occupation," in Sword, *The Soviet Takeover,* pp. 240–50. According to his sources, by the end of 1939, 2.75 million hectares (about 30 percent of the total land area) were confiscated by the Soviets in Eastern Poland. Of that, 1.31 million hectares were transferred to 474,000 peasants, and the state kept the rest (p. 241). By mid–1941, 2,866 collective farms

were established encompassing 800,000 hectares of land (14 percent of the total land area). Most of these collectives were located in Wołyń (21.5 percent) and Tarnopol (14.8 percent) (p. 247).

34. Grudzińska-Gross and Gross, *War Through Children's Eyes*, p. 13; Stefan Korboński, *The Jews and the Poles in World War II* (New York: Hippocrene Books, 1989), pp. 26–27.

35. This is a Polish government figure. See Gross, *Revolution from Abroad*, p. 227.

36. Aleksander Bregman, *Najlepszy sojusznik Hitlera: studium o współpracy Niemiecko-Sowieckiej 1939–1941*, 3d ed. (London: Orbis, 1967), p. 104. See his chapter 9, "Współpraca wojskowa i gospodarcza," pp. 94–108.

37. Documentary Survey by Vice-Admiral Ossman. *Trials of War Criminals Before the Nuremberg Military Tribunals* (hereafter: *TWC*), vol. 34 (Washington, DC: U.S. Government Printing Office, 1951–52), p. 674. See Ihor Kamenetsky, *Hitler's Occupation of Ukraine, 1941–1944: A Study of Totalitarian Imperialism* (Milwaukee: Marquette University Press, 1956), pp. 19–20.

38. Z. S. Siemaszko, in Sword, *The Soviet Takeover*, p. 234 n. 9.

39. Grudzińska-Gross and Gross, *War Through Children's Eyes*, p. 13.

40. Sword, *The Soviet Takeover*, p. 89.

41. Ibid., p. 100 n. 7.

42. Grudzińska-Gross and Gross, *War Through Children's Eyes*, p. 15.

43. From the Red Army newspaper, *Krasnaya Zvezda* (Red Star), September 18, 1940, as quoted in Sword, *The Soviet Takeover*, Appendix 2, p. 300.

44. The rate of collectivization established under the twenty-one-month Soviet rule at this time in Eastern Poland would not be surpassed until 1948, almost four years after Soviet reoccupation of that territory. Marples, in Sword, p. 249.

45. As quoted by Grudzińska-Gross and Gross, *War Through Children's Eyes*, p. 246 n. 12.

46. Ibid., n. 13.

47. Bogdan Czaykowski, "Soviet Policies in the Literary Sphere: Their Effects and Implications," in Sword, *The Soviet Takeover*, p. 118.

48. Davies, *God's Playground*, p. 451, uses the estimate of 1.5 million. According to estimates of Polish authorities (see Grudzińska-Gross and Gross, *War Through Childrn's Eyes*, pp. xxii and 239 n. 3), over 1.2 million Polish citizens were deported to the Soviet Union. Of these, 880,000 were civilian deportees.

According to Pobóg-Malinowski, pp. 110–11, at least 1.7 million people were forcefully resettled. Of these, 1.08 million were civilian deportees.

According to Z. S. Siemaszko, in Sword, *The Soviet Takeover*, pp. 217–18 and table on p. 230, the total of those deported was 1,646,000, of whom 1,450,000 were residents and refugees (excluding POWs).

Pobóg-Malinowski's estimates (p. 110) for the four massive deportations are as follows: February 1940, 220,000; April 1940, 320,000; June 1940, 240,000; and June 1941, 300,000. Z. S. Siemaszko's estimates (p. 228) for these four deportations are the same except for June 1941, for which he gives the range 200,000–300,000. These numbers amount to between 980,000 and 1,080,000 resident and refugee deportees.

The most recent (1997) Polish count, based on Soviet documents, for those deported is 320,000. This includes: 140,000 during the first, 60,000 during the second, 80,000 during the third, and 40,000 during the fourth deportation. These figures do not include those inducted into the Soviet army or POWs. *Zbrodnicza ewakuacja więzień i aresztów NKWD na Kresach wschodnich II Rzeczypospolitej w czerwcu-lipcu 1941 roku* (Warszawa: Główna Komisja Badania Zbrodni przeciwko Narodowi Polskiemu, 1997), pp. 8–9.

49. Keith Sword, *Deportation and Exile: Poles in the Soviet Union, 1939–48* (London: St. Martin's Press, 1994), pp. viii–ix, 17–18.

50. Grudzińska-Gross and Gross, *War Through Children's Eyes*, pp. xxii–xxiii.

51. Z. S. Siemaszko, in Sword, *The Soviet Takeover*, pp. 217–18.

52. These two tables can be found ibid., p. 230.

53. Grudzińska-Gross and Gross, *War Through Children's Eyes*, p. xxiii.

54. Apolonja Maria Kojder and Barbara Głogowska, *Marynia Don't Cry: Memoirs of Two Polish-Canadian Families* (Toronto: Multicultural History Society of Ontario, 1995), pp. 38–42.

55. Of the 18,632 prisoners mentioned in the March 5, 1940, "top secret" Soviet document — prisoners representing various nationalities and including 10,685 Poles (see Appendix, Document 7) — only the Poles were slated for death. KGB Chief Aleksander Shelepin's report prepared in 1959 for Nikita Khrushchev indicated that 21,857 Poles were executed in 1940. According to that report, of the 11,000 prisoners marked for execution in the occupied eastern territories of Poland, 7,305 were killed.

For an interesting article on Abraham Vidro (Wydra), a Polish Jew who was told about Katyn by Soviet Jewish officers and who kept "the secret" for thirty years, see "A Jewish Major [Yehoshua Sorokin] in the Soviet Security Service Confessed: 'What My Eyes Saw—The World Will Not Believe,'" *Ma'aariv* (Israel), July 21, 1971. According to Vidro's testimony, the massacre was so terrible that many of the Soviet soldiers doing the shooting threw themselves into the pit and committed suicide.

Despite Soviet lies and denials, soon after the discovery of the bodies by the Germans, the Poles had accumulated a substantial body of evidence that pointed directly to the Soviets as the perpetrators of this unprecedented atrocity. An early recapitulation of that evidence can be found in Zdzisław Stahl (ed.), *Zbrodnia katyńska w świetle dokumentów* (London: Gryf, 1948). See also Tadeusz Nieczuja, "Zbrodnia katyńska," *Przegląd Polski* 7, no. 25 (July 1948): 3–9, for a short summary of that work.

For a recent work containing documents and materials from the Soviet archives turned over to Poland in October 1992, see Wojciech Materski (ed.), *Katyn: Documents of Genocide* (Warsaw: Institute of Polish Studies, Polish Academy of Sciences, 1993). The Shelepin note referred to above is on p. 27. See also Vladimir Abarinov, *The Murderers of Katyn* (New York: Hippocrene, 1993).

Four years after the release of Stalin's order, some Russian authors are still attempting to deny the Soviet role in the Katyn executions. See the article on Jurii Muchin's latest work: Zdzisław Raczyński, "Antypolski paszkwil w Dumie," *Gazeta* (Toronto), January 25, 1996.

56. J. J. Danielski and M. Lubinski, "Polish Officers in Soviet Captivity, 1939–41: An Introduction to Postal History," *American Philatelist*, January 1996, pp. 48–49, 51.

57. Sławomir Kalbarczyk, *Wykaz łagrów sowieckich miejsc przymusowej pracy obywateli polskich w latach 1939–1943*, Part One (Warszawa: Główna Komisja Badania Zbrodni przeciwko Narodowi Polskiemu, Instytut Pamięci Narodowej, 1993), pp. 11–12. See also Kazimierz Zamorski, "Arrest and Imprisonment in the Light of Soviet Law," in Sword, *The Soviet Takeover*, pp. 201–16.

58. Aleksandr I. Solzhenitsyn, *The Gulag Archipelago, 1918–1956: An Experiment in Literary Investigation*, 1st ed. (New York: Harper and Row, 1973), p. 282.

59. As quoted by Zamorski, in Sword, *The Soviet Takeover*, p. 210.

60. As quoted by Jan Malanowski, "Sociological Aspects of the Annexation of Poland's Eastern Provinces to the USSR in 1939–41," in Sword, *The Soviet Takeover*, p. 78.

61. Kalbarczyk, p. 12.

62. Krzysztof Popiński, Aleksandr Kokurin, and Aleksandr Gurjanow, *Drogi śmierci* (Warszawa: Karta, 1995), p. 68. See also Gross, *Revolution from Abroad*, pp. 154–55, and Kalbarczyk, pp. 14, 24–25 nn. 22, 23, and 24.

63. Maria Wardzyńska, *Sytuacja ludności polskiej w Generalnym Komisariacie Litwy, czerwiec 1941–lipiec 1944* (Warszawa: Agencja Wydawnicza MAKO, 1993), p. 24.

64. Popiński, Kokurin, and Gurjanow, p. 23. For a list of ninety-nine POW camps in Eastern Poland, see Jan T. Gross, "Polish POW Camps in the Soviet-Occupied Western Ukraine," in Sword, *The Soviet Takeover*, pp. 53–54.

65. This summary comes from Zbigniew Schneigert, "Obozy NKWD jeńców polskich z lat 1939–1941 w Małopolsce Wschodniej," *Semper Fidelis* (Wrocław) 3, no. 4 (1992): 24–29; Gross, in Sword, *The Soviet Takeover*, pp. 44–52; and Popiński, Kokurin, and Gurjanow, pp. 7, 23–24. See also Zbigniew S. Siemaszko, *W sowieckim osaczeniu 1939–1943* (London: Polska Fundacja Kulturalna, 1991).

66. These three testimonies can be found in Schneigert, p. 29. For additional accounts, see Gross, *Revolution from Abroad*, pp. 183–84.

67. See Antoni Galiński, "Ewakuacja więzień kresowych," in *My, Sybiracy* 3 (1992). For a recent historical account of these Soviet executions, including copious documents and tables, see Popiński, Kokurin, and Gujanow,

68. Table 3 can be found in Popiński, Kokurin, and Gurjanow, pp. 31–32.

69. See AŻE, "Zapomniana zbrodnia," *Gazeta Wyborcza*, June 23, 1995, and Agnieszka Szyszko, "Ślady zbrodni," *Życie Warszawy*, June 23, 1995. German estimates for the number of prisoners in Łuck range from 1,600 to 1,800. Ukrainian estimates note 4,000 prisoners.

70. Gross, *Revolution from Abroad*, p. 181.

71. Popiński, Kokurin, and Gurjanow, p. 7.

72. Kalbarczyk, p. 24 n. 23.

73. Gross, *Revolution from Abroad*, p. 179. How was it possible for the Soviets to murder so many prisoners, especially in Eastern Poland, in such a short period of time? A highly placed individual with access to Soviet documents, Viktor

Suvorov, suggests that Stalin was mustering his forces near the Ribbentrop-Molotov line in preparation for *his own* attack on Germany scheduled for July 6, 1941. The Germans simply beat him to the punch by two weeks. The Soviet surprise, and the reason the Red Army was thrown back, he claims, lay in the fact that the Soviet Union was not prepared for a defensive war. See Viktor Suvorov, *Icebreaker: Who Started the Second World War?* trans. Thomas B. Beattie (London: Hamish Hamilton, 1990; New York: Viking Penguin, 1990).

74. Gross, *Revolution from Abroad,* p. 181.

75. Ibid., p. 182.

76. Popiński, Kokurin, and Gurjanow, pp. 25–26.

77. See Zygmunt Zieliński (ed.), *Życie religijne w Polsce pod okupacją 1939–1945. Metropolie wileńska i lwowska, zakony* (Katowice: Unia, 1992), pp. 493–502.

78. Zygmunt Mazur, "Męczeński klasztor dominikanów w Czortkowie," *Gazeta* (Toronto), April 1992.

79. Jan Karski, *The Great Powers and Poland, 1919–1945: From Versailles to Yalta* (New York: University Press of America, 1985), p. 489.

80. Ibid.

81. Davies, *God's Playground,* pp. 472–73. For three recent articles dealing with the fate of Poles in the Soviet Union, see the following: Czesław Madajczyk, "Badania losu ludności polskiej represjonowanej przez władze sowieckie w latach II wojny światowej (na wschód od Bugu)," in Hieronim Kubiak et al., *Mniejszości polskie i polonia w ZSRR* (Wrocław: Ossolineum — Wydawnictwo Polskiej Akademii Nauk, 1992), pp. 265–72; Elżbieta Trela Mazur, "Losy Polaków i dzieci polskich w ZSRR w latach 1941–1946 (z uwzględnieniem procesów repatriacji)," ibid., pp. 273–86; and Mieczysław Wieliczko, "Rozpoznanie przez Polski Czerwony Krzyż losu Polaków w Związku Radzieckim (listopad 1939–lipiec 1941 roku," ibid., pp. 287–300.

82. Davies, *God's Playground,* pp. 476–77. Roosevelt's words are found on p. 479.

83. Franciszek Proch, *Poland's Way of the Cross, 1939–1945* (New York: Polish Association of Former Political Prisoners of Nazi and Soviet Concentration Camps, 1987), p. 146.

Chapter 2: Nazi Terror

1. See Richard C. Lukas, *The Forgotten Holocaust: The Poles Under German Occupation, 1939–1944* (Lexington: University Press of Kentucky, 1986; New York: Hippocrene Books, 1990), pp. 1–39.

2. Łuczak, p. 685.

3. See table "Losses in Plant and Property in Poland (Post-War Frontiers) during the Second World War," in I. C. B. Dear (ed.), *The Oxford Companion to World War II* (New York: Oxford University Press, 1995), p. 896.

4. Adam Stebelski, *The Fate of Polish Archives during World War II* (Warsaw: Central Directorate of State Archives, 1964), p. 51, in Lukas, *The Forgotten Holocaust,* p. 11.

5. Lukas, *The Forgotten Holocaust,* p. 11.

6. In Dear, p. 894.

7. Lukas, *The Forgotten Holocaust,* pp. 11–12.

8. See Czesław Madajczyk, "Was *Generalplan Ost* Synchronous with the Final Solution?" in Asher Cohen et al. (eds.), *The Shoah and the War* (New York: Peter Lang, 1992), pp. 146–47, 150.

9. See Łuczak, pp. 141–46; Janusz Gumkowski and Kazimierz Leszczyński, *Poland under Nazi Occupation* (Warsaw: Polonia Publishing House, 1961), pp. 135–36; and Davies, *God's Playground,* p. 446. The following table is found on p. 146 of Łuczak.

TABLE 17. NUMBER OF POLES RESETTLED OR EVICTED BETWEEN 1939 AND 1944 IN GERMAN-OCCUPIED POLAND

Territory	***Number***
Wartheland (Kraj Warty)	630,000
Silesia (Śląsk)	81,000
Pomerania (Pomorze)	124,000
Białystok District	28,000
Ciechanów Regency	25,000
"Wild" Resettlement chiefly Pomorze	35,000
Including Annexed Territories(total)	**923,000**
Zamość area (Zamojszczyzna)	116,000
General Government	171,000
Warsaw (after uprising)	500,000
All Occupied Polish Territories (total)	**1,710,000**

10. Lukas, *The Forgotten Holocaust,* pp. 21–22. Another source lists *three* pacifications in this area: November 1941, which engulfed eight villages; November 1942–March 1943; and June-

August 1943 which resulted in the expulsion of over 100,000 Poles. The SS-ukrainische Wachmannschaften, trained in Trawniki, participated in these actions. See Maria Wardzyńska, *Formacja Wachmannschaften des SS- und Polizeiführers im Distrikt Lublin* (Warszawa: Główna Komisja Badania Zbrodni przeciwko Narodowi Polskiemu, 1992), p. 29. See also Gumkowski and Leszczyński, pp. 146–63. For a survivor's diary, see Zygmunt Klukowski, *Diary from the Years of Occupation, 1939–44,* trans. George Klukowski, eds. Andrew Klukowski and Helen Klukowski May (Chicago: University of Illinois Press, 1993).

11. Lukas, *The Forgotten Holocaust,* p. 26.

12. Roman Hrabar et al., *The Fate of Polish Children during the Last War* (Warsaw: Interpress, 1981), p. 206. Łuczak, on pp. 158 and 183, uses the same estimate, but in his "Szanse i trudności bilansu demograficznego Polski w latach 1939–1945," in Czesław Madajczyk (ed.), *Dzieje najnowsze* (Warszawa) 2 (1994): 12, which came out one year later, he lowers this number to 50,000 children.

13. Łuczak, pp. 149, 160.

14. Ibid., pp. 145–46.

15. Raul Hilberg, *The Destruction of the European Jews,* rev. ed., vol. 1 (New York: Holmes and Meier, 1985), p. 226.

16. John Keegan (ed.), *Times Atlas of the Second World War* (New York: Harper and Row, 1989), p. 207. According to Łuczak, pp. 178–79, 706,000 Poles (not counting POWs) were deported for forced labor from the annexed territories and 1,297,000 from the General Government and the district of Białystok. The following table appears on p. 180.

TABLE 18. NUMBER OF PERSONS DEPORTED FROM POLAND TO GERMANY FOR FORCED LABOR, 1939–1945

Territory	Number
General Government and District Białystok to July 7, 1944	1,214,000
Warsaw (after the uprising)	67,000
General Government in November and December 1944	16,000
Annexed territories	706,000
Eastern territories	500,000
Polish POWs	300,000
Wartheland (Kraj Warty) to France	23,500
Total	**2,826,500**

A table in Dear, p. 384, lists the total number of Poles who worked as forced laborers in August 1944 at 1,440,254 (civilians, 1,415,276; prisoners of war, 24,978). The total number of forced laborers in the German war economy in 1944 is given as 7,126,000 (civilians, 5,295,000; prisoners of war, 1,831,000). The German work force in that year was 29,800,000. See p. 381.

17. Dear, pp. 381–82. For a description of life in the forced labor camps, see Tadeusz Piotrowski, *Vengeance of the Swallows: Memoir of a Polish Family's Ordeal under Soviet Aggression, Ukrainian Ethnic Cleansing, and Nazi Enslavement and Their Emigration to America* (Jefferson, NC: McFarland, 1995), chapter 5, "In the Eye of Satan," pp. 115–34.

18. Łuczak, pp. 182–83.

19. Ibid., p. 99.

20. Korboński, *The Jews and the Poles in World War II,* p. 30. The *Oxford Companion to World War II* states that on this date, "182 members of academic staff of the Jagiellonian University and other higher education institutes in Cracow...were taken to Sachsenhausen where many subsequently died." Dear, p. 894.

21. Gumkowski and Leszczyński, p. 112.

22. Emmanuel Ringelblum, *Polish-Jewish Relations during the Second World War,* eds. Joseph Kermish and Shmuel Krakowski (Evanston, IL: Northwestern University Press, 1992), p. 6, editorial n. 13. This is a translation of Emanuel Ringelblum, *Stosunki polsko-żydowskie w czasie drugiej wojny światowej. Uwagi i spostrzeżenia* (Warszawa: Czytelnik, 1988).

23. Lukas, *The Forgotten Holocaust,* p. 9. An editorial note in Ringelblum, *Polish-Jewish Relations,* p. 6 n. 13, states, "In all, in the years of German occupation in Poland 28.5% of the professors, lecturers and teachers in institutions of higher learning were murdered, as well as 27.2% of the Catholic clergy."

24. Gumkowski and Leszczyński, p. 59.

25. Łuczak, pp. 101–2, 117. According to Eugeniusz Duraczyński, under the German occupation, 714 known executions of 16,376 people were carried out throughout Poland. Eugeniusz Duraczyński, *Wojna i opkupacja. Wrzesień 1939–Kwiecień 1943* (Warszawa: Wiedza Powszechna, 1974), pp. 36–38. For a similar estimate see Czesław Madajczyk, *Hitlerowski terror na wsi polskiej, 1939–1945* (Warszawa: Państwowe Wydawnictwo Naukowe, 1965), pp. 9–10. In my opinion, the number of those who died as the result of these executions is grossly underestimated. As we will

see shortly, the Piaśnica massacre alone resulted in over 12,000 deaths. See also Gumkowski and Leszczyński, pp. 110–30.

26. At the end of November 1939, there were 70,000 Selbstschutz members. Łuczak, p. 100.

27. Ibid., pp. 109, 117.

28. As reported by Gumkowski and Leszczyński, p. 128.

29. Korboński, *The Jews and the Poles in World War II,* p. 31.

30. See Lukas, *The Forgotten Holocaust,* pp. 182–219. Polish estimates of civilian casualties range from 150,000 to 200,000. In addition, Polish military losses included about 18,000 dead or missing and some 25,000 wounded. The German losses totaled about 17,000 killed or wounded. Andrzej Chmielarz, "Warsaw Fought Alone: Reflections on Aid to and the Fall of the 1944 Uprising," *Polish Review* 39, no. 4 (1994): 415.

31. Dear, p. 896.

32. Gumkowski and Leszczyński, pp. 112–14.

33. Ibid., p. 114.

34. See Władysław Bartoszewski, *Warszawski pierścień śmierci 1939–1944* (Warszawa: Zachodnia Agencja Prasowa, 1967). For Jewish victims in Pawiak, see Martin Gilbert, *The Holocaust: A History of the Jews of Europe during the Second World War* (New York: Holt, Rinehart and Winston, 1986), pp. 672–73, 700, 705.

35. Gumkowski and Leszczyński, p. 118.

36. Lukas, *The Forgotten Holocaust,* pp. 35, 98.

37. Records of the Main Commission for the Investigation of Nazi Crimes in Poland 649 z/OL, inw. 678, in Gumkowski and Leszczyński, p. 121.

38. Ibid., p. 122.

39. See Jerzy Biernacki, "Silence over the Graves," *Poland* (Warszawa, American Edition) 11, no. 267 (November 1976): 43, 46–47; and Tadeusz Bolduan, "Las Śmierci," *Myśl Polska* (London), September 1–15, 1985. Other sources on the Piaśnica massacre include Władysław K. Sasinowski, *Piaśnica, 1939–1944* (Committee for the Erection of a Memorial to the Victims of Piaśnica in Wejherowo, 1956), and Barbara Bojarska, *Piaśnica. Miejsce martyrologii i pamięci: z badań nad zbrodniami hitlerowskimi na Pomorzu,* 2d ed. (Gdańsk: Zrzeszenie Kaszubsko-Pomorskie, Oddział Gdański, 1989).

40. Adolf Lipschitz, a Jewish psychiatric patient from a mental hospital near Poznań, was one of the victims. In November 1939, his father was summoned to Gestapo headquarters and presented with a bill for Adolf's treatment covering the period from September 1, 1939 until October 19. When the father inquired why the treatment had ended on October 19, he was informed that on that day his son had been shot. After paying the bill, the father was handed a receipt as well as his son's death certificate signed by a doctor. Gilbert, p. 95.

41. Walter Mahlke, a German from Leśniewo, in Biernacki, p. 46.

42. Aleksander Jankowski, escapee from the prison in Wejherowo, ibid.

43. Elżbieta Ellwart, a resident of Wejherowo, nineteen years old, married, and six months pregnant at the time of her accidental discovery of this crime, ibid., pp. 46–47.

44. Sasinowski, ibid., p. 47.

45. Ibid.; Bolduan.

46. Łuczak, p. 114.

47. Henry Friedlander, *The Origins of Nazi Genocide: From Euthanasia to the Final Solution* (Chapel Hill: University of North Carolina Press, 1995), p. 137.

48. Łuczak, p. 115.

49. Ibid.

50. *Frank's Diary, Working Sessions and Addresses,* vol. 9, p. 440, as quoted by Gumkowski and Leszczyński, p. 117. For another edition of Frank's diary, see Stanisław Piotrowski, *Dziennik Hansa Franka* (Warszawa: Wydawnictwo Prawnicze, 1956).

51. *Protokół Posiedzenia Rady Narodowej R.P.,* July 1942, in A.5.2/32, General Sikorski Historical Institution, London, England.

52. Auschwitz I, the main camp, was primarily intended to serve as a concentration camp for Polish political prisoners. It was built in the early part of 1940 just on the outskirts of the town of Oświęcim after the surrounding area was cleared of its Polish population. The first transport, consisting of 728 Polish prisoners, arrived there on June 14, 1940. By the end of that year, Auschwitz I housed 7,879 predominantly Polish inmates. At the end of 1941, it had 18,000 prisoners. From 1942 on, it included many ethnic groups and Jews as well.

Construction for Birkenau (Auschwitz II) began in October 1941 after Hitler's mid–1941 order for the "Final Solution." This much larger subcamp, located about four kilometers from the main camp, functioned solely as an extermination center for Jews, although thousands of Gypsies and Soviet prisoners of war are said to have died there as well. The first transport of Polish Jews arrived at Birkenau in January 1942. That spring, the first two crematoria became operational. See Gumkowski and Leszczyński, pp. 76–82.

According to the estimate of Dr. Franciszek Piper, chief researcher at the Auschwitz museum, out of a total of 1.3 million inmates at the Auschwitz-Birkenau complex, there were 1.1 million Jews, 140,000—150,000 Poles, 23,000 Gypsies, 15,000 Soviet prisoners of war, and 25,000 prisoners of other nationalities. Of these, 1.1 million died, including half of all the Polish inmates. The first to be gassed by Zyklon B in September 1941 were Soviet POWs and Poles. For these statistics, see Franciszek Piper, "Weryfikacja strat osobowych w obozie koncentracyjnym w Oświęcimiu," in Madajczyk, *Dzieje najnowsze*, pp. 15–25.

The five crematoria of the Auschwitz-Birkenau complex were all destroyed before the war's end: crematorium IV, on October 7, 1944; crematoria II and III, on January 20, 1945; and crematorium V, on the night of January 25–26, 1945. A day later, the surviving inmates were liberated by the Red Army. See Główna Komisja Badania Zbrodni Hitlerowskich w Polsce — Rada Ochrony Pomników Walki i Męczeństwa, *Obozy hitlerowskie na ziemiach polskich 1939–1945: Informator encyklopedyczny* (Warszawa: Państwowe Wydawnictwo Naukowe, 1979), p. 369.

The original estimate of "four million" who supposedly died in the Auschwitz-Birkenau complex had its origins in the statements of the camp's German officials (Rudolf Hoess and others) and of the Jewish prisoners from the Sonderkommando. The 4 million figure, cited repeatedly at the Nuremberg Trials, was later adopted by the Soviets and became the "official" communist block estimate. However, the number of Jewish deaths was downplayed in favor of Soviet and other victims. In the west, between 2.5 and 4 million, mostly Jewish victims were said to have died there.

The breakup of the Soviet Union allowed Polish historians to question these original estimates. Their research confirmed a count that is remarkably consistent with Polish wartime intelligence reports: 1.1 million. This new estimate now appears in the camp literature and is displayed at the camp itself, which has been visited by over 20 million people and maintained by the Poles for decades without any external assistance.

53. Zygmunt Zieliński, with Richard Tyndorf, "Rescue Efforts on Behalf of Jews by the Roman Catholic Church in German-Occupied Poland" (unpublished 1997 manuscript). Zenon Fijałkowski, *Kościół katolicki na ziemiach polskich w latach okupacji hitlerowskiej* (Warszawa: Książka i Wiedza, 1983), p. 375, states:

> During the Nazi occupation, the Catholic Church in Poland experienced enormous clerical and material losses. According to the latest research by W. Jacewicz and J. Woś, in the years 1939–1945, 2,801 members of the clergy lost their lives; they were either murdered during the occupation or killed in military maneuvers. Among them were 6 bishops, 1,926 diocesan priests and clerics, 375 priests and clerics from monastic orders, 205 brothers, and 289 sisters. 599 diocesan priests and clerics were killed in executions, as well as 281 members of the monastic clergy (priests, brothers and sisters). Of the 1,345 members of the clergy murdered in death camps, 798 died in Dachau, 167 in Auschwitz, 90 in Działdowo, 85 in Sachsenhausen, 71 in Gusen, 40 in Stutthof, and the rest in camps such as Buchenwald, Gross-Rosen, Mauthausen, Majdanek, Bojanowo, and others.

According to *Encyklopedia Katolicka*, "Dachau," vol. 3 (Lublin: Towarzystwo Naukowe Katolickiego Uniwersytetu Lubelskiego, 1979), columns 965-67, 4,618 Christian clergymen were imprisoned in Nazi concentration camps. Of these, 2,796 were in Dachau, where almost 95 percent of the clergymen were Roman Catholics and almost 65 percent (1,807) were Poles. Of the 947 clergymen who died in Dachau, 866 were Poles. Several hundred Polish priests were selected for hypothermia and other medical experiments.

New Catholic Encyclopedia, "Poland: The Church in Poland, 1939–1945," vol. 11 (New York: McGraw-Hill, 1967), pp. 481–83, states: "In all, 13 Polish bishops were exiled or arrested and put in concentration camps.... There were 3,647 priests, 389 clerics, 341 brothers, and 1,117 sisters put in concentration camps, in which 1,996 priests, 113 clerics, and 238 sisters perished.... The diocesan clergy of the Polish Church, who at the beginning of World War II numbered 10,017, lost 25 percent (2,647)."

For one account of the experiences of Roman Catholic priests in concentration camps, see Bedřich Hoffmann, *And Who Will Kill You: The Chronicle of the Life and Sufferings of Priests in the Concentration Camps* (Poznań: Pallottinum, 1994).

54. In Richard C. Lukas (ed.), *Out of the Inferno: Poles Remember the Holocaust* (Lexington: University Press of Kentucky, 1989), p. 141.

55. Łuczak, pp. 132–33.

56. Ibid., pp. 122–23.

57. Ibid., p. 124.

58. Ibid., pp. 124–25.

59. Ibid.

60. Regarding Jewish reserves and maps of their location in Poland, see Gerald Reitlinger, *The Final Solution* (London: Vallentine, Mitchell, 1953), and the undated brochure in Italian, *La Chiesa "eroica" di Polonia* (Rome: ARS GRAF). An article on this topic, "Niedoszłe państwo żydowskie w Lubelszczyźnie," may also be found in Jędrzej Giertych (ed.), *Komunikaty Towarzystwa imienia Romana Dmowskiego,* vol. 2 (London: Veritas, 1979–80), pp. 25–99.

61. Łuczak, pp. 125–26.

62. These estimates come from Friedlander, table on p. 287. See also Hilberg, *The Destruction of the European Jews,* 3, p. 1219. According to Zygmunt Mańkowski, about 250,000 people died in Majdanek, including about 100,000 Poles. Zygmunt Mańkowski, "Problem weryfikacji strat w obozie na Majdanku," *Dzieje Najnowsze* (Warszawa) 26, no. 2 (1994): 27–31.

63. Under the German occupation, Poland was partitioned as follows:

a) The Government General, encompassing the central and south-eastern parts of the country, divided into five *Distrikte*: Warsaw, Lublin, Cracow, Radom, and Distrikt Galizien (added on August 1, 1941);

b) The *Wartheland,* consisting of the entire Poznań Województwo (province), almost the entire Łódź Województwo, five counties of the Pomorze Województwo, and one county of the Warsaw Województwo;

c) Danzig-West Preussen (Danzig-West Prussia), including the remaining area of the Pomorze Województwo;

d) Distrikt Zichenau (Ciechanów), consisting of the five northern counties of the Warsaw Województwo;

e) Ostoberschlesien (Eastern Upper Silesia), encompassing the counties of Sosnowiec, Będzin, and Chrzanów, and parts of the counties of Zawiercie, Olkusz, and Żywiec, i.e., the western part of the Cracow Województwo and of the former Polish Upper Silesia (Zagłębie) [units *b, c, d,* and *e* were incorporated —*eingegliedert*— into the Reich];

f) Bezirk Białystok (established after the invasion of the U.S.S.R. in June 1941), which consisted of seven *Kommissariate*: Białystok, Grajewo, Grodno, Bielsk-Podlaski, Łomża, Sokółki, and Wołkowysk. The town of Białystok was a separate administrative entity. This Bezirk was attached (*angeliedert*) to the jurisdiction of the *Gauleiter* of Eastern Prussia, Erich Koch;

g) Polish Byelorussia was in part included in the Bezirk Białystok and in part in the Reichskommissariat Ostland (concerning the Pinsk area, see below, Reichskommissariat Ukraine); and

h) The Polish part of Volhynia, included in the Reichskommissariat Ukraine.

The *Reichskommissariat Ostland* consisted of the areas of the former Baltic states (including the Vilna region) and of the greater part of Byelorussia, Polish and Soviet.

The *Reichskommissariat Ukraine* encompassed the following *Generalkommissariate*: Volhynia-Podolia, Zhitomir, Kiev, Dnepropetrovsk, and the Crimea, as well as the southern part of Polish Byelorussia and the town of Pińsk. All the conquered areas east of the Dnieper were under military administration until September 1942, when they were taken over, together with the northern parts of the Crimea, by the civil administration.

Isaiah Trunk, *Judenrat: The Jewish Councils in Eastern Europe under Nazi Occupation* (New York: Macmillan, 1972), pp. ix, xii.

64. Jürgen Thorwald, *Wen sie verderben wollen. Bericht des grossen Verrats* (Stuttgart: Steingrüben-Verlag, 1952), p. 75.

65. Erich Koch. See *Nazi Conspiracy and Aggression* (hereafter: *NCA*), vol. 3 (Washington, DC: U.S. Government Printing Office, 1946), pp. 798–99.

66. See Raul Hilberg, *Perpetrators, Victims, Bystanders: The Jewish Catastrophe, 1933–1945* (New York: HarperCollins, 1992), pp. 94–96, 199–201. A section on the Tuczyn ghetto also appears in Gilbert, pp. 463–64. "In the early hours of September 24 [1942]," he states, "German and Ukrainian policemen began shooting into the ghetto." For a table that provides the dates of establishment and liquidation of the ghettos in Wołyń, see Shmuel Spector, *The Holocaust of Volhynian Jews, 1941–1944* (Jerusalem: Yad Vashem — The Federation of Volhynian Jews, 1990), pp.

TABLE 19. EUROPEAN LOSSES DURING WORLD WAR II (IN THOUSANDS)

Country	*Population, End of 1938*	*War Losses*				
		Military	*Civilian*		*Total*	*% of Population*
			Non-Jewish	*Jewish*		
USSR	170,500	7,000	8,500	845	16,345	9.6%
Poland	28,400*	360**	3,230	2,500	6,090	21.4%
Germany	68,500	3,500	500	110	4,110	6.0%
Yugoslavia	15,490	300	1,150	63	1,513	9.8%
Rumania	16,070*	300	—	370	670	4.2%
France	41,680	250	250	70	570	1.4%
Czechoslovakia	14,610*	200	75	271	546	3.7%
Italy	43,780	330	80	17	427	1.0%
Hungary	9,200	140	50	200	390	4.2%
U.K.	47,814	326	62	—	388	0.8%
Austria	6,653	230	24	53	307	4.6%
Holland	8,729	12	94	105	211	2.4%
Lithuania	2,400	—	50***	125	175	7.3%
Greece	7,295	20	80	62	162	2.2%
Belgium	8,386	12	49	50	111	1.3%
Latvia	2,000	—	30***	80	110	5.5%
Bulgaria	6,270	10	—	3	13	0.2%
Denmark, Norway, Estonia, Danzig, Luxembourg	8,520	7	5	6	18	0.2%
TOTAL	**506,297**	**12,997**	**14,229**	**4,930**	**32,156**	**6.4%**

*Not including territories ceded to USSR but including, in the case of Poland, the Polish and Jewish populations of these territories.
**Including 32,000 Jews.
***Franciszek J. Proch's estimate.

366–67. Pp. 214–17 deal with the uprising in the Tuczyn ghetto during which two-thirds of the Jews escaped into the forest; of these, only a handful survived the war.

67. Zbigniew Studułł, "Relacja Zbigniewa G. Sudułła, zamieszkałego w Australii, o rzeziach ukraińskich w rejonie Tuczyna nad Horyniem w powiecie rówieńskim na Wołyniu," in Giertych, *Komunikaty,* p. 327.

68. See, for example, Leni Yahil, *The Holocaust: The Fate of European Jewry, 1932–1945* (New York: Oxford University Press, 1990), pp. 260ff.

69. Ryszard Torzecki, *Polacy i Ukraińcy. Sprawa ukraińska w czasie II wojny światowej na terenie II Rzeczypospolitej* (Warszawa: Wydawnictwo Naukowe PWN, 1993), pp. 134–35.

70. Hilberg, *Perpetrators, Victims, Bystanders,* p. 201.

71. Krystyna Kersten, "Szacunek strat osobowych w Polsce Wschodniej," in Madajczyk, *Dzieje najnowsze,* p. 45. The 5 million figure comes from Gumkowski and Leszczyński, p. 146.

72. Appendix to Aide Mémoire of August 5, 1943, no. 41746, RG226, Office of Strategic Services, National Archives, Washington, D.C.

73. *TWC,* 25: 331.

74. Kersten, "Szacunek strat osobowych w Polsce Wschodniej," p. 45.

75. In Duraczyński, p. 17. Emphasis added.

76. Karol Grünberg, *SS gwardia Hitlera* (Warszawa: Książka i Wiedza, 1975), photocopy between pp. 272–73. Emphasis mine. See also Hannah Arendt, *Eichmann in Jerusalem: A Report on the Banality of Evil* (New York: Viking Press, 1965), pp. 157–58.

77. Łuczak, pp. 135–37, 140.

78. According to ibid., p. 685, Warsaw was 84 percent destroyed; Białystok, 50 percent;

TABLE 20. POLAND'S LOSSES DURING WORLD WAR II (IN THOUSANDS)

Description		Germany			USSR			Total
A. War Activities:				1940	(Katyn &			
1. Milit. Losses	Non-Jewish	263			others	15		
	Jewish	32	295	1944	(AK)	50	65	360
2. Civil. Losses	Sept. 1939:							
	Non-Jewish	450						
	Jewish	50						
	Warsaw Uprising	100	600	1944-45			50	650
B. Nazi Terror	Non-Jewish	1,795						
	Jewish	2,350	4,145					4,145
C. Soviet Terror				Non-Jewish		835		
				Jewish		100	935	935
Total Losses			**5,040**				**1,050**	**6,090**

Gdynia, 48 percent; and Poznań, 45 percent. In addition, the following cities acquired from Germany by Poland after the war also sustained heavy damage: Wrocław (Breslau), 68 percent; Opole (Oppeln), 60 percent; and Szczecin (Stettin) 50 percent. Gdańsk (Danzig), a Free City during the interwar period, sustained 50 percent damage.

79. According to J. Tomaszewski's adjusted census figures for 1931 (*Rzeczpospolita wielu narodów,* p. 35), 20,644,000, or 64.7 percent (by religious affiliation), of Poland's total population (31,916,000) consisted of ethnic Poles. This would exclude anyone who was Jewish by religion (although fully assimilated culturally and linguistically) but would include tens of thousands of Jewish converts to Catholicism. It would also ex post facto exclude Polonized Ukrainians and Belorussians. If this percentage (64.7%) is applied to the 1939 population estimate of Poland (35,100,000), we would arrive at 22.7 million ethnic Poles. By the same token, the number of Jews in 1939 would stand at 3.4 million (9.8% of the 1931 population was Jewish; hence .098 × 35.1 = 3.4).

Jewish wartime losses in Poland are estimated to be in the 2.7–2.9 million range. (Many Polish Jews found refuge in the Soviet Union and other countries.) Ethnic Polish losses are currently estimated in the range of 2 million. (The number is probably higher if we add all those who died at the hands of the Ukrainian Nationalists.) Therefore, Jewish wartime losses in Poland were between 79 percent and 85 percent; ethnic Polish losses, between 9 percent and 10 percent. Tables 19 and 20 provide another comparison. These tables come from Proch, pp. 146–47.

Other estimates for World War II war losses by country can be found in Ruth Leger Sivard, *World Military and Social Expenditures, 1987–88* (Washington, DC: World Priorities, 1987), pp. 29–31; *New Encyclopaedia Britannica, Macropaedia,* vol. 29 (Chicago: Encyclopaedia Britannica, 1992), p. 1023; Roman Nurowski, *1939–1945: War Losses in Poland* (Poznań: Wydawnictwo Zachodnie, 1960); and Dear, p. 290. According to the last reference, approximately fifty million war-related deaths occurred during World War II (twenty-two million military and 28 million civilian). The entry for Poland lists 4,123,000 war-related deaths (123,000 military and 4,000,000 civilian).

For another recent estimate (1994) of Poland's overall losses, see Czesław Łuczak, "Szanse i trudności bilansu demograficznego Polski w latach 1939–1945," in Madajczyk, *Dzieje najnowsze,* pp. 9–14. For overall losses in Eastern Poland, see Krystyna Kersten, "Szacunek strat osobowych w Polsce Wschodniej," ibid., pp. 41–50. The former (pp. 12, 14) lists Poland's losses (out of a total prewar population of about 35 million, 8 million of whom were minorities): 2 million Poles; 2.9 million Jews; and 1 million "other" — for a total of close to 6 million. According to the latter (p. 43), in 1939–40 there were approximately 6.7–6.8 million Poles and Jews in Eastern Poland. Of these, either 1.3 million

TABLE 21. NUMBER OF JEWS IN POLAND, 1931 (IN THOUSANDS)

		Language given as:			
Province	***Population***	***Jewish***	***Hebrew***	***Other***	***Total***
Poland	31,915.8	2,489.0	243.5	381.4	3,113.9
Warsaw (city)	1,171.8	313.6	19.7	19.4	352.7
Warsaw	2,529.1	200.2	14.9	4.0	219.1
Łódź	2,632.0	336.2	23.2	19.1	378.5
Kielce	2,935.6	293.2	11.7	12.1	317.0
Lublin	2,464.9	246.0	13.5	54.8	314.3
Białystok	1,643.8	172.2	22.8	2.4	197.4
Wilno	1,275.9	95.2	13.6	2.0	110.8
Nowogródek	1,057.1	69.8	7.2	5.9	82.9
Polesie	1,131.9	96.5	16.5	1.0	114.0
Wołyń	2,085.6	174.2	31.4	2.2	207.8
Poznań	2,106.5	2.9	0.4	3.9	7.2
Pomorze	1,080.1	1.8	0.1	1.5	3.4
Śląsk	1,295.0	5.4	1.1	12.4	18.9
Kraków	2,297.8	97.8	30.2	45.6	173.6
Lwów	3,127.4	211.0	21.9	109.5	342.4
Stanisławów	1,480.3	101.3	8.1	30.3	139.7
Tarnopol	1,600.4	71.9	7.0	55.2	134.1

(according to the criterion of language) or 1.5 million (according to the criterion of religious affiliation) were Jews. In all (pp. 47, 49), 1 million Jews and 1 million "other" (mostly Poles) died in Poland's eastern territories. Soviet terror accounted for some 500,000 to 600,000 of these deaths. According to Teresa Prekerowa, "Wojna i Okupacja," in Jerzy Tomaszewski (ed.), *Najnowsze dzieje Żydów w Polsce w zarysie (do 1950 roku),* (Warszawa: Wydawnictwo Naukowe PWN, 1993), p. 384, Jewish losses in Poland were 85 to 89 percent (i.e., between 3 and 3.1 million) out of a total Jewish population of 3.5 million (stated earlier — from compilation on p. 275 — to have been 3.3 million, see n. 1 in Chapter 3 below).

For a brief overall assessment of comparative Nazi and Soviet damage to Poland from September 1939 to June 1941, see Gross, *Revolution from Abroad,* pp. 226ff.

80. Jerzy Zdzisław Holzer, "Bilans demograficzny Polski dla okresu 1939–1945," in Madajczyk, *Dzieje najnowsze,* p. 7. Some of these losses, of course, are attributed to the shift in borders after the war.

81. Łuczak, p. 683.

82. Lukas, *The Forgotten Holocaust,* p. 34.

83. For a lengthy analysis of the meaning of the term *collaboration* and types, see Werner Röhr, "Okkupation und Kollaboration," in Werner Röhr (ed.), *Okkupation und Kollaboration (1938–1945). Beiträge zu Konzepten und Praxis der Kollaboration in der deutschen Okkupationspolitik* (Berlin: Hüthig Verlagsgemeinschaft, 1994), pp. 59–84. According to Czesław Madajczyk (ibid.), the Germans did not use the word *collaborator* in their various memorandums and correspondence. Rather, they spoke of *willige Fremdvölkische, nationale Verwaltungen, antikommunistische Kräfte,* and of course, *agents* and *confidants.* For example, although the words *freiwillige Mitarbeit* appear many times in the voluminous *Diary of Hans Frank,* one is hard put to find even a single passage that contains the word *collaborator* or *collaboration.*

Chapter 3: Jewish Collaboration

1. Norman Davies, "Poles and Jews: An Exchange," *New York Review of Books,* April 9, 1987. Table 21 above comes from J. Tomaszewski, *Rzeczpospolita wielu narodów,* p. 148.

According to Teresa Prekerowa, in J. Tomaszewski, *Najnowsze dzieje Żydów w Polsce,* p. 275, in 1939 there were 600,000 Jews (out of 10 million residents) in the Polish territories annexed by the Third Reich, 1.5 million Jews (out of 12 million residents) in the General Government, and 1.2

million Jews (out of 13.4 million residents) in the Soviet-occupied eastern territories of Poland.

2. In Lukas, *Out of the Inferno,* p. 8.

3. Sholem Asch, *Kiddush Ha-Shem: An Epic of 1684* (New York: Arnoa Press, 1975), as quoted in *Polin* 7 (1992): ix.

4. As quoted by Teresa Prekerowa, in J. Tomaszewski, *Najnowsze dzieje Żydów w Polsce,* p. 273. For the reference to the Bund, see. p. 275.

5. Ibid., pp. 274–75. See also Simon Schochet, "Polscy oficerowie pochodzenia żydowskiego — jeńcy Katynia na tle walk o niepodległość (próba identyfikacji)," *Niepodległość* (New York, London) vol. 21 (1988): 152–66.

The military administration of occupied Poland was followed by a German civil administration. According to Wojciech Roszkowski (Andrzej Albert), *Historia Polski 1914–1993* (Warszawa: Wydawnictwo Naukowe PWN, 1994), p. 91, the Polish campaign of September 1939 (both fronts) exacted a heavy military toll.

Poland:	70,000	soldiers and officers killed
	133,000	wounded
	300,000	taken as prisoners by Germany
	180,000	taken as prisoners by the Soviet Union
	50,000	caught and interned by the Soviet Union after the end of the campaign
	83,000	soldiers and officers crossed into Rumania, Hungary, Lithuania, and Latvia
Germany:	90,000	soldiers and officers killed
	60,000	wounded

In reference to the German losses above, Roszkowski states that various estimates abound, and he presents these figures as probable. Many other sources, including Dear, pp. 903ff., say that there were fewer than 50,000 German casualties — killed, wounded, or missing.

No figures are available for the USSR. However, according to a speech (October 31, 1939) reported in *Pravda* (November 1, 1939) of Vyacheslav Molotov to the Supreme Soviet, 737 Soviet soldiers had lost their lives in the Polish campaign and 1,862 were wounded. He stated, "A brief strike against Poland, first by the German, and later by the Red Army, was enough to ensure that nothing remained of this ugly child of the Versailles Treaty." According to Szawłowski, in Sword, *The Soviet Takeover,* p. 42, the real Soviet losses amounted to between 8,000 and 10,000 men, including 2,500 to 3,000 killed.

6. In Krystyna Kersten, *Polacy, Żydzi, Komunizm. Anatomia półprawd 1939–68* (Warszawa: Niezależna Oficyna Wydawnicza, 1992), p. 30.

7. Davies, "Poles and Jews: An Exchange."

8. Smolar, "Jews as a Polish Problem," p. 58. The Jewish Bund, founded in 1897, was the first Marxist party with a mass following. See Christopher Andrew and Oleg Gordievsky, *KGB: The Inside Story of Its Foreign Operations from Lenin to Gorbachev* (New York: HarperCollins, 1990), p. 22.

9. Jaff Schatz, *The Generation: The Rise and Fall of the Jewish Communists of Poland* (Berkeley: University of California Press, 1991), p. 82. Schatz describes the focus of his work as follows: "Those whose experience is described here were born around 1910. They joined the Communist movement at the end of the 1920s and the beginning of the 1930s. They survived World War II in the USSR and after the war rebuilt their lives in Poland. On their final defeat two and a half decades later, they became refugees again, leaving Poland together with the remnants of Polish Jewry" (p. 3).

10. Andrzej Zwoliński, *Starsi bracia* (Kraków, 1994), p. 79. There is some controversy as to the number of communists actually imprisoned in Poland during the interwar years. For one statistical summary, see Schatz, pp. 87–88. Considering all types of arrests (temporary, those awaiting trial, those already sentenced), Schatz notes, "Indeed, there is reason to regard as only moderately exaggerated the statement that in the 1930s, of all the members of the Polish Communist party, 'three quarters were behind bars.'"

11. Henryk Cimek, *Komuniści, Polska, Stalin 1918–1939* (Białystok: Krajowa Agencja Wydawnicza, 1990), pp. 106–7. For tables of the percentage of Jews as compared with the percentages of other nationalities in the highest échelons of the Soviet government in 1917, 1917–22, and 1928–35, see Baltazar Podhorski's two articles "Na czerwonej fali" and "Udział Żydów w rewolucji komunistycznej w Rosji," *Biuletyn Informacyjny — Prawda o Komunizmie* (Warsaw) 1, no. 36 (1937): 28–31, and 4, no. 39 (1937): 127–32.

12. Isaac Bashevis Singer, *Love and Exile* (New York: Doubleday, 1984), p. 48.

13. Schatz, pp. 96–97.

14. Ibid., p. 2.

15. Ibid., p. 98.

16. Abel Kainer (Stanisław Krajewski), "Jews and Communism," in Michael Bernhard and Henryk Szlajfer (eds.), *From the Polish Underground: Selections from Krytyka, 1978–1993* (University Park: Pennsylvania State University Press, 1995), p. 359. Kainer was Krajewski's pseudonym for articles published in the underground political quarterly *Krytyka* during the communist era.

17. Ibid., p. 358.

18. Smolar, "Jews as a Polish Problem," p. 38, notes: "The Soviet Union, on the other hand, was seen as a country that allowed Jews full civil rights, or, more precisely, deprived them of rights in the same measure as it deprived others."

19. In the early 1920s, about 25 percent of all university students in Poland were Jewish. By 1930, Jews accounted for 40 percent of Poland's university graduates. See "The Golden Age," *Intercom* (Toronto) 12, no. 1 (spring 1993). In the United States, when the number of Jewish undergraduates rose from 6 percent in 1908 to 22 percent in 1922, Harvard University's president Lawrence Lowell declared that there was a "Jewish problem" and recommended an admissions quota. Other universities across the country soon followed Harvard's lead. In Poland, even with a *numerus clausus*, Jews continued to be overrepresented at some universities. In 1938–39, for example, about 13.5 percent of the student body at the Stefan Batory University in Wilno was Jewish, whereas all the other minorities taken together accounted for about 14 percent. See Piotr Łossowski (ed.), *Likwidacja Uniwersytetu Stefana Batorego przez władze litewskie w grudniu 1939 roku* (Warszawa: Wydawnictwo Interlibro, 1991), p. 74.

According to Bernard Weinryb, during the interwar years Jews accounted for 53 percent of all craftsmen and slightly over 50 percent of all lawyers and doctors in Eastern Poland. However, most of the Jews, like most of the other residents in this underdeveloped area of Poland, were very poor. Bernard Weinryb, "Polish Jews under Soviet Rule," in Peter Meyer et al., *The Jews in the Soviet Satellites* (Syracuse, NY: Syracuse University Press, 1953), p. 331. In Wołyń, 40 percent of the Jews engaged in handicrafts and made up 72.6 percent of all the artisans. Spector, *The Holocaust of Volhynian Jews,* p. 31.

20. For information on American anti-Semitism, see Leonard Dinnerstein, *Anti-Semitism in America* (New York: Oxford University Press, 1994), and Frederic Colpe Jaher, *A Scapegoat in the New Wilderness: The Origins and Rise of Anti-Semitism in America* (Cambridge: Harvard University Press, 1994).

21. In Lukas, *Out of the Inferno*, p. 9.

22. Ibid.

23. Rachmiel Frydland, *When Being Jewish Was a Crime* (New York: Thomas Nelson, 1978), pp. 17, 54.

24. Ibid., p. 55.

25. Abraham Sterzer, "We Fought for Ukraine!" *Ukrainian Quarterly* 20, no. 1 (1964): 38.

26. An interview with Dora Kacnelson, "Żydówka za karmelitenkami," *Głos Polski* (Toronto), October 9, 1993.

27. See Barbara Engelking, *Na łące popiołów: ocaleni z Holocaustu* (Warszawa: Cyklady, 1993), p. 126.

28. Słominski quoted in the prewar foremost literary weekly *Wiadomości Literackie*, no. 35 (1924).

29. Schatz, p. 34.

30. Israel Shahak, *Jewish History, Jewish Religion: The Weight of Three Thousand Years* (Boulder, CO: Pluto Press, 1994), p. 97.

31. Lukas, *Out of the Inferno,* p. 8.

32. Schatz, p. 34.

33. Gilbert, p. 22.

34. Israel Gutman and Shmuel Krakowski, *Unequal Victims: Poles and Jews during World War II* (New York: Holocaust Library, 1986), p. 11.

35. Gilbert, p. 51. For other pogroms between 1935 and 1937, see Ringelblum, *Polish-Jewish Relations,* pp. 11–12, editorial n. 2.

36. Schatz, p. 28.

37. Gilbert, pp. 55–56.

38. Zwoliński, p. 78.

39. Ringelblum, *Polish-Jewish Relations,* pp. 10–11.

40. Ben-Cion Pinchuk, *Shtetl Jews under Soviet Rule: Eastern Poland on the Eve of the Holocaust* (Cambridge, MA: Basil Blackwell, 1991), p. 18.

41. Rachela Walshaw and Sam Walshaw, *From out of the Firestone: A Memoir of the Holocaust* (New York: Shapolsky, 1991), pp. 7–8.

42. Ezra Mendelsohn, "Interwar Poland: Good for the Jews or Bad for the Jews?" in Chimen Abramsky et al. (eds.), *The Jews in Poland* (New York: Basil Blackwell, 1986), p. 130. Mendelsohn does not subscribe to this extreme position. See his "Jewish Historiography on Polish Jewry in the Interwar Period," in Antony Polonsky, Ezra Mendelsohn, and Jerzy Toma-

szewski (eds.), *Jews in Independent Poland, 1918–1939* (Washington, DC: Littleman Library of Jewish Civilization, 1994), pp. 3–13. This is vol. 8 of *Polin.*

43. Lukas, *The Forgotten Holocaust,* p. 125. See also Richard C. Lukas, "A Response," *Slavic Review,* fall/winter 1987, pp. 581–90. For reference to the events in Pińsk, see Jerzy Tomaszewski, "Pińsk, Saturday 5 April 1919," *Polin* 1 (1986): 227–51, and Józef Lewandowski, "History and Myth: Pińsk, April 1919," *Polin* 2 (1987): 50–72.

44. Ludwik Mroczka, "Przyczynek do kwestii żydowskiej w Galicji u progu II Rzeczysospolitej," in Feliks Kiryk, *Żydzi w Małopolsce. Studia z dziejów osadnictwa i życia społecznego* (Przemyśl: Południowo-Wschodni Instytut Naukowy w Przemyślu, 1991), p. 298.

45. See Kazimierz Kierski, *Ochrona praw mniejszości w Polsce* (Poznań, 1933), pp. 32–33. *Webster's New World Dictionary of the American Language* (New York: World Publishing Company, 1970) defines the word *pogrom* as "an organized persecution and massacre, often officially prompted, of a minority group, esp. of Jews (as in Czarist Russia)—*SYN.* see SLAUGHTER."

46. Adam Ciołkosz, "'Dzielnica żydowska' obozu w Jabłonnie," *Zeszyty Historyczne* (Paris) 20 (1971): 190–91.

47. Władysław Reymont, in *Gazeta Warszawska,* October 17, 1919, as quoted by Zwoliński, p. 76.

48. As quoted ibid.

49. Adam Penkulla, "The 'Przytyk Incidents' of 9 March 1936 from Archival Documents," *Polin* 5 (1990): 328–29. The quotation from the police report can be found on p. 336.

50. Ibid., p. 339.

51. See Kierski, pp. 32–33.

52. Zygmunt Zieliński, "Żydzi w społeczeństwie Polski międzywojennej" (unpublished 1995 manuscript).

53. Norman Davies, "Great Britain and the Polish Jews, 1918–20," *Journal of Contemporary History* 8, no. 2 (April 1973): 140–41.

54. Schatz, p. 338.

55. Mendelsohn, in Polonsky, Mendelsohn, and Tomaszewski, pp. 3–4.

56. In Kersten, *Polacy, Żydzi, Komunizm,* motto at the beginning of the work.

57. Smolar, "Jews as a Polish Problem," p. 33. According to Joseph Marcus, a British economist of Polish-Jewish descent, in 1929 the per-capita income was 830 zloty for Jews and 585 for non–Jews. The Jews, representing 10 percent of the country's population, controlled 20 percent of the nation's wealth. This favored economic status of the Jews, claims Marcus, continued through the 1930s as well. See Joseph Marcus, *Social and Political History of the Jews in Poland, 1919–1939* (New York: Mouton, 1983).

Iwo Cyprian Pogonowski, *Jews in Poland: A Documentary History* (New York: Hippocrene Books, 1993), p. 301, states:

> In 1937 Jewish business real estate was worth ten billion zlotys, or one-third of the total business real estate in Poland...the Jews paid 28% of income taxes, while they represented about 10% of the population.... In 1938, Jews represented 33.5% of Poland's physicians, 53% of lawyers, and about 24% of university students.... In 1938/39 Jewish press in Poland included 160 titles (11 scientific)—total daily circulation of 800,000, of which 180,000 were in Polish, the rest mainly in Yiddish. Among 103 professional theatres in Poland, 15 were Jewish.

See also Marian Fuks et al., *Żydzi polscy. Dzieje i kultura* (Warszawa: Wydawnictwo Interpress, 1982).

58. Mendelsohn, in Abramsky et al., pp. 136, 138–39. The sentence containing the latter phrase reads: "But, as we all know, such creativity is linked with oppression, with anti–semitism, with the refusal of Polish society to allow for Jewish integration."

59. See Gilbert, p. 53, and n. 15; see Jerzy Tomaszewski, "Niepodległa Rzeczpospolita," in J. Tomaszewski, *Najnowsze dzieje Żydów w Polsce,* p. 164.

60. See ibid., p. 165.

61. See Gilbert, p. 55, and n. 21.

62. See J. Tomaszewski, "Niepodległa Rzeczpospolita," in J. Tomaszewski, *Najnowsze dzieje Żydów w Polsce,* p. 164. The total in the "total" column on p. 164 is 8,956. The entries for "oversees" and "continental" emigration are 8,411 and 445, respectively. For my total (8,856), I have added the latter two figures.

63. See ibid., p. 165.

64. According to a 1943 Home Army document cited by Kermish and Krakowski, of the thirteen Polish political organizations associated with the Government Delegation for the Homeland, seven favored emigration of the Jews, four favored full integration (equal rights), and two favored removal. Among the three Polish organizations

opposed to the Government Delegation, two favored integration and one removal. In all, seven were for emigration, six for integration, and three for removal. Ringelblum, *Polish-Jewish Relations*, pp. 224–25.

65. In Eugenio Reale, *Raporty: Polska 1945-1946*, trans. Paweł Zdziechowski (Paris: Institut Littéraire, 1968), pp. 199–203. Reale was a communist until 1956. He served as the first Italian ambassador to postwar Poland from September 1945 until February 1947.

The seventh paragraph in this passage, the one that refers to the Jewish "solidarity with the Prussians," cannot pass without comment from a well-known authority on the subject matter, Prince Otto (Eduard Leopold) von Bismarck (1815–98), Prussian chancellor of the German Empire from 1871 to 1890. The date of his speech is May 15, 1847: "I do not believe that the Jews who settled in the Poznanian territory, even if they were allowed, would in great numbers gravitate to the German provinces, since — and here I do not wish to use an offensive term — the thoughtlessness endemic in the Polish character, under the guise of material gain, has always fashioned an Eldorado out of Poland for the Jews." On another occasion, the "Iron Chancellor" told A. Tatishchev, "Why did God create Polish Jews if not so that we may use them for espionage." As quoted by Zwoliński, p. 72.

66. Prekerowa, in J. Tomaszewski, *Najnowsze dzieje Żydów w Polsce*, p. 301. For other estimates, see Pinchuk, p. 107.

67. In Grudzińska-Gross and Gross, *War Through Children's Eyes*, p. 56.

68. Ibid., p. 9.

69. Spector, *The Holocaust of Volhynian Jews*, p. 246.

70. Arnold Zable, *Jewels and Ashes* (New York: Harcourt Brace, 1991), p. 111.

71. These testimonies, together with the Yad Vashem references, can be found in Grudzińska-Gross and Gross, *W czterdziestym nas matko na Sybir zesłali*, p. 29. They have been edited out of the shorter English version: *War Through Children's Eyes*.

72. See Felicja Wilczewska, *Nim minęło 25 lat* (Toronto: Century Publishing Company, 1983), pp. 18–19, 21, 33–34.

73. Grudzińska-Gross and Gross, *W czterdziestym nas matko na Sybir zesłali*, p. 29.

74. Sterzer, pp. 40–41. What is "difficult to believe" is that Dr. Abraham Sterzer, a Jew, not only willingly served as a medical doctor in the Ukrainian Insurgent Army (Ukrainska Povstanska Armiia, or UPA) but also has written about it under the title "*We* fought for Ukraine" (emphasis mine). Sterzer's article also appears in Modest Ripetsky, *UPA Medical Services* (Toronto: Litopys UPA, 1992), pp. 341–58.

75. Tennenbaum, p. 131.

76. In Gross, *Revolution from Abroad*, p. 33.

77. In Kersten, *Polacy, Żydzi, Komunizm*, p. 32.

78. Smolar, "Jews as a Polish Problem," p. 38.

79. In *The Rohatyn Jewish Community: A Town That Perished* (Israel: Rohatyn Association of Israel, 1962), p. 44.

80. In Alexander Manor (ed.), *The Book of Sambor and Stari-Sambor: A Memorial to the Jewish Communities of Sambor and Stari-Sambor. The Story of the Two Jewish Communities from Their Beginnings to Their End* (Tel Aviv: Hotsaat Irgun yotse Sambor-Stari-Sambor veha-sevivah be-Yisrael, 1980), p. xxxviii.

81. Our Jews here and there,
Will all go into government offices,
The Ukrainians to the kolkhozes,
And the Poles will be deported.

In Edward Rosa, *Wspomnienia lat przeżytych na Wołyniu* (Toronto: Alliance of the Polish Eastern Provinces, 1997), p. 16.

82. Daniel Golombka, in Gershon Zik (ed.), *Rożyszcze My Old Home* (Tel Aviv: Roshishcher Committee in Israel, 1976), p. 27.

83. Moshe Rabin, ibid., p. 45.

84. See Teresa Prekerowa, "Podziemie żydowskie a podziemie polskie," *Odra* (Wrocław), April 1991, pp. 30–35.

85. For example, see Grudzińska-Gross and Gross, *W czterdziestym nas matko na Sybir zesłali*; Liszewski, *Wojna polsko-sowiecka*; Krzysztof Rowiński (ed.), *Moje zderzenie z bolszewikami we wrześniu 1939 roku* (London: Polska Fundacja Kulturalna, 1986); Klara Mirska, *W cieniu wiecznego strachu: wspomnienia* (Paris: Imprimerie IM. PO, 1980); Marek Celt, *Biali kurierzy* (München: M. Celt, 1986); and Pinchuk.

Shmuel Spector notes of Wołyń:

> Communists, Jews among them, welcomed the Soviets with joy. They didn't waste time in joining the local civil militias and setting up a provisory administrative apparatus. The militias helped the new rulers to

> disarm Polish policemen and officials and placed them under arrest. These actions aroused the wrath of the Polish public. However, Jewish participation in the local administration and the militias did not last long. In November 1939 officials and policemen began arriving from the East and most Jews were dismissed from positions of responsibility.

Spector, *The Holocaust of Volhynian Jews*, p. 24. In the larger towns of Eastern Poland, the first citizens' committees and militias were predominantly Jewish. Grudzińska-Gross and Gross, *War Through Children's Eyes*, p. 9.

86. Aleksander Wat, *Mój wiek. Pamiętnik mówiony* (London: Polonia Book Fund, 1977), p. 298. This particular passage seems to have been edited out of the English version of Wat's work: *My Century: The Odyssey of a Polish Intellectual* (Berkeley: University of California Press, 1988).

87. Lukas, *The Forgotten Holocaust*, p. 81.

88. Davies, "Poles and Jews: An Exchange."

89. Pinchuk, pp. 34–35.

90. Max Wolfshaut-Dinkes, *Échec et mat. Récit d'un survivant de Przemysl en Galicie* (Paris: Association des fils et filles des déportés juifs de France, 1983), pp. 21–22, 36.

91. In Kersten, *Polacy, Żydzi, Komunizm*, p. 28. Kersten attributes these statements to the selective recall of those giving the testimonies; they concentrated exclusively on Jewish behavior that attested to Jewish pro-Soviet, anti-Polish dispositions. A closer analysis, Kersten maintains, reveals that not all Jews were so disposed but only the young, who were under the influence of the communists, and part of the Jewish poor — the part deprived of prospects and increasingly and brutally being pushed out of Poland, in other words, the part that had hoped to benefit the most from the Soviet occupation. This may explain, but does not change, the *fact* of collaboration. All collaborators hoped to gain something.

92. As quoted in Norman Davies and Antony Polonsky (eds.), *Jews in Eastern Poland and the USSR, 1939–46* (New York: St. Martin's Press, 1991), pp. 264–66. The original text and changes appear on pp. 260–72.

93. As quoted by Prekerowa, "Podziemie żydowskie a podziemie polskie," p. 31. Like Władysław Bartoszewski, Prekerowa was among those honored by Yad Vashem for her efforts in Żegota. Prekerowa's article confirms the Home Army reports about strong pro-communist leanings in the Jewish underground leadership. The passage quoted by Prekerowa appears in the English translation of Smolar, "Jews as a Polish Problem," p. 40.

94. Kersten, *Polacy, Żydzi, Komunizm*, p. 26.

95. Ibid., p. 31.

96. Ibid., p. 27.

97. Ibid., pp. 65–66.

98. See Spector, *The Holocaust of Volhynian Jews*, p. 247.

99. Karol Liszewski (Ryszard Szawłowski), "The Polish-Soviet War of 1939" (paper presented at the Conference on Soviet Rule in Eastern Poland, 1939–1941, held at the School of Slavonic and East European Studies, University of London, on April 12–14, 1989), p. 11.

100. Account of a schoolgirl from Grodno, in Liszewski, *Wojna polsko-sowiecka*, p. 206.

101. Account of K. T. Czelny, in Lukas, *Out of the Inferno*, pp. 39–40.

102. Report of Brigadier-General Jan Lachowicz, in Liszewski, *Wojna polsko-sowiecka*, pp. 265–66.

103. J. Rokicka, "Było sobie takie miasteczko na Pokucie," *Semper Fidelis* (Wrocław) 5, no. 22 (September-October 1994): 31.

104. Maria Borkowska, "Witali Sowietów chlebem i solą," *Gazeta Polska* (Warszawa), February 10, 1994.

105. Jędrzej Giertych, *In Defence of My Country* (London: Wydawnictwo Towarzystwa im. Romana Dmowskiego, 1981), p. 294 n. 87.

106. When I told this story to a friend of mine whose family is from the same general area of prewar Poland, he responded: "I don't doubt it at all. My father-in-law is from nearby Zamość county. There, he witnessed a Jewish woman, a proprietor of a prosperous restaurant, screaming fanatically to the Soviets to apprehend a Polish officer out of uniform whom she recognized."

107. Liszewski, *Wojna polsko-sowiecka*, p. 37.

108. Ibid., p. 44.

109. Ibid., pp. 60, 75.

110. Ibid., p. 63.

111. In Sword, *Deportation and Exile*, p. 17.

112. Liszewski, *Wojna polsko-sowiecka*, p. 122.

113. Ibid., p. 124.

114. Ibid., p. 156.

115. Zwoliński, p. 79.

116. Zieliński, *Życie religijne w Polsce pod okupacją, 1939–1945*, p. 494.

117. Wacław Szetelnicki, *Trembowla. Kresowy bastion wiary i polskości* (Wrocław: Rubikon, 1992), p. 213.

118. Mazur.

119. Davies, "Jews and Poles: An Exchange."

120. In Pinchuk, p. 98.

121. For one analysis, see Korzec and Szurek, pp. 204–25.

122. See Richard C. Lukas' response to David Engel: Lukas, "A Response," pp. 581–90.

123. Shmuel Krakowski, "Podziemie polskie wobec zagłady Żydów," *Odra* (Wrocław), April 1991, pp. 23–29.

124. See Prekerowa, in J. Tomaszewski, *Najnowsze dzieje Żydów w Polsce*, p. 276.

125. Arendt, p. 216.

126. David Shtockfish (ed.), *Memorial Book: Ostrow-Lubelski* (Israel: Ostrow-Lubelski Society, 1987), pp. 408(17)–407(18).

127. As quoted by Kainer (Krajewski), in Bernhard and Szlajfer, p. 374.

128. In Pinchuk, p. 114.

129. Tennenbaum, p. 179.

130. Czesław Madajczyk, *Faszyzm i okupacje 1938–1945. Wykonywanie okupacji przez państwa Osi w Europie*, vol. 1 (Poznań: Wydawnictwo Poznańskie, 1983), p. 546.

131. Association of Braslaw and Surroundings in Israel and America, *Darkness and Desolation: In Memory of the Communities of Braslaw Dubene Jaisi Jod Kislowszczizna Okmienic Opsa Plusy Rimszan Slobodka Zamosz Zaracz* (Tel Aviv: Ghetto Fighters' House and Hakibbutz Hameuchad Publishing House, n.d.), p. 612. Emphasis mine. According to the preface, this was published "forty years after the grim epoch." According to Mordechai Altshuler, "Historiography of the past few decades has largely based itself on a perspective articulated by Solomon Schwarz in his 1951 study:

'Throughout the period preceding the Soviet Union's entry into the war, readers of the Soviet press were kept in ignorance of the Nazi anti–Jewish policies; the government's neutrality blinded Soviet Jews to the mortal danger threatening them. When, on June 22, 1941, the Wehrmacht suddenly invaded the Soviet Union, the Jewish population was largely unaware of the persecution and extermination that awaited them; many of those who might have fled remained where they were and perished.'

Schwartz regards the press as the Soviet Jews' sole source of information, totally ignoring other media. But even if the Jews had had access to all the information available at that time, they could not have known of the danger of extermination, because the Reich kept the orders governing this action, which were evidently issued between March and May of 1941, as one of its darkest secrets; the annihilation of the Jews began only after the Nazi invasion of the Soviet Union. It may therefore be said that the Soviet Jews were inadequately informed as to discrimination against and persecution of Jews in Germany and the countries it had occupied." Mordechai Altshuler, "Escape and Evacuation of Soviet Jews at the Time of the Nazi Invasion: Policies and Realities" in Lucjan Dobroszycki and Jeffrey S. Gurock (eds.), *The Holocaust in the Soviet Union: Studies and Sources on the Destruction of the Jews in the Nazi-Occupied Territories of the USSR, 1941-1945* (Armonk, NY: M.E. Sharpe, 1993), p. 83.

132. German intelligence report, August 4, 1941, as quoted by Pinchuk, p. 118.

133. Lukas, *The Forgotten Holocaust*, p. 128.

134. See Pinchuk, chapter 4, "The Dissolution of the Old Order and Emergence of the Lonely Jew," pp. 28–40, as well as the "Conclusion," pp. 127–33. See also Spector, *The Holocaust of Volhynian Jews*, pp. 33–43.

135. Davies, "Jews and Poles: An Exchange."

136. Grudzińska-Gross and Gross, *War Through Children's Eyes*, p. 19. Sword, *Deportation and Exile*, p. 18, notes, "The fact that the 'resettled' community of Poles in the USSR was later found to have a large proportion of Jews (estimated by some as being 30 per cent — compared with the 8 per cent of the population in prewar eastern territories) can largely be attributed to this third wave of transports."

137. According to Z. S. Siemaszko, in Sword, *The Soviet Takeover*, table on p. 230, of the 281,000 Jewish deportees, 198,000 were refugees and 83,000 were local inhabitants.

138. Zdzisław Adamowicz, "Pięć lat wyroku wśród polarnych zórz: wspomnienia z lat 1939–1944," in Wiesław Myśliwski and Andrzej Garlicki (comps.), *Wschodnie losy Polaków*, vol. 4 (Łomża: Oficyna Wydawnicza "Stopka," 1991), pp. 284–85. A similar statement appears in *Gazeta Polska* (Warszawa), February 10, 1994. For names of some Jews arrested and imprisoned by the NKVD, see Marek Jan Chodakiewicz, "Szmulek chciał być sowieckim generałem," *Gazeta Polska* (Warszawa), December 1, 1994. The arrests of Polish, Jewish, Ukrainian, Belorussian, and other activists and

leaders in Eastern Poland (including local communists suspected of being Trotskyites) began immediately after the Soviet invasion and continued until the very end of the occupation. Prekerowa, in J. Tomaszewski, *Najnowsze dzieje Żydów w Polsce*, p. 302.

139. Smolar, "Jews as a Polish Problem," p. 40.

140. Not all members in Party leadership positions were ethnic Poles. Almost the entire staff of the Personnel Department, for example, consisted of Russians, Belorussians and Ukrainians. For an exceptionally revealing account dealing with the internal workings of the postwar Polish Communist Party, see Zbigniew Błażyński, *Mówi Józef Światło* (London: Polska Fundacja Kulturalna, 1986). Światło (Lichtstein, Licht, Fleischfarb, born in Medyna near Tarnopol) was a high-ranking Jewish functionary (vice-director of the infamous Tenth Department, the Ministry of State Security) in the Polish communist régime. The information regarding membership in the Personnel Department can be found on pp. 65, 68–69, 100.

Paczkowski's figures are cited in Leszek Żebrowski's summary "Żydzi w UB," *Gazeta Polska* (Warszawa), June 22, 1995. This article contains some statistical information on Jewish communists in the interwar years in Poland, as well as the Jewish and Polonized names of a number of Jews in Poland's postwar communist régime. The name changes were made at the urging of the Comintern.

141. Kainer (Krajewski), in Bernhard and Szlajfer, p. 337.

142. Czesław Miłosz, "Anti-Semitism in Poland," *Problems in Communism* 3 (1957): 37.

143. Smolar, "Jews as a Polish Problem," pp. 50, 59–60.

144. Schatz, pp. 208–9. In December 1948, the PPR and the PPS merged to form the PZPR. The PZPR, together with the marionette SL and SD, became the official political party system of communist Poland.

145. Korboński, *The Jews and the Poles in World War II*, chapter 5, "The Jews in Postwar Poland," pp. 71–86, *passim* with some name corrections. The passage in brackets in point number 6 is out of sequence with the rest of the quotation. It appears on p. 83 of Korboński. Regarding the penultimate paragraph, in a letter to the editor in *Najwyższy Czas* (Warszawa), no. 26 (1995), Antoni Zambrowski denies that his father's name was "Rubin Nussbaum."

146. John Sack, *An Eye for an Eye* (New York: BasicBooks, 1993), pp. 182–83. This reference deals only with Upper Silesia. For other regions of Poland where Jewish representation at the lower levels is also noted, see pp. 214–15, where, for example, Sack states:

> After the war, the Polish police were called the Militia. The police chief in Kattowitz [Katowice] was Pinek Pakanowski, and the police chief in Breslau [Wrocław] was Shmuel "Gross," who used the Polish name Mieczysław "Gross." Some other Jewish police chiefs in Poland and Poland-administered Germany were Yechiel Grynspan [Jechiel Grynszpan] in Hrubieszów, Ayzer Mąka in Bielsko-Biała, and an unidentified man in Żabkowice.... "Gross" became the police chief of Lublin (and was transferred to Breslau in May, 1945) and one of his eight precinct chiefs was Sever Rubinstein. According to "Gross," eighty percent of the police officers in Lublin and fifty percent of the policemen in Lublin were Jews.

That this was the prevailing state of affairs is acknowledged by a highly placed Jew: "In practically every little town and village the political police were Jews. It might have been a diabolical Russian plan originating in Stalin's days to give this ungrateful task to Jews. It might also have been motivated by Stalin's basic suspicion of Poles. In any case, this could not have happened had there not been countless Jewish candidates for this type of post." See "Poland Without Jews," *Bulletin of the Jewish Federation Council of Greater Los Angeles*, June 15, 1978.

147. Except for the final three sentences (my translation), this passage appears in Korboński, *The Jews and the Poles in World War II*, pp. 78–79. For the entire article, see Abel Kainer (Stanisław Krajewski), "Żydzi a komuna," *Krytyka* 15 (1983). An English version of that article is included in Bernhard and Szlajfer, pp. 353–94. The passage may be found on pp. 381–82.

148. See Irene Tomaszewski and Tecia Werbowski, *Zegota: The Rescue of Jews in Wartime Poland* (Montreal: Price-Patterson, 1994), p. 161.

149. Z.Z.Z. *Syndykat Zbrodni: Kartki z dziejów UB i SB w czterdziestoleciu PRL* (Paris: Editions Spotkania, 1986), p. 17.

150. In Gross, *Revolution from Abroad*, p. 144.

151. Mateusz Wyrwich, *Łagier Jaworzno: z*

dziejów czerwonego terroru (Warszawa: Editions Spotkania, 1995), pp. 36, 67. Shlomo (Solomon) Morel was the commandant of the Świętochłowice and Jaworzno concentration camps. He personally tortured and executed many Germans and Poles after the war, but he later claimed that he did it (in the case of the former) because of the way he had been treated in German concentration camps and (in the case of the latter) because the Poles had killed his brother for being a Jew. According to Wyrwich, both of these claims were false. Morel was never in a German concentration camp, and his brother, after a military trial for robbery, was sentenced to death by the AL commandant General Grzegorz Korczyński. Morel avoided a similar fate by testifying that his brother had been the leader of the captured robber band of which he had also been a part. Ibid., pp. 36, 66–69.

According to Henryk Pająk and Stanisław Żochowski, *Rządy zbirów 1940–1990* (Lublin: Retro, 1996), p. 66, between 60,000 and 80,000 Germans — men and women, children and the aged — were murdered by the Soviets and their collaborators in 1,255 concentration camps for Germans after the war. About 90 percent of them were innocent of any crime. In Świętochłowice and Jaworzno, where Morel presided, over 6,000 Germans and German nationals were executed in 1945–46.

152. Z.Z.Z., pp. 26–29. See also Aniela Steinsbergowa, *Widziane z ławy obrończej* (Paris: Institut Littéraire, 1977), and the following two issues of *Zeszyty Historyczne* (Paris): 53 (1980): 129–47; and 67 (1984): 37–70, 93–126.

153. Jerzy Poksiński, *"My sędziowie, nie od Boga..." Z dziejów Sądownictwa Wojskowego PRL 1944–1956. Materiały i dokumenty* (Warszawa: Gryf, 1996), pp. 14, 22. One of the military tribunal judges who passed sentences on members of the Polish underground was Stefan Michnik, who later emigrated to Sweden as Szwedowicz. See Leszek Żebrowski, *Paszkwil wyborczej (Michnik i Cichy o Powstaniu Warszawskim)* (Warszawa: Burchard Edition, 1995), pp. 36, 94.

Among the many victims of the Stalinist judiciary was the legendary Home Army leader General August Emil Fieldorf ("Nil"), who was prosecuted by Benjamin Wajbloch and sentenced by a court presided over by Maria Gurowska; his appeal was dismissed by E. Mertz, G. Auscaler, and I. Andrejew, with the assistance of P. Kernowa, the assistant prosecutor of the Chief Prosecutor's Office. See Pająk and Żochowski, pp. 212–15.

In March 1996, the almost eighty-year-old Adam Humer and eleven other functionaries of the UB were convicted as Poland's first postindependence Stalinist criminals for their role in the routine torturing of political prisoners during the Stalinist era. Humer was sentenced to nine years in prison. The rest received from two to eight years. There was a preindependence hearing in 1957 with sentences imposed on Anatol Fejgin, Józef Różański, Józef Dusza, and others for similar crimes.

154. Stanisław Burza-Karliński, "Poles Have Brave Record of Aiding Jewish Escapes," letter in *Toronto Star*, July 25, 1992.

155. Korboński, *The Jews and the Poles in World War II*, p. 86. As Schatz, p. 1, stated, the communist Jews had been both "triumphant builders of communism and victims of its wrath." For another perspective on the role of the Jews in postwar Poland, see Krystyna Kersten, "Jak było w latach 1944–1948: władza-komunizm-żydzi," *Polityka* (Warszawa), July 6, 1991.

156. For example, Jon Wiener's article "Jews, Germans, and 'Revenge,'" *The Nation*, June 20, 1994, p. 881, states:

> Still, the general point remains that many Polish Communists from Jewish families were more Communist than Jewish. As Adam Michnik, Poland's best-known dissident before the fall of Communism there, wrote in an underground periodical in 1987, "An overwhelming majority of communists of Jewish origin did not identify themselves with the Jewish nation. They saw themselves as Poles, or simply, as communists.... To the Jewish community they were renegades who had abandoned the language, religion and national identity of their fathers."

157. See Michał Borwicz, "Polish-Jewish Relations, 1944–1947," in Abramsky et al., pp. 194–95.

158. Sack, *An Eye for an Eye*, preface to the 1995 paperback edition, p. ix.

159. Krystyna Kersten, *The Establishment of Communist Rule in Poland, 1943–48* (Berkeley: University of California Press, 1991), p. 219.

160. Daniel Jonah Goldhagen, "False Witness," *New Republic*, December 27, 1993, pp. 31–32. Regarding Bierut's tabulation, Michael Checinski ("To the Editor," *New Republic*, February 14, 1994, p. 7), a Jew who served the Communist Party for twenty years, ten of which were

spent in the Office of Military Counterintelligence (code name: Informacja) set up by SMERSH in communist Poland, states: "The handwritten *internal* note of the president of Poland, which records that only 1.7 percent of the employees of the Office of State Security were Jews, can therefore without any doubt be taken to be absolutely accurate."

161. John Sack, "To the Editor," *New Republic*, February 14, 1994, p. 6, continues:

> On the same page ... he [Goldhagen] reports what he calls my "claim that 75 percent of those in the Office of State Security in Silesia were Jews," as a statistic he calls a "sheer invention." In fact, I never claim this. I report that 75 percent of the *officers*— the lieutenants, captains, etc. — in the Office in Silesia were Jews, and I cite the one source that would know it: the Jews themselves, including the one who was secretary of state security. On the national level, the chief of the Office was Jacob Berman, a Jew, and all or almost all the department heads were Jews.

162. Daniel Jonah Goldhagen, "Daniel Jonah Goldhagen Replies," *New Republic*, February 14, 1994, p. 7.

163. Kersten, *Polacy, Żydzi, Komunizm*, pp. 83–84, and 88 n. 15. Goldhagen's information came from Kersten's work (per author's phone conversation with him). Kersten reports that as of November 21, 1945, there were 28,000 people in the UB, not counting the militia and the KBW (Internal Security Corps). Of these, 12,000 were operatives (*pracowniki operacyjne*), and 2,500 worked in the MBP (Ministry of State Security). Kersten continues:

> According to Bierut's note, among the 25,600 engaged [workers] there were 438 Jews, or 1.7 percent of all the workers. In directorships (*stanowiska kierownicze*), for 500 persons there were 67 Jews — over 13 percent. It can be said — in reference to the number of Jews in Poland, less than 100,000 at this time, before the massive repatriation from the USSR — that they were overrepresented. But we must part ways with the myth that the UB was the Jews.

164. See Pająk and Żochowski, and also Henryk Pająk, *Strach być Polakiem* (Lublin: Retro, 1996). Kunert's estimate can be found in L. Żebrowski, "Żydzi w UB." In a series entitled "Lista bezpieczniaków" beginning on June 6, 1996, *Gazeta Polska* (Warszawa) published a comprehensive list of the highest-ranking communists in the security service of the PRL, along with their short biographies and nationality for the years 1944–78.

165. Błażyński, p. 100. Światło's words are on p. 93.

166. Władysław T. Bartoszewski, *The Convent at Auschwitz* (London: Bowerdean Press, 1990), p. 29. In recent years some Jews have come to a nascent and painful awareness that the normalization of Polish-Jewish relations also calls for some reciprocity on the part of the Jewish community: to acknowledge and seek forgiveness for the many wrongs that befell Poles at the hands of Jews in Soviet-occupied Eastern Poland and in the postwar Stalinist era — along the lines of the Polish bishops' and leaders' frequent statements of atonement and conciliation directed to the Jews. See, for example, Ruta Pragier, *Żydzi czy Polacy* (Warszawa: Rytm, 1992), and "Czy Żydzi także przeproszą Polaków?" *Słowo-Dziennik Katolicki* (Warszawa), December 4, 1995.

167. Józef Łyżwa, "Pomagałem a potem siedziałem," *Gazeta Polska* (Warszawa), February 10, 1994. For Łódź, Pabianice, and other towns, see Tadeusz Bednarczyk, *Życie codzienne warszawskiego getta. Warszawskie getto i ludzie (1939–1945 i dalej)* (Warszawa: Ojczyzna, 1995), p. 242. For Kraków, see Elinor J. Brecher, *Schindler's Legacy: True Stories of the List Survivors* (New York: Penguin, 1994), p. 56. For Oświcięm, see Moshe Wiess, "To Commemorate the 50th Anniversary of the Liberation from Auschwitz," *Jewish Press* (Brooklyn), January 27, 1995.

The Jews in Janów Lubelski also welcomed the Germans. According to one interviewee, when the group of men he was with entered the deserted town, people dressed in black appeared out of nowhere to greet them with flowers. But they had expected Germans, not Poles. Chagrined, they returned to whence they came.

In the previously cited June 30, 1946, report of the Italian Embassy in Poland on the Jewish question, the first secretary stated that although the Jews supported Poland during World War II (in contrast to their behavior during the First World War), there were reports that "in the first days of the conflict, numerous Jews greeted the entrance of the German armies into Polish cities with cries of joy." Reale, p. 204.

168. Chaim A. Kaplan, *Scroll of Agony: The*

Warsaw Diary of Chaim A. Kaplan (New York: Macmillan Company, 1965), pp. 19–21; see also pp. 160–61.

169. For references to Jewish collaboration, see: Tadeusz Bednarczyk, *Obowiązek silniejszy od śmierci: wspomnienia z lat 1939–1944 o polskiej pomocy dla Żydów w Warszawie* (Warszawa: Grunwald, 1986), *passim*; Bednarczyk, *Życie codzienne warszawskiego getta*, especially pp. 229–42; Kazimierz Iranek-Osmecki, *He Who Saves One Life* (New York: Crown Publishers, 1971), pp. 36–38; and Józef Garliński, *The Survival of Love: Memoir of a Resistance Officer* (New York: Blackwell, 1991), a translation of *Niezapomniane lata: dzieje Wywiadu Więziennego i Wywiadu Bezpieczeństwa Komendy Głównej Armii Krajowej* (London: Odnowa, 1987), p. 109.

For example of Jewish collaborators in Kraków, see Tadeusz Pankiewicz, *Apteka w getcie krakowskim* (Kraków: Wydawnictwo Literackie, 1982), pp. 82–90; Marek Arczyński and Wiesław Balcerak, *Kryptonym "Żegota." Z dziejów pomocy Żydom w Polsce 1939–1945,* 2d ed. (Warszawa: Czytelnik, 1983), pp. 173–74; Aleksander Bieberstein, *Zagłada Żydów w Krakowie* (Kraków: Wydawnictwo Literackie, 1985), pp. 86, 164–74; and Bednarczyk, *Życie codzienne warszawskiego getta*, p. 235.

170. The term *szmalcownik* designates someone who takes money for ransom. During the war, this term was applied by the Jews to blackmailers — those who demanded money in exchange for not reporting on the Jews in hiding. Among the *szmalcowniki* were Volksdeutsche, Poles, Ukrainians, and Jews. *Smalec* in Polish means "lard."

171. "I'm sorry Lilo," Stella said to one of her friends, "I have orders from the Gestapo to arrest you. Don't try any nonsense and don't try to escape. If you do, I'll have to use my pistol!" One weekend, Stella led the Gestapo to cabins housing sixty-two Jews. Peter Wyden, *Stella: One Woman's True Tale of Evil, Betrayal, and Survival in Hitler's Germany* (New York: Simon and Schuster, 1992), pp. 14, 156.

172. Davies, *God's Playground*, p. 265. I wonder why Steven Spielberg didn't use one of them for his steamy bedroom scene in *Schindler's List* rather than a Polish woman?

Albert B. Doyon, who was stationed in Europe from June 1944 to September 1945 as a U.S. Army artillery officer and served in U.S. foreign counterintelligence from 1946 to 1986, recalls that when his unit liberated Lager Dora (the home of the V-2 rocket) in the spring of 1945, a small group of emaciated Frenchmen waving a flag came out of the camp. A few days later, a group of "marching Jews" emerged. "We were amazed at their relatively good physical condition," states Doyon. "They didn't want anything from us except food and clothing and immediately set out in a westward direction. They told us that they were communists and proud of it. They were definitely on a mission." Still later, other prisoners of various nationalities came out or were carried out by the Americans. "Then, one day," continues Doyon, "five to seven beautiful, well-dressed and well-fed prostitutes appeared in our camp. They told us that they were Jewish. Since there was not much going on in the area [the American camp was just west of the town of Nordhausen], we assumed they had also come from Lager Dora." From an interview.

173. Simon Wiesenthal, *Justice Not Vengeance* (London: Weidenfeld and Nicolson, 1989), p. 232.

174. Bednarczyk, *Życie codzienne warszawskiego getta*, pp. 230, 235.

175. In Joachim Schoenfeld (ed.), *Holocaust Memoirs: Jews in the Lwów Ghetto, the Janowski Concentration Camp, and as Deportees in Siberia* (Hoboken, NJ: KTAV Publishing House, 1985), pp. 240–42, *passim.*

176. Dana I. Alvi, "Letters," *Los Angeles Times*, November 6, 1994.

177. Bednarczyk, *Życie codzienne warszawskiego getta,* p. 237. Nechama Tec, *In The Lion's Den: The Life of Oswald Rufeisen* (New York: Oxford University Press, 1990), pp. 254–55 n. 16, provides the following brief analysis of the complex bureaucratic structure of the Nazi police system:

> To simplify what in reality were complex and sometimes confusing arrangements, by 1941 the Nazi police was divided into two main parts: the regular police (Ordnungspolizei) and the secret police (Sicherheitspolizei). Each of these major branches was further subdivided. The first, the regular police, consisted of two main sections, the Schutzpolizei and the Gendarmerie. The Schutzpolizei was assigned to cities. One of their functions was to guard Jewish ghettos. The second, the Gendarmerie, stayed in the rural areas where it performed different police funcions, including the implementation of the policies of Jewish annihilation.

The secret police, the Sicherheitspolizei, was also subdivided into two main sections. One of them, Sipo or Gestapo, dealt with matters related to the security of the state. This was the political police. The second, Kripo, handled criminal rather than political matters. Penetrating into, and superimposed on, all these police sections was the SS (Schutzstaffel). Perceived as the expression of the Führer's will, the SS eventually assumed control over all police branches.

178. Hilberg, *Perpetrators, Victims, Bystanders*, p. 161.

179. For a fragment of a memoir written in 1943 by a Jewish policeman, see Calel Perechodnik, "Dzień ostatni," *Karta* (Warszawa) 9 (1992): 39–55. This fragment deals with the anti–Jewish action in Otwock (outside Warsaw) in August 1942. His memoir is *Czy ja jestem morderca?* (Warszawa: Karta, 1993); English edition: *Am I a Murderer? Testament of a Jewish Ghetto Policeman* (Boulder, CO: Westview Press, 1996).

180. Klukowski, *Diary*, pp. 195, 223.

181. Gilbert, p. 665.

182. Bieberstein, p. 165, as quoted by Jerzy Robert Nowak, "Jeszcze o Judenratach," *Słowo-Dziennik Katolicki* (Warszawa), December 26, 1994.

183. Emmanuel Ringelblum, *Notes from the Warsaw Ghetto: The Journal of Emmanuel Ringelblum* (New York: McGraw-Hill, 1958), pp. 329–32.

184. Blanca Rosenberg, *To Tell at Last: Survival under False Identity, 1941–45* (Chicago: University of Illinois Press, 1993), p. 34.

185. See Lucjan Dobroszycki (ed.), *The Chronicle of the Łódź Ghetto, 1941–1944* (New Haven: Yale University Press, 1984).

186. As quoted by Wyden, p. 118.

187. Arendt, p. 118.

188. H. R. Shapiro, "Schindler's Choice," *In These Times*, March 21, 1994. The passage from Arendt can be found in Arendt, p. 125. The reference to Kastner appears on p. 118. On p. 117 Arendt states, "Without Jewish help in administrative and police work — the final rounding up of Jews in Berlin was, as I have mentioned, done entirely by Jewish police — there would have been either complete chaos or an impossibly severe drain on German manpower."

189. Ringelblum, *Polish-Jewish Relations*, pp. 62–63, editorial n. 5. For one personal account, see *Canadian Jewish News*, April 26, 1993.

190. Klukowski, *Diary*, pp. 101–2.

191. Ibid., p. 112.

192. Ibid., p. 179.

193. Ibid., pp. 190–91.

194. Ibid., p. 195.

195. Ibid., pp. 209–10.

196. Ibid., p. 219.

197. Michael Diment, *The Lone Survivor: A Diary of the Lukacze Ghetto and Svyniukhy, Ukraine* (New York: Holocaust Library, 1992), pp. 79–80.

198. Tennenbaum, pp. 184, 199. Tennenbaum continues: "Paradoxically, at the same time, letters were received from the Warsaw ghetto that life there was quite normal. True, Jews were forbidden to leave the ghetto and gentiles were forbidden to enter, but it was all for the good. The Jews in the ghetto were left alone. Schools were established and there were theaters and night clubs." This was at a time when the smaller ghettos were being annihilated in the east.

199. Yeshayahu Austri-Dunn (ed.), *Memorial Book of Czortkow* (Tel Aviv: Irgun Yotzey Czortkow in Israel, 1967), pp. 16–17.

200. Baruch Milch, "Mój testament," *Karta* (Warszawa) 2 (February 1991): 5–7, 12, 15–16.

201. *Kronika Polska* 8 (July 1, 1944), cited in Paweł Szapiro (ed.), *Wojna żydowsko-niemiecka. Polska prasa konspiracyjna 1943–1944 o powstaniu w getcie Warszawy* (London: Aneks, 1992), p. 407.

202. Bednarczyk, *Życie codzienne warszawskiego getta*, p. 237; and Bednarczyk, *Obowiązek silniejszy od śmierci*, pp. 155–56. The 1,378 names mentioned by Bednarczyk can be found in Zespół akt Delegatury Rządu, sygn. 202/II–26, Centralne Archiwum KC PZPR.

203. Lukas, *The Forgotten Holocaust*, p. 118.

204. For example, Szaje Fastak, a Jewish Gestapo agent, was executed in Chmielnik for betraying two Poles, who were subsequently shot for the "crime of helping Jews." See Wacław Zajączkowski, *Martyrs of Charity: Christian and Jewish Response to the Holocaust*, Part One (Washington, DC: St. Maximilian Kolbe Foundation, 1987), entry no. 98, p. 136.

205. Ringelblum, *Notes from the Warsaw Ghetto*, p. 280.

206. Andrzej Leszek Szcześniak, "Kilka pytań do A. Michnika w sprawie Powstania Warszawskiego," *Polska Kontra. Pismo Konfederacji Obrońców Polski (KOP)* 2, no. 3, (April 23, 1994): 1. See L. Żebrowski, *Paszkwil Wyborczej*, pp. 94–95.

207. Arendt, p. 91.

208. Władysław Bartoszewski, *The Warsaw Ghetto: A Christian's Testimony* (Boston: Beacon Press, 1987), p. 89.

209. Israel Shahak, "'The Life of Death': An Exchange," *New York Review of Books*, January 29, 1987.

210. Wiesenthal, p. 231.

Chapter 4: Polish Collaboration

1. Włodzimierz Bonusiak, *Kto zabił profesorów lwowskich* (Rzeszów: Krajowa Agencja Wydawnicza Rzeszów, 1989), p. 10.

2. There were 8 Russians, 1,389 Ukrainians, 44 Poles, and 61 Jews. Gross, *Revolution from Abroad*, p. 107.

3. Kazimierz Podlaski (Bohdan Skaradziński), *Białorusini, Litwini, Ukraińcy* (London: Puls Publications, 1985), p. 37.

4. There were also 621 Belorussians, 72 Jews, 53 Ukrainians, and 43 Russians. Iwanow, in Sword, *The Soviet Takeover*, p. 264. Actually there were two counts. In the first there were 659 Belorussians, 105 Poles, 75 Jews, and 38 Russians. See Gross, *Revolution from Abroad*, p. 107.

5. Davies, "Poles and Jews: An Exchange."

6. This section on Polish writers is based on Czaykowski, in Sword, *The Soviet Takeover*, pp. 102–30. See also Mieczysław Inglot, "The Sociopolitical Role of the Polish Literary Tradition in the Cultural Life of Lwów: The Example of Adam Mickiewicz's Work," ibid., pp. 131–48, and Małgorzata Kosewska, "Poeci do wynajęcia," *Gazeta Polska* (Warszawa), November 2, 1995.

7. Aleksander Wat, "Polskiye Sovetskiye Pisateli," *Literaturnaya Gazeta*, December, 5, 1939, as quoted by Czaykowski, in Sword, *The Soviet Takeover*, p. 104. For Wat's personal criticism of the Soviet system, dictated to Czesław Miłosz in the mid–1960s in Berkeley, California, see Wat, *My Century*. Wat (1900–1967) was born in Warsaw to a family of Polish-Jewish intellectuals. He converted to Christianity in 1941 while in a Soviet prison.

8. A partial listing of Polish writers in Lwów can be found in Bonusiak, p. 10. For a partial listing of interwar Polish writers of Jewish origin, see Fuks et al., p. 55.

9. Z. S. Siemaszko, *W sowieckim osaczeniu*. pp. 118–19.

10. Ibid., p. 128.

11. Grudzińska-Gross and Gross, *War Through Children's Eyes*, p. 23.

12. This summary is based on Robert Szymczak, "Oskar Lange, American Polonia, and the Polish-Soviet Dilemma During World War II: The Public Partisan as Private Emissary," *Polish Review* 40, no. 1 (1995): 3–27. See also Charles Sadler, "Pro-Soviet Polish Americans: Oscar Lange and Russia's Friends in the Polonia, 1941–1945," *Polish Review* 22, no. 4 (1977): 25–39.

13. According to Pająk and Żochowski, p. 191, Oskar Lange was a Polish Jew. His parents were Artur and Zofia Rosner. The quote from Werth can be found in Alexander Werth, *Russia at War, 1941–1945* (New York: E. P. Dutton, 1964), p. 846.

14. Memorandum, Harriman to the Secretary of State, in *Foreign Relations of the United States: Diplomatic Papers, 1944*, vol. 3 (Washington, DC: U.S. G.P.O. 1965), pp. 1406–7.

15. For U.S. Ambassador (to Poland) Arthur Bliss Lane's reaction to the proposed appointment of an American citizen as Polish ambassador to the United States, see Arthur Bliss Lane, *I Saw Poland Betrayed* (Boston: Western Islands, 1948), pp. 102–3.

16. In Robert Szymczak, "Oskar Lange, American Polonia, and the Polish-Soviet Dilemma during World War II: Making the Case for a 'People's Poland,'" *Polish Review* 40, no. 2 (1995): 156.

17. The following summary is based on Z. S. Siemaszko, *W sowieckim osaczeniu*, pp. 120–33.

18. Grudzińska-Gross and Gross, *War Through Children's Eyes*, p. 174.

19. Keegan, p. 207.

20. According to Klemens Nussbaum, about 12,000 Jews served in Berling's army. Moreover, "In a situation where more than 50 percent of the officers corps was made up of Red Army Officers, every second officer of Polish citizenship was a Jew." In addition, "the most important posts in the political apparatus" of the army were occupied by Jews. In Davies and Polonsky, p. 51.

21. See *Gazeta Polska* (Warszawa, series beginning on January 11, 1996) for a published list of UB officers and their positions in Wrocław and Dolny Śląsk; the list is based on the doctoral dissertation of Krzysztof Szwagrzyk, "UB na Dolnym Śląsku 1945–1956." Szwagrzyk has identified over 800 officers by name.

22. W. T. Bartoszewski, p. 17.

23. Lukas, *The Forgotten Holocaust*, p. 114–15

24. Davies, *God's Playground*, p. 464.

25. Jerzy Turonek, *Białoruś pod okupacją niemiecką* (Warszawa: Książka i Wiedza, 1993), pp. 32–33.

26. See the June 9, 1994, summary statement of the Polish-Ukrainian conference of historians held at Podkowa Leśna, in *Lwów i Kresy* (London) 32 (March–August 1994); 11.

27. Joseph Rothschild, *Return to Diversity: A Political History of East Central Europe since World War II*, 2d ed. (New York: Oxford University Press, 1993), p. 28.

28. As quoted by Kazimierz Stys Nepean, "Letter of the Day," *Toronto Star*, December 8, 1992.

29. Ibid.

30. For a discussion on the nature and extent of Polish collaboration during the German occupation, see Czesław Madajczyk, "Kann man in Polen 1939–1945 von Kollaboration sprechen?" in Röhr, pp. 133–48.

31. See Ihor Kamenetsky, *Secret Nazi Plans for Europe: A Study of Lebensraum Policies* (New York: Bookman Associates, 1961), p. 89, and Report, May 31, 1943, no. 38399, RG226, Office of Strategic Services, National Archives, Washington, D.C.,

The Racial Register (Volksliste) contained four categories: Class I, Germans who had promoted the Nazi cause before the war; Class II, people who retained their German nationality but were passive in the prewar Nazi struggle; Class III, Germans and their children previously connected with Poland (e.g., through marriage) who were willing to become Germanized; and Class IV, Polonized Germans who resisted Germanization. See *Trial of the Major War Criminals before the International Military Tribunal (*hereafter: *TMWC)* (published at Nuremberg in 1949), vol. 4, pp. 715–16; U.S. Counsel, *NCA* 1: 1031ff.

32. Józef Garliński, *Poland in the Second World War* (London: Macmillan Press, 1985), p. 64.

33. Czesław Madajczyk, *Polityka III Rzeszy w okupowanej Polsce*, vol. 2 (Warszawa: Państwowe Wydawnictwo Naukowe, 1970), pp. 188–89.

34. Davies, *God's Playground*, p. 446.

35. All people in Nazi-occupied Europe were classified as belonging to one of the following categories: Reichsdeutsch — Germans born in prewar Germany; Volksdeutsch — German nationals who could claim German ancestry within their family for up to three generations; Nichtdeutsch — non-Germans free of Jewish blood; and Juden — the Jews. They were then treated accordingly.

36. Keegan, p. 207. According to Łuczak, p. 185, there were between 200,000 and 250,000 Poles induced into the German armed forces.

37. Stefan Korboński, *The Polish Underground State: A Guide to the Underground, 1939–1945* (New York: Hippocrene, 1981), p. 1.

38. Letter, Dormer to Eden with enclosures, June 11, 1942, FO371/31097/52481 C5951/954/55, Public Record Office, Kew, Richmond, England.

39. Keegan, p. 207.

40. Józef Garliński, *Fighting Auschwitz: The Resistance Movement in the Concentration Camp* (London: Orbis Books, 1994), p. 138. The Polish edition of this work (*Oświęcim walczący*) came out in 1974, followed by an English edition in 1975 published by Friedman, then a Fawcett paperpack.

41. Ibid., pp. 140–41. In Appendix 3, Item 15, Garliński provides the following names and nationalities of the best-known informers at Auschwitz: Wierusz-Kowalski (Pole), Stanisław Dorosiewicz (he called himself a Georgian), Ernst Malorny (German), Rudolf Kauer (German), Hersz Kurcwaig (Jew), Josef Rusin (Czech), and Zolotov (Russian). For more information on Stefan Ołpiński, see Władysław Żeleński, "W cieniu Stefana Ołpińskiego," *Zeszyty Historyczne* (Paris) 69 (1984): 149–222.

42. As quoted in Garliński, *Fighting Auschwitz*, p. 141.

43. In the SS: Dutch, 50,000; Belgians, 40,000; Hungarians, 40,000; Croatians, 40,000; Ukrainians, 25,000 (according to Himmler) of the over 80,000 who had volunteered just for the SS-Galizien; Cossacks, 30,000; Latvians, 30,000; French, 20,000; Albanians, 19,000; Russians, 18,000; Estonians, 15,000; Belorussians, 10,000; Italians, 10,000; Tatars, 10,000; Norwegians, 8,000; Danes, 6,000; Slovaks, 6,000; Czechs, 5,000; Rumanians, 5,000; Finns, 4,000; Serbs, 4,000; Bulgarians, 3,000; Armenians, 3,000; Georgians, 3,000; Uzbeks, 2,000; Greeks, 1,000; Swiss, 1,000; Swedes, 300; English, 100. See George H. Stein, *The Waffen SS: Hitler's Elite Guard at War, 1939–1945* (Ithaca, NY: Cornell University Press, 1966); Kurt-Georg Klietmann, *Die Waffen-SS. Eine Dokumentation* (Osnabrück: Verlag Der Freiwillige, 1965), pp. 499–515; and the four volumes of Littlejohn, *Foreign Legions of the Third Reich.*

44. Smolar, "Jews as a Polish Problem," p. 41.

45. Łuczak, p. 163.

46. Turonek, p. 231.

47. Ibid., p. 232.

48. Piotr Wandycz in an exchange with Jerzy Jastrzębowski, "Rozmowy o braciach," in *Zeszyty Historyczne* (Paris) 88 (1989): 20.

In this context it may be well to cite the short "Grapevine" article by Christopher John Farley, "A Pension Plan for Nazi Followers," which appeared in *Time* on May 10, 1993, p. 17:

> Fifty years after World War II, the Third Reich's Crack troops are cashing in. Many Czechs, Poles and other East Europeans served in Hitler's SS but hid their past after the end of World War II for fear of retribution from ruling communist governments. Now that communism is fading, SS veterans are going public to collect pensions from the German government. Germany's social security system has awarded $190-a-month payments (a small fortune in the Baltics) to more than 250 disabled SS veterans in Lithuania, Latvia and Estonia. Says Latvian SS veteran and pension receiver Boris Mikhailov: "Thank you, Germany, thank you." Latvian Jews who survived the Holocaust, it should be noted, haven't got a red cent.

Richard C. Lukas, "History in Loose-Leaf Notebooks," *Zgoda* (Chicago), August 1, 1994, commented:

> The deliberate attempt to create ambiguity between victims and victimizers of World War II was dramatized last year [1993] when TIME magazine claimed that "many Poles" served in Hitler's SS. The overwhelming weight of historical scholarship does not place ethnic Poles in the SS. That is why they are not included as SS members in the classic studies of Dr. George Stein and Dr. Gerald Reitlinger. I don't know one professional historian who has studied the SS who would agree with TIME's claim. Surely after more than 50 years, at least one respected historian would have surfaced to support TIME's assertion. But none has emerged.
>
> TIME distorted the historical record, which in this case is quite clear. Ethnic Germans who lived in Poland served in the SS but these were Germans, not Poles. TIME ignored the obvious and very important distinction.

The one-and-a-half-year furor caused by *Time*'s contention that "many ... Poles" served in the SS produced an interesting exchange of letters between the Canadian Polish Congress and the war crimes office in Ludwigsburg, Germany, the Polish Main Commission for the Investigation of Crimes Against the Polish Nation in Warsaw, and the German pension office in Ravensburg. (Copies of these letters are in the possession of the author.)

Letter from the war crimes office in Ludwigsburg (August 3, 1993):

> Since December 1, 1958, my office has been responsible for information on [clarification/ investigation of] Nazi crimes, which we have pursued systematically. In the context of this work, units that were recruited from [among] foreigners also have been examined. Predominantly, these were units of the Waffen-SS. Based on the knowledge gained herefrom, I can conclude that there was no Waffen-SS unit similar to the Latvian, Lithuanian, Ukrainian, etc., divisions that would have consisted solely of Polish volunteers or "conscripts."
>
> It has, however, come to our knowledge that many soldiers fought in the Waffen-SS who (at least prior to joining it) were of Polish nationality. To all intents and purposes, however, these were essentially Poles of German ancestry, who were later "Germanized," to use the parlance of the Nazi régime.
>
> I should also mention in this context that, after the attack on the Soviet Union, (ethnic) Poles showed an interest in joining the Waffen-SS or the Wehrmacht in order — as the saying went — to fight communism. While the Wehrmacht and the Waffen-SS (themselves) were pursuing such recruitment, Hitler or, rather, Himmler rejected the idea. Only on October 24, 1944, did Hitler agree to the enlistment of Poles as volunteers (see, in this connection, the decree of the Heeresgruppe Mitte [Central Army Squadron/Group] of November 4, 1944, concerning guidelines for the recruitment of Polish volunteers, Federal Archives Document MA 53-13/40). We have no knowledge about the formation, duty or attachment of these volunteer units — since, for the purposes of clarification of Nazi crimes (1944–1945), they did not become [never became] known and, therefore, we did not pursue these questions.
>
> Regardless of all else, there were Polish "willing helpers" (*Hilfswillige*) and Polish

police units (*polnische Polizeiverbände*) that became involved in SS operations (e.g., Polish police and "Trawniki people" [*Trawniki-Leute*] during the suppression of the Warsaw Ghetto Revolt, and "Trawniki people" serving as guards in concentration or annihilation camps).

Lastly, I cannot confirm that (ethnic) Poles who still live in Poland today and, presumably, were members of the Waffen-SS are receiving pensions from the Federal Republic, based on their former service in the Waffen-SS....

Considering the great number of inquiries, I cannot say [for certain] whether, among those inquiries, there were one or several that related to ethnic Poles. It could, theoretically, be checked out if one were to go through our [entire] central archives. In view of approximately 1.6 million registrations, however, this is impossible. The Bureau for Public Assistance in Ravensburg, moreover, did not seek our assistance at the time, which, however, we are now catching up with. So far, there have been no inquiries that related to ethnic Poles (only members of the Baltic states). This fact however, does not exclude the possibility that there may have been applications from Poles.

Letter from the Main Commission in Warsaw (September 14, 1993):

> In reference to your letter...I would like to inform you that a certain group of former Polish citizens in Silesia and Pomerania, who were placed or forced on to the *Deutsche Volksliste* did serve in the ranks of the SS. Enclosed you will find some references from K.G. Klietmann's *Die Waffen-SS* dealing with the number of volunteers serving in the SS. Since in the beginning only volunteers served in the SS, this means that they were ethnic Germans. The situation changed in 1943 when the Waffen-SS was complemented by conscription. Then, a small group (*niezbyt liczna grupa*) of Poles from Silesia and Pomarania chanced into the SS and was registered with Group III DVL (*Deutsche Volksliste*). Unfortunately, it is impossible to determine their number because in the statistics they were included with the Germans. The SS-Galizien division in which were also found Polish citizens of Ukrainian background is a separate matter.
>
> In any case, there was no Waffen-SS formation or German police consisting of [ethnic] Poles. [This presumably is not a reference to the "Blue Police."] The attempt to create a formation consisting of [ethnic] Poles within the SS or the Wehrmacht alluded to by [the war crimes office in Ludwigsburg] was not crowned with success.
>
> In the ranks of the "Trawnikileute" ["Trawniki people"] there were Polish citizens—mainly Ukrainians. Among the members of this formation tried by Polish courts after the war, there were a few who admitted to being of Polish nationality. You will find more information in the enclosed monograph [Maria Wardzyńska, *Formacja Wachmannschaften des SS- und Polizeiführers im Distrikt Lublin*—see p. 350 n. 35 below] dealing with this formation.
>
> There were no Poles in the personnel of the concentration camps; only a few former Polish citizens who acquired German citizenship.

Letter from the German pension office in Ravensburg (October 7, 1994):

> The contention by *Time* Magazine in New York that many Poles served in the SS, *allegedly* confirmed by our office is, on the basis of our information, *not* true.

After numerous additional letters from Canada and the United States, *Time* ran its retraction on November 21, 1994, p. 16:

> Correction
>
> In a brief item about pensions being paid by the German government to World War II veterans ["A Pension Plan for Nazi Followers," May 10, 1993], we wrote that among other nationalities, many Poles served in Hitler's SS. In the kind of vigorous dialogue with our readers that we welcome, many Americans and Canadians of Polish descent took umbrage at this assertion, citing not only historical studies but also reminding us of what Poland suffered under Hitler. Upon rechecking our sources, we found that precise information from that tragic period of history is elusive, but the number of ethnic Poles who may have actually served in the SS is almost certainly too small to warrant the use of *many*. We regret the error.

49. Prekerowa, in J. Tomaszewski, *Najnowsze dzieje Żydów w Polsce,* p. 349; Adam Hempel, *Pogrobowcy kl̨eski. Rzecz o policji "granatowej" w Generalnym Gubernatorstwie 1939–1945* (Warszawa: Państwowe Wydawnictwo Naukowe, 1990), p. 133.

50. Dear, p. 249.

51. Prekerowa, in J. Tomaszewski, *Najnowsze dzieje Żydów w Polsce,* p. 351.

52. See Lucjan Dobroszycki, *Reptile Journalism: The Official Polish-Language Press under the Nazis, 1939–1945* (New Haven: Yale University Press, 1994), and Czesław Miłosz, "Adders and Other Reptiles," *New York Review of Books,* May 11, 1995, pp. 15–18.

53. Korboński, *The Polish Underground State,* pp. 142–43.

54. According to Lukas, *The Forgotten Holocaust,* p. 198, Kamiński's first name was Mieczysław: "He was brought up a Russian, although his father was Polish and his mother German. Kamiński spent years in a Soviet labor camp." Turonek, p. 279, speaks of him as "Bronisław Kamiński." According to David Littlejohn, *The Patriotic Traitors: The History of Collaboration in German-Occupied Europe, 1940–45* (New York: Doubleday, 1972), p. 298, "Bronislav Kaminski" was a "gifted, if somewhat unscrupulous, character of Polish-Russian (also possibly Jewish) extraction." G. Stein, p. 264, refers to him as a "Russian engineer" (see also p. 265).

55. Lukas, *The Forgotten Holocaust,* pp. 194–206.

56. The quoted passages come from the editorial notes by Kermish and Krakowski, in Ringelblum, *Polish-Jewish Relations,* p. 42 n. 6 and p. 217 n. 2. For examples of Polish "informing" and "plunder and blackmail," see the sections so entitled in Gutman and Krakowski, pp. 220–25. For an account of Poles executed by the AK for denouncing Jews in southeastern Poland, see Adam Kazimierz Musiał, *Krwawe upiory: dzieje powiatu Dąbrowa Tarnowska w okresie okupacji hitlerowskiej* (Tarnów: Oficyna Wydawnicza Karat, 1993), pp. 32–69.

57. Korboński, *The Polish Underground State,* pp. 74–75; Lukas, *The Forgotten Holocaust,* p. 250 n. 100.

58. Łuczak, p. 499. For a work that deals with the alleged collaboration of Bishop Czesław Kaczmarek, see (Rev.) Jan Śledzianowski, *Ksiądz Czesław Kaczmarek biskup kielecki 1895–1963* (Kielce, 1991). Kaczmarek's September 24, 1939, pastoral letter that brought on the accusations of collaboration stated:

> Without law and order, without social discipline it is impossible to maintain the religious life, the life of the nation, and even the most ordinary life of human beings. For this reason, I call upon all of you—while first and foremost being obedient to the holy Commandments of God and the Church—to be obedient to the administrative authorities in all things that do not go against a Catholic conscience and our Polish dignity [*godność*].

Ibid., p. 67. Unfortunately, in the subsequent misreporting of the letter, the word *godność* (dignity, pride, honor, self-respect) was maliciously replaced with the word *gościnność* (hospitality) thus giving the letter a totally different tone from that originally intended by the bishop. This marked the beginning of Kaczmarek's troubles. His second pastoral letter, issued on October 2, 1939, repeated his previous admonition:

> I desire and call upon you to obey conscientiously all regulations and laws both of the administrative as well as the military authorities. We believe in the promises given to us, that nothing will be demanded of us which goes against Catholic conscience. There must be law and order in society. For this reason we must loyally cooperate with the aforementioned authorities; whosoever acts differently injures his society and makes more difficult the return to normal life and to better days.

Ibid., p. 69. Bishop Kaczmarek's logic (whether we agree with it or not) dictating this *counsel* (i.e., "to be obedient to the administrative authorities in all things that do not go against a Catholic conscience and our Polish dignity") is much more understandable than that which dictated the *actions* of the Judenräte in the ghettos, who with the help of the Judische Ordnungsdienst, often scrupulously *carried out* criminal orders that in fact constituted crimes against humanity, conscience, and national honor.

Bishop Sokołowski's case rested mostly on his failure to speak out against the German occupation policies, a sin of omission rather than a sin of commission. See Zygmunt Zieliński (ed.), *Życie religijne w Polsce pod okupacją hitlerowską 1939–1945* (Warszawa: Ośrodek Dokumentacji i Studiów Społecznych, 1982), p. 436.

Bishop Lorek is credited (also by Jews) for

intervening in behalf of Poles and Jews seized by Germans and for helping to hide Jews in the bell tower of the city's cathederal and the cellars of the seminary. His "collaboration" with the enemy also seems to have been minimal. See ibid., p. 444; Eva Feldenkreiz-Grinbal (ed.), *Eth Ezkera — Whenever I Remember: Memorial Book of the Jewish Community in Tzoyzmir (Sandomierz)* (n.p., n.d.), p. 553; and Carlo Falconi, *The Silence of Pius XII* (Boston: Little, Brown and Company, 1970), pp. 189–93.

59. See Władysław Bartoszewski and Zofia Lewin (eds.), *Righteous among Nations: How Poles Helped the Jews, 1939–1945* (London: Earlscourt Publications, 1969), document on p. 684.

60. Łuczak, pp. 315, 319. According to Łuczak, there was a Ukrainian Main Social Welfare Council. Danylo Husar Struk (ed.), *Encyclopedia of Ukraine,* vol. 5 (Toronto: University of Toronto Press, 1993), p. 368, however, states that the Ukrainian Relief Committees were under the umbrella of the Ukrainian Central Committee (Ukrainskyi Tsentralnyi Komitet, or UTsK).

61. Łuczak, pp. 316, 318.

62. Chaim Band of Brasław, in Association of Braslaw, *Darkness and Desolation,* p. 608. Zdzisław A. Siemaszko, "Wileńska AK a Niemcy," *Zeszyty Historyczne* (Paris) 110 (1994): 201, also states that initially the Poles welcomed the Germans. Similar observations were made by the commander-in-chief of the Polish Home Army, General Stefan Grot-Rowecki. See Smolar, "Jews as a Polish Problem," p. 40.

63. Turonek, pp. 65–66 and 250, notes 41–49.

64. See Mieczysław Suwała ("Oro," chaplain of AK forest units), "'Boże coś Polskę' w puszczy nalibockiej," in *Udział kapelanów wojskowych w drugiej wojnie światowej* (Warszawa: Akademia Teologii Katolickiej, 1984), pp. 371–74.

65. Turonek, pp. 65–66.

66. Chief of the Secret Police and the SD, "Operational Situation Report USSR No. 50," in Yitzhak Arad et al. (eds.), *Einsatzgruppen Reports: Selections from the Dispatches of the Nazi Death Squads' Campaign against the Jews, July 1941–January 1943* (New York: Holocaust Library, 1989), p. 83.

67. In Turonek, pp. 74–75. It may be mentioned that although he was careful to avoid the label of collaborator, Ian Stankevich himself— and the PBN, which he founded — attempted to take advantage of the German occupation to further the cause of the Belorussian independence movement by building up an indigenous armed forces and by filling administrative offices with Belorussians. See Longin Tomaszewski, *Kronika wileńska 1941–1945. Z dziejów polskiego państwa podziemnego* (Warszawa: Oficyna Wydawnicza Pomost, 1992), p. 79.

68. Turonek, pp. 203–4.

69. Ibid., p. 204.

70. Ibid., p. 205.

71. Ibid., p. 206. Nowogródek AK Commandant Janusz Prawdzic Szlaski stated, "I know that the 5th Wilno Brigade ["Łupaszka's" unit] cooperated with the Germans from the very beginning of its existence and, during the withdrawal of the Germans, left for the West." In Z. A. Siemaszko, p. 214.

72. Turonek, pp. 204–7.

73. Z. A. Siemaszko, *passim.*

74. In Turonek, pp. 206–7.

75. L. Tomaszewski, pp. 94–96.

76. Rothschild, p. 57.

77. See Z. A. Siemaszko, pp. 198–222, and J. Zdzisław Szyłeyko's response, "Współpraca wileńskiej AK z Niemcami — rzeczywistość czy fikcja?" *Zeszyty Historyczne* (Paris) 112 (1995): 233–36.

78. The Polish underground consisted of a number of clandestine organizations, including the Home Army, linked with the Polish government-in-exile, located from October 1939 to May 1940 in Paris and after that in England. The activities of these organizations were coordinated by the clandestine Government Delegation for the Homeland (Delegatura rządu) in occupied Poland.

79. Peter Silverman, David Smuschkowitz, and Peter Smuszkowicz, *From Victims to Victors* (Montmagny, Québec: Marquis; Toronto: Canadian Society for Yad Vashem, 1992), p. 113. This is a common refrain in Holocaust literature. For Poland's "official stance on the fate of [its] three million Jews," see Lukas, *The Forgotten Holocaust,* chapter 6: "The Polish Government, the Home Army, and the Jews," pp. 152–81.

80. Gutman and Krakowski, pp. 216–17. Tec (*In The Lion's Den,* pp. 183, 262 n. 5) also refers to the killing of Jews by "Polish partisans." The first reference (on p. 183) follows a paragraph dealing with the NSZ.

81. Ringelblum, *Polish-Jewish Relations,* editorial n. 35 on pp. 219–20. Krakowski cites that order in his *The War of the Doomed: Jewish Armed Resistance in Poland, 1942–1944* (New York: Holmes and Meier, 1984), p. 14.

82. In his review of Krakowski's *The War of the Doomed,* Stanislaus Blejwas states:

> The order cited by Krakowski was not nr. 116, but Bór-Komorowski's *Organizational Report nr. 220* (31 August 1943), which he dispatched *to the Government-in-Exile in London,* which *inter alia,* discusses the problem of uncontrolled bandits and partisan activity which provoked Nazi retaliation against the local civilian population. Krakowski not only misidentifies the order, which was not the text sent to local commanders, but summarizes Bór-Komorowski's report in a manner which could lead the reader to misunderstand its intent.

Krakowski's version reads:

> Well-armed gangs ramble endlessly in cities and villages, attack estates, banks, commercial and industrial companies, houses and large farms. The plunder is often accompanied by acts of murder which are carried out by Soviet partisan units hiding in the forests or by ordinary gangs of robbers. Men and women, especially Jewish women, participate in the assaults.... I have issued an order to the region for area commanders to go out with arms, when necessary, against these plunderers or revolutionary robbers.

The original reads:

> Well-armed gangs ramble endlessly in cities and villages, attack estates, banks, commercial and industrial companies, houses and apartments, and larger peasant farms. The plunder is often accompanied by acts of murder which are carried out by Soviet partisan units hiding in the forests or by ordinary gangs of robbers. The latter recruit from all kinds of criminal subversive elements.
>
> Men and women, especially Jewish women, participate in the assaults. This infamous action of demoralized individuals contributes in a considerable degree to the complete destruction of many citizens, who have already been tormented with the four year struggle against the enemy.
>
> The occupier has not basically opposed the existing state of affairs. When German security organs are sometimes called in, in the more serious instances, they refuse to help, avoiding the bandits. Often the reverse occurs — the greater act of banditism calls down repression upon the innocent population.
>
> In order to give some help and shelter to the defenseless population, I have issued an order — with the understanding of the Chief Delegate of the Government — to the commanders of regions and districts regarding local security. I have ordered the commanders of regions and districts, when necessary, to move with arms against these plundering or subversive bandit elements. I emphasized the need to liquidate the leaders of bands and not efforts to destroy entire bands. I recommend to the local commanders assuring the cooperation of the local population and of the representative of the Government's Delegate in organizing self-defence and of a warning system.

Blejwas notes, "A reading of the full text of this part of the Report in its correct context suggests that it is very debatable, at the least, to describe it as 'official permission' for *AK* commanders to attack Jewish partisan units, even if this was the text of an order (which it was not) sent to the local *AK* partisans commanders." Blejwas then quotes "a copy or version" of the September 15, 1943, Order No. 116 sent to local commanders. The order repeated the problem of partisan activity and counseled the elimination of the leaders but not the entire group; it did not refer specifically to Jews at all. Point number 2 of that order reads, "I recommend to the commanders of sub-districts and districts to step in where necessary against plundering or subversive bandit elements." This was interpreted by the communists as a carte blanche to kill communist partisans. Bór-Komorowski denied any such intent. In fact, in December 1943, he condemned an NSZ attack on the communist GL-AL units. See Stanislaus Blejwas, "Polemic as History: Shmuel Krakowski, the War of the Doomed. Jewish Armed Resistance in Poland, 1942–1944," *Polin,* 4 (1989): 357–58; Krakowski's "Response to Blejwas," ibid., pp. 362–67; and Blejwas' "Reply to Krakowski," ibid., pp. 368–69. See also Lukas, *The Forgotten Holocaust,* pp. 83, 242–43 n. 76.

John Lowell Armstrong (not to be confused with John A. Armstrong, the author of *Ukrainian Nationalism)* also addresses the claims that Bór-Komorowski's order was aimed against the Jews. After documenting the extent and serious nature of the banditry conducted by ethnic Poles (including some AK members), Soviet diversionary and partisan units, and the GL, as well as the AK's stringent measures against the bandits, including the issuance of numerous death sentences (estimated by Korboński at 920 in 1943 and the first half of 1944), Armstrong states:

> Therefore, it is clear from the foregoing that Order 116 and other Home Army orders against banditry were fully justified in the face of rampant robberies. As a result of these orders, the AK generally tried hard to put an end to banditry and robbery, not sparing ethnic Poles or even members of its own ranks in this struggle. The question becomes, then, whether or not Jews engaged in banditry, and, if they did, how did the Home Army react to this?
>
> Most Jewish historians, Krakowski and Ainsztein included, adamantly reject any suggestion of Jewish involvement in robberies of the Polish population. In Krakowski's case, this position is so stringent that he even ludicrously accuses Emmanuel Ringelblum of being under the influence of Polish "propaganda" when Ringelblum writes that Jews trying to survive in the forest were "condemned to the life of bandits who have to live by robbery." Actually, there were three ways in which Jews committed armed robbery of the Polish population during the Second World War: as members of partisan units, in order to survive, and in mixed Polish-Jewish professional bandit gangs.... [Examples follow.]
>
> In line with its basally uncompromising stand against banditry, the AK treated Jews who robbed with the same severity as it did Poles. Specific examples of death sentences carried out on Jews for robbery are found in Polish underground documents. For example, in a report on the Home Army's diversionary activities for August 1943, Bór-Komorowski noted that "for terrorist acts against the Polish population nine Jewish robber gangs were liquidated, killing seventy-six bandits." Another instance of the execution of Jews for robbery is found in a summary of actions carried out during the German occupation by a BCh unit in the Hrubieszów area. Here the Peasant Battalions shot a group of thirteen Jews for banditry. Certainly, these actions were severe, but they were not *a priori* anti–Semitic, as the Home Army generally treated all who robbed with the same harsh justice.... [An example follows: an AK unit led by Leon Szymbierski ("Orzeł") killed five Jewish partisans without orders, for which action Szymbierski was executed.]
>
> In the final analysis, Order 116 was aimed against bandits of all types without regard to nationality, including Jewish ones and those in the AK. The order, and others against banditry, were fully justified by the plague of robbery raging in German-occupied Poland. Although Order 116 was draconian, it was not intended to unleash a war against Jews and did not do so.

John Lowell Armstrong, "The Polish Underground and the Jews: A Reassessment of Home Army Commander Tadeusz Bór-Komorowski's Order 116 against Banditry," *Slavonic and East European Review,* 72, no. 2 (April 1994): 272, 275–76.

83. Joseph Kermish, "Postscript," in Ringelblum, *Polish-Jewish Relations,* pp. 311–12.

84. Prekerowa, in J. Tomaszewski, *Najnowsze dzieje Żydów w Polsce,* p. 367.

85. Richard Z. Chesnoff, "The Beginning of Redemption" *U.S. News and World Report,* April 3, 1995. A somewhat different version of Yaffa Eliach's story is presented by Edward Linenthal:

> On October 20, 1944, another baby brother — who had been born to Eliach's mother while they were in hiding was murdered along with his mother as they hid from Polish partisans who wanted to finish the work of killing Jews. When they discovered their hiding place, Eliach recalled, "there was my mother with the baby in her arms. She stood up, walked out...and I was just in back of her. And she said, "Have mercy on my baby. Please kill me first." She didn't ask for her life.... At that moment he shot my baby brother...and he shot my mother....She fell back on me and my brother, and my father. And they sprayed with the machine gun, but she protected us with her body, and the bullets went into her body. They shot very low, but her body got all the bullets...and I was covered with blood, and they left." Eliach's father was arrested a few days later by the Russians and sent to Siberia.

Edward T. Linenthal, *Preserving Memory: The Struggle to Create America's Holocaust Museum*

(New York: Viking Penguin, 1995), p. 176. According to Marjorie Rosen and Mary Huzinec, "Collector of Souls," *People Magazine* (interview with Yaffa Eliach, January 17, 1994), p. 38, in horrendous circumstances that call for a suspension of judgment, the first child was strangled by fellow Jews "in her mother's arms because they feared that he might cry and reveal their whereabouts." The attack in which Eliach's mother and brother were killed is described as follows: "After the liberation of Ejszyszki by the Russians, Eliach's family returned to her grandmother's house. One day, Polish partisans, believing that too many Jews had survived the war, broke in and shot to death Eliach's mother and new baby brother, who had been born in the cave. In 1944 her father was arrested by the KGB on trumped-up charges and exiled to Siberia for 17 years."

A version (copyrighted by Yaffa Eliach) similar to that of Linenthal but richer in details appears in André Stein, *Hidden Children: Forgotten Survivors of the Holocaust* (Toronto: Penguin Books Canada, 1993), pp. 64–65. This passage begins after the Sonensons reclaimed Chaim (Eliach's baby brother) from a priest with whom he was left:

> On October 20, there was a great party at the Sonensons' house to honour the baby's return from his Catholic home. They named him Chaim for "long life" and for his grandmother, Chaya. Yaffa and Yitzhak were allowed to stay up late for the special occasion. There was a great deal of eating, drinking, singing, dancing. Everybody was there, even some Russian soldiers. Then they all went to bed, the parents upstairs, and the children downstairs in their room.
>
> In the middle of the night, Yaffa was awakened by a noise that could have been a knock on the window next to her bed. She and Yitzhak leaped up and ran out of the room. The moment they crossed the threshold, a grenade crashed through the window and exploded.
>
> By the time the two children made it upstairs, Moshe and Zipporah and their guests were up, screaming and running around. Everyone else jumped out of the second-storey windows, but Yaffa's parents could not jump: they had the baby.
>
> Once again, the family had to hide. Moshe, faithful to his basic principle of never splitting up the family, looked for a place big enough to shelter all of them. There was a closet in the master bedroom. Moshe opened the door and found it suitable for all of them. The sloping ceiling allowed only for Zipporah to sit on the floor with her baby in her arms. Yaffa sat behind her. For Yitzhak and Moshe there was room only if they lay flat on the floor behind them. After having dragged a piece of furniture in front of the closet door, Moshe squeezed past it and hid with his family.
>
> For Yaffa, Yitzhak and their mother, who was holding Chaim in her arms, there was nothing to do but wait. They could hear loud voices coming closer to the stairs. Yaffa recognized the voice of the pharmacist's son, accompanied by white Partisans. "He came accompanied by some of his comrades who still wanted Poland free of Russians and Jews." Yaffa explains.
>
> Then she heard another voice: "There's no point looking for Sonenson and his wife. They must have escaped with the others."
>
> And another one said: "Let's just check upstairs."
>
> Upstairs they touched nothing. They were not interested in money or things. They wanted to kill Russians and Jews.
>
> "Look at the floor here!" Yaffa heard from inside the closet. "There's a fresh scratch on the floor from dragging a piece of furniture. Let's just see where it leads."
>
> They followed the scratch to the closet, moved the piece of furniture and opened the closet door.
>
> Inside they found Zipporah sitting on the floor with her head touching the ceiling. In her arms, she was holding her baby. She rose to her feet immediately and stepped into the room. The pharmacist's son had a gun.
>
> "Kill me first, not my baby!" she said calmly. She knew why he had come.
>
> But they shot the baby first. They put nine bullets into his tiny body. And then fifteen into the mother. "What made me count the bullets?" Yaffa asks herself in a scarcely audible voice. "To this day I don't understand."
>
> Zipporah's body fell back into the closet, on top of Yaffa. The child stumbled back under her mother's weight. She felt numb and heavy. She thought that the bullets had killed her. She felt that insects were already eating her flesh. So that's what it feels like being dead, she thought. Then she felt something warm and sticky on her skin. It was her mother's blood.

86. See Jarosław Wołkonowski, "Ejszyszki — zniekształcony obraz przeszłości," *Gazeta Wyborcza*, September 26, 1996. According to the testimony of Yitzhak Sonenson (Sonenshon in the document), Yaffa's older brother

> Korkuć was, one could say, an entrepreneur (*przedsiębiorca*) or a go-between. Not only did he hide Jews himself, he also sought out hiding places among other peasants in Korkociany and even in neighboring villages. I know that [my] father gave him money. How much? That I don't know. One night both of them went to the country town to dig up the money. There were four of us at his house: my father Moshe Sonenshon, my mother Zipporah, my sister Yaffa, and I.... Korkuć hid many Jews, I don't know how many. There were hiding places under his house, under the cow-shed, and even under the pigsty. I think that several dozen Jews were hidden by him; he hid many more that were under his care. He hid them among the neighbors and even in neighboring villages. He was accused of harboring Jews several times. They searched his premises a few times. Once he even sat in jail. But no one was ever found [Yad Vashem archive 03/2743, deposed on February 6, 1965].

In her *Hasidic Tales of the Holocaust* (New York: Oxford University Press, 1982), p. 216, Yaffa Eliach recalls being comforted by a Polish woman earlier in the war after Lithuanian collaborators slaughtered the Jews of Ejszyszki: "The big Polish woman picks up the little girl and covers her with a large woolen shawl. All is dark. The Polish woman whispers to her: 'He [a German] is probably calling to report that all the Jews in Eisysky are dead. But we fooled him, my little one, you are alive.'"

87. Michał Wołłejko, "Opowieści chasydzkie," *Gazeta Polska* (Warszawa), August 15, 1995.

88. This memo, dated July 27, 1995, was written in response to complaints received by *U.S. News and World Report* regarding the April 3 article. A copy of the memo is the possession of the author.

89. Wołłejko.

90. Leon Kahn, *No Time to Mourn: A True Story of a Jewish Partisan Fighter* (Vancouver: Laurelton Press, 1978), pp. 184–85.

91. Wołłejko. I have in my possession a copy of an undated, typed "Summary Report" (the original was undoubtedly handwritten) of perhaps this document translated into the English language. It is herein transcribed, without any grammatical corrections or changes. Source: Fond 3377, Opys 55, Box 216, Polish Home Army, former Party Archive of the Lithuanian Soviet Republic, p. 278).

THE SUMMARY REPORT

> After midnight, in the small hours of the night of October 20, 1944, bandits in the strength of about 150 men carried out armed assault on the town of Ejszyszki of Troki region where they destroyed everything in the building complex of the "volispolkom" [District Executive Committee of the City and District Council; it usually included district jail and police station in one building in "volost'"] destroyed all documents it contained and stole all official seals,
>
> At the time of the assault on the town of Ejszyszki, the bandits captured a captain of the Red Army in the domicile of citizen Moses SANIZON (Sonenson?) son of Shevelev (Shivas?); they disarmed him, took away his documents, and disrobed him, then they took him into the woods and shot him to death.
>
> In the process of disarming of a captain and a sergant of the Red Army, the hostess SANIZON [i.e. Moses' wife] was shot to death along with an infant of a suckling age. The bandits also captured a Red Army private who stayed in town of Ejszyszki and he was also disarmed, disrobed, taken outside of town and shot to death.
>
> Interrogation revealed that the assault on the town of Ejszyszki was organized and carried out by Polish burguois and insurgency organization, a northern group of the "Home Army" under the general command of BORYSEWICZ aka "Krys'" (Kristin).
>
> The assault was directly conducted under the command of:
>
> BABUL (Babula?) Michal son of Jan, aka "Gaj",
> CHINIEWICZ Jozef son of Jan aka "Grom",
> TAPPER Mikolaj son Piotra aka "Zaba",
> GOLMONT Henryk son of Peter (Holmont?) aka "Grunt",
>
> and for each of the above the Military Court issued death sentence.

Vice Chairman of the BB
[Anti-banditism Warfare]
Unit of the NKVD of
the Lithuanian SSR,
Junior Colonel signature /Eismont/

Note: the original of the Report is to be found in case N 14392/7 page 98.

ACCURACY OF TRANSCRIPTION CERTIFIED BY ASSOCIATE OFFICER OF THE KGB, BRANCH OF THE COUNCIL OF MINISTERS OF THE LITHUANIAN SSR
MAJOR signature /F. Chvanov/

92. Testimony (Yad Vashem archive 03/2743) of Yitzhak Sonenson. Emphasis mine.

Yaffa Sonenson Eliach also attests to the presence of Soviets on the premises. The following testimony comes from the PBS *Frontline* script for "Shtetl" (January 12, 1996), p. 43:

> At night, on the 20th of October, there was a bang on the window where my brother and I slept which was downstairs. And my brother grabbed me by the hand and we went upstairs to my parents who were sleeping upstairs.
>
> A minute later a grenade was thrown through the window and all the blankets, the covers and the pillows, everything exploded and all the feathers were all over and we heard shooting downstairs. There were Russians also living in our house. Two Russian officers that were sleeping downstairs.

Like her brother, Yaffa Eliach has stated (in 1993) that her father wanted to avenge the death of his wife and child but was arrested by the NKVD for "all kinds of crimes against the state." She continues: "Later we found out that his accusers were from among the twenty-nine Jewish survivors of our *shtetl*.... It was a banal case of settling accounts, animated by competition and business jealousy. Before the war, they were my father's competitors in the leather business, so they had him deported and made us into orphans. Those were not sentimental times." In A. Stein, p. 66.

93. For example, Zelda Metz in her 1945 testimony stated that some of those who escaped from Sobibór were killed by the AK. A year later, her story was modified and the acronym "AK" was changed to "NSZ." In the American work (1980) on Sobibór, the acronym "NSZ" was replaced by the phrase "Polish fascists." See Teresa Prekerowa, "Stosunek ludności polskiej do żydowskich uciekinierów z obozów zagłady w Treblince, Sobiborze i Bełżcu w świetle relacji żydowskich i polskich," *Biuletyn Głównej Komisji Badania Zbrodni przeciwko Narodowi Polskiemu—Instytut Pamięci Narodowej* (Warszawa) 35 (1993): 105. Incidentally, Tomasz Blatt, a survivor of the escape from Sobibór, has this to say about Sasha, the Russian officer who organized it all: "In the film and in all the documents [Sasha] is elevated to the rank of a hero, but this was not completely so. Certainly, he organized it all and we escaped. But one never hears that two or three days later, when our entire group was encamped in the forest, Sasha—under the pretext of going to search for food—took the strong and young people and all of our arms, and never returned, thus condemning those of us who remained to death." In Ewa Kurek, *Żydzi, Polacy, czy po prostu ludzie...* (Lublin: Takt, 1992), p. 136.

Regarding the point in question, the Polish ambassador to Israel, Jan Dowgiałło, noted:

> *Dowgiallo:* Many survivors told me that in their first years in Israel they didn't talk about their experiences. Only in the last three decades were they encouraged to talk about their feelings and experiences and the facts of Shoah.
>
> Very often I had the impression that there is literature in what they say. They somehow adjust their feelings and experiences to conform to the literature. It means many of them after having read books about the holocaust tell stories that seem to differ from reality. But, is it possible to describe their experiences by words?
>
> *[Harvey] Sarner:* Are you saying that over the years some survivors get confused between what they experienced and what they read?
>
> *Dowgiallo:* Exactly.

Jan Dowgiallo, *From Science to Diplomacy: A Pole's Experience in Israel* (Cathedral City, CA: Brunswick Press, 1995), p. 12. Yaffa Eliach adds:

> The first thing I learned was that if I wanted to establish oral history as a respectable discipline of Holocaust studies, I had to start

> with my childhood experiences. To do so, in spite of all the scepticism of my historian colleagues, I trusted my childhood memories. You don't forget when your mother's dead body falls on you. It was not a matter of what I did on Labor Day. Those were matters of life and death. To recall them I just had to choose to do so.

In A. Stein, p. 72.

94. Ringelblum, *Polish-Jewish Relations*, p. 218, editorial n. 34.

95. Leszek Żebrowski, *Narodowe Siły Zbrojne. Dokumenty, struktury, personalia* (Warszawa: Burchard Edition, 1994), pp. 6, 11–12.

96. Blejwas, pp. 355–56; Korboński, *The Polish Underground State*, pp. 104–9. According to Korboński, about ten to fifteen thousand NSZ members joined the Home Army in April 1944, and others joined later that year. The remainder (850 men) entrenched themselves in the Kielce district, were renamed the Holy Cross Brigade [Brygada Świętokrzyska], and collaborated for a time with the Germans before making their way to the American zone in Germany. There they served in the Guards' Battalions, a unit established by the Americans under Franciszek Sobolta, a colonel in the Polish army. Service in the non-merged military formations of the NSZ was never recognized by the Polish government-in-exile as service in the Polish armed forces. Korboński's book was published in 1981. On January 24, 1991, the Polish Seym did accord full combatant status to former members of the NSZ. See Leszek Żebrowski, "Brygada Świętokrzyska Narodowych Sił Zbrojnych — A Niemcy," *Kombatant* (Warszawa), 5, no. 6 [17–18] (1992): 17; Lukas, *The Forgotten Holocaust*, pp. 53–54, 236 n. 48; and Zbigniew S. Siemaszko, "Brygada Świętokrzyska 1945–1946," *Zeszyty Historyczne* (Paris) 38 (1976): 31–58.

97. *Szaniec* 15, no. 106 (December 4, 1943): 3. *Szaniec* was an underground publication of the Radical Nationalist Group (Obóz Narodowo-Radykalny, or ONR), which reflected the views of the NSZ. After April 1944, some members of the ONR merged with the NSZ together with the Związek Jaszczurczy and became known as the NSZ-ZJ (NSZ-ONR). The members who merged with the AK in March of that year were known as NSZ-AK. See L. Żebrowski, *Narodowe Siły Zbrojne*, p. 26.

98. From "Narodowe Siły Zbrojne: Deklaracja" (copy in the possession of the author).

99. *Szaniec* 15, no. 106 (December 4, 1943): 1.

100. Spector, *The Holocaust of Volhynian Jews*, pp. 265–66, states:

> There are two different accounts of this move [the eviction notice served to the Jews of Bielin to leave the village and move into two abandoned houses in Worczyn]. According to Schmuel Diamant, one of the fighters in the brigade, two Jewish young men left Bielin and were captured by the Germans. Under torture they gave the Germans the information they sought and the Germans promptly shelled the partisan formations. Nahum Weissman, who arrived in Bielin on March 19, 1944, heard from a Jewish woman that the Jews had been ordered to leave the areas controlled by the partisans, because of accusations of passing secrets to the Germans. On the other hand, Dr. [Eliyahu] Yakira heard from the division commander that it had been decided to concentrate the Jews in the village of Worczyn, situated on the periphery of the partisan-controlled area, due to the spread of typhoid epidemics.

In any case, according to testimonies, 120 Jews were murdered in Worczyn by the "Polish partisans." Dr. Yakira, the army physician, maintained that he did not hear about a mass murder but did hear of isolated cases of the killing of Jews. Spector notes, "According to him a partisan unit of the National Armed Forces — NSZ (*Narodowe Siły Zbrojne)*, the military arm of the anti-Semitic Endecja, joined the division in early 1944, and it was they who engaged in the killings. He himself saved two Jews from their hands."

101. L. Żebrowski, *Paszkwil wyborczej*, p. 99 n. 1; Leszek Żebrowski, "Mord w Drzewicy. Nieznane karty komunistycznej partyzantki," *Słowo-Dziennik Katolicki*, July 1–3, 1994; Leszek Żebrowski, "Moralistyka gen. Rozłubirskiego. Spór o 'Mord w Drzewicy,'" *Gazeta Polska*, January 5, 1995; Leszek Żebrowski, "PPR-owski bohater?" *Słowo-Dziennik Katolicki*, May 10, 1995; Edwin Rozłubirski "Polemika: 'Mord w Drzewicy.' Apologeta zbrodni NSZ," *Polityka*, September 10, 1994. See also Leszek Żebrowski, "Oddział specjalny czy 'banda pozorowana,'" *Słowo-Dziennik Katolicki*, January 12, 1995.

102. Leszek Żebrowski, "Zbrodnie komunistyczne na narodzie polskim w latach 1944–1989," *Ład* (Warszawa), November 1995.

103. Korboński, *The Polish Underground State*, pp. 105–6.

104. Lukas, *Out of the Inferno*, p. 5.

105. Czesław Czaplicki, in "Żydzi i Polacy: przerywamy milczenie," *Gazeta Polska* (Warszawa), February 10, 1994. Unfortunately, Czaplicki's short entry does not provide any other information beyond this general statement. His entry is entitled "Walczyliśmy ze zdrajcami, nie z Żydami" (We fought traitors, not Jews).

106. Letter dated November 7, 1995, copy in the author's possession.

107. Feliks Pisarewski-Parry, *Orły i Reszki* (Warszawa: Iskra, 1984), pp. 61–65, *passim.*

108. For additional references on the NSZ, see Jerzy Pilaciński, *Narodowe Siły Zbrojne: kulisy walki podziemnej 1939–1945* (London: Towarzystwo imienia Romana Dmowskiego, 1976); Zbigniew S. Siemaszko, *Narodowe Siły Zbrojne* (London: Odnowa, 1982); and Jerzy Olgierd Iłłakowicz, "O Narodowych Siłach Zbrojnych," *Zeszyty Historyczne* (Paris) 76 (1986): 89–112.

109. See Ringelblum, *Polish-Jewish Relations*, p. 312, the "Postscript" of Joseph Kermish. The number of the Jews who deserted in Palestine comes from Ryszard Terlecki. The Polish military authorities did not pursue the deserters. See Davies and Polonsky, p. 47.

110. Rafał Żebrowski, *Dzieje Żydów w Polsce. Kalendarium* (Warszawa: Żydowski Instytut Historyczny w Polsce, 1993), pp. 137, 149. See also Kersten, *Polacy, Żydzi, Komunizm*, pp. 63ff.

111. Lukas, *The Forgotten Holocaust*, p. 242 n. 71.

112. Wincenty Urban, *Droga krzyżowa Archidiecezji Lwowskiej w latach II wojny światowej 1939–1945* (Wrocław, 1983), "Dekanat Skałat," p. 113.

113. Turonek, pp. 97–98. Although the Germans should have known how many Jews they killed, the precise total for the number of Jews in Belorussia (169,828) has no correspondence to reality. According to J. Tomaszewski's (*Rzeczpospolita wielu narodów*, p. 116) adjusted census figures for 1931, there were 505,000 Jews in "Western Belorussia" alone.

114. In Silverman, Smuschkowitz, and Smuszkowicz, pp. 253–54. I trust that the author of this particularly revealing passage does not place the SS Brigade Kamiński in the same camp as the AK.

115. In Tec, *In the Lion's Den*, pp. 183–84.

116. In Mieczysław Juchniewicz, *Polacy w radzieckim ruchu partyzanckim* (Warszawa: MON, 1975), p. 302, and Turonek, pp. 121–22. See also Z. A. Siemaszko, p. 203.

117. Turonek, pp. 122, 124.

118. Zbigniew S. Siemaszko, "Komentarze," *Zeszyty Historyczne* (Paris) 86 (1988): 166.

119. Z.Z.Z., p. 13. For a reference to the arrest and liquidation of AK members in Wołyń at this time, see Władysław Kobylański, *W szponach trzech wrogów* (Chicago: Wici, 1988), pp. 70–71, see also pp. 139ff.

120. Ryszard Torzecki, "Gdzie Sicz, gdzie Wisła," *Gazeta Wyborcza*, September 19, 1995, also speaks about Stalin's order of October 1944 and Bierut's follow-up order of October 9, 1944, which called for the intensification of the battle against the underground forces, both Ukrainian and Polish, in "Western Belorussia" and "Western Ukraine."

The information in the following paragraphs and the quoted passages come from Pająk and Żochowski, pp. 64–69. Beria's report can be found in *Karta* 15 (1995): 39–40. See also the short Polish Press Agency (Polska Agencja Prasowa, or PAP) article by Zdzisław Raczyński, "Operacja rozbrajania oddziałów AK na Litwie w 1944 roku w świetle nowo ujawnionych dokumentów z rosyjskich archiwów," *Gazeta* (Toronto), November 4–6, 1994.

121. See Krystyna Kersten, *Narodziny systemu władzy: Polska 1943–1948* (Poznań: SAWW, 1990), p. 94. English edition: *The Establishment of Communist Rule in Poland, 1943–48,* p. 102. See also Roszkowski, pp. 131–33.

122. Łuczak, p. 407.

123. Turonek, p. 120.

124. Krakowski's suggestion that the Polish underground "could have easily solved the problem of feeding ten or twenty thousand Jews who were left in the forests" and thus could have prevented them from having to rob Polish farmsteads is extremely naive. See Shmuel Krakowski, "The Slaughter of Polish Jewry: A Polish 'Reassessment,'" *Wiener Library Bulletin 26* (1972): 19, and Krakowski, *The War of the Doomed*, pp. 15–16. For a critical review of the latter work, see John Stanley, "Book Reviews," *Polish Review*, 30, no. 4 (1985): 459–62.

125. Łuczak, p. 401. For a table showing estimates of the number of Jews living in family camps in Wołyń, see Spector, *The Holocaust of Volhynian Jews*, p. 332.

126. J. Rajgrodzki, "Jedenaście miesięcy w obozie zagłady w Treblince," *BŻIH* 25 (1958): 117, as quoted by Prekerowa, in J. Tomaszewski,

Najnowsze dzieje Żydów w Polsce, p. 367 n. 110. The reference to the AK paying for provisions is on p. 366.

127. Ibid., p. 365.

128. In J. L. Armstrong, p. 273.

129. Nicholas P. Vakar, *Belorussia: The Making of a Nation* (Cambridge: Harvard University Press, 1956), p. 195.

130. Yitzhak Arad, as quoted in J. Tomazewski, *Najnowsze dzieje Żydów w Polsce*, p. 366. This was not always the case, however, as Samuel Gruber, a Jewish partisan leader, noted in this episode from Pryszczowa Góra near Lublin:

> The partisans, the priest told the assembled mourners, were not robbers but fighting men, regardless of whether they were Christians or Jews. They were human beings who wanted to live and not be caught by the Germans. Accordingly, the priest warned his congregants, if a band of partisans came to your farmstead you should give them food and shelter for the night and not tip off the Germans, at least not immediately. You should always make the report the next morning after the partisans had left. Just be sure you don't inform the Germans while the partisans are still in your house, because if you do, you will end up having trouble from both sides, from the Germans for having taken in partisans, and from other underground fighters for having reported their friends.
>
> It seems that the villagers took the words of their priest to heart, for the next day they treated us with unusual deference and hospitality. They gave us food, clothing, and even shoes, "so you can march better," they said. However, this was not enough for some of our men. They went out on their own and, instead of asking peasants for what they wanted, acted the part of thieves and holdup men.

Samuel Gruber, *I Choose Life* (New York: Shengold Publishers, 1978), pp. 83–84.

131. Z. S. Siemaszko, "Komentarze," p. 165. Siemaszko attributes these thefts (in Belorussia) to the Soviet units that accepted the Jewish ghetto escapees into their ranks.

132. Prekerowa, in J. Tomaszewski, *Najnowsze dzieje Żydów w Polsce*, p. 369. According to Vakar, p. 195, there were about 10,000 to 11,000 Jewish partisans in Belorussia.

133. Prekerowa, in J. Tomaszewski, *Najnowsze dzieje Żydów w Polsce*, p. 366.

134. Filip Ożarowski, *Gdy płonął Wołyń* (Chicago: Wici, 1995), p. 31. The following Jewish anecdote comes from Święciany.

> On March 1, 1944, a Polish force of hundreds of fighters surrounded the fifty-man Kostas Kalinauskas unit of our brigade. The battle, near the village of Maironi in the vicinity of Podbrodzie, went on for several hours. About half of the partisans fell, among them the commander of the unit. The rest broke through the surrounding forces and retreated. The Poles murdered all the wounded who remained in the field. The unit had many Jews, and some of them were among those whom the Poles killed. The "Home Army" was anti-Semitic, particularly the units that operated in the east....
>
> [End of April] We were waiting out the daylight hours in a small woodland southeast of Swienciany and in the late afternoon entered a nearby farm to eat supper. The woman of the house was Polish. She and her two daughters seemed very upset at our appearance, which was not the usual reaction. While the mother was preparing our food, we conversed with the girls. Suddenly the door opened and a young man entered, a square Polish army cap on his head, captain's insignia on his epaulettes, and a pistol in his officer's belt. The last time I had seen such a uniform was on the day of the Warsaw's surrender at the end of September 1939. His entrance was so sudden that we all remained rooted to our seats. He too was surprised but was first to regain composure. He came to each of us, shook hands, and turned to leave. I was nearest the door. I pointed my submachine gun at him and ordered him not to move. We took his pistol away and, after very brief questioning, realized what he was doing there — he was the son of the landlady. As a Pole and a onetime officer, he had joined the Home Army a few months earlier. His unit of 300 fighters was temporarily camped in a village a few kilometers away, and he came to visit his mother and sisters every day. The family had known he would be coming, which was why our arrival had confused them. Lieutenant Seminov, the commander of our group, decided to leave the house lest other White

Poles [i.e., AK members] come, and we left without waiting for supper, taking the officer with us.

The following day in the forest we questioned the Pole about the Home Army and their collaborators in the area. At first he refused to talk, but after rather rough treatment he broke down and told us a great deal about their activities. It became clear that his unit was the one that had attacked the Kostas Kalinauskas partisans and caused them heavy losses. After intensive interrogation, the Pole was executed. He begged for mercy, but that did not help him. We could not take him with us and did not want to set him free. Semionov considered the death sentence an appropriate reprisal for the murder of our partisans.

"Clashes with the 'White Poles,'" in Isaac Kowalski (comp. and ed.), *Anthology on Armed Jewish Resistance, 1939–1945*, vol. 3 (New York: Jewish Combatants Publishing House, 1986), pp. 265–66. The term "White Poles" in the title is used as a synonym for members of the AK.

135. *Szaniec*, 15, no. 106 (December 4, 1943): 2.

136. Wacław Nowicki, *Żywe echa* (Warszawa: Antyk, 1993), pp. 98, 100. See also "Polskie Siły Zbrojne," *Armia Krajowa* vol. 3 (London, 1950), p. 529. It is strange that this particular incident is not mentioned in Nechama Tec, *Defiance: The Bielski Partisans* (New York: Oxford University Press, 1993).

137. In Prekerowa, in J. Tomaszewski, *Najnowsze dzieje Żydów w Polsce*, p. 368.

138. Marek Edelman, *Magazyn Gazety*, April 16, 1993.

139. Shmuel Krakowski, *The War of the Doomed*, pp. 135–36.

140. L. Żebrowski, *Paszkwil wyborczej*, p. 111.

141. *Powstanie w Ghetcie Warszawskim 1943 roku: zbiór dokumentów* (Warszawa, 1945), p. 9; Marek Chodakiewicz, Piotr Gontarczyk, and Leszek Żebrowski (eds.), *Tajne oblicze GL-AL i PPR*, vol. 1 (Warszawa: Burchard Edition, 1997), pp. 128–30. See also vol. 2, pp. 72–84.

142. L. Żebrowski, *Paszkwil wyborczej*, p. 113.

143. The July 7, 1943, GL report appears ibid., pp. 114–16.

144. Błażyński, p. 309.

145. Andrew and Gordievsky, pp. 310, 345.

146. In Leszek Żebrowski, "Z dziejów konspiracyjnej PPR 1942–1944: szczerzy komuniści lubili donosić," *Gazeta Polska* (Warszawa), February 2, 1995. This article documents the PPR-Gestapo connection.

147. Ibid.

148. Światło as quoted by Błażyński, pp. 102–3, see also pp. 31, 104.

149. Światło paraphrasing Romkowski, ibid., p. 116.

150. Roszkowski, p. 126. According to Lukas, *The Forgotten Holocaust*, p. 93, Grot-Rowecki's betrayers were Ludwik Kalkstein, an intelligence officer in the AK, Eugeniusz Świerczewski, his brother-in-law, and Blanka Karczorowski, Świerczewski's fiancée.

151. Photocopy in Marcin Zaborski, "Zbrodnia nie popełniona przez NSZ," *Gazeta Polska* (Warszawa), September 15, 1994. See also L. Żebrowski, "Oddział specjalny."

152. Andrew and Gordievsky, pp. 310, 345.

153. Światło, in Błażyński, pp. 112–13.

154. Sometimes mistakes were made, and sometimes people were executed under false pretenses. For example, on October 18, 1944, the NSZ condemned and executed its own commander, Lieutenant Colonel Stanisław Nakoniecznikoff-Klukowski ("Kmicic"), because he allegedly tried to sell out the NSZ to the communists but in reality because he intended to subordinate the NSZ to the AK. See Korboński, *The Polish Underground State*, p. 75, 106–7.

155. For a partial list of those executed by the ŻOB, see Ringelblum, *Polish-Jewish Relations*, pp. 250–51.

156. Piotr Jakucki, "Utrwalacz nagrodzony," *Gazeta Polska* (Warszawa), July 6, 1995.

157. See Shmuel Nizan (ed.), *Rachov-Annapol Testimony and Remembrance* (Tel-Aviv: Technosdar, 1978), pp. 73–76.

158. Światło, as quoted by Błażyński, pp. 120–21. Regarding Korczyński, see also Bożena Szaynok, *Pogrom Żydów w Kielcach 4 lipca 1946 r.* (Wrocław: Bellona, 1992), p. 104 n. 3.

159. Faye Schulman, *A Partisan's Memoir: Woman of the Holocaust* (Toronto: Second Story Press, 1995), p. 104.

160. As quoted by Tec, *In the Lion's Den*, p. 184. For Soviet documents attesting to the fact that the GL-AL killed scores of Jews see Chodakiewicz, Gontarczyk, and Żebrowski, vol. 2, pp. 43–71.

161. Pinchuk, p. 34. Emphasis mine.

162. As quoted by Anatol Wertheim, "Żydowska partyzantka na Białorusi," *Zeszyty Historyczne* (Paris) 86 (1988): 139.

163. Z. S. Siemaszko, "Komentarze," p. 164.

164. Schulman, p. 186. The passage reads:

> The frostbitten partisans had cried at my departure. Why the cold greeting now? I had to find out. After a few days had passed, I came across a Jewish boy and asked him, "What happened? What is going on? Where are the Jewish boys and girls?"
>
> He hung his head. "Most of the Jewish partisans were dismissed, sent away from the units into Nazi jaws because they did not have rifles." The order had been given by partisan headquarters. The partisans did not want the enemy to think that so many partisans were without rifles. A poorly armed opponent would be attacked with a stronger decisive force. The easiest solution was to expel the Jews. As always, when the Jews were not needed they were no longer wanted.
>
> ...Some of our Jewish former partisans had survived and were hiding defenceless in the woods.

The reader may want to note Schulman's earlier reference to the Soviet order to "kill every stranger in the woods who was not attached to a partisan group."

165. Z. S. Siemaszko, "Komentarze," p. 164.

166. Prekerowa, in J. Tomaszewski, *Najnowsze dzieje Żydów w Polsce*, p. 369.

167. Z. S. Siemaszko, "Komentarze," p. 164. According to Spector, *The Holocaust of Volhynian Jews*, p. 268, between 200 and 300 Jews participated in the Polish partisan movement there. Also, 1,096 Jews from the provinces of Wołyń and Tarnopol joined the Polish First Army (formed in the USSR) in the first week of May 1944 (p. 263). Gutman and Krakowski, p. 133, state:

> The dominant force in Volhynia were the Ukrainian nationalists who frequently assailed the Polish minority, slaughtering entire villages in the most atrocious manner. Under those circumstances the task of the Home Army was to defend the Polish villages against the Ukrainians. No wonder, then, that the outnumbered Home Army outposts which were stationed in vulnerable villages looked on the Jewish partisans as most desirable reinforcements. Accordingly, the Jewish partisans could rely on the support of the Polish villagers. The enemy of the Polish villagers and of the Jews was the same: the Ukrainians were murdering both.

168. See, for example, the story of Richard Kalinowicz, an AK unit leader from Sambor near Lwów, in Tomaszewski and Werbowski, pp. 144–51.

169. Prekerowa, in J. Tomaszewski, *Najnowsze dzieje Żydów w Polsce*, pp. 305, 355.

170. For a table listing various sabotage activities undertaken by the Home Army between January 1, 1941, and June 1944, see Dear, p. 901.

171. Prekerowa, in J. Tomaszewski, *Najnowsze dzieje Żydów w Polsce*, p. 382.

172. See Sheldon Kirshner, "Warsaw Ghetto Commander Forgives Tormentors" (an interview with Marek Edelman), *Canadian Jewish News* (Toronto), November 9, 1989.

173. Lukas, *The Forgotten Holocaust*, p. 175. See also his chapter on the Warsaw Uprising, pp. 182–219. For a listing of Polish military assistance to the Warsaw ghetto from April 19, 1943, to mid-June 1943, see Bednarczyk, *Życie codzienne warszawskiego getta*, p. 113–15.

174. Lukas, *The Forgotten Holocaust*, p. 175.

175. The foregoing analysis is based on Prekerowa, in J. Tomaszewski, *Najnowsze dzieje Żydów w Polsce*, pp. 360–61. See also Israel Gutman, "Polish Responses to the Liquidation of Warsaw Jewry," in Michael R. Marrus (ed.), *The Nazi Holocaust: Historical Articles on the Destruction of European Jews*, vol. 5, *Public Opinion and Relations to the Jews in Nazi Europe* (Westport, CT: Meckler, 1989) 1: 342–58. Gutman states (p. 350), "According to an authorized representative of the Polish government stationed in the United States, in the spring of 1943 the *AK* had in its possession 25,000 rifles, 6,000 revolver, 30,000 grenades, and other types of even heavier weapons." Adam Ciołkosz takes issue with this count in his "Broń dla getta Warszawy," *Zeszyty Historyczne* (Paris) 15 (1969): 15–44.

176. Hilberg, *Perpetrators, Victims, Bystanders*, p. 92–93.

177. Ringelblum, *Polish-Jewish Relations*, pp. 133–34. The editorial note (p. 133 n. 23) states:

> The Polish Police functioned only on the territories in central Poland forming the so-called General-Government — the regions of Warsaw, Lublin, Kielce, Cracow and Eastern Galicia. This police was subordinate to the German *Schutzpolizei* and constituted the

second-biggest armed force (after the German *Ordnungspolizei*) used for anti-Jewish measures. At the end of 1942, it numbered 14,300 men in all, about 3,000 of whom were stationed in Warsaw. The part played by the Polish Police in the liquidation of the Jews is confirmed from many sources.

For a study of the structure and function of the "Blue Police," see Hempel. According to this author (p. 91), at the end of 1942 the "Blue Police" consisted of 12,000 men. See also table on p. 92. According to Hempel (p. 161), by the end of 1942 the Germans gave up trying to use the "Blue Police" on a regular basis in the roundups and relegated their services to guard duties around the cordoned areas.

178. Gilbert, p. 361; Hempel, p. 184.

179. See *Opoka* (London) 11 (July 1975): 83.

180. Klukowski, *Diary*, p. 215.

181. Benjamin Mandelkern, *Escape from the Nazis* (Toronto: James Lorimer, 1988), pp. xi, 91ff.

182. Hempel, pp. 173, 262–69; Teresa Prekerowa, *Konspiracyjna Rada Pomocy Żydom w Warszawie 1942–1945* (Warszawa: Państwowy Instytut Wydawniczy, 1982), pp. 207–8; Prekerowa, in J. Tomaszewski, *Najnowsze dzieje Żydów w Polsce*, p. 352. One Polish policeman, Wacław Nowiński, was even awarded a medallion and a certificate of esteem by Yad Vashem for his active assistance to the Jews during the war. See Alexander Bronowski, *They Were Few* (New York: Pter Lang, 1991), p. 33. For a work dealing with the "Home of Father Boduen," see Adam Słomczyński, *Dom Ks. Boduena 1939–1945* (Warszawa: Państwowy Instytut Wydawniczy, 1975).

183. Lukas, *The Forgotten Holocaust*, p. 118; Bednarczyk, *Obowiązek silniejszy od śmierci*, pp. 107, 124.

184. In Hempel, p. 172.

185. Ringelblum, *Polish-Jewish Relations*, p. 154.

186. Chaim Kaplan, in Gilbert, p. 232; Hempel, p. 184. This was the first such execution. Thirty-two Polish policemen participated in this action. The preparatory work was handled by the Jewish police.

187. Hempel, p. 184.

188. Ibid., pp. 184–85.

189. Chaim Kaplan, in Gilbert, pp. 443, 446.

190. Hempel, p. 182. For additional anti-Jewish and anti-Gypsy actions by the "Blue Police," see pp. 166–89.

191. Klukowski, *Diary*, pp. 220–21.

192. Ibid., p. 222.

193. Korboński, *The Polish Underground State*, p. 75; Hempel, p. 163.

194. Hempel, p. 174.

195. Ibid., p. 133.

196. Ibid., pp. 124–36, 181–82.

197. Ibid., p. 295.

198. Klukowski, *Diary*, pp. 220–21.

199. Jacob Apenszlak (ed.), *The Black Book of Polish Jewry* (New York: Roy Publishers, 1943), pp. 30–31, as quoted by Lukas, *The Forgotten Holocaust*, p. 130. These young hoodlums were on the payroll of the Nazis, they attacked Polish people as well, and the Polish churches and underground press publicly denounced their behavior. Some Poles, in acts of pure heroism, tried to intervene and stop them. Lukas, *The Forgotten Holocaust*, pp. 253–54.

Ludwig Landau comments on this Warsaw episode in his chronicle, *Kronika lat wojny i okupacji* (Warszawa: Państwowe Wydawnictwo Naukowe, 1962), pp. 366–67: "Today a band of juveniles, mainly fourteen and fifteen-year-olds, was making the rounds of the Jewish stores in the vicinity of Marszałkowska Street breaking shopwindows and robbing the merchandise. The passers-by were indifferent, probably fearing that any demonstrative action on their part would cause them some unpleasantness or place them in danger. Neither the Polish nor the German police was to be seen." In an earlier entry, however, Landau stated: "There are instances of resolute reaction ... in the defense of the Jews on the part of non-Jewish passers-by" (p. 363).

200. In Gilbert, p. 408, and n. 29, which reads: "Klukowski diary, 8 August 1942: *Dziennik z lat okupacji Zamojszczyzny* (Lublin, 1959)]." This work, edited by Zygmunt Mańkowski, was first published in 1958 by Lubelska Spółdzielnia Wydawnicza in Lublin.

201. Klukowski, *Diary*, p. 209. In a comparison of these two translations with the 1958 Polish edition, Gilbert is clearly more faithful to the "original" than is the 1993 English edition. However, a note of caution must be added. In 1990, a supplement to Klukowski's *Dziennik* was published, spanning the years 1944–45. The "Editor's Note" states, "I have had a chance to compare, in part, the handwritten text of Dr. Klukowski with the text published in 1958. I found substantial differences having the character of tampering motivated by political considerations. Almost every critical comment

dealing with the PPR, communists, the Soviet Union and the Red Army has been omitted, for example, the fragment that states that Red Army soldiers liked to drink vodka. This, in part, compromises the value of the 1958 edition as a historical source." Zygmunt Klukowski, *Dziennik 1944–45*, ed. Wojciech Samoliński (Lublin: Oficyna Wydawnicza Federacji Solidarności Regionu Środkowowschodniego, 1990), p. 17.

To complicate matters even more, the verso in the English edition states that this edition is a translation of *Dziennik z lat okupacji Zamojszczyzny, 1939–1944* (presumably the 1958 Polish edition), and the translator (George Klukowski) notes (pp. xix–xx) that his father was too ill to personally supervise the editing and printing of the 1958 edition and that some changes were made. "I have restored," he continues, "those aspects of his original version that I believe best represent his intention." Furthermore, the English edition was abridged and edited and "is about 8 percent shorter than the Polish first edition." The translator's note ends with the following words: "But the historical integrity has been kept in tact. Never did we omit any historical or personal reference that might be considered relevant." The editors of the English edition were Andrew Klukowski and Helen Klukowski May.

Zygmunt Klukowski was arrested by the NKVD before and after his testimony at the International Military Tribunal trials in Nuremberg. In 1952, his twenty-one-year-old son, Tadeusz, was executed for his role in partisan activity linked to Operation "Martyka." When Zygmunt went to Warsaw to defend his son, he was arrested again and sentenced to ten years in Wronki prison. He was amnestied in 1956 and died in 1959.

202. In Gilbert, pp. 502–3, and n. 17, which states that this quotation comes from Kermish and Krakowski in Ringelblum, *Polish-Jewish Relations*, p. 220, editorial n. 37. Kermish and Krakowski list their source as "Zygmunt Klukowski, *Dziennik z lat okupacji Zamojszczyzny*, Lublin, 1959, p. 299."

203. Klukowski, *Diary*, p. 227. In a comparison of these two translations, clearly the Kermish and Krakowski version reflects the 1958 Polish edition more accurately than does the 1993 English edition. However, Gilbert (not Kermish and Krakowski) omits the first explanatory sentence, which is indispensable for the proper understanding of the words that follow. That short sentence reads: "Among the 'bandits,' there are quite a few Jews." This (my) translation differs substantively from the one in the English edition, which states: "There are several Jews active with the bandits." The passage in the 1958 edition reads: "*Wśród 'bandytów' sporo jest Żydów.*" The Polish adverb *sporo* in English means "quite a lot, quite a few, a good many, a considerable number" not "several." The quotation marks around the word "bandits" indicate that they were partisans.

204. Zemiński as quoted by Gilbert, p. 493.

205. Ringelblum as quoted ibid., p. 492.

206. Ibid., p. 717. Michał Cichy states that he is aware of sources indicating that "about 60 Jews were killed by [Warsaw ghetto] insurgents [i.e., by certain members belonging to the AK and the NSZ, or at least people dressed in the uniforms of the insurgents]; this includes 40 or 45 Jews in two mass murders one of which (involving 30 Jews killed by NSZ members) is very weakly documented." It is difficult, he says, to verify the "more than a hundred" figure given by Gilbert. See Michał Cichy's and Adam Michnik's articles, "Polacy — Żydzi: czarne karty powstania," *Gazeta Wyborcza*, January 29-30, 1994. These articles caused quite a stir in Poland and abroad. For a commentary based on documentary evidence that challenges these estimates, see L. Żebrowski, *Paszkwil wyborczej*. This work contains a letter to Adam Michnik, editor of *Gazeta Wyborcza*, from Stanisław Aronson ("Rysiek"), a Jew who served in the AK in 1942–44. The letter reads, in part: "After reading his book, I wrote to the above-mentioned professor Gilbert in 1990 stating that, as a participant in the uprising, I had never heard of such murders. He [Gilbert] agreed to a meeting with me which he subsequently cancelled for reasons unknown, as if to say: 'Please do not confuse me with the facts.'" Aronson then names several other Jews who also belonged to the AK and fought during the uprising and comments, "Could we have been members of the elite AK formation ["Kedyw"] if it was bound by a discriminatory policy?" (pp. 79–80).

207. For still other examples, see Gutman and Krakowski, pp. 208–25.

208. See Abraham Brumberg's "Letter to the Editor" and Czesław Miłosz's reply in *New York Review of Books*, June 22, 1995.

209. Jan Dobraczyński, "Traktowałem to jako swój obowiązek chrześcijański i polski" (interview) *Słowo-Dziennik Katolicki* (Warszawa) 67 (1993). For other anti-Semites who risked their lives to save the Jews, see Giertych, *In Defence of My Country*, pp. 305–8.

210. Smolar, "Jews as a Polish Problem," p. 36.

211. G. K. Chesterton, *The Well and the Shallows* (London: Sheed and Ward, 1935), p. 127.

212. See Zdzisław Przygoda, *Niezwykłe przygody w zwyczajnym życiu* (Warszawa: Ypsylon, 1994), p. 49.

213. As quoted by Smolar, "Jews as a Polish Problem," p. 36.

214. Gutman and Krakowski, pp. 208–37.

215. Gilbert, p. 493.

216. "I am indebted to the Poles for having saved my life twice during this war: once, in the winter of 1940, when the blessed arm of the Polish Underground saved me from certain death, and the second time when it got me out of an S.S. labour camp, where I would have met my death either in an epidemic or from a Ukrainian or S.S. bullet." Ringelblum, *Polish-Jewish Relations*, p. 1.

217. See Bartoszewski and Lewin, pp. 23–26, 35.

218. Gilbert, p. 654.

219. See Bednarczyk, *Obowiązek silniejszy od śmierci*, p. 147.

220. Gilbert, p. 660.

221. Ringelblum, *Polish-Jewish Relations*, p. 53.

222. Ibid., p. xxx.

223. Ibid., pp. 247–48.

224. Ibid, pp. 150–51.

225. See Franciszek Stopniak, "Pomoc kleru polskiego dla dzieci w II wojnie światowej," in Franciszek Stopniak (ed.), *Kośćiół katolicki na ziemiach Polski w czasie II wojny światowej: materiały i studia*, vol. 10, no. 5 (Warszawa: Akademia Teologii Katolickiej, 1981), pp. 3–63.

226. See Ciołkosz, "'Dzielnica żydowska,'" p. 196.

227. Ringelblum, *Polish-Jewish Relations*, pp. 2–3.

228. Lukas, *The Forgotten Holocaust*, p. 150.

229. Ciołkosz, "'Dzielnica żydowska,'" p. 196. On July 16, 1995, French President Jacques Chirac acknowledged the collective responsibility of the French state for the wartime deportations of the Jews during the Vichy régime of Marshal Pétain. Tony Judt, "French War Stories," *New York Times*, July 19, 1995, stated:

> Some 76,000 Jews from France died in death camps. A disproportionate number were foreign-born, people who had taken refuge from persecution elsewhere. The Germans could never have located them without the assistance of French bureaucrats and the police.
>
> Mr. Chirac's speech marked the anniversary of the largest roundup, which occurred on July 16, 1942, when 13,000 mostly non-French Jews were herded into a Parisian sports arena before being sent to the camps. The Nazis had specifically excluded young children from the deportation order, yet the French separated them from their parents and transferred them to a camp near Paris. There, 4,000 babies, toddlers and older children were pushed, dragged or carried by French officials into dark cattle cars for shipment to Auschwitz. Not one of them survived.

Most certainly, the Polish record of assistance to the Jews was better than that of the French.

230. A historian of Jewish origin, Walter Laqueur, *The Terrible Secret: Suppression of the Truth about Hitler's "Final Solution"* (London: Weidenfield and Nicolson, 1980), p. 200, notes: "The Polish underground played a pivotal role in the transmission of the news [of the Holocaust] to the West.... Most of the information about the Nazi policy of extermination reached Jewish circles abroad through the Polish underground." On p. 106 he continues: "The Polish case is very briefly that they did what they could, usually at great risk and in difficult conditions. If the news about the mass murders was not believed abroad this was not the fault of the Poles. It was, at least in part, the fault of the Polish Jews who, in the beginning, refused to believe it; it was also the responsibility of the Jewish leaders abroad who were initially quite skeptical." On p. 121 he adds, "No other Allied government was remotely as outspoken at the time and for a long time after."

231. In Władysław Bartoszewski, *The Blood Shed Unites Us: Pages from the History of Help to the Jews in Occupied Poland* (Warsaw: Interpress Publishers, 1970), p. 40.

232. Lukas, *The Forgotten Holocaust*, p. 140.

233. Ciołkosz, "'Dzielnica żydowska,'" p. 195.

234. Davies, *God's Playground*, p. 264.

235. In Gumkowski and Leszczyński, p. 59. Emphasis mine.

236. This passage also appears in Karol Pospieszalski, *Polska pod niemieckim prawem* (Poznań: Wydawnictwo Instytutu Zachodniego, 1946), p. 189.

237. Prekerowa, in J. Tomaszewski, *Najnowsze dzieje Żydów w Polsce*, pp. 304–5.

238. Madajczyk, *Polityka III Rzeszy w okupowanej Polsce*, 1: 45.

239. Szymon Danter, *Las sprawiedliwych: karta z dziejów ratowania Żydów w okupowanej Polsce* (Warszawa: Książka i Wiedza, 1968), p. 8.

240. See Jan T. Gross, *Polish Society under German Occupation: The Generalgouvernement, 1939–1944* (Princeton: Princeton University Press, 1979), pp. 185–86.

241. Hempel, p. 167.

242. From informal discussions with Wallace West, editor of *Polish Heritage*, and Anna Chrypińska, both of whom knew Szczeniowski (47th annual convention of the American Council for Polish Culture, Las Vegas, July 11–15, 1995).

243. Philip Friedman, *Their Brothers' Keepers* (New York: Holocaust Library, 1978), p. 37.

244. Ringelblum, *Notes from the Warsaw Ghetto*, p. 38.

245. Polish rescuers such as Władysława Choms(owa), many Jewish survivors such as Bruno Bettelheim, Ludwik Hirszfeld, and Oswald Rufeisen, Jewish prisoners such as Emanuel Ringelblum, and other Jews and Christians comment on the lack of resistance by the Jews. Lukas (*Out of the Inferno*, p. 11) quotes Choms(owa) as saying, "The greatest difficulty was the passivity of the Jews themselves." Hirszfeld's memoirs are published under the title *Historia jego życia* (Warszawa: Spółdzielnia Wydawnicza Czytelnik, 1946). For quotes from that work in English, see Iranek-Osmecki, p. 89. Rufeisen, who rescued a number of Jews after joining the German police and later as a partisan in Eastern Poland, stated: "I often saw [Jews] being led to the slaughter. I witnessed this with my own eyes. And indeed they went as lambs. One hardly heard a peep from them." See interview with Oswald Rufeisen, "Jako chrześcijanin, a nawet jako Żyd," *Polityka* (Warszawa) 2 (May 29, 1993). Bettelheim's statement is especially severe: "The Jews of Europe could have marched as free men against the SS, rather than to first grovel, then wait to be rounded up for their own extermination, and finally walk themselves to the gas chambers." As quoted by Neil Ascherson, "The Death Doctors," *New York Review of Books*, May 28, 1987.

246. See Richard C. Lukas, *Did the Children Cry? Hitler's War against Jewish and Polish Children, 1939–45* (New York: Hippocrene Books, 1994), and Lukas, "History in Loose-Leaf Notebooks."

247. See Gilbert, p. 667, and n. 23. "In all," states Gilbert, "seventy 'non-Aryan' men and thirty-one 'non-Aryan' women were seized: all were executed five days later." See also Tatiana Berenstein and Adam Rutkowski, *Assistance to the Jews in Poland, 1939–1945* (Warsaw: Polonia, 1963), pp. 42–43. According to the latter source, the hunt took place on Good Friday, April 7, 1944, in Żoliborz in Warsaw. It was carried out by "soldiers and police," who arrested 250 persons including 30 women. The authors continue, "Among them there were, of course, Jews and those who had given them shelter."

248. Lukas, *Out of the Inferno*, p. 4.

249. Łuczak, pp. 185, 196.

250. Lukas, "History in Loose-Leaf Notebooks." Spector, *The Holocaust of Volhynian Jews*, p. 263, notes cases of the AK providing Jews with forged Polish "Aryan" papers and issuing orders to protect and render assistance to the engineer Herman Friedrich Gräbe in his rescue efforts in behalf of the Jews.

251. Prekerowa, in J. Tomaszewski, *Najnowsze dzieje Żydów w Polsce*, pp. 356–58. For a short English version, see Teresa Prekerowa, "The Relief Council for Jews in Poland, 1942–1945," in Abramsky et al., pp. 161–75. See also Tomaszewski and Werbowski, and Bartoszewski and Lewin.

252. Łuczak, p. 128. See also Spector, *The Holocaust of Volhynian Jews*, pp. 248–49. For the role of the Roman Catholic Church in the rescue of Jews in the Warsaw area, see Bednarczyk, *Życie codzienne warszawskiego getta*, pp. 134–42.

253. Łuczak, p. 129.

254. Lukas, "History in Loose-Leaf Notebooks"; Łuczak, p. 128.

255. See Barbara Engelking, *Zagłada i pamięć* (Warszawa: Wydawnictwo FiS PAN, 1994), p. 9. According to Prekerowa, in J. Tomaszewski, *Najnowsze dzieje Żydów w Polsce*, p. 384, from 380,000 to 500,000 Jews survived the war. These would include the over 200,000 in the USSR, 30,000–60,000 in Poland with or without Christian assistance, 20,000–40,000 in German camps, 10,000–15,000 in the partisans or forests, those in the Polish army outside of Soviet territory, and those in the other lands to which they had emigrated early in the war.

256. Interview with Szymon Danter, in Małgorzata Niezabitowska, *Remnants: The Last Jews of Poland* (New York: Friendly Press, 1986), pp. 244–50.

257. Letter, dated February 7, 1996,

addressed to the National Chair of the Anti-Defamation League of B'nai B'rith in New York, in *Zgoda* (Chicago), April 1, 1996.

258. *Polityka* (Warszawa), April 20, 1968.

259. Danter, in Niezabitowska.

260. Władysław Żarski-Zajder, *Martyrologia ludności żydowskiej i pomoc społeczeństwa polskiego* (Warszawa: Związek Bojowników o Wolność i Demokrację, 1968), p. 16.

261. Hilberg, *The Destruction of the European Jews*, 2: 593–94.

262. P. Friedman, p. 63.

263. Livia Rothkirchen, "Czech Attitudes toward the Jews during Nazi Regime," *Yad Vashem Studies* 13 (1979): 314–15.

264. István Deák, "The Incomprehensible Holocaust: An Exchange," *New York Review of Books*, December 21, 1989.

265. István Deák, "Legends of King Christian: Another Exchange," *New York Review of Books*, September 27, 1990.

266. Deák, "The Incomprehensible Holocaust: An Exchange."

267. István Deák, "Who Saved Jews? An Exchange," *New York Review of Books*, April 25, 1991.

268. István Deák, "Holocaust Heroes," *New York Review of Books*, November 5, 1992.

269. Gilbert, p. 626.

270. Unless otherwise noted, this chronology is based on the following sources: Wacław Bielawski, *Zbrodnie na Polakach dokonane przez hitlerowców za pomoc udzielaną Żydom* (Warszawa: Główna Komisja Badania Zbrodni Hitlerowskich w Polsce—Instytut Pamięci Narodowej, 1987); Zajączkowski; and *Those Who Helped: Polish Rescuers of Jews during the Holocaust*, Part Two (Warsaw: Main Commission for the Investigation of Crimes Against the Polish Nation—Institute of National Memory, 1996). See also Lukas, *The Forgotten Holocaust*, 1997 edition, pp. 310–37; Korboński, *The Jews and the Poles in World War II*, pp. 64–68; and Mordecai Paldiel, *The Path of the Righteous: Gentile Rescuers of Jews during the Holocaust* (New York: Jewish Foundation for Christian Rescuers/ADL, 1993), pp. 176–235.

271. Proch, p. 112.

272. Główna Komisja Badania Zbrodni Hitlerowskich w Polsce—Rada Ochrony Pomników Walki i Męczeństwa, p. 230.

273. Kamil Barański, *Przeminęli zagończycy, chliborobi, chasydzi... Rzecz o ziemi stanisławowsko—kołomyjsko—stryjskiej* (London: Panda Press, 1988), pp. 83–84, 418; Leszek Jeżowski, "Ks. Edward Tobaczkowski," *Semper Fidelis* (Wrocław) 3, no. 16 (1993): 10.

274. Stanisław Wroński and Maria Zwolakowa, *Polacy Żydzi 1939–1945* (Warszawa: Książka i Wiedza, 1971), p. 361.

275. *Biuletyn Głównej Komisji Badania Zbrodni przeciwko Narodowi Polskiemu—Instytutu Pamięci Narodowej* (Warszawa) 35 (1993): 188–89.

276. Pogonowski, *Jews in Poland*, p. 118.

277. *Biuletyn Głównej Komisji*, pp. 189–90.

278. Ibid., pp. 186–87.

279. Ibid., pp. 191–92.

280. Pogonowski, *Jews in Poland*, p. 121.

281. *Głos Pracy* 20 (May 13, 1943), cited in Szapiro, p. 163.

282. Ibid.

283. Testimony of Irene Opdyke. See Carol Rittner and Sondra Myers (eds.), *The Courage to Care: Rescuers of Jews during the Holocaust* (New York: New York University Press, 1986), p. 48.

284. Bednarczyk, *Obowiązek silniejszy od śmierci*, p. 54.

285. Wroński and Zwolakowa, p. 433.

286. Bednarczyk, *Obowiązek silniejszy od śmierci*, p. 147.

287. Wroński and Zwolakowa, p. 433.

288. Bednarczyk, *Obowiązek silniejszy od śmierci*, pp. 146–47.

289. Rokicka, p. 32.

290. Reuben Ainsztein, *Jewish Resistance in Nazi-Occupied Eastern Europe: With a Historical Survey of the Jew as Fighter and Soldier in the Diaspora* (London: Elek, 1974), p. 441.

291. The sixty priests may not have been executed solely for the "crime of helping Jews." People were often executed for multiple reasons. These priests, however, were known to have assisted Jews. For a list of Polish clergy and religious killed in these circumstances, see Zieliński with Tyndorf, and Zajączkowski.

292. In Lukas, *Out of the Inferno*, p. 12.

293. "A Discussion," *Polin* 2 (1987): 341.

294. See "Czy Polacy są antysemitami?" *Głos Polski* (Toronto), May 14, 1994.

295. For example, Dr. Schneider, presumably Jewish, was a "well-known person and a good man" from Horodenka whom the Germans offered to free after a roundup. Instead he volunteered for the open-air execution, refused to undress with the rest, and threw his medical coat into the face of a Gestapo member. The doctor dared him to trample on this symbol of the medical profession and culture and told him to save the coat for the burial of Hitler, who, even with these Jewish

clothes, would lose the war and die like a wild dog. Dr. Schneider then jumped in front of another Gestapo member and stated that, as a lieutenant in the Polish army, he did not fear the bullets and demanded to be shot face to face. For this heroic insolence, Dr. Schneider was beaten to within an inch of his life and tossed, without being shot, into the pit, from whence he continued to abuse the Nazis until a machine-gun bullet silenced his harangues forever.

Heroism, however, was not without serious consequences for others. After a Jew in Stanisławów blinded a policeman by throwing acid in his face and escaped, the majority of the Jewish youth of that town, as well as the entire Jewish police force, were strung up on the city lampposts and telephone poles and were left hanging for three days. Such reprisal actions were far from rare. Milch, pp. 14, 17.

296. Ringelblum, *Polish-Jewish Relations*, p. 226–27.

297. Danter, in Niezabitowska. A February 17, 1996, signed statement of Wiktoria Procyk from Katowice (copy in author's possession) tells of one such incident, when a Jew "tapped on [her] window" in Eastern Poland:

> I know for certain that Fr. Franciszek [Bajer] helped the Jews. Perhaps I will begin with Chaja or Chajka, a Jewess who lived in Old Town (*Stare Miasto*) and owned a small variety store.... The winter of 1943–44 was terrible. The ghetto in Założce [in Podole] was already liquidated and the remainder of the Jews, who did not hide among the Poles, wandered through the forests where they were preyed upon by Ukrainian peasants with pitchforks, or the terrible butchers from the UPA [Ukrainska Povstanska Armiia—Ukrainian Insurgent Army], or the Ukrainian auxiliary police. Those apprehended were killed on the spot.
>
> It was on such a night, a night on which one would not turn out a dog, that someone knocked on our window. It was Chaja with two of her daughters, Ryfcia and Gitla. One of them was about twelve years old; the other younger. They were frozen to the bone, in dire poverty, hungry and full of lice. The priest took them in and hid them in the attic and later in a special shelter in the basement. In doing this he risked his own life, the life of his [widowed] mother, and my life as well as that of my son and my two daughters. [The home in question belonged to the narrator.] I agreed to this—commending my soul to God. Our entire family would recite the rosary on a daily basis with the priest and pray that the Virgin Mary would protect us from Ukrainian denouncers and also that she would protect Chaja and her children. The Most Holy Mother heard our prayers and all three Jewesses survived. Under the Soviets [after the war], Fr. Franciszek provided them with false birth certificates so they could pass for Polish women and they left the Soviet paradise and came to Poland. They lived for a while in Bytom and later emigrated to the United States.

298. Shahak, "'The Life of Death': An Exchange." One such instance of verbal opposition can be found in Zdzisław Przygoda, *The Way to Freedom* (Toronto: Lugus, 1995), p. 54:

> On my way home from work in the street car, I listened to the loud discussions amongst the passengers. "The ghetto is burning! The Jews are burning, and we will finally be rid of them!" said one. The majority of passengers reacted quickly by beating him as he made a quick exit from the moving carriage. It was clear that the majority of passengers were upset by the German action, and pleased that the ghetto inhabitants were beginning to fight.

299. The figure of 500,000 is an estimate. Daniel Jonah Goldhagen, "The People's Holocaust," *New York Times*, March 17, 1996, an article based on his book *Hitler's Willing Executioners: Ordinary Germans and the Holocaust* (New York: Alfred A. Knopf, 1996), states:

> The number of Germans working in concentration camps, ghettos, police battalions and other institutions involved in the genocide was far greater than people realize. Although a definitive estimate is difficult to make, it is clear that in excess of 100,000 Germans, and probably far more, helped exterminate European Jews....
>
> The German government agency in charge of investigating Nazi crimes has catalogued more than 330,000 people suspected of working in the various institutions that were used to kill Jews and others. For example, there were 38 police battalions, with a total

of at least 19,000 men, that participated in the genocide. Most of these men were not professional policemen or members of the Nazi Party or the SS.

The Nazi authorities, apparently acting on the assumption than any able-bodied German would consent to kill Jews, assigned virtually anyone who was available to the task. Their assumption was borne out....

The inescapable, fundamental truth is that for the Holocaust to have occurred, an enormous number of ordinary Germans had to become Hitler's willing executioners.

Is it unreasonable to assume that in addition to the 330,000 "people" mentioned above, at least 170,000 other "people" worked outside the institutional settings?

300. Milch, pp. 34–35.

301. Ibid., pp. 44–45. The two women in this narrative were shot by the Nazis in a raid on the hideout while the men were away. The Ukrainian family, which was preoccupied with various domestic chores outdoors, escaped. Dr. Milch died in Israel in 1989. "To this day," he wrote later, "I do not know exactly how this tragedy occurred, who perpetrated it, or where my wife is buried."

302. In T. Piotrowski, *Vengeance of the Swallows*, p. 197.

303. As cited in Szapiro, p. 415.

304. Lukas, *The Forgotten Holocaust*, p. 117. The 7,000 figure given by Lukas is a low estimate. As we have seen, the Polish auxiliary police and the Criminal Police alone numbered well over 15,000 at the end of 1942.

305. Shmuel Lerer's estimate can be found in Gilbert, p. 812. See also Gutman and Krakowski, pp. 370, 376 n. 41. Stanisław Meducki states:

> It was ... in March 1945 that the Ministry of State Administration recorded 117 cases of assaults on Jews, including 35 in the Provinces of Warsaw, in Lublin 33, in Rzeszów 23, in Białystok 21, and in Kielce 5. Men, women and children were murdered. During the next 5 months, from April to August 1945, 30 more cases of assault on Jewish families were recorded, including 11 robberies. It was also found out that some assaults had been committed as a result of claims made by the Jews to recover their property lost during the German occupation. 81 Jews lost their lives in those assaults. 15 persons were injured, and 5 persons were kidnapped.
>
> ... It should be noted that official statistics did not reflect the whole postwar reality because some of the murders, holdups, robberies, not to mention beatings, were dealt with by the weak state administration, which was [accepted] reluctantly by a considerable part of the society. Besides, apart from assaults and robbery, Jews were often assaulted for political reasons, as some of them were members of the security apparatus and the Communist régime.

Stanisław Meducki, *Antyżydowskie wydarzenia kieleckie 4 lipca 1946 roku: dokumenty i materiały*, vol. 2 (Kielce: Kieleckie Towarzystwo Naukowe, 1994), p. 9.

306. These incidents appear in Gilbert, pp. 816–19. The incident in Nowy Targ is attributed by Gilbert (p. 818) to former members of the AK: "As the five Jews approached the outskirts of Nowy Targ, their car was flagged down at what appeared to be a police check-point. The five Jews were ordered out of the car and shot. Their killers had been members of the former underground forces of the Polish Home Army. The five bodies were stripped of their clothing and left naked on the highway."

According to an account in a Jewish remembrance book, these five survivors "were shot by an NSZ gang." In this recounting of murders in the Nowy Targ area, only one was attributed to the AK: the murder of David Grassgreen on February 10, 1946. The rest were said to have been carried out by the NSZ. See Michael Walter Fass (ed.), *Nowy-Targ and Vicinity: Zakopane, Charni Dunaietz, Rabka, Yordanov, Shchavnitza, Kroshchenko, Yablonka, Makov Podhalanski* (Tel-Aviv: Townspeople Association of Nowy-Targ and Vicinity, 1979), pp. 71–73.

However, according to Stanisław Wałach, *Był w Polsce czas* (Kraków, 1971), p. 177, the attack in Nowy Targ, said to have taken place on April 20, 1945, was carried out by "Ogień," an independent underground organization not affiliated either with the AK or with the NSZ. At the time of the incident, members of "Ogień," dressed in the uniform of the Polish army, were patrolling the border. The five Jews who were killed were being transported to Czechoslovakia by an illegal Jewish organization called the Central Emigration Committee (Centralny Komitet Emigracyjny, or

CKE). When their car was stopped for routine inspection, a passenger supposedly opened fire and "Żbik" (nom de guerre) shot them all. See Bolesław Dereń, *Józef Kuraś "Ogień" partyzant Podhala* (Kraków: Secesja, 1995), pp. 123–24.

Gilbert's reference to Chaim Hirszman can be found on p. 817 of his work. According to Henryk Pająk, however, Hirszman was *not* killed because he was a Jew; rather, he was killed by the WiN (in his own house) because he was an "active and dangerous functionary of the Provincial UB in Lublin." A short description of the murder by one of the participants (based on court records) follows. See Henryk Pająk, *Konspiracja młodzieży szkolnej 1945–1955* (Lublin: Retro, 1994), pp. 130–31.

For a reference to the killing of a Jewish escapee (Hersz Blanke) from Sobibór who became a Soviet agent, see Anna Grażyna Kister, "Koniec donosiciela," *Gazeta Polska* (Warszawa), September 14, 1995. Surprisingly, Hersz Blanke's name does not appear among the forty-six Sobibór survivors listed by Richard Rashke in his work *Escape from Sobibor* (New York: Avon, 1982), p. 357.

307. Gilbert, p. 819.

308. As quoted by L. Żebrowski, *Paszkwil Wyborczej*, p. 100.

309. Kainer (Krajewski), in Bernhard and Szlajfer, pp. 375–76.

310. In Reale, p. 210.

311. George Lenczowski, *The Middle East in World Affairs*, 2d ed. (Ithaca, NY: Cornell University Press, 1956), pp. 329–30 (1st ed., 1952). According to Lt. Gen. Sir Frederick E. Morgan, chief of the United Nations Relief and Rehabilitation Administration in Germany, thousands of Polish Jews were winding up in the American occupation zone because of a "well-organized, positive plan to get out of Europe." He attributed this migration (some 2,000 Jews per week) to the efforts of an unknown secret Jewish organization. This statement was partly confirmed by the U.S. commander in Europe, Gen. Joseph T. McNarney, in a report written to the President and dated January 29, 1946. Officials in the State Department added, "A number of official and semi-official indications have been provided by the Warsaw government that it is encouraging the migration of part of its Jewish population." See ibid., n. 23.

312. See Jósef Orlicki, *Szkice z dziejów stosunków polsko-żydowskich 1918–1949*. (Warszawa: Krajowa Agencja Wydawnicza, 1983), pp. 251–54. According to Szaynok, p. 103, after the pogrom, 33,000 left in August, 12,000 in September, and 4,500 in November-December.

313. According to Gutman and Krakowski, pp. 370–71, an internal Polish government memorandum in their possession classifies these postwar anti–Jewish actions as follows: "1) those in the nature of provocations and pogroms (pogroms following blood libels in which Jews were accused of ritual murder of Gentile children took place in Rzeszow, Cracow, Tarnow and Sosnowiec); 2) blackmail with the purpose of driving Jews out of a community and depriving them of their possessions; 3) murder and robbery; 4) murder for its ownsake, usually accomplished by throwing grenades into Jewish shelters."

The date of this memorandum is given as the "beginning of 1947" in the text and as the "end of 1945" in the footnote. Its title is rather strange (or strangely translated, or a printer's error): "Manifestations of Anti-Semitism in Poland and the Battle Against It's." But the strangest thing of all is that whereas the memorandum "attributes these acts to forest-based gangs made up for the most part of members of the NSZ," the category of "anti–communist action" is not one that appears among the four mentioned above. As all historians know, the Polish underground drew up lists and executed Soviet agents, including Jewish Soviet agents.

314. Roszkowski, p. 147.

315. As quoted by Kersten, *The Establishment of Communist Rule in Poland*, p. 219.

316. As quoted ibid., p. 218.

317. Zwoliński, p. 90.

318. Roszkowski, p. 161.

319. Krzysztof Sidorkiewicz, "Polscy czekiści," *Gazeta Polska* (Warsaw), November 23, 1995; Błażyński, p. 116.

320. As quoted by Richard C. Lukas, *Bitter Legacy: Polish-American Relations in the Wake of World War II* (Lexington: University Press of Kentucky, 1982), p. 57.

321. No one connected with the Polish underground was spared. From time to time one comes across Jewish accounts that speak of the postwar arrest and/or execution of those Polish underground members who engaged in anti–Jewish actions during the war, especially in the forests. Yet even here, given the existential situation in the forests, this understandable desire for retribution didn't always conform to the traditional "Law of the Talon" justice. The story of Jerzy Filip is a case in point.

Filip ("Biga") served as a doctor in the

"Groma" AK unit in the Lublin area. One day his unit apprehended a man who "was weaving in between the trees around the axis of our march." The man was without documents. Because he answered direct questions by talking in circles, the captain of the unit took him for a German spy and ordered him shot. Dr. Filip intervened and suggested that perhaps twenty-five lashes would be enough to "make him sing." In the course of the beating the prisoner revealed that he was a Jew living with other Jewish families in an underground forest shelter near Józefów. Dr. Filip vouched for the fact that such family units existed in that area and that he himself often went to the shelters to administer to the sick. And so, the Jew's life was spared.

Shortly after the war, Dr. Filip was summoned to the Ministry of National Defense (Ministerstwo Obrony Narodowej, or MON) in Warsaw for a Virtuti Militari cross for his work and bravery during the German occupation. The ministry, he notes, was well guarded both inside and out. As the doctor was looking for the room, a man approached him in the hallway and asked twice whether Dr. Filip recognized him. Dr. Filip replied both times that he did not, since he had treated many people during the war. He was then asked whether he remembered the twenty-five lashes. A short order followed to one of the attendants: "Place the captain under guard!"

Realizing his plight, Dr. Filip managed to escape by overpowering the guard after his interrogator departed. He ends his tale with the following words: "If I were to have fulfilled the order of the leader of 'Groma,' I would not have had so much trouble later on. The moral of this story is that sometimes good deeds are repaid with evil." Jerzy Filip, "Listy do redakcji," *Głos Polski* (Toronto), December 2, 1978.

322. Wanda Lisowska, "Wspomnienia 'Grażyny,'" *Zeszyty Historyczne* (Paris) 36 (1976): 30–33.

323. Kaja Bogomilska, "Siedlecka UB mordowała młodzież," *Gazeta Polska* (Warszawa), June 8, 1995.

324. See Garliński, *Poland in the Second World War*, pp. 324–26.

325. See Tomaszewski and Werbowski, pp. 103–5.

326. Teresa Torańska, *"Them": Stalin's Polish Puppets* (New York: Harper and Row, 1987), pp. 321–22. Shortly after the war, Zofia Kossak-Szczucka was told by Berman: "I owe your family a debt which I want to repay. You rescued my brother's children from the ghetto ... I can assure your departure from the country.... I recommend that you go." She fled and died in exile. See Anna Bugnon-Rosset, "Z 'białych plam' w życiorysie Zofii Kossak," *Tygodnik Powszechny* (Kraków), April 3, 1988.

327. Sack, *An Eye for an Eye*, 1993 edition, p. 139.

328. Lukas, *Bitter Legacy*, p. 57.

329. Ibid.

330. Krzysztof Urbański, *Kieleccy Żydzi* (Kraków: Małopolska Oficyna Wydawnicza, 1993), p. 165.

331. Włodzimierz Kalicki, "Tajemnice pogromu," in Tadeusz Wiącek (ed.), *Zabić Żyda!: kulisy i tajemnice pogromu kieleckiego 1946* (Kraków: Oficyna Wydawnicza Temax, 1992), pp. 67–68; Krzysztof Urbański, "Pogrom," ibid., p. 142; Urbański, *Kieleccy Żydzi*, p. 176; Stanisław Meducki and Zenon Wrona (eds.), *Antyżydowskie wydarzenia kieleckie 4 lipca 1946 roku: dokumenty i materiały*, vol. 1 (Kielce: Urząd Miasta Kielce and Kieleckie Towarzystwo Naukowe, 1992), p. 11; Szaynok, pp. 25–26.

332. Meducki and Wrona, *op. cit.*, p. 12.

333. Krzysztof Kąkolewski, "Prawda o 'Pogromie kieleckim.' Przepraszam za Dariusza Rosatiego," *Nasza Polska*, March 14, 1996. This is the fourth in a series of five articles by Kąkolewski on the Kielce pogrom. The information contained in these articles also appears in his major work: *Umarły cmentarz* (Warszawa: Von Borowiecky, 1996).

334. Szaynok, p. 26.

335. Urbański, *Kieleccy Żydzi,* p. 191; Szaynok, pp. 27–28; Wiącek, p. 144.

336. As quoted in Meducki and Wrona, p. 14 n. 20, and Wiącek, in Wiącek, p. 144.

337. Szaynok, p. 27.

338. Kąkolewski, "Prawda o 'Pogromie kieleckim'" (March 21, 1996).

339. Urbański, *Kieleccy Żydzi*, p. 192.

340. Ibid.

341. Kalicki, in Wiącek, pp. 68–69; Szaynok, pp. 26–27.

342. Krystyna Kersten, "Kielce—4 lipca 1946 roku," in Wiącek, p. 108. The article originally appeared in *Tygodnik Solidarność,* December 4, 1981.

343. Ibid., p. 112, 115–16; Urbański, *Kieleccy Żydzi*, pp. 195–96.

344. Śledzianowski, p. 115.

345. Krzysztof Kąkolewski, "Prehistoria

dnia wczorajszego," *Tygodnik Solidarność*, December 16, 1994; Kąkolewski, "Prawda o 'Pogromie kieleckim'" (March 21, 1996).

346. Henryk's whereabouts is still a topic of debate. Relying on "official" sources, Zenon Wrona places him in the village of Zaborowice (hamlet of Bielaki near Mniów) some 25 kilometers from Kielce, where he was visiting his friend without his parents' knowledge. Zenon Wrona, "Tak było: kalendarium tragedii," *Gazeta Kielecka*, June 29, 1990. According to Eta Lewkowicz-Ajzenman, the chief of the Secretariat of the District State Security Office in Kielce, on the day after the pogrom investigation officers found out that Henryk had been abducted by two men and taken to Końskie. There he was instructed to accuse the Jews of kidnapping him. See Pogonowski, *Jews in Poland*, pp. 169–70. According to Antoni Czubiński, Henryk was abducted by Antoni Pasowski, a Jew who worked for the UB. Antoni Czubiński, *Dzieje najnowsze Polski: Polska Ludowa 1944–1989* (Poznań: Wielkopolska Agencja Wydawnicza, 1992), pp. 111, 113.

On the fifty-first anniversary of the Kielce pogrom, the following notice appeared in the July 4, 1997, Web page called "Donosy":

> Henryk Błaszczyk, whose alleged "abduction by Jews" was directly responsible for the Kielce pogrom, says that it was the functionaries of the UB who instructed him to relate the fabricated version of the events. In point of fact, the then ten-year-old boy ran away from his home for a few days to the home of acquaintances living near Kielce. After the pogrom, the UB imprisoned the entire Błaszczyk family and later threatened to kill them if at any time they told the truth. That is why Błaszczyk has decided to speak up only now.

Michał Jankowski, "Po 51 latach," *Donosy* no. 2101 (July 4, 1997), p. 1, Online, Internet, July 18, 1997, available: http://info.fuw.edu.pl/bin/donosy-select.

347. Kąkolewski, "Prawda o 'Pogromie kieleckim'" (March 28, 1996).

348. Lane, p. 206.

349. Szaynok, p. 104.

350. See Lane, pp. 199–211. Three days after the Kielce incident, the following declaration was issued by the Council and Executive Committee of the Society for the Promotion of Poland's Independence in New York:

A DECLARATION RE. THE KIELCE CRIME

While having but of most severe reprobation for any kind of oppression of the Jews in Poland — recognizing the absolute equality of rights of all Polish citizens — deeply moved by the horror of the Kielce events — and expressing our deepest sympathy to the Jews in Poland who are the victims of the monstrous policies of the Warsaw "government" aimed at attaining their perfidious inner as well as external political ends — we consider it our duty to declare in the name of Society for the Promotion of Poland's Independence, what follows:

The crimes committed in Kielce are the result of an infamous provocation planned by the secret police of the Warsaw regime. This is our inmost conviction.

Although all details of the diabolical plot are not known to us as yet, the reports of reliable American papers seem to justify that conviction of ours.

The motives of the policies of the Warsaw regime resulting in the Kielce events, may be summed up as follows:

1. The Warsaw regime is eager to turn away the world's public opinion from the tremendous difficulties of its administration, because it does not rest upon the will of the majority of the Polish Nation but its powerful secret police and the tremendous Soviet army of occupation. While public opinion of democratic countries begins to realize the abuses and frauds which the pro-Soviet regime is committing in Poland, to mention but the recent fraudulous referendum, the Warsaw powers provoke the Kielce murders, and successively appear in the role of defenders of the Jewish population to create the semblance of being the defenders of democracy.

2. The Warsaw regime has, from its very inauguration, endeavored to remove all Jews from Poland. Their Ghetto policies follow strictly the example of Hitler. Polish Jews, and quite particularly those who have been repatriated from Soviet Russia, are being forcibly settled in secluded areas, for instance in Lower Silesia where they are being kept isolated from the country's Christian population. Tens of thousands of Polish Jews are being transferred against their will to the city of Stettin, where they are being kept in

isolation camps and compelled to work at the construction of the port and of Soviet military bases.

While paralyzing the freedom of expression of the really democratic Polish press, organs of some antisemitic groups are being not only tolerated by the regime but enjoy its special favors.

All these are policies planned methodically by the pro-Soviet Warsaw regime, aimed at compelling the Jews to leave Poland.

3. The Warsaw regime receiving its orders from Moscow and acting strictly in obedience to them has its good reasons to adhere to such policies towards the Jews in Poland; it uses them as means to embarrass the British Government in matters pertaining to the Palestine problem, and, furthermore, to aggravate the political crisis in the Near East, to envenom Judaeo-Arab antagonisms. It is, indeed, for that purpose that the Warsaw regime endeavors to squeeze in the remnants of Poland's Jewish population which had succeeded in escaping the Hitler massacre, into the American and British zones of occupation in Germany and Austria.

The honor and good name of Poland and the Poles to whom thousands of Polish Jews owe their salvation in the period of the criminal Nazi occupation, require that the Kielce murder be fully avenged.

Yet the punishment of the guilty ones must, first of all, be dealt out on those who have plotted the Kielce provocation: one must, to that end, bare the criminal activities of the secret police of the Warsaw regime which had not only tolerated but, let us be clear about it, prepared the murders.

An investigation by the Warsaw regime will surely not find the real murderers. That regime cannot achieve it and does not want to do it. An investigation by an international Commission alone may reveal the real malefactors. But this must be done at once. Such a commission only will be able to corroborate the fact that the Kielce murders were inspired and organized by the secret political police of the Warsaw regime by means of provocatory methods following the pogrom standards of the ill-famed Tsarist Ochrana.

New York, July 7th, 1946.

Source: Teka "Związek Obrony Niepodległości Polski," teczka 1, Piłsudski Institute of America, Archiwum Rzeczowy (ARz).

351. Iwo Cyprian Pogonowski, "Holocaust Memorial Museum in Washington, DC," *New Horizon* 20 (November-December 1995): 10. See also his article in *Kielce—July 4, 1946: Background, Context, and Events, a Collective Work* (Toronto and Chicago: Polish Educational Foundation in North America, 1996), pp. 69–104.

352. Szaynok, p. 105; Kersten, in Wiącek, p. 115; Stanisław Mikołajczyk, *The Rape of Poland: Patterns of Soviet Aggression* (London: S. Low, Marston, 1948), p. 148. Władysław Kojder was a cousin of the father of Apolonia Maria Kojder, the Polish-Canadian coauthor of *Marynia Don't Cry*, cited in the first chapter. The following exchange between Czesław Miłosz and Alexander Wat (in Wat, *My Century*, pp. xxvii–xxviii) also sheds some light on the events in Kielce:

> Wat: In Ili, the head of the Union of Polish Patriots was an old prewar communist, a woman teacher, terribly doctrinaire....During the repatriation effort, she was in close contact with an old communist who had gotten through all the purges without a scratch because he was high up in the NKVD. This was a Pole named Spychaj [Sobczyński], a worker, a Chekist. Spychaj was one of the founders of the Union of Polish Patriots and had been in Russia for many years. His younger brother was in charge of the People's Army in the Kielce area, his name was Spychaj too. He was in charge of Kielce in 1946 when the pogrom took place there. He almost went to prison for that, but he was just transferred elsewhere, to another post.
>
> Miłosz: What do you think about that pogrom?
>
> Wat: On the basis of what I've heard from many quarters, the pogrom was launched—launched isn't the word, more like provoked—by the Kielce security forces (there wasn't a policeman in sight that day). Spychaj was in charge of those forces. It should be remembered that Spychaj had that older brother in the NKVD who hadn't returned to Poland. This is all conjecture of course but the instructions must have come from the Soviets. In other words, the younger Spychaj was acting on orders.

Miłosz: Yes, that's the same version I heard too. The point was to exploit Polish anti-Semitism in the international arena.

Wat: Yes, that was the point. Spychaj was supposed to stand trial but was transferred instead. And sometime in 1956 or 1957 when Poland started letting the first Jews emigrate to Israel, that same Spychaj was in charge of the security department that issued visas to the Jews. As an expert in such matters.

353. Zenon Wrona, in Wiącek, pp. 8, 12; Kalicki, ibid., pp. 97–98; see also Szaynok, pp. 37, 107.

354. See Michael Checinski, *Poland: Communism-Nationalism-Antisemitism* (New York: Karz-Cohl, 1982). See summary in Szaynok, pp. 106–7.

355. Meducki and Wrona, p. 18.

356. Kąkolewski, "Prawda o 'Pogromie kieleckim'" (March 7, 1996).

357. Ibid.

358. In Szaynok, p. 41.

359. Ibid.

360. Ibid., p. 49.

361. Ibid., p. 44.

362. Ibid.

363. Ibid.

364. In Checinski, *Poland*, p. 27. According to Kąkolewski, the telephone at the Jewish Center was deliberately disconnected at the local post office. Three Informacja officers were assigned to the task of executing Kahane. Kąkolewski, "Prawda o 'Pogromie kieleckim'" (March 14, 1996).

365. In Szaynok, p. 55.

366. Ibid., p. 46.

367. Ibid., p. 45.

368. Kąkolewski, "Prawda o 'Pogromie kieleckim'" (March 7, 1996).

369. Ibid. (March 14, 1996).

370. Ibid.

371. In Szaynok, p. 46.

372. Ibid., pp. 57–58, 77, 80. During the trial, Stefan Mazur happened to mention that he had belonged to an organization during the war. A bizarre exchange followed between Mazur and Adam Urbański Biegły, who wanted to know the name of that organization:

Mazur: It was the AL.
Biegły: Perhaps it was the AK?
Mazur: AL and AK. It's all the same.
Biegły: It is not the same at all.
Mazur: It was the AK.
Biegły: Does the defendant know the difference between the AL, AK, and NSZ?
Mazur: Certainly. There was the AL; there was also the BCh.
Biegły: Why, then, in light of this, does the defendant say AL and AK?
Mazur: I forgot. Anyway, I still belong to the AL even today.
Biegły: How can that be? The AL no longer exists.
Mazur: I apologize, I belong to the SL.

373. Ibid., p. 51.

374. Kąkolewski, "Prawda o 'Pogromie kieleckim'" (March 7, 1996).

375. As quoted by Kalicki, in Wiącek, p. 79.

376. See the 1946 "Center City" map of Kielce at the end of Meducki and Wrona.

377. Szaynok, p. 80, and n. 60.

378. Ibid., p. 60 n. 194; Kalicki, in Wiącek, p. 87. Arthur Bliss Lane stated, "But almost all sources agreed that the militia had been responsible to a great extent for the massacre, not only in failing to keep order, but in the actual killing of the victims, for many had been shot or bayoneted to death." Lane, p. 206.

379. Szaynok, p. 89, and n. 109.

380. See also the more recent article in Kersten, *Polacy, Żydzi, Komunizm*, pp. 89–142.

381. Kąkolewski, "Prehistoria dnia wczorajszego."

382. As quoted by John Micgiel, "Kościół katolicki i pogrom kielecki," *Niepodległość* (New York, London) 25 (1992): 137–39.

383. As quoted by Smolar, "Jews as a Polish Problem," pp. 47–48.

384. As quoted by Urbański, in Wiącek, p. 143, and in Urbański, *Kieleccy Żydzi*, pp. 225–26.

385. Michał Borwicz, "Polish-Jewish Relations, 1944–1947," in Abramsky et al., pp. 195–96.

386. See Kersten, *Polacy, Żydzi, Komunizm*, pp. 134–35.

387. "Poland Apologizes for Pogrom," *Forward* (New York), February 2, 1996.

388. At a meeting of the Central Committee of the Polish Workers' Party held in May 1945, Władysław Gomułka stated: "We are not in a position to combat the reactionary forces without the Red Army.... We do not have our own forces with which to replace them." Leszek Żebrowski,

TABLE 22. NUMBER OF BELORUSSIANS IN POLAND'S EASTERN PROVINCES, 1931 (IN THOUSANDS)

		According to Mother Tongue					
Province	***Total***	***Poles***	***Belorussians***	***Russians***	***Jews***	***Lithuanians***	***Germans***
			Official				
Białystok	1,643.8	1,182.3	205.6	35.1	194.9	13.1	7.3
Wilno	1,275.9	761.7	289.7	43.4	108.8	66.8	1.4
Nowogródek	1,057.1	553.9	413.5	6.8	77.0	2.5	0.4
Polesie	1,131.9*	164.1	75.3	16.2	113.0	0.0	1.1
			Adjusted				
Białystok	1,643.8	1,117	269	35	197	13	7
Wilno	1,275.9	641	409	43	111	67	1
Nowogródek	1,057.1	366	616	7	83	3	0
Polesie	1,131.9	127	654	16	114	0	1

*Including 54.0 Ukrainians and 707.4 local (*tutejsi*).

"Pretekst kielecki," *Gazeta Polska* (Warszawa), January 29, 1996.

389. Urban, pp. 90–91

390. Ibid., p. 96.

391. Ibid., p. 101.

392. Radio Free Europe (Munich), interview broadcast to Poland on January 7, 1989. See W. T. Bartoszewski, p. 30.

Chapter 5: Belorussian Collaboration

1. J. Tomaszewski, *Rzeczpospolita wielu narodów*, from the table (adjusted census) on p. 116 (see above). In the text, he gives a range for the Belorussian population: 1,948,000 to 2,226,000. Podlaski, p. 28, estimates that 2 million Belorussians lived in these territories. The 1931 official Polish census figures are much lower; Soviet figures (1939) are much higher. See Iwanow, in Sword, *The Soviet Takeover*, p. 255. According to Z. S. Siemaszko, ibid., table on p. 230, in 1939–41 the mother tongue of 1,945,000 people in the Soviet-occupied Polish provinces was Belorussian and "local." According to Aleksandra Bergman, *Sprawy białoruskie w II Rzeczypospolitej* (Warszawa: Państwowe Wydawnictwo Naukowe, 1984), p. 14, there were between 4 and 4.5 million people in "Western Belorussia," 2 to 2.5 million of whom were Belorussians.

2. Bergman, pp. 9, 53.

3. See Iwanow, in Sword, *The Soviet Takeover*, p. 253. For Soviet repressions against the Belorussians, see Vakar, pp. 145–54.

4. Iwanow, in Sword, *The Soviet Takeover*, p. 254.

5. According to David Marples, it was the soldiers of the Red Army, as well as the members of the Communist Party of Belorussia, who "played the dominant role in the Temporary Administrations and organized elections for the People's Assembly, which duly proclaimed the reunion of Western Belorussia with the Belorussian SSR." David R. Marples, *Stalinism in Ukraine in the 1940s* (New York: St. Martin's Press, 1992), p. 26.

6. Vladimir Aleksandrovich Poluian, *Revoliutsionno-demokraticheskoe dvizhenie v Zapadnoi Belorussii* (Minsk: Nauka i tekhnika, 1978), p. 352.

7. S. Kozhevnikov, in Sword, *The Soviet Takeover*, pp. 295–96.

8. In Grudzińska-Gross and Gross, *War Through Children's Eyes*, p. 56.

9. Podlaski, p. 28; Liszewski, *Wojna polsko-sowiecka*, p. 60, and the 1995 edition, vol. 1, pp. 353ff.; *Historia Belaruskai SSR*, vol. 4 (Minsk, 1975), p. 86; Nikolai Koditsa, *V edinoi sem'e bratskikh narodov* (Minsk, 1971), pp. 34–35.

10. Łuczak, p. 30.

11. As quoted in Jerzy Węgierski, *Lwów pod okupacją sowiecką 1939–1941* (Warszawa: Editions Spotkania, 1991), p. 218.

12. Gross, *Revolution from Abroad*, p. 29.

13. Erikson, in Sword, *The Soviet Takeover*, p. 19.

14. Łuczak, p. 511.

15. This and the following eyewitness accounts come from the Władysław Anders Collection and the Ministry of Information of the Republic of Poland in the London Collection located at the Hoover Institution Archives in Stanford, California, as quoted and referenced in Andrzej Guryn, "Zbrodnie Sowieckie wobec ludności cywilnej w Grodnie," *Gazeta* (Toronto), October 23–25, 1992.

16. Ibid.

17. Ibid.

18. Ibid.

19. Ibid.

20. Ibid.

21. Ibid.

22. Liszewski, *Wojna polsko-sowiecka*, p. 75.

23. Bugajski, p. 362. For other Polish discriminatory practices against the Belorussians, see Vakar, pp. 122–32. For a series of articles by Polish authors dealing with Belorussia from World War I to the 1921 Treaty of Riga, together with a series of articles by Belorussian authors dealing with repressions against the Belorussians in the 1930s and their deportation during the Soviet occupation, see Wiesław Balcerak (ed.), *Polska-Białoruś 1918–1945* (Warszawa: Instytut Historii PAN, 1994).

24. Davies, *God's Playground*, p. 409.

25. Andrzej Chojnowski, *Koncepcje polityki narodowościowej rządów polskich w latach 1921–1939* (Wrocław: Zakład Narodowy im. Ossolińskich, 1979), p. 228.

26. Korzec and Szurek, p. 212.

27. For a treatise on "military settlers" in Poland's eastern territories, see Henryk Lappo et al. (eds.), *Z Kresów Wschodnich Rzeczypospolitej: wspomnienia z osad wojskowych, 1921–1940* (London: Ognisko Rodzin Osadników Kresowych, 1992).

28. In Bergman, p. 16.

29. Iwanow, in Sword, *The Soviet Takeover*, *passim*.

30. Turonek, p. 38. That this was done primarily for propaganda reasons is made clear by the policy of forced deportation and Russification introduced in Belorussia just after the war. According to official statistics, from 1950 to the beginning of the 1960s about 900,000 people "left" Belorussia, mainly for Siberia and Kazakhstan.

Immediately after the war, with few exceptions, the entire curriculum in higher education was taught in the Russian language, a situation that forced students in primary and secondary schools to become greatly "motivated" to pursue their education in the Russian language as well. In the 1960s and 1970s, there was a massive attempt to transform all Belorussian schools into Russian ones. As a result, by the mid–1980s, Belorussian schools ceased to exist in the cities and were only nominally Belorussian in the villages, since most of the subjects in these village schools were taught in the Russian language.

Moreover, between 1950 and 1985, the number of books published in Belorussia went from 12.5 to 53.3 million, but those published in the Belorussian language fell from 10.7 to 5 million and the overall Belorussian involvement in the publishing business fell from 85 percent to 9 percent. Ibid., p. 240.

31. Sword, "Soviet Economic Policy," in Sword, *The Soviet Takeover*, pp. 86–101.

32. Turonek, p. 38.

33. Iwanow, in Sword, *The Soviet Takeover*, pp. 259–60.

34. According to one estimate based on a random sample of those arrested by the Soviet authorities in "Western Belorussia" between 1939 and 1941, 59 percent were Poles, 26 percent were Belorussians, 11 percent were Jews, 2 percent were Russians, 1 percent were Ukrainians, and 1 percent were "other" or "unknown." See Krzysztof Jaśkiewicz, "Obywatele polscy aresztowani na terytorium tzw. Zachodniej Białorusi w latach 1939–1941 w świetle dokumentacji NKWD/KGB," *Kwartalnik Historyczny* (Warszawa) 1 (1994): 125.

35. As quoted by Iwanow, in Sword, *The Soviet Takeover*, pp. 260–61.

36. Ibid., pp. 260–64.

37. Turonek, p. 54.

38. Ibid., p. 52. See also Vakar, p. 171.

39. Turonek, p. 58.

40. Ibid., p. 154; Vakar, p. 172. On April 2, 1996, Belorussian President Alexander Lukashenko and Russian President Boris Yeltsin signed a formal treaty to reunite their two countries politically and economically in a "Community of Sovereign Republics," which could eventually lead to a complete merger. The agreement was sealed with a shot of vodka, an act captured on film by a Reuters photographer. Lukashenko promised Belorussians that this treaty would "correct the historical error of 1991." See Geoffrey York, "Russia, Belorussia Celebrate Treaty," *Globe and Mail* (Toronto), April 3, 1996.

Whether the treaty would also "correct the

historical errors" of the 1930s and 1940s, when hundreds of thousands of Belorussians died at Soviet hands, Lukashenko did not say. Neither did he comment on the "historical error" of April 26, 1986, when 400,000 Belorussians had to be evacuated from the contaminated area around the Chernobyl nuclear-power plant lying just six miles south of the Belorussian border. On that day—the prevailing wind was northwesterly—reactor four exploded and spilled 70 percent of the total radioactivity (90 times greater than that of the atomic bombs dropped on Japan) on Belorussia and its 10 million inhabitants. Now, immune-system breakdowns ("Chernobyl AIDS") are widespread, the birthrate has fallen by 50 percent, thyroid cancer is on the rise, and fears are expressed that tens of thousands will contract some form of cancer in the future. According to Yevgeny Konopla, a biologist and leading authority on Chernobyl radiation, one-third of all Belorussian children are ill. Thanks to this Soviet "gift from hell," the entire Belorussia Republic will be contaminated for the next one hundred years, and no one will ever be able to live again in the fertile one-thousand-square-mile "exclusion zone," much of which lies in Belorussia. The half life of Plutonium 239 is 24,000 years. See Nell McCafferty, "Life after Chernobyl," *Audubon*, May-June 1996, pp. 66–75.

41. See Turonek, pp. 80–81, 85.
42. Ibid., p. 33.
43. Ibid., pp. 35–36, 39.
44. Ibid., pp. 39–40.
45. Ibid., p. 41.
46. Ibid., p. 42.
47. Ibid., pp. 43–44.
48. Ibid.
49. Ibid., p. 45.
50. Vakar, p. 177.
51. Turonek, p. 69.
52. Nuremberg Document E.C. 326, as quoted by John Loftus, *The Belarus Secret* (New York: Alfred A. Knopf, 1982), p. 87.
53. Turonek, p. 105.
54. Ibid., pp. 6, 71.
55. Ibid., pp. 46, 190–92, 219–20.
56. Ibid., p. 7. Tec, *In the Lion's Den*, p. 62, refers to the Belorussian police as having "a sprinkling of Poles."
57. In Turonek, p. 100.
58. Ibid., p. 100.
59. L. Tomaszewski, p. 225.
60. Turonek, p. 185.
61. Ibid.
62. Aleksander Zienkiewicz, *No Greater Love* (Rome, 1968), pp. 34–35.
63. In Turonek, p. 186.
64. Ibid.
65. Ibid.
66. Ibid.; Vakar, p. 264.
67. Turonek, p. 187.
68. Ibid.
69. Ibid., pp. 207–8. The Pilch reference is from Adolf Pilch, *Spotkania* (Paris), nos. 21–22 (1984): 80. The Belorussian estimate is from *Letapis* (New York) 28 (1985): 91.
70. Turonek, p. 207.
71. Vakar, p. 193.
72. For a recent article dealing, in part, with Belorussian collaboration under the German occupation, see Hans-Heinrich Wilhelm, "Die Rolle der Kollaboration für die deutsche Besatzungspolitik in Litauen und 'Weissruthenien,'" in Röhr, pp. 191–216.
73. Turonek, pp. 200–201.
74. Loftus, p. 27.
75. Ibid., pp. 28–29.
76. Ibid.
77. Gilbert, p. 298.
78. Ibid., pp. 298–99.
79. Ibid., pp. 446–47.
80. Ibid., p. 579.
81. Silverman, Smuschkowitz, and Smuszkowicz, p. 74.
82. Ibid., pp. 79, 82.
83. Ibid., p. 108.
84. Vakar, p. 267 n. 71.
85. Ibid., p. 187.
86. For the story of one such ethnic Belorussian rescuer in the Brest (Brześć) area, see Paldiel, pp. 285–88.
87. Silverman, Smuschkowitz, and Smuszkowicz p. 698; Hempel, p 133.
88. Turonek, pp. 200–202.
89. Władysław Kijuć, "Armia Krajowa na Litwie i Białorusi," *Zeszyty Historyczne* (Paris) 113 (1995): 162.
90. Turonek, 202–3.
91. Ibid., pp. 210, 212–13, 216.
92. Ibid., pp. 216–17.
93. Ibid., pp. 217, 225–26.
94. Ibid., pp. 208, 233–34.
95. Ibid., pp. 223–24.
96. Ibid., p. 224.
97. Littlejohn, *The Patriotic Traitors*, p. 364 n. 24.
98. Turonek, p. 232.
99. Ibid., p. 226.

100. Ibid., pp. 228–29.
101. Loftus, pp. 44–45.
102. Ibid., pp. 47, 51, 91.
103. Ibid., pp. 5, 105, 109.
104. Turonek, p. 236. Turonek considers this last estimate (reduced from the previous postwar estimate of 1,409,000 killed by Germans alone) still too high.

Chapter 6: Lithuanian Collaboration

1. See George Urbaniak, "Lithomania versus Panpolonism: The Roots of the Polish-Lithuanian Conflict before 1914," *Canadian Slavonic Papers* 31, no. 2 (June 1989): 107–27.
2. *Mały Rocznik Statystyczny 1939* (Warszawa: GUS, 1939), pp. 11, 36–37.
3. Łuczak, p. 525.
4. Ibid.
5. J. Tomaszewski, *Rzeczpospolita wielu narodów*, from the table (adjusted census) on p. 116. About 200,000 Poles lived in Lithuania at this time (p. 55). In 1931, the population of Wilno was 195,100. Of this total, 128,600 were Poles, 54,600 were Jews, 1,700 were Belorussians, and about 1 percent of the inhabitants were Lithuanian. *Mały Rocznik Statystyczny*, p. 37.
6. In Gross, *Revolution from Abroad*, p. 13. "The region should be awarded to Germany," said Stalin, "for her Foreign Minister [Ribbentrop] because of its fine stags."
7. Pobóg-Malinowski, p. 102.
8. Ibid., p. 103 n. 35.
9. Wardzyńska, *Sytuacja ludności polskiej w Generalnym Komisariacie Litwy*, p. 23. This study of the situation of Poles in the General Commissariat of Lithuania is based mostly on the documents that appear on pp. 129–274. See also Łuczak, p. 524.
10. Łossowski, *Likwidacja Uniwersytetu Stefana Batorego*, p. 13. This work, with a short introduction by the editor, contains various documents relating to the closure of the university.
11. Łuczak, pp. 525–26.
12. In Łossowski, *Likwidacja Universytetu Stefana Batorego*, pp. 98, 100. The university reopened in the fall of 1941 and was closed again in early 1943. See Romuald J. Misiunas and Rein Taagepera, *The Baltic States: Years of Dependence, 1940–1990*, rev. ed. (Berkeley: University of California Press, 1993), p. 54.
13. Stanisław Lagun, "W imię prawdy i przyjaźni," *Gazeta* (Toronto), July 12–14, 1991. See also Pobóg-Malinowski, p. 105; Roman Korab-Żebryk, *Biała Księga w obronie Armii Krajowej na Wileńszczyźnie* (Lublin: Wydawnictwo Lubelskie, 1991), p. 9; Wardzyńska, *Sytuacja ludności polskiej w Generalnym Komisariacie Litwy*, p. 25; and Łuczak, pp. 524–29.
14. Wardzyńska, *Sytuacja ludności polskiej w Generalnym Komisariacie Litwy*, pp. 21, 23–24.
15. V. Stanley Vardys, "The Baltic States under Stalin: The First Experiences, 1940–41," in Sword, *The Soviet Takeover*, pp. 279–81. For a table entitled "Communist Party Size and Ethnicity, 1930–80" for Lithuania and Eastern Latvia, see Misiunas and Taagepera, p. 359.
16. Wardzyńska, *Sytuacja ludności polskiej w Generalnym Komisariacie Litwy*, p. 24.
17. Korab-Żebryk, p. 10.
18. Wardzyńska, *Sytuacja ludności polskiej w Generalnym Komisariacie Litwy*, p. 24.
19. Lagun.
20. Wardzyńska, *Sytuacja ludności polskiej w Generalnym Komisariacie Litwy*, p. 29.
21. Ibid., p. 29.
22. Ibid., p. 30. For excerpts from the lengthy LAF "Directives for the Liberation of Lithuania, March 24, 1941," see Bronis J. Kaslas, *The USSR-German Aggression against Lithuania* (New York: Robert Speller and Sons, 1973), pp. 321–27.
23. From "Memorandum of the Lithuanian Activist Front for the Government of the Reich," in Kaslas, pp. 365–66.
24. Avraham Tory, *Surviving the Holocaust: The Kovno Ghetto Diary*, ed. Martin Gilbert, textual notes by Dina Porat, trans. Jerzy Michalowicz (Cambridge: Harvard University Press, 1990). See also István Deák's review of this work in *New York Review of Books*, November 8, 1990. For an article on Lithuanian collaboration under the German occupation, see the previously mentioned chapter by Wilhelm in Röhr. See also Karlis Kangeris, "Kollaboration vor der Kollaboration? Die baltischen Emigranten und ihre 'Befreiungskomitees' in Deutschland 1940/1941," ibid., pp. 174–75.
25. Hilberg, *Perpetrators, Victims, Bystanders*, p. 99.
26. In Wardzyńska, *Sytuacja ludności polskiej w Generalnym Komisariacie Litwy*, p. 30.
27. Four priests died in Wilno: Wacław Siekierko, Stanisław Staszewicz, Edward Jung and Tomasz Kamiński. Ibid., pp. 29–30.

28. After Škirpa, the designated prime minister, was detained in Berlin, Ambrazevičius became the acting prime minister. According to the *Encyclopedia Lituanica,* vol. 5 (Boston: J. Kapocius, 1976), p. 206, Škirpa was detained because "the Nazis, having understood his anti-collaborationist designs, refused to grant him permission to leave Berlin for Kaunas, placed him under home arrest, and later removed him to southern Germany." In 1944, he was sent to Bad Godesberg concentration camp.

29. In Estonia these indigenous directorates were called Landesdirektoren or "Country Directors," in Latvia, Generaldirektoren, or "General Directors."

30. Wardzyńska, *Sytuacja ludności polskiej w Generalnym Komisariacie Litwy*, p. 32.

31. Chief of the Security Police and the SD, "Operational Situational Report USSR No. 31," July 23, 1941, in Arad et al., p. 44.

32. Korab-Żebryk, p. 13; Wardzyńska, *Sytuacja ludności polskiej w Generalnym Komisariacie Litwy*, p. 58.

33. Wardzyńska, *Sytuacja ludności polskiej w Generalnym Komisariacie Litwy*, pp. 32–33; Korab-Żebryk, pp. 14–20. No known rosters exist of the Ypatingas Būys who were quartered in the army barracks. However, three lists have been preserved by the Lietuvos TSR Centrinis Valstybinis Archyvas, which provide the names, ranks, family status (names of wives, names and dates of birth of children), and addresses of sixty-nine Sonderkommando members who lived in their own homes in Wilno. Two of the documents are in the Lithuanian language and date from November 1941 and July 1942, respectively. The third, in the German language, is undated. The sixty-nine names can be found in Korab-Żebryk, pp. 17–19. Among them are the names of three women. A photocopy of the German list appears in Wardzyńska, *Sytuacja ludności polskiej w Generalnym Komisariacie Litwy*, in the unpaginated photo section at the end of the book. Thus far, only four members of the Ypatingas Būrys have been tried for war crimes in Poland, and that was in the 1970s. All four received death sentences, one of which was commuted to twenty-five years in prison.

Currently, federal officials in Canada are attempting to deport a ninety-year-old Lithuanian, Antanas Kenstavičius, on charges of war crimes. See David Vienneau, "B.C. Man Named as Alleged Nazi," *Toronto Star*, January 25, 1996.

34. Wardzyńska, *Sytuacja ludności polskiej w Generalnym Komisariacie Litwy*, pp. 33–34.

35. Ibid. and Wardzyńska, *Formacja Wachmannschaften*, p. 25. According to testimonies and court proceedings, there were no Poles in Trawniki, except for a few individual cases. Interestingly, in Trawniki there were also a few who, during the war, called themselves Volksdeutsch and Ukrainian but who, after the war, claimed to be Polish (p. 27).

36. Wardzyńska, *Sytuacja ludności polskiej w Generalnym Komisariacie Litwy*, p. 34. Miciunas and Taagepera, p. 57, state:

> In Lithuania, where almost the entire prewar army which had been turned into a Soviet unit surrendered *en masse* during the first days of the war, recruitment for the Defense Battalions was frequently presented to its members in the form of a choice between joining or being sent to a POW camp; thus it is not surprising that many joined. It has been estimated that during the period of their operation some 20,000 Lithuanians served in these battalions; this manpower averaged around 8,000 at any one time. In August 1941 there were 20 Lithuanian battalions with 8,388 officers and men; in March 1944 the figure stood at 8,000.

37. Hilberg, *Perpetrators, Victims, Bystanders*, p. 99.

38. Korab-Żebryk, pp. 23–24.

39. Gilbert, pp. 390–91. On March 5, 1942, the Lithuanian police also participated in the liquidation of the Baranowicze ghetto in Belorussia (p. 298).

40. Korab-Żebryk, pp. 58–59. Archbishop Skvireckas died in Austria in 1959. Bishop Brizgys emigrated to the United States.

41. Misiunas and Taagepera, pp. 58–59.

42. Korab-Żebryk, pp. 105–6; Wardzyńska, *Sytuacja ludności polskiej w Generalnym Komisariacie Litwy,* p. 34, 84.

43. Korab-Żebryk, pp. 109–10.

44. Misiunas and Taagepera, p. 59.

45. Wardzyńska, *Sytuacja ludności polskiej w Generalnym Komisariacie Litwy*, p. 34.

46. Ibid.

47. Ibid., p. 45.

48. Ibid., p. 39.

49. Ibid., p. 47.

50. Ibid., p. 54.

51. Korab-Żebryk, p. 58.

52. Wardzyńska, *Sytuacja ludności polskiej w Generalnym Komisariacie Litwy*, p. 54.

53. Report of the Eastern Bureau to the Polish government-in-exile in London, dated November 15, 1941, ibid., p. 158.

54. Ibid., p. 33; Korab-Żebryk, *op. cit.*, pp. 13, 15.

55. Table 4 along with another list of Ponary victims compiled from the journal of Kazimierz Sakowicz can be found in Wardzyńska, *Sytuacja ludności polskiej w Generalnym Komisariacie Litwy*, pp. 64–65.

56. L. Tomaszewski, p. 181.

57. Łuczak, p. 506.

58. Wardzyńska, *Sytuacja ludności polskiej w Generalnym Komisariacie Litwy*, pp. 181–86.

59. Report of the Polish Government Delegation, 1942, ibid., p. 223.

60. Ibid., p. 70 n. 14.

61. Korab-Żebryk, pp. 39–41. An AK report dated July 29, 1942, states that 1,200 Poles and 130 Polish prisoners were executed in connection with this affair. In Wardzyńska, *Sytuacja ludności polskiej w Generalnym Komisariacie Litwy*, pp. 202–3.

62. The notice appeared in *Goniec Codzienny*, September 18, 1943. It is reprinted in Korab-Żebryk, pp. 50–51.

63. Ibid., pp. 48–49.

64. For a list of the thirty-eight victims, see L. Tomaszewski, p. 226.

65. Korab-Żebryk, pp. 135–39.

66. L. Tomaszewski, p. 91.

67. Wardzyńska, *Sytuacja ludności polskiej w Generalnym Komisariacie Litwy*, pp. 99–108. The Eastern Bureau report appears on pp. 211–13.

68. Ibid., p. 116. The report is on p. 205.

69. See ibid., pp. 109–17.

70. Pobóg-Malinowski, pp. 324–25. For another revealing summary dated May 11, 1942, by Stefan Grot-Rowecki, see "Meldunek no. 121. Raport specjalny o 'sytuacji litewskiej,'" in Korab-Żebryk, pp. 28–35. This report is divided into the following sections: the period before the occupation of Wileńszczyzna, the period of occupation, the period of the Lithuanian SSR, the period during the German-Soviet War, the current situation, and the conclusion.

71. Wardzyńska, *Sytuacja ludności polskiej w Generalnym Komisariacie Litwy*, pp. 36–37.

72. Ibid., p. 37. Misiunas and Taagepera, p. 61, note: "Some outbreaks of indiscriminate killing of Jews occurred in Lithuania soon after the German attack, and several bands of *ad hoc* executioners are known to have perpetrated such massacres. The connection between their activity and the LAF's organized uprising is hard to establish, with no indication of any definite relationship except in time and circumstance." What, then, is one to make of these LAF anti-Semitic proclamations?

73. Michael Ignatieff, "In the New Republics (Lithuania's Role in the Extermination of Jews during World War II)," *New York Review of Books*, November 21, 1991.

74. Wardzyńska, *Sytuacja ludności polskiej w Generalnym Komisariacie Litwy*, p. 37.

75. Hilberg, *Perpetrators, Victims, Bystanders*, p. 99.

76. Wardzyńska, *Sytuacja ludności polskiej w Generalnym Komisariacie Litwy*, pp. 39–40. A "Special Report on the Political Situation and on Activity in the Area of Vilnius, Police Matters," issued by the Chief of SP and SD on July 7, 1941, states:

> The Lithuanian police branches in Vilnius, subordinated to the Einsatzkommando, were given the task of drawing up current lists of names of Jews in Vilnius: first the Intelligentsia, political activists, and wealthy Jews. Subsequently, searches and arrests were made and 54 Jews were liquidated on July 4, and 93 were liquidated on July 5. Sizeable property belonging to Jews were secured. With the help of Lithuanian police officials, a search was started for Communists and NKVD agents, most of whom, however, are said to have fled.
>
> A search was also started for hidden weapons of the Polish secret military organizations, of which the Lithuanian police has as yet not made an accurate estimate. The establishment of a Jewish quarter is being prepared.

Chief of Security Police and the SD, "Operational Situation Report USSR No 17," July 7, 1941, in Arad et al., p. 15. On the Wilno ghetto, see L. Tomaszewski, pp. 164–76.

77. Gilbert, pp. 217–18. A report from the regional commissar in Slutsk to the general commissar in Minsk — dated October 30, 1941— states that even the Belorussians were the objects of Nazi and Lithuanian police excesses. The following excerpt from that document can be found in Turonek, pp. 95–96.

> With indescribable brutality on the part of the German police, and especially the

> Lithuanian partisans [i.e., the Lithuanians in the service of the Nazis], Jews—and in their midst also Belorussians—were dragged out of their houses and brought together. There was shooting all over town and the bodies of shot Jews lay on the streets. The Belorussians had a great deal of difficulty in order to free themselves from the encirclement. The Jews, including the craftsmen, were very brutally maltreated in sight of the Belorussians. The Belorussians were also beaten with rubber truncheons and gun stocks. There could be no talk here of a Jewish action, rather it looked like a revolution. I was there in the middle of it all for the entire time with my officials in order to save what could be saved.... The Belorussian people who had full confidence in us are now frightened.... I am of the opinion that through this action much of what we have accomplished in the last few months has been negated and that much time will pass before we regain the lost trust of the people again.

78. Wardzyńska, *Sytuacja ludności polskiej w Generalnym Komisariacie Litwy*, pp. 40–41; Chief of the Security Police and Security Service, "Operational Situation Report USSR No. 155," January 11, 1942, in Arad et al., p. 277.

79. Gilbert, p. 170.

80. These excerpts can be found in Wardzyńska, *Sytuacja ludności polskiej w Generalnym Komisariacie Litwy*, pp. 133–46. The original journal is in the Central National Archive of Lithuania. Translated selections were published in the Lithuanian publication *Tiesa* (Truth) in 1959. Unfortunately, the Polish photocopy of the typed journal, produced in conjunction with the court proceedings against Viktoras Galvanauskas, has many lacunae, probably caused by the difficulty in transcribing the handwritten original.

81. As tabulated by Wardzyńska, *Sytuacja ludności polskiej w Generalnym Komisariacie Litwy*, p. 42.

82. Ibid. The 170,000 estimate is not one used by Wardzyńska, who speaks only in terms of "many thousands." A Polish Delegation report dated October 1941 states, "In Lithuania and the province of Wileńszczyzna, the Lithuanians—above all the Shaulists, the Lithuanian militia and the academic and *gimnazjum* youth—murdered almost the entire Jewish population, 170,000 persons." See ibid., p. 155. Misiunas and Taagepera, p. 64, use the same estimate. According to Ignatieff, 200,000 Lithuanian Jews died in 1941.

83. István Deák, "Heroism in Hell," *New York Review of Books*, November 8, 1990.

84. L. Tomaszewski, pp. 177–78.

85. Z. A. Siemaszko, p. 204.

86. In Korab-Żebryk, p. 15.

87. In Wardzyńska, *Sytuacja ludności polskiej w Generalnym Komisariacie Litwy*, p. 42.

88. Chief of the Security Police and Security Service, "Operational Situation Report No. 155," January 11, 1942, in Arad et al., p. 277.

89. Wardzyńska, *Sytuacja ludności polskiej w Generalnym Komisariacie Litwy*, p. 42. A Polish Government Delegation report dated October 1941 (p. 155) states that 30,000 of the 90,000 Wilno ghetto Jews had already been killed.

90. Gilbert, p. 612, see also pp. 668–69.

91. See P. Friedman, pp. 16–17, and Paldiel, pp. 216–17.

92. Wardzyńska, *Sytuacja ludności polskiej w Generalnym Komisariacie Litwy*, pp. 41–43. For some examples of Polish assistance to the Jews, see p. 44 n. 15.

93. For information regarding Lithuanian and Latvian rescuers, see Paldiel, pp. 237–64.

94. Deák, "Heroism in Hell."

Chapter 7: Ukrainian Collaboration

1. J. Tomaszewski, *Rzeczpospolita wielu narodów*, p. 86.

2. See Józef Turowski and Władysław Siemaszko, *Zbrodnie nacjonalistów ukraińskich dokonane na ludności polskiej na Wołyniu 1939–1945* (Warszawa: Główna Komisja Badania Zbrodni Hitlerowskich w Polsce, 1990), pp. 11–13, and Węgierski, *Lwów pod okupacją sowiecką*, p. 281.

3. See Tables 23 and 24 below. They come from Tomaszewski, *Reczpospolita wielu nasodów*, p. 78. Note discrepancy in the official number of Jews in Polesie in Table 23 and Table 22 on p. 346. J. Tomaszewski, *Rzeczpospolita wielu narodów*, p. 78.

4. Wołyń. Referat specjalny, February 1936, p. 70.

5. There were no elections in southeastern Poland to the first Seym because of military operations. In the 1922 General Elections, it was mostly the Ukrainians from former Russian Poland who participated, since, under pressure from the émigrés, Ukrainian political parties in Eastern Galicia boycotted the elections. The

TABLE 23. PROVINCES WITH UKRAINIAN POPULATION ACCORDING TO THE OFFICIAL 1931 CENSUS (IN THOUSANDS)

Province	*Population*	*Poles*	*Ukr.*	*Ruth.*	*Jews*	*Rus.*	*Ger.*	*Czechs*
Stanisławów	1,480.3	332.2	693.8	325.1	109.4	0.2	16.7	0.1
Tarnopol	1,600.4	789.1	402.0	326.2	78.9	0.2	2.7	0.1
Lwów	3,127.4	1,805.0	579.5	487.6	232.9	0.8	12.0	0.6
Lwów (city)	312.2	198.2	24.2	10.9	75.3	0.5	2.4	0.2
Wołyń	2,085.6	346.6	1,418.3	8.5	205.5	23.4	46.9	31.0
Polesie	1,131.9*	164.1	54.0	—	110.0	16.2	1.1	0.1
Lublin	2,464.9	2,109.2	63.1	10.7	259.5	2.8	15.9	0.0
Counties: Gorlice, Jasło, Nowy Sącz, Nowy Targ	534.3	452.4	1.0	57.8	21.0	0.1	0.8	0.0

*Including 75.3 Belorussians and 707.4 local (*tutejsi*).

TABLE 24. PROVINCES WITH UKRAINIAN POPULATION ACCORDING TO AN ADJUSTED 1931 CENSUS (IN THOUSANDS)

Province	*Population*	*Poles*	*Ukr.*	*Jews*	*Rus.*	*Ger.*	*Czechs*
Stanisławów	1,480.3	241	1,079	140	0	17	0
Tarnopol	1,600.4	590	872	134	0	3	0
Lwów	3,127.4	1,458	1,305	342	1	12	1
Lwów (city)	312.2	158	50	100	1	2	0
Wołyń	2,085.6	326	1,445	208	23	47	31
Polesie	1,131.9	127	219	114	16	1	0
Lublin	2,464.9	2,006	123	314	3	16	0
Kraków	2,297.8	2,053	59	174	0	9	0

reason for this was that whereas Poland's rights over Wołyń and Polesie were determined in 1921 by the Treaty of Riga, the situation of Eastern Galicia was still unresolved.

6. Table 6 comes from Skrzypek, *The Problem of Galicia*, p. 47.

7. Table 7 is from M. Feliński, *The Ukrainians in Poland* (London, 1931), p. 50. I have corrected one of the percent computations.

8. Skrzypek, *The Problem of Galicia*, p. 46.

9. Table 8 has been compiled from tables in Feliński, pp. 107–8.

10. Ibid., pp. 108–9.

11. Stanisław Wroński, "Introduction" to Henryk Cybulski, *Czerwone Noce* (1966; 4th ed., Warszawa: Wydawnictwo Ministerstwa Obrony Narodowej, 1977), p. 13.

12. Stanisław Srokowski, *Geografia gospodarcza Polski* (Warszawa, 1939), pp. 107–8, as summarized by Skrzypek, *The Problem of Galicia*, p. 54.

13. Myron B. Kuropas, *The Ukrainian Americans: Roots and Aspirations, 1884–1954* (Toronto: University of Toronto Press, 1991), p. 233; Bugajski, p. 361.

14. This is a relatively low standard for "large estates." During their occupation of Poland, the Russians defined "large landed estates" as those over 100 hectares (250 acres).

15. Skrzypek, *The Problem of Galicia*, p. 30.

16. Wroński, in Cybulski, pp. 8–9.

17. Kuropas, p. 233; Skrzypek, *The Problem of Galicia*, p. 54.

18. Wroński, in Cybulski, p. 9; Kubiak et al., p. 23.

19. In J. Tomaszewski, *Rzeczpospolita wielu narodów*, pp. 101–2.

20. Wroński, in Cybulski, p. 13.

21. Kuropas, p. 234. For a series of Ukrainian documents dealing with the demolition of Orthodox churches, see Mikołaj Siwicki, *Dzieje konfliktów polsko-ukraińskich*, vol. 1 (Warszawa, 1992), pp. 116–66.

22. J. Tomaszewski, *Rzeczpospolita wielu narodów*, p. 102.

23. See Maria Wiśniewska, "Rękopisy z Podlasia," *Gazeta Polska* (Warszawa), March 7, 1996. For uniate memoirs from Podlasie in the second half of the nineteenth century detailing the Russian persecution of the Catholic Church, see Tadeusz Krawczak (ed.), *Zanim wróciła Polska. Martyrologium ludności unickiej na Podlasiu w latach 1866–1905 w świetle wspomnień* (Warszawa: Neriton, 1994).

24. See Janusz Kania, "Likwidacja cerkwi na Lubelszczyźnie w okresie międzywojennym," *Chrześcijanin w Świecie* 14, no. 6, (1982): 50–89, and Janusz Kania, "Rozbiórki cerkwi na Lubelszczyźnie w roku 1938 a stanowisko Biskupa Fulmana," in Ryszard Łużny (ed.), *Chrześcijański wschód a kultura polska* (Lublin: Katolicki Uniwersytet Lubelski, 1989), pp. 31–53.

25. In Kania in Łużny, pp. 50–51. For one example of the difficulties currently confronting Poles in Eastern Galicia in getting some of their church property back, see H. Klancko, "Prosimy ale bez skutku," *Rota* (Lublin) 4, no. 12 (1993): 113. This statement reads, in part:

> On October 15, 1993 in Borysław, the Roman Catholic church of St. Barbara was renamed as the Greek-Catholic (Uniate) church of St. Anna and illegally handed over to the Lemkos.... In 1939 in Borysław there were 24,000 Poles, 7,000 Ukrainians, 9,000 other minorities, and three Catholic churches and six Uniate churches. Now for 48,000 people we have 9 Uniate churches and no Catholic churches, because they were illegally taken from us. According to the last census, there are 506 Polish families in Borysław. The pastor of the Greek-Catholic church (our Church of St. Barbara) is studying in Poland ... [and] we don't have a church.
>
> We requested permission to celebrate Mass in St. Barbara's on Sundays and major holy days. We do not have the possibility of teaching our children religion. We requested one hour per week for catechism lessons. We were always greeted with shouts, tears and grief. [*Zawsze był krzyk, płacz i skandał.*]

For a listing of Polish Catholic churches that have not been returned to Poles in the former Polish provinces of Lwów, Tarnopol, Stanisławów, and Wołyń, see "Informacja o sytuacji Kościoła rzymsko-katolickiego w Archidiecezji Lwowskiej, grudzień 1944," *Lwów i Kresy* (London) 79 (September 1995): 69–73.

26. The Polish Research Centre (ed.), *The Orthodox Eastern Church in Poland: Past and Present* (London: Polish Research Centre, 1942), pp. 47–49.

27. Skrzypek, *The Problem of Galicia*, p. 58.

28. Kubiak et al., p. 25; J. Tomaszewski, *Rzeczpospolita wielu narodów*, p. 93.

29. Feliński, p. 43.

30. J. Tomaszewski, *Rzeczpospolita wielu narodów*, pp. 93–94.

31. Table 9 has been compiled from tables in Feliński, p. 130. I have taken the liberty of correcting one small error of addition. The vast number of Polish, Ukrainian, and bilingual schools were public.

32. Skrzypek, *The Problem of Galicia*, p. 49.

33. Table 10 is from the report of the *voivode* of Wołyń. CA KC PZPR, zespół 1800/1, sygn. 277/I-1, found in Siwicki, 1: 188.

34. Wroński, in Cybulski, p. 13.

35. Orest Subtelny, *Ukraine: A History*, 2d ed. (Toronto: University of Toronto Press and Canadian Institute of Ukrainian Studies, 1994), p. 439.

36. Ibid., p. 439.

37. Feliński, p. 135.

38. Skrzypek, *The Problem of Galicia*, p. 49.

39. Table 11 and the figures in tables 12 and 13 are found ibid., p. 50.

40. Ibid., p. 51; Feliński, pp. 148–50.

41. Wroński, in Cybulski, p. 13.

42. Skrzypek, *The Problem of Galicia*, p. 23.

43. Ibid., p. 47. The speech by Father Mykola Ilkov, chairman of the "Ukrainian Peasants Club" (ibid., p. 83), reads in part:

> To-day, and in the light of what has taken place in the past few years, it seems to us that we have only one choice to make. We choose the support of Poland, which will enable us to maintain our national spirit and give us this expectation of the future, that in union with Poland, a union of two brother-nations, we may effect among other changes in history the unity of the whole Ukrainian nation. For the sake of such a vision we desire now in the Ukrainian territories joined to Poland, where for a thousand years the people have been united by blood and have lived in concord, to foster an even closer concord

> so that all who dwell there may have equal laws and equal obligations.

Vice-Marshal Vasyl Mudryi's speech delivered in the Seym on September 2, 1939 (ibid., p. 87), reads in part:

> At this historical juncture for the Polish Republic I have the honour to make the following declaration on behalf of the Ukrainian Parliamentary Representation:
>
> On August 24th, the National Congress of UNDO met in Lwów and unanimously adopted the resolution that in these present difficult times for the Republic the Ukrainian Nation will fulfill the citizen duties of blood and property towards the State. Further, the hope has been expressed that the political questions which hitherto had not been solved among the Ukrainians and Poles in the State shall be settled in an honourable and just manner in the interests of both nations in the near future. We, the Ukrainian Parliamentary Representation, on behalf of UNDO, and also the members of Ukrainian National Committee declare that there is not time to be lost on mutual political disputes and that we shall entirely fulfil the above decision together with the Ukrainian people and we shall sustain every sacrifice for the common defence of the State.

During the war, Mudryi became a Nazi collaborator who, at the same time, worked closely with the OUN-B. See Ryszard Torzecki, "Die Rolle der Zusammenarbeit mit der deutschen Besatzungsmacht in der Ukraine für deren Okkupationspolitik 1941 bis 1944," in Röhr, p. 242.

44. Skrzypek, *The Problem of Galicia*, p. 48.

45. The term *narodna* (in Galician dialect) is *narodnia* in literary Ukrainian. The Ukrainian National Rada resolution establishing the ZUNR was passed on October 9, 1918, in Lwów. On November 1, 1918, a ZUNR government was set up in Galicia, on November 6, in Bukovina, and on November 19, in Transcarpathia. The ZUNR constitution was approved on November 13, 1918. See Subtelny, *Ukraine: A History*, p. 352, and Struk, 5: 409–10, 694. Transcarpathia was the former Ruthenian province of Czechoslovakia.

For a Polish perspective (1921) on the inauguration and operation of the ZUNR in Złoczów — including oral history accounts, lists of Poles arrested, imprisoned, and/or executed, anti–Polish propaganda in *Zolochivske Slovo*, and a report on the exhumation by a judicial-forensic Polish Parliamentary Commission accompanied by an Allied (British and American) delegation (June 5–6, 1919) of twenty-two victims of Ukrainian excesses — see *Z krwawych dni Złoczowa 1919 roku* (Złoczów: Komitet Budowy Pomnika-Grobowca Dla Ofiar Mordów Ukraińskich, 1921).

46. In Feliński, p. 46. Petliura's recognition of the Polish boundaries may have cost Ukraine its independence. The attack on the Bolsheviks in behalf of Ukrainian independence by the combined Polish-Ukrainian forces began on April 25, 1920. Kiev fell on May 7. Were it not for the apathy of the Ukrainians from Galicia and the Ukrainian nation as a whole (there was no uprising to seize the reins of government, no volunteers to reinforce the victorious Ukrainian divisions), Ukraine would have been an independent state already in 1920. Since it would also have been an ally of Poland against the Soviet Union, the course of history would surely have been different. As it was, that military effort by Poland to help Ukraine achieve its freedom almost ended in disaster for Poland. In the counteroffensive, the Red Army reached the suburbs of Warsaw, only to be turned back by Polish forces on August 15.

47. For an early study on this topic and the delineation of these territorial ambitions, see Stanisław Skrzypek, *Ukraiński program państwowy* (London: Koło Lwowian, 1967), especially pp. 7–10 and the foldout map at the end of the work: "The Scope of the Territorial Aspirations of the Ukrainian Independence Movement." See also the maps in Wiktor Poliszczuk, *Gorzka prawda. Zbrodniczość OUN-UPA (spowiedź Ukraińca* (Toronto, 1995), p. 68, and the listing of "Ukrainian ethnographic" territories on p. 70.

In 1992 Bohdan Fedorak, the head of the OUN-B Ukrainian State Board (Ukrainske Derzhavne Pravlinnie), repeated the OUN-UPA territorial demands of the 1940s once more: "The present borders of Ukraine are the borders of the former USSR established by the authorities in Moscow. Almost one-third of all the ancient ethnographic territories settled from time immemorial by the Ukrainian nation lie beyond the borders of Ukraine. Ukraine cannot renounce including these lands and those Ukrainian people in the Ukrainian nation."

Bohdan Fedorak's article appeared in *Ukraina Molada* (Kiev) on June 30, 1992. The size of these "ethnographic Ukrainian territories" that remain to be incorporated into "Greater Ukraine," according to Fedorak, is approximately 200,000 square kilometers of land, or an area equivalent to approximately two-thirds of present-day Poland. This program of massive land acquisition, suggests Fedorak, "should be realized through [friendly] talks with the specified nations."

48. As quoted by Józef Garliński, "The Polish-Ukrainian Agreement, 1920," in Paul Latawski (ed.), *The Reconstruction of Poland, 1914–23* (New York: St. Martin's Press, 1992), pp. 57–58. Also in Skrzypek, *The Problem of Galicia*, p. 65.

49. In Skrzypek, *The Problem of Galicia*, pp. 72–73.

50. Kuropas, p. 234. See also Alexander J. Motyl, "Ukrainian Nationalist Political Violence in Inter-War Poland, 1921–1939," *East European Quarterly* 19, no. 1 (March 1985): 47.

51. See Feliński, pp. 55, 82–83, and Alexander J. Motyl, "The Rural Origins of the Communist and Nationalist Movements in Wołyń *Województwo*, 1921–1939," *Slavic Review* 37 (September 1978): 415.

52. See Skrzypek, *The Problem of Galicia*, p. 56, and Motyl, "The Rural Origins," pp. 412–20. According to the former author, the KPZU was dissolved because it was dominated by the OUN.

53. Skrzypek, *The Problem of Galicia*, p. 57.

54. Feliński, p. 51.

55. I fully recognize the self-evident fact that no country can be blamed for seeking independence, least of all Ukraine. (Whether it was realistic for the League of Nations to expect Poland to grant autonomy to "Western Ukraine" is another question.) I do not, therefore, condemn nationalism per se and realize that a degree of political terror will always accompany its more radical manifestations. In this political struggle, the underdog must take calculated risks and bear responsibility for the countermeasures that will surely follow. In fact, the underdog is counting on these countermeasures to follow! How else can it "rally the masses to the cause"? This is the nature of the game, and the Ukrainian Nationalists played it well.

I draw the line, however, between the "necessary" political terror of radical nationalism and the equally "necessary" repercussions it calls forth, on the one hand, and the ethnic cleansing of innocent civilians, on the other. In my estimation, the latter is always counterproductive and has no political or moral justification. It is tantamount to the immoral and tactically unproductive bombing of residential areas of cities during wartime.

One could speculate whether anything of a positive nature would or could have been gained by this radical movement were it not for the war. In all probability, some sort of a modus vivendi (with the Ukrainian people if not the OUN) would have been reached eventually. As it happened, neither side won that local battle, and the Soviet Union took the spoils. After fifty years of slavery, "Western Ukraine" is now a part of the Ukrainian nation. In this matter, nothing that the Poles or the Nationalists could have done or said would have made any difference in the least. The "fratricidal conflict," therefore, served no useful purpose. In hindsight, but also from the perspective of a rational appraisal of the political situation of the day, only one conclusion can be drawn: it was a price that did not need to have been paid by either side. Alexander Motyl states:

> In the twentieth century, Ukrainian nationalists have tried three times to build their own state: 1917–1921, when they failed; in 1941–1945, when they failed again; and it 1989–1991, when they finally succeeded. Success came the third time not because the nationalists tried harder or because they were stronger, but because the external conditions were right. Indeed, they were so right that sovereign Ukraine's leading nationalist proved to be the same person as Soviet Ukraine's leading antinationalist—Leonid Kravchuk. In a word, though Ukrainian nationalists, like all nationalists, would have us think otherwise, independence was not so much won by, as bequethed to, them.

Alexander J Motyl, *Dilemmas of Independence: Ukraine After Totalitarianism* (New York: Council of Foreign Relations Press, 1993), pp. 23–24.

56. The Dontsovian phrases in quotes can be found in Alexander J. Motyl, *The Turn to the Right: The Ideological Origins and Development of Ukrainian Nationalism, 1919–1929* (Boulder, CO: East European Monographs, 1980), chapter 6, "Dmytro Dontsov," pp. 61–85. See also Poliszczuk, *Gorzka prawda*, pp. 79–95, and Wiktor Poliszczuk, *Ideologia nacjonalizmu ukraińskiego według Dmytra Doncowa* (Warszawa, 1996). Among Dmytro Dontsov's works are the following: *Natsionalizm*, 3d ed. (London: Ukrainian Publishers, 1966); *Pidstavy nashoi polityky* (Vienna, 1921); and *Rik 1918, Kyiv* (Toronto: Homin Ukrainy, 1954).

57. For the distinction between "men of words," "fanatics," and "practical men of action," see Eric Hoffer, *The True Believer* (New York: Harper and Row, 1951), pp. 119–38.

58. Spector, *The Holocaust of Volhynian Jews*, p. 233.

59. "Nazrivaiuchi konflikty," *Surma* 2 (March 1927): 2, in Motyl, "Ukrainian Nationalist Political Violence," p. 53.

60. Włodzimierz Sławosz Dębski, *Antylitopys UPA* (Lublin, 1995), p. 14.

61. In Motyl, *The Turn to the Right*, p. 142. Volodymyr or Vladimir was a prince of Kievan Rus'. According to Motyl's source (B.K., an early SUNM activist, see p. 188 n. 263), "enslavement of foreigners" referred to non–Ukrainians living in Ukraine. Petro Mirchuk, *Narys istorii Orhanizatsii Ukrainskykh Natsionalistiv 1920–1939* (München: Ukrainske Vydavnytstvo, 1968), p. 127, explains, "This was the result of discussions of whether the Ukrainian State should give complete freedom to foreigners even when they act against it as in 1917–18 ... or should it, on the other hand, 'enslave' them, if this is what the security and growth of the Ukrainian State requires." Mirchuk also explains that the words "greatest crime" mean "murder, which the member of the revolutionary organization should not hesitate to commit if it be required for the good of the war of independence in behalf of the Ukrainian nation." See Poliszczuk, *Gorzka prawda*, p. 74.

62. "Permanentna revoliutsiia," *Surma* 37–10 (October 1930): 7.

63. Ibid.

64. Myroslav Yurkevich, "Organization of Ukrainian Nationalists," in Struk, 3: 708.

65. See Poliszczuk, *Gorzka prawda*, p. 74, and Marples, p. 74.

66. These passages can be found in Wiktor Poliszczuk, *Hirka pravda. Zlochynnist OUN-UPA (spovid ukraintsia)* (Toronto, 1995), p. 109, and in the Polish edition, *Gorzka prawda*, pp. 95–96.

67. The following passage — in B.F. Sabrin, *Alliance for Murder: The Nazi-Ukrainian Nationalist Partnership in Genocide* (New York: Sarpedon, 1991), p. 15 — comes from *Nash Klich*, a Ukrainian Nationalist newspaper. The date is June 3, 1938: "There is now a sociopolitical system which is developing the world over: in one country it manifests itself as Fascism, in another as Hitlerism, and we name it here Nationalism."

Kost Pankivskyi, chairman of the Ukrainian regional committe in Lwów, referred to OUN members as "people who for many years were connected with the Fascist and Nazi ideologies, preached totalitarian ideas and acted to realize them." Kost Pankivskyi, *Roky nimetskoi okupatsii: 1941–1944* (New York: Vydavnytstvo Kliuchi, 1965), p. 13.

John A. Armstrong, *Ukrainian Nationalism*, 3d ed. (Englewood, CO: Ukrainian Academic Press, 1990), p. 212, states, "The theory and teachings of the Ukrainian nationalists were very close to Fascism, and in some respects, such as the insistence on 'racial purity' even went beyond the original Fascist doctrines."

As to whether Ukrainian nationalism was fascist in its early phase (1919–21), see Motyl, *The Turn to the Right*, pp. 113–14, 162–69. 174–75.

68. Kuropas, pp. 238–39.

69. Subtelny, *Ukraine: A History*, p. 442.

70. Kuropas, p. 231.

71. This phrase became a motto of the Ukrainian Nationalists. Its formulation can be traced to Mykola Mikhnovskyi, the author of *Samostiina Ukraina* (Independent Ukraine) (Lwów: E. Kosevych, 1900), who stated therein: "All in Ukraine who are not for us are against us. Ukraine for the Ukrainians! So long as a single foreign enemy remains on our territory we do not have the right to lay down our arms." In John S. Reshetar, *The Ukrainian Revolution, 1917–1920: A Study in Nationalism* (New York: Arno Press, 1972), p. 2.

According to Motyl, *The Turn to the Right*, p. 9, the Kraków-based Revolutionary Ukrainian Party (Revoliutsiina Ukrainska Partiia, or RUP), which emerged in 1900 and whose program was based on Mikhnovskyi's pamphlet, was the first to echo the slogans: "Ukraine for Ukrainians" and "One, United, Indivisible, Free, Independent Ukraine from the Caucasus to the Carpathians." These slogans were adopted by the post-World War I Ukrainian Nationalists.

72. OUN (1929) proclamation in Mirchuk, p. 93.

73. Kuropas, p. 231.

74. *Ibid.*, p. 246. The phrase "join or die" was not used by the Ukrainian Nationalists. Rather, they said: "We either persuade or annihilate." Ryszard Torzecki, *Kwestia ukraińska w polityce III Rzeszy 1933–1945* (Warszawa: Książka i Wiedza, 1972), p. 241.

75. See, for example, Motyl, "Ukrainian Nationalist Political Violence," pp. 45–55, and Feliński, pp. 158–73.

76. Mirchuk names only three Ukrainian victims of the Polish pacification: Matvii Paranko,

Mykhailo Tutka, and Dmytro Pidhirnyi. Mirchuk, p. 252. Iaroslav Pelensky, *Vidnova* (Munich) 5 (1986), states that either nine or nineteen Ukrainians were killed, but he does not list the names or the reasons for the discrepancy. See Poliszczuk, *Gorzka prawda*, p. 119.

77. According to Feliński, 1,739 persons were arrested in the three provinces of Eastern Galicia between July 1 and November 30, 1930. Their various professions are listed in table 25.

TABLE 25. PERSONS ARRESTED IN EASTERN GALICIA FOR TERRORIST ACTIVITY BETWEEN JULY 1 AND NOVEMBER 30, 1930

University students	220
Secondary school boys	360
Peasants	510
Artisans	120
Workmen	45
Clerks	90
Merchants	6
Teachers	20
Government clerks	8
Journalists	5
Ukrainian clergy	30
Ukrainian seminarians	2
Other Clerics	3
Engineers	3
Doctors	2
Lawyers	6
Law students	6
Other professions	60
Without occupation	33
Occupation not defined	210
Total	1,739

Of this total, 914 were sent to trial. At the beginning of the following March, 211 persons were still in prison either awaiting trial or serving sentences. In the nineteen trials conducted to that date, of the 29 accused, 2 were found not guilty and the rest were sentenced. Feliński, pp. 170–71.

The trial for the murder of Bronisław Pieracki lasted from December 18, 1935, to January 13, 1936. Particularly revealing are the ages of these OUN élites hauled up on charges, who placed themselves in judgment over "traitors to the Ukrainian nation," killed, and gave orders to kill both prominent Poles and Ukrainians:

Stepan Bandera, 26, son of a Ukrainian Catholic priest, student of agronomy at the Lwów Politechnical Institute.
Mykola Lebed, 25, *gymnasium* graduate.
Daria Hnatkivska, 23, *gymnasium* graduate.
Iaroslav Karpynets, 30, student at Jagiellonian University.
Mykola Klymyshyn, 26, philosophy student at Jagiellonian University.
Bohdan Pidhainyi, 31, graduate of Danzig Polytechnical Institute.
Ivan Malutsa, 25, student at Lwów Polytechnical Institute.
Iakiv Chornii, 28, student at University of Lublin.
Ievhen Kachmarśkyi, 25, completed five years of *gymnazium.*
Roman Myhal, 24, student at University of Lwów.
Kateryna Zarytska, 21, student at Lwów Politechnical Institute.
Iaroslav Rak, 27, legal apprentice.

Their sentences read as follows: Bandera, Lebed, and Karpynets — death penalty commuted to life in prison; Klymyshyn and Pidhainyi — life in prison; Hnatkivska—15 years in prison; Malutsa, Myhal, and Kachmarskyi—12 years in prison; Zarytska — 8 years in prison; Rak and Chornii — 7 years in prison. For a revealing treatise first published in *Zeszyty Historyczne* (Paris) in 1973 which deals with the murder of Minister Pieracki, see Władysław Żeleński, *Zabójstwo Ministra Pierackiego* (Warszawa: Iskry, 1995).

A few months later, in May 1936, another trial began in Eastern Poland involving the leadership of the OUN. Among those indicted were Stepan Bandera, Roman Shukhevych, Volodymyr Ianiv, and Iaroslav Stetsko. Bandera was condemned to death for the second time, and again his sentence was commuted to life in prison. Mirchuk, pp. 389, 396. See Poliszczuk, *Gorzka prawda*, 120–21.

78. Feliński, p. 162; Motyl, "Ukrainian Nationalist Political Violence"; Osip Dumin (Osyp Dumyn), "Prawda o Ukraińskiej Organizacji Wojskowej," *Zeszyty Historyczne* (Paris) 30 (1974): p. 107, editorial n. 3.

79. Motyl, "Ukrainian Nationalist Political Violence," p. 50.

80. Ibid., p. 55 n. 13.

81. Ibid., p. 52.

82. Ibid., p. 48.

83. As quoted by Feliński, pp. 160–62.

84. These two sayings can be found in Antoni Szcześniak and Wiesław Szota, *Droga do nikąd. Działalność Organizacji Ukraińskich*

Nacjonalistów i jej likwidacja w Polsce (Warszawa: Ministerstwo Obrony Narodowej, 1973), p. 43.

85. In Torzecki, *Kwestia ukraińska w polityce III Rzeszy*, p. 136.

86. In Sabrin, p. 231.

87. As quoted by Feliński, pp. 171–72.

88. See Lubomyr Luciuk, "An Injustice That Won't Die: Ottawa Won't Admit Ukrainian Internment Was a Criminal Act," *Toronto Star*, August 11, 1995.

89. "The Report: A Minority in Poland — The Ukrainian Conflict," *Times* (London), December 12 and 18, 1930. This report is reprinted in the Appendix, Document 13.

90. Torzecki, *Kwestia ukraińska w polityce III Rzeszy*, p. 67; Pobóg-Malinowski, p. 728.

91. J. A. Armstrong, *Ukrainian Nationalism*, p. 13.

92. Dumin directed the UVO intelligence operation until March 23–24, 1926, when he announced that he did not recognize the leadership of the UVO and stormed out of an administrative meeting in the Free City of Danzig (Gdańsk), an act that cost him his position as well as his membership in the UVO. As an idealist, an officer in the Ukrainian army that fought for the independence of "Western Ukraine," he longed for action and battle and was put off by the procrastination, inefficiency, and money-grubbing practices of Konovalets (whom he called a "slick corruptionist") and the "dictator" Yurevich, who headed the UVO military detachments, which "did absolutely nothing," and whom he wanted prosecuted for mismanagement of funds (the unaccounted-for "2 x 100,000 dollars" he mentions in the report), for "demoralization of the UVO in the past 4 years," for "expropriation of Ukrainian peasants," for "illegal sale of the newspaper *Novyi Chas,*" and for "corruption of members of the leadership of the UVO."

Alexander Motyl notes, "Although unreliable as a source of information about the infighting within the UVO, the document does point out the degree to which the Konovalets' faction was dependent on the Germans." Motyl, *The Turn to the Right*, p. 123. This dependence is also noted by Lieutenant-Colonel Friedrich Preitner, one of the German instructors in the military training courses at Munich for the Ukrainians from Eastern Galicia. See Frank Golczewski, "Ukraińska karta niemieckiej akcji przeciwko Polsce," *Niepodległość* (New York, London, Wrocław). 26 (1993): 237–38. As the next two paragraphs indicate, Dumyn's report also paints an accurate picture of the nature and mission of the UVO.

93. Dumin, p. 104.

94. Ibid.

95. John Paul Himka, "Western Ukraine between the Wars," *Canadian Slavonic Papers* 34, no. 4 (December, 1992): 410.

96. One of these was Iaroslav Lubovych, an OUN member killed while robbing an unsuspecting Polish letter carrier. Thereafter, on every anniversary of his death, OUN articles appeared extolling his bravery in the "battle with oppression" and mourning his heroic death.

97. See Motyl, "Ukrainian Nationalist Political Violence," pp. 49–50.

98. Ibid.; Poliszczuk, *Gorzka prawda*, p. 131.

99. There is some controversy over the actual date of founding of this organization. In an article written in 1929, Konovalets gives the impression that the UVO was founded at the meeting of the Sharpshooters' Council in July 1920, when the Sich Sharpshooter Organization (*striltsi*) "in fact ceased to exist." See Ievhen Konovalets, *Prychynky do istorii ukrainskoi revoliutsii,* 2d ed. (Provid Ukrainskykh Natsionalistiv, 1948), p. 42. Whether these words mean "*officially* ceased to exist" and whether the UVO was formally established at that meeting, as Konovalets implies, are highly questionable. Szcześniak and Szota, pp. 31–32, state that the UVO was founded at the August 30, 1920, Prague meeting of the representatives of the Nationalist military organizations. The meeting was called by Konovalets, Melnyk, and Sushko.

100. Ibid., Szcześniak and Szota, p. 32; Motyl, *The Turn to the Right*, p. 108; Torzecki, *Kwestia ukraińska w polityce III Rzeszy*, p. 56.

101. Dumin, p. 108.

102. Torzecki, *Kwestia ukraińska w polityce III Rzeszy,* p. 88, and n. 111; Motyl, *The Turn to the Right,* pp. 124–25; and Motyl, "Ukrainian Nationalist Political Violence," p. 49.

103. Dumin, p. 109. For information regarding the OUN-Lithuanian connection based on the Emil Senyk archives, see Żeleński, *Zabójstwo Ministra Pierackiego*, pp. 56–59. According to the information contained in these UVO-OUN confiscated files, excluding the funds provided by the Abwehr for services rendered, half of the OUN operating funds came from Lithuania. An officer's testimony in the December 1935 trial for the murder of Minister Pieracki revealed that Lithuania still supported the OUN, in one way or another, as of that date (p. 59).

104. Dumin, p. 109.

105. Ibid., pp. 113–14.

106. See Appendix, Document 13, section: "Hostility to the State." Torzecki tells us that from 1918, the Nationalists "faithfully served German interests." Torzecki, *Kwestia ukraińska w politice III Rzeszy*, p. 322.

107. Ibid., p. 116.

108. Zynovii Knysh (Bohdan Mykhailuk), *Bunt Bandery* (Toronto: 1950), as cited by Petro Tereshchuk (Oleksander Matla), *Istorychni notatky* (Toronto, Homin Ukrainy, 1985), p. 47.

109. Szcześniak and Szota, p. 55. Alexander Dallin, *German Rule in Russia, 1941–1945: A Study of Occupation Policies* (London: Macmillan, 1955), p. 114, states: "Under Colonel Eugene Konovalets the OUN and its predecessor organizations had cultivated ties with German intelligence from as far back as 1921. After the assassination of Konovalets in 1938 by a Soviet agent, leadership of the OUN had passed to Colonel Andrew Mel'nyk, who continued the co-operation with Berlin."

110. Dumin, p. 107.

111. Ibid., pp. 111–12, and n. 11.

112. Poliszczuk, *Gorzka prawda*, p. 131; Szcześniak and Szota, p. 46.

113. Motyl, *The Turn to the Right*, p. 123.

114. Torzecki, *Kwestia ukraińska w polityce III Rzeszy*, p. 56.

115. Motyl, *The Turn to the Right*, p. 124.

116. Torzecki, *Kwestia ukraińska w polityce III Rzeszy*, pp. 126–27.

117. Szcześniak and Szota, pp. 47.

118. Torzecki, *Kwestia ukraińska w politice III Rzeszy*, p. 110.

119. Ibid., pp. 181–82.

120. Hrytsko Kupetskyi, *Tam, de sontse skhodyt. Spohady boiovyka OUN na Dalekomu Skhodi* (Toronto: Vydavnytstvo Viktora Polishchuka, 1988). See Poliszczuk, *Gorzka prawda*, p. 133.

121. Torzecki, *Kwestia ukraińska w politice III Rzeszy*, p. 182.

122. Poliszczuk, *Gorzka prawda*, p. 133; Dallin, pp. 115 n. 3, 116 n. 3; Torzecki, "Die Rolle der Zusammenarbeit," in Röhr, p. 247.

123. William Shirer, *The Rise and Fall of the Third Reich* (Greenwich, CT: Fawcett, 1960), p. 1481.

124. Alfred Rosenberg, *Der Zukunftsweg einer deutschen Aussenpolitik* (München: F. Eher, 1927), p. 97, in Dallin, p. 108.

125. Alfred Rosenberg, "Denkschrift Nr. 2" (April 7, 1941), Document 1018-PS, pp. 29–30, ibid., p. 109.

126. Ibid., p. 108.

127. Subtelny, *Ukraine: A History*, p. 444. This is an estimate; the real figure is unknown.

128. Kobylański, p. 11.

129. These words were uttered in the presence of Lev Shankovskyi, a teacher from a distinguished family of churchmen, who visited the Metropolitan shortly after the Soviet invasion. In Gross, *Revolution from Abroad*, p. 31.

According to Torzecki, during the June-July 1940 talks between Władysława Piechowska, the representative of the ZWZ, and Sheptytsky, the Metropolitan let it be known, in no uncertain terms, that "if the Soviets were to allow for the spread of the Uniate faith across the whole of Ukraine, he would be ready with the entire [Uniate] Church to cooperate with the USSR." Ryszard Torzecki, "Kontakty polsko-ukraińskie na tle problemu ukraińskiego w polityce polskiego rządu emigracyjnego i podziemia (1939–1944)," *Dzieje Najnowsze* (Warszawa) 1, no. 2 (1981): 328.

130. This passage and the ones that follow can be found in Skrzypek, *The Problem of Galicia*, annexes on pp. 88–93, see also p. 56.

131. Władysław Siemaszko, "Kto mordował Polaków na Wołyniu?" *Gazeta* (Toronto), February 28, 1995. Emphases mine.

132. See Władysław Siemaszko, "Stan badań nad terrorem ukraińskim na Wołyniu w latach 1939–1944," *Lwów i Kresy* (London) 72 (July–September 1992): 43.

133. Turowski and Siemaszko, p. 12. Emphasis mine.

134. Tennenbaum, pp. 100–101.

135. Turowski and Siemaszko, pp. 13–14. Emphasis mine.

136. Węgierski, *Lwów pod okupacją sowiecką*, p. 281.

137. Yitzhak Sternberg, *Under Assumed Identity* (Israel: Hakibbutz Hameuchad and Ghetto Fighters' House, 1986), p. 26. Sternberg goes on to say that in retribution, the Polish police and soldiers formed a company that went "from village to village systematically burning the houses of Ukrainians."

138. Łuczak, p. 26.

139. As quoted by Kersten, *Polacy, Żydzi, Komunizm*, p. 30.

140. In February 1940, for example, with the assistance of the local Ukrainian committee, several dozen Polish families (the "colonists") were deported to Siberia from the village of Pawłów.

Henryk Komański, "Eksterminacja polskiej ludności: powiat Radziechów," *Na Rubieży* (Wrocław) 4, no. 10, (1994): 5. See also Grudzińska-Gross and Gross, *War Through Children's Eyes*, pp. 9–10.

141. Grudzińska-Gross and Gross, *War Through Children's Eyes*, p. 10.

142. Ibid., pp. 63–64.

143. Ibid., p. 19.

144. Ibid., p. 10.

145. Orest Subtelny, "The Soviet Occupation of Western Ukraine, 1939–41: An Overview," in Yury Boshyk (ed.), *Ukraine during World War II: History and Its Aftermath, a Symposium* (Edmonton: Canadian Institute of Ukrainian Studies, 1986), p. 9. Boshyk's work is a collection of papers presented at a symposium in Toronto on March 12, 1985.

146. Subtelny, *Ukraine: A History*, p. 455.

147. Grudzińska-Gross and Gross, *War Through Children's Eyes*, p. 243.

148. In addition to ibid. and Turowski and Siemaszko, pp. 11–14, see Rowiński, pp. 33–36; Liszewski, *Wojna polsko-sowiecka*, pp. 119–26, 155, 171, 270–74; Wiktor Krzysztof Cygan, *Kresy w ogniu: wojna polsko-sowiecka 1939* (Warszawa: Warszawska Oficyna Wydawnicza, 1990), pp. 89, 111, 116–17, 131; and Myśliwski and Garlicki, 1: 188–204, and 2: 199–208.

149. In Grudzińska-Gross and Gross, *War Through Children's Eyes*, p. 56.

150. Ibid., pp. 65–66.

151. Ibid., p. 91.

152. Ibid., p. 104.

153. Ibid., pp. 118–19.

154. Ibid., pp. 131–32.

155. Ibid., p. 149.

156. Ibid., p. 139. Kobylański, p. 12, also refers to the murder by Ukrainians of Polish soldiers returning from the front in the province of Wołyń. "Later," he states, "the currents of the Horyń and Styr rivers washed up the bodies of dozens of murdered Polish soldiers."

157. In Grudzińska-Gross and Gross, *War Through Children's Eyes*, p. 169.

158. Ibid., p. 174.

159. Ibid., p. 193.

160. Ibid., pp. 194–95.

161. Ibid., pp. 197–98.

162. Ibid., pp. 149–50.

163. Gilbert, p. 157.

164. W. Siemaszko, p. 46.

165. One revealing testimony of what was transpiring in the early days of the German campaign, at least in the province of Tarnopol, comes from Dr. Milch. In 1939, there were approximately 1,100 Jews, 1,000 Poles, and 400 Ruthenians in the town of Tłuste. The population of the surrounding villages was 75 percent Ukrainian. The extermination of the Jews in this area began between five and ten months after the onset of their extermination in central Poland. The passage reads:

> There was no army in Tłuste or the surrounding area in the first 24 hours [after the German invasion]. One day, Hungarian soldiers appeared riding bicycles — the first patrol.... Meanwhile ... the Ukrainians began to show us what they were capable of. Right away they murdered all the Jews in almost every neighboring village. It was like this in all the counties.... In our area we were better off in one respect: the Hungarian army marched in first, not the Nazis, and they killed only those whom the Ukrainians pointed out as communists or state functionaries....
>
> In our town, what the enraged mob was unable to pillage, the Hungarian soldiers, after terrorizing us, at times raping even young girls, took at night the most valuable possessions.
>
> Such was the beginning at the hands of the newly-arrived although we did not see a single German or Gestapo in the first six weeks. We suffered even more from the local Ukrainians. They hoisted blue-yellow flags everywhere announcing the founding of independent Ukraine (*samostiina Ukraina*). Local Ukrainian committees were formed. They set up various administrative authorities; formed their own Ukrainian police — *Sich* — which consisted of young rustics and dark elements, and every other one was an elder or a commandant. As I already mentioned, they murdered almost all the Jews in the villages; in the smaller towns only those for whom they had an eye. In the large towns the Ukrainians launched large-scale pogroms and the Germans or Hungarians only played second fiddles.

Milch, p. 4. The statistics on Tłuste's population come from Andrzej Krawczyk, "Świadectwo Milcha," *Karta* (Warszawa) 2 (February 1991): 53.

166. Szcześniak and Szota repeat this thesis *three* times: pp. 155, 193, 202. Torzecki (*Kwestia*

ukraińska w politice III Rzeszy, p. 241) takes this position as well. Referring to events after June 30, 1941, in note 28 he states:

> To this point, that they [the Ukrainian Nationalists] did not renounce further collaboration, but rather supposedly transformed it into a so-called "limited cooperation," speaks Ilnytskyi in his work [Roman Ilnytskyi, *Deutschland und die Ukraine 1934–1945*, vol. 2 (München: Osteuropa Institut, 1958), pp. 190–258]. This also becomes evident from the cited SD (Einsatzgruppen and Einsatzkommando) reports and the reports contained in the collection: Kriegstagebuch des Kommandostabes Reichsführer SS, Tätigkeitsberichte der 1 und 2 SS—Inf. Brigade, der 1 SS Kaw., Verlag—Wien—Frankfurt—Zürich, 1965, a series published by "Europäische Perspektiven."

For a recent article on Ukrainian Nationalist collaboration see Ryszard Torzecki, "Die Rolle der Zusammenarbeit," in Röhr, pp. 239–72.

167. See Ribbentrop, memorandum on Msgr. Voloshyn, May 6, 1939, Document NG-3292; Michael Winch, *Republic for a Day* (London: Hale, 1939); W. E. D. Allen, *The Ukraine* (London: Cambridge University Press, 1940); and Dallin, p. 115.

Mykyta Kosakviskyi, "Z nedanoho minuloho," *Nashe Slovo* 5 (1977): 67–80, provides us with a glimpse of the nature of that government—a foretaste, perhaps, of the future Ukrainian Republic envisioned by the Nationalists. Sol Littman summarizes:

> A little-known sidebar to Ukrainian history is the brief period of a few weeks in which the nationalists took over the government in Transcarpathia before Hitler took it away from them and assigned it to the Hungarians. Mykyta Kosakivs'kyy's description of this blip on history's screen reveals that the Ukrainian regime was marked by severe legislation against the Jews, the end of freedom of the press, the abolishment of all competing political parties, and the establishment of German-style concentration camps.

Sol Littman, "The Ukrainian Halchyna Division: A Case Study of Historical Revisionism," in Saul S. Friedman (ed.), *Holocaust Literature: A Handbook of Critical, Historical, and Literary Writings* (Westport, CT: Greenwood Press, 1993), p. 297.

168. See Andrzej Szefer, "Dywersyjno-sabatażowa działalność wrocławskiej Abwehry na ziemiach polskich w przededniu agresji hitlerowskiej w 1939 r.," *Biuletyn Głównej Komisji Badania Zbrodni Hitlerowskich w Polsce* (Warszawa) 32 (1987): 274, 281–82. See German document "K—Organisation Ost-Galizien" verifying this on p. 317.

169. Myroslav Yurkevich, "Galician Ukrainians in German Military Formations and in the German Administration," in Boshyk, p. 70; Łuczak, p. 349.

170. Canaris, "Kriegstagebuchaufzeichnung über die Konferenz im Führerzug in Ilnau am 12.9.1939," Nuremberg Document 3047-PS. See also Lahousen, testimony, *TMWC*, 2: 448, 478, 3: 21, as cited by Dallin, p. 115.

171. Poliszczuk, *Gorzka prawda*, p. 132.

172. Łuczak, pp. 349–50; Tadeusz Olszański (Jan Łukaszów), *Historia Ukrainy XX wieku* (Warszawa: Oficyna Wydawnicza Volumen, 1993), p. 165; Szefer, p. 274.

173. Edward Prus, *Bluff XX wieku* (London: Koło Lwowian, 1992), pp. 101, 105.

174. Torzecki, "Die Rolle der Zusammenarbeit," in Röhr, p. 245; Joe Conason, "To Catch a Nazi," *Village Voice*, February 11, 1986, p. 19; Christopher Simpson, *Blowback: America's Recruitment of Nazis and Its Effects on the Cold War* (New York: Weidenfeld and Nicolson, 1988), p. 161.

175. Dallin, p. 115 n. 3. The feeling of the nationalist faction of the Ukrainian community in Canada is demonstrated by the following excerpt from an article entitled "In 1939 Poland Will Be Defeated," which appeared in *Novyi Shliakh* (Winnipeg), January 1939, as quoted by Torzecki, *Kwestia ukraińska w polityce III Rzeszy*, p. 178:

> We acknowledge only one banner; all others must give way because Ukraine is and will be nationalist.... Our program of liberating Western Ukraine and defeating Poland makes us, and only us, the sovereign leaders of the battle in all its stages and leads us directly to power without even any tentative provisions. For this, a swift and certain victory is needed.... We persuade or annihilate.

Naturally, the call to battle was on the German side against Poland.

176. Stolze, affidavit, Document USSR-231, *TMWC*, 7: 272–73, in Dallin, pp. 116–17.

177. J. A. Armstrong, p. 51.

178. After Konovalets' assassination (1938) by Norbert Valuch-Janenko, a Ukrainian NKVD agent (Dumin, p. 104, editorial n. 3), Melnyk was elected as the head of the OUN at the Second Grand Assembly of the OUN held in Rome on August 27, 1939. His title was *vozhd* (equivalent to *führer*), and like subsequent leaders, he was said to be responsible only to "God, the Nation, and his own conscience." Yurkevich, "Organization of Ukrainian Nationalists," in Struk, 3: 709. The term "Nation" in this quotation must surely refer to the OUN.

After their release from Bereza Kartuska (September 5–10, 1939), Bandera and the others contacted the Abwehr and, after a rest, returned to their operational base (called Kochstelle by Volodymyr Kubiiovych) in Kraków. There, they maintained close contact with Wehrmacht officials. Torzecki, "Die Rolle der Zusammenarbeit," in Röhr, pp. 242–44.

179. Łuczak, p. 349.

180. J. A. Armstrong, p. 71. Torzecki, *Polacy i Ukraińcy*, pp. 137, 155; Wolodymyr Kosyk, *The Third Reich and Ukraine* (New York: Peter Lang, 1993), p. 224. Littlejohn, *The Patriotic Traitors*, pp. 269–70, states, "German security forces armed and supplied such bodies as the Ukrainian Popular Self-Defence Force (U.N.S.) and the *Polis'ka Sich*." Document No. 129, Chief of SP and SD, "Report No. 4 from the Occupied Eastern Regions," May 22, 1942, in Kosyk, p. 573, states: "The Poliska Sich is a kind of Ukrainian free-corps under the leadership of a Taras Bulba. In the autumn of 1941, with the approval of the German authorities, B[ulba] set up a special unit to fight against the partisans. Although this free-corps was dissolved in November 1941, we believe it has been secretly reorganized and has accumulated a large number of weapons."

The formation of Borovets' unit was the brainchild of Andrii Livytskyi, the former president-in-exile of the UNR, who took an oath of allegiance to the Third Reich and received a monthly stipend from the Germans. The initiative group sent to Wołyń under Borovets consisted of former Petliura officers. See Torzecki, "Die Rolle der Zusammenarbeit," in Röhr, p. 242.

181. In J. A. Armstrong, p. 52.

182. FHQ and OKW/WFA, "Directive No. 4," September 25, 1939, U.S. Department of State, *Documents on German Foreign Policy*, series D, vol. 8 (Washington, DC: Government Printing Office, 1954), p. 135, in Dallin, p. 116.

183. Torzecki, *Kwestia ukraińska w polityce III Rzeszy*, p. 190.

184. Szcześniak and Szota, p. 96.

185. Ibid.

186. Olszański, *Historia Ukrainy XX wieku*, p. 165.

187. Szcześniak and Szota, p. 102.

188. Ihor Kamenetsky, "Some Aspects of Ukrainian Politics of National Self-Determination in View of Hitler's 'Drang Nach Osten,'" *Ukrainian Historian* 27 (1990): 107.

189. Szcześniak and Szota, pp. 102–3.

190. Kosyk, p. 129.

191. Szcześniak and Szota, p. 103.

192. O. Shtul and Ye. Stakhiv, "OUN Expeditionary Groups," in Struk, 3: 740–41; Kosyk, pp. 82, 94, 108–9, 121. See also Kamenetsky, *Hitler's Occupation of Ukraine*, p. 55, and Paul Robert Magocsi, *Galicia: A Historical Survey and Bibliographic Guide* (Toronto: University of Toronto Press, in association with the Canadian Institute of Ukrainian Studies and the Harvard Ukrainian Research Institute, 1983), p. 213. The phrase in quotation marks appears in Philip Friedman, "Ukrainian-Jewish Relations during the Nazi Occupation," in Marrus, p. 365.

193. Dallin, p. 118.

194. Ibid.

195. Document No. 55, "Memorandum of the Organization of Ukrainian Nationalists on the Solution to the Ukrainian Question," June 15, 1941, in Kosyk, pp. 503–4.

196. In Dallin, p. 115.

197. Document No. 42, "Letter from Schickendanz to von Stutterheim," September 17, 1940, in Kosyk, p. 490.

198. Document No. 43, September 18, 1940, "Letter from Schickendanz to Heydrich," ibid.

199. P. Friedman, in Marrus, p. 363. This committee was different from the UTsK (Ukrainian Central Committee), established in Kraków in the spring of 1940 under Volodymyr Kubiiovych, as well as from the UNK (Ukrainian National Committee), formed on March 12, 1945.

200. Littlejohn, *The Patriotic Traitors*, p. 296; Szcześniak and Szota, p. 104. Various authors state that the time of Nachtigall's arrival in Lwów was around 3:30 A.M. Kosyk, p. 134, places the time at 4:30 A.M.

201. Tsentralnyi Derzhavnyi Arkhiv Żhovtenvoi Revoliutsii i Sotsialistychnoho Budivnytstva

(Central State Archive of the October Revolution and Socialist Reconstruction) Kiev, f. 3833, op. 1, spr. 41, ark. 6. One eyewitness, in Wołyń, stated:

> When the Germans attacked Russia in June 1941, the Soviet army scrambled to get away without any semblance of order. Everyone was out for himself and tried to save his own skin. The NKVD and the militia were the first to run. Regular soldiers elicited sympathy among the Poles whom alone they trusted. Although they were hungry, they did not rob, and when they were certain that they were dealing with Poles, they pleaded: *Pozhaluista, daite kusochek khleba* [Please, give a piece of bread]. They avoided the Ukrainians, however, since they [the Ukrainians] dealt with them in the same way as they dealt with the scattered Polish soldiers returning in 1939, by shooting them in the back.
>
> The Ukrainians, then, made preparations for the glorious welcome of the Germans. They built a triumphant arch with a swastika and a trident, with German and yellow-blue colors, and tablets which read: *"Heil Hitler," "Khai zhyve samostiina Ukraina"* [Long live independent Ukraine].

Studułł, in Giertych, *Komunikaty*, p. 326.

202. Szcześniak and Szota, pp. 108–10, and n. 126. Aleksander Drożdżyński's and Jan Zaborowski's work is entitled *Oberländer, przez Ostforschung, "wywiad i NSDAP do rządu" NRF* (Poznań: Wydawnictwo Zachodnie, 1960). Cyprian Sawicki's work is *Ludzie i sprawy Norymbergi* (Poznań: Wydawnictwo Poznańskie, 1967).

203. Saul S. Friedman, *Pogromchik: The Assassination of Simon Petlura* (New York: Hart Publishing Company, 1976), p. 374.

204. Gerald Reitlinger, *The SS: Alibi of a Nation, 1922–1945* (New York: Viking Press, 1968), p. 204.

205. Drożdżyński and Zaborowski.

206. J. A. Armstrong, p. 54, and n. 12, and p. 56.

207. Gilbert, pp. 163–65, 168.

208. Ibid., p. 173.

209. Dallin, p. 119 and n. 2. Emphasis mine. His references on the excesses of the Banderowcy in respect to the Russians, Poles, and Jews include W. Diewerge (ed.), *Deutsche Soldaten sehen die Sowjetunion* (Berlin: Limpert, 1941), p. 45; Einsatzgruppen Reports, July 16, August 9, 28, 1941; and Petro Iarovyi, "K desiatoi godovshchine velikoi provokatsii," *Sotsialisticheskii Vestnik* (New York) 31 (1951): 138–49. For additional information on the role of this death battalion in the extermination of the Jews in Lwów and elsewhere, see Sabrin, p. 8, especially Dmytruk, p. 260; Stanisław Sławomir Nicieja, "Mord na Zboczu Kadeckim we Lwowie," *Miesięcznik społeczno-kulturalny* (Opole) 4 (1983); and Aleksander Korman, *Z krwawych dni Lwowa 1941 roku* (London: Koło Lwowian, 1989), pp. 17–23, who provides a listing of twenty-five names, dates, and short biographies of the murdered professors and family members. For another list and biographical information, see Bonusiak, pp. 85–104.

210. Torzecki, *Polacy i Ukraińcy*, pp. 118–19.

211. Popiński, Kokurin, and Gurjanow, p. 28. Andrzej Żbikowski, "Lokalne pogromy Żydów w czerwcu i lipcu 1941 roku na wschodnich rubieżach II Rzeczypospolitej," *Biuletyn ŻIH*, no. 162–63 (1992): 3–18, has identified over sixty pogroms occurring during June and July 1941 in Eastern Poland. In a listing of thirty-nine localities in Wołyń where pogroms took place in the first few weeks of the invasion, Spector (*The Holocaust of Volhynian Jews*, pp. 66–67) has identified twenty-two of them as having been carried out by "Ukrainians," two by "Ukrainian Police," and one by "Ukrainians and Germans." No Poles appear on this list of perpetrators. Gilbert, pp. 174–75, states:

> Throughout Eastern Galicia and the Volhynia, the Ukrainian population frequently provided an added dimension of danger for the local Jews. The Jewish historian Philip Friedman, who was in Lvov during these terrible months, and who subsequently carried out considerable historical research into the fate of the Jews of Eastern Galicia and the Volhynia, has recorded how, in Lvov, the Ukrainians themselves seized Jews and turned them over to the authorities. In Buczacz the pogrom was directed by the local Ukrainian intelligentsia. In Delatyn, the pogrom was largely the work of the music teacher Slawko Waszczuk; in Stanislawow, of Professor Lysiak, of the local teachers' seminary....
>
> [Similar events were said to have transpired in Dubno, Tarnopol, Kosów Hucułski, Skałat, Jabłonica, and Gliniany.]

212. Wiktor Poliszczuk, "Prawda musi być klarowana, oskarżenie precyzyjne," *Gazeta*

(Toronto), Christmas 1994; Poliszczuk, *Gorzka prawda*, p. 155.

213. Wiesenthal, p. 36.

214. Ibid., p. 7.

215. Ibid., p. 167.

216. Łuczak, p. 351.

217. In Węgierski, *Lwów pod okupacją sowiecką*, pp. 274–75. Rzepicki's testimony may be found in *Biuletyn Informacyjny* 2, no. 28 (1979): 70.

218. Bonusiak, pp. 37–38.

219. Ibid., p. 40.

220. In Wojciech Wrzesiński (ed.), *Kaźń profesorów lwowskich — lipiec 1941. Studia oraz relacje i dokumenty zebrane i opracowane przez Zygmunta Alberta* (Wrocław: Wydawnictwo Uniwersytetu Wrocławskiego, 1989), pp. 305–6, as quoted by Aleksander Korman in his letter to the editor, *Semper Fidelis* (Wrocław) 4, no. 5 (July–October 1990): 54. The last part of the passage reads: "An diesen Exzessen, bei denen es auch zu willkürlichen Totüngen gekommen ist, waren ukrainische Militz und Angehörige der 'ukrainischen Befreiunsarmee' beteiligt." The phrase "Ukrainian Liberation Army" must refer to *Nachtigall*, not the UPA, which was founded in the fall of 1942.

221. See Poliszczuk, *Gorzka prawda*, p. 157.

222. Werner Brockdorff, *Kollaboration oder Widerstand. Die Zusammenarbeit mit den Deutschen in den besetzten Ländern wahrend des zweiten Weltkrieges und deren schreckliche Folgen* (München: Wels Welsermuhl, 1968), p. 106.

223. Wolfdieter Bihl, "Ukrainians in the Armed Forces of the Reich: The 14th *Waffen* Grenadier Division of the SS," in Hans-Joachim Torke and John-Paul Himka (eds.), *German-Ukrainian Relations in Historical Perspective* (Toronto: Canadian Institute of Ukrainian Studies Press, 1994), p. 140.

224. Alfred Rosenberg, "Denkschrift Nr. 2," in Dallin, p. 109.

225. In Szcześniak and Szota, p. 106. According to Dallin, pp. 119–20 n. 4, the text of the declaration of independence is available in two versions. One concludes with the words: "Long live the leader of the OUN, Stepan Bandera!" The other includes the phrase: "Glory to the heroic German Army and its Führer, Adolf Hitler!" Actually, there are several versions of that proclamation. For a translation of an early typewritten copy of the "Act of Proclamation of the Ukrainian State," see J. A. Armstrong, pp. 56–57. However, almost none of the words quoted above or in the text appear in that version. See also S. V. Savchuk, "Akt proholoshennia Ukrainskoi Derzhavy 30-ho chervnia 1941 roku," *Novyi Litopys 1*, vol. 1 (1961): 3–25. According to Prus, *Bluff*, p. 141 and n. 142, copies of the original *Akt*, which circulated in Lwów, Stanisławów, Tarnopol, Złoczów, and Założce, have been preserved in Kiev in Tsentralnyi Derzhavnyi Arkhiv Zhovtenvoi Revoliutsii i Sotsialistychnoho Budivnytstva, f. 1, spr. 5, ark. 3. For a version in the Ukrainian language, see *Zborivski Visti* (Ukrainian Informative Newspaper, Zboriv), July 31, 1941, reprinted in *Ukrainian Historian* 27 (1990): pp. 112–13. See also Poliszczuk, *Gorzka prawda*, pp. 160–75. Two versions of the *Akt* appear on pp. 173–74.

226. In Sabrin, p. 245, including photocopy in the German language.

227. In J. A. Armstrong, p. 58.

228. Torzecki, "Die Rolle der Zusammenarbeit," in Röhr, p. 269.

229. Captured Nazi War Document no. 145, in Sabrin, p. 51.

230. Bandera, at his interrogation, was told by Ernst Kundt, undersecretary of state: "The German Wehrmacht and the Führer, who conquered this land, have the right to form a government. It is he who has the right to establish a government." Document No. 61, "Text of a Conversation between Representatives of the German Administration with Members of the Ukrainian National Committee and Stepan Bandera," July, 3, 1941, Kraków, in Kosyk, p. 511.

231. As quoted in Marples, p. 50.

232. Torzecki, *Kwestia ukraińska w polityce III Rzeszy*, p. 236. The interrogations took place in Kraków. Various Ukrainian émigrés, including Bandera, were placed under house arrest on July 2, 1941. Afterward, the Nationalist leaders were taken to Berlin. See Document No. 60, Chief of SP and SD, "Excerpt from the Report on Events in the USSR No. 11," July 3, 1941, in Kosyk, pp. 508–9, and Document No. 63, Chief of SP and SD, "Excerpt from the Report on Events in the USSR No. 13," July 5, 1941, ibid., p. 512–13. An aside in Document No. 65, "Hitler's Meeting with Rosenberg, Lammers, Keitel, Goering [*sic*], and Borman," July 16, 1941, The Führer's Headquarters, ibid., p. 516, notes, "(By the way: It has been shown several times that Rosenberg has a soft spot for the Ukrainians; he also wants to expand the old Ukraine considerably.)"

233. Torzecki, *Polacy i Ukraińcy*, pp. 124–25. Dallin, p. 120, states that Bandera was "treated with deference." Szcześniak and Szota, p. 119,

claim that from Zellenbau he still continued to direct the Nationalist movement. According to Torzecki, *Polacy i Ukraińcy, op. cit.*, p. 315, however, Bandera lost all contact with the OUN in the first quarter of 1942.

Torzecki adds an interesting aside: when mutually imprisoned, Poles and Ukrainians seemed to get along just fine. By way of illustration, he cites the case of Lech Sadowski, who helped Iaroslav Starukh, a known OUN-B activist, escape from a Lwów jail in December 1943 (p. 125).

234. Szcześniak and Szota, pp. 118–19.

235. Torzecki, *Kwestia ukraińska w polityce III Rzeszy*, p. 247.

236. Ibid., p. 256.

237. Ibid., p. 247.

238. Torzecki, *Polacy i Ukraińcy*, pp. 126–27. An excerpt from a telegram received on August 10, 1941, by the High Command of the Eleventh Army states, "After consultation with the Reich's minister for the eastern occupied territories, the organization *Roland* is to be withdrawn from the campaign for political reasons."According to Kosyk, only Nachtigall was placed under von dem Bach-Zelewski's "201 battalion of police protection." He states that before being sent to Vienna (Mayerling), Roland was first disarmed under German guns. On September 16, 1941, in a raid on the OUN-B Vienna bureau, some Ukrainian officers and noncommissioned officers of Roland, including Richard Jary, were arrested and interned in a concentration camp. He does not say what happened to Roland's enlisted soldiers after they reached Vienna. Kosyk, pp. 132–35.

239. A memorandum (July 16, 1941) dealing with a discussion between Hitler and Rosenberg, Lammers, Keitel, and Göring. *NCA*, 7: 1087; *TWC*, Nuremberg Document 221-L, in Kamenetsky, *Hitler's Occupation of Ukraine*, p. 68.

240. Littman, in S. Friedman, *Holocaust Literature*, p. 285.

241. See Poliszczuk, *Gorzka prawda*, p. 160.

242. As quoted by Szcześniak and Szota, p. 112.

243. Torzecki, *Kwestia ukraińska w polityce III Rzeszy*, pp. 292–93.

244. Torzecki, *Polacy i Ukraińcy*, p. 125.

245. J. A. Armstrong, p. 135; Szcześniak and Szota, p. 327. These arrests followed the seizure of an OUN-M anti–Nazi brochure.

246. Torzecki, *Kwestia ukraińska w polityce III Rzeszy*, p. 253.

247. J. A. Armstrong, p. 134. According to Michał Fijałka, *27. Wołyńska Dywizja Piechoty AK* (Warszawa: Instytut Wydawniczy Pax, 1986), p. 45, Borovets was arrested in August, 1943.

248. Chief of SP and SD, "Report on Events in the USSR, No. 15," July 7, 1941, NO 5154, in J. A. Armstrong, p. 63.

249. In Dallin, p. 121 n. 3.

250. Document No. 64, "Excerpt from the Report on Events in the USSR No. 23," July 15, 1941, in Kosyk, p. 513.

251. Bandera's letter (in German) can be found in *Ukrainian Historian* 25 (1988): 193.

252. Document No. 75, "Memorandum of the OUN Concerning German Demands to Dissolve the Ukrainian Government," August 14, 1941, in Kosyk, p. 526.

253. Chief of the Security Police and the SD, "Operational Situation Report USSR No. 56," August 18, 1941, in Arad et al., p. 92.

254. In Sabrin, p. 50. Source given as Archive of the History of the Party at the Central Committee of the Communist Party of Ukraine, fund 57, inventory 4, file 338, pp. 131–32.

255. Torzecki, *Polacy i Ukraińcy*, pp. 135–36.

256. In Szcześniak and Szota, p. 119. According to Kosyk, p. 207, this letter was written on January 14, 1942.

257. Kosyk.

258. Document No. 111, "Statement of Governor General Frank on the Subject of Ukrainians," December 16, 1941, in Kosyk, p. 553.

259. In Szcześniak and Szota, p. 121.

260. Torzecki, *Polacy i Ukraińcy*, p. 245.

261. Document No. 86, Chief of SP and SD, "Excerpt from the Report on Event in the USSR No. 79," September, 19, 1941, in Kosyk, p. 533.

262. Document No. 99, Chief of SP and SD, "Excerpts from the Report on Event in the USSR No. 126," October 29, 1941, ibid., p. 543.

263. Document No. 124, Chief of SP and SD, "Excerpt from the Report on Events in the USSR No. 191," April 10, 1942, ibid., pp. 567–68.

264. Yurkevich, "Organization of Ukrainian Nationalists," in Struk, 3: 708, states: "The OUN's membership consisted overwhelmingly of students and young people. There are no reliable figures, but estimates range as high as 20,000 (1939)."

265. In Szcześniak and Szota, p. 121.

266. See Document No. 135, Chief of SP

and SD, "Report No. 14 from the Occupied Eastern Regions," July 31, 1942, in Kosyk, p. 577.

267. See Document No. 158, "Report No. 32 from the Occupied Eastern Regions," December 1942, ibid., p. 604.

268. See Document No. 78, "From a Report on the Consequences of Partisan Activities," May 14, 1943, ibid., pp. 624–25, and Document No. 179, "German Losses Due to Resistance Activities in the Three Commissariats of Ukraine: Volhynia, Podolia, Zhytomyr," May 17, 1943, Zhytomyr, ibid., pp. 625–26.

269. See Paweł Chmielewski, "Hitlerowski terror wobec ludności cywilnej okupowanych obszarów Związku Radzieckiego," in Piotr Łossowski (ed.), *Związek Radziecki w latach Wielkiej Wojny Narodowej 1941–1945* (Wrocław: Zakład Narodowy im. Ossolińskich, 1979), p. 167.

270. See Document No. 143, Chief of SP and SD, "Report No. 22 from the Occupied Eastern Regions," September 25, 1942, in Kosyk, p. 589.

271. Document No. 158, "Report No. 32 from the Occupied Eastern Regions," December 1942, ibid., p. 604.

272. Szcześniak and Szota, p. 119.

273. Kosyk, p. 270.

274. J. A. Armstrong, p. 102.

275. Ibid., pp. 102–3.

276. Kosyk, p. 261.

277. Torzecki, *Kwestia ukraińska w polityce III Rzeszy*, pp. 246–47.

278. Szcześniak and Szota, pp. 120–21.

279. Wardzyńska, *Formacja Wachmannschaften*, pp. 10–31, *passim*.

280. Hilberg, *Perpetrators, Victims, Bystanders*, p. 96. In 1995, a former Trawniki graduate was deported from the United States for misrepresenting his past in order to obtain U.S. citizenship:

> Wasyl Lytwyn, 73, a retired shipping clerk from Chicago, was a member of the infamous guard units of the Trawniki SS training and base camp and its successor unit, the SS Streibel Battalion, from 1943 to April 1945, said the U.S. Justice Department's Office of Special Investigations (OSI).
>
> The Trawniki camp was used to train guards and police to assist in the Nazi's program of murdering the Jews of Europe.
>
> A complaint filed in court by the OSI in order to strip Lytwyn of his citizenship alleges he took part in the destruction of the Warsaw Ghetto in April and May 1943.
>
> The complaint also states that Lytwyn served in the guard detachment of the SS and Police Leader in Lublin and later in the Streibel Battalion.
>
> Between August 1944 and January 1945, the Streibel Battalion seized tens of thousands of Polish civilians and supervised them while they worked as slave laborers constructing fortifications in central Poland, the complaint states.
>
> Prior to departing the United States for Ukraine, Lytwyn signed an agreement with the OSI in which he admitted he obtained U.S. citizenship fraudulently and that he wilfully misrepresented his wartime activities. The court complaint to remove his citizenship was launched pursuant to the terms of that agreement.
>
> According to the complaint, Lytwyn immigrated to Canada in 1948 and obtained citizenship in 1955. He moved to the United States in 1957 and in 1994 became a U.S. citizen.
>
> Since its inception in 1979, the OSI has removed 44 Nazi persecutors from the United States while more than 300 are currently under investigation.

Canadian Jewish News, December 21, 1995.

281. See P. Friedman, in Marrus, p. 378.

282. In Gilbert, p. 426.

283. Chaim Hirszman's experiences as recorded by his wife, Pola, ibid., p. 306, see also pp. 304, 414–16, and 500.

284. Ibid., p. 326, see also pp. 344, 361, 375–76, 618–19.

285. Ibid., p. 399, see also pp. 408, 432–33, 456, 458–59, 512–13, 574, 597, and 603.

286. Ibid., p. 247.

287. Meir Peker, ibid., p. 490.

288. Interview, June 23, 1995, Freedom, N.H. Regina Gelb currently resides in New York City and is a professional translator.

289. In Gutman and Krakowski, p. 49. The forced-labor camps were located throughout Poland with most in the Central Industrial Area.

290. The Lagerschutz formations were set up by an order, dated February 27, 1941, of the Warsaw District governor. Volunteers were to be recruited from among the Poles, Belorussians, and Ukrainians. The Polish underground press put out a number of leaflets, with good results, urging Poles not to volunteer for this Nazi formation.

According to Regina Gelb, *all* the camp guards in Starachowice and in neighboring Skarżysko-Kammienna were Ukrainian. See Ringelblum, *Polish-Jewish Relations*, p. 41, editorial n. 5.

291. In the late 1940s, "Piorun" was spotted by one of the former residents of Starachowice on a street in Toronto. When some of the people began holding meetings on his account, he suddenly disappeared.

292. In Gutman and Krakowski, p. 50.

293. See Gilbert, p. 635.

294. Prekerowa, in J. Tomaszewski, *Najnowsze dzieje Żydów w Polsce*, p. 383.

295. P. Friedman, in Marrus, p. 378.

296. As quoted by Gilbert, pp. 150–51. Zuckerman's observation is on p. 150.

297. Spector, *The Holocaust of Volhynian Jews*, p. 175. Note 145 reads: "In early 1943 the local police stations in Volhyn-Podolia were manned by 453 Germans from the Order Police and 954 Germans from the gendarmerie. Thus there were 1,407 German policemen in the region, as compared to 11,870 Ukrainian policemen. In the Ukrainian mobile battalions served 3,500 policemen as compared with some 1,300 Germans."

298. Wardzyńska, *Formacja Wachmannschaften*, pp. 26, 29. The participation of the Ukrainians in the German resettlement campaign in the Lublin area is particularly noteworthy since this participation precipitated the political assassinations of Ukrainian activists by Poles in 1942. Ukrainian authors claim that this action by the Poles marks the beginning of the undeclared "Polish-Ukrainian War."

299. Four Einsatzgruppen were created just before the invasion of the Soviet Union. Numbering some three thousand men, they murdered nearly half a million people in six months time. G. Stein, p. 263.

Relying on Stefan Possony, "Anti-Semitism in the Russian Area," *Plural Societies* (winter 1974), pp. 91–92, Bohdan Vitvitsky states that the records of Israel's War Crimes Investigations Office suggest "that 11,000 Ukrainians were involved in some type of anti–Jewish measures, such as massacres or deportations." In light of what has been said and will be said in the present chapter, there is no justification for this extremely low estimate. Bohdan Vitvitsky, "Slavs and Jews: Consistent and Inconsistent Perspectives on the Holocaust," in Michael Berenbaum (ed.), *A Mosaic of Victims: Non-Jews Persecuted and Murdered by the Nazis* (New York: New York University Press, 1990), p. 105, see also pp. 106–7.

300. As quoted by P. Friedman, in Marrus, p. 364. Also in *UPA v svitli nimetskykh dokumentiv*, vol. 6 (Toronto: Litopys UPA, 1983), p. 41.

301. Einsatzgruppen report no. 24, July 16, 1941, p. 5, YVA 051/ER-24, as quoted in*UPA v svitli nimetskykh documentiu*, p. 111. This phrase also appears in the Chief of the Security Police and Security Services, "Operational Situation Report USSR No. 126," October 27, 1941, in Arad p. 210. See also P. Friedman, in Marrus, p. 367.

302. The eyewitness account of Dr. Otto Korfes, a former general of the Wehrmacht, describes one of the many crimes committed against the Polish and Jewish civilian populations by the Banderowcy, who assisted the SS and the Gestapo. "Mitellungsblatt," 1959, z. 11, in Szcześniak and Szota, p. 110. For another moving account of such an execution (October 5, 1942), in which 5,000 Jews were murdered by the Einsatzkommando units with the assistance of the Ukrainian militia in Dubno, Wołyń, see the Nuremberg testimony of Herman Gräbe, manager and engineer of a German construction firm in the Ukraine, in Shirer, pp. 1252–53.

303. Shtockfish, p. 405(20).

304. Bronisław Janik, *Było ich trzy* (Warszawa: Książka i Wiedza, 1970), p. 70. For example, in August, after being informed of the existence of an underground Jewish shelter by a group of Ukrainian "mushroom gatherers" from Kisorycz, the Ukrainian police under Himchak wasted no time coming to the location and shooting all of them (p. 71).

305. Torzecki, *Polacy i Ukraińcy*, p. 135.

306. Ainsztein, p. 252.

307. Torzecki, *Kwestia ukraińska w polityce III Rzeszy*, p. 290. An Einsatzgruppen report states: "In Volhynia, the Bandera group is particularly active. Ukrainians engaged by the German Army use their position for national and party purposes. They install members as mayors and exert strong influence on the entire Ukrainian Militia." Chief of Security Police and SD, "Operational Report USSR No. 50," August 12, 1941, in Arad et al., p. 83.

308. Torzecki, *Kwestia ukraińska w polityce III Rzeszy*, p. 242. Dmytro Paliiv served as a former leader of a small legal party in Poland. Later, he was the principal organizer and the highest ranking officer in the SS-Galizien. J. A. Armstrong, p. 128.

309. Shmuel Spector, "Ukrainische Hilfspolizei," in Israel Gutman (ed.), *Encyclopedia of the*

Holocaust, vol. 4 (New York: Macmillan, 1990), pp. 1530–31.

310. Tennenbaum, p. 181.

311. Hilberg, *Perpetrators, Victims, Bystanders,* p. 94.

312. See Gilbert, p. 206.

313. Hilberg, *The Destruction of the European Jews,* 1: 313–14.

314. Torzecki, *Polacy i Ukraińcy,* p. 136; Aharon Weiss, "The Holocaust and Ukrainian Victims," in Berenbaum, p. 112.

315. Hilberg, *Perpetrators, Victims, Bystanders,* pp. 93, 95.

316. See interview with Oswald Rufeisen, "Jako chrześcijanin, a nawet jako Żyd." *Polityka,* May 29, 1993.

317. Hilberg, *Perpetrators, Victims, Bystanders,* p. 94.

318. Torzecki, *Kwestia ukraińska w polityce III Rzeszy,* p. 242.

319. Operational Situation Report, USSR No. 47, August 9, 1941, Yad Vashem archive, as quoted by Gilbert, p. 182.

320. Maria Halina Horn, *A Tragic Victory* (Toronto: ECW Press, 1988), pp. 80–81.

321. In Hilberg, *Perpetrators, Victims, Bystanders,* pp. 95–96.

322. Wardzyńska, *Formacja Wachmannschaften,* pp. 9–10.

323. Bihl, in Torke and Himka, p. 141.

324. In Sabrin, pp. 209–10.

325. Ibid., p. 218.

326. Ibid., pp. 246–47.

327. Ibid., p. 247.

328. Ibid., p. 248.

329. Ibid., p. 249.

330. Ibid., p. 255.

331. Ibid., p. 258.

332. After the initial welcome of both the Soviet and the German occupation forces in Poland's eastern territories, the Ukrainians were somewhat better off than the Poles. Yet, for reasons stated below, those Ukrainians who risked their lives to help the Jews found themselves in an even more difficult predicament than the Poles. The Ukrainian rescuers in Eastern Poland also had to contend with the wrath of the Ukrainian Nationalists, whose ethnic-cleansing policies were aimed against all non–Ukrainians, including Jews. According to Weiss, in Berenbaum, p. 113:

> Thus, the situation of those Ukrainians whom I call "victims" was most difficult, if we bear in mind the background, the hostility of a remarkable large part of the Ukrainian population, the consistent anti-Jewish position of the Ukrainian leadership, and the German measures against anyone who attempted to rescue Jews. Indeed, about 100 Ukrainians from all the strata of the population were executed by the Germans in eastern Galicia due to their attempt to hide Jews.

For examples of individual Ukrainians who rendered assistance to the Jews, see Paldiel, pp. 268–83. This work also refers (p. 267) to the October 1943 execution of the 100 Ukrainians mentioned above.

Although he welcomed the German armies, was a staunch defender of Ukrainian nationalism, and supported the formation of the SS-Galizien, Metropolitan Sheptytsky condemned the use of the Ukrainian auxiliary police in the liquidation of the Jews and, through a network of some 550 monks and nuns, was able to save 150–200 Jewish children. Taras Hunczak, "Ukrainian-Jewish Relations during the Soviet and Nazi Occupations," in Boshyk, p. 49.

333. The name "UPA" was first used by Taras Borovets' partisans in Wołyń in December 1941. Its original title included a Polonism, "Ukrainska povstancha armiia," later changed to "Ukrainska povstanska armiia."

Also, the trident (*tryzub*), a symbol of Ukrainian independence and an emblem of the OUN-UPA, was the coat of arms of King Władysław Jagiełło (1386–1434). See any reference dealing with the coat of arms of Polish kings or see Jan Matejko's painting of Jagiełło. In this painting, the trident appears prominently on the upper left arm of the king's royal cloak. The 1992–93 publication *Good News* by the American Institute of Polish Culture of Miami, Florida, featured Matejko's portraits of the forty Polish kings. The painting of Jagiełło is on p. 73.

In late summer of 1942, the OUN-B sent Vasyl Sydor ("Shelest") to Wołyń and Polesie to establish, with the help of Roman Dmytro Klachkivskyi ("Klym Savur," "Okhrym," "Klym," "Krymskyi," "Omelian"— the regional military OUN-B commander), its own UPA. The founding date of the OUN-B UPA is said to be October 14, 1942, the day on which the first unit of this "army" came into existence. That summer and fall, numerous military Self-Defense Units (Samooboronnyi Kushchovi Viddily, or SKV) were established in Polesie and Wołyń. They consisted of local Ukrainians who took up arms at the bidding of the OUN-B.

Not wanting to be left out, the OUN-M formed a similar unit under the identical name in the spring of 1943. When attempts to unify these three UPAs failed, the OUN-B attacked Melnyk in July and Borovets in August 1943 and successfully coerced most of their followers, under penalty of death, to join the Bandera faction. In July 1943 military units called Ukrainian National Self-Defense (Ukrainska Natsionalna Samooborona, or UNS) were formed in Eastern Galicia. The UNS were similar in structure and function to the SKV.

The Security Service of the OUN (Sluzhba Bezpeky, or SB) was a police organ of terror similar in its functions to the Cheka and the Gestapo. After the split in the OUN, it served the OUN-B.It was headed by Mykola Lebed.

A central command for all UPA forces was established on or about November 22, 1943, under Roman Shukhevych as commander-in-chief. (According to Kosyk, p. 340, Shukhevych became the head of the OUN-B military staff in the spring of 1943 and the president of the OUN-B and the commander-in-chief of the UPA on August 25, 1943.)

The UPA in the Wołyń-Polesie region became the UPA-North (under Klachkivskyi), the military units in the Kamianets-Podilskyi/Vinnitsa area became the UPA-South (never formed), and those in Eastern Galicia became the UPA-West (under Sydor). This state of affairs lasted for the remainder of the war.

After the war, a remnant of the UPA moved into the Carpathian region, won support both by terrorizing the local inhabitants and by opposing the massive exchanges of borderland populations after the war, and continued to terrorize the Polish people and government until the group was liquidated by the Soviet, Czech, and Polish forces in 1947 during Operation "Wisła." In his May 10, 1946, report (No. 1597/608) to the Ministry of Foreign Affairs in Rome on the postwar exchange of populations, Ambassador Eugenio Reale noted the grave difficulties surrounding the repatriation of Ukrainians from Polish territories due to the fact that "many Ukrainians joined armed bands which spread political terror and live by robbery." He referred the Italian Ministry to his earlier reports (January 26, February 5, and February 10, 1946) regarding these matters. (Reale, pp. 170–71.)

Although Shukhevych formally dissolved the UPA on September 3, 1949 (he died during a battle with Soviet forces on March 5, 1950, in the village of Biłohorszcza near Lwów), small pockets of resistance lingered on under Vasyl Kuk ("Koval," "Medvid") and, after Kuk's arrest by the Soviet political police in October 1952, under Kostia Himmelraich, until 1954.

J. A. Armstrong, pp. 71, 113; Petro Sodol, "Ukrainian Insurgent Army," in Struk, 5: 392–95; Spector, "Ukrainska Povstanska Armyia," in Gutman, pp. 1531–32; and Torzecki, *Polacy i Ukraińcy*, p. 138. The reference to Kuk and Himmelraich comes from Edward Prus, *UPA. Armia powstańcza czy kurenie rizunów?* (Wrocław: Nortom, 1994), p. 106. The references to the SKV and the SB come from Poliszczuk, *Gorzka prawda*, pp. 220, 294–98. For a listing of UPA terrorist and diversionary activities from July 24, 1945, to December 6, 1946, see Szcześniak and Szota, pp. 530–36.

334. Ibid., p. 121.

335. Torzecki, *Kwestia Ukraińska w polityce III Rzeszy*, p. 302.

336. G. Stein, pp. 151, 185.

337. Torzecki, *Polacy i Ukraińcy*, p. 246.

338. Yurkevich, "Galician Ukrainians," in Boshyk, p. 76.

339. G. Stein, p. 185.

340. Volodymyr Kubiiovych, *Meni 85* (München: "Malode Zhyttia," 1985), pp. 113–14. Littman's phrase can be found in S. Friedman, *Holocaust Literature*, p. 290.

341. Kubiiovych, p. 169. See also Torzecki, "Die Rolle der Zusammenarbeit," in Röhr, p. 243.

342. Volodymyr Kubiiovych, "Appendix A: Origins of the Ukrainian Division 'Galicia,'" in Wolf-Dietrich Heike, *The Ukrainian Division "Galicia," 1943–45: A Memoir* (Toronto: Shevchenko Scientific Society, 1988), p. 144. According to Edward Prus, Melnyk sent Field Marshal Wilhelm Keitel on February 6, 1943, a letter that was referred to Himmler and that in part stated, "It seems that the time has come to include the Ukraine [i.e., Galicia] in the anti–Bolshevik front ... we long to take part [in the battle] and to give ourselves over to the disposition of the leadership of the [German] armed forces." In Edward Prus, *Melnykowcy. Kolaboracja czy opór?* (Wrocław: Stowarzyszenie Upamiętnienia Ofiar Zbrodni Ukraińskich Nacjonalistów, 1994), pp. 31–32.

343. In Bihl, in Torke and Himka, p. 156. Emphasis mine. This memo is undated, but from the context, it appears to have been sent to Himmler shortly after the formation of the SS-Galizien. The point of the memo is not to

convince Himmler of Ukrainian loyalty; rather, Wächter was simply trying to point out that there were Polish as well as Ukrainian "Galicians" and that since the division was "open only to the Ukrainians of Galicia and not to the Poles," it should have the word "Ukrainian" in it. This particular passage, however, reveals a great deal more. Could Wächter produce a similar list of Polish institutions "officially established and recognized by the German authorities"?

On April 12, 1943, Kurt Daluege, the head of the Ordnungspolizei, SS Oberstgruppenführer, wrote to SS Gruppenfüfrer Otto Winkelmann:

> There is now a new Order which includes the following: A new front division is to be created by and for the *Waffen SS,* which will be made up of Greek Catholic Ukrainians from Galicia and which will probably be called the "Galician Division" since these Ukrainians are from Galicia. The other Ukrainians in the Generalgouvernement, those from the Lublin area, are Greek Orthodox. These are to be used in the formation of police regiments with only a small German command.

Ibid., p. 142. Littlejohn, *The Patriotic Traitors,* p. 315, notes, "Volunteers for the new division were required to belong to the Eastern Catholic (uniate) faith." This was a convenient way, explains Littlejohn, of excluding all Poles and Russians who were Roman Catholic and Greek Orthodox, respectively.

344. Torzecki, "Die Rolle der Zusammenarbeit," in Röhr, p. 266.

345. Torzecki, *Polacy i Ukraińcy,* p. 247. According to Dallin, of the some 100,000 who volunteered, fewer than 30,000 were accepted. Dallin, p. 598. Littman, in S. Friedman, *Holocaust Literature,* pp. 281–82, states:

> German newsreel film of the period shows the volunteers of the newly formed Halychyna Division passing in review before Governor Wächter in Lviv on July 16, 1943. Still in their civilian clothes, they proudly display their SS and swastika insignia alongside the Halychyn Lion as they march by in ranks of four on their way to the railway station and boot camp. As they pass the swastika-bedecked reviewing stand, they raise their arms in the stiff-armed Nazi salute while the film's sound track intones: "One more train is departing the Fatherland with volunteers so that after training they can join the German army in defending Europe against the world Bolshevik enemy."
>
> In a similar ceremony in Kolomyea [Kołomyja], captured German film shows Wächter addressing the Ukrainian recruits as follows: "In joining the ranks of the volunteers you show that you are not indifferent to the struggle now taking place in Europe.... You wish, with arms in hand, to serve the Fatherland and the New Europe."

346. Littlejohn, *Foreign Legions of the Third Reich,* 4: 29.

347. In Bihl, in Torke and Himka, p. 145. This form of the oath is contained in the deployment order from SS Headquarters dated July 30, 1943. Wächter's minutes of the April 12, 1943, meeting state, "Form of oath: The oath will be in the form already in use for volunteer units" (p. 154). A slightly different translation of the same oath can be found in Littman, in S. Friedman, *Holocaust Literature,* p. 282.

348. In *Ridna Zemlia* (Lwów) 52 (December 26, 1943).

349. Heike, p. 4.

350. Yurkevich, "Galician Ukrainians," in Boshyk, p. 77.

351. Yury Boshyk's "Editor's Note," in Heike, p. xi. Mark Aarons and John Loftus, *Ratlines: How the Vatican's Nazi Networks Betrayed Western Intelligence to the Soviets* (London, England: Mandarin, 1991), p. 180, state: "By the beginning of 1943, nearly all of the 800,000 Ukrainian Jews had been murdered and their police executioners needed new assignments. There were so many ex-police volunteers that the Ukrainian unit [SS-Galizien] was originally named the 'Galician Police Division' before it was formally accepted by the SS."

Boshyk notes that in early 1945 the division's name was changed to ukrainische Nr. 1 (Ukrainian No. 1). So does Littlejohn (*Foreign Legions of the Third Reich,* 4: 32): "On November 12 [1944] its correct ethnic composition was acknowledged when its title was altered to: *14. Waffen-Grenadier-Division der S.S. (ukrainische Nr. 1).*" However, Boshyk, like so many other Ukrainian authors, also states that toward the end of the war, the division was renamed *1. Ukrainische Division der Ukrainischen National-Armee* (1st Ukrainian Division of the Ukrainian National Army, or UNA). Littlejohn (ibid., pp. 33, 45) states that it was "rechristened" as such after being handed over to Pavlo Shandruk. Littman, in S. Friedman, *Holocaust Literature*, pp. 286–87, comments: "On April 24, 1945—fifteen days before Germany's unconditional surrender—the division was renamed the First Ukrainian Division of the Ukrainian National Army. In practical terms the change in nomenclature meant little. General Fritz Freitag remained the division's commander, orders continued to be issued in German, and the men continued to be pawns in the German battle plan." No doubt, that was the *intended* course of action, but whether this name change was ever *formally* made remains an open question.

Major Heike, chief of staff of the SS-Galizien, stated that during its re-formation (1944), the division "was granted permission to officially call itself 'Ukrainian' and not simply 'Galician'" (Heike, p. 70). He also recalled that when defeat was inevitable, "Wächter wanted to merge the Ukrainian Division with the Polish army of General Władysław Anders because, from a legal standpoint, the Ukrainians in the Division were former citizens of Poland" (p. 120). Nowhere did he say, however, that the name of the SS-Galizien was changed either formally or informally to that of the 1st Ukrainian Division of the UNA—and he, of all people, should know.

In his penultimate chapter, "The End of Hostilities and the End of the Division," Heike did state, "General Shandruk brought trident insignia for the Ukrainian soldiers to wear on their caps" (p. 127). Undoubtedly, after surrendering to the Allies, all Ukrainian SS-Galizien collaborators said that they belonged to the 1st Ukrainian Division of the UNA. Heike himself attempted to refute the British claim that he had been an SS company commander (see p. vii).

See also Klietmann, p. 193. Other works about the division include G. Stein; Roman Krokhmaliuk, *Zahrava na skhodi: spohady i dokumenti z pratsi u Viiskovii upravi "Halychyna" v 1943–1945 rokakh* (Toronto: Bratstvo kol. Voiakiv 1-o Ukrainskoi Dyvizii UNA, 1978); Wasyl Veryha, *Dorohamy Druhoi Svitovoi viiny. Legendy pro uchast ukraintsiv u zdushuvanni vashavskoho povstannia v 1944 r. ta pro Ukrainsku Dyviziiu "Halychyna"* (Toronto: Brotherhood of Veterans of the I.UD UNA, 1981), pp. 181–208; and Pavlo Shandruk, "Historyczna prawda o Ukraińskiej Armii Narodowej," *Kultura*, no. 212 (June 1965): 86–103. The last is mostly about the UNA; after the war, Shandruk was the recipient of the Virtuti Militari cross of valor (Shandruk, pp. 106–7).

For Soviet works dealing with the SS-Galizien, see Valerii Styrkul, *The SS Werewolves* (Lviv: Kamenyar Publishers, 1982), and Valerii Styrkul, *We Accuse: Documentary Sketch* (Kiev: Dnipro Publishers, 1984).

For a German work by a foremost military historian, see Georg Tessin, *Verbände und Truppen der deutschen Wehrmacht und Waffen SS im Zweiten Weltkrieg, 1939–1945* (Frankfurt: Verlag E. S. Mittler und Sohh, 1974).

352. G. Stein, p. 186.

353. In Littlejohn, *Foreign Legions of the Third Reich*, 4: 29.

354. See John A. Armstrong's "Introduction," in Heike, p. xxii. Aarons and Loftus, p. 203, believe that the SS-Galizien archives are "presumably still in Vatican custody."

355. J. A. Armstrong, p. 128.

356. Heike, pp. ix–x.

357. Krokhmaliuk, p. 34.

358. Myroslav Kalba (comp.), *U lavakh druzhynnykiv. Spohady uchasnykiv* (Denver: Vyd. Druzhyn ukrainskykh natsionalistiv, 1982), p. 143.

359. Volodymyr Kubiiovych, "Appendix B: Appeal to Ukrainian Citizens and Youth by the Central Committee President on the Formation of the Ukrainian Division 6 May 1943," in Heike, pp. 146, 148. Emphases mine. There are two texts of Kubiiovych's appeal. One can be found in the Ukrainian Central Committee's organ, *Krakivski visti* (Kraków), May 16, 1943, and the other, containing the words "Muscovite-Jewish Bolshevism" and "Jewish-Bolshevik monster," can be found in the German-controlled *Lvivski visti* (Lwów), May 6, 1943. In all probability, the *Krakivski visti* version is the original.

360. Otto Wächter, "Appendix C: Appeal to the Able-Bodied Youth of Galicia," in Heike, p. 149. Emphases mine.

361. Ibid., pp. ix–x.

362. J. A. Armstrong, "Introduction," ibid., p. xix.

363. For the letter of transfer, see Sabrin, p. 258. The caption reads: "Photocopy of the letter describing the transfer of money from the Nazi Administration of the Generalgouvernement for the sum of 360,000 occupation zlotys to the treasury of Metropolitan Sheptytsky. 'My Office does not require an account for this money' reads the document significantly."

Łuczak also states that the Third Reich provided Metropolitan Sheptytsky with financial assistance. See Łuczak, pp. 500–503.

364. J. A. Armstrong, pp. 127, 131.

365. J. A. Armstrong, "Introduction," in Heike, p. xx.

366. J. A. Armstrong, pp. 127–28.

367. Ibid.

368. J. A. Armstrong, "Introduction," in Heike, p. xxi.

369. Ibid., p. 25.

370. Wasyl Veryha, *Visti Kombatanta* 5, no. 6, [36–37] (1968): 23. An AK field report dated May 4–5, 1944, also verifies the fact that the members of the SS-Galizien were joining the UPA. The report notes the "desertion of the *SS-Galizien* to the UPA." In Halina Czarnocka, et al. (eds.), *AK w dokumentach 1939–1945*, vol. 3, April 1943–July 1944 (London: Studium Polski Podziemnej, 1976), p. 430.

371. According to Torzecki, some 12,000 armed Ukrainian policemen from Wołyń joined the UPA from March 1943 onward. Torzecki, "Die Rolle der Zusammenarbeit," in Röhr, p. 267. Most of those from Eastern Galicia did too.

372. Łuczak, pp. 500–503, believes that both the Ukrainian Catholic Church and the Greek Orthodox Church cooperated with the Nazi régime.

According to Spector, *The Holocaust of Volhynian Jews*, pp. 242–43, the Ukrainian Orthodox Church was "an ally and partner of the Ukrainian nationalist movement." Spector adds:

> On February 12, 1942, Polikarp, the nationalist archbishop of Lutsk [Łuck] and Kovel was appointed "the head of the autocephalic [autonomous] church in the lands of the liberated Ukraine." His appointment was endorsed by the Germans, and Polikarp went out of his way to praise and extol his masters. He also staffed key posts in his jurisdiction with nationalist clergymen.... In a later stage they [Ukrainian priests] joined the Ukrainian Resistance Army (UPA) and, among other things, participated in attacks against Jewish family camps.

"In contrast," states Spector in n. 27, "A. Scheptitski [Sheptytsky], head of the Unitarian [Uniate] church in Galicia, who also welcomed the Nazi occupiers, regarding them as liberators from the Bolshevik yoke, nonetheless protested against the pogroms, and later even engaged in saving Jews. In Volhynia only a handful of Ukrainian priests endeavored to help the Jews."

373. J. A. Armstrong, pp. 130–31; Klym Dmytruk, "The Role of the Catholic and Orthodox Clergy during the Nazi Occupation," in Sabrin, p. 263. The reference to Bishop Kotsylovskyi can be found in Richard Landwehr, *Fighting for Freedom: The Ukrainian Volunteer Division of the Waffen-SS* (Silver Springs, MD: Bibliophile Legion Books, 1985), p. 40. The metropolitan's words can be found in Volodymyr Kubiiovych, "Appendix A: Origins of the Ukrainian Division 'Galicia,'" in Heike, p. 144.

374. Kubiiovych, ibid., p. 145.

375. Łuczak, p. 351.

376. G. Stein, pp. 186–87.

377. Torzecki, *Kwestia Ukraińska w polityce III Rzeszy*, p. 332.

378. Heike, p. x. The estimate for the losses at Brody is on p. 53. According to Littlejohn (*Foreign Legions of the Third Reich,* 4: 33), some "escaped eastward to join anti–Soviet partisan groups in the rear of the Red Army, then to continue the struggle for Ukrainian independence for years after the official end of the war in Europe." In other words, they joined the UPA.

In response to those who accused the SS of recruiting Ukrainians simply for cannon fodder, Himmler pointed out that they had been given a full year of training and that 250 Galicians in the SS-Galizien had been sent to attend the SS Junkerschule and had returned as officers. G. Stein, p. 186. In addition, others were trained in Hamburg, Osnabruch, Oldenberg, Neuhammer, Karlsruhe, and Koblens; and some 5,000 SS-Galizien recruits transferred from Ukrainian police regiments were given police combat training in France. Littman, in S. Friedman, *Holocaust Literature*, p. 282.

379. Heike, p. 63.

380. Ibid., p. x.

381. Ibid., pp. 80–81.

382. Torzecki, *Polacy i Ukraińcy*, p. 253. Hans von Krannhals confirms the presence of Ukrainian formations in Warsaw during the uprising. See his *Der Warshauer Aufstand 1944* (Frankfurt: Bernard und Graefe, 1964).

383. See Aleksander Korman, *Nieukarane zbrodnie SS-Galizien z lat 1943–1945* (London: Koło Lwowian, 1989), *passim.* Regarding the operation in Slovakia, Littman states:

> On October 1, 1944, the reconstituted Galician Division was ordered out of its barracks at Neuhammer and dispatched to Slovakia to assist in suppressing a popular, widespread revolt of the Slovak people against the puppet Tito regime and his Nazi sponsors.

The revolt was supported by important segments of the Slovak army.

Despite a spirited campaign, the Slovak forces were rapidly overpowered by vastly superior German forces. The defeated rebels fled toward the mountainous border areas, where they were readily mopped up by the Galician Division, stationed there for that purpose. Prisoners captured by the division were handed over to the Gestapo, which exacted a horrible revenge on the rebels. Czech military historians claim that the division behaved badly: "If we compare them to the regular Wehrmacht units, they way they behaved, the cruelty and pillage by the Galician Division was much worse."

Littman, in S. Friedman (ed.), *Holocaust Literature, op. cit.*, p. 285. This information is based on his interviews with Colonel Irvin Pauliak, Major V. F. Stefansky, and Dr. Pavel Simunic of the Military Historical institute of Slovakia, Bratislava, 1984.

384. *Na Rubieży* (Wrocław) 2, no. 12, (1995): 7–20, 22–24, 25–26. These villages are located in the county of Brody, the province of Tarnopol. The Huta Pieniacka article contains lists of victims and eyewitness accounts.

385. In Prus, *Melnykowcy*, p. 36.

386. Littman, in S. Friedman, *Holocaust Literature*, pp. 282–83. The references to Styrkul and his quote can be found in Styrkul, *We Accuse*, pp. 246–48, 134–35; Heike's words are in Heike, p. 22; the quote regarding Podkamień comes from Wacław Szetelnicki, *Zapomniany lwowski bohater ks. St. Frankl 1903–1944* (Rome: P.U.G., 1983), p. 132; the next quote can be found in Ainsztein (1975), p. 254; the reference to Huta Pieniacka comes from Zvi Weigler, "Two Polish Villages Razed for Extending Help to Jews and Partisans," *Yad Vashem Bulletin* (Jerusalem) 1 (April 1957): 18–20.

387. Littman, in S. Friedman, *Holocaust Literature*, p. 287.

388. Józef Fajkowski and Jan Religa, *Zbrodnie hitlerowskie na wsi polskiej 1939–1945* (Warszawa: Książka i Wiedza, 1981), pp. 142, 326, 407ff., 410ff., 414f., 429, 459, 464. All entries have archival references. The entries for June and July 1943 most probably involved the volunteer police regiments of the SS-Galizien, not the division itself. See Czesław Madajczyk (ed.), *Zamojszczyzna—Sonderlaboratorium SS. Zbiór dokumentów polskich i niemieckich z okresu okupacji hitlerowskiej* (Warszawa: Ludowa Spółdzielnia Wydawnicza, 1977), 2: 128 and editorial note 3.

389. Szcześniak and Szota, pp. 126–27; Komański, pp. 10, 13. The AK field reports that follow may be found in Czarnocka et al., pp. 383, 445, 447, 458, 507–8.

390. File T-175-94, National Military Archives, Washington, D.C.

391. Heike, p. 81.

392. Ibid., p. 5. See also Littlejohn, *Foreign Legions of the Third Reich*, 4: 29, 33ff.

393. Heike, p. 155 n. 13.

394. Ibid.

395. See Poliszczuk, *Gorzka prawda*, pp. 312 ff. Littman, in S. Friedman, *Holocaust Literature*, pp. 283–84, states:

> In the spring of 1944 five Ukrainian police regiments were incorporated into the division, police regiments 4, 5, 6, 7, and 8. The presence of these police regiments is of key importance in determining the true nature of the Halychyna Division. First, one must understand the special role of these German-recruited and German-directed police units. It was these locally recruited police groups that served as the chief executioners for the mobile killing squads known as *Einsatzgruppen*. They constituted the main force for tracking down those who fled to the forest and for wiping out entire villages suspected of sheltering partisans. Their ruthlessness and brutality were legend. In a period of eighteen months they succeeded in murdering one and a half million Jews in occupied Soviet territory. In some cases German officers, unable to stomach their cruelty, asked that the police regiments be withdrawn from their theater of operations.

396. Wiesenthal, pp. 34, 205.

397. Archiwum Zakładu Historii Partii, Delegatura Rządu RP na Kraj, 202 AM/1640/10, as quoted by Torzecki, *Kwestia Ukraińska w polityce III Rzeszy*, p. 326.

398. Littman, in S. Friedman, *Holocaust Literature*, p. 291. The title of Michael Yaremko's work is *From Separation to Unity* (Toronto: Shevchenko Scientific Society, 1967).

399. Himmler's talk in Neuhammer, May 16, 1944. See Torzecki, *Kwestia Ukraińska w polityce III Rzeszy, op. cit.*, p. 326.

400. Dear, p. 1047; G. Stein, pp. 187–88.

401. Agencja Informacyjna "*Wieś*" 33 (spec.) (Warszawa), September 9, 1943, in Szcześniak and Szota, p. 147.

402. See Kosyk, p. 308–10. Turowski and Siemaszko, p. 38, tell us that in March 1943 the Ukrainian Nationalists murdered a Polish family in Orżew. The only survivor was a small child who hid under a bed.

403. Kosyk, pp. 303–4.

404. Ibid., p. 304. According to Kamil Barański, beginning that fall the Germans shot the following number of UPA members in Stanisławów: 22 on October 23, 1943; 13 on October 30, 1943; 25 on November 17, 1943; 21 on March 11, 1944; and 30 between March 14 and March 20, 1944. Barański, p. 172. Similar executions were said to have occurred in Kołomyja: 32 on September 10, 1943; 15 on December 11, 1943; and 18 on Januray 11, 1944. Ibid., p. 214. Although Barański's work includes a large bibliography, unfortunately the author does not specifically reference these executions or provide any explanation for why they took place.

405. Peter J. Potichnyj, "The Ukrainian Insurgent Army (UPA) and the German Authorities," in Torke and Himka, p. 168. His note 18 on p. 174 contains references to a few underground publications from 1943–44 that provide information on this subject matter. See also Yuriy Tys-Krokhmaliuk, *UPA Warfare in Ukraine: Strategical, Tactical, and Organizational Problems of Ukrainian Resistance in World War II* (New York: Society of Veterans of Ukrainian Insurgent Army of the United States and Canada and St. George the Victorious Association of Veterans of Ukrainian Insurgent Army in Europe, 1972). Dębski, pp. 107–21 also has a section on UPA's skirmishes with the Germans — skirmishes that, he says, began toward the end of March 1943, right after the defection of the Ukrainian auxiliary police. His summary is based on the Ukrainian "Chronicle of the Ukrainian Insurgent Army," *Litopys Ukrainskoi Povstanskoi Armii* (Toronto: Vydavnytstvo Litopys UPA, 1977–83), which contains an analysis of reported encounters between the UPA and the Germans. According to Dębski, these accounts are lacking in detail and portray the UPA as always victorious, as always able to amass a great deal of German arms, and as always the protector of the people against pillage and extermination. According to his count (p. 117), based on *Litopys* data, the UPA was said to have eliminated 2,661 German soldiers!

406. Kamenetsky, *Hitler's Occupation of Ukraine*, pp. 80–81.

407. Ainsztein, pp. 359–60.

408. Kamenetsky, *Hitler's Occupation of Ukraine*, p. 72.

409. Kosyk, p. 309.

410. Heinz Hohne, *The Order of the Death's Head: The Story of Hitler's SS* (London: Pan Books, 1972), p. 385. Hohne bases his thesis on the Nazi source *Archiv für Publizistische Arbeit*, August 26, 1943.

411. Louis P. Lochner (ed.), *The Goebbels Diaries* (Garden City: Doubleday, 1948), p. 355.

412. Kobylański, p. 32.

413. J. A. Armstrong, pp. 134–35.

414. Łuczak, p. 350.

415. Spector, *The Holocaust of Volhynian Jews*, p. 270.

416. In Franciszek Połomski, *Aspekty rasowe w postępowaniu z robotnikami przymusowymi i jeńcami wojennymi III Rzeszy, 1933–1945* (Wrocław: Zakład Narodowy im. Ossolińskich, 1976), p. 97 n.

417. Spector, "Ukrainska Povstanska Armyia," in Gutman, pp. 1531–32; Torzecki, *Kwestia Ukraińska w polityce III Rzeszy*, p. 328. However, a May 10, 1944, AK field report, which speaks of the concentration of UPA forces in five regions of Eastern Poland, contradicts this position. According to that report, at least as of May 10, there was continued German-Ukrainian Nationalist collaboration. The report states: "It has been confirmed that the Germans are helping and cooperating with UPA units." In Czarnocka et al., p. 443.

418. In Dallin, p. 622.

419. Spector, *The Holocaust of Volhynian Jews*, p. 272.

420. Torzecki, *Kwestia Ukraińska w polityce III Rzeszy*, p. 326.

421. Littlejohn, *Foreign Legions of the Third Reich*, 4: 48.

422. Torzecki, *Kwestia Ukraińska w polityce III Rzeszy*, p. 336.

423. See J. A. Armstrong, pp. 140–41.

424. Torzecki, *Kwestia Ukraińska w polityce III Rzeszy*, p. 333.

425. Ibid., p. 334. Littlejohn, *The Patriotic Traitors*, p. 316, notes, "'Galician' workers in Germany were not required to submit to the indignity of wearing the detested *Ost* patch."

426. See Torzecki, *Kwestia Ukraińska w polityce III Rzeszy*, p. 335; J. A. Armstrong, pp. 135–36.

427. Torzecki, *Kwestia Ukraińska w polityce III Rzeszy*, pp. 337–38; J. A. Armstrong, p. 125. The Hiwis (Hilfswillige) were formed by Hitler's order of August 18, 1942. About 20 percent of

them were used for fighting, generally with the partisans. The remainder performed various services needed by the Wehrmacht and the SS. Torzecki, "Die Rolle der Zusammenarbeit," in Röhr, p. 259. Littlejohn, *The Patriotic Traitors*, p. 301, states: "In November 1941 six battalions of armed *Hiwis* were formed by Army Group Center. There were graced with the new title of *Osttruppen* (Eastern troops)—a term which became increasingly familiar. The *Wehrmacht* High Command then issued a secret order authorizing the setting up of *Osttruppen* combat groups of up to 200 men each (with indigenous officer compliment) for use against Soviet partisans."

428. Szcześniak and Szota, p. 199.

429. J. A. Armstrong, p. 142. Littlejohn, *The Patriotic Traitors*, p. 328, states:

> The Western Ukraine (Galicia), most collaborationist of all, had furnished an S.S. Division, while the German Army had established a Ukrainian equivalent of the R.O.A. known as the U.V.V.... Like its Russian counterpart the U.V.V. remained an army in name only. It was in fact only the generic term for the diverse Ukrainian military and security forces dispersed throughout the front. There may have been as many as 180,000 men in the U.V.V. (not necessarily ethnic Ukrainians, but from that region). They wore standard German army uniform distinguished by a blue and yellow arm shield bearing the Ukrainian national symbol—a trident.

430. Szcześniak and Szota, pp. 199, 202.

431. *TMWC*, 7: 273.

432. Torzecki, "Die Rolle der Zusammenarbeit," in Röhr, p. 267.

433. Heike, p. 136.

434. Dallin, p. 122.

435. Littlejohn, *Foreign Legions of the Third Reich*, 4: 41.

436. As quoted by J. A. Armstrong, p. 140.

437. Spector, *The Holocaust of Volhynian Jews*, p. 262.

438. Kamenetsky, *Hitler's Occupation of Ukraine*, p. 62. See also P. Friedman, in Marrus, p. 379, and Paldiel, p. 266.

439. According to Marples, pp. 58–59, 2.5 million Ukrainians were conscripted into the Red Army at the time of the German invasion and served on the Ukrainian front. An additional 750,000 were conscripted in the summer of 1944. See also Peter J. Potichnyj, "Ukrainians in World War II Military Formations: An Overview," in Boshyk, pp. 61–66. Potichnyj, pp. 61–62, states:

> Since the war's fiercest battles were on Ukrainian territory, it is not surprising that Ukrainians fought in various armies and military formations, in large numbers and on all fronts. In the Soviet army alone were 4.5 million citizens of Ukraine....
>
> Thousands of Ukrainians served in the Polish army of General Władysław Anders and fought with him on the British side in Egypt, Libya, and Italy. Ukrainians also joined the Polish units that advanced with the Soviet army into Poland. Czech units attached to the Allied forces and formed in the USSR had Ukrainian troops....
>
> A large number of Ukrainians served in the American and Canadian armed forces (an estimated 40,000 in the latter). They could also be found in the French Resistance.

440. I. Gartner, "Ukrainian Nationalism since World War II," in Sabrin, p. 230.

441. Loftus, p. 104.

442. Aarons and Loftus, p. 180. The authors state: "The screening was scanty. They interviewed only 200 men out of 8,272. They used camp inmates as interpreters, conducted no cross-examinations and basically asked the Ukrainians to tell them where they had been during World War II. Brigadier MacLean's 'screening team' cheerfully admitted that 'the short history of the Division was supplied entirely by the Ukrainians themselves and we had no information of any kind against which they could be checked'" (p. 194). The authors then point out, "Forty years later, in November 1988, a British All-Party Parliamentary Committee determined that the Galician SS had not received even the minimal screening required for normal immigration to Britain [from the British camp at Rimini, Italy], let alone the rigorous scrutiny promised in 1947" (p. 198).

443. The Ukrainian-American League wrote to the State Department to

> unequivocally protest plans to bring to our country people who cooperated with German fascists in terrorizing the Ukrainian, Polish and Jewish populations of Western Ukraine (formerly Poland), or who were soldiers in the SS Division "Halychyna" [Galician] which fought against the American and

> British armies in Italy, or who belonged to the armed bands which helped the German fascists in terrorizing and persecuting the people of our allied countries. They aided the Germans in the death camps in destroying not only Ukrainians, Poles and Jews, but citizens of Britain, France, and the United States.

Ibid., p. 194.

444. Christopher Simpson states:

> General Pavlo Shandruk, the leader of a Ukrainian liberation committee that had been founded under Nazi auspices, contacted Archbishop Ivan Buchko [called a "fanatical Ukrainian nationalist" by Aarons and Loftus, p. 175], a high ranking prelate in Rome specializing in Ukrainian matters for the Holy See. Shandruk pleaded with Buchko by letter to intervene on behalf of the Ukrainian soldiers who had served in SS units, particularly what Shandruk termed the "1st Ukrainian Division," which was in fact the 14th Waffen SS division "Galicia." Shandruk hoped that Archbishop Buchko might reach the Pope himself with the general's plea for mercy on behalf of his men.
>
> "Archbishop Ivan [Buchko] answered my letter very soon informing me that he had already visited the Division," Shandruk recalled later. "In a special audience (at night) the Archbishop had pleaded with His Holiness Pope Pius XII to intercede for the soldiers of the Division, who are the flower of the Ukrainian nation.... I learned from the Archbishop...that as a result of the intercession by His Holiness, the soldiers of the Division were reclassified merely as confinees [rather than prisoners of war] and Bolshevik agents were prohibited to visit their camps [*sic*]." Although the troops were still confined to the POW camp at Rimini, they were, according to Shandruk, "out of reach of Communist hands" and no longer subject to repatriation to the USSR. By the Spring of 1946 Shandruk, backed by Archbishop Buchko and the Ukrainian Relief Committee of Great Britain, had arranged with the British Government to extend "free settler" emigration status to the Ukrainian Waffen SS veterans at Rimini and to assist them in resettling in Canada, Australia, and other Commonwealth Countries.

Simpson, pp. 180–81 n. Except for the first set of brackets, the rest of the brackets are in the original note. Aarons and Loftus, p. 202, state: "The Americans quietly released their Galician SS prisoners and watched them happily track across the border to the British zone or quietly merge into the refugee population in their own zone. Across Germany the Ukrainian SS began drawing rations as 'victims of Nazi oppression.'"

445. Wiesenthal, pp. 204–5.

446. As quoted by Paul Lungin, "Author Outlines West's 'War Against the Jews,'" *Canadian Jewish News*, December 21, 1995. For an interesting report dealing with war criminals in Canada, see Honourable Jules Deschênes (Commissioner), *Commission of Inquiry on War Criminals, Report, Part I: Public* (Ottawa, Canada, December 30, 1986). The section on the SS-Galizien is on pp. 249–61.

447. Davies, *God's Playground*, p. 522. See Nicholas Bethell, *The Last Secret: The Delivery to Stalin of Over Two Million Russians by Britain and the United States* (New York: Basic Books, 1974), and Nikolai Tolstoy, *Victims of Yalta* (London: Hodder and Stoughton, 1977).

448. A related question concerns whether previously convicted felons, including UVO-OUN terrorists, should have been made to serve out the remainder of their prewar prison sentences after the war. Their "early release" was due to the German and Soviet invasions. In spite of the fact that some of them were sentenced for life, no one has ever been successfully extradited by the Polish communist government. Whether the current Polish government will attempt to reclaim those former criminals who are still alive remains to be seen.

449. "Refugee Screening Commission Report on Ukrainians in Surrendered Enemy Personnel (SEP) Camp No. 374 Italy, LACAB/18 RSC/RIC, 21 February 1947," in T. Piotrowski, *Vengeance of the Swallows*, pp. 110–11.

450. In Atle Grahl-Madsen, *The Status of Refugees in International Law*, vol. 1 (Leyden: A. W. Sijthoff, 1966), pp. 278–79. Emphasis mine.

451. Ibid., p. 279.

452. Ibid., p. 279 n. 177.

453. Ibid., pp. 279–80.

454. Littman, in S. Friedman, *Holocaust Literature*, pp. 288–89, states, "According to these criteria [i.e., those of Bradley F. Smith, *Reaching Judgment at Nuremberg* (New York: New American Library, 1979)], it is clear that a majority of the members of the Galician SS Division can be

regarded as war criminals since (1) they were volunteers, (2) they were aware of the criminal purposes for which they had been recruited, and (3) they participated in acts of violence against innocent civilians."

455. See Simpson, pp. 163–69; Conason, pp. 17–21; and Poliszczuk, *Gorzka prawda*, pp. 257–65.

456. See Gitta Sereny, "John Demjanjuk and the Failure of Justice," *New York Review of Books*, October 8, 1992, pp. 32–34.

457. In "Appendix A: Origins of the Ukrainian Division 'Galicia,'" in Heike, p. 140.

458. Document No. 129, Chief of SP and SD, "Report No. 4 from the Occupied Eastern Regions," May 22, 1942, in Kosyk, p. 572.

459. Document No. 149, Commander-in-Chief H. Geb. B., "Excerpt from Report No. 21 on the Enemy of Army Group B," October 29, 1942, Headquarters, ibid., p. 595.

460. Document No. 192, "German Memorandum on the Resistance Movement in Soviet Ukraine," November 3, 1944, ibid., p. 637.

461. Document No. 138, Chief of SP and SD, "Report No. 17 from the Occupied Eastern Regions," August 20, 1942, ibid., p. 581.

462. Document No. 182, "Letter from Koch to Rosenberg on the Subject of Resistance in the Reichskommissariat Ukraine," June 25, 1943, Równe, ibid., p. 628.

463. See, for example, Petro R. Sodol, *UPA: They Fought Hitler and Stalin: A Brief Overview of Military Aspects from the History of the Ukrainian Insurgent Army, 1942–1949* (New York: Committee for the World Convention and Reunion of Soldiers in the Ukrainian Insurgent Army, 1987).

464. Szcześniak and Szota, p. 471. According to Ukrainian Nationalist historians, Enemy No. 1 was the communists, Enemy No. 2 was the Poles who refused to leave ethnic Ukrainian lands, and enemy No 3 was the Germans in the police, the SD, and the administration. However, the OUN-UPA only attacked the Wehrmacht in "self-defense." See "U sorokovi rokovyny UPA," *Suchasnist*, no. 1–2 (261–262) (1983): 131–76, as summarized by Torzecki, "Die Rolle der Zusammenarbeit," in Röhr, pp. 267–68 n. 49.

465. Document No. 138, Chief of SP and SD, "Report No. 17 from the Occupied Eastern Regions," August 20, 1942, in Kosyk, p. 581.

466. Sabrin, pp. 241–42.

467. J. A. Armstrong, p. 219.

468. From Mykola Mikhnovskyi, *Samostiina Ukraina* (Independent Ukraine), in Reshetar, p. 2.

469. In Poliszczuk, *Gorzka prawda*, pp. 256–57.

470. Ibid., p. 224.

471. Ibid., p. 256.

472. Ibid., p. 90.

473. As quoted by Poliszczuk, *Hirka pravda*, p. 109, and Poliszczuk, *Gorzka prawda*, pp. 95–96. Poliszczuk, who is well-versed both in Polish and Ukrainian, argues that the Ukrainian phrase *povne usunennia* (complete removal) also means, in effect, "complete annihilation." The phrase corresponds to what we understand as "ethnic cleansing."

I have translated the terms *okupantiv* and *zaimantsiv*, occurring in the first line of the proclamation and resolution, respectively, as "occupants." The sense of the latter Ukrainian term, however, is better captured by the English word "squatters," or those who take or occupy a land illegally and unjustly.

474. In Poliszczuk, *Gorska prawda*, p. 105.

475. In Shmuel Spector, "The Jews of Volhynia and Their Reaction to Extermination," *Yad Vashem Studies* (Jerusalem) 15 (1983): 160, as quoted by Gilbert, p. 195.

476. Torzecki, *Kwestia ukraińska w polityce III Rzeszy*, pp. 192, 196. See also T. Piotrowski, *Vengeance of the Swallows*, p. 61, and Tadeusz Piotrowski, *Polish-Ukrainian Relations During World War II: Ethnic Cleansing in Volhynia and Eastern Galicia* (Toronto: Adam Mickiewicz Foundation, 1995). Spector, *The Holocaust of the Volhynian Jews*, p. 247, notes, "The nationalist Ukrainian administration was most hostile to the Poles; next to 'death to the Jews' the most popular slogan shouted during the popular marches and processions of the Ukrainians was 'death to the *lakhiv* (Poles).'"

477. A Chief of SP and SD report states that the Ukrainian Nationalist movement sought to create a Ukrainian state "governed by the Nationalists and unaffiliated with any other nation. It [the movement] was directed against the authorities *and citizens* of the nations which occupied ethnic Ukrainian lands." Bundesarchiv, sygn. R58/698, Der Chef der Sicherheistpolizei und des SD—Komandostab, Maldungen aus den besetzten Ostgebieten, as quoted by Władysław Filar, "Zbrodnicza działalność OUN-UPA przeciwko ludności polskiej na Wołyniu w latach 1942–1944," *Semper Fidelis* (Wrocław) 5, no. 28, (September-October 1995): 3–4. Emphasis mine.

478. In *Karta* 8 (1992): 65 and *Semper Fidelis* (Wrocław) 1, no. 18 (January-February 1994): 35.

479. Akcja "Wisła" involved the April-August 1947 forced resettlement of 140,000 Lemkos and Ukrainians from the southeastern borderlands of Communist Poland to the prewar German territories in the west and north of Poland. It was precipitated by the continued UPA terrorist activities therein, including the March 28, 1947, ambush which resulted in the death of General Karol Świerczewski. The following summary comes from Eugeniusz Misiło (ed.), "The UPA in Light of Polish Documents, Book One: The Military Court of the Operation Group 'Wisła,'" *LitopysUkrainskoi Povstanskoi Armii*, vol. 22 (1992), pp. 33–34:

> According to Polish Army General Staff's data 140,575 persons were exiled, 655 members of the UPA and OUN were killed and 1,466 captured before July 31, 1947. According to the Ministry of Public Security between the beginning of the operation "Wisła" and September 31, 1947, 2,274 Ukrainians accused of belonging to the armed underground were arrested. From among them 851 were arraigned in court, 1,648 were released and 115 were under interrogation. According to available information [from the Ukrainian Archive in Warsaw] 3,873 persons were sent to concentration camp in Jaworzno. Altogether 372 persons were sentenced to death in 1947. There were only 31 cases of pardon.
>
> In 1948 there were 75 death sentences — these were the summary trials in Przemysl and Rzeszow of 112 UPA soldiers, taken prisoner in summer of 1947 in Czechoslovakia while attempting to cross to the American occupation zone in Germany, and deported on May 22, 1948 to Poland. In Warsaw, the trial of 21 soldiers of the "Khrin" and "Stakh" units was held. They were accused of participation in gen Swierczewski's ambush and 9 of them were sentenced to death. In Olsztyn, 11 death sentences were pronounced against members of the underground's civilian network and those members of the dispersed UPA detachments from Tomaszow and Hrubieszow area, who succeeded in penetrating to Olsztyn area together with the exiled civilian population.
>
> The tragic list of UPA soldiers executed between 1944 and 1956 ends with Col. Myroslav Onyshkevych, "Orest," the UPA commander of "Zakerzon" area, who was sentenced to death on June 3 and executed on July 6, 1950 and with Petro Fedoriw, "Dalnych," chief of security service of "Zakerzon" area, sentenced on January 20 and executed on April 11, 1950. Mykhailo Soltys, "Woron," sentenced in 1951 and Wolodymyr Morochko, members of the security service (BSB), were both pardoned.
>
> The last famous UPA trial that ended with a death sentence, took place on March 1961 in Przemysl against Ivan Shpontak, "Zalizniak," commander of the 27th tactical military district, who was arrested in Slovakia and deported to Poland. The State Council commuted his death sentence to life imprisonment and, on February 26, 1970 to 25 years in prison. "Zalizniak" was released from prison on November 4, 1981. He was the last and the longest incarcerated UPA soldier in Poland.

Misilo presents the Ukrainian perspective on Akcja "Wisła." For a contrasting view, see Edward Prus, *Operacja "Wisła"* (Wrocław: Nortom, 1994), and Władysław Filar, *Przed akcją "Wisła" był Wołyń* (Warszawa: Światowy Związek Żołnierzy Armii Krajowej Okręg Wołyń, 1997).

480. Łuczak, p. 405. At its height the AK Wołyń had 7,326 men and 126 officers. It lost approximately 2,000 of its men in Wołyń.

481. Personal communiqué from Władysław Siemaszko. See also Łucjusz Włodkowski, "Bezustanne drażnienie," *Gazeta Wyborcza*, August 9, 1995. J. Dobrucka, who hails from the Równe area of Wołyń, "miraculously escaped death at the hands of the Ukrainians three times." She recalls that on one of those occassions, while she was hiding in the attic of a railway station with other women and children in Jeziorany, the men, with the assistance of a Hungarian unit, were able to repel an all-night Ukrainian Nationalist attack and thus save their lives. J. Dobrucka, "Letters to the Editor," *Gazeta* (Toronto), March 5, 1996.

482. Aleksander Korman, "Polscy 'Istriebitiele' z lat 1944–1945 w Małopolsce Wschodniej i na Wołyniu," *Semper Fidelis* (Wrocław) 3, no. 26 (May-June 1995): 7–11; Jerzy Węgierski, *Armia Krajowa na południowych i wschodnich przedpolach Lwowa* (Kraków: Platan, 1994), pp. 365–66; Adam Peretiatkowicz, *Polska samoobrona w okolicach Łucka* (Katowice: Ośrodek Badań Społeczno-

Kulturowych Towarzystwa Zachęty Kultury, 1995), pp. 98–100.

483. Janik, p. 286, refers to this forced migration eastward. Speaking of his own parents, but other Poles as well, he states, "Here they felt much safer than in the territories of Western Ukraine which were almost entirely under the control of the criminal underground of the Ukrainian Nationalists." Although tens of thousands of Poles lived in Soviet Ukraine, they were not subjected there to ethnic cleansing. See Wroński, in Cybulski, p. 14.

484. Władysław Filar, "Likwidatorzy z UPA," *Gazeta Wyborcza*, July 14, 1995.

485. In answer to Jan Łukaszów (Tadeusz Olszański), who states in his "Walki polsko-ukraińskie 1943–1947," *Zeszyty Historyczne* (Paris) 90 (1989): 166, 187, that neither the term "genocide" nor even the qualified term "selective genocide" should be used to describe the events in Eastern Poland during and after World War II (the UPA tried only to "depolonize, not exterminate the Polish population"), I quote this unanimously accepted article (II) of the United Nations Convention (December 9, 1948), with which he, a lawyer, should be familiar.

> In the present Convention, genocide means any of the following acts committed with the intent to destroy, in whole or in part, a national, ethnical, racial or religious group, as such:
> (a) killing members of the group;
> (b) causing serious bodily or mental harm to members of the group;
> (c) deliberately inflicting on the group conditions calculated to bring about its physical destruction in whole or in part;
> (d) imposing measures intended to prevent births within the group;
> (e) forcibly transferring children of the group to another group.

This reference appears in Ian A. Hunter, "Putting History on Trial: The Ukrainian Famine of 1932–33," in Honsberger, p. 158. Hunter's article deals with Stalin's starvation of the *Ukrainian* population during the 1930s. The petitioner was the World Congress of Free Ukrainians. The issue: Was it premeditated "genocide"?

Using the above-mentioned criteria, a seven-member commission identified the three essential elements required for "genocide":

> (1) a national, ethnical, racial, or religious group;
> (2) an intent to destroy, in whole or in part, this group "as such"; and
> (3) one or more of the specific acts enumerated in points (a) to (e) of Article II.

On deliberation, the commission concluded that the first and third conditions were "obviously fulfilled" in respect to the famine. There was some debate and dissension, however, regarding the second condition: whether there was really an "intent to destroy" the group "as such." In other words, was there "an intent to destroy" the Ukrainian people? (At that time, multitudes of non–Ukrainians within and outside Ukraine starved as well, for example, the 1 million in Kazakhstan and North Caucasus.)

The conclusion was that although there was no "serious evidence," no "decisive proof" of intent against an ethnic group "as such," the commission decided that "in view of all the substantiating data, it seems likely that such an intent existed" and that "the constituent elements of *genocide* were in existence at that time." The majority of the commission, therefore, determined that Joseph Stalin must bear personal responsibility for the *crime of genocide.*

If the great Ukrainian famine constituted an attempt at genocide, then the Polish slaughter (called "depolonization" by Łukaszów-Olszański) under the clear and unambiguous guidance and direction of the OUN, must certainly fit that description as well. If—in accordance with the wishes of the World Congress of Free Ukrainians, and rightfully so — the leader of the Soviet Union is to be held responsible for the deaths caused by the famine, should not the leadership of the OUN-UPA, in addition to the perpetrators themselves, also be held responsible for its members' atrocities?

It matters little that later, when things got out of hand, the OUN "made an effort" to stem the tide with its "peace negotiations" and "signed protocols" (Łukaszów-Olszański, "Walki polsko-ukraińskie 1943–1947," *Zeszyty Historyczne* [Paris] 90 [1989]: 176–77) with the nation which did not issue a similar death contract against the Ukrainians. Even if these efforts were made in good faith, pleading with the hungry lions (members of the UPA) once the Christians (civilians) were already in the arena did no good. As we know from Greek tragedy, once set loose, the cycle of evil must run its full course, and to paraphrase Shakespeare's Mark Antony, that evil will now always live on after them. These feeble attempts on the part of the OUN, however, were not made in good faith. They remind one of Hitler's similar and many public overtures to peace. We should forget about these public posturings and consider the actual and terrible deeds of the OUN-UPA up to the end of the war and beyond.

In the final analysis, these subtle distinctions drawn by academicians among words such as "depolonization," "genocide," "holocaust," and "ethnic cleansing" do not matter. What matters is that tens, if not hundreds, of thousands of innocent civilians were subjected to unimaginable terror, underwent unspeakable tortures, and met with grisly deaths simply because they happened to belong to the "wrong" nationality or religion. Let us forget about the words and remember the people, the people, and once more the people.

I offer that last thought in contradistinction to Mykola Stsiborskyi's (in Kuropas, p. 237) elaboration of Dmytro Andrievskyi's nationalistic agenda. "The nation, the nation, and once more the nation," wrote Stsiborskyi.

> The nation — rather than international and cosmopolitan delusion.
>
> The nation — instead of "eternal and universal human rights and brotherhood."
>
> The nation — with a will to self-government and a leadership which is not given to hysterical prostration and spiritual servility in the name of "humanity."
>
> The nation — as the conclusive and culminating objective of all political striving.

And what, pray tell, Mr. Stsiborskyi, is the nation *for*?

486. Turowski and Siemaszko, p. 158. The type of pioneering research done by Turowski and Siemaszko for Wołyń was carried out for Eastern Galicia by Urban and by Szetelnicki, *Zapomniany lwowski bohater*, pp. 117–39.

487. Report of an RP delegate from Wołyń, in Siwicki, 2: 137. It is unclear whether it was the Banderowcy or the Bulbowcy that began the slaughter. Various testimonies of survivors claim that Taras Bulba's group began the ethnic-cleansing campaign in the Sarny-Kostopol region. See, for example, Ewa Kujańska's story in T. Piotrowski, *Vengeance of the Swallows*, pp. 68–72. Torzecki, *Kwestia ukraińska w politice III Rzeszy*, p. 294, believes that it was the Bulbowcy who began it all. For a Jewish account of *Bulbowcy* attacks in Maciejów, a town halfway between Luboml and Kowel in the province of Wołyń, see Jacob Biber, *Survivors: A Personal Story of the Holocaust* (San Bernardino, CA: Borgo Press, 1986), pp. 145ff.

An AK field report (in Czarnocka et al., pp. 4–5) dated May 4, 1943, reads as follows:

> General Rowecki to Central Headquarters:
> Anarchy in Wołyń — Murder of Poles.
> Radiogram
>
> Wanda 6 — O. VI L. dz. 2366/43
> May 4, 1943 — Received: May 12, 1943
> Read: May 15, 1943
>
> The Situation in Wołyń
>
> In March [1943], the province of Wołyń was engulfed by anarchy which began at the end of February due to the activity of the nationalist, anti–Soviet bandits of Bulba-Borovets in the county of Sarny. They spread to the Kostopol county reaching a numerical strength of 4,000. This action was aimed primarily against the Poles: foresters and settlers. The toll of those murdered is estimated at 800.
>
> The Polish people are seeking shelter mainly in Sarny, Kostopol, Janowa Dolina and Łuck.
>
> Under German pressure, the Bulbowcy withdrew into the forest where they fight the Soviet partisans.
>
> On March 19–25 [1943], Ukrainians in the Schutzmannlandesdienst and Bahnschutz — about 6,000 in all — absconded into the forests. The wave of desertions began in the East. On March 14, the Ukrainian police school left Maciejów.
>
> The security service has ceased to exist. Reinforced German garrisons protect only railroad tracks and administrative centers.
>
> The Bulbowcy are deserting the police and peasants are attacking government properties and Polish settlers. About 200 Poles were killed.
>
> Up to now, things are quiet in the western counties.
>
> The Germans are taking almost no steps to control the anarchy. They are issuing proclamations to the deserters calling for their return and offering amnesty until April 25. They have appealed to the Poles to join the police — negative reaction.
>
> The Poles have gained control over the initial panic. They have placed the children in

the larger settlements. People capable of work and defense continue their spring field work [farming].

The commandant of the region is organizing self-defense centers. In answer to the Ukrainians, he has declared a willingness to live in peace with them. At the same time, he warned them that in the event of a repeat performance on their part, repressions would follow.

The Wołynian Ukrainian intelligentsia repudiates these actions calling them escapades of youth.

I am investigating the reasons for these actions.

The German version attributes these outbreaks to the Banderowcy whose organizational network was threatened by the anticipated disarming of the Ukrainian police.

Undoubtedly, the influence of Soviet propaganda, which is persistently urging the national elements in the occupied territories to launch a premature uprising, is also at play here.

Kalina 693

For additional references in AK field reports regarding the Ukrainian-Nationalist ethnic-cleansing campaign for the period April 1943 to July 1944, see Czarnocka et al., pp. 58–60, 63, 64, 68, 217, 258, 326, 345–50, 404, 417, 430, 437, 443, 445, 447, 458, 460, 465, 473, 482, 488, 544.

By the summer of 1943, the Banderowcy took complete charge of the ethnic cleansing campaign. By the fall of that year, after their attacks on Bulba's and Melnyk's men, only one faction of the UPA remained, that of the OUN-B.

488. Agnieszka Muzyka, "Relacja świadka Agnieszki Muzyki," *Na Rubieży* (Wrocław) 2, no. 3, (1993): 15.

489. P. Friedman, in Marrus, p. 391; Ryszard Torzecki, "Postawa metropolity," *Więź* (July-August 1988): 103.

490. In Giertych, *Komunikaty*, p. 349.

491. P. Friedman, in Marrus, p. 391, notes, "Only the last paragraph referred to the fratricidal wars among the Ukrainians (an allusion to the fight between the Bandera and Melnyk followers.)" Friedman also points out (p. 369), "In this fratricidal war several high dignitaries of the Greek-Orthodox Church lost their lives."

492. Torzecki, "Postawa metropolity," p. 103. For an exchange of correspondence between Archbishop Bolesław Twardowski and Archbishop Andrei Sheptytsky, as well as a commentary on this exchange, see Fr. Józef Wołczański, "Korespondencja Arcybiskupa Bolesława Twardowskiego z Arcybiskupem Andrzejem Szeptickim w latach 1943–1944," *Przegląd Wschodni* 2–6 (1992–93): pp. 465–84. See also Torzecki, "Kontakty polsko-ukraińskie," p. 343.

493. According to Olszański, *Historia Ukrainy XX wieku*, p. 185, the order to "depolonize" all Ukrainian "ethnographic" territories was issued by Roman Dmytro Klachkivskyi.

494. As quoted by Filar, *Zbrodnicza działalność OUN-UPA*, p. 5. The source of this report is given as Centralne Arch. MO Federacji Rosyjskiej, f. 1, op. 23, spr. 523.

495. Otaman Taras Bulba-Borovets, *Armiia bez derzhavy. Slava i trahediia ukrainskoho povstanskoho rukhu. Spohady* (Winnipeg: Nakladom Tovarystva "Volyn," 1981), p. 272, as quoted by Poliszczuk, *Gorzka prawda*, p. 260. Emphasis mine.

496. As quoted by P. Friedman, in Marrus, pp. 369–70 n. 19.

497. Mykola Lebed, *UPA: Ukrainska Povstanska Armiia* (Presove Biuro UHVR, 1946), p. 39, as quoted in Poliszczuk, *Gorzka prawda*, p. 260.

498. In Szcześniak and Szota, p. 173, and "Dokumenty z okresu mordowania Polaków w Małopolsce Wschodniej w czasie ostatniej wojny," *Biuletyn Koło Lwowian* no. 43 (June 1982): 8, respectively. The second notice, dated May 11, 1944, is a photocopy of the original notice, which was in Cyrillic.

499. Archiwum SBU Obwodu Wołyńskiego, d. no. 11315, I, pt. II, p. 16.

500. As quoted by Filar, "Zbrodnicza działalność OUN-UPA," p. 5. The source of this report is Archiwum Part. Instytutu Historii Partii przy CK Kompartii Ukrainy, "Osobyi Sektor—Sekretnaia Chast," f. 57, op. 4, spr. 191, s. 118.

501. Ibid. His source: Militararchiv, sygn. H 3/474, Amt Ausland/Abwehr Dienststelle Walli III, Nr. D 5800/43 g/B/AUSW. 273, Feststelungen zur Bandenlage, Q. U. den 13.7.1943.

502. In Siwicki, 2: 109, 173.

503. Petro R. Sodol, "UPA—The Ukrainian Insurgent Army: An Overview," *Ukrainian Quarterly* 51, no. 2–3 (summer-fall 1995): 146. The term "democratic" did not appear in OUN official documents until 1951.

504. Yurkevich, "Organization of Ukrainian Nationalists," in Struk, 3: 709.

505. For references on these exhumations, see *Na Rubieży* (Wrocław) 2, no. 3 (1993), pp. 17–24; Romuald Wernik, "Martytui viventes obligant," *Głos Polski* (Toronto), October 23, 1993, and Romuald Wernik, "Historyków obowiązuje prawda," ibid., October 15, 1994.

506. In Czarnocka et al., p. 417.

507. In Zdzisław Konieczny (ed.), *Źródła do dziejów regionu przemyskiego w latach 1944–1949* (Przemyśl: Wojewódzkie Archiwum Państwowe w Przemyślu, 1979), p. 67.

508. Subtelny, *Ukraine: A History*, p. 475, for example, states, "Ukrainians claim that massacres of their people began earlier, in 1942, when Poles wiped out thousands of Ukrainian villagers in the predominantly Polish areas of Kholm [Chełm], and that they continued in 1944–45 among the defenseless Ukrainian minority west of the San River." Peter Potichnyj, "'Akcja Wisła': The Forcible Relocation of the Ukrainian Population in Poland," *Ukrainian Quarterly* 44, no. 1–2 (spring-summer 1988): 78, states, "In Hrubeshiv [Hrubieszów] county alone more than 2,000 Ukrainians were killed by the Polish underground in 1942–1944." Unfortunately, the first author provides no supporting documentation for his claim, and the documentation of the second author does not support his claim that Poles began a campaign of ethnic cleansing of Ukrainians in 1942. See the following note. Moreover, a comparison of the adjusted 1931 census figures for Ukrainians in Lublin province (123,000) and the German wartime statistics with the number of Ukrainians "repatriated" to Soviet Ukraine in 1944–46 (190,734) and the number resettled in Akcja "Wisła" (44,726) does not support a conclusion of a widespread massacre or ethnic cleansing of the Ukrainian population of that province. The former number (123,000) is based on J. Tomaszewski, p. 78; the latter numbers are based on Eugeniusz Misiło (ed.), *Akcja "Wisła." Dokumenty* (Warszawa: Archiwum Ukraińskie, 1993), pp. 17, 32.

509. Evhen Pasternak provides a listing of the attacked Ukrainian villages in Hrubieszów county. No attacks were listed in 1942. There were five in 1943: the first four took place on May 26, the last on October 27. Evhen Pasternak, *Narys istorii Kholmshchyny i Pidliashshia (Novishi chasy)* (Winnipeg: Research Institute of Volyn, 1968), pp. 425–26, appendix 16. For a Polish translation, see Siwicki, 3: 126–28. See also Veryha, document no. 5, p. 225, which lists attacks on three villages in May 1943, at least two of which are the same as in Pasternak but with different dates (Mołożów, May 6, and Strzelce, May 29). According to Madajczyk, *Zamojszczyzna*, 1: 411–12, 443, the Polish population had been forcibly expelled from these villages.

510. See, "Do ludności ukraińskiej zamieszkałej na terenie pow. Hrubieszowskiego," in Veryha, document no. 2, pp. 214–15. For implementation, see document no. 5, pp. 224–26.

Torzecki states, "I have recently demonstrated that one cannot consider the occurrences in Lubelszczyzna [Lublin area] as the beginning of the bloody wars because they had a different background and were completely inspired by the Nazis of [SS General Odilo] Globocnik." Torzecki, "Postawa Metropolity," p. 105. See also his article "Z istorii polsko-ukrainskykh vzaiemovidnosyn na Lublinshchyni," *Nashe Slovo* (Warszawa) 25 (June 21, 1987) and 26 (June 28, 1987); Mikołaj Terleś, *Ethnic Cleansing of Poles in Volhynia and Eastern Galicia, 1942–1946* (Toronto: Alliance of the Polish Eastern Provinces, 1993), p. 67; Wojciech Sulewski, *Lasy w ogniu. Zamojszczyzna, 1939–1944* (Warszawa: Czytelnik, 1962), pp. 182–85; Wardzyńska, *Formacja Wachmannschaften des SS-*, pp. 29–31; and especially Madajczyk, *Zamojszczyzna*, vol. 1.

The Poles were expelled from Zamojszczyzna by the SS, Gestapo, German gendarmes, the Volksdeutsche, and Ukrainians in German service. See "Zbrodnie niemieckie w Zamojszczyźnie," in *Biuletyn Głównej Komisji Badania Zbrodni Niemieckich w Polsce* 2 (1947): 45–120. Some of them wound up in transit camps and holding camps, many in concentration camps and prisons; others were left to fend for themselves as best they could. In addition, many Poles were sent to the Reich for forced labor, and children with Aryan characteristics were abducted for Germanization programs. Madajczyk, *Zamojszczyzna*, 1: 7, states:

> In all, tens of thousands of Polish peasants were deported to [concentration] camps: 16,000 to Majdanek, 2,000 to Auschwitz; tens of thousands, partly from the camps, were diverted for forced labor in the Reich. 4,500 children were deported to Germany for Germanization. Persons who were in no condition to report to collection centers were killed. In order to terrorize the people or in reprisal for opposition, public executions "for show" were conducted or entire villages were pacified. Several dozen villages shared the lot of the Czech Lidice and worse, since all of

their inhabitants were murdered and the settlements burned.

The Ukrainians from these areas were also resettled, but mostly on the seized Polish farmsteads in the surrounding areas. (By German order, the collaborators and their families received preferential treatment. The order stated, "It is forbidden to treat them like Poles." See document in "Zbrodnie Niemieckie w Zamojszczyźnie," p. 110 and p. 97.) Concurrently, German settlers were brought in from Rumania, Bulgaria, Bessarabia, Yugoslavia, Croatia, and the Soviet Union and given the vacated households and farms. To protect their people, the Germans planned to leave a cordon of Ukrainian population to the north (Chełm county), to the east (the eastern part of Hrubieszów county), and to the south (the southern part of Tomaszów county)—areas that already contained a significant Ukrainian minority. (This was to be a temporary arrangement to facilitate German colonization. Later, like the Poles, the Ukrainians were to be removed from this entire area.) The Ukrainian police and local Ukrainian authorities (appointed by the Germans) collaborated in this German ethnic-cleansing program (see pp. 54–58, 78-83, 86, 88–90, 93–96, 98–100), hence the Polish underground's decision to strike at these agents. This is verified in Veryha, documents no. 5 (pp. 224–26) and no. 10 (pp. 236–37).

In addition, Poles who were released from transit and holding camps often made their way back to the area of the villages from which they had been expelled and joined displaced Poles who had escaped to the forests to avoid being seized by the Germans. From there, hoping to drive off the Germans *and* Ukrainians who had taken over the farms, the Poles engaged in harassment and raids directed against them.

I take exception, therefore, to the unsubstantiated claims of those Ukrainian writers who falsely accuse the Poles of conducting ethnic cleansing of Ukrainians in Zamojszczyzna at this time (1942) and of starting the "fratricidal conflict" ("Polish-Ukrainian War") that engulfed Poland's southeastern territories. See, for example, Pasternak, pp. 273–74; Veryha, p. 185; Lev Shankovskyi, "Ukrainska Povstancha Armiia," in *Istoriia ukrainskoho viiska* (Winnipeg: Ivan Tyktor, 1953), pp. 697–98; and Kosyk, p. 381.

To be sure, Polish-Ukrainian relations in Zamojszczyzna deteriorated considerably during the following summer, when the expulsions of Poles resumed. A Polish document dated July 29, 1943 (No. 317 in Madajczyk, *Zamojszczyzna*, 2: 128, noted: "In place of the expelled Poles, the Germans are bringing in Ukrainians from Eastern Galicia (Małopolska Wschodnia) to Biłgoraj county, who argue and fight among themselves for the best farmsteads. Unverified sources report that about 4,000 Ukrainians from the SS-Schützendivision 'Galizien' are taking part in the pacification action in the Lublin region." (Ibid., editorial note 3, states, "The 1st battalion of the 5th volunteer police regiment of the SS 'Galicia' participated in this action.")

That fall, events in eastern Zamojszczyzna took a further turn for the worse when UPA forces, having decimated the non-Ukrainian population of Wołyń, began to penetrate that region as well. By that time, no doubt, their reputation (as in Eastern Galicia, the next target of their atrocities) had preceded them. According to Madajczyk, atrocities were also perpetrated by that part of the Ukrainian police remaining in the service of the Germans. Ibid., 1: 7.

511. Klukowski, *Diary*, p. 229.

512. Ibid., p. 254.

513. Ibid., p. 258.

514. Ibid., p. 272.

515. Ibid., p. 273.

516. Ibid., p. 305.

517. Ibid., p. 310.

518. Ibid., p. 324.

519. With the exception of the first point (see T. Piotrowski, *Vengeance of the Swallows*, p. 37), this summary is based on Torzecki, *Kwestia ukraińska w polityce III Rzeszy*, pp. 170, 290–92, and Prus, *UPA*, pp. 14–20. Prus bases his comments in point no. 9 on the work of a former UPA officer, Kostiantyn Smovskyi: "He [Smovskyi] states emphatically that the Banderowcy were firmly convinced from the outset that their actions would bring great devastation. For this reason, as 'local patriots,' they did not want to turn Galicia into charred ruins, preferring instead that that ruined territory would be 'Orthodox' Wołyń." The title of Smovskyi's work is *Spohady uchasnyka banderivskoi UPA* (Mt. Dale, NY: Nasha Batkivshchyna, 1982). The passage to which Prus refers is on p. 10. Smovskyi also states that the population of Wołyń was unfavorably disposed (*neprykhylna*) toward the Banderowcy.

520. Peretiatkowicz, p. 138.

521. Ibid., p. 52.

522. In a recent article, Ryszard Torzecki, "Gdzie Sicz, gdzie Wisła," *Gazeta Wyborcza*, Sep-

tember 19, 1995, submits the estimate of 80,000 to 100,000.

523. The editors of *Na Rubieży*, a historical quarterly published by the Wrocław-based Stowarzyszenie Upamiętnienia Zbrodni Ukraińskich Nacjonalisów, have been gathering and publishing information on specific counties, villages, and towns for several years now. For testimonies, see Myśliwski and Garlicki, and Stanisław Biskupski (comp.), *Świadkowie mówią* (Warszawa: Światowy Związek Żołnierzy Armii Krajowej Okręg Wołyń, 1996). Six recent memoirs are Józef Anczarski, *Kronikarskie zapisy z lat cierpień i grozy w Małopolsce Wschodniej, 1939–1946* (Kraków, 1996); Tadeusz Bagiński, *Lipniki Wołynia polskiego* (Elbląg, 1995); Jan Białowąs, *Zdawało się, że pomarli a oni wciąż żyją. Wspomńienia z życia Polaków i Ukraińców w Ihrowicy oraz tragicznej nocy wigilijnej 1944 roku* (n.p., 1995); Ożarowski; Czesław Piotrowski, *Krwawe żniwa za Styrem, Horyniem i Słuczą* (Warszawa: Światowy Związek Żołnierzy Armii Krajowej Okręg Wołyński, 1995); and T. Piotrowski, *Vengeance of the Swallows*.

524. W. Siemaszko, p. 46. The full text of Siemaszko's conference paper, delivered at the University of Gdańsk on May 9, 1992, appears on pp. 37–47.

525. Table 14 comes from Turowski and Siemaszko. The estimates appear on p. 158. The documented figures are gleaned from pp. 160–65. These (1990) figures have recently been updated by Siemaszko. As of June 1995, the documented cases stand at 34,650. See Filar, "Likwidatorzy z UPA."

526. Diment, pp. 201–4.

527. Tennenbaum, p. 238.

528. Szcześniak and Szota, pp. 185–88, 346; Poliszczuk, *Gorzka prawda*, pp. 286–90; Węgierski, *Armia Krajowa*, pp. 79, 103, 142, 182, 193, 336–37; Giertych, *Komunikaty*, pp. 350–52. For a Ukrainian listing of villages attacked in 1944–45 by the Poles and for victim tolls, see Siwicki, 3: 307–8. A list of names of those murdered in Pawłokoma appears on pp. 295–96. It may be noted that the Polish assault on Pawłokoma was carried out by an AK group in retaliation for the earlier abduction and murder of Polish villagers and that later, in retaliation, the UPA carried out an assault on the Polish population of Pawłokoma. For Wierzchowiny see Dariusz Goszczyński, "Zagadka Wierzchowin," *Nasza Polska*, July 11, 1996, and Piotr Kipiński, "Czerwone dalie," *Gazeta Wyborcza*, February 10-11, 1996.

529. Poliszczuk, *Gorzka prawda*, p. 287.

530. Mirchuk, p. 408, in Motyl, "Ukrainian Nationalist Political Violence," pp. 50–51.

531. Both decrees can be found in Siwicki, 2: 111–12; the second is also in Szcześniak and Szota, p. 482.

532. Janik, p. 120.

533. Poliszczuk, *Gorzka prawda*, p. 79.

534. Ibid., pp. 188–89.

535. In T. Piotrowski, *Vengeance of the Swallows*, p. 79.

536. Peretiatkowicz, p. 20.

537. "Zbrodnie banderowskich bojówek OUN-UPA w powiecie Buczacz, województwo tarnopolskie," *Na Rubieży* (Wrocław) 4, no. 14 (1995): 24. See also Peretiatkowicz, p. 137 for other examples.

538. Janik, p. 114.

539. Helena Piotrowiak as quoted in T. Piotrowski, *Vengeance of the Swallows*, p. 235.

540. Szcześniak and Szota, p. 150 n. 29. The article "Zbrodnie banderowskich bójówek OUN-UPA w powiecie Buczacz," pp. 4–25, provides information regarding twenty-five Ukrainians (mostly listed by name and location) killed by the UPA in the county of Buczacz. Some reasons are listed for the murders: "for open condemnation of the UPA" (p. 8); "for condemning the methods of the Banderowcy out loud" (p. 12); "for opposing the murders of Poles" (p. 12); "for being a *sołtys* during the Soviet occupation" (p. 12); "for refusing to cooperate with local Ukrainian chauvinists" (p. 14); "for refusing to participate in the murder of Poles" (p. 14); "probably by mistake, due to the fact that a Pole was to have been on duty at the time [at a train station in Korościatyn]" (pp. 14–15); "for calling the Banderowcy criminals" — this by three mothers whose sons died in attacks on Polish villages — and for their "insolence" (all three of these elderly women were hung by the UPA) (p. 23); "for refusing to assist in the murder of Poles" (p. 23); "for warning Poles of imminent [UPA] attacks and for saving Polish lives" (p. 23); "for refusing to participate in the murder of Poles" — the previously mentioned Slavko Hulub (p. 24); "for refusing to kill his Polish mother" (p. 25); and "for discovering the remains [of Bronisława Drozda's father] and reporting the finding of the remains ... to the authorities" (pp. 17–18). The last case involved the death of Maryska Kurmylo, whose father was Ukrainian and whose mother was Polish. Maryska was in an advanced state of pregnancy at the time of her vicious murder. Her stomach was cut open, the unborn child was removed, and stones were placed inside. She

was then thrown into the same place, by the dam in the river, where Bronisława's father's body was retrieved. This article also lists the names of numerous Poles who died at the hands of the UPA in Buczacz.

541. See Poliszczuk, *Gorzka prawda*, p. 177.

542. Ibid., p. 201.

543. For statements regarding OUN-B SB atrocities against Ukrainians, see Poliszczuk, *Gorzka prawda*, pp. 294–98; Danylo Shumuk, *Za skhidnym obriiem. Spomyny* (Paris: Persha Ukrainska Drukarnia u Frantsii, 1974), especially p. 106; Hryhorii Stetsiuk, *Nepostavlenyi pamiatnyk. Spohady* (Winnipeg: Instytut Doslidiv Volyni, 1988), pp. 82, 88, 91, 98, 105, 119; Vasyl Mykhalchuk (ed.), *Tudy, de bii za voliu. Zbirnyk viiskovo-politychnykh materialiv u pamiat' Maksyma Skorupskoho-Maksa kurinnoho UPA* (London-Paris: Fundatsiia im. O. Olzhycha, 1989; Kyiv: "Kozaky," 1992), pp. 144–45, 158–59, 174– 75, 192–95.

For a short work dealing with one of the leaders of the SB, Dmytro Kupiak, see Bronisław Szeremeta, *Watażka. Wspomnienie nierozstrzelanego i jego zbrodnie* (Wrocław, 1995). Kupiak's sanitized memoir is *Spohady nerostrilanoho* (Toronto, 1991). Kupiak died in 1995 while under investigation, by the Canadian Department of Justice, for war crimes.

544. Mykhailo Podvorniak, *Viter z Volyni. Spohady* (Winnipeg: T-vo "Volyn," 1981), p. 197.

545. In Tadeusz Piotrowski, *Ukrainian Integral Nationalism: Chronological Assessment and Bibliography* (Toronto: Alliance of the Polish Eastern Provinces, with The Polish Educational Foundation in North America, 1997), pp. 80-83; and in Wiktor Poliszczuk, *Legal and Political Assessment of the OUN and UPA* (Toronto, 1997), a trilingual publication, pp. 6-10 (English), 64-68 (Polish), 118-22 (Ukrainian). A photocopy of the original appeal with all 95 signatures is in the possession of the author.

Conclusion

1. Hieronim Kubiak, "Polacy i polonia w ZSRR: kwestie terminologiczne, periodyzacja, rozmieszczenie przestrzenne, szacunki ilościowe," in Kubiak et al., table on p. 31. See also Roman Dzwonkowski, *Polacy na dawnych Kresach Wschodnich: z problematyki narodowościowej i religijnej* (Lublin: Wspólnota Polska, 1994), tables on pp. 16, 18, 21.

2. Zakład Badań Etnicznych Wydziału Politologii Uniwersytetu im. Marii Curie-Skłodowskiej in Lublin and *Forum Polonijne,* 1 (1995) published by the Komisja Spraw Emigracji Polaków za Granicą.

According to Andrzej Jankowski and Medard Masłowski, "Kierunki działań Ministerstwa Edukacji Narodowej na rzecz Polonii w ZSRR (stan w dniu 31 XII 1990 roku)," in Kubiak et al., pp. 191–92, in Belorussia there are about 135 schools and educational centers where at least some instruction is provided in the Polish language by teachers who are not always qualified; in Lithuania there are 111— in the Polish language (44), Polish-Russian (37), Polish-Russian-Lithuanian (23), and Polish-Lithuanian (7); in Ukraine, however, there are only 2 Polish schools in Lviv and an additional 80 schools in which some instruction is given in the Polish language. In 1990, both Ukraine and Belorussia refused to accept additional Polish teachers.

The number of Poles living in Ukraine is about the same as the number of Ukrainians living in Poland (i.e., between 200,000 and 500,000); whereas in 1958–59 there were 9 Ukrainian schools in Poland and 152 centers of instruction in the Ukrainian language, in 1990 there were only 5 Ukrainian schools left, 2 Polish-Ukrainian schools, and 56 centers of instruction in the Ukrainian language in the Polish school system. (Since 1990 several more Ukrainian high schools have been opened, including one in Przemyśl.) There is also a chair of Ukrainian philology at the University of Warsaw and one at the Jagiellonian University in Kraków. Since 1957, from ten to twenty Ukrainian teachers have traveled to Kiev each year to attend professional-development courses. See Myroslaw Truchan, "Ukrainians in Poland," in Ann Lencyk Pawliczko (ed.), *Ukraine and Ukrainians throughout the World: A Demographic and Sociological Guide to the Homeland and Its Diaspora* (Toronto: University of Toronto Press, 1994), pp. 176, 181.

See also Z. Anthony Kruszewski, "The Revival of the Polish Diaspora in Lithuania, Belorussia, and Ukraine," *Polish Review* 41, no. 3 (1996): 293–308.

3. Kubiak, in Kubiak et al., pp. 30–31. Less emphasis was placed on the exchange in Belorussia by the Soviets for fear of depopulization of large areas. In Lithuania, the exchange was well publicized, but only half of those who signed up were allowed to leave. According to Jacek Borkowicz, 380,000 Poles registered for the exchange program in Lithuania, 197,000 of whom were allowed

to leave between 1945 and 1947. By the end of 1946, according to this author, about 1.7 million Poles were repatriated: 1.24 million on the basis of the Polish-Soviet agreements; 200,000 fleeing the eastern territories of Poland for fear of the Ukrainian Nationalists; about as many returning from the forced-labor camps in the west; and about 70,000 demobilized soldiers. Jacek Borkowicz, "1945 wypędzeni Polacy," *Więź*, September 1995, pp. 45, 49.

4. Gabriele Simoncini, "Polyethnic Poland?" Presentation at the 55th Annual Meeting (June 20-21, 1997) of The Polish Institute of Arts and Sciences of America at Fordham University, New York. Handout. The Seym Commission estimates come from the Sejm RP Komisja Mniejszości Narodowych i Etnicznych. There are over 200 ethnic organizations registered with the Polish government. The category of illegal aliens is probably vastly underestimated. There may be twice that number. The last time official census statistics were gathered on minorities in Poland was 1946.

5. Recently, Lviv became the focus of Polish and Jewish concerns once more. On October 23, 1994, in a segment entitled "The Ugly Face of Freedom," the CBS television program *60 Minutes* showed the reunion of the veterans of the SS-Galizien and the UNA-UNSO (Ukrainska Natsionalna Asambleia — Ukrainian National Assembly — and its paramilitary arm, Ukrainska Natsionalna Samooborona — Ukrainian National Self-Defense) "soldiers" marching through the city streets and chanting racist slogans.

Morley Safer, of *60 Minutes*, commented on the *SS-Galizien* reunion:

> Many of the Ukrainian men of Lvov who marched off as members of the SS never returned, killed fighting for Hitler. But last summer, a good number of the survivors, veterans of the SS Galician Division, did return for a reunion laid on by the Lvov City Council. Ukrainian SS veterans now living in Canada, the United States and Ukraine. Nowhere, certainly not in Germany, are the SS so openly celebrated. And for this reunion, Cardinal Lubachivsky, head of the Ukrainian Catholic Church, gave his blessing, just as a predecessor did to the SS more than 50 years ago.

On the UNA-UNSO march, Safer noted: "The group marching is Una Unso, a political party whose motto is 'force and order.' Three of its members, including the man shouting orders, were elected members of Ukraine's national parliament. A sister party, the Social Nationalists, calls for the need to liquidate certain people." Safer asked Simon Wiesenthal, "What's your reaction to this?" Wiesenthal answered, "They have not changed." CBS *60 Minutes* transcript, vol. 27, no. 7 (October 23, 1994): 15, 17, 19. For more information on the UNA-UNSO, see Bohdan Nahaylo, "Ukraine," *RFE/RL Research Report* 3, no. 16 (April 22, 1994): 42–49.

On June 29, 1997, the eve of the fifty-sixth anniversary of the OUN-B declaration of independence in Lwów — just weeks after President Kuchma's visit with Pope John Paul II — the UNA and former veterans of the UPA marched down the streets of Lviv again. They halted before the memorial to Taras Shevchenko, threw Polish, Russian, Rumanian, and other flags onto the pavement, and with shouts "Death to the enemies!" proceeded to wipe their high boots with them in plain view of the gathered crowd and reporters.

6. The recently released results of a national survey conducted at the end of 1994 conjointly by Polish and Lithuanian statistical departments revealed that although a substantial majority of Poles in Lithuania and Lithuanians in Poland are bilingual, each group tends to use its native language at home and continues to identify itself in terms of its ethnic background and religion. More important, neither side feels itself to be discriminated against by the other either socially or economically. Only 3 to 5 percent of the 8,000 respondents (4,000 Poles in Lithuania and 4,000 Lithuanians in Poland) stated that Polish-Lithuanian relations in both nations are "hostile or conflictive." See "Nie ma większych konfliktów między Polakami i Litwinami," *Gazeta* (Toronto), January 23, 1996. This study has been questioned on methodological grounds. Whereas the 4,000 Lithuanians sampled in Poland represent about one-fourth of all Lithuanians, the 4,000 Poles sampled in Lithuania represent less than 1 percent of the Poles living there.

For a chronology dealing with Polish-Lithuanian conflicts from February 24, 1990, to May 10, 1996, see Piotr Bączek, "Kalendarium konfliktu polsko-litewskiego," *Gazeta Polska* (Warszawa), May 30, 1996.

Bibliography

Archives

Archiwum Akt Nowych (Warsaw)
Archiwum Głownej Komisji Badania Zbrodni przeciwko Narodowi Polskiemu — Instytutu Pamięci Narodowej (formerly, Archiwum Głównej Komisji Zbrodni Hitlerowskich w Polsce)
Archiwum i Muzeum Imienia gen. Władysława Sikorskiego
Archiwum Państwowe (Przemyśl)
Archiwum Państwowe (Warsaw)
Archiwum Państwowe Kielce, 1945–1950
Archiwum SBU Obwodu Wołyńskiego
Archiwum Ukraińskie (Warsaw)
Archiwum Zakładu Historii Partii
Bundesarchiv
Centralne Archiwum KC PZPR
Hoover Institution Archives (Stanford, CA)
Lietuvos TSR Centrinis Valstybinis Archyvas
Militararchiv
National Archives (Washington, DC)
National Archives of Canada
National Military Archives (Washington, DC)
Piłsudski Institute of America, Archiwum Rzeczowy
State Archives of the Russian Federation
Tsentralnyi Derzhavnyi Arkhiv Zhovtenvoi Revoliutsii i Sotsialistychnoho Budivnytstva (Kiev)
Yad Vashem (Jerusalem)
Żydowski Instytut Historyczny (Warsaw)

Newspapers

Canadian Jewish News
Chrześcijanin w Świecie
Czerwony Sztandar
Die Welt
Forward
Gazeta
Gazeta Kielecka
Gazeta Polska
Gazeta Warszawska
Gazeta Wyborcza
Globe and Mail
Głos Polski
Głos Pracy
Goniec Codzienny
Jewish Chronicle
Kombatant
Krakivski Visti
Krasnaya Zvezda
Literaturnaya Gazeta
Los Angeles Times
Lvivski Visti
Ma'aariv
Magazyn Gazety
Myśl Polska
Najwyższy Czas
Nash Klich
Nasz Przegląd
Nasza Polska
Natsionalna Trybuna
New York Times

Novyi Chas
Novyi Shliakh
Polityka
Pravda
Przegląd Tygodniowy
Reporter
Ridna Zemlia
Samostiina Ukraina
Słowo-Dziennik Katolicki
Surma
Szaniec
Times (London)
Toronto Star
Tygodnik Powszechny
Tygodnik Solidarność
Ukraina
Ukraina Molada
Ukrainski Shchodenni Visti
Vidnova
Village Voice
Volyn
Wiadomości Literackie
Zborivski Visti
Zgoda
Zolochivske Slovo
Życie Warszawy

Books and Articles

Aarons, Mark, and John Loftus. *Ratlines: How the Vatican's Nazi Networks Betrayed Western Intelligence to the Soviets.* London, England: Mandarin, 1991.

Abarinov, Vladimir. *The Murderers of Katyn.* New York: Hippocrene, 1993.

Abramsky, Chimen, et al., eds. *The Jews in Poland.* New York: Basil Blackwell, 1986.

Ainsztein, Reuben. *Jewish Resistance in Nazi-Occupied Eastern Europe: With a Historical Survey of the Jew as Fighter and Soldier in the Diaspora.* London: Elek, 1974; New York: Barnes and Noble Books, 1975.

Allen, W. E. D. *The Ukraine.* London: Cambridge University Press, 1940.

Anczarski, Józef. *Kronikarskie zapisy z lat cierpień i grozy w Małopolsce Wschodniej, 1939–1946.* Kraków, 1996.

Andrew, Christopher, and Oleg Gordievsky. *KGB: The Inside Story of Its Foreign Operations from Lenin to Gorbachev.* New York: HarperCollins, 1990.

Apenszlak, Jacob, ed. *The Black Book of Polish Jewry.* New York: Roy Publishers, 1943.

Arad, Yitzhak, et al., eds. *The Einsztzgruppen Reports: Selections from the Dispatches of the Nazi Death Squads' Campaign against the Jews, July 1941–January 1943.* New York: Holocaust Library, 1989.

Arczyński, Marek, and Wiesław Balcerak. *Kryptonym "Żegota." Z dziejów pomocy Żydom w Polsce 1939–1945.* 2d ed. Warszawa: Czytelnik, 1983.

Arendt, Hannah. *Eichmann in Jerusalem: A Report on the Banality of Evil.* New York: Viking Press, 1965.

Armstrong, John A. *Ukrainian Nationalism.* 3d ed. Englewood, CO: Ukrainian Academic Press, 1990.

Armstrong, John Lowell. "The Polish Underground and the Jews: A Reassessment of Home Army Commander Tadeusz Bór-Komorowski's Order 116 Against Banditry." *Slavonic and East European Review* 72, no. 2 (April 1994): 259–76.

Asch, Sholem. *Kiddush Ha-Shem: An Epic of 1684.* New York: Arnoa Press, 1975.

Ascherson, Neil. "The Death Doctors." *New York Review of Books,* May 28, 1987, pp. 29–34.

Association of Braslaw and Surroundings in Israel and America. *Darkness and Desolation: In Memory of the Communities of Braslaw Dubene Jaisi Jod Kislowszczizna Okmienic Opsa Plusy Rimszan Slobodka Zamosz Zaracz.* Tel Aviv: Ghetto Fighters' House and Hakibbutz Hameuchad Publishing House, n.d.

Austri-Dunn, Yeshayahu, ed. *Memorial Book of Czortkow.* Tel Aviv: Irgun Yotzey Czortkow in Israel, 1967.

Bagiński, Tadeusz. *Lipniki Wołynia polskiego.* Elbląg, 1995.

Balcerak, Wiesław, ed. *Polska-Białoruś 1918-1945.* Warszawa: Instytut Historii PAN, 1994.

Barański, Kamil. *Przeminęli zagończycy, chliborobi, chasydzi… Rzecz o ziemi stanisławowsko–kołomyjsko — stryjskiej.* London: Panda Press, 1988.

Bartoszewski, Władysław. *The Blood Shed Unites Us: Pages from the History of Help to the Jews in Occupied Poland.* Warsaw: Interpress Publishers, 1970.

_____. *The Warsaw Ghetto: A Christian's Testimony.* Boston: Beacon Press, 1987.

_____. *Warszawski pierścień śmierci 1939–1944.* Warszawa: Zachodnia Agencja Prasowa, 1967.

_____, and Zofia Lewin, eds. *Righteous Among Nations: How Poles Helped the Jews, 1939-1945.* London: Earlscourt Publications, 1969.

Bartoszewski, Władysław T. *The Convent at Auschwitz.* London: Bowerdean Press, 1990.

Bednarczyk, Tadeusz. *Obowiązek silniejszy od śmierci: wspomnienia z lat 1939–1944 o polskiej pomocy dla Żydów w Warszawie.* Warszawa: Grunwald, 1986.

_____. *Życie codzienne warszawskiego getta. Warszawskie getto i ludzie (1939–1945 i dalej).* Warszawa: Ojczyzna, 1995.

Berenbaum, Michael, ed. *A Mosaic of Victims: Non-Jews Persecuted and Murdered by the Nazis.* New York: New York University Press, 1990.

Berenstein, Tatiana, and Adam Rutkowski. *Assistance to the Jews in Poland, 1939–1945.* Warsaw: Polonia, 1963.

Bergman, Aleksandra. *Sprawy białoruskie w II Rzeczypospolitej.* Warszawa: Państwowe Wydawnictwo Naukowe, 1984.

Bernhard, Michael, and Henryk Szlajfer, eds. *From the Polish Underground: Selections from Krytyka, 1978–1993.* University Park: Pennsylvania State University Press, 1995.

Bethell, Nicholas. *The Last Secret: The Delivery to Stalin of Over Two Million Russians by Britain and the United States.* New York: Basic Books, 1974.

Białowąs, Jan. *Zdawało się, Że pomarli a oni wciąż żyją. Wspomńienia z życia Polaków i Ukraińców w Ihrowicy oraz tragicznej nocy wigilijnej 1944 roku.* N.p., 1995.

Biber, Jacob. *Survivors: A Personal Story of the Holocaust.* San Bernardino, CA: Borgo Press, 1986.

Bieberstein, Aleksander. *Zagłada Żydów w Krakowie.* Kraków: Wydawnictwo Literackie, 1985.

Bielawski, Wacław. *Zbrodnie na Polakach dokonane przez hitlerowców za pomoc udzielaną Żydom.* Warszawa: Główna Komisja Badania Zbrodni Hitlerowskich w Polsce—Instytut Pamięci Narodowej, 1987.

Biernacki, Jerzy. "Silence over the Graves." *Poland* (Warszawa, American Edition) 11, no. 267 (November 1976): 42–47.

Biskupski, Stanisław, comp. *Świadkowie mówią.* Warszawa: Światowy Związek Żołnierzy Armii Krajowej Okręg Wołyń, 1996.

Błażyński, Zbigniew. *Mówi Józef Światło.* London: Polska Fundacja Kulturalna, 1986.

Blejwas, Stanislaus. "Polemic as History: Shmuel Krakowski, the War of the Doomed. Jewish Armed Resistance in Poland, 1942-1944." *Polin* 4 (1989): 354–62.

Bojarska, Barbara. *Piaśnica. Miejsce martyrologii i pamięci: z badań nad zbrodniami hitlerowskimi na Pomorzu.* 2d ed. Gdańsk: Zrzeszenie Kaszubsko-Pomorskie, Oddział Gdański, 1989.

Bonusiak, Włodzimierz. *Kto zabił profesorów lwowskich?* Rzeszów: Krajowa Agencja Wydawnicza Rzeszów, 1989.

Borkowicz, Jacek. "1945 wypędzeni Polacy." *Więź,* September 1995, pp. 37–55.

Boshyk, Yury, ed. *Ukraine during World War II: History and Its Aftermath, a Symposium.* Edmonton: Canadian Institute of Ukrainian Studies, 1986.

Brayer, Lynda. Sworn affidavit, Jerusalem. December 5, 1993.

_____. Address to the Canadian Immigration and Refugee Board, Conference on Israel, Montreal, August 19, 1994.

Brecher, Elinor J. *Schindler's Legacy: True Stories of the List Survivors.* New York: Penguin, 1994.

Bregman, Aleksander. *Najlepszy sojusznik Hitlera: studium o współpracy Niemiecko-Sowieckiej 1939–1941.* 3d ed. London: Orbis, 1967.

Brockdorff, Werner. *Kollaboration oder Widerstand. Die Zusammenarbeit mit den Deutschen in den besetzten Ländern wahrend des zweiten Weltkrieges und deren schreckliche Folgen.* München: Wels Welsermuhl, 1968.

Bronowski, Alexander. *They Were Few.* New York: Peter Lang, 1991.

Bugajski, Janusz. *Ethnic Politics in Eastern Europe: A Guide to Nationality Policies, Organizations, and Parties.* New York: M. E. Sharpe, 1994.

Bulba-Borovets, Otaman Taras. *Armiia bez derzhavy. Slava i trahediia ukrainskoho povstanskoho rukhu. Spohady.* Winnipeg: Nakladom Tovarystva "Volyn," 1981.

Celt, Marek. *Biali kurierzy.* München: M. Celt, 1986.

Checinski, Michael. *Poland: Communism-Nationalism-Antisemitism.* New York: Karz-Cohl, 1982.

Chesnoff, Richard Z. "The Beginning of Redemption." *U.S. News and World Report,* April 3, 1995, pp. 66-67.

Chesterton, G. K. *The Well and the Shallows.* London: Sheed and Ward, 1935.

Chiesa "eroica" di Polonia, La. Rome: ARS GRAF, n.d.

Chmielarz, Andrzej. "Warsaw Fought Alone: Reflections on Aid to and the Fall of the 1944 Uprising." *Polish Review* 39, no. 4 (1994): 415–33.

Chodakiewicz, Marek, Piotr Gontarczyk, and Leszek Żebrowski, eds. *Tajne oblicze GL-AL i PPR.* 2 vols. Warszawa: Burchard Edition, 1997.

Chojnowski, Andrzej. *Koncepcje polityki narodowościowej rządów polskich w latach 1921–1939.* Wrocław: Zakład Narodowy im. Ossolińskich, 1979.

Cimek, Henryk. *Komuniści, Polska, Stalin 1918–1939.* Białystok: Krajowa Agencja Wydawnicza, 1990.

Ciołkosz, Adam. "Broń dla getta Warszawy." *Zeszyty Historyczne* (Paris) 15 (1969): 15–44.

_____. "'Dzielnica żydowska' obozu w Jabłonnie." *Zeszyty Historyczne* (Paris) 20 (1971): 178–200.

Cohen, Asher, et al., eds. *The Shoah and the War.* New York: Peter Lang, 1992.

Concise Statistical Year-Book. London: Polish Ministry of Information, London, 1941.

Cybulski, Henryk. *Czerwone Noce.* 1966. 4th ed., Warszawa: Wydawnictwo Ministerstwa Obrony Narodowej, 1977.

Cygan, Wiktor Krzysztof. *Kresy w ogniu: wojna polsko-sowiecka 1939.* Warszawa: Warszawska Oficyna Wydawnicza, 1990.

Czarnocka, Halina, et al., eds. *AK w dokumentach 1939–1945.* Vol. 3, April 1943–July 1944. London: Studium Polski Podziemnej, 1976.

Czubiński, Antoni. *Dzieje najnowsze Polski: Polska Ludowa 1944–1989.* Poznań: Wielkopolska Agencja Wydawnicza, 1992.

Dallin, Alexander. *German Rule in Russia, 1941–1945: A Study of Occupation Policies.* New York: London: Macmillan, 1955; New York: St. Martin's Press, 1957.

Danielski, J. J. and M. Lubinski. "Polish Officers in Soviet Captivity, 1939–41: An Introduction to Postal History." *American Philatelist,* January 1996, pp. 48–60.

Danter, Szymon. *Las sprawiedliwych: karta z dziejów ratowania Żydów w okupowanej Polsce.* Warszawa: Książka i Wiedza, 1968.

Davies, Norman. *God's Playground: A History of Poland.* 2 vols. New York: Columbia University Press, 1982.

_____. "Great Britain and the Polish Jews, 1918–20." *Journal of Contemporary History* 8, no. 2 (April 1973): 119–42.

_____. "The Misunderstood Victory in Europe." *New York Review of Books,* May 25, 1995, pp. 7–10.

_____. "Poles and Jews: An Exchange." *New York Review of Books,* April 9, 1987.

_____, and Antony Polonsky, eds. *Jews in Eastern Poland and the USSR, 1939–46.* New York: St. Martin's Press, 1991.

Deák, István. "Heroism in Hell." *New York Review of Books,* November 8, 1990, pp. 52–57.

_____. "Holocaust Heroes." *New York Review of Books,* November 5, 1992, pp. 22–26.

_____. "The Incomprehensible Holocaust: An Exchange." *The New York Review of Books* (December 21, 1989), pp. 62-65.

_____. "Legends of King Christian: Another Exchange." *New York Review of Books,* September 27, 1990, pp. 67–68.

_____. "Who Saved Jews? An Exchange." *New York Review of Books,* April 25, 1991, pp. 60–62.

Dear, I. C. B., ed. *The Oxford Companion to World War II.* New York: Oxford University Press, 1995.

Dębski, Włodzimierz Sławosz. *Antylitopys UPA.* Lublin, 1995.

Dereń, Bolesław. *Józef Kuraś "Ogień" partyzant Podhala.* Kraków: Secesja, 1995.

Deschênes, Honourable Jules. *Commission of Inquiry on War Criminals, Report, Part I: Public.* Ottawa, Canada. December 30, 1986.

Diewerge, W., ed. *Deutsche Soldaten sehen die Sowjetunion.* Berlin: Limpert, 1941.

Diment, Michael. *The Lone Survivor: A Diary of the Lukacze Ghetto and Svyniukhy, Ukraine.* New York: Holocaust Library, 1992.

Dinnerstein, Leonard. *Anti-Semitism in America.* New York: Oxford University Press, 1994.

Dobroszycki, Lucjan. *Reptile Journalism: The Official Polish-Language Press under the Nazis, 1939–1945.* New Haven: Yale University Press, 1994.

_____, ed. *The Chronicle of the Łódź Ghetto, 1941–1944.* New Haven: Yale University Press, 1984.

_____, and Jeffrey S. Gurock, eds. *The Holocaust in the Soviet Union: Studies and Sources on the Destruc-*

tion of the Jews in the Nazi-Occupied Territories of the USSR, 1941–1945. Armonk, NY: M. E. Sharpe, 1993.

"Dokumenty z okresu mordowania Polaków w Małopolsce Wschodniej w czasie ostatniej wojny," *Biuletyn Koło Lwowian,* no. 43 (June 1982): 8.

Dontsov, Dmytro. *Natsionalizm.* 3d ed. London: Ukrainian Publishers, 1966.

Dowgiallo, Jan. *From Science to Diplomacy: A Pole's Experience in Israel.* Cathedral City, CA: Brunswick Press, 1995.

Drożdżyński, Aleksander, and Jan Zaborowski. *Oberländer, przez Ostforschung, "wywiad i NSDAP do rządu" NRF.* Poznań: Wydawnictwo Zachodnie, 1960.

Dumin, Osip. "Prawda o Ukraińskiej Organizacji Wojskowej." Dated May 1926. Berlin. Translated from German. *Zeszyty Historyczne* (Paris) 30 (1974): 103–37.

Duraczyński, Eugeniusz. *Wojna i opkupacja. Wrzesień 1939–Kwiecień 1943.* Warszawa: Wiedza Powszechna, 1974.

Dzwonkowski, Roman. *Polacy na dawnych Kresach Wschodnich: z problematyki narodowościowej i religijnej.* Lublin: Wspólnota Polska, 1994.

Eberhardt, Piotr. *Polska granica wschodnia, 1939–1945.* Warszawa: Editions Spotkania, n.d.

Eliach, Yaffa. *Hasidic Tales of the Holocaust.* New York: Oxford University Press, 1982.

Encyclopedia Lituanica. Vol. 5. Boston: J. Kapocius, 1976.

Encyklopedia Katolicka. Vol. 3. Lublin: Towarzystwo Naukowe Katolickiego Uniwersytetu Lubelskiego, 1979.

Engelking, Barbara. *Na łące popiołów: ocaleni z Holocaustu.* Warszawa: Cyklady, 1993.

_____. *Zagłada i pamięć.* Warszawa: Wydawnictwo FIS PAN, 1994.

Fajkowski, Józef, and Jan Religa. *Zbrodnie hitlerowskie na wsi polskiej 1939–1945.* Warszawa: Książka i Wiedza, 1981.

Falconi, Carlo. *The Silence of Pius XII.* Boston: Little, Brown and Company, 1970.

Farley, Christopher John. "A Pension Plan for Nazi Followers." *Time,* May 10, 1993, p. 17.

Fass, Michael Walter, ed. *Nowy-Targ and Vicinity: Zakopane, Charni Dunaietz, Rabka, Yordanov, Shchavnitza, Kroshchenko, Yablonka, Makov Podhalanski.* Tel-Aviv: Townspeople Association of Nowy-Targ and Vicinity, 1979.

Feldenkreiz-Grinbal, Eva, ed. *Eth Ezkera— Whenever I Remember: Memorial Book of the Jewish Community in Tzoyzmir (Sandomierz).* N.p., n.d.

Feliński, M. *The Ukrainians in Poland.* London, 1931.

Fijałka, Michał. *27. Wołyńska Dywizja Piechoty AK.* Warszawa: Instytut Wydawniczy Pax, 1986.

Fijałkowski, Zenon. *Kościół katolicki na ziemiach polskich w latach okupacji hitlerowskiej.* Warszawa: Książka i Wiedza, 1983.

Filar, Władysław. *Przed akcją "wisła" był Wołyń.* Warszawa: Światowy Związek Żołnierzy armii Krajowej Okręg Wołyń, 1997.

_____. "Zbrodnicza działalność OUN-UPA przeciwko ludności polskiej na Wołyniu w latach 1942–1944." *Semper Fidelis* (Wrocław) 5, no. 28 (September-October 1995): 3–5.

Friedlander, Henry. *The Origins of Nazi Genocide: From Euthanasia to the Final Solution.* Chapel Hill: University of North Carolina Press, 1995.

Friedman, Philip. *Their Brothers' Keepers.* New York: Holocaust Library, 1978.

Friedman, Saul S. *Pogromchik: The Assassination of Simon Petlura.* New York: Hart Publishing Company, 1976.

_____, ed. *Holocaust Literature: A Handbook of Critical, Historical, and Literary Writings.* Westport, CT: Greenwood Press, 1993.

Frydland, Rachmiel. *When Being Jewish Was a Crime.* New York: Thomas Nelson, 1978.

Fuks, Marian, et al. *Żydzi polscy. Dzieje i kultura.* Warszawa: Interpress, 1982.

Galiński, Antoni. "Ewakuacja więzień kresowych." *My, Sybiracy* 3 (1992): 63–75.

Garlicki, Andrzej, ed. *Z dziejów Drugiej Rzeczypospolitej.* Warszawa: Wydawnictwa Szkolne in Pedagogiczne, 1986.

Garliński, Józef. *Fighting Auschwitz: The Resistance Movement in the Concentration Camp.* London: Orbis Books, 1994.

_____. *Niezapomniane lata: dzieje Wywiadu Więziennego i Wywiadu Bezpieczeństwa Komendy Głównej Armii Krajowej.* London: Odnowa, 1987.

_____. *Oświęcim walczący.* London: Odnowa, 1974.
_____. *Poland in the Second World War.* London: Macmillan Press, 1985.
_____. *Polska w drugiej wojnie światowej.* London: Odnowa, 1982.
_____. *The Survival of Love: Memoir of a Resistance Officer.* New York: Blackwell, 1991.

Giertych, Jędrzej. *In Defence of My Country.* London: Wydawnictwo Towarzystwa im. Romana Dmowskiego, 1981.

_____, ed. *Komunikaty Towarzystwa imienia Romana Dmowskiego,* vol. 2. London: Veritas, 1979–80.

Gilbert, Martin. *The Holocaust: A History of the Jews of Europe during the Second World War.* New York: Holt, Rinehart and Winston, 1986; Glasgow: Fontana/Collins, 1987.

Główna Komisja Badania Zbrodni Hitlerowskich w Polsce—Rada Ochrony Pomników Walki i Męczeństwa. *Obozy hitlerowskie na ziemiach polskich 1939–1945: Informator encyklopedyczny.* Warszawa: Państwowe Wydawnictwo Naukowe, 1979.

Golczewski, Frank. "Ukraińska karta niemieckiej akcji przeciwko Polsce." *Niepodległość* (New York, London, Wrocław) 26 (1993): 231–38.

Goldhagen, Daniel Jonah. "False Witness." *New Republic,* December 27, 1993, pp. 28–34.

_____. *Hitler's Willing Executioners: Ordinary Germans and the Holocaust.* New York: Alfred A. Knopf, 1996.

Grahl-Madsen, Atle. *The Status of Refugees in International Law.* Vol. 1. Leyden: A. W. Sijthoff, 1966.

Gross, Jan T. *Polish Society under German Occupation: The Generalgouvernement, 1939–1944.* Princeton: Princeton University Press, 1979.

_____. *Revolution from Abroad: The Soviet Conquest of Poland's Western Ukraine and Western Belorussia.* Princeton: Princeton University Press, 1988.

Gruber, Samuel. *I Choose Life.* New York: Shengold Publishers, 1978.

Grudzińska-Gross, Irena, and Jan Tomasz Gross, eds. *W czterdziestym nas matko na Sybir zesłali... Polska a Rosja 1939–1942.* London: Aneks, 1983.

_____. *War Through Children's Eyes: The Soviet Occupation of Poland and the Deportations, 1939–1941.* Stanford, CA: Hoover Institution Press, 1985.

Grünberg, Karol. *SS gwardia Hitlera.* Warszawa: Książka i Wiedza, 1975.

Gumkowski, Janusz, and Kazimierz Leszczyński. *Poland under Nazi Occupation.* Warsaw: Polonia Publishing House, 1961.

Gutman, Israel, ed. *Encyclopedia of the Holocaust.* 4 vols. New York: Macmillan, 1990.

_____, and Shmuel Krakowski. *Unequal Victims: Poles and Jews During World War II.* New York: Holocaust Library, 1986.

Heike, Wolf-Dietrich. *The Ukrainian Division "Galicia," 1943–45: A Memoir.* Toronto: Shevchenko Scientific Society, 1988.

Hempel, Adam. *Pogrobowcy klęski. Rzecz o policji "granatowej" w Generalnym Gubernatorstwie 1939–1945.* Warszawa: Państwowe Wydawnictwo Naukowe, 1990.

Hilberg, Raul. *The Destruction of the European Jews.* 3 vols. Rev. ed. New York: Holmes and Meier, 1985.

_____. *Perpetrators, Victims, Bystanders: The Jewish Catastrophe 1933–1945.* New York: HarperCollins, 1992.

Himka, John Paul. "Western Ukraine between the Wars." *Canadian Slavonic Papers* 34, no. 4 (December 1992): 391–412.

Hirszfeld, Ludwik. *Historia jego życia.* Warszawa: Spółdzielnia Wydawnicza Czytelnik, 1946.

Historia Belaruskai SSR. Minsk, 1975.

Hoffer, Eric. *The True Believer.* New York: Harper and Row, 1951.

Hoffmann, Bedřich. *And Who Will Kill You: The Chronicle of the Life and Sufferings of Priests in the Concentration Camps.* Poznań: Pallottinum, 1994.

Hohne, Heinz. *The Order of the Death's Head: The Story of Hitler's SS.* London: Pan Books, 1972.

Honsberger, John D., ed. *Gazette* (Toronto) 26 (1992): 138–62.

Horn, Maria Halina. *A Tragic Victory.* Toronto: ECW Press, 1988.

Hrabar, Roman, et al. *The Fate of Polish Children during the Last War.* Warsaw: Interpress, 1981.

Iarovyi, Petro. "K desiatoi godovshchine velikoi provokatsii." *Sotsialisticheskii Vestnik* (New York) 31 (1951): 138-49.

Ignatieff, Michael. "In the New Republics (Lithuania's Role in the Extermination of Jews during World War II)." *New York Review of Books,* November 21, 1991, pp. 30-34.

Iłłakowicz, Jerzy Olgierd. "O Narodowych Siłach Zbrojnych." *Zeszyty Historyczne* (Paris) 76 (1986): 89–112.

Ilnytskyi, Roman. *Deutschland und die Ukraine 1934–1945.* München: Osteuropa Institut, 1958.

"Informacja o sytuacji Kościoła rzymsko-katolickiego w Archidiecezji Lwowskiej, grudzien 1944." *Lwów i Kresy* (London) 79 (September 1995): 69–73.

Iranek-Osmecki, Kazimierz. *He Who Saves One Life.* New York: Crown Publishers, 1971.

Istoriia ukrainskoho viiska. Winnipeg: Ivan Tyktor, 1953.

Iwanow, Mikołaj. "The First Punished Nation: Excerpts from the Study *Poles in the Soviet Union, 1917–1990.*" *Panorama Polska* (Warszawa) 502 (November 1991): 9–11, English section, pp. iv–v.

_____. *Pierwszy naród ukarany: stalinizm wobec polskiej ludności kresowej 1921–1938.* Warszawa: Agencja Omnipress, 1991.

Jaher, Frederic Colpe. *A Scapegoat in the New Wilderness: The Origins and Rise of Anti-Semitism in America.* Cambridge: Harvard University Press, 1994.

Janik, Bronisław. *Było ich trzy.* Warszawa: Książka i Wiedza, 1970.

Jankowski, Jan, and Antoni Serafiński, comp. *Polska w liczbach: Poland in Numbers.* London: Polish Lawyers Association in the United Kingdom, 1941.

Jaśkiewicz, Krzysztof. "Obywatele polscy aresztowani na terytorium tzw. Zachodniej Białorusi w latach 1939–1941 w świetle dokumentacji NKWD/KGB." *Kwartalnik Historyczny* (Warszawa) 1 (1994): 105–34.

Jastrzębowski, Jerzy. "Rozmowy o braciach." *Zeszyty Historyczne* (Paris) 88 (1989): 3–33.

Jeżowski, Leszek. "Ks. Edward Tobaczkowski." *Semper Fidelis* (Wrocław) 3, no. 16 (1993): 9–10.

Juchniewicz, Mieczysław. *Polacy w radzieckim ruchu partyzanckim.* Warszawa: MON, 1975.

Kahn, Leon. *No Time to Mourn: A True Story of a Jewish Partisan Fighter.* Vancouver: Laurelton Press, 1978.

Kainer, Abel (Stanisław Krajewski). "Żydizi a komuna." *Krytyka* 15 (1983).

Kąkolewski, Krzysztof. *Umarły cmentarz.* Warszawa: Von Borowiecky, 1996.

Kalba, Myroslav, comp. *U lavakh druzhynnykiv. Spohady uchasnykiv.* Denver: Vyd. Druzhyn ukrainskykh natsionalistiv, 1982.

Kalbarczyk, Sławomir. *Wykaz łagrów sowieckich miejsc przymusowej pracy obywateli polskich w latach 1939–1943.* Part One. Warszawa: Główna Komisja Badania Zbrodni przeciwko Narodowi Polskiemu, Instytut Pamięci Narodowej, 1993.

Kamenetsky, Ihor. *Hitler's Occupation of Ukraine, 1941–1944: A Study of Totalitarian Imperialism.* Milwaukee: Marquette University Press, 1956.

_____. *Secret Nazi Plans for Europe: A Study of Lebensraum Policies.* New York: Bookman Associates, 1961.

_____. "Some Aspects of Ukrainian Politics of National Self-Determination in View of Hitler's 'Drang Nach Osten.'" *Ukrainian Historian* 27 (1990): 104–12.

Kania, Janusz. "Likwidacja cerkwi na Lubelszczyźnie w okresie międzywojennym." *Chrześcijanin w Świecie* 14, no. 6 (1982): 50–89.

Kaplan, Chaim A. *Scroll of Agony: The Warsaw Diary of Chaim A. Kaplan.* New York: Macmillan Company, 1965.

Karski, Jan. *The Great Powers and Poland, 1919–1945: From Versailles to Yalta.* New York: University Press of America, 1985.

Kaslas, Bronis J. *The USSR-German Aggression against Lithuania.* New York: Robert Speller and Sons, 1973.

Keegan, John, ed. *Times Atlas of the Second World War.* New York: Harper and Row, 1989.

Kersten, Krystyna. *The Establishment of Communist Rule in Poland, 1943–48.* Berkeley: University of California Press, 1991.

_____. *Narodziny systemu władzy: Polska 1943–1948.* Poznań: SAWW, 1990.

_____. *Polacy, Żydzi, Komunizm. Anatomia półprawd 1939–68.* Warszawa: Niezależna Oficyna Wydawnicza, 1992.

Khrushchev, Nikita. "Krushchev's Secret Tapes." *Time,* October 1, 1990, p. 47.

Kielce—July 4, 1946: Background, Context, and Events, a Collective Work. Toronto and Chicago: Polish Educational Foundation in North America, 1996.

Kierski, Kazimierz. *Ochrona praw mniejszości w Polsce.* Poznań, 1933.

Kijuć, Władysław. "Armia Krajowa na Litwie i Białorusi." *Zeszyty Histroyczne* (Paris) 113 (1995): 160–65.

Kiryk, Feliks. *Żydzi w Małopolsce. Studia z dziejów osadnictwa i życia społecznego.* Przemyśl: Południowo-Wschodni Instytut Naukowy w Przemyślu, 1991.

Klietmann, Kurt-Georg. *Die Waffen-SS. Eine Dokumentation.* Osnabrück: Verlag Der Freiwillige, 1965.

Klukowski, Zygmunt. *Diary from the Years of Occupation, 1939–44.* Trans. George Klukowski. Eds. Andrew Klukowski and Helen Klukowski May. Chicago: University of Illinois Press, 1993.

_____. *Dziennik 1944–45.* Ed. Wojciech Samoliński. Lublin: Oficyna Wydawnicza Federacji Solidarności Regionu Środkowowschodniego, 1990.

_____. *Dziennik z lat okupacji Zamojszczyzny, 1939–44.* Ed. Zygmunt Mańkowski. Lublin: Lubelska Spółdzielnia Wydawnicza, 1958, 1959.

Knysh, Zynovii (Bohdan Mykhailuk). *Bunt Bandery.* Toronto, 1950.

Kobylański, Władysław. *W szponach trzech wrogów.* Chicago: Wici, 1988.

Koditsa, Nikolai. *V edinoi sem'e bratskikh narodov.* Minsk, 1971.

Kojder, Apolonja Maria, and Barbara Głogowska. *Marynia Don't Cry: Memoirs of Two Polish-Canadian Families.* Toronto: Multicultural History Society of Ontario, 1995.

Komański, Henryk. "Eksterminacja polskiej ludności: powiat Radziechów." *Na Rubieży* (Wrocław) 4, no. 10 (1994): 4–14.

Konieczny, Zdzisław, ed. *Źródła do dziejów regionu przemyskiego w latach 1944–1949.* Przemyśl: Wojewódzkie Archiwum Państwowe w Przemyślu, 1979.

Konovalets, Ievhen. *Prychynky do istorii ukrainskoi revoliutsii.* 2d ed. Provid Ukrainskykh Natsionalistiv, 1948.

Korab-Żebryk, Roman. *Biała Księga w obronie Armii Krajowej na Wileńszczyźnie.* Lublin: Wydawnictwo Lubelskie, 1991.

Korboński, Stefan. *The Jews and the Poles in World War II.* New York: Hippocrene Books, 1989.

_____. *The Polish Underground State: A Guide to the Underground, 1939–1945.* New York: Hippocrene, 1981.

Korman, Aleksander. *Nieukarane zbrodnie SS-Galizien z lat 1943–1945.* London: Koło Lwowian, 1989.

_____. "Polscy "Istriebitiele" z lat 1944–1945 w Małopolsce Wschodniej i na Wołyniu." *Semper Fidelis* (Wrocław) 3, no. 26 (May–June 1995): 7–11.

_____. *Z krwawych dni Lwowa 1941 roku.* London: Koło Lwowian, 1989.

Korzec, Paweł, and Jean-Charles Szurek. "Jews and Poles under Soviet Occupation (1939–1941): Conflicting Interests." *Polin* 4 (1989): 204–25.

Kosakviskyi, Mykyta. "Z nedanoho minuloho." *Nashe Slovo* 5 (1977): 67–80.

Kosyk, Wolodymyr. *The Third Reich and Ukraine.* New York: Peter Lang, 1993.

Kowalski, Isaac, comp. and ed. *Anthology on Armed Jewish Resistance, 1939–1945.* Vol. 3. New York: Jewish Combatants Publishing House, 1986.

Krakowski, Shmuel. "Podziemie polskie wobec zagłady Żydów." *Odra* (Wrocław), April 1991, pp. 23–29.

_____. *The War of the Doomed: Jewish Armed Resistance in Poland, 1942–1944.* New York: Holmes and Meier, 1984.

Krannhals, Hans von. *Der Warshauer Aufstand 1944.* Frankfurt: Bernard und Graefe, 1964.

Krawczak, Tadeusz, ed. *Zanim wróciła Polska. Martyrologium ludności unickiej na Podlasiu w latach 1866–1905 w świetle wspomnień.* Warszawa: Neriton, 1994.

Krawczyk, Andrzej. "Świadectwo Milcha." *Karta* (Warszawa) 2 (February 1991): 53–56.

Krokhmaliuk, Roman. *Zahrava na skhodi: spohady i dokumenti z pratsi u Viiskovii upravi "Halychyna" v 1943–1945 rokakh.* Toronto: Bratstvo kol. Voiakiv 1-o Ukrainskoi Dyvizii UNA, 1978.

Kruszewski, Z. Anthony. "The Revival of the Polish Diaspora in Lithuania, Belarus, and Ukraine." *Polish Review* 41, no. 3 (1996): 293–308.

Kubiak, Hieronim, et al., *Mniejszości polskie i polonia w ZSRR.* Wrocław: Ossolineum — Wydawnictwo Polskiej Akademii Nauk, 1992.

Kubiiovych, Volodymyr. *Meni 85.* München: "Malode Zhyttia," 1985.

Kupetskyi, Hrytsko. *Tam, de sontse skhodyt. Spohady boiovyka OUN na Dalekomu Skhodi.* Toronto: Vydavnytstvo Viktora Polishchuka, 1988.

Kupiak, Dmytro. *Spohady nerostrilanoho.* Toronto, 1991.

Kurek, Ewa. *Żydzi, Polacy, czy po prostu ludzie...* Lublin: Takt, 1992.
Kuropas, Myron B. *The Ukrainian Americans: Roots and Aspirations, 1884–1954*. Toronto: University of Toronto Press, 1991.
Landau, Ludwig. *Kronika lat wojny i okupacji*. Warszawa: Państwowe Wydawnictwo Naukowe, 1962.
Landwehr, Richard. *Fighting for Freedom: The Ukrainian Volunteer Division of the Waffen-SS*. Silver Springs, MD: Bibliophile Legion Books, 1985.
Lane, Arthur Bliss. *I Saw Poland Betrayed*. Boston: Western Islands, 1948.
Lappo, Henryk et al., eds. *Z Kresów Wschodnich Rzeczypospolitej: wspomnienia z osad wojskowych, 1921–1940*. London: Ognisko Rodzin Osadników Kresowych, 1992.
Laqueur, Walter. *The Terrible Secret: Suppression of the Truth about Hitler's "Final Solution."* London: Weidenfield and Nicolson, 1980.
Latawski, Paul, ed. *The Reconstruction of Poland, 1914–23*. New York: St. Martin's Press, 1992.
Lebed, Mykola. *UPA: Ukrainska Povstanska Armiia*. Presove Biuro UHVR, 1946.
Lenczowski, George. *The Middle East in World Affairs*. 2d ed. Ithaca, NY: Cornell University Press, 1956.
Lewandowski, Józef. "History and Myth: Pińsk, April 1919." *Polin* 2 (1987): 50–72.
Linenthal, Edward T. *Preserving Memory: The Struggle to Create America's Holocaust Museum*. New York: Viking Penguin, 1995.
Lisowska, Wanda. "Wspomnienia 'Grażyny.'" *Zeszyty Historyczne* (Paris) 36 (1976): 27–35.
Liszewski, Karol [Ryszard Szawłowski]. "The Polish-Soviet War of 1939." Paper presented at the Conference on Soviet Rule in Eastern Poland, 1939–1941, held at the School of Slavonic and East European Studies, University of London, on April 12–14, 1989.
_____. *Wojna polsko-sowiecka 1939 roku*. London: Polska Fundacja Kulturalna, 1986. 2 vols., Warszawa: Neriton, 1995.
Litopys Ukrainskoi Povstanskoi Armii. Toronto: Vydavnytstvo Litopys UPA, 1977–83.
Littlejohn, David. *Foreign Legions of the Third Reich*. 4 vols. San Jose, CA: R. James Bender Publishing, 1985.
_____. *The Patriotic Traitors: The History of Collaboration in German-Occupied Europe, 1940–45*. New York: Doubleday, 1972.
Lochner, Louis P., ed. *The Goebbels Diaries*. Garden City: Doubleday, 1948.
Loftus, John. *The Belarus Secret*. New York: Alfred A. Knopf, 1982.
Łossowski, Piotr, ed. *Likwidacja Uniwersytetu Stefana Batorego przez władze litewskie w grudniu 1939 roku*. Warszawa: Wydawnictwo Interlibro, 1991.
_____. *Związek Radziecki w latach Wielkiej Wojny Narodowej 1941–1945*. Wrocław: Zakład Narodowy im. Ossolińskich, 1979.
Łuczak, Czesław. *Polska i Polacy w drugiej wojnie światowej*. Poznań: Wydawnictwo Naukowe Uniwersytetu imienia Adama Mickiewicza, 1993.
Lukas, Richard C. *Bitter Legacy: Polish-American Relations in the Wake of World War II*. Lexington: University Press of Kentucky, 1982.
_____. *Did the Children Cry? Hitler's War against Jewish and Polish Children, 1939–45*. New York: Hippocrene Books, 1994.
_____. *The Forgotten Holocaust: The Poles under German Occupation, 1939–1944*. Lexington: University Press of Kentucky, 1986; New York: Hippocrene Books, 1990, 1997.
_____. "A Response." *Slavic Review*, fall/winter 1987, pp. 581–90.
_____, ed. *Out of the Inferno: Poles Remember the Holocaust*. Lexington: University Press of Kentucky, 1989.
Łużny, Ryszard, ed. *Chrześcijański wschód a kultura polska*. Lublin: Katolicki Uniwersytet Lubelski, 1989.
Lwów i Kresy (London) 32 (March-August 1994) and (September 1995): 69–73.
McCafferty, Nell. "Life after Chernobyl." *Audubon*, May-June 1996, pp. 66–75.
Madajczyk, Czesław. *Faszyzm i okupacje 1938–1945. Wykonywanie okupacji przez państwa Osi w Europie*. Poznań: Wydawnictwo Poznańskie, 1983.
_____. *Hitlerowski terror na wsi polskiej, 1939–1945*. Warszawa: Państwowe Wydawnictwo Naukowe, 1965.
_____. *Polityka III Rzeszy w okupowanej Polsce*. 2 vols. Warszawa: Państwowe Wydawnictwo Naukowe, 1970.
_____, ed. *Dzieje najnowsze* (Warszawa) 2 (1994).

_____. *Zamojszczyzna—Sonderlaboratorium SS. Zbiór dokumentów polskich i niemieckich z okresu okupacji hitlerowskiej.* 2 vols. Warszawa: Ludowa Spółdzielnia Wydawnicza, 1977.

Magocsi, Paul Robert. *Galicia: A Historical Survey and Bibliographic Guide.* Toronto: University of Toronto Press, in association with the Canadian Institute of Ukrainian Studies and the Harvard Ukrainian Research Institute, 1983.

Mały Rocznik Statystyczny, 1939. Warszawa: *GUS,* 1939.

Mandelkern, Benjamin. *Escape from the Nazis.* Toronto: James Lorimer, 1988.

Mańkowski, Zygmunt. "Problem weryfikacji strat w obozie na Majdanku." *Dzieje Najnowsze* (Warszawa) 26, no. 2 (1994): 27–31.

Manor, Alexander, ed. *The Book of Sambor and Stari-Sambor: A Memorial to the Jewish Communities of Sambor and Stari-Sambor. The Story of the Two Jewish Communities from Their Beginnings To Their End.* Tel Aviv: Hotsaat Irgun yotse Sambor-Stari-Sambor veha-sevivah be-Yisrael, 1980.

Marcus, Joseph. *Social and Political History of the Jews in Poland, 1919–1939.* New York: Mouton, 1983.

Marples, David R. *Stalinism in Ukraine in the 1940s.* New York: St. Martin's Press, 1992.

Marrus, Michael R., ed. *The Nazi Holocaust: Historical Articles on the Destruction of European Jews. Vol. 5, Public Opinion and Relations to the Jews in Nazi Europe* (2 vols). Westport, CT: Meckler, 1989.

Materski, Wojciech, ed. *Katyn: Documents of Genocide.* Warsaw: Institute of Polish Studies, Polish Academy of Sciences, 1993.

Meducki, Stanisław. *Antyżydowskie wydarzenia kieleckie 4 lipca 1946 roku: dokumenty i materiały.* Vol. 2. Kielce: Kieleckie Towarzystwo Naukowe, 1994.

_____, and Zenon Wrona, eds. *Antyżydowskie wydarzenia kieleckie 4 lipca 1946 roku: dokumenty i materiały.* Vol. 1. Kielce: Urząd Miasta Kielce and Kieleckie Towarzystwo Naukowe, 1992.

Meyer, Peter, et al. *The Jews in the Soviet Satellites.* Syracuse, NY: Syracuse University Press, 1953.

Micgiel, John. "Kościół katolicki i pogrom kielecki." *Niepodległość* (New York, London) 25 (1992): 134–72.

Mikhnovskyi, Mykola. *Samostiina Ukraina.* Lwów: E. Kosevych, 1900.

Mikołajczyk, Stanisław. *The Rape of Poland: Patterns of Soviet Aggression.* London: S. Low, Marston, 1948.

Milch, Baruch. "Mój testament." *Karta* (Warszawa) 2 (February 1991): 3–52.

Miłosz, Czesław. "Adders and Other Reptiles." *New York Review of Books,* May 11, 1995, pp. 15–18; and reply to Abraham Brumberg, June 22, 1995.

_____. "Anti-Semitism in Poland." *Problems in Communism* 3 (1957): 35–40.

Mirchuk, Petro. *Narys istorii Orhanizatsii Ukrainskykh Natsionalistiv 1920–1939.* München: Ukrainske Vydavnytstvo, 1968.

Mirska, Klara. *W cieniu wiecznego strachu: wspomnienia.* Paris: Imprimerie IM. PO, 1980.

Misiło, Eugeniusz, ed. *Akcja "Wisła." Dokumenty.* Warszawa: Archiwum Ukraińskie, 1993.

Misiunas, Romuald J., and Rein Taagepera. *The Baltic States: Years of Independence, 1940–1990.* Rev. ed. Berkeley: University of California Press, 1993.

Motyl, Alexander J. *Dilemmas of Independence: Ukraine after Totalitarianism.* New York: Council of Foreign Relations Press, 1993.

_____. "The Rural Origins of the Communist and Nationalist Movements in Wołyń *Województwo,* 1921–1939." *Slavic Review* 37 (September 1978): 412–20.

_____. *The Turn to the Right: The Ideological Origins and Development of Ukrainian Nationalism, 1919–1929.* Boulder, CO: East European Monographs, 1980.

_____. "Ukrainian Nationalist Political Violence in Inter-War Poland, 1921–1939." *East European Quarterly* 19, no. 1 (March 1985): 45–55.

Musiał, Adam Kazimierz. *Krwawe upiory: dzieje powiatu Dąbrowa Tarnowska w okresie okupacji hitlerowskiej.* Tarnów: Oficyna Wydawnicza Karat, 1993.

Muzyka, Agnieszka. "Relacja świadka Agnieszki Muzyki." *Na Rubieży* (Wrocław) 2, no. 3 (1993): 15–16.

Mykhalchuk, Vasyl, ed. *Tudy, de bii za voliu. Zbirnyk viiskovo-politychnykh materialiv u pamiat' Maksyma Skorupskoho-Maksa kurinnoho UPA.* London-Paris: Fundatsiia im. O. Olzhycha, 1989; Kyiv: "Kozaky," 1992.

Myśliwski, Wiesław, and Andrzej Garlicki, comps. *Wschodnie losy Polaków.* 4 vols. Łomża: Oficyna Wydawnicza "Stopka," 1991.

Nahaylo, Bohdan. "Ukraine." *RFE/RL Research Report* 3, no. 16 (April 22, 1994): 42–49.

New Catholic Encyclopedia. Vol. 11. New York: McGraw-Hill, 1967.

New Encyclopaedia Britannica. Macropaedia. Vol. 29. Chicago: Encyclopaedia Britannica, 1992.

Nieczuja, Tadeusz. "Zbrodnia katyńska." *Przegląd Polski* 7, no. 25 (July 1948): 3–9.

Niezabitowska, Małgorzata. *Remnants: The Last Jews of Poland*. New York: Friendly Press, 1986.

Nowicki, Wacław. *Żywe echa*. Warszawa: Antyk, 1993.

Nurowski, Roman. *1939–1945: War Losses in Poland*. Poznań: Wydawnictwo Zachodnie, 1960.

Okupacja i rozbiór Polski we wrześniu 1939 r. Warszawa: Wojskowy Instytut Historyczny, 1992. Map and text prepared for a historical-military atlas, *Polacy na frontach II wojny światowej*.

Olszański, Tadeusz [Jan Łukaszów]. *Historia Ukrainy XX wieku*. Warszawa: Oficyna Wydawnicza Volumen, 1993.

_____. "Walki polsko-ukraińskie 1943–1947." *Zeszyty Historyczne* (Paris) 90 (1989): 159–99.

Orlicki, Józef. *Szkice z dziejów stosunków polsko-żydowskich 1918–1949*. Warszawa: Krajowa Agencja Wydawnicza, 1983.

Ożarowski, Filip. *Gdy płonął Wołyń*. Chicago: Wici, 1995.

Pająk, Henryk. *Konspiracja młodzieży szkolnej 1945–1955*. Lublin: Retro, 1994.

_____. *Strach być Polakiem*. Lublin: Retro, 1996.

_____, and Stanisław Żochowski. *Rządy zbirów 1940–1990*. Lublin: Retro, 1996.

Paldiel, Mordecai. *The Path of the Righteous: Gentile Rescuers of Jews during the Holocaust*. New York: Jewish Foundation for Christian Rescuers/ADL, 1993.

Pankiewicz, Tadeusz. *Apteka w getcie krakowskim*. Kraków: Wydawnictwo Literackie, 1982.

Pankivskyi, Kost. *Roky nimetskoi okupatsii: 1941–1944*. New York: Vydavnytstvo Kliuchi, 1965.

Pasternak, Evhen. *Narys istorii Kholmshchyny i Pidliashshia (Novishi chasy)*. Winnipeg: Research Institute of Volyn, 1968.

Pawliczko, Ann Lencyk, ed. *Ukraine and Ukrainians throughout the World: A Demographic and Sociological Guide to the Homeland and Its Diaspora*. Toronto: University of Toronto Press, 1994.

Penkulla, Adam. "The 'Przytyk Incidents' of 9 March 1936 from Archival Documents." *Polin* 5 (1990): 327–59.

Perechodnik, Calel. *Am I a Murderer? Testament of a Jewish Ghetto Policeman*. Boulder, CO: Westview Press, 1996.

_____. "Dzień ostatni." *Karta* (Warszawa) 9 (1992): 39–55.

Peretiatkowicz, Adam. *Polska samoobrona w okolicach Łucka*. Katowice: Ośrodek Badań Społeczno-Kulturowych Towarzystwa Zachęty Kultury, 1995.

Pilaciński, Jerzy. *Narodowe Siły Zbrojne: kulisy walki podziemnej 1939–1945*. London: Towarzystwo imienia Romana Dmowskiego, 1976.

Piłsudski, Józef. *Pisma zbiorowe: wydanie prac dotychczas drukiem ogłoszonych*. Warszawa: Instytut Józefa Piłsudskiego, 1937.

Pinchuk, Ben-Cion. *Shtetl Jews under Soviet Rule: Eastern Poland on the Eve of the Holocaust*. Cambridge, MA: Basil Blackwell, 1991.

Piotrowski, Czesław. *Krwawe żniwa za Styrem, Horyniem i Słuczą*. Warszawa: Światowy Związek Żołnierzy Armii Krajowej Okręg Wołyński, 1995.

Piotrowski, Stanisław. *Dziennik Hansa Franka*. Warszawa: Wydawnictwo Prawnicze, 1956.

Piotrowski, Tadeusz. "Polish-Ukrainian Relations During World War II: Ethnic Cleansing in Volhynia and Eastern Galicia." Toronto: Adam Mickiewicz Foundation, 1995. (A talk.)

_____. *Ukrainian Integral Nationalism: Chronological Assessment and Bibliography*. Toronto: Alliance of the Polish Eastern Provinces, with The Polish Educational Foundation in North America, 1997.

_____. *Vengeance of the Swallows: Memoir of a Polish Family's Ordeal Under Soviet Aggression, Ukrainian Ethnic Cleansing, and Nazi Enslavement and Their Emigration to America*. Jefferson, NC: McFarland, 1995.

Pisarewski-Parry, Felix. *Orły i Reszki*. Warszawa: Iskra, 1984.

Pobóg-Malinowski, Władysław. *Najnowsza historia polityczna Polski, 1864-1945*. 3 vols. London, 1983.

Podhorski, Baltazar. "Na czerwonej fali." *Biuletyn Informacyjny—Prawda o Komunizmie* (Warsaw) 1, no. 36 (1937): 28–31.

_____. "Udział Żydów w rewolucji komunistycznej w Rosji." *Biuletyn Informacyjny—Prawda o Komunizmie* (Warsaw) 4, no. 39 (1937): 127–32.

Podlaski, Kazimierz [Bohdan Skaradziński]. *Białorusini, Litwini, Ukraińcy.* London: Puls Publications, 1985.

Podvorniak, Mykhailo. *Viter z Volyni. Spohady.* Winnipeg: T-vo "Volyn," 1981.

Pogonowski, Iwo Cyprian. "Holocaust Memorial Museum in Washington, DC." *New Horizon* 20 (November-December 1995): 9–11.

_____. *Jews in Poland: A Documentary History.* New York: Hippocrene Books, 1993.

Poksiński, Jerzy. *"My sędziowie, nie od Boga..." Z dziejów Sądownictwa Wojskowego PRL 1944–1956. Materiały i dokumenty.* Warszawa: Gryf, 1996.

Polish Research Centre, ed. *The Orthodox Eastern Church in Poland: Past and Present.* London: Polish Research Centre, 1942.

Poliszczuk, Wiktor. *Gorzka Prawda. Zbrodniczość OUN-UPA (spowiedź Ukraińca).* Toronto, 1995.

_____. *Hirka pravda. Zlochynnist OUN-UPA (spovid ukraintsia).* Toronto, 1995.

_____. *Ideologia nacjonalizmu ukraińskiego według Dmytra Doncowa.* Warszawa, 1996.

_____. *Legal and Political Assessment of the OUN and UPA.* Toronto, 1997. A trilingual publication.

Połomski, Franciszek. *Aspekty rasowe w postępowaniu z robotnikami przymusowymi i jeńcami wojennymi III Rzeszy, 1933–1945.* Wrocław: Zakład Narodowy im. Ossolińskich, 1976.

Polonsky, Antony, Ezra Mendelsohn, and Jerzy Tomaszewski, eds. *Jews in Independent Poland, 1918–1939.* Washington, DC: The Littleman Library of Jewish Civilization, 1994. (This is vol. 8 of *Polin.*)

Poluian, Vladimir Aleksandrovich. *Revoliutsionno-demokraticheskoe dvizhenie v Zapadnoi Belorussii.* Minsk: Nauka i tekhnika, 1978.

Popiński, Krzysztof, Aleksandr Kokurin, and Aleksandr Gurjanow. *Drogi śmierci.* Warszawa: Karta, 1995.

Pospieszalski, Karol. *Polska pod niemieckim prawem.* Poznań: Wydawnictwo Instytutu Zachodniego, 1946.

Potichnyj, Peter. "'Akcja Wisła': The Forcible Relocation of the Ukrainian Population in Poland." *Ukrainian Quarterly* 44, no. 1–2 (spring-summer 1988): 72–90.

Pragier, Ruta. *Żydzi czy Polacy.* Warszawa: Rytm, 1992.

Prekerowa, Teresa. *Konspiracyjna Rada Pomocy Żydom w Warszawie 1942–1945.* Warszawa: Państwowy Instytut Wydawniczy, 1982.

_____. "Podziemie żydowskie a podziemie polskie." *Odra* (Wrocław), April 1991, pp. 30-35.

_____. "Stosunek ludności polskiej do żydowskich uciekinierów z obozów zagłady w Treblince, Sobiborze i Bełżcu w świetle relacji żydowskich i polskich." *Biuletyn Głównej Komisji Badania Zbrodni przeciwko Narodowi Polskiemu—Instytut Pamięci Narodowej* (Warszawa) 35 (1993).

Proch, Franciszek. *Poland's Way of the Cross, 1939–1945.* New York: Polish Association of Former Political Prisoners of Nazi and Soviet Concentration Camps, 1987.

Prus, Edward. *Bluff XX wieku.* London: Koło Lwowian, 1992.

_____. *Melnykowcy. Kolaboracja czy opór?* Wrocław: Stowarzyszenie Upamiętnienia Ofiar Zbrodni Ukraińskich Nacjonalistów, 1994.

_____. *Operacja "Wisła."* Wrocław: Nortom, 1994.

_____. *UPA. Armia powstańcza czy kurenie rizunów?* Wrocław: Nortom, 1994.

Przygoda, Zdzisław. *Niezwykłe przygody w zwyczajnym życiu.* Warszawa: Ypsylon, 1994.

_____. *The Way to Freedom.* Toronto: Lugus, 1995.

Rashke, Richard. *Escape from Sobibor.* New York: Avon, 1982.

Reale, Eugenio. *Raporty: Polska 1945–1946.* Trans. Paweł Zdziechowski. Paris: Institut Littéraire, 1968.

Reitlinger, Gerald. *The Final Solution.* London: Vallentine, Mitchell, 1953.

_____. *The SS: Alibi of a Nation, 1922–1945.* New York: Viking Press, 1968.

Reshetar, John S. *The Ukrainian Revolution, 1917–1920: A Study in Nationalism.* New York: Arno Press, 1972.

Ringelblum, Emanuel. *Kronika getta warszawskiego: wrzesień 1939—styczeń 1943.* Warszawa: Czytelnik, 1983.

_____. *Notes from the Warsaw Ghetto: The Journal of Emmanuel Ringelblum.* New York: McGraw-Hill, 1958.

_____. *Polish-Jewish Relations during the Second World War.* Eds. Joseph Kermish and Shmuel Krakowski. Evanston, IL: Northwestern University Press, 1992.

_____. *Stosunki polsko-żydowskie w czasie drugiej wojny światowej. Uwagi i spostrzeżenia.* Warszawa: Czytelnik, 1988.

Ripetsky, Modest. *UPA Medical Services.* Toronto: Litopys UPA, 1992.

Rittner, Carol, and Sondra Myers, eds. *The Courage to Care: Rescuers of Jews during the Holocaust.* New York: New York University Press, 1986.

The Rohatyn Jewish Community: A Town That Perished. Israel: Rohatyn Association of Israel, 1962.

Röhr, Werner, ed. *Okkupation und Kollaboration (1938–1945). Beiträge zu Konzepten und Praxis der Kollaboration in der deutschen Okkupationspolitik.* Berlin: Hüthig Verlagsgemeinschaft, 1994.

Rokicka, J. "Było sobie takie miasteczko na Pokucie." *Semper Fidelis* (Wrocław) 5, no. 22 (September-October 1994): 29–32.

Rosa, Edward. *Wspomnienia lat przeżytych na Wołyniu.* Toronto: Alliance of the Polish Eastern Provinces, 1997.

Rosen, Marjorie, and Mary Huzinec. "Collector of Souls." *People Magazine,* January 17, 1994, pp. 36–39. (Interview with Yaffa Eliach.)

Rosenberg, Alfred. *Der Zukunftsweg einer deutschen Aussenpolitik.* München: F. Eher, 1927.

Rosenberg, Blanca. *To Tell at Last: Survival under False Identity, 1941–45.* Chicago: University of Illinois Press, 1993.

Roszkowski, Wojciech [Andrzej Albert]. *Historia Polski 1914–1993.* Warszawa: Wydawnictwo Naukowe PWN, 1994.

Rothkirchen, Livia. "Czech Attitudes toward the Jews during Nazi Regime." *Yad Vashem Studies* 13 (1979): 287–320.

Rothschild, Joseph. *Return to Diversity: A Political History of East Central Europe since World War II.* 2d Ed. New York: Oxford University Press, 1993.

Rowiński, Krzysztof, ed. *Moje zderzenie z bolszewikami we wrześniu 1939 roku.* London: Polska Fundacja Kulturalna, 1986.

Sabrin, B. F. *Alliance for Murder: The Nazi-Ukrainian Nationalist Partnership in Genocide.* New York: Sarpedon, 1991.

Sack, John. *An Eye for an Eye.* New York: BasicBooks, 1993, 1995.

Sadler, Charles. "Pro-Soviet Polish Americans: Oscar Lange and Russia's Friends in the Polonia, 1941–1945." *Polish Review* 22, no. 4 (1977): 25–39.

Sasinowski, Władysław K. *Piaśnica, 1939–1944.* Committee for the Erection of a Memorial to the Victims of Piaśnica in Wejherowo, 1956.

Savchuk, S. V. "Akt proholoshennia Ukrainskoi Derzhavy 30-ho chervnia 1941 roku." *Novyi Litopys 1,* vol. 1 (1961): 3–25.

Sawicki, Cyprian. *Ludzie i sprawy Norymbergi.* Poznań: Wydawnictwo Poznańskie, 1967.

Schatz, Jaff. *The Generation: The Rise and Fall of the Jewish Communists of Poland.* Berkeley: University of California Press, 1991.

Schneigert, Zbigniew. "Obozy NKWD jeńców polskich z lat 1939–1941 w Małopolsce Wschodniej." *Semper Fidelis* (Wrocław) 3, no. 4 (1992): 24–29.

Schochet, Simon. "Polscy oficerowie pochodzenia żydowskiego — jeńcy Katynia na tle walk o niepodległość (próba identyfikacji)." *Niepodległość* (New York, London) 21 (1988): 152–66.

Schoenfeld, Joachim, ed. *Holocaust Memoirs: Jews in the Lwów Ghetto, the Janowski Concentration Camp, and as Deportees in Siberia.* Hoboken, NJ: KTAV Publishing House, 1985.

Schulman, Faye. *A Partisan's Memoir: Woman of the Holocaust.* Toronto: Second Story Press, 1995.

Sereny, Gitta. "John Demjanjuk and the Failure of Justice." *New York Review of Books,* October 8, 1992, pp. 32–34.

Shahak, Israel. *Jewish History, Jewish Religion: The Weight of Three Thousand Years.* Boulder, CO: Pluto Press, 1994.

_____. "'The Life of Death': An Exchange." *New York Review of Books,* January 29, 1987, pp. 45-50.

Shandruk, Pavlo. "Historyczna prawda o Ukraińskiej Armii Narodowej." *Kultura,* no. 212 (June 1965): 86–103.

Shankovskyi, Lev. "Ukrainska Povstancha Armiia." In *Istoriia ukrainskoho viiska.* Winnipeg: Ivan Tyktor, 1953, pp. 635–821.

Shirer, William. *The Rise and Fall of the Third Reich.* Greenwich, CT: Fawcett, 1960.

Shoup, Paul S. *The East European and Soviet Data Handbook: Political, Social, and Developmental Indicators, 1945–1975.* New York: Columbia University Press, 1981.

Shtockfish, David, ed., *Memorial Book: Ostrow-Lubelski.* Israel: Ostrow-Lubelski Society, 1987.

Shumuk, Danylo. *Za skhidnym obriiem. Spomyny.* Paris: Persha ukrainska drukarnia u Frantsii, 1974.

Siemaszko, Władysław. "Stan badań nad terrorem ukraińskim na Wołyniu w latach 1939–1944." *Lwów i Kresy* (London) 72 (July-September 1992): 37–47.

Siemaszko, Zbigniew S. "Brygada Świętokrzyska 1945–1946." *Zeszyty Historyczne* (Paris) 38 (1976): 31–58.

_____. "Komentarze." *Zeszyty Historyczne* (Paris) 86 (1988): 162–69.

_____. *Narodowe Siły Zbrojne.* London: Odnowa, 1982.

_____. *W sowieckim osaczeniu 1939–1943.* London: Polska Fundacja Kulturalna, 1991.

Siemaszko, Zdzisław A. "Wileńska AK a Niemcy." *Zeszyty Historyczne* (Paris) 110 (1994): 198–222.

Silverman, Peter, David Smuschkowitz, and Peter Smuszkowicz. *From Victims to Victors.* Montmagny, Québec: Marquis; Toronto: Canadian Society for Yad Vashem, 1992.

Simpson, Christopher. *Blowback, America's Recruitment of Nazis and Its Effects on the Cold War.* New York: Weidenfeld and Nicolson, 1988.

Singer, Isaac Bashevis. *Love and Exile.* New York: Doubleday, 1984.

Sivard, Ruth Leger. *World Military and Social Expenditures, 1987–88.* Washington, DC: World Priorities, 1987.

Siwicki, Mikołaj. *Dzieje konfliktów polsko-ukraińskich.* Warszawa, 1992(vols. 1 and 2), 1994 (vol. 3).

Skrzypek, Stanisław. *The Problem of Galicia.* London: Polish Association for the South-Eastern Provinces, 1948.

_____. *Ukraiński program państwowy.* London: Koło Lwowian, 1967.

Śledzianowski, Jan. *Ksiądz Czesław Kaczmarek biskup kielecki 1895–1963.* Kielce, 1991.

Słomczyński, Adam. *Dom Ks. Boduena 1939–1945.* Warszawa: Państwowy Instytut Wydawniczy, 1975.

Smith, Bradley F. *Reaching Judgment at Nuremberg.* New York: New American Library, 1979.

Smolar, Aleksander. "Jews as a Polish Problem." *Daedelus,* spring 1987, pp. 31–73.

_____. "Tabu i niewinnosć." *Aneks* (London) 41/42 (1986): 89–133.

Smovskyi, Kostiantyn. *Spohady uchasnyka banderivskoi UPA.* Mt. Dale, NY: Nasha Batkivshchyna, 1982.

Sodol, Petro R. "UPA — The Ukrainian Insurgent Army: An Overview." *Ukrainian Quarterly* 51, no. 2–3 (summer-fall 1995): 139–75.

_____. *UPA: They Fought Hitler and Stalin: A Brief Overview of Military Aspects from the History of the Ukrainian Insurgent Army, 1942–1949.* New York: Committee for the World Convention and Reunion of Soldiers in the Ukrainian Insurgent Army, 1987.

Solzhenitsyn, Aleksandr I. *The Gulag Archipelago, 1918–1956: An Experiment in Literary Investigation.* New York: Harper and Row, 1973.

Spector, Shmuel. *The Holocaust of Volhynian Jews, 1941–1944.* Jerusalem: Yad Vashem — The Federation of Volhynian Jews, 1990.

Srokowski, Stanisław. *Geografia gospodarcza Polski.* Warszawa, 1939.

Stahl, Zdzisław, ed. *Zbrodnia katyńska w świetle dokumentów.* London: Gryf, 1948.

Stanley, John. "Book Reviews." *Polish Review* 30, no. 4 (1985): 459–62.

Stebelski, Adam. *The Fate of Polish Archives during World War II.* Warsaw: Central Directorate of State Archives, 1964.

Stein, André. *Hidden Children: Forgotten Survivors of the Holocaust.* Toronto: Penguin Books Canada, 1993.

Stein, George H. *The Waffen SS: Hitler's Elite Guard at War, 1939–1945.* Ithaca, NY: Cornell University Press, 1966.

Steinsbergowa, Aniela. *Widziane z ławy obrończej.* Paris: Institut Littéraire, 1977.

Sternberg, Yitzhak. *Under Assumed Identity.* Israel: Hakibbutz Hameuchad and Ghetto Fighters' House, 1986.

Sterzer, Abraham. "We Fought for Ukraine!" *Ukrainian Quarterly* 20, no. 1 (1964): 37–41.

Stetsiuk, Hryhorii. *Nepostavlenyi pamiatnyk. Spohady.* Winnipeg: Instytut Doslidiv Volyni, 1988.

Stopniak, Franciszek, ed. *Kościół katolicki na ziemiach Polski w czasie II wojny światowej: materiały i studia.* Vol. 10, no. 5. Warszawa: Akademia Teologii Katolickiej, 1981.

Struk, Danylo Husar, ed. *Encyclopedia of Ukraine.* Vols. 3–5. Toronto: University of Toronto Press, 1993.

Styrkul, Valerii. *The SS Werewolves.* Lviv: Kamenyar Publishers, 1982.

_____. *We Accuse: Documentary Sketch.* Kiev: Dnipro Publishers, 1984.

Subtelny, Orest. *Ukraine: A History.* 2d ed. Toronto: University of Toronto Press and Canadian Institute of Ukrainian Studies, 1994.

Sulewski, Wojciech. *Lasy w ogniu. Zamojszczyzna, 1939-1944.* Warszawa: Czytelnik, 1962.

Suvorov, Viktor. *Icebreaker: Who Started the Second World War?* Trans. Thomas B. Beattie. London: Hamish Hamilton, 1990; New York: Viking Penguin, 1990.

Sword, Keith. *Deportation and Exile: Poles in the Soviet Union, 1939–48.* London: St. Martin's Press, 1994.

_____, ed. *The Soviet Takeover of the Polish Eastern Provinces, 1939–1941.* New York: St. Martin's Press, 1991.

Szapiro, Paweł, ed. *Wojna żydowsko-niemiecka. Polska prasa konspiracyjna 1943–1944 o powstaniu w getcie Warszawy.* London: Aneks, 1992.

Szaynok, Bożena. *Pogrom Żydów w Kielcach 4 lipca 1946 r.* Wrocław: Bellona, 1992.

Szcześniak, Antoni, and Wiesław Szota. *Droga do nikąd. Działalność Organizacji Ukraińskich Nacjonalistów i jej likwidacja w Polsce.* Warszawa: Ministerstwo Obrony Narodowej, 1973.

Szefer, Andrzej. "Dywersyjno-sabatażowa działalność wrocławskiej Abwehry na ziemiach polskich w przededniu agresji hitlerowskiej w 1939 r." *Biuletyn Głównej Komisji Badania Zbrodni Hitlerowskich w Polsce* (Warszawa) 32 (1987): 271–372.

Szeremeta, Bronisław. *Watażka. Wspomnienie nierozstrzelanego i jego zbrodnie.* Wrocław, 1995.

Szetelnicki, Wacław. *Trembowla. Kresowy bastion wiary i polskości.* Wrocław: Rubikon, 1992.

_____. *Zapomniany lwowski bohater ks. St. Frankl 1903–1944.* Rome: P.U.G., 1983.

Szwagrzyk, Krzysztof. "UB na Dolnym Śląsku 1945-1956." Ph.D. diss.

Szyłeyko, J. Zdzisław. "Współpraca wileńskiej AK z Niemcami — rzeczywistość czy fikcja?" *Zeszyty Historyczne* (Paris) 112 (1995): 233–36.

Szymczak, Robert. "Oskar Lange, American Polonia, and the Polish-Soviet Dilemma during World War II: Making the Case for a 'People's Poland.'" *Polish Review* 40. no. 2 (1995): 131–57.

_____. "Oskar Lange, American Polonia, and the Polish-Soviet Dilemma during World War II: The Public Partisan as Private Emissary." *Polish Review* 40, no. 1 (1995): 3–27.

Tec, Nechama. *Defiance: The Bielski Partisans.* New York: Oxford University Press, 1993.

_____. *In the Lion's Den: The Life of Oswald Rufeisen.* New York: Oxford University Press, 1990.

Tennenbaum, Samuel Lipa. *Zloczow Memoir.* New York: Shengold Publishers, 1986.

Tereshchuk, Petro [Oleksander Matla]. *Istorychni notatky.* Toronto: Homin Ukrainy, 1985.

Terleś, Mikołaj. *Ethnic Cleansing of Poles in Volhynia and Eastern Galicia, 1942–1946.* Toronto: Alliance of the Polish Eastern Provinces, 1993.

Tessin, Georg. *Verbände und Truppen der deutschen Wehrmacht und Waffen SS im Zweiten Weltkrieg, 1939–1945.* Frankfurt: Verlag E. S. Mittler und Sohh, 1974.

Thorwald, Jürgen. *Wen sie verderben wollen. Bericht des grossen Verrats.* Stuttgart: Steingrüben-Verlag, 1952.

Those Who Helped: Polish Rescuers of Jews during the Holocaust. Part Two. Warsaw: Main Commission for the Investigation of Crimes Against the Polish Nation — Institute of National Memory, 1996.

Tolstoy, Nikolai. *Victims of Yalta.* London: Hodder and Stoughton, 1977.

Tomaszewski, Irene, and Tecia Werbowski. *Zegota: The Rescue of Jews in Wartime Poland.* Montreal: Price-Patterson, 1994.

Tomaszewski, Jerzy, ed. *Najnowsze dzieje Żydów w Polsce w zarysie (do 1950 roku).* Warszawa: Wydawnictwo Naukowe PWN, 1993.

_____. "Pińsk, Saturday 5 April 1919." *Polin* 1 (1986): 227–51.

_____. *Rzeczpospolita wielu narodów.* Warszawa: Czytelnik, 1985.

Tomaszewski, Longin. *Kronika wileńska 1941–1945. Z dziejów polskiego państwa podziemnego.* Warszawa: Oficyna Wydawnicza Pomost, 1992.

Torańska, Teresa. *"Them": Stalin's Polish Puppets.* New York: Harper and Row, 1987.

Torke, Hans-Joachim, and John Paul Himka, eds. *German-Ukrainian Relations in Historical Perspective.* Toronto: Canadian Institute of Ukrainian Studies Press, 1994.

Tory, Avraham. *Surviving the Holocaust: The Kovno Ghetto Diary*. Ed. Martin Gilbert. Textual notes by Dina Porat. Trans. Jerzy Michalowicz. Cambridge: Harvard University Press, 1990.

Torzecki, Ryszard. "Kontakty polsko-ukraińskie na tle problemu ukraińskiego w polityce polskiego rządu emigracyjnego i podziemia (1939–1944)." *Dzieje Najnowsze* (Warszawa) 1, no. 2 (1981): 319–46.

_____. *Kwestia ukraińska w polityce III Rzeszy 1933–1945*. Warszawa: Książka i Wiedza, 1972.

_____. *Polacy i Ukraińcy. Sprawa ukraińska w czasie II wojny światowej na terenie II Rzeczypospolitej*. Warszawa: Wydawnictwo Naukowe PWN, 1993.

_____. "Postawa metropolity." *Więź* (July-August 1988): 99–115.

Trunk, Isaiah. *Judenrat: The Jewish Councils in Eastern Europe under Nazi Occupation*. New York: Macmillan, 1972.

Turonek, Jerzy. *Białoruś pod okupacją niemiecką*. Warszawa: Książka i Wiedza, 1993.

Turowski, Józef, and Władysław Siemaszko. *Zbrodnie nacjonalistów ukraińskich dokonane na ludności polskiej na Wołyniu 1939–1945*. Warszawa: Główna Komisja Badania Zbrodni Hitlerowskich w Polsce, 1990.

Tys-Krokhmaliuk, Yuriy. *UPA Warfare in Ukraine: Strategical, Tactical, and Organizational Problems of Ukrainian Resistance in World War II*. New York: Society of Veterans of Ukrainian Insurgent Army of the United States and Canada and St. George the Victorious Association of Veterans of Ukrainian Insurgent Army in Europe, 1972.

Udział kapelanów wojskowych w drugiej wojnie światowej. Warszawa: Akademia Teologii Katolickiej, 1984.

"The Ugly Face of Freedom," CBS *60 Minutes* transcript, vol. 27, no. 7 (October 23, 1994): 14-19.

UPA v svitli nimetskykh dokumentiv. Toronto: Litopys UPA, 1983.

Urban, Wincenty. *Droga krzyżowa Archidiecezji Lwowskiej w latach II wojny światowej 1939–1945*. Wrocław, 1983.

Urbaniak, George. "Lithomania versus Panpolonism: The Roots of the Polish-Lithuanian Conflict before 1914." *Canadian Slavonic Papers* 31, no. 2 (June 1989): 107–27.

Urbański, Krzysztof. *Kieleccy Żydzi*. Kraków: Małopolska Oficyna Wydawnicza, 1993.

Vakar, Nicholas P. *Belorussia: The Making of a Nation*. Cambridge: Harvard University Press, 1956.

Veryha, Wasyl. *Dorohamy Druhoi Svitovoi viiny. Legendy pro uchast ukraintsiv u zdushuvanni vashavskoho povstannia v 1944 r. ta pro Ukrainsku Dyviziiu "Halychyna."* Toronto: Brotherhood of Veterans of the I.UD UNA, 1981.

Vinton, Louisa. "The Katyn Documents: Politics and History." *RFE/RL Research Report* 2, no. 4 (January 22, 1993): 19–31.

Wałach, Stanisław. *Był w Polsce czas*. Kraków, 1971.

Walshaw, Rachela, and Sam Walshaw. *From out of the Firestone: A Memoir of the Holocaust*. New York: Shapolsky, 1991.

Wardzyńska, Maria. *Formacja Wachmannschaften des SS- und Polizeiführers im Distrikt Lublin*. Warszawa: Główna Komisja Badania Zbrodni przeciwko Narodowi Polskiemu, 1992.

_____. *Sytuacja ludnośći polskiej w Generalnym Komisariacie Litwy, czerwiec 1941–lipiec 1944*. Warszawa: Agencja Wydawnicza MAKO, 1993.

Wat, Aleksander. *Mój wiek. Pamiętnik mówiony*. London: Polonia Book Fund, 1977.

_____. *My Century: The Odyssey of a Polish Intellectual*. Berkeley: University of California Press, 1988.

Węgierski, Jerzy. *Armia Krajowa na południowych i wschodnich przedpolach Lwowa*. Kraków: Platan, 1994.

_____. *Lwów pod okupacją sowiecką 1939–1941*. Warszawa: Editions Spotkania, 1991.

Werth, Alexander. *Russia at War, 1941–1945*. New York: E. P. Dutton, 1964.

Wertheim, Anatol. "Żydowska partyzantka na Białorusi." *Zeszyty Historyczne* (Paris) 86 (1988): 96–162.

Wącek, Tadeusz, ed. *Zabić Żyda!: kulisy i tajemnice pogromu kieleckiego 1946*. Kraków: Oficyna Wydawnicza Temax, 1992.

Wiener, Jon. "Jews, Germans, and 'Revenge.'" *The Nation*, June 20, 1994, pp. 878–82.

Wiesenthal, Simon. *Justice Not Vengeance*. London: Weidenfeld and Nicolson, 1989.

_____. *Prawo czy zemsta*. Warszawa, 1993.

Wilczewska, Felicja. *Nim minęło 25 lat*. Toronto: Century Publishing Company, 1983.

Winch, Michael. *Republic for a Day*. London: Hale, 1939.

Wołczański, Józef. "Korespondencja Arcybiskupa Bolesława Twardowskiego z Arcybiskupem Andrzejem Szeptickim w latach 1943–1944." *Przegląd Wschodni* 2-6 (1992–93): 465–84.

Wolfshaut-Dinkes, Max. *Échec et mat. Récit d'un survivant de Przemysl en Galicie.* Paris: Association des fils et filles des déportés juifs de France, 1983.

Wroński, Stanisław, and Maria Zwolakowa. *Polacy Żydzi 1939–1945.* Warszawa: Książka i Wiedza, 1971.

Wrzesiński, Wojciech, ed. *Kaźń profesorów lwowskich — lipiec 1941. Studia oraz relacje i dokumenty zebrane i opracowane przez Zygmunta Alberta.* Wrocław: Wydawnictwo Uniwersytetu Wrocławskiego, 1989.

Wyden, Peter. *Stella: One Woman's True Tale of Evil, Betrayal, and Survival in Hitler's Germany.* New York: Simon and Schuster, 1992.

Wyrwich, Mateusz. *Łagier Jaworzno: z dziejów czerwonego terroru.* Warszawa: Editions Spotkania, 1995.

Yahil, Leni. *The Holocaust: The Fate of European Jewry, 1932–1945.* New York: Oxford University Press, 1990.

Yaremko, Michael. *From Separation to Unity.* Toronto: Shevchenko Scientific Society, 1967.

Zable, Arnold. *Jewels and Ashes.* New York: Harcourt Brace, 1991.

Zajączkowski, Wacław. *Martyrs of Charity: Christian and Jewish Response to the Holocaust.* Part One. Washington, DC: St. Maximilian Kolbe Foundation, 1987.

Żarski-Zajder, Władysław. *Martyrologia ludności Żydowskiej i pomoc społeczeństwa polskiego.* Warszawa: Związek Bojowników o Wolność i Demokrację, 1968.

Żbikowski, Andrzej. "Lokalne pogromy Żydów w czerwcu i lipcu 1941 roku na wschodnich rubieżach II Rzeczypospolitej." *Biuletyn ŻIH*, no. 162–63 (1992): 3–18.

Zbrodnicza ewakuacja więzień i aresztów NKWD na Kresach Wschodnich II Rzeczypospolitej w czerwcu-lipcu 1941 roku. Warszawa: Główna Komisja Badania Zbrodni przeciwko Narodowi Polskiemu, 1997.

"Zbrodnie banderowskich bojówek OUN-UPA w powiecie Buczacz, województwo tarnopolskie." *Na Rubieży* (Wrocław) 4, no. 14 (1995): 4–25.

"Zbrodnie niemieckie w Zamojszczyźnie." *Biuletyn Głównej Komisji Badania Zbrodni Niemieckich w Polsce* 2 (1947): 45–120.

Żebrowski, Leszek. "Brygada Świętokrzyska Narodowych Sił Zbrojnych — A Niemcy." *Kombatant* (Warszawa), 5 no. 6 [17–18] (1992): 15–17.

_____. *Narodowe Siły Zbrojne. Dokumenty, struktury, personalia.* Warszawa: Burchard Edition, 1994.

_____. *Paszkwil Wyborczej (Michnik i Cichy o Powstaniu Warszawskim).* Warszawa: Burchard Edition, 1995.

Żebrowski, Rafał. *Dzieje Żydów w Polsce. Kalendarium.* Warszawa: Żydowski Instytut Historyczny w Polsce, 1993.

Żeleński, Władysław. "W cieniu Stefana Ołpińskiego." *Zeszyty Historyczne* (Paris) 69 (1984): 149–222.

_____. *Zabójstwo Ministra Pierackiego.* Warszawa: Iskry, 1995.

Zieliński, Zygmunt. "Żydzi w społeczeństwie Polski międzywojennej." Unpublished 1995 manuscript.

_____, ed. *Życie religijne w Polsce pod okupacją 1939–1945. Metropolie wileńska i lwowska, zakony.* Katowice: Unia, 1992.

_____, ed. *Życie religijne w Polsce pod okupacją hitlerowską 1939–1945.* Warszawa: Ośrodek Dokumentacji i Studiów Społecznych, 1982.

_____, with Richard Tyndorf. "Rescue Efforts on Behalf of Jews by the Roman Catholic Church in German-Occupied Poland." Unpublished 1997 manuscript.

Zienkiewicz, Aleksander. *No Greater Love.* Rome, 1968.

Zik, Gershon, ed. *Rożyszcze My Old Home.* Tel Aviv: Roshishcher Committee in Israel, 1976.

Z krwawych dni Złoczowa 1919 roku. Złoczów: Komitet Budowy Pomnika-Grobowca Dla Ofiar Mordów Ukraińskich, 1921.

Zwoliński, Andrzej. *Starsi bracia.* Kraków, 1994.

Z.Z.Z. *Syndykat Zbrodni: Kartki z dziejów UB i SB w czterdziestoleciu PRL.* Paris: Editions Spotkania, 1986.

Index

Aarons, Mark 371–72, 376–77, 390
Abakumov, Viktor S. 99
Abarinov, Vladimir 298, 390
Abholer (retrievers) 66
Abrahamsen, Samuel 119
Abramchyk, Mikola 156
Abramsky, Chimen 308–9, 314, 337, 345, 390
Abwehr (German intelligence) 74, 88–89, 149, 155, 194–97, 205–6, 212, 235–36, 359, 363
Ackerfeld, Lola Potok 61
act of July 31, 1924 184
Act of Proclamation of the Ukrainian State 365
"active center" (*aktyw centralny*) 36
Adamowicz, Zdzisław 58, 312
Adamski, Stanisław 83
Adder Press 85
"Adolf" (Jewish) partisan unit 101
Adryan, Andrzej 81
African Americans 5, 38
agents 74, 104, 107; communist 289; Gestapo 109–110, 125, 216, 232; Israeli 70; Jewish 100; of the Jewish agency in Palestine 70; Jewish Gestapo 66, 74, 86, 105, 112, 120, 122, 317; Jewish Soviet 341; NKVD 351; OUN 193; among the Polish population 86; Polish Gestapo 86, 89; Polish Kripo 86; Polish NKVD 103; Polish prostitutes as 85; of SMERSH 93; Soviet 58, 103, 232, 265; Ukrainian 206; Ukrainian Nationalist 205; Ukrainian NKVD 363
Agrarian Party of Ukraine 255
Agudat Israel (Union of Israel) 6, 293
Ainsztein, Reuben 123, 221, 233, 325, 338, 368, 374–75, 390
air force auxiliaries (Luftwaffen-Helfer) 156
Ajzenman (Kaniewski), Julian 95
AK (Armia Krajowa, or Home Army) 54, 59–60, 62, 81, 83, 87–96, 105, 109, 112, 116–117, 122, 129, 132, 134, 155, 166, 175, 216, 237, 240–41, 249, 252, 322–24, 327–32, 340, 345, 385; anti-Belorussian actions of the 152; anti-Lithuanian reprisals of the 169; and anti-Semitism 90, 100, 102–3; assistance to Jews by the 337; assistance to the Warsaw Ghetto Revolt by the 107–8; attack on ŻOB by the 91, 325; Belorussians in the 150; "Brasławska" Brigade of the 169; "cecylia" unit of the 89; and Ejszyszki 91–94; Fifth (Wilno) Brigade of the 168, 323; fight against "bandits" of the 102; "Groma" unit of the 342; Jews in the 107, 333; Jews posing as members of the 101; "Kedyw" unit of the 335; liquidation by Soviets of the 19, 92, 98–100, 104, 130–31; "Łupaszka" Brigade of the 169; members as collaborators 85, 88–90, 100, 323; "Narocz" Brigade of the 169; reasons for not accepting Jews by the 106–7; Soviet orders to destabilize the 19, 58, 88, 98–100, 103–4, 150, 153, 330 (*see also* order: of Beria, of Moscow, of Stalin); strength and losses in Wołyń 379; Wołyń (27th Infantry Division) 245, 251, 379. *See also* Polish: underground
Akcja "Wisła" *see* Operation: "Wisła"
Akinchyts, Fabian 148–50
"Akinchyts School" 149
Aktion A-B 23
Aktion Petliura 208–9;
Aktion of summer 1942 116
Aktiubinsk 13
AL (Gwardia Ludowa, or People's Army) 58, 95, 97, 100–104, 106, 130, 134, 136, 314, 324, 332, 345 (*see also* GL); killing of Jews by *see* executions and murders: of Jews by GL-AL
Albert, Andrzej *see* Roszkowski, Wojciech
Albertine Sisters 109
"All Lithuanian Conference" 166
Allen, W. E. D. 362, 390
Allgemeine SS 238
Alliance of Belorussian Students 148–49;
Alliance of Free Poles 89
Allied Air Force 19
Allies 30, 81–83, 106, 118, 149, 215, 232, 235, 237, 241, 259, 372
Alpert, Jechiel 137–38, 277
Altai Mountains 13
Altshuler, Mordechai 312
Alvi, Dana I. 67, 316
Amalgamated Clothing Workers Union 79
Ambrazevičius (Brazaitis), Juozas 164, 167, 350
America *see* United States
American: Council for Polish Culture 337; Institute of Polish Culture 369; Polonia 80; Slav Congress 79
"amnesty" (August 12, 1941) 16, 81
Ancerewicz, Czesław 85, 89
Anczarski, Józef 385, 390
Anders, Władysław 52–53, 156–57, 372, 376; army of 80, 84, 97, 135, 279
Andrejew, I. 314
Andrew, Christopher 307, 332, 390
Andrievskyi, Dmytro 381
Angel, Jan 27
Anglo-American Investigating Commission *see* Morgenthau Commission

Anielewicz, Mordechai 51, 118
annexed territories 22–23, 28, 294, 299–300
Anti-Comintern Pact 119
anti-Semitism 40–41, 43, 45–47, 53, 61, 63–65, 91–92, 100, 106, 113, 115, 119, 124, 128–30, 140–142, 280, 308–9, 345; in America 38. *See also* AK: and anti-Semitism *and also* LAF: and anti-Semitism
antikommunistische Kräfte 306
Antolin 254
Anvier (France) 53
APA (Aussenpolitisches Amt, or Department of Foreign Politics) 148
Apartheid 273
Apenszlak, Jacob 334, 390
Appeal (of Ukrainian parliamentarians, 1996) 255–56
Arad, Yitzhak 323, 331, 350–52, 366, 368, 390
Arbeitsjuden (Jewish workers) 175
Archangel 13
archives: AK 88; department of the MBP 60; Kielce 140; Warsaw 21; Yad Vashem *see* Yad Vashem
Archutowski, Roman 122
Arciszewski, Mikołaj 81
arcs de triomphe (triumphal arches) 49, 145, 198
Arctic Circle 13
Arczyński, Marek 316, 390
Arendt, Hannah 69–70, 75, 304, 312, 317, 390
Arezzana, Romano 263
Argentina 157
Armia Krajowa *see* AK
Armstrong, John A. 194–95, 205, 209, 216, 227, 233, 242, 324, 357, 359, 363–68, 370, 372–73, 375–76, 378, 390
Armstrong, John Lowell 324–25, 331, 390
Army Group: Center 376; North 166, 234; South 294
Aronson, Stanisław 335
Asch, Sholem 307, 390
Ascherson, Neil 337, 390
assistance to Jews: by AK 337; by Belorussians 154, 348; by Bishop Lorek 323; by Father Franciszek Bajer 339; by Latvians 352; by Lithuanians 176, 352; by NSZ 96; Polish 62, 112–23 (*see also the following:* Association of Polish Syndicalists; Community Self-Defence Organization; PCK; Provisional Committee of Conrad Żegota; Special Committee for Assistance to Jews; RGO; RPŻ; Zamość-Lublin Committee for Rendering Assistance to Jews; Żegota); by Polish clergy 175; by Polish police 109; by Roman Catholic Church 337; by Sheptytsky 369; by Ukrainians 224, 369
Association of Polish Syndicalists 117
Astroŭski, Radaslaŭ 150, 154–57
Auerswald, Heinz 109
Aufbaudienst (Lithuanian forces) 164–65
Augustów 17; Forest 160–61
Auscaler, G. 314
Auschwitz (Oświęcim) 28, 83–84, 112, 115, 120, 129, 220, 301–2, 315, 319, 336, 377, 383; informers in 319
Auschwitz-Birkenau 29
Ausrottung (annihilation) 247
Aussenpolitisches Amt *see* APA
Ausserordentliche Befriedungsaktion *see* Aktion: A-B
Australia 129
Austria 3, 155, 176, 197, 205, 212, 228, 286–88, 304, 344
Austria-Hungary 188, 288
Austri-Dunn, Yeshayahu 317, 390
Auswärtiges Amt (Ministry of Foreign Affairs) 194
Avross (from Wołyń) 252
AŻE 298

Babi Yar 222, 255
Babii, Ivan 192
Babul, Mikołaj 93–94, 327
Bachynskyi, Myhkhalo 189, 286–87
Bach-Zelewski, Erich von dem 85, 232–33, 366; Schutzmannschtaft Bataillon 201 of *see* Schutzmannschaften Bataillonen: no. 201
Bączek, Piotr 387
Bad Godesberg 350
Badyan, Gustav 176
Bagiński, Tadeusz 385, 390
Bahnschutz (railway security police) 133, 237, 381
Bajer, Franciszek 339
Bąkowski, Władysław 229
Balcerak, Wiesław 316, 347, 390
Balkans 46
Baltic: republics 148, 266; states 7, 16, 70, 321
Baltics 320
Band, Chaim 57, 323
Bandera, Aleksy 212
Bandera, Stepan 197, 205–7, 209–10, 212, 214, 221, 227, 234, 237, 240, 252–53, 358, 363, 365–66, 368, 370, 382. *See also the following:* Banderowcy; Consul: II; OUN-B
Bandera, Vasyl 212
Banderowcy 105, 199, 245, 247–48, 252–54, 364, 368, 381–82, 384–85. *See also* Bandera, Stepan *and also* OUN-B
Bank of Poland 21
Baran, Stefan 182
Baranowicze 81, 87, 148–49, 154–56, 350
Barański, Kamil 338, 375, 390
Barasz, Efraim 69
"Barbarossa" 150
Bartomaitis, J. 165
Bartosiński, Jan 276
Bartoszewski, Władysław 75, 116, 132, 301, 311, 318, 323, 336–37, 390
Bartoszewski, Władysław T. 65, 82, 315, 318, 346, 390
Bashtakov (*troika* member) 270
Basilian Fathers 189
Bataliony Chłopskie *see* BCh
Battle of Britain 82
Baudienst (compulsory labor service) 237
Bauminger, Róża 219
BBH (Bergbauernhilfe, or Mountain-Peasants' Help) 205, 236
BCh (Bataliony Chłopskie, or Peasant Legions) 100, 252, 325, 345
Beattie, Thomas B. 299
Beck, Joseph 168
Beck, Józef 4, 264
Beck (major) 105
Bednarczyk, Tadeusz 66, 74, 112, 122, 315–17, 333–34, 336–38, 391
Bednarz, Bronisław 277
Będzin 61, 303
Belarus Brigade 156–57; *see also* Waffen-SS: Grenadier-brigade "Weissruthenian"
Belaruskaya: Abarona *see* BKA; Narodnaya Samapomach *see* BNS; Nezalezhnitskaya Partyia *see* BNP; Republika Ludova *see* BR; Tsentralnaya Rada *see* BTsR
Belaruskaye Narodnaye Abyednannye *see* BNA
Belaruski Kamitet Samapomachy *see* BKS
Belgium 173, 193, 232, 285, 304
Belorussia-East 148, 150, 153
Belorussia-West 148, 150, 153–55
Belorussian: "Affair" 196; Central Council *see* BTsR; Committee 149; Commissariat *see* General:

Commissariat of Belorussia; Committee of Mutual Assistance *see* BKS; Front 99; Home Defense Corps *see* BKA; Independent Party *see* BNP; National Organization of Mutual Assistance *see* BNS; National Union *see* BNA; National Socialist Party 148; Nationalist Party *see* PBN; nationalists 5, 100, 150; People's Republic *see* BRL; Representation *see* Weissruthenische Vertrauenstelle; SS Brigade *see* Belarus Brigade *and see* Waffen-SS: Grenadierbrigade "Weissruthenian"; SSR 9, 79, 99, 143, 161, 259–60, 270, 296, 346 (*see also* Soviet: Belorussia)
Belov, von (procurator in Hamburg) 210
Bełżec 29, 71–2, 74, 109, 129, 217, 223
Berenbaum, Michael 368–69, 391
Berenstein, Tatiana 337, 391
Bereza Kartuska 193, 363
Berezów Niżny 253–54
Berezwecz 17–18
Bergbauernhilfe *see* BBH
Berger, Gottlob 224, 234
Bergman, Aleksandra 346–47, 391
Bergman, Frydel 123
Beria, Lavrenti 7, 80, 99–100, 269–70, 330
Berkeley CA 318
Berlin 9, 66, 104, 148–49, 155–56, 163, 175, 193–98, 204, 210–11, 214–16, 221, 233, 235, 288, 317, 350, 360, 365
Berling, Zygmunt 80; army of 19, 81; Jews in army of 318
Berman, Adolf 123, 132, 279–80
Berman, Jakub 60, 130, 132–35, 141, 315, 342
Bernhard, Michael 308, 312–13, 341, 391
Bertrand, G. 82
Bessarabia 7, 214, 384
Besstelung (requisitions) 73
Besstelungsmann 73
Betar 50
Bethell, Nicholas 377, 391
Bettelheim, Bruno 337
Beuthen *see* Bytom
Beyersdorff, Friedrich 220, 229–30, 236
Bezirk Bialystok 30, 303
Beznowski, Helena *see* Kojder, Helena
Biała Podlaska 56, 129, 149
Białobrzegi 120
Białopolacy *see* White: Poles
Białowąs, Jan 385, 391
Białozórka 254
Białystok 9–10, 17, 19, 22, 27, 30–31, 39–40, 48–49, 55–56, 69–70, 81, 87, 94, 100–101, 122, 143, 145, 148, 152, 155, 160, 184, 202, 218, 223, 261, 294, 296, 299–300, 303–4, 306, 340, 346
Biber, Jacob 381, 391
Bidaczów Nowy 120–21
Bieberstein, Aleksander 68, 316–17, 391
Biegły, Adam Urbański 345
Bielaki 275, 343
Bielawski, Wacław 338, 391
Bielicka 153
Bielin 329
Bielsk-Podlaski 303
Bielski, Tuvia 100; brigade of 102
Bielsko-Biała 61, 313
Bier, Janina 77
Biernacki, Jerzy 2, 301, 391
Bierut, Bolesław 61, 64, 103–4, 130, 134, 141, 279, 314–15, 330
Bihl, Wolfdieter 365, 369–71
Biłgoraj 110, 120–21, 181, 248, 250, 384
bilingual schools (*szkoły utrakwistyczne*) 185, 354
Biłka Szlachecka 142
Biłohorszcza 370
BIP (Biuro Informacji i Propagandy, or Bureau of Information and Propaganda) 95
Birkenau 301–2. *See also* Auschwitz-Birkenau
Birontas (colonel) 166
Bishops' Council (of Kielce) 279
Biskupski, Stanisław 385, 391
Bismarck, Otto von (Eduard Leopold) 310
Biuro Informacji i Propagandy *see* BIP
BKA (Belaruskaya Krayovaya Abarona, or Belorussian Home Defense Corps) 89, 150, 153, 155–56
BKS (Belaruski Kamitet Samapomachy Belorussian Committee of Mutual Assistance) 149–50
blackmailers 97 104, 117, 128, 142; Jewish 66, 70, 75; Polish 66–67, 75, 85–86, 123. *See also* szmalcowniki
Blanke, Hersz 341
Błaszczyk, Henryk 135, 275–76, 343
Błaszczyk, Walenty 136, 275–76
Blatt, Tomasz 328
Błażejewski (UB member in Kielce) 278
Błażyński, Zbigniew 65, 105, 313, 315, 332, 341, 391
Blejwas, Stanislaus 324, 329, 391
Blobel, Paul 175; "Special Commando 1005" of 175
Blome, Kurt 28
Blond, Szlomo 120
blood-libel 135
"Blue Police" (Policja granatowa) 67, 71, 85, 109–10, 122–23, 321, 334. *See also* police: Polish
BNA (Belaruskaye Narodnaye Abyednannye, or Belorussian National Union) 149
BNP (Belaruskaya Nezalezhnitskaya Partyia, or Belorussian Independent Party) 153, 155
BNS (Belaruskaya Narodnaya Samapomach, or Belorussian National Organization of Mutual Assistance) 152, 155
Bobihushchy, Ievhen 213
Bóbrka 17–18, 289
Bochnia 109
Bogomilska, Kaja 342
Bohun-Dąbrowski, Antoni 96
Bojanowo 302
Bojarska, Barbara 301, 391
Bolduan, Tadeusz 301
Bolesławiec 128
Bolotny (doctor in Szczebrzeszyn) 71
Bolshevik: Asiatics 170; Party 12; Revolution 38; youth associations 10. *See also* Bolsheviks *and also* Bolshevism
Bolsheviks 41, 49, 52–53, 56, 89, 143, 145–46, 153, 164, 166–67, 173–74, 187–88, 196, 199, 203, 209, 212, 214, 225, 227, 232, 234, 246, 288, 355
Bolshevism 7, 214, 225–26, 228, 236
Bonusiak, Włodzimierz 210, 318, 364–65, 391
Bór Kunowski 122
Bór-Komorowski, Tadeusz 91, 102, 104, 324–25
Borejsza, Jerzy 60, 78
Borisov 148, 153
Borkowicz, Jacek 386–87, 391
Borkowska, Maria 311
Bormann, Martin 31, 365
Boroŭski, Andrei 149
Borovets, Taras 199, 206–7, 213, 216–17, 228, 233–36, 246, 250, 363, 366, 369–70, 381–82, 391; Brigade for Special Tasks of 230, 235; partisans of 369. *See also* Bulbowcy
Borów 95, 230
Borowski, Henryk 89
Boruny 151
Borwicz, Michał 117, 141, 314, 345

Borysewicz (Kristin) 327
Borysław 17, 18, 354
Boshyk, Yury 361–62, 369–71, 376, 391
Bosnia 251, 261
Bot (gendarme) 110
boycott: of Jewish businesses 42, 46; of 1921 Polish census by Ukrainians 187; of 1921 Polish elections by Ukrainians 187, 352
Boy-Żeleński, Tadeusz 78
Brandenburg regiment 208
Brasław 57, 322
"Brasławska" *see* AK: "Brasławska" Brigade
Bratislava 374
Brayer, Lynda 40, 270, 274–75, 391
Brazaitis, Juozas *see* Ambrazevičius, Juozas
Brazauskas, Algirdas 176
Brecher, Elinor J. 315, 391
Bregman, Aleksander 297, 391
Bremen 197
Breslau *see* Wrocław
Brest Litovsk 47
Brigade for Special Tasks *see* Borovets, Taras: Brigade for Special Tasks of
Brinskiy's [Brinskyi's] brigade 233
Brisk 56
Bristot (commander) 229
British: blockade 11; Empire 263; Foreign Office 129; mandate 136
Brizgys, Vincentas 164, 166, 350
BRL (Belaruskaya Republika Ludova, or Belorussian People's Republic) 155
Brockdorff, Werner 210, 365, 391
Brodacka, Maria 120
Brody 121, 123, 227–30, 232, 373–74
Broner, Hersz 101
Broniewski, Janina 78
Broniewski, Władysław 78
Bronowski, Alexander 334, 391
Brooklyn College 119
Brumberg, Abraham 335
Brunner, Alois 66
Brygada Świętokrzyska *see* Holy Cross Brigade
Brygidki *see* prisons, Soviet: Brygidki
Brygidki Street 53
Brystygier, Luna (Julia) 60
Brystygier, Nathan 60
Brześć (Brest) 53, 87, 148, 233, 348
Brzeżany 17, 19, 200, 289
Brzoza, Jan 78
BTsR (Belaruskaya Tsentralnaya Rada, or Belorussian Central Council) 150, 153, 155–56
Buchenwald 28, 115, 129, 302
Buchko, Ivan 377
Buczacz 200, 254, 364, 385–86
Buczyński, Władysław 136, 277–78
Budanov (professor) 281
Buenos Aires 238
Bugajski, Janusz 293, 347, 353, 391
Bugnon-Rosset, Anna 342
Bujnicki, Teodor 78
Bukojemski, Leon 80
Bukovina 183, 188, 207, 214, 355
Bukovinian Battalion of 1941 214, 236
"Bulba," Taras *see* Borovets, Taras
Bulbowcy 105, 199, 253, 381. *See also* Taras Borovets
Bulgaria 7, 304, 384
Bund 35, 44, 117, 307
Bundists 6
Burdecki, Feliks 85
Bureau of Information and Propaganda *see* BIP
"Burza" *see* Operation: "Burza"
Burza-Karliński, Stanisław 314
Burzec 111
Burzyński, Antoni 99
Busk 17
"Butcher of Borisov" 153
Butyrki *see* prisons, Soviet: in Butyrki
Bytom (Beuthen) 61, 339

Canada 62, 116, 193, 195, 205, 237–38, 321, 350, 362, 367, 377, 387. *See also* Canadian
Canadian: Immigration and Refugee Board 274; Polish Congress 320
Canaris, Wilhelm 197, 205, 212, 235, 362
Carpathian: Mountains 177, 205, 235, 237; region, 188, 260, 270. *See also* Carpathians
Carpathians 357
Catholic Church 302, 354; Greek (Ukrainian), or Uniate 180–83, 198, 203, 211, 214, 261, 360, 373, 282, 287–88; Roman 63, 86, 117, 181–82, 261, 282, 337
Catholic clergy: arrest of in Wileńszczyzna 168; denunciation by Orthodox clergy of 151; Fulman's directive (June 2, 1938) to 182; German atrocities against 28, 151; Lithuanian actions against 162, 164; losses of during World War II 302; medical experiments on 302; memorandum regarding Kielce pogrom 140–41; proposal to rescue Jewish children 113; from Śląsk (Silesia) who died in concentration camps 83. *See also* executions and murders: of Catholic clergy
Catholicism 74
Caucasus 172, 357; North 380
"Cecylia" *see* AK: "Cecylia" unit
Celt, Marek 310, 391
"Center" 149
Central: Army Squadron/Group *see* Heeresgruppe Mitte; Europe 3; Emigration Committee *see* CKE; Committee of Polish Jews *see* CKŻP; Committee of the Communist Party of Belorussia, Lithuania and Ukraine 98; Industrial Area *see* COP; Poland 13, 21, 36, 41, 58, 66, 106, 142, 230
Centralny: Komitet Emigracyjny *see* CKE; Komitet Żydów w Polsce *see* CKŻP; Okręg Przemysłowy *see* COP
Chachaj, Aleksander 280
Charles I 286
Checinski, Michael 136, 314, 345, 391
Cheka 82, 370
Chełchowski, Hilary 105, 136, 277, 278
Chełm (Kholm) 27, 39, 47, 177, 181, 229, 248, 254, 281–84, 383–84. *See also* Chełmszczyzna
Chełmno (Kulmhof) 29, 32, 218
Chełmszczyzna (Chełm region) 182, 188, 231, 244, 248. *See also* Chełm
Cherniakovsky, I.D. 99
Chernobyl 348
"Chernobyl Aids" 348
Chesnoff, Richard Z. 91, 92, 325, 391
Chesterton, G. K. 112, 336, 391
Chicago 55, 79, 192, 367
"Chicago Poles" 79
Chief Social Welfare Council *see* NRO
Chiniewicz, Jozef 327
Chirac, Jacques 336
Chlebowice Świrskie 252
Chmielarz, Andrzej 301, 392
Chmielewski, Paweł 367
Chmielewski, Zygmunt 280
Chmielnik 120, 317
Chodaczów Wielki 229
Chodakiewicz, Marek Jan 312, 332, 392
Chojnowski, Andrzej 293, 347, 392

Chomsowa, Władysława 337
Chordzieżka 25
Chorka, W. 224
Chornii, Iakiv 358
Chornomorets, Iaroslav 253
Chorzów (Königshütte) 61
Christian Democrats (Lithuanian) 163, 265
Christian III (King) 119
Christiansen, Julian 88
Chrypińska, Anna 337
Chrzanów 43, 303
Churchill, Winston 19, 236
Chvanov, F. 328
CIA (Central Intelligence Agency) 239
CIC (Counter-Intelligence Corps) 237
Cichowski, Roman 280
Cichy, Michał 335
Ciechanów Regency (Distrikt Zichenau) 22, 299, 303
Ciechanowiec 17
Ciechanowski, Jan 80
Ciepielów Stary 121
Ciesie 122
Ciesielszuk, Jerzy 192
Cieszyn (Teschen) 47
Cimek, Henryk 36, 307, 392
Ciołkosz, Adam 42, 115, 309, 333, 336, 392
citizens': committees 48–49, 51, 311; militias 48–49, 51, 201, 311
City Supervisory Council *see* MRN
civil rights act 3
Civil Militia *see* MO
civil-defense centers 245
CKE (Centralny Komitet Emigracyjny, or Central Emigration Committee) 341
CKŻP (Centralny Komitet Żydów w Polsce, or Central Committee of Polish Jews) 279
Clinton, Bill 194
Cohen, Asher 299, 392
Colburn, Mary Jean 2
collectivization: in Eastern Poland 9, 11–12, 203, 296; in Soviet Ukraine 203; in Western Belorussia 147, 151
colonization: by Germans of eastern territories *see* Generalplan Ost; by Poles of Eastern Poland 4
Comintern (Communist International) *see* Communist: International
Commando 1005 *see* Paul Blobel: "Special Commando 1005"
Committeefor Civilian Struggle 86
Communist: International (Comintern) 77, 144, 189, 313; Union of Polish Youth *see* KZMP; Workers' Party of Poland *see* KPRP; underground 95. *See also* Communist Party
Communist Party 16, 59–60, 63, 153, 260–1, 265, 314; of Belorussia 99, 346; (Bolshevik) of Belorussia *see* KP(b)B; of Lithuania 162; of Poland *see* KPP, KPRP; of Ukraine 255; of Western Belorussia *see* KPZB; of Western Ukraine *see* KPZU
Community Self-Defence Organization 117
Conason, Joe 362, 378
concentration camps: American 193; Canadian 193; German 23–25, 28–31, 67, 75, 83–84, 115, 119, 121, 124, 157, 206, 211–12, 217, 230, 235, 301–2, 314, 321, 339, 350, 366, 383 (*see also under specific names*); Polish *see* Bereza Kartuska, Jaworzno; Soviet 15, 199; Stalinist (in Poland) 59, 131, 314; Ukrainian Nationalist 362
Conference of Ambassadors 3, 159, 188, 190, 263, 293
confidants: Jewish 132; Polish 85; Ukrainian 101
Constitution: Lithuanian 162; Polish 3–5, 184, 264, 283; Soviet 11–12; United States 5, 38; ZUNR 188
Consul: I 197, 205 (*see also* Melnyk, Andrii); II 197, 205 (*see also* Bandera, Stepan)
COP (Centralny Okręg Przemysłowy, or Central Industrial Area) 218, 367
corrective labor camps (Soviet) 13
Cotler, Irwin 275
Coughlin, Charles 38
Council for Aid to Jews *see* RPŻ
Council of Belorussian People's Republic 149
"Council of Sages" 293
Counter-Intelligence Corps *see* CIC
County Office of State Security *see* PUBP
Court Medical Commission 27
Cracow *see* Kraków
"creative coercion" 191
Crimea 303
Criminal Police *see* Kripo
Croatia 176, 384
cryptoanalysts (Polish) 82
"cultural Jerusalem" 159
Cumań 246
Cybulski, Henryk 353–54, 380, 392
Cygan, Wiktor Krzysztof 361, 392
Cyprian (brother) 244
Czaplicki (colonel) 60
Czaplicki, Czesław 330
Czarna Łoża 254
Czarnocka, Halina 373, 374–75, 381, 383, 392
Czarnomski (BIP member) 95
Czartorysk 254
Czaykowski, Bogdan 297, 318
Czech Protectorate 119
Czechoslovakia 3, 5, 64, 118, 130, 141, 181, 188, 195, 294, 304, 340, 355, 379
Czechowski, Emilian 192
Czecowski, Kasper 168
Czelny, K. T. 311
Czerepin 252
Czerlany 17
Czernicy 230
Czernowitz 188
Częstochowa 41, 43, 61, 86, 91, 94, 280
Czortków 17–19, 56, 72
Czubiński, Antoni 343, 392
Czuszel, Romuald 145

Dąb (chief prosecutor) 279
Dąbrowski, Józef 120
Dachau 23, 28, 302
Dahlwitz 155
Dallin, Alexander 209, 235, 360, 362–66, 371, 375–76, 392
Daluege, Kurt 371
Dan, Aleksander 78
Danielski, J. J. 298, 392
Danilewicz, Jan 278–79
Danter, Szymon 115, 118, 124, 337–39, 392
Danzig *see* Gdańsk
Danzig-West Prussia (Danzig-West Preussen) 25, 303
Davies, Norman 9, 36, 43, 51, 56–57, 82, 115, 238, 293, 295–97, 299, 306–7, 309, 311–12, 316, 318–19, 330, 336, 347, 377, 392
Day of Atonement 171
Days of Awe 49
Deák, István 2, 118, 174, 176, 338, 349, 352, 392
Dear, I. C. B. 299–301, 305, 322, 333, 374, 392
"Death to Spies" *see* SMERSH
"Death's Head" 115
Dębica 121
Dębski, Włodzimierz Sławosz 357, 375, 392
Decalogue (Dekaloh) 190–91
Declaration of Independence (Israeli) 275
Dederkały 243

Defense Battalions (Lithuanian) 350
Delatyn 364
Delegatura Rządu *see* Polish: Government Delegation for the Homeland
Delmenhorst 197
Demin, Mikhail A. *see* Dyomin, Mikhail A.
Demjanjuk, Ivan 239
Demko, Mikołaj (Mieczysław Moczar) 130–31
Democratic Left 81
Denmark 116, 118–19, 304
Department: "A" 276; of Civil Servants (Polish) 134; of Criminal Institutions in Katowice 61; of Foreign Politics *see* APA; of Justice (Canadian) 386; Justice (United States) 156; Legalization (Legalizacja) 175; Organizational (of the PPR) 134; Personnel (Polish) 313; Political (German) 31, 83; Provincial (in Kielce) 42; of Service to Justice (Department Służby Sprawiedliwości) 62; Social Services (Warsaw) 112; State (United States) 80, 140, 376
depolonization 159, 199, 380–81
deportation:
of AK members to the Soviet Union 100
of Belorussian residents to the Soviet Union 148, 347
from Eastern Poland: to Germany 22, 31, 206, 248; to the Soviet Union 13–15, 55, 203, 248; to Germany 19, 32, 67
of Jews: from Chmielnik 120; from Eastern Poland by Soviets 312; from France 336; from other German-occupied nations to Poland 32; to Soviet Union 51, 58, 106
of Poles: from annexed territories to Germany 300; from the eastern territories 297; from GG to Germany 300; from the Lithuanian Commissariat with assistance of Lithuanian police 169; from Zamojszczyzna with Ukrainian assistance 220, 249; to Germany with Belorussian assistance 151; to Germany with BNS assistance 152; to the Soviet Union with Jewish assistance 51, 56, 58, 65, 123, 131, 161
of Polish soldiers to the Soviet Union 16, 19
of Ukrainians and Lemkos during Operation "Wisła" 379
from Wileńszczyzna by Soviets 163
Deraźne 252, 254
Dereń, Bolesław 341, 392
Derewno 87
Deschênes, Jules 377, 392
Dessau 155
Detachments of Ukrainian Nationalists *see* DUN
Detective Forces *see* Kripo
Detroit 79
"Detroit Poles" 79
Deutscherein 133
Diachenko, P. 235
Diamant, Schmuel 329
Diewerge, W. 364, 392
Dillon, Thomas P. 140
Diment, Michael 252, 317, 385, 392
Dinnerstein, Leonard 308, 392
Dionysius (metropolitan) 211, 281–82
Directorate of Civil Resistance 110
Dirlewanger [Oscar] Police Brigade 85, 231
Distrikt: Galizien 30, 215, 303; Lublin 217
Dmowski, Roman 293
Dmytruk, Klym 364, 373
Dnepropetrovsk 303
Dnieper 213, 303
Dniestr 17
Dobcza 252
Dobra 252
Dobraczyński, Jan 112, 114, 335
Dobromil 17
Dobromirski, Franciszek 25
Dobroszycki, Lucjan 312, 317, 322, 392
Dobrucka, J. 379
Dobrzyńska, Zofia 87
"doctors plot" 61
Dog's Hill (Psia Góra) 146
Dolny Śląsk *see* Śląsk: Lower
Domagała, Czesław 77
Dominican: Priests, murder of 19, 56; Sisters 175
Dontsov, Dmytro 189, 190–91, 240, 242, 356, 393
Dorfman, Baruch 137
Dorosiewicz, Stanisław 319
Dowgiałło, Bronisław 146
Dowgiałło, Jan 328, 393
Doyon, Albert B. 316
Draby 151
Draskienki 168
Drohobycz 17–18
Drozda, Bronisława 385–386
Drożdżyński, Aleksander 208–9, 364, 393
Druskieniki 162
Druzhyny Ukrainskykh Natsionalistiv *see* DUN
Drzewica 95
Dubinki 169
Dubno 17, 251, 364, 368
Dudziński, Kazimierz 80
Dukla 207
Dumyn, Osyp 194–96, 358–60, 363, 393
DUN (Druzhyny Ukrainskykh Natsionalistiv, or Detachments of Ukrainian Nationalists) 207, 213, 236. *See also* Nachtigall, Roland
Duraczyński, Eugeniusz 300, 304, 393
Dusza, Józef 314
Dygnarowicz, Jan 135, 276
Dym (ropemaker in Szczebrzeszyn) 110
Dyomin (Demin), Mikhail A. 136
Działdowo 30, 302
Działoszyce 109
Dziedzic, Emil 78
Dzielna Street 25, 116
Dziekanka 27
Dzierżyński, Feliks 82
Dzierżyński, Zofia 78
Dziewieniszki 162
Dzisna 55
Dzwonkowski, Roman 386, 393

"Eagle" *see* NSZ: "Eagle" unit
EastCentral Europe 256, 261
Eastern: Europe 3, 46, 91–92, 108, 129–30, 181, 215, 221, 249, 285–86; Galicia (Eastern Małopolska, Małopolska Wschodnia) 3, 4, 9, 30, 39, 41, 50, 72, 99, 110, 177, 179–80, 183–89, 193, 195–96, 213, 217, 221–22, 225, 227, 233–34, 236, 244, 246, 248–51, 258–59, 286–90, 293, 333, 352–54, 358–59, 364, 369–70, 373, 381, 384 (*see also* Galicia); Latvia 349; Poland (Kresy Wschodnie) 1, 3, 6, 9–12, 15–16, 18, 21, 38, 40–41, 43, 48, 52–53, 57–59, 70, 75, 77, 79, 91, 97, 107, 122, 124, 150, 157, 160–61, 177, 183, 187, 189–91, 195, 198–99, 201–2, 204–5, 207–9, 223, 229, 231, 234, 239, 245, 258–60, 295–98, 305, 308, 311, 313, 315, 337, 339, 358, 369,375, 380; Turkish Battle Group *see* Osttürkischer Waffenverband; Ukraine *see* Soviet: Ukraine, *and see* Ukrainian: SSR
Eberhardt, Piotr 296, 393
Ebner (chairman of the Judenrat in Chortków) 72
"economic action" 101–2

Edelman, Marek 102, 107, 332–33
Egypt 376
Eichmann, Adolf 66, 69–70
Einsatzgruppen 23, 30, 104, 115, 125, 153–54, 213, 220–21, 229, 237, 362, 368, 374; A 170, 222; B 170; C 209, 222; D 222
Einsatzkommando 23, 210, 216, 220–23, 237, 351, 362, 368; no. 2 170; no. 3 167, 170, 174–75; no. 4-a 222; no. 9 170; zur besonderen Verwendung 209
Eisenman, Edka 134
Eisenstein, Barek 61
Eismont (junior colonel) 328
Ejszyszki 91–94, 132, 148, 162, 168, 326–27
Eliach (née Sonenson), Yaffa 91–4, 325–28, 393
Ellwart, Elżbieta 301
emigration of Jews from postwar Poland 134, 259, 341; after Kielce pogrom 129, 341; reasons for 129–31; Soviet pressure to enhance 136, 141
Endecja 329
Endlösung der Judenfrage *see* Final Solution
Engel, David 56, 312
Engelking, Barbara 308, 337, 393
England 7, 43, 97, 161, 323. *See also* Great Britain *and also* United Kingdom
ENIGMA 82
Eretz Israel (Land of Israel) 35, 44
Erikson, John 295, 346
Erwachendes Deutschland 117
Estonia 15, 22, 148, 266, 304, 320, 350
ethnic cleansing 6, 31, 177, 191, 195, 200, 204, 231, 237, 380, 384; campaign of OUN-UPA 179, 187, 234, 241–58, 369, 378, 381–83
euthanasia program (Gnadentod) 27–28
exchange of populations *see* Polish-Soviet: agreements on exchange of populations
executions and murders:
of AK members: in Ponary 175; by Soviets 19; by UB 132
of Belorussians: by AK 152; in Soviet Belorussia in the 1930s 143; by Soviets and Germans 157
in Białystok by Germans 31
of Bolshevik infiltrators in Pińsk by Poles 41
of Catholic clergy: in Czortków by NKVD 19; by Germans 28, 120, 122, 150, 302; by "Lithuanian partisans" 164; in Ponary 175; by Soviets 12
of Czech children by Germans 32
of Germans by Stalinist régime in postwar Poland 314
of Gypsies: by Germans 32; by Polish police 109
of Jews 29–30; in Babi Yar 222, 255; in Belorussia 153; in Dubno with Ukrainian assistance 368; in Eastern Poland 30–31; by the GL-AL 105, 332; in Kisorycz by Ukrainian police 368; in Lithuania 351; by Lithuanian partisans 170; in Łowicz by Germans with Ukrainian assistance 220; in Lubiaż by Ukrainians 204; in Łuków by Germans 25; in Lwów by Ukrainian police 223–24; (partisans) by AK 325; in Poland (from German occupied territories) 32; by Poles during the Warsaw Ghetto Revolt 111, 335; by "Polish partisans" 323; by Polish police 109; in Ponary 170–75; by SS and Lithuanians in the Seventh Fort in Kaunas 165; in Tarnopol by Ukrainians 361; by Ukrainian guards in labor camps 218; by Ukrainian police 250; in Wilno 174, 351; in Wołyń 222; in Žagarė 170
in Kampinos woods by Germans with Ukrainian assistance 220
of Lithuanians by AK 169
in Lwów 208–10
of members of the Polish National Defense by German army 23
of non-Ukrainians by OUN-UPA 251–54
of NSZ members by UB 132
in occupied Poland by Germans 23, 300
in Palmiry by Germans 24–25
of PCK women by Soviets 146
in Piaśnica by Germans 25–27, 301
of Poles: by Germans 23, 151; in Grodno by Red Army 145; in Lwów 208–10, 364; by OUN-UPA 243–53; by Polish police 109; in Ponary 167–68, 175; by Soviets 12, 15, 16, 17, 80, 298; by Ukranians 203; by UVO-ON 192; in Wilejka by Germans 151; in Wilenszczyzna 167–68, 351; in Wilno by Lithuanian police and SS 169; in Wola Ostrowiecka and Ostrówki by UPA 247; who assisted Jews 175–76, 120–23
of prisoners: by Germans 25, 32, 351; by Polish police 109; by Soviets 17–19, 163, 210;
of psychiatric patients by Germans 27, 32, 301
by Roland in Belorussia 213
of Ukrainians: by Germans 216, 375; by OUN-B 192; by OUN-UPA-SB 253–54; by Poles in reprisals 252; by Polish police and soldiers 360; by Polish underground in Zamość region 249
in Warsaw by Germans 24
in Wawer by Germans 25
in Złoczów by OUN-B 221
exposure (*ujawnienie*) 104
expropriations 195
extermination camps 28–31, 67, 69, 116, 217. *See also under specific names*
Extraordinary Pacification Action *see* Aktion: A-B

Fahnder (scouts) 66
Fajkowski, Józef 230–31, 374, 393
Fajtel, Berek 137
Falange 45
Falconi, Carlo 323, 393
family camps (Jewish) 98, 100, 330, 373
Farley, Christopher John 320, 393
Fass, Michael Walter 340, 393
Fastak, Szaje 317
Federal: Building in Oklahoma City 194; Republic of Germany 209
Fedorak, Bohdan 355–56
Fedoriw, Petro 379
Fejgin, Anatol 60, 141, 314
Feldbach 228
Feldenkreiz-Grinbal, Eva 323, 393
Feldgestapo 210
Feliński, M. 189, 286–87, 353–56, 358–59, 393
Fermann (Luftwaffe lieutenant) 156
Fiedorowicz, Antoni 78
Fieldorf, August Emil 314
Fifth (Wilno) Brigade of the AK *see* AK: Fifth (Wilno) Brigade
Fijałka, Michał 366, 393
Fijałkowski, Zenon 302, 393
Fik (from Turobin) 250

Filar, Władysław 247, 378–80, 382, 385, 393
Filip, Jerzy 341–42
Filipkowski, Władysław 99
Film Polski (Polish Film) 279
"Final Solution" 29, 56, 67, 119, 123, 125, 170, 220–22, 301
Finder, Paweł 81, 103, 105
Firger, Oziasz 224
First Ukrainian: Division 238, 371–72, 377; Front 234
First World War *see* World War I
Fischer, Ludwig 29, 120
Fisz, Abram 138;
Fisz, Regina 138
Flakartillerie (Flak) 156, 234
Flossenburg 239
Flurbereinigung (uprising) 205
forced-labor camps, German 24, 28, 30, 67, 69, 117, 151–52, 165, 169, 254, 367, 387; conditions in 22; condition of Jews in 29; Poles in 22; in Pravieniškės 168; in Skarżysko-Kamienna 218–19; in Starachowice 218–19; total workers in 300; Ukrainians in 23
forced-labor camps, Soviet 13; conditions in 16; liquidation of 16; Soviet citizens in 22; in Eastern Poland 15–16
Forest: Augustów *see* Augustów: Forest; Kabacki *see* Kabacki Forest; Klamocha *see* Klamocha Forest; Lasy Janowskie *see* Janowskie Forest; Parczew *see* Parczew Forest; Poniemuń *see* Poniemuń Forest
Forster, Albert 83
fortified villages *see* Wehrdörfer
14. Freiwilligen-Grenadier-Division der SS *see* SS-Galizien
Fourteenth German Army 205, 294
14. Waffen-Grenadier-Division der SS *see* SS-Galizien
Fourth: Fort in Kaunas *see* Kaunas: Fourth Fort in; Geneva Convention 273
France 7, 32, 53, 82, 114, 116, 119, 161, 173, 176, 225, 232, 263, 293, 300, 304, 336, 373, 377
Frank, Hans 21, 28, 30, 38, 74
Frankfurt on the Oder 213
Franko, Ivan 202
"Free Frenchmen" division 114
Freedom and Independence *see* WiN
Freedom NH 367
Freedom-Equality-Independence *see* WRN
Freitag, Fritz 226, 372
freiwillige Mitarbeit 306
French Resistance 376
Friedlander, Henry 301, 303, 393
Friedman, Philip 116, 118, 337–38, 352, 363–64, 367–68, 376, 382, 393
Friedman, Saul S. 208, 362, 364, 366, 370–74, 377, 393
Fróg, Gracjan 89
Frontier Defense Corps *see* KOP
Frydland, Rachmiel 38–39, 308, 393
Frydman (Jewish commandant at Bethuen) 61
Frymer (gendarmerie commandant) 110
Fuks, Marian 309, 318, 393
Fulman, Marian Leon 182
Fyodorov-Chernigovskiy [Fyodorov-Chernihovskyi], Aleksei 233

Gaik, Stanisław 103
Gailiūnas 172
Gal, Jan 110
Galicia 31, 40–41, 194, 199, 207–8, 214–15, 217, 220, 222–23, 225–26, 230–31, 240, 255, 263, 370–71, 355, 376. *See also* Eastern: Galicia
Galiński, Antoni 298, 393
Galvanauskas, Viktoras 352
Gancwajch, Abraham 66
Ganswagens 229
Garlicki, Andrzej 293, 312, 361, 385, 393
Garliński, Józef 83, 316, 319, 342, 356, 393
Garnowski, Władysław 281
Gartner, I. 237, 376
gas vans 31
Gazda, Stanisław 61
Gdańsk (Danzig) 23, 26, 47, 83, 197, 304–5, 359
Gdynia 26, 305
Gebler, Julius 121
Gęborski, Czesław 61
Geheime Staatspolizei *see* Gestapo
Gelb (née Laks), Regina 2, 218–20, 367–68
General: Belorussian Congress 155; Commissariat of Lithuania (Generalkommissariat Litauen) 148, 164, 166, 169, 174–76, 349; Commissaariat of Belorussia (Generalkommissariat Weissruthenien) 148, 150, 152; Government *see* GG
Generaldirektoren (General Directors) 350
Generalgouvernement *see* GG
Generalplan Ost 22, 181, 204
Generalräte (Directorate, or "General Counselors") 164–65
Geneva 196, 288
Genghis Khan 115
genocide 1, 23, 29–32, 70, 82, 177, 204, 221, 239, 255, 258, 339–40, 380–81
Gens, Jakub 69
Gering, Daniel 25
German: Security Police *see* Sipo; Nationals *see* Volksdeutsche; Workers' Party 241
German-Soviet: Boundary and Friendship Treaty (September 28, 1939) 11, 57, 160, 206; Supplementary Protocol of 57; Non-Aggression Pact (August 23, 1939) 7, 50, 160; pact (February 10, 1940) 11; War 351
Germanization 22, 319, 383
Gerstein, Kurt 217
Gęsla Street 109
Gestapo (Geheime Staatspolizei, or Secret State Police) 9, 19, 22–5, 58, 60, 62, 65–66, 68–69, 71, 73–74, 84–87, 89–91, 95, 97, 102–5, 109–10, 114–16, 120–22, 134, 151–52, 154, 165, 168–69, 172–74, 197, 205, 207–8, 210, 215–16, 220, 232, 237, 254, 295, 301, 316–17, 332, 338–39, 361, 368, 370, 374, 383. *See also* police: German
GG (Generalgouvernement, General Government) 8, 22–23, 27–30, 36, 69, 74, 78, 83, 86–87, 101, 108, 110, 114, 145, 149–50, 154, 205–6, 213–14, 225, 227, 234, 236, 244, 250, 299–300, 303, 306, 333, 371;Germans in 116
ghetto: in Baranowicze 154, 350; in Belorussia 154; in Chmielnik, 120; in Kaunas 170; in Kielce 120, 133; in Kołomyja 109; in Lachwa 154; in Łódź 29, 69; in Łukacze 71; in Minsk 154; in Nowogródek 154; in Piotrków Trybunalski 29; in Starachowice, 218; in Tłumacz 120; in Tuczyn 30–31, 303–4; Warsaw 22, 24, 29, 40, 66–67, 74–75, 105, 109, 112, 114, 120–22, 124–125, 165, 217, 317, 333, 335, 367 (*see also* Warsaw Ghetto Revolt); in Wilno 170, 175, 351–52; in Wołyń 303; in Założce 339
Gienek, Anna 253–54
Gienek, Antek 253–54
Gienek, Vasyl 253–54
Giertych, Jędrzej 303–4, 311, 335, 364, 382, 385, 394
Gieysztor, Józef 181

Gilbert, Martin 40, 111–12, 119, 128–29, 165, 170–71, 209, 301, 303, 308–9, 317, 334–38, 340–41, 348, 350–52, 361, 364, 367–69, 378, 394, 404
GL (Gwardia Ludowa, or People's Guard) 58, 81, 95, 97, 100–106, 108, 110, 134, 324–25, 332 (*see also* AL); killing of Jews by the *see* executions/murders of Jews: by the GL-AL; "Lew" unit of 95; "Waryński" unit of 95
Głębocki, Mirosław 89
Głębokie 17, 89, 148, 156
Gleichenberg 228
Gleiwitz *see* Gliwice
Glinciszki 168–69
Gliniany 364
Gliwice (Gleiwitz) 61, 133
Globocnik, Odilo 217, 383
Głogów Małopolski 121
Głogowska, Barbara 297, 396
Głowacki, Aleksander 95
Gnadentod *see* euthanasia program
Gochniak, Franciszek 17
Godlewski, Marceli 112, 149
Godomski (school superintendent) 192
Godzów 230
Goebbels, Paul Joseph 85
Goetel, Ferdynand 85
Golczewski, Frank 359, 394
Goldhagen, Daniel Jonah 63–64, 314–15, 339, 394
Goldschlag, Stella 66, 316
Goldstein, Maurice 129
Golmont, Henryk 327
Golombka, Daniel 310
Gomułka, Władysław 61, 77, 103, 105, 117, 130, 135, 277, 345
Gontarczyk, Piotr 332, 392
Góra Kalwaria 277–78
Górale "legion" 84
Goralenvolk *see* "mountaineer nation"
Gorczyński, Eustachy 80
Gordievsky, Oleg 307, 332, 390
Göring, Hermann 25, 196, 365–66
Gorlice 353
Górny Śląsk *see* Śląsk: Upper
Górski, Halina 78
Górski, Juliusz 56
Górski, Konrad 161
Goszczyński, Dariusz 385
Gottberg, Curt von 88–89, 148, 155–56
Government Bloc 187
Gräbe, Herman Friedrich 337, 368
Grabowiec 2, 54–55, 62
Grahl-Madsen, Atle 377, 394
Grajewo 303
Granat factory 279
Grand Duchy of Lithuania 5, 159
Granosieckie 151
Grassgreen, David 340
Graużyszki 166
gravediggers 102–3
Great: Assembly 293; Britain 32, 38, 116, 129, 205, 337, 376–77; (*see also* England *and also* United Kingdom); Commandments 190; Conference of Ukrainian Nationalists *see* VZUN; Depression 38; Terror 9; Ukraine 290
Greater: Germany (Grossdeutschland) 30, 148, 226; Ukraine 5, 191, 199, 261, 355
Grecki, Zdzisław 121
Greece 304
Greek: Catholic Theological Academy 185; Civil War 260; (Ukrainian) Catholic Church *see* Catholic Church: Greek (Ukrainian)
Greifer (catchers) 66
Greiser, Arthur 28
Grenon, Rose 2
Grenzschutz (border guard) 205, 237
Griazovets 15
Grinewize, Mordko 137
Gródek Jagielloński 17, 201, 289
Grodno 17, 49, 53, 55, 87, 146, 184, 281, 303, 311; Soviet occupation of 145
Grojecka Street 122
"Groma" *see* AK: "Groma" unit
Gross, Jan Tomasz 2, 5, 18, 48, 58, 78, 145, 293–99, 306, 310–13, 318, 337, 346, 349, 360–61, 394
"Gross," Shmuel (Mieczyslaw) 313
Grossdeutschland *see* Greater: Germany
Gross-Rosen 302
Grosz, Wiktor 60
Grot, Paul 217
Grot-Rowecki, Stefan 104, 108, 145, 212, 323, 332, 351, 381
Gruber, Samuel 331, 394
Grudzińska-Gross, Irena 2, 48, 78, Irena 294–97, 310–12, 318, 346, 361, 394
Grünberg, Karol 304, 394
Grünsapan-Kikiel, Natan *see* Roman Romkowski
Gruszczyński, Maksymilian 120
Grygorcewiczówna, Marysia 102
Grynbaum, Albert 134, 136–38
Grynszpan, Jechiel 100, 313
Grzesik, Ferdynand 120
Grzywaczewski, Stefan 280
guards: Belorussian 154; border *see* Grenzschutz; camp *see* Lagerschutz; communist 61; German 175, 218; Lithuanian 19, 91, 165, 171, 175; LVR members as 166; Nazi 25; Polish 110; Polish, in PRL 133; railway *see* Bahnschutz; Ukrainian 68, 102, 205–6, 213, 217–20, 222, 237
Guards' Battalions 329
Gulag 16, 53, 116, 161, 163, 181, 193, 202–3, 243, 248
Gumkowski, Janusz 24, 299–302, 304, 336, 394
Gunatów 121
Gurjanow, Aleksandr 2, 298–99, 364, 400
Gurock, Jeffrey, S. 312, 392
Gurowska, Maria 314
Guryn, Andrzej 347
Gusen 302
Gutman, Israel 40–41, 90, 112, 123, 308, 322–23, 333, 335–36, 340–41, 367–68, 370, 375, 394
Gwardia Ludowa *see* GL
Gwiazdowicz, Kazimierz 276–77, 279, 281
Gwoździec 53, 122
Gypsies 1, 3, 29–30, 32, 109–10, 154, 159, 174, 229, 244, 259 276, 301–2

Hajduczak ("Blue Police" member) 110
Hałaburda, Kazimierz 78
Hamburg 197, 210, 373
Hancewicze 148
Handelsman, Marceli 96
Hapsburg, Wilhelm (Wasyl Wyszywany) 286
hard-labor camps *see* forced-labor camps, German *and see* forced labor camps, Soviet
Harrison, Averell 79
Hatza'ir, Hashomer 50, 293
Hautval, Adeleide 84
Hawelland 197
haydamaks 244
Heeresgruppe Mitte (Central Army Squadron/Group) 320
Heike, Wolf-Dietrich 226–29, 231, 235, 370–74, 376, 378, 394
Heimatdienst (work service) 206, 220, 237
Hel Peninsula 26
Helsinki: Accords agreement 256; Final Act (August 1, 1975) 256
Hemelingen 197
Hempel, Adam 322, 334, 337, 348, 394

Hening (Jewish collaborator in Warsaw) 74
Herbska Street 276
Herzl, Theodore 5
Herzner, Albrecht 207
Heu-Aktion (recruitment action) 156
Heydrich, Reinhard 23, 69, 207, 209
Hibner, Juliusz 60
High Command of the German Armed Forces *see* OKW
Hilberg, Raul 31, 67, 108, 165, 170, 222, 300, 303–4, 317, 333, 338, 349–51, 367, 369, 394
Hilfspolizei 165, 237; Ukrainische 221–22
Hilfspolizeitruppe (auxiliary police units) 164
Hilfswillige (Hiwis, or volunteer auxiliaries) 234–35, 237, 320, 375
Himchak (Ukrainian police leader) 368
Himka, John Paul 195, 359, 365, 369–71, 375, 394, 403
Himler (German gendarme) 71
Himmelraikh, Kostia 370
Himmler, Heinrich 22, 26, 28, 31, 85, 181, 213, 217, 221–22, 224–25, 228, 231–32, 235, 320, 370–1, 373–74; plan for the Poles of 23, 115
Hindenburg *see* Zabrze
Hiroshima 107, 136
Hirszfeld, Ludwik 337, 394
Hirszman, Chaim 129, 341, 367
Hirszman, Pola 367
Hitler, Adolf 1, 7, 11, 18–19, 23, 27, 31–32, 56, 58, 60, 72, 84, 86, 90, 113, 125, 129, 149–50, 161, 171, 178, 195, 198, 207, 210–15, 224–25, 228, 231, 233–36, 240–41, 294, 301, 320–21, 338, 340, 343–44, 362, 364–66, 375, 381, 387; plan for the Poles of 115
Hitlerjügend (Hitler Youth) 84, 234; statistics on 156
Hitler Youth *see* Hitlerjügend
Hiwis *see* Hilfswillige
Hiżowa, Emilia 280
Hlakoŭski, Stanislaŭ 151
Hlebowicz, Henryk 151
Hlond, August 131, 280
Hnatkivska, Daria 358
Hobbes, Thomas 33
Hoduciszki 162
Hoess, Rudolf 302
Hoffer, Eric 357, 394
Hoffmann, Bedřich 302, 394
Hohne, Heinz 375, 394
Holder, Henryk 62
holding camps, German 383–84
Holiszów 96
Holland 118, 304
Holocaust 1–2, 29–30, 40–41, 44, 52, 63, 69, 91–92, 114, 116, 118–19, 123, 129, 133, 142, 153, 243, 258, 320, 336, 340, 381
Hołówko, Tadeusz 192
Holszany 151
Holy Cross Brigade (Brygada Świłtokrzyska) 85, 96, 241, 329
Holzer, Jerzy Zdzisław 32, 306
Home Army *see* AK
"Home of Father Boduen" 109, 334
Honsberger, John D. 296, 380, 394
Höppner, Heinz Rolf 29
Horn, Maria Halina 223, 369, 394
Horochów 11, 251
Horodenka 17, 338
Hotel: Polonia 135; Polski affair 74
Hrabar, Roman 300, 394
Hramada 146, 150
Hrubieszów 54, 62, 181, 207, 230, 248–50, 313, 325, 379, 383–84
Hryniewicz, Antoni 281
Hryniokh, Ivan 211
Hryshchenko, Vasyl 198
Hucisko 121
Hulub, Slavko 254, 385
Humer, Adam 136, 276, 314
Hunczak, Taras 369
"Hundred Group" 223
Hungar (head of the OD in Czortków) 72
Hungarian White Terror 44
Hungary 7, 23, 44, 64, 70, 117, 130, 176, 188, 304, 307
Hunter, Ian A. 296, 380
Huta Pieniacka 122–23, 229–30, 374
Huta Stepańska 198, 233
Huta Werchobuska 122–23, 229
Huzinec, Mary 326, 394

Ianiv, Volodymyr 358
Iarovyi, Petro 364, 394
Iaşi 207
Iatsiv, Dmytro 207, 212
Ignatieff, Michael 2, 170, 351–52, 395
Ili 344
Ilkov, Mykola 187, 354
Iłłakowicz, Jerzy Olgierd 330, 395
Ilnytskyi, Roman 212–13, 362, 395
Imach, Roman 80
Immergrun 229
index of "anti-Soviet elements" 14
Informacja (Information, code name for the Stalinist Office of Military Counterintelligence) 64, 136, 315, 345
Inglot, Mieczysław 318
"iniative groups" 103
"initiative minority" 189, 195
Institute of Military History 93
integral nationalism 204, 258
Interim: National Political Council *see* TNRP; National Unity Council *see* TRJN
Internal: Army (Wojsko Wewnętrzne) 130; Security Corps *see* KBW
International: Commission 256; Committee of Auschwitz 129; Military Tribunal 10, 238, 241, 335; Organization for Help to the Revolutionaries *see* MOPR; Tribunal 255–56
internment camps (Zivilinterniertenlager) 39
Intifada 273
Iranek-Osmecki, Kazimierz 316, 337, 395
Irkutsk 13
"Iron Guard" 212
"Iron Wolf" 265
Israel 40, 44–45, 60, 63, 70, 129, 132, 135–36, 176, 223, 239, 255, 270–75, 328, 340, 345
Israeli: Journalists Association 274; War Crime Commission 128
istrebitelnyye (destruction) battalions 148, 245
Italian Embassy 46, 129, 315
Italy 82, 197, 235, 263, 304, 376–77
"Ivan the Terrible" 239
Ivanoŭski, Vatslaŭ 149–50
Iwańczyk-Wiślicz, Eugeniusz 105, 134, 279
Iwanow, Mikołaj 296, 318, 346–47, 395
Iwański, Henryk 108

Jabłonica 364
Jabłonna 41
Jacewicz, W. 302
Jacewicze 174
Jacobowitz (Jewish commendant in Śląsk) 61
Jagiełło, (King) Władysław 369
Jagiellońska Street 54
Jagoda, Henryk 82
Jaher, Frederic Colpe 308, 395
Jakavonis, A. 165
Jakucewicz (Belorussian collaborator) 152

Jakucki, Piotr 105, 134, 332
Jałbrzykowski (bishop) 282
Jamna 230
Janik, Bronisław 253, 368, 380, 385, 395
Jankowski, Aleksander 301
Jankowski, Andrzej 386
Jankowski, Jan 294, 395
Jankowski, Michał 343
Janów Lubelski 315
Janowa Dolina 381
Janowskie Forest (Lasy Janowskie) 105, 130
Japan 9, 197, 263, 348
Jarosław 207, 247–48
Jary, Richard ("Riko") 196–97, 205, 207, 366
Jasiński (chief of police) 87
Jaśkiewicz, Krzysztof 347, 395
Jasło 353
Jastrębowski, Jerzy 320, 395
Jastrun, Mieczysław 78
Jastrzębice 61
Jaszuny 168
Jaworów 17, 49
Jaworzno 314, 379
Jęczmieniszki 165
Jędrzejczak (lieutenant) 277
Jehovah's Witnesses 1
Jeleński, Konstanty A. 45
Jelsk 148
Jermachenko, Ivan 149–50
Jerusalem 118, 123, 176, 270, 274
"Jerusalem of Lithuania" 40
Jerusalemites (Jerozolimy) *see* Tuvia Bielski: brigade of
Jewish: Combat Organization *see* ŻOB; communists 37, 44, 51–52, 61, 63, 65, 82, 130, 134, 142, 146, 161; Councils *see* Judenräte; ethnocentrism 38–39; Gestapo brigades 66, 74; Guard of Liberty *see* Żagiew; Historical Institute 115, 118; Military Union *see* ŻZW; National Committee 117, 128; per capita income in interwar Poland 309; police *see* police: Jewish; professionals in Poland during the interwar years 308–9; reserves 29, 303; Social Welfare Mutual Assistance (Society) *see* ŻSS; Socialists 44; students in Polish universities during the interwar years 307; underground 66, 107, 311; wealth in interwar Poland 309
Jews in the Soviet government 307
Jeziorany 379
Jeżowski, Leszek 338, 395
Jodl, Alfred 205
Jody 90, 97–98, 154
Joint Distribution Committee 279
Josefov (in Czechoslovakia) 196
Józefów (near Warsaw) 24–25, 91, 342
Jóźwiak, Franciszek 103, 277
Jóźwiak, Witold 105
Juchniewicz, Mieczysław 330, 395
"Judaistic (*ažidavely*) Kremlin" 154
Judenaltester 73
Judenherbergerung (harboring Jews) 121
Judenräte (Jewish Councils) 29, 66–67, 69–74, 322
Judenreferent 73
Judt, Tony 336
Jugo-Grodnicki (attorney) 281
Jung, Edward 349
Junkerschule 373
Jupo (Jewish police force) 66. *See also* police: Jewish
Jurkowski (lieutenant) 64
Juszkiewicz, Paweł 145

Kabacki Forest 109
Kabajda (soten) 224
Kabulov (*troika* member) 270
Kachmarskyi, Ievhen 358
Kacnelson, Dora 39, 308
Kaczmarek, Czesław 86, 140; pastoral letters of 322
Kaczorowski, Michał 279
Kadzielnia 279
Kaganovich, Lazar 7
Kahane, Dawid 279
Kahane, Seweryn 137, 276–77, 345
Kahn, Leon 92, 327, 395
Kainer, Abel *see* Stanisław Krajewski
Kąkolewski, Krzysztof 134, 136–39, 142, 342–43, 345, 395
Kalba, Myroslav 372, 395
Kalbarczyk, Sławomir 18, 298, 395
Kalicki, Włodzimierz 342, 345
Kalinauskas, Kostas 331–32
Kalinin 15
Kalinowicz, Richard 333
Kalinowski, Józef (first secretary of the KW PPR in Kielce) 134, 278, 280
Kalinowski, Józef (victim at Chordzieżka) 25
Kalisz 132
Kalkstein, Ludwik 332
Kalubovič, A. 154
Kałusz 17
Kamenetsky, Ihor 233, 297, 319, 363, 366, 375–76, 395
Kamianets-Podilskyi 370
Kamiński, Bronisław 98, 322; brigade of 85, 155, 330
Kamiński, Tomasz 349
Kamionka 230; Strumiłowa 17
Kampinos woods 23, 220
Kangeris, Karlis 349
Kania, Janusz 182, 354, 395
Kaniewski, Julian *see* Julian Ajzenman
Kaplan, Chaim A. 66, 315, 334, 395
Kapos (trusties) 66
Karaganda 13
Karaites 3, 159, 260
Karczorowski, Blanka 332
Karlsruhe 373
Karpynets, Iaroslav 358
Karski, Jan 52, 299, 395
Kartuzy 26
Kashub nationals 83
Kashubians 3
Kaslas, Bronis J. 349, 395
Kasman, Leon 60
Kastner, Adolf 25
Kastner, Rudolf 70, 317
Katowice (Kattowitz) 61, 313, 339
Katyn 15, 19, 79, 82, 98, 135, 255, 269–70, 298, 305
Kauer, Rudolf 319
Kaunas 19, 42, 67, 162–65, 168, 170, 196, 350; Fourth Fort in 173, 175; Ninth Fort in 175; Seventh Fort in 165, 175
Kazakhstan 13, 93, 347, 380
Kazimierz III (king) 46
KB (Korpus Bezpieczeństwa, or Security Corps) 108
KBW (Korpus Bezpieczeństwa Wewnętrznego, or Internal Security Corps) 130, 135–36, 277, 280, 315
KC PPR (Komitet Centralny of the PPR, or Central Committee of the PPR) 278–79
"Kedyw" *see* AK: "Kedyw" unit
Keegan, John 300, 318–19, 395
Keitel, Wilhelm 23, 205, 365–66, 370
Keith, Gerald 131
Kellog-Briand Pact 295
Kemnitz, Edward 96
Kenstavičius, Antanas 350
Kermish, Joseph 70, 86, 90–91, 118, 300, 309, 322, 325, 330, 335
Kernowa, P. 314
Kersten, Krystyna 63–64, 140, 304–5, 307, 309–11, 314–15, 330, 341–42, 344–45, 360, 395
KGB (Komitet Gosudarstvennoi Bezopasnosti, or Committee for State Security) 82, 297, 326,

328, 347. *See also* police: Soviet security
Khalkhin-Gol armistice 9
Kharkov 15, 172, 196
Khatyn 255
Kholm *see* Chełm
Khomyshyn, Hryhorii 187
"Khrin" *see* UPA: "Khrin" unit
Khrushchev, Nikita 296–97, 395
Kiddush Ha-Shem 113, 126
kidnapping of Polish children by Germans 22
Kielce 41–43, 81, 86, 91, 94, 105, 120–21, 129–31, 133–36, 138–42, 159, 230, 275–81, 294, 306, 329, 333, 340, 342–45; Jews in governance structure of 134
Kielecki, Krzysztof Komar 295
Kierczyńska, Melania 78
Kierski, Kazimierz 309, 396
Kiev 30, 78–79, 183, 188, 197, 201, 211–12, 214, 216, 228–29, 256, 258, 288, 303, 355, 365, 386
"Kievan Rus" 357
Kijuć, Władysław 348, 396
Kiliński, Jan 95
Kinkelins, Wilhelm 234
Kirichuk, Y. W. 224
Kirov 13
Kirsanov, S. 77
Kirshner, Sheldon 333
Kiryk, Feliks 309, 396
Kisorycz 368
Kister, Anna Grażyna 341
Kiszyński, Lesław 146
Klachkivskyi, Roman Dmytro 246–47, 369–70, 382
Klaipėda (Memel) 169
Klamocha Forest 121
Klancko, H. 354
Kleck 145
Klehr, Josef 84
Kleinhaut, Shmuel 61
Klepaczów 254
Klietmann, Kurt-Georg 319, 321, 372, 396
Klimov, Ivan 147
Kliszko, Zenon 77, 279
Kłosiewicz, Wiktor 60
Klukowski, Andrew 300, 335, 396
Klukowski, George 300, 335, 396
Klukowski, Helen *see* May, Helen Klukowski
Klukowski, Tadeusz 335
Klukowski, Zygmunt 67, 70, 109–11, 249, 300, 317, 334–35, 384, 396
Klymiv, Ivan 208
Klymyshyn, Mykola 358
Kmicic 98–99
KNAPP (Komitet Narodowy Amerykanów Polskiego Pochodzenia, or National Committee of Americans of Polish Descent) 79
Knesset 176, 275
Knysh, Zynovii (Bohdan Mykhailuk) 254, 360, 396
Koblens 373
Kobylański, Władysław 233, 330, 360–61, 375, 396
Koch, Erich 30, 206, 212–13, 217, 235–36, 240, 303, 378
Koch, Hans 211, 212, 214
Kochstelle 363
Koditsa, Nikolai 346, 396
Kohn-Heller streetcars 68
Kojder, Apolonja Maria 297, 344, 396
Kojder (née Beznowski), Helena 15
Kojder, Władysław 136, 344
Kokhanivka (Kochanówka) 229
Kokurin, Aleksandr 2, 298–99, 364, 400
Kolaciński, Władysław 96
Kolbuszowa 42
Kolkhoz 148
Kołodno 244
Kołomyja 9, 17, 53, 109, 253, 371, 375
Kolonia Wileńska 175
Komański, Henryk 230–31, 361, 374, 396
Komarno 17
Komi 13
Komisja Polskiego Sztabu Głównego w Londynie 128
Komitet: Centralny PPR *see* KC PPR; Gosudarstvennoi Bezopasnosti *see* KGB; Narodowy Amerykanów Polskiego Pochodzenia *see* KNAPP; Narodowy Polski *see* Polish: National Committee; Rady Narodowej *see* KRN; Walki Cywilnej *see* Committee for Civilian Struggle; Wojewódzki Polskiej Partii Robotniczej *see* KW PPR; Zamojsko-Lubelski Niesienia Pomocy Żydom *see* Zamość-Lublin Committee for Rendering Assistance to Jews
Kommunisticheskaya Partiia (bolsheviki) Belaruskaya *see* KP(b)B
Komorowski, Tadeusz *see* Tadeusz Bór-Komorowski
Komsomol (Kommunisticheskii Soyuz Molodezhi, or Communist League of Youth) 49, 147
Komunistyczna: Partia (bolszewików) Białorusi *see* KP(b)B; Partia Polski *see* KPP; Partia Robotnicza Polski *see* KPRP; Partia Zachodniej Białorusi *see* KPZB; Partia Zachodniej Ukrainy *see* KPZU
Komunistyczne Zjednoczenie Młodych Polaków *see* KZMP
Koniecpol 91
Konieczny, Kazimierz 277, 280
Konieczny, Zdzisław 383, 396
Königshütte *see* Chorzów
Konopla, Yevgeny 348
Konovalets, Ievhen 190, 194–97, 201, 288, 359–60, 363, 396
Końskie 343
KOP (Korpus Ochrony Pogranicza, or Frontier Defense Corps) 12
Korab-Żebryk, Roman 174, 349–52, 396
Koral, Tadeusz 120
Korboński, Stefan 60, 63, 83, 86, 95, 131, 135, 297, 300–301, 313–14, 319, 322, 325, 329–30, 332, 334, 338, 396
Korczyński, Grzegorz 105, 130, 135, 314, 332
Korfes, Otto 368
Korkociany 327
Korkuć, Kazimierz 91, 327
Korman, Aleksander 299–31, 364–65, 373, 379, 396
Kornecki, Adam 134
Korneychuk, Aleksandr 78
Korościatyn 385
Korpus: Bezpieczeństwa *see* KB; Bezpieczeństwa Wewnętrznego *see* KBW; Ochrony Pogranicza *see* KOP
Korzec, Paweł 295, 312, 347, 396
Kosakviskyi, Mykyta 362, 396
Kościerzyna 26
Kościuszko, Tadeusz 95
Kościuszko League 79
Kościuszko Street 279
Kosewska, Małgorzata 318
Kosów Huculski 364
Kosów Lacki 128
Kossak-Szczucka, Zofia 117, 243, 342; "Protest" of 112
Kostopol 251–52, 381
Kosyk, Wolodymyr 232–33, 363, 365–67, 370, 375, 378, 384, 396
Koszów 254
Kot, Stanisław 201
Kotsylovskyi, Iosafat 228, 373
Kott, Jan 78
Kovel *see* Kowel
Kowalski, Isaac 332, 396
Kowalski (mayor) 87
Kowel (Kovel) 56, 221, 233, 251, 373, 381

Kozak, Ivan 223
Kożera, Wacław 61
Kozhevnikov, S. 12, 144, 346
Kozielsk 15, 80
Kozłowski (victim in Borysław) 18
Kozowa 289
KP(b)B [Komunistyczna Partia (bolszewików) Białorusi, Kommunisticheskaya Partiia (bolsheviki) Belaruskaya, or Communist (Bolshevik) Party of Belorussia] 147
KPP (Komunistyczna Partia Polski, or Polish Communist Party) 36–38, 58–59, 77–78, 143, 307; Jewish membership in 36–38, 59; reasons Jews joined 38
KPRP (Komunistyczna Partia Robotnicza Polski, or Communist Workers' Party of Poland) 37, 143, 313. *See also* PPR
KPZB (Komunistyczna Partia Zachodniej Białorusi, or Communist Party of Western Belorussia) 37, 143–44, 147, 149
KPZU (Komunistyczna Partia Zachodniej Ukrainy, or Communist Party of Western Ukraine) 37, 143, 189, 200, 356
Krahelska, Halina 96
Krahelska-Filipowiczowa, Wanda 117
Kraj Warty *see* Wartheland
Kraj Wileński *see* Wileńszczyzna
Krajewski, Kazimierz 93
Krajewski, Stanisław (Abel Kainer) 38, 58, 61, 129, 308, 312–13, 341, 395
Kraków (Cracow) 23, 42, 86, 115, 117, 119–20, 122, 129, 133, 136, 149, 185, 206, 208, 212, 215, 220, 243, 300, 303, 306, 315–16, 333, 341, 353, 357, 363, 365, 386
Krakowski, Shmuel 40–41, 56, 70, 86, 90, 100, 102, 112, 300, 308–9, 312, 322–25, 330, 332–33, 335–36, 340–41, 367–68, 394, 396
Krall, Hanna 118
Kramer 56
Kranc, Leon 224
Krannhals, Hans von 373, 396
Krasicki, Jan 77
Krasne 97
Krasnodębska, J. *see* Rokicka, J.
Krasnodębska, Stefania 123
Krasnovodsk 80
Kravchuk, Leonid 356
Krawczak, Tadeusz 354, 396
Krawczyk, Andrzej 361, 396
Krawczyk, Eugeniusz 140
"Krawecki," Adam 61
Kręglicki 276
Kremlin 7
Kresy Wschodnie *see* Eastern: Poland
Krew 151
Kriegseinsatz-kommando Süd, H. J. 234
Kriminalpolizei *see* Kripo
Kripo (Kriminalpolizei, or Criminal Police, Detective Forces) 85–86, 110, 125, 154, 164, 237, 317, 340. *See also* police: German
Kristallnacht 243
KRN (Komitet Rady Narodowej, or Committee of the National Council) 279–80
Krokhmaliuk, Roman 226, 372, 396
Krongold, Fajgel *see* Felicja Kwiatkowska
Krosno 206
Kruczek, Władysław 77
Krüger, Wlater 205
Krukowska, Anna 210
Krupavičius, Mykolas 163
Krusze 174
Kruszewski, Z. Anthony 386, 396
Krynica 207
Krystynopol 207
Krzemieniec 17, 243–44, 251, 281
Krzeptowski, Wacław 85
Krzeszowicz, Janina 123
Krzeszowicz, Karol 123
Krzeszowski, Lubosław 90
Krzycki, Leo 79
Krzymiński, Ludwik 134
Krzyżanowski, Aleksander 88–89, 99, 152, 169
Kube, Wilhelm 97–98, 148
Kubiak, Hieronim 299, 353–54, 386, 396
Kubiak, Stanisław 43
Kubiiovych, Volodymyr 215, 224–28, 234, 240, 363, 370, 372–73, 396
Kubiliūnas, Petras 164, 167
Kubina, Teodor 86
Kuchma, Leonid 256, 258, 387
Kujańska, Ewa 381
Kuk, Vasyl 370
Kukliński, Franciszek 80
Kukliński, Józef 139
Kulaks 9
Kulmhof *see* Chełmno
Kümel, Dawid 56
Kundt, Ernst 365
Kunert, Andrzej K. 64, 315
Kupetskyi, Hrytsko 197, 360, 396
Kupiak, Dmytro 386, 396
Kupsza, Stanisław 277–79
Kurcwaig, Hersz 319
Kurek, Ewa 328, 397
Kurmylo, Maryska 385
Kuropas, Myron B. 180, 182, 188, 353, 356–7, 381, 397
Kursk 172
Kuryluk, Karol 78
Kuś (family from Młynów) 244
Kushch Self-Defense Units *see* SKV
Kushel, Frantsishak 155, 157
Kustanay 13
Kutrzeba, Joseph S. 118
Kuty 243–44
Kuźmiński, Stefan 276
Kuźnicki, Wiktor 139, 276–77, 279, 281
Kwasek, Edward 138
Kwaśniewski, Aleksander 256, 258;
Kwaśniewski, Jolanta 258
Kwiatkowska, Felicja (Fajgel Krongold) 134
Kwiek, Rudolf 29
KW PPR (Komitet Wojewódzki of the PPR, or Provincial Committee of the PPR) 134, 278, 280
KZMP (Komunistyczne Zjednoczenie Młodych Polaków, or Communist Union of Polish Youth) 37

Laba, Vasyl 228
Lachowicz, Jan 311
Lachwa 154
Łącki *see* prisons (Soviet): Łącki
LAF (Lietuviu Aktyvistu Frontas, or Lithuanian Activist Front) 163–65, 349, 351; and anti-Semitism 170; call for erection of Polish ghettos by 162; March 19, 1941, directive of 163–4, 167
Lager Dora 316
Lagerschutz (camp guards) 102, 218, 237, 367; "Trawniki people" as *see* "Trawniki people"
Łagowski, Stefan 17
Lagun, Stanisław 162–63, 349
Lahousen, Erwin 362
Lake Quenz (Austria) 197
Laks, Anna *see* Wilson, Anna
Laks, Krystyna *see* Lerman, Krystyna
Laks, Regina *see* Gelb, Regina
Łambinowice (Lamsdorf) 61, 149
Lammers, Hans 207, 365–66
Lamsdorf *see* Łambinowice
land-grant: policies in Eastern Poland 4, 146–47; act, abrogation of 181

land reform policies in Eastern Poland 180
Landau, Ludwig 334, 397
Landesdirektoren (Country Directors) 350
Landwehr, Richard 373, 397
Lane, Arthur Bliss 130, 135, 140, 318, 343, 345, 397
Lange, Oskar 79–80, 318
Lanota, Anna 39
Łanowce 243
Laos 281
Lappo, Henryk 347, 397
Laqueur, Walter 336, 397
Laskovich, V.P. 147
Lasy Janowskie *see* Janowskie Forest
Latawski, Paul 356, 397
Latin America 129
Latvia 3, 13, 15, 22, 80, 148, 154–55, 159, 166, 266, 304, 307, 320, 350; Eastern 349
Lauenburg 26
Lauterbach 74
Law of Reasons 273
Law of Return 273
Lazebnik, Fayna *see* Schulman, Faye
League of Nations 3–4, 161, 187–88, 193–94, 196, 239, 264, 295, 356
Lebed, Mykola (Maksym Ruban) 205–6, 210, 224, 239, 246, 254, 358, 370, 382, 397
Lechthaler's 11th Reserve Police Battalion 165
Legalizacja (Legalization Department) *see* Department: Legalization
Legionowa Street 53
Leipzig 149
Lemberg *see* Lwów
Łemkowszczyzna (Łemko region) 177, 188, 207
Lenczowski, George 129, 341, 397
Lenin, Vladimir 9, 43
Leningrad 169, 172
Lenk, Janina 146
Lenkavskyi, Stepan 190, 207
Leonarda Street 139
Leonówka 246
Lepel 85
Lerer, Shmuel 128, 340
Lerman (née Laks), Krystyna 220
lesaviki (wood demons) 101
Leśniewo 26, 301
Leszczyński, Kazimierz 24, 299–302, 304, 336, 394
letter: from Bandera (August 3, 1941) to Hitler 214; from Bandera (June 23, 1941) to Hitler 211; of Bishop Khomyshyn (pastoral, 1931) 187; from Brother Cyprian (June 7, 1943) to Adam Sapieha 243–44; from the elders of Lubaczów (April 12, 1945) to Warsaw 247–48; from Jermachenko (1939) to Hitler 149; of Kaczmarek *see* Czesław kaczmarek: pastoral letters; from Melnyk (January 18, 1943) to Hitler 224; from Melnyk (July 6, 1941) to Hitler 213–14; from Melnyk and other Nationalists (November 1944) to Hitler 234; from Melnyk, Sheptytsky and others (February 2, 1942) to Hitler 214–15; from Omelchenko, T. (January 12, 1942), to Hitler 215; from OUN (October 1941) to the Gestapo 215; of Sheptytsky (various) *see* Andrei Sheptytsky; from Stetsko (July 4, 1941) to Hitler 211–12; from the "Ukrainian government" to Hitler (telegram, June 30, 1941) 211
"Lew" *see* GL: "Lew" unit
Lewandowski, Józef 309, 397
Lewica Demokratyczna *see* Democratic Left
Lewickowski, Wacław 77
Lewin, Efraim 61
Lewin, Julian 134, 278
Lewin, Leopold 78
Lewin, Zofia 323, 336–37, 390
Lewkowicz-Ajzenman, Eta 343
Libya 376
Lida 17, 32, 42, 87–89, 132, 148, 152–53, 241
Lidice 32, 384
Lietuvių Aktyvistų Frontas *see* LAF
Lietzow, Paul 26
Limanowa 120
Linenthal, Edward T. 325–26, 397
Lipiński, Piotr 385
Lipschitz, Adolf 301
Lipszowicz, Eliahu 129
Lisowska, Wanda 131, 342, 397
List, Wilhelm 205, 294
Liszewski, Karol 296, 310–11, 346–47, 361, 397. *See also* Szawłowski, Ryszard
Litauische Sonderverbände *see* LVR
Literary Club 77
"Lithuania for Lithuanians" 163
Lithuanian: Activist Front *see* LAF; Commissariat *see* General: Commissariat of Lithuania; communists 161, 167; Legion *see* LVR; Local Detachments *see* LVR; People's Diet 162; SSR 99, 162, 162, 259–60, 328, 351 (*see also* Soviet: Lithuania)
Lithuanianization 161–62, 167
Littlejohn, David 234–35, 294, 319, 322, 348, 363, 371–76, 397
Littman, Sol 213, 225, 229, 231–32, 362, 366, 370–74, 377
Litvaks (Litwaki) 43
Litvinov, Maxim 295
Livytskyi, Andrii 363
Lochne, Louis P. 375, 397
Łódź 21, 28–29, 46, 67, 69, 129–130, 133, 149, 279, 294, 303, 306, 315
Loftus, John 153, 156–57, 237–38, 348–49, 371–72, 376–77, 397
Lohse, Heinrich 30
Lokot 85
Łomża 303
London 19, 53, 88, 100, 112, 156, 181, 194–95; Charter 238; Convention 295; Poles 78–79
Lontski (captain) 66
Łopatyn 17
Lorek, Jan Kanty 86, 322; assistance to Jews by 323
Łossowski, Piotr 308, 349, 367, 397
Lowell, Lawrence 308
Lower Rhine 82
Lower Silesia *see* Śląsk: Lower
Łowicz 220
Łoziński (bishop) 282
Lubachivsky (cardinal) 387
Lubaczów 201, 247–48
Lubartów 103, 120
Lubelszczyzna (Lublin region) 229, 231, 383–84. *See also* Lublin
Lubianka *see* prisons (Soviet): Lubianka
Lubiaż 204
Lubieszow 204
Lubinski, M. 298, 392
Lublin 19, 25, 27, 29, 54, 67, 70, 94–96, 99–101, 105, 129–130, 160, 165, 177, 181–82, 217, 219–20, 230, 244, 247–51, 281–83, 303, 306, 313, 331, 333–34, 340–42, 353, 367–68. *See also* Lubelszczyzna
Luboml 251, 381
Luborzyce 86
Lubovych, Iaroslav 359
Luby 186
Luciuk, Lubomyr 359
Łuck 11, 17–18, 55–56, 120, 199, 200, 211, 251, 298, 373, 381
Łuczak, Czesław 2, 100, 118, 168, 210, 233, 294, 296, 299–301, 303–6, 319, 322–23, 330, 337,

346–47, 349, 351, 360, 362–63, 365, 372–73, 375, 379, 397
Łuczyce 254
Ludmiłówka 105
Ludwigsburg 320–21
"Ludwików" 279; steelworkers 138
Luftwaffe 155–56, 166, 234
Łukacze 71
Lukas, Richard C. 23, 32, 39, 41, 51, 96–97, 108, 114–16, 118, 128, 133, 299–301, 303, 306–9, 311–12, 317–18, 320, 322–24, 329–30, 332–34, 336–38, 340–42, 397
Lukashenko, Alexander 347–48
Łukaszów, Jan *see* Tadeusz Olszańaski
Łukiszki *see* prisons, German and Stalinist: Łukiszki
Łuków 25; woods 111
Lungin, Paul 377
Łuniniec 12
"Łupaszka" *see* AK: "Łupaszka" Brigade
Lutyk, Taras 224
Lutze, Viktor 233
Luxembourg 304
Luzhynski, Mikhal 156
Łużny, Ryszard 354, 397
Lviv *see* Lwów
Lvov *see* Lwów
LVR (Lietuvos Vietinė Rinktinė, or Lithuanian Local Detachments) 164; atrocities against Polish civilians by 166
Lwów (Lemberg, Lviv, Lvov) 9–12, 15, 17–19, 31, 40–43, 47, 49–54, 56–57, 60, 77–79, 99, 120, 133, 177, 180, 183–87, 192, 199–202, 204, 207–17, 223, 225, 228–30, 234, 236, 242, 250, 261, 287, 289, 291, 296, 306, 318, 333, 353–55, 357, 363–66, 370–71, 386–87
Łyczki 254
Łyntupy 168; Stare 168
Łysa Góra 142
Lysiak (professor) 364
Lytwyn, Wasyl 367
Łyżwa, Józef 315

McCafferty, Nell 348, 397
McClennen, Eliza 2
Machajek, Zofia 280
Machine-Tractor Stations 12
Maciejów 381
Maciulevičius, Jonas 168
Mackiewicz, Józef 85, 69
MacLean (brigadier) 376
McLoughlin, Merrill 92
McNarrey, Joseph T. 341
Madagascar 29
Madajczyk, Czesław 115, 299–300, 302, 304–6, 312, 319, 337, 374, 383–84, 397
Mądro, Roman 247
Magocsi, Paul Robert 363, 398
Magyars (Hungarians) 209
Mahlke, Walter 27, 301
Mahlke, Werner 26
Maigewitter 229
Mailov, Aleksei 192
Main: Commission for the Investigation of [formerly: Nazi] Crimes Against the Polish Nation 24, 251, 320–21; Social Welfare Council *see* RGO
Maironi 331
Maisky, Ivan 81
Majdan Nowy 121
Majdan Stary 230
Majdanek 19, 28–29, 122, 165, 302–03, 383
Majewski, Tadeusz 277
Majówka 218–19
Mąka, Ayzer 313
Mąka, Moshe 61
Mąka, Pinek 61
Makowiecki, Jerzy 95
Maksymchuk-Kardash, Mykola 212
Malakhovka 80–81
Malanowski, Jan 298
Malenkov, Georgi 7
Malets, Dionizy 151
Malińska 230
Małopolska Wschodnia *see* Eastern: Galicia
Malorny, Ernst 319
Malutsa, Ivan 358
Maly Trostenets 154
Manchuria 197
Mandelkern, Benjamin 109, 334, 398
"Manifesto of Prague" 234
Mankovskyi, I. 78
Mańkowski, Zygmunt 277, 303, 334, 398
Manor, Alexander 310, 398
Mao Tse-tung 64
MAP (Ministerstwo Administracji Publicznej, or Ministry of State Administration) 280, 340
Marcinkańce 162
Marcus, Joseph 309, 398
Marczak (street peddler) 122
Marczak, Władysław (gardner) 122
Marek, Wacława 77
Maria Wola 254
Markiewicz (UB commandant in Kielce) 137, 277–78
Markov Brigade 98
Markwita, Kazimierz 134
Marmurowa Street 279
Marples, David R. 296–97, 346, 357, 365, 376, 398
Marrus, Michael R. 333, 363, 367–68, 376, 382, 398
Marszałkowska Street 111, 334
martial law 261
Martynets, Volodymyr 196
Martyrs' and Heroes' Remembrance Authority in Jerusalem 123
Marusarzówna, Helena 295
Marxism 80
Maślanko, Mieczysław 281
Maśliński, Józef 78
Masłowski, Medard 386
Master Race 30
Masurian nationals 83
Matejko, Jan 369
Materski, Wojciech 298, 398
Matla, Oleksander *see* Tereshchuk, Petro
Matsuda, M. 263
Matysiak (policeman from Sułowo) 110
Mauthausen 28, 115, 129, 302
May, Helen Klukowski 300, 335, 396
Mayerling 366
Mazowsze 94
Mazur, Elżbieta Trela 299
Mazur, Stefan 138, 345
Mazur, Zygmunt 299, 312
MBP (Ministerstwo Bezpieczeństwa Publicznego, or Ministry of State Security) 58, 61, 64, 132, 136, 138, 276–77, 279, 313, 315; Fifth Department of 60; Investigation Department of 60; Special Commission 279; Tenth Department of 60, 141, 313; Third Department of 60. *See also* UB
Mechowo 27
medical experiments 28–29, 302
Mediterranean 82
Mednoye 15
Meducki, Stanisław 2, 281, 340, 342, 345, 398
Medyna 313
Mein Kampf 240
Melnica 233
Melnyk, Andrii 197, 205–6, 208–9, 213–15, 221, 224, 227, 234, 236, 359–60, 363, 370, 382. *See also* Consul I *and also* OUN-M
Memorandum on the Development of the Jewish National Home 45
Mende, G. von 212
Mendel (of Gwoździec) 123
Mendelsohn, Ezra 41, 44–45, 308–9, 400

Mendykowski (gendarme) 110
Merin, Mojsze 69
Merkulov (*troika* member) 270
Mertz, E. 314
Metz, Zelda 328
Meyer, Peter 308, 398
Meyers, Sondra 338, 401
Miadziel 98
Micgiel, John 345, 398
Michalewicz, Aleksander 280
Michalowicz, Jerzy 349, 404
Michnik, Adam 314, 335
Michnik, Stefan 314
Miciunas 350
Mickiewicz, Adam 79; Foundation in Canada 2; Gimnazjum 162
Mickuny 168
Middle East 92, 97, 136
Miechów 86, 121
"Miecz i Pług" 86, 104
Mieczysław Karłowicz Conservatory of Music 162
Międzynarodowa Organizacja Pomocy Rewolucjonistom *see* MOPR
Miejska Rada Nadzorcza *see* MRN
Mielnica 254
Mikhailov, Boris 320
Mikhnovskyi, Mykola 242, 357, 378, 398
Mikołaj Rej Street 66
Mikołajczyk, Stanisław 133, 135, 141, 344, 398
Mikołajów 17
Mikołów, (Nikolai) 61
Mikoyan, Anastas 269
Miłaszewski, Kacpar 99, 106
Milch, Baruch 2, 72, 74, 317, 339–40, 361, 398; testament of 126–28
Milicja Obywatelska *see* MO
"military settlers" 146–47, 180
militia: Belorussian 147; Civil (in Kielce) *see* MO; civilian *see* civilian: militias; Jewish 49–51, 53–55, 57, 62, 66, 71–72, 74, 201, 203; Lithuanian 176, 352; Polish 248, 276–80, 313, 315, 345; Soviet 231; Ukrainian 30–31, 50, 55, 71, 201–3, 207–10, 214, 217, 221–23, 237, 249, 368; School (in Kielce) 139
Miłosz, Czesław 59, 313, 318, 322, 335, 344–45, 398
Minc, Hilary 60, 77, 130, 134
Ministry: of Defense (Israeli) 273; of Education (Polish) 59; of Foreign Affairs (in Rome) 46, 59, 370; of the Interior (Israeli) 273; of Justice (in Germany) 32, (in Poland) 59, 62; of Justice Commission (Polish) 279; of National Defense (Obrony Narodowej) *see* MON; of State Administration (Administracji Publicznej) *see* MAP; of State Security (Bezpieczeństwa Publicznego) *see* MBP
Mińkowski, Chaja 43
Mińkowski, Josek 43
Minsk 42, 88, 143, 148, 154–55, 165, 351
Minsk Mazowiecki 122, 132
Mir 222
Mirchuk, Petro 357–58, 385, 398
Mirska, Klara 310, 398
Misiło, Eugeniusz 379, 383, 398
Misiunas, Romuald J. 166, 349–52, 398
Mitteleuropa 47
Mitzveh 39
Mława 120
Młynów 244
Mniów 275, 343
MO (Milicja Obywatelska, or Civil Militia) 130, 136–41, 275–77, 279–80
Moczar, Mieczysław *see* Demko, Mikołaj
Moderówka 229
Modlin 24
Mohyla, Peter 183
Mohylan Academy 183
Mołodeczno 156
Mołodów 53
Mołojec, Bolesław 103
Molotov, Vyacheslav 7, 9, 160, 269, 307
Molotov: Brigade 107; cocktails 108; -Ribbentrop agreement *see* German-Soviet: Non-Aggression Pact
Mołożów 383
MON (Ministerstwo Obrony Narodowej, or Ministry of National Defense) 62, 342
Mongolia 9
Montreal 96, 275
MOPR (Międzynarodowa Organizacja Pomocy Rewolucjonistom, or International Organization for Help to the Revolutionaries) 37
Morel, Shlomo (Solomon) 61–62, 130, 314
Morgan, Frederick E. 341
Morgenthau [Henry] Commission 42
Morochko, Wolodymyr 379
Moroz, Valentyn 197
Moscow 7, 9, 15, 19, 58, 60, 64, 77–81, 94, 98–99, 102–4, 132, 135, 142, 150, 161–2, 183, 199, 204, 207, 209, 212, 215, 221, 235, 260, 269, 284–85, 344, 355
Mosdorf, Jan 112
Moszek (of Gwoździec) 123
Moszek, Leska 43
Moszkowicz, Abram 138
Motol 54
Motyl, Alexander J. 192, 356–60, 385, 398
Mountain-Peasants' Help *see* BBH
"mountaineer nation" (Goralenvolk) 85
MRN (Miejska Rada Nadzorcza, or City Supervisory Council) 279
Mroczka, Ludwik 309
Mruckowski 98
Mstislav (Stepan Skrypnyk) 228
Mucha, Jan 138, 276
Muchin, Jurii 298
Mudryi, Vasyl 180, 187, 355
Munich 149, 196–97, 359
Muranowski ("Blue Police" member) 110
murders *see* executions and murders
Murowana Oszmianka 166
Museum of the National House 185
Musiał, Adam Kazimierz 322, 398
Musiał, Józef 61
Mussolini, Benito 32
Mutual Declaration of the Presidents of the Republic of Poland and Ukraine (May 21, 1997) 256–57
Muzyka, Agnieszka 245, 382, 398
Myers, Sondra 338, 398
Myhal, Roman 358
Mykhailuk, Bohdan *see* Zynovii Knysh
Mykhalchuk, Vasyl 386, 398
Myron, Dmytro 212
Myśliwski, Wiesław 312, 361, 385, 398
Mysłowice (Myslowitz) 61

Nabiałczyk, Stefan 277
Nachtigall 207–13, 217, 224, 226, 228, 230, 232, 236, 248, 255, 363, 365–66. *See also* DUN
Naczelna Rada Opiekuńcza *see* NRO
Nadwór 55
Nadwórna 17
Nagasaki 107, 136
Naglerowa, Herminia 78
Nahaylo, Bohdan 387, 399
Najwyższy Sąd Wojskowy *see* NSW

Nakoniecznikoff-Klukowski, Stanisław 332
Naliboki 100, 102
"Narocz" *see* AK: "Narocz" Brigade
Narodnyi: Komissariat Gosudarstvennoi Bezopasnosti *see* NKGB; Komissariat Vnutrennikh Del *see* NKVD
Narodowa Organizacja Wojskowa *see* NOW
Narodowe Siły Zbrojne *see* NSZ
Narodowy Związek Wojskowy *see* NZW
Nasutów 120
National: Armed Forces *see* NSZ; Committee of Americans of Polish Descent *see* KNAPP; Council (Polish) 59; Defense (Obrona Narodowa) 23; Forces of Poland (Siły Zbrojne w Kraju) 95; Military Organization *see* NOW; Military Union *see* NZW; Party *see* SN; Socialism 1, 22, *see also* NSDAP; Socialist German Workers' Party *see* NSDAP; Unionists *see* Tautininkai
"national dictatorship" 191
nationale Verwaltungen 306
Nationalist Military Detachments *see* VVN
nationalization decrees 11
Nationalsozialistische Deutsche Arbeiter Partei *see* NSDAP
Native Americans 5, 38
naval auxiliaries (Marine-Helfer) 156
Nawóz 200, 203
Near East 344
Neisse *see* Nysa
Nepean, Kazimierz Stys 319
Netreby 254
Neubarger 123
Neuhammer 207, 213, 373–74
New Hampshire 2, 38
"New Reich" 8
New York 48, 79, 119, 193, 239, 343–44, 367
Nichtdeutsch 319
Nicieja, Stanisław Sławomir 364
Nickel, Siegfried 156
Nieczuja, Tadeusz 298, 399
Niemenczyn 167
Niezabitowska, Małgorzata 337–39, 399
Nikolai *see* Mikołów
Ninth Fort in Kaunas *see* Kaunas: Ninth Fort in
Nizan, Shmuel 332
NKGB (Narodnyi Komissariat Gosudarstvennoi Bezopasnosti, or People's Commissariat for State Security) 60, 81, 92, 99, 132, 267–69. *See also* police: Soviet security
NKVD (Narodnyi Komissariat Vnutrennikh Del, or People's Commissariat for Internal Affairs) 9, 14–19, 49, 51, 56, 62, 81–82, 92–94, 99, 103, 131–32, 141, 143, 147, 163, 167, 199, 201, 210, 254, 265, 269–70, 295, 312, 328, 335, 344, 351, 363–64. *See also* police: Soviet security
Norden, A. 210
Nordhausen 316
Normandy 82
North: Africa 82; Bukovina 214; Carolina 38; Caucasus 380
Norway 82, 88, 118–19, 166, 232, 304
Nosal, Aniela 123
Nosal, Piotr 123
Novosibirsk 13
NOW (Narodowa Organizacja Wojskowa, or National Military Organization) 94
Nowa Wilejka 167
Nowak, Jerzy Robert 317
Nowakowski, Irena 129
Nowe Święcany 168
Nowicki, Wacław 332, 399
Nowinarska Street 122
Nowiński, Wacław 334
Nowogród Wołyński 16
Nowogródek 9, 12, 17, 30, 79, 85, 88–90, 92, 98, 100, 102, 131, 143, 146, 148, 150–55, 160, 184, 202, 223, 241, 281, 296, 306, 323, 346
Nowogródska Street 111
Nowotko, Marceli 81, 103
Nowy Sącz 353
Nowy Targ 129, 340, 353
NRO (Naczelna Rada Opiekuńcza, or Chief Social Welfare Council) 86
NSDAP (Nationalsozialistische Deutsche Arbeiter Partei, or National Socialist German Workers' Party) 28, 148, 190, 241–42. *See also* National: Socialism
NSW (Najwyższy Sąd Wojskowy, or Supreme Military Court) 139, 280–81
NSZ (Narodowe Siły Zbrojne, or National Armed Forces) 85, 90–91, 94–97, 100, 102, 111, 131–32, 134–36, 220, 241, 252, 280, 323–24, 328–30, 332, 335, 340–41 345; "Eagle" unit of the 91
numerus: nullus 47; *clausus* 38, 42, 47, 308
Nuremberg 1 205, 235, 258, 335, 368; Laws (1935) 45, 48, 243; Trials 302; Tribunal 10, 135, 255
Nurowski, Roman 305, 399
Nussbaum, Klemens 318
Nussbaum, Rubin *see* Zambrowski, Antoni
Nysa (Neisse) 61
NZW (Narodowy Związek Wojskowy, or National Military Union) 131

Oberkommando der Wehrmacht *see* OKW
Oberländer, Theodor 207, 209
Obertyńska, Beata 78
Obórki 120
Obóz Narodowo-Radykalny *see* ONR
Obrona Narodowa *see* National: Defense
Ochab, Edward 77
Ochotnicza Rezerwa Milicji Obywatelskiej *see* ORMO
Ochrana 344
OD (Ordnungsdienst, or Order Service, Order Police) 67–69, 72–74, 87, 222, 316, 322, 334, 368, 371. *See also* police: Jewish
oddziały pozorowane *see* "sham units"
Odessa 207, 212
Odra, Jerzy 78
Office of (State) Security *see* UB
"Ogień" 340
Okięczyc, Józef 280
Okręg Wileński *see* Wileńszczyzna
Okręt (Okrent), Zygmunt 60
Okulicki, Leopold 100
OKW (Oberkommando der Wehrmacht, or High Command of the German Armed Forces) 207
Oldenberg 373
Oleksiniec 244
Oleszyce 17
Oliner, Samuel 38
Olkusz 303
Ołpiński, Stefan 84, 319
Olshanskyi, Teofil 197
Olszanica 17, 252
Olszański, Tadeusz (Jan Łukaszów) 362–63, 380, 382, 399
Olsztyn 379
Omelchenko, T. 215
ONR (Obóz Narodowo-Radykalny, or Radical Nationalist Group) 45, 96, 329
Onyshkevych, Myroslav 379
Opdyke, Irene 338
open-air shootings 29, 31, 123
Operation: "Burza" (Tempest)

100, 171; "Martyka" 335; "Ostra Brama" 89–90, 93; "Swamp Fever" 165;"Wisła" (Vistula) 244, 257–58, 260, 261, 370, 379, 383
Operational Groups: German *see* Einsatzkommando, Einsatzgruppen; Soviet 104
Opoczno 120
Opole (Oppeln) 47, 61, 149, 305
Opole Lubelskie 109
Oranienberg 115
Orany 167
Orawa 294
order: to arrest 1,000 Poles in Wileńszczyzna (May 19, 1942) 168; of Beria (No. 0016, January 11, 1945) 100; of Beria (No. 00315, April 1945) 100; of Bór-Komorowski (No. 116, September 12, 1943) 91, 102, 324, 325; of Chief of SP and SD (July 1, 1941) on cleansing of Jews, Bolsheviks and Polish intelligentsia 166; for creating the SS-Galizien 225, 371; of German authorities for preferential treatment of Ukrainian collaborators in Zamojszczyzna 384; of German occupation authorities on the treatment of Poles in Eastern Poland (November 26, 1942) 150; of Gottberg for the formation of the BKA (February 23, 1944); of Hitler to form the Hiwis (August 18, 1942) 375; of Krzyżanowski (April 12, 1944, no. 5) forbidding AK reprisals against civilians 169; of Moscow (June 22, 1943) 19, 58, 98, 150, 153; of Moscow to liquidate the Polish underground (Marceli Nowotko's secret mission, December 1941) 58, 103–4; No. 001223 (deportation) 266; of OUN-B commanding Ukrainians to desert German police and official posts (April 4, 1943) 253; of OUN-B commanding Ukrainians to join the OUN (April 5, 1943) 253; of OUN-UPA for ethnic cleansing 245–47; of OUN-UPA nailed to Polish doors commanding them to leave Eastern Poland 246; of Polish Ministry of Education (April 12, 1927, no. 155 2334/27) 184; of Radkiewicz (December 4, 1945) regarding "sham units" 104; of SS and police chief in Radom prohibiting assistance to Jews (September 21, 1942) 114; of Stalin for a scorched earth in Belorussia (July 3, 1941) 147–48; of Stalin (July 14, 1944, No. 220145) 19, 58, 99, 153 148; of Stalin (October 1944) 330
Order: Police *see* OD; Service *see* OD
Ordner (raiders) 66
Ordnungsdienst *see* OD
Organization: Todt, Poles in 83; to Help Children (in southern France) 114; of Ukrainian Nationalists *see* OUN
Organizational Report nr. 220 (August 31, 1943) 324
Orhanizatsiia Ukrainskykh Natsionalistiv *see* OUN
Orle 26–27
Orlemański, Stanisław 79–80
Orlicki, Józef 341, 399
ORMO (Ochotnicza Rezerwa Milicji Obywatelskiej, or Volunteer Reserve of the Civil Militia) 138
Orthodox: Belorussians 89; Jews 44, 49, 113
Orthodox Church 4, 146 155, 180, 185, 203, 250, 281–83, 373, 382; Autocephalous 182–83, 228, 284; Polish revindication policies against 181–83; Russian 183
Orthodoxy 44
Orżew 232, 375
OSI (Office of Special Investigation) 156, 238, 367
Osmólski, Mieczysław 96
Osnabruch 373
Ossman (vice admiral) 297
Ossów 122
Ossowska, Wanda 210
Ostashkov 15, 80, 99
Ostministerium 31
"Ostra Brama" *see* Operation: "Ostra Brama"
Ostróg 12
Ostrów-Lubleski 56
Ostrowiec Świętokrzyski 134
Ostrówki 198, 245, 247
Ostrowsky, Radaslaŭ *see* Astroŭski, Radaslaŭ
Osttruppen (eastern troops) 224, 376
Osttürkischer Waffenverband (Eastern Turkish Battle Group) 231
Oświęcim *see* Auschwitz
Oszmiana 17, 148, 151, 162
Ottynia 17
Otwock 317
OUN (Orhanizatsiia Ukrainskykh Natsionalistiv, or Organization of Ukrainian Nationalists) 117, 185, 188, 190–98, 200, 205–9, 214–17, 220–1, 223, 225, 229, 231, 235–38, 240–43, 245–47, 250–56, 355–60, 363, 365, 369–70, 377–83, 385; founding of 190; membership as of 1939, 366; Provid 196–97, 207, 212, 258; support and training by Germany of 196–97, 206; terrorist campaign in interwar Eastern Poland of 191–95; ethnic cleansing by *see* ethnic cleansing: campaign of OUN-UPA. *See also the following:* OUN-B; OUN-M; Ukrainian Nationalists; UPA
OUN-B (Organization of Ukrainian Nationalists, Bandera faction) 192, 199, 204, 206–8, 210–17, 220–1, 224, 227–28, 232, 234, 236–37, 241, 245–48, 250, 254, 355, 366, 369–70, 382, 386–87; declaration of Ukrainian independence by 211–12. *See also the following:* Bandera; Banderowcy; OUN; Ukrainian Nationalists; UPA
OUN-M (Organization of Ukrainian Nationalists, Melnyk faction) 204–7, 213–17, 225, 227–28, 233, 236, 250, 366, 370. *See also the following:* Melnyk; OUN; Ukrainian Nationalists
Our Lady of Ostra Brama 159
Owczarnia 95
Ożarowski, Filip 101, 331, 385, 399

Pabianice 315
pacification: of Belorussia by Germans 148, 157, 213; of Belorussian SSR by Soviets 144; of Eastern Galicia (1930) by Poles 4, 191, 194–95, 287–91, 357; of Eastern Poland by Soviets with Ukrainian assistance 202; of Lublin/Zamość district by Germans with Ukrainian assistance 22, 220, 299–300, 384; of Poland by Germans 23; of Polish villages by Nachtigall 208; of Polish villages by Ukrainian police 250; of Wołyń by Germans with Borovests' assistance 206, 217. *See also* Aktion: A-B
Pacula, Wojciech 109
Paczkowski, Andrzej 58, 64, 313
Pająk, Henryk 64, 314–15, 318, 330, 341, 399
Pakanowski, Pinek 313
Pakosz Street 279

Paldiel, Mordecai 338, 348, 352, 369, 376, 399
Palestine 5, 44–45, 70, 129–30, 136, 330, 344
Paliiv, Dmytro 221, 226, 368
Palikrowy 229–30
Pallotine Sisters 151–52
Palmiry 23–24
Panevėžys 165
Pankiewicz, Tadeusz 316, 399
Pankivskyi, Kost 357, 399
Paranko, Matvii 357
Parchacz 15
Parczew Forest 129
Paris 156, 263, 323
parliament: of Denmark 119; Jewish *see* Knesset; Polish 5, 59 (*see also* Seym); Ukrainian 255–56
Parnicki, Teodor 78
partisans: attack on Jews by Soviet 105–6; communist 324; Jewish 58, 94–95, 97–98, 100–102, 105, 130, 237, 240, 324–25, 331, 333; Jewish "mercenary" 103; Lithuanian 92, 164–5, 167, 170, 352; Polish 91–92, 95, 98–100, 102–3, 107, 121, 155, 228, 323–26, 329, 331, 335; Soviet 19, 58, 81, 88–89, 97–98, 100–103, 105–7, 150, 153, 166, 168, 175, 206, 214, 216, 229, 231, 235, 237, 240, 254, 250, 253, 324–25, 376, 381; Tito's 228; Ukrainian 100, 206–7, 227–28, 233, 252
Partyia Belaruskikh Natsianalistov *see* PBN
Pasieczna 17
Pasowski, Antoni 135, 276, 343
Passover 110
Pasternak, Evhen 383–84, 399
Pasternak, Leon 78
Patton's Third Army 157
Pauker, Ana 130
Paul (German Jew) 28–29
Pauliak, Irvin 374
Pavlishchev Bor 15, 80
Pavlodar 13
Pavlov (or Požėlas, Lithuanian NKVD member) 167
Pawiak *see the following:* prisons: German: Pawiak; executions and murders: of prisoners by Germans; executions and murders: of prisoners by Polish police
"Pawiak project" 96
Pawliczko, Ann Lencyk 386, 399
Pawlik (teacher) 87
Pawłokoma 252, 385
Pawłów 166, 360
PBN (Partyia Belaruskikh Natsianalistov, or Belorussian Nationalist Party) 87, 149, 323
PCK (Polski Czerwony Krzyż, or Polish Red Cross) 24, 84, 86, 117, 279. *See also* executions and murders: of PCK women by Soviets
Peasant: Legions *see* BCh; Populist Union (Lithuanian) 163
Peasants' Party of Ukraine 255
Pedowski, Ryszard 2, 54–55, 62
Peker, Meir 218, 367
Pelensky, Iaroslav 357
penal camps: German 28; Soviet 52
Penkulla, Adam 42, 309, 399
People's: Army *see* AL; Assembly of Western Belorussia 77, 346; Assembly of Western Ukraine 11, 77–78; Commissariat for Internal Affairs *see* NKVD; Commissariat for State Security *see* NKGB; Guard *see* GL; Palace 40; Party *see* SL
Perechodnik, Calel 317, 399
Peretiatkowicz, Adam 379, 384–85, 399
Pergamen ("Kuka," the *woziwoda*) 55
Pesach 63
Pest 70
Pétain, Henri Philippe 84, 336
Petliura, Symon 5, 187–88, 208–9, 288, 355, 363; Aktion *see* Aktion: Petliura; alliance with Piłsudski of *see* Piłsudski-Petliura Agreement
Petropavlosk 13
Pevnyi, Petro 189, 283, 286
Phipps, Eric 263
Piaseczne 109
Piaśnica 26–27, 301; Wielka 25
Pidhainyi, Bohdan 358
Pidhirnyi, Dmytro 357
Piechowska, Władysława 360
Piecuch, Henryk 141
Piękna Street 96
Pieracki, Bronisław 192, 239, 358–59
Pilaciński, Jerzy 330, 399
Pilch, Adolf 88, 153, 348
Pilica-Zamek 121
Piłsudski, Józef 4, 6, 10, 38, 42, 47, 146, 159, 182, 187, 192, 283, 288, 293–94, 399
Piłsudski-Petliura Agreement 5, 187
Pinchuk, Ben-Cion 40–41, 51, 106, 308, 310–12, 332, 399
Pinkertons (Pinkertowcy) 103
Pińsk 17, 40–42, 49, 53–54, 105, 148, 282, 303
"Piorun" (Ukrainian guard) 218, 368
Piotrków Trybunalski 29
Piotrkowska Street 278
Piotrowiak, Helena 254, 385
Piotrowski, Ala 2
Piotrowski, Andrzej 2
Piotrowski, Czesław 385, 399
Piotrowski, Janina 128
Piotrowski, Renia 2
Piotrowski, Stanisław 301, 399
Piotrowski, Tadeusz 2, 300, 340, 377–78, 381, 385–86, 399
Piotrowski, Terri 2
Piper, Franciszek 302
Piramowicz, Grzegorz, Elementary School 275
Pisarewski-Parry, Feliks 96–97, 330, 399
Piskorowice 252
Piskunowicz 93
PLAN (Polska Ludowa Akcja Niepodległości, or Polish People's Independence Action) 108
Planty Street 134–39, 141, 276–78
Płaszów 28
Plater-Gajewski, Jan 13
Plechavičius, Povelas 166
"Pobieda" Brigade 102
Poblihushchy, Ievhen 207
Pobóg-Malinowski, Władysław 169, 294–97, 349, 351, 359, 399
Poczajów 281
Podabas, Marijonas 89, 168
Podborze 174
Podbrodzie 331
Podgaje 23
Podhajce 200, 289
Podhirskyi (deputy) 187
Podhorski, Baltazar 307, 399
Podkamień 229–30, 374
Podkowa Leśna 319
Podlasie 94, 181–2, 188, 354
Podlaski, Kazimierz (Bohdan Skaradziński) 318, 346, 400
Podole (Podolia) 217, 220–21, 240, 258, 303, 339, 368
Podvorniak, Mykhailo 254, 386, 400
Podwalna Street 275
Poel (general) 90
Pogonowski, Iwo Cyprian 28, 135, 309, 338, 343–44, 400
pogroms: in Białystok 40; in Czechoslovakia 141; in Częstochowa 41, 43; in East Europe 46; in Eastern Poland 40–41, 43, 209, 222; in Ejszyszki 91–94; in Galicia 40; in Hungary 141; in Kaunas 170; in Kielce 41, 43, 129–42, 275–81, 341–45; in Kolbuszowa 42; in Kraków 136; in Lida 42; in Lithuanian Commissariat 170; in Lwów 40–43,

208–10, 223–24; in Minsk 42; in Pińsk 41–42; in postwar Poland 128–29, 340; in Przytyk 40, 42–43; in Russia 46; in Rzeszów 136, 141; in Tarnopol 361; in Ukraine 230; in Warsaw 110–12; in Wileńszczyzna 170; in Wilno 40, 42; in Wołyń 364; in Worczyn 329
Poincaré, R. 263
pokhidni hrupy (marching, or expeditionary groups) 207, 221, 228, 236, 248
Pokrzywiński, Józef 139
Poksiński, Jerzy 62, 314, 400
Polak, Kazimierz 120
Polak, Henryk 17
"Poland for the Poles" 260
Poleneinsatz (employment of Poles) 22
Polesie 9, 17, 30–31, 36, 101, 105, 107, 143, 145–46, 148, 177, 184, 202, 233, 246, 281, 296, 306, 346, 352–53, 369–70
Polewka, Adam 78
police: Belorussian 87, 125, 150, 153–54, 348 (*see also* "Ravens"); Bolshevik 52; French 336; German 75, 120–22, 125, 152, 154, 209, 221, 223, 316, 321, 334, 337, 351, 368 (*see also* Gestapo, Kripo, SD — German *and also* Sipo); German field 152; German gendarmes 25, 27, 30–31, 67, 71, 89, 102, 109–10, 121, 316, 383; German military 120–22; Jewish 49, 64, 66–69, 70–75, 87, 110, 123, 125, 154, 172, 313, 317, 334, 339 (*see also* Jupo, OD); LAF 164; Latvian 125, 218; Lithuanian 125, 154, 162, 168–70, 172, 222, 350–51 (*see also* Saugumo); Polish 16, 25, 49, 54, 68, 75, 85–86, 108–9, 121, 125, 152, 161, 192, 311, 313, 321, 333–34, 340, 360 (*see also* "Blue Police," Polnische Polizeiverbände); Slovak 295; Soviet 55; Soviet security 51 (*see also* KGB, NKGB, NKVD); Stalinist (in Poland) political 60–61, 65, 344; Ukrainian 30, 73–74, 101, 120, 125–26, 142, 154, 199, 205, 209–10, 216, 218, 221–25, 228, 230–33, 237, 241, 248–50, 252, 303, 339, 361, 364, 368–69, 373, 375, 381–82, 384
Policja granatowa *see* "Blue Police"
Polikarp (Sikorskyi) 211, 373
Polish: Accord of Independence *see* PPN; American Congress 79; army *see* WP; Bar Association 120; Committee of National Liberation 19; Commonwealth 35; (communist labor) Party *see* SP; "concentration camps" 45; "Corridor" 3, 26; Council of Christians and Jews 38; Democratic Party *see* SD: Polish; Embassy 16, 81; First Army, Jews in 333; Government Delegation for the Homeland (Delegatura Rządu) 97, 99, 117, 169, 175, 200, 245, 251, 309–10, 323–24; government-in-exile 19, 53, 79–80, 87–88, 97–98, 100, 107, 112, 117, 156, 169, 251, 323–24, 329, 351; Legion in Belorussia 106; museums 21; National Alliance 79; National Assembly 189; National Committee (Komitet Narodowy Polski) 42; nationalists 288; October of 1956 60; parliament *see* parliament: Polish; People's Independence Action *see* PLAN; People's Party *see* PSL; People's Republic *see* PRL; "pogroms" 44–45; police *see* police: Polish; Red Cross *see* PCK; Roman Catholic Union 79; Settlement Commission (Polska Komisja Likwidacyjna) 41; Socialist Party *see* PPS; underground 19, 32, 58, 74, 81, 83, 85–86, 90, 93–95, 98–100, 102–4, 106–8, 112, 116, 125, 128, 130–31, 133–35, 138, 141, 314, 323, 330, 336, 341, 383–84; underground, dissemination of news about the Holocaust by 107, 114, 150, 152–53, 162–63, 166–67, 237, 248–49, 336 (*see also* AK); Underground Scouting Organization 121; United Workers' Party *see* PZPR; Workers' Party *see* PPR; writers 77–79, 318
Polish-Czechoslovak War 293
Polish-Lithuanian: Commonwealth 159; War 293
Polish-Poznanian War 293
Polish-Silesian War 293
Polish-Soviet: agreements on exchange of populations 259; Non-Aggression Pact of 1932, 295; (Sikorski-Maisky) Agreement (July 30, 1941) 79, 81; War (1919–1920) 3, 40, 43–44, 293
Polish-Ukrainian: Accord of 1933 187; (Galician) War (November 1918–July 1919) 3, 6, 43, 188
Poliska Sich 206, 213, 216, 228, 236, 250, 363
Poliszczuk, Wiktor 209, 252–53, 355–60, 362, 364–66, 370, 374, 378, 382, 385–86, 400
Politburo 132
Political: Bureau of the Central Committee of the Communist Party 7; cleansing of the territory (Politische Flurbereinigung) 23; Department (German) *see* Department: Political (German)
Pollak (colonel) 278
Polnische Polizeiverbände 321; *see also* police: Polish
Połomski, Franciszek 375, 400
Polonization 40
Polonsky, Antony 308–9, 311, 318, 330, 392, 400
Polotsk 148
Polska: Komisja Likwidacyjna *see* Polish: Settlement Commission; Ludowa Akcja Niepodległości *see* PLAN; Partia Robotnicza *see* PPR; Partia Socjalistyczna *see* PPS; Rzeczpospolita Ludowa *see* PRL; Zjednoczona Partia Robotnicza *see* PZPR
Polski Czerwony Krzyż *see* PCK
Polskie: Porozumienie Niepodległościowe *see* PPN; Stronnictwo Ludowe *see* PSL
Poluian, Vladimir Aleksandrovich 346, 400
Polytechnical Institute: in Danzig 358; in Lwów 358
Pomorze (Pomerania) 22, 25, 46, 83, 294, 299, 303, 306, 321
Ponary 89, 165–66, 168, 170–72, 174–75; Riflemen *see* Ypatingas Bārys
Poniemuń Forest 146
Ponomarenko, Pantelemon 98–99
Pope John Paul II 387
Pope Pius XII 377
Popiński, Krzysztof 2, 18, 209, 298–99, 364, 400
Popowski Ostrów 200
Porat, Dina 349, 404
posëlki (settlements) 13
Pospieszalski, Karol 336, 400
Possony, Stefan 368
Potichnyj, Peter J. 233, 375–76, 383, 400
Potsdam 233, 259
POW (Prisoners of War) camps: in Eastern Poland 16, 298; German 16, 28, 223, 350; in Griazovets 15; in Kozielsk 15, 80; in Latvia 15, 80; liquidation of Soviet 16; in Lithuania 15, 80, 99, 161; in Ostashkov 80; in Pavlishchev Bor 15, 80; in Rimini 377; in Starobielsk 80

Powiatowy Urząd Bezpieczeństwa Publicznego *see* PUBP
POWs (Prisoners of war): American 32; British 32; French 32; Italian 32; Lithuanian 165; Polish 13, 15–16, 20, 22–23, 52, 80–81, 174, 300; Polish, in Latvia 13; Polish, in Lithuania 13; Polish, in Soviet Union 13; and prisoners killed in Soviet-occupied Poland 17; Soviet 16, 32, 154, 174–75, 217, 302; Soviet deportation of Polish 13
Poželas see Pavlov
Poznań 27, 29–30, 47, 133, 301, 303, 305–6
Pozniak, Zenon 143
PPN (Polskie Porozumienie Niepodległościowe, or Polish Accord of Independence) 141
PPR (Polska Partia Robotnicza, or Polish Workers' Party) 19, 77, 81, 94, 97, 108, 130–31, 133–36, 138, 141, 278–80, 313, 332, 335, 345; founding of 103; Jews in 134. *See also* KPRP
PPS (Polska Partia Socjalistyczna, or Polish Socialist Party) 117, 135, 189, 313, 279–80
Pragier, Adam 135
Pragier, Ruta 315, 400
Prague 28, 149, 190, 193, 195, 213, 294, 359
Prasa gadzinowa *see* Adder Press
Pravieniškės (Prawieniszki) *see* prisons (Soviet and German): Pravieniškės
Preitner, Friedrich 359
Prekerowa, Teresa 108, 115, 306–7, 310–13, 322, 325, 328, 330–34, 337, 368, 400
Presidium of the Council of Ministers 132
Prestlaw (gendarme) 110
Preszel 123
Preussisch-Holland 196–97
prisons:
German 30, 32, 115; Gestapo 115, 174; Łukiszki 165, 167–68, 170, 173; Pawiak 24–25, 96, 109, 116, 121, 220; Pawiak, Jewish victims in 301; Pravieniškės (Prawieniszki) 168
Soviet 13, 15–16, 58; atrocities in 17–19; Brygidki 18, 210; in Butyrki 80; Łącki 210; liquidation of 16, 18; Lubianka 80; Pravieniškės (Prawieniszki) 19; in Tarnopol 56
Stalinist era in Poland 61; in Ejszyszki 132; in Hrubieszów 62; in Kielce 134; Łukiszki 132; in Radun 132; torture in 62, 132; in Wejherowo 301; in Wilno 132; in Wronki 335
PRL (Polska Rzeczpospolita Ludowa, or Polish People's Republic) 20, 80, 106, 129–31; Jews in government positions in 60–61, 63–65, 82, 97, 130–31, 133, 142, 313, 315
proces monstrum 143
Proch, Franciszek J. 2, 299, 304–5, 338, 400
Procyk, Wiktoria 339
Proskurov 208
prostitutes: Jewish 66, 316; Polish 85
Prosvita 186, 285
Protection Squad *see* SS
Protectorate of Czechoslovakia and Moravia 28
Protocols of the Elders of Zion 44
Provid *see* OUN: Provid
Provincial: Committee of the Polish Socialist Party *see* WK PPS; Committee of the Polish Workers' Party *see* KW PPR; Department in Kielce *see* Department: Provincial (in Kielce); Office of State Security *see* WUBP
Provisional Committee of Konrad Żegota 117. *See also* RPŻ, Żegota
Prus, Edward 362, 365, 370, 374, 379, 384, 400
Prussia 3, 116; East 3, 194; Eastern 303; West 155, 303
Pruszków 19, 105
Pruszyński, Ksawery 52
Pryczing (gendarme) 110
Pryszczowa Góra 331
Pryszniewo 27
Przemyśl 17, 51, 177, 208, 228, 379, 386
Przemyślany 17–18, 200
Przesiołka 146
Przeworsk 121
Przewrotne 121
Przyboś, Julian 78
Przygoda, Zdzisław 336, 339, 400
Przymusiński, Franciszek Augustyn 109
Przysieka 230
Przytyk 40, 42
PSL (Polskie Stronnictwo Ludowe, or Polish People's Party) 133, 135–36, 141, 279–80
Pszczółkowski, Edmund 77
PUBP (Powiatowy Urząd Bezpieczeństwa Publicznego, or County Office of State Security) 134
Puck 26
Puławy 109, 121
Pułstoki 174
Purim 154
Putrament, Jerzy 78
Pyatikhatki 15
PZPR (Polska Zjednoczona Partia Robotnicza, or Polish United Workers' Party) 64, 313; Jews in 59

Quisling, Vidkun 84, 88

Rabin, Moshe 310
Rabin, Yitzhak 176
Racial Register *see* Volksliste
Raczyński, Zdzisław 298, 330
Rada: Pomocy Żydom *see* RPŻ; Główna Opiekuńcza *see* RGO
Radical Nationalist Group *see* ONR
radio-telegraph operators 81
Radkiewicz, Stanisław 64, 104, 134, 141, 277, 279
Radom 43, 66, 91, 114, 133, 280, 303
Radstadt 228
Radstädter Tauern 235
Raduń 132
Radymno 207
Rajbrot 230
Rajca 151
Rajgrodzki, J. 330
Rak, Iaroslav 358
Rákosi, Mátyás 130
Rasch 209
Rashid, Harum al 231
Rashke, Richard 341, 400
Raszeja, Franciszek 120
"Ravens" 153–54. *See also* Police: Belorussian
Ravensbrück 28, 220, 320–21
Ravlyk, Ivan 207
Rawa Ruska 250
Reale, Eugenio 2, 46, 310, 315, 341, 370, 400
Rebet, Lev 207, 212
recovered (odzyskane) territories 259
Redliński, Kazimierz 140
referendum 9; in Eastern Poland 144; in Kielce 135–36, 138, 141; in Western Belorussia and Western Ukraine 9, 78
Refugee Aid Committee 200
Regensburg 157
Regional Action Committee 93
Regula (Belorussian collaborator) 152
Reichsarbeitsdienst (Reich Labor Service) 205, 207, 236
Reichsdeutsch 84, 319
Reichsgetto 29
Reichskommissariat: Ostland (Eastern Reich Commissariat)

30, 148, 303; Ukraine (Ukrainian Commissariat) 30, 148, 213, 216, 223, 236, 240, 250, 303
Reichsstelle für Raumordnung 150
Reichswehr 196
Reiner, Emil 26
Reitlinger, Gerald 84, 209, 303, 320, 364, 400
Rejewski, Marian 82
Rejowiec 230
Rejtanów 254
Religa, Jan 230–31, 374, 393
Rembertów 104, 131
Remmels, Hans-Hermann 223
Repucha, Józef 146
requisitions *see* Besstelung
Research Centre for a Solution to the Jewish Problem 45
Reshetar, John S. 357, 378, 400
"revindication campaign" 182
Reviuk, Osyp 196
Revoliutsiina Ukrainska Partiia *see* RUP
Revolutionary: Directory (OUN-B) 206; Ukrainian Party *see* RUP
Reymont, Władysław 42, 309
RGO (Rada Główna Opiekuńcza, or Main Social Welfare Council) 85–87, 117
Rhode Island 38
Ribbentrop, Joachim von 9, 160, 349, 362
Ribbentrop-Molotov: agreement *see* German-Soviet: Non-Aggression Pact; line of demarcation 208, 299
Ridna Shkola 186
Rieše *see* Rzesza
Riga 166. *See also* Treaty: of Riga
Righteous: Among the Nations 123; Christians 118, 123
Rimini 235, 376–77
Ringelblum, Emanuel 2, 40–41, 68, 90–91, 109, 111, 114–17, 124, 128, 220, 300, 308, 310, 317, 322–23, 325, 329–30, 332–37, 339, 368, 400; betrayal of 112, 122; on placing Jewish children in convents 113; on Polish rescue efforts 113; rescue by Polish underground of 112, 336; on the Warsaw pogroms 112
Ripetsky, Modest 310, 401
Rittner, Carol 338, 401
River: Bug 56–58, 160, 251; Horyń 31, 361; Oder 213; San 188, 207, 221, 246, 383; Silnica 139; Styr 361; Wisła (Vistula) 19, 100; Zbrucz 177, 188–89, 198, 245, 288, 293
ROA [Russkaya Osvoboditelnaya Armiia, or (Vlasov's) Russian Liberation Army] 84–85, 234–35, 237, 376
Rodzhko, Vsyevolod 155
Rodźko, Wacław 56
Rogozińska, Maria 121
Rohatyn 50, 200, 289–90
Röhm, Ernst 196–97
Röhr, Werner 306, 319, 348–49, 355, 360, 362–63, 365, 370–1, 373, 376, 378, 401
Rokicka (née Krasnodębska), J. 123, 311, 338, 401
Rokiny Nowe 254
Rokitno 221
Roland 207, 212–13, 217, 224, 226, 228, 230, 232, 236, 248, 255, 366. *See also* DUN
Romanowicz (Belorussian collaborator) 152
Rome 196, 243, 363, 370, 377
Rome-Warsaw Concordat 182
Romein, Judy 2
Romkowski, Roman (Natan Grünsapan-Kikiel) 60, 64, 104, 332
RONA (Russkaya Osvoboditelnaya Narodnaya Armiia, or Russian National Liberation Army) 85
Ronikier, Adam 86
Roosevelt, Franklin 19, 79, 236, 299
Rosa, Edward 310, 401
Rosalszczyzna 56
Rosati, Dariusz 142
Rosen, Marjorie 326, 401
Rosenbaum, Wilhelm 205
Rosenberg, Alfred 148, 150, 156, 196–98, 212, 215, 234, 240, 360, 365–66, 378, 401
Rosenberg, Blanca 68, 317, 401
Rosenberg, Dawid 56
Rosenfeld, Seidler von 88
Rosh Hashanah 63
Rosner, Artur 318
Rosner, Zofia 318
Rostov 172
Roszkowski, Wojciech (Andrzej Albert) 307, 330, 332, 341, 401
Rothkirchen, Livia 338, 401
Rothschild, Joseph 90, 319, 323, 401
Rowecki, Stefan *see* Grot-Rowecki, Stefan
Rowiński, Krzysztof 310, 361, 401
Równe (Rivne) 11–12, 16–17, 30–31, 212, 216, 228, 232–34, 236, 251, 378–79
Różański (Goldberg), Józef 60, 64, 314
Rozen-Zawadzki, Kazimierz 80
Rozłubirski, Edwin 329
Różycki, Jerzy 82
Rożyszcze 50, 200
RPŻ (Rada Pomocy Żydom, or Council for Aid to Jews, code name: Żegota) 75, 97, 112; functions of 117. *See also* Provisional Committee of Konrad Żegota *and also* Żegota
Ruban, Maksym *see* Lebed, Mykola
Rubin (from Wołomin) 121
Rubinstein, Sever 313
Rudka 252
Rudki 17
Rudziński pit 173
Rudziński Street 174
Rufeisen, Oswald 98, 106, 222, 337, 369
Rumania 5, 7, 15, 44, 64, 78, 130, 176, 188, 201, 207, 250, 290, 304, 307, 384
Rumbold, Horace 44
Rumkowski, Mordechai Chaim 69
Rumszyszki 19
RUP (Revoliutsiina Ukrainska Partiia, or Revolutionary Ukrainian Party) 357
Rusin, Josef 319
Russian: National Liberation Army *see* RONA; Liberation Army *see* ROA; Federation 5
Russification 159, 183, 347
Russkaya: Osvoboditelnaya Armiia *see* ROA; Osvoboditelnaya Narodnaya Armiia *see* RONA
Rutkowski, Adam 337, 391
Rýchla Divizia *see* Swift Group
Rypist, Marian 277
Ryświanka 12, 125
Rzeczyca 30–31
Rzepicki, A. 210, 365
Rzesza (Rieše) 168
Rzeszów 115, 120–21, 136, 141, 177, 230, 340–41, 379
Rzymowski, Wincenty 133

SA (Sturmabteilung, or Storm Troopers) 197, 233
Sabrin, B. F. 223, 242, 357, 359, 364–66, 369, 372–73, 376, 378, 401
Sachsenhausen 23, 28, 104, 115, 212–13, 300, 302
Sack, John 60, 63–64, 131, 133, 313–15, 342, 401
Sadler, Charles 318, 401
Sądowa Wisznia 17
Sadowski, Lech 366
Safer, Morley 387
Sahryń 252
Saint Germain-en-Laye 263

Saków 252
Sakowicz, Kazimierz 171, 351
Sałapa, Ryszard 277
Sambor 17–18, 50, 333
Samchuk, Ulas 236, 243
Samoliński, Wojciech 335
Samooboronnyi Kushchovi Viddily *see* SKV
samostiina Ukraina 191, 254, 361, 364
Samuel, Stuart M. 42
Sanacja 146, 182
Sandomierz 86
Sanok 206–7
sapery (battalions of engineers) 155
Sapieha, Adam 243
Sarner, Harvey 328
Sarny 10, 17, 19, 217, 240, 244, 251, 381
Sasha (of Sobibór) 328
Sasinowski, Władysław K. 301, 401
Satanów 208
Saubersdorf 207, 213
Saugumo (secret security police) 164–65, 168–70. *See also* police: Lithuanian
Savchuk, S. V. 365, 401
Sawicki, Cyprian 208, 364, 401
Sayuz Belaruskay Moladzi *see* SBM
SB: (OUN-B) Sluzhba Bezpeky, or Security Service 210, 254, 370, 379, 386; (Polish) Służba Bezpieczeństwa, or Security Service 140
SBM (Sayuz Belaruskay Moladzi, or Union of Belorussian Youth) 153, 155–56
Schaff, Adam 60
Schatz, Jaff 2, 36–37, 39–40, 44, 64, 307–9, 313–14, 401
Schickedanz, Arno 207
Schiller, Henryk 78
Schimana, Walter 226
Schindler, Oskar 69–70
Schneider (doctor from Horodenka) 338
Schneigert, Zbigniew 298, 401
Schnelle Division *see* Swift Group
Schochet, Simon 307, 401
Schoenfeld, Joachim 316, 401
Schöngarth, Karl Eberhard 209
Schörner's pancer army group 235
Schulenburg, Friedrich Werner von der 161
Schulman (née Fayna Lazebnik), Faye 105, 107, 332–33, 401
Schultz (gendarme) 110
Schuschnigg, Kurt von 212
Schutzmannlandesdienst 381
Schutzmannschaft, Ukrainische Hilfspolizei (Ukrainian Auxiliary Police Constabluary) 222
Schutzmannschaften Bataillonen (police battalions) 154, 164–66, 217, 222–23, 237; Belorussian 153–55, 222; Estonian 222; Latvian 154, 222; Lithuanian 154, 222; no. *201* 213, 223, 230, 236, 366; no. *202* (Polish) 154; no. *203* 217; no. *207* 230; nos. *201–12* 223; nos. *251–65* 165; nos. *301–10* 165; Russian 154, 222; Ukrainian 154, 222
Schutzpolizei 223, 316, 333
Schutzstaffel *see* SS
Schwartz, Dawid *see* Hibner, Juliusz
Schwarz, Solomon 312
Schwientochlowitz *see* Świętochłowice
SD: [(Polish) Stronnictwo Demokratyczne, or Democratic Party] 117, 279, 313; [(German) Sicherheitsdienst, or Security Service] 87–88, 90, 98, 149, 151, 165, 205, 207, 221, 230, 232, 378 (*see also* police: German)
Second: General Congress of the OUN-B (April 1941) 220; Warsaw Infantry Division 277, 280
Secret State Police *see* Gestapo
Security Corps *see* KB
Sędek, Stefan 276, 279
sekretnooperatsionnyie dokument 93
Selbstschutz 23, 170, 301; Baltic 222
Selbstschutzabteilung (self-defense units) 165
Sel-Rob (Ukrainian Peasants' and Workers' Socialist Organization) 189; Union (Ukrainian Peasants' and Workers' Socialist Union) 189
"*selsovet*" 93
Semik, Jan 120
Seminov (lieutenant) 331
Semipalatynsk 13
Sendłak, Stefan 117
Senyk, Emil 359
Serafiński, Antoni 294, 395
Serbia 124
Sereny, Gitta 378, 401
Seret (town) 188
Serov, Ivan 99–100, 269
Service for Polish Victory *see* SZP
Seventeenth German Army 294
Seventh Fort in Kaunas *see* Kaunas: Seventh Fort in
Seweryński, Tadeusz 278
Seym (*Sejm*) 23, 37, 146, 179–80, 187, 229, 260–61, 283, 286, 329, 352, 355. *See also* parliament: Polish
Shahak, Israel 2, 39, 75, 125, 308, 318, 339, 401
Shalom, Yehoram Ben 275
"sham units" 104
Shandruk, Pavlo 230, 235, 237, 372, 377, 401
Shankovskyi, Lev 360, 384, 401
Shapiro, H.R. 69, 317
Shapiro, Sleima 98
Sharpshooter's Council 359
Shaulists 162–63, 171–74, 352
Shchors, Mikola 149
Shelepin, Aleksander 297–98
Sheptytsky, Andrei 165, 198, 209, 228, 246, 360, 369, 373, 382; German financial assistance to the treasury 227, 372; letter to Himmler (January 1942) 214, 222; letter to Hitler (August 1941) 214; letter (with Melnyk and others) to Hitler (February 2, 1942) 214–15; pastoral letter of (August 3, 1936) 199; pastoral letter of (June 1941) in support of the "Ukrainian government" 211; pastoral letter of (March 27, 1942) 214; pastoral letter of (November 1942) 214, 245; rescue of Jews by 369
Shevchenko Scientific Society 185
Shirer, William 197, 360, 368, 401
Shklarek, Moshe 217
Shoah 66
Shoup, Paul S. 294, 402
Shpilevoi 136–38, 276–78
Shpontak, Ivan 379
shtetlach 39
Shtockfish, David 312, 368, 402
Shtul, O. 363
Shukhevych, Roman 206–7, 210–11, 213, 227, 241, 248, 358, 370
Shumuk, Danylo 386, 402
Šiauliai 165
Siberia 9, 51, 55, 123, 132, 142, 285, 295, 325–26, 347, 360
Sich Sharpshooter Organization 359. *See also* Sichovi Striltsi
Sicherheitsdienst *see* SD (German)
Sicherheitspolizei *see* Sipo
Sichovi Striltsi (Sich Riflemen) 194, 227
Sidor, Dionizy 279
Sidorkiewicz, Krzysztof 341
Siedlce 49, 86, 132
Siedlecki, Władysław 277
Siedliska 111
Siedlisko 198
Siegling's 30. Waffen-Grenadier-

Division *see* Waffen-SS: 30. Waffen-Grenadier-Division der SS (russiche Nr 2)
Siekierko, Wacław 349
Siemaszko, Władysław 2, 18, 199, 245, 251, 352, 360–61, 375, 379, 381, 385, 402
Siemaszko, Zbigniew S. 13, 58, 81, 148, 163, 203, 296–98, 312, 318, 329–31, 333, 346, 402
Siemaszko, Zdzisław A. 174, 323, 330, 352, 402
Siemianówka 229
Siemiatycze 17
Siemieliszki 168
Sienkiewicz, Henryk 243
Sienkiewicz Street 136, 275, 277–78
Sieńkowszczyzna 166
Siewierski, Janusz 80
Sikorski, Władysław 36, 53, 57, 79, 81, 83, 201, 236; Maisky agreement with *see* Polish-Soviet: (Sikorski-Maisky) Agreement
Sikorskyi *see* Polikarp
Silberman, Abraham 221
Silberman, Malka 221
Silesia *see* Śląsk
Silesian nationals 83
silrada (village council) 126
Silskyi Hospodar (Village Husbandman) 186
Silverman, Peter 323, 330, 348, 402
Siły Zbrojne w Kraju *see* National: Forces of Poland
Sima, Horia 212
Simoncini, Gabriele 2, 387
Simpson, Christopher 362, 377–78, 402
Simunic, Pavel 374
Singer, Isaac Bashevis 37, 307, 402
Singer, Kalman 276, 279
Sipo (Sicherheitspolizei, or Security Police) 25, 87, 110, 165, 221, 316–17, 317. *See also* police: German
Sisters: of Charity 122; of the Holy Family of Nazareth 151–52
Sivard, Ruth Leger 305, 402
Siwicki, Mikołaj 353–54, 381–83, 385, 402
Skałat 364
Skaradziński, Bohdan *see* Podlaski, Kazimierz
Skarga, Piotr 35
Skarżysko-Kamienna 218–19, 368
Skhodni 81
"skhody" 81
Skidel 55, 145
Skirmunt, Henryk 54
Škirpa, Kazys 163, 350
Skiwski, Jan Emil 85
Skniłów 17
Skoczyński, Antoni 86
Skorupskyi, Maksym 254
Skorzak (city janitor in Szczebrzeszyn) 110
Skrypnyk, Stepan *see* Mstislav
Skrzypek, Stanisław 2, 183, 187, 263–65, 293, 295, 353–56, 360, 402
SKV (Samooboronnyi Kushchovi Viddily, or Kushch Self-Defense Units) 245, 252, 369–70
Skvireckas, Juozapas 166, 350
SL (Stronnictwo Ludowe, or People's Party) 117, 279, 313, 345
Slánský, Rudolf 130
Śląsk (Silesia) 22, 61, 83, 129, 213, 299, 306, 315, 321; Eastern Upper (Ostoberschlesien) 303; Lower (Dolny) 318, 343; Upper (Górny) 3, 69, 85 294, 303, 313
Slavs 30, 234–35, 240
Śledzianowski, Jan 322, 342, 402
Slipyi, Iosafat 228
Slodkowski, Andrew 2
Słomczyński, Adam 334, 402
Słominski, Antoni 39, 308
Słonim 17, 87, 148, 151, 155
Slovak: Air Force 294; Republic 228
Slovakia 8, 163–64, 176, 229, 231, 255, 294, 373–74, 379
Slovenia 228
Słowacki Street 279
Słowików 43
Slutsk 148, 351
Służba: Zwycięstwu Polski *see* SZP; Bezpieczeństwa *see* SB (Polish)
Sluzhba Bezpeky *see* SB (OUN-B)
Smerdyń 199
SMERSH (Smert' Shpionam, Sovetskii Metod Rozoblacheniia Shpionov, or Death to Spies, Soviet Method of Detecting Spies) 93, 99–100, 315
Smith, Bradley F. 377, 402
Smolar, Aleksander 6, 36, 45, 50, 52, 58–59, 84, 293, 307–11, 313, 319, 323, 336, 345, 402
Smorgonie 151
Smovskyi, Kostiantyn 384, 402
Smuschkowitz, David 323, 330, 348, 402
Smuszkowicz, Peter 323, 330, 348, 402
SN (Stronnictwo Narodowe, or National Party) 42, 45, 47, 94
SOB (Socjalistyczna Organizacja Bojowa, or Socialist Combat Organization) 100
Sobczyński (Spychaj), Władysław 136, 138, 276–79, 281, 344–45
Sobibór 29, 217, 239, 328, 341
Sobiński, Stanisław 192
Soból, Adam 138, 278
Sobolta, Franciszek 329
Soboń, Jan 140
Social: Democrats (Lithuanian) 163; Nationalists (Ukrainian) 387
Socialist: Combat Organization *see* SOB; Party of Ukraine 255
Society: of Free Jews (Towarzystwo Wolnych Żydów) 66, 74; of St. Ives 270; for the Promotion of Poland's Independence 343; of Ukrainian Secondary School Teachers 186
Socjalistyczna Organizacja Bojowa *see* SOB
Sodol, Petro R. 370, 378, 382, 402
Soiuz: Ukrainek (Union of Ukrainian Women) 186; Ukrainskoi Natsionalistychnoi Molodi *see* SUNM
Sokil 186
Sokółki 303
Sokołów 121
Sokołowski, Czesław 86, 322
Sokołowski, Władysław 78
Sokul 199–200
Solidarity 133, 260
Soltys, Mykhailo 379
Soły 151
Solzhenitsyn, Aleksandr I. 16, 298, 402
Sonderdienst 71, 73
Sonderkommando (special security police units) 66, 75, 164–65, 167, 169–71, 175, 302, 350; Sonderkommando AS 74
Sonenson, Chaim 326
Sonenson, Moshe 92, 326–27
Sonenson, Yaffa *see* Yaffa Eliach
Sonenson, Yitzhak 93, 326–28
Sonenson, Zipporah 92, 94, 326–27
Sophie's Choice 124
Sorokin, Yehoshua 298
Sosnowiec 61, 303, 341
Sośwa 15
"soul-snatching" 113
South River, New Jersey 157, 159
Southeastern Poland 178, 189–90, 209, 231, 251, 258, 260
Southern Ireland 288
Sovetskii Metod Rozoblacheniia Shpionov *see* SMERSH
Soviet: Belorussia 143–44, 157,

259 (*see also* Belorussian: SSR); (East, Eastern) Ukraine, 188, 195, 198, 203, 207, 223, 235, 239, 257, 259, 296, 356, 380, 383 (*see also* Ukrainian: SSR); espionage schools in Belorussia 153; Lithuania 259 (*see also* Lithuanian: SSR); -Lithuanian Friendship Treaty 161; Method of Detecting Spies *see* SMERSH; organs of oppression 19, 32, 51, 59, 61, 64–5, 92, 94, 97, 106, 130–1; Penal Code 16; purges of communist Jews 65, 106, 130; support of German war effort 11–12
Sovietization 79, 183
SP: [Stronnictwo Polskie, or Polish (communist labor) Party] 279; SP (Sicherheitspolizei, or Security Police) *see* Sipo
Spain 197
Special: Commando 1005 *see* Paul Blobel: "Special Commando 1005"; Committee for Assistance to Jews 117; Civil Courts of Warsaw and Kraków Regions 86
Spector, Shmuel 49, 220, 233, 303, 308, 310–12, 329–30, 333, 337, 357, 364, 368, 370, 373, 375–76, 378, 402
Spielberg, Steven 316
Spilker, Alfred 74
"Spilker's boys" 75
Spisz 294
Spitzel (stool pigeons) 66
Społeczna Organizacja Samoobrony *see* Community Self-Defence Organization
Społem 277, 279
"Społem" Bank 110
Springfield MA 79
Spychaj, Władysław *see* Władysław Sobczyński
Spychalski, Marian 103
Srokowski, Stanisław 353, 402
SS (Schutzstaffel, or Protection Squad) 22, 25–27, 31–32, 83–84, 89, 91, 114, 116, 121–122, 125 153–54, 156, 165–66, 169, 208–10, 220–23, 225–28, 233–34, 237–38, 241, 317, 319, 337, 340, 367–68, 371, 373, 376, 383, 387; antiaircraft defense corps 237; auxiliaries (SS-Helfer) 156; controversy over Poles in 320–21
SS-Galizien 87, 121, 165, 220, 225–41, 249, 252, 319, 321, 368–74, 376–77, 384, 387; atrocities committed by 229–31; defeat of 228; formation of 225–28; oath sworn by members of 371; police regiments of 225, 228–29, 231, 236, 249, 371, 373–74, 384; in Slovakia, Slovenia and at the Austrian front 228; subunits of 229; surrender of 228, 235; training in France of 232; Ukrainian leadership support for 227–28
SS-Kampfgruppe 229
SS-Totenkopf-Verbände 238
Saint Anna (church) 354
Saint Barbara (church) 354
Saint Euphrosynia's Church 157
Saint George Cathedral 228
Stahl, Zdzisław 298, 402
Stahle, Rainer 90
"Stakh" *see* UPA: "Stakh" unit
Stakhiv, Ievhen 212, 363
Stakhiv, Volodymyr 212
Stalin, Josef 1, 7, 9–12, 15, 19–20, 32, 37, 50, 57–61, 64, 77, 79–80, 99, 103, 130, 133–134, 148, 153, 160–61, 171, 178, 198, 204, 236, 240, 269, 298–99, 313, 330, 349, 380
Stalingrad 224, 241
Stalinist methods of torture 62
Stańczyk, Jan 53
Stanisławów 9, 17–18, 31, 50, 53, 55, 120, 177, 184, 200, 202, 236, 253, 287, 296, 306, 339, 353–354, 365, 375
Stankevich, Ian 87–88, 149–50, 323;
Stankevich, Stanislaŭ 153
Stanley, John 330, 402
Star of David 29, 73; trade in 116
Starachowice 2, 41, 122, 218–19, 368
Stare Święcany 168
Starewicz, Artur 60
Starobielsk 15, 17, 80
Starukh, Iaroslav 207, 366
Staszewicz, Stanisław 349
State Department *see* Department: State (United States)
Stebelski, Adam 299, 402
Steblychyn, Bohdan 254
Steca, Stanisław 279
Stefanówka 95
Stefansky, V. F. 374
Steiger, Stanisław 197
Stein, André 326, 328–29, 402
Stein, George H. 84, 226, 228, 319–20, 322, 368, 370, 372–74, 402
Steinberg, Lucien 38
Steinsbergowa, Aniela 314, 402
Stella (of Gwoździec) 123
Stępień, Michał 140
Sterdyń 121
Sternberg, Yitzhak 200–201, 360, 402
Sterzer, Abraham 39, 49, 308, 310, 402
Stetsiuk, Hryhorii 386, 402
Stetsko, Iaroslav 206–7, 211–12, 221, 358
Stöckel (forester in Warszkowo) 26
Stolin 148
Stołkiewicz, Ryszard 109
Stołpce 12, 149
Stolze (Abwehr officer) 363
Stopniak, Franciszek 336, 402
Storm Troopers *see* SA
Storozinetz 188
Stowarzyszenie Upamiętnienia Zbrodni Ukraińskich Nacjonalistów 385
Stralsund 26
Streibel Battalion 367
Stronnictwo: Demokratyczne *see* SD (Polish); Ludowe *see* SL; Narodowe *see* SN; Polskie *see* SP
Struk, Danylo Husar 323, 355, 357, 363, 366, 370, 383, 403
Stryj 17–18, 56
Strzelce 383
strzelcy ponarskie (Ponary Riflemen) *see* Ypatingas Būrys
Strzelnica 218
Stsiborskyi, Mykola 381
Studencki (captain) 64
Studniberg, Chaim 61
Studułł, Zbigniew 304, 364
Studzieniec 120
Sturmabteilung *see* SA
Sturmwind: I 229; II 229
Stutterheim, von (Reich cabinet advisor) 207
Stuttgart 157
Stutthof 26–28, 302
Stypułowski, Zbigniew 96
Styrkul, Valerii 229, 231, 372, 374, 403
Stys Nepean, Kazimierz 82
Subtelny, Orest 354–55, 357, 360–61, 383, 403
Sucha Łoża 254
Sulaspils (Kircholm) 166
Sulewski, Wojciech 383, 403
Sulowo 110
SUNM (Soiuz Ukrainskoi Natsionalistychnoi Molodi, or Union of Ukrainian Nationalist Youth) 190, 357
Supreme: Military Court *see* NSW; Council (League of Nations) 4, 188, 190, 293
Surkonty 132
Surowiec 278
Sushko, Roman 196, 359; Ukrainian Legion of 205–6

Suvorov, Viktor 299, 403
Suwała, Mieczysław 323
Suwałki 169
Sverdlovsk 13, 15
Sweden 118–19, 173, 314
Światło (Licht, Lichtstein, Fleischfarb), Józef 60, 65, 103–5, 131, 313, 315, 332
Świda, Józef 88
Święciany 101, 162, 168, 331
Święcicki, Roman Leon 110
Świerczewski, Eugeniusz 332
Świerczewski, Karol 379
Świętochłowice (Schwientochlowitz) 61, 314
Swift Group 8, 294
Świniuchy 71
Świr 148, 162
Switzerland 114, 156, 193
Sword, Keith 2, 265, 269, 295–98, 307, 311–12, 318, 346–47, 349, 403
Sydor, Vasyl 369–70
sylna liudyna 189
Sym, Igo 85
Symkiewicz, Henryk 140
Syring (gendarme) 110
"Szaniec" 86
Szapiro (from Ossów) 122
Szapiro, Paweł 317, 338, 340, 403
Szare Szeregi *see* Polish: Underground Scouting Organization
Szawłowski, Ryszard 146, 295–96, 307. *See also* Liszewski, Karol
Szaynok, Bożena 332, 341–45, 403
Szczebrzeszczyn 70–71, 110–11, 249
Szczecin (Stettin) 305, 343
Szczecyn 230
Szczeniowski, Olgierd 116, 337
Szczerzec 17
Szcześniak, Andrzej Leszek 317
Szcześniak, Antoni 208, 217, 230–31, 240–41, 358–61, 363–68, 370, 374–76, 378, 382, 385, 403
Szczuczyn 90
Szczypiorski, Stanisław 80
Szebnie 229
Szefer, Andrzej 362, 403
Szemplińska, Ewa 78
Szendzielarz, Zygmunt 89, 169; "Łupaszka" Brigade of *see* AK: "Łupaszka" Brigade
Szenwald, Lucjan 78
Szepietówka 16
Szeple 254
Szeremeta, Bronisław 386, 403
Szetelnicki, Wacław 312, 374, 381, 403
szkoły utrakwistyczne see bilingual schools
szlachta 147; *zagrodowa* (minor nobility) 146
Szlajfer, Henryk 308, 312–13, 341, 391
Szlamka, Karol 146
Szlaski, Janusz Prawdzic 323
Szliachczik (prison superintendent) 87
szmalcowniki 109: definition of 316; Jewish 66, 86, 100, 103, 125; Polish 66–67, 85,-86, 125, 142. *See also* blackmailers
Sznajder, Mejer 128
Szołomyja 252
Szota, Wiesław 208, 217, 230–31, 240–41, 358–61, 363–68, 370, 374–76, 378, 382, 385, 403
SZP (Służba Zwycięstwu Polski, or Service for Polish Victory) 163
Szpondarski, Czesław 277, 280
Sztablewski (MBP officer) 136, 276
Szucha Street 74
Szuchman, Ewa 137, 280
Szulman (Jewish collaborator in Dzisna) 55
Szumigalski, Włodzimierz 80
Szumsk 243–44
Szurek, Jean-Charles 295, 312, 347
Szwagrzyk, Krzysztof 318, 403
Szyłeyko, J. Zdzisław 323, 403
Szymbierski, Leon 91, 325
Szymczak, Robert 318, 403
Szyr, Eugeniusz 60
Szyszko, Agnieszka 298

T., Maximilian (of Warsaw) 66
Taagepera, Rein 166, 349–52, 398
Tapper, Mikolaj 327
Tarnobrzeg 230
Tarnogród 250
Tarnopol 9–10, 17, 50, 56, 72, 121–22, 177, 184, 200, 202–3, 208, 221, 229–31, 254, 287, 289–90, 296–97, 306, 313, 333, 353–54, 361, 364–65, 374
Tarnów 120, 206, 230, 341
Tarnowskie Góry (Tarnowitz) 61
Tarwid, Mieczysław 109
Tatars 3, 174
Tatishchev, A. 310
Tatuliński ("Blue Police" member) 110
Tautininkai (National Unionists) 163
Tchórznicki, Konstanty 86
Tec, Nechama 92, 316, 323, 330, 332, 348, 403
"technical apparatus" (*technika*) 36–37
Teheran 79
"Tempest" *see* Operation: "Burza"
Tenenbaum-Tamaroff, M. 70
Tennenbaum, Samuel Lipa 57, 72, 200, 222, 252, 293, 310, 312, 317, 360, 369, 385, 403
Tenth Department *see* MBP: Tenth Department of
Tereshchuk, Petro (Oleksander Matla) 360, 403
Terkieltaub, Israel 137
Terlecki, Ryszard 330
Terleś, Mikołaj 383, 403
Teschen *see* Cieszyn
Tessin, Georg 372, 403
Thierack, Otto 31
Third Ordinance 114
Third World War 240–41. *See also* World War III
Thorwald, Jürgen 303, 403
Tito 228, 374
Tłumacz 120
Tłuste 72, 74, 126, 361
TNRP (Tymczasowa Narodowa Rada Polityczna, or Interim National Political Council) 96
Tobaczkowski, Edward 120
Todt Organization auxiliaries (O.T.-Helfer) 156
Tolstoy, Nikolai 377, 403
Tomala, Michał 80
Tomaszewski, Irene 313, 333, 337, 342, 403
Tomaszewski, Jerzy 2, 143, 180, 182, 293–94, 296, 305–7, 309–10, 312–13, 322, 325, 330–34, 337, 346, 349, 352–54, 368, 383, 400, 403
Tomaszewski, Longin 174, 323, 348, 351–52, 403
Tomaszów 181, 379, 384
Tomaszów Mazowiecki 79
Torańska, Teresa 60, 132, 342, 403
Torke, Hans-Joachim 365, 369–71, 375, 403
Toronto 238, 368
Toruń 149
Tory, Avraham 164, 349, 404
Torzecki, Ryszard 209, 217, 228, 246, 304, 330, 355, 357, 359–71, 373–76, 378, 381–84, 404
Towarzystwo Wolnych Żydów *see* Society: of Free Jews
"Tower of Faces" 92
Traby 56
Transcarpathia 355, 362
Transcarpathian government 204
transit camps (Durchgangslager) 28, 30, 169, 218–19; Soviet 16, 383–84
Trawniki 165, 217, 300, 350, 367
"Trawniki people" (Trawniki-Leute) 321

Treaty: German-Soviet Boundary and Friendship *see* German-Soviet: Boundary and Friendship Treaty; of Good Neighborliness, Friendly Relations and Cooperation of May 18, 1992 256; for the Protection of Minorities 3, 4, 184, 263; on the Renunciation of War 295; of Riga 94–95, 143, 188, 190, 293, 295, 347, 353; Soviet-Lithuanian Friendship *see* Soviet-Lithuanian Friendship Treaty; Versailles 3, 263, 307
Treblinka 29, 102, 116, 121–22, 217–18, 223, 239
Tremblay, Cindy 2
Treptow 26
Treuhänder 21
Treuhandstelle Ost 21
"trial" of the sixteen 19, 132
triumphal arches *see arcs de triomphe*
TRJN (Tymczasowa Rada Jedności Narodowej, or Interim National Unity Council) 279
"troika" 266–68, 270
Troki 168, 327
Trościaniec 199
Trotsky, Leon 43
Trotskyites 313
Truchan, Myroslaw 386
Trunk, Isaiah 70, 303, 404
Tsanava, Lavrenti 99–100
Tuczyn 12, 30–31, 303–4
Turek 128
Turobin 250
Turonek 84, 87–88, 153, 319, 322–23, 330, 347–49, 351, 404
Turowski, Józef 245, 251, 352, 360–61, 375, 381, 385, 404
Tutka, Mykhailo 357
Tverdokhlib, Sydor 192
Twardowski, Bolesław 382
Twenty-ninth (Lithuanian) Territorial Corps of the Red Army 162, 164
Twenty-seventh Infantry Division of the AK *see* AK: Wołyń
Tymczasowa: Narodowa Rada Polityczna *see* TNRP; Rada Jedności Narodowej *see* TRJN
Tyndorf, Richard 2, 302, 405
Tys-Krokhmaliuk, Yuriy 375, 404
Tyszyński, Leon 80

UB [Urząd Bezpieczeństwa, or Office of (State) Security] 104, 130–41, 275–76, 278–79, 314–15, 318, 341, 343; Jews in 58, 61–65, 133–34. *See also* MBP
Ückermünde 26
UDKs (Ukrainskyi Dopomohovyi Komitety, or Ukrainian Relief Committees) 86, 225, 323
UHA (Ukrainska Halytska Armiia, or Ukrainian Galician Army) 196, 226
UHVR (Ukrainska Holovna Vyzvolna Rada, or Ukrainian Supreme Liberation Council) 234
ujawnienie see exposure
"Ukraine for Ukrainians" 189, 191, 243, 247, 357
Ukrainian: Central Committee *see* UTsK; Central Council 188; Civil War 44; Committee for Help to the Suffering Ukraine 198; Educational Societies *see* UOT; famine 9, 380; Galician Army *see* UHA; Gymnasium in Lwów 192; Insurgent Army *see* UPA; Labor Party *see* URP; Legion 205–6, 213, 236; Liberation Army 210 (*see also* UVV); Main Social Welfare Council 86–87, 323; Medical Society 186; Military Organization *see* UVO; National Army *see* UNA (Ukrainian National Army); National Committee *see* UNK; National Democratic Union *see* UNDO; National Museum 185; National Rada 187; National Republic *see* UNR; National Self-Defense *see* UNS *and see* UNSO; nationalism 49, 189–90, 193, 196, 212, 241, 248, 255–56; Nationalists 4–6, 31, 88, 100–101, 122, 177–78, 180, 187, 190–91, 193–94, 196, 198–201, 204–13, 215–17, 220–21, 223–24, 226, 229, 231–33, 235–43, 246–51, 253, 255, 258, 305, 333, 356–57, 362, 369, 375, 380, 387 (*see also the following:* Banderowcy; Bulbowcy; OUN; OUN-B; OUN-M; UPA); neo-Nationalists 178, 191, 204, 212, 240, 261; parliament *see* parliament: Ukrainian; Parliamentary Representation 187, 355; Party 187; Peasant Party 187; Radical-Socialist Party *see* USRP; Relief Committee of Great Britain 377; Relief Committees *see* UDKs; Scientific Institute 186; Sich 126; Social Democratic Party 198; Social Democratic Labor Party 199; Socialist Democratic Party *see* USDP; Socialist Radical Party 198; SSR 9, 189, 259–60, 270, 296 (*see also* Soviet: Ukraine); State Board 355; Supreme Liberation Council *see* UHVR
Ukrainian-American League 237, 376
Ukrainization 78
Ukrainska: Halytska Armiia *see* UHA; Holovna Vyzvolna Rada *see* UHVR; Narodna Respublika *see* UNR; Natsionalna Armiia *see* UNA (Ukrainian National Army); Natsionalna Samooborona *see* UNS, *and also* UNSO; Povstanska Armiia *see* UPA; Robotnicha Partiia *see* URP; Sotsialistychna Demokratychna Partiia *see* USDP; Sotsialistychna Radykalna Partiia *see* USRP; Viiskova Orhanizatsiia *see* UVO
Ukrainske: Derzhavne Pravlinnie *see* Ukrainian: State Board; Natsionalne-Demokratychne Obiednannie *see* UNDO; Osvitne Tovaristva *see* UOT; Vyzvolne Viisko *see* UVV
Ukrainskyi: Dopomohovyi Komitety *see* UDKs; Natsionalnyi Komitet *see* UNK; Tsentralnyi Komitet *see* UTsK
Ulster 288
Umschlagplatz 68
UNA (Ukrainska Natsionalna Armiia, or Ukrainian National Army) 235, 237; First Ukrainian Division of the 371–72, 377
UNA(*Ukrainska Natsionalna Asambleia,* or Ukrainian National Assembly) 387
underground court 84–86, 93; condemnation of "Blue Police" by 110
UNDO (Ukrainske Natsionalne-Demokratychne Obiednannie or, Ukrainian National Democratic Union) 187, 189, 198–99, 201, 355
Uniate Church *see* Catholic Church: Greek
Union: for Armed Struggle *see* ZWZ; of Belorussian Youth *see* SBM; of Israel *see* Agudat Israel; of Polish Patriots 19, 79, 142, 344; of Ukrainian Lawyers 186; of Ukrainian Merchants 186; of Ukrainian Nationalist Youth *see* SUNM; of Ukrainian Soviet Writers 78–79
United Kingdom 24, 304 (*see also* Great Britain *and also* England)
United Nations 238; Convention

380; Relief and Rehabilitation Administration 341
United States 3, 5, 24, 32, 38, 40, 44, 47, 60, 80, 116, 123–24, 129, 157, 183–84, 188, 193, 195, 202, 205, 237, 263, 318, 321, 333, 339, 350, 367, 377, 387
University: of California 63; of Chicago 79; Harvard 38, 308; Ivan Franko 202; Jagiellonian 23, 42, 79, 300, 358, 386; of Kharkov 287; of Lublin 182, 358; of Lwów 57, 202, 358; of New Hampshire 2; Ohio State 38; Polytechnical Division of Lwów 210; of Poznań 120; Princeton 38; secret Ukrainian 185; Stanford 52; Stefan Batory (USB) 161, 168, 308; of Warsaw 185, 386
UNK (Ukrainskyi Natsionalnyi Komitet, or Ukrainian National Committee) 208, 230, 235, 363
UNR (Ukrainska Narodna Respublika, or Ukrainian National Republic) 187–88, 194, 363; government-in-exile 189
UNS (Ukrainska Natsionalna Samooborona, or Ukrainian National Self-Defense) 240, 245, 252, 363, 370
UNSO Ukrainska Natsionalna Samooborona, or Ukrainian National Self-Defense) 387
Untermensch(en) 30, 224, 227, 235
UOT (Ukrainske Osvitne Tovaristva, or Ukrainian Educational Societies) 225
UPA (Ukrainska Povstanska Armiia, or Ukrainian Insurgent Army) 177, 188, 213, 216–17, 220, 224, 227–35, 237, 240–42, 245–48, 250–56, 258, 260, 310, 339, 355, 365, 373, 375, 378–81, 384–87; dissolution of 370; ethnic cleansing by *see* ethnic cleansing: campaign of OUN-UPA; founding of the OUN-B 369; founding of the OUN-M 369; founding of Taras-Borovets' 369; "Khrin" unit of 379; military core of 228; North 246, 370; South 370; "Stakh" unit of 379; West 370. *See also the following:* Taras Borovets; OUN; OUN-B; OUN-M; Ukrainian Nationalists
Upper Silesia *see* Śląsk: Upper
Ural Mountains 13, 15
Urban, Wincenty 97, 330, 346, 381, 404
Urbaniak, George 349, 404
Urbanowicz, Henryk 278–80
Urbański, Krzysztof 342, 345, 404
URP (Ukrainska Robotnicha Partiia, or Ukrainian Labor Party) 189
Urząd Bezpieczeństwa *see* UB
U.S. Holocaust Memorial Museum 1, 92, 142
USB *see* University: Stefan Batory
Uście Zielone 254
USDP (Ukrainska Sotsialistychna Demokratychna Partiia or, Ukrainian Socialist Democratic Party) 189
Usiejewicz, Helena 78
USRP (Ukrainska Sotsialistychna Radykalna Partiia, or Ukrainian Radical-Socialist Party) USRP 189
Ustashi 207
UTsK (Ukrainskyi Tsentralnyi Komitet, or Ukrainian Central Committee) 215, 225, 323, 363, 372
UVO (Ukrainska Viiskova Orhanizatsiia, or Ukrainian Military Organization) 177, 190–92, 194–97, 241, 243, 286, 288, 359, 377; Bolshevik support of 196; Czechoslovakian support of 195–96; founding of 190, 195; German support of 196–97; Lithuanian support of of 196; terrorist campaign in interwar Eastern Poland 191–95; UVV (Ukrainske Vyzvolne Viisko, or Ukrainian Liberation Army) 235, 237, 376

V-2 rocket 82
Vadis, Aleksander 100
Vagabund 229
Vakar, Nicholas P. 154, 331, 346–48, 404
Valuch-Janenko, Norbert 363
Vardys, V. Stanley 349
Vatican 118, 237
Vatutin, Nikolai 234
Velykyi Zbir Ukrainskykh Natsionalistiv *see* VZUN
Versailles Treaty *see* Treaty: Versailles
Veryha, Wasyl 227, 372–73, 383–84, 404
Vichy 88, 336
Vidro (Wydra), Abraham 298
Vienna 133, 190, 213, 286, 366
Vienneau, David 350
Viiskovi Viddily Natsionalistiv *see* VVN
"Villa of Happiness" or "Villa of Pleasure" 80–81
Vilna *see* Wilno
Vilniaus Kraštas *see* Wileńszczyzna
Vilnius *see* Wilno
Vilno *see* Wilno
Vinnista 9, 208, 212, 370
Vinton, Louisa 270, 404
Virtuti Militari 342, 372
Viryušhka, Mikhal 155
Vitebsk 148
Vitvitsky, Bohdan 368
Vladimir (prince of Kievan Rus') 357
Vladimir (saint) 190
Vlasov, Andrei 84–85, 156, 232–35, 237; army of *see* ROA
Voldemaras, Augustinas 163
Volhynia *see* Wołyń
"volispolkom" 327
Volksdeutsch (German Nationals) 16, 22, 83, 85, 124–25, 128, 150, 165, 205–6, 217, 259, 314, 316, 319, 321, 350, 383
Volksliste (Racial Register) 22, 83, 319, 321
Vołogda 13
Voloshyn, Avhustyn 362
Volunteer Reserve of the Civil Militia *see* ORMO
Volya 177, 241
Volyn *see* Wołyń
Voroshilov, Kliment 7, 269
VVN (Viiskovi Viddily Natsionalistiv, or Nationalist Military Detachments) 205, 236
VZUN (Velykyi Zbir Ukrainskykh Natsionalistiv, or Great Conference of Ukrainian Nationalists): First (January 28–Ferbruary 3, 1929) 190, 242, 255; Second (August 27, 1939) 243, 363; Third (August 21–25, 1943) 247

Wachmannschaften (guard units) 164–65, 237; des SS- und Polizeiführers im Distrikt Lublin 217; SS-ukrainische 217, 220, 300
Wąchock 41
Wächter, Otto 215, 225–26, 232, 371–72
Waffen-SS 22, 84–85, 114, 156, 166, 224–25, 228, 232, 234, 238–39, 241, 320–21, 371, 377; Grenadier-brigade "Weissruthenian" (Belorussian Grenadier Brigade) 156 (*see also* Belarus Brigade); SS-Freiwilligen-Division "Galizien" (SS Volunteer Division "Galician") *see* SS-Galizien; statistics on

nationalities in 319; Ukrainians in 232; 14. Freiwilligen-Grenadier-Division der SS (galizische Nr 1) (14th Volunteer Grenadier Division of the SS, 1st Galician) *see* SS-Galizien; 14. Waffen-Grenadier-Division der SS (galizische Nr 1) *see* SS-Galizien; 24. Waffen-Gebirgskarstjäger-Division der SS 232, 236; 29. Waffen-Grenadier-Division der SS (russische Nr 1) 232, 236; 30. Waffen-Grenadier-Division der SS (russiche Nr 2) 84, 153, 156, 232, 237; 30. Waffen-Grenadier-Division der SS (weissruthenische Nr 1) 84, 156
Wajbloch, Benjamin 314
Wajnrauch, Herschel 55
Wałach, Stanisław 340, 404
Waldman, Yaakov 128
Walshaw, Rachela 41, 308, 404
Walshaw, Sam 308, 404
"Wanda" (NSZ member) 96
Wandycz, Piotr 85, 320
Wannsee conference 29
War Crimes Investigations Office (Israeli) 368
Wardzyńska, Maria 2, 166, 298, 300, 321, 349–52, 367–69, 383, 404
Warsaw: ghetto *see* ghettos: in Warsaw *and see* Warsaw Ghetto Revolt; Social Services Department *see* Department: Social Services (Warsaw); Uprising 19, 23, 67, 75, 85, 100, 107–8, 111, 229–30, 333
Warsaw Ghetto Revolt 51, 120, 134, 321; Polish assistance to 107–8; Lithuanian battalion in 165; murder of Jews by Poles during the 335
Warski, Adolf 146
Warszawska Street 43
Warszkowo 26
Wartheland (Kraj Warty, Warta region) 22, 28–29, 299–300, 303
"Waryński" *see* GL: "Waryński" unit
Washington DC 1, 140
Wasilewska, Wanda 78–79
Wasserpolen nationals 83
Wasylewski, Stanisław 78
Waszczuk, Slavko 364
Wat, Aleksander 51, 77–78, 311, 318, 344–45, 404
Wawel Castle 206
Wawer 24–25
Ważyk, Adam 78
"Węgielny" (AK leader) 169
Węgierski, Jerzy 200, 346, 352, 360, 365, 379, 385, 404
Węgrów 121, 132
Wehrdörfer (fortified villages) 153, 155–56
Wehrmacht 9, 11, 15, 19, 22–23, 26, 36, 49, 82, 85, 87, 91, 115, 163–64, 168, 206–8, 210–11, 214–15, 217–18, 224–26, 230, 233–35, 312, 320–21, 363, 365, 368, 374, 376, 378; Poles in the 83, 319; Ukrainians in 237
Wehrwolf 229
Weigler, Zvi 374
Weinryb, Bernard 308
Weiss, Aharon 369
Weiss, Martin 165
Weissman, Nahum 329
Weissruthenische Vertrauenstelle (Belorussian Representation or, White Ruthenian Nazi Party) 149
Wejherowo 26, 301
Wejsiaty 174
Werbowski, Tecia 313, 333, 337, 342, 403
Werfel, Roman 60, 78
Werkschutz (work security) 206, 237
Wernik, Romuald 383
Werth, Alexander 79, 318, 404
Wertheim, Anatol 332, 404
West, Wallace 337
Western: Belorussia (Western Byelorussia) 9–10, 12, 87, 90, 99, 143, 145–48, 153, 157, 183, 196, 208, 295, 330, 346–47; Europe 7, 46–47, 115, 129, 183, 256; Germany 130; Poland 13, 21, 31, 52, 58, 87; Ukraine 5, 9–12, 47, 49, 143–45, 177, 179–80, 183, 187, 189–90, 196–98, 202, 206, 208, 235, 237, 239, 241, 245–47, 254–55, 295, 330, 356, 359, 362, 376, 380; Ukrainian National Republic *see* ZUNR
White: Poles (Białopolacy) 93, 151, 332; -Russian Welfare Society 152; Russians (Belorussians) 151–52; Ruthenia 188, 199; Ruthenian Nazi Party *see* Weissruthenische Vertrauenstelle; Steed 265
Whitehead Avenue 157
Wiącek, Tadeusz 342, 344–45, 404
Wiatr, Zenon 280
Wicherkiewicz, Tadeusz 80
Wicyń 229
Widerszal, Ludwik 95
Wieliczko, Mieczysław 299
Wielkie Oczy 49
Wielkopolska 294
Wiener, Jon 314, 404
Wiener-Neustadt 197, 207
Wierusz-Kowalski 319
Wierzbica 121
Wierzchowiny 252, 385
Wiesenthal, Simon 66, 75, 142, 209–10, 231, 238, 316, 318, 365, 374, 377, 387, 404
Wieśniak, Stanisław 43
Wiess, Moshe 315
Wilbersturm 229
Wilczewska, Felicja 310, 404
Wilejka 17, 87–89, 148, 151
Wileńszczyzna (Wilno region, Kraj Wileński, Okręg Wileński, Vilniaus Kraštas, Ziemia Wileńska) 9, 100, 159, 161–70, 177, 351–52. *See also* Wilno
Wilhelm, Hans-Heinrich 348–49
willige Fremdvölkische 306
Wilno (Vilna, Vilnius, Vilno) 3, 5, 9, 16–17, 19, 30, 41–42, 47, 55–57, 69, 81, 85, 87–90, 92–93, 99, 102, 132–133, 143, 147–52, 159–65, 167–72, 174–75, 180, 196, 281–82, 288, 293, 296, 303, 306, 308, 346, 349, 350–52; Cathedral 176. *See also* Wileńszczyzna
Wilson (née Laks), Anna 220
WiN (Wolność i Niezawisłość, or Freedom and Independence) 131, 135–36, 252, 280, 341
Winch, Michael 362, 404
Winkelmann, Otto 371
Wirth 84
Wisenburg (gendarme) 110
Wiśniewska, Maria 354
Wiśniowiec 243–44
Witkowski 27
Wittenmayer 229
Wittke (Oberwachmeister) 26
WK PPS (Wojewódzki Komitet Polskiej Partii Socjalistycznej or, Provincial Committee of the Polish Socialist Party) 280
Włodawa 181
Włodkowski, Łucjusz 379
Włodzimierz 50, 251
Włodzimierz Wołyński 17
Wojciechowski, Stanisław 192, 197
Wojewódzki: Komitet Polskiej Partii Socjalistycznej *see* WK PPS; Urząd Bezpieczeństwa Publicznego *see* WUBP
Wojsko Polskie *see* WP
Wojsko Wewnętrzne *see* Internal: Army
Wola Ostrowiecka 247
Wołczański, Józef 382, 404

Wolfshaut-Dinkes, Max 51, 311, 405
Wólka Profecka 217
Wólka Szczecka 230
Wołkonowski, Jarosław 93–94, 327
Wołkowysk 184, 303
Wołłejko, Michał 93, 327
Wolność i Niezawisłość *see* WiN
Wolność-Równość-Niepodległość *see* WRN
Wołomin 121
Wołowysk 17
Wołożyn 17
Wolski, Mieczysław 122
Wołyń (Volhynia, Volyn) 3, 9–12, 17, 19, 30–31, 49–50, 53, 71, 81, 99, 101, 125, 177, 179–81, 184–85, 187–89, 195, 199–200, 203, 206–7, 212, 215–17, 220–22, 229–30, 233, 239–40, 244–52, 254–55, 257–58,281, 283–88, 290, 293, 296, 303, 306, 308, 310, 330, 333, 352–54, 361, 363–64, 368–70, 373, 379, 381, 384
Worczyn 95, 329
World: Congress of Free Ukrainians 380; Jewish Congress 142; Federation of Soldiers of the Home Army 93
World Trade Center 193
World War I 3, 5, 40, 43, 46, 159, 181, 196, 226, 94, 347
World War II losses: in Belorussia 157; in Poland 305; of Catholic clergy 300, 302; ethnic Polish 32, 305; ethnic Polish and Jewish during the September campaign 36; ethnic Polish and Jewish in 1939–1940 115; ethnic Polish in Eastern Poland 305–6; at German hands 32; at German hands of Polish professionals 23; at the hands of the OUN-UPA 251; Jewish 32, 305–6; Jewish in Eastern Poland 306; Polish, German and Soviet during the September campaign 307; at Soviet hands 20, 32; in Warsaw 24, 301
World War III 260. *See also* Third World War
Woś, J. 302
WP (Wojsko Polskie, or Polish Army) 136, 139, 277
WRN (Wolność-Równość-Niepodległość, or Freedom-Equality-Independence) 117
Wrocław (Breslau) 61, 197, 207, 305, 313, 318
Wrona, Zenon 2, 281, 342–43, 345, 398
Wronki 335
Wroński, Stanisław 338, 353–54, 380, 405
Wrzesiński, Wojciech 365, 405
Wrzeszcz, Jan 139, 278–80
Wrzos 43
Wszędobył, Jan 145
WUBP (Wojewódzki Urząd Bezpieczeństwa Publicznego, or Provincial Office of State Security) 130, 134, 139, 276–80
Wulff, Horst 89
Wyden, Peter 316–17, 405
Wygoda 91, 168
Wyrka 198
Wyrwich, Mateusz 313–14, 405
Wyszków 102; report from 103
Wyszywany, Wasyl *see* Wilhelm Hapsburg

Yacov 98
Yad Vashem 49, 60, 75, 96, 118, 123, 310–11, 334
Yahil, Leni 70, 119, 304, 405
Yakira, Eliyahu 329
Yaremko, Michael 232, 374, 405
Yedunov, Yakov 100
Yeltsin, Boris 15, 347
YIVO 159
Yom Kippur 49, 63
York, Geoffrey 347
Ypatingas Būrys 165, 174, 350
Yugoslavia 7, 124, 229, 231, 255, 304, 384
Yurkevich, Myroslav 224, 357, 362–63, 366, 370–71, 383

Zabecki, Franciszek 218
Żabkowice 313
Zable, Arnold 49, 310, 405
Zabłudowski, Tadeusz 60
Zaborowice 275, 343
Zaborowski, Jan 208–9, 364, 393
Zaborski, Marcin 332
Zabrze (Hindenburg) 61
Žagarė 171
Żagiew (Żydowska Gwardia Wolności, or Jewish Guard of Liberty) 66, 74
Zagłębie 303
Zagłębie Dąbrowskie 294
Zagórska Street 277
Zagórski, Edmund 276, 279
Zagórski, S.D. 141
Zając (general) 81
Zajączkowski, Stanisław 78
Zajączkowski, Wacław 317, 338, 405
"Zakerzon" area 379
Zakharka, Vasil 149
Zakhidno-Ukrainska Narodna Respublika *see* ZUNR
Zakłodzie 71
Zakopane 85, 205–6, 254
Zaleszczyki 17, 72
Założce 339, 365
Zambrowski, Antoni 313
Zambrowski, Roman 60, 134, 277, 279
Zamojszczyzna (Zamość region) 28, 177, 244, 248–9, 299, 383–84. *See also* Zamość
Zamorski, Kazimierz 298
Zamość 22, 28, 54, 67, 70–71, 110, 177, 230, 248–49, 311. *See also* Zamojszczyzna
Zamość-Lublin Committee for Rendering Assistance to Jews (Komitet Zamojsko-Lubelski Niesienia Pomocy Żydom) 117
Zamoyski, Maurice 263
Zarecki, Tadeusz 134
Żarski-Zajder, Władysław 118, 338, 405
Żaruk-Michalski, Aleksander 280
Zarytska, Kateryna 358
Zarzetka 121
Zawadzki, Aleksander 130
Zawiercie 61, 303
"Żbik" (member of "Ogień") 341
Żbikowski, Andrzej 364, 405
Zborów 17
Zdołbunów 199, 251
Zdziechowski, Paweł 310
Żebrowski, Leszek 96, 102, 313–15, 317, 329, 332, 335, 341, 345, 392, 405
Żebrowski, Rafał 330, 405
Żegota 106, 108, 112, 117–18, 131–32, 311. *See also* Provisional Committee of Konrad Żegota *and also* RPŻ
Zehnpfenig (captain) 168
Żeidzina (reverend) 165
Zeif, Aharon 57
Zelek, Roman 278
Żeleński, Władysław 319, 358–59, 405
Zelicki, Paweł 279
Zellenbau 212, 365
Zelwa 145
Zemiński 335
Zgórsko 278
Zhitomir 216, 303
Zieliński, Zygmunt 299, 302, 309, 311, 322, 338, 405
Zielonkiewicz, Aleksander 122
Zielony Dąb 254
Ziemia Wileńska *see* Wilełszczyzna
Zienkiewicz, Aleksander 151, 348, 405
Zik, Gershon 310, 405

Zimkiewicz, Henryk 26
Zionism 44, 293. *See also* Zionist: movement *and also* Zionists
Zionist: Jewish Agency 70; movement 129
Zionists 5–6, 44
Zivilabteilung 69
Złoczów 17–18, 57, 72, 123, 208, 221, 229, 252, 355, 365
ŻOB (Żydowska Organizacja Bojowa, or Jewish Combat Organization) 91, 102, 104, 108, 332
Żochowski, Stanisław 64, 314–15, 318, 330
Żoliborz 112, 337
Żółkiew 17
Żółkiewka 250
Żółkwia 49
Zolotov (informer in Auschwitz) 319
ŻSS [Żydowska Samopomoc Społeczna, or Jewish Social Welfare Mutual Assistance (Society)] 86–87
Zubiak, Leon 62
Zuckerman, Yitzhak 220, 368
ZUNR (Zakhidno-Ukrainska Narodna Respublika, or Western Ukrainian National Republic) 187–8, 288, 293, 355
Żuprany 151
Związek: Jaszczurczy 329; Patriotów Polskich *see* Union: of Polish Patriots; Syndykalistów Polskich *see* Association of Polish Syndicalists; Walki Zbrojnej *see* ZWZ; Wolnych Polaków *see* Alliance: of Free Poles
Zwięczyce 121, 230
Zwieczyniec 173
Zwolakowa, Maria 338, 405
Zwoliński, Andrzej 36, 131, 307–11, 341, 405
ZWZ (Związek Walki Zbrojnej, or Union for Armed Struggle) 94, 163, 360
Żydaczów 17
żydokomuna 37, 97, 130
Żydowska: Gwardia Wolności *see* Żagiew; Organizacja Bojowa *see* ŻOB; Samopomoc Społeczna *see* ŻSS
Żydowski: Komitet Narodowy *see* Jewish: National Committee; Związek Wojskowy *see* ŻZW
Zygalski, Henryk 82
Zyklon B 31, 302
Żymierski, Michał 103
Żywiec 286, 303
ŻZW (Żydowski Związek Wojskowy, or Jewish, Military Union) 108
Z.Z.Z. 313–14, 330, 405